MyEconLab and Hubbard/O'Brien, *Macroeconomics*, Fourth Edition:
The Power of Practice.

MyEconLab creates the perfect pedagogical loop that provides not only text-specific assessment and practice problems, but also tutorial support to make sure students learn from their mistakes.

Auto-generated Test and Assignments. MyEconLab comes with preloaded assignments, all of which are automatically graded and include select end-of-chapter questions and problems from the textbook.

Study Plan. A Study Plan is generated from each student's results on quizzes and tests. Students can clearly see which topics they have mastered and, more importantly, which they need to work on.

MyEconLab www.myeconlab.com

Learning Resources. To further reinforce understanding, Study Plan and Homework problems link to additional learning resources:

- A *step-by-step Guided Solution* helps students break down a problem much the same way as an instructor would do during office hours.

- *The eText page* on which the topic of the exercise is explained promotes reading the text when further explanation is needed.

- A *graphing tool* encourages students to draw and manipulate graphs and deepen their understanding by illustrating economic relationships and ideas.

Unlimited Practice. Many Study Plan and Instructor-assigned exercises contain algorithms to ensure students get as much practice as they need.

As students work through Study Plan or Homework exercises, instant feedback and tutorial resources guide them towards understanding.

Macroeconomics

Macroeconomics

Fourth Edition

R. Glenn Hubbard
Columbia University

Anthony Patrick O'Brien
Lehigh University

PEARSON

Boston   Columbus   Indianapolis   New York   San Francisco   Upper Saddle River
Amsterdam   Cape Town   Dubai   London   Madrid   Milan   Munich   Paris   Montréal   Toronto
Delhi   Mexico City   São Paulo   Sydney   Hong Kong   Seoul   Singapore   Taipei   Tokyo

Editorial Director: Sally Yagan
Editor in Chief: Donna Battista
AVP/Executive Editor: David Alexander
VP/Development Director: Stephen Deitmer
Executive Development Editor:
    Lena Buonanno
Editorial Project Manager: Lindsey Sloan
Editorial Assistant: Emily Brodeur
Marketing Director: Patrice Jones
AVP/Executive Marketing Manager:
    Lori DeShazo
Marketing Assistant: Courtney Kamauf
Senior Managing Editor: Nancy H. Fenton
Production Project Manager:
    Carla Thompson
Manufacturing Director: Evelyn Beaton
Senior Manufacturing Buyer: Carol Melville
Senior Media Buyer: Ginny Michaud

Creative Director: Christy Mahon
Senior Art Director, Cover: Jonathan Boylan
Image Manager: Rachel Youdelman
Text Permissions Project Supervisor:
    Michael Joyce
Media Director: Susan Schoenberg
Content Lead, MyEconLab: Noel Lotz
Senior Media Producer:
    Melissa Honig
Associate Production Project Manager:
    Alison Eusden
Full-Service Project Management/Interior
Design/Photo Research/Composition:
    PreMediaGlobal, Inc.
Printer/Binder: Courier, Kendallville
Cover Printer: Courier, Kendallville
Text Font: Minion

Credits and acknowledgments borrowed from other sources and reproduced, with
permission, in this textbook appear on appropriate page within text (or on page C-1).

Microsoft® and Windows® are registered trademarks of the Microsoft Corporation in
the U.S.A. and other countries. Screen shots and icons reprinted with permission from the
Microsoft Corporation. This book is not sponsored or endorsed by or affiliated with the
Microsoft Corporation.

Many of the designations by manufacturers and sellers to distinguish their products are claimed
as trademarks. Where those designations appear in this book, and the publisher was aware of a
trademark claim, the designations have been printed in initial caps or all caps.

Cataloging-in-Publication Data is on file at the Library of Congress

10 9 8 7 6 5 4 3 2 1

ISBN 13: 978-0-13-283224-3
ISBN 10: 0-13-283224-0

PEARSON

For Constance, Raph, and Will
—*R. Glenn Hubbard*

For Cindy, Matthew, Andrew, and Daniel
—*Anthony Patrick O'Brien*

Glenn Hubbard, policymaker, professor, and researcher.
R. Glenn Hubbard is the dean and Russell L. Carson Professor of Finance and Economics in the Graduate School of Business at Columbia University and professor of economics in Columbia's Faculty of Arts and Sciences. He is also a research associate of the National Bureau of Economic Research and a director of Automatic Data Processing, Black Rock Closed-End Funds, KKR Financial Corporation, and MetLife. He received his Ph.D. in economics from Harvard University in 1983. From 2001 to 2003, he served as chairman of the White House Council of Economic Advisers and chairman of the OECD Economy Policy Committee, and from 1991 to 1993, he was deputy assistant secretary of the U.S. Treasury Department. He currently serves as co-chair of the nonpartisan Committee on Capital Markets Regulation. Hubbard's fields of specialization are public economics, financial markets and institutions, corporate finance, macroeconomics, industrial organization, and public policy. He is the author of more than 100 articles in leading journals, including *American Economic Review, Brookings Papers on Economic Activity, Journal of Finance, Journal of Financial Economics, Journal of Money, Credit, and Banking, Journal of Political Economy, Journal of Public Economics, Quarterly Journal of Economics, RAND Journal of Economics*, and *Review of Economics and Statistics*. His research has been supported by grants from the National Science Foundation, the National Bureau of Economic Research, and numerous private foundations.

Tony O'Brien, award-winning professor and researcher.
Anthony Patrick O'Brien is a professor of economics at Lehigh University. He received his Ph.D. from the University of California, Berkeley, in 1987. He has taught principles of economics for more than 15 years, in both large sections and small honors classes. He received the Lehigh University Award for Distinguished Teaching. He was formerly the director of the Diamond Center for Economic Education and was named a Dana Foundation Faculty Fellow and Lehigh Class of 1961 Professor of Economics. He has been a visiting professor at the University of California, Santa Barbara, and the Graduate School of Industrial Administration at Carnegie Mellon University. O'Brien's research has dealt with such issues as the evolution of the U.S. automobile industry, sources of U.S. economic competitiveness, the development of U.S. trade policy, the causes of the Great Depression, and the causes of black-white income differences. His research has been published in leading journals, including *American Economic Review, Quarterly Journal of Economics, Journal of Money, Credit, and Banking, Industrial Relations, Journal of Economic History*, and *Explorations in Economic History*. His research has been supported by grants from government agencies and private foundations. In addition to teaching and writing, O'Brien also serves on the editorial board of the *Journal of Socio-Economics*.

BRIEF CONTENTS

CONTENTS

*These end-of-chapter resource materials repeat in all chapters.

PART 2: Firms in the Domestic and International Economies

PART 6: The International Economy

Chapter 18: Macroeconomics in
an Open Economy   608

FLEXIBILITY CHART

The following chart helps you organize your syllabus based on your teaching preferences and objectives:

Core	Optional	Policy
Chapter 1: Economics: Foundations and Models	**Chapter 1 Appendix:** Using Graphs and Formulas	
Chapter 2: Trade-offs, Comparative Advantage, and the Market System		
Chapter 3: Where Prices Come From: The Interaction of Demand and Supply		
	Chapter 4 Appendix: Quantitative Demand and Supply Analysis	**Chapter 4:** Economic Efficiency, Government Price Setting, and Taxes
		Chapter 5: The Economics of Health Care
	Chapter 6: Firms, the Stock Market, and Corporate Governance	
	Chapter 6 Appendix: Tools to Analyze Firms' Financial Information	
Chapter 7: Comparative Advantage and the Gains from International Trade		
Chapter 8: GDP: Measuring Total Production and Income		
Chapter 9: Unemployment and Inflation		
Chapter 10: Economic Growth, the Financial System, and Business Cycles		
Chapter 11: Long-Run Economic Growth: Sources and Policies		

When George Lucas was asked why he made *Star Wars*, he replied, "It's the kind of movie I like to see, but no one seemed to be making them. So, I decided to make one." We realized that no one seemed to be writing the kind of textbook we wanted to use in our classes. So, after years of supplementing texts with fresh, lively, real-world examples from newspapers, magazines, Web sites, and professional journals, we decided to write an economics text that delivers complete economics coverage with many real-world business examples. Our goal was to keep our classes "widget free."

New to the Fourth Edition

The severe economic downturn that began in 2007 with the bursting of the housing bubble was still affecting the economy in 2011. Unemployment had risen to levels not seen in decades and remained above 9 percent for more than two and a half years. The crisis in the financial system was the worst since the Great Depression of the 1930s. Policy debates intensified as Congress passed and President Barack Obama enacted the American Recovery and Reinvestment Act of 2009, the largest package of spending increases and tax cuts in history. The Federal Reserve sailed into uncharted waters as it developed new policy tools to deal with the unprecedented financial turmoil. Other long-running policy debates continued as well, as comprehensive health care legislation, looming cost increases for Social Security and Medicare, huge long-run budget deficits, environmental problems, income inequality, and changes to the tax system all received attention from economists, policymakers, and the public.

In this new edition, we help students understand recent economic events and the policy responses to them. As in the earlier editions, we place applications at the forefront of the discussion. We believe that students find the study of economics more interesting and easier to master when they see economic analysis applied to real-world issues that concern them.

Here is a summary of the changes in this fourth edition. Please see the next section, starting on the next page, for details on each of these changes:

- A new Chapter 5, "The Economics of Health Care," covers health care around the world, information problems and externalities in the market for health care, and the debate over President Obama's Patient Protection and Affordable Care Act.
- There is new coverage of the slow recovery from the recession and financial crisis of 2007–2009.
- There is new coverage of initiatives by the Federal Reserve, including quantitative easing and Operation Twist.
- There is new coverage of fiscal policy, including analysis of the debate over fiscal stimulus and the magnitude of multipliers for government spending and taxes.
- All companies in the chapter openers have been either replaced with new companies or updated with current information.
- All chapters include new *An Inside Look* newspaper articles and analyses to help students apply economic thinking to current events and policy debates.
- There are 21 new *Making the Connection* features to help students tie economic concepts to current events and policy issues.
- Figures and tables have been updated, using the latest data available.
- Many of the end-of-chapter problems have been either replaced or updated.

In this new edition, we have taken the opportunity to make many changes throughout the text, while concentrating on the key areas described in the following sections.

Policy debates, including health care, trade, and pollution. The number of jobs in the health care sector continues to increase. In Chapter 1, "Economics: Foundations and Models," we use the debate about whether public policy is resulting in physicians leaving private practice to introduce students to positive and normative economic analysis. In Chapter 7, "Comparative Advantage and the Gains from International Trade," we explore the "Buy American" provision in the 2009 stimulus package.

As this book goes to press, the debate continues over the consequences of the 2010 overhaul of the U.S. health care system. In Chapter 2, "Trade-offs, Comparative Advantage, and the Market System," we discuss the trade-offs involved in health care spending and the Medicare and Medicaid programs. We revisit the topic of health care in the new Chapter 5, "The Economics of Health Care," where we discuss projections of health care spending and the role of the U.S. government in the health care system.

The recession and financial crisis of 2007–2009 and its aftermath. Today's students feel the effects of the slow recovery from the worst economic crisis since the Great Depression of the 1930s. The problems in the financial system in the United States and the euro zone have proven that it is important for students in both microeconomics and macroeconomics courses to understand the basics of how financial markets work and the role of government in financial regulation. In Chapter 6, "Firms, the Stock Market, and Corporate Governance," we cover the basics of the stock and bond markets, discuss why stock prices fluctuate, and examine the role of the principal–agent problem in the financial meltdown of 2007–2009. Chapter 13, "Aggregate Demand and Aggregate Supply Analysis," covers the origins of the recession and includes a new discussion of how long it takes the economy to return to potential GDP. The housing bust and subprime crisis are discussed in Chapter 14, "Money, Banks, and the Federal Reserve System," and Chapter 15, "Monetary Policy."

New initiatives by the Federal Reserve. During 2008, the Fed dramatically broke with precedent by setting up a number of new "lending facilities" and by participating in actions such as the purchase of Bear Stearns by JPMorgan Chase. In this new edition, we provide students with a basic background on investment banks and the process of securitization; the mortgage-backed securities market, including the roles of Fannie Mae and Freddie Mac; and the debate among economists concerning the Fed's two rounds of quantitative easing and "Operation Twist."

Real-world company examples and newspaper articles. As in previous editions, we open each chapter by highlighting a company to establish a real-world context for learning and to spark students' interest in economics. We have chosen new companies for some chapters and updated the information in the other chapters. As in previous editions, each chapter closes with the *An Inside Look* feature, which shows students how to apply the concepts from the chapter to the analysis of a news article. We have replaced all the *An Inside Look* features in this edition. Here is a snapshot of some of these changes:

Chapter 3, "Where Prices Come From: The Interaction of Demand and Supply," opens with a discussion of the iPad and the tablet reader revolution. The *An Inside Look* feature presents an article and analysis of how a shortage of display screens could affect the sale of tablet readers.

Chapter 5, "The Economics of Health Care," opens with a discussion of the rising health care costs for small businesses. The *An Inside Look* feature presents an article and analysis of health care spending and the Patient Protection and Affordable Care Act of 2010.

Chapter 6, "Firms, the Stock Market, and Corporate Governance," opens with a discussion of the runaway success of the private company Facebook and how some of the company's stock is available for sale in private markets. *An Inside Look* features Internet companies that allow qualified investors a chance to buy stock in private companies.

Chapter 8, "GDP: Measuring Total Production and Income," opens with a discussion of Ford Motor Company's performance following the 2007–2009 recession. The *An*

Inside Look feature presents an analysis of how uncertain economic conditions in 2011 and 2012 kept demand for automobiles below initial sales estimates

Chapter 15, "Monetary Policy," opens with a discussion of homebuilder Toll Brothers. The *An Inside Look* feature presents an analysis of the effects of "Operation Twist," the Federal Reserve's attempt to boost the economy in late 2011 by stimulating the sluggish housing market.

Further changes to the fourth edition

The following are further changes to the fourth edition:

- This edition provides many new *Making the Connection* features, which help students tie economic concepts to current events and policy issues, as well as updated sections, figures, and tables:

  Chapter 1 opens with a new discussion of doctors in private practice and includes two new *Making the Connections*, "Does Health Insurance Give People an Incentive to Become Obese?" and "Should Medical School Be Free?"

  Chapter 2 includes a new *Making the Connection*, "A Story of the Market System in Action: How Do You Make an iPad?"

  Chapter 3 opens with discussion of the tablet computer industry and includes three new *Making the Connections*: "The Aging of the Baby Boom Generation," "Forecasting the Demand for iPads," and "Are Quiznos Sandwiches Normal Goods and Subway Sandwiches Inferior Goods?"

  Chapter 5 is new to this edition and covers health care around the world; information problems and externalities in the market for health care; and the Patient Protection and Affordable Care Act in the United States. The chapter contains *Making the Connections* titled "How Much Is That MRI Scan?" and "Health Exchanges, Small Businesses, and Rising Medical Costs."

  Chapter 6 has a new section on the financial crisis of 2007–2009 and two new *Making the Connections*: "The Rating Game: Is the U.S. Treasury Likely to Default on Its Bonds?" and "Are Buyers of Facebook Stock Getting a Fair Deal?"

  Chapter 9 opens with a new discussion of Bank of America's 2011 announcement to lay off 30,000 workers and includes two new *Making the Connections*: "How Unusual Was the Unemployment Situation Following the 2007–2009 Recession?" and "How Should We Categorize Unemployment at Bank of America?"

  Chapter 11 includes two new *Making the Connections*: "Is Income All That Matters?" and "Will China's Standard of Living Ever Exceed That of the United States?"

  Chapter 13 includes two new *Making the Connections*: "Which Components of Aggregate Demand Changed the Most during the 2007–2009 Recession?" and "How Long Does It Take to Return to Potential GDP? Economic Forecasts Following the Recession of 2007–2009."

  Chapter 15 includes two new *Making* the *Connections*: "Too Low for Zero: The Fed Tries 'Quantitative Easing' and 'Operation Twist'" and "Trying to Hit a Moving Target: Making Policy with "Real-Time Data."'

  Chapter 16 opens with a new discussion of the role of government in creating jobs, and includes a new section on "Fiscal Policy in Action: Did the Fiscal Stimulus Package Work?"; a new table showing competing estimates of the size of the government spending and tax multipliers; and a new *Making the Connection*: "Why Was the Recession of 2007–2009 So Severe?"

  Chapter 17 opens with a new discussion of CarMax.

  Chapter 19 opens with a new discussion of Airbus and includes updated information about the euro debt crisis.

- Figures and tables have been updated using the latest data available.

- Many of the end-of-chapter problems have been either replaced or updated.
- Finally, we have gone over the text literally line-by-line, tightening the discussion, re-writing unclear points, and making many other small changes. We are grateful to the many instructors and students who made suggestions for improvements in the previous edition. We have done our best to incorporate as many of those suggestions as possible.

The Foundation:
Contextual Learning and Modern Organization

Students come to study macroeconomics with a strong interest in understanding events and developments in the economy. We try to capture that interest and develop students' economic intuition and understanding in this text. We present macroeconomics in a way that is modern and based in the real world of business and economic policy. And we believe we achieve this presentation without making the analysis more difficult. We avoid the recent trend of using simplified versions of intermediate models, which are often more detailed and more complex than what students need to understand the basic macroeconomic issues. Instead, we use a more realistic version of the familiar aggregate demand and aggregate supply model to analyze short-run fluctuations and monetary and fiscal policy. We also avoid the "dueling schools of thought" approach often used to teach macroeconomics at the principles level. We emphasize the many areas of macroeconomics where most economists agree. And we present throughout real business and policy situations to develop students' intuition.

- **A broad discussion of macro statistics.** Many students pay at least some attention to the financial news and know that the release of statistics by federal agencies can cause movements in stock and bond prices. A background in macroeconomic statistics helps clarify some of the policy issues encountered in later chapters. In Chapter 8, "GDP: Measuring Total Production and Income," and Chapter 9, "Unemployment and Inflation," we provide students with an understanding of the uses and potential shortcomings of the key macroeconomic statistics, without getting bogged down in the minutiae of how the statistics are constructed. So, for instance, we discuss the important differences between the payroll survey and the household survey for understanding conditions in the labor market. We explain why financial markets react more strongly to news from the payroll survey. New to this edition is a discussion of the employment–population ratio, which some economists regard as a key measure of labor market performance. Chapter 15, "Monetary Policy," discusses why the Federal Reserve prefers to measure inflation using the personal consumption expenditures price index rather than the consumer price index.

- **Early coverage of long-run topics.** We place key macroeconomic issues in their long-run context in Chapter 10, "Economic Growth, the Financial System, and Business Cycles," and Chapter 11, "Long-Run Economic Growth: Sources and Policies." Chapter 10 puts the business cycle in the context of underlying long-run growth and discusses what actually happens during the phases of the business cycle. We believe this material is important if students are to have the understanding of business cycles they will need to interpret economic events; this material is often discussed only briefly or omitted entirely in other books. We know that many instructors prefer to have a short-run orientation to their macro courses, with a strong emphasis on policy. Accordingly, we have structured Chapter 10 so that its discussion of long-run growth would be sufficient for instructors who want to move quickly to short-run analysis. Chapter 11 uses a simple neoclassical growth model to explain important growth issues. We apply the model to topics such as the decline of the Soviet economy, the surprisingly strong growth performance of Botswana, and the failure of many developing countries to sustain high growth rates. And we challenge students with the discussion "Why Isn't the Whole World Rich?"

- **A dynamic model of aggregate demand and aggregate supply.**
  We take a fresh approach to the standard aggregate demand and
  aggregate supply (*AD–AS*) model. We realize there is no good,
  simple alternative to using the *AD–AS* model when explaining movements in the price level and in real GDP. But we know
  that more instructors are dissatisfied with the *AD–AS* model
  than with any other aspect of the macro principles course. The
  key problem, of course, is that *AD–AS* is a static model that attempts to account for dynamic changes in real GDP and the
  price level. Our approach retains the basics of the *AD–AS* model
  but makes it more accurate and useful by making it more dynamic. We emphasize two points: First, changes in the position
  of the short-run (upward-sloping) aggregate supply curve depend mainly on the state of expectations of the inflation rate.
  Second, the existence of growth in the economy means that the
  long-run (vertical) aggregate supply curve shifts to the right every year. This "dynamic" *AD–AS* model provides students with
  a more accurate understanding of the causes and consequences
  of fluctuations in real GDP and the price level. Chapter 13, "Aggregate Demand and Aggregate Supply Analysis," includes a
  three-layer, full-color acetate for the key introductory dynamic
  AD–AS graph (Figure 13.8, "A Dynamic Aggregate Demand and
  Aggregate Supply Model," on page 439 and reproduced on the
  right). We created this acetate to help students see how the graph
  builds step by step and to help make the graph easier for instructors to present. The acetate will help instructors who want to use
  dynamic *AD–AS* in class but believe the model needs to be developed carefully. We introduce this model in Chapter 13 and use
  it to discuss monetary policy in Chapter 15, "Monetary Policy,"
  and fiscal policy in Chapter 16, "Fiscal Policy." Instructors may
  safely omit the sections on the dynamic *AD–AS* model without
  any loss in continuity to the discussion of macroeconomic theory
  and policy.

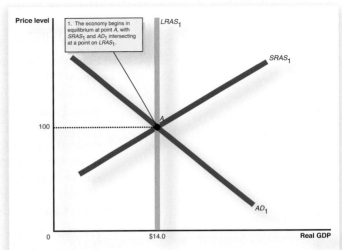

The first acetate overlay adds the shifts in the long-run
and short-run aggregate supply curves.

The second acetate overlay adds the shifts in the aggregate
demand curve to complete the dynamic model.

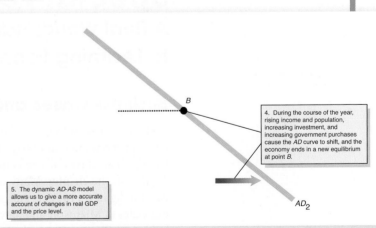

- **Extensive coverage of monetary policy.** Because of the central
  role monetary policy plays in the economy and in students' curiosity about business and financial news, we devote
  two chapters—Chapters 15, "Monetary Policy," and
  17, "Inflation, Unemployment, and Federal Reserve
  Policy"—to the topic. We emphasize the issues involved in the Fed's choice of monetary policy targets, and we include coverage of the Taylor rule.
  The fourth edition includes coverage of the Fed's
  new policies aimed at dealing with the housing crisis and its effects on financial markets.

- **Coverage of both the demand-side and supply-
  side effects of fiscal policy.** Our discussion of fiscal
  policy in Chapter 16, "Fiscal Policy," carefully dis-
  tinguishes between automatic stabilizers and discretionary fiscal policy. We also provide significant
  coverage of the supply-side effects of fiscal policy.

- **A self-contained but thorough discussion of the Keynesian income-expenditure
  approach.** The Keynesian income-expenditure approach (the "45°-line diagram," or
  "Keynesian cross") is useful for introducing students to the short-run relationship between spending and production. Many instructors, however, prefer to omit this material.

Therefore, we use the 45°-line diagram only in Chapter 12, "Aggregate Expenditure and Output in the Short Run." The discussion of monetary and fiscal policy in later chapters uses only the *AD–AS* model, making it possible to omit Chapter 12.

- **Extensive international coverage.** We include three chapters devoted to international topics: Chapter 7, "Comparative Advantage and the Gains from International Trade," Chapter 18, "Macroeconomics in an Open Economy," and Chapter 19, "The International Financial System." Having a good understanding of the international trading and financial systems is essential to understanding the macroeconomy and to satisfying students' curiosity about the economic world around them. In addition to the material in our three international chapters, we weave international comparisons into the narratives of several other chapters, including our discussion of labor market policies in Chapter 17, "Inflation, Unemployment, and Federal Reserve Policy," and central banking in Chapter 14, "Money, Banks, and the Federal Reserve System."

- **Flexible chapter organization.** Because we realize that there are a variety of approaches to teaching principles of macroeconomics, we have structured our chapters for maximum flexibility. For example, our discussion of long-run economic growth in Chapter 10, "Economic Growth, the Financial System, and Business Cycles," makes it possible for instructors to omit the more thorough discussion of these issues in Chapter 11, "Long-Run Economic Growth: Sources and Policies." Our discussion of the Keynesian 45°-line diagram is confined to Chapter 12 so that instructors who do not use this approach can proceed directly to aggregate demand and aggregate supply analysis in Chapter 13, "Aggregate Demand and Aggregate Supply Analysis." While we devote two chapters to monetary policy, the first of these—Chapter 15, "Monetary Policy"—is a self-contained discussion, so instructors may safely omit the material in Chapter 17, "Inflation, Unemployment, and Federal Reserve Policy," if they choose to. Finally, instructors may choose to omit all three of the international chapters (Chapter 7, "Comparative Advantage and the Gains from International Trade," Chapter 18, "Macroeconomics in an Open Economy," and Chapter 19, "The International Financial System"), cover just Chapter 9 on international trade; cover just Chapter 18; or cover Chapter 18 and Chapter 19 while omitting Chapter 7. Please refer to the flexibility chart on pages xviii–xix to help select the chapters and order best suited to your classroom needs.

Special Features:
A Real-World, Hands-on Approach to Learning Economics

Business Cases and *An Inside Look* News Articles

Each chapter-opening case provides a real-world context for learning, sparks students' interest in economics, and helps to unify the chapter. The case describes an actual company facing a real situation. The company is integrated in the narrative, graphs, and pedagogical features of the chapter. Many of the chapter openers focus on the role of entrepreneurs in developing new products and bringing them to the market. For example, Chapter 3 covers Bill Gates of Microsoft and Steve Jobs of Apple, Chapter 6 covers Mark Zuckerberg of Facebook, and Chapter 13 covers Fred Smith of FedEx. Here are a few examples of companies we explore in the chapter openers in this new edition:

- Apple (Chapter 3, "Where Prices Come From: The Interaction of Demand and Supply")
- Facebook (Chapter 6, "Firms, the Stock Market, and Corporate Governance")
- FedEx (Chapter 13, "Aggregate Demand and Aggregate Supply Analysis")

An Inside Look is a two-page feature that shows students how to apply the concepts from the chapter to the analysis of a news article. Select articles deal with policy issues and are titled *An Inside Look at Policy*. Articles are from sources such as the *Wall Street Journal*, the *Economist*, and *BusinessWeek*. The *An Inside Look* feature presents an excerpt from an article, analysis of the article, a graph(s), and critical thinking questions.

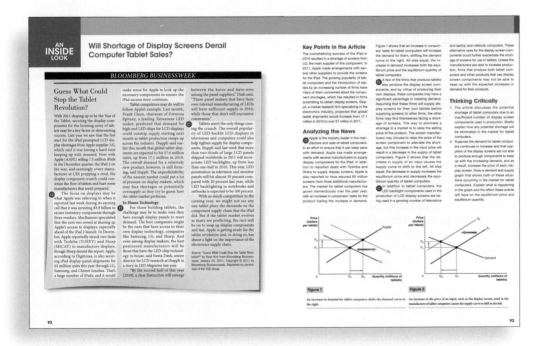

Here are some examples of the articles featured in *An Inside Look*:

- "Guess What Could Stop the Tablet Revolution?" *Bloomberg Businessweek* (Chapter 3, "Where Prices Come From: The Interaction of Demand and Supply")
- "How to Buy into Facebook Before It Goes Public," *Kiplinger* (Chapter 6, "Firms, the Stock Market, and Corporate Governance")

- "Will the Fed's New Policies Revitalize the Housing Market?" *Atlantic* (Chapter 15, "Monetary Policy")
- "Obama Proposes Additional Spending to Stimulate the Economy" *U.S. News & World Report* (Chapter 16, "Fiscal Policy")

Economics in Your Life

After the chapter-opening real-world business case, we have added a personal dimension to the chapter opener, with a feature titled *Economics in Your Life*, which asks students to consider how economics affects their own lives. The feature piques the interest of students and emphasizes the connection between the material they are learning and their own experiences.

Economics in Your Life

Will You Buy an Apple iPad or a Samsung Galaxy Tab?

Suppose you are considering buying a tablet computer and that you are choosing between an Apple iPad and a Samsung Galaxy Tab. Apple introduced the iPad in April 2010, and Samsung introduced the Galaxy Tab in November 2010; seven months is a long time in the world of high-tech gadgets. Apple products have become very fashionable, and if you buy an iPad, you will have access to many more applications—or "apps"—that can increase the enjoyability and productivity of your tablet. One strategy Samsung can use to overcome those advantages is to compete based on price and value. Would you choose to buy a Galaxy Tab if it had a lower price than an iPad? If your income increased, would it affect your decision about which tablet to buy? As you read the chapter, see if you can answer these questions. You can check your answers against those we provide **page 91** at the end of this chapter.

At the end of the chapter, we use the chapter concepts to answer the questions asked at the beginning of the chapter.

Continued from page 69

Economics in Your Life

Will You Buy an Apple iPad or a Samsung Galaxy Tab?

At the beginning of the chapter, we asked you to consider two questions: Would you choose to buy a Samsung Galaxy Tab tablet if it had a lower price than an Apple iPad? and Would your decision be affected if your income increased? To determine the answer to the first question, you have to recognize that the iPad and the Galaxy Tab are substitutes. If you consider the two tablets to be very close substitutes, then you are likely to buy the one with the lower price. In the market, if consumers generally believe that iPad and the Galaxy Tab are close substitutes, a fall in the price of the iPad will increase the quantity of iPads demanded and decrease the demand for Galaxy Tabs. Suppose that you are currently leaning toward buying the Galaxy Tab because its price is lower than the price of the iPad. If an increase in your income would cause you to change your decision and buy the iPad, then the Galaxy Tab is an inferior good for you.

The following are examples of the topics we cover in the *Economics in Your Life* feature:

- Will you buy an Apple iPad or a Samsung Galaxy tablet? (Chapter 3, "Where Prices Come From: The Interaction of Demand and Supply")
- Do corporate managers act in the best interests of shareholders? (Chapter 6, "Firms, the Stock Market, and Corporate Governance.")
- Is an employer likely to cut your pay during a recession? (Chapter 13, "Aggregate Demand and Aggregate Supply Analysis")

Solved Problems

Many students have great difficulty handling applied economics problems. We help students overcome this hurdle by including two or three worked-out problems tied to select chapter-opening learning objectives. Our goals are to keep students focused on the main ideas of each chapter and to give students a model of how to solve an economic problem by breaking it down step by step. Additional exercises in the end-of-chapter *Problems and Applications* section are tied to every *Solved Problem*. Additional *Solved Problems* appear in the Instructor's Manual and the print Study Guide. In addition, the Test Item Files include problems tied to the *Solved Problems* in the main book.

Don't Let This Happen to You

We know from many years of teaching which concepts students find most difficult. Each chapter contains a box feature called *Don't Let This Happen to You* that alerts students to the most common pitfalls in that chapter's material. We follow up with a related question in the end-of-chapter *Problems and Applications* section.

Making the Connection

Each chapter includes two to four *Making the Connection* features that provide real-world reinforcement of key concepts and help students learn how to interpret what they read on the Web and in newspapers. Most *Making the Connection* features use relevant, stimulating, and provocative news stories focused on businesses and policy issues. One-third of the *Making the Connection* features are new to this edition, and most others have been updated. Several *Making the Connection* features discuss health care, which remains a pressing policy issue. Each *Making the Connection* has at least one

Don't Let This Happen to You

Remember: A Change in a Good's Price Does *Not* Cause the Demand or Supply Curve to Shift

Suppose a student is asked to draw a demand and supply graph to illustrate how an increase in the price of oranges would affect the market for apples, other variables being constant. He draws the graph on the left below and explains it as follows: "Because apples and oranges are substitutes, an increase in the price of oranges will cause an initial shift to the right in the demand curve for apples, from D_1 to D_2. However, because this initial shift in the demand curve for apples results in a higher price for apples, P_2, consumers will find apples less desirable, and the demand curve will shift to the left, from D_2 to D_3, resulting in a final equilibrium price of P_3." Do you agree or disagree with the student's analysis?

You should disagree. The student has correctly understood that an increase in the price of oranges will cause the demand curve for apples to shift to the right. But the second

demand curve shift the student describes, from D_2 to D_3, will not take place. Changes in the price of a product do not result in shifts in the product's demand curve. Changes in the price of a product result only in movements along a demand curve.

The graph on the right below shows the correct analysis. The increase in the price of oranges causes the demand curve for apples to increase from D_1 to D_2. At the original price, P_1, the increase in demand initially results in a shortage of apples equal to $Q_3 - Q_1$. But, as we have seen, a shortage causes the price to increase until the shortage is eliminated. In this case, the price will rise to P_2, where the quantity demanded and the quantity supplied are both equal to Q_2. Notice that the increase in price causes a decrease in the *quantity demanded*, from Q_3 to Q_2, but does *not* cause a decrease in demand.

MyEconLab

Your Turn: Test your understanding by doing related problems 4.13 and 4.14 on pages 98–99 at the end of this chapter.

Making the Connection

Forecasting the Demand for iPads

One of the most important decisions that the managers of any large firm face is which new products to develop. A firm must devote people, time, and money to designing a new product, negotiating with suppliers, formulating a marketing campaign, and many other tasks. But any firm has only limited resources and so faces a trade-off: Resources used to develop one product will not be available to develop another product. Ultimately, the products a firm chooses to develop will be those that it believes will be the most profitable. So, to decide which products to develop, firms need to forecast the demand for those products.

We saw at the beginning of the chapter that in 2001, Bill Gates predicted that within five years, a majority of computers sold would be tablets. If Gates had been correct about the way the computer market was changing, then any computer firm that didn't develop a tablet would have run the risk of being left behind. David Sobotta, who worked at Apple for 20 years and eventually became its national sales manager, has described discussions at Apple during 2002 about whether to develop a tablet. According to Sobotta, representatives of the federal government's National Institutes of Health urged Apple to develop a tablet computer, arguing that it would be particularly useful to doctors, nurses, and hospitals. Apple's managers decided not to develop a tablet, however, because they believed the technology available at that time was too complex for the average computer user and they also believed that the demand from doctors and nurses would be small. As we saw in the chapter opener, Apple's forecast was correct. Despite Bill Gates's prediction, in 2006,

Will the future demand for tablets such as the iPad continue to grow?

supporting end-of-chapter problem to allow students to test their understanding of the topic discussed. Here are some of the new *Making the Connection* features:

- Chapter 2: "A Story of the Market System in Action: How Do You Make an iPad?"
- Chapter 3: "The Aging of the Baby Boom Generation"
- Chapter 9: "How Should We Categorize Unemployment at Bank of America?"
- Chapter 10: "The Connection between Economic Prosperity and Health"
- Chapter 13: "How Long Does It Take to Return to Potential GDP? Economic Forecasts Following the Recession of 2007–2009"
- Chapter 16: "Why Was the Recession of 2007–2009 So Severe?"
- Chapter 19: "Can the Euro Survive?"

Graphs and Summary Tables

Graphs are an indispensable part of a principles of economics course but are a major stumbling block for many students. Every chapter except Chapter 1 includes end-of-chapter problems that require students to draw, read, and interpret graphs. Interactive graphing exercises appear on the book's supporting Web site. We use four devices to help students read and interpret graphs:

1. Detailed captions
2. Boxed notes

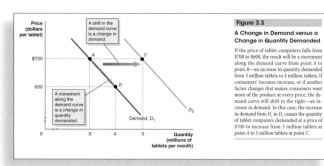

Figure 3.3

A Change in Demand versus a Change in Quantity Demanded

If the price of tablet computers falls from $700 to $600, the result will be a movement along the demand curve from point A to point B—an increase in quantity demanded from 3 million tablets to 4 million tablets. If consumers' incomes increase, or if another factor changes that makes consumers want more of the product at every price, the demand curve will shift to the right—an increase in demand. In this case, the increase in demand from D_1 to D_2 causes the quantity of tablet computers demanded at a price of $700 to increase from 3 million tablets at point A to 5 million tablets at point C.

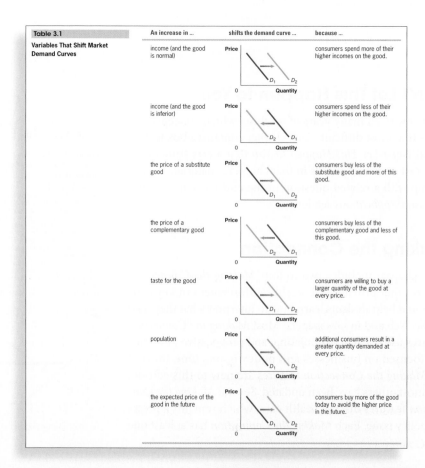

Table 3.1	An increase in ...	shifts the demand curve ...	because ...
Variables That Shift Market Demand Curves	income (and the good is normal)		consumers spend more of their higher incomes on the good.
	income (and the good is inferior)		consumers spend less of their higher incomes on the good.
	the price of a substitute good		consumers buy less of the substitute good and more of this good.
	the price of a complementary good		consumers buy less of the complementary good and less of this good.
	taste for the good		consumers are willing to buy a larger quantity of the good at every price.
	population		additional consumers result in a greater quantity demanded at every price.
	the expected price of the good in the future		consumers buy more of the good today to avoid the higher price in the future.

3. Color-coded curves
4. Summary tables with graphs (see pages 76, 81, and 425 for examples)

Review Questions and Problems and Applications— Grouped by Learning Objective to Improve Assessment

All the end-of-chapter material—*Summary, Review Questions,* and *Problems and Applications*—is grouped under learning objectives. The goals of this organization are to make it easier for instructors to assign problems based on learning objectives, both in the book and in MyEconLab, and to help students efficiently review material that they find difficult. If students have difficulty with a particular learning objective, an instructor can easily identify which end-of-chapter questions and problems support that objective and assign them as homework or discuss them in class. Every exercise in a chapter's *Problems and Applications* section is available in MyEconLab. Using MyEconLab, students can complete these and many other exercises online, get tutorial help, and receive instant feedback and assistance on exercises they answer incorrectly. Also, student learning will be enhanced by having the summary material and problems grouped together by learning objective, which will allow students to focus on the parts of the chapter they found most challenging. Each major section of the chapter, paired with a learning objective, has at least two review questions and three problems.

As in the previous editions, we include one or more end-of-chapter problems that test students' understanding of the content presented in the *Solved Problem, Making the Connection,* and *Don't Let This Happen to You* special features in the chapter. Instructors can cover a feature in class and assign the corresponding problem for homework. The Test Item Files also include test questions that pertain to these special features.

Integrated Supplements

The authors and Pearson Education/Prentice Hall have worked together to integrate the text, print, and media resources to make teaching and learning easier.

MyEconLab is a unique online course management, testing, and tutorial resource.

MyEconLab

For the Instructor

Instructors can choose how much or how little time to spend setting up and using MyEconLab. Here is a snapshot of what instructors are saying about MyEconLab:

"MyEconLab offers [students] a way to practice every week. They receive immediate feedback and a feeling of personal attention. As a result, my teaching has become more targeted and efficient."—Kelly Blanchard, Purdue University

"Students tell me that offering them MyEconLab is almost like offering them individual tutors."—Jefferson Edwards, Cypress Fairbanks College

"MyEconLab's eText is great—particularly in that it helps offset the skyrocketing cost of textbooks. Naturally, students love that."—Doug Gehrke, Moraine Valley Community College

Each chapter contains two preloaded homework exercise sets that can be used to build an individualized study plan for each student. These study plan exercises contain tutorial resources, including instant feedback, links to the appropriate learning objective in the eText, pop-up definitions from the text, learning objective summaries, and step-by-step guided solutions, where appropriate. After the initial setup of the course by the instructor, student use of these materials requires no further instructor setup. The online grade book records each student's performance and time spent on the tests and study plan and generates reports by student or by chapter.

Alternatively, instructors can fully customize MyEconLab to match their course exactly, including reading assignments, homework assignments, video assignments, current news assignments, and quizzes and tests. Assignable resources include:

- Preloaded homework exercise sets for each chapter that include the student tutorial resources mentioned above
- Preloaded quizzes for each chapter that are unique to the text and not repeated in the study plan or homework exercise sets
- Study plan problems that are similar to the end-of-chapter problems and numbered exactly like the book to make assigning homework easier
- *Economics in the News* articles that are updated weekly with appropriate exercises
- ABC News clips, which explore current economic applications and policy issues, along with exercises
- Real-Time Data Exercises continuously update with real-time data.
- **Real-Time Data** The real-time data problems are new. These problems load the latest available data from FRED, a comprehensive up-to-date data set maintained by the Federal Reserve Bank of St. Louis. The questions are graded with feedback in exactly the same way as those based on static data.
- **Experiments in MyEconLab** Experiments are a fun and engaging way to promote active learning and mastery of important economic concepts. Pearson's Experiments program is flexible and easy for instructors and students to use.
  - Single-player experiments allow your students to play against virtual players from anywhere at anytime so long as they have an Internet connection.
  - Multiplayer experiments allow you to assign and manage a real-time experiment with your class.
  - Pre- and post-questions for each experiment are available for assignment in MyEconLab.

For a complete list of available experiments, visit **www.myeconlab.com**

- Test Item File questions that allow you to assign quizzes or homework that will look just like your exams
- Econ Exercise Builder, which allows you to build your own customized exercises

Exercises include multiple-choice, graph drawing, and free-response items, many of which are generated algorithmically so that each time a student works them, a different variation is presented.

MyEconLab grades every problem type except essays, even problems with graphs. When working homework exercises, students receive immediate feedback, with links to additional learning tools.

Customization and Communication

MyEconLab in MyLab/Mastering provides additional optional customization and communication tools. Instructors who teach distance-learning courses or very large lecture sections find the MyLab/Mastering format useful because they can upload course documents and assignments, customize the order of chapters, and use communication features such as Document Sharing, Chat, ClassLive, and Discussion Board.

For the Student

MyEconLab puts students in control of their learning through a collection of testing, practice, and study tools tied to the online, interactive version of the textbook and other media resources. Here is a snapshot of what students are saying about MyEconLab:

"It was very useful because it had EVERYTHING, from practice exams to exercises to reading. Very helpful."—student, Northern Illinois University

"I would recommend taking the quizzes on MyEconLab because it gives you a true account of whether or not you understand the material."—student, Montana Tech

"It made me look through the book to find answers, so I did more reading."—student, Northern Illinois University

Students can study on their own, or they can complete assignments created by their instructor. In MyEconLab's structured environment, students practice what they learn, test their understanding, and pursue a personalized study plan generated from their performance on sample tests and from quizzes created by their instructors. In Homework or Study Plan mode, students have access to a wealth of tutorial features, including:

- Instant feedback on exercises that helps students understand and apply the concepts

- Links to the eText to promote reading of the text just when the student needs to revisit a concept or an explanation

- Step-by-step guided solutions that force students to break down a problem in much the same way an instructor would do during office hours

- Pop-up summaries of the appropriate learning objective to remind students of key ideas while studying

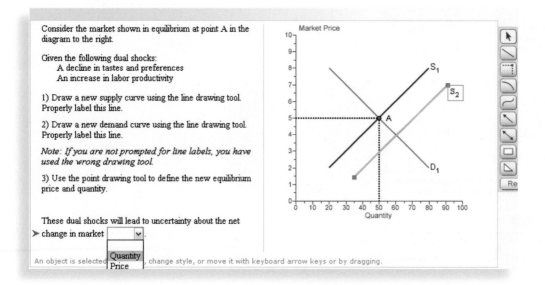

- Pop-up key term definitions from the eText to help students master the vocabulary of economics

- Links to the important features of the eText, such as *Solved Problem*, *Making the Connection*, *An Inside Look*, and *Don't Let This Happen to You*

- A graphing tool that is integrated into the various exercises to enable students to build and manipulate graphs to better understand how concepts, numbers, and graphs connect

Additional MyEconLab Tools

MyEconLab includes the following additional features:

- **eText**—In addition to the portions of eText available as pop-ups or links, a fully searchable eText is available for students who wish to read and study in a fully electronic environment.

- **Print upgrade**—For students who wish to complete assignments in MyEconLab but read in print, Pearson offers registered MyEconLab users a loose-leaf version of the print text at a significant discount.

- **Glossary flashcards**—Every key term is available as a flashcard, allowing students to quiz themselves on vocabulary from one or more chapters at a time.

- **MySearchLab**—Research **MySearchLab** provides extensive help on the research process and four exclusive databases of credible and reliable source material, including the *New York Times*, the *Financial Times*, and peer-reviewed journals.

MyEconLab content has been created through the efforts of Chris Annala, State University of New York–Geneseo; Charles Baum, Middle Tennessee State University; Carol Dole, Jacksonville University; Sarah Ghosh, University of Scranton; Satyajit Ghosh, University of Scranton; Melissa Honig, Pearson Education; Woo Jung, University of Colorado; Courtney Kamauf, Pearson Education; Chris Kauffman, University of Tennessee–Knoxville; Russell Kellogg, University of Colorado–Denver; Noel Lotz, Pearson Education; Katherine McCann, University of Delaware; Daniel Mizak, Frostburg State University; Christine Polek, University of Massachusetts–Boston; Mark Scanlan, Stephen F. Austin State University; Leonie L. Stone, State University of New York–Geneseo; and Bert G. Wheeler, Cedarville University.

Other Resources for the Instructor

Instructor's Manual

Edward Scahill of the University of Scranton prepared the Instructor's Manual, which includes chapter-by-chapter summaries grouped by learning objectives, teaching outlines incorporating key terms and definitions, teaching tips, topics for class discussion, new *Solved Problems*, new *Making the Connection* features, new *Economics in Your Life* scenarios, and solutions to all review questions and problems in the book. The Instructor's Manual is available in print and for download from the Instructor's Resource Center (**www.pearsonhighered.com/hubbard**). The authors, Harry Ellis of the University of North Texas, and Robert Gillette of the University of Kentucky prepared the solutions to the end-of-chapter review questions and problems.

Two Test Item Files

Randy Methenitis of Richland College prepared two Test Item Files. Each Test Item File includes 2,000 multiple-choice, true/false, short-answer, and graphing questions. There are questions to support each key feature in the book. The Test Item Files are available in print and for download from the Instructor's Resource Center (www.pearsonhighered.com/hubbard). Test questions are annotated with the following information:

- **Difficulty:** 1 for straight recall, 2 for some analysis, 3 for complex analysis
- **Type:** multiple-choice, true/false, short-answer, essay
- **Topic:** the term or concept the question supports
- **Learning outcome**
- **AACSB** (see description that follows)
- **Page number**
- **Special feature in the main book:** chapter-opening business example, *Economics in Your Life*, *Solved Problem*, *Making the Connection*, *Don't Let This Happen to You*, and *An Inside Look*

The Association to Advance Collegiate Schools of Business (AACSB)

The Test Item File author has connected select questions to the general knowledge and skill guidelines found in the AACSB Assurance of Learning Standards.

What Is the AACSB?

AACSB is a not-for-profit corporation of educational institutions, corporations, and other organizations devoted to the promotion and improvement of higher education in business administration and accounting. A collegiate institution offering degrees in business administration or accounting may volunteer for AACSB accreditation review. The AACSB makes initial accreditation decisions and conducts periodic reviews to promote continuous quality improvement in management education. Pearson Education is a proud member of the AACSB and is pleased to provide advice to help you apply AACSB Assurance of Learning Standards.

What Are AACSB Assurance of Learning Standards?

One of the criteria for AACSB accreditation is the quality of curricula. Although no specific courses are required, the AACSB expects a curriculum to include learning experiences in the following categories of Assurance of Learning Standards:

- Communication
- Ethical Reasoning
- Analytic Skills
- Use of Information Technology
- Multicultural and Diversity
- Reflective Thinking

Questions that test skills relevant to these standards are tagged with the appropriate standard. For example, a question testing the moral questions associated with externalities would receive the Ethical Reasoning tag.

How Can Instructors Use the AACSB Tags?

Tagged questions help you measure whether students are grasping the course content that aligns with the AACSB guidelines noted above. This in turn may suggest enrichment activities or other educational experiences to help students achieve these skills.

TestGen

The computerized TestGen package allows instructors to customize, save, and generate classroom tests. The test program permits instructors to edit, add, or delete questions from the Test Item Files; analyze test results; and organize a database of tests and student results. This software allows for extensive flexibility and ease of use. It provides many options for organizing and displaying tests, along with search and sort features. The software and the Test Item Files can be downloaded from the Instructor's Resource Center (www.pearsonhighered.com/hubbard).

PowerPoint Lecture Presentation

Three sets of PowerPoint slides, prepared by Fernando Quijano, Dickinson State University, are available:

1. A comprehensive set of PowerPoint slides can be used by instructors for class presentations or by students for lecture preview or review. These slides include all the graphs, tables, and equations in the textbook. Two versions are available—step-by-step mode, in which you can build graphs as you would on a blackboard, and automated mode, in which you use a single click per slide.

2. A comprehensive set of PowerPoint slides have Classroom Response Systems (CRS) questions built in so that instructors can incorporate CRS "clickers" into their classroom lectures. For more information on Pearson Education's partnership with CRS, see the description below. Instructors can download these PowerPoint presentations from the Instructor's Resource Center (www.pearsonhighered.com/hubbard).

3. A student version of the PowerPoint slides is available as .pdf files. This version allows students to print the slides and bring them to class for note taking. Instructors can download these PowerPoint presentations from the Instructor's Resource Center (www.pearsonhighered.com/hubbard).

Instructor's Resource Disk

The Instructor's Resource Disk contains all the faculty and student resources that support this text. Instructors can access and edit the Instructor's Manual, Test Item Files, TestGen files, and PowerPoint presentations. By simply clicking a chapter, faculty can access an interactive library of resources. They can then pick and choose from the various supplements and export them to their hard drives.

Classroom Response Systems

Classroom Response Systems (CRS) is an exciting new wireless polling technology that increases the interactivity of large and small classrooms by enabling instructors to pose questions to their students, record results, and display the results instantly. Students can answer questions easily, using compact remote-control transmitters. Pearson Education has partnerships with leading CRS providers and can show you everything you need to know about setting up and using CRS. Pearson Education will provide the classroom hardware, text-specific PowerPoint slides, software, and support, and will also show you how your students can benefit! Please contact your local Pearson Education sales representative for more information.

Blackboard and WebCT Course Content

Pearson Education offers fully customizable course content for the Blackboard and WebCT Course Management Systems.

Other Resources for the Student

In addition to MyEconLab, Pearson provides the following resources.

Study Guide

Jim Lee of Texas A&M University, Corpus Christi, prepared the Study Guide, which reinforces the textbook and provides students with the following resources:

- Chapter summary
- Discussion of each learning objective
- Section-by-section review of the concepts presented
- Helpful study hints
- Additional *Solved Problems* to supplement those in the text
- Key terms with definitions
- A self-test, including 40 multiple-choice questions plus a number of short-answer and true/false questions, with accompanying answers and explanations

PowerPoint Slides

For student use as a study aid or note-taking guide, PowerPoint slides, prepared by Fernando Quijano, Dickinson State University, and Shelly Tefft, can be downloaded from MyEconLab or the Instructor's Resource Center and made available to students. The slides include:

- All graphs, tables, and equations in the text
- Figures in step-by-step mode and automated modes, using a single click per graph curve
- End-of-chapter key terms with hyperlinks to relevant slides

Instructors

CourseSmart goes beyond traditional expectations, providing instant online access to the textbooks and course materials you need, at a lower cost to students. And, even as students save money, you can save time and hassle with a digital textbook that allows you to search the most relevant content at the very moment you need it. Whether it's evaluating textbooks or creating lecture notes to help students with difficult concepts, CourseSmart can make life a little easier. See how when you visit www.coursesmart.com.

Students

CourseSmart goes beyond traditional expectations, providing instant, online access to the textbooks and course materials students need, at lower cost. They can also search, highlight, and take notes anywhere, any time. See all the benefits to students at www.coursesmart.com.

Consultant Board, Accuracy Review Board, and Reviewers

The guidance and recommendations of the following instructors helped us develop the revision plans for the fourth edition and the supplements package. While we could not incorporate every suggestion from every consultant board member, reviewer, or accuracy checker, we do thank each and every one of you and acknowledge that your feedback was indispensable in developing this text. We greatly appreciate your assistance in making this the best text it could be; you have helped teach a whole new generation of students about the exciting world of economics.

Consultant Board

Sherman T. Folland, Oakland University
Robert Gillette, University of Kentucky
William Goffe, State University of New York–Oswego
Edward Scahill, University of Scranton
Stephen Snyder, University of Pittsburgh
Robert Whaples, Wake Forest University

Accuracy Review Board

Our accuracy checkers did a particularly painstaking and thorough job of helping us proof the graphs, equations, and features of the text and the supplements. We are grateful for their time and commitment:

Fatma Abdel-Raouf, Goldey-Beacom College
Cynthia Bansak, St. Lawrence University
Kelly Hunt Blanchard, Purdue University
Harry Ellis, University of North Texas
Mark Gius, Quinnipiac University
William Goffe, State University of New York–Oswego
Anthony Gyapong, Pennsylvania State University
Randy Methenitis, Richland College
David Mitch, University of Maryland–Baltimore County
Fernando Quijano, Dickinson State University
Ratha Ramoo, Diablo Valley College
Edward Scahill, University of Scranton
Michael Stone, Quinnipiac University
Arlena Sullivan, Jones County Junior College
Julianne Treme, University of North Carolina
  –Wilmington

Reviewers

The guidance and thoughtful recommendations of many instructors helped us develop and implement a revision plan that expanded the book's content, improved the figures, and strengthened assessment features. We extend special thanks to Edward Scahill of the University of Scranton for helping us revise the chapter openers, to Randy Methenitis of Richland College for helping us revise the *An Inside Look* feature, and to Robert Gillette of the University of Kentucky for helping us revise the end-of-chapter questions. We are grateful for the comments and many helpful suggestions received from the following reviewers:

Sindy Abadie, Southwest Tennessee Community College
Shawn Abbott, College of the Siskiyous
Bradley Andrew, Juniata College
Rita Balaban, University of North Carolina
Annette Chamberlin, National College
James D'Angelo, Xavier University
Alexander Deshkovski, North Carolina Central University
Kirk Doran, University of Notre Dame
Debbie Evercloud, University of Colorado–Denver
Lydia Gan, School of Business, University of North
  Carolina–Pembroke
Edgar Ghossoub, University of Texas at San Antonio
Scott Houser, Colorado School of Mines
Peng Huang, Ripon College
James Ibe, Morris College
Jean Kujawa, Lourdes College
Larry Landrum, Virginia Western Community College
Jim Lee, Texas A&M University–Corpus Christi
Solomon Namala, Cerritos College
Eugene Bempong Nyantakyi, West Virginia University
Curtis Price, University of Southern Indiana
Bobby Puryear, North Carolina State University
Denis Raihall, West Chester University
Robert Rycroft, University of Mary Washington
Peter Schuhmann, University of North Carolina–
  Wilmington
Abdulhamid Sukar, Cameron University
Yaqin Wang, Youngstown State University
Tara Westerhold, Western Illinois University
Anne Williams, Gateway Community College

Previous Edition Class Testers, Accuracy Reviewers, and Consultants

Class Testers

We are grateful to both the instructors who class-tested manuscript of the first edition and their students for providing clear-cut recommendations on how to make chapters interesting, relevant, and comprehensive:

Charles A. Bennett, Gannon University

Anne E. Bresnock, University of California–Los Angeles, and California State Polytechnic University–Pomona

Linda Childs-Leatherbury, Lincoln University, Pennsylvania

John Eastwood, Northern Arizona University

David Eaton, Murray State University

Paul Elgatian, St. Ambrose University

Patricia A. Freeman, Jackson State University

Robert Godby, University of Wyoming

Frank Gunter, Lehigh University

Ahmed Ispahani, University of LaVerne

Brendan Kennelly, Lehigh University and National University of Ireland–Galway

Ernest Massie, Franklin University

Carol McDonough, University of Massachusetts–Lowell

Shah Mehrabi, Montgomery College

Sharon Ryan, University of Missouri–Columbia

Bruce G. Webb, Gordon College

Madelyn Young, Converse College

Susan Zumas, Lehigh University

Accuracy Review Boards

We are grateful to the following accuracy checkers of the previous editions for their hard work on the book and supplements:

Fatma Abdel-Raouf, Goldey-Beacom College

Anne Alexander, University of Wyoming

Mohammad Bajwa, Northampton Community College

Hamid Bastin, Shippensburg University

Kelly Hunt Blanchard, Purdue University

Don Bumpass, Sam Houston State University

Charles Callahan III, State University of New York–Brockport

Mark S. Chester, Reading Area Community College

Kenny Christianson, Binghamton University

Ishita Edwards, Oxnard College

Harold Elder, University of Alabama

Harry Ellis, University of North Texas

Can Erbil, Brandeis University

Marc Fusaro, Arkansas Tech University

Sarah Ghosh, University of Scranton

Robert Gillette, University of Kentucky

Maria Giuili, Diablo Valley College

Robert Godby, University of Wyoming

William L. Goffe, State University of New York–Oswego

Travis Hayes, University of Tennessee–Chattanooga

Carol Hogan, University of Michigan–Dearborn

Anisul M. Islam, University of Houston–Downtown

Aaron Jackson, Bentley College

Nancy Jianakoplos, Colorado State University

Thomas C. Kinnaman, Bucknell University

Mary K. Knudson, University of Iowa

Faik A. Koray, Louisiana State University

Stephan Kroll, California State University–Sacramento

Tony Lima, California State University–East Bay

Randy Methenitis, Richland College

Normal C. Miller, Miami University

David Mitch, University of Maryland–Baltimore County

James A. Moreno, Blinn College

Michael Potepan, San Francisco State University

Mary L. Pranzo, California State University–Fresno

Matthew Rafferty, Quinnipiac University

Jeff Reynolds, Northern Illinois University

Brian Rosario, University of California–Davis

Joseph M. Santos, South Dakota State University

Edward Scahill, University of Scranton

Mark V. Siegler, California State University–Sacramento

Rachel Small, University of Colorado–Boulder

Stephen Smith, Bakersfield College

Rajeev Sooreea, Pennsylvania State University–Altoona

Rebecca Stein, University of Pennsylvania

Ed Steinberg, New York University

Arlena Sullivan, Jones County Junior College

Wendine Thompson–Dawson, University of Utah

Robert Whaples, Wake Forest University

Consultant Boards

We received guidance from a dedicated consultant board during the development of the previous editions at several critical junctures. We relied on the board for input on content, figure treatment, and design:

Kate Antonovics, University of California–San Diego

Robert Beekman, University of Tampa

Valerie Bencivenga, University of Texas–Austin

Kelly Blanchard, Purdue University

Susan Dadres, Southern Methodist University

Harry Ellis, Jr., University of North Texas

Robert Gillette, University of Kentucky
Robert Godby, University of Wyoming
William L. Goffe, State University of New York–Oswego
Jane S. Himarios, University of Texas–Arlington
Donn M. Johnson, Quinnipiac University
Mark Karscig, Central Missouri State University
Jenny Minier, University of Kentucky
David Mitch, University of Maryland–Baltimore County
Nicholas Noble, Miami University
Michael Potepan, San Francisco State University
Matthew Rafferty, Quinnipiac University
Helen Roberts, University of Illinois–Chicago
Robert Rosenman, Washington State University
Joseph M. Santos, South Dakota State University
Martin C. Spechler, Indiana University–Purdue University Indianapolis
Robert Whaples, Wake Forest University
Jonathan B. Wight, University of Richmond

Reviewers

The guidance and recommendations of the following instructors helped us shape the previous editions.

ALABAMA
Doris Bennett, Jacksonville State University
Harold W. Elder, University of Alabama–Tuscaloosa
Wanda Hudson, Alabama Southern Community College
Edward Merkel, Troy University
James L. Swofford, University of Southern Alabama

ARIZONA
Doug Conway, Mesa Community College
John Eastwood, Northern Arizona University
Price Fishback, University of Arizona

ARKANSAS
Jerry Crawford, Arkansas State University
Marc Fusaro, Arkansas Tech University
Randall Kesselring, Arkansas State University
Dan Marburger, Arkansas State University

CALIFORNIA
Renatte Adler, San Diego State University
Ercument Aksoy, Los Angeles Valley College
Maneeza Aminy, Golden Gate University
Kate Antonovics, University of California–San Diego
Becca Arnold, Mesa College
Asatar Bair, City College of San Francisco
Diana Bajrami, College of Alameda
Robert Bise, Orange Coast Community College
Victor Brajer, California State University–Fullerton
Anne E. Bresnock, University of California–Los Angeles, and California State Polytechnic University–Pomona
David Brownstone, University of California–Irvine

Maureen Burton, California State Polytechnic University–Pomona
Anoshua Chaudhuri, San Francisco State University
James G. Devine, Loyola Marymount University
Jose Esteban, Palomar College
Roger Frantz, San Diego State University
Craig Gallet, California State University–Sacramento
Andrew Gill, California State University–Fullerton
Maria Giuili, Diablo Valley College
Julie Gonzalez, University of California–Santa Cruz
Lisa Grobar, California State University–Long Beach
Steve Hamilton, California State University–Fullerton
Dewey Heinsma, Mt. San Jacinto Community College
Jessica Howell, California State University–Sacramento
Greg Hunter, California State University–Pomona
John Ifcher, Santa Clara University
Ahmed Ispahani, University of LaVerne
George A. Jouganatos, California State University–Sacramento
Jonathan Kaplan, California State University–Sacramento
Leland Kempe, California State University–Fresno
Philip King, San Francisco State University
Lori Kletzer, University of California, Santa Cruz
Stephan Kroll, California State University–Sacramento
David Lang, California State University–Sacramento
Carsten Lange, California State Polytechnic University–Pomona
Don Leet, California State University–Fresno
Rose LeMont, Modesto Junior College
Tony Lima, California State University–East Bay
Solina Lindahl, California Polytechnic State University–San Luis Obispo
Roger Mack, DeAnza College
Michael Marlow, California Polytechnic State University
Kristen Monaco, California State University–Long Beach
W. Douglas Morgan, University of California, Santa Barbara
Nivedita Mukherji, Oakland University
Andrew Narwold, University of San Diego
Hanna Paulson, West Los Angeles College
Joseph M. Pogodzinksi, San Jose State University
Michael J. Potepan, San Francisco State University
Mary L. Pranzo, California State University–Fresno
Sasha Radisich, Glendale Community College
Ratha Ramoo, Diablo Valley College
Scott J. Sambucci, California State University–East Bay
Ariane Schauer, Marymount College
Frederica Shockley, California State University–Chico
Mark Siegler, California State University–Sacramento
Jonathan Silberman, Oakland University
Lisa Simon, California Polytechnic State University–San Louis Obispo
Stephen Smith, Bakersfield College

Rodney B. Swanson, University of California–Los Angeles

Martha Stuffler, Irvine Valley College

Lea Templer, College of the Canyons

Kristin A. Van Gaasbeck, California State University–Sacramento

Va Nee Van Vleck, California State University–Fresno

Michael Visser, Sonoma State University

Steven Yamarik, California State University–Long Beach

Guy Yamashiro, California State University–Long Beach

Kevin Young, Diablo Valley College

Anthony Zambelli, Cuyamaca College

COLORADO

Mohammed Akacem, Metropolitan State College of Denver

Rhonda Corman, University of Northern Colorado

Dale DeBoer, University of Colorado–Colorado Springs

Karen Gebhardt, Colorado State University

Murat Iyigun, University of Colorado at Boulder

Nancy Jianakoplos, Colorado State University

Jay Kaplan, University of Colorado–Boulder

William G. Mertens, University of Colorado–Boulder

Rachael Small, University of Colorado–Boulder

Stephen Weiler, Colorado State University

CONNECTICUT

Christopher P. Ball, Quinnipiac University

Mark Gius, Quinnipiac University

Donn M. Johnson, Quinnipiac University

Robert Martel, University of Connecticut

Judith Mills, Southern Connecticut State University

Matthew Rafferty, Quinnipiac University

Christian Zimmermann, University of Connecticut

DISTRICT OF COLUMBIA

Colleen Callahan, American University

Robert Feinberg, American University

Walter Park, American University

DELAWARE

Fatma Abdel-Raouf, Goldey-Beacom College

Ali Ataiifar, Delaware County Community College

Andrew T. Hill, University of Delaware

FLORIDA

Herman Baine, Broward Community College

Robert L. Beekman, University of Tampa

Eric P. Chiang, Florida Atlantic University

Martine Duchatelet, Barry University

Hadley Hartman, Santa Fe Community College

Richard Hawkins, University of West Florida

Brad Kamp, University of South Florida

Brian Kench, University of Tampa

Thomas McCaleb, Florida State University

Barbara A. Moore, University of Central Florida

Augustine Nelson, University of Miami

Jamie Ortiz, Florida Atlantic University

Deborah Paige, Santa Fe Community College

Robert Pennington, University of Central Florida

Bob Potter, University of Central Florida

Jerry Schwartz, Broward Community College–North

William Stronge, Florida Atlantic University

Nora Underwood, University of Central Florida

Zhiguang Wang, Florida International University

Joan Wiggenhorn, Barry University

GEORGIA

Greg Brock, Georgia Southern University

Donna Fisher, Georgia Southern University

Shelby Frost, Georgia State University

John King, Georgia Southern University

Constantin Ogloblin, Georgia Southern University

Dr. Greg Okoro, Georgia Perimeter College–Clarkston

Michael Reksulak, Georgia Southern University

Bill Yang, Georgia Southern University

IDAHO

Cynthia Hill, Idaho State University

Don Holley, Boise State University

Tesa Stegner, Idaho State University

ILLINOIS

Teshome Abebe, Eastern Illinois University

Ali Akarca, University of Illinois–Chicago

Zsolt Becsi, Southern Illinois University–Carbondale

James Bruehler, Eastern Illinois University

Louis Cain, Loyola University Chicago and Northwestern University

Rosa Lea Danielson, College of DuPage

Kevin Dunagan, Oakton Community College

Scott Gilbert, Southern Illinois University

Rajeev K. Goel, Illinois State University

David Gordon, Illinois Valley Community College

Alan Grant, Eastern Illinois University

Rik Hafer, Southern Illinois University–Edwardsville

Alice Melkumian, Western Illinois University

Christopher Mushrush, Illinois State University

Jeff Reynolds, Northern Illinois University

Helen Roberts, University of Illinois–Chicago

Thomas R. Sadler, Western Illinois University

Eric Schulz, Northwestern University

Dennis Shannon, Southwestern Illinois College

Charles Sicotte, Rock Valley Community College

Neil T. Skaggs, Illinois State University

Kevin Sylwester, Southern Illinois University–Carbondale

Wendine Thompson-Dawson, Monmouth College

Mark Witte, Northwestern University

Laurie Wolff, Southern Illinois University–Carbondale

Paula Worthington, Northwestern University

INDIANA

Kelly Blanchard, Purdue University

Cecil Bohanon, Ball State University

Thomas Gresik, University of Notre Dame

Robert B. Harris, Indiana University–Purdue University, Indianapolis

Fred Herschede, Indiana University–South Bend

John Pomery, Purdue University

Rob Rude, Ivy Tech Community College

James K. Self, Indiana University–Bloomington

Esther-Mirjam Sent, University of Notre Dame

Virginia Shingleton, Valparaiso University

Martin C. Spechler, Indiana University–Purdue University Indianapolis

Arun K. Srinivasan, Indiana University–Southeast Campus

Geetha Suresh, Purdue University–West Lafayette

IOWA

Terry Alexander, Iowa State University

Paul Elgatian, St. Ambrose University

Jennifer Fuhrman, University of Iowa

Ken McCormick, University of Northern Iowa

Andy Schuchart, Iowa Central Community College

John Solow, University of Iowa

Jonathan Warner, Dordt College

KANSAS

Guatam Bhattacharya, University of Kansas

Amanda Freeman, Kansas State University

Dipak Ghosh, Emporia State University

Alan Grant, Baker University

Wayne Oberle, St. Ambrose University

Jodi Messer Pelkowski, Wichita State University

Martin Perline, Wichita State University

Joel Potter, Kansas State University

Joshua Rosenbloom, University of Kansas

Shane Sanders, Kansas State University

Bhavneet Walia, Kansas State University

KENTUCKY

Tom Cate, Northern Kentucky University

Nan-Ting Chou, University of Louisville

David Eaton, Murray State University

Ann Eike, University of Kentucky

Robert Gillette, University of Kentucky

Barry Haworth, University of Louisville

Gail Hoyt, University of Kentucky

Donna Ingram, Eastern Kentucky University

Waithaka Iraki, Kentucky State University

Hak Youn Kim, Western Kentucky University

Martin Milkman, Murray State University

Jenny Minier, University of Kentucky

David Shideler, Murray State University

John Vahaly, University of Louisville

LOUISIANA

Lara Gardner, Southeastern Louisiana University

Jay Johnson, Southeastern Louisiana University

Faik Koray, Louisiana State University

Paul Nelson, University of Louisiana–Monroe

Sung Chul No, Southern University and A&M College

Tammy Parker, University of Louisiana–Monroe

Wesley A. Payne, Delgado Community College

Nancy Rumore, University of Louisiana at Lafayette

MARYLAND

Carey Borkoski, Anne Arundel Community College

Kathleen A. Carroll, University of Maryland–Baltimore County

Jill Caviglia-Harris, Salisbury University

Dustin Chambers, Salisbury University

Karl Einolf, Mount Saint Mary's University

Marsha Goldfarb, University of Maryland–Baltimore City

Bruce Madariaga, Montgomery College

Shah Mehrabi, Montgomery College

Gretchen Mester, Anne Arundel Community College

David Mitch, University of Maryland–Baltimore County

John Neri, University of Maryland

Henry Terrell, University of Maryland

MASSACHUSETTS

William L. Casey, Jr., Babson College

Arthur Schiller Casimir, Western New England College

Michael Enz, Western New England College

Can Erbil, Brandeis University

Lou Foglia, Suffolk University

Gerald Friedman, University of Massachusetts

Todd Idson, Boston University

Aaron Jackson, Bentley College

Russell A. Janis, University of Massachusetts–Amherst

Anthony Laramie, Merrimack College

Carol McDonough, University of Massachusetts–Lowell

William O'Brien, Worcester State College

Ahmad Saranjam, Bridgewater State College

Howard Shore, Bentley College

Janet Thomas, Bentley College

Gregory H. Wassall, Northeastern University

Bruce G. Webb, Gordon College

Gilbert Wolpe, Newbury College

Jay Zagorsky, Boston University

MICHIGAN

Eric Beckman, Delta College

Jared Boyd, Henry Ford Community College

Victor Claar, Hope College

Dr. Sonia Dalmia, Grand Valley State University

Daniel Giedeman, Grand Valley State University

Steven Hayworth, Eastern Michigan University

Gregg Heidebrink, Washtenaw Community College

Carol Hogan, University of Michigan–Dearborn

Marek Kolar, Delta College

Susan J. Linz, Michigan State University

James Luke, Lansing Community College

Ilir Miteza, University of Michigan–Dearborn

John Nader, Grand Valley State University

Norman P. Obst, Michigan State University
Laudo M. Ogura, Grand Valley State University
Robert J. Rossana, Wayne State University
Michael J. Ryan, Western Michigan University
Charles A. Stull, Kalamazoo College
Michael J. Twomey, University of Michigan–Dearborn
Mark Wheeler, Western Michigan University
Wendy Wysocki, Monroe County Community College

MINNESOTA

Mary Edwards, Saint Cloud State University
Phillip J. Grossman, Saint Cloud State University
Monica Hartman, University of St. Thomas
Matthew Hyle, Winona State University
David J. O'Hara, Metropolitan State University–Minneapolis
Kwang Woo (Ken) Park, Minnesota State University–Mankato
Artatrana Ratha, Saint Cloud State University
Ken Rebeck, Saint Cloud State University
Katherine Schmeiser, University of Minnesota

MISSISSIPPI

Becky Campbell, Mississippi State University
Randall Campbell, Mississippi State University
Patricia A. Freeman, Jackson State University
Arlena Sullivan, Jones County Junior College

MISSOURI

Chris Azevedo, University of Central Missouri
Ariel Belasen, Saint Louis University
Catherine Chambers, University of Central Missouri
Paul Chambers, University of Central Missouri
Kermit Clay, Ozarks Technical Community College
Ben Collier, Northwest Missouri State University
John R. Crooker, University of Central Missouri
Jo Durr, Southwest Missouri State University
Julie H. Gallaway, Southwest Missouri State University
Terrel Gallaway, Southwest Missouri State University
Mark Karscig, Central Missouri State University
Nicholas D. Peppes, Saint Louis Community College–Forest Park
Steven T. Petty, College of the Ozarks
Sharon Ryan, University of Missouri–Columbia
Ben Young, University of Missouri–Kansas City

MONTANA

Agnieszka Bielinska-Kwapisz, Montana State University–Bozeman
Jeff Bookwalter, University of Montana–Missoula

NEBRASKA

Allan Jenkins, University of Nebraska–Kearney
James Knudsen, Creighton University
Craig MacPhee, University of Nebraska–Lincoln
Kim Sosin, University of Nebraska–Omaha
Mark E. Wohar, University of Nebraska–Omaha

NEVADA

Bernard Malamud, University of Nevada–Las Vegas
Bill Robinson, University of Nevada–Las Vegas

NEW HAMPSHIRE

Evelyn Gick, Dartmouth College
Neil Niman, University of New Hampshire

NEW JERSEY

Len Anyanwu, Union County College
Maharuk Bhiladwalla, Rutgers University–New Brunswick
Giuliana Campanelli-Andreopoulos, William Paterson University
Gary Gigliotti, Rutgers University–New Brunswick
John Graham, Rutgers University–Newark
Berch Haroian, William Paterson University
Paul Harris, Camden County College
Jeff Rubin, Rutgers University
Henry Ryder, Gloucester County College
Donna Thompson, Brookdale Community College

NEW MEXICO

Donald Coes, University of New Mexico
Kate Krause, University of New Mexico
Curt Shepherd, University of New Mexico

NEW YORK

Seemi Ahmad, Dutchess Community College
Chris Annala, State University of New York–Geneseo
Erol Balkan, Hamilton College
John Bockino, Suffolk County Community College–Ammerman
Charles Callahan III, State University of New York–Brockport
Michael Carew, Baruch College
Sean Corcoran, New York University
Ranjit S. Dighe, City University of New York–Bronx Community College
Debra Dwyer, Stony Brook University
Glenn Gerstner, Saint John's University–Queens
Susan Glanz, Saint John's University–Queens
William L. Goffe, State University of New York–Oswego
Wayne A. Grove, LeMoyne College
Nancy Howe, Hudson Valley Community College
Christopher Inya, Monroe Community College
Ghassan Karam, Pace University
Clifford Kern, State University of New York–Binghamton
Mary Lesser, Iona College
Anna Musatti, Columbia University
Theodore Muzio, St. John's University, New York
Emre Ozsoz, Fashion Institute of Technology
Howard Ross, Baruch College
Ed Steinberg, New York University
Leonie Stone, State University of New York–Geneseo
Ganti Subrahmanyam, University of Buffalo
Jogindar S. Uppal, State University of New York–Albany
Susan Wolcott, Binghamton University

NORTH CAROLINA

Otilia Boldea, North Carolina State University
Robert Burrus, University of North Carolina–Wilmington
Lee A. Craig, North Carolina State University
Kathleen Dorsainvil, Winston–Salem State University
Michael Goode, Central Piedmont Community College
Salih Hakeem, North Carolina Central University
Melissa Hendrickson, North Carolina State University
Haiyong Liu, East Carolina University
Kosmas Marinakis, North Carolina State University
Todd McFall, Wake Forest University
Shahriar Mostashari, Campbell University
Jonathan Phillips, North Carolina State University
Jeff Sarbaum, University of North Carolina–Greensboro
Peter Schuhmann, University of North Carolina–Wilmington
Robert Shoffner, Central Piedmont Community College
Catherine Skura, Sandhills Community College
Carol Stivender, University of North Carolina–Charlotte
Vera Tabakova, East Carolina University
Eric Taylor, Central Piedmont Community College
Hui-Kuan Tseng, University of North Carolina at Charlotte
Robert Whaples, Wake Forest University
John Whitehead, Appalachian State University
Gary W. Zinn, East Carolina University
Rick Zuber, University of North Carolina at Charlotte

OHIO

John P. Blair, Wright State University
Bolong Cao, Ohio University–Athens
Kyongwook Choi, Ohio University
James D'Angelo, University of Cincinnati
Darlene DeVera, Miami University
Tim Fuerst, Bowling Green University
Harley Gill, Ohio State University
Leroy Gill, Ohio State University
Steven Heubeck, Ohio State University
Daniel Horton, Cleveland State University
Ernest Massie, Franklin University
Ida A. Mirzaie, Ohio State University
Jay Mutter, University of Akron
Mike Nelson, University of Akron
Nicholas Noble, Miami University
Dennis C. O'Neill, University of Cincinnati
Joseph Palardy, Youngstown State University
Charles Reichheld, Cuyahoga Community College
Teresa Riley, Youngstown State University
Rochelle Ruffer, Youngstown State University
Kate Sheppard, University of Akron
Richard Stratton, University of Akron
Albert Sumell, Youngstown State University
Steve Szheghi, Wilmington College

Melissa Thomasson, Miami University
Yaqin Wang, Youngstown State University
Bert Wheeler, Cedarville University
Kathryn Wilson, Kent State University
Sourushe Zandvakili, University of Cincinnati

OKLAHOMA

David Hudgins, University of Oklahoma
Bill McLean, Oklahoma State University
Denny Myers, Oklahoma City Community College
Ed Price, Oklahoma State University
Abdulhamid Sukar, Cameron University

OREGON

Bill Burrows, Lane Community College
Tom Carroll, Central Oregon Community College
Tim Duy, University of Oregon
B. Starr McMullen, Oregon State University
Ted Scheinman, Mount Hood Community College
Larry Singell, University of Oregon
Ayca Tekin-Koru, Oregon State University

PENNSYLVANIA

Bradley Andrew, Juniata College
Mohammad Bajwa, Northampton Community College
Gustavo Barboza, Mercyhurst College
Charles A. Bennett, Gannon University
Cynthia Benzing, West Chester University
Howard Bodenhorn, Lafayette College
Milica Bookman, St. Joseph's University
Robert Brooker, Gannon University
Eric Brucker, Widener University
Linda Childs-Leatherbury, Lincoln University
Scott J. Dressler, Villanova University
Satyajit Ghosh, University of Scranton
Anthony Gyapong, Pennsylvania State University–Abington
Mehdi Haririan, Bloomsburg University
Andrew Hill, Federal Reserve Bank of Philadelphia
Steven Husted, University of Pittsburgh
James Jozefowicz, Indiana University of Pennsylvania
Stephanie Jozefowicz, Indiana University of Pennsylvania
Nicholas Karatjas, Indiana University of Pennsylvania
Mary Kelly, Villanova University
Brendan Kennelly, Lehigh University
Thomas C. Kinnaman, Bucknell University
Christopher Magee, Bucknell University
Katherine McCann, Penn State
Judy McDonald, Lehigh University
Ranganath Murthy, Bucknell University
Hong V. Nguyen, University of Scranton
Cristian Pardo, Saint Joseph's University
Iordanis Petsas, University of Scranton
Adam Renhoff, Drexel University
Nicole Sadowski, York College of Pennsylvania
Edward Scahill, University of Scranton

Ken Slaysman, York College of Pennsylvania

Rajeev Sooreea, Pennsylvania State University–Altoona

Rebecca Stein, University of Pennsylvania

Sandra Trejos, Clarion University

Peter Zaleski, Villanova University

Ann Zech, Saint Joseph's University

Lei Zhu, West Chester University of Pennsylvania

Susan Zumas, Lehigh University

RHODE ISLAND

Jongsung Kim, Bryant University

Leonard Lardaro, University of Rhode Island

Nazma Latif-Zaman, Providence College

SOUTH CAROLINA

Calvin Blackwell, College of Charleston

Ward Hooker, Orangeburg–Calhoun Technical College

Woodrow W. Hughes, Jr., Converse College

John McArthur, Wofford College

Chad Turner, Clemson University

Madelyn Young, Converse College

SOUTH DAKOTA

Joseph M. Santos, South Dakota State University

Jason Zimmerman, South Dakota State University

TENNESSEE

Sindy Abadie, Southwest Tennessee Community College

Charles Baum, Middle Tennessee State University

John Brassel, Southwest Tennessee Community College

Bichaka Fayissa, Middle Tennessee State University

Michael J. Gootzeit, University of Memphis

Travis Hayes, University of Tennessee–Chattanooga

Christopher C. Klein, Middle Tennessee State University

Leila Pratt, University of Tennessee at Chattanooga

Millicent Sites, Carson-Newman College

TEXAS

Carlos Aguilar, El Paso Community College

Rashid Al-Hmoud, Texas Tech University

William Beaty, Tarleton State University

Klaus Becker, Texas Tech University

Alex Brown, Texas A&M University

Jack A. Bucco, Austin Community College–Northridge and Saint Edward's University

Don Bumpass, Sam Houston State University

Marilyn M. Butler, Sam Houston State University

Mike Cohick, Collin County Community College

Cesar Corredor, Texas A&M University

Steven Craig, University of Houston

Patrick Crowley, Texas A&M University–Corpus Christi

Richard Croxdale, Austin Community College

Susan Dadres, Southern Methodist University

Harry Ellis, Jr., University of North Texas

Paul Emberton, Texas State University

Diego Escobari, Texas A&M University

Nicholas Feltovich, University of Houston–Main

Charles Harold Fifield, Baylor University

Mark Frank, Sam Houston State University

Richard Gosselin, Houston Community College–Central

Sheila Amin Gutierrez de Pineres, University of Texas–Dallas

Tina J. Harvell, Blinn College–Bryan Campus

James W. Henderson, Baylor University

Jane S. Himarios, University of Texas–Arlington

James Holcomb, University of Texas–El Paso

Jamal Husein, Angelo State University

Ansul Islam, University of Houston–Downtown

Karen Johnson, Baylor University

Kathy Kelly, University of Texas–Arlington

Thomas Kemp, Tarrant County College–Northwest

Jim Lee, Texas A&M University–Corpus Christi

Ronnie W. Liggett, University of Texas–Arlington

Akbar Marvasti, University of Houston–Downtown

James Mbata, Houston Community College

Kimberly Mencken, Baylor University

Randy Methenitis, Richland College

Carl Montano, Lamar University

James Moreno, Blinn College

Camille Nelson, Texas A & M University

Michael Nelson, Texas A&M University

Charles Newton, Houston Community College–Southwest College

John Pisciotta, Baylor University

Sara Saderion, Houston Community College–Southwest College

George E. Samuels, Sam Houston State University

David Schutte, Mountain View College

Ivan Tasic, Texas A&M University

David Torres, University of Texas–El Paso

Ross vanWassenhove, University of Houston

Roger Wehr, University of Texas–Arlington

Jim Wollscheid, Texas A&M University–Kingsville

J. Christopher Wreh, North Central Texas College

David W. Yoskowitz, Texas A&M University–Corpus Christi

Inske Zandvliet, Brookhaven College

UTAH

Chris Fawson, Utah State University

Lowell Glenn, Utah Valley State College

Aric Krause, Westminster College

Arden Pope, Brigham Young University

VERMONT

Nancy Brooks, University of Vermont

VIRGINIA

Lee Badgett, Virginia Military Institute

Lee A. Coppock, University of Virginia

Janelle Davenport, Hampton University

Philip Heap, James Madison University

George E. Hoffer, Virginia Commonwealth University

Oleg Korenok, Virginia Commonwealth University

Frances Lea, Germanna Community College

Carrie Meyer, George Mason University

John Min, Northern Virginia Community College

James Roberts, Tidewater Community College–Virginia Beach

Araine A. Schauer, Mary Mount College

Sarah Stafford, The College of William & Mary

Bob Subrick, James Madison University

Susanne Toney, Hampton University

Michelle Vachris, Christopher Newport University

James Wetzel, Virginia Commonwealth University

George Zestos, Christopher Newport University

WASHINGTON

Andrew Ewing, University of Washington

Stacey Jones, Seattle University

Dean Peterson, Seattle University

Robert Rosenman, Washington State University

WEST VIRGINIA

Jacqueline Agesa, Marshall University

Richard Agesa, Marshall University

WISCONSIN

Marina Karabelas, Milwaukee Area Technical College

Elizabeth Sawyer Kelly, University of Wisconsin–Madison

Pascal Ngoboka, University of Wisconsin–River Falls

Kevin Quinn, St. Norbert College

John R. Stoll, University of Wisconsin–Green Bay

WYOMING

Robert Godby, University of Wyoming

DISTRICT OF COLUMBIA

Leon Battista, American Enterprise Institute

Michael Bradley, George Washington University

Colleen M. Callahan, American University

INTERNATIONAL

Minh Quang Dao, Carleton University–Ottawa, Canada

A Word of Thanks

Once again, we benefited greatly from the dedication and professionalism of the Pearson Economics team. Executive Editor David Alexander's energy and support were indispensable. David helped mold the presentation and provided words of encouragement whenever our energy flagged. Executive Development Editor Lena Buonanno worked tirelessly to ensure that this text was as good as it could be and to coordinate the many moving parts involved in a project of this magnitude. This new edition posed particular challenges, and we remain astonished at the amount of time, energy, and unfailing good humor she brings to this project. As we worked on the first edition, Director of Key Markets David Theisen provided invaluable insight into how best to structure a principles text. His advice helped shape nearly every chapter. We have worked with Executive Marketing Manager Lori DeShazo on three different books: principles of economics, money and banking, and intermediate macroeconomics, and we continue to be amazed at her energy and creativity in promoting the field of economics. Steve Deitmer, Director of Development, brought sound judgment to the many decisions required to create this book. Alison Eusden and Lindsey Sloan managed the extensive supplement package that accompanies the book. Carla Thompson, Kristin Ruscetta, and Jonathan Boylan turned our manuscript pages into a beautiful published book. We received excellent research assistance from Ed Timmons, Matthew Saboe, David Van Der Goes, and Jason Hockenberry. We thank Pam Smith, Elena Zeller, and Jennifer Brailsford for their careful proofreading of first- and second-round page proofs.

A good part of the burden of a project of this magnitude is borne by our families. We appreciate the patience, support, and encouragement of our wives and children.

Economics:
Foundations and Models

Chapter Outline and Learning Objectives

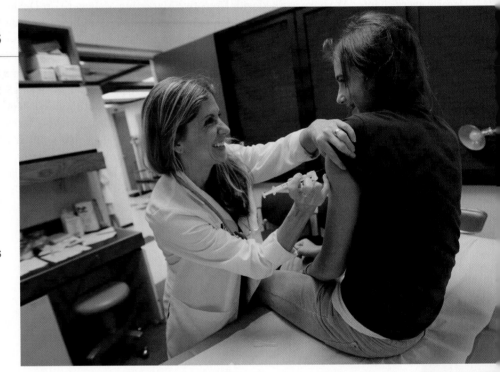

Why Are Some Doctors Leaving Private Practice?

When you visit a doctor's office, you probably don't think of it as a small business, but that's what it is. Like other businesspeople, a doctor hires workers—nurses, physician's assistants, and receptionists—and buys or rents machinery and equipment. A doctor's income represents the profits from his or her practice, or the difference between the revenue received from patients and their health insurance plans and the costs to the doctor of wages, rent, loans, and insurance. For many years, the typical doctor operated his or her practice either alone or in partnership with other doctors. Lately, though, an increasing number of doctors have given up their practices and become salaried employees of hospitals. Although as recently as 2002 more than three times as many medical practices were owned by doctors as by hospitals, by 2008 more medical practices were owned by hospitals.

The movement of many doctors from running their own businesses to being salaried employees of hospitals is due to changes occurring within the U.S. health care system. Soaring health care costs have led many private health care insurers, as well as the federal and state governments, to reduce the payments they make to doctors in return for treating patients. President Barack Obama's package of health care changes, sometimes referred to as "Obamacare," was passed by Congress in 2010 and is being gradually phased in through 2014. The package will result in major changes in how some people will receive health insurance and how doctors will be compensated. Policymakers are also considering changes to Medicare, the federal government program that provides health care to people over age 65, because the costs of the program have been rising very rapidly. Over time, these changes have increased the amount of paperwork doctors must complete in order to be paid for treating patients. This paperwork has raised the costs doctors incur in running their practices, which makes becoming a salaried employee of a hospital more attractive.

Throughout this book, we will see that many policy issues, including changes in the U.S. medical system, involve economics. In fact, knowledge of economics can help you to better understand and analyze many policy issues.

AN INSIDE LOOK on **page 20** discusses how health professionals may be delaying retirement because they are concerned about their finances.

Based on Robert Kocher, M.D., and Nikhil R. Sahni, "Hospitals' Race to Employ Physicians—The Logic Behind a Money-Losing Proposition," *New England Journal of Medicine*, May 12, 2011; and Uwe E. Reinhardt, "Producing More Primary-Care Doctors," *New York Times*, June 10, 2011.

Economics in Your Life

Will There Be Plenty of Jobs Available in the Health Care Industry?

The U.S. Health Resources and Services Administration (HRSA) forecasts that the number of doctors in the United States will increase from about 808,000 in 2010 to 866,400 in 2020. But the HRSA also forecasts that the number of doctors needed to provide patient care will rise from about 805,000 in 2010 to 922,000 in 2020. In other words, this federal government agency forecasts that there will be a shortage of about 56,000 doctors in 2020. The U.S. Bureau of Labor Statistics projects that four of the six fastest growing occupations over the next 10 years will be in the medical field. It would seem that plenty of jobs should be available in health care during the next few years. But the availability of these jobs depends on the reliability of the forecasts. What is the basis for the forecasts on the availability of jobs in health care, and how reliable are the forecasts? As you read this chapter, see if you can answer this question. You can check your answer against the one we provide on **page 18** at the end of this chapter.

I n this book, we use economics to answer questions such as the following:

- How are the prices of goods and services determined?
- How does pollution affect the economy, and how should government policy deal with these effects?
- Why do firms engage in international trade, and how do government policies affect international trade?
- Why does government control the prices of some goods and services, and what are the effects of those controls?

Economists do not always agree on the answers to every question. In fact, as we will see, economists engage in lively debate on some issues. In addition, new problems and issues are constantly arising. So, economists are always at work developing new methods to analyze economic questions.

Scarcity A situation in which unlimited wants exceed the limited resources available to fulfill those wants.

All the issues we discuss in this book illustrate a basic fact of life: People must make choices as they try to attain their goals. We must make choices because we live in a world of **scarcity**, which means that although our wants are unlimited, the resources available to fulfill those wants are limited. You might like to own a BMW and spend each summer in five-star European hotels, but unless Bill Gates is a close and generous relative, you probably lack the money to fulfill these dreams. Every day, you make choices as you spend your limited income on the many goods and services available. The finite amount of time you have also limits your ability to attain your goals. If you spend an hour studying for your economics midterm, you have one hour less to study for your history midterm. Firms and the government are in the same situation as you: They also must attain their goals with limited resources. **Economics** is the study of the choices consumers, business managers, and government officials make to attain their goals, given their scarce resources.

Economics The study of the choices people make to attain their goals, given their scarce resources.

We begin this chapter by discussing three important economic ideas that we will return to many times in this book: *People are rational, people respond to incentives, and optimal decisions are made at the margin.* Then we consider the three fundamental questions that any economy must answer: *What* goods and services will be produced? *How* will the goods and services be produced? and *Who* will receive the goods and services produced? Next, we consider the role of *economic models* in analyzing economic issues. **Economic models** are simplified versions of reality used to analyze real-world economic situations. We will explore why economists use models and how they construct them. Finally, we will discuss the difference between microeconomics and macroeconomics, and we will preview some important economic terms.

Economic model A simplified version of reality used to analyze real-world economic situations.

1.1 LEARNING OBJECTIVE

Explain these three key economic ideas: People are rational, people respond to incentives, and optimal decisions are made at the margin.

Market A group of buyers and sellers of a good or service and the institution or arrangement by which they come together to trade.

Three Key Economic Ideas

As you try to achieve your goals, whether they involve buying a new computer or finding a part-time job, you will interact with other people in *markets*. A **market** is a group of buyers and sellers of a good or service and the institution or arrangement by which they come together to trade. Most of economics involves analyzing what happens in markets. Throughout this book, as we study how people make choices and interact in markets, we will return to three important ideas:

1. People are rational.
2. People respond to economic incentives.
3. Optimal decisions are made at the margin.

People Are Rational

Economists generally assume that people are rational. This assumption does *not* mean that economists believe everyone knows everything or always makes the "best" decision. It means that economists assume that consumers and firms use all available information as they act to achieve their goals. Rational individuals weigh the benefits and costs of each action, and they choose an action only if the benefits outweigh the costs. For example, if Microsoft charges a price of $239 for a copy of Windows, economists assume that the managers at Microsoft have estimated that a price of $239 will earn Microsoft the most profit. The managers may be wrong; perhaps a price of $265 would be more profitable, but economists assume that the managers at Microsoft have acted rationally, on the basis of the information available to them, in choosing the price. Of course, not everyone behaves rationally all the time. Still, the assumption of rational behavior is very useful in explaining most of the choices that people make.

People Respond to Economic Incentives

Human beings act from a variety of motives, including religious belief, envy, and compassion. Economists emphasize that consumers and firms consistently respond to *economic* incentives. This fact may seem obvious, but it is often overlooked. For example, according to an article in the *Wall Street Journal*, the FBI couldn't understand why banks were not taking steps to improve security in the face of an increase in robberies: "FBI officials suggest that banks place uniformed, armed guards outside their doors and install bullet-resistant plastic, known as a 'bandit barrier,' in front of teller windows." FBI officials were surprised that few banks took their advice. But the article also reported that installing bullet-resistant plastic costs $10,000 to $20,000, and a well-trained security guard receives $50,000 per year in salary and benefits. The average loss in a bank robbery is only about $1,200. The economic incentive to banks is clear: It is less costly to put up with bank robberies than to take additional security measures. FBI agents may be surprised by how banks respond to the threat of robberies—but economists are not.

In each chapter, the *Making the Connection* feature discusses a news story or another application related to the chapter material. Read the following *Making the Connection* for a discussion of whether people respond to economic incentives even when deciding how much to eat and how much exercise to undertake.

| Making the Connection | ## Does Health Insurance Give People an Incentive to Become Obese? |

Obesity is an increasing problem in the United States. The U.S. Centers for Disease Control (CDC) defines obesity for an adult as having a body mass index (BMI) of 30 or greater. The body mass index measures a person's weight relative to the person's height. (The exact formula is: BMI = (Weight in pounds/(Height in inches)^2) $\times$ 703.) A BMI of 30 is equivalent to a person 5'4" being 30 pounds overweight. Obesity is related to a variety of diseases, including heart disease, stroke, diabetes, and hypertension.

The two maps below show the striking increase in obesity in the 15 years between 1994 and 2009. In 1994, in a majority of states the population was between 10 percent and 14 percent obese, and in no state was more than 20 percent of the population obese. By 2009, only in Colorado was less than 20 percent of the population obese, and in about two-thirds of the states, 25 percent or more of the population was obese, including nine states where more than 30 percent of the population was obese.

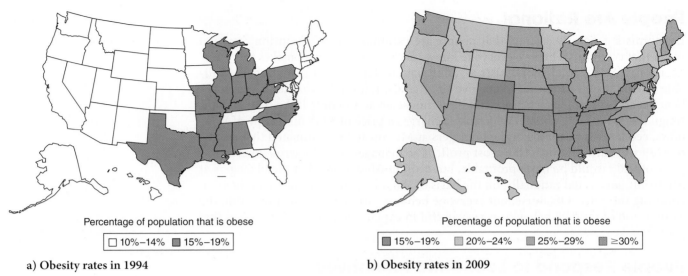

Percentage of population that is obese

☐ 10%–14% ■ 15%–19%

a) Obesity rates in 1994

Percentage of population that is obese

■ 15%–19% ☐ 20%–24% ■ 25%–29% ■ ≥30%

b) Obesity rates in 2009

Data from Centers for Disease Control and Prevention, "Behavior Risk Factor Surveillance System."

Many people who suffer from obesity have underlying medical conditions. For these people, obesity is an unfortunate medical problem that they cannot control. The fact that obesity is increasing, though, indicates that for some people obesity is the result of diet and lifestyle choices. Potential explanations for the increase in obesity include greater intake of high-calorie fast foods, insufficient exercise, and a decline in the physical activity associated with many jobs. The CDC recommends that teenagers get a minimum of 60 minutes of aerobic exercise per day, a standard that only 15 percent of high school students were meeting in 2011. In 1960, 50 percent of jobs in the United States required at least moderate physical activity. By 2010, only 20 percent of jobs did. As a result, the typical worker was burning off about 130 fewer calories per workday.

In addition to eating too much and not exercising enough, could health insurance be a cause of obesity? Obese people tend to suffer more medical problems than do people who are not overweight and so incur higher medical costs. Overweight people with health insurance that will reimburse them for only part of their medical bills or who have no health insurance must pay some or all of these higher medical bills themselves. Overweight people with health insurance that covers most of their medical bills will not suffer as large a monetary cost from being obese. In other words, by reducing some of the costs of obesity, health insurance may give people an economic incentive to gain weight. At first glance, this argument may seem implausible. Some people suffer from medical conditions that can make physical activity difficult or that can cause weight gain even with moderate eating, so they may become overweight whether they have health insurance or not. Some people are overweight due to poor eating habits, and they probably don't consider health insurance when deciding whether to have another slice of chocolate cake or to watch television instead of going to the gym. But if economists are correct about the importance of economic incentives, then we would expect that if we hold all other personal characteristics—such as age, gender, and income—constant, people with health insurance will be more likely to be overweight than people without health insurance.

Jay Bhattacharya and Kate Bundorf of Stanford University, Noemi Pace of University College London, and Neeraj Sood of the RAND Corporation, a research center, have analyzed the effects of health insurance on weight. Using a sample that followed nearly 80,000 people during the years 1989–2004, they found that after controlling for income, education, race, gender, age, and other factors, people with health insurance are significantly more likely to be overweight than are people without health insurance. Having private health insurance increased BMI by 1.3 points, and having public health insurance, such as *Medicaid*, which is a program under which the government provides health care to low-income people, increased BMI by 2.3 points. These findings suggest that people respond to economic incentives even when making decisions about what they eat and how much they exercise.

Based on Centers for Disease Control and Prevention, "Obesity Trends Among U.S. Adults Between 1985 and 2009," www.cdc.gov; Katherine M. Flegal, Margaret D. Caroll, Cynthia L. Ogden, and Lester R. Curtin, "Prevalence and Trends in Obesity Among U.S. Adults, 1999–2008," *Journal of the American Medical Association*, Vol. 303, No. 3, January 20, 2010, pp. 235–41; Jay Bhattacharya, Kate Bundorf, Noemi Pace, and Neeraj Soodin, "Does Health Insurance Make You Fat?" in Michael Grossman and Naci H. Mocan, eds., *Economic Aspects of Obesity*, (Chicago: University of Chicago Press, 2011); and Tara Parker-Pope, "Less Active at Work, Americans Have Packed on Pounds," *New York Times*, May 25, 2011.

Your Turn: Test your understanding by doing related problems 1.5 and 1.6 on page 22 at the end of this chapter.   MyEconLab

Optimal Decisions Are Made at the Margin

Some decisions are "all or nothing": For instance, when an entrepreneur decides whether to open a new restaurant, she either starts the new restaurant or she doesn't. When you decide whether to enter graduate school or to take a job, you either enter graduate school or you don't. But rather than being all or nothing, most decisions in life involve doing a little more or a little less. If you are trying to decrease your spending and increase your saving, the decision is not really between saving all the money you earn or spending it all. Rather, many small choices are involved, such as whether to buy a caffè mocha at Starbucks every day or just three times per week.

Economists use the word *marginal* to mean "extra" or "additional." Should you watch another hour of TV or spend that hour studying? The *marginal benefit* (or, in symbols, *MB*) of watching more TV is the additional enjoyment you receive. The *marginal cost* (or *MC*) is the lower grade you receive from having studied a little less. Should Apple produce an additional 300,000 iPhones? Firms receive *revenue* from selling goods. Apple's marginal benefit is the additional revenue it receives from selling 300,000 more iPhones. Apple's marginal cost is the additional cost—for wages, parts, and so forth—of producing 300,000 more iPhones. *Economists reason that the optimal decision is to continue any activity up to the point where the marginal benefit equals the marginal cost—in symbols, where* MB = MC. Often we apply this rule without consciously thinking about it. Usually you will know whether the additional enjoyment from watching a television program is worth the additional cost involved in not spending that hour studying, without giving the decision a lot of thought. In business situations, however, firms often have to make careful calculations to determine, for example, whether the additional revenue received from increasing production is greater or less than the additional cost of the production. Economists refer to analysis that involves comparing marginal benefits and marginal costs as **marginal analysis**.

In each chapter of this book, you will see the special feature *Solved Problem*. This feature will increase your understanding of the material by leading you through the steps of solving an applied economic problem. After reading the problem, you can test your understanding by working the related problems that appear at the end of the chapter and in the study guide that accompanies this book. You can also complete Solved Problems on **www.myeconlab.com** and receive tutorial help.

Marginal analysis Analysis that involves comparing marginal benefits and marginal costs.

Solved Problem 1.1

A Doctor Makes a Decision at the Margin

A doctor is considering keeping her office open 9 hours per day rather than 8 hours. The doctor's office manager argues, "Keeping the office open an extra hour is a good idea because your practice will make a total profit of $300,000 per year when the office is open 9 hours per day." Do you agree with the office manager's reasoning? What, if any, additional information do you need to decide whether the doctor should keep her office open an additional hour per day?

Solving the Problem

Step 1: **Review the chapter material.** This problem is about making decisions, so you may want to review the section "Optimal Decisions Are Made at the Margin," which begins on page 7.

Step 2: **Explain whether you agree with the manager's reasoning.** We have seen that any activity should be continued to the point where the marginal benefit is equal to the marginal cost. In this case, that involves a doctor continuing to keep her office open up to the point where the additional revenue she receives from seeing more patients is equal to the marginal cost of keeping her office open an additional hour. The office manager has not done a marginal analysis, so you should not agree with the manager's reasoning. The statement about the total profit of keeping the office open for 9 hours is not relevant to the decision of whether to stay open an additional hour.

Step 3: **Explain what additional information you need.** You will need additional information to make a correct decision. You will need to know the marginal revenue and the marginal cost of keeping the practice open an extra hour. The marginal revenue would depend on how many more patients the doctor can see in the extra hour. The marginal cost would include the additional salary to be paid to the office staff, any additional medical supplies that would be used, as well as any additional electricity or other utilities. The doctor would also need to take into account the nonmonetary cost of spending another hour working rather than spending time with her family and friends or in other leisure activities.

MyEconLab   **Your Turn:** For more practice, do related problems 1.7, 1.8, and 1.9 on page 23 at the end of this chapter.

1.2 LEARNING OBJECTIVE

Discuss how an economy answers these questions: What goods and services will be produced? How will the goods and services be produced? Who will receive the goods and services produced?

Trade-off The idea that because of scarcity, producing more of one good or service means producing less of another good or service.

Opportunity cost The highest-valued alternative that must be given up to engage in an activity.

The Economic Problem That Every Society Must Solve

Because we live in a world of scarcity, any society faces the *economic problem* that it has only a limited amount of economic resources—such as workers, machines, and raw materials—and so can produce only a limited amount of goods and services. Therefore, every society faces **trade-offs**: Producing more of one good or service means producing less of another good or service. In fact, the best way to measure the cost of producing a good or service is the value of what has to be given up to produce it. The **opportunity cost** of any activity—such as producing a good or service—is the highest-valued alternative that must be given up to engage in that activity. The concept of opportunity cost is very important in economics and applies to individuals as much as it does to firms or to society as a whole. Consider the example of a doctor who could receive a salary of $100,000 per year working as an employee of a hospital but decides to open his own private practice instead. In that case, the opportunity cost of the physician services he supplies to his own firm is the $100,000 he gives up by not working for the hospital, even if he does not explicitly pay himself a salary.

Trade-offs force society to make choices when answering the following three fundamental questions:

1. *What* goods and services will be produced?
2. *How* will the goods and services be produced?
3. *Who* will receive the goods and services produced?

Throughout this book, we will return to these questions many times. For now, we briefly introduce each question.

What Goods and Services Will Be Produced?

How will society decide whether to produce more economics textbooks or more Blu-ray players? More daycare facilities or more football stadiums? Of course, "society" does not make decisions; only individuals make decisions. The answer to the question of what will be produced is determined by the choices that consumers, firms, and the government make. Every day, you help decide which goods and services firms will produce when you choose to buy an iPhone instead of a BlackBerry or a caffè mocha rather than a chai tea. Similarly, Apple must choose whether to devote its scarce resources to making more iPhones or more iPad tablet computers. The federal government must choose whether to spend more of its limited budget on breast cancer research or on repairing highways. In each case, consumers, firms, and the government face the problem of scarcity by trading off one good or service for another. And each choice made comes with an opportunity cost, measured by the value of the best alternative given up.

How Will the Goods and Services Be Produced?

Firms choose how to produce the goods and services they sell. In many cases, firms face a trade-off between using more workers or using more machines. For example, a local service station has to choose whether to provide car repair services using more diagnostic computers and fewer auto mechanics or more auto mechanics and fewer diagnostic computers. Similarly, movie studios have to choose whether to produce animated films using highly skilled animators to draw them by hand or fewer animators and more computers. In deciding whether to move production offshore to China, firms may need to choose between a production method in the United States that uses fewer workers and more machines and a production method in China that uses more workers and fewer machines.

Who Will Receive the Goods and Services Produced?

In the United States, who receives the goods and services produced depends largely on how income is distributed. Individuals with the highest income have the ability to buy the most goods and services. Often, people are willing to give up some of their income—and, therefore, some of their ability to purchase goods and services—by donating to charities to increase the incomes of poorer people. Each year, Americans donate about $300 billion to charity, or an average donation of $2,650 for each household in the country. An important policy question, however, is whether the government should intervene to make the distribution of income more equal. Such intervention already occurs in the United States, because people with higher incomes pay a larger fraction of their incomes in taxes and because the government makes payments to people with low incomes. There is disagreement over whether the current attempts to redistribute income are sufficient or whether there should be more or less redistribution.

Centrally Planned Economies versus Market Economies

Centrally planned economy An economy in which the government decides how economic resources will be allocated.

Market economy An economy in which the decisions of households and firms interacting in markets allocate economic resources.

To answer the three questions—what, how, and who—societies organize their economies in two main ways. A society can have a **centrally planned economy** in which the government decides how economic resources will be allocated. Or a society can have a **market economy** in which the decisions of households and firms interacting in markets allocate economic resources.

From 1917 to 1991, the most important centrally planned economy in the world was that of the Soviet Union, which was established when Vladimir Lenin and the Communist Party staged a revolution and took over the Russian Empire. In the Soviet Union, the government decided what goods to produce, how the goods would be produced, and who would receive the goods. Government employees managed factories and stores. The objective of these managers was to follow the government's orders rather than to satisfy the wants of consumers. Centrally planned economies like that of the Soviet Union have not been successful in producing low-cost, high-quality goods and services. As a result, the standard of living of the average person in a centrally planned economy tends to be low. All centrally planned economies have also been political dictatorships. Dissatisfaction with low living standards and political repression finally led to the collapse of the Soviet Union in 1991. Today, only a few small countries, such as Cuba and North Korea, still have completely centrally planned economies.

All the high-income democracies, such as the United States, Canada, Japan, and the countries of Western Europe, have market economies. Market economies rely primarily on privately owned firms to produce goods and services and to decide how to produce them. Markets, rather than the government, determine who receives the goods and services produced. In a market economy, firms must produce goods and services that meet the wants of consumers, or the firms will go out of business. In that sense, it is ultimately consumers who decide what goods and services will be produced. Because firms in a market economy compete to offer the highest-quality products at the lowest price, they are under pressure to use the lowest-cost methods of production. For example, in the past 10 years, some U.S. firms, particularly in the electronics and furniture industries, have been under pressure to reduce their costs to meet competition from Chinese firms.

In a market economy, the income of an individual is determined by the payments he receives for what he has to sell. If he is a civil engineer, and firms are willing to pay a salary of $85,000 per year for engineers with his training and skills, that is the amount of income he will have to purchase goods and services. If the engineer also owns a house that he rents out, his income will be even higher. One of the attractive features of markets is that they reward hard work. Generally, the more extensive the training a person has received and the longer the hours the person works, the higher the person's income will be. Of course, luck—both good and bad—also plays a role here, as elsewhere in life. We can conclude that market economies respond to the question "Who receives the goods and services produced?" with the answer "Those who are most willing and able to buy them."

The Modern "Mixed" Economy

In the nineteenth and early twentieth centuries, the U.S. government engaged in relatively little regulation of markets for goods and services. Beginning in the middle of the twentieth century, government intervention in the economy dramatically increased in the United States and other market economies. This increase was primarily caused by the high rates of unemployment and business bankruptcies during the Great Depression of the 1930s. Some government intervention was also intended to raise the incomes of the elderly, the sick, and people with limited skills. For example, in the 1930s, the United States established the Social Security system, which provides government payments to retired and disabled workers, and minimum wage legislation, which sets a floor on the wages employers can pay workers in many occupations. In more recent years, government intervention in the economy has also expanded to meet such goals as protection of the environment, the promotion of civil rights, and the provision of medical care to low-income people and the elderly.

Some economists argue that the extent of government intervention makes it no longer accurate to refer to the U.S., Canadian, Japanese, and Western European economies as pure market economies. Instead, they should be referred to as *mixed economies*. A **mixed economy** is still primarily a market economy because most economic decisions result from the interaction of buyers and sellers in markets. However, the government plays a significant role in the allocation of resources. As we will see in later chapters, economists continue to debate the role government should play in a market economy.

One of the most important developments in the international economy in recent years has been the movement of China from being a centrally planned economy to being a more mixed economy. The Chinese economy suffered decades of economic stagnation following the takeover of the government in 1949 by Mao Zedong and the Communist Party. Although China remains a political dictatorship, production of most goods and services is now determined in the market rather than by the government. The result has been rapid economic growth that in the near future may lead to total production of goods and services in China surpassing total production in the United States.

> **Mixed economy** An economy in which most economic decisions result from the interaction of buyers and sellers in markets but in which the government plays a significant role in the allocation of resources.

Efficiency and Equity

Market economies tend to be more efficient than centrally planned economies. There are two types of efficiency: *productive efficiency* and *allocative efficiency*. **Productive efficiency** occurs when a good or service is produced at the lowest possible cost. **Allocative efficiency** occurs when production is in accordance with consumer preferences. Markets tend to be efficient because they promote competition and facilitate voluntary exchange. With **voluntary exchange**, both the buyer and seller of a product are made better off by the transaction. We know that the buyer and seller are both made better off because, otherwise, the buyer would not have agreed to buy the product or the seller would not have agreed to sell it. Productive efficiency is achieved when competition among firms in markets forces the firms to produce goods and services at the lowest cost. Allocative efficiency is achieved when the combination of competition among firms and voluntary exchange between firms and consumers results in firms producing the mix of goods and services that consumers prefer most. Competition will force firms to continue producing and selling goods and services as long as the additional benefit to consumers is greater than the additional cost of production. In this way, the mix of goods and services produced will match consumer preferences.

Although markets promote efficiency, they don't guarantee it. Inefficiency can arise from various sources. To begin with, it may take some time to achieve an efficient outcome. When Blu-ray players were introduced, for example, firms did not instantly achieve productive efficiency. It took several years for firms to discover the lowest-cost method of producing this good. As we will discuss in Chapter 4, governments sometimes reduce efficiency by interfering with voluntary exchange in markets. For example, many governments limit the imports of some goods from foreign countries. This limitation reduces efficiency by keeping goods from being produced at the lowest cost. The production of some goods damages the environment. In this case, government intervention can increase efficiency because without such intervention, firms may ignore the costs of environmental damage and thereby fail to produce the goods at the lowest possible cost.

An economically efficient outcome is not necessarily a desirable one. Many people prefer economic outcomes that they consider fair or equitable, even if those outcomes

> **Productive efficiency** A situation in which a good or service is produced at the lowest possible cost.
>
> **Allocative efficiency** A state of the economy in which production is in accordance with consumer preferences; in particular, every good or service is produced up to the point where the last unit provides a marginal benefit to society equal to the marginal cost of producing it.
>
> **Voluntary exchange** A situation that occurs in markets when both the buyer and seller of a product are made better off by the transaction.

Equity The fair distribution of economic benefits.

are less efficient. **Equity** is harder to define than efficiency, but it usually involves a fair distribution of economic benefits. For some people, equity involves a more equal distribution of economic benefits than would result from an emphasis on efficiency alone. For example, some people support raising taxes on people with higher incomes to provide the funds for programs that aid the poor. Although governments may increase equity by reducing the incomes of high-income people and increasing the incomes of the poor, efficiency may be reduced. People have less incentive to open new businesses, to supply labor, and to save if the government takes a significant amount of the income they earn from working or saving. The result is that fewer goods and services are produced, and less saving takes place. As this example illustrates, *there is often a trade-off between efficiency and equity*. Government policymakers often confront this trade-off.

1.3 LEARNING OBJECTIVE

Understand the role of models in economic analysis.

Economic Models

Economists rely on economic theories, or models (the words *theory* and *model* are used interchangeably), to analyze real-world issues, such as those involved with health care. As mentioned earlier, economic models are simplified versions of reality. Economists are certainly not alone in relying on models: An engineer may use a computer model of a bridge to help test whether it will withstand high winds, or a biologist may make a physical model of a nucleic acid to better understand its properties. One purpose of economic models is to make economic ideas sufficiently explicit and concrete so that individuals, firms, or the government can use them to make decisions. For example, we will see in Chapter 3 that the model of demand and supply is a simplified version of how the prices of products are determined by the interactions among buyers and sellers in markets.

Economists use economic models to answer questions. For example, will the United States have a sufficient number of doctors in 2020? For a complicated question like this one, economists often use several models to examine different aspects of the issue. For example, economists at the U.S. Bureau of Labor Statistics (BLS) build models that allow them to forecast future employment in different occupations. These models allow the BLS to forecast how many doctors there are likely to be at a future date. Economists can use different models to forecast the demand for medical services. Together these models can be used to determine whether there will be a sufficient number of doctors in 2020. As mentioned on page 3, economists at the U.S. Health Resources and Services Administration (HRSA) have used models to forecast that there will be a shortage of about 56,000 doctors in 2020.

Sometimes economists use an existing model to analyze an issue, but in other cases, they must develop a new model. To develop a model, economists generally follow these steps:

1. Decide on the assumptions to use in developing the model.
2. Formulate a testable hypothesis.
3. Use economic data to test the hypothesis.
4. Revise the model if it fails to explain the economic data well.
5. Retain the revised model to help answer similar economic questions in the future.

The Role of Assumptions in Economic Models

Any model is based on making assumptions because models have to be simplified to be useful. We cannot analyze an economic issue unless we reduce its complexity. For example, economic models make behavioral assumptions about the motives of consumers and firms. Economists assume that consumers will buy the goods and services that will maximize their well-being or their satisfaction. Similarly, economists assume that firms act to maximize their profits. These assumptions are simplifications because they do not describe the motives of every consumer and every firm. How can we know if the assumptions in a model are too simplified or too limiting? We discover this when we form hypotheses based on these assumptions and test these hypotheses using real-world information.

Forming and Testing Hypotheses in Economic Models

An **economic variable** is something measurable that can have different values, such as the incomes of doctors. A hypothesis in an economic model is a statement that may be either correct or incorrect about an economic variable. An example of a hypothesis in an economic model is the statement that the falling incomes earned by primary care physicians—often referred to as "family doctors"—will result in a decline in the number of physicians choosing to enter primary care in the United States in 2020. An economic hypothesis is usually about a causal relationship; in this case, the hypothesis states that lower incomes cause, or lead to, fewer doctors entering primary care.

Economic variable Something measurable that can have different values, such as the incomes of doctors.

We have to test a hypothesis before we can accept it. To test a hypothesis, we analyze statistics on the relevant economic variables. In our primary care doctor example, we would gather statistics on the incomes of primary care physicians, the number of primary care physicians, and perhaps other variables as well. Testing a hypothesis can be tricky. For example, showing that the number of primary care physicians declined at a time when the average income of these physicians declined would not be enough to demonstrate that the decline in income *caused* the decline in the number of physicians. Just because two things are correlated—that is, they happen at the same time—does not mean that one caused the other. For example, before entering practice, a doctor spends time in a teaching hospital as a resident in his or her field. Teaching hospitals determine how many residencies they will offer in a particular field. Suppose that teaching hospitals decreased the number of residencies in primary care at the same time that the incomes of primary care physicians were declining. In that case, the declining number of residencies, rather than the declining incomes, might have caused the decline in the number of primary care physicians. Over a period of time, many economic variables change, which complicates the testing of hypotheses. In fact, when economists disagree about a hypothesis, such as the effect of falling incomes on the supply of primary care physicians, it is often because of disagreements over interpreting the statistical analysis used to test the hypothesis.

Note that hypotheses must be statements that could, in principle, turn out to be incorrect. Statements such as "Increasing the number of primary care physicians is good" or "Increasing the number of primary care physicians is bad" are value judgments rather than hypotheses because it is not possible to disprove them.

Economists accept and use an economic model if it leads to hypotheses that are confirmed by statistical analysis. In many cases, the acceptance is tentative, however, pending the gathering of new data or further statistical analysis. In fact, economists often refer to a hypothesis having been "not rejected," rather than having been "accepted," by statistical analysis. But what if statistical analysis clearly rejects a hypothesis? For example, what if a model leads to a hypothesis that declining incomes of primary care physicians will lead to a decline in the number of these physicians, but the data reject this hypothesis? In this case, the model must be reconsidered. It may be that an assumption used in the model was too simplified or too limiting. For example, perhaps the model ignored the fact that primary care physicians were moving from owning their own practices to become salaried employees of hospitals, where they would be freed from the responsibilities involved in running their own businesses. This change in how primary care physicians are employed might explain why the data rejected the hypothesis.

In 2010, the BLS analyzed the accuracy of the projections it had made in 1996 of employment levels in 2006. Some projections were quite accurate, while others were less so. For instance, the BLS had projected that 677,917 physicians and surgeons would be employed in 2006, but actual employment was only 633,292, or about 7 percent less than projected. The error with respect to physician's assistants was much larger, with the projection being that 93,485 physician's assistants would be employed in 2006, but employment was actually only 65,628, or about 30 percent less than expected. Analyzing the errors in these projections helps the BLS to improve the models it uses to make projections of occupational employment.

The process of developing models, testing hypotheses, and revising models occurs not just in economics but also in disciplines such as physics, chemistry, and biology. This process is often referred to as the *scientific method*. Economics is a *social science* because it applies the scientific method to the study of the interactions among individuals.

Normative and Positive Analysis

Throughout this book, as we build economic models and use them to answer questions, we need to bear in mind the distinction between *positive analysis* and *normative analysis*. **Positive analysis** is concerned with *what is*, and **normative analysis** is concerned with *what ought to be*. Economics is about positive analysis, which measures the costs and benefits of different courses of action.

Positive analysis Analysis concerned with what is.

Normative analysis Analysis concerned with what ought to be.

We can use the federal government's minimum wage law to compare positive and normative analysis. In 2012, under this law, it was illegal for an employer to hire a worker at a wage less than $7.25 per hour. Without the minimum wage law, some firms and some workers would voluntarily agree to a lower wage. Because of the minimum wage law, some workers have difficulty finding jobs, and some firms end up paying more for labor than they otherwise would have. A positive analysis of the federal minimum wage law uses an economic model to estimate how many workers have lost their jobs because of the law, its effect on the costs and profits of businesses, and the gains to workers receiving the minimum wage. After economists complete this positive analysis, the decision as to whether the minimum wage law is a good idea or a bad idea is a normative one and depends on how people evaluate the trade-off involved. Supporters of the law believe that the losses to employers and to workers who are unemployed as a result of the law are more than offset by the gains to workers who receive higher wages than they would without the law. Opponents of the law believe the losses are greater than the gains. The assessment by any individual depends, in part, on that person's values and political views. The positive analysis an economist provides would play a role in the decision but can't by itself decide the issue one way or the other.

In each chapter, you will see a *Don't Let This Happen to You* box like the one on the next page. These boxes alert you to common pitfalls in thinking about economic ideas. After reading this box, test your understanding by working the related problem that appears at the end of the chapter.

Economics as a Social Science

Because economics studies the actions of individuals, it is a social science. Economics is therefore similar to other social science disciplines, such as psychology, political science, and sociology. As a social science, economics considers human behavior—particularly decision-making behavior—in every context, not just in the context of business. Economists have studied such issues as how families decide on the number of children to have, why people have difficulty losing weight or attaining other desirable goals, and why people often ignore relevant information when making decisions. Economics also has much to contribute to questions of government policy. As we will see throughout this book, economists have played an important role in formulating government policies in areas such as the environment, health care, and poverty.

Don't Let This Happen to You

Don't Confuse Positive Analysis with Normative Analysis

"Economic analysis has shown that the minimum wage law is a bad idea because it causes unemployment." Is this statement accurate? As of 2012, the federal minimum wage law prevents employers from hiring workers at a wage of less than $7.25 per hour. This wage is higher than some employers are willing to pay some workers. If there were no minimum wage law, some workers who currently cannot find any firm willing to hire them at $7.25 per hour would be able to find employment at a lower wage. Therefore, positive economic analysis indicates that the minimum wage law causes unemployment (although economists disagree about how much unemployment the minimum wage causes). *But*, some of those workers who have jobs benefit from the minimum wage because they are paid a higher wage than they otherwise would be. In other words, the minimum wage law creates both losers (the workers who become unemployed and the firms that have to pay higher wages) and winners (the workers who receive higher wages).

Should we value the gains to the winners more than we value the losses to the losers? The answer to this question involves normative analysis. Positive economic analysis can show the consequences of a particular policy, but it cannot tell us whether the policy is "good" or "bad." So, the statement at the beginning of this box is inaccurate.

MyEconLab

Your Turn: Test your understanding by doing related problem 3.9 on page 25 at the end of this chapter.

Making the Connection | Should Medical School Be Free?

The U.S. population continues to increase, which by itself would increase the demand for medical services. In addition, though, the average age of the population is rising, and older people need more medical care than do younger people. So, over time, the number of doctors needs to increase. As mentioned at the beginning of the chapter, the Health Resources and Services Administration (HRSA) estimates that the number of doctors needed to provide patient care will rise from about 805,000 in 2010 to 922,000 in 2020.

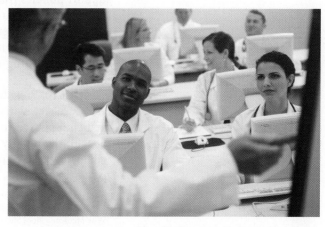

Should these medical students have to pay tuition?

Can we be sure that these additional doctors will be available in 2020? The HRSA forecasts that, in fact, there will be a shortage of 56,000 doctors in 2020. The bulk of that shortage is likely to be in primary care physicians, or family doctors. As we will discuss in later chapters, ordinarily we expect that when consumers want more of a product, higher wages and salaries and more job openings will attract workers to that industry. For example, during the U.S. housing boom of the mid-2000s, the number of workers in the building trades—carpenters, plumbers, roofers, and others—increased rapidly. But producing more doctors is a long process. After completing his or her undergraduate education, a doctor spends four years in medical school and then three to five years at a teaching hospital, pursuing a residency in a particular field of medicine. Apparently convinced that hospitals will not train enough doctors unless they get help, Congress contributes $10 billion per year to teaching hospitals, based on the number of residents they train.

Recently, Peter Bach of the Sloan-Kettering Cancer Center and Robert Kocher of the Brookings Institution have proposed that medical schools should charge no tuition. They argue that nearly all students graduate from medical school owing money on student loans, with the average student owing more than $150,000. We might expect that these debts, although large, would not deter students from applying to medical school, because in 2011, the average income of physicians was more than $250,000 per year. Bach and Kocher argue, though, that the high cost of medical school has two bad outcomes: Some good students do not apply because they either do not want to be saddled with such large debts or because they are unable to borrow sufficient money, and many students avoid going into primary care—where average incomes are $190,000—in favor of specialties such as plastic surgery or anesthesiology—where average incomes are $325,000. Teaching hospitals pay doctors a salary of about $50,000 per year during their residencies. Bach and Kocher propose that hospitals continue to pay residents who pursue primary care but not pay residents who specialize. The money that hospitals would otherwise pay to these residents would be paid to medical schools instead to finance the free tuition. The plan would give residents an incentive to pursue primary care rather than to specialize. Critics of the Bach and Kocher proposal have questioned whether many students capable of being admitted to medical school actually are deterred by medical school tuition. They also question whether many residents who intend to specialize would choose primary care instead, even if specializing means they have to borrow to meet living expenses rather than paying for them with a hospital salary.

Like many other policy debates, the debate over whether changes should be made in how medical school is paid for has positive and normative elements. By gathering data and using economic models, it is possible to assess some of the quantitative claims made by each side in the debate: What role does tuition play in a student's decision about whether to attend medical school? Have tuition increases had a large effect or a small effect on the number of applications to medical school? How do changes in expected future incomes affect the decisions of medical students about which specialty to choose? These are all positive questions, so it is possible to formulate quantitative answers. Ultimately, though, this debate also has a normative element. For instance, some doctors, economists, and policymakers argue that it is important that people living in low-income or rural areas have improved access to health care, so they are willing to support policies that would redirect medical students away from specialized fields and toward primary care. Other doctors, economists, and policymakers believe that medical students who enter specialized fields make a larger contribution to society than do students who enter primary care. A disagreement of this type is unlikely to be resolved by building models and analyzing data because the issue involved is essentially normative.

In 2010, President Obama and Congress enacted the Patient Protection and Affordable Care Act, which made major changes to the U.S. health care system. The changes are being phased in through 2014. Additional changes are likely as policymakers grapple with the rapidly escalating costs of health care. Whether Congress and the president will enact policies intended to increase the number of primary care physicians remains to be seen.

Based on Suzanne Sataline and Shirley S. Wang, "Medical Schools Can't Keep Up," *Wall Street Journal*, April 12, 2010; Uwe E. Reinhardt, "Producing More Primary-Care Doctors," *New York Times*, June 10, 2011; and Peter B. Bach and Robert Kocher, "Why Medical School Should Be Free," *New York Times*, May 28, 2011.

MyEconLab   **Your Turn:** Test your understanding by doing related problem 3.7 on page 25 at the end of this chapter.

1.4 LEARNING OBJECTIVE

Distinguish between microeconomics and macroeconomics.

Microeconomics and Macroeconomics

Economic models can be used to analyze decision making in many areas. We group some of these areas together as *microeconomics* and others as *macroeconomics*. **Microeconomics** is the study of how households and firms make choices, how they interact in markets, and how the government attempts to influence their choices. Microeconomic issues include explaining how consumers react to changes in product prices and how firms decide what prices to charge for the products they sell. Microeconomics also involves policy issues, such as analyzing the most efficient way to reduce teenage smoking, analyzing the costs and benefits of approving the sale of a new prescription drug, and analyzing the most efficient way to reduce air pollution.

Macroeconomics is the study of the economy as a whole, including topics such as inflation, unemployment, and economic growth. Macroeconomic issues include explaining why economies experience periods of recession and increasing unemployment and why, over the long run, some economies have grown much faster than others. Macroeconomics also involves policy issues, such as whether government intervention can reduce the severity of recessions.

The division between microeconomics and macroeconomics is not hard and fast. Many economic situations have *both* a microeconomic and a macroeconomic aspect. For example, the level of total investment by firms in new machinery and equipment helps to determine how rapidly the economy grows—which is a macroeconomic issue. But to understand how much new machinery and equipment firms decide to purchase, we have to analyze the incentives individual firms face—which is a microeconomic issue.

Microeconomics The study of how households and firms make choices, how they interact in markets, and how the government attempts to influence their choices.

Macroeconomics The study of the economy as a whole, including topics such as inflation, unemployment, and economic growth.

A Preview of Important Economic Terms

1.5 LEARNING OBJECTIVE

Define important economic terms.

In the following chapters, you will encounter certain important terms again and again. Becoming familiar with these terms is a necessary step in learning economics. Here we provide a brief introduction to some of these terms. We will discuss them all in greater depth in later chapters:

- **Entrepreneur.**   An *entrepreneur* is someone who operates a business. In a market system, entrepreneurs decide what goods and services to produce and how to produce them. An entrepreneur starting a new business puts his or her own funds at risk. If an entrepreneur is wrong about what consumers want or about the best way to produce goods and services, the entrepreneur's funds can be lost. This is not an unusual occurrence: In the United States, about half of new businesses close within four years. Without entrepreneurs willing to assume the risk of starting and operating businesses, economic progress would be impossible in a market system.

- **Innovation.**   There is a distinction between an *invention* and *innovation*. An *invention* is the development of a new good or a new process for making a good. An *innovation* is the practical application of an invention. (*Innovation* may also be used more broadly to refer to any significant improvement in a good or in the means of producing a good.) Much time often passes between the appearance of a new idea and its development for widespread use. For example, the Wright brothers first achieved self-propelled flight at Kitty Hawk, North Carolina, in 1903, but the Wright brothers' plane was very crude, and it wasn't until the introduction of the DC-3 by Douglas Aircraft in 1936 that regularly scheduled intercity airline flights became common in the United States. Similarly, the first digital electronic computer—the ENIAC—was developed in 1945, but the first IBM personal computer was not introduced until 1981, and widespread use of computers did not have a significant effect on the productivity of U.S. business until the 1990s.

- **Technology.**   A firm's *technology* is the processes it uses to produce goods and services. In the economic sense, a firm's technology depends on many factors, such as the skill of its managers, the training of its workers, and the speed and efficiency of its machinery and equipment.

- **Firm, company, or business.**   A *firm* is an organization that produces a good or service. Most firms produce goods or services to earn profits, but there are also nonprofit firms, such as universities and some hospitals. Economists use the terms *firm*, *company*, and *business* interchangeably.

- **Goods.**   *Goods* are tangible merchandise, such as books, computers, or Blu-ray players.

- *Services.* *Services* are activities done for others, such as providing haircuts or investment advice.

- *Revenue.* A firm's *revenue* is the total amount received for selling a good or service. It is calculated by multiplying the price per unit by the number of units sold.

- *Profit.* A firm's *profit* is the difference between its revenue and its costs. Economists distinguish between *accounting profit* and *economic profit*. In calculating accounting profit, we exclude the cost of some economic resources that the firm does not pay for explicitly. In calculating economic profit, we include the opportunity cost of all resources used by the firm. When we refer to *profit* in this book, we mean economic profit. It is important not to confuse *profit* with *revenue*.

- *Household.* A *household* consists of all persons occupying a home. Households are suppliers of factors of production—particularly labor—used by firms to make goods and services. Households also demand goods and services produced by firms and governments.

- *Factors of production or economic resources.* Firms use factors of production to produce goods and services. The main factors of production are labor, capital, natural resources—including land—and entrepreneurial ability. Households earn income by supplying to firms the factors of production.

- *Capital.* The word *capital* can refer to *financial capital* or to *physical capital*. Financial capital includes stocks and bonds issued by firms, bank accounts, and holdings of money. In economics, though, *capital* refers to physical capital, which includes manufactured goods that are used to produce other goods and services. Examples of physical capital are computers, factory buildings, machine tools, warehouses, and trucks. The total amount of physical capital available in a country is referred to as the country's *capital stock*.

- *Human capital.* Human capital refers to the accumulated training and skills that workers possess. For example, college-educated workers generally have more skills and are more productive than workers who have only high school degrees.

Continued from page 3

Economics in Your Life

Will There Be Plenty of Jobs Available in the Health Care Industry?

At the beginning of the chapter, we posed the question "What is the basis for the forecasts on the availability of jobs in health care, and how reliable are the forecasts?" As the U.S. population increases and as the average age of the population rises, it seems likely that there will be an increase in the numbers of doctors, nurses, physician's assistants, and other health care workers. The U.S. Bureau of Labor Statistics (BLS) publishes the most widely used occupational forecasts. Economists at the BLS base these forecasts on economic models. The forecasts can be inaccurate, however. For example, in 1996, the BLS forecast that 93,485 physician's assistants would be employed in 2006, when in fact only 65,628 were. The BLS analyzes errors like these in attempting to improve its forecasts. So, it is likely that the BLS's forecasts will become more accurate over time, but it would be a mistake to expect the forecasts to be exact.

for firms that have employer-provided health insurance receive lower wages than people working at those firms who are not obese. At firms that do not provide health insurance, obese workers do not receive lower wages than workers who are not obese.

   a. Why might firms that provide workers with health insurance pay a lower wage to obese workers than to workers who are not obese?

   b. Is Bhattacharya and Bundorf's finding relevant to the question of whether health insurance provides people with an incentive to become obese? Briefly explain.

Based on Jay Bhattacharya and M. Kate Bundorf, "The Incidence of the Health Care Costs of Obesity," *Journal of Health Economics*, Vol. 28, No. 3, May 2009, pp. 649–58.

1.7 **[Related to** Solved Problem 1.1 **on page 8]** During 2009, movie studios began to release a substantial number of films in 3-D format. To show films in this format, theater owners have to invest in 3-D equipment that costs $75,000 for each projector. Typically, theater owners can charge about $3 more for a ticket to a 3-D movie than for a movie in the conventional 2-D format. If you owned a movie theater, discuss how you would go about deciding whether to invest in 3-D equipment. How would your analysis change, given information that the proportion of total box-office spending on 3-D movies has been relatively flat since 2009?

Based on Lauren A. E. Schuker, "Can 3-D Save Hollywood?" *Wall Street Journal*, March 20, 2009; and "3D Films Struggle," *The Economist*, July 23–29, 2011.

1.8 **[Related to** Solved Problem 1.1 **on page 8]** Two students are discussing Solved Problem 1.1:

Joe: "I think the key additional information you need to know in deciding whether the doctor should keep the medical practice open 9 hours per day rather than 8 hours is the amount of profit she is currently making while being open 8 hours. Then she can compare the profit earned from being open 9 hours with the profit earned from

being open 8 hours. This information is more important than the additional revenue and additional cost of being open 1 more hour."

Jill: "Actually, Joe, knowing how much profits change when the medical practice stays open 1 more hour is exactly the same as knowing the additional revenue and the additional cost."

   Briefly evaluate their arguments.

1.9 **[Related to** Solved Problem 1.1 **on page 8]** Late in the semester, a friend tells you, "I was going to drop my psychology course so I could concentrate on my other courses, but I had already put so much time into the course that I decided not to drop it." What do you think of your friend's reasoning? Would it make a difference to your answer if your friend has to pass the psychology course at some point to graduate? Briefly explain.

1.10 In a paper written by Bentley College economists Patricia M. Flynn and Michael A. Quinn, the authors state:

> We find evidence that Economics is a good choice of major for those aspiring to become a CEO [chief executive officer]. When adjusting for size of the pool of graduates, those with undergraduate degrees in Economics are shown to have had a greater likelihood of becoming an S&P 500 CEO than any other major.

A list of famous economics majors published by Marietta College includes business leaders Warren Buffett, Donald Trump, Ted Turner, Diane von Furstenberg, and Sam Walton, as well as former presidents George H.W. Bush, Gerald Ford, and Ronald Reagan. Why might studying economics be particularly good preparation for being the top manager of a corporation or a leader in government?

Based on Patricia M. Flynn and Michael A. Quinn, "Economics: A Good Choice of Major for Future CEOs," *Social Science Research Network*, November 28, 2006; and *Famous Economics Majors*, Marietta College, Marietta, Ohio, May 22, 2010.

 1.2

The Economic Problem That Every Society Must Solve, pages 8–12

LEARNING OBJECTIVE: Discuss how an economy answers these questions: What goods and services will be produced? How will the goods and services be produced? Who will receive the goods and services produced?

Summary

Society faces **trade-offs**: Producing more of one good or service means producing less of another good or service. The **opportunity cost** of any activity—such as producing a good or service—is the highest-valued alternative that must be given up to engage in that activity. The choices of consumers, firms, and governments determine what goods and services will be produced. Firms choose how to produce the goods and services they sell. In the United States, who receives the goods and services produced depends largely on how income is distributed in the marketplace. In a **centrally planned economy**, most economic decisions are made by the government. In a **market economy**, most economic decisions are made by consumers and firms. Most economies, including that of the United States, are **mixed economies** in which

most economic decisions are made by consumers and firms but in which the government also plays a significant role. There are two types of efficiency: productive efficiency and allocative efficiency. **Productive efficiency** occurs when a good or service is produced at the lowest possible cost. **Allocative efficiency** occurs when production is in accordance with consumer preferences. **Voluntary exchange** is a situation that occurs in markets when both the buyer and seller of a product are made better off by the transaction. **Equity** is more difficult to define than efficiency, but it usually involves a fair distribution of economic benefits. Government policymakers often face a trade-off between equity and efficiency.

MyEconLab   Visit **www.myeconlab.com** to complete these exercises online and get instant feedback.

Review Questions

2.1 Why does scarcity imply that every society and every individual face trade-offs?

2.2 What are the three economic questions that every society must answer? Briefly discuss the differences in how centrally planned, market, and mixed economies answer these questions.

2.3 What is the difference between productive efficiency and allocative efficiency?

2.4 What is the difference between efficiency and equity? Why do government policymakers often face a trade-off between efficiency and equity?

Problems and Applications

2.5 Does Bill Gates, one of the richest people in the world, face scarcity? Does everyone? Are there any exceptions?

2.6 In a market economy, why does a firm have a strong incentive to be productively efficient and allocatively efficient? What does the firm earn if it is productively and allocatively efficient, and what happens if it is not?

2.7 Would you expect new and better machinery and equipment to be adopted more rapidly in a market economy or in a centrally planned economy? Briefly explain.

2.8 Centrally planned economies have been less efficient than market economies.
   a. Has this difference in efficiency happened by chance, or is there some underlying reason?
   b. If market economies are more economically efficient than centrally planned economies, would there ever be a reason to prefer having a centrally planned economy rather than a market economy?

2.9 Relative to a market economy, would you expect a centrally planned economy to be better at productive efficiency or allocative efficiency? Briefly explain.

2.10 Leonard Fleck, a philosophy professor at Michigan State University, has written:

> When it comes to health care in America, we have limited resources for unlimited health care needs. We want everything contemporary medical technology can offer that will improve the length or quality of our lives as we age. But as presently healthy taxpayers, we want costs controlled.

Why is it necessary for all economic systems to limit services such as health care? How does a market system prevent people from getting as many goods and services as they want?

From Leonard Fleck, *Just Caring: Health Care Rationing and Democratic Deliberation*, (New York: Oxford University Press, 2009).

2.11 Suppose that your local police department recovers 100 tickets to a big NASCAR race in a drug raid. Police decide to distribute the tickets to residents and announces that tickets will be given away at 10 A.M. Monday at City Hall.
   a. What groups of people will be most likely to try to get the tickets? Think of specific examples and then generalize.
   b. What is the opportunity cost of distributing the tickets this way?
   c. Productive efficiency occurs when a good or service (such as the distribution of tickets) is produced at the lowest possible cost. Is this an efficient way to distribute the tickets? If possible, think of a more efficient method of distributing the tickets.
   d. Is this an equitable way to distribute the tickets? Explain.

1.3 Economic Models, pages 12–16

LEARNING OBJECTIVE: Understand the role of models in economic analysis.

Summary

An **economic variable** is something measurable that can have different values, such as the wages of software programmers. Economists rely on economic models when they apply economic ideas to real-world problems. **Economic models** are simplified versions of reality used to analyze real-world economic situations. Economists accept and use an economic model if it leads to hypotheses that are confirmed by statistical analysis. In many cases, the acceptance is tentative, however, pending the gathering of new data or further statistical analysis. Economics is a *social science* because it applies the scientific method to the study of the interactions among individuals. Economics is concerned with positive analysis rather than normative analysis. **Positive analysis** is concerned with what is. **Normative analysis** is concerned with what ought to be. Because economics is based on studying the actions of individuals, it is a social science. As a social science, economics considers human behavior in every context of decision making, not just in business.

 Visit **www.myeconlab.com** to complete these exercises online and get instant feedback.

Review Questions

3.1 Why do economists use models? How are economic data used to test models?

3.2 Describe the five steps by which economists arrive at a useful economic model.

3.3 What is the difference between normative analysis and positive analysis? Is economics concerned mainly with normative analysis or with positive analysis? Briefly explain.

Problems and Applications

3.4 Do you agree with the following assertion: "The problem with economics is that it assumes that consumers and firms always make the correct decision. But we know everyone's human, and we all make mistakes."

3.5 Suppose an economist develops an economic model and finds that "it works great in theory, but it fails in practice." What should the economist do next?

3.6 Dr. Strangelove's theory is that the price of mushrooms is determined by the activity of subatomic particles that exist in another universe parallel to ours. When the subatomic particles are emitted in profusion, the price of mushrooms is high. When subatomic particle emissions are low, the price of mushrooms is also low. How would you go about testing Dr. Strangelove's theory? Discuss whether this theory is useful.

3.7 **[Related to the** Making the Connection **on page 15]** The *Making the Connection* explains that there are both positive and normative elements to the debate over whether medical schools should charge tuition and whether hospitals should continue to pay residents who pursue primary care but not residents who specialize. What economic statistics would be most useful in evaluating the positive elements in this debate? Assuming that these statistics are available or could be gathered, are they likely to resolve the normative issues in this debate?

3.8 **[Related to the** Chapter Opener **on page 3]** In recent years, many doctors have decided to give up running their practices as small businesses and have become salaried employees of hospitals.

    a. What important differences exist between doctors' practices and other small businesses, such as restaurants and hardware stores?

    b. How have the economic incentives for operating a private practice as opposed to becoming a salaried employee of a hospital changed over the years for doctors?

3.9 **[Related to the** Don't Let This Happen to You **on page 15]** Explain which of the following statements represent positive analysis and which represent normative analysis.

    a. A 50-cent-per-pack tax on cigarettes will lead to a 12 percent reduction in smoking by teenagers.

    b. The federal government should spend more on AIDS research.

    c. Rising paper prices will increase textbook prices.

    d. The price of coffee at Starbucks is too high.

3.10 In the United States, to receive a medical license, a doctor must complete a residency program at a hospital. Hospitals are not free to expand their residency programs in a particular medical specialty without approval from a Residency Review Committee (RRC), which is made up of physicians in that specialty. A hospital that does not abide by the rulings of the RRC runs the risk of losing its accreditation from the Accreditation Council for Graduate Medical Education (ACGME). The ACGME and the RRCs argue that this system makes it possible to ensure that residency programs do not expand to the point where they are not providing residents with high-quality training.

    a. How does this system help protect consumers?

    b. How might this system protect the financial interests of doctors more than the well-being of consumers?

    c. Briefly discuss whether you consider this system to be a good one.

Based on Brian Palmer, "We Need More Doctors, Stat!" *Slate*, June 27, 2011; and Sean Nicholson, "*Barriers to Entering Medical Specialties*," Wharton School, September 2003.

 1.4 **Microeconomics and Macroeconomics,** pages 16–17

LEARNING OBJECTIVE: Distinguish between microeconomics and macroeconomics.

Summary

Microeconomics is the study of how households and firms make choices, how they interact in markets, and how the government attempts to influence their choices. **Macroeconomics** is the study of the economy as a whole, including topics such as inflation, unemployment, and economic growth.

MyEconLab Visit **www.myeconlab.com** to complete these exercises online and get instant feedback.

Review Question

4.1 Briefly discuss the difference between microeconomics and macroeconomics.

Problems and Applications

4.2 Briefly explain whether each of the following is primarily a microeconomic issue or a macroeconomic issue.

    a. The effect of higher cigarette taxes on the quantity of cigarettes sold

    b. The effect of higher income taxes on the total amount of consumer spending

    c. The reasons for the economies of East Asian countries growing faster than the economies of sub-Saharan African countries

    d. The reasons for low rates of profit in the airline industry

4.3 Briefly explain whether you agree with the following assertion: "Microeconomics is concerned with things that happen in one particular place, such as the unemployment rate in one city. In contrast, macroeconomics is concerned with things that affect the country as a whole, such as how the rate of teenage smoking in the United States would be affected by an increase in the tax on cigarettes."

 1.5 **A Preview of Important Economic Terms,** pages 17–19

LEARNING OBJECTIVE: Define important economic terms.

Summary

Becoming familiar with important terms is a necessary step in learning economics. These important economic terms include *capital, entrepreneur, factors of production, firm, goods, household, human capital, innovation, profit, revenue, services,* and *technology.*

Appendix

Using Graphs and Formulas

Graphs are used to illustrate key economic ideas. Graphs appear not just in economics textbooks but also on Web sites and in newspaper and magazine articles that discuss events in business and economics. Why the heavy use of graphs? Because they serve two useful purposes: (1) They simplify economic ideas, and (2) they make the ideas more concrete so they can be applied to real-world problems. Economic and business issues can be complicated, but a graph can help cut through complications and highlight the key relationships needed to understand the issue. In that sense, a graph can be like a street map.

For example, suppose you take a bus to New York City to see the Empire State Building. After arriving at the Port Authority Bus Terminal, you will probably use a map similar to the one shown below to find your way to the Empire State Building.

Maps are very familiar to just about everyone, so we don't usually think of them as being simplified versions of reality, but they are. This map does not show much more than the streets in this part of New York City and some of the most important buildings. The names, addresses, and telephone numbers of the people who live and work in the area aren't given. Almost none of the stores and buildings those people work and live in are shown either. The map doesn't indicate which streets allow curbside parking and which don't. In fact, the map shows almost nothing about the messy reality of life in this section of New York City, except how the streets are laid out, which is the essential information you need to get from the Port Authority to the Empire State Building.

Street map of New York City. Copyright © 2011 City Maps Inc. Reprinted by permission.

Think about someone who says, "I know how to get around in the city, but I just can't figure out how to read a map." It certainly is possible to find your destination in a city without a map, but it's a lot easier with one. The same is true of using graphs in economics. It is possible to arrive at a solution to a real-world problem in economics and business without using graphs, but it is usually a lot easier if you do use them.

Often, the difficulty students have with graphs and formulas is a lack of familiarity. With practice, all the graphs and formulas in this text will become familiar to you. Once you are familiar with them, you will be able to use them to analyze problems that would otherwise seem very difficult. What follows is a brief review of how graphs and formulas are used.

Graphs of One Variable

Figure 1A.1 displays values for *market shares* in the U.S. automobile market, using two common types of graphs. Market shares show the percentage of industry sales accounted for by different firms. In this case, the information is for groups of firms: the "Big Three"—Ford, General Motors, and Chrysler—as well as Japanese firms, European firms, and Korean firms. Panel (a) displays the information on market shares as a *bar graph*, where the market share of each group of firms is represented by the height of its bar. Panel (b) displays the same information as a *pie chart*, with the market share of each group of firms represented by the size of its slice of the pie.

Information on economic variables is also often displayed in *time-series graphs*. Time-series graphs are displayed on a coordinate grid. In a coordinate grid, we can measure the value of one variable along the vertical axis (or *y*-axis) and the value of another variable along the horizontal axis (or *x*-axis). The point where the vertical axis intersects the horizontal axis is called the *origin*. At the origin, the value of both variables is zero. The points on a coordinate grid represent values of the two variables. In Figure 1A.2, we measure the number of automobiles and trucks sold worldwide by Ford Motor Company on the vertical axis, and we measure time on the horizontal axis. In time-series

(a) Bar graph

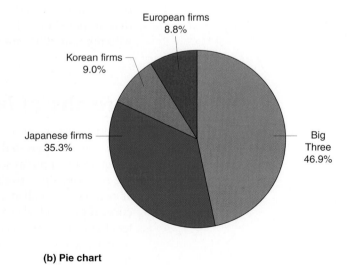

(b) Pie chart

Figure 1A.1 Bar Graphs and Pie Charts

Values for an economic variable are often displayed as a bar graph or as a pie chart. In this case, panel (a) shows market share data for the U.S. automobile industry as a bar graph, where the market share of each group of firms is represented by the height of its bar. Panel (b) displays the same information as a pie chart, with the market share of each group of firms represented by the size of its slice of the pie. Data from "Auto Sales," *Wall Street Journal*, July 1, 2011.

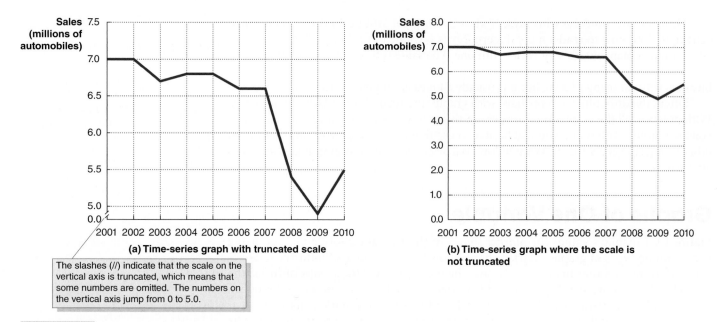

(a) Time-series graph with truncated scale

The slashes (//) indicate that the scale on the vertical axis is truncated, which means that some numbers are omitted. The numbers on the vertical axis jump from 0 to 5.0.

(b) Time-series graph where the scale is not truncated

Figure 1A.2 **Time-Series Graphs**

Both panels present time-series graphs of Ford Motor Company's worldwide sales during each year from 2001 to 2010. Panel (a) has a truncated scale on the vertical axis, and panel (b) does not. As a result, the fluctuations in Ford's sales appear smaller in panel (b) than in panel (a).
Data from Ford Motor Company, *Annual Report*, various years.

graphs, the height of the line at each date shows the value of the variable measured on the vertical axis. Both panels of Figure 1A.2 show Ford's worldwide sales during each year from 2001 to 2010. The difference between panel (a) and panel (b) illustrates the importance of the scale used in a time-series graph. In panel (a), the scale on the vertical axis is truncated, which means it does not start with zero. The slashes (//) near the bottom of the axis indicate that the scale is truncated. In panel (b), the scale is not truncated. In panel (b), the decline in Ford's sales during 2008 and 2009 appears smaller than in panel (a). (Technically, the horizontal axis is also truncated because we start with the year 2001, not the year 0.)

Graphs of Two Variables

We often use graphs to show the relationship between two variables. For example, suppose you are interested in the relationship between the price of a pepperoni pizza and the quantity of pizzas sold per week in the small town of Bryan, Texas. A graph showing the relationship between the price of a good and the quantity of the good demanded at each price is called a *demand curve*. (As we will discuss later, in drawing a demand curve for a good, we have to hold constant any variables other than price that might affect the willingness of consumers to buy the good.) Figure 1A.3 shows the data collected on price and quantity. The figure shows a two-dimensional grid on which we measure the price of pizza along the *y*-axis and the quantity of pizza sold per week along the *x*-axis. Each point on the grid represents one of the price and quantity combinations listed in the table. We can connect the points to form the demand curve for pizza in Bryan, Texas. Notice that the scales on both axes in the graph are truncated. In this case, truncating the axes allows the graph to illustrate more clearly the relationship between price and quantity by excluding low prices and quantities.

Price (dollars per pizza)	Quantity (pizzas per week)	Points
$15	50	A
14	55	B
13	60	C
12	65	D
11	70	E

Figure 1A.3

Plotting Price and Quantity Points in a Graph

The figure shows a two-dimensional grid on which we measure the price of pizza along the vertical axis (or *y*-axis) and the quantity of pizza sold per week along the horizontal axis (or *x*-axis). Each point on the grid represents one of the price and quantity combinations listed in the table. By connecting the points with a line, we can better illustrate the relationship between the two variables.

As you learned in Figure 1A-2, the slashes (///) indicate that the scales on the axes are truncated, which means that numbers are omitted: On the horizontal axis numbers jump from 0 to 50, and on the vertical axis numbers jump from 0 to 11.

Slopes of Lines

Once you have plotted the data in Figure 1A.3, you may be interested in how much the quantity of pizza sold increases as the price decreases. The *slope* of a line tells us how much the variable we are measuring on the *y*-axis changes as the variable we are measuring on the *x*-axis changes. We can use the Greek letter delta (Δ) to stand for the change in a variable. The slope is sometimes referred to as the rise over the run. So, we have several ways of expressing slope:

$$\text{Slope} = \frac{\text{Change in value on the vertical axis}}{\text{Change in value on the horizontal axis}} = \frac{\Delta y}{\Delta x} = \frac{\text{Rise}}{\text{Run}}.$$

Figure 1A.4 reproduces the graph from Figure 1A.3. Because the slope of a straight line is the same at any point, we can use any two points in the figure to calculate the slope of the line. For example, when the price of pizza decreases from $14 to $12, the quantity of pizza sold increases from 55 per week to 65 per week. Therefore, the slope is:

$$\text{Slope} = \frac{\Delta\,\text{Price of pizza}}{\Delta\,\text{Quantity of pizza}} = \frac{(\$12 - \$14)}{(65 - 55)} = \frac{-2}{10} = -0.2.$$

The slope of this line gives us some insight into how responsive consumers in Bryan, Texas, are to changes in the price of pizza. The larger the value of the slope (ignoring the negative sign), the steeper the line will be, which indicates that not many additional pizzas are sold when the price falls. The smaller the value of the slope, the flatter the line will be, which indicates a greater increase in pizzas sold when the price falls.

Taking into Account More Than Two Variables on a Graph

The demand curve graph in Figure 1A.4 shows the relationship between the price of pizza and the quantity of pizza demanded, but we know that the quantity of any good demanded depends on more than just the price of the good. For example, the quantity

Figure 1A.4

Calculating the Slope of a Line

We can calculate the slope of a line as the change in the value of the variable on the y-axis divided by the change in the value of the variable on the x-axis. Because the slope of a straight line is constant, we can use any two points in the figure to calculate the slope of the line. For example, when the price of pizza decreases from \$14 to \$12, the quantity of pizza demanded increases from 55 per week to 65 per week. So, the slope of this line equals -2 divided by 10, or -0.2.

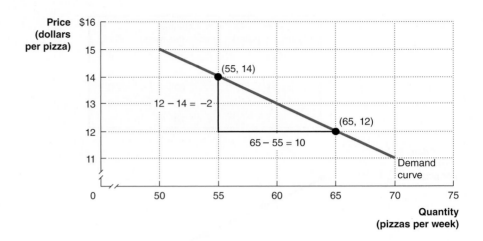

of pizza demanded in a given week in Bryan, Texas, can be affected by other variables, such as the price of hamburgers, whether an advertising campaign by local pizza parlors has begun that week, and so on. Allowing the values of any other variables to change will cause the position of the demand curve in the graph to change.

Suppose, for example, that the demand curve in Figure 1A.4 were drawn holding the price of hamburgers constant, at \$1.50. If the price of hamburgers rises to \$2.00, some consumers will switch from buying hamburgers to buying pizza, and more pizzas will be demanded at every price. The result on the graph will be to shift the line representing the demand curve to the right. Similarly, if the price of hamburgers falls from \$1.50 to \$1.00, some consumers will switch from buying pizza to buying hamburgers, and fewer pizzas will be demanded at every price. The result on the graph will be to shift the line representing the demand curve to the left.

The table in Figure 1A.5 shows the effect of a change in the price of hamburgers on the quantity of pizza demanded. For example, suppose that at first we are on the line labeled *Demand curve₁*. If the price of pizza is \$14 (point A), an increase in the price of hamburgers from \$1.50 to \$2.00 increases the quantity of pizzas demanded from 55 to 60 per week (point B) and shifts us to *Demand curve₂*. Or, if we start on *Demand curve₁* and the price of pizza is \$12 (point C), a decrease in the price of hamburgers from \$1.50 to \$1.00 decreases the quantity of pizzas demanded from 65 to 60 per week (point D) and shifts us to *Demand curve₃*. By shifting the demand curve, we have taken into account the effect of changes in the value of a third variable—the price of hamburgers. We will use this technique of shifting curves to allow for the effects of additional variables many times in this book.

Positive and Negative Relationships

We can use graphs to show the relationships between any two variables. Sometimes the relationship between the variables is *negative*, meaning that as one variable increases in value, the other variable decreases in value. This was the case with the price of pizza and the quantity of pizzas demanded. The relationship between two variables can also be *positive*, meaning that the values of both variables increase or decrease together. For example, when the level of total income—or *disposable personal income*—received by households in the United States increases, the level of total *consumption spending*, which is spending by households on goods and services, also increases. The table in Figure 1A.6 shows the values (in billions of dollars) for income and consumption spending for the years 2007–2010. The graph plots the data from the table, with disposable personal income measured along the horizontal axis and consumption spending measured along the vertical axis. Notice that the four points do not all fall exactly on the line. This is often the case with real-world data. To examine the relationship between two variables, economists often use the straight line that best fits the data.

Quantity (pizzas per week)			
Price (dollars per pizza)	When the Price of Hamburgers = $1.00	When the Price of Hamburgers = $1.50	When the Price of Hamburgers = $2.00
$15	45	50	55
14	50	55	60
13	55	60	65
12	60	65	70
11	65	70	75

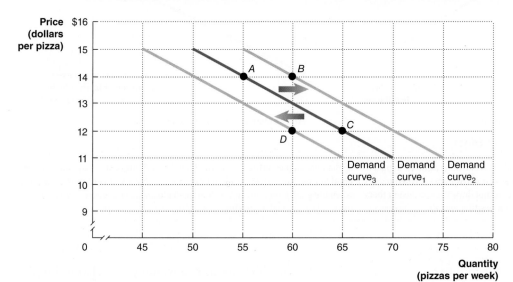

Figure 1A.5

Showing Three Variables on a Graph

The demand curve for pizza shows the relationship between the price of pizzas and the quantity of pizzas demanded, *holding constant other factors that might affect the willingness of consumers to buy pizza.* If the price of pizza is $14 (point *A*), an increase in the price of hamburgers from $1.50 to $2.00 increases the quantity of pizzas demanded from 55 to 60 per week (point *B*) and shifts us to *Demand curve₂*. Or, if we start on *Demand curve₁* and the price of pizza is $12 (point *C*), a decrease in the price of hamburgers from $1.50 to $1.00 decreases the quantity of pizza demanded from 65 to 60 per week (point *D*) and shifts us to *Demand curve₃*.

Determining Cause and Effect

When we graph the relationship between two variables, we often want to draw conclusions about whether changes in one variable are causing changes in the other variable. Doing so, however, can lead to incorrect conclusions. For example, suppose you graph the number of homes in a neighborhood that have a fire burning in the fireplace and

Year	Disposable Personal Income (billions of dollars)	Consumption Spending (billions of dollars)
2007	$10,424	$9,806
2008	10,953	10,105
2009	11,035	10,001
2010	11,375	10,349

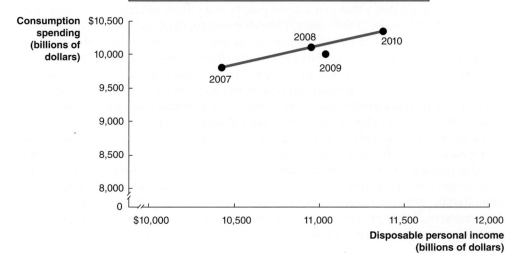

Figure 1A.6

Graphing the Positive Relationship between Income and Consumption

In a positive relationship between two economic variables, as one variable increases, the other variable also increases. This figure shows the positive relationship between disposable personal income and consumption spending. As disposable personal income in the United States has increased, so has consumption spending.

Data from U.S. Department of Commerce, Bureau of Economic Analysis.

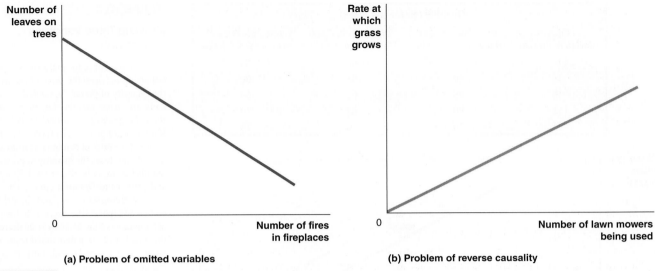

(a) Problem of omitted variables

(b) Problem of reverse causality

Figure 1A.7 **Determining Cause and Effect**

Using graphs to draw conclusions about cause and effect can be hazardous. In panel (a), we see that there are fewer leaves on the trees in a neighborhood when many homes have fires burning in their fireplaces. We cannot draw the conclusion that the fires cause the leaves to fall because we have an *omitted variable*—the season of the year. In panel (b), we see that more lawn mowers are used in a neighborhood during times when the grass grows rapidly and fewer lawn mowers are used when the grass grows slowly. Concluding that using lawn mowers *causes* the grass to grow faster would be making the error of *reverse causality*.

the number of leaves on trees in the neighborhood. You would get a relationship like that shown in panel (a) of Figure 1A.7: The more fires burning in the neighborhood, the fewer leaves the trees have. Can we draw the conclusion from this graph that using a fireplace causes trees to lose their leaves? We know, of course, that such a conclusion would be incorrect. In spring and summer, there are relatively few fireplaces being used, and the trees are full of leaves. In the fall, as trees begin to lose their leaves, fireplaces are used more frequently. And in winter, many fireplaces are being used and many trees have lost all their leaves. The reason that the graph in Figure 1A.7 is misleading about cause and effect is that there is obviously an *omitted variable* in the analysis—the season of the year. An omitted variable is one that affects other variables, and its omission can lead to false conclusions about cause and effect.

Although in our example the omitted variable is obvious, there are many debates about cause and effect where the existence of an omitted variable has not been clear. For instance, it has been known for many years that people who smoke cigarettes suffer from higher rates of lung cancer than do nonsmokers. For some time, tobacco companies and some scientists argued that there was an omitted variable—perhaps a failure to exercise or a poor diet—that made some people more likely to smoke and more likely to develop lung cancer. If this omitted variable existed, then the finding that smokers were more likely to develop lung cancer would not have been evidence that smoking *caused* lung cancer. In this case, however, nearly all scientists eventually concluded that the omitted variable did not exist and that, in fact, smoking does cause lung cancer.

A related problem in determining cause and effect is known as *reverse causality*. The error of reverse causality occurs when we conclude that changes in variable X cause changes in variable Y when, in fact, it is actually changes in variable Y that cause changes in variable X. For example, panel (b) of Figure 1A.7 plots the number of lawn mowers being used in a neighborhood against the rate at which grass on lawns in the neighborhood is growing. We could conclude from this graph that using lawn mowers *causes* the grass to grow faster. We know, however, that in reality, the causality is in the other direction: Rapidly growing grass during the spring and summer causes the increased use of lawn mowers. Slowly growing grass in the fall or winter or during periods of low rainfall causes decreased use of lawn mowers.

Once again, in our example, the potential error of reverse causality is obvious. In many economic debates, however, cause and effect can be more difficult to determine. For example, changes in the money supply, or the total amount of money in the economy, tend to occur at the same time as changes in the total amount of income people in the economy earn. A famous debate in economics was about whether the changes in the money supply caused the changes in total income or whether the changes in total income caused the changes in the money supply. Each side in the debate accused the other side of committing the error of reverse causality.

Are Graphs of Economic Relationships Always Straight Lines?

The graphs of relationships between two economic variables that we have drawn so far have been straight lines. The relationship between two variables is *linear* when it can be represented by a straight line. Few economic relationships are actually linear. For example, if we carefully plot data on the price of a product and the quantity demanded at each price, holding constant other variables that affect the quantity demanded, we will usually find a curved—or *nonlinear*—relationship rather than a linear relationship. In practice, however, it is often useful to approximate a nonlinear relationship with a linear relationship. If the relationship is reasonably close to being linear, the analysis is not

(a) The slope of a nonlinear curve is not constant

(b) The slope of a nonlinear curve is measured by the slope of the tangent line

Figure 1A.8 The Slope of a Nonlinear Curve

The relationship between the quantity of iPhones produced and the total cost of production is curved rather than linear. In panel (a), in moving from point *A* to point *B*, the quantity produced increases by 1 million iPhones, while the total cost of production increases by $50 million. Farther up the curve, as we move from point *C* to point *D*, the change in quantity is the same—1 million iPhones—but the change in the total cost of production is now much larger: $250 million.

Because the change in the *y* variable has increased, while the change in the *x* variable has remained the same, we know that the slope has increased. In panel (b), we measure the slope of the curve at a particular point by the slope of the tangent line. The slope of the tangent line at point *B* is 75, and the slope of the tangent line at point *C* is 150.

significantly affected. In addition, it is easier to calculate the slope of a straight line, and it also is easier to calculate the area under a straight line. So, in this textbook, we often assume that the relationship between two economic variables is linear, even when we know that this assumption is not precisely correct.

Slopes of Nonlinear Curves

In some situations, we need to take into account the nonlinear nature of an economic relationship. For example, panel (a) of Figure 1A.8 shows the hypothetical relationship between Apple's total cost of producing iPhones and the quantity of iPhones produced. The relationship is curved rather than linear. In this case, the cost of production is increasing at an increasing rate, which often happens in manufacturing. Put a different way, as we move up the curve, its slope becomes larger. (Remember that with a straight line, the slope is always constant.) To see this effect, first remember that we calculate the slope of a curve by dividing the change in the variable on the y-axis by the change in the variable on the x-axis. As we move from point A to point B, the quantity produced increases by 1 million iPhones, while the total cost of production increases by $50 million. Farther up the curve, as we move from point C to point D, the change in quantity is the same—1 million iPhones—but the change in the total cost of production is now much larger: $250 million. Because the change in the y variable has increased, while the change in the x variable has remained the same, we know that the slope has increased.

To measure the slope of a nonlinear curve at a particular point, we must measure the slope of the *tangent line* to the curve at that point. A tangent line will touch the curve only at that point. We can measure the slope of the tangent line just as we would the slope of any other straight line. In panel (b), the tangent line at point B has a slope equal to:

$$\frac{\Delta \text{Cost}}{\Delta \text{Quantity}} = \frac{75}{1} = 75.$$

The tangent line at point C has a slope equal to:

$$\frac{\Delta \text{Cost}}{\Delta \text{Quantity}} = \frac{150}{1} = 150.$$

Once again, we see that the slope of the curve is larger at point C than at point B.

Formulas

We have just seen that graphs are an important economic tool. In this section, we will review several useful formulas and show how to use them to summarize data and to calculate important relationships.

Formula for a Percentage Change

One important formula is the percentage change. The *percentage change* is the change in some economic variable, usually from one period to the next, expressed as a percentage. An important macroeconomic measure is the real gross domestic product (GDP). GDP is the value of all the final goods and services produced in a country during a year. "Real" GDP is corrected for the effects of inflation. When economists say that the U.S. economy grew 3.0 percent during 2010, they mean that real GDP was 3.0 percent higher in 2010 than it was in 2009. The formula for making this calculation is:

$$\frac{\text{GDP}_{2010} - \text{GDP}_{2009}}{\text{GDP}_{2009}} \times 100$$

or, more generally, for any two periods:

$$\text{Percentage change} = \frac{\text{Value in the second period} - \text{Value in the first period}}{\text{Value in the first period}} \times 100.$$

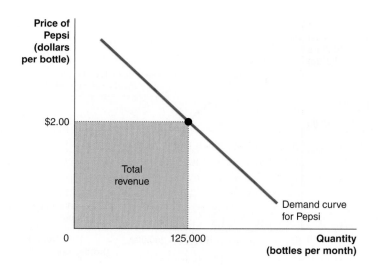

Figure 1A.9

Showing a Firm's Total Revenue on a Graph

The area of a rectangle is equal to its base multiplied by its height. Total revenue is equal to quantity multiplied by price. Here, total revenue is equal to the quantity of 125,000 bottles times the price of $2.00 per bottle, or $250,000. The area of the green-shaded rectangle shows the firm's total revenue.

In this case, real GDP was $12,703 billion in 2009 and $13,088 billion in 2010. So, the growth rate of the U.S. economy during 2010 was:

$$\left(\frac{\$13,088 - \$12,703}{\$12,703} \right) \times 100 = 2.8\%.$$

Notice that it doesn't matter that in using the formula, we ignored the fact that GDP is measured in billions of dollars. In fact, when calculating percentage changes, *the units don't matter*. The percentage increase from $12,703 billion to $13,088 billion is exactly the same as the percentage increase from $12,073 to $13,088.

Formulas for the Areas of a Rectangle and a Triangle

Areas that form rectangles and triangles on graphs can have important economic meaning. For example, Figure 1A.9 shows the demand curve for Pepsi. Suppose that the price is currently $2.00 and that 125,000 bottles of Pepsi are sold at that price. A firm's *total revenue* is equal to the amount it receives from selling its product, or the quantity sold multiplied by the price. In this case, total revenue will equal 125,000 bottles times $2.00 per bottle, or $250,000.

The formula for the area of a rectangle is:

$$\text{Area of a rectangle} = \text{Base} \times \text{Height}.$$

In Figure 1A.9, the green-shaded rectangle also represents the firm's total revenue because its area is given by the base of 125,000 bottles multiplied by the price of $2.00 per bottle.

We will see in later chapters that areas that are triangles can also have economic significance. The formula for the area of a triangle is:

$$\text{Area of a triangle} = \frac{1}{2} \times \text{Base} \times \text{Height}.$$

The blue-shaded area in Figure 1A.10 is a triangle. The base equals 150,000 − 125,000, or 25,000. Its height equals $2.00 − $1.50, or $0.50. Therefore, its area equals 1/2 × 25,000 × $0.50, or $6,250. Notice that the blue area is a triangle only if the demand curve is a straight line, or linear. Not all demand curves are linear. However, the formula for the area of a triangle will usually still give a good approximation, even if the demand curve is not linear.

Summary of Using Formulas

You will encounter several other formulas in this book. Whenever you must use a formula, you should follow these steps:

1. Make sure you understand the economic concept the formula represents.

Figure 1A.10

The Area of a Triangle

The area of a triangle is equal to 1/2 multiplied by its base multiplied by its height. The area of the blue-shaded triangle has a base equal to 150,000 − 125,000, or 25,000, and a height equal to $2.00 − $1.50, or $0.50. Therefore, its area equals 1/2 × 25,000 × $0.50, or $6,250.

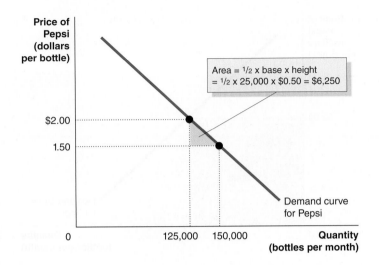

2. Make sure you are using the correct formula for the problem you are solving.
3. Make sure the number you calculate using the formula is economically reasonable. For example, if you are using a formula to calculate a firm's revenue and your answer is a negative number, you know you made a mistake somewhere.

 Using Graphs and Formulas, pages 26–36

LEARNING OBJECTIVE: Review the use of graphs and formulas.

MyEconLab   Visit **www.myeconlab.com** to complete these exercises online and get instant feedback.

Problems and Applications

1A.1 The following table shows the relationship between the price of custard pies and the number of pies Jacob buys per week:

Price	Quantity of Pies	Week
$3.00	6	July 2
2.00	7	July 9
5.00	4	July 16
6.00	3	July 23
1.00	8	July 30
4.00	5	August 6

   a. Is the relationship between the price of pies and the number of pies Jacob buys a positive relationship or a negative relationship?
   b. Plot the data from the table on a graph similar to Figure 1A.3 on page 29. Draw a straight line that best fits the points.
   c. Calculate the slope of the line.

1A.2 The following table gives information on the quantity of glasses of lemonade demanded on sunny and overcast days:

Price (dollars per glass)	Quantity (glasses of lemonade per day)	Weather
$0.80	30	Sunny
0.80	10	Overcast
0.70	40	Sunny
0.70	20	Overcast
0.60	50	Sunny
0.60	30	Overcast
0.50	60	Sunny
0.50	40	Overcast

Plot the data from the table on a graph similar to Figure 1A.5 on page 31. Draw two straight lines representing the two demand curves—one for sunny days and one for overcast days.

1A.3 Using the information in Figure 1A.2 on page 28, calculate the percentage change in auto sales from one year to the next. Between which years did sales fall at the fastest rate?

1A.4 Real GDP in 2008 was $13,162 billion. Real GDP in 2009 was $12,703 billion. What was the percentage change in real GDP from 2008 to 2009? What do economists call the percentage change in real GDP from one year to the next?

1A.5 Assume that the demand curve for Pepsi passes through the following two points:

Price per Bottle of Pepsi	Number of Bottles Demanded
$2.50	100,000
1.25	200,000

a. Draw a graph with a linear demand curve that passes through these two points.
b. Show on the graph the areas representing total revenue at each price. Give the value for total revenue at each price.

1A.6 What is the area of the blue triangle shown in the following figure?

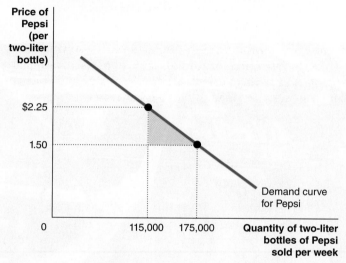

1A.7 Calculate the slope of the total cost curve at point A and at point B in the following figure.

2

Trade-offs, Comparative Advantage, and the Market System

Chapter Outline and Learning Objectives

Managers Making Choices at BMW

When you think of cars that combine fine engineering, high performance, and cutting-edge styling, you are likely to think of BMW. Founded in Germany in 1916, BMW today has 23 factories in 15 countries and worldwide sales of more than 1.5 million cars.

To compete in the automobile market, the managers of BMW must make many strategic decisions, such as whether to introduce new car models. BMW has begun selling a hydrogen-powered version of the 7-Series sedan and is also working on fuel cell–powered cars. Another strategic decision BMW's managers face is where to advertise. Although some of BMW's managers did not believe the company could sell cars in China, BMW decided to advertise heavily there. The advertising paid off: China has become the company's third-largest market, after Germany and the United States, with sales increasing by more than 85 percent in 2010 alone.

BMW's managers have also faced the strategic decision of whether to concentrate production in factories in Germany or to build new factories in overseas markets. Keeping production in Germany makes it easier for BMW's managers to supervise production and to employ German workers, who generally have high levels of technical training. By building factories in other countries, BMW can benefit from paying lower wages and can reduce political friction by producing vehicles in the same country in which it sells them. BMW opened a plant in Shenyang, in northeast China and a plant in Chennai in India. It also opened a U.S. factory in Spartanburg, South Carolina, which currently produces the X3, X5, and X6 models for sale both in the United States and worldwide.

Managers also face smaller-scale—or tactical—business decisions. For instance, in scheduling production at BMW's Spartanburg plant, managers must decide each month the quantity of X3, X5, and X6 models to produce. Like other decisions managers make, this one involves a trade-off: Producing more of one of these three models means producing fewer of the others.

AN INSIDE LOOK on **page 60** discusses the trade-off GM faces when deciding how to allocate resources between producing powertrains for its two electric cars—the Chevy volt and the Cadillac Converj.

Based on Christoph Rauwald, "BMW's Quarterly Profit Soars," *The Wall Street Journal*, May 4, 2011; and BMW, *Annual Report, 2010.*

Economics in Your Life

The Trade-offs When You Buy a Car

When you buy a car, you probably consider factors such as safety and fuel efficiency. To increase fuel efficiency, automobile manufacturers make cars small and light. Large cars absorb more of the impact of an accident than do small cars. As a result, people are usually safer driving large cars than small cars. What can we conclude from these facts about the relationship between safety and fuel efficiency? Under what circumstances would it be possible for automobile manufacturers to make cars safer and more fuel efficient? As you read the chapter, see if you can answer these questions. You can check your answers against those provided on **page 58** at the end of this chapter.

Scarcity A situation in which unlimited wants exceed the limited resources available to fulfill those wants.

In a market system, managers at most firms must make decisions like those made by BMW's managers. The decisions managers face reflect a key fact of economic life: *Scarcity requires trade-offs.* **Scarcity** exists because we have unlimited wants but only limited resources available to fulfill those wants. Goods and services are scarce. So, too, are the economic resources, or *factors of production*—workers, capital, natural resources, and entrepreneurial ability—used to make goods and services. Your time is scarce, which means you face trade-offs: If you spend an hour studying for an economics exam, you have one less hour to spend studying for a psychology exam or going to the movies. If your university decides to use some of its scarce budget to buy new computers for the computer labs, those funds will not be available to buy new books for the library or to resurface the student parking lot. If BMW decides to devote some of the scarce workers and machinery in its Spartanburg assembly plant to producing more X6 hybrid cars, those resources will not be available to produce more X5 SUVs.

Households and firms make many of their decisions in markets. Trade is a key activity that takes place in markets. Trade involves the decisions of millions of households and firms spread around the world. By engaging in trade, people can raise their standard of living. In this chapter, we provide an overview of how the market system coordinates the independent decisions of these millions of households and firms. We begin our analysis of the economic consequences of scarcity and the working of the market system by introducing an important economic model: the *production possibilities frontier*.

Production Possibilities Frontiers and Opportunity Costs

As we saw in the chapter opener, BMW operates an automobile factory in Spartanburg, South Carolina, where it assembles several car models. Because the firm's resources—workers, machinery, materials, and entrepreneurial skills—are limited, BMW faces a trade-off: Resources devoted to producing one model are not available for producing other models. Chapter 1 explained that economic models can be useful in analyzing many questions. We can use a simple model called the *production possibilities frontier* to analyze the trade-offs BMW faces in its Spartanburg plant. A **production possibilities frontier (*PPF*)** is a curve showing the maximum attainable combinations of two products that may be produced with available resources and current technology. In BMW's case, we simplify by assuming that the company produces only X6 hybrids and X5 SUVs at the Spartanburg plant, using workers, materials, robots, and other machinery.

Production possibilities frontier (*PPF*) A curve showing the maximum attainable combinations of two products that may be produced with available resources and current technology.

Graphing the Production Possibilities Frontier

Figure 2.1 uses a production possibilities frontier to illustrate the trade-offs that BMW faces. The numbers from the table are plotted in the graph. The line in the graph is BMW's production possibilities frontier. If BMW uses all its resources to produce hybrids, it can produce 800 per day—point *A* at one end of the production possibilities frontier. If BMW uses all its resources to produce SUVs, it can produce 800 per day—point *E* at the other end of the production possibilities frontier. If BMW devotes resources to producing both vehicles, it could be at a point like *B*, where it produces 600 hybrids and 200 SUVs.

All the combinations either on the frontier—like *A*, *B*, *C*, *D*, and *E*—or inside the frontier—like point *F*—are *attainable* with the resources available. Combinations on the frontier are *efficient* because all available resources are being fully utilized, and the

BMW's Production Choices at Its Spartanburg Plant		
Choice	Quantity of Hybrids Produced	Quantity of SUVs Produced
A	800	0
B	600	200
C	400	400
D	200	600
E	0	800

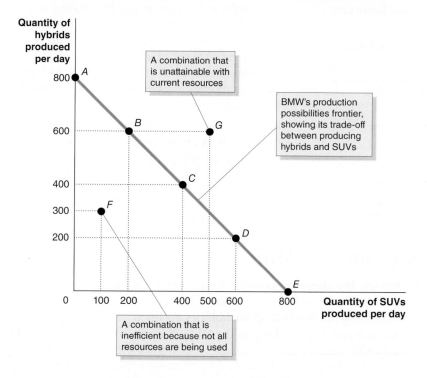

Figure 2.1

BMW's Production Possibilities Frontier

BMW faces a trade-off: To build one more hybrid, it must build one less SUV. The production possibilities frontier illustrates the trade-off BMW faces. Combinations on the production possibilities frontier—like points *A*, *B*, *C*, *D*, and *E*—are *technically efficient* because the maximum output is being obtained from the available resources. Combinations inside the frontier—like point *F*—are *inefficient* because some resources are not being used. Combinations outside the frontier—like point *G*—are *unattainable* with current resources.

fewest possible resources are being used to produce a given amount of output. Combinations inside the frontier—like point *F*—are *inefficient* because maximum output is not being obtained from the available resources—perhaps because the assembly line is not operating at capacity. BMW might like to be beyond the frontier—at a point like *G*, where it would be producing 600 hybrids and 500 SUVs—but points beyond the production possibilities frontier are *unattainable*, given the firm's current resources. To produce the combination at *G*, BMW would need more machines or more workers.

Notice that if BMW is producing efficiently and is on the production possibilities frontier, the only way to produce more of one vehicle is to produce fewer of the other vehicle. Recall from Chapter 1 that the **opportunity cost** of any activity is the highest-valued alternative that must be given up to engage in that activity. For BMW, the opportunity cost of producing one more SUV is the number of hybrids the company will not be able to produce because it has shifted those resources to producing SUVs. For example, in moving from point *B* to point *C*, the opportunity cost of producing 200 more SUVs per day is the 200 fewer hybrids that can be produced.

What point on the production possibilities frontier is best? We can't tell without further information. If consumer demand for SUVs is greater than the demand for hybrids, the company is likely to choose a point closer to *E*. If demand for hybrids is greater than demand for SUVs, the company is likely to choose a point closer to *A*.

Opportunity cost The highest-valued alternative that must be given up to engage in an activity.

Solved Problem 2.1

Drawing a Production Possibilities Frontier for Rosie's Boston Bakery

Rosie's Boston Bakery specializes in cakes and pies. Rosie has 5 hours per day to devote to baking. In 1 hour, Rosie can prepare 2 pies or 1 cake.

a. Use the information given to complete the following table:

Choice	Hours Spent Making		Quantity Made	
	Cakes	Pies	Cakes	Pies
A	5	0		
B	4	1		
C	3	2		
D	2	3		
E	1	4		
F	0	5		

b. Use the data in the table to draw a production possibilities frontier graph illustrating Rosie's trade-offs between making cakes and making pies. Label the vertical axis "Quantity of cakes made." Label the horizontal axis "Quantity of pies made." Make sure to label the values where Rosie's production possibilities frontier intersects the vertical and horizontal axes.

c. Label the points representing choice *D* and choice *E*. If Rosie is at choice *D*, what is her opportunity cost of making more pies?

Solving the Problem

Step 1: Review the chapter material. This problem is about using production possibilities frontiers to analyze trade-offs, so you may want to review the section "Graphing the Production Possibilities Frontier," which begins on page 40.

Step 2: Answer part (a) by filling in the table. If Rosie can produce 1 cake in 1 hour, then with choice *A*, she will make 5 cakes and 0 pies. Because she can produce 2 pies in 1 hour, with choice *B*, she will make 4 cakes and 2 pies. Using similar reasoning, you can fill in the remaining cells in the table as follows:

Choice	Hours Spent Making		Quantity Made	
	Cakes	Pies	Cakes	Pies
A	5	0	5	0
B	4	1	4	2
C	3	2	3	4
D	2	3	2	6
E	1	4	1	8
F	0	5	0	10

Step 3: Answer part (b) by drawing the production possibilities frontier graph. Using the data in the table in Step 2, you should draw a graph that looks like this:

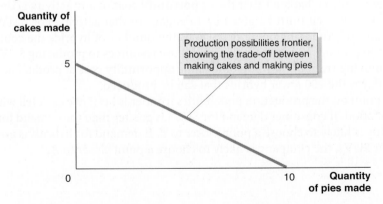

If Rosie devotes all 5 hours to making cakes, she will make 5 cakes. There-fore, her production possibilities frontier will intersect the vertical axis at 5 cakes made. If Rosie devotes all 5 hours to making pies, she will make 10 pies. Therefore, her production possibilities frontier will intersect the hori-zontal axis at 10 pies made.

Step 4: **Answer part (c) by showing choices D and E on your graph.** The points for choices D and E can be plotted using the information from the table:

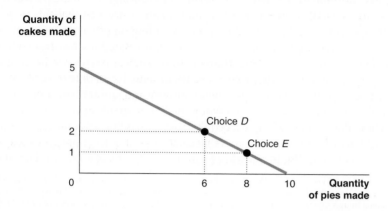

Moving from choice D to choice E increases Rosie's production of pies by 2 but lowers her production of cakes by 1. Therefore, her opportunity cost of making 2 more pies is making 1 less cake.

Your Turn: For more practice, do related problem 1.9 on page 63 at the end of this chapter.   MyEconLab

---

Making the Connection	**Facing Trade-offs in Health Care Spending**

Households have limited incomes. If the price of health care rises, households have to choose whether to buy less health care or spend less on other goods and services. The same is true of the federal government's spending on health care. The government provides health insurance to about 30 percent of the population through programs such as Medicare for people over age 65 and Medicaid for low-income peo-ple. If the price of health care rises, the government has to either cut back on the services provided through Medicare and Medicaid or cut spending in another part of the government's budget. (Of course, both households and the government can borrow to pay for some of their spending, but ultimately the funds they can borrow are also limited.)

About 54 percent of the population has private health insur-ance, often provided by an employer. When the fees doctors charge, the cost of prescription drugs, and the cost of hospital stays rise, the cost to employers of providing health insurance increases. As a result, employers will typically increase the amount they withhold from employees' paychecks to pay for the insurance. Some employers—particularly small firms—will even stop of-fering health insurance to their employees. In either case, the price employees pay for health care will rise. How do people respond to rising health care costs? Isn't health care a necessity that people continue to consume the same amount of, no matter how much its price increases? In fact, studies have shown that rising health care costs cause people to cut back their spending on medical services, just as people cut back their spending on other goods and services when their prices rise. One academic study indicates that for every 1 percent increase in the amount employers charge employees for insurance,

Spending more on health care means spending less on other goods and services for both households and governments.

164,000 people become uninsured. Of course, people without health insurance can still visit the doctor and obtain prescriptions, but they have to pay higher prices than do people with insurance. Although the consequences of being uninsured can be severe, particularly if someone develops a serious illness, economists are not surprised that higher prices for health insurance lead to less health insurance being purchased: Faced with limited incomes, people have to make choices among the goods and services they buy.

The Congressional Budget Office estimates that as the U.S. population ages and medical costs continue to rise, federal government spending on Medicare will more than double over the next 10 years. Many policymakers are concerned that this rapid increase in Medicare spending will force a reduction in spending on other government programs. Daniel Callahan, a researcher at the Hastings Center for Bioethics, has argued that policymakers should consider taking some dramatic steps, such as having Medicare stop paying for open-heart surgery and other expensive treatments for people over 80 years of age. Callahan argues that the costs of open-heart surgery and similar treatments for the very old exceed the benefits, and the funds would be better spent on treatments for younger patients, where the benefits would exceed the costs. Spending less on prolonging the lives of the very old in order to save resources that can be used for other purposes is a very painful trade-off to consider. But in a world of scarcity, trade-offs of some kind are inevitable.

Based on Daniel Callahan, "The Economic Woes of Medicare," *The New York Times*, November 13, 2008; Ezekiel J. Emanuel, "The Cost–Coverage Trade-off," *Journal of the American Medical Association*, Vol. 299, No. 8, February 27, 2008, pp. 947–949; and Congressional Budget Office, *A Preliminary Analysis of the President's Budget and an Update of CBO's Budget and Economic Outlook*, March 2009.

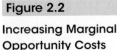 **Your Turn:** Test your understanding by doing related problems 1.10, 1.11, 1.12, and 1.13 on page 63 at the end of this chapter.

Increasing Marginal Opportunity Costs

We can use the production possibilities frontier to explore issues concerning the economy as a whole. For example, suppose we divide all the goods and services produced in the economy into just two types: military goods and civilian goods. In Figure 2.2, we let tanks represent military goods and automobiles represent civilian goods. If all the country's resources are devoted to producing military goods, 400 tanks can be produced in one year. If all resources are devoted to producing civilian goods, 500 automobiles can be produced in one year. Devoting resources to producing both goods results in the economy being at other points along the production possibilities frontier.

Notice that this production possibilities frontier is bowed outward rather than being a straight line. Because the curve is bowed out, the opportunity cost of automobiles in terms of tanks depends on where the economy currently is on the production possibilities frontier. For example, to increase automobile production from 0 to 200—moving from point *A* to point *B*—the economy has to give up only 50 tanks. But to increase

Figure 2.2

Increasing Marginal Opportunity Costs

As the economy moves down the production possibilities frontier, it experiences *increasing marginal opportunity costs* because increasing automobile production by a given quantity requires larger and larger decreases in tank production. For example, to increase automobile production from 0 to 200—moving from point *A* to point *B*—the economy has to give up only 50 tanks. But to increase automobile production by another 200 vehicles—moving from point *B* to point *C*—the economy has to give up 150 tanks.

automobile production by another 200 vehicles—moving from point *B* to point *C*—the economy has to give up 150 tanks.

As the economy moves down the production possibilities frontier, it experiences *increasing marginal opportunity costs* because increasing automobile production by a given quantity requires larger and larger decreases in tank production. Increasing marginal opportunity costs occur because some workers, machines, and other resources are better suited to one use than to another. At point *A*, some resources that are well suited to producing automobiles are forced to produce tanks. Shifting these resources into producing automobiles by moving from point *A* to point *B* allows a substantial increase in automobile production, without much loss of tank production. But as the economy moves down the production possibilities frontier, more and more resources that are better suited to tank production are switched into automobile production. As a result, the increases in automobile production become increasingly smaller, while the decreases in tank production become increasingly larger. We would expect in most situations that production possibilities frontiers will be bowed outward rather than linear, as in the BMW example discussed earlier.

The idea of increasing marginal opportunity costs illustrates an important economic concept: *The more resources already devoted to an activity, the smaller the payoff to devoting additional resources to that activity.* For example, the more hours you have already spent studying economics, the smaller the increase in your test grade from each additional hour you spend—and the greater the opportunity cost of using the hour in that way. The more funds a firm has devoted to research and development during a given year, the smaller the amount of useful knowledge it receives from each additional dollar—and the greater the opportunity cost of using the funds in that way. The more funds the federal government spends cleaning up the environment during a given year, the smaller the reduction in pollution from each additional dollar—and, once again, the greater the opportunity cost of using the funds in that way.

Economic Growth

At any given time, the total resources available to any economy are fixed. Therefore, if the United States produces more automobiles, it must produce less of something else—tanks in our example. Over time, though, the resources available to an economy may increase. For example, both the labor force and the capital stock—the amount of physical capital available in the country—may increase. The increase in the available labor force and the capital stock shifts the production possibilities frontier outward for the U.S. economy and makes it possible to produce both more automobiles and more

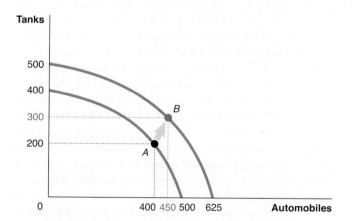

(a) Shifting out the production possibilities frontier

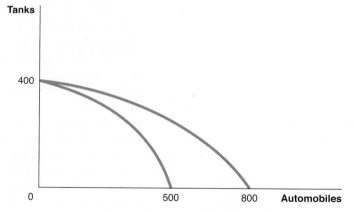

(b) Technological change in the automobile industry

Figure 2.3 Economic Growth

Panel (a) shows that as more economic resources become available and technological change occurs, the economy can move from point *A* to point *B*, producing more tanks and more automobiles. Panel (b) shows the results of technological change in the automobile industry that increases the quantity of vehicles workers can produce per year while leaving unchanged the maximum quantity of tanks that can be produced. Shifts in the production possibilities frontier represent *economic growth.*

tanks. Panel (a) of Figure 2.3 shows that the economy can move from point *A* to point *B*, producing more tanks and more automobiles.

Similarly, technological change makes it possible to produce more goods with the same number of workers and the same amount of machinery, which also shifts the production possibilities frontier outward. Technological change need not affect all sectors equally. Panel (b) of Figure 2.3 shows the results of technological change in the automobile industry that increases the quantity of automobiles workers can produce per year while leaving unchanged the quantity of tanks that can be produced.

Economic growth The ability of the economy to increase the production of goods and services.

Shifts in the production possibilities frontier represent **economic growth** because they allow the economy to increase the production of goods and services, which ultimately raises the standard of living. In the United States and other high-income countries, the market system has aided the process of economic growth, which over the past 200 years has greatly increased the well-being of the average person.

2.2 LEARNING OBJECTIVE

Understand comparative advantage and explain how it is the basis for trade.

Trade The act of buying and selling.

Comparative Advantage and Trade

We can use the ideas of production possibilities frontiers and opportunity costs to understand the basic economic activity of *trade*. Markets are fundamentally about **trade**, which is the act of buying and selling. Sometimes we trade directly, as when children trade one baseball card for another baseball card. But often we trade indirectly: We sell our labor services as, say, an accountant, a salesperson, or a nurse for money, and then we use the money to buy goods and services. Although in these cases, trade takes place indirectly, ultimately the accountant, salesperson, or nurse is trading his or her services for food, clothing, and other goods and services. One of the great benefits of trade is that it makes it possible for people to become better off by increasing both their production and their consumption.

Specialization and Gains from Trade

Consider the following situation: You and your neighbor both have fruit trees on your property. Initially, suppose you have only apple trees and your neighbor has only cherry trees. In this situation, if you both like apples and cherries, there is an obvious opportunity for both of you to gain from trade: You trade some of your apples for some of your neighbor's cherries, making you both better off. But what if there are apple and cherry trees growing on both of your properties? In that case, there can still be gains from trade. For example, your neighbor might be very good at picking apples, and you might be very good at picking cherries. It would make sense for your neighbor to concentrate on picking apples and for you to concentrate on picking cherries. You can then trade some of the cherries you pick for some of the apples your neighbor picks. But what if your neighbor is actually better at picking both apples and cherries than you are?

We can use production possibilities frontiers (*PPFs*) to show how your neighbor can benefit from trading with you *even though she is better than you are at picking both apples and cherries*. (For simplicity, and because it will not have any effect on the conclusions we draw, we will assume that the *PPFs* in this example are straight lines.) The table in Figure 2.4 shows how many apples and how many cherries you and your neighbor can pick in one week. The graph in the figure uses the data from the table to construct *PPFs*. Panel (a) shows your *PPF*. If you devote all your time to picking apples, you can pick 20 pounds of apples per week. If you devote all your time to picking cherries, you can pick 20 pounds per week. Panel (b) shows that if your neighbor devotes all her time to picking apples, she can pick 30 pounds. If she devotes all her time to picking cherries, she can pick 60 pounds.

The production possibilities frontiers in Figure 2.4 show how many apples and cherries you and your neighbor can consume, *without trade*. Suppose that when you don't trade with your neighbor, you pick and consume 8 pounds of apples and 12 pounds of cherries per week. This combination of apples and cherries is represented by point *A* in panel (a) of Figure 2.5. When your neighbor doesn't trade with you, she picks and consumes 9 pounds of apples and 42 pounds of cherries per week. This combination of apples and cherries is represented by point *C* in panel (b) of Figure 2.5.

	You		Your Neighbor	
	Apples	Cherries	Apples	Cherries
Devote all time to picking apples	20 pounds	0 pounds	30 pounds	0 pounds
Devote all time to picking cherries	0 pounds	20 pounds	0 pounds	60 pounds

Figure 2.4   **Production Possibilities for You and Your Neighbor, without Trade**

The table in this figure shows how many pounds of apples and how many pounds of cherries you and your neighbor can each pick in one week. The graphs in the figure use the data from the table to construct production possibilities frontiers (*PPFs*) for you and your neighbor. Panel (a) shows your *PPF*. If you devote all your time to

picking apples and none of your time to picking cherries, you can pick 20 pounds. If you devote all your time to picking cherries, you can pick 20 pounds. Panel (b) shows that if your neighbor devotes all her time to picking apples, she can pick 30 pounds. If she devotes all her time to picking cherries, she can pick 60 pounds.

After years of picking and consuming your own apples and cherries, suppose your neighbor comes to you one day with the following proposal: She offers to trade you 15 pounds of her cherries for 10 pounds of your apples next week. Should you accept this offer? You should accept because you will end up with more apples and more cherries to consume. To take advantage of her proposal, you should specialize in picking only apples rather than splitting your time between picking apples and picking cherries. We know this will allow you to pick 20 pounds of apples. You can trade 10 pounds

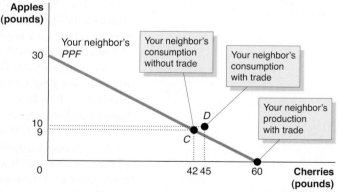

Figure 2.5   **Gains from Trade**

When you don't trade with your neighbor, you pick and consume 8 pounds of apples and 12 pounds of cherries per week—point *A* in panel (a). When your neighbor doesn't trade with you, she picks and consumes 9 pounds of apples and 42 pounds of cherries per week—point *C* in panel (b). If you specialize in picking apples, you can pick 20 pounds. If your neighbor specializes in picking cherries,

she can pick 60 pounds. If you trade 10 pounds of your apples for 15 pounds of your neighbor's cherries, you will be able to consume 10 pounds of apples and 15 pounds of cherries—point *B* in panel (a). Your neighbor can now consume 10 pounds of apples and 45 pounds of cherries—point *D* in panel (b). You and your neighbor are both better off as a result of the trade.

Table 2.1

A Summary of the Gains from Trade

	You		Your Neighbor	
	Apples (in pounds)	Cherries (in pounds)	Apples (in pounds)	Cherries (in pounds)
Production *and* consumption *without* trade	8	12	9	42
Production *with* trade	20	0	0	60
Consumption *with* trade	10	15	10	45
Gains from trade (increased consumption)	2	3	1	3

of apples to your neighbor for 15 pounds of her cherries. The result is that you will be able to consume 10 pounds of apples and 15 pounds of cherries (point *B* in panel (a) of Figure 2.5). You are clearly better off as a result of trading with your neighbor: You now can consume 2 more pounds of apples and 3 more pounds of cherries than you were consuming without trading. You have moved beyond your *PPF*!

Your neighbor has also benefited from the trade. By specializing in picking only cherries, she can pick 60 pounds. She trades 15 pounds of cherries to you for 10 pounds of apples. The result is that she can consume 10 pounds of apples and 45 pounds of cherries (point *D* in panel (b) of Figure 2.5). This is 1 more pound of apples and 3 more pounds of cherries than she was consuming before trading with you. She also has moved beyond her *PPF*. Table 2.1 summarizes the changes in production and consumption that result from your trade with your neighbor. (In this example, we chose one specific rate of trading cherries for apples—15 pounds of cherries for 10 pounds of apples. There are, however, many other rates of trading cherries for apples that would also make you and your neighbor better off.)

Absolute Advantage versus Comparative Advantage

Perhaps the most remarkable aspect of the preceding example is that your neighbor benefits from trading with you even though she is better than you at picking both apples and cherries. **Absolute advantage** is the ability of an individual, a firm, or a country to produce more of a good or service than competitors, using the same amount of resources. Your neighbor has an absolute advantage over you in producing both apples and cherries because she can pick more of each fruit than you can in the same amount of time. Although it seems that your neighbor should pick her own apples *and* her own cherries, we have just seen that she is better off specializing in cherry picking and leaving the apple picking to you.

We can consider further why both you and your neighbor benefit from specializing in picking only one fruit. First, think about the opportunity cost to each of you of picking the two fruits. We saw from the *PPF* in Figure 2.4 that if you devoted all your time to picking apples, you would be able to pick 20 pounds of apples per week. As you move down your *PPF* and shift time away from picking apples to picking cherries, you have to give up 1 pound of apples for each pound of cherries you pick (the slope of your *PPF* is −1. For a review of calculating slopes, see the appendix to Chapter 1.) Therefore, your opportunity cost of picking 1 pound of cherries is 1 pound of apples. By the same reasoning, your opportunity cost of picking 1 pound of apples is 1 pound of cherries. Your neighbor's *PPF* has a different slope, so she faces a different trade-off: As she shifts time from picking apples to picking cherries, she has to give up 0.5 pound of apples for every 1 pound of cherries she picks (the slope of your neighbor's *PPF* is −0.5). As she shifts time from picking cherries to picking apples, she gives up 2 pounds of cherries for every 1 pound of apples she picks. Therefore, her opportunity cost of picking 1 pound of apples is 2 pounds of cherries, and her opportunity cost of picking 1 pound of cherries is 0.5 pound of apples.

Absolute advantage The ability of an individual, a firm, or a country to produce more of a good or service than competitors, using the same amount of resources.

	Opportunity Cost of Picking 1 Pound of Apples	Opportunity Cost of Picking 1 Pound of Cherries
You	1 pound of cherries	1 pound of apples
Your Neighbor	2 pounds of cherries	0.5 pound of apples

Table 2.2

Opportunity Costs of Picking Apples and Cherries

Table 2.2 summarizes the opportunity costs for you and your neighbor of picking apples and cherries. Note that even though your neighbor can pick more apples in a week than you can, the *opportunity cost* of picking apples is higher for her than for you because when she picks apples, she gives up more cherries than you do. So, even though she has an absolute advantage over you in picking apples, it is more costly for her to pick apples than it is for you. The table also shows that her opportunity cost of picking cherries is lower than your opportunity cost of picking cherries. **Comparative advantage** is the ability of an individual, a firm, or a country to produce a good or service at a lower opportunity cost than competitors. In apple picking, your neighbor has an *absolute advantage* over you, but you have a *comparative advantage* over her. Your neighbor has both an absolute advantage and a comparative advantage over you in picking cherries. As we have seen, you are better off specializing in picking apples, and your neighbor is better off specializing in picking cherries.

Comparative advantage The ability of an individual, a firm, or a country to produce a good or service at a lower opportunity cost than competitors.

Comparative Advantage and the Gains from Trade

We have just derived an important economic principle: *The basis for trade is comparative advantage, not absolute advantage.* The fastest apple pickers do not necessarily do much apple picking. If the fastest apple pickers have a comparative advantage in some other activity—picking cherries, playing Major League Baseball, or being industrial engineers—they are better off specializing in that other activity. Individuals, firms, and countries are better off if they specialize in producing goods and services for which they have a comparative advantage and obtain the other goods and services they need by trading. We will return to the important concept of comparative advantage in Chapter 7, which is devoted to the subject of international trade.

Don't Let This Happen to You

Don't Confuse Absolute Advantage and Comparative Advantage

First, make sure you know the definitions:

- **Absolute advantage.** The ability of an individual, a firm, or a country to produce more of a good or service than competitors, using the same amount of resources. In our example, your neighbor has an absolute advantage over you in both picking apples and picking cherries.
- **Comparative advantage.** The ability of an individual, a firm, or a country to produce a good or service at a lower opportunity cost than competitors. In our example, your neighbor has a comparative advantage in picking cherries, but you have a comparative advantage in picking apples.

Keep these two key points in mind:

1. It is possible to have an absolute advantage in producing a good or service without having a comparative advantage. This is the case with your neighbor picking apples.
2. It is possible to have a comparative advantage in producing a good or service without having an absolute advantage. This is the case with you picking apples.

MyEconLab

Your Turn: Test your understanding by doing related problem 2.5 on page 64 at the end of this chapter.

Solved Problem 2.2

Comparative Advantage and the Gains from Trade

Suppose that Canada and the United States both produce maple syrup and honey, which sell for the same prices in both countries. These are the combinations of the two goods that each country can produce in one day using the same amounts of capital and labor:

Canada		United States	
Honey (in tons)	Maple Syrup (in tons)	Honey (in tons)	Maple Syrup (in tons)
0	60	0	50
10	45	10	40
20	30	20	30
30	15	30	20
40	0	40	10
		50	0

a. Who has a comparative advantage in producing maple syrup? Who has a comparative advantage in producing honey?

b. Suppose that Canada is currently producing 30 tons of honey and 15 tons of maple syrup, and the United States is currently producing 10 tons of honey and 40 tons of maple syrup. Demonstrate that Canada and the United States can both be better off if they specialize in producing only one good and engage in trade.

c. Illustrate your answer to question (b) by drawing a *PPF* for the United States and a *PPF* for Canada. Show on your *PPF*s the combinations of honey and maple syrup produced and consumed in each country before and after trade.

Solving the Problem

Step 1: **Review the chapter material.** This problem is about comparative advantage, so you may want to review the section "Absolute Advantage versus Comparative Advantage," which begins on page 48.

Step 2: **Answer part (a) by calculating who has a comparative advantage in each activity.** Remember that a country has a comparative advantage in producing a good if it can produce the good at the lowest opportunity cost. When Canada produces 1 more ton of honey, it produces 1.5 tons less of maple syrup. When the United States produces 1 more ton of honey, it produces 1 ton less of maple syrup. Therefore, the United States' opportunity cost of producing honey—1 ton of maple syrup—is lower than Canada's—1.5 tons of maple syrup. When Canada produces 1 more ton of maple syrup, it produces 0.67 ton less of honey. When the United States produces 1 more ton of maple syrup, it produces 1 ton less of honey. Therefore, Canada's opportunity cost of producing maple syrup—0.67 ton of honey—is lower than that of the United States—1 ton of honey. We can conclude that the United States has a comparative advantage in the production of honey and Canada has a comparative advantage in the production of maple syrup.

Step 3: **Answer part (b) by showing that specialization makes Canada and the United States better off.** We know that Canada should specialize where it has a comparative advantage, and the United States should specialize where it has a comparative advantage. If both countries specialize, Canada will produce 60 tons of maple syrup and 0 tons of honey, and the United States will produce 0 tons of maple syrup and 50 tons of honey. After both countries specialize, the United States could then trade 30 tons of honey to Canada in exchange for 40 tons of maple syrup. (Other mutually beneficial trades are possible as well.) We can summarize the results in a table:

	Before Trade		After Trade	
	Honey (in tons)	Maple Syrup (in tons)	Honey (in tons)	Maple Syrup (in tons)
Canada	30	15	30	20
United States	10	40	20	40

The United States is better off after trade because it can consume the same amount of maple syrup and 10 more tons of honey. Canada is better off after trade because it can consume the same amount of honey and 5 more tons of maple syrup.

Step 4: **Answer part (c) by drawing the *PPFs*.**

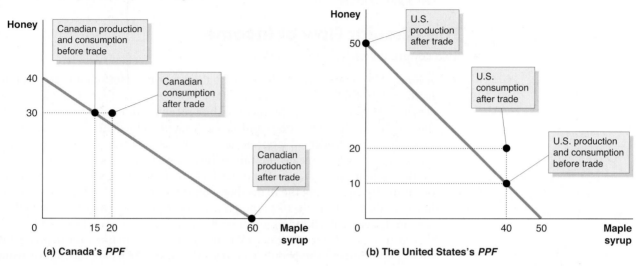

(a) Canada's *PPF*

(b) The United States's *PPF*

Your Turn: For more practice, do related problems 2.6 and 2.7 on page 65 at the end of this chapter.

MyEconLab

The Market System

We have seen that households, firms, and the government face trade-offs and incur opportunity costs because resources are scarce. We have also seen that trade allows people to specialize according to their comparative advantage. By engaging in trade, people can raise their standard of living. Of course, trade in the modern world is much more complex than the examples we have considered so far. Trade today involves the decisions of millions of people around the world. But how does an economy make trade possible, and how are the decisions of these millions of people coordinated? In the United States and most other countries, trade is carried out in markets. Markets also determine the answers to the three fundamental questions discussed in Chapter 1: What goods and services will be produced? How will the goods and services be produced? and Who will receive the goods and services produced?

Recall that the definition of **market** is a group of buyers and sellers of a good or service and the institution or arrangement by which they come together to trade. Markets take many forms: They can be physical places, such as a local pizza parlor or the New York Stock Exchange, or virtual places, such as eBay. In a market, the buyers are demanders of goods or services, and the sellers are suppliers of goods or services. Households and firms interact in two types of markets: *product markets* and *factor markets*. **Product markets** are markets for goods—such as computers—and services—such as medical treatment. In product markets, households are demanders and firms are suppliers. **Factor markets** are markets for the *factors of production*. **Factors of production** are the inputs used to make goods and services. Factors of production are divided into four broad categories:

- *Labor* includes all types of work, from the part-time labor of teenagers working at McDonald's to the work of senior managers in large corporations.

- *Capital* refers to physical capital, such as computers and machine tools, that is used to produce other goods.

2.3 LEARNING OBJECTIVE

Explain the basic idea of how a market system works.

Market A group of buyers and sellers of a good or service and the institution or arrangement by which they come together to trade.

Product market A market for goods—such as computers—or services—such as medical treatment.

Factor market A market for the factors of production, such as labor, capital, natural resources, and entrepreneurial ability.

Factors of production The inputs used to make goods and services.

- *Natural resources* include land, water, oil, iron ore, and other raw materials (or "gifts of nature") that are used in producing goods.

- An *entrepreneur* is someone who operates a business. *Entrepreneurial ability* is the ability to bring together the other factors of production to successfully produce and sell goods and services.

The Circular Flow of Income

Two key groups participate in markets:

- A *household* consists of all the individuals in a home. Households are suppliers of factors of production—particularly labor—employed by firms to make goods and services. Households use the income they receive from selling the factors of production to purchase the goods and services supplied by firms. We are familiar with households as suppliers of labor because most people earn most of their income by going to work, which means they are selling their labor services to firms in the labor market. But households own the other factors of production as well, either directly or indirectly, by owning the firms that have these resources. All firms are owned by households. Small firms, like a neighborhood restaurant, might be owned by one person. Large firms, like Microsoft or BMW, are owned by millions of households that own shares of stock in them. (We discuss the stock market in Chapter 6.) When firms pay profits to the people who own them, the firms are paying for using the capital and natural resources that are supplied to them by those owners. So, we can generalize by saying that in factor markets, households are suppliers and firms are demanders.

- *Firms* are suppliers of goods and services. Firms use the funds they receive from selling goods and services to buy the factors of production needed to make the goods and services.

Circular-flow diagram A model that illustrates how participants in markets are linked.

We can use a simple economic model called the **circular-flow diagram** to see how participants in markets are linked. Figure 2.6 shows that in factor markets, households supply labor and other factors of production in exchange for wages and other payments from firms. In product markets, households use the payments they earn in factor markets to purchase the goods and services supplied by firms. Firms produce these goods and services using the factors of production supplied by households. In the figure, the blue arrows show the flow of factors of production from households through factor markets to firms. The red arrows show the flow of goods and services from firms through product markets to households. The green arrows show the flow of funds from firms through factor markets to households and the flow of spending from households through product markets to firms.

Like all economic models, the circular-flow diagram is a simplified version of reality. For example, Figure 2.6 leaves out the important role of government in buying goods from firms and in making payments, such as Social Security or unemployment insurance payments, to households. The figure also leaves out the roles played by banks, the stock and bond markets, and other parts of the *financial system* in aiding the flow of funds from lenders to borrowers. Finally, the figure does not show that some goods and services purchased by domestic households are produced in foreign countries and some goods and services produced by domestic firms are sold to foreign households. (We explore the government, the financial system, and the international sector further in later chapters.) Despite these simplifications, the circular-flow diagram in Figure 2.6 is useful for seeing how product markets, factor markets, and their participants are linked together. One of the great wonders of the market system is that it manages to successfully coordinate the independent activities of so many households and firms.

The Gains from Free Markets

Free market A market with few government restrictions on how a good or service can be produced or sold or on how a factor of production can be employed.

A **free market** exists when the government places few restrictions on how goods and services can be produced or sold or on how factors of production can be employed.

Figure 2.6

The Circular-Flow Diagram

Households and firms are linked together in a circular flow of production, income, and spending. The blue arrows show the flow of the factors of production. In factor markets, households supply labor, entrepreneurial ability, and other factors of production to firms. Firms use these factors of production to make goods and services that they supply to households in product markets. The red arrows show the flow of goods and services from firms to households. The green arrows show the flow of funds. In factor markets, households receive wages and other payments from firms in exchange for supplying the factors of production. Households use these wages and other payments to purchase goods and services from firms in product markets. Firms sell goods and services to households in product markets, and they use the funds to purchase the factors of production from households in factor markets.

Governments in all modern economies intervene more than is consistent with a fully free market. In that sense, we can think of the free market as being a benchmark against which we can judge actual economies. There are relatively few government restrictions on economic activity in the United States, Canada, the countries of Western Europe, Hong Kong, Singapore, and Estonia. So these countries come close to the free market benchmark. In countries such as Cuba and North Korea, the free market system has been rejected in favor of centrally planned economies with extensive government control over product and factor markets. Countries that come closest to the free market benchmark have been more successful than countries with centrally planned economies in providing their people with rising living standards.

The Scottish philosopher Adam Smith is considered the father of modern economics because his book *An Inquiry into the Nature and Causes of the Wealth of Nations*, published in 1776, was an early and very influential argument for the free market system. Smith was writing at a time when extensive government restrictions on markets were still common. In many parts of Europe, the *guild system* still prevailed. Under this system, governments would give guilds, or organizations of producers, the authority to control the production of a good. For example, the shoemakers' guild controlled who was allowed to produce shoes, how many shoes they could produce, and what price they could charge. In France, the cloth makers' guild even dictated the number of threads in the weave of the cloth.

Smith argued that such restrictions reduced the income, or wealth, of a country and its people by restricting the quantity of goods produced. Some people at the time supported the restrictions of the guild system because it was in their financial interest to do so. If you were a member of a guild, the restrictions served to reduce the competition you faced. But other people sincerely believed that the alternative to the guild system was economic chaos. Smith argued that these people were wrong and that a country could enjoy a smoothly functioning economic system if firms were freed from guild restrictions.

The Market Mechanism

In Smith's day, defenders of the guild system worried that if, for instance, the shoemakers' guild did not control shoe production, either too many or too few shoes would be produced. Smith argued that prices would do a better job of coordinating the activities of buyers and sellers than the guilds could. A key to understanding Smith's argument is the assumption that *individuals usually act in a rational, self-interested way.* In particular, individuals take those actions most likely to make themselves better off financially. This assumption of rational, self-interested behavior underlies nearly all economic analysis. In fact, economics can be distinguished from other fields that study human behavior—such as sociology and psychology—by its emphasis on the assumption of self-interested behavior. Adam Smith understood—as economists today understand—that people's motives can be complex. But in analyzing people in the act of buying and selling, the motivation of financial reward usually provides the best explanation for the actions people take.

For example, suppose that a significant number of consumers switch from buying regular gasoline-powered cars to buying gasoline/electric-powered hybrid cars, such as the Toyota Prius, as in fact has happened in the United States during the past 10 years. Firms will find that they can charge relatively higher prices for hybrid cars than they can for regular cars. The self-interest of these firms will lead them to respond to consumers' wishes by producing more hybrids and fewer regular cars. Or suppose that consumers decide that they want to eat less bread, pasta, and other foods high in carbohydrates, as many did following the increase in popularity of the Atkins and South Beach diets. Then the prices firms can charge for bread and pasta will fall. The self-interest of firms will lead them to produce less bread and pasta, which in fact is what happened.

Note that for the market mechanism to work in responding to changes in consumers' wants, *prices must be flexible.* Changes in *relative prices*—that is, the price of one good or service relative to other goods or services—provides information, or a signal, to both consumers and firms. For example, in 2010, consumers worldwide increased their demand for cattle and poultry. Because corn is fed to cattle and poultry, prices for corn soared relative to prices for other crops. Many farmers in the United States received this price signal and responded by increasing the amount of corn they planted and decreasing the amount of soybeans and wheat. One Kansas farmer was quoted as saying, "It seemed to me there was $100 to $150 per acre more money in the corn than there was in the beans. That's the kind of math that a lot of guys were using." Similarly, falling prices for DVDs or music CDs in the 2000s was a signal to movie studios and record companies to devote fewer resources to these products and more resources to making movies and music available online. In the United States today, governments at the federal, state, and local levels set or regulate the price of only about 10 to 20 percent of goods and services. The prices of other goods and services are free to change as consumer wants change and as costs of production change.

In the case where consumers want more of a product, and in the case where they want less of a product, the market system responds without a guild or the government giving orders about how much to produce or what price to charge. In a famous phrase, Smith said that firms would be led by the "invisible hand" of the market to provide consumers with what they want. Firms respond *individually* to changes in prices by making decisions that *collectively* end up satisfying the wants of consumers.

Making the Connection

A Story of the Market System in Action: How Do You Make an iPad?

Apple produces the iPad 2. Because Apple's headquarters is in Cupertino, California, it seems reasonable to assume that iPads are also manufactured in that state. In fact, although engineers at Apple designed the iPad, the company produces none of the components of the iPad, nor does it assemble the components into a finished product. Far from being produced entirely by one company in one place, the iPad requires the coordinated activities of thousands of workers and dozens of firms spread around the world.

Foxconn, which is based in Taiwan, assembles the iPad in factories in Shenzhen and Chengdu, China, and ships them to Apple for sale in the United States. Foxconn has announced plans to begin assembling some iPads in a new factory in Brazil by 2012. Although Foxconn does final assembly, it doesn't make any of the components and, in fact, charges Apple less than $15 for assembling each iPad.

The table below lists just some of the many suppliers of components for the iPad 2.

The market coordinates the activities of the many people spread around the world who contribute to the making of an iPad.

Firm	Location of the Firm	iPad Component the Firm Supplies
ARM	Great Britain	Processor design
Broadcom	United States (California)	Touchscreen controller
Infineon Technologies	Germany	Semiconductors
LG Electronics	South Korea	Screen
Samsung	South Korea	Flash memory and processor
Texas Instruments	United States (Texas)	Touchscreen controller

Each of these suppliers in turn relies on its own suppliers. For example, Broadcom designs the touchscreen controller for the iPad and supplies it to Apple, but it does not manufacture the components of the controller or assemble them. To manufacture the components, Broadcom relies on SilTerra, based in Malaysia; SMIC, based in mainland China; and Taiwan Semiconductor Manufacturing Corporation (TSMC) and UMC, based in Taiwan. TSMC's factories are for the most part not in Taiwan but in mainland China and Eastern Europe. To assemble the components, Broadcom uses several companies, including Amkor Technology, based in Chandler, Arizona, and STATS ChipPAC, based in Singapore.

All told, an iPad contains hundreds of parts that are designed, manufactured, and assembled by firms around the world. Many of these firms are not even aware of which other firms are also producing components for the iPad. Few of the managers of these firms have met managers of the other firms or shared knowledge of how their particular components are produced. In fact, no one person from Tim Cook, the chief executive officer of Apple, on down possesses the knowledge of how to produce all the components that are assembled into an iPad. Instead, the invisible hand of the market has led these firms to contribute their knowledge and resources to the process that ultimately results in an iPad available for sale in a store in the United States. Apple has so efficiently organized the process of producing the iPad that you can order a custom iPad with a personal engraving and have it delivered from an assembly plant in China to your doorstep in the United States in as little as three days.

Based on Andrew Rassweiler, "iPad 2 Carries Bill of Materials of $326.60, IHS iSuppli Teardown Analysis Shows," iSuppli.com, March 13, 2011; Arik Hesseldahl, "Apple iPad Components Cost At Least $259," *Bloomberg Businessweek*, April 7, 2010; and Chinmei Sung, "Foxconn Faces Limited Impact from Chengdu Fire, Analysts Say," *Bloomberg Businessweek*, May 22, 2011.

Your Turn: Test your understanding by doing related problems 3.8 and 3.9 on page 66 at the end of this chapter.   MyEconLab

The Role of the Entrepreneur

Entrepreneur Someone who operates a business, bringing together the factors of production—labor, capital, and natural resources—to produce goods and services.

Entrepreneurs are central to the working of the market system. An **entrepreneur** is someone who operates a business. Entrepreneurs must first determine what goods and services they believe consumers want, and then they must decide how to produce those goods and services most profitably, using the available factors of production—labor, capital, and natural resources. Successful entrepreneurs are able to search out opportunities to provide new goods and services. Often these opportunities are created by new technology. Consumers and existing businesses typically do not at first realize that the new technology makes new products feasible. For example, even after the development of the internal combustion engine had made automobiles practicable, Henry Ford remarked, "If I had asked my customers what they wanted, they would have said a faster horse." Because consumers often cannot evaluate a new product before it exists, some of the most successful entrepreneurs, such as the late Steve Jobs of Apple, rarely use *focus groups*, or meetings with consumers in which the customers are asked what new products they would like to see. Instead, entrepreneurs think of products that consumers may not even realize they need, such as, in Jobs's case, an MP3 player—iPod—or a tablet computer—iPad.

Entrepreneurs are of great importance to the economy because they are often responsible for making new products widely available to consumers, as Henry Ford did with the automobile and Steve Jobs did with the iPod. Table 2.3 lists some of the important products entrepreneurs at small firms introduced during the twentieth century.

Table 2.3 **Important Products Introduced by Entrepreneurs at Small Firms**	Product	Inventor
	Air conditioning	William Haviland Carrier
	Airplane	Orville and Wilbur Wright
	Biomagnetic imaging	Raymond Damadian
	Biosynthetic insulin	Herbert Boyer
	DNA fingerprinting	Alec Jeffries
	FM radio	Edwin Howard Armstrong
	Helicopter	Igor Sikorsky
	High-resolution CAT scanner	Robert Ledley
	Hydraulic brake	Malcolm Lockheed
	Integrated circuit	Jack Kilby
	Microprocessor	Ted Hoff
	Optical scanner	Everett Franklin Lindquist
	Oral contraceptives	Carl Djerassi
	Overnight delivery service	Fred Smith
	Personal computer	Steve Jobs and Steve Wozniak
	Quick-frozen foods	Clarence Birdseye
	Safety razor	King Gillette
	Soft contact lens	Kevin Tuohy
	Solid fuel rocket engine	Robert Goddard
	Supercomputer	Seymour Cray
	Vacuum tube	Philo Farnsworth
	Zipper	Gideon Sundback

Based on William J. Baumol, *The Microtheory of Innovative Entrepreneurship*, (Princeton, NJ: Princeton University Press, 2010) and various sources. Note that the person who first commercially developed a particular product is sometimes disputed by historians.

Entrepreneurs put their own funds at risk when they start businesses. If they are wrong about what consumers want or about the best way to produce goods and services, they can lose those funds. In fact, it is not unusual for entrepreneurs who eventually achieve great success to fail at first. For instance, early in their careers, both Henry Ford and Sakichi Toyoda, who eventually founded the Toyota Motor Corporation, started companies that quickly failed. Research by Richard Freeman of Harvard University has shown that the typical entrepreneur earns less than someone with the same education and other characteristics who is an employee at a large firm. Few entrepreneurs make the fortunes earned by Henry Ford, Steve Jobs, or Bill Gates.

Entrepreneurs make a vital contribution to economic growth through their roles in responding to consumer demand and in introducing new products. So, government policies that encourage entrepreneurship are also likely to increase economic growth and raise the standard of living. In the next section, we consider the legal framework required for a successful market in which entrepreneurs can succeed.

The Legal Basis of a Successful Market System

In a free market, government does not restrict how firms produce and sell goods and services or how they employ factors of production. But the absence of government intervention is not enough for the market system to work well. Government has to take active steps to provide a *legal environment* that will allow the market system to succeed.

Protection of Private Property For the market system to work well, individuals must be willing to take risks. Someone with $250,000 can be cautious and keep it safely in a bank—or even in cash, if the person doesn't trust banks. But the market system won't work unless a significant number of people are willing to risk their funds by investing them in businesses. Investing in businesses is risky in any country. Many businesses fail every year in the United States and other high-income countries. But in high-income countries, someone who starts a new business or invests in an existing business doesn't have to worry that the government, the military, or criminal gangs might decide to seize the business or demand payments for not destroying the business. Unfortunately, in many poor countries, owners of businesses are not well protected from having their businesses seized by the government or from having their profits taken by criminals. Where these problems exist, opening a business can be extremely risky. Cash can be concealed easily, but a business is difficult to conceal and difficult to move.

Property rights are the rights individuals or firms have to the exclusive use of their property, including the right to buy or sell it. Property can be tangible, physical property, such as a store or factory. Property can also be intangible, such as the right to an idea. Two amendments to the U.S. Constitution guarantee property rights: The 5th Amendment states that the federal government shall not deprive any person "of life, liberty, or property, without due process of law." The 14th Amendment extends this guarantee to the actions of state governments: "No state . . . shall deprive any person of life, liberty, or property, without due process of law." Similar guarantees exist in every high-income country. Unfortunately, in many developing countries, such guarantees do not exist or are poorly enforced.

Property rights The rights individuals or firms have to the exclusive use of their property, including the right to buy or sell it.

In any modern economy, *intellectual property rights* are very important. Intellectual property includes books, films, software, and ideas for new products or new ways of producing products. To protect intellectual property, the federal government grants a *patent* that gives an inventor—which is often a firm—the exclusive right to produce and sell a new product for a period of 20 years from the date the patent was filed. For instance, because Microsoft has a patent on the Windows operating system, other firms cannot sell their own versions of Windows. The government grants patents to encourage firms to spend money on the research and development necessary to create new products. If other companies could freely copy Windows, Microsoft would not have spent the funds necessary to develop it. Just as a new product or a new method of making a product receives patent protection, books, films, and software receive *copyright* protection. Under U.S. law, the creator of a book, film, or piece of music has the exclusive right to use the creation during the creator's lifetime. The creator's heirs retain this exclusive right for 50 years after the death of the creator.

Enforcement of Contracts and Property Rights Business activity often involves someone agreeing to carry out some action in the future. For example, you may borrow $20,000 to buy a car and promise the bank—by signing a loan contract—that you will pay back the money over the next five years. Or Microsoft may sign a licensing agreement with a small technology company, agreeing to use that company's technology for a period of several years in return for a fee. Usually these agreements take the form of legal contracts. For the market system to work, businesses and individuals have to rely on these contracts being carried out. If one party to a legal contract does not fulfill its obligations—perhaps the small company had promised Microsoft exclusive use of its technology but then began licensing it to other companies—the other party can go to court to have the agreement enforced. Similarly, if property owners in the United States believe that the federal or state government has violated their rights under the 5th or 14th Amendments, they can go to court to have their rights enforced.

But going to court to enforce a contract or private property rights will be successful only if the court system is independent and judges are able to make impartial decisions on the basis of the law. In the United States and other high-income countries, the court systems have enough independence from other parts of the government and enough protection from intimidation by outside forces—such as criminal gangs—that they are able to make their decisions based on the law. In many developing countries, the court systems lack this independence and will not provide a remedy if the government violates private property rights or if a person with powerful political connections decides to violate a business contract.

If property rights are not well enforced, fewer goods and services will be produced. This reduces economic efficiency, leaving the economy inside its production possibilities frontier.

Continued from page 39

Economics in Your Life

The Trade-offs When You Buy a Car

At the beginning of the chapter, we asked you to think about two questions: When buying a new car, what is the relationship between safety and fuel efficiency? and Under what circumstances would it be possible for automobile manufacturers to make cars safer and more fuel efficient? To answer the first question, you have to recognize that there is a trade-off between safety and fuel efficiency. With the technology available at any particular time, an automobile manufacturer can increase fuel efficiency by making a car smaller and lighter. But driving a lighter car increases your chances of being injured if you have an accident. The trade-off between safety and fuel efficiency would look much like the relationship in Figure 2.1 on page 41. To get more of both safety and gas mileage, automobile makers would have to discover new technologies that allow them to make cars lighter and safer at the same time. Such new technologies would make points like G in Figure 2.1 attainable.

1.8 Use the following production possibilities frontier for a country to answer the questions.

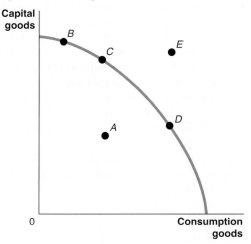

a. Which point or points are unattainable? Briefly explain why.

b. Which point or points are efficient? Briefly explain why.

c. Which point or points are inefficient? Briefly explain why.

d. At which point is the country's future growth rate likely to be the highest? Briefly explain why.

1.9 **[Related to** Solved Problem 2.1 **on page 42]** You have exams in economics and chemistry coming up, and you have five hours available for studying. The following table shows the trade-offs you face in allocating the time you will spend in studying each subject:

	Hours Spent Studying		Midterm Score	
Choice	Economics	Chemistry	Economics	Chemistry
A	5	0	95	70
B	4	1	93	78
C	3	2	90	84
D	2	3	86	88
E	1	4	81	90
F	0	5	75	91

a. Use the data in the table to draw a production possibilities frontier graph. Label the vertical axis "Score on economics exam," and label the horizontal axis "Score on chemistry exam." Make sure to label the values where your production possibilities frontier intersects the vertical and horizontal axes.

b. Label the points representing choice C and choice D. If you are at choice C, what is your opportunity cost of increasing your chemistry score?

c. Under what circumstances would choice A be a sensible choice?

1.10 **[Related to the** Making the Connection **on page 43]** Suppose the U.S. president is attempting to decide whether the federal government should spend more on research to find a cure for heart disease. He asks you, one of his economic advisors, to prepare a report discussing the relevant factors he should consider. Use the concepts of opportunity cost and trade-offs to discuss some of the main issues you would deal with in your report.

1.11 **[Related to the** Making the Connection **on page 43]** Uwe Reinhardt, an economist at Princeton University, wrote the following in a column in the *New York Times*:

> [Cost-effectiveness analysis] seeks to establish which of several alternative strategies capable of achieving a given therapeutic goal is the least-cost strategy. It seems a sensible form of inquiry in a nation that is dismayed over the rising cost of health care. . . . Opponents of cost-effectiveness analysis include individuals who sincerely believe that health and life are "priceless."

Are health and life priceless? Are there any decisions you make during your everyday life that indicate whether you consider health and life to be priceless?

From Uwe E. Reinhardt, "'Cost-Effectiveness Analysis' and U.S. Health Care," *The New York Times*, March 13, 2009.

1.12 **[Related to the** Making the Connection **on page 43]** Suppose that the federal government is deciding which of two cancer treatment therapies it will allow Medicare to pay for (assuming that only one treatment therapy will be funded): Therapy A, which will prolong the average life span of patients receiving the treatment by 24 months and will cost $750,000 per patient treated, and Therapy B, which will prolong the average life span of patients receiving the treatment by 20 months and will cost $25,000 per patient treated. What factors should the federal government take into consideration in making its decision?

1.13 **[Related to the** Making the Connection **on page 43]** Lawrence Summers served as secretary of the treasury in the Clinton administration from 1999 to 2001 and as director of the National Economic Council in the Obama administration from 2009 to 2010. He has been quoted as giving the following moral defense of the economic approach:

> There is nothing morally unattractive about saying: We need to analyze which way of spending money on health care will produce more benefit and which less, and using our money as efficiently as we can. I don't think there is anything immoral about seeking to achieve environmental benefits at the lowest possible costs.

Would it be more ethical to reduce pollution without worrying about the cost or by taking the cost into account? Briefly explain.

From "Precepts from Professor Summers," *The Wall Street Journal*, October 17, 2002.

1.14 In *The Wonderful Wizard of Oz* and his other books about the Land of Oz, L. Frank Baum observed that if people's wants were limited enough, most goods would not be scarce. According to Baum, this was the case in Oz:

> There were no poor people in the Land of Oz, because there was no such thing as money. . . . Each person was given freely by his neighbors whatever he required for his use, which is as much as anyone may reasonably desire. Some tilled the lands and raised great crops of grain, which was divided equally among the whole population, so that all had enough. There were many tailors and dressmakers and shoemakers and the like, who made things that any who desired them might wear. Likewise there were jewelers who made ornaments for the person, which pleased and beautified the people, and these ornaments also were free to those who asked for them. Each man and woman, no matter what he or she produced for the good of the community, was supplied by the neighbors with food and clothing and a house and furniture and ornaments and games. If by chance the supply ever ran short, more was taken from the great storehouses of the Ruler, which were afterward filled up again when there was more of any article than people needed. . . .

> You will know, by what I have told you here, that the Land of Oz was a remarkable country. I do not suppose such an arrangement would be practical with us.

Do you agree with Baum that the economic system in Oz wouldn't work in the contemporary United States? Briefly explain why or why not.

From *The Emerald City of Oz* by L. Frank Baum, pp. 30–31. First published in 1910.

Comparative Advantage and Trade, pages 46–51
LEARNING OBJECTIVE: Understand comparative advantage and explain how it is the basis for trade.

Summary

Fundamentally, markets are about **trade**, which is the act of buying or selling. People trade on the basis of comparative advantage. An individual, a firm, or a country has a **comparative advantage** in producing a good or service if it can produce the good or service at the lowest opportunity cost. People are usually better off specializing in the activity for which they have a comparative advantage and trading for the other goods and services they need. It is important not to confuse comparative advantage with absolute advantage. An individual, a firm, or a country has an **absolute advantage** in producing a good or service if it can produce more of that good or service using the same amount of resources. It is possible to have an absolute advantage in producing a good or service without having a comparative advantage.

 Visit **www.myeconlab.com** to complete these exercises online and get instant feedback.

Review Questions

2.1 What is absolute advantage? What is comparative advantage? Is it possible for a country to have a comparative advantage in producing a good without also having an absolute advantage? Briefly explain.

2.2 What is the basis for trade: absolute advantage or comparative advantage? How can an individual or a country gain from specialization and trade?

Problems and Applications

2.3 Look again at the information in Figure 2.4 on page 47. Choose a rate of trading cherries for apples different from the rate used in the text (15 pounds of cherries for 10 pounds of apples) that will allow you and your neighbor to benefit from trading apples and cherries. Prepare a table like Table 2.1 on page 48 to illustrate your answer.

2.4 Using the same amount of resources, the United States and Canada can both produce lumberjack shirts and lumberjack boots, as shown in the following production possibilities frontiers:

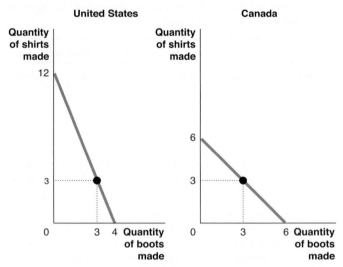

a. Who has a comparative advantage in producing lumberjack boots? Who has a comparative advantage in producing lumberjack shirts? Explain your reasoning.

b. Does either country have an absolute advantage in producing both goods? Explain.

c. Suppose that both countries are currently producing three pairs of boots and three shirts. Show that both can be better off if they each specialize in producing one good and then engage in trade.

2.5 **[Related to** Don't Let This Happen to You **on page 49]** In the 1950s, the economist Bela Balassa compared 28 manufacturing industries in the United States and Britain. In every one of the 28 industries, Balassa found that the United States had an absolute advantage. In these circumstances, would there have been any gain to the United States from importing any of these products from Britain? Explain.

2.6 [Related to Solved Problem 2.2 **on page 50**] Suppose Iran and Iraq both produce oil and olive oil, which sell for the same prices in both countries. The following table shows combinations of both goods that using the same amounts of capital and labor each country can produce in a day, measured in thousands of barrels:

Iraq		Iran	
Oil	Olive Oil	Oil	Olive Oil
0	8	0	4
2	6	1	3
4	4	2	2
6	2	3	1
8	0	4	0

a. Who has the comparative advantage in producing oil? Explain.

b. Can these two countries gain from trading oil and olive oil? Explain.

2.7 [Related to Solved Problem 2.2 **on page 50**] Suppose that France and Germany both produce schnitzel and wine. The following table shows combinations of the goods that each country can produce in a day:

France		Germany	
Wine (bottles)	Schnitzel (pounds)	Wine (bottles)	Schnitzel (pounds)
0	8	0	15
1	6	1	12
2	4	2	9
3	2	3	6
4	0	4	3
		5	0

a. Who has a comparative advantage in producing wine? Who has a comparative advantage in producing schnitzel?

b. Suppose that France is currently producing 1 bottle of wine and 6 pounds of schnitzel, and Germany is currently producing 3 bottles of wine and 6 pounds of schnitzel. Demonstrate that France and Germany can both be better off if they specialize in producing only one good and then engage in trade.

2.8 Can an individual or a country produce beyond its production possibilities frontier? Can an individual or a country consume beyond its production possibilities frontier? Explain.

2.9 If Country A can produce with the same amount of resources twice as much coffee as Country B, explain how Country B could have the comparative advantage in producing coffee.

2.10 Imagine that the next time the Indianapolis Colts play the New England Patriots at Lucas Oil Stadium in Indianapolis, Colts star quarterback Peyton Manning has a temporary lack of judgment and plans to sell Colts memorabilia during the game because he realizes that he can sell five times more Colts products than any other player. Likewise, imagine that you are a creative and effective manager at work and that you tell your employees that during the next six months, you plan to clean the offices because you can clean five times better than the cleaning staff. What error in judgment are both Peyton and you making? Why shouldn't you do what you are better than anyone else at doing?

2.11 Is specialization and trade between individuals and countries more about having a job or about obtaining a higher standard of living? Individually, if you go from a situation of not trading with others (you produce everything yourself) to a situation of trading with others, do you still have a job? Does your standard of living increase? Likewise, if a country goes from not trading with other countries to trading with other countries, does it still have jobs? Does its standard of living increase?

2.12 In colonial America, the population was spread thinly over a large area, and transportation costs were very high because it was difficult to ship products by road for more than short distances. As a result, most of the free population lived on small farms, where they not only grew their own food but also usually made their own clothes and very rarely bought or sold anything for money. Explain why the incomes of these farmers were likely to rise as transportation costs fell. Use the concept of comparative advantage in your answer.

2.13 During the 1928 presidential election campaign, Herbert Hoover, the Republican candidate, argued that the United States should import only products that could not be produced here. Do you believe that this would be a good policy? Explain.

2.3	**The Market System, pages 51–58**

LEARNING OBJECTIVE: Explain the basic idea of how a market system works.

Summary

A **market** is a group of buyers and sellers of a good or service and the institution or arrangement by which they come together to trade. **Product markets** are markets for goods and services, such as computers and medical treatment. **Factor markets** are markets for the **factors of production**, such as labor, capital, natural resources, and entrepreneurial ability. A **circular-flow diagram** shows how participants in product markets and factor markets are linked. Adam Smith argued in his 1776 book *The Wealth of Nations* that in a **free market**, where the government does not control the production of goods and services, changes in prices lead firms to produce the goods and services most desired by consumers. If consumers demand more of a good, its price will rise. Firms respond to rising prices by increasing production. If consumers demand less of a good, its price will fall. Firms respond to falling prices by producing less of a good. An **entrepreneur** is someone who operates a business. In the market system, entrepreneurs are responsible for organizing the production of goods and services. The market system will work well only if there is protection for **property rights**, which are the rights of individuals and firms to use their property.

MyEconLab   Visit **www.myeconlab.com** to complete these exercises online and get instant feedback.

Review Questions

3.1 What is a circular-flow diagram, and what does it demonstrate?

3.2 What are the two main categories of participants in markets? Which participants are of greatest importance in determining what goods and services are produced?

3.3 What is a free market? In what ways does a free market economy differ from a centrally planned economy?

3.4 What is an entrepreneur? Why do entrepreneurs play a key role in a market system?

3.5 Under what circumstances are firms likely to produce more of a good or service? Under what circumstances are firms likely to produce less of a good or service?

3.6 What are private property rights? What role do they play in the working of a market system? Why are independent courts important for a well-functioning economy?

Problems and Applications

3.7 Identify whether each of the following transactions will take place in the factor market or in the product market and whether households or firms are supplying the good or service or demanding the good or service:

a. George buys a BMW X6 hybrid.

b. BMW increases employment at its Spartanburg plant.

c. George works 20 hours per week at McDonald's.

d. George sells land he owns to McDonald's so it can build a new restaurant.

3.8 **[Related to the** Making the Connection **on page 55]** In *The Wealth of Nations*, Adam Smith wrote the following (Book I, Chapter II): "It is not from the benevolence of the butcher, the brewer, or the baker, that we expect our dinner, but from their regard to their own interest." Briefly discuss what he meant by this.

3.9 **[Related to the** Making the Connection **on page 55]** According to an article in the *Wall Street Journal*, the parts contained in the BlackBerry Torch smartphone include a power management chip made by Texas Instruments (United States), a memory chip made by Samsung (South Korea), a GPS receiver made by CSR (United Kingdom), a radio frequency (RF) transceiver made by Dialog Semiconductor (Germany), an RF transceiver made by Renesas (Japan), an application and communications processor made by Marvell (United States), a video image processor made by STMicroelectronics (Switzerland), and plastic and stamped metal parts made by several firms in China. A firm in Mexico carries out final assembly of the Torch before it is shipped to BlackBerry for sale in the United States and other countries. Is it necessary for the managers in all of these firms to know how the components of the Torch are manufactured and how the components are assembled into a smartphone? Is it necessary for the chief executive officer (CEO) of BlackBerry to know this information? Briefly explain.

Based on Jennifer Valentino-DeVries and Phred Dvorak, "Piece by Piece: The Suppliers behind the New BlackBerry Torch Smartphone." *The Wall Street Journal*, August 16, 2010.

3.10 In many parts of Europe during the mid-1770s, governments gave guilds, or organizations of producers, the authority to control who was allowed to produce a good, the amount of the good produced, and the price charged for the good. Would you expect more competition among producers in a *guild system* or in a market system? Was the consumer or the producer at the center of the guild system, and which is at the center of the market system? How would the two systems compare over time in terms of innovation of new products and technologies?

3.11 In a speech at the New York University Law School, Federal Reserve Chairman Ben Bernanke stated:

> Writing in the eighteenth century, Adam Smith conceived of the free-market system as an "invisible hand" that harnesses the pursuit of private interest to promote the public good. Smith's conception remains relevant today, notwithstanding the enormous increase in economic complexity since the Industrial Revolution.

Briefly explain the idea of the invisible hand. What's so important about the idea of the invisible hand?

From Ben S. Bernanke, "Financial Regulation and the Invisible Hand," speech made at the New York University Law School, New York, New York, April 11, 2007.

3.12 Evaluate the following argument: "Adam Smith's analysis is based on a fundamental flaw: He assumes that people are motivated by self-interest. But this isn't true. I'm not selfish, and most people I know aren't selfish."

3.13 Writing in the *New York Times*, Michael Lewis argued that "a market economy is premised on a system of incentives designed to encourage an ignoble human trait: self-interest." Do you agree that self-interest is an "ignoble human trait"? What incentives does a market system provide to encourage self-interest?

From Michael Lewis, "In Defense of the Boom," *The New York Times*, October 27, 2002.

3.14 Some economists have been puzzled that although entrepreneurs take on the risk of losing time and money by starting new businesses, on average their incomes are lower than those of people with similar characteristics who go to work at large firms. Economist William Baumol believes part of the explanation for this puzzle may be that entrepreneurs are like people who buy lottery tickets. On average, people who don't buy lottery tickets are left with more money than people who buy tickets because lotteries take in more money than they give out. Baumol argues that "the masses of purchasers who grab up the [lottery] tickets are not irrational if they receive an adequate payment in another currency: psychic rewards."

a. What are "psychic rewards"?

b. What psychic rewards might an entrepreneur receive?

c. Do you agree with Baumol that an entrepreneur is like someone buying a lottery ticket? Briefly explain.

From William J. Baumol, *The Microtheory of Innovative Entrepreneurship*, (Princeton, NJ: Princeton University Press, 2010).

3.15 The 2009 International Property Rights Index study states:

Data shows that countries that protect the physical and intellectual property of their people enjoy nearly nine times higher [income per person] . . . than countries ranking lowest in property rights protections. The study . . . compared the protections of physical and intellectual property to economic stability in 115 countries. . . .

How would the creation of property rights be likely to affect the economic opportunities available to citizens of those countries ranking lowest in property rights protections?

Based on Kelsey Zahourek, "Report: Property Rights Linked to Economic Security," *International Property Rights Index 2009 Report*.

Where Prices Come From: The Interaction of Demand and Supply

Chapter Outline and Learning Objectives

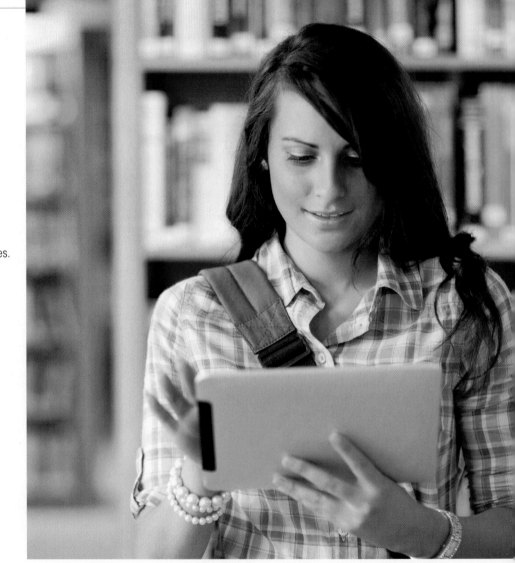

The Tablet Computer Revolution

Bill Gates, who was then chairman of Microsoft, made a famous—but wrong!—prediction in 2001. At a computer industry trade show, he predicted that tablet computers would make up a majority of personal computer sales within five years. Microsoft had developed new software that made it possible to use a stylus to write on a laptop computer screen, and Gates hoped that consumers would respond to compact lightweight computers. But many consumers found them awkward to use and thought that the prices, at $2,000 or more, were too high. As a result, rather than making up a majority of computer sales in 2006, tablets were just 1 percent of the market.

Fast forward to 2010: After years of stating that his company would not enter the market for netbooks—or lightweight computers smaller than laptops—Apple CEO Steve Jobs introduced the iPad in April. The iPad was an immediate success, selling nearly 15 million units by the end of the year. The iPad 2, released in early 2011, experienced similarly rapid sales.

The iPad was very different from the tablet computers that had failed to win favor with consumers a few years earlier. The iPad was more awkward to use for word processing or working on spreadsheets, but it was lighter than earlier tablets, and its wireless connectivity and portability made it better for Web surfing, checking e-mail, texting, and watching videos.

Although initially Apple had the market for new-style tablets largely to itself, competitors appeared rapidly. Toshiba, Samsung, Dell, LG, Motorola, Lenovo, Amazon, and ZTE all introduced tablets running on Google's Android operating system. Research in Motion (RIM) introduced the BlackBerry Playbook, based on its operating system.

The intense competition among firms selling the new tablets is a striking example of how the market responds to changes in consumer tastes. As many consumers indicated that they would buy small tablets, firms scrambled to meet the demand for this new product. Although intense competition is not always good news for firms trying to sell products, it is a boon to consumers because it increases the available choice of products and lowers the prices consumers pay for those products.

AN INSIDE LOOK on **page 92** discusses how the many tablet producers are concerned about component shortages.

Based on Matt Berger and James Niccolai, "Gates Unveils Portable Tablet PC," *PC World*, November 12, 2001; Wolfgang Gruener, "240 Million Tablets: The Gazillion-Dollar Forecast Game," www.fool.com, February 6, 2011; David Pogue, "Pretty Tablet, Though Late for the Ball," *New York Times*, June 29, 2011; and Stu Woo and Yukari Iwatani Kane, "Amazon to Battle Apple iPad with Tablet," *Wall Street Journal*, July 14, 2011.

Economics in Your Life

Will You Buy an Apple iPad or a Samsung Galaxy Tab?

Suppose you are considering buying a tablet computer and that you are choosing between an Apple iPad and a Samsung Galaxy Tab. Apple introduced the iPad in April 2010, and Samsung introduced the Galaxy Tab in November 2010; seven months is a long time in the world of high-tech gadgets. Apple products have become very fashionable, and if you buy an iPad, you will have access to many more applications—or "apps"—that can increase the enjoyability and productivity of your tablet. One strategy Samsung can use to overcome those advantages is to compete based on price and value. Would you choose to buy a Galaxy Tab if it had a lower price than an iPad? If your income increased, would it affect your decision about which tablet to buy? As you read the chapter, see if you can answer these questions. You can check your answers against those we provide **page 91** at the end of this chapter.

I n Chapter 1, we explored how economists use models to predict human behavior. In Chapter 2, we used the model of production possibilities frontiers to analyze scarcity and trade-offs. In this chapter and the next, we explore the model of demand and supply, which is the most powerful tool in economics, and use it to explain how prices are determined.

Recall from Chapter 1 that because economic models rely on assumptions, the models are simplifications of reality. In some cases, the assumptions of the model may not seem to describe exactly the economic situation being analyzed. For example, the model of demand and supply assumes that we are analyzing a *perfectly competitive market*. In a **perfectly competitive market**, there are many buyers and sellers, all the products sold are identical, and there are no barriers to new firms entering the market. These assumptions are very restrictive and apply exactly to only a few markets, such as the markets for wheat and other agricultural products. Experience has shown, however, that the model of demand and supply can be very useful in analyzing markets where competition among sellers is intense, even if there are relatively few sellers and the products being sold are not identical. In fact, in recent studies, the model of demand and supply has been successful in analyzing markets with as few as four buyers and four sellers. In the end, the usefulness of a model depends on how well it can predict outcomes in a market. As we will see in this chapter, this model is often very useful in predicting changes in quantities and prices in many markets.

We begin considering the model of demand and supply by discussing consumers and the demand side of the market, before turning to firms and the supply side. Throughout the book we will apply this model to understand business, the economy, and economic policy.

Perfectly competitive market A market that meets the conditions of (1) many buyers and sellers, (2) all firms selling identical products, and (3) no barriers to new firms entering the market.

The Demand Side of the Market

Chapter 2 explained that in a market system, consumers ultimately determine which goods and services will be produced. The most successful businesses are the ones that respond best to consumer demand. But what determines consumer demand for a product? Certainly, many factors influence the willingness of consumers to buy a particular product. For example, consumers who are considering buying a tablet computer, such as an Apple iPad or an Samsung Galaxy Tab, will make their decisions based on, among other factors, the income they have available to spend and the effectiveness of the advertising campaigns of the companies that sell tablets. The main factor in most consumer decisions, though, is the price of the product. So, it makes sense to begin with price when analyzing the decisions of consumers to buy a product. It is important to note that when we discuss demand, we are considering not what a consumer *wants* to buy but what the consumer is both willing and *able* to buy.

Demand Schedules and Demand Curves

Demand schedule A table that shows the relationship between the price of a product and the quantity of the product demanded.

Tables that show the relationship between the price of a product and the quantity of the product demanded are called **demand schedules**. The table in Figure 3.1 shows the number of tablet computers consumers would be willing to buy over the course of a day at five different prices. The amount of a good or a service that a consumer is willing and able to purchase at a given price is referred to as the **quantity demanded**. The graph in Figure 3.1 plots the numbers from the table as a **demand curve**, a curve that shows the relationship between the price of a product and the quantity of the product demanded. (Note that for convenience, we made the demand curve in Figure 3.1 a straight line, or linear. There is no reason that all demand curves need to be straight lines.) The demand curve in Figure 3.1 shows the **market demand**, or the demand by all the consumers of a given good or service. The market for a product, such as restaurant meals, that is

Quantity demanded The amount of a good or service that a consumer is willing and able to purchase at a given price.

Demand curve A curve that shows the relationship between the price of a product and the quantity of the product demanded.

Market demand The demand by all the consumers of a given good or service.

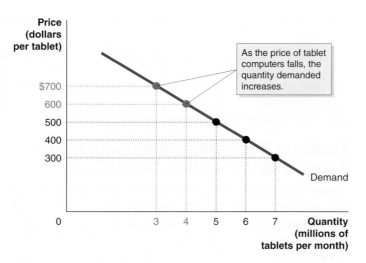

Demand Schedule	
Price (dollars per tablet)	Quantity (millions of tablets per month)
$700	3
600	4
500	5
400	6
300	7

As the price of tablet computers falls, the quantity demanded increases.

Figure 3.1

A Demand Schedule and Demand Curve

As the price changes, consumers change the quantity of tablet computers they are willing to buy. We can show this as a *demand schedule* in a table or as a *demand curve* on a graph. The table and graph both show that as the price of tablet computers falls, the quantity demanded increases. When the price of tablet computers is $700, consumers buy 3 million tablets per month. When the price drops to $600, consumers buy 4 million tablets. Therefore, the demand curve for tablet computers is downward sloping.

purchased locally would include all the consumers in a city or a relatively small area. The market for a product that is sold internationally, such as tablet computers, would include all the consumers in the world.

The demand curve in Figure 3.1 slopes downward because consumers will buy more tablets as the price falls. When the price of a tablet is $700, consumers buy 3 million tablets per month. If the price of a tablet falls to $600, consumers buy 4 million tablets. Buyers demand a larger quantity of a product as the price falls because the product becomes less expensive relative to other products and because they can afford to buy more at a lower price.

The Law of Demand

The inverse relationship between the price of a product and the quantity of the product demanded is called the **law of demand**: Holding everything else constant, when the price of a product falls, the quantity demanded of the product will increase, and when the price of a product rises, the quantity demanded of the product will decrease. The law of demand holds for any market demand curve. Economists have found only a very few exceptions to this law.

Law of demand The rule that, holding everything else constant, when the price of a product falls, the quantity demanded of the product will increase, and when the price of a product rises, the quantity demanded of the product will decrease.

What Explains the Law of Demand?

It makes sense that consumers will buy more of a good when the price falls and less of a good when the price rises, but let's look more closely at why this is true. When the price of tablet computers falls, consumers buy a larger quantity because of the *substitution effect* and the *income effect*.

Substitution Effect The **substitution effect** refers to the change in the quantity demanded of a good that results from a change in price, making the good more or less expensive *relative* to other goods that are *substitutes*. When the price of tablet computers falls, consumers will substitute buying tablet computers for buying other goods, such as laptop computers, netbook computers, or even smartphones.

Substitution effect The change in the quantity demanded of a good that results from a change in price, making the good more or less expensive relative to other goods that are substitutes.

The Income Effect The **income effect** of a price change refers to the change in the quantity demanded of a good that results from the effect of a change in the good's price on consumers' purchasing power. Purchasing power is the quantity of goods a consumer can buy with a fixed amount of income. When the price of a good falls, the increased purchasing power of consumers' incomes will usually lead them to purchase a larger quantity of the good. When the price of a good rises, the decreased purchasing

Income effect The change in the quantity demanded of a good that results from the effect of a change in the good's price on consumers' purchasing power.

power of consumers' incomes will usually lead them to purchase a smaller quantity of the good.

Note that although we can analyze them separately, the substitution effect and the income effect happen simultaneously whenever a price changes. So, a fall in the price of tablet computers leads consumers to buy more tablet computers, both because the tablets are now less expensive relative to substitute products and because the purchasing power of the consumers' incomes has increased.

Holding Everything Else Constant: The *Ceteris paribus* Condition

Ceteris paribus ("all else equal") condition The requirement that when analyzing the relationship between two variables—such as price and quantity demanded—other variables must be held constant.

Notice that the definition of the law of demand contains the phrase *holding everything else constant*. In constructing the market demand curve for tablet computers, we focused only on the effect that changes in the price of tablet computers would have on the quantity consumers would be willing and able to buy. We were holding constant other variables that might affect the willingness of consumers to buy tablets. Economists refer to the necessity of holding all variables other than price constant in constructing a demand curve as the **ceteris paribus** condition; *ceteris paribus* is Latin for "all else equal."

What would happen if we allowed a change in a variable—other than price—that might affect the willingness of consumers to buy tablet computers? Consumers would then change the quantity they demanded at each price. We can illustrate this effect by shifting the market demand curve. A shift of a demand curve is *an increase or a decrease in demand*. A movement along a demand curve is *an increase or a decrease in the quantity demanded*. As Figure 3.2 shows, we shift the demand curve to the right if consumers decide to buy more of the good at each price, and we shift the demand curve to the left if consumers decide to buy less at each price.

Variables That Shift Market Demand

Many variables other than price can influence market demand. These five are the most important:

- Income
- Prices of related goods
- Tastes
- Population and demographics
- Expected future prices

We next discuss how changes in each of these variables affect the market demand curve.

Figure 3.2

Shifting the Demand Curve

When consumers increase the quantity of a product they want to buy at a given price, the market demand curve shifts to the right, from D_1 to D_2. When consumers decrease the quantity of a product they want to buy at a given price, the demand curve shifts to the left, from D_1 to D_3.

Income The income that consumers have available to spend affects their willingness and ability to buy a good. Suppose that the market demand curve in Figure 3.1 on page 71 represents the willingness of consumers to buy tablet computers when average household income is $50,000. If household income rises to $52,000, the demand for tablets will increase, which we show by shifting the demand curve to the right. A good is a **normal good** when demand increases following a rise in income and decreases following a fall in income. Most goods are normal goods, but the demand for some goods falls when income rises and rises when income falls. For instance, as your income rises, you might buy less canned tuna or fewer hot dogs and buy more shrimp or prime rib. A good is an **inferior good** when demand decreases following a rise in income and increases following a fall in income. So, for you, canned tuna and hot dogs would be examples of inferior goods—not because they are of low quality but because you buy less of them as your income increases.

Normal good A good for which the demand increases as income rises and decreases as income falls.

Inferior good A good for which the demand increases as income falls and decreases as income rises.

Making the Connection | Are Quiznos Sandwiches Normal Goods and Subway Sandwiches Inferior Goods?

In recent years, as American families juggle busy schedules, they have increasingly relied on eating out rather than preparing meals at home. According to a survey by *Restaurants and Institutions* magazine, adults eat an average of nearly four meals per week outside the home. Nearly one-third of consumers frequently eat lunch away from home, and on weekdays more than 15 percent frequently eat dinner away from home, a proportion that rises to more than 35 percent on weekends.

Does this behavior change during a recession? We might expect that it would because recessions result in declining incomes, as some people lose their jobs and others are forced to work fewer hours or have their wages reduced. Dining out is more expensive than preparing meals at home, so one way to save during a recession is to cut back on restaurant meals. In fact, during the 2007–2009 recession, many restaurants had a difficult time. Particularly hard hit were "casual dining" restaurants that provide table service and serve moderately priced food. Among other restaurants, Ruby Tuesday, Olive Garden, Red Lobster, and LongHorn Steakhouse all experienced declining demand, while Bennigan's and Steak and Ale filed for bankruptcy.

Subway experienced increased sales during 2008 and 2009, while sales of Quiznos sandwiches fell.

However, the recession hurt some restaurants more than others. McDonald's restaurants experienced increased sales during 2008 and 2009. In the market for fast-food sandwiches, Subway reported increasing sales, while sales of Quiznos sandwiches, which are higher-priced, fell. So, Big Macs and Subway sandwiches seem to fit the economic definition of an inferior good because demand increases as income falls, while Quiznos sandwiches fit the definition of a normal good. But remember that inferior goods are not necessarily of low quality; they are just goods for which consumers increase their demand as their incomes fall.

Based on Julie Jargon and Mike Spector, "LBO, Recession Singe Quiznos," *Wall Street Journal*, July 21, 2011; Melodie Warner, "McDonald's Profit Rises 15%," *Wall Street Journal*, July 22, 2011; and "The New American Diner," *Restaurants and Institutions*, January 1, 2008.

Your Turn: For more practice, do related problem 1.11 on page 95 at the end of this chapter.

MyEconLab

Prices of Related Goods The prices of other goods can also affect consumers' demand for a product. Goods and services that can be used for the same purpose—such as tablet computers and laptop computers—are **substitutes**. When two goods are

Substitutes Goods and services that can be used for the same purpose.

substitutes, the more you buy of one, the less you will buy of the other. A decrease in the price of a substitute causes the demand curve for a good to shift to the left. An increase in the price of a substitute causes the demand curve for a good to shift to the right.

Suppose that the market demand curve in Figure 3.1 on page 71 represents the willingness and ability of consumers to buy laptop computers during a week when the average price of a laptop computer is $800. If the average price of laptops falls to $700, how will the market demand for tablets change? Consumers will demand fewer tablets at every price. We show this by shifting the demand curve for tablets to the left.

Complements Goods and services that are used together.

Goods and services that are used together—such as hot dogs and hot dog buns— are **complements**. When two goods are complements, the more consumers buy of one, the more they will buy of the other. A decrease in the price of a complement causes the demand curve for a good to shift to the right. An increase in the price of a complement causes the demand curve for a good to shift to the left.

Many people use applications, or "apps," on their tablet computers. So, tablets and apps are complements. Suppose the market demand curve in Figure 3.1 represents the willingness of consumers to buy tablets at a time when the average price of an app is $2.99. If the average price of apps drops to $0.99, consumers will buy more apps *and* more tablets: The demand curve for tablets will shift to the right.

Tastes Consumers can be influenced by an advertising campaign for a product. If Apple, Samsung, Amazon, and other firms making tablet computers begin to advertise heavily online, consumers are more likely to buy tablets at every price, and the demand curve will shift to the right. An economist would say that the advertising campaign has affected consumers' *taste* for tablet computers. Taste is a catchall category that refers to the many subjective elements that can enter into a consumer's decision to buy a product. A consumer's taste for a product can change for many reasons. Sometimes trends play a substantial role. For example, the popularity of low-carbohydrate diets caused a decline in demand for some goods, such as bread and donuts, and an increase in demand for beef. In general, when consumers' taste for a product increases, the demand curve will shift to the right, and when consumers' taste for a product decreases, the demand curve for the product will shift to the left.

Demographics The characteristics of a population with respect to age, race, and gender.

Population and Demographics Population and demographic factors can affect the demand for a product. As the population of the United States increases, so will the number of consumers, and the demand for most products will increase. The **demographics** of a population refers to its characteristics, with respect to age, race, and gender. As the demographics of a country or region change, the demand for particular goods will increase or decrease because different categories of people tend to have different preferences for those goods. For instance, Hispanics are expected to increase from 16 percent of the U.S. population in 2010 to 29 percent in 2050. This increase will expand demand for Spanish-language books and cable television channels, among other goods and services.

Making the Connection | **The Aging of the Baby Boom Generation**

The average age of the U.S. population is increasing. After World War II in 1945, the United States experienced a "baby boom," as birthrates rose and remained high through the early 1960s. Falling birthrates after 1965 mean that the baby boom generation is larger than the generation before it and the generations after it. The figure on the next page uses projections from the U.S. Census Bureau to show that as boomers age, they are increasing the fraction of the U.S. population that is older than 65.

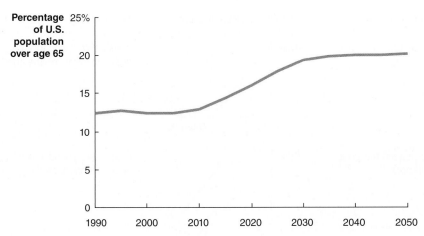

Data from U.S. Census Bureau.

What effects will the aging of the baby boom generation have on the economy? Older people have a greater demand for medical care than do younger people. So, in coming years, the demand for doctors, nurses, and hospital facilities should all increase. The increasing demand for health care is so strong that between the beginning of the 2007–2009 recession and June 2011, 1 million new jobs were created in health care—at the same time as total employment in the United States *declined* by 7 million jobs. As we mentioned in Chapter 2, the increased demand for medical care will also drive up the federal government's costs under the Medicare program, which pays part of the medical bills of people who are 65 and older.

Aging boomers will also have an effect on the housing market. Older people often "downsize" their housing by moving from large, single-family homes, whose maintenance can be difficult and expensive, to smaller homes, condominiums, or apartments. So, in coming years, the demand for large homes may decrease, while the demand for smaller homes and apartments may increase. Older people also tend to drive less often and for shorter distances than do younger drivers. So, their cars wear out more slowly and, therefore, need to be replaced less often, reducing the total demand for cars.

Based on U.S. Bureau of Labor Statistics, "Employment, Hours, and Earnings from the Current Employment Statistics Survey," July 2011; Liam Denning, "Car Makers Hit the Age Speed Bump," *Wall Street Journal*, September 18, 2010; Kendra Marr, "The Economy's Steady Pulse—Health-Care Sector Is Poised to Keep Expanding, but So Are Its Costs," *Washington Post*, June 13, 2008; and Peter Francese, "The Changing Face of the U.S. Consumer," *Advertising Age*, July 7, 2008.

Your Turn: For more practice, do related problems 1.12 and 1.13 on page 95 at the end of this chapter.   MyEconLab

Expected Future Prices Consumers choose not only which products to buy but also when to buy them. For instance, if enough consumers become convinced that houses will be selling for lower prices in three months, the demand for houses will decrease now, as some consumers postpone their purchases to wait for the expected price decrease. Alternatively, if enough consumers become convinced that the price of houses will be higher in three months, the demand for houses will increase now, as some consumers try to beat the expected price increase.

Table 3.1 on page 76 summarizes the most important variables that cause market demand curves to shift. Note that the table shows the shift in the demand curve that results from an *increase* in each of the variables. A *decrease* in these variables would cause the demand curve to shift in the opposite direction.

A Change in Demand versus a Change in Quantity Demanded

It is important to understand the difference between a *change in demand* and a *change in quantity demanded*. A change in demand refers to a shift of the demand curve. A shift occurs if there is a change in one of the variables, *other than the price of the product*, that

Table 3.1	An increase in ...	shifts the demand curve ...	because ...
Variables That Shift Market Demand Curves	income (and the good is normal)		consumers spend more of their higher incomes on the good.
	income (and the good is inferior)		consumers spend less of their higher incomes on the good.
	the price of a substitute good		consumers buy less of the substitute good and more of this good.
	the price of a complementary good		consumers buy less of the complementary good and less of this good.
	taste for the good		consumers are willing to buy a larger quantity of the good at every price.
	population		additional consumers result in a greater quantity demanded at every price.
	the expected price of the good in the future		consumers buy more of the good today to avoid the higher price in the future.

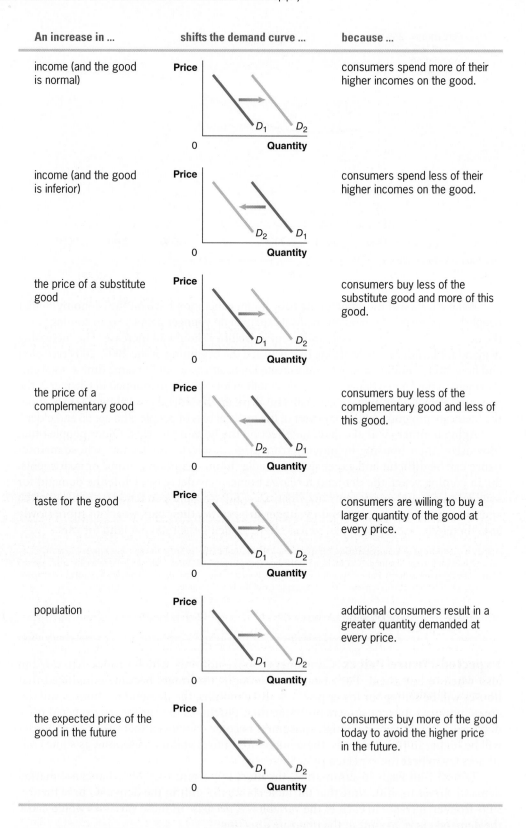

affects the willingness of consumers to buy the product. A change in quantity demanded refers to a movement along the demand curve as a result of a change in the product's price. Figure 3.3 illustrates this important distinction. If the price of tablet computers falls from $700 to $600 per tablet, the result will be a movement along the demand curve from point *A* to point *B*—an increase in quantity demanded from 3 million to 4 million. If consumers' incomes increase, or if another factor changes that makes consumers want more of the product at every price, the demand curve will shift to the right—an increase

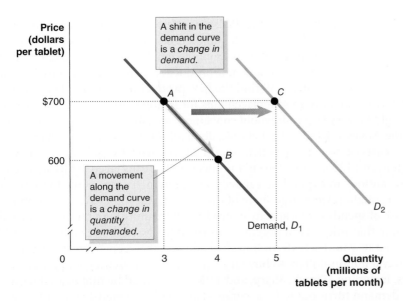

Figure 3.3

A Change in Demand versus a Change in Quantity Demanded

If the price of tablet computers falls from $700 to $600, the result will be a movement along the demand curve from point *A* to point *B*—an increase in quantity demanded from 3 million tablets to 4 million tablets. If consumers' incomes increase, or if another factor changes that makes consumers want more of the product at every price, the demand curve will shift to the right—an increase in demand. In this case, the increase in demand from D_1 to D_2 causes the quantity of tablet computers demanded at a price of $700 to increase from 3 million tablets at point *A* to 5 million tablets at point *C*.

in demand. In this case, the increase in demand from D_1 to D_2 causes the quantity of tablet computers demanded at a price of $700 to increase from 3 million at point *A* to 5 million at point *C*.

| Making the Connection | ## Forecasting the Demand for iPads |

One of the most important decisions that the managers of any large firm face is which new products to develop. A firm must devote people, time, and money to designing a new product, negotiating with suppliers, formulating a marketing campaign, and many other tasks. But any firm has only limited resources and so faces a trade-off: Resources used to develop one product will not be available to develop another product. Ultimately, the products a firm chooses to develop will be those that it believes will be the most profitable. So, to decide which products to develop, firms need to forecast the demand for those products.

We saw at the beginning of the chapter that in 2001, Bill Gates predicted that within five years, a majority of computers sold would be tablets. If Gates had been correct about the way the computer market was changing, then any computer firm that didn't develop a tablet would have run the risk of being left behind. David Sobotta, who worked at Apple for 20 years and eventually became its national sales manager, has described discussions at Apple during 2002 about whether to develop a tablet. According to Sobotta, representatives of the federal government's National Institutes of Health urged Apple to develop a tablet computer, arguing that it would be particularly useful to doctors, nurses, and hospitals. Apple's managers decided not to develop a tablet, however, because they believed the technology available at that time was too complex for the average computer user and they also believed that the demand from doctors and nurses would be small. As we saw in the chapter opener, Apple's forecast was correct. Despite Bill Gates's prediction, in 2006, tablets made up only 1 percent of the computer market. According to Sobotta, "Apple executives had a theory that the route to success will not be through selling thousands of relatively expensive things, but millions of very inexpensive things like iPods."

Apple continued to work on tablets, though, developing the technology to eliminate keyboards in favor of touchscreen displays. Rather than proceed immediately to building a tablet, Steve Jobs, who was then Apple's CEO, realized he could use this technology in a different way: "I thought 'My God we can build a phone out of this.'" After the technology had been successfully embodied in the iPhone, Apple and Jobs turned back to developing

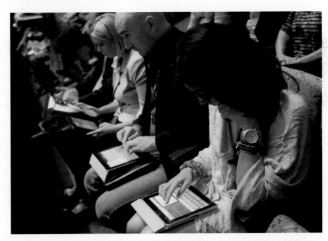

Will the future demand for tablets such as the iPad continue to grow?

a tablet computer. The result was the iPad, first offered for sale in April 2010. The iPad was an immediate success, selling nearly 15 million units by the end of 2010 and leading other firms to introduce competing products. But how rapidly would demand for tablets grow?

Forecasting the demand for any new product is challenging because it is difficult to gauge how many consumers will find the new product to be useful. For instance, would consumers see tablets as good replacements for laptop computers? If so, the demand for tablets might be very large. Or would consumers see tablets as being more like e-readers, such as the Amazon Kindle? In that case, demand was likely to be much smaller. In mid-2011, forecasts of how many tablets would be sold worldwide in 2012 ranged between 54.8 million and 120 million. Given this uncertainty, firms faced a difficult choice: If they were too cautious in expanding capacity or in buying components for a new product, other firms might seize a large share of the market. But if they were too optimistic, they ran the risk of spending on capacity to produce more units than they could actually sell—an outcome that might turn potential profits into losses. For example, in 2011, Apple forecast that it would sell 40 million iPads during the year. Accordingly, the company spent several billion dollars to buy large quantities of touchscreen panels from manufacturers, including Wintek, Sharp, and TPK. That would be money well spent . . . if the forecast demand turns out to be accurate. Time will tell whether the future demand for tablets will be as large as Apple and other firms were forecasting it would be during 2011.

Based on Wolfgang Gruener, "240 Million Tablets: The Gazillion-Dollar Forecast Game," www.fool.com, February 6, 2011; "Apple Conference Call on Q1 2011 Financial Results," www.apple.com, January 18, 2011; David Sobotta, "What Jobs Told Me on the iPhone," *The Guardian* (London), January 3, 2007, p. 1; "Jobs Says iPad Idea Came Before iPhone," *Associated Press*, January 2, 2010; and Laura June, "The Apple Tablet: A Complete History, Supposedly," endgadget.com, January 26, 2010.

MyEconLab   **Your Turn:** For more practice, do related problem 1.16 on page 95 at the end of this chapter.

3.2 LEARNING OBJECTIVE

Discuss the variables that influence supply.

Quantity supplied The amount of a good or service that a firm is willing and able to supply at a given price.

Supply schedule A table that shows the relationship between the price of a product and the quantity of the product supplied.

Supply curve A curve that shows the relationship between the price of a product and the quantity of the product supplied.

The Supply Side of the Market

Just as many variables influence the willingness and ability of consumers to buy a particular good or service, many variables also influence the willingness and ability of firms to sell a good or service. The most important of these variables is price. The amount of a good or service that a firm is willing and able to supply at a given price is the **quantity supplied**. Holding other variables constant, when the price of a good rises, producing the good is more profitable, and the quantity supplied will increase. When the price of a good falls, the good is less profitable, and the quantity supplied will decrease. In addition, as we saw in Chapter 2, devoting more and more resources to the production of a good results in increasing marginal costs. If, for example, Apple, Toshiba, Samsung, LG, and other firms increase production of tablet computers during a given time period, they are likely to find that the cost of producing additional tablets increases as their suppliers run existing factories for longer hours and pay higher prices for components and higher wages for workers. With higher marginal costs, firms will supply a larger quantity only if the price is higher.

Supply Schedules and Supply Curves

A **supply schedule** is a table that shows the relationship between the price of a product and the quantity of the product supplied. The table in Figure 3.4 is a supply schedule showing the quantity of tablet computers that firms would be willing to supply per month at different prices. The graph in Figure 3.4 plots the numbers from the supply schedule as a *supply curve*. A **supply curve** shows the relationship between the price of a product and the quantity of the product supplied. The supply schedule and supply curve both show that as the price of tablet computers rises, firms will increase the quantity they supply. At a price of $600 per tablet, firms will supply 6 million tablets per month. At the higher price of $700, firms will supply 7 million. (Once again, we are assuming for convenience that the supply curve is a straight line, even though not all supply curves are actually straight lines.)

Supply Schedule	
Price (dollars per tablet)	Quantity (millions of tablets per month)
$700	7
600	6
500	5
400	4
300	3

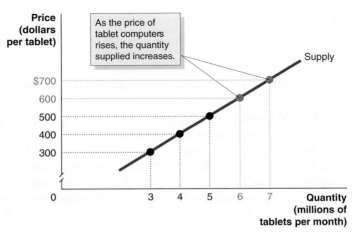

As the price of tablet computers rises, the quantity supplied increases.

Figure 3.4

A Supply Schedule and Supply Curve

As the price changes, Apple, Toshiba, Samsung, LG, and other firms producing tablet computers change the quantity they are willing to supply. We can show this as a *supply schedule* in a table or as a *supply curve* on a graph. The supply schedule and supply curve both show that as the price of tablet computers rises, firms will increase the quantity they supply. At a price of $600 per tablet, firms will supply 6 million tablets. At a price of $700, firms will supply 7 million tablets.

The Law of Supply

The *market supply curve* in Figure 3.4 is upward sloping. We expect most supply curves to be upward sloping, according to the **law of supply**, which states that, holding everything else constant, increases in price cause increases in the quantity supplied, and decreases in price cause decreases in the quantity supplied. Notice that the definition of the law of supply—like the definition of the law of demand—contains the phrase *holding everything else constant*. If only the price of the product changes, there is a movement along the supply curve, which is *an increase or a decrease in the quantity supplied*. As Figure 3.5 shows, if any other variable that affects the willingness of firms to supply a good changes, the supply curve will shift, which is *an increase or a decrease in supply*. When firms increase the quantity of a product they want to sell at a given price, the supply curve shifts to the right. The shift from S_1 to S_3 represents *an increase in supply*. When firms decrease the quantity of a product they want to sell at a given price, the supply curve shifts to the left. The shift from S_1 to S_2 represents *a decrease in supply*.

Law of supply The rule that, holding everything else constant, increases in price cause increases in the quantity supplied, and decreases in price cause decreases in the quantity supplied.

Variables That Shift Market Supply

The following are the most important variables that shift market supply:

- Prices of inputs
- Technological change

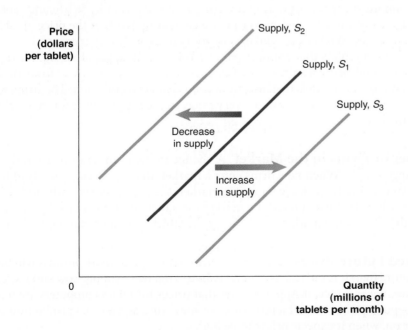

Figure 3.5

Shifting the Supply Curve

When firms increase the quantity of a product they want to sell at a given price, the supply curve shifts to the right. The shift from S_1 to S_3 represents an *increase in supply*. When firms decrease the quantity of a product they want to sell at a given price, the supply curve shifts to the left. The shift from S_1 to S_2 represents a *decrease in supply*.

- Prices of substitutes in production
- Number of firms in the market
- Expected future prices

We next discuss how each of these variables affects the market supply curve.

Prices of Inputs The factor most likely to cause the supply curve for a product to shift is a change in the price of an *input*. An input is anything used in the production of a good or service. For instance, if the price of a component of tablet computers, such as Flash memory, rises, the cost of producing tablet computers will increase, and tablets will be less profitable at every price. The supply of tablets will decline, and the market supply curve for tablets will shift to the left. Similarly, if the price of an input declines, the supply of tablets will increase, and the supply curve will shift to the right.

Technological change A positive or negative change in the ability of a firm to produce a given level of output with a given quantity of inputs.

Technological Change A second factor that causes a change in supply is *technological change*. **Technological change** is a positive or negative change in the ability of a firm to produce a given level of output with a given quantity of inputs. Positive technological change occurs whenever a firm is able to produce more output using the same amount of inputs. This shift will happen when the *productivity* of workers or machines increases. If a firm can produce more output with the same amount of inputs, its costs will be lower, and the good will be more profitable to produce at any given price. As a result, when positive technological change occurs, the firm will increase the quantity supplied at every price, and its supply curve will shift to the right. Normally, we expect technological change to have a positive effect on a firm's willingness to supply a product.

Negative technological change is relatively rare, although it could result from an earthquake or another natural disaster or from a war that reduces firms' ability to supply as much output with a given amount of inputs. Negative technological change will raise firms' costs, and the good will be less profitable to produce. Therefore, negative technological change will cause the market supply curve to shift to the left.

Prices of Substitutes in Production Firms often choose which good or service they will produce. Alternative products that a firm could produce are called *substitutes in production*. To this point, we have considered the market for all types of tablet computers. A key feature of tablet computers is whether they connect to the Internet just by Wi-Fi or by either Wi-Fi or a cellular network. Suppose we consider as separate markets tablet computers capable of only connecting to the Internet by Wi-Fi and tablet computers that can connect either by Wi-Fi or a cellular network. If the price of tablets that connect by either Wi-Fi or a cellular network increases, these tablets will become more profitable than tablets that connect only by Wi-Fi, and Apple, Toshiba, and the other firms making tablets will shift some of their productive capacity away from Wi-Fi–only models and toward models that also allow for a cellular connection. The firms will offer fewer Wi-Fi–only models for sale at every price, so the supply curve for these tablets will shift to the left.

Number of Firms in the Market A change in the number of firms in the market will change supply. When new firms *enter* a market, the supply curve shifts to the right, and when existing firms leave, or *exit*, a market, the supply curve shifts to the left. For instance, when Toshiba entered the market for tablet computers in July 2011 by introducing the Thrive, the market supply curve for tablet computers shifted to the right.

Expected Future Prices If a firm expects that the price of its product will be higher in the future than it is today, it has an incentive to decrease supply now and increase it in the future. For instance, if Apple believes that prices for tablet computers are temporarily low—perhaps because of a recession—it may store some of its production today to sell later on, when it expects prices to be higher.

An increase in ...	shifts the supply curve ...	because ...	Table 3.2

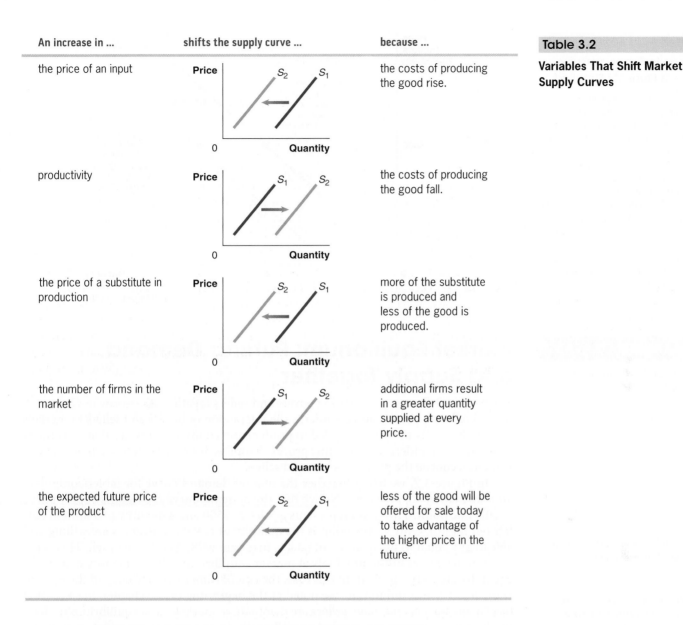

An increase in ...	shifts the supply curve ...	because ...
the price of an input		the costs of producing the good rise.
productivity		the costs of producing the good fall.
the price of a substitute in production		more of the substitute is produced and less of the good is produced.
the number of firms in the market		additional firms result in a greater quantity supplied at every price.
the expected future price of the product		less of the good will be offered for sale today to take advantage of the higher price in the future.

Table 3.2 summarizes the most important variables that cause market supply curves to shift. Note that the table shows the shift in the supply curve that results from an *increase* in each of the variables. A *decrease* in these variables would cause the supply curve to shift in the opposite direction.

A Change in Supply versus a Change in Quantity Supplied

We noted earlier the important difference between a change in demand and a change in quantity demanded. There is a similar difference between a *change in supply* and a *change in quantity supplied*. A change in supply refers to a shift of the supply curve. The supply curve will shift when there is a change in one of the variables, *other than the price of the product*, that affects the willingness of suppliers to sell the product. A change in quantity supplied refers to a movement along the supply curve as a result of a change in the product's price. Figure 3.6 illustrates this important distinction. If the price of tablet computers rises from $500 to $600 per tablet, the result will be a movement up the supply curve from point *A* to point *B*—an increase in quantity supplied from 5 million tablets to 6 million tablets. If the price of an input decreases or another factor changes that causes sellers to supply more of the product at every price, the supply curve will shift to the right—an increase in supply. In this case, the increase in supply from S_1 to S_2 causes the quantity of tablet computers supplied at a price of $600 to increase from 6 million at point *B* to 8 million at point *C*.

Figure 3.6

A Change in Supply versus a Change in Quantity Supplied

If the price of tablet computers rises from $500 to $600 per tablet, the result will be a movement up the supply curve from point *A* to point *B*—an increase in quantity supplied by Apple, Toshiba, Samsung, and the other firms from 5 million to 6 million tablets. If the price of an input decreases or another factor changes that causes sellers to supply more of the product at every price, the supply curve will shift to the right—an increase in supply. In this case, the increase in supply from S_1 to S_2 causes the quantity of tablet computers supplied at a price of $600 to increase from 6 million at point *B* to 8 million at point *C*.

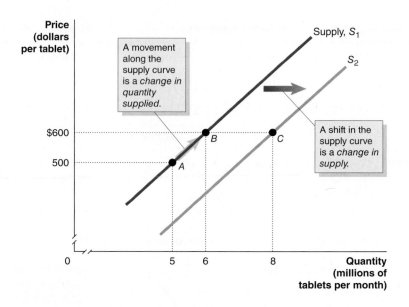

3.3 LEARNING OBJECTIVE

Use a graph to illustrate market equilibrium.

Market equilibrium A situation in which quantity demanded equals quantity supplied.

Competitive market equilibrium A market equilibrium with many buyers and many sellers.

Market Equilibrium: Putting Demand and Supply Together

The purpose of markets is to bring buyers and sellers together. As we saw in Chapter 2, instead of being chaotic and disorderly, the interaction of buyers and sellers in markets ultimately results in firms being led to produce the goods and services that consumers want most. To understand how this process happens, we first need to see how markets work to reconcile the plans of buyers and sellers.

In Figure 3.7, we bring together the market demand curve for tablet computers and the market supply curve. Notice that the demand curve crosses the supply curve at only one point. This point represents a price of $500 and a quantity of 5 million tablets per month. Only at this point is the quantity of tablets consumers are willing and able to buy equal to the quantity of tablets firms are willing and able to sell. This is the point of **market equilibrium**. Only at market equilibrium will the quantity demanded equal the quantity supplied. In this case, the *equilibrium price* is $500, and the *equilibrium quantity* is 5 million. As we noted at the beginning of the chapter, markets that have many buyers and many sellers are competitive markets, and equilibrium in these markets is a **competitive market equilibrium**. In the market for tablet computers,

Figure 3.7

Market Equilibrium

Where the demand curve crosses the supply curve determines market equilibrium. In this case, the demand curve for tablet computers crosses the supply curve at a price of $500 and a quantity of 5 million tablets. Only at this point is the quantity of tablet computers consumers are willing to buy equal to the quantity that Apple, Amazon, Samsung, and the other firms are willing to sell: The quantity demanded is equal to the quantity supplied.

there are many buyers but only about 20 firms. Whether 20 firms is enough for our model of demand and supply to apply to this market is a matter of judgment. In this chapter, we are assuming that the market for tablet computers has enough sellers to be competitive.

How Markets Eliminate Surpluses and Shortages

A market that is not in equilibrium moves toward equilibrium. Once a market is in equilibrium, it remains in equilibrium. To see why, consider what happens if a market is not in equilibrium. For instance, suppose that the price in the market for tablet computers was $600, rather than the equilibrium price of $500. As Figure 3.8 shows, at a price of $600, the quantity of tablets supplied would be 6 million, and the quantity of tablets demanded would be 4 million. When the quantity supplied is greater than the quantity demanded, there is a **surplus** in the market. In this case, the surplus is equal to 2 million tablets (6 million − 4 million = 2 million). When there is a surplus, firms have unsold goods piling up, which gives them an incentive to increase their sales by cutting the price. Cutting the price will simultaneously increase the quantity demanded and decrease the quantity supplied. This adjustment will reduce the surplus, but as long as the price is above $500, there will be a surplus, and downward pressure on the price will continue. Only when the price has fallen to $500 will the market be in equilibrium.

Surplus A situation in which the quantity supplied is greater than the quantity demanded.

If, however, the price were $300, the quantity demanded would be 7 million, and the quantity supplied would be 3 million, as shown in Figure 3.8. When the quantity demanded is greater than the quantity supplied, there is a **shortage** in the market. In this case, the shortage is equal to 4 million tablets (7 million − 3 million = 4 million). When a shortage occurs, some consumers will be unable to buy tablet computers at the current price. In this situation, firms will realize that they can raise the price without losing sales. A higher price will simultaneously increase the quantity supplied and decrease the quantity demanded. This adjustment will reduce the shortage, but as long as the price is below $500, there will be a shortage, and upward pressure on the price will continue. Only when the price has risen to $500 will the market be in equilibrium.

Shortage A situation in which the quantity demanded is greater than the quantity supplied.

At a competitive market equilibrium, all consumers willing to pay the market price will be able to buy as much of the product as they want, and all firms willing to accept the market price will be able to sell as much of the product as they want. As a result, there will be no reason for the price to change unless either the demand curve or the supply curve shifts.

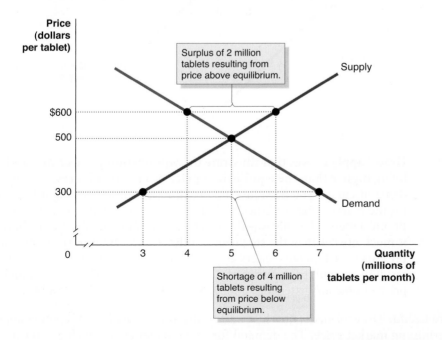

Figure 3.8

The Effect of Surpluses and Shortages on the Market Price

When the market price is above equilibrium, there will be a *surplus*. In the figure, a price of $600 for tablet computers results in 6 million tablets being supplied but only 4 million tablets being demanded, or a surplus of 2 million. As Apple, Toshiba, Dell, and other firms cut the price to dispose of the surplus, the price will fall to the equilibrium of $500. When the market price is below equilibrium, there will be a *shortage*. A price of $300 results in 7 million tablets being demanded but only 3 million tablets being supplied, or a shortage of 4 million tablets. As firms find that consumers who are unable to find tablet computers available for sale are willing to pay higher prices to get them, the price will rise to the equilibrium of $500.

Demand and Supply Both Count

Keep in mind that the interaction of demand and supply determines the equilibrium price. Neither consumers nor firms can dictate what the equilibrium price will be. No firm can sell anything at any price unless it can find a willing buyer, and no consumer can buy anything at any price without finding a willing seller.

Solved Problem 3.3

Demand and Supply Both Count: A Tale of Two Letters

Which letter is likely to be worth more: one written by Abraham Lincoln or one written by his assassin, John Wilkes Booth? Lincoln is one of the greatest presidents, and many people collect anything he wrote. The demand for letters written by Lincoln surely would seem to be much greater than the demand for letters written by Booth. Yet when R. M. Smythe and Co. auctioned off on the same day a letter written by Lincoln and a letter written by Booth, the Booth letter sold for $31,050, and the Lincoln letter sold for only $21,850. Use a demand and supply graph to explain how the Booth letter has a higher market price than the Lincoln letter, even though the demand for letters written by Lincoln is greater than the demand for letters written by Booth.

Solving the Problem

Step 1: **Review the chapter material.** This problem is about prices being determined at market equilibrium, so you may want to review the section "Market Equilibrium: Putting Demand and Supply Together," which begins on page 82.

Step 2: **Draw demand curves that illustrate the greater demand for Lincoln's letters.** Begin by drawing two demand curves. Label one "Demand for Lincoln's letters" and the other "Demand for Booth's letters." Make sure that the Lincoln demand curve is much farther to the right than the Booth demand curve.

Step 3: **Draw supply curves that illustrate the equilibrium price of Booth's letters being higher than the equilibrium price of Lincoln's letters.** Based on the demand curves you have just drawn, think about how it might be possible for the market price of Lincoln's letters to be lower than the market price of Booth's letters. The only way this can be true is if the supply of Lincoln's letters is much greater than the supply of Booth's letters. Draw on your graph a supply curve for Lincoln's letters and a supply curve for Booth's letters that will result in an equilibrium price of Booth's letters of $31,050 and an equilibrium price of Lincoln's letters of $21,850. You have now solved the problem.

Extra Credit: The explanation for this puzzle is that both demand and supply count when determining market price. The demand for Lincoln's letters is much greater than the

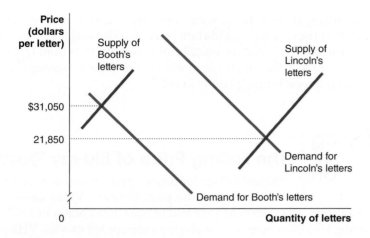

demand for Booth's letters, but the supply of Booth's letters is very small. Historians believe that only eight letters written by Booth exist today. (Note that the supply curves for letters written by Booth and by Lincoln are upward sloping, even though only a fixed number of each of these types of letters is available and, obviously, no more can be produced. The upward slope of the supply curves occurs because the higher the price, the larger the quantity of letters that will be offered for sale by people who currently own them.)

Your Turn: For more practice, do related problems 3.5 and 3.6 on page 97 at the end of this chapter.   MyEconLab

---

The Effect of Demand and Supply Shifts on Equilibrium

3.4 LEARNING OBJECTIVE

Use demand and supply graphs to predict changes in prices and quantities.

We have seen that the interaction of demand and supply in markets determines the quantity of a good that is produced and the price at which it sells. We have also seen that several variables cause demand curves to shift and other variables cause supply curves to shift. As a result, demand and supply curves in most markets are constantly shifting, and the prices and quantities that represent equilibrium are constantly changing. In this section, we look at how shifts in demand and supply curves affect equilibrium price and quantity.

The Effect of Shifts in Supply on Equilibrium

When Toshiba entered the market for tablet computers by introducing the Thrive, the market supply curve for tablet computers shifted to the right. Figure 3.9 shows the

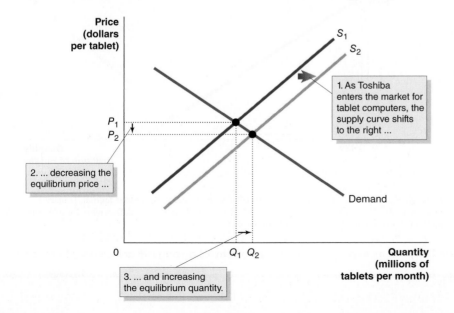

Figure 3.9

The Effect of an Increase in Supply on Equilibrium

If a firm enters a market, as Toshiba entered the market for tablet computers when it introduced the Thrive, the equilibrium price will fall, and the equilibrium quantity will rise:

1. As Toshiba enters the market for tablet computers, a larger quantity of tablets will be supplied at every price, so the market supply curve shifts to the right, from S_1 to S_2, which causes a surplus of tablets at the original price, P_1.
2. The equilibrium price falls from P_1 to P_2.
3. The equilibrium quantity rises from Q_1 to Q_2.

supply curve shifting from S_1 to S_2. When the supply curve shifts to the right, there will be a surplus at the original equilibrium price, P_1. The surplus is eliminated as the equilibrium price falls to P_2, and the equilibrium quantity rises from Q_1 to Q_2. If existing firms exit the market, the supply curve will shift to the left, causing the equilibrium price to rise and the equilibrium quantity to fall.

Making the Connection

The Falling Price of Blu-ray Players

The technology for playing prerecorded movies has progressed rapidly during the past 30 years. Video cassette recorders (VCRs) were introduced in Japan in 1976 and in the United States in 1977. As the first way of recording television programs or playing prerecorded movies, VHS players were immensely popular. In 1997, though, digital video disc (DVD) players became available in the United States. DVDs could store more information than could the VHS tapes played on VCRs and could produce a crisper picture. Within a few years, sales of DVD players were greater than sales of VCRs, and by 2006 the movie studios had stopped releasing films on VHS tapes. In 2006, Blu-ray players were introduced. Because Blu-ray discs can store 25 gigabytes of data, compared with fewer than 5 gigabytes on a typical DVD, Blu-ray players can reproduce high-definition images that DVD players cannot.

When firms first began selling VCRs, DVD players, and Blu-ray players, they initially charged high prices that declined rapidly within a few years. As the figure below shows, the average price of a Blu-ray player was about $800 in May 2006, but it had declined to about $120 in December 2010. Sales of Blu-ray players rose from about 425,000 in 2006 to 11.25 million in 2010. The figure shows that the decline in price and increase in quantity resulted from a large shift to the right of the supply curve. The supply curve in 2010 was much farther to the right than the supply curve in 2006 for two reasons: First, after Samsung introduced the first Blu-ray player—at a price of $999—other firms entered the industry, increasing the quantity supplied at every price. Second, the prices of the parts used in manufacturing Blu-ray players, particularly the laser components, declined sharply. As the cost of manufacturing the players declined, the quantity supplied at every price increased.

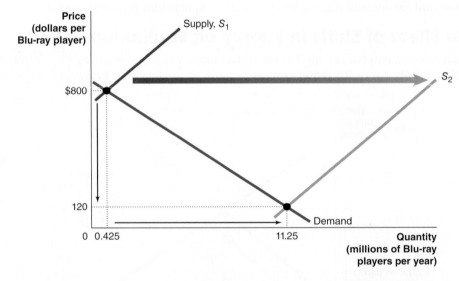

Based on Sarah McBride, "New DVD Players Resolve Battle of Formats," *Wall Street Journal*, January 4, 2007; Yukari Iwatani Kane and Miguel Bustillo, "Dreaming of a Blu Christmas," *Wall Street Journal*, December 23, 2009; and "DEG 2010 Year-End Home Entertainment Report," www.degonline.com.

MyEconLab **Your Turn:** For more practice, do related problem 4.6 on page 98 at the end of this chapter.

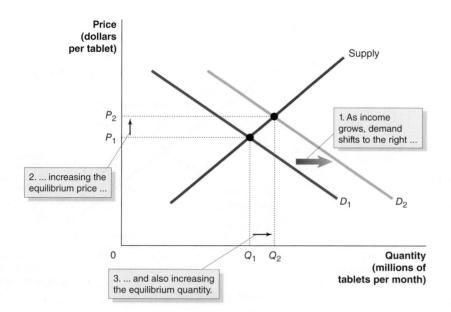

Figure 3.10

The Effect of an Increase in Demand on Equilibrium

Increases in income will cause the equilibrium price and quantity to rise:

1. Because tablet computers are a normal good, as income grows, the quantity demanded increases at every price, and the market demand curve shifts to the right, from D_1 to D_2, which causes a shortage of tablet computers at the original price, P_1.

2. The equilibrium price rises from P_1 to P_2.

3. The equilibrium quantity rises from Q_1 to Q_2.

The Effect of Shifts in Demand on Equilibrium

Because tablet computers are a normal good, when incomes increase, the market demand curve for tablet computers shifts to the right. Figure 3.10 shows the effect of a demand curve shifting to the right, from D_1 to D_2. This shift causes a shortage at the original equilibrium price, P_1. To eliminate the shortage, the equilibrium price rises to P_2, and the equilibrium quantity rises from Q_1 to Q_2. In contrast, if the price of a substitute good, such as laptop computers, were to fall, the demand for tablet computers would decrease, shifting the demand curve for tablets to the left. When the demand curve shifts to the left, the equilibrium price and quantity will both decrease.

The Effect of Shifts in Demand and Supply over Time

Whenever only demand or only supply shifts, we can easily predict the effect on equilibrium price and quantity. But what happens if *both* curves shift? For instance, in many markets, the demand curve shifts to the right over time as population and income grow. The supply curve also often shifts to the right as new firms enter the market and positive technological change occurs. Whether the equilibrium price in a market rises or falls over time depends on whether demand shifts to the right more than does supply. Panel (a) of Figure 3.11 shows that when demand shifts to the right more than supply, the equilibrium price rises. But, as panel (b) shows, when supply shifts to the right more than demand, the equilibrium price falls.

Table 3.3 summarizes all possible combinations of shifts in demand and supply over time and the effects of the shifts on equilibrium price (P) and quantity (Q). For example, the entry in red in the table shows that if the demand curve shifts to the right and the supply curve also shifts to the right, the equilibrium quantity will increase, while the equilibrium price may increase, decrease, or remain unchanged. To make sure you understand each entry in the table, draw demand and supply graphs to check whether you can reproduce the predicted changes in equilibrium price and quantity. If the entry in the table says the predicted change in equilibrium price or quantity can be either an increase or a decrease, draw two graphs similar to panels (a) and (b) of Figure 3.11, one showing the equilibrium price or quantity increasing and the other showing it decreasing. Note also that in the ambiguous cases where either price or quantity might increase or decrease, it is also possible that price or quantity might remain unchanged. Be sure you understand why this is true.

(a) Demand shifting more than supply

(b) Supply shifting more than demand

Figure 3.11   **Shifts in Demand and Supply over Time**

Whether the price of a product rises or falls over time depends on whether demand shifts to the right more than supply.

In panel (a), demand shifts to the right more than supply, and the equilibrium price rises:

1.   Demand shifts to the right more than supply.
2.   The equilibrium price rises from P_1 to P_2.

In panel (b), supply shifts to the right more than demand, and the equilibrium price falls:

1.   Supply shifts to the right more than demand.
2.   The equilibrium price falls from P_1 to P_2.

Table 3.3 **How Shifts in Demand and Supply Affect Equilibrium Price (P) and Quantity (Q)**	Supply Curve Unchanged	Supply Curve Shifts to the Right	Supply Curve Shifts to the Left
Demand Curve Unchanged	Q unchanged P unchanged	Q increases P decreases	Q decreases P increases
Demand Curve Shifts to the Right	Q increases P increases	Q increases P increases or decreases	Q increases or decreases P increases
Demand Curve Shifts to the Left	Q decreases P decreases	Q increases or decreases P decreases	Q decreases P increases or decreases

Solved Problem 3.4

High Demand and Low Prices in the Lobster Market?

During a typical spring, when demand for lobster is relatively low, Maine lobstermen can typically sell their lobster catches for about $6.00 per pound. During the summer, when demand for lobster is much higher, Maine lobstermen can typically sell their lobster catches for only about $3.00 per pound. One recent July, a lobster-boat captain noted, "Per pound, it's less expensive than hot dogs right now." It may seem strange that the market price is higher when demand is low than when demand is high. Resolve this paradox, with the help of a demand and supply graph.

Solving the Problem

Step 1: **Review the chapter material.** This problem is about how shifts in demand and supply curves affect the equilibrium price, so you may want to review the section "The Effect of Shifts in Demand and Supply over Time," which begins on page 87.

Step 2: **Draw the demand and supply graph.** Draw a demand and supply graph, showing the market equilibrium in the spring. Label the equilibrium price $6.00. Label both the demand and supply curves "in spring."

Step 3: **Add to your graph a demand curve for summer.**

Step 4: **Explain the graph.** After studying the graph, it is possible to see how the equilibrium price can fall from $6.00 to $3.00, despite the increase in demand: The supply curve must have shifted to the right by enough to cause the equilibrium price to fall to $3.00. Draw the new supply curve, label it "in summer," and label the new equilibrium price $3.00. The demand for lobster does increase in summer compared with spring. But the increase in the supply of lobster between spring and summer is even greater. So, the equilibrium price falls.

Based on Beth D'Addono, "With Prices Falling, Lobster Is No Longer a Splurge," *Philadelphia Daily News*, June 16, 2011; and Jon Birger, "Looking for a Bargain Dinner: Try Lobster," cnnmoney.com, July 18, 2009.

MyEconLab   **Your Turn:** For more practice, do related problems 4.7 and 4.8 on page 98 at the end of this chapter.

Don't Let This Happen to You

Remember: A Change in a Good's Price Does *Not* Cause the Demand or Supply Curve to Shift

Suppose a student is asked to draw a demand and supply graph to illustrate how an increase in the price of oranges would affect the market for apples, other variables being constant. He draws the graph on the left below and explains it as follows: "Because apples and oranges are substitutes, an increase in the price of oranges will cause an initial shift to the right in the demand curve for apples, from D_1 to D_2. However, because this initial shift in the demand curve for apples results in a higher price for apples, P_2, consumers will find apples less desirable, and the demand curve will shift to the left, from D_2 to D_3, resulting in a final equilibrium price of P_3." Do you agree or disagree with the student's analysis?

You should disagree. The student has correctly understood that an increase in the price of oranges will cause the demand curve for apples to shift to the right. But the second

demand curve shift the student describes, from D_2 to D_3, will not take place. Changes in the price of a product do not result in shifts in the product's demand curve. Changes in the price of a product result only in movements along a demand curve.

The graph on the right below shows the correct analysis. The increase in the price of oranges causes the demand curve for apples to increase from D_1 to D_2. At the original price, P_1, the increase in demand initially results in a shortage of apples equal to $Q_3 - Q_1$. But, as we have seen, a shortage causes the price to increase until the shortage is eliminated. In this case, the price will rise to P_2, where the quantity demanded and the quantity supplied are both equal to Q_2. Notice that the increase in price causes a decrease in the *quantity demanded*, from Q_3 to Q_2, but does *not* cause a decrease in demand.

MyEconLab

Your Turn: Test your understanding by doing related problems 4.13 and 4.14 on pages 98–99 at the end of this chapter.

1.9 Imagine that the table below shows the quantity demanded of UGG boots at five different prices in 2012 and in 2013:

Price	Quantity Demanded	
	2012	2013
$160	5,000	4,000
170	4,500	3,500
180	4,000	3,000
190	3,500	2,500
200	3,000	2,000

Name two different variables that could cause the quantity demanded of UGG boots to change as indicated from 2012 to 2013.

1.10 Suppose that the curves in the graph below represent two demand curves for rib eye steaks. What would cause a movement from point A to point B on D_1? Name two variables that would cause a movement from point A to point C.

1.11 [**Related to the** Making the Connection **on page 73**] A student makes the following argument:

> The chapter says that for consumers as a group, Quiznos sandwiches are normal goods, and Subway sandwiches are inferior goods. But I like the taste of Subway sandwiches better than I like the taste of Quiznos sandwiches, so for me Quiznos sandwiches are inferior goods, and Subway sandwiches are normal goods.

Do you agree with the student's reasoning? Briefly explain.

1.12 [**Related to the** Making the Connection **on page 74**] Name three products whose demand is likely to increase rapidly if the following demographic groups increase at a faster rate than the population as a whole:

a. Teenagers

b. Children under age five

c. Recent immigrants

1.13 [**Related to the** Making the Connection **on page 74**] Since 1979, China has had a policy that allows couples to have only one child. This policy has caused a change in the demographics of China. Between 2000 and 2010, the share of the population under age 14 decreased from 23 percent to 17 percent, and, as parents attempt to ensure that the lone child is a son, the number of newborn males relative to females has increased. How has the one-child policy changed the relative demand for goods and services in China?

Based on "China's Family Planning: Illegal Children Will Be Confiscated" and "China's Population: Only and Lonely," *The Economist*, July 21, 2011.

1.14 Suppose the following table shows the price of a base model Toyota Prius hybrid and the quantity of Priuses sold for three years. Do these data indicate that the demand curve for Priuses is upward sloping? Explain.

Year	Price	Quantity
2010	$24,880	35,265
2011	24,550	33,250
2012	25,250	36,466

1.15 Richard Posner is a federal court judge who also writes on economic topics. A newspaper reporter summarized Posner's views on the effect of online bookstores and e-books on the demand for books:

> Posner's [argument] is that the disappearance of bookstores is to be celebrated and not mourned, partly because e-books and online stores will reduce the cost of books and thus drive up demand for them.

Do you agree with Posner's statement, as given by the reporter? Briefly explain.

From Christopher Shea, "Judge Posner Hails the Demise of Bookstores," *Wall Street Journal*, January 13, 2011.

1.16 [**Related to the** Making the Connection **on page 77**] In early 2011, financial journalist Wolfgang Gruener made the following observation about forecasts of the future demand for tablet computers:

> The conclusion can only be that the market is too young to sustain a reliable short-, mid- or long-term forecast. If you trust any number at this time, good luck with that. Only a fool would bet the farm and a business on any forecast for the tablet market right now.

Why might it be particularly difficult to forecast the demand for a new product? Which issues might make it particularly difficult to forecast the demand for tablet computers?

From Wolfgang Gruener, "240 Million Tablets: The Gazillion-Dollar Forecast Game," ConceivablyTech.com, February 6, 2011.

3.2 The Supply Side of the Market, pages 78–82

LEARNING OBJECTIVE: Discuss the variables that influence supply.

Summary

The **quantity supplied** is the amount of a good that a firm is willing and able to supply at a given price. A **supply schedule** is a table that shows the relationship between the price of a product and the quantity of the product supplied. A **supply curve** shows on a graph the relationship between the price of a product and the quantity of the product supplied. When the price of a product rises, producing the product is more profitable, and a greater amount will be supplied. The **law of supply** states that, holding everything else constant, the quantity of a product supplied increases when the price rises and decreases when the price falls. Changes in the prices of inputs, technology, the prices of substitutes in production, expected future prices, and the number of firms in a market all cause the supply curve to shift. **Technological change** is a positive or negative change in the ability of a firm to produce a given level of output with a given quantity of inputs. A change in supply refers to a shift of the supply curve. A change in quantity supplied refers to a movement along the supply curve as a result of a change in the product's price.

MyEconLab   Visit **www.myeconlab.com** to complete these exercises online and get instant feedback.

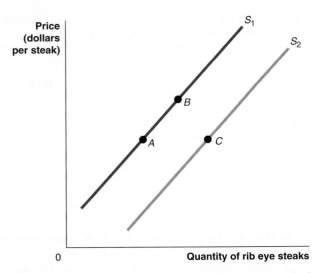

Review Questions

2.1 What is a supply schedule? What is a supply curve?

2.2 What is the difference between a change in supply and a change in the quantity supplied?

2.3 What is the law of supply? What are the main variables that will cause a supply curve to shift? Give an example of each.

Problems and Applications

2.4 Briefly explain whether each of the following statements describes a change in supply or a change in the quantity supplied:

   a. To take advantage of high prices for snow shovels during a snowy winter, Alexander Shovels, Inc., decides to increase output.

   b. The success of the Apple iPad leads more firms to begin producing tablet computers.

   c. In the six months following the Japanese earthquake and tsunami in 2011, production of automobiles in Japan declined by 20 percent.

2.5 Suppose that the curves at the top of the next column represent two supply curves for rib eye steaks. What would cause a movement from point A to point B on S_1? Name two variables that would cause a movement from point A to point C.

2.6 Suppose that the following table shows the quantity supplied of UGG boots at five different prices in 2012 and in 2013:

| Price | Quantity Supplied | |
	2012	2013
$160	300,000	200,000
170	350,000	250,000
180	400,000	300,000
190	450,000	350,000
200	500,000	400,000

Name two different variables that would cause the quantity supplied of UGG boots to change as indicated in the table from 2012 to 2013.

2.7 Will each firm in the tablet computer industry always supply the same quantity as every other firm at each price? What factors might cause the quantity of tablet computers supplied by different firms to be different at a particular price?

2.8 If the price of a good increases, is the increase in the quantity of the good supplied likely to be smaller or larger, the longer the time period being considered? Briefly explain.

<table>
<tr><td>**3.3**</td><td>

Market Equilibrium: Putting Demand and Supply Together, pages 82–85
LEARNING OBJECTIVE: Use a graph to illustrate market equilibrium.

</td></tr>
</table>

Summary

Market equilibrium occurs where the demand curve intersects the supply curve. A **competitive market equilibrium** has a market equilibrium with many buyers and many sellers. Only at this point is the quantity demanded equal to the quantity supplied. Prices above equilibrium result in **surpluses**, with the quantity supplied being greater than the quantity demanded. Surpluses cause the market price to fall. Prices below equilibrium result in **shortages**, with the quantity demanded being greater than the quantity supplied. Shortages cause the market price to rise.

MyEconLab   Visit **www.myeconlab.com** to complete these exercises online and get instant feedback.

Review Questions

3.1 What do economists mean by *market equilibrium*?

3.2 What do economists mean by a *shortage*? By a *surplus*?

3.3 What happens in a market if the current price is above the equilibrium price? What happens if the current price is below the equilibrium price?

Problems and Applications

3.4 Briefly explain whether you agree with the following statement: "When there is a shortage of a good, consumers eventually give up trying to buy it, so the demand for the good declines, and the price falls until the market is finally in equilibrium."

3.5 **[Related to** Solved Problem 3.3 **on page 84]** In *The Wealth of Nations*, Adam Smith discussed what has come to be known as the "diamond and water paradox":

> Nothing is more useful than water: but it will purchase scarce anything; scarce anything can be had in exchange for it. A diamond, on the contrary, has scarce any value in use; but a very great quantity of other goods may frequently be had in exchange for it.

Graph the market for diamonds and the market for water. Show how it is possible for the price of water to be much lower than the price of diamonds, even though the demand for water is much greater than the demand for diamonds.

From Adam Smith, *An Inquiry into the Nature and Causes of the Wealth of Nations*, Vol. I, (Oxford, UK: Oxford University Press, 1976 original edition, 1776).

3.6 **[Related to** Solved Problem 3.3 **on page 84]** An article discusses the market for autographs by Mickey Mantle, the superstar centerfielder for the New York Yankees during the 1950s and 1960s: "At card shows, golf outings, charity dinners, Mr. Mantle signed his name over and over." One expert on sport autographs is quoted as saying: "He was a real good signer. . . . He is not rare." Yet the article quotes another expert as saying: "Mr. Mantle's autograph ranks No. 3 of most-popular autographs, behind Babe Ruth and Muhammad Ali." A baseball signed by Mantle is likely to sell for the relatively high price of $250 to $400. By contrast, baseballs signed by Whitey Ford, a teammate of Mantle's on the Yankees, typically sell for less than $150. Use one graph to show both the demand and supply for autographs by Whitey Ford and the demand and supply for autographs by Mickey Mantle. Show how it is possible for the price of Mantle's autographs to be higher than the price of Ford's autographs, even though the supply of Mantle autographs is larger than the supply of Ford autographs.

Based on Beth DeCarbo, "Mantle Autographs Not Rare, but Collectors Don't Care," *Wall Street Journal*, August 4, 2008.

3.7 If a market is in equilibrium, is it necessarily true that all buyers and all sellers are satisfied with the market price? Briefly explain.

3.8 During the summer of 2011, General Motors (GM) had trouble selling pickup trucks. According to an article in *USA Today*:

> General Motors dealers had a 122-day supply of Chevrolet Silverado and GMC Sierra pickups in June, more than 50% above what's considered optimum. . . . Behind the glut: The year started strong and makers pumped up production. Then the economy slowed faster than they cut back.

a. What does a glut imply about the quantity demanded of GM pickup trucks relative to the quantity supplied?

b. Would prices of GM pickup trucks be expected to rise or fall in the summer of 2011?

c. Why did the slowing economy help cause the glut of pickup trucks?

From Chris Woodyard, "Pickup Truck Glut Brings Hot Deals This Summer," *USA Today*, July 11, 2011.

3.4 The Effect of Demand and Supply Shifts on Equilibrium, pages 85–91

LEARNING OBJECTIVE: Use demand and supply graphs to predict changes in prices and quantities.

Summary

In most markets, demand and supply curves shift frequently, causing changes in equilibrium prices and quantities. Over time, if demand increases more than supply, equilibrium price will rise. If supply increases more than demand, equilibrium price will fall.

 Visit **www.myeconlab.com** to complete these exercises online and get instant feedback.

Review Questions

4.1 Draw a demand and supply graph to show the effect on the equilibrium price in a market in the following two situations:
a. The demand curve shifts to the right.
b. The supply curve shifts to the left.

4.2 If, over time, the demand curve for a product shifts to the right more than the supply curve does, what will happen to the equilibrium price? What will happen to the equilibrium price if the supply curve shifts to the right more than the demand curve? For each case, draw a demand and supply graph to illustrate your answer.

Problems and Applications

4.3 The following is from an article in the *Wall Street Journal*:

> Fuel prices tend to rise [during the summer] for a number of reasons, from the use of more expensive fuel additives in warm weather to maintenance shutdowns at refineries that tend to tighten the supply. Demand for gasoline also traditionally rises during the summer driving season as more people head out on long vacation road trips.

Draw a demand and supply graph of the market for gasoline to analyze the situation described in this article. Be sure to indicate the equilibrium price of gasoline at the beginning of summer, the equilibrium price of gasoline during summer, and any shifts in the demand curve and supply curve for gasoline.

"Is $4 per Gallon the New 'Normal' for Gas?" by Jonathan Welsh from *The Wall Street Journal*, June 11, 2011. Copyright © 2011 by *Dow Jones & Company, Inc.* Reproduced with permission of *Dow Jones & Company, Inc.*

4.4 According to an article in the *Wall Street Journal* about the effect of increases in the demand for corn: "Farmers are likely to cut back on some crops, such as soybeans and rice, to make room for the additional corn." Use a demand and supply graph to analyze the effect on the equilibrium price of soybeans resulting from the increase in the demand for corn.

From Scott Kilman, "Corn Planting to Surge as Farmers Chase High Prices," *Wall Street Journal*, March 31, 2011.

4.5 As oil prices rose during 2006, the demand for alternative fuels increased. Ethanol, one alternative fuel, is made from corn. According to an article in the *Wall Street Journal*, the price of tortillas, which are made from corn, also rose during 2006: "The price spike [in tortillas] is part of a ripple effect from the ethanol boom."

a. Draw a demand and supply graph for the corn market and use it to show the effect on this market of an increase in the demand for ethanol. Be sure to indicate the equilibrium price and quantity before and after the increase in the demand for ethanol.

b. Draw a demand and supply graph for the tortilla market and use it to show the effect on this market of an increase in the price of corn. Once again, be sure to indicate the equilibrium price and quantity before and after the increase in the demand for ethanol.

c. During 2009, the demand for gasoline had fallen, lowering its price. The demand for ethanol had declined as well. Ethanol producers, though, were asking the Environmental Protection Agency (EPA) to raise the allowable amount of ethanol in gasoline blends from 10 percent to 15 percent. If the EPA were to agree to this proposal, what would be the likely effect on tortilla prices?

Based on Stephen Power, "Industry Seeks to Raise Ethanol Levels in Fuel," *Wall Street Journal*, March 7, 2009; and Mark Gongloff, "Tortilla Soup," *Wall Street Journal*, January 25, 2007.

4.6 **[Related to the** Making the Connection **on page 86]** During 2009, the demand for LCD televisions appeared to be falling. At the same time, some industry observers expected that several smaller television manufacturers might exit the market. Use a demand and supply graph to analyze the effects of these factors on the equilibrium price and quantity of LCD televisions. Clearly show on your graph the old equilibrium price and quantity and the new equilibrium price and quantity. Can you tell for certain whether the new equilibrium price will be higher or lower than the old equilibrium price? Briefly explain.

4.7 **[Related to** Solved Problem 3.4 **on page 88]** The demand for watermelons is highest during summer and lowest during winter. Yet watermelon prices are normally lower in summer than in winter. Use a demand and supply graph to demonstrate how this is possible. Be sure to carefully label the curves in your graph and to clearly indicate the equilibrium summer price and the equilibrium winter price.

4.8 **[Related to** Solved Problem 3.4 **on page 88]** According to one observer of the lobster market: "After Labor Day, when the vacationers have gone home, the lobstermen usually have a month or more of good fishing conditions, except for the occasional hurricane." Use a demand and supply graph to explain whether lobster prices are likely to be higher or lower during the fall than during the summer.

Based on Jay Harlow, "Lobster: An Affordable Luxury," Sallybernstein.com.

4.9 Years ago, an apple producer argued that the United States should enact a tariff, or a tax, on imports of bananas. His reasoning was that "the enormous imports of cheap bananas into the United States tend to curtail the domestic consumption of fresh fruits produced in the United States."

a. Was the apple producer assuming that apples and bananas are substitutes or complements? Briefly explain.

b. If a tariff on bananas acts as an increase in the cost of supplying bananas in the United States, use two demand and supply graphs to show the effects of the apple producer's proposal. One graph should show the effect on the banana market in the United States, and the other graph should show the effect on the apple market in the United States. Be sure to label the change

in equilibrium price and quantity in each market and any shifts in the demand and supply curves.

From Douglas A. Irwin, *Peddling Protectionism: Smoot-Hawley and the Great Depression*, (Princeton, NJ: Princeton University Press, 2011), p. 22.

4.10 An article in the *Wall Street Journal* noted that the demand for Internet advertising was declining at the same time that the number of Internet sites accepting advertising was increasing. After reading the article, a student argues: "From this information, we know that the price of Internet ads should fall, but we don't know whether the total quantity of Internet ads will increase or decrease." Is the student's analysis correct? Illustrate your answer with a demand and supply graph.

Based on Martin Peers, "Future Shock for Internet Ads?" *Wall Street Journal*, February 17, 2009.

4.11 Historically, the production of many perishable foods, such as dairy products, was highly seasonal. Thus, as the supply of those products fluctuated, prices tended to fluctuate tremendously—typically by 25 to 50 percent or more—over the course of the year. One impact of mechanical refrigeration, which was commercialized on a large scale in the last decade of the nineteenth century, was that suppliers could store perishables from one season to the next. Economists have estimated that as a result of refrigerated storage, wholesale prices rose by roughly 10 percent during peak supply periods, while they fell by almost the same amount during the off season. Use a demand and supply graph for each season to illustrate how refrigeration affected the market for perishable food.

Based on Lee A. Craig, Barry Goodwin, and Thomas Grennes, "The Effect of Mechanical Refrigeration on Nutrition in the U.S.," *Social Science History*, Vol. 28, No. 2, Summer 2004, pp. 327–328.

4.12 Briefly explain whether each of the following statements is true or false.

a. If the demand and supply for a product both increase, the equilibrium quantity of the product must also increase.

b. If the demand and supply for a product both increase, the equilibrium price of the product must also increase.

c. If the demand for a product decreases and the supply of the product increases, the equilibrium price of the product may increase or decrease, depending on whether supply or demand has shifted more.

4.13 **[Related to the** Don't Let This Happen to You **on page 90]** A student writes the following: "Increased production leads to a lower price, which in turn increases demand." Do you agree with his reasoning? Briefly explain.

4.14 **[Related to the** Don't Let This Happen to You **on page 90]** A student was asked to draw a demand and supply graph to illustrate the effect on the tablet computers market of a fall in the price of displays used in tablet computers, holding everything else constant. She drew the graph below and explained it as follows:

Displays are an input to tablet computers, so a fall in the price of displays will cause the supply curve for tablets to shift to the right (from S_1 to S_2). Because this shift in the supply curve results in a lower price (P_2), consumers will want to buy more tablets, and the demand curve will shift to the right (from D_1 to D_2). We know that more tablets will be sold, but

we can't be sure whether the price of tablets will rise or fall. That depends on whether the supply curve or the demand curve has shifted farther to the right. I assume that the effect on supply is greater than the effect on demand, so I show the final equilibrium price (P_3) as being lower than the initial equilibrium price (P_1).

Explain whether you agree or disagree with the student's analysis. Be careful to explain exactly what—if anything—you find wrong with her analysis.

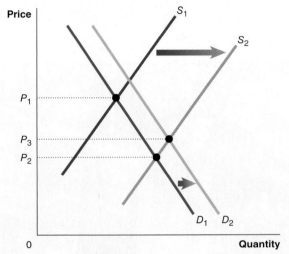

4.15 Following are four graphs and four market scenarios, each of which would cause either a movement along the supply curve for Pepsi or a shift of the supply curve. Match each scenario with the appropriate graph.

  a. A decrease in the supply of Coke

  b. A drop in the average household income in the United States from $52,000 to $50,000

  c. An improvement in soft drink bottling technology

  d. An increase in the prices of sugar and high-fructose corn syrup

4.16 Proposals have been made to increase government regulation of firms providing childcare services by, for instance, setting education requirements for childcare workers. Suppose that these regulations increase the quality of childcare and cause the demand for childcare services to increase. At the same time, assume that complying with the new government regulations increases the costs of firms providing childcare services. Draw a demand and supply graph to illustrate the effects of these changes in the market for childcare services. Briefly explain whether the total quantity of childcare services purchased will increase or decrease as a result of regulation.

4.17 The following graphs show the supply and demand curves for two markets. One of the markets is for BMW automobiles, and the other is for a cancer-fighting drug, without which lung cancer patients will die. Briefly explain which graph most likely represents which market.

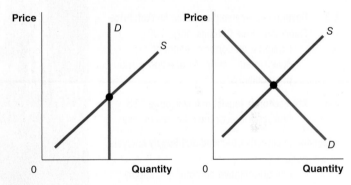

Economic Efficiency, Government Price Setting, and Taxes

Chapter Outline and Learning Objectives

Should the Government Control Apartment Rents?

Robert F. Moss owns an apartment building in New York City. Unlike most other business owners, he is not free to charge the prices he would like for the service he offers. In New York, San Francisco, Los Angeles, and nearly 200 smaller cities, apartments are subject to rent control by the local government. Rent control puts a legal limit on the rent that landlords can charge for an apartment.

New York City has 2 million apartments, about half of which are subject to rent control. The other 1 million apartments have their rents determined in the market by the demand and supply for apartments. Mr. Moss's building includes apartments that are rent controlled and apartments that are not. The market-determined rents are usually far above the controlled rents. The government regulations that determine what Mr. Moss can charge for a rent-controlled apartment are very complex. The following is Mr. Moss's description:

> When [an apartment] is vacated, state rent laws entitle landlords to raise rents in three primary ways: a vacancy increase of 20 percent for a new tenant's two-year lease (a bit less for a one-year lease); one-fortieth per month of the cost of any improvements, and a "longevity bonus" for longtime residents (calculated at six-tenths of 1 percent times the tenant's last legal rent multiplied by the number of years of residency beyond eight). . . . Apartments renting for $2,000 a month are automatically deregulated if they are vacant. Occupied apartments whose rent reaches that figure can be deregulated if the income of the tenants has been $175,000 or more for two years.

As this description shows, someone earning a living by renting out apartments in New York City has to deal with much more complex government regulation of prices than someone who owns, for instance, a McDonald's restaurant.

Tenants in rent-controlled apartments in New York are reluctant to see rent control end because rents for those apartments are much lower than rents for apartments that aren't rent controlled. Although rent control laws are intended to make housing more affordable for people with low incomes, high-income people can end up benefiting. For example, in New York City, rent control has resulted in actress Mia Farrow and television host Alistair Cooke living for many years in large apartments overlooking Central Park, while paying rents far below market levels. When the FBI arrested James "Whitey" Bulger, a former Boston crime boss, in 2011, they discovered that he had been living for more than 15 years in a rent-controlled apartment in Santa Monica.

AN INSIDE LOOK AT POLICY on **page 122** discusses a legal battle between Oscar-winning actress Faye Dunaway and the landlord of her rent-controlled New York City apartment.

Based on Robert F. Moss, "A Landlord's Lot Is Sometimes Not an Easy One," *New York Times*, August 3, 2003; and Lynda Gorov, "Whitey Bulger Used Rent-Controlled Apartment Since Mid-1990s, Property Manager Says," *The Boston Globe*, June 23, 2011.

Economics in Your Life

Does Rent Control Make It Easier for You to Find an Affordable Apartment?

Suppose you have job offers in two cities. One factor in deciding which job to accept is whether you can find an affordable apartment. If one city has rent control, are you more likely to find an affordable apartment in that city, or would you be better off looking for an apartment in a city without rent control? As you read the chapter, see if you can answer this question. You can check your answer against the one we provide on **page 121** at the end of this chapter.

W e saw in Chapter 3 that in a competitive market the price adjusts to ensure that the quantity demanded equals the quantity supplied. Stated another way, in equilibrium, every consumer willing to pay the market price is able to buy as much of the product as the consumer wants, and every firm willing to accept the market price can sell as much as it wants. Even so, consumers would naturally prefer to pay a lower price, and sellers would prefer to receive a higher price. Normally, consumers and firms have no choice but to accept the equilibrium price if they wish to participate in the market. Occasionally, however, consumers succeed in having the government impose a **price ceiling**, which is a legally determined maximum price that sellers may charge. Rent control is an example of a price ceiling. Firms also sometimes succeed in having the government impose a **price floor**, which is a legally determined minimum price that sellers may receive. In markets for farm products such as milk, the government has been setting price floors that are above the equilibrium market price since the 1930s.

Another way the government intervenes in markets is by imposing taxes. The government relies on the revenue raised from taxes to finance its operations. Unfortunately, whenever the government imposes a price ceiling, a price floor, or a tax, there are predictable negative economic consequences. It is important for government policymakers and voters to understand the negative consequences when evaluating these policies. Economists have developed the concepts of *consumer surplus*, *producer surplus*, and *economic surplus* to analyze the economic effects of price ceilings, price floors, and taxes.

Price ceiling A legally determined maximum price that sellers may charge.

Price floor A legally determined minimum price that sellers may receive.

Consumer Surplus and Producer Surplus

Consumer surplus measures the dollar benefit consumers receive from buying goods or services in a particular market. Producer surplus measures the dollar benefit firms receive from selling goods or services in a particular market. Economic surplus in a market is the sum of consumer surplus plus producer surplus. As we will see, *when the government imposes a price ceiling or a price floor, the amount of economic surplus in a market is reduced*—in other words, price ceilings and price floors reduce the total benefit to consumers and firms from buying and selling in a market. To understand why this is true, we need to understand how consumer surplus and producer surplus are determined.

Consumer Surplus

Consumer surplus is the difference between the highest price a consumer is willing to pay for a good or service and the price the consumer actually pays. For example, suppose you are in Wal-Mart, and you see a DVD of *Harry Potter and the Deathly Hallows, Part 2* on the rack. No price is indicated on the package, so you take it over to the register to check the price. As you walk to the register, you think to yourself that $18 is the highest price you would be willing to pay. At the register, you find out that the price is actually $12, so you buy the DVD. Your consumer surplus in this example is $6: the difference between the $18 you were willing to pay and the $12 you actually paid.

We can use the demand curve to measure the total consumer surplus in a market. Demand curves show the willingness of consumers to purchase a product at different prices. Consumers are willing to purchase a product up to the point where the marginal benefit of consuming a product is equal to its price. The **marginal benefit** is the additional benefit to a consumer from consuming one more unit of a good or service. As a simple example, suppose there are only four consumers in the market for chai tea: Theresa, Tom, Terri, and Tim. Because these four consumers have different tastes for tea and different incomes, the marginal benefit each of them receives

Consumer surplus The difference between the highest price a consumer is willing to pay for a good or service and the price the consumer actually pays.

Marginal benefit The additional benefit to a consumer from consuming one more unit of a good or service.

Consumer	Highest Price Willing to Pay
Theresa	$6
Tom	5
Terri	4
Tim	3

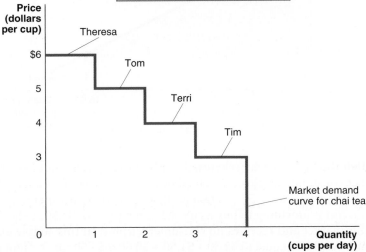

Figure 4.1

Deriving the Demand Curve for Chai Tea

With four consumers in the market for chai tea, the demand curve is determined by the highest price each consumer is willing to pay. For prices above $6, no tea is sold because $6 is the highest price any consumer is willing to pay. For prices of $3 and below, every one of the four consumers is willing to buy a cup of tea.

from consuming a cup of tea will be different. Therefore, the highest price each is willing to pay for a cup of tea is also different. In Figure 4.1, the information from the table is used to construct a demand curve for chai tea. For prices above $6 per cup, no tea is sold because $6 is the highest price any of the consumers is willing to pay. At a price of $5, both Theresa and Tom are willing to buy tea, so two cups are sold. At prices of $3 and below, all four consumers are willing to buy tea, and four cups are sold.

Suppose the market price of tea is $3.50 per cup. As Figure 4.2 shows, the demand curve allows us to calculate the total consumer surplus in this market. In panel (a),

(a) Consumer surplus with a market price of $3.50

(b) Consumer surplus with a market price of $3.00

Figure 4.2 **Measuring Consumer Surplus**

Panel (a) shows the consumer surplus for Theresa, Tom, and Terri when the price of tea is $3.50 per cup. Theresa's consumer surplus is equal to the area of rectangle A and is the difference between the highest price she would pay—$6—and the market price of $3.50. Tom's consumer surplus is equal to the area of rectangle B, and Terri's consumer surplus is equal to the area of rectangle C. Total consumer surplus in this market is equal to the sum of the areas of rectangles A, B, and C, or the total area below the demand curve and above the market price. In panel (b), consumer surplus increases by the shaded area as the market price declines from $3.50 to $3.00.

Figure 4.3

Total Consumer Surplus in the Market for Chai Tea

The demand curve tells us that most buyers of chai tea would have been willing to pay more than the market price of $2.00. For each buyer, consumer surplus is equal to the difference between the highest price he or she is willing to pay and the market price actually paid. Therefore, the total amount of consumer surplus in the market for chai tea is equal to the area below the demand curve and above the market price. Consumer surplus represents the benefit to consumers in excess of the price they paid to purchase the product.

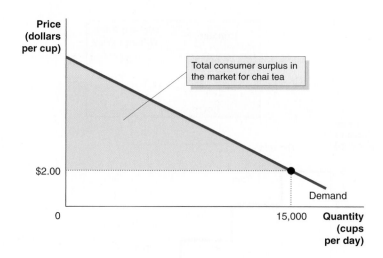

we can see that the highest price Theresa is willing to pay is $6, but because she pays only $3.50, her consumer surplus is $2.50 (shown by the area of rectangle *A*). Similarly, Tom's consumer surplus is $1.50 (rectangle *B*), and Terri's consumer surplus is $0.50 (rectangle *C*). Tim is unwilling to buy a cup of tea at a price of $3.50, so he doesn't participate in this market and receives no consumer surplus. In this simple example, the total consumer surplus is equal to $2.50 + $1.50 + $0.50 = $4.50 (or the sum of the areas of rectangles *A*, *B*, and *C*). Panel (b) shows that a lower price will increase consumer surplus. If the price of tea drops from $3.50 per cup to $3.00, Theresa, Tom, and Terri each receive $0.50 more in consumer surplus (shown by the shaded areas), so total consumer surplus in the market rises to $6.00. Tim now buys a cup of tea but doesn't receive any consumer surplus because the price is equal to the highest price he is willing to pay. In fact, Tim is indifferent between buying the cup or not—his well-being is the same either way.

The market demand curves shown in Figures 4.1 and 4.2 do not look like the smooth curves we saw in Chapter 3. This is because this example uses a small number of consumers, each consuming a single cup of tea. With many consumers, the market demand curve for chai tea will have the normal smooth shape shown in Figure 4.3. In this figure, the quantity demanded at a price of $2.00 is 15,000 cups per day. We can calculate total consumer surplus in Figure 4.3 the same way we did in Figures 4.1 and 4.2: by adding up the consumer surplus received on each unit purchased. Once again, we can draw an important conclusion: *The total amount of consumer surplus in a market is equal to the area below the demand curve and above the market price.* Consumer surplus is shown as the blue area in Figure 4.3 and represents the benefit to consumers in excess of the price they paid to purchase the product—in this case, chai tea.

| Making the Connection | The Consumer Surplus from Broadband Internet Service |

The Consumer Surplus from Broadband Internet Service

Consumer surplus allows us to measure the benefit consumers receive in excess of the price they paid to purchase a product. Recently, Shane Greenstein and Ryan McDevitt, economists at Northwestern University, estimated the consumer surplus that households receive from subscribing to broadband Internet service. To do this, they estimated the demand curve for broadband Internet service and then computed the shaded area shown in the graph on the next page.

In 2006, 47 million consumers paid an average price of $36 per month to subscribe to a broadband Internet service. The demand curve shows the marginal benefit consumers

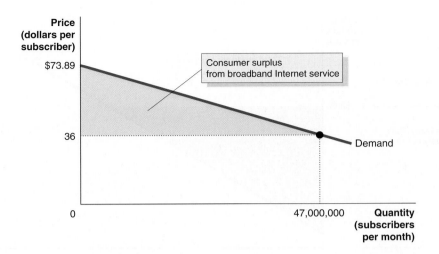

receive from subscribing to a broadband Internet service rather than using dialup or doing without access to the Internet. The area below the demand curve and above the $36 price line represents the difference between the price consumers would have paid rather than do without broadband service and the $36 they did pay. The shaded area on the graph represents the total consumer surplus in the market for broadband Internet service. Greenstein and McDevitt estimate that the value of this area is $890.5 million. This is one month's benefit to the consumers who subscribe to a broadband Internet service.

Based on Shane Greenstein and Ryan C. McDevitt, "The Broadband Bonus: Accounting for Broadband Internet's Impact on U.S. GDP," National Bureau of Economic Research Working Paper 14758, February 2009.

Your Turn: Test your understanding by doing related problem 1.9 on page 124 at the end of this chapter.

MyEconLab

Producer Surplus

Just as demand curves show the willingness of consumers to buy a product at different prices, supply curves show the willingness of firms to supply a product at different prices. The willingness to supply a product depends on the cost of producing it. Firms will supply an additional unit of a product only if they receive a price equal to the additional cost of producing that unit. **Marginal cost** is the additional cost to a firm of producing one more unit of a good or service. Consider the marginal cost to the firm Heavenly Tea of producing one more cup: In this case, the marginal cost includes the ingredients to make the tea and the wages paid to the worker preparing the tea. Often, the marginal cost of producing a good increases as more of the good is produced during a given period of time. This is the key reason—as we saw in Chapter 3—that supply curves are upward sloping.

Panel (a) of Figure 4.4 shows Heavenly Tea's producer surplus. For simplicity, we show Heavenly producing only a small quantity of tea. The figure shows that Heavenly's marginal cost of producing the first cup of tea is $1.25. Its marginal cost of producing the second cup is $1.50, and so on. The marginal cost of each cup of tea is the lowest price Heavenly is willing to accept to supply that cup. The supply curve, then, is also a marginal cost curve. Suppose the market price of tea is $2.00 per cup. On the first cup of tea, the price is $0.75 higher than the lowest price Heavenly is willing to accept. **Producer surplus** is the difference between the lowest price a firm would be willing to accept for a good or service and the price it actually receives. Therefore, Heavenly's

Marginal cost The additional cost to a firm of producing one more unit of a good or service.

Producer surplus The difference between the lowest price a firm would be willing to accept for a good or service and the price it actually receives.

Figure 4.4 **Measuring Producer Surplus**

Panel (a) shows Heavenly Tea's producer surplus. Producer surplus is the difference between the lowest price a firm would be willing to accept and the price it actually receives. The lowest price Heavenly Tea is willing to accept to supply a cup of tea is equal to its marginal cost of producing that cup. When the market price of tea is $2.00, Heavenly receives producer surplus of $0.75 on the first cup (the area of rectangle A), $0.50 on the second cup (rectangle B), and $0.25 on the third cup (rectangle C). In panel (b), the total amount of producer surplus tea sellers receive from selling chai tea can be calculated by adding up for the entire market the producer surplus received on each cup sold. In the figure, total producer surplus is equal to the area above the supply curve and below the market price, shown in red.

producer surplus on the first cup is $0.75 (shown by the area of rectangle A). Its producer surplus on the second cup is $0.50 (rectangle B). Its producer surplus on the third cup is $0.25 (rectangle C). Heavenly will not be willing to supply the fourth cup because the marginal cost of producing it is greater than the market price. Heavenly Tea's total producer surplus is equal to $0.75 + $0.50 + $0.25 = $1.50 (or the sum of rectangles A, B, and C). A higher price will increase producer surplus. For example, if the market price of chai tea rises from $2.00 to $2.25, Heavenly Tea's producer surplus will increase from $1.50 to $2.25. (Make sure you understand how the new level of producer surplus was calculated.)

The supply curve shown in panel (a) of Figure 4.4 does not look like the smooth curves we saw in Chapter 3 because this example uses a single firm producing only a small quantity of tea. With many firms, the market supply curve for chai tea will have the normal smooth shape shown in panel (b) of Figure 4.4. In panel (b), the quantity supplied at a price of $2.00 is 15,000 cups per day. We can calculate total producer surplus in panel (b) the same way we did in panel (a): by adding up the producer surplus received on each cup sold. Therefore, *the total amount of producer surplus in a market is equal to the area above the market supply curve and below the market price.* The total producer surplus tea sellers receive from selling chai tea is shown as the red area in panel (b) of Figure 4.4.

What Consumer Surplus and Producer Surplus Measure

We have seen that consumer surplus measures the benefit to consumers from participating in a market, and producer surplus measures the benefit to producers from participating in a market. It is important, however, to be clear about what this means. In a sense, consumer surplus measures the *net* benefit to consumers from participating in a market rather than the *total* benefit. That is, if the price of a product were zero, the consumer surplus in a market would be all of the area under the demand curve. When the price is not zero, consumer surplus is the area below the demand curve and above the market price. So, consumer surplus in a market is equal to the total benefit received by consumers minus the total amount they must pay to buy the good or service.

Similarly, producer surplus measures the *net* benefit received by producers from participating in a market. If producers could supply a good or service at zero cost, the producer surplus in a market would be all of the area below the market price. When cost is not zero, producer surplus is the area below the market price and above the supply curve. So, producer surplus in a market is equal to the total amount firms receive from consumers minus the cost of producing the good or service.

The Efficiency of Competitive Markets

4.2 LEARNING OBJECTIVE

Understand the concept of economic efficiency.

In Chapter 3, we defined a *competitive market* as a market with many buyers and many sellers. An important advantage of the market system is that it results in efficient economic outcomes. But what do we mean by *economic efficiency*? The concepts we have developed so far in this chapter give us two ways to think about the economic efficiency of competitive markets. We can think in terms of marginal benefit and marginal cost. We can also think in terms of consumer surplus and producer surplus. As we will see, these two approaches lead to the same outcome, but using both can increase our understanding of economic efficiency.

Marginal Benefit Equals Marginal Cost in Competitive Equilibrium

Figure 4.5 again shows the market for chai tea. Recall from our discussion that the demand curve shows the marginal benefit received by consumers, and the supply curve shows the marginal cost of production. To achieve economic efficiency in this market, the marginal benefit from the last unit sold should equal the marginal cost of production. The figure shows that this equality occurs at competitive equilibrium where 15,000 cups per day are produced and marginal benefit and marginal cost are both equal to $2.00. Why is this outcome economically efficient? Because every cup of chai tea has been produced where the marginal benefit to buyers is greater than or equal to the marginal cost to producers.

Another way to see why the level of output at competitive equilibrium is efficient is to consider what the situation would be if output were at a different level. For instance, suppose that output of chai tea were 14,000 cups per day. Figure 4.5 shows that at this level of output, the marginal benefit from the last cup sold is $2.20, whereas the marginal cost is only $1.80. This level of output is not efficient because 1,000 more cups could be produced for which the additional benefit to consumers would be greater than the additional cost of production. Consumers would willingly purchase those cups, and

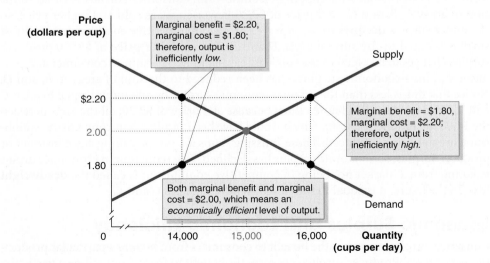

Figure 4.5

Marginal Benefit Equals Marginal Cost Only at Competitive Equilibrium

In a competitive market, equilibrium occurs at a quantity of 15,000 cups and a price of $2.00 per cup, where marginal benefit equals marginal cost. This is the economically efficient level of output because every cup has been produced where the marginal benefit to buyers is greater than or equal to the marginal cost to producers.

Figure 4.6

Economic Surplus Equals the Sum of Consumer Surplus and Producer Surplus

The economic surplus in a market is the sum of the blue area, representing consumer surplus, and the red area, representing producer surplus.

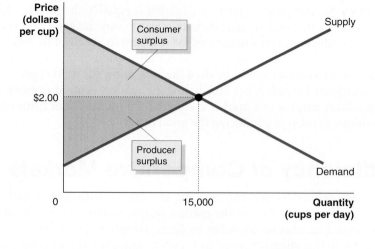

tea sellers would willingly supply them, making both consumers and sellers better off. Similarly, if the output of chai tea were 16,000 cups per day, the marginal cost of the 16,000th cup is $2.20, whereas the marginal benefit is only $1.80. Tea sellers would only be willing to supply this cup at a price of $2.20, which is $0.40 higher than consumers would be willing to pay. In fact, consumers would not be willing to pay the price tea sellers would need to receive for any cup beyond the 15,000th.

To summarize, we can say this: *Equilibrium in a competitive market results in the economically efficient level of output, where marginal benefit equals marginal cost.*

Economic Surplus

Economic surplus The sum of consumer surplus and producer surplus.

Economic surplus in a market is the sum of consumer surplus and producer surplus. In a competitive market, with many buyers and sellers and no government restrictions, economic surplus is at a maximum when the market is in equilibrium. To see this, let's look one more time at the market for chai tea shown in Figure 4.6. The consumer surplus in this market is the blue area below the demand curve and above the line indicating the equilibrium price of $2.00. The producer surplus is the red area above the supply curve and below the price line.

Deadweight Loss

Deadweight loss The reduction in economic surplus resulting from a market not being in competitive equilibrium.

To show that economic surplus is maximized at equilibrium, consider a situation in which the price of chai tea is *above* the equilibrium price, as shown in Figure 4.7. At a price of $2.20 per cup, the number of cups consumers are willing to buy per day drops from 15,000 to 14,000. At competitive equilibrium, consumer surplus is equal to the sum of areas A, B, and C. At a price of $2.20, fewer cups are sold at a higher price, so consumer surplus declines to just the area of A. At competitive equilibrium, producer surplus is equal to the sum of areas D and E. At the higher price of $2.20, producer surplus changes to be equal to the sum of areas B and D. The sum of consumer and producer surplus—economic surplus—has been reduced to the sum of areas A, B, and D. Notice that this is less than the original economic surplus by an amount equal to areas C and E. Economic surplus has declined because at a price of $2.20, all the cups between the 14,000th and the 15,000th, which would have been produced in competitive equilibrium, are not being produced. These "missing" cups are not providing any consumer or producer surplus, so economic surplus has declined. The reduction in economic surplus resulting from a market not being in competitive equilibrium is called the **deadweight loss**. In the figure, it is equal to the sum of yellow triangles C and E.

Economic Surplus and Economic Efficiency

Consumer surplus measures the benefit to consumers from buying a particular product, such as chai tea. Producer surplus measures the benefit to firms from selling a particular

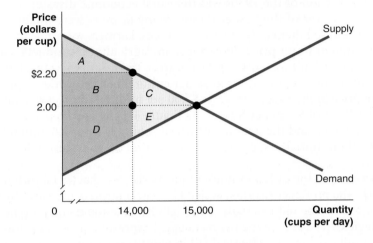

	At Competitive Equilibrium	At a Price of $2.20
Consumer Surplus	A + B + C	A
Producer Surplus	D + E	B + D
Deadweight Loss	None	C + E

Figure 4.7

When a Market Is Not in Equilibrium, There Is a Deadweight Loss

Economic surplus is maximized when a market is in competitive equilibrium. When a market is not in equilibrium, there is a deadweight loss. When the price of chai tea is $2.20 instead of $2.00, consumer surplus declines from an amount equal to the sum of areas *A*, *B*, and *C* to just area *A*. Producer surplus increases from the sum of areas *D* and *E* to the sum of areas *B* and *D*. At competitive equilibrium, there is no deadweight loss. At a price of $2.20, there is a deadweight loss equal to the sum of areas *C* and *E*.

product. Therefore, economic surplus—which is the sum of the benefit to firms plus the benefit to consumers—is the best measure we have of the benefit to society from the production of a particular good or service. This gives us a second way of characterizing the economic efficiency of a competitive market: *Equilibrium in a competitive market results in the greatest amount of economic surplus, or total net benefit to society, from the production of a good or service.* Anything that causes the market for a good or service not to be in competitive equilibrium reduces the total benefit to society from the production of that good or service.

Now we can give a more general definition of *economic efficiency* in terms of our two approaches: **Economic efficiency** is a market outcome in which the marginal benefit to consumers of the last unit produced is equal to its marginal cost of production and in which the sum of consumer surplus and producer surplus is at a maximum.

Economic efficiency A market outcome in which the marginal benefit to consumers of the last unit produced is equal to its marginal cost of production and in which the sum of consumer surplus and producer surplus is at a maximum.

Government Intervention in the Market: Price Floors and Price Ceilings

Notice that we have *not* concluded that every *individual* is better off if a market is at competitive equilibrium. We have only concluded that economic surplus, or the *total* net benefit to society, is greatest at competitive equilibrium. Any individual producer would rather receive a higher price, and any individual consumer would rather pay a lower price, but usually producers can sell and consumers can buy only at the competitive equilibrium price.

Producers or consumers who are dissatisfied with the competitive equilibrium price can lobby the government to legally require that a different price be charged. In the United States, the government only occasionally overrides the market outcome by setting prices. When the government does intervene, it can either attempt to aid sellers by requiring that a price be above equilibrium—a price floor—or aid buyers by requiring that a price be below equilibrium—a price ceiling. To affect the market outcome, the government must set a price floor that is above the equilibrium price or set a price ceiling that is below the equilibrium price. Otherwise, the price ceiling or price floor will not be *binding* on buyers and sellers. The preceding section demonstrates that moving away from competitive equilibrium will reduce economic efficiency. We can use

4.3 LEARNING OBJECTIVE

Explain the economic effect of government-imposed price floors and price ceilings.

the concepts of consumer surplus, producer surplus, and deadweight loss to see more clearly the economic inefficiency of price floors and price ceilings.

Price Floors: Government Policy in Agricultural Markets

The Great Depression of the 1930s was the worst economic disaster in U.S. history, affecting every sector of the U.S. economy. Many farmers were unable to sell their products or could sell them only at very low prices. Farmers were able to convince the federal government to set price floors for many agricultural products. Government intervention in agriculture—often referred to as the *farm program*—has continued ever since. To see how a price floor in an agricultural market works, suppose that the equilibrium price in the wheat market is $3.00 per bushel, but the government decides to set a price floor of $3.50 per bushel. As Figure 4.8 shows, the price of wheat rises from $3.00 to $3.50, and the quantity of wheat sold falls from 2.0 billion bushels per year to 1.8 billion. Initially, suppose that production of wheat also falls to 1.8 billion bushels.

Just as we saw in the earlier example of the market for chai tea (shown in Figure 4.7 on page 109), the producer surplus received by wheat farmers increases by an amount equal to the area of the red rectangle A and falls by an amount equal to the area of the yellow triangle C. The area of the red rectangle A represents a transfer from consumer surplus to producer surplus. The total fall in consumer surplus is equal to the area of the red rectangle A plus the area of the yellow triangle B. Wheat farmers benefit from this program, but consumers lose. There is also a deadweight loss equal to the areas of the yellow triangles B and C, which represents the decline in economic efficiency due to the price floor. There is a deadweight loss because the price floor has reduced the amount of economic surplus in the market for wheat. Or, looked at another way, the price floor has caused the marginal benefit of the last bushel of wheat to be greater than the marginal cost of producing it. We can conclude that a price floor reduces economic efficiency.

We assumed initially that farmers reduce their production of wheat to the amount consumers are willing to buy. In fact, as Figure 4.8 shows, a price floor will cause the quantity of wheat that farmers want to supply to increase from 2.0 billion to 2.2 billion bushels. Because the higher price also reduces the amount of wheat consumers want to buy, the result is a surplus of 0.4 billion bushels of wheat (the 2.2 billion bushels supplied minus the 1.8 billion demanded).

Figure 4.8

The Economic Effect of a Price Floor in the Wheat Market

If wheat farmers convince the government to impose a price floor of $3.50 per bushel, the amount of wheat sold will fall from 2.0 billion bushels per year to 1.8 billion. If we assume that farmers produce 1.8 billion bushels, producer surplus then increases by the red rectangle A—which is transferred from consumer surplus—and falls by the yellow triangle C. Consumer surplus declines by the red rectangle A plus the yellow triangle B. There is a deadweight loss equal to the yellow triangles B and C, representing the decline in economic efficiency due to the price floor. In reality, a price floor of $3.50 per bushel will cause farmers to expand their production from 2.0 billion to 2.2 billion bushels, resulting in a surplus of wheat.

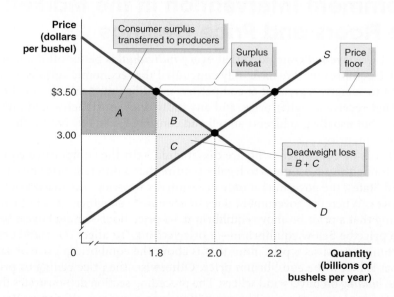

The federal government's farm programs have often resulted in large surpluses of wheat and other agricultural products. In response, the government has usually either bought the surplus food or paid farmers to restrict supply by taking some land out of cultivation. Because both of these options are expensive, Congress passed the Freedom to Farm Act of 1996. The intent of the act was to phase out price floors and government purchases of surpluses and return to a free market in agriculture. To allow farmers time to adjust, the federal government began paying farmers *subsidies*, or cash payments based on the number of acres planted. Although the subsidies were originally scheduled to be phased out, Congress has passed additional Farm Acts that have resulted in the continuation of subsidies.

Making the Connection	Price Floors in Labor Markets: The Debate over Minimum Wage Policy

The minimum wage may be the most controversial "price floor." Supporters see the minimum wage as a way of raising the incomes of low-skilled workers. Opponents argue that it results in fewer jobs and imposes large costs on small businesses.

Since July 2009, the national minimum wage as set by Congress has been $7.25 per hour for most occupations. It is illegal for an employer to pay less than this wage in those occupations. For most workers, the minimum wage is irrelevant because it is well below the wage employers are voluntarily willing to pay them. But for low-skilled workers—such as workers in fast-food restaurants—the minimum wage is above the wage they would otherwise receive. The following figure shows the effect of the minimum wage on employment in the market for low-skilled labor.

Without a minimum wage, the equilibrium wage would be W_1 and the number of workers hired would be L_1. With a minimum wage set above the equilibrium wage, the number of workers demanded by employers declines from L_1 to L_2, and the quantity of labor supplied increases to L_3, leading to a surplus of workers unable to find jobs equal to $L_3 - L_2$. The quantity of labor supplied increases because the higher wage attracts more people to work. For instance, some teenagers may decide that working after school is worthwhile at the minimum wage of $7.25 per hour but would not be worthwhile at a lower wage.

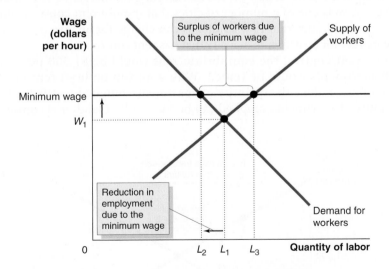

This analysis is very similar to our analysis of the wheat market in Figure 4.8. Just as a price floor in the wheat market leads to less wheat being consumed, a price floor in the labor market should lead to fewer workers being hired. Views differ sharply among economists, however, concerning how large a reduction in employment the minimum wage causes. For instance, David Card of the University of California, Berkeley, and Alan Krueger of Princeton University, who in 2011 was appointed by President Barack Obama to chair the Council of Economic Advisers, conducted a study of fast-food restaurants in New Jersey and Pennsylvania. Their study indicated that the effect of minimum wage increases on employment is very small. This study has been very controversial, however. Other economists have examined similar data and have come to the different conclusion that the minimum wage leads to a significant decrease in employment.

Whatever the extent of employment losses from the minimum wage, because it is a price floor, it will cause a deadweight loss, just as a price floor in the wheat market does. Therefore, many economists favor alternative policies for attaining the goal of raising the incomes of low-skilled workers. One policy many economists support is the *earned income tax credit*. The earned income tax credit reduces the amount of tax that low-income wage earners would otherwise pay to the federal government. Workers with very low incomes who do not owe any tax receive a payment from the government. Compared with the minimum wage, the earned income tax credit can increase the incomes of low-skilled workers without reducing employment. The earned income tax credit also places a lesser burden on the small businesses that employ many low-skilled workers, and it may cause a smaller loss of economic efficiency.

Based on David Card and Alan B. Krueger, *Myth and Measurement: The New Economics of the Minimum Wage*, (Princeton, NJ: Princeton University Press, 1995); David Neumark and William Wascher, "Minimum Wages and Employment: A Case Study of the Fast-Food Industry in New Jersey and Pennsylvania: Comment," *American Economic Review*, Vol. 90, No. 5, December 2000, pp. 1362–1396; and David Card and Alan B. Krueger, "Minimum Wages and Employment: A Case Study of the Fast-Food Industry in New Jersey and Pennsylvania: Reply," *American Economic Review*, Vol. 90, No. 5, December 2000, pp. 1397–1420.

MyEconLab   **Your Turn:** Test your understanding by doing related problem 3.12 on page 127 at the end of this chapter.

Price Ceilings: Government Rent Control Policy in Housing Markets

Support for governments setting price floors typically comes from sellers, and support for governments setting price ceilings typically comes from consumers. For example, when there is a sharp increase in gasoline prices, there are often proposals for the government to impose a price ceiling on the market for gasoline. As we saw in the chapter opener, New York is one of a number of cities that impose rent control, which puts a ceiling on the maximum rent that landlords can charge for an apartment. Figure 4.9 shows the market for apartments in a city that has rent control.

Without rent control, the equilibrium rent would be $1,500 per month, and 2,000,000 apartments would be rented. With a maximum legal rent of $1,000 per month, landlords reduce the quantity of apartments supplied to 1,900,000. The fall in the quantity of apartments supplied can be the result of landlords converting some

Figure 4.9

The Economic Effect of a Rent Ceiling

Without rent control, the equilibrium rent is $1,500 per month. At that price, 2,000,000 apartments would be rented. If the government imposes a rent ceiling of $1,000, the quantity of apartments supplied falls to 1,900,000, and the quantity of apartments demanded increases to 2,100,000, resulting in a shortage of 200,000 apartments. Producer surplus equal to the area of the blue rectangle *A* is transferred from landlords to renters, and there is a deadweight loss equal to the areas of yellow triangles *B* and *C*.

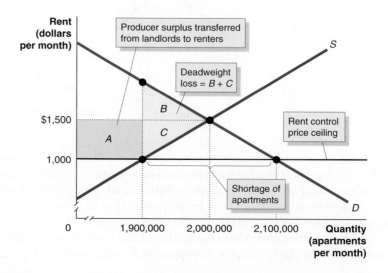

Don't Let This Happen to You

Don't Confuse "Scarcity" with "Shortage"

At first glance, the following statement seems correct: "There is a shortage of every good that is scarce." In everyday conversation, we describe a good as "scarce" if we have trouble finding it. For instance, if you are looking for a gift for a child, you might call the latest hot toy "scarce" if you are willing to buy it at its listed price but can't find it online or in any store. But recall from Chapter 2 that economists have a broad definition of *scarce*. In the economic sense, almost everything—except undesirable things like garbage—is scarce. A shortage of a good occurs only if the quantity demanded is greater than the quantity supplied at the current price. Therefore, the preceding statement—"There is a shortage of every good that is scarce"—is incorrect. In fact, there is no shortage of most scarce goods.

MyEconLab

Your Turn: Test your understanding by doing related problem 3.15 on page 128 at the end of this chapter.

apartments into offices, selling some off as condominiums, or converting some small apartment buildings into single-family homes. Over time, landlords may even abandon some apartment buildings. At one time in New York City, rent control resulted in landlords abandoning whole city blocks because they were unable to cover their costs with the rents the government allowed them to charge. In London, when rent controls were applied to rooms and apartments located in a landlord's own home, the quantity of these apartments supplied dropped by 75 percent.

In Figure 4.9, with the rent ceiling of $1,000, the quantity of apartments demanded rises to 2,100,000. There is a shortage of 200,000 apartments. Consumer surplus increases by rectangle *A* and falls by triangle *B*. Rectangle *A* would have been part of producer surplus if rent control were not in place. With rent control, it is part of consumer surplus. Rent control causes the producer surplus received by landlords to fall by rectangle *A* plus triangle *C*. Triangles *B* and *C* represent the deadweight loss. There is a deadweight loss because rent control has reduced the amount of economic surplus in the market for apartments. Rent control has caused the marginal benefit of the last apartment rented to be greater than the marginal cost of supplying it. We can conclude that a price ceiling, such as rent control, reduces economic efficiency. The appendix to this chapter shows how we can make quantitative estimates of the deadweight loss, and it provides an example of the changes in consumer surplus and producer surplus that can result from rent control.

Renters as a group benefit from rent controls—total consumer surplus is larger—but landlords lose. Because of the deadweight loss, the total loss to landlords is greater than the gain to renters. Notice also that although renters as a group benefit, the number of renters is reduced, so some renters are made worse off by rent controls because they are unable to find an apartment at the legal rent.

Black Markets

To this point, our analysis of rent controls is incomplete. In practice, renters may be worse off and landlords may be better off than Figure 4.9 makes it seem. We have assumed that renters and landlords actually abide by the price ceiling, but sometimes they don't. Because rent control leads to a shortage of apartments, renters who would otherwise not be able to find apartments have an incentive to offer landlords rents above the legal maximum. When governments try to control prices by setting price ceilings or price floors, buyers and sellers often find a way around the controls. The result is a **black market** where buying and selling take place at prices that violate government price regulations.

In a housing market with rent controls, the total amount of consumer surplus received by renters may be reduced and the total amount of producer surplus received by landlords may be increased if apartments are being rented at prices above the legal price ceiling.

Black market A market in which buying and selling take place at prices that violate government price regulations.

Solved Problem 4.3

What's the Economic Effect of a Black Market for Apartments?

In many cities that have rent controls, the actual rents paid can be much higher than the legal maximum. Because rent controls cause a shortage of apartments, desperate tenants are often willing to pay landlords rents that are higher than the law allows, perhaps by writing a check for the legally allowed rent and paying an additional amount in cash. Look again at Figure 4.9 on page 112. Suppose that competition among tenants results in the black market rent rising to $2,000 per month. At this rent, tenants demand 1,900,000 apartments. Use a graph showing the market for apartments to compare this situation with the one shown in Figure 4.9. Be sure to note any differences in consumer surplus, producer surplus, and deadweight loss.

Solving the Problem

Step 1: **Review the chapter material.** This problem is about price controls in the market for apartments, so you may want to review the section "Price Ceilings: Government Rent Control Policy in Housing Markets," which begins on page 112.

Step 2: **Draw a graph similar to Figure 4.9, with the addition of the black market price.**

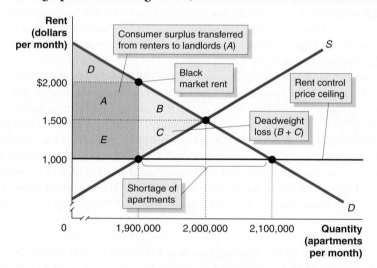

Step 3: **Analyze the changes from Figure 4.9.** The black market rent is now $2,000—even higher than the original competitive equilibrium rent shown in Figure 4.9. So, consumer surplus declines by an amount equal to the red rectangle *A* plus the red rectangle *E*. The remaining consumer surplus is the blue triangle *D*. Note that the rectangle *A*, which would have been part of consumer surplus without rent control, represents a transfer from renters to landlords. Compared with the situation shown in Figure 4.9, producer surplus has increased by an amount equal to rectangles *A* and *E*, and consumer surplus has declined by the same amount. Deadweight loss is equal to triangles *B* and *C*, the same as in Figure 4.9.

Extra Credit: This analysis leads to a surprising result: With an active black market in apartments, rent control may leave renters as a group worse off—with less consumer surplus—than if there were no rent control. There is one more possibility to consider, however. If enough landlords become convinced that they can get away with charging rents above the legal ceiling, the quantity of apartments supplied will increase. Eventually, the market could even end up at the competitive equilibrium, with an equilibrium rent of $1,500 and equilibrium quantity of 2,000,000 apartments. In that case, the rent control price ceiling becomes nonbinding, not because it was set below the equilibrium price but because it was not legally enforced.

MyEconLab **Your Turn:** For more practice, do related problem 3.14 on page 127 at the end of this chapter.

Rent controls can also lead to an increase in racial and other types of discrimination. With rent controls, more renters are looking for apartments than there are apartments to rent. Landlords can afford to indulge their prejudices by refusing to rent to people they don't like. In cities without rent controls, landlords face more competition, which makes it more difficult to turn down tenants on the basis of irrelevant characteristics, such as race.

The Results of Government Price Controls: Winners, Losers, and Inefficiency

When the government imposes price floors or price ceilings, three important results occur:

- Some people win.

- Some people lose.

- There is a loss of economic efficiency.

The winners with rent control are the people who are paying less for rent because they live in rent-controlled apartments. Landlords may also gain if they break the law by charging rents above the legal maximum for their rent-controlled apartments, provided that those illegal rents are higher than the competitive equilibrium rents would be. The losers from rent control are the landlords of rent-controlled apartments who abide by the law and renters who are unable to find apartments to rent at the controlled price. Rent control reduces economic efficiency because fewer apartments are rented than would be rented in a competitive market (refer again to Figure 4.9, on page 112). The resulting deadweight loss measures the decrease in economic efficiency.

Positive and Normative Analysis of Price Ceilings and Price Floors

Are rent controls, government farm programs, and other price ceilings and price floors bad? As we saw in Chapter 1, questions of this type have no right or wrong answers. Economists are generally skeptical of government attempts to interfere with competitive market equilibrium. Economists know the role competitive markets have played in raising the average person's standard of living. They also know that too much government intervention has the potential to reduce the ability of the market system to produce similar increases in living standards in the future.

But recall from Chapter 1 the difference between positive and normative analysis. Positive analysis is concerned with *what is*, and normative analysis is concerned with *what should be*. Our analysis of rent control and of the federal farm programs in this chapter is positive analysis. We discussed the economic results of these programs. Whether these programs are desirable or undesirable is a normative question. Whether the gains to the winners more than make up for the losses to the losers and for the decline in economic efficiency is a matter of judgment and not strictly an economic question. Price ceilings and price floors continue to exist partly because people who understand their downside still believe they are good policies and therefore support them. The policies also persist because many people who support them do not understand the economic analysis in this chapter and so do not understand the drawbacks to these policies.

The Economic Impact of Taxes

4.4 LEARNING OBJECTIVE

Analyze the economic impact of taxes.

Supreme Court Justice Oliver Wendell Holmes once remarked, "Taxes are what we pay for a civilized society." When the government taxes a good or service, however, it affects the market equilibrium for that good or service. Just as with a price ceiling or price floor, one result of a tax is a decline in economic efficiency. Analyzing taxes is an important part of the field of economics known as *public finance*. In this section, we will use the model of demand and supply and the concepts of consumer surplus, producer surplus, and deadweight loss to analyze the economic impact of taxes.

The Effect of a Tax on the Market for Cigarettes

Without the tax, market equilibrium occurs at point *A*. The equilibrium price of cigarettes is $4.00 per pack, and 4 billion packs of cigarettes are sold per year. A $1.00-per-pack tax on cigarettes will cause the supply curve for cigarettes to shift up by $1.00, from S_1 to S_2. The new equilibrium occurs at point *B*. The price of cigarettes will increase by $0.90, to $4.90 per pack, and the quantity sold will fall to 3.7 billion packs. The tax on cigarettes has increased the price paid by consumers from $4.00 to $4.90 per pack. Producers receive a price of $4.90 per pack (point *B*), but after paying the $1.00 tax, they are left with $3.90 (point *C*). The government will receive tax revenue equal to the green-shaded box. Some consumer surplus and some producer surplus will become tax revenue for the government, and some will become deadweight loss, shown by the yellow-shaded area.

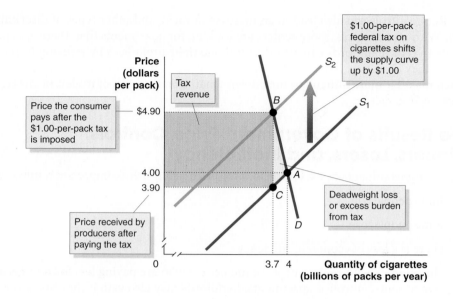

The Effect of Taxes on Economic Efficiency

Whenever a government taxes a good or service, less of that good or service will be produced and consumed. For example, a tax on cigarettes will raise the cost of smoking and reduce the amount of smoking that takes place. We can use a demand and supply graph to illustrate this point. Figure 4.10 shows the market for cigarettes.

Without the tax, the equilibrium price of cigarettes would be $4.00 per pack, and 4 billion packs of cigarettes would be sold per year (point *A*). If the federal government requires sellers of cigarettes to pay a $1.00-per-pack tax, then their cost of selling cigarettes will increase by $1.00 per pack. This increase in costs causes the supply curve for cigarettes to shift up by $1.00 because sellers will now require a price that is $1.00 greater to supply the same quantity of cigarettes. In Figure 4.10, the supply curve shifts up by $1.00 to show the effect of the tax, and there is a new equilibrium price of $4.90 and a new equilibrium quantity of 3.7 billion packs (point *B*).

The federal government will collect tax revenue equal to the tax per pack multiplied by the number of packs sold, or $3.7 billion. The area shaded in green in Figure 4.10 represents the government's tax revenue. Consumers will pay a higher price of $4.90 per pack. Although sellers appear to be receiving a higher price per pack, once they have paid the tax, the price they receive falls from $4.00 per pack to $3.90 per pack. There is a loss of consumer surplus because consumers are paying a higher price. The price producers receive falls, so there is also a loss of producer surplus. Therefore, the tax on cigarettes has reduced *both* consumer surplus and producer surplus. Some of the reduction in consumer and producer surplus becomes tax revenue for the government. The rest of the reduction in consumer and producer surplus is equal to the deadweight loss from the tax, shown by the yellow-shaded triangle in the figure.

We can conclude that the true burden of a tax is not just the amount consumers and producers pay the government but also includes the deadweight loss. The deadweight loss from a tax is referred to as the *excess burden* of the tax. *A tax is efficient if it imposes a small excess burden relative to the tax revenue it raises.* One contribution economists make to government tax policy is to advise policymakers on which taxes are most efficient.

Tax Incidence: Who Actually Pays a Tax?

The answer to the question "Who pays a tax?" seems obvious: Whoever is legally required to send a tax payment to the government pays the tax. But there can be an important difference between who is legally required to pay the tax and who actually *bears*

Price (dollars per gallon)

Price the consumers of gasoline pay after the 10-cents-per-gallon tax is imposed

S_2

S_1

$3.08

3.00

2.98

10-cents-per-gallon federal excise tax on gasoline shifts the supply curve up

Price the sellers of gasoline receive after the 10-cents-per-gallon tax is imposed

D

0   140 144   **Quantity (billions of gallons per year)**

Figure 4.11

The Incidence of a Tax on Gasoline

With no tax on gasoline, the price would be $3.00 per gallon, and 144 billion gallons of gasoline would be sold each year. A 10-cents-per-gallon excise tax shifts up the supply curve from S_1 to S_2, raises the price consumers pay from $3.00 to $3.08, and lowers the price sellers receive from $3.00 to $2.98. Therefore, consumers pay 8 cents of the 10-cents-per-gallon tax on gasoline, and sellers pay 2 cents.

the burden of the tax. The actual division of the burden of a tax between buyers and sellers is referred to as **tax incidence**. The federal government currently levies an excise tax of 18.4 cents per gallon of gasoline sold. Gas station owners collect this tax and forward it to the federal government, but who actually bears the burden of the tax?

Tax incidence The actual division of the burden of a tax between buyers and sellers in a market.

Determining Tax Incidence on a Demand and Supply Graph Suppose that currently the federal government does not impose a tax on gasoline. In Figure 4.11, equilibrium in the retail market for gasoline occurs at the intersection of the demand curve and supply curve, S_1. The equilibrium price is $3.00 per gallon, and the equilibrium quantity is 144 billion gallons. Now suppose that the federal government imposes a 10-cents-per-gallon tax. As a result of the tax, the supply curve for gasoline will shift up by 10 cents per gallon. At the new equilibrium, where the demand curve intersects the supply curve, S_2, the price has risen by 8 cents per gallon, from $3.00 to $3.08. Notice that only in the extremely unlikely case that demand is a vertical line will the market price rise by the full amount of the tax. Consumers are paying 8 cents more per gallon. Sellers of gasoline receive a new higher price of $3.08 per gallon, but after paying the 10-cents-per-gallon tax, they are left with $2.98 per gallon, or 2 cents less than they were receiving in the old equilibrium.

Although the sellers of gasoline are responsible for collecting the tax and sending the tax receipts to the government, they do not bear most of the burden of the tax. In this case, consumers pay 8 cents of the tax because the market price has risen by 8 cents, and sellers pay 2 cents of the tax because after sending the tax to the government, they are receiving 2 cents less per gallon of gasoline sold. Expressed in percentage terms, consumers pay 80 percent of the tax, and sellers pay 20 percent of the tax.

Solved Problem 4.4

When Do Consumers Pay All of a Sales Tax Increase?

A student makes the following statement: "If the federal government raises the sales tax on gasoline by $0.25, then the price of gasoline will rise by $0.25. Consumers can't get by without gasoline, so they have to pay the whole amount of any increase in the sales tax." Under what circumstances will the student's statement be true? Illustrate your answer with a graph of the market for gasoline.

Solving the Problem

Step 1: **Review the chapter material.** This problem is about tax incidence, so you may want to review the section "Tax Incidence: Who Actually Pays a Tax?" that begins on page 116.

Step 2: **Draw a graph like Figure 4.11 to illustrate the circumstances when consumers will pay all of an increase in a sales tax.**

Step 3: **Use the graph to evaluate the statement.** The graph shows that consumers will pay all of an increase in a sales tax only if the demand curve is a vertical line. It is very unlikely that the demand for gasoline would look like this because we expect that for every good, an increase in price will cause a decrease in the quantity demanded. Because the demand curve for gasoline is not a vertical line, the statement is incorrect.

MyEconLab **Your Turn:** For more practice, do related problem 4.7 on page 130 at the end of the chapter.

Does It Make a Difference Whether the Government Collects a Tax from Buyers or Sellers? We have already seen the important distinction between the true burden of a tax and whether buyers or sellers are legally required to pay a tax. We can reinforce this point by noting explicitly that the incidence of a tax does *not* depend on whether the government collects a tax from the buyers of a good or from the sellers. Figure 4.12 illustrates this point by showing the effect on equilibrium in the market for gasoline if a 10-cents-per-gallon tax is imposed on buyers rather than on sellers. That is, we are now assuming that instead of sellers having to collect the 10-cents-per-gallon tax at the pump, buyers are responsible for keeping track of how many gallons of gasoline they purchase and sending the tax to the government. (Of course, it would be very difficult for buyers to keep track of their purchases or for the government to check whether they were paying all of the taxes they owe. That is why the government collects the tax on gasoline from sellers.)

Figure 4.12 is similar to Figure 4.11 except that it shows the gasoline tax being imposed on buyers rather than sellers. In Figure 4.12, the supply curve does not shift because nothing has happened to change the quantity of gasoline sellers are willing to supply at any given price. The demand curve has shifted, however, because consumers now have to pay a 10-cent tax on every gallon of gasoline they buy. Therefore, at every

Figure 4.12

The Incidence of a Tax on Gasoline Paid by Buyers

With no tax on gasoline, the demand curve is D_1. If a 10-cents-per-gallon tax is imposed that consumers are responsible for paying, the demand curve shifts down by the amount of the tax, from D_1 to D_2. In the new equilibrium, consumers pay a price of $3.08 per gallon, including the tax. Producers receive $2.98 per gallon. This is the same result we saw when producers were responsible for paying the tax.

quantity, they are willing to pay a price 10 cents less than they would have without the tax. In the figure, we indicate the effect of the tax by shifting the demand curve down by 10 cents, from D_1 to D_2. Once the tax has been imposed and the demand curve has shifted down, the new equilibrium quantity of gasoline is 140 billion gallons, which is exactly the same as in Figure 4.11.

The new equilibrium price after the tax is imposed appears to be different in Figure 4.12 than in Figure 4.11, but if we include the tax, buyers will pay the same price and sellers will receive the same price in both figures. To see this, notice that in Figure 4.11, buyers pay sellers a price of $3.08 per gallon. In Figure 4.12, they pay sellers only $2.98, but they must also pay the government a tax of 10 cents per gallon. So, the total price buyers pay remains $3.08 per gallon. In Figure 4.11, sellers receive $3.08 per gallon from buyers, but after they pay the tax of 10 cents per gallon, they are left with $2.98, which is the same amount they receive in Figure 4.12.

Making the Connection	Is the Burden of the Social Security Tax Really Shared Equally between Workers and Firms?

Most people who receive paychecks have several different taxes withheld from them by their employers, who forward these taxes directly to the government. In fact, many people are shocked after getting their first job when they discover the gap between their gross pay and their net pay after taxes have been deducted. The largest tax many people of low or moderate income pay is FICA, which stands for the Federal Insurance Contributions Act. FICA funds the Social Security and Medicare programs, which provide income and health care to the elderly and disabled. FICA is sometimes referred to as the *payroll tax*. When Congress passed the act, it wanted employers and workers to equally share the burden of the tax. Currently, FICA is 15.3 percent of wages, with 7.65 percent paid by workers by being withheld from their paychecks and the other 7.65 percent paid by employers.

But does requiring workers and employers to each pay half the tax mean that the burden of the tax is also shared equally? Our discussion in this chapter shows that the answer is no. In the labor market, employers are buyers, and workers are sellers. As we saw in the example of the federal tax on gasoline, whether the tax is collected from buyers or from sellers does not affect the incidence of the tax. Most economists believe, in fact, that the burden of FICA falls almost entirely on workers. The following figure, which shows the market for labor, illustrates why.

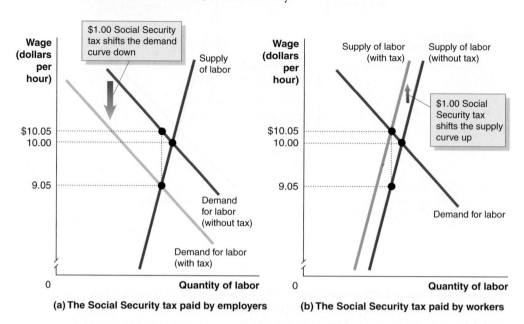

(a) The Social Security tax paid by employers

(b) The Social Security tax paid by workers

In the market for labor, the demand curve represents the quantity of labor de-manded by employers at various wages, and the supply curve represents the quantity of labor supplied by workers at various wages. The intersection of the demand curve and the supply curve determines the equilibrium wage. In both panels, the equilibrium wage without a Social Security payroll tax is $10 per hour. For simplicity, let's assume that the payroll tax equals $1 per hour of work. In panel (a), we assume that employers must pay the tax. The tax causes the demand for labor curve to shift down by $1 at every quantity of labor because firms now must pay a $1 tax for every hour of labor they hire. We have drawn the supply curve for labor as being very steep because most economists believe the quantity of labor supplied by workers does not change much as the wage rate changes. Workers pay $0.95 of the tax because their wages fall from $10 before the tax to $9.05 after the tax. Firms pay only $0.05 of the tax because the amount they pay for an hour of labor increases from $10 before the tax to $10.05 after the tax. In panel (a), after the tax is imposed, the equilibrium wage declines from $10 per hour to $9.05 per hour. Firms are now paying a total of $10.05 for every hour of work they hire: $9.05 in wages to workers and $1 in tax to the government. In other words, workers have paid $0.95 of the $1 tax, and firms have paid only $0.05.

Panel (b) shows that this result is exactly the same if the tax is imposed on workers rather than on firms. In this case, the tax causes the supply curve for labor to shift up by $1 at every quantity of labor because workers must now pay a tax of $1 for every hour they work. After the tax is imposed, the equilibrium wage increases to $10.05 per hour. But workers receive only $9.05 after they have paid the $1.00 tax. Once again, workers have paid $0.95 of the $1 tax, and firms have paid only $0.05.

Although the figure presents a simplified analysis, it reflects the conclusion of most economists who have studied the incidence of FICA: Even though Congress requires employers to pay half the tax and workers to pay the other half, in fact, the burden of the tax falls almost entirely on workers. This conclusion would not be changed even if Congress revised the law to require either employers or workers to pay all of the tax. The forces of demand and supply working in the labor market, and not Congress, determine the incidence of the tax.

MyEconLab **Your Turn:** Test your understanding by doing related problems 4.8 and 4.9 on page 130 at the end of this chapter.

Continued from page 101

Economics in Your Life

Does Rent Control Make It Easier for You to Find an Affordable Apartment?

At the beginning of the chapter, we posed the following question: If you have two job offers in different cities, one with rent control and one without, will you be more likely to find an afford-able apartment in the city with rent control? In answering the question, this chapter has shown that although rent control can keep rents lower than they might otherwise be, it can also lead to a permanent shortage of apartments. You may have to search for a long time to find a suitable apart-ment, and landlords may even ask you to give them payments "under the table," which would make your actual rent higher than the controlled rent. Finding an apartment in a city without rent control should be much easier, although the rent may be higher.

Conclusion

The model of demand and supply introduced in Chapter 3 showed that markets free from government intervention eliminate surpluses and shortages and do a good job of responding to the wants of consumers. We have seen in this chapter that both consum-ers and firms sometimes try to use the government to change market outcomes in their favor. The concepts of consumer and producer surplus and deadweight loss allow us to measure the benefits consumers and producers receive from competitive market equi-librium. These concepts also allow us to measure the effects of government price floors and price ceilings and the economic impact of taxes.

Read *An Inside Look at Policy* on the next page for an example of how celebrity Faye Dunaway and her son have financially benefited from rent-control laws in New York City.

...and the Rent-Controlled Apartment Goes to ... Actress Faye Dunaway!

NEW YORK TIMES

For Faye Dunaway, Real-Life Role in Housing Court

She was a brazen bank robber in "Bonnie and Clyde," the mysterious Evelyn Mulwray in "Chinatown" and a scheming television executive in "Network," for which she won an Oscar.

Now Faye Dunaway is a defendant in case No. 76667/11 in Manhattan housing court, just another rent-stabilized tenant facing eviction.

In a lawsuit filed Tuesday, her landlord claims that Ms. Dunaway, who pays $1,048.72 a month for a one-bedroom walk-up apartment in a century-old tenement building on East 78th Street, does not actually live there, but rather lives in California. The suit also names her son, Liam Dunaway O'Neill, whose father is the photographer Terry O'Neill, as a subtenant in the apartment.

As proof, the landlord, unnamed in court papers, states that Ms. Dunaway owns a home in West Hollywood, and has her voter and automobile registrations there. The suit also cites three moving violations she received in California from May 2009 to December 2010.

Rent stabilization rules require tenants to live in the apartment they are renting as a primary residence, not as a second home. Ms. Dunaway, 70, does not appear to be living glamorously. The home in California is a nice but not flashy house on which she still carries a mortgage, according to the lawsuit. Her car is a 2007 Toyota Corolla.

Ms. Dunaway is one of the many celebrities who have fought to keep rent-regulated apartments in New York over the years. But Ms. Dunaway's current apartment is also a vast departure from the 20th-floor apartment she inhabited at the Eldorado earlier in her career. ...

If Ms. Dunaway leaves, the landlord is likely to get far more rent. According to rental data tracked by the brokerage Citi Habitats, one-bedroom walk-up apartments on the Upper East Side currently rent for an average of $2,318 a month.

Ms. Dunaway rented her current apartment on the Upper East Side on Aug. 1, 1994, in a six-story yellow brick building with fire escapes in the front. The name next to the outdoor buzzer reads "F. Dunaway." The building's hallway floors are green linoleum. Its cream walls are chipped, and pink marble steps lead up to her third-floor unit. Her front door is painted aquamarine and has the names "Dunaway/ONeill" and "PT Bascom" listed by the black doorbell. There is a simple brown doormat with black trim. No one answered the door on Tuesday afternoon.

Ms. Dunaway had problems in the past with her landlord, who filed a notice in 2009 in Civil Court in Manhattan for nonpayment of rent. That case appeared to have been resolved, and she signed a lease in April 2009 to remain in her apartment until July 31, 2011.

Court papers show that the landlord investigated earlier this year to determine where she actually lived and contacted Ms. Dunaway in March with its findings. The landlord asked her to leave when her lease expired on July 31.

Neighbors said that while they had seen Ms. Dunaway in the past, they had not seen her much lately. Keith Cohen, owner of Orwasher's Bakery near Ms. Dunaway's apartment, said that employees had told him when he arrived in 2007 that Ms. Dunaway lived nearby, but that he had never seen her.

Rosane Franco, manager of the nearby Tiny Doll House shop, said she had seen Ms. Dunaway a few times in the past two years, but that the last time was "many months ago."

The occupant of an apartment next door, who would not give her name, said through her door, "I've never met her."

Ms. Dunaway's Twitter feed shows no mention of her being in New York recently. Her son, Mr. O'Neill, has written on his Twitter feed, "I live in LA."

Ms. Dunaway is scheduled for a hearing in Civil Court on Aug. 11 at 2 P.M.

If she departs, it may not have much effect on her sleepy block between First and Second Avenues.

"She's not that glamorous person everybody saw in the movies," Ms. Franco said. "We were surprised that she lived here in the first place."

Key Points in the Article

In July 2011, Oscar-winning actress Faye Dunaway found herself embroiled in a legal battle as the defendant in a lawsuit filed by the landlord of her rent-controlled New York City apartment. According to the lawsuit, Dunaway faced eviction from her apartment based on the landlord's claim that she had violated the New York rent stabilization rule that requires the apartment be the primary residence of the tenant. Dunaway first moved into the apartment in 1994, and as recently as 2009 renewed her lease through July 2011. Following an investigation, the landlord concluded that Dunaway's primary residence is actually in Los Angeles, and based on these findings, asked her to leave the apartment when the lease expired on July 31. Dunaway's refusal to leave prompted the landlord to file the lawsuit in Manhattan housing court following the expiration of her lease.

Analyzing the News

(a) According to her landlord, Dunaway's monthly rent on the rent-controlled apartment is $1,048.72. Rent-controlled apartments generally rent for an amount below what the equilibrium price would be were the market not subject to this government-set price. Rent control not only reduces the potential revenue that could be received by landlords if the market were not

regulated, but also results in a shortage of apartments.

(b) In the case of Dunaway's apartment, the controlled rent is apparently significantly below the amount that could be charged in an unregulated market. Rental data show that in the same neighborhood, apartments of a similar size and layout rent for an average of $2,318 per month, more than double the rent Dunaway is paying. The figure below shows an example of rent control in the New York City apartment market, using the average rent of $2,318 as the equilibrium price. At the rent-controlled price of $1,048.72, a shortage of apartments will exist, represented by the distance from Q_1 to Q_2. The shortage indicates that more people will want to rent apartments at the rent controlled price than there will be apartments available for rent. It is understandable why Dunaway's landlord would like to take advantage of the primary residency restriction in the New York rent stabilization rules and have her evicted from the apartment. As described in the chapter opener, current rent control laws in New York are quite complex, but landlords can raise the rent on vacant apartments, and apartments renting for $2,000 a month are automatically deregulated if they are vacant. Based on these laws, the monthly revenue the landlord could receive by renting this apartment to a new tenant would definitely increase.

(c) Dunaway's landlord filed a legal notice against her for nonpayment of rent in 2009, so this is not the first time the two parties have engaged in legal wrangling. That issue was apparently resolved, but this time the landlord definitely seems to want Dunaway out and is using the residency restriction as the means. Neighborhood residents have stated that they have not seen Dunaway much lately, supporting the landlord's claim that the New York apartment is not the actor's primary residence. No matter what methods landlords use in an attempt to reclaim rent-controlled apartments, if their efforts are successful, they will be able to increase their revenues so long as demand remains strong for these properties.

Thinking Critically About Policy

1. One consequence of rent control is a shortage of apartments, which is shown in the figure. Suppose rent control also leads to a reduction in the supply of affordable apartments. Use the figure on this page to illustrate the effects of a reduction in supply, and explain what will happen to the shortage of apartments.

2. One reason some economists are critical of rent control laws is that they create a deadweight loss. Using the figure on this page, identify the area representing the deadweight loss. What causes the deadweight loss? What would the supply curve have to look like for the deadweight loss to equal zero?

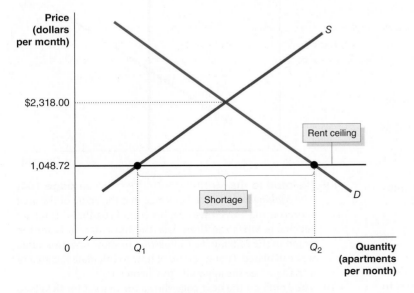

The effect of rent control laws on the supply of affordable apartments.

Chapter Summary and Problems

Key Terms

Black market, p. 113

Consumer surplus, p. 102

Deadweight loss, p. 108

Economic efficiency, p. 109

Economic surplus, p. 108

Marginal benefit, p. 102

Marginal cost, p. 105

Price ceiling, p. 102

Price floor, p. 102

Producer surplus, p. 105

Tax incidence, p. 117

 4.1 **Consumer Surplus and Producer Surplus,** pages 102–107

LEARNING OBJECTIVE: Distinguish between the concepts of consumer surplus and producer surplus.

Summary

Although most prices are determined by demand and supply in markets, the government sometimes imposes *price ceilings* and *price floors*. A **price ceiling** is a legally determined maximum price that sellers may charge. A **price floor** is a legally determined minimum price that sellers may receive. Economists analyze the effects of price ceilings and price floors using *consumer surplus* and *producer surplus*. **Marginal benefit** is the additional benefit to a consumer from consuming one more unit of a good or service. The demand curve is also a marginal benefit curve. **Consumer surplus** is the difference between the highest price a consumer is willing to pay for a good or service and the price the consumer actually pays. The total amount of consumer surplus in a market is equal to the area below the demand curve and above the market price. **Marginal cost** is the additional cost to a firm of producing one more unit of a good or service. The supply curve is also a marginal cost curve. **Producer surplus** is the difference between the lowest price a firm is willing to accept for a good or service and the price it actually receives. The total amount of producer surplus in a market is equal to the area above the supply curve and below the market price.

MyEconLab Visit **www.myeconlab.com** to complete these exercises online and get instant feedback.

Review Questions

1.1 What is marginal benefit? Why is the demand curve referred to as a marginal benefit curve?

1.2 What is marginal cost? Why is the supply curve referred to as a marginal cost curve?

1.3 What is consumer surplus? How does consumer surplus change as the equilibrium price of a good rises or falls?

1.4 What is producer surplus? How does producer surplus change as the equilibrium price of a good rises or falls?

Problems and Applications

1.5 Suppose that a frost in Florida reduces the size of the orange crop, which causes the supply curve for oranges to shift to the left. Briefly explain whether consumer surplus will increase or decrease and whether producer surplus will increase or decrease. Use a demand and supply graph to illustrate your answers.

1.6 A student makes the following argument: "When a market is in equilibrium, there is no consumer surplus. We know this because in equilibrium, the market price is equal to the price consumers are willing to pay for the good." Briefly explain whether you agree with the student's argument.

1.7 How does consumer surplus differ from the total benefit consumers receive from purchasing products? Similarly, how does producer surplus differ from the total revenue that firms receive from selling products? Under what special case will consumer surplus equal the total benefit consumers receive from consuming a product? Under what special case will producer surplus equal the total revenue firms receive from selling a product?

1.8 The following graph illustrates the market for a breast cancer–fighting drug, without which breast cancer patients cannot survive. What is the consumer surplus in this market? How does it differ from the consumer surplus in the markets you have studied up to this point?

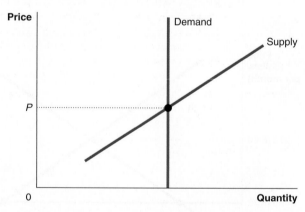

1.9 [**Related to the** Making the Connection **on page 104**] The *Making the Connection* states that the value of the area representing consumer surplus from broadband Internet service is $890.5 million. Use the information from the graph in the *Making the Connection* to show how this value was calculated. (For a review of how to calculate the area of a triangle, see the appendix to Chapter 1.)

1.10 The graph on the next page shows the market for tickets to a concert that will be held in a local arena that seats 15,000 people. What is the producer surplus in this market? How does it differ from the producer surplus in the markets you have studied up to this point?

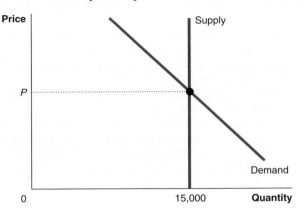

1.11 A study estimates that the total consumer surplus gained by people participating in auctions on eBay in a recent year was $7 billion. Is it likely that the total consumer surplus for the items bought in these auctions was higher or lower than it would have been if consumers had purchased these items for fixed prices in retail stores?

Based on Ravi Bapna, Wolfgang Jank, and Galit Shmueli, "Consumer Surplus in Online Auctions," *Information Systems Research*, Vol. 19, No. 4, December 2008, pp. 400–416.

1.12 Movies, songs, and books are covered by copyrights, which allow the creators of these works to keep other people from reproducing them without permission. Many people, though, violate copyright laws by using file-sharing services that allow them to download copies of songs and movies at a zero price.

a. Does file sharing increase the consumer surplus from consuming existing songs and movies? Draw a demand curve to illustrate your answer. The demand curve should indicate the price when file sharing is not possible, the zero price with file sharing, and the amount of consumer surplus with and without file sharing.

b. What are the likely effects of file sharing in the long run? Is file sharing likely to increase the total consumer surplus from consuming songs and movies in the long run? Briefly explain.

Based on Joel Waldfogel, "Bye, Bye, Miss American Pie? The Supply of New Recorded Music Since Napster," National Bureau of Economic Research Working Paper 16882, March 2011.

4.2 The Efficiency of Competitive Markets, pages 107–109

LEARNING OBJECTIVE: Understand the concept of economic efficiency.

Summary

Equilibrium in a competitive market is **economically efficient**. **Economic surplus** is the sum of consumer surplus and producer surplus. Economic efficiency is a market outcome in which the marginal benefit to consumers from the last unit produced is equal to the marginal cost of production and where the sum of consumer surplus and producer surplus is at a maximum. When the market price is above or below the equilibrium price, there is a reduction in economic surplus. The reduction in economic surplus resulting from a market not being in competitive equilibrium is called the **deadweight loss**.

 MyEconLab   Visit **www.myeconlab.com** to complete these exercises online and get instant feedback.

Review Questions

2.1 Define *economic surplus* and *deadweight loss*.
2.2 What is economic efficiency? Why do economists define *efficiency* in this way?

Problems and Applications

2.3 Briefly explain whether you agree with the following statement: "A lower price in a market always increases economic efficiency in that market."
2.4 Briefly explain whether you agree with the following statement: "If at the current quantity marginal benefit is greater than marginal cost, there will be a deadweight loss in the market. However, there is no deadweight loss when marginal cost is greater than marginal benefit."
2.5 Using a demand and supply graph, illustrate and briefly explain the effect on consumer surplus and producer surplus of a price below the equilibrium price. Show any deadweight loss on your graph.
2.6 Briefly explain whether you agree with the following statement: "If consumer surplus in a market increases, producer surplus must decrease."
2.7 Does an increase in economic surplus in a market always mean that economic efficiency in the market has increased? Briefly explain.
2.8 Using the graph below, explain why economic surplus would be smaller if Q_1 or Q_3 were the quantity produced than if Q_2 is the quantity produced.

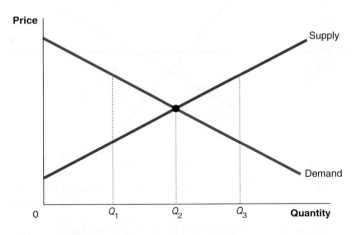

4.3 Government Intervention in the Market: Price Floors and Price Ceilings, pages 109-115

LEARNING OBJECTIVE: Explain the economic effect of government-imposed price floors and price ceilings.

Summary

Producers or consumers who are dissatisfied with the market outcome can attempt to convince the government to impose price floors or price ceilings. Price floors usually increase producer surplus, decrease consumer surplus, and cause a deadweight loss. Price ceilings usually increase consumer surplus, reduce producer surplus, and cause a deadweight loss. The results of the government imposing price ceilings and price floors are that some people win, some people lose, and a loss of economic efficiency occurs. Price ceilings and price floors can lead to a **black market**, where buying and selling take place at prices that violate government price regulations. Positive analysis is concerned with what is, and normative analysis is concerned with what should be. Positive analysis shows that price ceilings and price floors cause deadweight losses. Whether these policies are desirable or undesirable, though, is a normative question.

MyEconLab   Visit **www.myeconlab.com** to complete these exercises online and get instant feedback.

Review Questions

3.1 Why do some consumers tend to favor price controls while others tend to oppose them?

3.2 Do producers tend to favor price floors or price ceilings? Why?

3.3 What is a black market? Under what circumstances do black markets arise?

3.4 Can economic analysis provide a final answer to the question of whether the government should intervene in markets by imposing price ceilings and price floors? Briefly explain.

Problems and Applications

3.5 The graph below shows the market for apples. Assume that the government has imposed a price floor of $10 per crate.

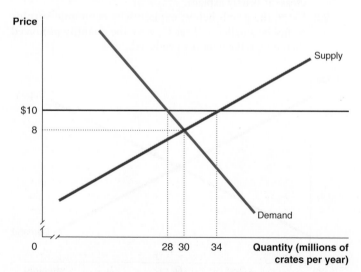

a. How many crates of apples will be sold after the price floor has been imposed?

b. Will there be a shortage or a surplus? If there is a shortage or a surplus, how large will it be?

c. Will apple producers benefit from the price floor? If so, explain how they will benefit.

3.6 Use the information on the kumquat market in the table to answer the following questions:

Price (per Crate)	Quantity Demanded (Millions of Crates per Year)	Quantity Supplied (Millions of Crates per Year)
$10	120	20
15	110	60
20	100	100
25	90	140
30	80	180
35	70	220

a. What are the equilibrium price and quantity? How much revenue do kumquat producers receive when the market is in equilibrium? Draw a graph showing the market equilibrium and the area representing the revenue received by kumquat producers.

b. Suppose the federal government decides to impose a price floor of $30 per crate. Now how many crates of kumquats will consumers purchase? How much revenue will kumquat producers receive? Assume that the government does not purchase any surplus kumquats. On your graph from question (a), show the price floor, the change in the quantity of kumquats purchased, and the revenue received by kumquat producers after the price floor is imposed.

c. Suppose the government imposes a price floor of $30 per crate and purchases any surplus kumquats from producers. Now how much revenue will kumquat producers receive? How much will the government spend on purchasing surplus kumquats? On your graph from question (a), show the area representing the amount the government spends to purchase the surplus kumquats.

3.7 Suppose that the government sets a price floor for milk that is above the competitive equilibrium price.

a. Draw a graph showing this situation. Be sure your graph shows the competitive equilibrium price, the price floor, the quantity that would be sold in competitive equilibrium, and the quantity that would be sold with the price floor.

b. Compare the economic surplus in this market when there is a price floor and when there is no price floor.

3.8 A newspaper headline reads: "State Officials Take on Pricing Regulations to Try to Provide Better, Dependable Income to Dairy Farmers." Is providing dependable income to dairy farmers a good policy goal for government officials? How are government officials likely to try to achieve this goal using pricing regulations? Should government officials use regulations to try to provide dependable incomes to every business in the country?

Based on Tim Darragh, "Thirsty for More Milk," *Morning Call*, (Allentown, PA) July 12, 2010.

3.9 During 2007, the Venezuelan government allowed consumers to buy only a limited quantity of sugar. The government also imposed a ceiling on the price of sugar. As a result, both the quantity of sugar consumed and the market price of sugar were below the competitive equilibrium price and quantity. Draw a graph to illustrate this situation. On your graph, be sure to indicate the areas representing consumer surplus, producer surplus, and deadweight loss.

3.10 Refer to problem 3.9. An article in the *New York Times* contained the following (Hugo Chávez is the president of Venezuela):

> José Vielma Mora, the chief of Seniat, the government's tax agency, oversaw a raid this month on a warehouse here where officials seized about 165 tons of sugar. Mr. Vielma said the raid exposed hoarding by vendors who were unwilling to sell the sugar at official prices. He and other officials in Mr. Chávez's government have repeatedly blamed the shortages on producers, intermediaries and grocers.

Do you agree that the shortages in the Venezuelan sugar market are the fault of "producers, intermediaries and grocers"? Briefly explain.

From Simon Romero, "Chavez Threatens to Jail Price Control Violators," *New York Times*, February 17, 2007.

3.11 To drive a taxi legally in New York City, you must have a medallion issued by the city government. City officials have issued only 13,200 medallions. Let's assume that this puts an absolute limit on the number of taxi rides that can be supplied in New York City on any day because no one breaks the law by driving a taxi without a medallion. Let's also assume that each taxi can provide 6 trips per day. In that case, the supply of taxi rides is fixed at 79,200 (or 6 rides per taxi × 13,200 taxis). We show this in the following graph, with a vertical line at this quantity. *Assume that there are no government controls on the prices that drivers can charge for rides.* Use the graph below to answer the following questions.

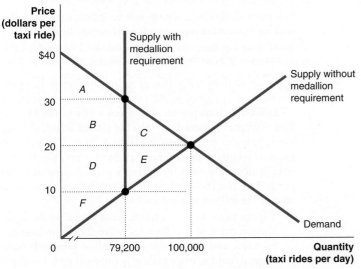

a. What would the equilibrium price and quantity be in this market if there were no medallion requirement?

b. What are the price and quantity with the medallion requirement?

c. Indicate on the graph the areas representing consumer surplus and producer surplus if there were no

medallion requirement. Calculate the values of consumer and producer surplus.

d. Indicate on the graph the areas representing consumer surplus, producer surplus, and deadweight loss with the medallion requirement. Calculate the values of consumer surplus, producer surplus, and deadweight loss.

e. In 2011, the state of New York allowed New York City to sell 1,500 new taxi medallions. Assuming that each of the new taxis can also provide 6 rides per day, what is the new quantity of taxi rides per day? On the graph, show the effects of the new medallions on consumer surplus, producer surplus, and deadweight loss. You do not have to calculate the values.

Based on Jeremy Smerd, "Taxi Plan Breakthrough in Albany," www .crainsnewyork.com, June 24, 2011.

3.12 [**Related to the** Making the Connection **on page 111**] Some economists studying the effects of the minimum wage law have found that it tends to reduce the employment of black teenagers relative to white teenagers. Does the graph in the *Making the Connection* help you understand why black teenagers may have been disproportionately affected by the minimum wage law? Briefly explain.

3.13 [**Related to the** Chapter Opener **on page 101**] Writing in the *New York Times*, economist Paul Krugman commented on an article he read that concerned the trials of people who were searching for apartments in San Francisco. Krugman recounted the story's "tales of would-be renters, pounding the pavements, of dozens of desperate applicants arriving at a newly offered apartment, trying to impress the landlord with their credentials. And yet there was something . . . missing . . . two words I knew had to be part of the story." What two words do you think were missing from the story?

Based on Paul Krugman, "Reckonings; A Rent Affair," *New York Times*, June 7, 2000.

3.14 [**Related to** Solved Problem 4.3 **on page 114**] Use the information on the market for apartments in Bay City in the table to answer the following questions:

Rent	Quantity Demanded	Quantity Supplied
$500	375,000	225,000
600	350,000	250,000
700	325,000	275,000
800	300,000	300,000
900	275,000	325,000
1,000	250,000	350,000

a. In the absence of rent control, what is the equilibrium rent, and what is the equilibrium quantity of apartments rented? Draw a demand and supply graph of the market for apartments to illustrate your answer. In equilibrium, will there be any renters who are unable to find an apartment to rent or any landlords who are unable to find a renter for an apartment?

b. Suppose the government sets a ceiling on rents of $600 per month. What is the quantity of apartments demanded, and what is the quantity of apartments supplied?

c. Assume that all landlords abide by the law. Use a demand and supply graph to illustrate the effect of this price ceiling on the market for apartments. Be sure to indicate on your graph each of the following: (i) the area representing consumer surplus after the price ceiling has been imposed, (ii) the area representing producer surplus after the price ceiling has been imposed, and (iii) the area representing the deadweight loss after the ceiling has been imposed.

   d. Assume that the quantity of apartments supplied is the same as you determined in (b). But now assume that landlords ignore the law and rent this quantity of apartments for the highest rent they can get. Briefly explain what this rent will be.

3.15 [Related to the Don't Let This Happen to You **on page 113**] Briefly explain whether you agree or disagree with the following statement: "If there is a shortage of a good, it must be scarce, but there is not a shortage of every scarce good."

3.16 A student makes the following argument:

> A price floor reduces the amount of a product that consumers buy because it keeps the price above the competitive market equilibrium. A price ceiling, on the other hand, increases the amount of a product that consumers buy because it keeps the price below the competitive market equilibrium.

Do you agree with the student's reasoning? Use a demand and supply graph to illustrate your answer.

3.17 University towns with major football programs experience an increase in demand for hotel rooms during home football weekends. Hotel management responds to the increase in demand by increasing the price they charge for a room. Periodically, there is an outcry against the higher prices and accusations of "price gouging."

   a. Draw a demand and supply graph of the market for hotel rooms in Boostertown for weekends with home football games and another graph for weekends without home football games. If the Boostertown city council passes a law stating that prices for rooms are not allowed to rise, what would happen to the market for hotel rooms during home football game weekends? Show your answer on your graph.

   b. If the prices of hotel rooms are not allowed to increase, what will be the effect on out-of-town football fans?

   c. How might the city council's law affect the supply of hotel rooms over time? Briefly explain.

   d. University towns are not the only places that face peak and non-peak "seasons." Can you think of other locations that face a large increase in demand for hotel rooms during particular times of the year? Why do we typically not see laws limiting the prices hotels can charge during peak seasons?

3.18 An advocate of medical care system reform makes the following argument:

> The 15,000 kidneys that are transplanted in the United States each year are received for free from organ donors. Despite this, because of hospital and doctor fees, the average price of a kidney transplant is $250,000. As a result, only rich people or people with very good health insurance can afford these transplants. The government should put a ceiling of $100,000 on the price of kidney transplants. That way, middle-income people will be able

to afford them, the demand for kidney transplants will increase, and more kidney transplants will take place.

Do you agree with the advocate's reasoning? Use a demand and supply graph to illustrate your answer.

3.19 [Related to the Chapter Opener **on page 101**] The cities of Peabody and Woburn are 5 miles apart. Woburn enacts a rent control law that puts a ceiling on rents well below their competitive market value. Predict the effect of this law on the competitive equilibrium rent in Peabody, which does not have a rent control law. Illustrate your answer with a demand and supply graph.

3.20 [Related to the Chapter Opener **on page 101**] The competitive equilibrium rent in the city of Lowell is currently $1,000 per month. The government decides to enact rent control and to establish a price ceiling for apartments of $750 per month. Briefly explain whether rent control is likely to make each of the following people better or worse off:

   a. Someone currently renting an apartment in Lowell

   b. Someone who will be moving to Lowell next year and who intends to rent an apartment

   c. A landlord who intends to abide by the rent control law

   d. A landlord who intends to ignore the law and illegally charge the highest rent possible for his apartments

3.21 [Related to the Chapter Opener **on page 101**] The following newspaper article describes a journalist's experience renting an apartment about thirteen years ago:

> . . . [A] lawyer suggested that I withhold my rent because my landlord had consistently failed to provide adequate heat, and my building was infested with mice and roaches. When the landlord took me to court for not paying rent, ... I won an abatement and did not have to pay any rent for six months.
>
> [I didn't realize] that allowing the landlord to take me to Housing Court would make it almost impossible for me to rent another apartment. . . anywhere in the United States.

Is it more likely that a tenant will be "blacklisted" in a city with rent control or one without rent control? Briefly explain.

Based Susan Lippman, "Blacklist Blues: Landlords Use Dodgy Database to Fend Off Feisty Tenants," *The Indypendent*, December 12, 2008.

3.22 Suppose that initially the gasoline market is in equilibrium, at a price of $3.00 per gallon and a quantity of 45 million gallons per month. Then a war in the Middle East disrupts imports of oil into the United States, shifting the supply curve for gasoline from S_1 to S_2. The price of gasoline begins to rise, and consumers protest. The federal government responds by setting a price ceiling of $3.00 per gallon. Use the graph at the top of the next column to answer the following questions.

   a. If there were no price ceiling, what would be the equilibrium price of gasoline, the quantity of gasoline demanded, and the quantity of gasoline supplied? Now assume that the price ceiling is imposed and that there is no black market in gasoline. What are the price of gasoline, the quantity of gasoline demanded, and the quantity of gasoline supplied? How large is the shortage of gasoline?

b. Assume that the price ceiling is imposed, and there is no black market in gasoline. Show on the graph the areas representing consumer surplus, producer surplus, and deadweight loss.

c. Now assume that there is a black market, and the price of gasoline rises to the maximum that consumers are willing to pay for the amount supplied by producers at $3.00 per gallon. Show on the graph the areas representing producer surplus, consumer surplus, and deadweight loss.

d. Are consumers made better off with the price ceiling than without it? Briefly explain.

3.23 An editorial in the *Economist* magazine discusses the fact that in most countries—including the United States—it is illegal for individuals to buy or sell body parts, such as kidneys.

a. Draw a demand and supply graph for the market for kidneys. Show on your graph the legal maximum price of zero and indicate the quantity of kidneys supplied at this price. (*Hint:* Because we know that some kidneys are donated, the quantity supplied will not be zero.)

b. The editorial argues that buying and selling kidneys should be legalized:

> With proper regulation, a kidney market would be a big improvement over the current sorry state of affairs. Sellers could be checked for disease and drug use, and cared for after operations. . . . Buyers would get better kidneys, faster. Both sellers and buyers would do better than in the illegal market, where much of the money goes to middlemen.

Do you agree with this argument? Should the government treat kidneys like other goods and allow the market to determine the price?

From "Psst, Wanna Buy a Kidney?" *The Economist*, November 18, 2006, p. 15.

4.4 | **The Economic Impact of Taxes, pages 115–120**
LEARNING OBJECTIVE: Analyze the economic impact of taxes.

Summary

Most taxes result in a loss of consumer surplus, a loss of producer surplus, and a deadweight loss. The true burden of a tax is not just the amount paid to government by consumers and producers but also includes the deadweight loss. The deadweight loss from a tax is the excess burden of the tax. **Tax incidence** is the actual division of the burden of a tax. In most cases, consumers and firms share the burden of a tax levied on a good or service.

 Visit **www.myeconlab.com** to complete these exercises online and get instant feedback.

Review Questions

4.1 What is meant by *tax incidence*?
4.2 What do economists mean by an *efficient tax*?
4.3 Does who is legally responsible for paying a tax—buyers or sellers—make a difference in the amount of tax each pays? Briefly explain.

Problems and Applications

4.4 Suppose the current equilibrium price of a quarter-pound hamburger is $5, and 10 million quarter-pound hamburgers are sold per month. After the federal government imposes a tax of $0.50 per hamburger, the equilibrium price of hamburgers rises to $5.20, and the equilibrium quantity falls to 9 million. Illustrate this situation with a demand and supply graph. Be sure your graph shows the equilibrium price before and after the tax, the equilibrium quantity before and after the tax, and the areas representing consumer surplus after the tax, producer surplus after the tax, tax revenue collected by the government, and deadweight loss.

4.5 Use the graph of the market for cigarettes below to answer the following questions.

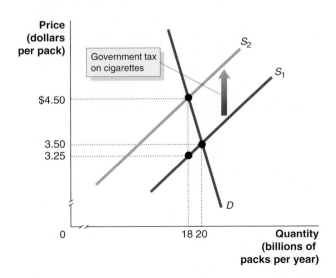

a. According to the graph, how much is the government tax on cigarettes?

b. What price do producers receive after paying the tax?

c. How much tax revenue does the government collect?

4.6 Consider the graph of the market for cigarettes in problem 4.5, where it is assumed that the government collects the tax from the producers of cigarettes.

a. How would the graph be different if the tax were collected from the buyers of cigarettes?

b. What would be the new equilibrium price that buyers pay producers of cigarettes?

c. Including the tax, what would be the total amount that cigarette buyers pay per pack?

4.7 **[Related to** Solved Problem 4.4 **on page 117]** Suppose the federal government decides to levy a sales tax on pizza of $1.00 per pie. Briefly explain whether you agree with the following statement, made by a representative of the pizza industry:

> The pizza industry is very competitive. As a result, pizza sellers will have to pay the whole tax because they are unable to pass any of it on to consumers in the form of higher prices. Therefore, a sales tax of $1.00 per pie will result in pizza sellers receiving $1.00 less on each pie sold, after paying the tax.

Illustrate your answer with a graph.

4.8 **[Related to the** Making the Connection **on page 119]** If the price consumers pay and the price sellers receive are not affected by whether consumers or sellers collect a tax on a good or service, why does the government usually require sellers and not consumers to collect a tax?

4.9 **[Related to the** Making the Connection **on page 119]** Suppose the government imposes a payroll tax of $1 per hour of work and collects the tax from employers. Use a graph for the market for labor to show the effect of the payroll tax, assuming the special case of a vertical supply curve of labor. By how much does the new equilibrium wage that employers pay workers fall?

Appendix

Quantitative Demand and Supply Analysis

LEARNING OBJECTIVE

Use quantitative demand and supply analysis.

Graphs help us understand economic change *qualitatively*. For instance, a demand and supply graph can tell us that if household incomes rise, the demand curve for a normal good will shift to the right, and its price will rise. Often, though, economists, business managers, and policymakers want to know more than the qualitative direction of change; they want a *quantitative estimate* of the size of the change.

In this chapter, we carried out a qualitative analysis of rent controls. We saw that imposing rent controls involves a trade-off: Renters as a group gain, but landlords lose, and the market for apartments becomes less efficient, as shown by the deadweight loss. To better evaluate rent controls, we need to know more than just that these gains and losses exist; we need to know how large they are. A quantitative analysis of rent controls will tell us how large the gains and losses are.

Demand and Supply Equations

The first step in a quantitative analysis is to supplement our use of demand and supply curves with demand and supply *equations*. We noted briefly in Chapter 3 that economists often statistically estimate equations for demand curves. Supply curves can also be statistically estimated. For example, suppose that economists have estimated that the demand for apartments in New York City is:

$$Q^D = 3,000,000 - 1,000P$$

and the supply of apartments is:

$$Q^S = -450,000 + 1,300P.$$

We have used Q^D for the quantity of apartments demanded per month, Q^S for the quantity of apartments supplied per month, and P for the apartment rent, in dollars per month. In reality, both the quantity of apartments demanded and the quantity of apartments supplied will depend on more than just the rental price of apartments in New York City. For instance, the demand for apartments in New York City will also depend on the average incomes of families in the New York area and on the rents of apartments in surrounding cities. For simplicity, we will ignore these other factors.

With no government intervention, we know that at competitive market equilibrium, the quantity demanded must equal the quantity supplied, or:

$$Q^D = Q^S.$$

We can use this equation, which is called an *equilibrium condition*, to solve for the equilibrium monthly apartment rent by setting the quantity demanded from the demand equation equal to the quantity supplied from the supply equation:

$$3,000,000, - 1,000P = -450,000 + 1,300P$$
$$3,450,000 = 2,300P$$
$$P = \frac{3,450,000}{2,300} = \$1,500.$$

Figure 4A.1

Graphing Supply and Demand Equations

After statistically estimating supply and demand equations, we can use the equations to draw supply and demand curves. In this case, the equilibrium rent for apartments is $1,500 per month, and the equilibrium quantity of apartments rented is 1,500,000. The supply equation tells us that at a rent of $346, the quantity of apartments supplied will be zero. The demand equation tells us that at a rent of $3,000, the quantity of apartments demanded will be zero. The areas representing consumer surplus and producer surplus are also indicated on the graph.

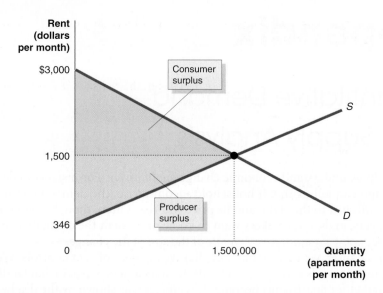

We can then substitute this price back into either the supply equation or the demand equation to find the equilibrium quantity of apartments rented:

$$Q^D = 3{,}000{,}000 - 1{,}000P = 3{,}000{,}000 - 1{,}000(1{,}500) = 1{,}500{,}000$$

$$Q^S = -450{,}000 + 1{,}300P = -450{,}000 + 1{,}300(1{,}500) = 1{,}500{,}000.$$

Figure 4A.1 illustrates the information from these equations in a graph. The figure shows the values for rent when the quantity supplied is zero and when the quantity demanded is zero. These values can be calculated from the demand equation and the supply equation by setting Q^D and Q^S equal to zero and solving for price:

$$Q^D = 0 = 3{,}000{,}000 - 1{,}000P$$

$$P = \frac{3{,}000{,}000}{1{,}000} = \$3{,}000$$

and:

$$Q^S = 0 = -450{,}000 + 1{,}300P$$

$$P = \frac{-450{,}000}{-1{,}300} = \$346.15.$$

Calculating Consumer Surplus and Producer Surplus

Figure 4A.1 shows consumer surplus and producer surplus in this market. Recall that the sum of consumer surplus and producer surplus equals the net benefit that renters and landlords receive from participating in the market for apartments. We can use the values from the demand and supply equations to calculate the value of consumer surplus and producer surplus. Remember that consumer surplus is the area below the demand curve and above the line representing market price. Notice that this area forms a right triangle because the demand curve is a straight line—it is *linear*. As we noted in the appendix to Chapter 1, the area of a triangle is equal to ½ × Base × Height. In this case, the area is:

$$\frac{1}{2} \times (1{,}500{,}000) \times (3{,}000 - 1{,}500) = \$1{,}125{,}000{,}000.$$

So, this calculation tells us that the consumer surplus in the market for rental apartments in New York City would be about $1.125 billion.

We can calculate producer surplus in a similar way. Remember that producer surplus is the area above the supply curve and below the line representing market price.

Because our supply curve is also a straight line, producer surplus in the figure is equal to the area of the right triangle:

$$\tfrac{1}{2} \times 1,500,000 \times (1,500 - 346) = \$865,500,000.$$

This calculation tells us that the producer surplus in the market for rental apartments in New York City is about $865.5 million.

We can use this same type of analysis to measure the impact of rent control on consumer surplus, producer surplus, and economic efficiency. For instance, suppose the city imposes a rent ceiling of $1,000 per month. Figure 4A.2 can help guide us as we measure the impact.

First, we can calculate the quantity of apartments that will actually be rented by substituting the rent ceiling of $1,000 into the supply equation:

$$Q^S = -450,000 + (1,300 \times 1,000) = 850,000.$$

We also need to know the price on the demand curve when the quantity of apartments is 850,000. We can do this by substituting 850,000 for quantity in the demand equation and solving for price:

$$850,000 = 3,000,000 - 1,000P$$

$$P = \frac{-2,150,000}{-1,000} = \$2,150.$$

Compared with its value in competitive equilibrium, consumer surplus has been reduced by a value equal to the area of the yellow triangle B but increased by a value equal to the area of the blue rectangle A. The area of the yellow triangle B is:

$$\tfrac{1}{2} \times (1,500,000 - 850,000) \times (2,150 - 1,500) = \$211,250,000,$$

and the area of the blue rectangle A is Base × Height, or:

$$(\$1,500 - \$1,000) \times (850,000) = \$425,000,000.$$

The value of consumer surplus in competitive equilibrium was $1,125,000,000. As a result of the rent ceiling, it will be increased to:

$$(\$1,125,000,000 + \$425,000,000) - \$211,250,000 = \$1,338,750,000.$$

Compared with its value in competitive equilibrium, producer surplus has been reduced by a value equal to the area of the yellow triangle C plus a value equal to the area of the blue rectangle. The area of the yellow triangle C is:

$$\tfrac{1}{2} \times (1,500,000 - 850,000) \times (1,500 - 1,000) = \$162,500,000.$$

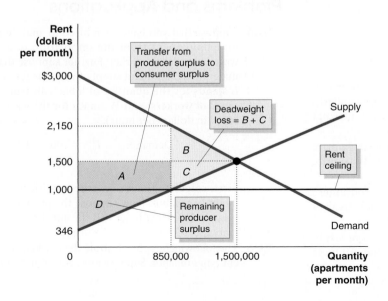

Figure 4A.2

Calculating the Economic Effect of Rent Controls

Once we have estimated equations for the demand and supply of rental housing, a diagram can guide our numerical estimates of the economic effects of rent control. Consumer surplus falls by an amount equal to the area of the yellow triangle B and increases by an amount equal to the area of the blue rectangle A. The difference between the values of these two areas is $213,750,000. Producer surplus falls by an amount equal to the area of the blue rectangle A plus the area of the yellow triangle C. The value of these two areas is $587,500,000. The remaining producer surplus is equal to the area of triangle D, or $278,000,000. Deadweight loss is equal to the area of triangle B plus the area of triangle C, or $373,750,000.

We have already calculated the area of the blue rectangle *A* as $425,000,000. The value of producer surplus in competitive equilibrium was $865,500,000. As a result of the rent ceiling, it will be reduced to:

$$\$865,500,000 - \$162,500,000 - \$425,000,000 = \$278,000,000.$$

The loss of economic efficiency, as measured by the deadweight loss, is equal to the value represented by the areas of the yellow triangles *B* and *C*, or:

$$\$211,250,000 + \$162,500,000 = \$373,750,000.$$

The following table summarizes the results of the analysis (the values are in millions of dollars):

Consumer Surplus		Producer Surplus		Deadweight Loss	
Competitive Equilibrium	Rent Control	Competitive Equilibrium	Rent Control	Competitive Equilibrium	Rent Control
$1,125	$1,338.75	$865.50	$278	$0	$373.75

Qualitatively, we know that imposing rent control will make consumers better off, make landlords worse off, and decrease economic efficiency. The advantage of the analysis we have just gone through is that it puts dollar values on the qualitative results. We can now see how much consumers have gained, how much landlords have lost, and how great the decline in economic efficiency has been. Sometimes the quantitative results can be surprising. Notice, for instance, that after the imposition of rent control, the deadweight loss is actually greater than the remaining producer surplus.

Economists often study issues where the qualitative results of actions are apparent, even to non-economists. You don't have to be an economist to understand who wins and who loses from rent control or that if a company cuts the price of its product, its sales will increase. Business managers, policymakers, and the general public do, however, need economists to measure quantitatively the effects of different actions—including policies such as rent control—so that they can better assess the results of these actions.

4A | **Quantitative Demand and Supply Analysis, pages 131–134**
LEARNING OBJECTIVE: Use quantitative demand and supply analysis.

 MyEconLab Visit **www.myeconlab.com** to complete these exercises online and get instant feedback.

Review Questions

4A.1 In a linear demand equation, what economic information is conveyed by the intercept on the price axis? Similarly, what economic information is conveyed by the intercept on the price axis in a linear supply equation?

4A.2 Suppose you were assigned the task of choosing a price that maximizes economic surplus in a market. What price would you choose? Why?

4A.3 Consumer surplus is used as a measure of a consumer's net benefit from purchasing a good or service. Explain why consumer surplus is a measure of net benefit.

4A.4 Why would economists use the term *deadweight loss* to describe the impact on consumer surplus and producer surplus from a price control?

Problems and Applications

4A.5 Suppose that you have been hired to analyze the impact on employment from the imposition of a minimum wage in the labor market. Further suppose that you estimate the demand and supply functions for labor, where *L* stands for the quantity of labor (measured in thousands of workers) and *W* stands for the wage rate (measured in dollars per hour):

Demand: $L^D = 100 - 4W$

Supply: $L^S = 6W$

First, calculate the free market equilibrium wage and quantity of labor. Now suppose the proposed minimum wage is $12. How large will the surplus of labor in this market be?

4A.6 The following graphs illustrate the markets for two different types of labor. Suppose an identical minimum wage is

imposed in both markets. In which market will the minimum wage have the largest impact on employment? Why?

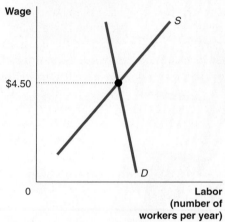

4A.7 Suppose that you are the vice president of operations of a
manufacturing firm that sells an industrial lubricant in a

competitive market. Further suppose that your economist
gives you the following demand and supply functions:

$$\text{Demand: } Q^D = 45 - 2P$$
$$\text{Supply: } Q^S = -15 + P$$

What is the consumer surplus in this market? What is the
producer surplus?

4A.8 The following graph shows a market in which a price
floor of $3.00 per unit has been imposed. Calculate the
values of each of the following:

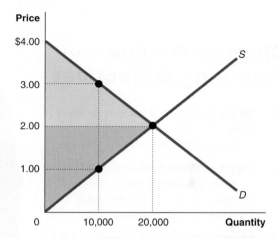

a. The deadweight loss
b. The transfer of producer surplus to consumers or
the transfer of consumer surplus to producers
c. Producer surplus after the price floor is imposed
d. Consumer surplus after the price floor is imposed

4A.9 Construct a table like the one in this appendix on page
134, but assume that the rent ceiling is $1,200 rather than
$1,000.

5

The Economics of Health Care

Chapter Outline and Learning Objectives

Small Businesses Feel the Pinch of Escalating Health Care Costs

Elizabeth Crowell and her husband, Robert Wilson, own two antique stores in Brooklyn, New York. Like other small business owners, they face various challenges as they compete with the many similar stores in their area. But in 2011, Elizabeth and Robert were most concerned with paying Empire Blue Cross for health insurance for their family and their employees. In 2010, the premium—the payment a firm or an individual makes to buy health insurance—increased by 20 percent, and in 2011, the premium increased by 25 percent. Elizabeth said that: "It's the only cost in my business that's unmanageable. . . . If you have a cost to a business that jumps 20% to 25% a year, it's unsustainable."

Elizabeth and Robert were not alone in worrying about escalating health care costs. For several decades, health care spending has been steadily increasing as a fraction of gross domestic product (GDP), which is the value of the total production of goods and services in the economy. Health care spending increased from 5.2 percent of GDP in 1960 to 17.5 percent in 2011, an upward trend that is expected to continue. The federal government provides medical insurance to people aged 65 and older under the Medicare program, and the federal and state governments provide medical insurance to low-income people under the Medicaid program. The U.S. Congressional Budget Office projects that Medicare and Medicaid spending will increase from 5.6 percent of GDP in 2011 to nearly 12 percent in 2050. If governments do not reduce spending on these programs, they will have to sharply increase taxes or reduce spending on other programs.

In 2010, President Obama and Congress enacted the Patient Protection and Affordable Care Act, which made major changes to the U.S. health care system. The changes are being phased in through 2014. Included in the act is a provision for each state to set up health insurance exchanges to make health insurance less expensive for small businesses and individuals by allowing them to enter an insurance pool where both healthy and sick people will be in the same insurance plan and pay the same insurance premium. In 2011, economists and policymakers debated whether the health insurance exchanges would succeed in lowering health care premiums for small businesses and individuals.

AN INSIDE LOOK AT POLICY on **page 162** discusses government projections of future health care costs.

Based on Judith Messina, "Small Businesses Wary on Health Insurance Exchange," www.crainsnewyork.com, June 12, 2011; Celia Barbour, "The Ultimate Recyclers," *New York Times*, October 21, 2007; "Antique and Gift Store Owner Sold on Affordable Care Act," www.smallbusinessmajority.org; U.S. Center for Medicare and Medicaid Studies, "National Health Expenditure Data;" and U.S. Congressional Budget Office, "CBO's 2011 Long-Term Budget Outlook," June 2011.

Economics in Your Life

Why Is It Difficult for People Who Are Seriously Ill to Buy Health Insurance?

If you become ill and don't have health insurance, you are likely to be stuck paying large medical bills. Even a brief stay in a hospital can result in a bill of thousands of dollars. You may conclude that people with chronic illnesses are most likely to buy health insurance to help reduce their medical bills. But if you are chronically ill and don't currently have health insurance, buying it can be very difficult. Usually, people who demand a service can easily find a provider of that service. So, why is it difficult for people who are seriously ill to buy health insurance? As you read the chapter, see if you can answer this question. You can check your answer against the one we provide on **page 161** at the end of this chapter.

137

Health care The goods and services, such as prescription drugs and consultations with a doctor, that are intended to maintain or improve a person's health.

Health care refers to the goods and services, such as prescription drugs and consultations with a doctor, that are intended to maintain or improve a person's health. Improvements in health care are an important part of the tremendous increase in living standards people in the United States and other high-income countries have experienced over the past 100 years. Health care has seen rapid technological change with new products, such as MRI units and other diagnostic equipment; prescription drugs to treat cancer, high blood pressure, and AIDS; vaccinations for meningitis; and new surgical techniques, such as cardiac catheterizations for treatment of heart disease.

Health care is provided through markets, just as are most other goods and services such as hamburgers or haircuts. So, we can apply the tools of economic analysis we used in previous chapters to health care. But the market for health care has interesting features that make it different from other markets. In the United States, the doctors and hospitals that supply most health care are primarily private firms, but the government also provides some health care services directly through the Veterans Health Administration, which is part of the U.S. Department of Veterans Affairs. The government also provides health care indirectly through the *Medicare* and *Medicaid* programs. In addition to having a large government role, the market for health care differs from most markets in other ways. Most importantly, the typical consumer of health care doesn't pay its full price. Most people either have private medical insurance—most often provided through their employer—or they are enrolled in the Medicare or Medicaid programs. Consumers who have insurance make different decisions about the quantity of health care they wish to consume than they would if they were paying the full cost of the services they receive. As we will see, to analyze the market for health care we will need to use economic tools beyond those introduced in previous chapters. We begin our analysis of health care with an overview of health care around the world.

5.1 LEARNING OBJECTIVE

Discuss trends in U.S. health over time.

The Improving Health of People in the United States

Two hundred years ago, the whole world was very poor by modern standards. Today, the average person in high-income countries has a standard of living well beyond what even the richest people in the past could have dreamed of. One aspect of this higher standard of living is the improved health the average person enjoys. For example, in the late 1700s, England had the highest level of income per person of any large country. But the average person in England had a short life span and suffered from diseases, such as cholera, yellow fever, dysentery, and smallpox, that have disappeared from high-income countries today. The average life expectancy at birth was only 38 years, and 30 percent of the population died before reaching the age of 30. Even people who survived to age 20 could only expect to live an average of 34 more years. In 2011, the average life expectancy at birth in the United Kingdom and other high-income countries was around 80 years. People in eighteenth century England were also short by modern standards. The average height of an adult male was 5 feet, 5 inches compared with 5 feet, 9 inches today.

In this section, we discuss the health of the average person in the United States. In section 5.2, we discuss the health of people in other countries.

Changes over Time in U.S. Health

When economists measure changes over time in the standard of living in a country, they usually look first at increases in income per person. Changes in the health of the average person, though, are also an important indicator of changes in well-being and, therefore,

Variable	1850	2011
Life expectancy at birth	38.3 years	78.4 years
Average height (adult males)	5'7"	5'9"
Infant mortality (death of a person aged one year or less)	228.9 per 1,000 live births	6.1 per 1,000 live births

Table 5.1

Health in the United States, 1850 and 2011

Note: The data on heights for 1850 include only native-born white and black citizens. The data on heights for 2011 were gathered in 2003–2006.
Based on Susan B. Carter, et al., eds., *Historical Statistics of the United States: Millennium Edition*; U.S. National Center for Health Statistics, *Anthropometric Reference Data for Children and Adults: United States, 2003–2006*, October 22, 2008; U.S. Central Intelligence Agency, *World Factbook*.

changes in the standard of living. The health of the average person in the United States improved significantly during the nineteenth and twentieth centuries, and, by and large, it continues to improve today.

Table 5.1 compares some indicators of health in the United States in 1850 and 2011. Individuals in the United States today are taller, they live much longer, and they are much less likely to die in the first months of life than was true 150 years ago.

The Rise and Fall and Rise of American Heights

A person's height relies partly on genetics—that is, tall parents tend to have tall children—but also on a person's *nutritional status*. Nutritional status depends on a person's food intake relative to the work the person has to perform, whether the person is able to remain warm in cold weather, and the diseases to which the person is exposed. Over time, people in high-income countries have, on average, become taller, just as people in high-income countries today are taller than people in low-income countries. Height, then, can be used as a measure of health and well-being in situations when other direct measures may not be available.

Take the case of the United States: Figure 5.1 shows changes in the average height of adult males born in the given years in the United States between 1710–1970, measured in centimeters. The trend has been upward, except for the period from 1830–1890, when the average adult male became about two inches shorter. This decline in height did not occur because incomes were falling during these years and people had to reduce their food purchases. Quite the opposite: The income of the average person in the United States was almost three times greater in 1890 than it had been in 1830. Instead, the nutritional status of the average person deteriorated as people moved from farms to cities. At that time, a lack of refrigeration made distributing meat and dairy products difficult in cities, so many people did not consume enough protein. More importantly, U.S. cities were very unhealthy places in the late nineteenth century. Most cities lacked basic sanitation, including sewers, clean drinking water, and regular garbage removal. People often dumped garbage into the streets and left it to rot. Not surprisingly, cities suffered from periodic epidemics of diseases such as cholera, dysentery, scarlet fever, diphtheria, and yellow fever that are largely unknown in the modern United States. The widespread acceptance in the late nineteenth century that diseases were caused by bacteria helped lead to the *public health movement* in the late nineteenth and early twentieth centuries, which eventually brought sewers, clean drinking water, and regular garbage removal to all U.S. cities. The improvement in sanitary conditions in cities and improvements in food distribution caused the increases in height that began around 1890. So, changes in the height of the average American over time can give us insight into health and well-being that we could not obtain by looking only at income.

Figure 5.1

The Average Height of Adult Males in the United States, 1710–1970

The average height of adult males has increased over time in the United States, with the exception of the period from 1830 to 1890, when the average male born in those years lost 2 inches in height in part due to limited distribution of food, particularly protein, and poor sanitation in cities.

Note: Values are for native-born adult males. Data from "The Average Height of Adult Males in the United States, 1710–1970" from *Historical Statistics of the United States: Millennium Edition*, Series Bd653 (Cambridge University Press, 2003); and Centers for Disease Control and Prevention.

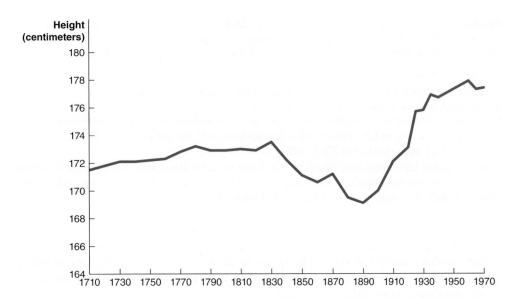

Reasons for Long-Run Improvements in U.S. Health

Apart from the temporary setback in the mid-nineteenth century, the health of people in the United States has steadily improved, with heights and life expectancies increasing and death rates decreasing. Panel (a) of Figure 5.2 shows the increase in life expectancy from 1900 to 2009 and the decline in the mortality rate, or death rate, measured as deaths per 100,000 people for the same years. Note that the mortality rate is "age adjusted," which means that it is not affected by changes in the age structure of the population. Life expectancy at birth in the United States increased from 47.3 years in 1900 to 78.2 years in 2009. Panel (b) in Figure 5.2 shows for recent years the change in the overall mortality rate of the U.S. population, measured as deaths per 100,000 people, and the age-adjusted mortality rates for several diseases. The overall mortality

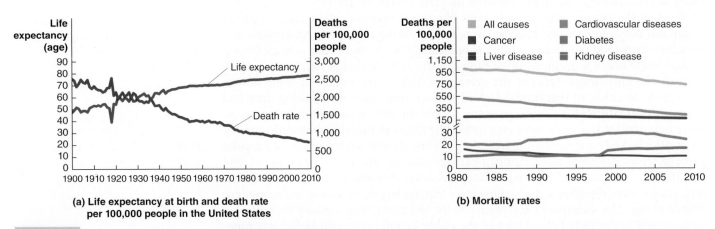

(a) Life expectancy at birth and death rate per 100,000 people in the United States

(b) Mortality rates

Figure 5.2 **The Improving Health of the U.S. Population**

Since 1900, life expectancy in the United States has increased and mortality rates have decreased. Since 1981, there have been significant decreases in rates of death due to cancer, cardiovascular diseases, and diseases of the liver. Rates of death due to kidney disease and diabetes have increased as obesity have increased slightly. Note that in panel (a), the increase in mortality and decrease in life expectancy in 1918 are due to the severe influenza epidemic of that year.

Data from [Panel (a)]: Susan B. Carter et al., eds., *Historical Statistics of the United States: Millennium Edition*, Series Ab644; and Centers for Disease Control and Prevention, National Vital Statistics Reports, various issues; [Panel (b)]: "Age-Adjusted Mortality per 100,000 by Underlying and Multiple Cause, Ages 181: US, 1981–2009"; Centers for Disease Control and Prevention, National Center for Health Statistics, "VitalStats: Mortality," www.cdc.gov/nchs/vitalstats.htm.

rate decreased by more than 25 percent between 1981 and 2009. Over this same period, deaths from cancer, from cardiovascular disease, such as heart attacks and strokes, and from diseases of the liver all declined substantially. Deaths from diabetes and from kidney disease both increased slightly during this period, largely due to the effects of increasing obesity. The overall decline in death rates in the United States since 1981, was due to changes in lifestyle, particularly a decline in smoking, and advances in new diagnostic equipment, new prescription drugs, and new surgical techniques.

What explains the long-run increases in life expectancy and declines in death rates? We have already seen that improvements in sanitation and in the distribution of food during the late nineteenth and early twentieth centuries led to better health during that period. Nobel Laureate Robert Fogel of the University of Chicago and Roderick Floud of Gresham College, along with coauthors, have described a process by which better health makes it possible for people to work harder as they become taller, stronger, and more resistant to disease. Working harder raises a country's total income, making it possible for the country to afford better sanitation, more food, and a better system for distributing the food. In effect, improving health shifts out a country's production possibilities frontier. Higher incomes also allow the country to devote more resources to research and development, including medical research.

Health Care around the World

5.2 LEARNING OBJECTIVE

Compare the health care systems and health care outcomes in the United States and other countries.

In the United States, most health care is provided by private firms, either through doctors' practices or hospitals. The main exception is the care the government provides through the network of hospitals operated by the federal government's Veterans Administration, although some cities also own and operate hospitals. Governments in most countries outside of the United States have a more substantial direct role in paying for or providing health care. Policymakers and economists debate the effects of greater government involvement in the health care system on health outcomes such as life expectancy, infant mortality, and successful treatment of diseases.

The U.S. Health Care System

One important difference among health care systems in different countries is how people pay for the health care they receive. Most people in the United States have *health insurance* that helps them to pay their medical bills. **Health insurance** is a contract under which a buyer agrees to make payments, or *premiums*, in exchange for the provider's agreeing to pay some or all of the buyer's medical bills. Figure 5.3 shows the sources of health insurance in the United States in 2009. About 54 percent of people have private health insurance. Most people who have private health insurance receive it through their employer. In 2010, about 99 percent of firms employing more than 200 workers and

Health insurance A contract under which a buyer agrees to make payments, or *premiums*, in exchange for the provider's agreeing to pay some or all of the buyer's medical bills.

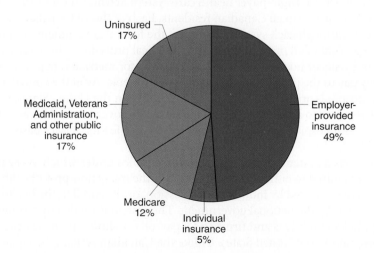

Figure 5.3

Sources of Health Insurance in the United States, 2009

A majority of people in the United States live in households that have private health insurance (provided by an employer or purchased directly). Government programs insure about 29 percent of the population.

Data from Kaiser Commission on Medicaid and the Uninsured; the Urban Institute; and the U.S. Bureau of the Census.

Fee-for-service A system under which doctors and hospitals receive a separate payment for each service that they provide.

about 68 percent of firms employing between 3 and 199 workers offered health insurance as a fringe benefit (that is, a type of non-wage compensation) to their employees. Private health insurance companies can be either not-for-profit firms, such as some of the Blue Cross and Blue Shield organizations, or for-profit firms, such as Aetna and John Hancock, which typically also sell other types of insurance. Private health insurance firms sell *group plans* to employers to cover all of their employees or individual plans directly to the public. Some health insurance plans reimburse doctors and hospitals on a **fee-for-service** basis, which means that doctors and hospitals receive a payment for each service they provide. Other health insurance plans are organized as *health maintenance organizations (HMOs)*, which typically reimburse doctors mainly by paying a flat fee per patient, rather than paying a fee for each individual office visit or other service provided.

In 2009, 29 percent of people received health insurance either through Medicare, Medicaid, the Veterans Administration, or through some other government program. Seventeen percent of people were not covered by health insurance in 2009. Many people lack health insurance because their incomes are low, and they believe they cannot afford to buy private health insurance. Some low-income people either do not qualify for Medicaid or they choose not to participate in that program. About two-thirds of the uninsured live in families where at least one member has a job. These individuals either were not offered health insurance through their employers or chose not to purchase it. Some young people opt out of employer-provided health insurance because they are healthy and do not believe that the cost of the premium their employer charges for the insurance is worth the benefit of having the insurance. In 2009, 57 percent of the uninsured were younger than 34. Although 99 percent of firms with 200 or more employees offer health insurance to their employees, only about 63 percent of employees accept the coverage. The remaining employees are either covered by a spouse's policy or have decided to go uninsured because they do not want to pay the premium for the insurance. The uninsured must pay for their own medical bills *out-of-pocket*, with money from their own income, just as they pay their other bills, or receive care from doctors or hospitals either free or below the normal price. As we will see, addressing the problems of the uninsured was one of the motivations for the federal government's health care legislation enacted in 2010.

The Health Care Systems of Canada, Japan, and the United Kingdom

In many countries, such as Canada, Japan, and the United Kingdom, the government either supplies health care directly by operating hospitals and employing doctors and nurses, or pays for most health care expenses, even if hospitals are not government owned and doctors are not government employees. In this section, we look briefly at the health care system in several countries.

Single-payer health care system A system, such as the one in Canada, in which the government provides health insurance to all of the country's residents.

Canada Canada has a **single-payer health care system** in which the government provides *national health insurance* to all Canadian residents. Each of the 10 Canadian provinces has its own system, although each system must meet the federal government's requirement of covering 100 percent of all medically necessary medical procedures. Individuals pay nothing for doctor's visits or hospital stays; instead they pay for medical care indirectly through the taxes they pay to the provincial and federal governments. As in the United States, most doctors and hospitals are private businesses, but unlike in the United States, doctors and hospitals are required to accept the fees that are set by the government. Also as in the United States, doctors and hospitals are typically reimbursed on a fee-for-service basis.

Japan Japan has a system of *universal health insurance* under which every resident of the country is required to either (a) enroll in one of the many non-profit health insurance societies that are organized by industry or profession, or (b) enroll in the health insurance program provided by the national government. The system is funded by a combination of premiums paid by employees and firms and a payroll tax similar to the tax that funds the Medicare program in the United States. Unlike the Canadian system, the Japanese system requires substantial *co-payments* under which patients pay as much as 30 percent of their medical bills, while health insurance pays for the rest. Japanese health insurance does not pay for most preventive care, such as annual physical exams, or for medical expenses connected with pregnancies, unless complications result. Health insurance in the United States and Canada typically does cover these expenses. As in the United States, most doctors in Japan do not work for the government and there are many privately owned hospitals. The number of government-run hospitals, though, is greater than in the United States.

The United Kingdom In the United Kingdom the government, through the National Health Service (NHS), owns nearly all hospitals and directly employs nearly all doctors. This is unlike in the United States, Canada, and Japan, where the government employs relatively few doctors and owns relatively few hospitals. Because there is only a small system of private insurance and private hospitals in the United Kingdom, its health care system is often referred to as **socialized medicine**. With 1.7 million employees, the NHS is the largest government-run health care system in the world. Apart from a small co-payment for prescriptions, the NHS supplies health care services without charge to patients, receiving its funding from income taxes. The NHS concentrates on preventive care and care for acute conditions. Elective care—such as hip replacements or reconstructive surgery following a mastectomy—is a low priority. The NHS's goals result in waiting lists for elective procedures that can be very long, with patients sometimes waiting a year or more for a procedure that would available in a few weeks or less in the United States. To avoid the waiting lists, more than 10 percent of the population also has private health insurance, frequently provided by employers, which the insured use to pay for elective procedures. The NHS essentially trades off broader coverage for longer waiting times and performing fewer procedures, particularly non-emergency surgeries.

> **Socialized medicine** A health care system under which the government owns most of the hospitals and employs most of the doctors.

Comparing Health Care Outcomes around the World

We have seen that the way health care systems are organized varies significantly across countries. Health care outcomes and the amounts countries spend on health care are also quite different. As Figure 5.4 shows, typically, the higher the level of income per person in a country, the higher the level of spending per person on health care. This is not surprising, because health care is a *normal good*. As we saw in Chapter 3, as income increases, so does spending on normal goods. The line in the figure shows the average relationship between income per person and health care spending per person. The dots for most countries are fairly close to the line, but note that the dot representing the United States is significantly above the line. Being well above the line indicates that health care spending

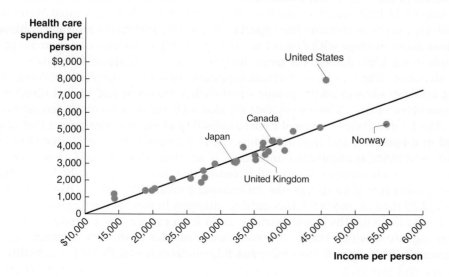

Figure 5.4

Levels of Income per Person and Spending per Person on Health Care, 2009

The United States is well above the line showing the average relationship between income per person and health care spending per person, which indicates that the United States spends more per person on health care than do other countries, even taking into account the relatively high levels of income in the United States.

Note: Income per person is measured as real GDP per person.

Data from the Organization for Economic Co-operation and Development, *OECD Health Data 2011,* June 2011.

Table 5.2 Health Outcomes in High-Income Countries

Health Care Outcome	United States	Canada	Japan	United Kingdom	OECD average
Life Expectancy					
Life expectancy at birth	78.2 years	80.7 years	83.0 years	80.4 years	79.3 years
Male life expectancy at age 65	17.3 years	18.1 years	18.2 years	18.1 years	17.1 years
Female life expectancy at age 65	20.0 years	21.3 years	24.0 years	20.8 years	20.4 years
Infant mortality (deaths per 1,000 live births)	6.5	5.1	2.6	4.7	4.7
Health Problems					
Obesity (percentage of the population self-reported)	27.7%	16.5%	n/a	n/a	15.5%
Diabetes hospital admissions per 100,000 population	57	23	n/a	32	21
Diagnostic Equipment					
MRI units and CT scanners per 1,000,000 population	60.2	19.4	n/a	n/a	27.2
Cancer					
Deaths from cancer per 100,000 population	104.1	113.3	94.8	115.8	114.7
Risk of dying of cancer before age 75	11.2%	11.8%	9.7%	11.9%	12.0%
Mortality ratio for cancer	39.5%	40.4%	52.3%	47.6%	48.1%

Note: The data for the first six rows are the most recent available, typically 2009. For cancer, the data are for 2008, and the last column presents data for the 27 countries in the European Union rather than for the OECD. Cancer mortality rates are age adjusted, which means they are not affected by differences in age structure across countries. n/a means that there are no data available.

Data from the Organization for Economic Cooperation and Development, *OECD Health Data 2011*; J. Ferlay, H.R. Shin, F. Bray, D. Forman, C. Mathers, and D.M. Parkin, *Globocan 2008* v1.2, Cancer Incidence and Mortality Worldwide: IARC CancerBase No. 10, Lyon, France: International Agency for Research on Cancer, 2010, http://globocan.iarc.fr; and Mark Pearson, "Why Does the United States Spend So Much More Than other Countries?" Written Statement of Mark Pearson, Head, Health Division, OECD, to Senate Special Committee on Aging, September 30, 2009.

per person in the United States is higher than in other countries, even taking into account the relatively high income levels in the United States. Later in this chapter, we will discuss explanations for the high levels of health care spending in the United States.

Have the high levels of spending on health care in the United States resulted in better health outcomes? Are people in the United States healthier, and do they have their medical problems addressed more rapidly than do people in the other countries? Table 5.2 compares several health care outcomes for the countries that are members of the Organization for Economic Cooperation and Development (OECD), a group of 34 high-income countries. The table shows that the United States does relatively poorly in terms of life expectancy at birth, and infant mortality, although it does about average with respect to life expectancy of women and men at age 65. People in the United States are more likely to have complications from diabetes and are also more likely to be obese than are people in other countries, although these data are from surveys asking people whether they are obese and are not direct measurements of obesity. The obesity data are also available for a relatively few countries.

The United States rates well in the availability of medical equipment that can be used in diagnosing and treating illness. Table 5.2 shows that the United States has more than twice as many MRI units and CT scanners than the OECD average. The United States also appears to do well in cancer treatment. People in the United States have a lower rate of cancer deaths and a lower probability of dying from cancer before age 75 than in most OECD countries, although higher than in Japan. The United States also has a relatively low mortality ratio from cancer. The mortality ratio measures the rate at which people die from cancer relative to the rate at which they are diagnosed with cancer. A low cancer mortality ratio indicates that the U.S. health care system does a relatively good job of reducing the death rate among people diagnosed with cancer.

How useful are cross-country comparisons of health care outcomes in measuring the effectiveness of different health care systems? Health economists and other researchers disagree strongly about the answer to this question. We can consider some of the difficulties in making cross-country comparisons in health care outcomes:

- *Data problems.* Countries do not always collect data on diseases and other health problems in the same way. So, there are not enough consistent data available to compare health care outcomes for more than a few diseases.

- *Problems with measuring health care delivery.* The easiest outcomes to measure are deaths because a specific event has occurred. So, measures of life expectancy, infant mortality, and mortality rates from some diseases, such as cancer, are available across countries. But much of health care involves care of injuries, simple surgical procedures, writing pharmaceutical prescriptions, and other activities where outcomes are difficult to measure. For example, although the United Kingdom does well in many of the measures shown in Table 5.2, patients there have long waiting times for elective surgical procedures that can be arranged much more quickly in some other countries, including the United States. Measuring the cost of these waiting times to patients is difficult, however.

- *Problems with distinguishing health care effectiveness from lifestyle choices.* Health care outcomes depend partly on the effectiveness of doctors and hospitals in delivering medical services. But they also depend on the choices of individuals. So, for example, in the United States the high rates of obesity and hospitalizations for diabetes—which can be a complication of obesity—may be caused more by the decisions individuals make about diet and exercise than by the effectiveness of the U.S. health care system.

- *Problems with determining consumer preferences.* In most markets, we can assume that the quantities and prices we observe reflect the interactions of the preferences of consumers (demand) with the costs to firms of producing goods and services (supply). Given their incomes and their preferences, consumers compare the prices of different goods and services when making their buying decisions. The prices firms charge represent the costs of providing the good or service. In the market for health care, however, the government plays the dominant role in supplying the service in most countries other than the United States, so the cost of the service is not fully represented in its price, which in some countries is zero. Even in countries where consumers must pay for medical services, the prices they pay usually do not represent the cost of providing the service. In the United States, for instance, consumers with private health insurance typically pay only 10 percent to 20 percent of the price as a co-payment. For these reasons, it is difficult to determine whether some countries do a better job than others in providing health care services whose cost and effectiveness are consistent with consumer preferences.

Information Problems and Externalities in the Market for Health Care

5.3 LEARNING OBJECTIVE

Discuss how information problems and externalities affect the market for health care.

The market for health care is significantly affected by the problem of **asymmetric information**, which occurs when one party to an economic transaction has less information than the other party. Understanding the concept of asymmetric information can help us analyze the actions of buyers and sellers of health care and health care insurance and the actions of the government in the health care market. The consequences of asymmetric information may be easier to understand if we first consider its effect on the market for used automobiles, which was the market in which economists first began to carefully study the problem of asymmetric information.

Asymmetric information A situation in which one party to an economic transaction has less information than the other party.

Adverse Selection and the Market for "Lemons"

Nobel Laureate George Akerlof, of the University of California, Berkeley, pointed out that the seller of a used car will always have more information on the true condition of the car than will potential buyers. A car that has been poorly maintained—by, for instance, not having its oil changed regularly—may have damage that even a trained mechanic would have difficulty detecting.

If potential buyers of used cars know that they will have difficulty separating the good used cars from the bad used cars, or "lemons," they will take this into account in the prices they are willing to pay. Consider the following simple example: Suppose that half of the 2010 Volkswagen Jettas offered for sale have been well maintained and are good, reliable used cars. The other half have been poorly maintained and are lemons that will be unreliable. Suppose that potential buyers of 2010 Jettas would be willing to pay $10,000 for a reliable one but only $5,000 for an unreliable one. The sellers know how well they have maintained their cars and whether they are reliable, but the buyers do not have this information and so have no way of telling the reliable cars from the unreliable ones.

In this situation, buyers will generally offer a price somewhere between the price they would be willing to pay for a good car and the price they would be willing to pay for a lemon. In this case, with a 50–50 chance of buying a good car or a lemon, buyers might offer $7,500, which is halfway between the price they would pay if they knew for certain the car was a good one and the price they would pay if they knew it was a lemon.

Unfortunately for used car buyers, a major glitch arises at this point. From the buyers' perspective, given that they don't know whether any particular car offered for sale is a good car or a lemon, an offer of $7,500 seems reasonable. But the sellers do know whether the cars they are offering are good cars or lemons. To a seller of a good car, an offer of $7,500 is $2,500 below the true value of the car, and the seller will be reluctant to sell. But to a seller of a lemon, an offer of $7,500 is $2,500 above the true value of the car, and the seller will be quite happy to sell. As sellers of lemons take advantage of knowing more about the cars they are selling than buyers do, the used car market will fall victim to **adverse selection**: Most used cars offered for sale will be lemons. In other words, because of asymmetric information, the market has selected adversely the cars that will be offered for sale. Notice as well that the problem of adverse selection reduces the total quantity of used cars bought and sold in the market because few good cars are offered for sale.

Adverse selection The situation in which one party to a transaction takes advantage of knowing more than the other party to the transaction.

Asymmetric Information in the Market for Health Insurance

Asymmetric information problems are particularly severe in the markets for all types of insurance, including health care insurance. To understand this point, first consider how insurance works. Insurance companies provide the service of *risk pooling* when they sell policies to households. For example, if you own a $150,000 house but do not have a fire insurance policy, a fire that destroys your house can be a financial catastrophe. But an insurance company can pool the risk of your house burning down by selling fire insurance policies to you and thousands of other homeowners. Homeowners are willing to pay the certain cost represented by the premium they pay for insurance in return for eliminating the uncertain—but potentially very large—cost should their house burn down. Notice that for the insurance company to cover all of its costs, the total amount it receives in premiums must be greater than the amount it pays out in claims to policyholders. To survive, insurance companies have to predict accurately the amount they are likely to pay out to policyholders. For instance, if an insurance company predicts that the houses of only 2 percent of policyholders will burn down during a year when 5 percent of houses actually burn down, the company will suffer losses. On the other hand, if the company predicts that 8 percent of houses will burn down when only 5 percent actually do, the company will have charged premiums that are too high. A company that charges premiums that are too high will lose customers to other companies and may eventually be driven out of business.

Adverse Selection in the Market for Health Insurance One obstacle to health insurance companies accurately predicting the number of claims policyholders will make is that buyers of health insurance policies always know more about the state of their health—and, therefore, how likely they are to submit medical bills for payment—than will the insurance companies. In other words, insurance companies face an adverse selection problem because sick people are more likely to want health insurance than are healthy people. If insurance companies have trouble determining who is healthy and who is sick, they will end up setting their premiums too low and will fail to cover their costs. An insurance company that finds that the premiums it is charging are too low to cover the costs of the claims being submitted faces a problem. The company might try to increase the premiums it charges, but this runs the risk of making the adverse selection problem worse. If premiums rise, then younger, healthier people who rarely visit the doctor or have to be hospitalized may respond to the increase in premiums by dropping their insurance. The insurance company will then find its adverse selection problem has been made worse because its policyholders will be less healthy on average than they were before the premium increase. The situation is similar to that facing a used car buyer who knows that adverse selection is a problem in the used car market and decides to compensate for it by lowering the price he is willing to pay for a car. The lower price will reduce the number of sellers of good cars willing to sell to him, making his adverse selection problem worse.

One controversial way to deal with the problem of adverse selection is to require individuals to buy health insurance. Most states require drivers to buy automobile insurance, so that both high-risk and low-risk drivers will carry insurance. The Patient Protection and Affordable Care Act (PPACA) passed in 2010 requires that beginning in 2014 residents of the United States must carry insurance or pay a fine. This provision of the law is known as the *individual mandate*. We discuss it further later in the chapter.

Moral Hazard in the Market for Health Insurance The insurance market is subject to a second consequence of asymmetric information. **Moral hazard** refers to actions people take after they have entered into a transaction that make the other party to the transaction worse off. Moral hazard in the insurance market occurs when people change their behavior after becoming insured. For example, once a firm has taken out a fire insurance policy on a warehouse, it might be reluctant to install an expensive sprinkler system. Similarly, someone with health insurance may visit the doctor for treatment of a cold or other minor illness, when he would not do so without the insurance. Or someone with health insurance might engage in risky activities, such as riding a motorcycle, that she would avoid if she lacked insurance.

> **Moral hazard** The actions people take after they have entered into a transaction that make the other party to the transaction worse off.

One way to think about the basic moral hazard problem with insurance is to note that normally there are two parties to an economic transaction: the buyer and the seller. The insurance company becomes a third party to the purchase of medical services because the insurance company, rather than the patient, pays for some or all of the service. For this reason, economists refer to traditional health insurance as a *third-party payer* system. The third-party payer system means that consumers of health care do not pay a price that reflects the full cost of providing the service. This lower price leads consumers to use more health care than they otherwise would.

Third-party payer health insurance can also lead to another consequence of moral hazard known as the *principal–agent problem* because doctors may be led to take actions that are not necessarily in the best interests of their patients, such as prescribing unnecessary tests or other treatments. The **principal–agent problem** results from agents—in this case, doctors—pursuing their own interests rather than the interests of the principals—in this case, patients—who hired them. If patients had to pay the full price of lab tests, MRI scans, and other procedures, they would be more likely to question whether the procedures were really necessary. Because health insurance pays most of the bill for these procedures, patients are more likely to accept them. Note that the fee-for-service aspect of most health insurance can make the principal–agent problem worse because doctors and hospitals are paid for each service performed,

> **Principal–agent problem** A problem caused by agents pursuing their own interests rather than the interests of the principals who hired them.

Don't Let This Happen to You

Don't Confuse Adverse Selection with Moral Hazard

The two key consequences of asymmetric information are adverse selection and moral hazard. It is easy to get these concepts mixed up. One way to keep the concepts straight is to remember that adverse selection refers to what happens at the time of entering into the transaction. An example would be an insurance company that sells a life insurance policy to a terminally ill person because the company lacks full information on the person's health. Moral hazard refers to what happens after entering into the transaction. For example, a nonsmoker buys a life insurance policy and then starts smoking four packs of cigarettes a day. (It may help to remember that *a* comes before *m* in the alphabet just as *a*dverse selection comes before *m*oral hazard.)

MyEconLab

Your Turn: Test your understanding by doing related problem 3.9 on page 166 at the end of this chapter.

whether or not the service was effective. Many doctors argue that the increasing number of medical procedures is not the result of third-party payer health insurance. Instead the increase reflects the improved effectiveness of the procedures in diagnosing illness and the tendency of some doctors to practice "defensive medicine" because they fear that if they fail to diagnose an illness, a patient may file a malpractice lawsuit against them.

How Insurance Companies Deal with Adverse Selection and Moral Hazard
Insurance companies can take steps to reduce adverse selection and moral hazard problems. For example, insurance companies can use deductibles and coinsurance to reduce moral hazard. A deductible requires the policyholder to pay a certain dollar amount of a claim. With coinsurance, the insurance company pays only a percentage of any claim. Suppose you have a health insurance policy with a $200 deductible and 20 percent coinsurance, and you have a medical bill of $1,000. You must pay the first $200 of the bill and 20 percent of the remaining $800. Deductibles and coinsurance make the policies less attractive to people who intend to file many claims, thereby reducing the adverse selection problem. Deductibles and coinsurance also provide policyholders with an incentive to avoid filing claims, thereby reducing the moral hazard problem. Notice, though, that deductibles and coinsurance reduce, but do not eliminate, adverse selection and moral hazard. People who anticipate having large medical bills will still have a greater incentive than healthy people to buy insurance, and people with health insurance are still more likely to file claims than are people without health insurance.

To reduce the problem of adverse selection, someone applying for an individual health insurance policy is usually required to submit his or her medical records to the insurance company. Insurance companies usually also carry out their own medical examinations. Companies have often limited coverage of *pre-existing conditions*, which are medical problems, such as heart disease or cancer, that the buyer already has before purchasing the insurance. The limits that health insurance companies placed on pre-existing conditions typically lasted for one or two years or, occasionally, were permanent. Limits on pre-existing conditions have been very common in health insurance policies for individuals, but were also sometimes included in group policies, such as the policies companies sell to businesses providing coverage to their employees. Exclusions and limits on coverage of pre-existing conditions have been controversial. Critics argue that by excluding coverage of pre-existing conditions, insurance companies were forcing people with serious illnesses to pay the entire amount of what might be very large medical bills or to go without medical care. Some people with chronic or terminal illnesses found it impossible to buy an individual health insurance policy. The insurance companies argue that if they do not exclude coverage of pre-existing conditions, then adverse selection problems might make it difficult to offer any health insurance policies or might force the companies to charge premiums that are so high as to cause relatively healthy people to not renew their policies, which would make adverse selection problems worse. To some extent, the debate over coverage of pre-existing conditions is a normative one. Ordinarily, in a market system, people who cannot afford a good or service must do without it. Many people, though, are reluctant to see people not have access to health insurance because they cannot afford it. As we will discuss in the next section, the Patient Protection and Affordable Care Act passed by Congress in 2010 included significant restrictions on the ability of insurance companies to limit coverage of pre-existing conditions.

Solved Problem 5.3

Dealing with Adverse Selection

Private health insurance that has deductibles and co-payments can generate a lot of paper work for patients: insurance companies send patients statements indicating how much they owe doctors, doctors send bills asking for payment, and disagreements arise over which treatments are eligible for insurance. In 2011, the company Off Your Desk was offering consumers a service that would handle all the paperwork involved with health insurance for a fee of $65 per month. A newspaper article on the service noted that: "Still, the service does have an adverse selection problem. . . ."

a. What adverse selection problem does the firm face? Be sure to define adverse selection in your answer.

b. How might the firm attempt to deal with this adverse selection problem?

Solving the Problem

Step 1: **Review the chapter material.** This problem is about adverse selection, so you may want to review the section "Adverse Selection in the Market for Health Insurance," which appears on page 147, and the section "How Insurance Companies Deal with Problems of Adverse Selection and Moral Hazard," which begins on page 148.

Step 2: **Answer part a by defining adverse selection and explaining how the concept applies in this example.** Adverse selection is the situation in which one party to a transaction takes advantage of knowing more than the other party to the transaction. In this example, Off Your Desk runs the risk of attracting a disproportionate number of customers who have extensive paperwork needs that will cost the company more than $65 per month to process.

Step 3: **Answer part b by explaining how the firm might deal with the problem of adverse selection.** The firm has strategies available: It could restrict its service to only covering bills its customers receive after they sign up. This strategy would reduce adverse selection by limiting the attractiveness of the service to customers who already had complicated billing questions that they needed help with and that would be likely to cost more than $65 per month to resolve. The strategy would be similar to health insurance plans that exclude coverage of patients' pre-existing conditions. The firm could also put a limit on the number of bills that it would process for the flat fee of $65. That strategy would avoid attracting customers who anticipate having many bills. In fact, Off Your Desk uses both strategies: It does not cover bills customers received before signing up for the service, and it will only cover the paperwork involved with 10 medical claims over a three-month period.

Based on Jennifer Saranow Schultz, "Outsourcing Insurance Paperwork," *New York Times*, January 19, 2011.

Your Turn: For more practice, do related problem 3.11 on page 166 at the end of this chapter.   MyEconLab

Externalities in the Market for Health Care

For most goods and services, we assume that the consumer receives all the benefits from consuming the good and that the firm producing the good bears all of the costs of production. Some goods or services, though, involve an *externality*, which is a benefit or cost that affects someone who is not directly involved in the production or consumption of a good or service. For example, if a utility burns coal to produce electricity, the result will be air pollution, which causes a *negative externality* because people with asthma or other breathing problems may bear a cost even though they were not involved in buying or selling the electricity that caused the pollution. College education may result in a *positive externality* because college-educated people are less likely to commit crimes and, by being better-informed voters, more likely to contribute to better government policies. So, although you receive most of the benefits of your college education, other people also receive some of the benefits.

Externalities interfere with the economic efficiency of a market equilibrium. We saw in Chapter 4 that a competitive market achieves economic efficiency by maximizing the sum of consumer surplus and producer surplus. But when there is a negative externality in production, as with air pollution, the market will produce more than the efficient quantity. When there is a positive externality in consumption, as with college educations, the market will produce less than the efficient quantity.

Are there externalities involved with medicine and health care? There are several aspects of health care that many economists believe involve externalities. For example, anyone vaccinated against a communicable disease protects not just himself or herself but also reduces the chances that people who have not been vaccinated will contract the disease. There is some debate over whether obesity may involve a negative externality. People who are obese are more likely to suffer from heart disease, diabetes, or other medical problems. Obesity may involve an externality because people who are *not* obese may pay for some of the health care costs obese people incur.

Economists and policymakers debate whether the existence of externalities requires significant government involvement in health care.

<table>
<tr><td>Making
the
Connection</td><td>Should the Government Run
the Health Care System?</td></tr>
</table>

During the debate over President Barack Obama's health care plan during 2009 and 2010, some members of Congress proposed expanding the federal government's role in health care by adopting a system similar to the single-payer system used in Canada under which the government would provide health care to all residents of the United States. What role the federal government should play in health care remains a controversial public policy issue.

Economists categorize goods on the basis of whether they are *rival* and *excludable*. Rivalry occurs when one person's consuming a unit of a good means no one else can consume it. If you consume a taco, for example, no one else can consume it. Excludability means that anyone who does not pay for a good cannot consume it. If you don't pay for a taco, for example, Taco Bell can exclude you from consuming it. A *public good* is both nonrival and nonexcludable. Public goods are often, although not always, supplied by a government rather than by private firms. The classic example of a public good is national defense. Your consuming national defense does not interfere with your neighbor's consuming it, so consumption is nonrivalrous. You also cannot be excluded from consuming it, whether you pay for it or not. No private firm would be willing to supply national defense because everyone can consume national defense without paying for it.

Is health care a public good that government should supply—or, at least, pay for? Is it a private good, like furniture, clothing, or computers, that private firms should supply and consumers should pay for without government aid? Should private firms supply most health care, subject to some government regulation? Economists differ in their answers to these questions because the delivery of health care involves a number of complex issues, but we can consider briefly some of the most important points. Because public goods are both nonrivalrous and nonexcludable, health care does not qualify as a public good under the usual definition. More than one person cannot simultaneously consume the same surgical operation, for example. And someone who will not pay for an operation can be excluded from consuming it. (Most states require hospitals to treat patients who are too poor to pay for treatment, and many doctors will treat poor people at a reduced price. But because there is nothing in the nature of health care that keeps people who do not pay for it from being excluded from consuming it, health care does not fit the definition of a public good.)

Congress passed, and President Obama signed, the Patient Protection and Affordable Care Act in 2010.

There are aspects of the delivery of health care that have convinced some economists that government intervention is justified, however. For example, consuming certain types of health care generates positive externalities. Being vaccinated against a communicable disease, such as influenza or meningitis, not only reduces the chance that the person vaccinated will catch the disease but also reduces the probability that an epidemic of the disease will occur. Therefore, the market may supply an inefficiently small quantity of vaccinations unless vaccinations receive a government subsidy.

Information problems can also be important in the market for private health insurance. Consumers as buyers of health insurance often know much more about the state of their health than do the companies selling health insurance. This information problem may raise costs to insurance companies when the pool of people being insured is small, making insurance companies less willing to offer health insurance to consumers the companies suspect may file too many claims. Economists debate how important information problems are in health care markets and whether government intervention is required to reduce them.

Many economists believe that market-based solutions are the best approach to improving the health care system. As we saw in Table 5.2 on page 144, the United States has a mixed record with respect to health care outcomes. The United States is, however, a world leader in innovation in medical technology and prescription drugs. The market-oriented approach to reforming health care starts with the goal of improving health care outcomes while preserving incentives for U.S. firms to continue with innovations in medical screening equipment, surgical procedures, and prescription drugs. Presently, markets are delivering inaccurate signals to consumers because when buying health care, unlike when buying most other goods and services, consumers pay a price well below the true cost of providing the service. Under current tax laws, individuals do not pay taxes on health insurance benefits they receive from their employers, and this encourages them to want very generous coverage that reduces incentives to control costs. As we will discuss later in the chapter, market-based approaches to health care reform attempt to address these issues.

It remains an open question whether the U.S. health care system will continue to move toward greater government intervention, which is the approach adopted in most other countries, or whether market-based reforms will be implemented. Because health care is so important to consumers and because health care spending looms so large in the U.S. economy, the role of the government in the health care system is likely to be the subject of intense debate for some time to come.

Your Turn: Test your understanding by doing related problems 3.13 and 3.14 on page 166 at the end of this chapter.

MyEconLab

5.4 LEARNING OBJECTIVE

Explain the major issues
involved in the debate over
health care policy in the
United States.

The Debate over Health Care Policy in the United States

Shortly after taking office in January 2009, President Barack Obama proposed far-reaching changes in the U.S. health care system. The result was the Patient Protection and Affordable Care Act (PPACA), which Congress passed in March 2010. The act was controversial, with every Republican member of Congress and 34 Democratic members of Congress voting against it. Economists vigorously debated its likely effects on health care and the economy. In the next section, we explore the issue of rising health care costs, which played an important role in the health care debate, before discussing the details of the PPACA and the debate over the legislation's effect.

The Rising Cost of Health Care

Figure 5.5 illustrates a key fact underlying the debate over health care policy in the United States: Health care's share of gross domestic product, which is the total value of output in the economy, is increasing. Panel (a) shows that spending on health care was less than 6 percent of GDP in 1965, but had risen to about 17.5 percent in 2011, and was projected to rise to about 19.5 percent in 2019. In other words, an increasing percentage of total production in the United States is being devoted to health care. Panel (b) shows increases in health care spending per person in the United States and 10 other high-income countries. Spending on health care has grown faster in the United States than in other countries.

Does it matter that spending on health care is an increasing share of total spending and output in the U.S. economy? The shares of different products in total spending change frequently. For instance, in the United States, the shares of spending on cell

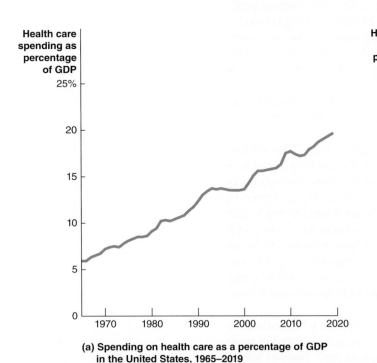

(a) Spending on health care as a percentage of GDP in the United States, 1965–2019

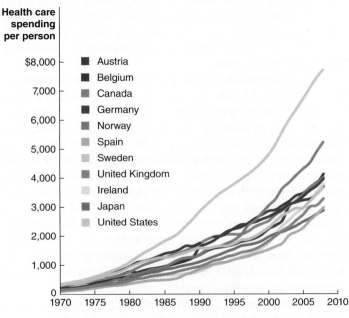

(b) Health care spending per person, 1970–2008

Figure 5.5 Spending on Health Care around the World

Panel (a) shows that health care spending has been a rising percentage of GDP in the United States. Health care spending rose from less than 6 percent of GDP in 1965 to about 17.5 percent in 2011, and it is projected to rise to about 19.5 percent in 2019. Panel (b) shows that health care spending per person has been growing faster in the United States than in other high-income countries.

Data from [Panel (a)]: U.S. Department of Health and Human Services, Centers for Medicare and Medicaid Services; panel (b): Organization for Economic Cooperation and Development, *OECD Health Data 2011*, June 2011.

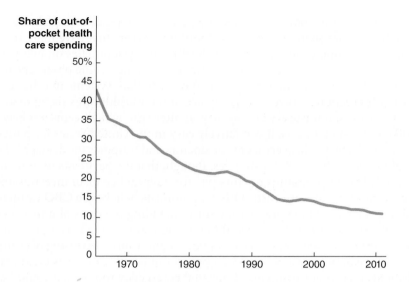

Figure 5.6

The Declining Share of Out-of-Pocket Health Care Spending

Out-of-pocket spending on health care has declined sharply as a fraction of all health care spending.

Data from U.S. Department of Health and Human Services, Centers for Medicare and Medicaid Services.

phones or LCD televisions were much greater in 2012 than in 2000. Spending on food as a share of total spending has been declining for decades. Economists interpret these changes as reflecting consumers' preferences—consumers choose to devote relatively more of their incomes to spending on cell phones and relatively less to spending on food. As we have seen, though, most people pay for health care by relying on third-party payers, such as employer-provided health insurance or government-provided Medicare or Medicaid. Out-of-pocket spending, spending on health care that consumers pay out of their own incomes rather than through health insurance, has been declining.

Figure 5.6 shows that out-of-pocket spending on health care as a percentage of all spending on health care has steadily declined since 1965. In 1965, 45 percent of all health care spending was out-of-pocket, while in 2011, only 11 percent was. As a result, in recent years, consumers of health care have been directly paying for only a small fraction of the true cost of providing health care, with third-party payers picking up the remainder. As average incomes rise, consumers might be expected to spend a rising share of the increase on health care. But because consumers do not pay the full cost of increases in health care spending, they may not be willing to buy as much health care as they currently receive if they had to pay the full price.

Because the federal and state governments in the United States pay for just over half of health care spending through Medicare, Medicaid, and other programs, increases in health care spending can cause problems for government budgets. The Medicare and Medicaid programs began in 1965. By 2010, spending on these programs had grown to 5.5 percent of GDP. That percentage is expected to more than double over the next 40 years unless health care costs begin to grow at a slower rate. In 2011, the federal government was struggling to find ways to pay for the projected increases in Medicare and Medicaid without severely cutting other federal spending or sharply raising taxes.

Explaining Rapid Increases in Health Care Spending

In this section we briefly discuss some reasons economists believe that health care spending has been increasing rapidly in the United States. We start by reviewing explanations that are sometimes offered by policymakers and journalists, but that are unlikely to account for most of the increases in health care costs.

Factors That Do Not Explain Sustained Increases in Health Care Spending
The two panels of Figure 5.5 show that spending on health care has been growing faster

than the economy as a whole for at least the past several decades. Explaining the rapid growth of health care spending requires identifying factors that have more than a one-time effect. For example, because the U.S. health care system relies on many independent hospitals, medical practices, and insurance companies, some observers argue that it generates more paperwork, duplication, and waste than systems in other countries. Even if this observation is correct, it cannot account for health care's rising share of GDP unless paperwork and waste are *increasing* year after year, which seems unlikely.

Unlike in most countries, it is relatively easy in the United States for patients who have been injured by medical errors to sue doctors and hospitals for damages. The Congressional Budget Office (CBO) estimates, though, that the payments to settle malpractice lawsuits plus the premiums doctors pay for malpractice insurance amount to less than 1 percent of health care costs. Other economists believe the CBO estimate is too low and that the costs of malpractice lawsuits, including the costs of unnecessary tests and procedures doctors order to avoid being sued, are as much as 7 percent of total health care costs. Still, these costs have not been significantly increasing over time.

Somewhere between 1 percent and 4 percent of health care costs are due to uninsured patients receiving treatments at hospital emergency rooms that could have been provided less expensively in doctors' offices. But once again, this cost has not been increasing rapidly enough to account for much of the increase in health care as a percentage of GDP.

"Cost Disease" in the Health Care Sector

Some economists argue that health care suffers from a problem often encountered in service industries. In some sectors of the economy, particularly manufacturing and the production of goods, *productivity*, or the amount of output each worker can produce in a given period, increases steadily. These increases in productivity occur because over time firms provide workers with more machinery and equipment, including computers, with which to work, and because technological progress results in improvements in machinery and equipment and other parts of the production process. As workers produce more goods, firms are able to pay them higher wages. In service-producing industries, though, increasing output per worker is more difficult. In education, for instance, computers and the Internet have been useful, but most of education still involves a teacher standing in front of a classroom of students. Increasing the number of students per teacher year after year is not feasible. The same is true of medicine, where MRI units, CT scanners, and other medical technology have improved diagnosis and treatment, but most medicine still requires a face-to-face meeting between a doctor and a patient. As wages rise in industries in which productivity is increasing rapidly, service industries in which productivity is increasing less rapidly must match these wage increases or lose workers. Because increases in wages are not offset by increases in productivity in service industries, the cost to firms of supplying services increases.

William Baumol of New York University has labeled the tendency for low productivity in service industries to lead to higher costs in those industries as "the cost disease of the service sector." There is good reason to think that health care suffers from this cost disease because growth in labor productivity in health care has been less than half as fast as labor productivity growth in the economy as a whole. This slow growth in productivity can help explain why the cost of health care has been rising so rapidly, thereby increasing health care's share of total spending and output.

The Aging of the Population and Advances in Medical Technology

As people age, they increase their spending on health care. Firms continue to develop new prescription drugs and new medical equipment that typically have higher costs than the drugs and equipment they replace. The aging of the U.S. population and the introduction of higher cost drugs and medical equipment interact to drive up spending on the federal government's Medicare program and on health care generally. Many newly introduced drugs and diagnostic tools are used disproportionately by people over age 65. Partly as a result, health care spending on people over age 65 is six times greater than spending on people aged 18 to 24 and four times greater than on people aged 25 to 44.

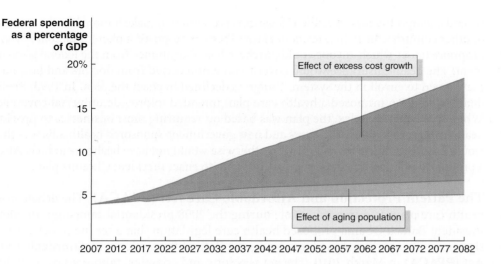

Figure 5.7

Reasons for Rising Federal Spending on Medicare and Medicaid

Although the aging of the U.S. population will increase federal government spending on the Medicare and Medicaid programs, increases in the cost of providing health care will have a larger effect on government spending on these programs.

Data from U.S. Congressional Budget Office, *Long-Term Outlook for Health Care Spending*, Washington, DC: U.S. Government Printing Office, November 2007.

In 2010, there were 47 million people receiving Medicare, and that number is expected to grow to 80 million by 2030. As we have seen, even in the absence of the development of new drugs and other medical technology, low rates of productivity in the health care sector could be expected to drive up costs. In fact, as Figure 5.7 illustrates, the CBO estimates that most of the increase in federal spending on the Medicare and Medicaid programs will be due to increases in the cost of providing health care, rather than to the aging of the population. In the figure, "effect of excess cost growth" refers to the extent to which health care costs per person grow faster than GDP per person. So, the combination of an aging population and increases in the cost of providing health care are an important reason why health care spending is an increasing percentage of GDP.

Distorted Economic Incentives As we noted earlier, some part of the increase in health care spending shown in Figure 5.5 on page 152 represents consumers choosing to allocate more of their incomes to health care as their incomes rise. But as we have also seen, consumers usually pay less than the true cost of medical treatment because a third party—typically, an insurance company or the government—often pays most of the bill. For example, consumers who have health insurance provided by their employers usually pay only a small amount—perhaps $20—for a visit to a doctor's office, when the true cost of the visit might be $80 or $90. The result is that consumers demand a larger quantity of health care services than they would if they paid a price that better represented the cost of providing the services. Doctors and other health care providers also have a reduced incentive to control costs because they know that an insurance company will pick up most of the bill.

In some important ways, health insurance is different from other types of insurance. As we discussed earlier, the basic idea of insurance is that the risk of an unpredictable, high-cost event—a house fire or a serious car accident—is pooled among the many consumers who buy insurance. Health insurance, though, also typically covers many planned expenses, such as routine checkups, annual physicals, vaccinations, and other low-cost events, such as treatment for minor illnesses. By disguising the true cost of these routine expenses, health insurance encourages overuse of health care services.

We discuss further the role of economic incentives in health care in the next section.

The Debate over Health Care Policy

As we have seen, the United States has been unusual among high-income countries in relying on private health insurance—largely from firms—to provide health care coverage to the majority of the population. Most other high-income countries either provide health care directly, as the United Kingdom does, through government-owned hospitals and government-employed doctors, or they provide health insurance to all residents, as Canada does, without directly employing doctors or owning hospitals. There have been several attempts to reorganize the U.S. health care system to make it more like the systems in other countries. In 1945, President Harry Truman proposed a plan for *national health insurance* under which anyone could purchase health insurance from the federal government. The health insurance would cover treatment received from doctors and hospitals that agreed to enroll in the system. Congress declined to enact the plan. In 1993, President Bill Clinton proposed a health care plan intended to provide universal coverage. While somewhat complex, the plan was based on requiring most businesses to provide health insurance to their employees and new government-sponsored health alliances that would ensure coverage for anyone who otherwise would not have health insurance. After a prolonged political debate, Congress chose not to enact President Clinton's plan.

The Patient Protection and Affordable Care Act (PPACA) The debate over health care played an important role during the 2008 presidential campaign. In 2009, President Barack Obama proposed health care legislation that after much debate and significant changes was signed into law as the **Patient Protection and Affordable Care Act (PPACA)** in March 2010. The act was long and complex, taking up over 20,000 pages and touching nearly every aspect of health care in the United States. Here is a summary of only the act's main provisions:

Patient Protection and Affordable Care Act (PPACA) Health care reform legislation passed by Congress and signed by President Barack Obama in 2010.

- *Individual mandate* The act required that, with limited exceptions, every resident of the United States have health insurance that meets certain basic requirements. Beginning in 2014, individuals who do not acquire health insurance will be subject to a fine. The fine will rise over time, reaching $895 per person or 2.5 percent of income, whichever is greater, by 2018.

- *State health exchanges* Beginning in 2014, each state is to establish an Affordable Insurance Exchange. Separate exchanges are to be established for individuals and small businesses with fewer than 50 employees. The exchanges will be run by a state government agency or by a non-profit firm and will offer health insurance policies that meet certain specified requirements. The intention is that private insurance companies will compete by offering policies on the exchanges to individuals and small businesses. Low-income individuals and small businesses with 25 or fewer employees will be eligible for tax credits to offset the costs of buying health insurance.

- *Employer mandate* Beginning in 2014, every firm with more than 200 employees must offer health insurance to its employees and must automatically enroll them in the plan. Firms with more than 50 employees must offer health insurance or pay a fee of $3,000 to the federal government for every employee who receives a tax credit from the federal government for obtaining health insurance through a health exchange.

- *Regulation of health insurance* Insurance companies are required to participate in a high-risk pool that will insure individuals with pre-existing medical conditions who have been unable to buy health insurance for at least six months. All individual and group policies must provide coverage for dependent children up to age 26. Beginning in 2014, lifetime dollar maximums on coverage are prohibited. Limits are also placed on the size of deductibles and on the waiting period before coverage becomes effective.

- *Medicare and Medicaid* Eligibility for Medicaid was expanded to persons with incomes up to 400 percent of the federal poverty line; in 2011, the federal poverty line was an annual income of $10,890 for an individual. In an attempt to control increases in health care costs, an Independent Payment Advisory Board (IPAB) was established with the power to reduce Medicare payments for prescription drugs and for the use of diagnostic equipment and other technology if Medicare spending exceeds certain levels. Some Medicare reimbursements to hospitals and doctors were reduced.

- *Taxes* Several new taxes will help fund the program. Beginning in 2013, workers earning more than $200,000 will have their share of the Medicare payroll tax increase from 1.45 percent to a 2.35 percent, and investors who earn more than $200,000 will pay a new 3.8 percent tax on their investment income. Beginning in 2018, a tax will be imposed on employer-provided health insurance plans that have a value above $10,200 for an individual or $27,500 for a family. Pharmaceutical firms, health insurance firms, and firms producing medical devices will also pay new taxes.

The PPACA is scheduled to be fully implemented by 2019 at which point more than 30 million additional individuals are expected to have health care coverage. The Congressional Budget Office (CBO) has estimated that the law will increase federal government spending by about $938 billion over 10 years. The CBO estimates that the additional taxes and fees enacted under the law will raise over $1 trillion, which would be enough to pay for the plan and reduce the federal government's budget deficit by more than $100 billion over 10 years. Many economists have disputed this estimate, arguing that the law's new spending will increase the deficit.

The Debate over the PPACA Any law as far-reaching and complex as the PPACA is bound to draw criticism. As noted earlier in the chapter, the congressional debate over the law was highly partisan with every Republican ultimately voting against it and all Democrats in the Senate and all but 34 Democrats in the House voting in favor of it. Critics of the act can be divided into two broad groups: Those who argue that health care reform should involve a greater movement toward a system similar to the European, Canadian, and Japanese systems, and those who argue that health care reform should include more market-based changes.

As we discussed in the *Making the Connection* on page 150, some economists and policymakers believe that information problems and externalities in the market for health care are sufficiently large that the government should either provide health care directly through government-owned hospitals and government-employed doctors or pay for health care through national health insurance, sometimes referred to as a *single-payer system*. Although the PPACA significantly increased the federal government's involvement in the health care system, it stopped short of the degree of government involvement that exists in the Canadian, Japanese, or European systems. Critics in favor of moving toward greater government involvement typically argue that doing so would reduce the paperwork and waste caused by the current system or the system as it will be under PPACA. They argue that the current Medicare system—which is essentially a single-payer system for people over age 65—has proved to have lower administrative costs than have private health insurance companies. Supporters of greater government involvement in the health care system have also argued that the Canadian and European systems have had lower levels of health care spending per person and lower rates of increase in total health care spending, while providing good health care outcomes.

Market-based reforms of health care involve changing the market for health care so that it becomes more like the markets for other goods and services. As in other markets, the prices consumers pay and suppliers receive would do a better job of conveying information on consumer demand and supplier costs. The expectation is that increased competition among doctors, hospitals, pharmaceutical companies, and other providers of health care would reduce costs and increase economic efficiency. Economists who support market-based reforms as the best approach to improving the health care system were disappointed that the PPACA did not adopt this approach. Currently, markets are delivering inaccurate signals to consumers because when buying health care, unlike when buying most other goods and services, consumers pay a price well below the true cost of providing the service.

Market-based reforms Changes in the market for health care that would make it more like the markets for other goods and services.

Making the Connection | **How Much Is That MRI Scan?**

Magnetic Resonance Imaging (MRI) units play an important role in modern medicine. First introduced in the early 1980s, MRI units allow doctors to see inside the body's soft tissues to identify tumors, torn muscles, and other medical problems.

As we noted earlier, MRI units are more widely available in the United States than in most other countries. We would normally expect that when a product is widely available, competition among firms results in the price of the product being about the same everywhere. Customers would not buy a bestselling book from Amazon.com if the price was 50 percent higher than on BarnesandNoble.com.

Does competition equalize the prices of medical services? The data in the table below indicates that the prices of abdominal MRI scans vary widely. In most cities in the United States, the most expensive MRI scan has a price that is more than double the least expensive scan. Two reporters looking at prices for shoulder MRI scans in Pensacola, Florida, found that Sacred Heart Hospital was charging $800 for a shoulder MRI scan, while Pensacola Open MRI & Imaging, a private firm located less than one mile away, was charging $450 for the same scan. Pensacola Open MRI & Imaging was actually using newer MRI units that give higher resolution images, so they were charging less for a better service.

City	Highest price	Lowest price	Difference
New York, New York	$9,300	$2,400	$6,900
Orlando, Florida	6,800	2,250	4,550
Dallas, Texas	6,500	2,100	4,400
San Francisco, California	7,200	2,850	4,350
Chicago, Illinois	6,100	2,100	4,000
Omaha, Nebraska	5,700	2,000	3,700
Baton Rouge, Louisiana	5,600	2,025	3,575
Atlanta, Georgia	5,500	2,100	3,400
Lexington, Kentucky	5,100	2,000	3,100
Charlotte, North Carolina	4,500	2,100	2,400

How can some providers of medical services charge hundreds or thousands of dollars more than competitors and remain in business? The answer is that most patients are unconcerned about prices because they do not pay them or pay only a fraction of them. Patients typically rely on doctors to refer them to a facility for an MRI scan or other procedure and make little or no effort to determine the price the facility charges. A goal of market-based reforms of the health care system is to give patients an incentive to pay more attention to the prices of medical services.

Based on Caitlin Kenney, "Shopping for an MRI," npr.org, November 6, 2009; MRI prices from newchoicehealth.com, August 21, 2011.

MyEconLab **Your Turn:** Test your understanding by doing related problem 4.10 and on page 167 at the end of this chapter.

Supporters of market-based reforms note that employees have to pay federal income and payroll taxes on the wages their employers pay them, but in most circumstances they do not pay taxes on the value of the health insurance their employers provide them. This feature of the tax laws encourages employees to want very generous health care coverage; in fact, if offered the choice between a $1,000 salary increase or increased health care coverage that was worth $1,000, many people would choose the increased health care coverage because it would be tax free (although someone who was young and healthy and did not expect to have medical bills would probably still choose the increase in salary). The size of this tax break is quite substantial—more than $250 billion in 2011. But individuals typically get no tax break when buying an individual health insurance policy or when they spend money on health care out-of-pocket.[1] Some economists have proposed making the tax treatment of employer-provided health insurance the same as the tax treatment of individually purchased health insurance and out-of-pocket health care spending. They argue that this change could, potentially, significantly reduce spending on health care without reducing the effectiveness of the health care received. Such tax law changes would make it more likely that employer-provided health insurance would focus on large medical bills—such as those resulting from hospitalizations—while consumers would pay prices closer to the costs of providing routine medical care. John Cogan of the Hoover Institution, R. Glenn Hubbard of Columbia University, and Daniel Kessler of Stanford estimate that repealing the tax preference for employer-provided health insurance would reduce spending by people enrolled in these programs by 33 percent.

Currently, the U.S. health care system is a world leader in innovation in medical technology and prescription drugs. About two-thirds of pharmaceutical patents are issued to U.S. firms and about two-thirds of research on new medicines is carried out in the United States. One goal of market-based reforms would be to ensure that U.S. firms continue with innovations in medical screening equipment, surgical procedures, and prescription drugs. Executives of U.S. pharmaceutical firms have voiced concern over whether aspects of PPACA will affect their ability to profitably bring new prescription drugs to market. In particular, managers at these firms worry that the new Independent Payment Advisory Board might reduce the payments Medicare would make for new prescription drugs.

Both critics of the PPACA who favor greater government involvement in health care and those who favor market reforms raise questions about the act's individual mandate. The individual mandate requires every U.S. resident to have health insurance. The mandate was considered necessary because otherwise healthy people might avoid buying insurance until they become ill. Because insurance companies would not be allowed to deny coverage for pre-existing conditions, they would end up paying large medical bills for people who had not been paying premiums to support the system while they were healthy. There were questions, though, about whether the requirement to buy health insurance would be enforceable. Although people who do not buy insurance are subject to fines under the act, there was no mechanism set up to collect the fines if people refused to pay them voluntarily.

Making the Connection	**Health Exchanges, Small Businesses, and Rising Medical Costs**

We saw at the beginning of the chapter that for many small businesses, the cost of providing health insurance to their employees has become a heavy burden. A key provision of the PPACA was intended to address this problem. As noted earlier, by 2014, every state is obligated to set up an Affordable Insurance Exchange. Each exchange must operate a Small Business Health Options Program (SHOP) where private insurance companies will offer small firms health insurance plans that the firms can purchase for their workers. Small firms with up to 100 employees will be eligible to purchase health insurance through their state's SHOP. In addition, firms with fewer than 25 employees will receive a tax credit to offset up to 50 percent of the cost of providing health insurance to their workers.

The plan is intended to get over one of the key disadvantages small firms face when buying health insurance: limited risk pooling. When an insurance company sells health insurance to a large firm, the risk of illness and large medical bills is spread across many employees. Adverse selection problems are also reduced when a plan covers a large number of workers. When a firm employs only a few workers, as is the case with the New York antique store we discussed in the chapter opener, a single illness

---

[1]Individuals receive a deduction on their federal income tax only if their medical expenses are greater than 7.5 percent of their income. Only a relatively small number of individuals have expenses high enough to make use of that deduction. The threshold is being raised under the PPACA to 10 percent.

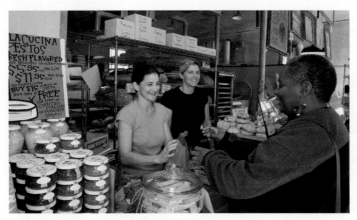

Will the Small Business Health Options Program (SHOP) help small businesses keep health insurance costs down?

can cause an insurance company to make payments far above the premiums it has received from the firm. Typically, the insurance company will then substantially raise the premiums the firm will pay. Even if none of the employees of a firm becomes ill, insurance companies concerned about adverse selection problems may raise premiums substantially over time. The owners of the antique store had to pay premium increases of more than 20 percent per year. Under the SHOP plan, a small firm's employees would be pooled with the employees of other small firms and premiums could differ across firms only on the basis of the age of the employees and whether the employees smoke. The federal government has given the states significant flexibility in designing the exchanges.

Will SHOP provide a solution to the difficulties small firms encounter in providing health insurance for their employees? Initially, the New York antique store owner was optimistic: "In the short run, the tax credits definitely give me money to potentially hire another employee. . . . I'm hopeful we'll see other benefits, especially all of the savings from the exchanges, in the long run." It is difficult to say how effective the exchanges will be, however, because they will not begin operating until 2014, and as of 2011 many states had not yet announced the rules under which their exchanges would operate. The failure of a health insurance exchange that the state of California ran from 1993 to 2006 shows one potential problem. Firms with relatively healthy workers found that they could buy health insurance more cheaply outside of the exchange. As they left the exchange, insurers needed to raise rates to cover the remaining pool of companies with less healthy workers. Higher rates led more firms to withdraw until finally the exchange collapsed. This process is sometimes referred to as an *adverse selection death spiral*. To succeed, the new health exchanges need to avoid this spiral.

The federal government hopes that the exchanges will improve the choices available to small businesses by requiring that insurance companies meet guidelines for the types of insurance they offer and the information they provide to these businesses. Supporters of the exchanges also hope that they will reduce administrative costs, which will allow insurance companies to offer plans with lower premiums. Some economists and policymakers, however, argue that by increasing the number of people covered by health insurance the exchanges were likely to increase the demand for medical services, further driving up their costs. If health care costs rise as a result, the exchanges would have to pass the costs along to businesses in the form of higher insurance premiums.

As of 2011, the health exchanges, as well as other aspects of the PPACA, were subject to lawsuits from states that claimed that the act violated the U.S. Constitution. Some members of Congress were also attempting to amend the act before it went fully into effect in 2014. The outcome of these political debates could potentially alter how the health exchanges would be run.

Based on "Affordable Insurance Exchanges: Choices, Competition and Clout for Small Businesses," healthcare.gov, July 11, 2011; Judith Messina, "Health Care Reform for Small Business: This Is Going to Hurt," *Crain's New York Business*, 2010; and Kaiser Family Foundation, "Establishing Health Insurance Exchanges: An Update on State Efforts," July 2011; "Antique and Gift Store Owner Sold on Affordable Care Act," www.smallbusinessmajority.org; and Michael Sanerino, "California Offers Lessons on Insurance Exchanges," *Wall Street Journal*, August 3, 2009.

MyEconLab   **Your Turn:** Test your understanding by doing related problem 4.12 on page 167 at the end of this chapter.

Continued from page 137

Economics in Your Life

Why Is It Difficult for People Who Are Seriously Ill to Buy Health Insurance?

At the beginning of this chapter, we asked: Why is it difficult for people who are seriously ill to buy health insurance? Someone who is seriously ill can face frighteningly large medical bills. It is natural that such a person would like to purchase health insurance to help pay those bills. Unfortunately, insurance works best when it involves risk pooling for people who face an uncertain and high-cost event, such as their house burning down or being diagnosed with cancer. Insurance companies are naturally reluctant to provide insurance to someone who is already seriously ill because the premiums they receive from the person are certain to be less than the person's medical bills—which the insurance company will have to pay. In order to remain in business, insurance companies will either not insure people with preexisting medical conditions or will insure them only after a waiting period of perhaps years. The Patient Protection and Affordable Care Act (PPACA), which became law in 2010, attempts to make it easier for people with preexisting conditions to buy health insurance. Under the act, each state will run a health exchange that will offer individual health insurance policies to individuals who cannot be excluded because of preexisting conditions and who will pay premiums that can vary only by the buyer's age and whether the buyer is a smoker. Economists and policymakers debate whether the act will be effective.

Conclusion

In this chapter, we have seen that economic analysis can provide important insights into the market for health care. As with many other policy issues, though, economic analysis can help inform the debate, but cannot resolve it. Because health care is so important to consumers and because health care spending looms so large in the U.S. economy, the role of the government in the health care system is likely to be the subject of intense debate for years to come.

Before moving on to Chapter 6, read *An Inside Look at Policy* on the next page for a discussion of health care spending and the Patient Protection and Affordable Care Act.

Health Care Spending Expected to Increase 70 Percent by End of Decade

ASSOCIATED PRESS

U.S. Health Care Tab to Hit $4.6T in 2020

The nation's health care tab is on track to hit $4.6 trillion in 2020, accounting for about $1 of every $5 in the economy, government number crunchers estimate in a report out Thursday.

(a) How much is that? Including government and private money, health care spending in 2020 will average $13,710 for every man, woman and child, says Medicare's Office of the Actuary.

By comparison, U.S. health care spending this year is projected to top $2.7 trillion, or about $8,650 per capita, roughly $1 of $6 in the economy. Most of that spending is for care for the sickest people.

The report from Medicare economists and statisticians is an annual barometer of a trend that many experts say is unsustainable but doesn't seem to be slowing down. A political compromise over the nation's debt and deficits might succeed in tapping the brakes on health care, but polarized lawmakers have been unable to deliver a deal.

(b) The analysis found that President Barack Obama's health care overhaul would only be a modest contributor to growing costs, even though an additional 30 million people who would be otherwise uninsured stand to gain coverage.

The main reasons that health care spending keeps growing faster than the economy are the high cost of medical innovations and an aging society that consumes increasing levels of service.

Many of the newly insured people under the health care law will be younger and healthier. As a result, they are expected to use more doctor visits and prescription drugs and relatively less of pricey hospital care. Health care spending will jump by 8 percent in 2014, when the law's coverage expansion kicks in. But over the 2010–2020 period covered by the estimate, the average yearly growth in health care spending will be only 0.1 percentage point higher than without Obama's overhaul.

Part of the reason for that optimistic prognosis is that cuts and cost controls in the health care law start to bite down late in the decade. However, the same nonpartisan Medicare experts who produced Thursday's estimate have previously questioned whether that austerity will be politically sustainable if hospitals and other providers start going out of business as a result. The actuary's office is responsible for long-range cost estimates.

The report found that health care spending in 2010 grew at a historically low rate of 3.9 percent, partly because of the sluggish economy. That will change as the economy shakes off the lingering effects of the recession.

(c) Government, already the dominant player because of Medicare and Medicaid, will become even more important. By 2020, federal, state and local government health care spending will account for just under half the total tab, up from 45 percent currently. As the health care law's coverage expansion takes effect, "health care financing is anticipated to further shift toward governments," the report said.

Estimates from previous years had projected that the government share would already be at the 50 percent mark, but the actuary's office changed its method for making the complex calculations. Under the previous approach, some private payments such as worker's compensation insurance had been counted in the government column. Technical accuracy—not political pressure—was behind that change, said Stephen Heffler, one of the experts who worked on the estimates.

Separately, another new report finds that the United States continues to spend far more on health care than other economically developed countries. The study by the Commonwealth Fund found that U.S. health care spending per person in 2008 was more than double the median—or midpoint—for other leading economies. Although survival rates for some cancers were higher in the U.S., the report found that quality of care overall was not markedly better.

Key Points in the Article

Government analysts predict that the cost of health care will reach $4.6 trillion in 2020, an average of $13,710 per person. The total cost in 2011 is expected to exceed $2.7 trillion, or about $8,650 per person. The high costs of medical innovation and an aging population are cited as the primary reasons for the rapid increase in health care costs. The implementation of health care reform is expected to contribute only modestly to this increase, with the government's share of spending rising from 45 percent to just under 50 percent of the total cost. A majority of this increase will be for Medicare and Medicaid payments, with the health care overhaul expected to account for an increase of only one-tenth of one percent. A number of analysts believe the continued increases in health care costs are unsustainable for the economy.

Analyzing the News

a Spending on health care in the United States is increasing at a rapid pace, and it is expected to be roughly 20 percent of GDP by 2020. This means that one-fifth of total production in the United States will be devoted to health care, compared to one-twentieth in the mid-1960s. While health care spending as a percentage of GDP has been steadily growing, the percentage of this spending that is being paid directly by consumers has been steadily declining. The figure below shows both the increase in health

care spending as a percentage of GDP and the decrease in out-of-pocket health care spending by consumers as a percentage of all health care spending in the United States since 1965. These data show that while increasing amounts of production are being devoted to health care, consumers are directly paying a smaller and smaller percentage of the cost. The declining out-of-pocket spending, and subsequent increasing percentage of third-party payouts, is often cited as one of the reasons for the overall increase in health care spending.

b The rapid increase in health care spending is thought by many to be unsustainable without increases in taxes or decreases in other areas of spending. In 2009, President Obama proposed sweeping changes for the U.S. health care system, and the following year, he signed the Patient Protection and Affordable Care Act (PPACA) into law. There has been much debate as to whether this health care overhaul package will increase or decrease overall spending on health care, but an analysis by Medicare officials claims that the PPACA will result in only a 0.1 percent additional increase in annual health care spending over the next decade. If this projection is accurate, the PPACA will not significantly contribute to the continued increases in health care spending.

c One of the biggest concerns over the rise in health care spending in the United States is the government's increasingly large share of the overall cost. Due

primarily to Medicare and Medicaid, federal, state, and local governments already account for 45 percent of the nation's annual health care spending, and with the passage of the PPACA, this share is expected to rise to nearly 50 percent by 2020. If the current rate of increase in spending is truly unsustainable and the government will be responsible for a larger share of these increasing costs, major changes to government spending or taxes will need to be implemented to get health care costs under control. This will no doubt continue to be a topic of heated debate in Washington in years to come.

Thinking Critically about Policy

1. Under the Patient Protection and Affordable Care Act (PPACA), every resident of the United States will be required to have health insurance, so up to 30 million people who would otherwise be uninsured will potentially have insurance coverage. Explain the effect that this increase in the number of insured people may have on the adverse selection problem and the moral hazard problem in the market for health insurance. How might this change affect total spending on health care?

2. Analysts and policymakers have described rapid increases in health care spending as unsustainable for the economy. In what sense are these increases unsustainable?

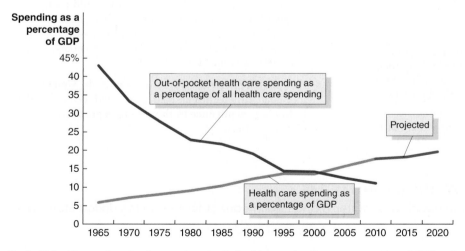

In the United States, there has been an increase in health care spending as a percentage of GDP and a decrease in out-of-pocket health care spending by consumers since 1965.

Chapter Summary and Problems

Key Terms

Adverse selection, p. 146

Asymmetric information, p. 145

Fee-for-service, p. 142

Health care, p. 138

Health insurance, p. 141

Market-based reforms, p. 157

Moral hazard, p. 147

Patient Protection and Affordable Care Act (PPACA), p. 156

Principal–agent problem, p. 147

Single-payer health care
system, p. 142

Socialized medicine, p. 143

5.1 **The Improving Health of People in the United States,** pages 138–141
LEARNING OBJECTIVE: Discuss trends in U.S. health over time.

Summary

Health care refers to goods and services, such as prescription drugs
and consultations with a doctor, that are intended to maintain or
improve health. Over time, the health of people in most countries
has improved. In the United States, as a result of improving health,
life expectancy has increased, death rates have decreased, infant
mortality has decreased, and the average person has become taller.

 Visit **www.myeconlab.com** to complete these
exercises online and get instant feedback.

Review Questions

1.1 Briefly discuss the ways in which the market for health
care is different from and the ways in which it is similar to
the markets for other goods and services.

1.2 Briefly describe changes over time in the health of the average person in the United States.

1.3 How can changes over time in the average height of the
people in a country be a measure of the country's living
standards?

1.4 How can improvements in health increase a country's total
income? How can increases in a country's total income improve health?

Problems and Applications

1.5 Consider the following statement: "To some economists,
nutritional status—measured for example by heights—
suffers as a measure of living standards because height is
not normally seen . . . as something that can be bought."
a. What is meant by "nutritional status"?
b. Is income per person the only good measure of living
standards? Briefly explain.

c. Why might nutritional status be used as a measure of
living standards? Does it matter that it isn't possible to
buy a greater height? Briefly explain.
From Roderick Floud, et al., *The Changing Body: Health, Nutrition, and
Human Development in the Western World Since 1700,* (Cambridge:
Cambridge University Press, 2011), p. 13.

1.6 In what sense have improvements in the health of the
average American caused the U.S. production possibilities
frontier to shift out? Panel (a) in Figure 5.2 on page 140
indicates that life expectancy in the United States declined
between 1916 and 1918. What effect did this decline in life
expectancy likely have on the U.S. production possibilities
frontier? Briefly explain.

1.7 In *The Elusive Quest for Growth*, William Easterly describes
the bottom poor in Malawi as "the stunted poor, with thin
bodies, short stature . . . , who experience frequent illnesses
and a severe lack of food." He reports that "In the poorest
nations like Burundi, Madagascar, and Uganda, nearly half
of all children under the age of three are abnormally short
because of nutritional deficiency."
a. Why do a "severe lack of food" and "nutritional deficiency" have anything to do with adults being of short
stature and children being abnormally short?
b. Easterly states, "Poverty is not just low GDP; it is dying
babies, starving children . . ." How could rising GDP
per capita decrease the number of dying babies?
Based on William Easterly, *The Elusive Quest for Growth: Economists'
Adventures and Misadventures in the Tropics,* (Cambridge: The MIT
Press, 2001), p. 11 and 14–15.

1.8 How was the public health movement in the United States
in the late nineteenth and early twentieth centuries like a
technological advance to the country's production possibilities frontier?

5.2 **Health Care Around the World,** pages 141–145
LEARNING OBJECTIVE: Compare the health care systems and health care outcomes in the United States and
other countries.

Summary

Health insurance is a contract under which a buyer agrees to make
payments, or premiums, in exchange for the provider's agreeing to
pay some or all of the buyer's medical bills. A majority of people

in the United States live in households that have private health insurance, which they typically obtain through an employer. Other
people have health insurance through the government's Medicare
and Medicaid programs. In 2009, about 17 percent of people in
the United States lacked health insurance. Many health insurance

plans operate on a **fee-for-service** basis under which doctors and hospitals receive a payment for each service they provide. Most countries outside of the United States have greater government involvement in their health care systems. Canada has a **single-payer health care system**, in which the government provides national health insurance to all Canadian residents. In the United Kingdom, the government owns most hospitals and employs most doctors, and the health care system is referred to as **socialized medicine**. The United States spends more per person on health care than do other high-income countries. The United States has lower life expectancy, higher infant mortality, and a greater incidence of obesity than do other high-income countries. The United States has more medical technology per person and has lower mortality rates for people diagnosed with cancer than do other high-income countries. Various problems make it difficult to compare health care outcomes across countries.

MyEconLab   Visit **www.myeconlab.com** to complete these exercises online and get instant feedback.

Review Questions

2.1 Define the following terms:
 a. Health insurance
 b. Fee-for-service
 c. Single-payer health care system
 d. Socialized medicine

2.2 What are the main sources of health insurance in the United States?

2.3 Briefly compare the health care systems in Canada, Japan, and the United Kingdom with the health care system in the United States.

2.4 What is meant by the phrase "health care outcome"? How do health care outcomes in the United States compare with those of other high-income countries? What problems arise in attempting to compare health care outcomes across countries?

Problems and Applications

2.5 If health care is a normal good, would we expect that spending on health care would increase or decrease over time? Briefly explain.

2.6 Why do comparisons in health care outcomes across countries often concentrate on measures such as life expectancy and infant mortality? Are there other measures of the quality of health care systems? Briefly explain.

2.7 Two health care analysts argue that in the United States, "we have arrived at a moment where we are making little headway in defeating various kinds of diseases. Instead, our main achievements today consist of devising ways to marginally extend the lives of the very sick."
 a. Should "marginally extend[ing] the lives of the very sick" be an important goal of a health care system? What other goals should have a higher priority? (*Note:* This question is basically a normative one without a definitive correct or incorrect answer. You are being asked to consider what the goals of a health care system *should be.*)
 b. Would it be possible to measure how successful the health care systems of different countries are in extending the lives of the very sick? If so, how might it be done?

From David Brooks, "Death and Budgets," *New York Times*, July 14, 2011.

5.3

Information Problems and Externalities in the Market for Health Care, pages 145–151
LEARNING OBJECTIVE: Discuss how information problems and externalities affect the market for health care.

Summary

The market for health care is affected by the problem of **asymmetric information**, which occurs when one party to an economic transaction has less information than the other party. **Adverse selection**, the situation in which one party to a transaction takes advantage of knowing more than the other party to the transaction, is a problem for firms selling health insurance policies because it results in less healthy people being more likely to buy insurance than are healthier people. **Moral hazard**, actions people take after they have entered into a transaction that make the other party to the transaction worse off, is also a problem for insurance companies because once people have health insurance they are likely to make more visits to their doctors and in other ways increase their use of medical services. Moral hazard can also involve a **principal–agent problem** in which doctors may order more lab tests, MRI scans, and other procedures than they would if their patients lacked health insurance. Insurance companies use deductibles, copayments, and restrictions on coverage of patients with preexisting conditions to reduce the problems of adverse selection and moral hazard. There may be externalities involved with medicine and health care because, for example,

people who are vaccinated against influenza or other diseases may not receive all of the benefits from having been vaccinated and people who become obese may not bear all of the costs from their obesity.

MyEconLab   Visit **www.myeconlab.com** to complete these exercises online and get instant feedback.

Review Questions

3.1 Define the following terms:
 a. Asymmetric information
 b. Adverse selection
 c. Moral hazard
 d. Principal–agent problem

3.2 What are the asymmetric information problems in the market for health insurance?

3.3 How do health insurance companies deal with asymmetric information problems?

3.4 What is an externality? Are there externalities in the market for health care? Briefly explain.

Problems and Applications

3.5 Suppose you see a 2006 Volkswagen Jetta GLS Turbo Sedan advertised in the campus newspaper for $10,000. If you knew the car was reliable, you would be willing to pay $12,000 for it. If you knew the car was unreliable, you would only be willing to pay $8,000 for it. Under what circumstances should you buy the car?

3.6 What is the "lemons problem"? Is there a lemons problem with health insurance? Briefly explain.

3.7 Michael Kinsley, a political columnist, observes, "The idea of insurance is to share the risks of bad outcomes." In what sense does insurance involve sharing risks? How does the problem of adverse selection affect the ability of insurance to provide the benefit of sharing risk?

From Michael Kinsley, "Congress on Drugs," *Slate*, August 1, 2002.

3.8 Under the Social Security retirement system, the federal government collects a tax on most people's wage income and makes payments to retired workers above a certain age who are covered by the system. (The age to receive full Social Security retirement benefits varies based on the year the worker was born.) The Social Security retirement system is sometimes referred to as a program of social insurance. Is Social Security an insurance program in the same sense as a health insurance policy that a company provides to its workers? Briefly explain.

3.9 **[Related to the** Don't Let This Happen to You **on page 148]** Briefly explain whether you agree with the following statement: "The reluctance of healthy young adults to buy medical insurance creates a moral hazard problem for insurance companies."

3.10 A newspaper editorial observes:

Doctors complain that high malpractice awards drive up their insurance premiums and that they are forced to practice "defensive medicine," ordering unnecessary tests and procedures to protect themselves from possible lawsuits.

Is there another economic explanation for why doctors may end up ordering unnecessary tests and other medical procedures? Briefly explain.

From "Medicaid and the N.Y. Budget: A Bad Deal on Malpractice," *New York Times*, March 12, 2011.

3.11 **[Related to** Solved Problem 5.3 **on page 149]** An article in the *Economist* magazine argues that the real problem with health insurance is:

The healthy people who decide not to buy insurance out of rational self-interest, and who turn out to be right. By not buying insurance, those (largely young) healthy people will be failing to subsidize the people insurance is meant for: the ones who end up getting sick.

a. Why is it rational for healthy people not to buy health insurance?

b. Do you agree that health insurance is meant for people who end up getting sick?

c. Why is the situation described here a problem for a system of health insurance? If it is a problem, suggest possible solutions.

From "Romney on Health Care: To Boldly Go Where He Had Already Been Before," *Economist*, May 13, 2011.

3.12 An article in the *Economist* magazine contains the following description of the "classic adverse selection spiral": "because [health insurance] premiums go higher, healthy people become even less likely to buy insurance, which drives premiums higher yet, and so on until the whole thing winks out. . . ." Why does an adverse selection spiral develop? What steps can insurance companies take to avoid it?

From "Romney on Health Care: To Boldly Go Where He Had Already Been Before," *Economist*, May 13, 2011.

3.13 **[Related to the** Making the Connection **on page 150]** Is health care a public good? Briefly explain. Why does the government directly provide health care in some countries, such as the United Kingdom, but not in others?

3.14 **[Related to the** Making the Connection **on page 150]** Explain whether you agree with the following statement:

Providing health care is obviously a public good. If one person becomes ill and doesn't receive treatment, that person may infect many other people. If many people become ill, then the output of the economy will be negatively affected. Therefore, providing health care is a public good that should be supplied by the government.

5.4   The Debate over Health Care Policy in the United States, pages 152–160

LEARNING OBJECTIVE: Explain the major issues involved in the debate over health care policy in the United States.

Summary

In March 2010, Congress passed the Patient Protection and Affordable Care Act (PPACA), which significantly reorganized the U.S. health care system. Spending on health care in the United States has been growing rapidly as a percentage of GDP, and spending per person on health care has been growing more rapidly than in other high-income countries. Third-party payers, such as employer-provided health insurance and the Medicare and Medicaid programs, have financed an increasing fraction of health care spending, while out-of-pocket payments have sharply declined as a fraction of total health care spending. Several explanations have been offered for the rapid increase in health care spending in the United States: Slow rates of growth of labor productivity in health care may be driving up costs, the U.S. population is becoming older, medical technology and new prescription drugs have higher costs, and the tax system and the reliance on third-party payers have distorted the economic incentives of consumers and suppliers of health care. The PPACA has several important provisions: (1) an individual mandate that requires every resident of the United States to obtain health insurance or be fined; (2) the establishment of health exchanges that will be run by the state governments and provide a means for individuals and small businesses to purchase health insurance; (3) an employer mandate that requires every firm with more than 200 employees to offer health insurance to them; (4) increased regulation of health insurance companies; (5) expansion of eligibility for Medicaid and the establishment of the Independent Payment Advisory Board, which has the power to reduce Medicare payments for prescription drugs and for the use of diagnostic equipment and other technology if Medicare spending exceeds certain levels; and (6) increased taxes on workers with incomes above $200,000. Some critics of the PPACA argue that it does not go far enough in increasing government involvement in the health care system, while other critics argue that health care reform should rely more heavily on **market-based reforms**, which involve changing the market for health care so that it becomes more like the markets for other goods and services.

MyEconLab   Visit **www.myeconlab.com** to complete these exercises online and get instant feedback.

Review Questions

4.1 What is the Patient Protection and Affordable Care Act (PPACA)? Briefly list its major provisions.

4.2 In the United States, what has been the trend in health care spending as a percentage of GDP? Compare the increases in health care spending per person in the United States with the increases in health care spending per person in other high-income countries. What implications do current trends in health care spending have for the growth of federal government spending in the United States?

4.3 Briefly discuss how economists explain the rapid increases in health care spending.

4.4 What arguments do economists and policymakers make who believe that the federal government should have a larger role in the health care system criticize the PPACA?

4.5 What arguments do economists and policymakers make who believe that market-based reforms are the key to improving the health care system criticize the PPACA?

Problems and Applications

4.6 Figure 5.7 on page 155 shows that the Congressional Budget Office forecasts that only about 10 percent of the PPACA-related increase in spending on Medicare as a percentage of GDP will be due to the aging of the population. What factors explain the other 90 percent of the increase?

4.7 Some economists and policymakers have argued that one way to control federal government spending on Medicare is to have a board of experts decide whether new medical technologies are worth their higher costs. If the board decides that they are *not* worth the costs, Medicare would not pay for them. Other economists and policymakers argue that the costs to beneficiaries should more closely represent the costs of providing medical services. This result might be attained by raising premiums, deductibles, and copayments or by "means testing," which would limit the Medicare benefits high-income individuals receive. Political columnist David Brooks has summarized these two ways to restrain the growth of spending on Medicare: "From the top, a body of experts can be empowered to make rationing decisions. . . . Alternatively, at the bottom, costs can be shifted to beneficiaries with premium supports to help them handle the burden."

a. What are "rationing decisions"? How would these decisions restrain the growth of Medicare spending?

b. How would shifting the costs of Medicare to beneficiaries restrain the growth of Medicare spending? What does Brooks mean by "premium supports"?

c. Should Congress and the president be concerned about the growth of Medicare spending? If so, which of these approaches should they adopt or is there a third approach that might be better? (*Note:* This last question is normative and has no definitive answer. It is intended to lead you to consider possible approaches to the Medicare program.)

Based on David Brooks, "The Missing Fifth," *New York Times*, May 9, 2011.

4.8 Ross Douthat, a political columnist, offers the following observations about the Medicare program:

Certainly telling seniors to buy all their own health care is a complete political (and ethical) non-starter. But telling seniors to pay for more of their own health care—well, it's hard to see how else we can hope to reduce Medicare's fiscal burden.

a. What does Douthat mean by Medicare's "fiscal burden"?

b. How could the government change the Medicare program so that seniors would pay for more of their own health care? How would this change restrain growth in the spending on Medicare? How would this change affect very low-income seniors?

Based on Ross Douthat, "We're All Rationers," *New York Times*, May 19, 2011.

4.9 Nobel Laureate Robert Fogel of the University of Chicago has argued, "Expenditures on healthcare are driven by demand, which is spurred by income and by advances in biotechnology that make health interventions increasingly effective."

a. If Fogel is correct, should policymakers be concerned by projected increases in health care spending as a percentage of GDP?

b. What objections do some economists raise to Fogel's analysis of what is driving increases in spending on health care?

Based on Robert Fogel, "Forecasting the Cost of U.S. Healthcare," *The American*, September 3, 2009.

4.10 [**Related to the** Making the Connection **on page 157**] How can providers of some medical services charge hundreds or thousands of dollars more than competitors and remain in business? Why don't patients go to the providers that charge the lower price for the same medical service?

4.11 [**Related to the** Chapter Opener **on page 137**] Why do small firms face more of a problem with risk pooling when buying insurance than do large firms?

4.12 [**Related to the** Making the Connection **on page 159**] How are the state insurance exchanges with the Small Business Health Option Program (SHOP) intended to help small businesses with their problem of limited risk pooling when buying health insurance for their employees? What is the adverse selection death spiral that led to the collapse of the health insurance exchange run by the state of California from 1993 to 2006?

Chapter Outline and Learning Objectives

How Can You Buy a Piece of Facebook?

When Mark Zuckerberg started Facebook in 2004, he was a sophomore in college. Just 5 years later, Facebook had 150 million users. By contrast, it took cell phone companies 15 years to reach 150 million users and 7 years for Apple's iPod to reach that many users. Zuckerberg started Facebook because he believed that people were less interested in meeting new friends online—the assumption built into other sites—than they were in finding a better way of staying in touch with the friends they already had. On Facebook, pages would typically be visible only to people the user had linked to, or "friended," which helped to reduce the problem of fake identities that plagued other sites.

Any business experiencing the runaway success of Facebook quickly develops a need to raise money to finance its expansion. Some businesses raise the funds they need by borrowing from banks. Large firms, as Facebook has become, have the ability to sell stocks and bonds to investors in financial markets. By selling stock, a firm trades partial ownership of the firm in exchange for the funds needed for growth and expansion. Firms that sell stock that is traded in financial markets such as the New York Stock Exchange are called *public firms*, whereas firms that do not sell stock are called *private firms*.

In late 2011, Facebook remained a private firm. However, a small number of its shares are available for sale on private markets but not on public financial markets. Companies such as Facebook often issue shares to their founders, some of their employees, and some private investors. Under federal regulations, holders of these shares can sell them under certain conditions. In mid-2011, stock in Facebook was selling for about $35 per share, which made the total value of the firm about $80 billion.

Because the buying and selling of stock in Facebook was not being done on the public financial markets, the firm was not subject to the usual federal regulations that apply to public firms. Some economists and policymakers argued that the result was less protection for investors. As we will see in this chapter, financial markets are crucial to the health of the economy, and how financial markets should be regulated is an important policy issue.

AN INSIDE LOOK on **page 188** discusses how two new Internet companies allow qualified investors a chance to buy stock in private companies.

Based on Shayndi Raice, "Is Facebook Worth $100 Billion?" *Wall Street Journal*, July 14, 2011; Sarah Morgan, "How to Buy Shares of Facebook," *Wall Street Journal*, January 5, 2011; Jessi Hempel, "How Facebook Is Taking Over Our Lives," *Fortune*, March 11, 2009.

Economics in Your Life

Do Corporate Managers Act in the Best Interests of Shareholders?

Although stockholders legally own corporations, managers often have a great deal of freedom in deciding how corporations are run. As a result, managers can make decisions, such as spending money on large corporate headquarters or decorating their offices with expensive paintings, that are in their interests but not in the interests of the shareholders. If managers make decisions that waste money and lower the profits of a firm, the price of the firm's stock will fall, which hurts the investors who own the stock. Suppose you own stock in a corporation. Why is it difficult to get the managers to act in your interests rather than in their own? Given this problem, should you ever take on the risk of buying stock? As you read the chapter, see if you can answer these questions. You can check your answers against those we provide on **page 187** at the end of this chapter.

I n this chapter, we look at firms: how they are organized, how they raise funds, and the information they provide to investors. As we have discussed in earlier chapters, firms in a market system are responsible for organizing the factors of production to produce goods and services. Firms are the vehicles entrepreneurs use to earn profits. To succeed, entrepreneurs must meet consumers' wants by producing new or better goods and services or by finding ways of producing existing goods and services at a lower cost so they can be sold at a lower price. Entrepreneurs also need access to sufficient funds, and they must be able to efficiently organize production. As the typical firm in many industries has become larger over the past 100 years, the task of efficiently organizing production has become more difficult. In the final section of this chapter, we look at problems of corporate governance that have occurred in recent years. We also look at the steps firms and the government have taken to avoid similar problems in the future.

Categorize the major types of firms in the United States.

Sole proprietorship A firm owned by a single individual and not organized as a corporation.

Partnership A firm owned jointly by two or more persons and not organized as a corporation.

Corporation A legal form of business that provides owners with protection from losing more than their investment should the business fail.

Asset Anything of value owned by a person or a firm.

Limited liability The legal provision that shields owners of a corporation from losing more than they have invested in the firm.

Types of Firms

In studying a market economy, it is important to understand the basics of how firms operate. In the United States, there are three legal categories of firms: *sole proprietorships*, *partnerships*, and *corporations*. A **sole proprietorship** is a firm owned by a single individual. Although most sole proprietorships are small, some employ many workers and earn large profits. **Partnerships** are firms owned jointly by two or more—sometimes many—persons. Most law and accounting firms are partnerships. Some of them can be quite large. For instance, in 2011, the Baker & McKenzie law firm based in Chicago had 1,350 partners. Most large firms, though, are organized as *corporations*. A **corporation** is a legal form of business that provides owners with protection from losing more than their investment should the business fail.

Who Is Liable? Limited and Unlimited Liability

A key distinction among the three types of firms is that the owners of sole proprietorships and partnerships have unlimited liability. Unlimited liability means there is no legal distinction between the personal assets of the owners of the firm and the assets of the firm. An **asset** is anything of value owned by a person or a firm. If a sole proprietorship or a partnership owes a lot of money to the firm's suppliers or employees, the suppliers and employees have a legal right to sue the firm for payment, even if this requires the firm's owners to sell some of their personal assets, such as stocks or bonds. In other words, with sole proprietorships and partnerships, the owners are not legally distinct from the firms they own.

It may only seem fair that the owners of a firm be responsible for a firm's debts. But early in the nineteenth century, it became clear to many state legislatures in the United States that unlimited liability was a significant problem for any firm that was attempting to raise funds from large numbers of investors. An investor might be interested in making a relatively small investment in a firm but be unwilling to become a partner in the firm, for fear of placing at risk all of his or her personal assets if the firm were to fail. To get around this problem, state legislatures began to pass *general incorporation laws*, which allowed firms to be organized as corporations. Under the corporate form of business, the owners of a firm have **limited liability**, which means that if the firm fails, the owners can never lose more than the amount they have invested in the firm. The personal assets of the owners of the firm are not affected by the failure of the firm. In fact, in the eyes of the law, a corporation is a legal "person," separate from its owners. Limited liability has made it possible for corporations to raise funds by issuing shares of stock to large numbers of investors. For example, if you buy a share of Google stock, you are a part owner of the firm, but even if Google were to go bankrupt, you would not be personally responsible

Table 6.1

Differences among Business Organizations

	Sole Proprietorship	Partnership	Corporation
Advantages	• Control by owner • No layers of management	• Ability to share work • Ability to share risks	• Limited personal liability • Greater ability to raise funds
Disadvantages	• Unlimited personal liability • Limited ability to raise funds	• Unlimited personal liability • Limited ability to raise funds	• Costly to organize • Possible double taxation of income

for any of Google's debts. Therefore, you could not lose more than the amount you paid for the stock.

Organizing a firm as a corporation also has some disadvantages. In the United States, corporate profits are taxed twice—once at the corporate level and again when investors receive a share of corporate profits. Corporations generally are larger than sole proprietorships and partnerships and are therefore more difficult to organize and run. Table 6.1 reviews the advantages and disadvantages of different forms of business organization.

Corporations Earn the Majority of Revenue and Profits

Figure 6.1 gives basic statistics on the three types of business organizations. Panel (a) shows that almost three-quarters of all firms are sole proprietorships. Panels (b) and (c) show that although only 18 percent of all firms are corporations, corporations account for a large majority of the revenue and profits earned by all firms. *Profit* is the difference between revenue and the total cost to a firm of producing the goods and services it offers for sale.

There are more than 5.8 million corporations in the United States, but only 35,000 have annual revenues of more than $50 million. We can think of these 35,000 firms—including Microsoft, McDonald's, and Google—as representing "big business." These large firms earn 84 percent of the total profits of all corporations in the United States.

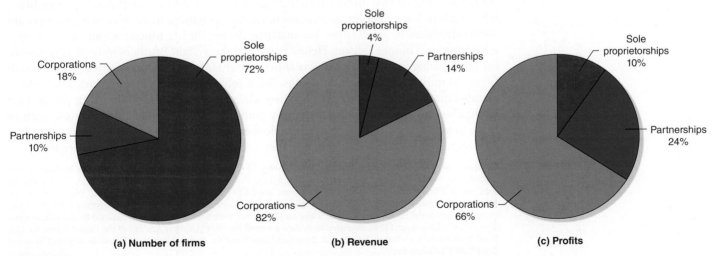

(a) Number of firms   **(b) Revenue**   **(c) Profits**

Figure 6.1   **Business Organizations: Sole Proprietorships, Partnerships, and Corporations**

The three types of firms in the United States are sole proprietorships, partnerships, and corporations. Panel (a) shows that only 18 percent of all firms are corporations. Yet, as panels (b) and (c) show, corporations account for a large majority of the total revenue and profits earned by all firms.

Data from U.S. Census Bureau, *The 2011 Statistical Abstract of the United States.*

Making the Connection | How Important Are Small Businesses to the U.S. Economy?

We have seen that although a large majority of all firms are sole proprietorships, they account for only a small fraction of total revenues and profits earned by all firms. And while 85 percent of all firms employ fewer than 20 workers, fewer than 20 percent of all workers are employed by these firms.

In a typical year, 40 percent of new jobs are created by small firms.

Does this mean that small businesses are unimportant to the U.S. economy?

To the contrary, most economists would argue that small firms are vital to the health of the economy. Starting a small firm provides an entrepreneur with a vehicle for bringing a new product or process to market. Locating the funding to start a small firm is often difficult, though, because a new firm lacks a record of operating profitably, so banks and other lenders are worried that the firm won't be able to pay back borrowed money. As a result, more than 80 percent of small firms are started using funds provided by the founders and their families, by credit cards, or by loans taken out against the value of the founders' homes. While anyone starting a new firm hopes to become successful, perhaps even wealthy, the act of founding a company can also provide employment opportunities for workers and new goods and services for consumers. In a typical year, more than 600,000 new firms open in the United States, and of these, more than 95 percent employ fewer than 20 workers. In a typical year, new small firms create 3.3 million jobs; 40 percent of all new jobs are created by small firms, and in some years more than half are. Strikingly, more than 85 percent of all jobs created by new firms are created by small firms.

Although, on average, jobs at small firms pay lower wages than jobs at large firms and are less likely to provide fringe benefits, such as health insurance and retirement accounts, workers at small firms tend to be younger and, in fact, the first job for many workers is often with a small firm. Small firms are also less likely to lay off workers during a recession than are large firms.

Entrepreneurs founding small firms have been the source of many of the most important new goods and services available to consumers. This is true even though large firms spend much more on research and development than do small firms. Some economists have argued that although spending on research and development by large firms often leads to important improvements in existing products, innovative new products are often introduced by small firms. For instance, during the late nineteenth and early twentieth centuries, Thomas Edison, Henry Ford, and the Wright Brothers were all responsible for introducing important products shortly after starting what were initially very small firms. In more recent years, Bill Gates, Steve Jobs, Michael Dell, and Mark Zuckerberg decided that the best way to develop their ideas was by founding Microsoft, Apple, Dell Computer, and Facebook rather than by going to work for large corporations. Each of these firms began with a handful of employees, and the key products and processes they pioneered were developed long before they evolved into the large firms they are today.

Based on David Neumark, Brandon Wall, and Junfu Zhang, "Do Small Businesses Create More Jobs? New Evidence for the United States from the National Establishment Time Series," *Review of Economics and Statistics*, Vol. 93, No. 1, February 2011, pp. 16-29; Conor Dougherty and Pui-Wing Tam, "Start-Ups Chase Cash as Funds Trickle Back," *Wall Street Journal*, April 1, 2010; Amar Bhidé, *The Origins and Evolution of New Businesses*, New York: Oxford University Press, 2003; Giuseppe Moscarini and Fabien Postel-Vinay, "Large Employers Are More Cyclically Sensitive," National Bureau of Economic Research, Working Paper 14740, February 2009; data are from the 2009 Statistical Abstract of the United States, the U.S. Small Business Administration, and the U.S. Bureau of Labor Statistics. National Bureau of Economic Research Working Paper 13818, February 2008.

MyEconLab   **Your Turn:** Test your understanding by doing related problem 1.8 on page 190 at the end of this chapter.

The Structure of Corporations and the Principal-Agent Problem

6.2 LEARNING OBJECTIVE

Describe the typical management structure of corporations and understand the concepts of separation of ownership from control and the principal-agent problem.

Because large corporations account for most sales and profits in the economy, it is important to know how they are managed. Most large corporations have a similar management structure. The way in which a corporation is structured and the effect that structure has on the corporation's behavior is referred to as **corporate governance**.

Corporate governance The way in which a corporation is structured and the effect that structure has on the corporation's behavior.

Corporate Structure and Corporate Governance

Corporations are legally owned by their *shareholders*, the owners of the corporation's stock. Unlike with a sole proprietorship, a corporation's shareholders, although they are the firm's owners, do not manage the firm directly. Instead, they elect a *board of directors* to represent their interests. The board of directors appoints a *chief executive officer* (CEO) to run the day-to-day operations of the corporation. Sometimes the board of directors also appoints other members of *top management*, such as the *chief financial officer* (CFO). At other times, the CEO appoints other members of top management. Members of top management, including the CEO and CFO, often serve on the board of directors. Members of management serving on the board of directors are referred to as *inside directors*. Members of the board of directors who do not have a direct management role in the firm are referred to as *outside directors*. The outside directors are intended to act as checks on the decisions of top managers, but the distinction between an outside director and an inside director is not always clear. For example, the CEO of a firm that sells a good or service to a large corporation may sit on the board of directors of that corporation. Although technically an outside director, this person may be reluctant to oppose the top managers because they have the power to stop purchasing from his or her firm. In some instances, top managers have effectively controlled their firms' boards of directors.

Unlike the owners of family businesses or private firms such as Facebook, the top management of a large corporation does not generally own a large share of the firm's stock, so large corporations have a **separation of ownership from control**. Although the shareholders actually own the firm, top management controls the firm's day-to-day operations. Because top managers do not own the entire firm, they may decrease the firm's profits by spending money to purchase private jets or schedule management meetings at luxurious resorts. Economists refer to the conflict between the interests of shareholders and the interests of top management as a **principal-agent problem**.[1] This problem occurs when agents—in this case, a firm's top management—pursue their own interests rather than the interests of the principal who hired them—in this case, the shareholders of the corporation. To reduce the effect of the principal-agent problem, many boards of directors in the 1990s began to tie the salaries of top managers to the profits of the firm or to the price of the firm's stock. They hoped this would give top managers an incentive to make the firm as profitable as possible, thereby benefiting its shareholders. Sometimes, though, top managers would take steps that increased the profits of the firm in the short run—and the salaries and bonuses of the top managers—but that actually reduced the profits of the firm in the long run.

Separation of ownership from control A situation in a corporation in which the top management, rather than the shareholders, control day-to-day operations.

Principal-agent problem A problem caused by an agent pursuing his own interests rather than the interests of the principal who hired him.

---

[1]In Chapter 5, we saw that the principal-agent problem arises from moral hazard that can occur because of asymmetric information. In this case, the asymmetric information involves top managers knowing more about how the firm is actually run than do the firm's shareholders.

Solved Problem 6.2

Does the Principal–Agent Problem Apply to the Relationship between Managers and Employees?

Briefly explain whether you agree with the following argument:

> The principal–agent problem applies not just to the relationship between shareholders and top managers. It also applies to the relationship between managers and workers. Just as shareholders have trouble monitoring whether top managers are earning as much profit as possible, managers have trouble monitoring whether employees are working as hard as possible.

Solving the Problem

Step 1: Review the chapter material. This problem concerns the principal–agent problem, so you may want to review the section "Corporate Structure and Corporate Governance" on page 173.

Step 2: Evaluate the argument. You should agree with the argument. A corporation's shareholders have difficulty monitoring the activities of top managers. In practice, they attempt to do so indirectly through the corporation's board of directors. But the firm's top managers may influence—or even control—the firm's board of directors. Even if top managers do not control a board of directors, it may be difficult for the board to know whether actions managers take—such as opening a branch office in Paris—will increase the profitability of the firm or just increase the enjoyment of the top managers.

To answer the problem, we must extend this analysis to the relationship between managers and workers: Managers would like employees to work as hard as possible. Employees would often rather not work hard, particularly if they do not see a direct financial reward for doing so. Managers can have trouble monitoring whether employees are working hard or goofing off. (Is that employee in his cubicle diligently staring at a computer screen because he is hard at work on a report or because he is surfing the Web for sports scores or posting to his Facebook page?) So, the principal–agent problem does apply to the relationship between managers and employees.

Extra Credit: Boards of directors try to reduce the principal–agent problem by designing compensation policies for top managers that give them financial incentives to increase profits. Similarly, managers try to reduce the principal–agent problem by designing compensation policies that give workers an incentive to work harder. For example, some manufacturers pay factory workers on the basis of how much they produce rather than on the basis of how many hours they work.

MyEconLab **Your Turn:** For more practice, do related problems 2.7 and 2.8 on page 191 at the end of this chapter.

6.3 LEARNING OBJECTIVE

Explain how firms raise the funds they need to operate and expand.

How Firms Raise Funds

Owners and managers of firms try to earn a profit. To earn a profit, a firm must raise funds to pay for its operations, including paying its employees and buying or renting computers and other machinery and equipment. Indeed, a central challenge for anyone running a firm, whether that person is a sole proprietor or a top manager of a large corporation, is raising the funds needed to operate and expand the business. Suppose you decide to open an online social networking site, using $100,000 you have saved in a bank.

You use the $100,000 to rent a building for your firm, to buy computers, and to pay other start-up expenses. Your firm is a great success, and you decide to expand by moving to a larger building and buying more computers. As the owner of a small business, you can raise the funds for this expansion in three ways:

1. If you are making a profit, you could reinvest the profits back into your firm. Profits that are reinvested in a firm rather than taken out of a firm and paid to the firm's owners are *retained earnings*.
2. You could raise funds by recruiting additional owners to invest in the firm. This arrangement would increase the firm's *financial capital*.
3. Finally, you could borrow the funds from relatives, friends, or a bank.

The managers of a large public firm have some additional ways to raise funds, as we will see in the next section.

Sources of External Funds

Unless firms rely on retained earnings, they have to raise the *external funds* they need from others who have funds available to invest. It is the role of an economy's *financial system* to transfer funds from savers to borrowers—directly through financial markets or indirectly through financial intermediaries such as banks.

Most firms raise external funds in two ways. The first way relies on financial intermediaries such as banks and is called **indirect finance**. If you put $1,000 in a checking account or a savings account, or if you put money in a $1,000 certificate of deposit (CD), the bank will loan most of those funds to borrowers. The bank will combine your funds with those of other depositors and, for example, make a $100,000 loan to a local business. Small businesses rely heavily on bank loans as their primary source of external funds.

> **Indirect finance** A flow of funds from savers to borrowers through financial intermediaries such as banks. Intermediaries raise funds from savers to lend to firms (and other borrowers).

A second way for firms to acquire external funds is through *financial markets*. Raising funds in these markets, such as the New York Stock Exchange on Wall Street in New York, is called **direct finance**. Direct finance usually takes the form of the borrower selling the lender a *financial security*. A financial security is a document—sometimes in electronic form—that states the terms under which the funds have passed from the buyer of the security (who is lending funds) to the borrower. *Bonds* and *stocks* are the two main types of financial securities. Typically, only large corporations are able to sell bonds and stocks on financial markets. Investors are generally unwilling to buy securities issued by small and medium-sized firms because the investors lack sufficient information on the financial health of smaller firms.

> **Direct finance** A flow of funds from savers to firms through financial markets, such as the New York Stock Exchange.

Bonds **Bonds** are financial securities that represent promises to repay a fixed amount of funds. When General Electric (GE) sells a bond to raise funds, it promises to pay the purchaser of the bond an interest payment each year for the term of the bond, as well as a final payment of the amount of the loan, or the *principal*, at the end of the term. GE may need to raise many millions of dollars to build a factory, but each individual bond has a principal, or *face value*, of $1,000, which is the amount each bond purchaser is lending GE. So, GE must sell many bonds to raise all the funds it needs. Suppose GE promises it will pay interest of $60 per year to anyone who buys one of its bonds. The interest payments on a bond are referred to as **coupon payments**. The **interest rate** is the cost of borrowing funds, usually expressed as a percentage of the amount borrowed. If we express the coupon as a percentage of the face value of the bond, we find the interest rate on the bond, called the *coupon rate*. In this case, the interest rate is:

> **Bond** A financial security that represents a promise to repay a fixed amount of funds.

> **Coupon payment** An interest payment on a bond.

> **Interest rate** The cost of borrowing funds, usually expressed as a percentage of the amount borrowed.

$$\frac{\$60}{\$1,000} = 0.06, \text{ or } 6\%$$

Many bonds that corporations issue have terms, or *maturities*, of 30 years. In this example, if you bought a bond from GE, GE would pay you $60 per year for 30 years, and at the end of the thirtieth year, GE would repay the $1,000 principal to you.

The interest rate that a borrower selling a bond has to pay depends on how likely bond buyers—investors—think that the bond seller is to default, or not make the promised coupon or principal payments. The higher the *default risk* on a bond, the higher the interest rate. For example, investors see the federal government as being very unlikely to default on its bonds, so federal government bonds pay a lower interest rate than do bonds of a firm such as GE. In turn, GE pays a lower interest rate on its bonds than does a corporation that investors believe is not as likely to make its bond payments.

| Making the Connection | **The Rating Game: Is the U.S. Treasury Likely to Default on Its Bonds?** |

Federal regulations require that before they can sell bonds to investors, firms and governments must first have bonds rated by one of the credit rating agencies. The three largest rating agencies are Moody's Investors Service, Standard & Poor's Corporation, and Fitch Ratings. These private firms rate bonds by giving them letter grades—AAA or Aaa being the highest—that reflect the probability that the firm or government will be able to make the payments on the bond. The following table shows the ratings:

	Moody's Investors Service	Standard & Poor's (S&P)	Fitch Ratings	Meaning of the Ratings
Investment-grade bonds	Aaa	AAA	AAA	Highest credit quality
	Aa	AA	AA	Very high credit quality
	A	A	A	High credit quality
	Baa	BBB	BBB	Good credit quality
Non-investment-grade bonds	Ba	BB	BB	Speculative
	B	B	B	Highly speculative
	Caa	CCC	CCC	Substantial default risk
	Ca	CC	CC	Very high levels of default risk
	C	C	C	Exceptionally high levels of default risk
	—	D	D	Default

Note: The entries in the "Meaning of the Ratings" column are slightly modified from those that Fitch uses. The other two rating agencies have similar descriptions. For each rating from Aa to Caa, Moody's adds a numerical modifier of 1, 2, or 3. The rating Aa1 is higher than the rating Aa2, and the rating Aa2 is higher than the rating Aa3. Similarly, Standard & Poor's and Fitch Ratings add a plus (+) or minus (–) sign. The rating AA+ is higher than the rating AA, and the rating AA is higher than the rating AA–.

Source: *Money, Banking, and the Financial System* 1st edition by R. Glenn Hubbard and Anthony P. O'Brien. Copyright © 2012 by Pearson Education, Inc. Reprinted and Electronically reproduced by permission of Pearson Education, Inc., Upper Saddle River, New Jersey.

Investors can use the ratings in deciding how much risk they are willing to take on when buying a bond. Generally, the lower the rating, the higher the interest rate an investor will receive, but also the higher the risk that the issuer of the bond will default.

The ratings agencies charge firms and governments—rather than investors—for their services. This arrangement raises the question of whether rating agencies face a conflict of interest. Because firms issuing bonds can choose which of the agencies to hire to rate their bonds, the agencies may have an incentive to give higher ratings than might be justified in order to keep the firms' business. During the housing boom of the mid-2000s, some financial firms issued *mortgage-backed bonds*. These bonds were similar to regular corporate bonds except that the interest payments came from mortgage loans people had taken out to buy houses. The money from those mortgage payments was passed along to investors who had bought the mortgage-backed bonds. The rating agencies gave many of these bonds AAA ratings, even though when housing prices began to decline in 2006, the issuers of many of these bonds defaulted on them. Some economists and policymakers believe the rating agencies provided the high ratings primarily to ensure that the firms that issued them would continue to hire them.

Standard & Poor's (S&P) became involved in another controversy in August 2011, when it downgraded U.S. Treasury bonds from AAA to AA+. This was the first time since the rating agencies had begun rating Treasury bonds that any of them had given Treasury bonds less than a AAA rating. The reason for the rating downgrade was the state of the federal government's budget deficit. Whenever the federal government runs a budget deficit, the Treasury must borrow an amount equal to the deficit by issuing bonds. In 2011, the federal government was spending much more than it was collecting in taxes, resulting in a large budget deficit. The budget deficit reflected the lower tax receipts and increased government spending resulting from the 2007–2009 economic recession. But forecasts from the U.S. Congressional Budget Office indicated that even after the effects of the recession had disappeared, large budget deficits would remain because spending on Social Security, Medicare, Medicaid, and other government programs were expected to increase faster than tax revenues. When prolonged negotiations between President Barack Obama and Congress failed to make much of a dent in the problem, S&P announced the rating downgrade. In the days following the announcement, interest rates on Treasury bonds actually fell rather than rising, as might have been expected if investors had believed that a default was possible.

So, is it likely that the U.S. Treasury will default on its bonds? S&P argued that while a default is still unlikely, the continuing large deficits increased the chance that someday the Treasury might not make the interest payments on its bonds. Like the Ghost of Christmas Yet to Come in Charles Dickens's *A Christmas Carol*, S&P was giving a warning of something that might happen rather than something that necessarily must happen.

Based on Tom Lauricella, Matt Phillips and Serena Ng, "Markets Brace for Downgrade's Toll," *Wall Street Journal*, August 8, 2011; and Andrew Ross Sorkin, "S.E.C. Urges Changes to Ratings-Agency Rules," *New York Times*, August, 29, 2010.

Your Turn: Test your understanding by doing related problem 3.8 on page 192 at the end of this chapter.

MyEconLab

Stocks When you buy a newly issued bond from a firm, you are lending funds to that firm. When you buy **stock** issued by a firm, you are actually buying part ownership of the firm. When a corporation sells stock, it is doing the same thing the owner of a small business does when she takes on a partner: The firm is increasing its financial capital by bringing additional owners into the firm. Any individual shareholder usually owns only a small fraction of the total shares of stock issued by a corporation.

> **Stock** A financial security that represents partial ownership of a firm.

A shareholder is entitled to a share of the corporation's profits, if there are any. Corporations generally keep some of their profits—known as retained earnings—to finance future expansion. The remaining profits are paid to shareholders as **dividends**. Investors hope that a firm will earn economic profits by using its retained earnings to grow, causing the firm's share price to rise, and providing a *capital gain* for investors. If a corporation is unable to make a profit, it usually does not pay a dividend. Under the law, corporations must make payments on any debt they have before making payments to their owners. That is, a corporation must make promised payments to bondholders before it can make any dividend payments to shareholders. In addition, when firms sell stock, they acquire from investors an open-ended commitment of funds to the firm.

> **Dividends** Payments by a corporation to its shareholders.

Unlike bonds, stocks do not have a maturity date, so the firm is not obliged to return the investor's funds at any particular date.

Stock and Bond Markets Provide Capital— and Information

The original purchasers of stocks and bonds may resell them to other investors. In fact, most of the buying and selling of stocks and bonds that takes place each day involves investors reselling existing stocks and bonds to each other rather than corporations selling new stocks and bonds to investors. The buyers and sellers of stocks and bonds together make up the *stock and bond markets*. There is no single place where stocks and bonds are bought and sold. Some trading of stocks and bonds takes place in buildings known as *exchanges*, such as the New York Stock Exchange or the Tokyo Stock Exchange. In the United States, the stocks and bonds of the largest corporations are traded on the New York Stock Exchange. The development of computer technology has spread the trading of stocks and bonds outside exchanges to *securities dealers* linked by computers. These dealers comprise the *over-the-counter market*. The stocks of many computer and other high-technology firms—including Apple, Google, and Microsoft—are traded in the most important of the over-the-counter markets, the *National Association of Securities Dealers Automated Quotations* system, which is referred to by its acronym, NASDAQ.

Shares of stock represent claims on the profits of the firms that issue them. Therefore, as the fortunes of the firms change and they earn more or less profit, the prices of the stock the firms have issued should also change. Similarly, bonds represent claims to receive coupon payments and one final payment of principal. Therefore, a particular bond that was issued in the past may have its price go up or down, depending on whether the coupon payments being offered on newly issued bonds are higher or lower than on existing bonds. If you hold a bond with a coupon of $40 per year, and newly issued bonds have coupons of $50 per year, the price of your bond will fall because it is less attractive to investors. The price of a bond will also be affected by changes in default risk, or the investors' perceptions of the issuing firm's ability to make the coupon payments. For example, if investors begin to believe that a firm may soon go out of business and stop making coupon payments to its bondholders, the price of the firm's bonds will fall to very low levels.

Changes in the value of a firm's stocks and bonds offer important information for a firm's managers, as well as for investors. An increase in the stock price means that investors are more optimistic about the firm's profit prospects, and the firm's managers might want to expand the firm's operations as a result. By contrast, a decrease in the firm's stock price indicates that investors are less optimistic about the firms' profit

Don't Let This Happen to You

When Google Shares Change Hands, Google Doesn't Get the Money

Google is a popular investment, with investors buying and selling shares often as their views about the value of the firm shift. That's great for Google, right? Think of all that money flowing into Google's coffers as shares change hands and the stock price goes up. *Wrong.* Google raises funds in a primary market, but shares change hands in a secondary market. Those trades don't put money into Google's hands, but they do give important information to the firm's managers. Let's see why.

Primary markets are those in which newly issued claims are sold to initial buyers by the issuer. Businesses can raise funds in a primary financial market in two ways—by borrowing (selling bonds) or by selling shares of stock—which result in different types of claims on the borrowing firm's future income. Although you may hear about the stock market fluctuations every day in news updates, bonds actually account for more of the funds raised by borrowers. The total value of bonds in the United States is typically about twice the value of stocks.

In *secondary markets*, stocks and bonds that have already been issued are sold by one investor to another. If

Google sells shares to the public, it is turning to a primary market for new funds. Once Google shares are issued, investors trade the shares in the secondary market. Google does not receive any new funds when Google shares are traded on secondary markets. The initial seller of a stock or bond raises funds from a lender only in the primary market. Secondary markets convey information to firms' managers and to investors by determining the price of stocks and bonds. For example, a major increase in Google's stock price conveys the market's good feelings about the firm, and the firm may decide to raise funds to expand. So, secondary markets are valuable sources of information for corporations that are considering raising funds.

Primary and secondary markets are both important, but they play different roles. As an investor, you principally trade stocks and bonds in a secondary market. As a corporate manager, you may help decide how to raise new funds to expand the firm where you work.

MyEconLab

Your Turn: Test your understanding by doing related problem 3.12 on page 192 at the end of this chapter.

prospects, so management may want to shrink the firm's operations. Likewise, changes in the value of the firm's bonds imply changes in the cost of external funds to finance the firm's investment in research and development or in new factories. A higher bond price indicates a lower cost of new external funds, while a lower bond price indicates a higher cost of new external funds.

Why Do Stock Prices Fluctuate So Much?

The performance of the U.S. stock market is often measured using *stock market indexes*. Stock market indexes are averages of stock prices with the value of the index set equal to 100 in a particular year, called the *base year*. Because the stock indexes are intended to show movements in prices from one year to the next, rather than the actual dollar values of the underlying stocks, the year chosen for the base year is unimportant. Figure 6.2 shows movements from January 1995 to September 2011 in the three most widely followed stock indexes:

- The Dow Jones Industrial Average, which is an index of the stock prices of 30 large U.S. corporations.

- The S&P 500, which is an index prepared by Standard & Poor's Corporation and includes the stock prices of 500 large U.S. firms.

- The NASDAQ Composite Index, which includes the stock prices of the more than 4,000 firms whose shares are traded in the NASDAQ stock market. NASDAQ is an "over-the-counter" market, meaning that buying and selling on NASDAQ is carried out between dealers who are linked together by computer. The listings on NASDAQ are dominated by high-tech firms such as Apple, Microsoft, and Google.

As we have seen, ownership of a firm's stock represents a claim on the firm's profits. So, the larger the firm's profits are, the higher its stock price will be. When the overall economy is expanding, incomes, employment, and spending will all increase, as will corporate profits. When the economy is in a recession, incomes, employment, and spending will fall, as will corporate profits. We would expect that stock prices will rise when the economy is expanding and fall when the economy is in recession. We see this pattern reflected in the three stock market indexes in Figure 6.2. All three indexes follow a roughly similar pattern: Increases in stock prices during the economic expansion of the late 1990s, declines after the "dot-com crash" of 2000 and the recession of 2001, increases from late 2001 to late 2007, declines as the U.S. economy entered a recession at the end of 2007, and then increases beginning in early 2009.

The stock prices of many early Internet companies soared in the late 1990s, as some analysts made what turned out to be overly optimistic predictions about how rapidly

(a) Dow Jones Industrial Average   (b) S&P 500   (c) NASDAQ

Figure 6.2 Movements in Stock Market Indexes, January 1995 to September 2011

The performance of the U.S. stock market is often measured by market indexes, which are averages of stock prices. The three most important indexes are the Dow Jones Industrial Average, the S&P 500, and the NASDAQ. During the period from 1995 to 2011, the three indexes followed similar patterns, rising when the U.S. economy was expanding and falling when the economy was in recession.

online retailing would grow. In 2000, when investors came to believe that many dot-coms would never be profitable, their stock prices crashed. Because the NASDAQ is dominated by high-tech stocks, it experienced greater swings during the dot-com boom and bust of the late 1990s and early 2000s than did the other two indexes. The sharp declines in all three indexes beginning in late 2007 reflected the severity of the recession that began in December of that year. The severity of the recession was due in part to problems with financial firms, which we will discuss later in this chapter.

Making the Connection	**Following Abercrombie & Fitch's Stock Price in the Financial Pages**

If you read the online stock listings on the *Wall Street Journal's* web site or on another site, you will notice that the listings pack into a small space a lot of information about what happened to stocks during the previous day's trading. The figure on the next page reproduces a small portion of the listings from the *Wall Street Journal* from August 9, 2011, for stocks listed on the New York Stock Exchange. The listings provide information on the buying and selling of the stock of five firms during the previous day. Let's focus on the highlighted listing for Abercrombie & Fitch, the clothing store, and examine the information in each column:

- The first column gives the name of the company.
- The second column gives the firm's "ticker" symbol (ANF), which you may have seen scrolling along the bottom of the screen on cable financial news channels.
- The third column (Open) gives the price (in dollars) of the stock at the time that trading began, which is 9:30 A.M. on the New York Stock Exchange. Abercrombie & Fitch opened for trading at a price of $67.85.
- The fourth column (High) and the fifth column (Low) give the highest price and the lowest price the stock sold for during the day.
- The sixth column (Close) gives the price the stock sold for the last time it was traded before the close of trading (4:00 P.M.), which in this case was $61.05.
- The seventh column (Net Chg) gives the amount by which the closing price changed from the closing price the day before. In this case, the price of Abercrombie & Fitch's stock had fallen by $9.25 per share from its closing price the day before. Changes in Abercrombie & Fitch's stock price give the firm's managers a signal that they may want to expand or contract the firm's operations.
- The eighth column (%Chg) gives the change in the price in percentage terms rather than in dollar terms.
- The ninth column (Vol) gives the number of shares of stock traded on the previous day.
- The tenth column (52 Week High) and the eleventh column (52 Week Low) give the highest price the stock has sold for and the lowest price the stock has sold for during the previous year. These numbers tell how *volatile* the stock price is—that is, how much it fluctuates over the course of the year. In this case, Abercrombie's stock had been quite volatile, rising as high as $78.25 per share and falling as low as $33.97 per share. These large fluctuations in price are an indication of how risky investing in the stock market can be.
- The twelfth column (Div) gives the dividend, expressed in dollars. In this case, 0.70 means that Abercrombie paid a dividend of $0.70 per share.
- The thirteenth column (Yield) gives the *dividend yield*, which is calculated by dividing the dividend by the *closing price* of the stock—that is, the price at which Abercrombie's stock last sold before the close of trading on the previous day.
- The fourteenth column (PE) gives the *P-E ratio* (or *price–earnings ratio*), which is calculated by dividing the price of the firm's stock by its earnings per share. (Remember that because firms retain some earnings, earnings per share is not necessarily the same as dividends per share.) Abercrombie's P-E ratio was 37, meaning that its price per share was 37 times its earnings per share. So, you would have to pay $37 to buy $1 of Abercrombie & Fitch's earnings.

- The final column (Year-To-Date %Chg) gives the percentage change in the price of the stock from the beginning of the year to the previous day. In this case, the price of Abercrombie's stock had fallen by 5.9 percent since the beginning of 2011.

	Symbol	Open	High	Low	Close	Net Chg	%Chg	Vol	52 Week High	52 Week Low	Div	Yield	PE	Year-To-Date %Chg
ABB ADS	ABB	20.60	20.89	19.59	19.59	-2.00	-9.26	7,134,463	27.58	18.53	0.64	3.3	16	-12.7
ABBOTT LABORATORIES	ABT	49.30	50.13	47.56	48.06	-2.17	-4.32	18,398,789	54.24	45.07	1.92	4.0	17	0.3
ABERCROMBIE & FITCH CO.	ANF	67.85	68.93	58.84	61.05	-9.25	-13.16	6,891,113	78.25	33.97	0.70	1.15	37	-5.9
ABITIBIBOWATER	ABH	16.11	16.18	15.58	15.72	-0.96	-5.76	1,703,003	30.54	15.58	...	...	...	-33.6
ABM INDUSTRIES	ABM	19.79	20.72	17.29	17.29	-3.34	-16.19	1,762,427	27.14	17.29	0.56	3.2	16	-34.26

Source: "Abercrombie and Fitch Stock History" from *The Wall Street Journal*. Copyright © 2011 by *Dow Jones & Company, Inc.* Reproduced with permission of *Dow Jones & Company, Inc.*

Your Turn: Test your understanding by doing related problems 3.13 and 3.14 on pages 192–193 at the end of this chapter.

MyEconLab

Using Financial Statements to Evaluate a Corporation

6.4 LEARNING OBJECTIVE

Understand the information provided in corporations' financial statements.

To raise funds, a firm's managers must persuade banks or buyers of its stocks or bonds that it will be profitable. Before a firm can sell new issues of stocks or bonds, it must first provide investors and financial regulators with information about its finances. To borrow from a bank or another financial intermediary, the firm must disclose financial information to the lender as well.

In most high-income countries, government agencies require firms to disclose specific financial information to the public before they are allowed to sell securities such as stocks or bonds in financial markets. In the United States, the Securities and Exchange Commission requires publicly owned firms to report their performance in financial statements prepared using standard accounting methods, often referred to as *generally accepted accounting principles*. Such disclosure reduces information costs, but it doesn't eliminate them—for two reasons. First, some firms may be too young to have much information for potential investors to evaluate. Second, managers may try to present the required information in the best possible light so that investors will overvalue their securities.

Private firms also collect information on business borrowers and sell the information to lenders and investors. If the information-gathering firm does a good job, lenders and investors purchasing the information will be better able to judge the quality of borrowing firms. Firms specializing in information—including Moody's Investors Service, Standard & Poor's Corporation, Value Line, and Dun & Bradstreet—collect information from businesses and sell it to subscribers. Buyers include individual investors, libraries, and financial intermediaries. You can find some of these publications in your college library or through online information services.

What kind of information do investors and firm managers need? A firm must answer three basic questions: What to produce? How to produce it? and What price to charge? To answer these questions, a firm's managers need two pieces of information: The first is

Liability Anything owed by a person or a firm.

the firm's revenues and costs, and the second is the value of the property and other assets the firm owns and the firm's debts, or other **liabilities**, that it owes to other persons and firms. Potential investors in the firm also need this information to decide whether to buy the firm's stocks or bonds. This information is contained in the firm's *financial statements*, principally its income statement and balance sheet, which we discuss next.

The Income Statement

Income statement A financial statement that sums up a firm's revenues, costs, and profit over a period of time.

A firm's **income statement** sums up its revenues, costs, and profit over a period of time. Corporations issue annual income statements, although the 12-month *fiscal year* covered may be different from the calendar year to better represent the seasonal pattern of the business. We explore income statements in greater detail in the appendix to this chapter.

Getting to Accounting Profit An income statement shows a firm's revenue, costs, and profit for the firm's fiscal year. To determine profitability, the income statement starts with the firm's revenue and subtracts its operating expenses and taxes paid. The remainder, *net income*, is the **accounting profit** of the firm.

Accounting profit A firm's net income, measured as revenue minus operating expenses and taxes paid.

. . . And Economic Profit Accounting profit provides information on a firm's current net income, measured according to accepted accounting standards. Accounting profit is not, however, the ideal measure of a firm's profits because it neglects some of the firm's costs. By taking into account all costs, *economic profit* provides a better indication than accounting profit of how successful a firm is. Firms making an economic profit will remain in business and may even expand. Firms making an *economic loss* are unlikely to remain in business in the long run. To understand how economic profit is calculated, remember that economists always measure cost as *opportunity cost*. The **opportunity cost** of any activity is the highest-valued alternative that must be given up to engage in that activity. Costs are either *explicit* or *implicit*. When a firm spends money, an **explicit cost** results. If a firm incurs an opportunity cost but does not spend money, an **implicit cost** results. For example, firms incur an explicit labor cost when they pay wages to employees. Firms have many other explicit costs as well, such as the cost of the electricity used to light their buildings or the costs of advertising or insurance.

Opportunity cost The highest-valued alternative that must be given up to engage in an activity.

Explicit cost A cost that involves spending money.

Implicit cost A nonmonetary opportunity cost.

Some costs are implicit, however. The most important of these is the opportunity cost to investors of the funds they have invested in the firm. Economists use the term *nominal rate of return* to refer to the minimum amount that investors must earn on the funds they invest in a firm, expressed as a percentage of the amount invested. If a firm fails to provide investors with at least a normal rate of return, it will not be able to remain in business over the long run because investors will not continue to invest their funds in the firm. For example, Bethlehem Steel was once the second-leading producer of steel in the United States and a very profitable firm, with stock that sold for more than $50 per share. By 2002, investors became convinced that the firm's uncompetitive labor costs in world markets meant that the firm would never be able to provide investors with a normal rate of return. Many investors expected that the firm would eventually have to declare bankruptcy, and as a result, the price of Bethlehem Steel's stock plummeted to $1 per share. Shortly thereafter, the firm declared bankruptcy, and its remaining assets were sold off to a competing steel firm. The return (in dollars) that investors require to continue investing in a firm is a true cost to the firm and should be subtracted from the firm's revenues to calculate its profits.

The necessary rate of return that investors must receive to continue investing in a firm varies from firm to firm. If the investment is risky—as would be the case with a biotechnology start-up—investors may require a high rate of return to compensate them for the risk. Investors in firms in more established industries, such as electric utilities, may require lower rates of return. The exact rate of return investors require to invest in any particular firm is difficult to calculate, which also makes it difficult for an accountant to include the return as a cost on an income statement. Firms have other implicit costs besides the return investors require that can also be difficult to calculate. As a result, the rules of accounting generally require that only explicit costs be included in the firm's financial records. *Economic costs* include both explicit costs *and* implicit costs. **Economic profit** is equal to a firm's revenues minus its economic costs. Because accounting profit excludes some implicit costs, it is larger than economic profit.

Economic profit A firm's revenues minus all of its implicit and explicit costs.

The Balance Sheet

A firm's **balance sheet** sums up its financial position on a particular day, usually the end of a quarter or year. Recall that an asset is anything of value that a firm owns, and a liability is a debt or an obligation owed by a firm. Subtracting the value of a firm's liabilities from the value of its assets leaves its *net worth*. We can think of the net worth as what the firm's owners would be left with if the firm were closed, its assets were sold, and its liabilities were paid off. Investors can determine a firm's net worth by inspecting its balance sheet. We analyze a balance sheet in more detail in the appendix to this chapter, which begins on page 195.

Balance sheet A financial statement that sums up a firm's financial position on a particular day, usually the end of a quarter or year.

Corporate Governance Policy and the Financial Crisis of 2007–2009

6.5 LEARNING OBJECTIVE

Discuss the role that corporate governance problems may have played in the financial crisis of 2007–2009.

A firm's financial statements provide important information on the firm's ability to create value for investors and the economy. Accurate and easy-to-understand financial statements are inputs to decisions by the firm's managers and by investors. Indeed, the information in accounting statements helps guide resource allocation in the economy.

Firms disclose financial statements in periodic filings to the federal government and in *annual reports* to shareholders. An investor is more likely to buy a firm's stock if the firm's income statement shows a large after-tax profit and if its balance sheet shows a large net worth. The top management of a firm has at least two reasons to attract investors and keep the firm's stock price high. First, a higher stock price increases the funds the firm can raise when it sells a given amount of stock. Second, to reduce the principal–agent problem, boards of directors often tie the salaries of top managers to the firm's stock price or to the profitability of the firm.

Top managers clearly have an incentive to maximize the profits reported on the income statement and the net worth reported on the balance sheet. If top managers make good decisions, the firm's profits will be high, and the firm's assets will be large relative to its liabilities. Problems that surfaced during the early 2000s, however, revealed that some top managers have inflated profits and hidden liabilities that should have been listed on their balance sheets. At other firms, managers took on more risk than they disclosed to investors. We will explore recent problems with corporate governance, and the government's reaction to these problems, by discussing the accounting scandals of the early 2000s and problems that many financial firms encountered during 2007–2009.

The Accounting Scandals of the Early 2000s

In the early 2000s, the top managers of several large and well-known firms, including Enron, an energy trading firm, and WorldCom, a telecommunications firm, were shown to have falsified their firms' financial statements in order to mislead investors about how profitable the firms actually were. Several top managers were sentenced to long jail terms, and some of the firms, including Enron, went out of business.

How was it possible for corporations such as Enron and WorldCom to falsify their financial statements? The federal government regulates how financial statements are prepared, but this regulation cannot by itself guarantee the accuracy of the statements. All firms that issue stock to the public have certified public accountants *audit* their financial statements. Unfortunately, as the Enron and WorldCom scandals revealed, top managers who are determined to deceive investors about the true financial condition of their firms can also deceive outside auditors.

To guard against future scandals, new federal legislation was enacted in 2002. The landmark *Sarbanes-Oxley Act of 2002* requires that CEOs personally certify the accuracy of financial statements. The Sarbanes-Oxley Act also requires that financial analysts and auditors disclose whether any conflicts of interest might exist that would limit their independence in evaluating a firm's financial condition. On balance, most observers acknowledge that the Sarbanes-Oxley Act increased confidence in the U.S. corporate governance system. However, as we will discuss in the next section, problems during 2007–2009 at financial firms again raised questions of whether corporations were adequately disclosing information to investors.

The Financial Crisis of 2007–2009

Beginning in 2007 and lasting into 2009, the U.S. economy suffered the worst financial crisis since the Great Depression of the 1930s. At the heart of the crisis was a problem in the market for home mortgages. When people buy houses, they typically borrow the money by taking out a mortgage loan from a bank or another financial institution. The house they are buying is pledged as collateral for the loan, meaning that the bank can take possession of the house and sell it if the borrower defaults by failing to make the payments on the loan.

For many years, the bank or other financial institution granting a mortgage would keep the loan until the borrower had paid it off. Beginning in the 1970s, financial institutions began *securitizing* some mortgage loans, which means that groups of mortgages were bundled together and sold to investors. These *mortgage-backed securities* are very similar to bonds in that the investor who buys one receives regular interest payments, which in this case come from the payments being made on the original mortgage loans. At first, the securitization process was carried out by the Federal National Mortgage Association ("Fannie Mae") and the Federal Home Loan Mortgage Corporation ("Freddie Mac"), which Congress had established to help increase the volume of lending in the home mortgage market. Fannie Mae and Freddie Mac would buy mortgages granted to credit-worthy borrowers and bundle them into securities that were then sold to investors.

Beginning in the 1990s, private financial firms, primarily investment banks, started to securitize mortgages. By the early 2000s, many mortgages were being granted by banks and other financial institutions to "subprime" borrowers, who are borrowers whose credit histories include failures to make payments on bills, and "Alt-A" borrowers, who failed to document that their incomes were high enough to afford their mortgage payments. Both subprime and Alt-A borrowers were more likely to default on loans than were conventional borrowers. Fueled by the ease of obtaining a mortgage, housing prices in the United States soared before beginning a sharp downturn in mid-2006. By 2007, many borrowers—particularly subprime and Alt-A borrowers—began to default on their mortgages. This was bad news for anyone owning mortgage-backed securities because the value of these securities depended on steady payments being made on the underlying mortgages. As prices of these securities plunged, many financial institutions suffered heavy losses, and some of the largest of them remained in business only because they received aid from the federal government.

During the financial crisis, many investors complained that they weren't aware of the riskiness of some of the assets—particularly mortgage-backed securities—on the balance sheets of financial firms. Some observers believed that the managers of many financial firms had intentionally misled investors about the riskiness of these assets. Others argued that the managers themselves had not understood how risky the assets were. In the fall of 2008, Fannie Mae and Freddie Mac were brought under direct control of the government. As the crisis passed, in July 2010, Congress overhauled regulation of the financial system with the passage of the **Wall Street Reform and Consumer Protection Act**, referred to as the Dodd-Frank Act. Among its provisions, the act created the Consumer Financial Protection Bureau, housed in the Federal Reserve, to write rules intended to protect consumers in their borrowing and investing activities. The act also established the Financial Stability Oversight Council, which includes representatives from all the major federal financial regulatory bodies, including the SEC and the Federal Reserve. The council is intended to identify and act on risks to the financial system. Economists are divided in their opinions about whether the Dodd-Frank Act would significantly reduce the risk of future financial crises.

Wall Street Reform and Consumer Protection Act (Dodd-Frank Act) Legislation passed during 2010 that was intended to reform regulation of the financial system.

Did Principal–Agent Problems Help Bring on the Financial Crisis?

As we have seen, the process of securitizing mortgages played an important role in the financial crisis of 2007–2009. Beginning in the 1990s, private investment banks began to securitize mortgages. Unlike commercial banks, whose main activities are accepting deposits and making loans, investment banks had traditionally concentrated on providing advice to corporations on selling new stocks and bonds and on *underwriting* the issuance of stocks and bonds by guaranteeing a price to the firm selling them. Investment banking is considered more risky than commercial banking because investment banks can suffer heavy losses on underwriting. To address this greater risk, Congress passed the Glass-Steagall Act in 1933. The act prevented financial firms from being both commercial banks and investment banks.

Some economists and policymakers argued that Glass-Steagall reduced competition for investment banking services by prohibiting commercial banks from offering these services. Congress repealed the Glass-Steagall Act in 1999, after which some commercial banks began engaging in investment banking. Many of the largest, best-known investment banks, such as Lehman Brothers, Bear Stearns, Goldman Sachs, Merrill Lynch, and Morgan Stanley, remained exclusively investment banks. The mortgage-backed securities originated by the investment banks were mostly sold to investors, but some were retained as investments by these firms. As a result, when the prices of these securities declined beginning in 2007, the investment banks suffered heavy losses. Lehman Brothers was forced to declare bankruptcy, Merrill Lynch and Bear Stearns were sold to commercial banks in deals arranged by the U.S. government, and Goldman Sachs and Morgan Stanley became bank holding companies, which allowed them to engage in commercial banking activity. With these developments, the era of the large Wall Street investment bank came to an end.

Why did the investment banks take on so much risk by originating securities backed by mortgages granted to borrowers who had a high likelihood of defaulting on the loans? Michael Lewis, a financial journalist and former Wall Street bond salesman, has argued that a key reason was a change in how the investment banks were organized. Traditionally, Wall Street investment banks had been organized as partnerships, but by 2000 they had all converted to being publicly traded corporations. As we have seen, in a partnership the funds of the relatively small group of owners are put directly at risk, and the principal–agent problem is reduced because there is little separation of ownership from control. With a publicly traded corporation, on the other hand, the principal–agent problem can be severe. Lewis argues:

> No investment bank owned by its employees would have . . . bought and held $50 billion in [exotic mortgage-backed securities]. . . . or even allow [these securities] to be sold to its customers. The hoped-for short-term gain would not have justified the long-term hit.

Issues of corporate governance will clearly continue to be a concern for economists, policymakers, and investors.

Making the Connection | Are Buyers of Facebook Stock Getting a Fair Deal?

Many technology firms, including Facebook, turn to *venture capital firms* for funds. These firms raise funds from investors and use the funds to make investments in small start-up firms. A venture capital firm frequently takes a large ownership stake in a start-up firm, often placing its own employees on the board of directors or even having them serve as managers. These steps can reduce principal–agent problems because the venture capital firm has a greater ability to closely monitor the managers. The firm's managers will probably be attentive to

Was buying stock in Facebook a good investment?

the wishes of a large investor because having a large investor sell its stake in the firm may make it difficult to raise funds from new investors.

Several venture capital funds, including Accel Partners, invested in Facebook. If a start-up firm becomes successful, then it will typically become a public firm by issuing stock. The first issue of stock by a firm is called an *initial public offering (IPO)*. The IPO makes it possible for the venture capital firm to easily sell its ownership share of the firm to other investors. In the case of Facebook, though, CEO Mark Zuckerberg was reluctant to allow an IPO because he wanted to keep the company private rather than bring in many additional investors, which could reduce his control of the firm. The lack of an IPO meant that Accel, other venture capital firms, and Facebook employees who had received stock could not easily "cash out" by selling their shares. As we saw at the beginning of the chapter, though, it is possible for private firms to sell a limited amount of stock. These sales don't take place on the New York Stock Exchange or NASDAQ but are arranged by firms such as SharesPost and SecondMarket, which match up sellers of stock in private firms with buyers. These sales are sometimes called *private placements*, and the market for shares of private firms is sometimes referred to as the *shadow market* to distinguish it from the stock markets on which shares of public firms are traded. Trading in private-company shares has been increasing rapidly; it doubled from 2009 to 2010 and was expected to grow by 50 percent during 2011.

Only so-called accredited investors are eligible to buy shares of private firms. An investor is accredited if he or she has an income of $200,000 or more for at least the previous two years or has a net worth of $1 million. A private company cannot have more than 499 individual shareholders. Because the Securities and Exchange Commission (SEC) assumes that accredited investors are experienced and sophisticated, the market for shares of private firms is not closely regulated. In particular, private firms do not have to disclose their financial statements, such as their income statements and balance sheets, as public firms do. Some economists and policymakers, though, worry that there is potential for sellers of shares in a private firm to take advantage of buyers because the insiders selling the shares have information about the firm's financial statements that the investors do not. For instance, in mid-2011, stock in Facebook was selling for about $35 per share, which would make the total value of the firm about $80 billion. Was Facebook really worth that much? It was difficult to tell because the firm did not have to make public its revenue or profits.

As the SEC considered changing the regulations governing the sale of shares in private firms, it faced conflicting pressures. Some economists and policymakers wanted the SEC to require private firms to disclose more information to potential investors. Others argued that the SEC should relax some of the existing regulations to make it easier for start-ups to raise funds without having to meet all of the requirements to become a publicly traded firm. In late 2011, it was unclear which way the SEC would move, although it did appear to be favoring a proposal to raise the limit on the number of shareholders allowed in a private firm.

Based on Shayndi Raice, "Is Facebook Worth $100 Billion?" *Wall Street Journal*, July 14, 2011; Pui-Wing Tam, "As Web IPOs Hit, Few Share the Spoils," *Wall Street Journal*, July 8, 2011; Miguel Helft, "Facebook Deal Offers Freedom From Scrutiny," *New York Times*, January 3, 2011; Jean Eaglesham, "U.S. Eyes New Stock Rules," *Wall Street Journal*, April 6, 2011; and Michael Hickins, "Investor Criticizes 'Shadow Market,'" *Wall Street Journal*, March 17, 2011.

MyEconLab **Your Turn:** Test your understanding by doing related problem 5.7 on page 194 at the end of this chapter.

Continued from page 169

Economics in Your Life

Do Corporate Managers Act in the Best Interests of Shareholders?

At the beginning of the chapter, we asked you to consider two questions: Why is it difficult to get the managers of a firm to act in your interests rather than in their own? and Given this problem, should you ever take on the risk of buying stock? The reason managers may not act in shareholders' interest is that in large corporations there is separation of ownership from control: The shareholders own the firm, but the top managers actually control it. This results in the principal–agent problem discussed in the chapter. The principal–agent problem clearly adds to the risk you would face by buying stock rather than doing something safe with your money, such as putting it in the bank. But the rewards to owning stock can also be substantial, potentially earning you far more over the long run than a bank account. Buying the stock of well-known firms, such as Google, that are closely followed by Wall Street investment analysts helps to reduce the principal–agent problem. It is less likely that the managers of these firms will take actions that are clearly not in the best interests of shareholders because the managers' actions are difficult to conceal. Buying the stock of large, well-known firms certainly does not completely eliminate the risk from the principal–agent problem, however. Enron, WorldCom, and some of the other firms that were involved in the scandals discussed in this chapter were all well known and closely followed by Wall Street analysts, as were the large financial firms that ran into difficulties during the financial crisis of 2007–2009, but their stock turned out to be very poor investments.

Conclusion

In a market system, firms make independent decisions about which goods and services to produce, how to produce them, and what prices to charge. In modern high-income countries, such as the United States, large corporations account for a majority of the sales and profits earned by firms. Generally, the managers of these corporations do a good job of representing the interests of stockholders while providing the goods and services demanded by consumers. As the business scandals of the early 2000s and the problems with financial firms in 2007–2009 showed, however, the principal–agent problem can sometimes become severe. Economists debate the costs and benefits of regulations proposed to address these problems.

An *Inside Look* on the next page discusses how the Web sites SecondMarket and SharesPost help qualified investors buy shares of private companies.

Shares of Private Companies Available to Qualified Investors

KIPLINGER

How to Buy Into Facebook Before It Goes Public

Goldman Sachs caused a stir in early January when word broke that it would invest $450 million in Facebook. Even more intriguing, though, was the news that Goldman would create a fund through which its clients could buy some $1.5 billion worth of shares in the fast-growing, privately held social-networking company.

(a) But you don't have to be a well-heeled Goldman client to get in on Facebook or other hot, privately held companies before they go public. Two Web sites—SharesPost.com and SecondMarket.com—provide electronic platforms that allow qualified investors to buy shares from company insiders and employees who want to cash out before a company goes public. By offering a way to enter an area previously open only to Wall Street's elite, "we democratize the opportunity to invest in private company stocks," says David Weir, chief executive of SharesPost.

(b) Since 2004, SecondMarket, a registered brokerage, has been offering a marketplace for alternative investments, such as asset-backed securities, mortgage securities and limited-partnership interests. Last year, $400 million worth of transactions closed on SecondMarket, up from $100 million in 2009. At present, 40 private stock issues trade on the platform, with Facebook, Twitter and LinkedIn the most active.

SharesPost, founded in June 2009, is not a brokerage but works with brokers to manage transactions. Currently, it lists 150 privately held companies, with the total number of buy and sell orders available (not actual trades) worth roughly $400 million.

Why would you want to invest in a nonpublic company? You could become an insider before a firm goes public, presumably at a much higher price than you paid for your shares. Facebook is at the center of attention because of its extraordinary growth and the perception that its initial public offering could be as successful as that of Google (symbol GOOG). Facebook hasn't yet announced plans for an IPO, but many market watchers expect the Palo Alto, Cal., company to go public next year. . . .

(c) Signing up with the secondary-market services is as easy as joining Facebook; actually getting to trade is another matter. Neither outfit requires clients to pony up $2 million or more and hold the shares until 2013, as Goldman is stipulating for its Facebook offering. However, both companies require clients to be accredited investors. According to the Securities and Exchange Commission, this means investors must have enough knowledge and experience to evaluate an investment's risks and be able to bear them, and they must have a net worth of at least $1 million or income exceeding $200,000 per year for the preceding two years. After the company verifies your information, a process that typically takes 48 hours, you're ready to trade. In addition, once you make a purchase, both SharesPost and SecondMarket require you to hold the shares for at least one year.

Privately held stocks don't trade quickly, or even every day. Typically, the seller sets a price, but buyers and sellers can—and do—haggle. And agreeing to a price doesn't mean the trade will actually go through. Mark Murphy, a spokesman for Second-Market, says companies have the right of first refusal. So even if the seller accepts the deal, his or her company has 30 days to check you out to determine if they want you as a shareholder. If not, the company can deny the trade and buy the shares from the seller itself. If a trade goes through, you can expect to pay a commission of 2% to 5% of the size of the transaction. Murphy says the typical SecondMarket transaction is about $2 million. SharesPost says its transactions range from $10,000 to millions of dollars.

Key Points in the Article

When Goldman Sachs invested in Facebook in 2011, it also offered some of its best clients a chance to purchase shares in the company. In addition to companies such as Goldman Sachs, two relatively new companies, SecondMarket and SharesPost, offer qualified investors the chance to purchase private company stock from company insiders and employees who want to sell their personal shares. These new firms give investors an opportunity to purchase stock before a company goes public. Signing up with SecondMarket and SharesPost is a relatively quick process, but both companies require their clients to meet the qualifications of the Securities and Exchange Commission's (SEC's) definition of an accredited investor.

Analyzing the News

(a) Some companies are publicly traded, and others are privately held. Most large corporations are owned by stockholders, who through boards of directors have the right to hire or fire top managers. Publicly traded companies sell stock as a way to raise funds. Some large corporations, such as Facebook, are privately held. With a private company, upper management has more control of the company than if the company were publicly traded, but the company must look to alternatives such as taking on private investors to raise capital. In 2011, Facebook turned to investment banking firm Goldman Sachs,

which invested $450 million in the social networking company. Goldman Sachs then offered an opportunity to some of its best clients to purchase shares in Facebook. Private offerings to top clients are one of the few ways investors can buy into private companies. Two Web sites, however, are now offering investors the opportunity to buy shares of private companies from company insiders and employees, opening the door a little wider to investment in private companies.

(b) SecondMarket and SharesPost are two Web sites that list for sale shares in privately held companies. Offerings are limited to a total of 190 private stocks but include well-known companies such as Facebook and Twitter. The figure below shows that these numbers are tiny compared to the roughly 15,000 publicly traded companies represented by the New York Stock Exchange, NASDAQ, and stocks traded over-the-counter. The chapter discusses the principal–agent problem, which normally does not occur in privately held companies where the founder and majority shareholder typically runs the company. Management and ownership are one and the same, so they do not have differing interests. When private companies take on investors, ownership interests can start to vary from those of management, and the principal–agent problem can become a reality. With shares of privately held companies now being offered to a wider variety of investors, the principal–agent problem has the potential of becoming more significant.

(c) Because privately held companies are not legally required to release financial statements, these investments have the potential of being quite risky. Both SecondMarket and SharesPost abide by SEC guidelines for accredited investors and require investors to meet qualifications, which include experience in evaluating an investment's risk and having a minimum net worth of $1 million or having annual income of at least $200,000 over the preceding two years. Both companies also require purchased shares to be held for at least one year, so these opportunities are designed for serious, knowledgeable investors and not for casual investors.

Thinking Critically

1. Explain why purchasing shares of a privately held company such as Facebook could be much more risky for investors than purchasing shares of a publicly traded company.

2. In January 2011, Goldman Sachs announced it would invest $450 million in Facebook. An executive at Facebook who knew when this deal would be announced could have made money quickly by buying Goldman Sachs stock and selling it at a higher price a few days later. (Goldman Sachs stock went up almost $7 a share over a seven-day period surrounding the investment.) Such "insider trading" is illegal, however. Do you think that insider trading should be illegal? Are there benefits to other investors or to the economy as a whole associated with insider trading? Are there problems associated with insider trading?

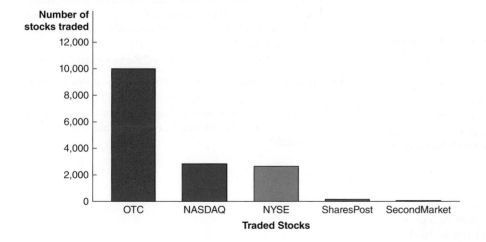

SecondMarket and SharesPost offer 190 private stocks, which is a small number compared with the number of stock that are publicly traded.

Chapter Summary and Problems

Key Terms

Accounting profit, p. 182

Asset, p. 170

Balance sheet, p. 183

Bond, p. 175

Corporate governance, p. 173

Corporation, p. 170

Coupon payment, p. 175

Direct finance, p. 175

Dividends, p. 177

Economic profit, p. 183

Explicit cost, p. 182

Implicit cost, p. 182

Income statement, p. 182

Indirect finance, p. 175

Interest rate, p. 175

Liability, p. 182

Limited liability, p. 170

Opportunity cost, p. 182

Partnership, p. 170

Principal–agent problem, p. 173

Separation of ownership from control, p. 173

Sole proprietorship, p. 170

Stock, p. 177

Wall Street Reform and Consumer Protection Act (Dodd-Frank Act), p. 184

 Types of Firms, pages 170-172

LEARNING OBJECTIVE: Categorize the major types of firms in the United States.

Summary

There are three types of firms: A **sole proprietorship** is a firm owned by a single individual and not organized as a corporation. A **partnership** is a firm owned jointly by two or more persons and not organized as a corporation. A **corporation** is a legal form of business that provides the owners with limited liability. An **asset** is anything of value owned by a person or a firm. The owners of sole proprietorships and partners have unlimited liability, which means there is no legal distinction between the personal assets of the owners of the business and the assets of the business. The owners of corporations have **limited liability**, which means they can never lose more than their investment in the firm. Although only 20 percent of firms are corporations, they account for the majority of revenue and profit earned by all firms.

MyEconLab   Visit **www.myeconlab.com** to complete these exercises online and get instant feedback.

Review Questions

1.1 What are the three major types of firms in the United States? Briefly discuss the most important characteristics of each type.

1.2 What is limited liability? Why does the government grant limited liability to the owners of corporations?

1.3 Why is limited liability more important for firms trying to raise funds from a large number of investors than for firms trying to raise funds from a small number of investors?

Problems and Applications

1.4 Suppose that shortly after graduating from college, you decide to start your own business. Will you be likely to organize the business as a sole proprietorship, a partnership, or a corporation? Explain your reasoning.

1.5 How would the establishment of limited liability for the owners of corporations affect the production possibilities frontier of a country over time?

1.6 Evaluate the following argument:

> I would like to invest in the stock market, but I think that buying shares of stock in a corporation is too risky. Suppose I buy $10,000 of General Electric stock, and the company ends up going bankrupt. Because as a stockholder I'm part owner of the company, I might be responsible for paying hundreds of thousands of dollars of the company's debts.

1.7 According to an article in the *Economist* magazine, historian David Faure has argued that the Chinese economy failed to grow rapidly during the nineteenth century because "family-run companies . . . could not raise sufficient capital to exploit the large-scale opportunities tied to the rise of the steam engine, notably railways and (with limited exceptions) global shipping and automated manufacturing." How did the United States solve the problem of firms raising enough funds to operate railroads and other large-scale businesses?

Based on "The PCCW Buy-out in Court," *Economist*, April 21, 2009.

1.8 **[Related to the** Making the Connection **on page 172]** Why might large existing firms be more likely to focus on improving existing goods and services than on introducing new ones? Why might small new firms take the opposite approach?

6.2 **The Structure of Corporations and the Principal-Agent Problem,** pages 173–174

LEARNING OBJECTIVE: Describe the typical management structure of corporations and understand the concepts of separation of ownership from control and the principal–agent problem.

Summary

Corporate governance refers to the way in which a corporation is structured and the impact a corporation's structure has on the firm's behavior. Most corporations have a similar management structure: The shareholders elect a board of directors that appoints the corporation's top managers, such as the chief executive officer (CEO). Because the top management often does not own a large fraction of the stock in the corporation, large corporations have a **separation of ownership from control**. Because top managers have less incentive to increase the corporation's profits than to increase their own salaries and their own enjoyment, corporations can suffer from the **principal-agent problem**. The principal–agent problem exists when the principals—in this case, the shareholders of the corporation—have difficulty getting the agent—the corporation's top management—to carry out their wishes.

MyEconLab   Visit **www.myeconlab.com** to complete these exercises online and get instant feedback.

Review Questions

2.1 What does it mean to say that there is a separation of ownership from control in large corporations?

2.2 How is the separation of ownership from control related to the principal–agent problem?

2.3 Why is it important for a board of directors to have outside directors, as opposed to only inside directors?

Problems and Applications

2.4 The principal–agent problem arises almost everywhere in the business world, and it also crops up even closer to home. Discuss the principal–agent problem that exists in the college classroom. Who is the principal? Who is the agent? What potential conflicts in objectives are there between this principal and this agent?

2.5 The principal–agent problem in a public corporation between ownership and top management results from asymmetric information. What information, if known, would prevent this principal–agent problem?

2.6 Sales personnel, whether selling life insurance, automobiles, or magazine subscriptions, typically get paid on commission instead of a straight hourly wage. How does paying a commission help solve the principal–agent problem between the owner of a business and the sales force?

2.7 **[Related to** Solved Problem 6.2 **on page 174]** Briefly explain whether you agree with the following argument: "The separation of ownership from control in large corporations and the principal–agent problem mean that top managers can work short days, take long vacations, and otherwise slack off."

2.8 **[Related to** Solved Problem 6.2 **on page 174]** The members of many corporate boards of directors have to be reelected by the firm's stockholders every year. Some corporations, though, have staggered elections for their boards of directors, with only one-half or one-third of the members being up for election each year. According to an article in the *Economist* magazine, studies have found that firms that have staggered elections for their boards of directors are less profitable than similar firms where all members of the boards of directors are elected each year. Provide a possible explanation for this finding.

Based on "A Different Class," *Economist*, February 18, 2011.

2.9 An article in *BusinessWeek* states that members of boards of directors believe that, in general, the compensation of CEOs is too high. However, most board members believe that the compensation of the CEO of their firm is appropriate. The article concludes: "Given this and that they work for the CEO, it is not surprising that boards continue to support high levels of CEO compensation." How does this statement relate to the principal–agent problem?

Based on "Fixing Executive Compensation Excesses," by Edward E. Lawler from *BusinessWeek*, February 5, 2009.

6.3 **How Firms Raise Funds,** pages 174–181

LEARNING OBJECTIVE: Explain how firms raise the funds they need to operate and expand.

Summary

Firms rely on retained earnings—which are profits retained by the firm and not paid out to the firm's owners—or on using the savings of households for the funds they need to operate and expand. With **direct finance**, the savings of households flow directly to businesses when investors buy **stocks** and **bonds** in financial markets. With **indirect finance**, savings flow indirectly to businesses when households deposit money in saving and checking accounts in banks and the banks lend these funds to businesses. Federal, state, and local governments also sell bonds in financial markets, and households also borrow funds from banks. When a firm sells a bond, it is borrowing money from the buyer of the bond. The firm makes a **coupon payment** to the buyer of the bond. The **interest rate** is the cost of borrowing funds, usually expressed as a percentage of the amount borrowed. When a firm sells stock, it is selling part ownership of the firm to the buyer of the stock. **Dividends** are payments by a corporation to its shareholders. The original purchasers of stocks and bonds may resell them in stock and bond markets, such as the New York Stock Exchange. The performance of the U.S. stock market is often measured using stock market indexes. The three most widely followed stock indexes are the Dow Jones Industrial Average, the S&P 500, and the NASDAQ Composite Index.

MyEconLab   Visit **www.myeconlab.com** to complete these exercises online and get instant feedback.

Review Questions

3.1 What is the difference between direct finance and indirect finance? If you borrow money from a bank to buy a new car, are you using direct finance or indirect finance?

3.2 Why is a bond considered to be a loan but a share of stock is not? Why do corporations issue both bonds and shares of stock?

3.3 How do the stock and bond markets provide information to businesses? Why do stock and bond prices change over time?

Problems and Applications

3.4 Suppose that a firm in which you have invested is losing money. Would you rather own the firm's stock or the firm's bonds? Explain.

3.5 Suppose you originally invested in a firm when it was small and unprofitable. Now the firm has grown to be large and profitable. Would you be better off if you had bought the firm's stock or the firm's bonds? Explain.

3.6 If you deposit $20,000 in a savings account at a bank, you might earn 1 percent interest per year. Someone who borrows $20,000 from a bank to buy a new car might have to pay an interest rate of 6 percent per year on the loan. Knowing this, why don't you just lend your money directly to the car buyer, cutting out the bank?

3.7 **[Related to the** Chapter Opener **on page 169]** The owners of Facebook have had several opportunities to sell the company to larger firms or to make the firm a public corporation by selling stock. In 2009, the value of Facebook was estimated to be somewhere between $2 billion and $5 billion. So, selling Facebook or making it a public corporation would make Mark Zuckerberg and its other owners very wealthy. In those circumstances, why might a firm such as Facebook choose to remain a private company?

Based on Felix Salmon, "Facebook Eyes Additional Funding," Reuters. com, April 30, 2009.

3.8 **[Related to the** Making the Connection **on page 176]** The following is from an article in the *Wall Street Journal*:

> Moody's Investors Service. . . . said it was cutting Japan's government bond rating to Aa3 from Aa2, citing "large budget deficits and the build-up in Japanese government debt since the 2009 global recession."

a. Moody's downgraded Japan's government debt from Aa2 to Aa3. What is Moody's top bond rating?

b. Why would "large budget deficits and the build-up in Japanese government debt" be a reason to downgrade Japan's debt rating?

"Moody's Downgrades Japan Debt, But Offers A Stable Outlook," by William Sposato from *Wall Street Journal*, August 24, 2011. Copyright © 2011 by Dow Jones & Company, Inc.. Reproduced with permission of Dow Jones & Company, Inc.

3.9 What effect would the following events be likely to have on the price of Google's stock?

a. A competitor launches a search engine that's just as good as Google's.

b. The corporate income tax is abolished.

c. Google's board of directors becomes dominated by close friends and relatives of its top management.

d. The price of wireless Internet connections unexpectedly drops, so more and more people use the Internet.

e. Google announces a huge profit of $1 billion, but everybody anticipated that Google would earn a huge profit of $1 billion.

3.10 The French government issues bonds with 50-year maturities. Would such bonds be purchased only by very young investors who expect to still be alive when the bond matures? Briefly explain.

3.11 The following appeared in an article in the *Wall Street Journal* about the bond market in high-income (or "developed") countries (that is, the United States and countries in Europe) and the emerging-market countries (that is, Latin American and Asian countries):

> "In the developed markets, it's been about analyzing the business cycle, and in emerging markets, it's been about solvency," says David Rolley, the co-manager of the Loomis Sayles Global Bond fund. "Now it's not. You have to do both for both." . . . It could ultimately mean that developed economies, the U.S. included, could face extra penalties for the perceived, even if ever-so-slight, risk that they may not repay their debts.

a. What does it mean to say that the emerging markets have been about "solvency"?

b. What are the "extra penalties" the developed economies could face from the increase in perceived risk?

From Matthieu Wirz and Matt Phillips, "Sea Change in Map of Global Risk," *Wall Street Journal*, August 1, 2011.

3.12 **[Related to the** Don't Let This Happen to You **on page 178]** Briefly explain whether you agree or disagree with the following statement: "The total value of the shares of Microsoft stock traded on the NASDAQ last week was $250 million, so the firm actually received more revenue from stock sales than from selling software."

3.13 **[Related to the** Making the Connection **on page 180]** Loans from banks are the most important external source of funds to businesses because most businesses are too small to borrow in financial markets by issuing stocks or bonds. Most investors are reluctant to buy the stocks or bonds of small businesses because of the difficulty of gathering accurate information on the financial strength and profitability of the businesses. Nevertheless, news about the stock market is included in nearly every network news program and is often the lead story in the business section of most newspapers. Is there a contradiction here? Why is the average viewer of TV news or the average reader of a newspaper interested in the fluctuations in prices in the stock market?

3.14 **[Related to the** Making the Connection **on page 180]** The following table shows information from August 26, 2011, about the stock price of Starbucks Corporation:

Symbol	Open	High	Low	Close	Net Chg	Volume	52-Week High	52-Week Low	Div
SBUX	36.28	37.67	35.73	37.39	0.97	8,195,104	41.11	22.69	0.52

a. How much did the price of Starbucks stock go up or down from the day before?

b. Did the Starbucks stock price vary much during the day's trading period?

c. Did the price of Starbucks stock vary much over the preceding 52 weeks?

d. How many shares of Starbucks stock were traded on the previous day?

6.4 **Using Financial Statements to Evaluate a Corporation, pages 181–183**
LEARNING OBJECTIVE: Understand the information provided in corporations' financial statements.

Summary

A firm's **income statement** sums up its revenues, costs, and profit over a period of time. A firm's **balance sheet** sums up its financial position on a particular day, usually the end of a quarter or year. A balance sheet records a firm's assets and liabilities. A **liability** is anything owed by a person or a firm. Firms report their **accounting profit** on their income statements. Accounting profit does not always include all of a firm's **opportunity cost**. **Explicit cost** is a cost that involves spending money. **Implicit cost** is a nonmonetary opportunity cost. Because accounting profit excludes some implicit costs, it is larger than **economic profit**.

 Visit **www.myeconlab.com** to complete these exercises online and get instant feedback.

Review Questions

4.1 What is the difference between a firm's assets and its liabilities? Give an example of an asset and an example of a liability.

4.2 What is the difference between a firm's balance sheet and a firm's income statement?

4.3 Distinguish between a firm's explicit costs and its implicit costs and between a firm's accounting profit and its economic profit.

4.4 Would a business be expected to survive in the long run if it earned a positive accounting profit but a negative economic profit? Explain.

Problems and Applications

4.5 Paolo currently has $100,000 invested in bonds that earn him 10 percent interest per year. He wants to open a pizza restaurant and is considering either selling the bonds and

using the $100,000 to start his restaurant or borrowing the $100,000 from a bank, which would charge him an annual interest rate of 7 percent. He finally decides to sell the bonds and not take out the bank loan. He reasons, "Because I already have the $100,000 invested in the bonds, I don't have to pay anything to use the money. If I take out the bank loan, I have to pay interest, so my costs of producing pizza will be higher if I take out the loan than if I sell the bonds." What do you think of Paolo's reasoning?

4.6 Paolo and Alfredo are twins who both want to open pizza restaurants. Their parents have always liked Alfredo best, and they buy two pizza ovens and give both to him. Unfortunately, Paolo must buy his own pizza ovens. Does Alfredo have a lower cost of producing pizza than Paolo does because Alfredo received his pizza ovens as a gift, while Paolo had to pay for his? Briefly explain.

4.7 Dane decides to give up a job earning $100,000 per year as a corporate lawyer and converts the duplex that he owns into a UFO museum. (He had been renting out the duplex for $20,000 a year.) His direct expenses include $50,000 per year paid to his assistants and $10,000 per year for utilities. Fans flock to the museum to see his collection of extraterrestrial paraphernalia, which he could easily sell on eBay for $1,000,000. Over the course of the year, the museum brings in revenues of $100,000.

a. How much is Dane's accounting profit for the year?

b. Is Dane earning an economic profit? Explain.

4.8 The Securities and Exchange Commission requires that every firm that wishes to issue stocks and bonds to the public make available its balance sheet and income statement. Briefly explain how information useful to investors can be found in these financial statements.

6.5

Corporate Governance Policy and the Financial Crisis of 2007–2009, pages 183-186

LEARNING OBJECTIVE: Discuss the role that corporate governance problems may have played in the financial crisis of 2007–2009.

Summary

Because their compensation often rises with the profitability of the corporation, top managers have an incentive to overstate the profits reported on their firm's income statements. During the early 2000s, it became clear that the top managers of several large corporations had done this, even though intentionally falsifying financial statements is illegal. The *Sarbanes-Oxley Act* of 2002 took several steps intended to increase the accuracy of financial statements and increase the penalties for falsifying them. The financial crisis of 2007–2009 revealed that many financial firms held assets that were far riskier than investors had realized. Congress passed the Wall Street Reform and Consumer Protection Act (Dodd-Frank Act) in July 2010 to address some of the issues raised by the financial crisis of 2007–2009.

MyEconLab   Visit **www.myeconlab.com** to complete these exercises online and get instant feedback.

Review Questions

5.1 What is the Sarbanes-Oxley Act? Why was it passed?

5.2 What was the source of the problems encountered by many financial firms during the crisis of 2007–2009?

Problems and Applications

5.3 The board of directors of Advanced Micro Devices, Inc., issued guidelines on company stock ownership by executive officers and members of the board of directors, effective February 7, 2008. This statement details the number of required common stock shares of Advanced Micro Devices that should be held by the company's executives and board members. The details of these guidelines are shown in the following table:

Officer Level	Ownership Guideline (number of shares)
Chairman and CEO	312,500
President and COO	125,000
Executive vice presidents	78,125
Senior vice presidents	35,000
Board of Directors	
Board members	15,000

What reason would the board of directors have for requiring top executives of a company to own shares of the company's stock? Why would the board of directors include themselves in these stock ownership requirements? Would potential investors view these stock ownership requirements favorably?

Stock Ownership Guidelines, Advanced Micro Devices Board of Directors, 2008. Copyright © 2008 by AMD. Reprinted by permission.

5.4 The following is from an article in *USA Today*:

> In what some call a worldwide corporate-governance movement, shareholders are pushing for stronger corporate-governance laws, teaming with investors from different countries and negotiating behind the scenes with businesses.

What is corporate governance? Why would shareholders push for stronger corporate governance laws?

From Edward Iwata, "Corporate governance gets more transparent worldwide," *USA Today*, February 17, 2008.

5.5 An article in *BusinessWeek* stated that the Allstate Corporation, a large insurance company, would begin to require a simple majority vote of shareholders, rather than a two-thirds majority vote, to elect members to its board of directors and to remove directors in between annual meetings when elections are held. The article also stated that the price of Allstate's stock rose following the announcement. Briefly discuss whether there may have been a connection between these changes in Allstate's corporate governance and the increase in the firm's stock price.

Based on "Allstate Announces Changes to Governance," *BusinessWeek*, February 20, 2007.

5.6 According to a survey in 2007, 78 percent of corporate executives responding believed that the costs of complying with the Sarbanes-Oxley Act outweighed the benefits. The total costs of compliance were about $2.92 million per company. Is it possible to put a dollar value on the benefits of complying with Sarbanes-Oxley? Which groups are likely to receive the most benefits from Sarbanes-Oxley: investors, corporations, or some other group?

Based on Kara Scannell, "Costs to Comply with Sarbanes-Oxley Decline Again," *Wall Street Journal*, May 16, 2007, p. C7.

5.7 **[Related to the** Making the Connection **on page 185]** According to an article in the *Wall Street Journal*, "Currently, companies can issue shares privately without incurring onerous reporting obligations if they have fewer than 500 shareholders. The SEC is considering raising that limit, though it's unclear by how much." The article also says, "Some investors say the SEC should stop companies from getting around the rule, which they say remains an essential safeguard." Who is being safeguarded by the current rule? What are they being safeguarded from?

From Jean Eaglesham, "U.S. Eyes New Stock Rules," *Wall Street Journal*, April 8, 2011.From Jean Eaglesham, "U.S. Eyes New Stock Rules," *Wall Street Journal*, April 8, 2011.

Appendix

Tools to Analyze Firms' Financial Information

LEARNING OBJECTIVE

Understand the concept of present value and the information contained on a firm's income statement and balance sheet.

As we saw in the chapter, modern business firms are not just "black boxes" transforming inputs into output. Most business revenues and profits are earned by large corporations. Unlike founder-dominated firms, the typical large corporation is run by managers who generally do not own a controlling interest in the firm. Large firms raise funds from outside investors, and outside investors seek information on firms and the assurance that the managers of firms will act in the interests of the investors.

This chapter shows how corporations raise funds by issuing stocks and bonds. This appendix provides more detail to support that discussion. We begin by analyzing *present value* as a key concept in determining the prices of financial securities. We then provide greater information on *financial statements* issued by corporations, using Google as an example.

Using Present Value to Make Investment Decisions

Firms raise funds by selling equity (stock) and debt (bonds and loans) to investors and lenders. If you own shares of stock or a bond, you will receive payments in the form of dividends or coupons over a number of years. Most people value funds they already have more highly than funds they will receive some time in the future. For example, you would probably not trade $1,000 you already have for $1,000 you will not receive for one year. The longer you have to wait to receive a payment, the less value it will have for you. One thousand dollars you will not receive for two years is worth less to you than $1,000 you will receive after one year. The value you give today to money you will receive in the future is called the future payment's **present value**. The present value of $1,000 you will receive in one year will be less than $1,000.

Present value The value in today's dollars of funds to be paid or received in the future.

Why is this true? Why is the $1,000 you will not receive for one year less valuable to you than the $1,000 you already have? The most important reason is that if you have $1,000 today, you can use that $1,000 today. You can buy goods and services with the money and receive enjoyment from them. The $1,000 you receive in one year does not have direct use to you now.

Also, prices will likely rise during the year you are waiting to receive your $1,000. So, when you finally do receive the $1,000 in one year, you will not be able to buy as much with it as you could with $1,000 today. Finally, there is some risk that you will not receive the $1,000 in one year. The risk may be very great if an unreliable friend borrows $1,000 from you and vaguely promises to pay you back in one year. The risk may be very small if you lend money to the federal government by buying a U.S. Treasury bond. In either case, though, there is at least some risk that you will not receive the funds promised.

When someone lends money, the lender expects to be paid back both the amount of the loan and some additional interest. Say that you decide that you are willing to lend your $1,000 today if you are paid back $1,100 one year from now. In this case, you are charging $100/$1,000 = 0.10, or 10 percent interest on the funds you have loaned. Economists would say that you value $1,000 today as equivalent to the $1,100 to be received one year in the future.

Notice that $1,100 can be written as $1,000 $(1 + 0.10)$. That is, the value of money received in the future is equal to the value of money in the present multiplied by 1 plus the interest rate, with the interest rate expressed as a decimal. Or:

$$\$1,100 = \$1,000(1 + 0.10).$$

Notice, also, that if we divide both sides by $(1 + 0.10)$, we can rewrite this formula as:

$$\$1,000 = \frac{\$1,100}{(1 + 0.10)}.$$

The rewritten formula states that the present value is equal to the future value to be received in one year divided by 1 plus the interest rate. This formula is important because you can use it to convert any amount to be received in one year into its present value. Writing the formula generally, we have:

$$\text{Present value} = \frac{\text{Future value}_1}{(1 + i)}.$$

The present value of funds to be received in one year—Future value$_1$—can be calculated by dividing the amount of those funds to be received by 1 plus the interest rate. With an interest rate of 10 percent, the present value of $1,000,000 to be received one year from now is:

$$\frac{\$1,000,000}{(1 + 0.10)} = \$909,090.91.$$

This method is a useful way of calculating the value today of funds that will be received in one year. But financial securities such as stocks and bonds involve promises to pay funds over many years. Therefore, it would be even more useful if we could expand this formula to calculate the present value of funds to be received more than one year in the future.

This expansion is easy to do. Go back to the original example, where we assumed you were willing to loan out your $1,000 for one year, provided that you received 10 percent interest. Suppose you are asked to lend the funds for two years and that you are promised 10 percent interest per year for each year of the loan. That is, you are lending $1,000, which at 10 percent interest will grow to $1,100 after one year, and you are agreeing to loan that $1,100 out for a second year at 10 percent interest. So, after two years, you will be paid back $1,100 $(1 + 0.10)$, or $1,210. Or:

$$\$1,210 = \$1,000(1 + 0.10)(1 + 0.10),$$

or:

$$\$1,210 = \$1,000(1 + 0.10)^2.$$

This formula can also be rewritten as:

$$\$1,000 = \frac{\$1,210}{(1 + 0.10)^2}.$$

To put this formula in words, the $1,210 you receive two years from now has a present value equal to $1,210 divided by the quantity 1 plus the interest rate squared. If you agree to lend out your $1,000 for three years at 10 percent interest, you will receive:

$$\$1,331 = \$1,000(1 + 0.10)^3.$$

Notice, again, that:

$$\$1,000 = \frac{\$1,331}{(1 + 0.10)^3}.$$

You can probably see a pattern here. We can generalize the concept to say that the present value of funds to be received n years in the future—whether n is 1, 20, or 85 does not matter—equals the amount of the funds to be received divided by the quantity 1 plus the interest rate raised to the *n*th power. For instance, with an interest rate of 10 percent, the value of $1,000,000 to be received 25 years in the future is:

$$\text{Present value} = \frac{\$1,000,000}{(1 + 0.10)^{25}} = \$92,296.$$

Or, more generally:

$$\text{Present value} = \frac{\text{Future value}_n}{(1 + i)^n}$$

where Future value$_n$ represents funds that will be received in *n* years.

Solved Problem 6A.1

How to Receive Your Contest Winnings

Suppose you win a contest and are given the choice of the following prizes:

Prize 1: $50,000 to be received right away, with four additional payments of $50,000 to be received each year for the next four years

Prize 2: $175,000 to be received right away

Explain which prize you would choose and the basis for your decision.

Solving the Problem

Step 1: Review the material. This problem involves applying the concept of present value, so you may want to review the section "Using Present Value to Make Investment Decisions," which begins on page 195.

Step 2: Explain the basis for choosing the prize. Unless you need cash immediately, you should choose the prize with the highest present value.

Step 3: Calculate the present value of each prize. Prize 2 consists of one payment of $175,000 received right away, so its present value is $175,000. Prize 1 consists of five payments spread out over time. To find the present value of the prize, we must find the present value of each of these payments and add them together. To calculate present value, we must use an interest rate. Let's assume an interest rate of 10 percent. In that case, the present value of Prize 1 is:

$$\$50,000 + \frac{\$50,000}{(1 + 0.10)} + \frac{\$50,000}{(1 + 0.10)^2} + \frac{\$50,000}{(1 + 0.10)^3} + \frac{\$50,000}{(1 + 0.10)^4} =$$

$$\$50,000 + \$45,454.55 + \$41,322.31 + \$37,565.74 + \$34,150.67 = \$208,493.$$

Step 4: State your conclusion. Prize 1 has the greater present value, so you should choose it rather than Prize 2.

Your Turn: For more practice, do related problems 6A.6, 6A.7, 6A.8, and 6A.9 on page 202 at the end of this appendix.   MyEconLab

Using Present Value to Calculate Bond Prices

Anyone who buys a financial asset, such as shares of stock or a bond, is really buying a promise to receive certain payments—dividends in the case of shares of stock or coupons in the case of a bond. The price investors are willing to pay for a financial asset should be equal to the value of the payments they will receive as a result of owning the asset. Because most of the coupon or dividend payments will be received in the future, it is their present value that matters. Put another way, we have the following important idea: *The price of a financial asset should be equal to the present value of the payments to be received from owning that asset.*

Let's consider an example. Suppose that in 1982, General Electric issued a bond with an $80 coupon that will mature in 2012. It is now 2010, and that bond has been bought and sold by investors many times. You are considering buying it. If you buy the bond, you will receive two years of coupon payments plus a final payment of the bond's principal, or face value, of $1,000. Suppose, once again, that you need an interest rate of 10 percent to invest your funds. If the bond has a coupon of $80, the present value of the payments you receive from owning the bond—and, therefore, the present value of the bond—will be:

$$\text{Present value} = \frac{\$80}{(1 + 0.10)} + \frac{\$80}{(1 + 0.10)^2} + \frac{\$1,000}{(1 + 0.10)^2} = \$965.29.$$

That is, the present value of the bond will equal the present value of the three payments you will receive during the two years you own the bond. You should, therefore, be willing to pay $965.29 to own this bond and have the right to receive these payments from GE. This process of calculating present values of future payments is used to determine bond prices, with one qualification: The relevant interest rate used by investors in the bond market to calculate the present value and, therefore, the price of an existing bond is usually the coupon rate on comparable newly issued bonds. Therefore, the general formula for the price of a bond is:

$$\text{Bond price} = \frac{\text{Coupon}_1}{(1 + i)} + \frac{\text{Coupon}_2}{(1 + i)^2} + \dots + \frac{\text{Coupon}_n}{(1 + i)^n} + \frac{\text{Face value}}{(1 + i)^n},$$

where Coupon_1 is the coupon payment to be received after one year, Coupon_2 is the coupon payment to be received after two years, up to Coupon_n, which is the coupon payment received in the year the bond matures. The ellipsis takes the place of the coupon payments—if any—received between the second year and the year when the bond matures. Face value is the amount that will be received when the bond matures. The interest rate on comparable newly issued bonds is i.

Using Present Value to Calculate Stock Prices

When you own a firm's stock, you are legally entitled to your share of the firm's profits. Remember that the profits a firm pays out to its shareholders are referred to as *dividends*. The price of a share of stock should be equal to the present value of the dividends investors expect to receive as a result of owning that stock. Therefore, the general formula for the price of a stock is:

$$\text{Stock price} = \frac{\text{Dividend}_1}{(1 + i)} + \frac{\text{Dividend}_2}{(1 + i)^2} + \dots$$

Notice that this formula looks very similar to the one we used to calculate the price of a bond, with a couple important differences. First, unlike a bond, stock has no maturity date, so we have to calculate the present value of an infinite number of dividend payments. At first, it may seem that the stock's price must be infinite as well, but remember that dollars you don't receive for many years are worth very little today. For instance, a dividend payment of $10 that will be received 40 years in the future is worth only a little more than $0.20 today at a 10 percent interest rate. The second difference between the stock price formula and the bond price formula is that whereas the coupon payments you receive from owning the bond are known with certainty—they are written on the bond and cannot be changed—you don't know for sure what the dividend payments from owning a stock will be. How large a dividend payment you will receive depends on how profitable the company will be in the future.

Although it is possible to forecast the future profitability of a company, this cannot be done with perfect accuracy. To emphasize this point, some economists rewrite the basic stock price formula by adding a superscript *e* to each dividend term to emphasize that these are *expected* dividend payments. Because the future profitability of companies is often very difficult to forecast, it is not surprising that differences of opinion exist over what the price of a particular stock should be. Some investors will be very optimistic about the future profitability of a company and will, therefore, believe that the company's stock should have a high price. Other investors might be very pessimistic and believe that the company's stock should have a low price.

A Simple Formula for Calculating Stock Prices

It is possible to simplify the formula for determining the price of a stock, if we assume that dividends will grow at a constant rate:

$$\text{Stock price} = \frac{\text{Dividend}}{(i - \text{Growth rate})}.$$

In this equation, Dividend is the dividend expected to be received one year from now, and Growth rate is the rate at which those dividends are expected to grow. If a company pays a dividend of $1 per share to be received one year from now and Growth rate is 10 percent, the company is expected to pay a dividend of $1.10 the following year, $1.21 the year after that, and so on.

Now suppose that IBM will pay a dividend of $5 per share at the end of year, the consensus of investors is that these dividends will increase at a rate of 5 percent per year for the indefinite future, and the interest rate is 10 percent. Then the price of IBM's stock should be:

$$\text{Stock price} = \frac{\$5.00}{(0.10 - 0.05)} = \$100.00.$$

Particularly during the years 1999 and 2000, there was much discussion of whether the high prices of many Internet stocks—such as the stock of Amazon.com—were justified, given that many of these companies had not made any profit yet and so had not paid any dividends. Is there any way that a rational investor would pay a high price for the stock of a company currently not earning profits? The formula for determining stock prices shows that it is possible, provided that the investor's assumptions are optimistic enough! For example, during 1999, one stock analyst predicted that Amazon.com would soon be earning $10 per share of stock. That is, Amazon.com's total earnings divided by the number of shares of its stock outstanding would be $10. Suppose Amazon.com pays out that $10 in dividends and that the $10 will grow rapidly over the years, by, say, 7 percent per year. Then our formula indicates that the price of Amazon.com stock should be:

$$\text{Stock price} = \frac{\$10.00}{(0.10 - 0.07)} = \$333.33.$$

If you are sufficiently optimistic about the future prospects of a company, a high stock price can be justified even if the company is not currently earning a profit. But investors in growth stocks must be careful. Suppose investors believe that growth prospects for Amazon are only 4 percent per year instead of 7 percent because the firm turns out not to be as profitable as initially believed. Then our formula indicates that the price of Amazon.com stock should be:

$$\text{Stock price} = \frac{\$10.00}{(0.10 - 0.04)} = \$166.67.$$

This price is only half the price determined assuming a more optimistic growth rate. Hence investors use information about a firm's profitability and growth prospects to determine what the firm is worth.

Going Deeper into Financial Statements

Corporations disclose substantial information about their business operations and financial position to actual and potential investors. Some of this information meets the demands of participants in financial markets and of information-collection agencies, such as Moody's Investors Service, which develops credit ratings that help investors judge how risky corporate bonds are. Other information meets the requirements of the U.S. Securities and Exchange Commission.

Key sources of information about a corporation's profitability and financial position are its principal financial statements—the *income statement* and the *balance sheet*. These important information sources were first introduced in the chapter. In the following section we go into more detail, using recent data for Google as an example.

Analyzing Income Statements

As discussed in the chapter, a firm's income statement summarizes its revenues, costs, and profit over a period of time. Figure 6A.1 shows Google's income statement for 2010.

Google's income statement presents the results of the company's operations during the year. Listed first are the revenues it earned, largely from selling advertising on its Web site, from January 1, 2010, to December 31, 2010: $29,321 million. Listed next are Google's operating expenses, the most important of which is its *cost of revenue*—which is commonly known as *cost of sales* or *cost of goods sold*: $10,417 million. Cost of revenue is the direct cost of producing the products sold, including in this case the salaries of the computer programmers Google hires to write the software for its Web site. Google also has substantial costs for researching and developing its products ($3,762 million) and for advertising and marketing them ($2,799 million). General and administrative expenses ($1,962 million) include costs such as the salaries of top managers.

The difference between a firm's revenue and its costs is its profit. Profit shows up in several forms on an income statement. A firm's *operating income* is the difference between its revenue and its operating expenses. Most corporations, including Google, also have investments, such as government and corporate bonds, that normally generate some income for them. In this case, Google earned $415 million on its investments, which

Note: All numbers are in millions of dollars.

Figure 6A.1 Google's Income Statement for 2010

Google's income statement shows the company's revenue, costs, and profit for 2010. The difference between its revenue ($29,321 million) and its operating expenses ($18,940 million) is its operating income ($10,381 million). Most corporations also have investments, such as government or corporate bonds, that generate some income for them. In this case, Google earned $415 million, giving the firm an income before taxes of $10,796 million. After paying taxes of $2,291 million, Google was left with a net income, or accounting profit, of $8,505 million for the year.

Data from Google Inc. (2010) 10-K Annual Report. SEC EDGAR website www.sec.gov/edgar.shtml.

increased its *income before taxes* to $10,796 million. The federal government taxes the profits of corporations. During 2010, Google paid $2,291 million—or about 21 percent of its profits—in taxes. *Net income* after taxes was $8,505 million. The net income that firms report on their income statements is referred to as their after-tax *accounting profit*.

Analyzing Balance Sheets

As discussed in the chapter, while a firm's income statement reports the firm's activities for a period of time, a firm's balance sheet summarizes its financial position on a particular day, usually the end of a quarter or year. To understand how a balance sheet is organized, first recall that an asset is anything of value that the firm owns, and a liability is a debt or an obligation that the firm owes. Subtracting the value of a firm's liabilities from the value of its assets leaves its *net worth*. Because a corporation's stockholders are its owners, net worth is often listed as **stockholders' equity** on a balance sheet. Using these definitions, we can state the balance sheet equation (also called the basic accounting equation) as follows:

$$\text{Assets} - \text{Liabilities} = \text{Stockholders Equity},$$

or:

$$\text{Assets} = \text{Liabilities} + \text{Stockholders Equity}.$$

This formula tells us that the value of a firm's assets must equal the value of its liabilities plus the value of stockholders' equity. An important accounting rule dating back to the beginning of modern bookkeeping in fifteenth-century Italy holds that balance sheets should list assets on the left side and liabilities and net worth, or stockholders' equity, on the right side. Notice that this means that *the value of the left side of the balance sheet must always equal the value of the right side*. Figure 6A.2 shows Google's balance sheet as of December 31, 2010.

A couple of the entries on the asset side of the balance sheet may be unfamiliar: *Current assets* are assets that the firm could convert into cash quickly, such as the balance in its checking account or its accounts receivable, which is money currently owed to the firm for products that have been delivered but not yet paid for. *Goodwill* represents the difference between the purchase price of a company and the market value of its assets. It represents the ability of a business to earn an economic profit from its assets. For example, if you buy a restaurant that is located on a busy intersection and you employ a chef with a reputation for preparing delicious food, you may pay more than the market value of the tables, chairs, ovens, and other assets. This additional amount you pay will be entered on the asset side of your balance sheet as goodwill.

Current liabilities are short-term debts such as accounts payable, which is money owed to suppliers for goods received but not yet paid for, or bank loans that will be paid back in less than one year. Long-term bank loans and the value of outstanding corporate bonds are *long-term liabilities*.

Stockholders' equity The difference between the value of a corporation's assets and the value of its liabilities; also known as *net worth*.

Assets		Liabilities and Stockholders' Equity	
Current Assets	$41,562	Current Liabilities	$9,996
Property and Equipment	7,759	Long-term Liabilities	1,614
Investments	523	Total Liabilities	11,610
Goodwill	6,256	Stockholders' Equity	46,241
Other long-term assets	1,751		
Total Assets	57,851	Total liabilities and stockholders' equity	57,851

Note: All values are in millions of dollars.

Figure 6A.2

Google's Balance Sheet as of December 31, 2010

Corporations list their assets on the left of their balance sheets and their liabilities on the right. The difference between the value of a firm's assets and the value of its liabilities equals the net worth of the firm, or stockholders' equity. Stockholders' equity is listed on the right side of the balance sheet. Therefore, the value of the left side of the balance sheet must always equal the value of the right side.

Data from Google Inc. (2010) 10-K Annual Report. SEC EDGAR website www.sec.gov/edgar.shtml.

Key Terms

Present value, p. 195

Stockholders' equity, p. 201

 6A **Tools to Analyze Firms' Financial Information,** pages 195–201

LEARNING OBJECTIVE: Understand the concept of present value and the information contained on a firm's income statement and balance sheet.

MyEconLab Visit **www.myeconlab.com** to complete these exercises online and get instant feedback.

Review Questions

6A.1 Why is money you receive at some future date worth less to you than money you receive today? If the interest rate rises, what effect does this have on the present value of payments you receive in the future?

6A.2 Give the formula for calculating the present value of a bond that will pay a coupon of $100 per year for 10 years and that has a face value of $1,000.

6A.3 Compare the formula for calculating the present value of the payments you will receive from owning a bond to the formula for calculating the present value of the payments you will receive from owning a stock. What are the key similarities? What are the key differences?

6A.4 How is operating income calculated? How does operating income differ from net income? How does net income differ from accounting profit?

6A.5 What is the key difference between a firm's income statement and its balance sheet? What is listed on the left side of a balance sheet? What is listed on the right side?

Problems and Applications

6A.6 **[Related to** Solved Problem 6A.1 **on page 197]**
If the interest rate is 10 percent, what is the present value of a bond that matures in two years, pays $85 one year from now, and pays $1,085 two years from now?

6A.7 **[Related to** Solved Problem 6A.1 **on page 197]**
Before the 2008 season, the New York Yankees signed second baseman Robinson Cano to a contract that would pay him the following amounts: $3 million for the 2008 season, $6 million for the 2009 season, $9 million for the 2010 season, and $10 million for the 2011 season, with an option for $14 million for the 2012 season and an option for $15 million for the 2013 season. Assume that Cano plays all six seasons for the Yankees and that he receives each of his six seasonal salaries as a lump-sum payment at the end of the season and he receives his 2008 salary one year after he signs the contract.

  a. Some newspaper reports described Cano as having signed a $57 million contract with the Yankees. Do you agree that $57 million was the value of this contract? Briefly explain.

  b. What was the present value of Cano's contract at the time he signed it (assuming an interest rate of 10 percent)?

  c. If you use an interest rate of 5 percent, what was the present value of Cano's contract?

Based on Joel Sherman, "Robinson Cano Deal Final," *New York Post*, January 8, 2008.

6A.8 **[Related to** Solved Problem 6A.1 **on page 197]**
A winner of the Pennsylvania Lottery was given the choice of receiving $18 million at once or $1,440,000 per year for 25 years.

  a. If the winner had opted for the 25 annual payments, how much in total would she have received?

  b. At an interest rate of 10 percent, what would be the present value of the 25 payments?

  c. At an interest rate of 5 percent, what would be the present value of the 25 payments?

  d. What interest rate would make the present value of the 25 payments equal to the one payment of $18 million? (This question is difficult and requires the use of a financial calculator or a spreadsheet. *Hint:* If you are familiar with the Excel spreadsheet program, use the RATE function. You can answer parts b and c by using the Excel NPV [Net Present Value] function.)

6A.9 **[Related to** Solved Problem 6A.1 **on page 197]**
Before the start of the 2000 baseball season, the New York Mets decided they didn't want Bobby Bonilla playing for them any longer. But Bonilla had a contract with the Mets for the 2000 season that would have obliged the Mets to pay him $5.9 million. When the Mets released Bonilla, he agreed to take the following payments in lieu of the $5.9 million the Mets would have paid him in the year 2000: He would receive 25 equal payments of $1,193,248.20 each July 1 from 2011 to 2035. If you were Bobby Bonilla, which would you rather have had, the lump-sum $5.9 million or the 25 payments beginning in 2011? Explain the basis for your decision.

6A.10 Suppose that eLake, an online auction site, is paying a dividend of $2 per share. You expect this dividend to grow 2 percent per year, and the interest rate is 10 percent. What is the most you would be willing to pay for a share of stock in eLake? If the interest rate is 5 percent, what is the most you would be willing to pay? When interest rates in the economy decline, would you expect stock prices in general to rise or fall? Explain.

6A.11 Suppose you buy the bond of a large corporation at a time when the inflation rate is very low. If the inflation rate increases during the time you hold the bond, what is likely to happen to the price of the bond?

6A.12 Use the information in the following table for calendar year 2010 to prepare an income statement for McDonald's Corporation's. Be sure to include entries for operating income and net income.

Revenue from company restaurants	$16,233 million
Revenue from franchised restaurants	7,841 million
Cost of operating company-owned restaurants	13,060 million
Income taxes	2,054 million
Interest expense	451 million
General and administrative cost	2,333 million
Cost of restaurant leases	1,378 million

Data from McDonalds Corp. (2010) 10-K Annual Report. SEC EDGAR (www.sec.gov/edgar.shtml).

6A.13 Use the information in the following table on the financial situation of Starbucks Corporation as of October 3, 2010, to prepare a balance sheet for the firm. Be sure to include an entry for stockholders' equity.

Current assets	$2,756 million
Current liabilities	1,779 million
Property and equipment	2,417 million
Long-term liabilities	925 million
Goodwill	262 million
Other assets	951 million

Data from Starbucks Corp. (2010) 10-K Annual Report. SEC EDGAR (www.sec.gov/edgar.shtml).

6A.14 The *current ratio* is equal to a firm's current assets divided by its current liabilities. Use the information in Figure 6A.2 on page 201 to calculate Google's current ratio on December 31, 2010. Investors generally prefer that a firm's current ratio be greater than 1.5. What problems might a firm encounter if the value of its current assets is low relative to the value of its current liabilities?

Comparative Advantage and the Gains from International Trade

Chapter Outline and Learning Objectives

Does the Federal Government's "Buy American" Policy Help U.S. Firms?

In response to the economic recession of 2007–2009, Congress and President Barack Obama passed the American Recovery and Reinvestment Act of 2009, a bill that included tax cuts and increased government spending, particularly on infrastructure such as bridges and roads. The bill included a "Buy American" provision that required all manufactured goods bought with these funds to be made in the United States. The intention was to increase the number of jobs the bill would create by preventing foreign companies from participating in the new spending projects.

Some U.S. firms, though, were opposed to the Buy American provision. These firms had two concerns: First, they were afraid that foreign governments would retaliate. Canada and China in particular, protested before the bill was passed that the United States had signed international agreements in which it had promised not to impose new barriers to foreign companies selling in the United States. Once the bill passed, retaliation did take place. China passed a similar bill that increased infrastructure spending, while specifying that only Chinese firms could participate. Illinois-based Caterpillar, which makes bulldozers and other construction equipment, and other U.S. firms were excluded. One executive at Caterpillar was quoted as saying, "The so-called Buy American amendment is really an anti-export provision."

U.S. firms were also concerned because in the modern business world, foreign-based firms often buy from U.S. suppliers, and U.S. suppliers often buy from foreign firms. As one executive for General Electric put it, "The supply chains are so integrated, it is crazy to try to impose a Buy American provision. Some components cross the border four or five times."

Are Buy American provisions and other attempts to protect U.S. firms from foreign competition good ideas? As we will see in this chapter, these policies create winners— the firms that are sheltered from foreign competition—but they also create losers— U.S. firms that rely on exports to foreign countries, as well as U.S. consumers and taxpayers who must pay higher prices for goods that could have been purchased at lower prices from foreign companies.

AN INSIDE LOOK on **page 230** examines a federal lawsuit against Home Depot, alleging that the company violated the Buy American provision.

Based on Keith Bradsher, "Pentagon Must 'Buy American,' Barring Chinese Solar Panels," *New York Times*, January 9, 2011; Peter Fritsch and Corey Boles, "How 'Buy American' Can Hurt U.S. Firms," *Wall Street Journal*, September 17, 2009; and Mark Drajem, "GE, Caterpillar Fight 'Buy American' Rule in Stimulus," Bloomberg.com, January 22, 2009.

Economics in Your Life

Have You Heard of the "Buy American" Provision?

Politicians often support restrictions on trade to convince people to vote for them. The workers in the industries these restrictions protect are likely to vote for the politicians because the workers think trade restrictions will protect their jobs. But most people are not workers in industries protected from foreign competition by trade restrictions. Many people work for firms, such as Caterpillar, that sell goods in foreign markets. These workers risk losing their jobs if foreign countries retaliate against U.S. attempts to reduce imported goods. How, then, did some U.S. companies convince Congress to include the Buy American provision in the American Recovery and Reinvestment Act of 2009, and why have relatively few people even heard of this provision? As you read the chapter, see if you can answer these questions. You can check your answers against those we provide on **page 229** at the end of this chapter.

Trade is simply the act of buying or selling. Is there a difference between trade that takes place within a country and international trade? Within the United States, domestic trade makes it possible for consumers in Ohio to eat salmon caught in Alaska and for consumers in Montana to drive cars built in Michigan or Kentucky. Similarly, international trade makes it possible for consumers in the United States to drink wine from France and use Blu-ray players from Japan. But one significant difference between domestic trade and international trade is that international trade is more controversial. At one time, nearly all the televisions, shoes, clothing, and toys bought in the United States were also produced in the United States. Today, firms in other countries produce most of these goods. This shift has benefited U.S. consumers because foreign-made goods have lower prices or higher quality than the U.S.-made goods they have replaced. But at the same time, many U.S. firms that produced these goods have gone out of business, and their workers have had to find other jobs. Not surprisingly, opinion polls show that many Americans favor reducing international trade because they believe doing so will preserve jobs in the United States. But is this belief accurate?

We can use the tools of demand and supply developed in Chapter 3 to analyze markets for internationally traded goods and services. We saw in Chapter 2 that trade in general—whether within a country or between countries—is based on the principle of comparative advantage. In this chapter, we look more closely at the role of comparative advantage in international trade. We also use the concepts of consumer surplus, producer surplus, and deadweight loss from Chapter 4 to analyze government policies that interfere with trade. With this background, we can return to the political debate over whether the United States benefits from international trade. We begin by looking at how large a role international trade plays in the U.S. economy.

7.1 LEARNING OBJECTIVE

Discuss the role of international trade in the U.S. economy.

The United States in the International Economy

International trade has grown tremendously over the past 50 years. The increase in trade is the result of the falling costs of shipping products around the world, the spread of inexpensive and reliable communications, and changes in government policies. Firms can use large container ships to send their products across oceans at low cost. Businesspeople today can travel to Europe or Asia, using fast, inexpensive, and reliable air transportation. The Internet, cell phones, and text messaging allow managers to communicate instantaneously and at a very low cost with customers and suppliers around the world. These and other improvements in transportation and communication have created an integrated global marketplace that earlier generations of businesspeople could only dream of.

Tariff A tax imposed by a government on imports.

Imports Goods and services bought domestically but produced in other countries.

Exports Goods and services produced domestically but sold in other countries.

Over the past 50 years, many governments have changed policies to facilitate international trade. For example, tariff rates have fallen. A **tariff** is a tax imposed by a government on *imports* of a good into a country. **Imports** are goods and services bought domestically but produced in other countries. In the 1930s, the United States charged an average tariff rate above 50 percent. Today, the rate is less than 2 percent. In North America, most tariffs between Canada, Mexico, and the United States were eliminated following the passage of the North American Free Trade Agreement (NAFTA) in 1994. Twenty-seven countries in Europe have formed the European Union, which has eliminated all tariffs among member countries, greatly increasing both imports and **exports**, which are goods and services produced domestically but sold in other countries.

The Importance of Trade to the U.S. Economy

U.S. consumers buy increasing quantities of goods and services produced in other countries. At the same time, U.S. businesses sell increasing quantities of goods and services to consumers in other countries. Figure 7.1 shows that since 1970, both exports and imports have been steadily increasing as a fraction of U.S. gross domestic product (GDP).

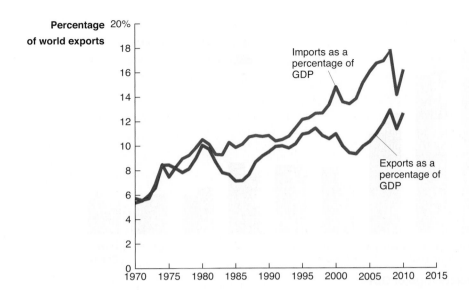

Figure 7.1

International Trade Is of Increasing Importance to the United States

Exports and imports of goods and services as a percentage of total production—measured by GDP—show the importance of international trade to an economy. Since 1970, both imports and exports have been steadily rising as a fraction of U.S. GDP.

Data from the U.S. Department of Commerce, Bureau of Economic Analysis.

Recall that GDP is the value of all the final goods and services produced in a country during a year. In 1970, exports and imports were both less than 6 percent of GDP. In 2010, exports were about 13 percent of GDP, and imports were about 16 percent.

Not all sectors of the U.S. economy are affected equally by international trade. For example, although it's difficult to import or export some services, such as haircuts and appendectomies, a large percentage of U.S. agricultural production is exported. Each year, the United States exports about 50 percent of its wheat and rice crops and 20 percent of its corn crop.

Many U.S. manufacturing industries also depend on trade. About 20 percent of U.S. manufacturing jobs depend directly or indirectly on exports. In some industries, such as computers, the products these workers make are directly exported. In other industries, such as steel, the products are used to make other products, such as bulldozers or machine tools, that are then exported. In all, about two-thirds of U.S. manufacturing industries depend on exports for at least 10 percent of jobs.

U.S. International Trade in a World Context

The United States is the largest exporter in the world, as Figure 7.2 illustrates. Six of the other seven leading exporting countries are also high-income countries. Although China is still a relatively low-income country, the rapid growth of the Chinese economy over the past 30 years has resulted in its becoming the third-largest exporter.

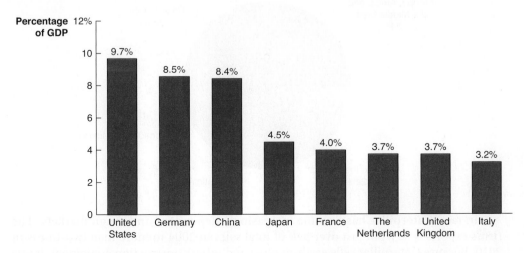

Figure 7.2

The Eight Leading Exporting Countries, 2010

The United States is the leading exporting country, accounting for 9.7 percent of total world exports. The values are the shares of total world exports of merchandise and commercial services.

Data from World Trade Organization, *International Trade Statistics*, 2010.

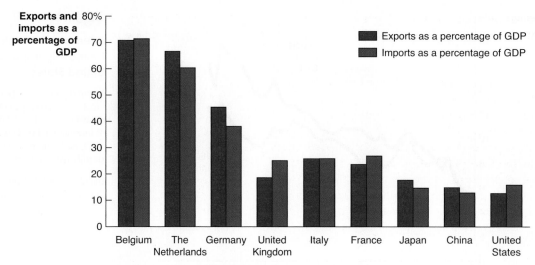

Figure 7.3 **International Trade as a Percentage of GDP**

International trade is still less important to the United States than to most other countries.
Data from Organization for Economic Cooperation and Development, *Country Statistical Profile*, 2011.

Figure 7.3 shows that international trade is less important to the United States than to many other countries, with imports and exports being smaller percentages of GDP. In some smaller countries, such as Belgium and the Netherlands, imports and exports make up more than half of GDP. In the larger European economies, imports and exports make up one-quarter to one-half of GDP.

Making the Connection | How Caterpillar Depends on International Trade

We saw in the chapter opener that Caterpillar, Inc., was opposed to the Buy American provision in the American Recovery and Reinvestment Act. Jim Owens, Caterpillar's CEO, argued, "We need to avoid things like . . . 'Buy American.' . . . If we turn inward, it sends a terrible signal to the rest of the world, and I'm concerned that other countries will adopt even more protectionist measures for their countries." Owens had cause to be concerned because, as the graph below shows, in 2010, 68 percent of Caterpillar sales were outside North America. This dependence on exports made Caterpillar vulnerable to foreign governments responding to the Buy American provision by restricting exports from the United States.

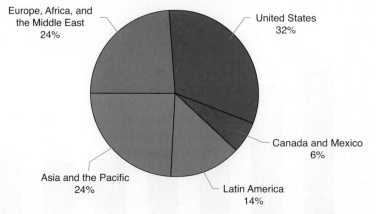

In fact, Caterpillar has become increasingly dependent on foreign markets. The firm's exports rose from just over half of total sales in 2004 to more than two-thirds in 2010. Because Caterpillar sells earth-moving and other construction equipment, it was severely affected by the decline in the U.S. housing market that began in 2006. Although sales in the United States declined by more than half between 2006 and 2008, increases in exports were enough to make 2008 a record sales year for Caterpillar. By 2009, however, the slowdown in the world economy had begun to affect the company, and sales declined 37 percent. Sales rose by 31 percent in 2010, but the increase came largely from higher sales outside of the United States.

Although Caterpillar now sells more outside the United States than inside, it still remains a major employer in the United States. At the end of 2010, Caterpillar employed more than 41,000 workers in 278 offices and factories in the United States. In addition, Caterpillar dealers in the United States employed more than 50,000 people. Thousands of other workers are employed at the many U.S. firms that supply Caterpillar with parts and components for its products. Problems at Caterpillar result in problems in the U.S. communities where the company and its suppliers are located. Caterpillar employs more than 20,000 people in the area around its headquarters in Peoria, Illinois. When sales declines led to layoffs in early 2009, the local real estate market, local stores and businesses, and the tax revenues of local governments were all affected. Like many U.S. firms that depend on exports, Caterpillar and its employees are vulnerable to disruptions in world trade caused by foreign retaliation against U.S. exports or other political problems.

Based on Geoff Colvin, "Caterpillar Is Absolutely Crushing It," *Fortune*, May 12, 2011; Steve Tarter, "Cat Raises the Possibility of Leaving Illinois," *Journal Star*, March 25, 2011; Steven Gray, "Caterpillar Layoffs: How They're Playing in Peoria," *Time*, January 29, 2009; and Caterpillar, 2010 *Annual Report*.

Your Turn: Test your understanding by doing related problem 1.7 on page 232 at the end of this chapter.

MyEconLab

Comparative Advantage in International Trade

7.2 LEARNING OBJECTIVE

Understand the difference between comparative advantage and absolute advantage in international trade.

Why have businesses around the world increasingly looked for markets in other countries? Why have consumers increasingly purchased goods and services made in other countries? People trade for one reason: Trade makes them better off. Whenever a buyer and seller agree to a sale, they must both believe they are better off; otherwise, there would be no sale. This outcome must hold whether the buyer and seller live in the same city or in different countries. As we will see, governments are more likely to interfere with international trade than they are with domestic trade, but the reasons for the interference are more political than economic.

A Brief Review of Comparative Advantage

In Chapter 2, we discussed the key economic concept of *comparative advantage*. **Comparative advantage** is the ability of an individual, a firm, or a country to produce a good or service at a lower opportunity cost than competitors. Recall that **opportunity cost** is the highest-valued alternative that must be given up to engage in an activity. People, firms, and countries specialize in economic activities in which they have a comparative advantage. In trading, we benefit from the comparative advantage of other people (or firms or countries), and they benefit from our comparative advantage.

A good way to think of comparative advantage is to recall the example in Chapter 2 of you and your neighbor picking fruit. Your neighbor is better at picking both apples and cherries than you are. Why, then, doesn't your neighbor pick both types of fruit? Because the opportunity cost to your neighbor of picking her own apples is very high: She is a particularly skilled cherry picker, and every hour spent picking apples is an hour taken away from picking cherries. You can pick apples at a much lower opportunity cost than your neighbor, so you have a comparative advantage in picking apples. Your neighbor can pick cherries at a much lower opportunity cost than you can, so she has a comparative advantage in picking cherries. Your neighbor is better off specializing in picking cherries, and you are better off specializing in picking apples. You can then trade some of your apples for some of your neighbor's cherries, and both of you will end up with more of each fruit.

Comparative advantage The ability of an individual, a firm, or a country to produce a good or service at a lower opportunity cost than competitors.

Opportunity cost The highest-valued alternative that must be given up to engage in an activity.

Table 7.1

An Example of Japanese Workers Being More Productive Than American Workers

	Output per Hour of Work	
	Cell Phones	Tablet Computers
Japan	12	6
United States	2	4

Comparative Advantage in International Trade

The principle of comparative advantage can explain why people pursue different occupations. It can also explain why countries produce different goods and services. International trade involves many countries importing and exporting many different goods and services. Countries are better off if they specialize in producing the goods for which they have a comparative advantage. They can then trade for the goods for which other countries have a comparative advantage.

We can illustrate why specializing on the basis of comparative advantage makes countries better off with a simple example involving just two countries and two products. Suppose the United States and Japan produce only cell phones and tablet computers, like Apple's iPad or Samsung's Galaxy Tab. Assume that each country uses only labor to produce each good and that Japanese and U.S. cell phones and tablet computers are exactly the same. Table 7.1 shows how much each country can produce of each good with one hour of labor.

Notice that Japanese workers are more productive than U.S. workers in making both goods. In one hour of work, Japanese workers can make six times as many cell phones and one and one-half times as many tablet computers as U.S. workers. Japan has an *absolute advantage* over the United States in producing both goods. **Absolute advantage** is the ability to produce more of a good or service than competitors when using the same amount of resources. In this case, Japan can produce more of both goods using the same amount of labor as the United States.

It might seem at first that Japan has nothing to gain from trading with the United States because it has an absolute advantage in producing both goods. However, Japan should specialize and produce only cell phones and obtain the tablet computers it needs by exporting cell phones to the United States in exchange for tablet computers. The reason that Japan benefits from trade is that although it has an *absolute advantage* in the production of both goods, it has a *comparative advantage* only in the production of cell phones. The United States has a comparative advantage in the production of tablet computers.

If it seems contrary to common sense that Japan should import tablet computers from the United States even though Japan can produce more tablets per hour of work, think about the opportunity cost to each country of producing each good. If Japan wants to produce more tablet computers, it has to switch labor away from cell phone production. Every hour of labor switched from producing cell phones to producing tablet computers increases tablet computer production by 6 and reduces cell phone production by 12. Japan has to give up 12 cell phones for every 6 tablet computers it produces. Therefore, the opportunity cost to Japan of producing one more tablet computer is 12/6, or 2 cell phones.

If the United States switches one hour of labor from cell phones to tablet computers, production of cell phones falls by 2, and production of tablet computers rises by 4. Therefore, the opportunity cost to the United States of producing one more tablet computer is 2/4, or 0.5 cell phone. The United States has a lower opportunity cost of producing tablet

Absolute advantage The ability to produce more of a good or service than competitors when using the same amount of resources.

Table 7.2

The Opportunity Costs of Producing Cell Phones and Tablet Computers

The table shows the opportunity cost each country faces in producing cell phones and tablet computers. For example, the entry in the first row and second column shows that Japan must give up 2 cell phones for every tablet computer it produces.

	Opportunity Costs	
	Cell Phones	Tablet Computers
Japan	0.5 tablet computer	2 cell phones
United States	2 tablet computers	0.5 cell phone

	Production and Consumption	
	Cell Phones	Tablet Computers
Japan	9,000	1,500
United States	1,500	1,000

Table 7.3

Production without Trade

computers and, therefore, has a comparative advantage in making this product. By similar reasoning, we can see that Japan has a comparative advantage in producing cell phones. Table 7.2 summarizes the opportunity cost each country faces in producing these goods.

How Countries Gain from International Trade

Can Japan really gain from producing only cell phones and trading with the United States for tablet computers? To see that it can, assume at first that Japan and the United States do not trade with each other. A situation in which a country does not trade with other countries is called **autarky**. Assume that in autarky, each country has 1,000 hours of labor available to produce the two goods, and each country produces the quantities of the two goods shown in Table 7.3. Because there is no trade, these quantities also represent consumption of the two goods in each country.

Increasing Consumption through Trade

Suppose now that Japan and the United States begin to trade with each other. The **terms of trade** is the ratio at which a country can trade its exports for imports from other countries. For simplicity, let's assume that the terms of trade end up with Japan and the United States being willing to trade one cell phone for one tablet computer.

Once trade has begun, the United States and Japan can exchange tablet computers for cell phones or cell phones for tablet computers. For example, if Japan specializes by using all 1,000 available hours of labor to produce cell phones, it will be able to produce 12,000. It then could export 1,500 cell phones to the United States in exchange for 1,500 tablet computers. (Remember that we are assuming that the terms of trade are one cell phone for one tablet computer.) Japan ends up with 10,500 cell phones and 1,500 tablet computers. Compared with the situation before trade, Japan has the same number of tablet computers but 1,500 more cell phones. If the United States specializes in producing tablet computers, it will be able to produce 4,000. It could then export 1,500 tablet computers to Japan in exchange for 1,500 cell phones. The United States ends up with 2,500 tablet computers and 1,500 cell phones. Compared with the situation before trade, the United States has the same number of cell phones but 1,500 more tablet computers. Trade has allowed both countries to increase the quantities of goods consumed. Table 7.4 summarizes the gains from trade for the United States and Japan.

By trading, Japan and the United States are able to consume more than they could without trade. This outcome is possible because world production of both goods increases after trade. (In this example, our "world" consists of just the United States and Japan.)

Why does total production of cell phones and tablet computers increase when the United States specializes in producing tablet computers and Japan specializes in producing cell phones? A domestic analogy helps to answer this question: If a company shifts production from an old factory to a more efficient modern factory, its output will increase. In effect, the same thing happens in our example. Producing tablet computers in Japan and cell phones in the United States is inefficient. Shifting production to the more efficient country—the one with the comparative advantage—increases total production. The key point is this: *Countries gain from specializing in producing goods in which they have a comparative advantage and trading for goods in which other countries have a comparative advantage.*

7.3 LEARNING OBJECTIVE

Explain how countries gain from international trade.

Autarky A situation in which a country does not trade with other countries.

Terms of trade The ratio at which a country can trade its exports for imports from other countries.

Table 7.4

Gains from Trade for Japan and the United States

Without Trade

Production and Consumption

	Cell Phones	Tablet Computers
Japan	9,000	1,500
United States	1,500	1,000

With Trade

	Production with Trade		Trade		Consumption with Trade	
	Cell Phones	Tablet Computers	Cell Phones	Tablet Computers	Cell Phones	Tablet Computers
Japan	12,000	0	Export 1,500	Import 1,500	10,500	1,500
United States	0	4,000	Import 1,500	Export 1,500	1,500	2,500

With trade, the United States and Japan specialize in the good they have a comparative advantage in producing . . .

. . . and export some of that good in exchange for the good the other country has a comparative advantage in producing.

Gains from Trade

Increased Consumption

Japan	1,500 Cell Phones
United States	1,500 Tablet Computers

The increased consumption made possible by trade represents the gains from trade.

Solved Problem 7.3

The Gains from Trade

The first discussion of comparative advantage appears in *On the Principles of Political Economy and Taxation*, a book written by David Ricardo in 1817. Ricardo provided a famous example of the gains from trade, using wine and cloth production in Portugal and England. The following table is adapted from Ricardo's example, with cloth measured in sheets and wine measured in kegs:

	Output per Year of Labor	
	Cloth	Wine
Portugal	100	150
England	90	60

a. Explain which country has an absolute advantage in the production of each good.
b. Explain which country has a comparative advantage in the production of each good.

c. Suppose that Portugal and England currently do not trade with each other. Each country has 1,000 workers, so each has 1,000 years of labor time to use producing cloth and wine, and the countries are currently producing the amounts of each good shown in the following table:

	Cloth	Wine
Portugal	18,000	123,000
England	63,000	18,000

Show that Portugal and England can both gain from trade. Assume that the terms of trade are that one sheet of cloth can be traded for one keg of wine.

Solving the Problem

Step 1: **Review the chapter material.** This problem is about absolute and comparative advantage and the gains from trade, so you may want to review the section "Comparative Advantage in International Trade," which begins on page 210, and the section "How Countries Gain from International Trade," which begins on page 211.

Step 2: **Answer part a. by determining which country has an absolute advantage.**
Remember that a country has an absolute advantage over another country when it can produce more of a good using the same resources. The first table in the problem shows that Portugal can produce more cloth *and* more wine with one year's worth of labor than can England. Thus, Portugal has an absolute advantage in the production of both goods and, therefore, England does not have an absolute advantage in the production of either good.

Step 3: **Answer part b. by determining which country has a comparative advantage.**
A country has a comparative advantage when it can produce a good at a lower opportunity cost. To produce 100 sheets of cloth, Portugal must give up producing 150 kegs of wine. Therefore, the opportunity cost to Portugal of producing 1 sheet of cloth is 150/100, or 1.5 kegs of wine. England has to give up producing 60 kegs of wine to produce 90 sheets of cloth, so its opportunity cost of producing 1 sheet of cloth is 60/90, or 0.67 keg of wine. The opportunity costs of producing wine can be calculated in the same way. The following table shows the opportunity cost to Portugal and England of producing each good.

	Opportunity Costs	
	Cloth	Wine
Portugal	1.5 kegs of wine	0.67 sheet of cloth
England	0.67 keg of wine	1.5 sheets of cloth

Portugal has a comparative advantage in wine because its opportunity cost is lower. England has a comparative advantage in cloth because its opportunity cost is lower.

Step 4: **Answer part c. by showing that both countries can benefit from trade.** By now it should be clear that both countries will be better off if they specialize where they have a comparative advantage and trade for the other product. The following table is very similar to Table 7.4 and shows one example of trade making both countries better off. (To test your understanding, construct another example.)

Without Trade

	Production and Consumption	
	Cloth	Wine
Portugal	18,000	123,000
England	63,000	18,000

With Trade

	Production with Trade		Trade		Consumption with Trade	
	Cloth	Wine	Cloth	Wine	Cloth	Wine
Portugal	0	150,000	Import 18,000	Export 18,000	18,000	132,000
England	90,000	0	Export 18,000	Import 18,000	72,000	18,000

Gains from Trade

	Increased Consumption
Portugal	9,000 wine
England	9,000 cloth

Your Turn: For more practice, do related problems 3.5 and 3.6 on page 234 at the end of this chapter. MyEconLab

Why Don't We See Complete Specialization?

In our example of two countries producing only two products, each country specializes in producing one of the goods. In the real world, many goods and services are produced in more than one country. For example, the United States, Japan, Germany, Canada, Mexico, India, China, and other countries produce automobiles. We do not see complete specialization in the real world for three main reasons:

- *Not all goods and services are traded internationally.* Even if, for example, Japan had a comparative advantage in the production of medical services, it would be difficult for Japan to specialize in producing medical services and then export them. There is no easy way for U.S. patients who need appendectomies to receive them from surgeons in Japan.

- *Production of most goods involves increasing opportunity costs.* Recall from Chapter 2 that production of most goods involves increasing opportunity costs. So, in our example, if the United States devotes more workers to producing tablet computers, the opportunity cost of producing more tablet computers will increase. At some point, the opportunity cost of producing tablet computers in the United States may rise to the level of the opportunity cost of producing tablet computers in Japan. When that happens, international trade will no longer push the United States further toward specialization. The same will be true of Japan: Increasing opportunity cost will cause Japan to stop short of complete specialization in producing cell phones.

- *Tastes for products differ.* Most products are *differentiated*. Cell phones, tablet computers, cars, and televisions—to name just a few products—come with a wide variety of features. When buying automobiles, some people look for reliability and fuel efficiency, others look for room to carry seven passengers, and still others want styling and high performance. So, some car buyers prefer Toyota Prius hybrids, some prefer Chevy Suburbans, and others prefer BMWs. As a result, Japan, the United States, and Germany may each have a comparative advantage in producing different types of automobiles.

Does Anyone Lose as a Result of International Trade?

In our cell phone and tablet computer example, consumption increases in both the United States and Japan as a result of trade. Everyone gains, and no one loses. Or do

---

Don't Let This Happen to You

Remember That Trade Creates Both Winners and Losers

The following statement is from a Federal Reserve publication: "Trade is a win–win situation for all countries that participate." People sometimes interpret statements like this to mean that there are no losers from international trade. But notice that the statement refers to *countries*, not individuals. When countries participate in trade, they make their consumers better off by increasing the quantity of goods and services available to them. As we have seen, however, expanding trade eliminates the jobs of workers employed at companies that are less efficient than foreign companies. Trade also creates new jobs at companies that export to foreign markets. It may be difficult, though, for workers who lose their jobs because of trade to easily find others. That is

why in the United States, the federal government uses the Trade Adjustment Assistance program to provide funds for workers who have lost their jobs due to international trade. Qualified unemployed workers can use these funds to pay for retraining, for searching for new jobs, or for relocating to areas where new jobs are available. This program—and similar programs in other countries—recognizes that there are losers from international trade as well as winners.

Based on Federal Reserve Bank of Dallas, "International Trade and the Economy," www.dallasfed.org/educate/everyday/ev7.html.

MyEconLab

Your Turn: Test your understanding by doing related problem 3.12 on page 235 at the end of this chapter.

they? In our example, we referred repeatedly to "Japan" or the "United States" producing cell phones or tablet computers. But countries do not produce goods—firms do. In a world without trade, there would be cell phone and tablet computer firms in both Japan and the United States. In a world with trade, there would be only Japanese cell phone firms and U.S. tablet computer firms. Japanese tablet computer firms and U.S. cell phone firms would close. Overall, total employment would not change, and production would increase as a result of trade. Nevertheless, the owners of Japanese tablet computer firms, the owners of U.S. cell phone firms, and the people who work for them are worse off as a result of trade. The losers from trade are likely to do their best to convince the Japanese and U.S. governments to interfere with trade by barring imports of the competing products from the other country or by imposing high tariffs on them.

Where Does Comparative Advantage Come From?

Among the main sources of comparative advantage are the following:

- *Climate and natural resources.* This source of comparative advantage is the most obvious. Because of geology, Saudi Arabia has a comparative advantage in the production of oil. Because of climate and soil conditions, Costa Rica has a comparative advantage in the production of bananas, and the United States has a comparative advantage in the production of wheat.

- *Relative abundance of labor and capital.* Some countries, such as the United States, have many highly skilled workers and a great deal of machinery. Other countries, such as China, have many unskilled workers and relatively little machinery. As a result, the United States has a comparative advantage in the production of goods that require highly skilled workers or sophisticated machinery to manufacture, such as aircraft, semiconductors, and computer software. China has a comparative advantage in the production of goods, such as tools, clothing, and children's toys, that require unskilled workers and small amounts of simple machinery.

- *Technology.* Broadly defined, *technology* is the process firms use to turn inputs into goods and services. At any given time, firms in different countries do not all have access to the same technologies. In part, this difference is the result of past investments countries have made in supporting higher education or in providing support for research and development. Some countries are strong in *product technologies*, which involve the ability to develop new products. For example, firms in the United States have pioneered the development of such products as radios, televisions, digital computers, airliners, medical equipment, and many prescription drugs. Other countries are strong in *process technologies*, which involve the ability to improve the processes used to make existing products. For example, Japanese-based firms, such as Toyota and Honda, have succeeded by greatly improving the processes for designing and manufacturing automobiles.

- *External economies.* It is difficult to explain the location of some industries on the basis of climate, natural resources, the relative abundance of labor and capital, or technology. For example, why does southern California have a comparative advantage in making movies or Switzerland in making watches or New York in providing financial services? The answer is that once an industry becomes established in an area, firms that locate in that area gain advantages over firms located elsewhere. The advantages include the availability of skilled workers, the opportunity to interact with other firms in the same industry, and proximity to suppliers. These advantages result in lower costs to firms located in the area. Because these lower costs result from increases in the size of the industry in an area, economists refer to them as **external economies**.

External economies Reductions in a firm's costs that result from an increase in the size of an industry.

Making
the
Connection

Leave New York City? Risky for Financial Firms

The name "Wall Street" is shorthand for the whole U.S. financial system of banks, brokerage houses, and other financial firms. Wall Street is also, of course, an actual street in the New York City borough of Manhattan. The New York Stock Exchange is located on Wall Street, and many financial firms have their headquarters in Manhattan. There are also a lot of financial firms located outside Manhattan, but many of the largest firms believe that there are advantages to being located close to Wall Street. For instance, in 1997, UBS, a large Swiss bank, moved its North American headquarters from Manhattan to Stamford, Connecticut, where it built the largest facility for trading financial securities in the world. By 2011, UBS had begun moving many of its bankers back to Manhattan and was expected to occupy more than 1 million square feet of the 3 World Trade Center building once construction was complete. Other financial firms have also moved some operations out of Manhattan only to move them back.

Financial firms benefit from the external economies of being located in New York City.

The original concentration of financial firms in Manhattan was something of a historical accident. In colonial times and up through the early nineteenth century, Philadelphia and Boston were at least close rivals to New York City as business and financial centers. In fact, Philadelphia had both a larger population than New York and was the headquarters of the federal government's first two central banks. New York City received a boost in its rivalry with other cities when the Erie Canal was completed in upstate New York in 1825. The canal resulted in crops and other raw materials being shipped to New York City rather than to other ports. This inflow led to the development of banking, insurance, and other financial firms. Coupled with the gradual increase in trading on the New Stock Exchange, the increase in business resulting from the completion of the canal established New York City as the leading financial center in the country.

But the Erie Canal has long since ceased to operate, and most stock trading takes place electronically rather than on the floor of the New York Stock Exchange. So, why has New York continued to see a high concentration of financial firms, with some firms that temporarily left deciding to return? The answer is that financial firms benefit from the external economies of being located in New York City. Even in the Internet age, many financial deals are still conducted face-to-face, so not having a physical presence in Manhattan puts a firm at a disadvantage. Many people pursuing careers in finance also want to be physically located in Manhattan because that is where most of the highest-paying financial jobs are. Firms that have moved out of Manhattan have had more difficulty attracting and retaining the most productive workers. In addition, Manhattan also has a large concentration of firms that provide support services, such as software programming for running financial firms' computer systems.

Large financial firms located outside Manhattan, particularly those that heavily trade securities or attempt to make deals that involve mergers between firms, may have higher costs than firms located in Manhattan. Having many financial firms originally located in Manhattan was a historical accident, but external economies gave the area a comparative advantage in providing financial services once the industry began to grow there.

Based on Brett Philbin, "UBS Shifts Staff to New York," *Wall Street Journal*, July 13, 2011; and Charles V. Bagli, "Regretting Move, Bank May Return to Manhattan," *New York Times*, June 8, 2011.

MyEconLab **Your Turn:** Test your understanding by doing related problem 3.13 on page 235 at the end of this chapter.

Comparative Advantage over Time: The Rise and Fall—and Rise—of the U.S. Consumer Electronics Industry

A country may develop a comparative advantage in the production of a good, and then, as time passes and circumstances change, the country may lose its comparative advantage in producing that good and develop a comparative advantage in producing other goods. For several decades, the United States had a comparative advantage in the production of consumer electronic goods, such as televisions, radios, and stereos. The comparative advantage of the United States in these products was based on having developed most of the underlying technology, having the most modern factories, and having a skilled and experienced workforce. Gradually, however, other countries, particularly Japan, gained access to the technology, built modern factories, and developed skilled workforces. As mentioned earlier, Japanese firms have excelled in process technologies, which involve the ability to improve the processes used to make existing products. By the 1970s and 1980s, Japanese firms were able to produce many consumer electronic goods more cheaply and with higher quality than could U.S. firms. Japanese firms Sony, Panasonic, and Pioneer replaced U.S. firms Magnavox, Zenith, and RCA as world leaders in consumer electronics.

By 2011, however, as the technology underlying consumer electronics had evolved, comparative advantage had shifted again, and several U.S. firms had surged ahead of their Japanese competitors. For example, Apple had developed the iPod, iPhone, and iPad; Linksys, a division of Cisco Systems, took the lead in home wireless networking technology; and TiVo pioneered the digital video recorder (DVR). As pictures and music converted to digital data, process technologies became less important than the ability to design and develop new products. These new consumer electronic products required skills similar to those in computer design and software writing, where the United States had long maintained a comparative advantage.

Once a country has lost its comparative advantage in producing a good, its income will be higher and its economy will be more efficient if it switches from producing the good to importing it, as the United States did when it switched from producing televisions to importing them. As we will see in the next section, however, there is often political pressure on governments to attempt to preserve industries that have lost their comparative advantage.

Government Policies That Restrict International Trade

Free trade, or trade between countries that is without government restrictions, makes consumers better off. We can expand on this idea by using the concepts of consumer surplus and producer surplus from Chapter 4. Figure 7.4 shows the market in the United States for the bio-fuel ethanol, which can be used as a substitute for gasoline. The figure shows the situation of autarky, where the United States does not trade with other countries. The equilibrium price of ethanol is $2.00 per gallon, and the equilibrium quantity is 6.0 billion gallons per year. The blue area represents consumer surplus, and the red area represents producer surplus.

Now suppose that the United States begins importing ethanol from Brazil and other countries that produce ethanol for $1.00 per gallon. Because the world market for ethanol is large, we will assume that the United States can buy as much ethanol as it wants without causing the *world price* of $1.00 per gallon to rise. Therefore, once imports of ethanol are permitted into the United States, U.S. firms will not be able to sell ethanol at prices higher than the world price of $1.00, and the U.S. price will become equal to the world price.

Figure 7.5 shows the result of allowing imports of ethanol into the United States. With the price lowered from $2.00 to $1.00, U.S. consumers increase their purchases

7.4 LEARNING OBJECTIVE

Analyze the economic effects of government policies that restrict international trade.

Free trade Trade between countries that is without government restrictions.

Figure 7.4

The U.S. Market for Ethanol under Autarky

This figure shows the market for ethanol in the United States, assuming autarky, where the United States does not trade with other countries. The equilibrium price of ethanol is $2.00 per gallon, and the equilibrium quantity is 6.0 billion gallons per year. The blue area represents consumer surplus, and the red area represents producer surplus.

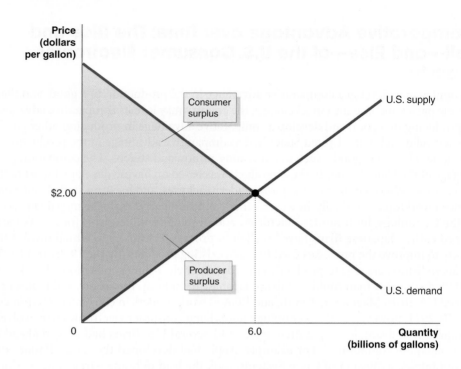

from 6.0 billion gallons to 9.0 billion gallons. Equilibrium moves from point *F* to point *G*. In the new equilibrium, U.S. producers have reduced the quantity of ethanol they supply from 6.0 billion gallons to 3.0 billion gallons. Imports will equal 6.0 billion gallons, which is the difference between U.S. consumption and U.S. production.

Under autarky, consumer surplus would be area *A* in Figure 7.5. With imports, the reduction in price increases consumer surplus, so it is now equal to the sum of areas *A*, *B*, *C*, and *D*. Although the lower price increases consumer surplus, it reduces producer surplus. Under autarky, producer surplus was equal to the sum of the areas *B* and *E*.

Figure 7.5

The Effect of Imports on the U.S. Ethanol Market

When imports are allowed into the United States, the price of ethanol falls from $2.00 to $1.00. U.S. consumers increase their purchases from 6.0 billion gallons to 9.0 billion gallons. Equilibrium moves from point *F* to point *G*. U.S. producers reduce the quantity of ethanol they supply from 6.0 billion gallons to 3.0 billion gallons. Imports equal 6.0 billion gallons, which is the difference between U.S. consumption and U.S. production. Consumer surplus equals the areas *A*, *B*, *C*, and *D*. Producer surplus equals the area *E*.

	Under Autarky	With Imports
Consumer Surplus	*A*	*A* + *B* + *C* + *D*
Producer Surplus	*B* + *E*	*E*
Economic Surplus	*A* + *B* + *E*	*A* + *B* + *C* + *D* + *E*

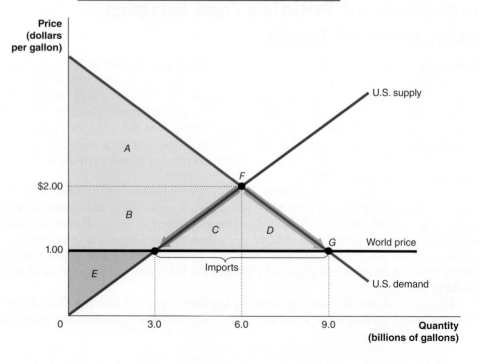

With imports, producer surplus is equal to only area *E*. Recall that economic surplus equals the sum of consumer surplus and producer surplus. Moving from autarky to allowing imports increases economic surplus in the United States by an amount equal to the sum of areas *C* and *D*.

We can conclude that international trade helps consumers but hurts firms that are less efficient than foreign competitors. As a result, these firms and their workers are often strong supporters of government policies that restrict trade. These policies usually take one of two forms: *tariffs* or *quotas* and *voluntary export restraints*.

Tariffs

The most common interferences with trade are *tariffs*, which are taxes imposed by a government on goods imported into a country. Like any other tax, a tariff increases the cost of selling a good. Figure 7.6 shows the effect of a tariff of $0.50 per gallon on ethanol imports into the United States. The $0.50 tariff raises the price of ethanol in the United States from the world price of $1.00 per gallon to $1.50 per gallon. At this higher price, U.S. ethanol producers increase the quantity they supply from 3.0 billion gallons to 4.5 billion gallons. U.S. consumers, though, cut back their purchases of ethanol from 9.0 billion gallons to 7.5 billion gallons. Imports decline from 6.0 billion gallons (9.0 billion − 3.0 billion) to 3.0 billion gallons (7.5 billion − 4.5 billion). Equilibrium moves from point *G* to point *H*.

By raising the price of ethanol from $1.00 to $1.50, the tariff reduces consumer surplus by the sum of areas *A*, *T*, *C*, and *D*. Area *A* is the increase in producer surplus from the higher price. The government collects tariff revenue equal to the tariff of $0.50 per gallon multiplied by the 3.0 billion gallons imported. Area *T* represents the government's tariff revenue. Areas *C* and *D* represent losses to U.S. consumers that are not captured by anyone. These areas are deadweight loss and represent the decline in economic efficiency resulting from the ethanol tariff. Area *C* shows the effect on U.S. consumers of being forced to buy from U.S. producers who are less efficient than foreign producers, and area *D* shows the effect of U.S. consumers buying less ethanol than they would have at the world price. As a result of the tariff, economic surplus has been reduced by the sum of areas *C* and *D*.

We can conclude that the tariff succeeds in helping U.S. ethanol producers but hurts U.S. consumers and the efficiency of the U.S. economy.

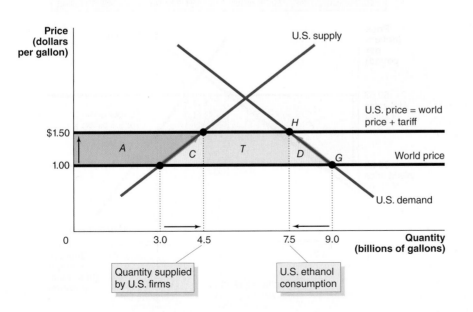

Loss of Consumer Surplus	=	Increase in Producer Surplus	+	Government Tariff Revenue	+	Deadweight Loss
A + C + T + D		A		T		C + D

Figure 7.6

The Effects of a Tariff on Ethanol

Without a tariff on ethanol, U.S. producers will sell 3.0 billion gallons of ethanol, U.S. consumers will purchase 9.0 billion gallons, and imports will be 6.0 billion gallons. The U.S. price will equal the world price of $1.00 per gallon. The $0.50-per-gallon tariff raises the price of ethanol in the United States to $1.50 per gallon, and U.S. producers increase the quantity they supply to 4.5 billion gallons. U.S. consumers reduce their purchases to 7.5 billion gallons. Equilibrium moves from point *G* to point *H*. The ethanol tariff causes a loss of consumer surplus equal to the area *A* + *C* + *T* + *D*. The area *A* is the increase in producer surplus due to the higher price. The area *T* is the government's tariff revenue. The areas *C* and *D* represent deadweight loss.

Quotas and Voluntary Export Restraints

Quota A numerical limit a government imposes on the quantity of a good that can be imported into the country.

A **quota** is a numerical limit on the quantity of a good that can be imported, and it has an effect similar to that of a tariff. A quota is imposed by the government of the importing country. A **voluntary export restraint (VER)** is an agreement negotiated between two countries that places a numerical limit on the quantity of a good that can be imported by one country from the other country. In the early 1980s, the United States and Japan negotiated a VER that limited the quantity of automobiles the United States would import from Japan. The Japanese government agreed to the VER primarily because it was afraid that if it did not, the United States would impose a tariff or quota on imports of Japanese automobiles. Quotas and VERs have similar economic effects.

Voluntary export restraint (VER) An agreement negotiated between two countries that places a numerical limit on the quantity of a good that can be imported by one country from the other country.

The main purpose of most tariffs and quotas is to reduce the foreign competition that domestic firms face. For many years, Congress has imposed a quota on sugar imports to protect U.S. sugar producers. Figure 7.7 shows the actual statistics for the U.S. sugar market in 2010. The effect of a quota is very similar to the effect of a tariff. By limiting imports, a quota forces the domestic price of a good above the world price. In this case, the sugar quota limits sugar imports to 5.3 billion pounds (shown by the bracket in Figure 7.7), forcing the U.S. price of sugar up to $0.53 per pound, or $0.25 higher than the world price of $0.28 per pound. The U.S. price is above the world price because the quota keeps foreign sugar producers from selling the additional sugar in the United States that would drive the price down to the world price. At a price of $0.53 per pound, U.S. producers increase the quantity of sugar they supply from the 4.7 billion pounds they would supply at the world price to 15.9 billion pounds, and U.S. consumers cut back their purchases of sugar from the 27.5 billion pounds they would purchase at the world price to the 21.2 billion pounds they are willing to purchase at the higher U.S. price. If there were no import quota, equilibrium would be at the world price (point *E*), but with the quota equilibrium is at the U.S. price (point *F*).

Measuring the Economic Effect of the Sugar Quota

We can use the concepts of consumer surplus, producer surplus, and deadweight loss to measure the economic impact of the sugar quota. Without a sugar quota, the world price of $0.28 per pound would also be the U.S. price. In Figure 7.7, without a sugar

Figure 7.7

The Economic Effect of the U.S. Sugar Quota

Without a sugar quota, U.S. sugar producers would have sold 4.7 billion pounds of sugar, U.S. consumers would have purchased 27.5 billion pounds of sugar, and imports would have been 22.8 billion pounds. The U.S. price would have equaled the world price of $0.28 per pound. Because the sugar quota limits imports to 5.3 billion pounds (the bracket in the graph), the price of sugar in the United States rises to $0.53 per pound, and U.S. producers supply 15.9 billion pounds. U.S. consumers purchase 21.2 billion pounds rather than the 27.5 billion pounds they would purchase at the world price. Without the import quota, equilibrium would be at point *E*; with the quota, equilibrium is at point *F*. The sugar quota causes a loss of consumer surplus equal to the area *A* + *B* + *C* + *D*. The area *A* is the gain to U.S. sugar producers. The area *B* is the gain to foreign sugar producers. The areas *C* and *D* represent deadweight loss. The total loss to U.S. consumers in 2010 was $6.08 billion.

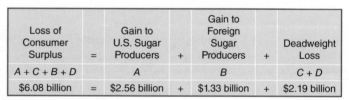

Loss of Consumer Surplus	=	Gain to U.S. Sugar Producers	+	Gain to Foreign Sugar Producers	+	Deadweight Loss
A + C + B + D	=	A	+	B	+	C + D
$6.08 billion	=	$2.56 billion	+	$1.33 billion	+	$2.19 billion

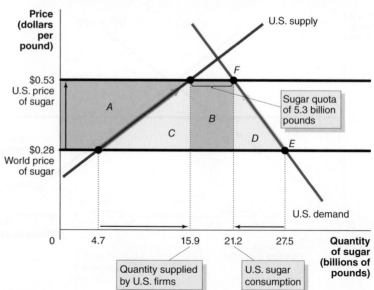

quota, consumer surplus would equal the area above the $0.28 price line and below the demand curve. The sugar quota causes the U.S. price to rise to $0.53 and reduces consumer surplus by the area $A + B + C + D$. Without a sugar quota, producer surplus received by U.S. sugar producers would be equal to the area below the $0.28 price line and above the supply curve. The higher U.S. price resulting from the sugar quota increases the producer surplus of U.S. sugar producers by an amount equal to area A.

A foreign producer must have a license from the U.S. government to import sugar under the quota system. Therefore, a foreign sugar producer that is lucky enough to have an import license also benefits from the quota because it is able to sell sugar in the U.S. market at $0.53 per pound instead of $0.28 per pound. The gain to foreign sugar producers is area B. Areas A and B represent transfers from U.S. consumers of sugar to U.S. and foreign producers of sugar. Areas C and D represent losses to U.S. consumers that are not captured by anyone. These areas are deadweight loss and represent the decline in economic efficiency resulting from the sugar quota. Area C shows the effect of U.S. consumers being forced to buy from U.S. producers that are less efficient than foreign producers, and area D shows the effect of U.S. consumers buying less sugar than they would have at the world price.

Figure 7.7 provides enough information to calculate the dollar value of each of the four areas. The table in the figure shows the results of these calculations. The total loss to consumers from the sugar quota was $6.08 billion in 2010. About 42 percent of the loss to consumers, or $2.56 billion, was gained by U.S. sugar producers as increased producer surplus. About 22 percent, or $1.33 billion, was gained by foreign sugar producers as increased producer surplus, and about 36 percent, or $2.19 billion, was a deadweight loss to the U.S. economy. The U.S. International Trade Commission estimates that eliminating the sugar quota would result in the loss of about 3,000 jobs in the U.S. sugar industry. The cost to U.S. consumers of saving these jobs is equal to $6.08 billion/3,000, or about $2,026,667 per job. In fact, this cost is an underestimate because eliminating the sugar quota would result in new jobs being created, particularly in the candy industry. Over the years, several U.S. candy companies—including the makers of Life Savers and Star Brite mints—have moved factories to other countries to escape the effects of the sugar quota.

Solved Problem 7.4

Measuring the Economic Effect of a Quota

Suppose that the United States currently both produces and imports apples. The U.S. government then decides to restrict international trade in apples by imposing a quota that allows imports of only 4 million boxes of apples into the United States each year. The figure shows the results of imposing the quota.

Fill in the following table, using the prices, quantities, and letters in the figure:

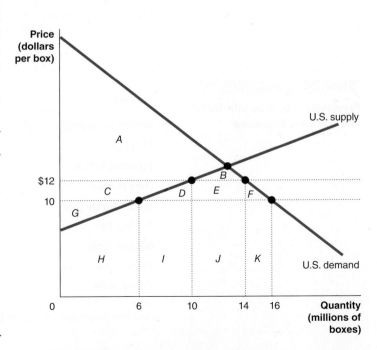

	Without Quota	With Quota
World price of apples		
U.S. price of apples		
Quantity supplied by U.S. firms		
Quantity demanded by U.S. consumers		
Quantity imported		
Area of consumer surplus		
Area of producer surplus		
Area of deadweight loss		

Solving the Problem

Step 1: **Review the chapter material.** This problem is about measuring the economic effects of a quota, so you may want to review the section "Quotas and Voluntary Export Restraints," and "Measuring the Economic Effect of the Sugar Quota," which begin on page 220.

Step 2: **Fill in the table.** After studying Figure 7.7, you should be able to fill in the table. Remember that consumer surplus is the area below the demand curve and above the market price:

	Without Quota	With Quota
World price of apples	$10	$10
U.S. price of apples	$10	$12
Quantity supplied by U.S. firms	6 million boxes	10 million boxes
Quantity demanded by U.S. consumers	16 million boxes	14 million boxes
Quantity imported	10 million boxes	4 million boxes
Area of consumer surplus	$A + B + C + D + E + F$	$A + B$
Area of domestic producer surplus	G	$G + C$
Area of deadweight loss	No deadweight loss	$D + F$

MyEconLab **Your Turn:** For more practice, do related problem 4.14 on page 237 at the end of this chapter.

The High Cost of Preserving Jobs with Tariffs and Quotas

The sugar quota is not alone in imposing a high cost on U.S. consumers to save jobs at U.S. firms. Table 7.5 shows, for several industries, the costs tariffs and quotas impose on U.S. consumers per year for each job saved.

Many countries besides the United States also use tariffs and quotas to try to protect jobs. Table 7.6 shows the cost to Japanese consumers per year for each job saved as a result of tariffs and quotas in the listed industries. Note the staggering cost of $51 million for each job saved that is imposed on Japanese consumers by their government's restrictions on imports of rice.

Table 7.5

Preserving U.S. Jobs with Tariffs and Quotas Is Expensive

Product	Number of Jobs Saved	Cost to Consumers per Year for Each Job Saved
Benzenoid chemicals	216	$1,376,435
Luggage	226	1,285,078
Softwood lumber	605	1,044,271
Dairy products	2,378	685,323
Frozen orange juice	609	635,103
Ball bearings	146	603,368
Machine tools	1,556	479,452
Women's handbags	773	263,535
Canned tuna	390	257,640

Data from Federal Reserve Bank of Dallas, 2002 *Annual Report*, Exhibit 11.

Product	Cost to Consumers per Year for Each Job Saved
Rice	$51,233,000
Natural gas	27,987,000
Gasoline	6,329,000
Paper	3,813,000
Beef, pork, and poultry	1,933,000
Cosmetics	1,778,000
Radio and television sets	915,000

Table 7.6

Preserving Japanese Jobs with Tariffs and Quotas Is Also Expensive

"Preserving Japanese Jobs with Tariffs and Quotas Is Also Expensive" by Yoko Sazabami, Shujiro Urata, and Hiroki Kawai from *Measuring the Cost of Protection in Japan.* Copyright © 1995 by the Institute for International Economics. Reprinted by permission.

Just as the sugar quota costs jobs in the candy industry, other tariffs and quotas cost jobs outside the industries immediately affected. For example, in 1991, the United States imposed tariffs on flat-panel displays used in laptop computers. This was good news for U.S. producers of these displays but bad news for companies producing laptop computers. Toshiba, Sharp, and Apple all closed their U.S. laptop production facilities and moved production overseas. In fact, whenever one industry receives tariff or quota protection, jobs are lost in other domestic industries.

Making the Connection

Save Jobs Making Hangers ... and Lose Jobs in Dry Cleaning

When supporters of tariffs and quotas argue that these interferences with trade save jobs, they are referring to jobs in the industry protected by the tariffs and quotas. We have seen that a tariff or quota makes it easier for domestic firms to compete against foreign firms that may have lower costs. More production by domestic firms means more employment at those firms, thereby saving jobs in that industry. But as we have also seen, other industries can see their costs rise as a result of the tariff or quota, causing firms in these industries to raise prices. Higher prices will reduce the quantity demanded resulting in lower production and fewer jobs in those industries.

This is just what happened when the United States raised the tariff on wire garment hangers imported from China. Under trade agreements signed with other countries, the United States is allowed to impose tariffs on imports if foreign firms are selling products in the United States at below their production cost. The U.S. International Trade Commission (ITC) determined that Chinese firms had, in fact, been selling wire garment hangers in the United States at below the firms' production cost and so imposed a tariff on imports of the hangers. Dry cleaners in the United States use a lot of wire hangers, so the tariff sharply increased the cleaners' costs. For example, a dry cleaner in East Harlem in New York City found that the price of a box of 500 hangers rose from $17.50 to $40. The dry cleaner uses 4,000 hangers per week, so his costs rose by $180 per week, or by $9,360 per year. The dry cleaning industry is made up of thousands of mostly small firms and is highly competitive. Small dry cleaners had difficulty absorbing the increased cost. The owner of the East Harlem dry cleaner was quoted as saying, "We can't do this business any more."

At the time the tariff was imposed, the dry cleaning industry employed 221,230 workers. Over the following two years, employment declined by about 17,000 workers, although not all of this decline was due to the increase in the cost of hangers. The ITC

A tariff on hangers increased the cost of doing business for U.S. dry cleaners.

estimated that the tariff would save about 300 jobs in U.S. factories producing wire hangers, and it would raise the average cost per dry cleaner by about $4,000 per year. At the time the tariff was imposed, there were about 30,000 dry cleaners in the United States, so the total cost of the tariff was about $120,000,000. The cost each year per job saved was about $120,000,000/300 = $400,000. At the time, the typical worker making wire hangers was earning about $31,000 per year.

As dry cleaners, their employees, and consumers buying wire hangers found out, tariffs can be both an expensive and ineffective way to attempt to preserve jobs.

Based on Jennifer Bleyer, "Dry Cleaners Feel an Ill Wind from China," *New York Times*, April 27, 2008; Gigi Douban, "Costs Up, So Dry Cleaners Want Their Hangers Back," npr.org, May 8, 2008; U.S. International Trade Commission, *Steel Wire Garment Hangers from China: Investigation No. 731-TA-1123 (Final)*, Publication 4034, September 2008; and U.S. Bureau of Labor Statistics, *Occupational Employment Statistics*, May 17, 2011.

MyEconLab **Your Turn:** Test your understanding by doing related problem 4.15 on page 237 at the end of this chapter.

Gains from Unilateral Elimination of Tariffs and Quotas

Some politicians argue that eliminating U.S. tariffs and quotas would help the U.S. economy only if other countries eliminated their tariffs and quotas in exchange. It is easier to gain political support for reducing or eliminating tariffs or quotas if it is done as part of an agreement with other countries that involves their eliminating some of their tariffs or quotas. But as the example of the sugar quota shows, *the U.S. economy would gain from the elimination of tariffs and quotas even if other countries did not reduce their tariffs and quotas.*

Other Barriers to Trade

In addition to tariffs and quotas, governments sometimes erect other barriers to trade. For example, all governments require that imports meet certain health and safety requirements. Sometimes, however, governments use these requirements to shield domestic firms from foreign competition. This can be true when a government imposes stricter health and safety requirements on imported goods than on goods produced by domestic firms.

Many governments also restrict imports of certain products on national security grounds. The argument is that in time of war, a country should not be dependent on imports of critical war materials. Once again, these restrictions are sometimes used more to protect domestic companies from competition than to protect national security. For example, for years, the U.S. government would buy military uniforms only from U.S. manufacturers, even though uniforms are not a critical war material.

7.5 LEARNING OBJECTIVE

Evaluate the arguments over trade policies and globalization.

The Arguments over Trade Policies and Globalization

The argument over whether the U.S. government should regulate international trade dates back to the early days of the country. One particularly controversial attempt to restrict trade took place during the Great Depression of the 1930s. At that time, the United States and other countries attempted to help domestic firms by raising tariffs on foreign imports. The United States started the process by passing the Smoot-Hawley Tariff in 1930, which raised average tariff rates to more than 50 percent. As other countries retaliated by raising their tariffs, international trade collapsed.

By the end of World War II in 1945, government officials in the United States and Europe were looking for a way to reduce tariffs and revive international trade. To help achieve this goal, they set up the General Agreement on Tariffs and Trade (GATT) in 1948. Countries that joined GATT agreed not to impose new tariffs or import quotas. In addition, a series of *multilateral negotiations*, called *trade rounds*, took place, in which countries agreed to reduce tariffs from the very high levels of the 1930s.

In the 1940s, most international trade was in goods, and the GATT agreement covered only goods. In the following decades, trade in services and in products incorporating *intellectual property*, such as software programs and movies, grew in importance. Many GATT members pressed for a new agreement that would cover services and intellectual property, as well as goods. A new agreement was negotiated, and in January 1995, GATT was replaced by the **World Trade Organization (WTO)**, headquartered in Geneva, Switzerland. More than 150 countries are currently members of the WTO.

World Trade Organization (WTO) An international organization that oversees international trade agreements.

Why Do Some People Oppose the World Trade Organization?

During the years immediately after World War II, many low-income, or developing, countries enacted high tariffs and restricted investment by foreign companies. When these policies failed to produce much economic growth, many of these countries decided during the 1980s to become more open to foreign trade and investment. This process became known as **globalization**. Most developing countries joined the WTO and began to follow its policies.

Globalization The process of countries becoming more open to foreign trade and investment.

During the 1990s, opposition to globalization began to increase. In 1999, this opposition took a violent turn at a meeting of the WTO in Seattle, Washington. A large number of protestors assembled in Seattle to meet the WTO delegates. Protests started peacefully but quickly became violent. Protesters looted stores and burned cars, and many delegates were unable to leave their hotel rooms. Similar incidents have occurred at most WTO meetings in the years since.

Why would attempts to reduce trade barriers with the objective of increasing income around the world cause such a furious reaction? The opposition to the WTO comes from three sources. First, some opponents are specifically against the globalization process that began in the 1980s and became widespread in the 1990s. Second, other opponents have the same motivation as the supporters of tariffs in the 1930s—to erect trade barriers to protect domestic firms from foreign competition. Third, some critics of the WTO support globalization in principle but believe that the WTO favors the interests of the high-income countries at the expense of the low-income countries. Let's look more closely at the sources of opposition to the WTO.

Anti-globalization Many of those who protest at WTO meetings distrust globalization. Some believe that free trade and foreign investment destroy the distinctive cultures of many countries. As developing countries began to open their economies to imports from the United States and other high-income countries, these imports of food, clothing, movies, and other goods began to replace the equivalent local products. So, a teenager in Thailand might be sitting in a McDonald's restaurant, wearing Levi's jeans and a Ralph Lauren shirt, listening to a recording by Lady Gaga on his iPod, before downloading *The Dark Knight Rises* to his iPad. Globalization has increased the variety of products available to consumers in developing countries, but some people argue that this is too high a price to pay for what they see as damage to local cultures.

Globalization has also allowed multinational corporations to relocate factories from high-income countries to low-income countries. These new factories in Indonesia, Malaysia, Pakistan, and other countries pay much lower wages than are paid in the United States, Europe, and Japan and often do not meet the environmental or safety regulations that are imposed in high-income countries. Some factories use child labor, which is illegal in high-income countries. Some people have argued that firms with factories in developing countries should pay workers wages as high as those paid in high-income countries. They also believe these firms should abide by the health, safety, and environmental regulations that exist in the high-income countries.

The governments of most developing countries have resisted these proposals. They argue that when the currently rich countries were poor, they also lacked environmental or safety standards, and their workers were paid low wages. They argue that it is easier for rich countries to afford high wages and environmental and safety regulations than it is for poor countries. They also point out that many jobs that seem to have very low wages based on the standards of high-income countries are often better than the alternatives available to workers in low-income countries.

<table>
<tr><td>Making
the
Connection</td><td>

The Unintended Consequences of Banning Goods Made with Child Labor

</td></tr>
</table>

In many developing countries, such as Indonesia, Thailand, and Peru, children as young as seven or eight work 10 or more hours a day. Reports of very young workers laboring long hours, producing goods for export, have upset many people in high-income countries. In the United States, boycotts have been organized against stores that stock goods made in developing countries with child labor. Many people assume that if child workers in developing countries weren't working in factories making clothing, toys, and other products, they would be in school, as are children in high-income countries.

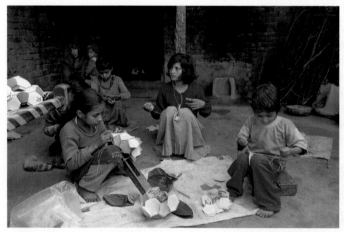

Would eliminating child labor, such as stitching soccer balls, improve the quality of children's lives?

In fact, children in developing countries usually have few good alternatives to work. Schooling is frequently available for only a few months each year, and even children who attend school rarely do so for more than a few years. Poor families are often unable to afford even the small costs of sending their children to school. Families may rely on the earnings of very young children to survive, as poor families once did in the United States, Europe, and Japan. There is substantial evidence that as incomes begin to rise in poor countries, families rely less on child labor. The United States eventually outlawed child labor, but not until 1938. In developing countries where child labor is common today, jobs producing export goods are usually better paying and less hazardous than the alternatives.

As preparations began in France for the 1998 World Cup, there were protests that Baden Sports—the main supplier of soccer balls—was purchasing the balls from suppliers in Pakistan that used child workers. France decided to ban all use of soccer balls made by child workers. Bowing to this pressure, Baden Sports moved production from Pakistan, where the balls were hand-stitched by child workers, to China, where the balls were machine-stitched by adult workers in factories. There was some criticism of the boycott of hand-stitched soccer balls at the time. In a broad study of child labor, three economists argued:

> Of the array of possible employment in which impoverished children might engage, soccer ball stitching is probably one of the most benign. . . . [In Pakistan] children generally work alongside other family members in the home or in small workshops. . . . Nor are the children exposed to toxic chemicals, hazardous tools or brutal working conditions. Rather, the only serious criticism concerns the length of the typical child stitcher's work-day and the impact on formal education.

In fact, the alternatives to soccer ball stitching for child workers in Pakistan turned out to be extremely grim. According to Keith Maskus, an economist at the University of Colorado and the World Bank, a "large proportion" of the children who lost their jobs stitching soccer balls ended up begging or in prostitution.

Based on Tom Wright, "Pakistan Defends Its Soccer Industry," *Wall Street Journal*, April 26, 2010; Drusilla K. Brown, Alan V. Deardorff, and Robert M. Stern, "U.S. Trade and Other Policy Options to Deter Foreign Exploitation of Child Labor," in Magnus Blomstrom and Linda S. Goldberg, eds., *Topics in Empirical International Economics: A Festchrift in Honor of Bob Lispey*, (Chicago: University of Chicago Press, 2001); Tomas Larsson, *The Race to the Top: The Real Story of*

Globalization, (Washington, DC: Cato Institute, 2001), p. 48; and Eric V. Edmonds and Nina Pavcnik, "Child Labor in the Global Economy," *Journal of Economic Perspectives*, Vol. 19, No. 1, Winter 2005, pp. 199–220.

Your Turn: Test your understanding by doing related problem 5.5 on page 238 at the end of this chapter.

MyEconLab

"Old-Fashioned" Protectionism

The anti-globalization argument against free trade and the WTO is relatively new. Another argument against free trade, called *protectionism*, has been around for centuries. **Protectionism** is the use of trade barriers to shield domestic firms from foreign competition. For as long as international trade has existed, governments have attempted to restrict it to protect domestic firms. As we saw with the analysis of the sugar quota, protectionism causes losses to consumers and eliminates jobs in the domestic industries that buy the protected product. In addition, by reducing the ability of countries to produce according to comparative advantage, protectionism reduces incomes.

Protectionism The use of trade barriers to shield domestic firms from foreign competition.

Why, then, does protectionism attract support? Protectionism is usually justified on the basis of one of the following arguments:

- *Saving jobs.* Supporters of protectionism argue that free trade reduces employment by driving domestic firms out of business. It is true that when more-efficient foreign firms drive less-efficient domestic firms out of business, jobs are lost, but jobs are also lost when more-efficient domestic firms drive less-efficient domestic firms out of business. These job losses are rarely permanent. In the U.S. economy, jobs are lost and new jobs are created continually. No economic study has ever found a long-term connection between the total number of jobs available and the level of tariff protection for domestic industries. In addition, trade restrictions destroy jobs in some industries at the same time that they preserve jobs in others. The U.S. sugar quota may have saved jobs in the U.S. sugar industry, but it has also destroyed jobs in the U.S. candy industry.

- *Protecting high wages.* Some people worry that firms in high-income countries will have to start paying much lower wages to compete with firms in developing countries. This fear is misplaced, however, because free trade actually raises living standards by increasing economic efficiency. When a country practices protectionism and produces goods and services it could obtain more inexpensively from other countries, it reduces its standard of living. The United States could ban imports of coffee and begin growing it domestically. But this would entail a very high opportunity cost because coffee could only be grown in the continental United States in greenhouses and would require large amounts of labor and equipment. The coffee would have to sell for a very high price to cover these costs. Suppose the United States did ban coffee imports: Eliminating the ban at some future time would eliminate the jobs of U.S. coffee workers, but the standard of living in the United States would rise as coffee prices declined and labor, machinery, and other resources moved out of coffee production and into production of goods and services for which the United States has a comparative advantage.

- *Protecting infant industries.* It is possible that firms in a country may have a comparative advantage in producing a good, but because the country begins production of the good later than other countries, its firms initially have higher costs. In producing some goods and services, substantial "learning by doing" occurs. As workers and firms produce more of the good or service, they gain experience and become more productive. Over time, costs and prices will fall. As the firms in the "infant industry" gain experience, their costs will fall, and they will be able to compete successfully with foreign producers. Under free trade, however, they may not get a chance. The established foreign producers can sell the product at a lower price and drive domestic producers out of business before they gain enough experience to compete. To economists, this is the most persuasive of the protectionist arguments. It has a significant drawback, however. Tariffs used to protect an infant industry eliminate the need for the firms in the industry to become productive enough to compete with foreign firms. After World War II, the governments of many developing countries used the "infant industry" argument to justify high tariff rates. Unfortunately, most of their infant industries never grew up, and they continued for years as inefficient drains on their economies.

- *Protecting national security.* As already discussed, a country should not rely on other countries for goods that are critical to its military defense. For example, the United States would probably not want to import all its jet fighter engines from China. The definition of which goods are critical to military defense is a slippery one, however. In fact, it is rare for an industry to ask for protection without raising the issue of national security, even if its products have mainly nonmilitary uses.

Dumping

Dumping Selling a product for a price below its cost of production.

In recent years, the United States has extended protection to some domestic industries by using a provision in the WTO agreement that allows governments to impose tariffs in the case of *dumping*. **Dumping** is selling a product for a price below its cost of production. Although allowable under the WTO agreement, using tariffs to offset the effects of dumping is very controversial.

In practice, it is difficult to determine whether foreign companies are dumping goods because the true production costs of a good are not easy for foreign governments to calculate. As a result, the WTO allows countries to determine that dumping has occurred if a product is exported for a lower price than it sells for on the home market. There is a problem with this approach, however. Often there are good business reasons for a firm to sell a product for different prices to different consumers. For example, the airlines charge business travelers higher ticket prices than leisure travelers. Firms also use "loss leaders"—products that are sold below cost, or even given away free—when introducing a new product or, in the case of retailing, to attract customers who will also buy full-price products. For example, during the holiday season, Wal-Mart sometimes offers toys at prices below what they pay to buy them from manufacturers. It's unclear why these normal business practices should be unacceptable when used in international trade.

Positive versus Normative Analysis (Once Again)

Economists emphasize the burden on the economy imposed by tariffs, quotas, and other government restrictions on free trade. Does it follow that these interferences are bad? Remember from Chapter 1 the distinction between *positive analysis* and *normative analysis*. Positive analysis concerns what *is*. Normative analysis concerns what *ought to be*. Measuring the effect of the sugar quota on the U.S. economy is an example of positive analysis. Asserting that the sugar quota is bad public policy and should be eliminated is normative analysis. The sugar quota—like all other interferences with trade—makes some people better off and some people worse off, and it reduces total income and consumption. Whether increasing the profits of U.S. sugar companies and the number of workers they employ justifies the costs imposed on consumers and the reduction in economic efficiency is a normative question.

Most economists do not support interferences with trade, such as the sugar quota. Few people become economists if they don't believe that markets should usually be as free as possible. But the opposite view is certainly intellectually respectable. It is possible for someone to understand the costs of tariffs and quotas but still believe that tariffs and quotas are a good idea, perhaps because they believe unrestricted free trade would cause too much disruption to the economy.

The success of industries in getting the government to erect barriers to foreign competition depends partly on some members of the public knowing the costs of trade barriers but supporting them anyway. However, two other factors are also at work:

1. The costs tariffs and quotas impose on consumers are large in total but relatively small per person. For example, the sugar quota imposes a total burden of about $6.08 billion per year on consumers. Spread across 310 million Americans, the burden is less than $20 per person: too little for most people to worry about, even if they know the burden exists.
2. The jobs lost to foreign competition are easy to identify, but the jobs created by foreign trade are less easy to identify.

In other words, the industries that benefit from tariffs and quotas benefit a lot—for example, the sugar quota increases the profits of U.S. sugar producers by $2.28 billion—whereas each consumer loses relatively little. This concentration of benefits and widely spread burdens makes it easy to understand why members of Congress receive strong pressure from some industries to enact tariffs and quotas and relatively little pressure from the general public to reduce them.

Continued from page 205

Economics in Your Life

Have You Heard of the "Buy American" Provision?

At the beginning of the chapter, we asked you to consider how some U.S. companies convinced Congress to include the Buy American provision in the American Recovery and Reinvestment Act and why relatively few people have heard of this provision. In the chapter, we saw that trade restrictions tend to preserve relatively few jobs in the protected industries, while leading to job losses in other industries and costing consumers billions per year in higher prices. This might seem to increase the mystery of why Congress enacted the Buy American provision. We have also seen, though, that *per person*, the burden of specific trade restrictions can be small. The sugar quota, for instance, imposes a per-person cost on consumers of only about $19 per year. Not many people will take the trouble of writing a letter to their member of Congress or otherwise make their views known in the hope of saving $19 per year. In fact, few people will even spend the time to become aware that a specific trade restriction exists. So, if before you read this chapter you had never heard of the Buy American provision, you are certainly not alone.

Conclusion

There are few issues economists agree upon more than the economic benefits of free trade. However, there are few political issues as controversial as government policy toward trade. Many people who would be reluctant to see the government interfere with domestic trade are quite willing to see it interfere with international trade. The damage high tariffs inflicted on the world economy during the 1930s shows what can happen when governments around the world abandon free trade. Whether future episodes of that type can be avoided is by no means certain.

Read *An Inside Look at Policy* on the next page for a discussion of a legal dispute between Home Depot and the government in connection with the Buy American provision.

ABC NEWS

Home Depot Accused of Violating Buy American Act

Home Depot is the target of a lawsuit for allegedly selling goods manufactured in China and other prohibited countries to U.S. government agencies in violation of the Buy American Act, according to court documents.

The suit was filed in 2008 by two employees of another government contractor and alleges that "Home Depot had major sourcing operations in China for many years," as well as India, and that the company knew that certain brands and products were to be excluded from sale to U.S. government agencies because they were not compliant with the Trade Agreements Act.

The suit also says, "Home Depot affirmatively misrepresented to federal government customers that its GSA-scheduled contract 'covered everything in our store.'"

GSA is the federal General Services Administration, which supplies products for U.S. government offices.

(a) The Buy American Act and Trade Agreements Act work together to promote the purchase of U.S. goods or goods manufactured in countries when it serves the nation's economic interest.

The Atlanta-based home improvement retailer, with more than 2,200 locations in four countries (including China), denies the allegations.

"We would never knowingly sell prohibited goods under any circumstances, and we have been cooperating with the government to provide requested information," Home Depot spokesman Ron wrote in a statement. "We believe the plaintiffs have an inaccurate view of the facts, so we look forward to presenting our side of this case as the process moves forward."

The plaintiffs' attorney, Paul D. Scott, said, "We're looking forward to having our day in court and having a jury of American citizens decide what they think of this case."

The U.S. Department of Justice had no comment about the allegations.

The Great Depression–era Buy American Act of 1933 was intended to produce jobs and keep the economy afloat.

(b) "It's faulty logic to think that's going to benefit the United States to favor U.S. products if the government could buy foreign made products for lower prices," Stephen Bronars, senior economist with Welch Consulting, said.

"The view that if you do something yourself you're going to have closer to full employment ignores [the fact that] if you can get something more cheaply, it frees up resources you can allocate to something else."

(c) But some disagree. This view "ignores the effect of trade on jobs and ignores the effect of trade on business," Robert E. Scott of the Economic Policy Institute said. "Globalization: Everybody wins except for most of us. That is in fact what happened."

While the Home Depot fends off the suit, the company continues to offer government buyers a look at how "Federal Dollars Go Farther at the Home Depot."

According to Scott's research, Americans lost 2.4 million jobs from 2001 to 2008 because U.S. multinational corporations outsourced production companies to China.

"It's not in the interest of the United States," Scott said. "It has hurt us as producer of goods. It has hurt wages and it has hurt GDP," Scott said.

"I tend to think that U.S. companies are increasingly outsourcing production and I think that has hurt the American economy," said Scott, who views the Buy American Act as a net benefit to the U.S. economy.

Key Points in the Article

A lawsuit filed against Home Depot, alleged that the Atlanta-based home improvement company knowingly violated the Buy American provision of the American Recovery and Reinvestment Act of 2009 by selling to U.S. government agencies products prohibited by the legislation. A spokesman for Home Depot denied the allegations, claiming that the company would never intentionally sell prohibited goods and that the plaintiffs in the lawsuit had misinterpreted the facts surrounding the case.

Analyzing the News

(a) Part of the American Recovery and Reinvestment Act of 2009, the Buy American provision required that all manufactured goods purchased with funds authorized under the act be made in the United States. In 1979, the United States passed the Trade Agreements Act, which mandates that the government only purchase end products valued over a specific dollar amount if they are made in the United States or come from a list of designated countries, unless the desired product is not available from these countries. Some view the Buy American provision as a partner of the Trade Agreements Act in the promotion of U.S. produced goods. The Home Depot case is not the first filed against a major U.S. corporation for violating the Buy American provi-

sion. The table below lists several major companies that made settlement payments to the U.S. government following litigation for allegedly violating the Buy American provision or the Trade Agreements Act.

Company	Settlement	Date
Fastenal	$6.25 million	2011
Corporate Express Office Products	5.02 million	2006
Staples	7.4 million	2005
Office Depot	4.75 million	2005
Office Max	9.72 million	2005
Invacare	2.6 million	1998

(b) Critics of the Buy American provision argue that paying more for U.S.-produced products when lower-priced products are available from other countries misallocates resources and drives up the costs of some projects being funded with federal money. Because the total amount of spending under the American Recovery and Reinvestment Act of 2009 was fixed, the more costly each project was, the fewer projects that would be funded. The Buy American provision was intended to increase employment in the United States, but if resources are being misallocated and, as a result, fewer projects can be funded, the number of new jobs created would be reduced.

(c) Proponents of the Buy American provision believe that the provision does, indeed, create jobs and benefit American businesses and workers.

The figure shows the effect of the Buy American provision on the steel market in the United States. (For simplicity, we assume that there are no barriers to foreign steel producers selling to the United States, apart from the Buy American provision. We also assume that the figure represents the whole market for steel in the United States, not just the market for steel to be used in projects funded by the American Recovery and Reinvestment Act of 2009.) In the absence of the Buy American provision, the price of steel in the United States is P_1, which is both the U.S. price and the world price. By limiting the amount of steel that can be imported into the United States, the Buy American provision raises the price of steel in the United States to P_2, which is above the world price, and equilibrium moves from point A to point B. U.S. consumption of steel falls from Q_4 to Q_3, the quantity of steel supplied by U.S. steel producers increases from Q_1 to Q_2, and imports of foreign steel decline from $Q_4 - Q_1$ to $Q_3 - Q_2$. U.S. steel companies—and their workers—gain from the provision, as do foreign steel companies still able to sell in the United States because they receive a price higher than the world price. However, U.S. consumers—and taxpayers—lose because they must now pay a price above the world price.

Thinking Critically about Policy

1. The Buy American provision, as well as tariffs and quotas on foreign imports, are intended to save jobs in the United States. Do they, in fact, save jobs? Do you support these trade restrictions? Briefly explain.

2. Consumers lose when the government interferes with trade as it did with the Buy American provision. Why, then, does Congress enact such legislation?

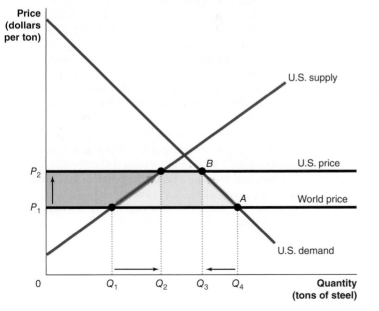

The effect of the "Buy American" provision on the steel market in the United States.

Chapter Summary and Problems

Key Terms

Absolute advantage, p. 210

Autarky, p. 211

Comparative advantage, p. 209

Dumping, p. 228

Exports, p. 206

External economies, p. 215

Free trade, p. 217

Globalization, p. 225

Imports, p. 206

Opportunity cost, p. 209

Protectionism, p. 227

Quota, p. 220

Tariff, p. 206

Terms of trade, p. 211

Voluntary export restraint (VER), p. 220

World Trade Organization (WTO), p. 225

7.1 **The United States in the International Economy, pages 206–209**
LEARNING OBJECTIVE: Discuss the role of international trade in the U.S. economy.

Summary

International trade has been increasing in recent decades, in part because of reductions in *tariffs* and other barriers to trade. A **tariff** is a tax imposed by a government on imports. The quantity of goods and services the United States imports and exports has been continually increasing. **Imports** are goods and services bought domestically but produced in other countries. **Exports** are goods and services produced domestically and sold to other countries. Today, the United States is the leading exporting country in the world, and about 20 percent of U.S. manufacturing jobs depend on exports.

MyEconLab　Visit www.myeconlab.com to complete these exercises online and get instant feedback.

Review Questions

1.1 Briefly explain whether the value of U.S. exports is typically larger or smaller than the value of U.S. imports.

1.2 Are imports and exports a smaller or larger fraction of GDP than they were 40 years ago?

1.3 Briefly explain whether you agree with the following statement: "International trade is more important to the U.S. economy than to most other economies."

Problems and Applications

1.4 If the United States were to stop trading goods and services with other countries, which U.S. industries would be likely to see their sales decline the most? Briefly explain.

1.5 Briefly explain whether you agree with the following statement: "Japan has always been much more heavily involved in international trade than are most other nations. In fact, today Japan exports a larger fraction of its GDP than Germany, Great Britain, or the United States."

1.6 Why might a smaller country, such as the Netherlands, be more likely to import and export larger fractions of its GDP than would a larger country, such as China or the United States?

1.7 **[Related to the** Making the Connection **on page 208]** Douglas Irwin, a professor of economics at Dartmouth College, wrote the following in a column in the *New York Times*:

> General Electric and Caterpillar have opposed the Buy American provision because they fear it will hurt their ability to win contracts abroad. . . . Once we get through the current economic mess, China, India and other countries are likely to continue their large investments in building projects. If such countries also adopt our preferences for domestic producers, then America will be at a competitive disadvantage in bidding for those contracts.

What are "preferences for domestic producers"? Why would these preferences put U.S. firms at a "competitive disadvantage"? Why might having difficulty making sales in China and India be a particular problem for Caterpillar?

"If We Buy American, No One Else Will", by Douglas A. Irwin from *New York Times*, January 31, 2009. Copyright © 2009 by Douglas A. Irwin. Reprinted by permission of the author.

7.2

Comparative Advantage in International Trade, pages 209-211

LEARNING OBJECTIVE: Understand the difference between comparative advantage and absolute advantage in international trade.

Summary

Comparative advantage is the ability of an individual, a business, or a country to produce a good or service at the lowest **opportunity cost**. **Absolute advantage** is the ability to produce more of a good or service than competitors when using the same amount of resources. Countries trade on the basis of comparative advantage, not on the basis of absolute advantage.

MyEconLab   Visit **www.myeconlab.com** to complete these exercises online and get instant feedback.

Review Questions

2.1 What is the difference between absolute advantage and comparative advantage? Will a country always be an exporter of a good where it has an absolute advantage in production? Briefly explain.

2.2 A WTO publication calls comparative advantage "arguably the single most powerful insight in economics." What is comparative advantage? What makes it such a powerful insight?

Based on World Trade Organization, "Understanding the WTO," www.wto.org/english/thewto_e/whatis_e/tif_e/fact3_e.htm.

Problems and Applications

2.3 Why do the goods that countries import and export change over time? Use the concept of comparative advantage in your answer.

2.4 In a newspaper column, Frank Wolak, a professor of economics at Stanford, referred to "the economic forces that lead to most children's toys being developed in the United States and mass-produced in China and other developing countries." What economic forces is he referring to? If a U.S. company develops a toy, why is a Chinese company likely to end up manufacturing the toy?

Source: Frank A. Wolak, "Our Comparative Advantage," *New York Times*, January 19, 2011.

2.5 Briefly explain whether you agree with the following argument: "Unfortunately, Bolivia does not have a comparative advantage with respect to the United States in the production of any good or service." (*Hint:* You do not need any specific information about the economies of Bolivia or the United States to be able to answer this question.)

2.6 The following table shows for Greece and Italy the hourly output per worker measured as quarts of olive oil and pounds of pasta:

| | Output per Hour of Work | |
	Olive Oil	Pasta
Greece	4	2
Italy	4	8

Calculate the opportunity cost of producing olive oil and pasta in both Greece and in Italy.

2.7 In January 2008, the Bank of France published a report, stating that in 2006, hourly labor productivity in the United States was higher than the productivity in Japan. If U.S. workers can produce more goods and services per hour than Japanese workers, why does the United States continue to import from Japan some products it could produce at home?

Based on Gilbert Cette, Yusuf Kocoglu, and Jacques Mairesse, "A Comparison of Productivity in France, Japan, The United Kingdom and the United States over the Past Century," Banque de France, January 8, 2008.

2.8 Patrick J. Buchanan, a former presidential candidate, argued in his book on the global economy that there is a flaw in David Ricardo's theory of comparative advantage:

> Classical free trade theory fails the test of common sense. According to Ricardo's law of comparative advantage . . . if America makes better computers and textiles than China does, but our advantage in computers is greater than our advantage in textiles, we should (1) focus on computers, (2) let China make textiles, and (3) trade U.S. computers for Chinese textiles. . . .
>
> The doctrine begs a question. If Americans are more efficient than Chinese in making clothes . . . why surrender the more efficient American industry? Why shift to a reliance on a Chinese textile industry that will take years to catch up to where American factories are today?

Do you agree with Buchanan's argument? Briefly explain.

From Patrick J. Buchanan, *The Great Betrayal: How American Sovereignty and Social Justice Are Being Sacrificed to the Gods of the Global Economy*, (Boston: Little, Brown & Company), 1998, p. 66.

2.9 In a 2007 debate among Democratic presidential candidates, Barack Obama made the following statement: "Well, look, people don't want a cheaper T-shirt if they're losing a job in the process." What did Obama mean by the phrase "losing a job in the process"? Using the economic concept of comparative advantage, explain under what circumstances it would make sense for the United States to produce all of the T-shirts purchased in the United States. Do you agree with Obama's statement? Briefly explain.

Based on James Pethokoukis, "Democratic Debate Spawns Weird Economics," *U.S. News & World Report*, August 8, 2007.

7.3 How Countries Gain from International Trade, pages 211–217

LEARNING OBJECTIVE: Explain how countries gain from international trade.

Summary

Autarky is a situation in which a country does not trade with other countries. The **terms of trade** is the ratio at which a country can trade its exports for imports from other countries. When a country specializes in producing goods where it has a comparative advantage and trades for the other goods it needs, the country will have a higher level of income and consumption. We do not see complete specialization in production for three reasons: Not all goods and services are traded internationally, production of most goods involves increasing opportunity costs, and tastes for products differ across countries. Although the population of a country as a whole benefits from trade, companies—and their workers—that are unable to compete with lower-cost foreign producers lose. Among the main sources of comparative advantage are climate and natural resources, relative abundance of labor and capital, technology, and external economies. **External economies** are reductions in a firm's costs that result from an increase in the size of an industry. A country may develop a comparative advantage in the production of a good, and then as time passes and circumstances change, the country may lose its comparative advantage in producing that good and develop a comparative advantage in producing other goods.

MyEconLab Visit **www.myeconlab.com** to complete these exercises online and get instant feedback.

Review Questions

3.1 Briefly explain how international trade increases a country's consumption.

3.2 What is meant by a country specializing in the production of a good? Is it typical for countries to be completely specialized? Briefly explain.

3.3 What are the main sources of comparative advantage?

3.4 Does everyone gain from international trade? If not, explain which groups lose.

Problems and Applications

3.5 **[Related to** Solved Problem 7.3 **on page 212]** The following table shows the hourly output per worker in two industries in Chile and Argentina:

| | Output per Hour of Work | |
	Hats	Beer
Chile	8	6
Argentina	1	2

a. Explain which country has an absolute advantage in the production of hats and which country has an absolute advantage in the production of beer.

b. Explain which country has a comparative advantage in the production of hats and which country has a comparative advantage in the production of beer.

c. Suppose that Chile and Argentina currently do not trade with each other. Each has 1,000 hours of labor to use producing hats and beer, and the countries are currently producing the amounts of each good shown in the following table:

	Hats	Beer
Chile	7,200	600
Argentina	600	800

Using this information, give a numerical example of how Chile and Argentina can both gain from trade. Assume that after trading begins, one hat can be exchanged for one barrel of beer.

3.6 **[Related to** Solved Problem 7.3 **on page 212]** A political commentator makes the following statement:

The idea that international trade should be based on the comparative advantage of each country is fine for rich countries like the United States and Japan. Rich countries have educated workers and large quantities of machinery and equipment. These advantages allow them to produce every product more efficiently than poor countries can. Poor countries like Kenya and Bolivia have nothing to gain from international trade based on comparative advantage.

Do you agree with this argument? Briefly explain.

3.7 Briefly explain whether you agree with the following statement: "Most countries exhaust their comparative advantage in producing a good or service before they reach complete specialization."

3.8 Is free trade likely to benefit a large, populous country more than a small country with fewer people? Briefly explain.

3.9 An article in the *New Yorker* magazine states, "the main burden of trade-related job losses and wage declines has fallen on middle- and lower-income Americans. But . . . the very people who suffer most from free trade are often, paradoxically, among its biggest beneficiaries." Explain how it is possible that middle- and lower-income Americans are both the biggest losers and at the same time the biggest winners from free trade.

Based on James Surowiecki, "The Free-Trade Paradox," *New Yorker*, May 26, 2008.

3.10 Hal Varian, an economist at the University of California, Berkeley, has made two observations about international trade:

a. Trade allows a country "to produce more with less."

b. There is little doubt who wins [from trade] in the long run: consumers.

Briefly explain whether you agree with either or both of these observations.

Based on Hal R. Varian, "The Mixed Bag of Productivity," *New York Times*, October 23, 2003.

3.11 Imagine that the graph below shows Tanzania's production possibilities frontier for cashew nuts and mangoes. Assume that the output per hour of work is 8 bushels of cashew nuts or 2 bushels of mangoes, and that Tanzania has 1,000 hours of labor. Without trade, Tanzania evenly splits its labor hours between cashews and mangoes and produces and consumes at point *A*.

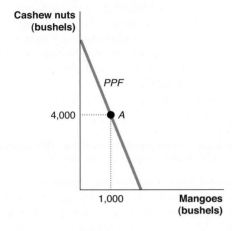

a. Suppose Tanzania opens trade with Kenya, and Kenya's output per hour of work is 1 bushel of cashew nuts or 1 bushel of mangoes. Having the comparative advantage, Tanzania completely specializes in cashew nuts. How many bushels of cashew nuts can Tanzania produce? Denote this point on the graph as point *B*.

b. Suppose Tanzania keeps 5,000 bushels of cashew nuts and exports the remaining 3,000 bushels. If the terms of trade are 1 bushel of mangoes for 2 bushels of cashew nuts, how many bushels of mangoes will Tanzania get in exchange? Denote on the graph the quantity of cashew nuts and mangoes that Tanzania consumes with trade and label this point as point *C*. How does point *C* with trade compare to point *A* without trade?

c. With trade, is Tanzania producing on its production possibilities frontier? With trade, is Tanzania consuming on its production possibilities frontier?

3.12 **[Related to the** Don't Let This Happen to You **on page 214]** In 2011, President Barack Obama described a trade agreement reached with the government of Colombia as a "'win-win' for both our countries." Is everyone in both countries likely to win from the agreement? Briefly explain.

Based on Kent Klein, "Obama: Free Trade Agreement a 'Win-Win' for US, Colombia," Voice of America (voanews.com), accessed April 7, 2011.

3.13 **[Related to the** Making the Connection **on page 216]** Explain why there are advantages to a movie studio operating in southern California, rather than in, say, Florida.

7.4 Government Policies That Restrict International Trade, pages 217–224

LEARNING OBJECTIVE: Analyze the economic effects of government policies that restrict international trade.

Summary

Free trade is trade between countries without government restrictions. Government policies that interfere with trade usually take the form of *tariffs*, *quotas*, or *voluntary export restraints* (VERs). A **tariff** is a tax imposed by a government on imports. A **quota** is a numeric limit imposed by a government on the quantity of a good that can be imported into the country. A **voluntary export restraint (VER)** is an agreement negotiated between two countries that places a numerical limit on the quantity of a good that can be imported by one country from the other country. The federal government's sugar quota costs U.S. consumers $6.08 billion per year, or about $2,026,667 per year for each job saved in the sugar industry. Saving jobs by using tariffs and quotas is often very expensive.

 MyEconLab Visit **www.myeconlab.com** to complete these exercises online and get instant feedback.

Review Questions

4.1 What is a tariff? What is a quota? Give an example, other than a quota, of a non-tariff barrier to trade.

4.2 Who gains and who loses when a country imposes a tariff or a quota on imports of a good?

Problems and Applications

4.3 In a public opinion poll, 47 percent of people responding believed that free trade hurts the U.S. economy, while only 23 percent believed that it helps the economy. (The remaining people were uncertain about the effects of free trade or believed that it did not make much difference.) What is "free trade"? Do you believe it helps or hurts the economy? (Be sure to define what you mean by "helps" or "hurts.") Why do you think that more Americans appear to believe that free trade hurts the economy than believe that it helps the economy?

Based on Gallup Poll, February 2–5, 2011, www.pollingreport.com/trade.

4.4 The G20 is a group of central bankers and finance ministers from 19 countries and the European Union who have a common goal of promoting global economic stability. In a letter to the editor of the *New York Times*, Victor K. Fung, the chairman of the International Chamber of Commerce, comments on the 2009 G20 summit in London: "While global leaders promise to fight protectionism when they gather at summit meetings, they must also resist intense pressure back home to adopt populist policies that will most certainly protract the recession." What does Fung mean by "fighting protectionism"? What does he mean by "populist policies"? How might populist trade policies extend a period of high unemployment and low production, such as the 2007–2009 recession?

Based on Victor K. Fung, "Resist Protectionism," Letter to the Editor, *New York Times*, March 30, 2009.

4.5 Political commentator B. Bruce-Briggs once wrote the following in the *Wall Street Journal*: "This is not to say that the case for international free trade is invalid; it is just irrelevant. It is an 'if only everybody . . .' argument. . . . In the real world almost everybody sees benefits in economic nationalism." What do you think he means by "economic nationalism"? Do you agree that a country benefits from free trade only if every other country also practices free trade? Briefly explain.

Based on B. Bruce-Biggs, "The Coming Overthrow of Free Trade," *Wall Street Journal*, February 24, 1983, p. 28.

4.6 Two U.S. senators made the following argument against allowing free trade: "Fewer and fewer Americans support our government's trade policy. They see a shrinking middle class, lost jobs and exploding trade deficits. Yet supporters of free trade continue to push for more of the same—more job-killing trade agreements." Do you agree with these senators that reducing barriers to trade reduces the number of jobs available to workers in the United States? Briefly explain.

Based on Byron Dorgan and Sherrod Brown, "How Free Trade Hurts," *Washington Post*, December 23, 2006, p. A21.

4.7 The United States produces beef and also imports beef from other countries.

a. Draw a graph showing the demand and supply of beef in the United States. Assume that the United States can import as much as it wants at the world price of beef without causing the world price of beef to increase. Be sure to indicate on the graph the quantity of beef imported.

b. Now show on your graph the effect of the United States imposing a tariff on beef. Be sure to indicate on your graph the quantity of beef sold by U.S. producers before and after the tariff is imposed, the quantity of beef imported before and after the tariff, and the price of beef in the United States before and after the tariff.

c. Discuss who benefits and who loses when the United States imposes a tariff on beef.

4.8 **[Related to the** Chapter Opener **on page 205]** Which U.S. firms are most likely to be unfavorably affected by a provision which states that only U.S. firms can participate in programs financed by federal spending?

4.9 When Congress was considering a bill to impose quotas on imports of textiles, shoes, and other products, the late Milton Friedman, a Nobel Prize–winning economist, made the following comment: "The consumer will be forced to spend several extra dollars to subsidize the producers [of these goods] by one dollar. A straight handout would be far cheaper." Why would a quota result in consumers paying much more than domestic producers receive? Where do the other dollars go? What does Friedman mean by a "straight handout"? Why would this be cheaper than a quota?

Based on Milton Friedman, "Free Trade," *Newsweek Magazine*, August 27, 1970.

4.10 The United States has about 9,000 rice farmers. In 2006, these rice farmers received $780 million in subsidy payments from the U.S. government (or nearly $87,000 per farmer). These payments result in U.S. farmers producing much more rice than they otherwise would, a substantial amount of which is exported. According to an article in the *Wall Street Journal*, Kpalagim Mome, a farmer in the African country of Ghana, can no longer find buyers in Ghana for his rice:

"We can't sell our rice anymore. It gets worse every year," Mr. Mome says. . . . Years of economic hardship have driven three of his brothers to walk and hitchhike 2,000 miles across the Sahara to reach the Mediterranean and Europe. His sister plans to leave next year. Mr. Mome's plight is repeated throughout farm communities in Africa and elsewhere in the developing world.

Why would subsidies paid by the U.S. government to U.S. rice farmers reduce the incomes of rice farmers in Africa?

From Juliane von Reppert-Bismarck, "How Trade Barriers Keep Africans Adrift," *Wall Street Journal*, December 27, 2006.

4.11 A student makes the following argument:

Tariffs on imports of foreign goods into the United States will cause the foreign companies to add the amount of the tariff to the prices they charge in the United States for those goods. Instead of putting a tariff on imported goods, we should ban importing them. Banning imported goods is better than putting tariffs on them because U.S. producers benefit from the reduced competition, and U.S. consumers don't have to pay the higher prices caused by tariffs.

Briefly explain whether you agree with the student's reasoning.

4.12 Suppose China decides to pay large subsidies to any Chinese company that exports goods or services to the United States. As a result, these companies are able to sell products in the United States at far below their cost of production. In addition, China decides to bar all imports from the United States. The dollars that the United States pays to import Chinese goods are left in banks in China. Will this strategy raise or lower the standard of living in China? Will it raise or lower the standard of living in the United States? Briefly explain. Be sure to provide a definition of "standard of living" in your answer.

4.13 According to an editorial in the *Washington Post*: "Sugar protectionism is a burden on consumers and a job-killer."

a. In what sense does the United States practice "sugar protectionism"?

b. In what way is sugar protectionism a burden on consumers? In what way is it a job-killer?

c. If sugar protectionism has the bad effects stated in the editorial, why don't Congress and the president eliminate it?

Based on "Sourball," *Washington Post*, March 22, 2010.

4.14 [**Related to** Solved Problem 7.4 **on page 221**] Suppose that the United States currently both produces kumquats and imports them. The U.S. government then decides to restrict international trade in kumquats by imposing a quota that allows imports of only 6 million pounds of kumquats into the United States each year. The figure shows the results of imposing the quota.

Fill in the table in the next column using the letters in the figure:

	Without Quota	With Quota
World price of kumquats	_____	_____
U.S. price of kumquats	_____	_____
Quantity supplied by U.S. firms	_____	_____
Quantity demanded	_____	_____
Quantity imported	_____	_____
Area of consumer surplus	_____	_____
Area of domestic producer surplus	_____	_____
Area of deadweight loss	_____	_____

4.15 [**Related to the** Making the Connection **on page 223**] An economic analysis of a proposal to impose a quota on steel imports into the United States indicated that the quota would save 3,700 jobs in the steel industry but cost about 35,000 jobs in other U.S. industries. Why would a quota on steel imports cause employment to fall in other industries? Which other industries are likely to be most affected?

Based on Study cited in Douglas A. Irwin, *Free Trade Under Fire*, (Princeton, NJ: Princeton University Press, 2002), p. 82.

7.5	**The Arguments over Trade Policies and Globalization,** pages 224–229

LEARNING OBJECTIVE: Evaluate the arguments over trade policies and globalization.

Summary

The **World Trade Organization (WTO)** is an international organization that enforces international trade agreements. The WTO has promoted **globalization**, the process of countries becoming more open to foreign trade and investment. Some critics of the WTO argue that globalization has damaged local cultures around the world. Other critics oppose the WTO because they believe in **protectionism**, which is the use of trade barriers to shield domestic firms from foreign competition. The WTO allows countries to use tariffs in cases of **dumping**, when an imported product is sold for a price below its cost of production. Economists can point out the burden imposed on the economy by tariffs, quotas, and other government interferences with free trade. But whether these policies should be used is a normative decision.

Review Questions

5.1 What events led to the General Agreement on Tariffs and Trade (GATT)? Why did the WTO eventually replace GATT?

5.2 What is globalization? Why are some people opposed to globalization?

5.3 What is protectionism? Who benefits and who loses from protectionist policies? What are the main arguments people use to justify protectionism?

5.4 What is dumping? Who benefits and who loses from dumping? What problems arise when anti-dumping laws are implemented?

Problems and Applications

5.5 **[Related to the** Making the Connection **on page 226]**
The following excerpt is from a newspaper story on President Bill Clinton's proposal to create a group within the Word Trade Organization (WTO) responsible for developing labor standards. The story was published just before the 1999 WTO meeting in Seattle that ended in rioting:

> [President Clinton proposed that] core labor standards . . . become "part of every trade agreement. And ultimately I would favor a system in which sanctions would come for violating any provision of a trade agreement. . . ." But the new U.S. stand is sure to meet massive resistance from developing countries, which make up more than 100 of the 135 countries in the WTO. They are not interested in adopting tougher U.S. labor standards.

What did Clinton mean by "core labor standards"? Why would developing countries resist adopting these standards?

From Terence Hunt, "Salute to Trade's Benefits Turns into 'Kind of Circus,'" *Associated Press*, December 2, 1999.

5.6 Steven Landsburg, an economist at the University of Rochester, wrote the following in an article in the *New York Times*:

> Free trade is not only about the right of American consumers to buy at the cheapest possible price; it's also about the right of foreign producers to earn a living. Steelworkers in West Virginia struggle hard to make ends meet. So do steelworkers in South Korea. To protect one at the expense of the other, solely because of where they happened to be born, is a moral outrage.

How does the U.S. government protect steelworkers in West Virginia at the expense of steelworkers in South Korea? Is Landsburg making a positive or a normative statement? A few days later, Tom Redburn published an article disagreeing with Landsburg:

> It is not some evil character flaw to care more about the welfare of people nearby than about that of those far away—it's human nature. And it is morally—and economically—defensible. . . . A society that ignores the consequences of economic disruption on those among its citizens who come out at the short end of the stick is not only heartless, it also undermines its own cohesion and adaptability.

Which of the two arguments do you find most convincing?

Based on Steven E. Landsburg, "Who Cares if the Playing Field Is Level?" *The New York Times*, June 13, 2001; and Tom Redburn, "Economic View: Of Politics, Free Markets, and Tending to Society," *The New York Times*, June 17, 2001.

5.7 Suppose you are explaining the benefits of free trade and someone states, "I don't understand all the principles of comparative advantage and gains from trade. I just know that if I buy something produced in America, I create a job for an American, and if I buy something produced in Brazil, I create a job for a Brazilian." Do you agree with this statement? When the United States imports products in which it does not have a comparative advantage, does that mean that there are fewer jobs in the United States? In the example in the text with Japan and America producing and trading cell phones and tablet computers, when the United States imports cell phones from Japan, does the number of jobs in the United States decline?

5.8 **[Related to the** Chapter Opener **on page 205]** In a forum in the *New York Times* on the Buy American provision in the American Recovery and Reinvestment Act, the editors posed the following question: "Why is the buy-American idea objectionable, or, alternatively, under what circumstances should it be promoted?" Roger Simmermaker, the author of *How Americans Can Buy American*, responded:

> The buy-American provision in the economic stimulus bill isn't as much about a return to protectionism as it is about a return to the American virtues and values—self-sufficiency, self-reliance and independence—that this country was founded on. Workers in foreign countries don't pay taxes to America. Only American workers pay taxes to America. We need to employ American steelworkers, ironworkers and autoworkers so we need to . . . keep and create American jobs.

Burton Folsom Jr., a professor at Hillsdale College, offered an opposing view:

> "Slap a tariff on China and save American jobs," the protectionists say. This tempting line of reasoning is flawed for two reasons. First, if Americans pay more for, say, American-made shoes or shirts, then they have less to spend for other things they might need—they are simply subsidizing inefficient local producers. And those American manufacturers, who are protected from foreign competitors, have little incentive to innovate and cut prices. Second, if we refuse to buy China's imports, China will refuse to buy our exports, including our first-rate computers and iPods. Our export market collapses.

Which of the two arguments do you find the most convincing?

From "That 'Buy American' Provision" series. *New York Times*, February 11, 2009. Reprinted with kind permission from Roger Simmermaker and Burton Folsom, Jr.

5.9 President George W. Bush and President Barack Obama had trouble getting Congress to ratify free trade agreements the United States had negotiated with South Korea, Colombia, and Panama. According to an article in the *New York Times*, "When the Democrats controlled Congress, they resisted the trade agreements because they feared they would harm American workers." Is it likely that trade agreements that reduce tariffs and quotas will harm American workers? Briefly explain.

Based on Mark Drajem, "Obama to Pursue Trade Deals, Avoid Turning 'Inward,'" Bloomberg.com, April 23, 2009.

5.10 The following appeared in an article in *BusinessWeek* that argued against free trade: "The U.S. is currently in a precarious position. In addition to geopolitical threats, we face a severe economic shock. We have already lost trillions of dollars and millions of jobs to foreigners." If a country engages in free trade, is the total number of jobs in the country likely to decline? Briefly explain.

Based on Vladimir Masch, "A Radical Plan to Manage Globalization," *BusinessWeek*, February 14, 2007.

GDP: Measuring Total Production and Income

Chapter Outline and Learning Objectives

Ford Motor Company Feels the Effects of the Recession

In the more than 100 years that Ford Motor Company has been in business, its experiences have often mirrored those of the U.S. economy. So, it was no surprise that in the spring of 2009, with the U.S. economy suffering from its worst downturn since the 1930s, sales of Ford cars and trucks plummeted. In May 2009, Ford's sales were down 20 percent from a year earlier. Still, Ford was doing better than General Motors and Chrysler, Ford's two great American rivals, which had both declared bankruptcy. Those firms survived largely because the federal government invested more than $62 billion in them. While Ford suffered heavy losses, it did not require direct government aid.

By 2011, as the economy was slowly recovering from the downturn, Ford's sales were rising. Ford and the automobile industry as a whole were experiencing the effects of the *business cycle*, which refers to alternating periods of economic expansion and recession. Production and employment increase during expansions and fall during recessions.

Whether the general level of economic activity is increasing is important not just to firms such as Ford but also to workers wondering whether they will be able to keep their jobs and to college students wondering whether they will be able to find jobs when they graduate. One study found that during the slow recovery from the 2007–2009 recession, of those students who graduated from college in the spring of 2010, only 56 percent had found a job a year later. The average salary of those who did find a job was $27,000, down from an average of $30,000 for the classes of 2006 to 2008. What's more, students who graduate during recessions will continue to earn less for as long as 15 years after they graduate. The overall state of the economy is clearly important!

AN INSIDE LOOK AT POLICY on **page 260** discusses how uncertain economic conditions in 2011 and 2012 kept demand for automobiles below initial sales estimates.

Based on Sharon Terlep and Mike Ramsey, "August Auto Sales Perk Up," *The Wall Street Journal*, September 2, 2011; Catherine Rampell, "Many with New College Degrees Find the Job Market Humbling," *The New York Times*, May 18, 2011; and Lisa B. Kahn, "The Long-Term Labor Market Consequences of Graduating from College in a Bad Economy," *Labour Economics*, Vol. 17, No. 2, April 2010, pp. 303–316.

Economics in Your Life

What's the Best Country for You to Work In?

Suppose that an airline offers you a job after graduation in 2012. The firm has offices in Canada and China, and because you are fluent in English and Mandarin, you get to choose the country in which you will work and live. Gross domestic product (GDP) is a measure of an economy's total production of goods and services, so one factor in your decision is likely to be the growth rate of GDP in each country. Based on the International Monetary Fund's forecasts for 2012, GDP would increase by 2.6 percent in Canada but expand 9.5 percent in China. What effect do these two very different growth rates have on your decision to work and live in one country or the other? If China's much larger growth rate does not necessarily lead you to decide to work and live in China, why not? As you read this chapter, see if you can answer these questions. You can check your answers against those we provide on **page 259** at the end of this chapter.

Microeconomics The study of how households and firms make choices, how they interact in markets, and how the government attempts to influence their choices.

Macroeconomics The study of the economy as a whole, including topics such as inflation, unemployment, and economic growth.

Business cycle Alternating periods of economic expansion and economic recession.

Expansion The period of a business cycle during which total production and total employment are increasing.

Recession The period of a business cycle during which total production and total employment are decreasing.

Economic growth The ability of an economy to produce increasing quantities of goods and services.

Inflation rate The percentage increase in the price level from one year to the next.

As we saw in Chapter 1, we can divide economics into the subfields of microeconomics and macroeconomics. **Microeconomics** is the study of how households and firms make choices, how they interact in markets, and how the government attempts to influence their choices.

Macroeconomics is the study of the economy as a whole, including topics such as inflation, unemployment, and economic growth. In microeconomic analysis, economists generally study individual markets, such as the market for personal computers. In macroeconomic analysis, economists study factors that affect many markets at the same time. As we saw in the chapter opener, one important macroeconomic issue is the business cycle. The **business cycle** refers to the alternating periods of expansion and recession that the U.S. economy has experienced since at least the early nineteenth century. A business cycle **expansion** is a period during which total production and total employment are increasing. A business cycle **recession** is a period during which total production and total employment are decreasing. In the following chapters, we will discuss the factors that influence the business cycle and policies the government may use to reduce its effects.

Another important macroeconomic topic is **economic growth**, which refers to the ability of an economy to produce increasing quantities of goods and services. Economic growth is important because an economy that grows too slowly fails to raise living standards. In some countries in Africa, very little economic growth has occurred in the past 50 years, and many people remain in severe poverty. Macroeconomics analyzes both what determines a country's rate of economic growth and the reasons growth rates differ so greatly across countries.

Macroeconomics also analyzes what determines the total level of employment in an economy. As we will see, in the short run, the level of employment is significantly affected by the business cycle, but in the long run, the effects of the business cycle disappear, and other factors determine the level of employment. A related issue is why some economies are more successful than others at maintaining high levels of employment over time. Another important macroeconomic issue is what determines the **inflation rate**, or the percentage increase in the average level of prices from one year to the next. As with employment, inflation is affected both by the business cycle and by other long-run factors. Finally, macroeconomics is concerned with the linkages among economies: international trade and international finance.

Macroeconomic analysis provides information that consumers and firms need in order to understand current economic conditions and to help predict future conditions. A family may be reluctant to buy a house if employment in the economy is declining because some family members may be at risk of losing their jobs. Similarly, firms may be reluctant to invest in building new factories or to undertake major new expenditures on information technology if they expect that future sales may be weak. For example, in 2011, H. J. Heinz announced that it would close three of its factories in the United States. Heinz made that decision because macroeconomic forecasts indicated that consumer demand for its ketchup and other food products would increase only slowly. Macroeconomic analysis can also aid the federal government in designing policies that help the U.S. economy perform more efficiently.

In this chapter and Chapter 9, we begin our study of macroeconomics by considering how best to measure key macroeconomic variables. As we will see, there are important issues involved in measuring macroeconomic variables. We start by considering measures of total production and total income in an economy.

Gross Domestic Product Measures Total Production

"Anemic GDP Figures Rattle Stocks"

"U.K. GDP Weak, but Could Have Been Worse"

"Concern Looms after Japan GDP Surprise"

"Malaysia's GDP Rises 4%"

"Indonesia's GDP Tops Forecast"

These headlines are from articles that appeared in the *Wall Street Journal* during 2011. Why is GDP so often the focus of news stories? In this section, we explore what GDP is and how it is measured. We also explore why knowledge of GDP is important to consumers, firms, and government policymakers.

Measuring Total Production: Gross Domestic Product

Economists use **gross domestic product (GDP)** to measure total production. GDP is the market *value* of all *final* goods and services produced in a country during a period of time, typically one year. In the United States, the Bureau of Economic Analysis (BEA) in the Department of Commerce compiles the data needed to calculate GDP. The BEA issues reports on the GDP every three months. GDP is a central concept in macroeconomics, so we need to consider its definition carefully.

Gross domestic product (GDP) The market value of all final goods and services produced in a country during a period of time, typically one year.

GDP Is Measured Using Market Values, Not Quantities The word *value* is important in the definition of GDP. In microeconomics, we measure production in quantity terms: the number of cars Ford produces, the tons of wheat U.S. farmers grow, or the number of passengers American Airlines transports. When we measure total production in the economy, we can't just add together the quantities of every good and service because the result would be a meaningless jumble. Tons of wheat would be added to gallons of milk, numbers of passengers on flights, and so on. Instead, we measure production by taking the *value*, in dollar terms, of all the goods and services produced.

GDP Includes Only the Market Value of Final Goods In measuring GDP, we include only the value of *final goods and services*. A **final good or service** is one that is purchased by its final user and is not included in the production of any other good or service. Examples of final goods are a hamburger purchased by a consumer and a computer purchased by a business. Some goods and services, though, become part of other goods and services. For example, Ford does not produce tires for its cars and trucks; it buys them from tire companies, such as Goodyear and Michelin. The tires are an **intermediate good**, while a Ford truck is a final good. In calculating GDP, we include the value of the Ford truck but not the value of the tire. If we included the value of the tire, we would be *double counting*: The value of the tire would be counted once when the tire company sold it to Ford and a second time when Ford sold the truck, with the tire installed, to a consumer.

Final good or service A good or service purchased by a final user.

Intermediate good or service A good or service that is an input into another good or service, such as a tire on a truck.

GDP Includes Only Current Production GDP includes only production that takes place during the indicated time period. For example, GDP in 2012 includes only the goods and services produced during that year. In particular, GDP does *not* include the value of used goods. If you buy a DVD of *The Dark Knight Rises* from Amazon.com, the purchase is included in GDP. If six months later you resell the DVD on eBay, that transaction is not included in GDP.

Solved Problem 8.1

Calculating GDP

Suppose that a very simple economy produces only four goods and services: eye examinations, pizzas, textbooks, and paper. Assume that all the paper in this economy is used in the production of textbooks. Use the information in the following table to compute GDP for the year 2013:

Production and Price Statistics for 2013		
(1) Product	(2) Quantity	(3) Price per Unit
Eye examinations	100	$50.00
Pizzas	80	10.00
Textbooks	20	100.00
Paper	2,000	0.10

Solving the Problem

Step 1: Review the chapter material. This problem is about gross domestic product, so you may want to review the section "Measuring Total Production: Gross Domestic Product" on page 243.

Step 2: Determine which goods and services listed in the table should be included in the calculation of GDP. GDP is the value of all final goods and services. Therefore, we need to calculate the value of the final goods and services listed in the table. Eye examinations, pizzas, and textbooks are final goods. Paper would also be a final good if, for instance, a consumer bought it to use in a printer. However, here we are assuming that publishers purchase all the paper to use in manufacturing textbooks, so the paper is an intermediate good, and its value is not included in GDP.

Step 3: Calculate the value of the three final goods and services listed in the table. Value is equal to the quantity produced multiplied by the price per unit, so we multiply the numbers in column (1) by the numbers in column (2).

Product	(1) Quantity	(2) Price per Unit	(3) Value
Eye examinations	100	$50	$5,000
Pizzas	80	10	800
Textbooks	20	100	2,000

Step 4: Add the value for each of the three final goods and services to find GDP. GDP = Value of eye examinations produced + Value of pizzas produced + Value of textbooks produced = $5,000 + $800 + $2,000 = $7,800.

MyEconLab   **Your Turn:** For more practice, do related problem 1.10 on page 263 at the end of this chapter.

Production, Income, and the Circular-Flow Diagram

When we measure the value of total production in the economy by calculating GDP, we are simultaneously measuring the value of total income. To see why the value of total production is equal to the value of total income, consider what happens to the money you spend on a single product. Suppose you buy an Apple iPad for $499 at a Best Buy store. *All* of that $499 must end up as someone's income. Apple and Best Buy will receive some of the $499 as profits, workers at Apple will receive some as wages, the salesperson who sold you the iPad will receive some as salary, the firms that sell parts to Apple will receive some as profits, the workers for those firms will receive some as wages, and so on. Every penny must end up as someone's income. (Note, though, that any sales tax on the iPad will be collected by the store and sent to the government, without ending up as anyone's income.) Therefore, if we add up the value of every good and service sold in the economy, we must get a total that is exactly equal to the value of all the income in the economy.

The circular-flow diagram in Figure 8.1 was introduced in Chapter 2 to illustrate the interaction of firms and households in markets. We use it here to illustrate the flow of spending and money in the economy. Firms sell goods and services to three groups: domestic households, foreign firms and households, and the government. Expenditures by foreign firms and households (shown as "Rest of the World" in the diagram) on domestically produced goods and services are called *exports*. For example, American Airlines sells many tickets to passengers in Europe and Asia. As noted at the bottom of Figure 8.1, we can measure GDP by adding up the total expenditures of these groups on goods and services.

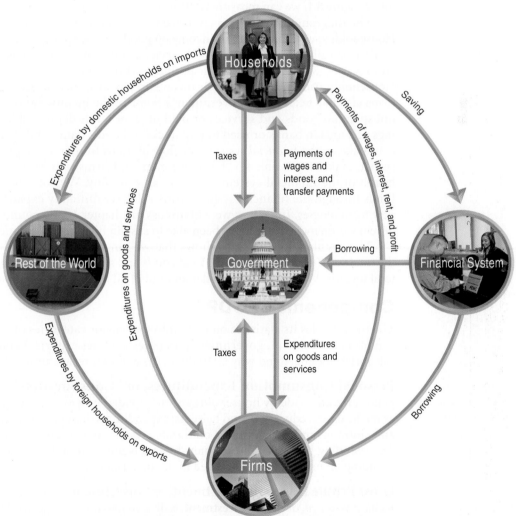

GDP can be measured by total wages, interest, rent, and profits received by households.

GDP can be measured by total expenditures on goods and services by households, firms, government, and the rest of the world.

Figure 8.1 **The Circular Flow and the Measurement of GDP**

The circular-flow diagram illustrates the flow of spending and money in the economy. Firms sell goods and services to three groups: domestic households, foreign firms and households, and the government. To produce goods and services, firms use factors of production: labor, capital, natural resources, and entrepreneurship. Households supply the factors of production to firms in exchange for income in the form of wages, interest, profit, and rent. Firms make payments of wages and interest to households in exchange for hiring workers and other factors of production. The sum of wages, interest, rent, and profit is total income in the economy. We can measure GDP as the total income received by households. The diagram also shows that households use their income to purchase goods and services, pay taxes, and save. Firms and the government borrow the funds that flow from households into the financial system. We can measure GDP either by calculating the total value of expenditures on final goods and services or by calculating the value of total income.

Firms use the *factors of production*—labor, capital, natural resources, and entrepreneurship—to produce goods and services. Households supply the factors of production to firms in exchange for income. We divide income into four categories: wages, interest, rent, and profit. Firms pay wages to households in exchange for labor services, interest for the use of capital, and rent for natural resources such as land. Profit is the income that remains after a firm has paid wages, interest, and rent. Profit is the return to entrepreneurs for organizing the other factors of production and for bearing the risk of producing and selling goods and services. As Figure 8.1 shows, federal, state, and local governments make payments of wages and interest to households in exchange for hiring workers and other factors of production. Governments also make *transfer payments* to households. **Transfer payments** include Social Security payments to retired and disabled people and unemployment insurance payments to unemployed workers. These payments are not included in GDP because they are not received in exchange for production of a new good or service. The sum of wages, interest, rent, and profit is total income in the economy. As noted at the top of Figure 8.1, we can measure GDP as the total income received by households.

Transfer payments Payments by the government to households for which the government does not receive a new good or service in return.

The diagram also allows us to trace the ways that households use their income. Households spend some of their income on goods and services. Some of this spending is on domestically produced goods and services, and some is on foreign-produced goods and services. Spending on foreign-produced goods and services is known as *imports*. Households also use some of their income to pay taxes to the government. (Note that firms also pay taxes to the government.) Some of the income earned by households is not spent on goods and services or paid in taxes but is deposited in checking or savings accounts in banks or used to buy stocks or bonds. Banks and stock and bond markets make up the *financial system*. The flow of funds from households into the financial system makes it possible for the government and firms to borrow. As we will see, the health of the financial system is vital to an economy. Without the ability to borrow funds through the financial system, firms will have difficulty expanding and adopting new technologies. In fact, as we will discuss in Chapter 10, no country without a well-developed financial system has been able to sustain high levels of economic growth.

The circular-flow diagram shows that we can measure GDP either by calculating the total value of expenditures on final goods and services or by calculating the value of total income. We get the same dollar amount of GDP with both approaches.

Components of GDP

The BEA divides its statistics on GDP into four major categories of expenditures: consumption, investment, government purchases, and net exports. Economists use these categories to understand why GDP fluctuates and to forecast future GDP.

Personal Consumption Expenditures, or "Consumption" Consumption expenditures are made by households and are divided into expenditures on *services*, such as medical care, education, and haircuts; expenditures on *nondurable goods*, such as food and clothing; and expenditures on *durable goods*, such as automobiles and furniture. The spending by households on new houses is not included in consumption. Instead, spending on new houses is included in the investment category, which we discuss next.

Consumption Spending by households on goods and services, not including spending on new houses.

Gross Private Domestic Investment, or "Investment" Spending on *gross private domestic investment*, or simply **investment**, is divided into three categories. *Business fixed investment* is spending by firms on new factories, office buildings, and machinery used to produce other goods. *Residential investment* is spending by households and firms on new single-family and multi-unit houses. *Changes in business inventories* are also included in investment. Inventories are goods that have been produced but not yet sold. If Ford has $200 million worth of unsold cars at the beginning of the year and $350 million worth of unsold cars at the end of the year, then the firm has spent $150 million on inventory investment during the year.

Investment Spending by firms on new factories, office buildings, machinery, and additions to inventories, plus spending by households and firms on new houses.

Government Consumption and Gross Investment, or "Government Purchases" **Government purchases** are spending by federal, state, and local governments on goods and services, such as teachers' salaries, highways, and aircraft carriers. Again, government spending on transfer payments is not included in government purchases because it does not result in the production of new goods and services.

Government purchases Spending by federal, state, and local governments on goods and services.

Don't Let This Happen to You

Remember What Economists Mean by *Investment*

Notice that the definition of *investment* in this chapter is narrower than in everyday use. For example, people often say they are investing in the stock market or in rare coins. As we have seen, economists reserve the word *investment* for purchases of machinery, factories, and houses. Economists don't include purchases of stock or rare coins or deposits in savings accounts in the definition of investment because these activities don't result in the production of new goods. For example, a share of Microsoft stock

represents part ownership of that company. When you buy a share of Microsoft stock, nothing new is produced; there is just a transfer of that small piece of ownership of Microsoft. Similarly, buying a rare coin or putting $1,000 into a savings account does not result in an increase in production. GDP is not affected by any of these activities, so they are not included in the economic definition of investment.

MyEconLab

Your Turn: Test your understanding by doing related problem 1.11 on page 263 at the end of this chapter.

Net Exports of Goods and Services, or "Net Exports" Net exports are equal to *exports* minus *imports*. Exports are goods and services produced in the United States and purchased by foreign firms, households, and governments. We add exports to our other categories of expenditures because otherwise we would not be including all spending on new goods and services produced in the United States. For example, if a farmer in South Dakota sells wheat to China, the value of the wheat is included in GDP because it represents production in the United States. Imports are goods and services produced in foreign countries and purchased by U.S. firms, households, and governments. We subtract imports from total expenditures because otherwise we would be including spending that does not result in production of new goods and services in the United States. For example, if U.S. consumers buy $1 billion worth of furniture manufactured in China, that spending is included in consumption expenditures. But the value of those imports is subtracted from GDP because the imports do not represent production in the United States.

Net exports Exports minus imports.

An Equation for GDP and Some Actual Values

A simple equation sums up the components of GDP:

$$Y = C + I + G + NX.$$

The equation tells us that GDP (denoted as Y) equals consumption (C) plus investment (I) plus government purchases (G) plus net exports (NX). Figure 8.2 shows the values of the components of GDP for the year 2010. The graph in the figure highlights the fact that consumption is by far the largest component of GDP. The table provides a more detailed breakdown and shows several interesting points:

- Consumer spending on services is greater than the sum of spending on durable and nondurable goods. This greater spending on services reflects the continuing trend in the United States and other high-income countries away from the production of goods and toward the production of services. As the populations of these countries have become, on average, both older and wealthier, their demand for services such as medical care and financial advice has increased faster than their demand for goods.
- Business fixed investment is the largest component of investment. As we will see in later chapters, spending by firms on new factories, computers, and machinery can fluctuate. For example, a decline in business fixed investment played an important role in the 2007–2009 recession.
- Purchases made by state and local governments are greater than purchases made by the federal government. Because basic government activities, such as education and law enforcement, occur largely at the state and local levels, state and local government spending is greater than federal government spending.

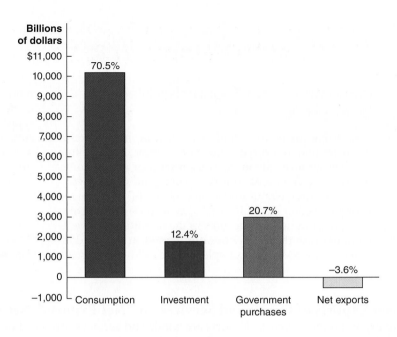

COMPONENTS OF GDP (billions of dollars)		
Consumption		$10,246
Durable goods	$1,086	
Nondurable goods	2,302	
Services	6,859	
Investment		1,795
Business fixed investment	1,390	
Residential construction	338	
Change in business inventories	67	
Government Purchases		3,003
Federal	1,223	
State and local	1,780	
Net Exports		−517
Exports	1,840	
Imports	2,357	
Total GDP		$14,527

Figure 8.2   Components of GDP in 2010

Consumption accounts for 70.5 percent of GDP, far more than any of the other components. In recent years, net exports typically have been negative, which reduces GDP. Note that the subtotals may not sum to the totals for each category because of rounding.
Data from U.S. Bureau of Economic Analysis.

- Imports are greater than exports, so net exports are negative. We will discuss in Chapter 18 why imports have typically been larger than exports for the U.S. economy.

Making the Connection

Will U.S. Consumers Be Spending Less?

We saw in Figure 8.2 that in 2010, consumption was 70.5 percent of GDP in the United States. As the figure below shows, consumption is a larger fraction of GDP in the United States than in most other high-income countries or in rapidly growing countries such as China and India.

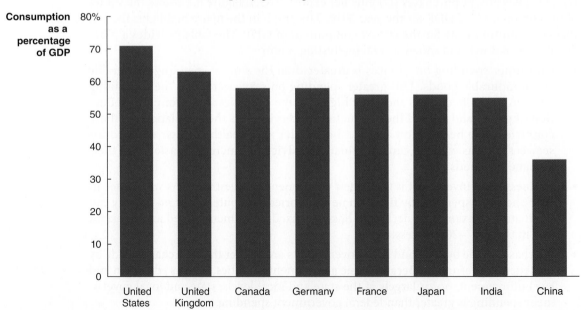

As shown in the following figure, over time, consumption in the United States has increased as a fraction of GDP. Through the mid-1980s, consumption was less than 65 percent of GDP. By the early 2000s, consumption had increased to 70 percent of GDP.

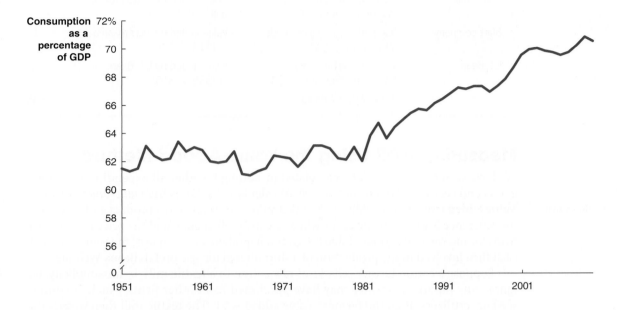

U.S. households financed this increased consumption partly by reducing saving and partly by increasing borrowing. While households were saving about 10 percent of their income in the mid-1980s, saving dropped to about 1 percent by 2005. Low saving rates were partly due to an increase in household wealth resulting from rising housing prices and rising stock prices. In many parts of the country, housing prices increased rapidly between 2001 and 2006. Stock prices, as measured by the Dow Jones Industrial Average and the S&P 500, reached record highs in October 2007. Some households felt less need to save out of their current incomes because their homes and their investments in the stock market were increasing in value.

During the early 2000s, many households borrowed against the increased value of their homes by taking out home equity loans, which many banks were increasingly willing to grant. Banks and other financial firms also loosened the requirements for issuing credit cards, so some households with flawed credit histories were able to borrow against their credit cards to finance their spending. The ratio of loans and other household debt to household income, which had been about 65 percent in the mid-1980s, rose to a record 133 percent in 2007 before declining to 102 percent in mid-2011.

Housing prices began to decline in 2006, and that decline accelerated with the start of the recession in December 2007. Stock prices also declined sharply. The combination of falling housing prices and falling stock prices wiped out trillions of dollars in household wealth. Banks and other financial institutions also tightened lending standards, making it more difficult for many households to borrow money. In the face of declining wealth and with reduced access to loans, household saving rates began to increase, rising above 6 percent by 2009.

As we will see in later chapters, increased household saving can be good news for the economy in the long run because it provides more funds that firms can borrow to finance investment, which can lead to more rapid rates of economic growth. But in the short run, in 2011, many firms—particularly firms such as Ford that sell consumer durables—worried that the slow recovery from the 2007–2009 recession was due in part to the determination of U.S. households to cut back on spending and increase saving.

Data from U.S. Bureau of Economic Analysis; Organization for Economic Cooperation and Development; and United Nations.

Your Turn: Test your understanding by doing related problem 1.12 on page 263 at the end of this chapter. MyEconLab

Table 8.1
Calculating Value Added

Firm	Value of Product	Value Added	
Cotton farmer	Value of raw cotton = $1	Value added by cotton farmer	= 1
Textile mill	Value of raw cotton woven into cotton fabric = $3	Value added by cotton textile mill = ($3 − $1)	= 2
Shirt company	Value of cotton fabric made into a shirt = $15	Value added by shirt manufacturer = ($15 − $3)	= 12
L.L.Bean	Value of shirt for sale on L.L.Bean's Web site = $35	Value added by L.L.Bean = ($35 − $15)	= 20
		Total Value Added	= **$35**

Measuring GDP Using the Value-Added Method

We have seen that GDP can be calculated by adding together all expenditures on final goods and services. An alternative way of calculating GDP is the *value-added method.* **Value added** refers to the additional market value a firm gives to a product and is equal to the difference between the price for which the firm sells a good and the price it paid other firms for intermediate goods. Table 8.1 gives a hypothetical example of the value added by each firm involved in the production of a shirt offered for sale on L.L.Bean's Web site.

Value added The market value a firm adds to a product.

Suppose a cotton farmer sells $1 of raw cotton to a textile mill. If, for simplicity, we ignore any inputs the farmer may have purchased from other firms—such as cottonseed or fertilizer—then the farmer's value added is $1. The textile mill then weaves the raw cotton into cotton fabric, which it sells to a shirt company for $3. The textile mill's value added ($2) is the difference between the price it paid for the raw cotton ($1) and the price for which it can sell the cotton fabric ($3). Similarly, the shirt company's value added is the difference between the price it paid for the cotton fabric ($3) and the price it receives for the shirt from L.L.Bean ($15). L.L.Bean's value added is the difference between the price it pays for the shirt ($15) and the price for which it can sell the shirt on its Web site ($35). Notice that *the price of the shirt on L.L.Bean's Web site is exactly equal to the sum of the value added by each firm involved in the production of the shirt.* We can calculate GDP by adding up the market value of every final good and service produced during a particular period. Or, we can arrive at the same value for GDP by adding up the value added of every firm involved in producing those final goods and services.

Does GDP Measure What We Want It to Measure?

8.2 LEARNING OBJECTIVE

Discuss whether GDP is a good measure of well-being.

Economists use GDP to measure total production in the economy. For that purpose, we would like GDP to be as comprehensive as possible, not overlooking any significant production that takes place in the economy. Most economists believe that GDP does a good—but not flawless—job of measuring production. GDP is also sometimes used as a measure of well-being. Although it is generally true that the more goods and services people have, the better off they are, we will see that GDP provides only a rough measure of well-being.

Shortcomings in GDP as a Measure of Total Production

When the BEA calculates GDP, it does not include two types of production: production in the home and production in the underground economy.

Household Production With few exceptions, the BEA does not attempt to estimate the value of goods and services that are not bought and sold in markets. If a carpenter makes and sells bookcases, the value of those bookcases will be counted in GDP. If the carpenter makes a bookcase for personal use, it will not be counted in GDP. *Household production* refers to goods and services people produce for themselves. The most important type of household production is the services a homemaker provides to the homemaker's family. If a person has been caring for children, cleaning the house, and preparing the family meals, the value of such services is not included in GDP. If the person then decides to work outside the home, enrolls the children in day care, hires a cleaning service, and begins buying the family's meals in restaurants, the value of GDP will rise by the amount paid for day care, cleaning services, and restaurant meals, even though production of these services has not actually increased.

The Underground Economy Individuals and firms sometimes conceal the buying and selling of goods and services, in which case their production isn't counted in GDP. Individuals and firms conceal what they buy and sell for three basic reasons: They are dealing in illegal goods and services, such as drugs or prostitution; they want to avoid paying taxes on the income they earn; or they want to avoid government regulations. This concealed buying and selling is referred to as the **underground economy**. Estimates of the size of the underground economy in the United States vary widely, but it is probably at most 10 percent of measured GDP, or about $1.5 trillion. The underground economy in some low-income countries, such as Zimbabwe or Peru, may be more than half of measured GDP.

Is not counting household production or production in the underground economy a serious shortcoming of GDP? Most economists would answer "no" because the most important use of GDP is to measure changes in how the economy is performing over short periods of time, such as from one year to the next. For this purpose, omitting household production and production in the underground economy doesn't matter because there is not likely to be much change in household production or the size of the underground economy from one year to the next.

We also use GDP to measure how production of goods and services grows over fairly long periods of a decade or more. For this purpose, omitting household production and production in the underground economy may be more important. For example, beginning in the 1970s, the number of women working outside the home increased dramatically. Some of the goods and services—such as childcare and restaurant meals—produced in the following years were not true additions to total production; rather, they were replacing what had been household production.

Underground economy Buying and selling of goods and services that is concealed from the government to avoid taxes or regulations or because the goods and services are illegal.

| Making the Connection | Why Do Many Developing Countries Have Such Large Underground Economies? |

Recent estimates put the size of the underground economy at 8 percent of measured GDP in the United States and 13 percent in Western Europe. The underground economy is much larger in many developing countries—perhaps 50 percent or more of measured GDP. In developing countries, the underground economy is often referred to as the *informal sector*, as opposed to the *formal sector*, in which output of goods and services is measured. Although it might not seem to matter whether production of goods and services is measured and included in GDP or unmeasured, a large informal sector can be a sign of government policies that are retarding economic growth.

Because firms in the informal sector are acting illegally, they tend to be smaller and have less capital than firms acting legally. The entrepreneurs who start firms in the informal sector may be afraid the government could someday close or confiscate their firms. Therefore, the entrepreneurs limit their investments in these firms. As a consequence, workers in these firms have less machinery and equipment to work with and so can produce fewer goods and services. Entrepreneurs in the informal sector also have to pay the costs of avoiding government authorities. For example, construction firms operating in the informal sector in Brazil have to employ lookouts who can warn workers to hide when government inspectors come around. In many countries, firms in the informal sector have to pay substantial bribes to government officials to remain in business. The informal sector is large

In some developing countries, more than half the workers may be in the underground economy.

in some developing economies because taxes are high and government regulations are extensive. For example, firms in Brazil pay 85 percent of all taxes collected, as compared with 41 percent in the United States. Not surprisingly, about half of all Brazilian workers are employed in the informal sector. In Zimbabwe and Peru, the fraction of workers in the informal sector may be as high as 60 or 70 percent. One estimate put the size of the informal sector in India at nearly 50 percent.

Many economists believe taxes in developing countries are so high because these countries are attempting to pay for government sectors that are as large relative to their economies as the government sectors of industrial economies. Including transfer payments, government spending in Brazil, for example, is 41 percent of measured GDP, compared to 36 percent in the United States. In the early twentieth century, when the United States was much poorer than it is today, government spending was only about 8 percent of GDP, so the tax burden on U.S. firms was much lower. In countries such as Brazil, bringing firms into the formal sector from the informal sector may require reductions in government spending and taxes. In most developing countries, however, voters are reluctant to see government services reduced.

Based on "Dynamic but Dirty," *Economist*, December 2, 2010; "Notes from the Underground," *Economist*, April 2, 2009; Mary Anastasia O'Grady, "Why Brazil's Underground Economy Grows and Grows," *Wall Street Journal*, September 10, 2004; and the International Monetary Fund.

MyEconLab **Your Turn:** Test your understanding by doing related problem 2.8 on page 264 at the end of this chapter.

Shortcomings of GDP as a Measure of Well-Being

The main purpose of GDP is to measure a country's total production. GDP is also frequently used, though, as a measure of well-being. For example, newspaper and magazine articles often include tables that show the levels of GDP per person for different countries, which is usually referred to as *GDP per capita*. GDP per capita is calculated by dividing the value of GDP for a country by the country's population. These articles imply that people in the countries with higher levels of GDP per capita are better off. Although increases in GDP often do lead to increases in the well-being of the population, it is important to be aware that GDP is not a perfect measure of well-being for several reasons.

The Value of Leisure Is Not Included in GDP
If an economic consultant decides to retire, GDP will decline even though the consultant may value increased leisure more than the income he or she was earning running a consulting firm. The consultant's well-being has increased, but GDP has decreased. In 1890, the typical American worked 60 hours per week. Today, the typical American works fewer than 40 hours per week. If Americans still worked 60-hour weeks, GDP would be much higher than it is, but the well-being of the typical person would be lower because less time would be available for leisure activities.

GDP Is Not Adjusted for Pollution or Other Negative Effects of Production
When a dry cleaner cleans and presses clothes, the value of this service is included in GDP. If the chemicals the dry cleaner uses pollute the air or water, GDP is not adjusted to compensate for the costs of the pollution. Similarly, the value of cigarettes produced is included in GDP, with no adjustment made for the costs of the lung cancer that some smokers develop.

We should note, though, that increasing GDP often leads countries to devote more resources to pollution reduction. For example, in the United States between 1970 and 2011, as GDP was steadily increasing, emissions of the six main air pollutants declined by more than 50 percent. Developing countries often have higher levels of pollution than high-income countries because the lower GDPs of the developing countries make them more reluctant to spend resources on pollution reduction. Levels of pollution in China are much higher than in the United States, Japan, or the countries of Western

Europe. According to the World Health Organization, 7 of the 10 most polluted cities in the world are in China, but as Chinese GDP continues to rise, the country is likely to devote more resources to reducing pollution.

GDP Is Not Adjusted for Changes in Crime and Other Social Problems

An increase in crime reduces well-being but may actually increase GDP if it leads to greater spending on police, security guards, and alarm systems. GDP is also not adjusted for changes in divorce rates, drug addiction, or other factors that may affect people's well-being.

GDP Measures the Size of the Pie but Not How the Pie Is Divided Up When a country's GDP increases, the country has more goods and services, but those goods and services may be very unequally distributed. Therefore, GDP may not provide good information about the goods and services consumed by the typical person.

To summarize, we can say that a person's well-being depends on many factors that are not considered in calculating GDP. Because GDP is designed to measure total production, it should not be surprising that it does an imperfect job of measuring well-being.

Making the Connection | **Did World War II Bring Prosperity?**

The Great Depression of the 1930s was the worst economic downturn in U.S. history. GDP declined by more than 25 percent between 1929 and 1933 and did not reach its 1929 level again until 1938. The unemployment rate remained at very high levels of 10 percent or more through 1940. Then, in 1941, the United States entered World War II. The graph below shows that GDP rose dramatically during the war years of 1941 to 1945. (The graph shows values for real GDP, which, as we will see in the next section, corrects measures of GDP for changes in the price level.) The unemployment rate also fell to very low levels—below 2 percent.

Traditionally, historians have argued that World War II brought prosperity back to the U.S. economy. But did it? Economist Robert Higgs argued that if we look at the well-being of the typical person, the World War II years were anything but prosperous. Higgs pointed out that increased production of tanks, ships, planes, and munitions accounted for most of the increase in GDP during those years. Between 1943 and 1945, more than 40 percent of the labor force was either in the military or producing war goods. As a result, between 1939 and 1944, production of clothing, radios, books, and other consumption goods per person increased only about 2 percent, leaving the quantity of consumption goods available to the typical person in 1944 still below what it had been in 1929. With the end of the war, true prosperity did return to the U.S. economy, and by 1946, production of consumption goods per person had risen by more than 25 percent from what it had been in 1929.

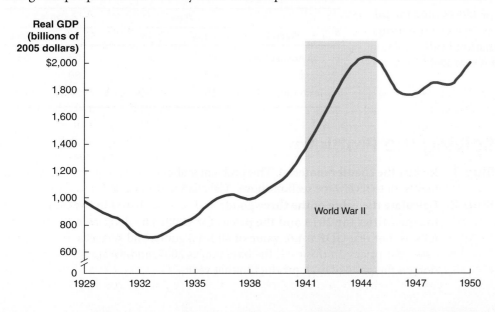

World War II was a period of extraordinary sacrifice and achievement by the "greatest generation." But statistics on GDP may give a misleading indication of whether it was also a period of prosperity.

Based on Robert Higgs, "Wartime Prosperity? A Reassessment of the U.S. Economy in the 1940s," *Journal of Economic History*, Vol. 52, No. 1, March 1992; Robert Higgs, "From Central Planning to the Market: The American Transition, 1945–1947," *Journal of Economic History*, Vol. 59, No. 3, September 1999; and data from the U.S. Bureau of Economic Analysis.

MyEconLab **Your Turn:** Test your understanding by doing related problem 2.10 on page 264 at the end of this chapter.

8.3 LEARNING OBJECTIVE

Discuss the difference between real GDP and nominal GDP.

Real GDP versus Nominal GDP

Because GDP is measured in value terms, we have to be careful about interpreting changes over time. To see why, consider interpreting an increase in the total value of pickup truck production from $40 billion in 2012 to $44 billion in 2013. Can we be sure that because $44 billion is 10 percent greater than $40 billion, the number of trucks produced in 2013 was 10 percent greater than the number produced in 2012? We can draw this conclusion only if the average price of trucks did not change between 2012 and 2013. In fact, when GDP increases from one year to the next, the increase is due partly to increases in production of goods and services and partly to increases in prices. Because we are mainly interested in GDP as a measure of production, we need a way of separating the price changes from the quantity changes.

Calculating Real GDP

Nominal GDP The value of final goods and services evaluated at current-year prices.

Real GDP The value of final goods and services evaluated at base-year prices.

The BEA separates price changes from quantity changes by calculating a measure of production called *real GDP*. **Nominal GDP** is calculated by summing the current values of final goods and services. **Real GDP** is calculated by designating a particular year as the *base year* and then using the prices of goods and services in the base year to calculate the value of goods and services in all other years. For instance, if the base year is 2005, real GDP for 2013 would be calculated by using prices of goods and services from 2005. By keeping prices constant, we know that changes in real GDP represent changes in the quantity of goods and services produced in the economy.

Solved Problem 8.3

Calculating Real GDP

Suppose that a very simple economy produces only the following three final goods and services: eye examinations, pizzas, and textbooks. Use the information in the table on the right to compute real GDP for the year 2013. Assume that the base year is 2005.

Product	2005		2013	
	Quantity	Price	Quantity	Price
Eye examinations	80	$40	100	$50
Pizzas	90	11	80	10
Textbooks	15	90	20	100

Solving the Problem

Step 1: **Review the chapter material.** This problem is about calculating real GDP, so you may want to review the section above, "Calculating Real GDP."

Step 2: **Calculate the value of the three goods and services listed in the table, using the quantities for 2013 and the prices for 2005.** The definition on this page tells us that real GDP is the value of all final goods and services, evaluated at base-year prices. In this case, the base year is 2005, and we are given information on the price of each product in that year:

Product	2013 Quantity	2005 Price	Value
Eye examinations	100	$40	$4,000
Pizzas	80	11	880
Textbooks	20	90	1,800

Step 3: **Add up the values for the three products to find real GDP.** Real GDP for 2013 equals the sum of:

Quantity of eye examination in 2013 $\times$ Price of eye examinations in 2005 $= \$4,000$
Quantity of pizza produced in 2013 $\times$ Price of pizzas in 2005 $= \$880$
Quantity of textbooks produced in 2013 $\times$ Price of textbooks in 2005 $= \$1,800$
or, $6,680

Extra Credit: Notice that the quantities of each good produced in 2005 were irrelevant for calculating real GDP in 2013. Notice also that the value of $6,680 for real GDP in 2013 is lower than the value of $7,800 for nominal GDP in 2013 that we calculated in Solved Problem 8.1 on page 244.

Your Turn: For more practice, do related problem 3.4 on pages 264–265 at the end of this chapter. MyEconLab

---

One drawback to calculating real GDP using base-year prices is that, over time, prices may change relative to each other. For example, the price of cell phones may fall relative to the price of milk. Because this change is not reflected in the fixed prices from the base year, the estimate of real GDP is somewhat distorted. The further away the current year is from the base year, the worse the problem becomes. To make the calculation of real GDP more accurate, in 1996, the BEA switched to using *chain-weighted prices*, and it now publishes statistics on real GDP in "chained (2005) dollars."

The details of calculating real GDP using chain-weighted prices are more complicated than we need to discuss here, but the basic idea is straightforward: Starting with the base year, the BEA takes an average of prices in that year and prices in the following year. It then uses this average to calculate real GDP in the year following the base year (currently the year 2005). For the next year—in other words, the year that is two years after the base year—the BEA calculates real GDP by taking an average of prices in that year and the previous year. In this way, prices in each year are "chained" to prices from the previous year, and the distortion from changes in relative prices is minimized.

Holding prices constant means that the *purchasing power* of a dollar remains the same from one year to the next. Ordinarily, the purchasing power of the dollar falls every year, as price increases reduce the amount of goods and services that a dollar can buy.

Comparing Real GDP and Nominal GDP

Real GDP holds prices constant, which makes it a better measure than nominal GDP of changes in the production of goods and services from one year to the next. In fact, growth in the economy is almost always measured as growth in real GDP. If a headline in the *Wall Street Journal* states "U.S. Economy Grew 2.3% Last Year," the article will report that real GDP increased by 2.3 percent during the previous year.

We describe real GDP as being measured in "base-year dollars." For example, with a base year of 2005, nominal GDP in 2010 was $14,527 billion, and real GDP in 2010 was $13,088 billion in 2005 dollars. Because, on average, prices rise from one year to the next, real GDP is greater than nominal GDP in years before the base year and less than nominal GDP for years after the base year. In the base year, real GDP and nominal GDP are the same because both are calculated for the base year using the same prices and quantities. Figure 8.3 shows movements in nominal GDP and real GDP between 1990 and 2010. In the years before 2005, prices were, on average, lower than in 2005, so nominal GDP was lower than real GDP. In 2005, nominal and real GDP were equal. Since 2005, prices have been, on average, higher than in 2005, so nominal GDP is higher than real GDP.

Figure 8.3

Nominal GDP and Real GDP, 1990–2010

Currently, the base year for calculating GDP is 2005. In the years before 2005, prices were, on average, lower than in 2005, so nominal GDP was lower than real GDP. In 2005, nominal and real GDP were equal. Since 2005, prices have been, on average, higher than in 2005, so nominal GDP is higher than real GDP.

Data from U.S. Bureau of Economic Analysis.

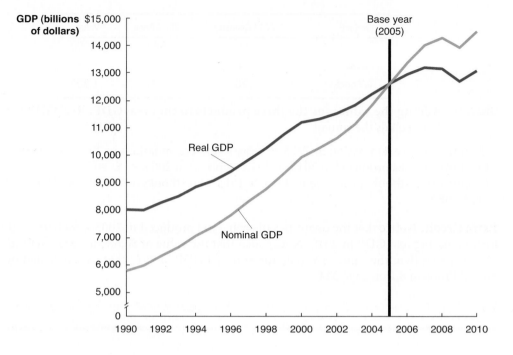

Price level A measure of the average prices of goods and services in the economy.

GDP deflator A measure of the price level, calculated by dividing nominal GDP by real GDP and multiplying by 100.

The GDP Deflator

Economists and policymakers are interested not just in the level of total production, as measured by real GDP, but also in the *price level*. The **price level** measures the average prices of goods and services in the economy. One of the goals of economic policy is a stable price level. We can use values for nominal GDP and real GDP to compute a measure of the price level called the *GDP deflator*. We can calculate the **GDP deflator** by using this formula:

$$\text{GDP deflator} = \frac{\text{Nominal GDP}}{\text{Real GDP}} \times 100.$$

To see why the GDP deflator is a measure of the price level, think about what would happen if prices of goods and services rose while production remained the same. In that case, nominal GDP would increase, but real GDP would remain constant, so the GDP deflator would increase. In reality, both prices and production usually increase each year, but the more prices increase relative to the increase in production, the more nominal GDP increases relative to real GDP, and the higher the value for the GDP deflator. Increases in the GDP deflator allow economists and policymakers to track increases in the price level over time.

Remember that in the base year (currently 2005), nominal GDP is equal to real GDP, so the value of the GDP price deflator will always be 100 in the base year. The following table gives the values for nominal and real GDP for 2009 and 2010:

	2009	2010
Nominal GDP	$13,939 billion	$14,527 billion
Real GDP	$12,703 billion	$13,088 billion

We can use the information from this table to calculate values for the GDP price deflator for 2009 and 2010:

Formula	Applied to 2009	Applied to 2010
GDP deflator $= \dfrac{\text{Nominal GDP}}{\text{Real GDP}} \times 100$	$\left(\dfrac{\$13,939\,\text{billion}}{\$12,703\,\text{billion}}\right) \times 100 = 110$	$\left(\dfrac{\$14,527\,\text{billion}}{\$13,088\,\text{billion}}\right) \times 100 = 111$

From these values for the deflator, we can calculate that the price level increased by 0.9 percent between 2009 and 2010:

$$\left(\frac{111 - 110}{110} \right) \times 100 = 0.9\%.$$

In Chapter 9, we will see that economists and policymakers also rely on another measure of the price level, known as the consumer price index. In addition, we will discuss the strengths and weaknesses of different measures of the price level.

Other Measures of Total Production and Total Income

8.4 LEARNING OBJECTIVE

Understand other measures of total production and total income.

National income accounting refers to the methods the BEA uses to track total production and total income in the economy. The statistical tables containing this information are called the *National Income and Product Accounts (NIPA)* tables. Every quarter, the BEA releases NIPA tables containing data on several measures of total production and total income. We have already discussed the most important measure of total production and total income: gross domestic product (GDP). In addition to computing GDP, the BEA computes the following four measures of production and income: gross national product, national income, personal income, and disposable personal income.

Gross National Product (GNP)

We have seen that GDP is the value of final goods and services produced within the United States. *Gross national product (GNP)* is the value of final goods and services produced by residents of the United States, even if the production takes place *outside* the United States. U.S. firms have facilities in foreign countries, and foreign firms have facilities in the United States. Ford, for example, has assembly plants in the United Kingdom, and Toyota has assembly plants in the United States. GNP includes foreign production by U.S. firms but excludes U.S. production by foreign firms. For the United States, GNP is almost the same as GDP. For example, in 2010, GDP was $14,527 billion, and GNP was $14,716 billion, or only about 1 percent more than GDP.

For many years, GNP was the main measure of total production compiled by the federal government and used by economists and policymakers in the United States. However, in many countries other than the United States, a significant percentage of domestic production takes place in foreign-owned facilities. For those countries, GDP is much larger than GNP and is a more accurate measure of the level of production within the country's borders. As a result, many countries and international agencies had long preferred using GDP to using GNP. In 1991, the United States joined those countries in using GDP as its main measure of total production.

National Income

In producing goods and services, some machinery, equipment, and buildings wear out and have to be replaced. The value of this worn-out machinery, equipment, and buildings is *depreciation*. In the NIPA tables, depreciation is referred to as the *consumption of fixed capital*. If we subtract this value from GDP, we are left with *national income*.

Previously in this chapter, we stressed that the value of total production is equal to the value of total income. This point is not strictly true if by "value of total production" we mean GDP and by "value of total income" we mean national income because national income will always be smaller than GDP by an amount equal to depreciation. In practice, though, the difference between the value of GDP and value of national income does not matter for most macroeconomic issues.

Personal Income

Personal income is income received by households. To calculate personal income, we subtract the earnings that corporations retain rather than pay to shareholders in the form of dividends. We also add in the payments received by households from the government in the form of *transfer payments* or interest on government bonds.

Disposable Personal Income

Disposable personal income is equal to personal income minus personal tax payments, such as the federal personal income tax. It is the best measure of the income households actually have available to spend.

Figure 8.4 shows the values of these measures of total production and total income for the year 2010 in a table and a graph.

The Division of Income

Figure 8.1 on page 245 illustrates the important fact that we can measure GDP in terms of total expenditure or as the total income received by households. GDP calculated as the sum of income payments to households is sometimes referred to as *gross domestic income*. Figure 8.5 shows the division of total income among wages, interest, rent, profit, and certain non-income items. The non-income items are included in gross domestic income because sales taxes, depreciation, and a few other small items are included in the value of goods and services produced but are not directly received by households as income. *Wages* include all compensation received by employees, including fringe benefits such as health insurance. *Interest* is net interest received by households, or the difference between the interest received on savings accounts, government bonds, and other investments and the interest paid on car loans, home mortgages, and other debts. *Rent* is rent received by households. *Profits* include the profits of sole proprietorships, which are usually small businesses, and the profits of corporations. Figure 8.5 shows that the largest component of gross domestic income is wages, which are about three times as large as profits.

Measure	Billions of dollars
GDP	$14,527
GNP	14,716
National income	12,840
Personal income	12,374
Disposable personal income	11,180

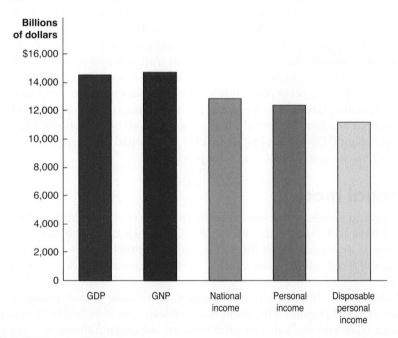

Figure 8.4 Measures of Total Production and Total Income, 2010

The most important measure of total production and total income is gross domestic product (GDP). As we will see in later chapters, for some purposes, the other measures of total production and total income shown in the figure turn out to be more useful than GDP.
Data from U.S. Bureau of Economic Analysis.

	Billions of dollars	
Wages		$7,981
Interest		748
Rent		350
Profit		2,455
Profits of sole proprietors	1,036	
Profits of corporations	1,418	
Taxes, depreciation, and statistical discrepancy		2,993

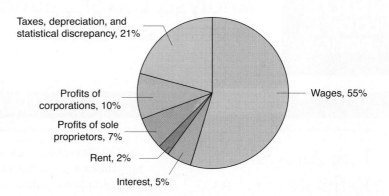

Figure 8.5 The Division of Income, 2010

We can measure GDP in terms of total expenditure or as the total income received by households. The largest component of income received by households is wages, which are more than three times as large as the profits received by sole proprietors and the profits received by corporations combined.

Data from U.S. Bureau of Economic Analysis.

Continued from page 241

Economics in Your Life

What's the Best Country for You to Work In?

At the beginning of the chapter, we posed two questions: What effect should Canada's and China's two very different growth rates of GDP have on your decision to work and live in one country or the other? And if China's much higher growth rate does not necessarily lead you to decide to work and live in China, why not? This chapter has shown that although it is generally true that the more goods and services people have, the better off they are, GDP provides only a rough measure of well-being. GDP does not include the value of leisure; nor is it adjusted for pollution and other negative effects of production or crime and other social problems. So, in deciding where to live and work, you would need to balance China's much higher growth rate of GDP against these other considerations. You would also need to take into account that although China's *growth rate* is higher than Canada's, Canada's current *level* of real GDP is higher than China's.

Conclusion

In this chapter, we have begun the study of macroeconomics by examining an important concept: how a nation's total production and income can be measured. Understanding GDP is important for understanding the business cycle and the process of long-run economic growth. In the next chapter, we discuss the issues involved in measuring two other key economic variables: the unemployment rate and the inflation rate.

Read *An Inside Look at Policy* on the next page for a discussion of how declining consumer confidence led analysts to lower their estimates of new automobile sales for 2011 and 2012.

BLOOMBERG

U.S. Auto Sales Estimates Cut as Confidence Slows Rebound

Analysts are reducing estimates for U.S. automobile sales for 2011 and 2012, citing weak consumer confidence that has slowed the pace of recovery since May.

J.D. Power & Associates lowered its estimate for U.S. auto sales in 2011 by 300,000 light vehicles to 12.6 million, the Westlake Village, California-based researcher said today in a statement. J.D. Power reduced its estimate for next year by 600,000 cars and light trucks to 14.1 million.

The reduction by J.D. Power follows analysts at IHS Automotive in cutting expectations below the sales forecasts given by General Motors Co. (GM) and Ford Motor Co. (F), the largest U.S. automakers. JPMorgan Chase & Co., Goldman Sachs Group Inc. and RBC Capital Markets LLC also shaved estimates this month.

ⓐ "The thought of a second-half recovery is just not in the cards," Jeff Schuster, J.D. Power's executive director of global forecasting, said today in a phone interview. "It really comes down to consumer confidence and consumers just don't have any right now. There just really isn't a strong reason to go make that big-ticket purchase."

Consumer confidence in the U.S. economic outlook slumped in August to the lowest level since the recession, raising the risk that spending will dry up. The Bloomberg Consumer Comfort Index's monthly expectations gauge dropped to minus 34, the weakest since March 2009, from minus 22 in July.

Applications for unemployment benefits climbed last week to the highest level in a month, Labor Department figures showed today in Washington.

Goldman Cuts

Goldman Sachs today lowered its 2012 U.S. auto sales estimate by 1 million light vehicles to 13.5 million. The New York–based investment bank sees 12.8 million deliveries this year. RBC Capital earlier this week lowered its estimates for 2011 by 200,000 units to 12.5 million and by 700,000 to 13.3 million for next year.

"Fragile U.S. consumer sentiment and recently tempered economic expectations" led to the reductions, Seth Weber, an RBC Capital analyst based in New York, said in an Aug. 16 research note. . . .

GM, Ford Estimates

ⓑ GM and Dearborn, Michigan–based Ford forecast at least 13 million new-vehicle sales in 2011, including medium- and heavy- duty trucks. The U.S. averaged annual light-vehicle deliveries of 16.8 million vehicles from 2000 to 2007, according to Autodata Corp., a Woodcliff Lake, New Jersey–based research company.

"There's a lot of turmoil in the business and turmoil means uncertainty, so we're a little unsure of these numbers," Chief Executive Officer Dan Akerson of Detroit-based GM, told analysts Aug. 9. . . .

No 'Snap Back'

ⓒ J.D. Power sees a 12.1 million seasonally adjusted annualized rate for August. Analysts and automakers had been predicting a "snap back" in demand once inventories recovered from the March earthquake and tsunami in Japan, which disrupted production and led to shortages of parts and finished vehicles.

"We're not seeing that snap back, and given all the variables out there it's a lower probability that we're going to see that happen this year," Schuster said today.

Sales ran at a seasonally adjusted annualized rate of 12.2 million through the first two weeks of August, Edmunds.com said in an e-mailed statement. The Santa Monica, California–based researcher still predicts 12.9 million deliveries this year and 13.9 million in 2012.

J.D. Power's estimate for full-year sales assumes that the industry will average a 12.8 million seasonally adjusted annualized rate in the last four months of the year, Schuster said. Lower gasoline prices and higher spending on sales incentives may help the sales pace accelerate to those levels late this year, he said.

If the pace of deliveries stays about flat, sales may finish the year at 12.4 million, according to J.D. Power's estimates.

"If August comes in at the level we're expecting, that gives us a really clear indication that we're running out" of time in 2011 "to get going again," Schuster said.

Key Points in the Article

Citing declining consumer confidence in the economy, J.D. Power & Associates reduced its estimates for car and light truck sales in the United States by 300,000 vehicles for 2011 and by 600,000 for 2012. Other companies also announcing lower estimated sales include Goldman Sachs, RBC Capital, IHS Automotive, and JPMorgan Chase. Automakers and analysts had initially predicted an increase in new vehicle demand once inventories of new automobiles and auto parts stabilized following the March 2011 earthquake and tsunami in Japan, but uncertain economic conditions kept demand below the initial sales estimates.

Analyzing the News

(a) Jeff Schuster of J.D. Power & Associates cited the lack of consumer confidence as a main reason for the decline in auto sales during the first half of 2011 and the lower estimates for the remainder of the year. In August, Bloomberg's consumer comfort index was the weakest it has been since March 2009, and consumer confidence in the economic outlook for the United States dropped to its lowest level since the recession. As you read in this chapter, automobiles are durable goods, and consumers are more likely to reduce purchases of durable goods when they are not confident about their jobs or their future

incomes. Automobiles have high prices, and as Schuster stated in the article, "There just really isn't a strong reason to go make that big-ticket purchase." Falling automobile sales reduce total consumption. Recall that consumption accounts for about 70 percent of GDP. The figure below shows that by June 2009, GDP had fallen for four consecutive quarters. Falling consumption contributed to the decline in GDP during that period. GDP began to rise again by September 2009, but the increases in GDP began to slow down in 2010, dropping to only 1 percent by June 2011. The significant slowdown in the growth of real GDP in 2011, as shown in the figure, reflects the lack of consumer confidence mentioned in the article and helps explain the lowered estimates for new car sales for the year.

(b) Following an increase in sales during 2010, both General Motors and Ford initially estimated that U.S. sales of new cars and trucks would increase to more than 13 million in 2011. Although the article does not mention any specific revised estimates from these companies, General Motors's CEO Dan Akerson was quoted on August 9 as saying, "There's a lot of turmoil in the business and turmoil means uncertainty, so we're a little unsure of these numbers." His statement seems to summarize the economic uncertainty discussed in the article.

(c) Initial estimates for new vehicle sales were lowered following the earthquake and tsunami that struck Japan in March

2011 and led to shortages of parts and new vehicles worldwide. Analysts and automakers had predicted that the market would "snap back" once these shortages had been eliminated, with demand for new vehicles increasing in the second half of the year. According to J.D. Power's Jeff Schuster, "We're not seeing that snap back, and given all the variables out there it's a lower probability that we're going to see that happen this year," again reflecting uncertainty and the lack of consumer confidence in the U.S. economy.

Thinking Critically about Policy

1. The auto industry is cyclical: Auto sales rise during economic expansions and fall during economic recessions. Would you expect the same to be true of the markets for used vehicles and for vehicle repairs?

2. Ford and General Motors estimated that new vehicle sales in the United States would top 13 million in 2011. This sales number included medium- and heavy-duty trucks, which are more often purchased by businesses than households. Which component of GDP is affected by purchases of new vehicles by businesses? Which component of GDP is affected by purchases of new vehicles by households?

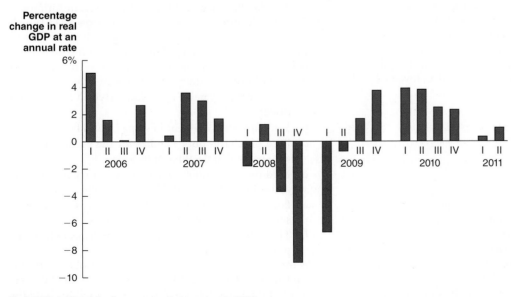

Real GDP declined for four consecutive quarters in 2009.

Chapter Summary and Problems

Key Terms

Business cycle, p. 242

Consumption, p. 246

Economic growth, p. 242

Expansion, p. 242

Final good or service, p. 243

GDP deflator, p. 256

Government purchases, p. 246

Gross domestic product (GDP), p. 243

Inflation rate, p. 242

Intermediate good or service, p. 243

Investment, p. 246

Macroeconomics, p. 242

Microeconomics, p. 242

Net exports, p. 247

Nominal GDP, p. 254

Price level, p. 256

Real GDP, p. 254

Recession, p. 242

Transfer payments, p. 246

Underground economy, p. 251

Value added, p. 250

 8.1 **Gross Domestic Product Measures Total Production,** pages 243–250
LEARNING OBJECTIVE: Explain how total production is measured.

Summary

Economics is divided into the subfields of **microeconomics**—which studies how households and firms make choices—and **macroeconomics**—which studies the economy as a whole. An important macroeconomic issue is the **business cycle**, which refers to alternating periods of economic expansion and economic recession. An **expansion** is a period during which production and employment are increasing. A **recession** is a period during which production and employment are decreasing. Another important macroeconomic topic is **economic growth**, which refers to the ability of the economy to produce increasing quantities of goods and services. Macroeconomics also studies the **inflation rate**, or the percentage increase in the price level from one year to the next. Economists measure total production by **gross domestic product (GDP)**, which is the value of all *final goods and services* produced in an economy during a period of time. A **final good or service** is purchased by a final user. An **intermediate good or service** is an input into another good or service and is not included in GDP. When we measure the value of total production in the economy by calculating GDP, we are simultaneously measuring the value of total income. GDP is divided into four major categories of expenditures: consumption, investment, government purchases, and net exports. Government **transfer payments** are not included in GDP because they are payments to individuals for which the government does not receive a good or service in return. We can also calculate GDP by adding up the **value added** of every firm involved in producing final goods and services.

MyEconLab Visit **www.myeconlab.com** to complete these exercises online and get instant feedback.

Review Questions

1.1 Why in microeconomics do we measure production in terms of quantity, but in macroeconomics we measure production in terms of market value?

1.2 If the U.S. Bureau of Economic Analysis added up the values of every good and service sold during the year, would the total be larger or smaller than GDP?

1.3 In the circular flow of income, why must the value of total production in an economy equal the value of total income?

1.4 Describe the four major components of expenditures in GDP and write the equation used to represent the relationship between GDP and the four expenditure components.

1.5 What is the difference between the value of a firm's final product and the value added by the firm to the final product?

Problems and Applications

1.6 A student remarks: "It doesn't make sense that intermediate goods are not counted in GDP. A computer chip is an intermediate good, and without it a PC won't work. So why don't we count the computer chip in GDP?" Provide an answer for the student's question.

1.7 Briefly explain whether each of the following transactions represents the purchase of a final good.
a. The purchase of wheat from a wheat farmer by a bakery
b. The purchase of an aircraft carrier by the federal government
c. The purchase of French wine by a U.S. consumer
d. The purchase of a new airliner by American Airlines

1.8 **[Related to the** Chapter Opener **on page 241]** Which component of GDP will be affected by each of the following transactions involving Ford Motor Company? If you believe that none of the components of GDP will be affected by the transactions, briefly explain why.
a. You purchase a new Ford Escape Hybrid from a Ford dealer.
b. You purchase a 2010 Ford Escape Hybrid from a friend.
c. Ford purchases door handles for the Escape from an auto parts manufacturer in Indiana.
d. Ford produces 1,000 Escapes in a factory in Missouri and ships them to a car dealer in Shanghai, China.
e. Ford purchases new machine tools to use in its Missouri Escape factory.
f. The state of Missouri builds a new highway to help improve access to the Ford Escape plant.

1.9 Is the value of a house built in 2000 and resold in 2013 included in the GDP of 2013? Briefly explain. Would the services of the real estate agent who helped sell (or buy) the house in 2013 be counted in GDP for 2013? Briefly explain.

1.10 [**Related to** Solved Problem 8.1 **on page 244**] Suppose that a simple economy produces only four goods: textbooks, hamburgers, shirts, and cotton. Assume that all the cotton is used in the production of shirts. Use the information in the following table to calculate nominal GDP for 2013:

Production and Price Statistics for 2013		
Product	Quantity	Price
Textbooks	100	$60.00
Hamburgers	100	2.00
Shirts	50	25.00
Cotton	80	0.60

1.11 [**Related to the** Don't Let This Happen to You **on page 247**] Briefly explain whether you agree with the following statement: "In years when people buy many shares of stock, investment will be high and, therefore, so will GDP."

1.12 [**Related to the** Making the Connection **on page 248**] An article on USAToday.com observed: "Consumer spending, once the driving force of the U.S. economy, is likely to remain stagnant for years as households struggle to cut debt and build up savings, economists say." Why does cutting debt and building up savings affect consumer spending? If consumer spending remains stagnant, what will be the likely effect on the economy?

Based on Karina Frayter, "Economists: Consumers Won't Save the Economy," USAToday.com, October 2, 2011.

1.13 For the total value of expenditures on final goods and services to equal the total value of income generated from producing those final goods and services, all the money that a business receives from the sale of its product must be paid out as income to the owners of the factors of production. How can a business make a profit if it pays out as income all the money it receives?

1.14 An artist buys scrap metal from a local steel mill as a raw material for her metal sculptures. Last year, she bought $5,000 worth of the scrap metal. During the year, she produced 10 metal sculptures that she sold for $800 each to a local art store. The local art store sold all of the sculptures to local art collectors, at an average price of $1,000 each. For the 10 metal sculptures, what was the total value added of the artist, and what was the total value added of the local art store?

8.2 Does GDP Measure What We Want It to Measure? pages 250–254

LEARNING OBJECTIVE: Discuss whether GDP is a good measure of well-being.

Summary

GDP does not include household production, which refers to goods and services people produce for themselves, nor does it include production in the **underground economy**, which consists of concealed buying and selling. The underground economy in some developing countries may be more than half of measured GDP. GDP is not a perfect measure of well-being because it does not include the value of leisure, it is not adjusted for pollution or other negative effects of production, and it is not adjusted for changes in crime and other social problems.

MyEconLab   Visit www.myeconlab.com to complete these exercises online and get instant feedback.

Review Questions

2.1 Why does the size of a country's GDP matter? How does it affect the quality of life of the country's people?

2.2 What is the underground economy? Why do some countries have larger underground economies than do other countries?

2.3 Why is GDP an imperfect measure of economic well-being? What types of production does GDP not measure? Even if GDP included these types of production, why would it still be an imperfect measure of economic well-being?

Problems and Applications

2.4 Which of the following are likely to increase measured GDP, and which are likely to reduce it?

a. The fraction of women working outside the home increases.

b. There is a sharp increase in the crime rate.

c. Higher tax rates cause some people to hide more of the income they earn.

2.5 Michael Burda of Humboldt University in Germany and Daniel Hamermesh of the University of Texas examined how workers in the United States who lost their jobs between 2003 and 2006 spent their time. They discovered that during the period when they were unemployed, the decline in the number of hours of paid work done by these workers was almost the same as the increase in the number of hours these workers devoted to household production. Do Burda and Hamermesh's findings allow us to draw any conclusions about whether total production in the economy—whether that production is included in GDP or not—fell when these workers became unemployed? Does your answer depend on whether the household production they carried out while unemployed involved activities, such as child care, that the workers had been paying other people to perform before the workers lost their jobs? Briefly explain.

Based on Michael Burda and Daniel S. Hamermesh, "Unemployment, Market Work, and Household Production," *Economic Letters*, Vol. 107, May 2010, pp. 131–133.

2.6 Does the fact that the typical American works less than 40 hours per week today and worked 60 hours per week in 1890 make the difference between the economic well-being of Americans today versus 1890 higher or lower than indicated by the difference in real GDP per capita today versus in 1890? Explain.

2.7 Roger Ransom and Richard Sutch, economic historians at the University of California, Riverside, have estimated that African-American farmers in the U.S. South after the Civil War worked about 30 percent fewer hours per year than they had as slaves during the years before the Civil War. If after the Civil War, African-American farmers had continued to work these additional hours, their production and income would have been higher and so would have been U.S. GDP. Would the farmers' well-being also have been higher as a result of working these additional hours? Does your answer affect how we should interpret changes in U.S. GDP from before the Civil War to after the Civil War? Briefly explain.

Based on Roger L. Ransom and Richard Sutch, *One Kind of Freedom: The Economic Consequences of Emancipation*, Second Edition, (New York: Cambridge University Press), 2001.

2.8 **[Related to the** Making the Connection **on page 251]** A report of the World Bank, an international organization devoted to increasing economic growth in developing countries, included the following statement: "Informal economic activities pose a particular measurement problem [in calculating GDP], especially in developing countries, where much economic activity may go unrecorded." What does the World Bank mean by "informal economic activities"? Why would these activities make it harder to measure GDP? Why might they make it harder to evaluate the standard of living in developing countries relative to the standard of living in the United States?

Based on The World Bank, *World Development Indicators*, (Washington, DC: The World Bank, 2003), p. 189.

2.9 Each year, the United Nations publishes the Human Development Report, which provides information on the standard of living in nearly every country in the world. The report includes data on real GDP per person and also contains a broader measure of the standard of living called the Human Development Index (HDI). The HDI combines data on gross national income (GNI) per person with data on life expectancy at birth, average years of schooling, and expected years of schooling. (GNI is a measure of the total income per person in a country.) The following table shows values for GNI per person and the HDIs for several countries. Prepare one list that ranks countries from highest GNI per person to lowest and another list that ranks countries from highest HDI to lowest. Briefly discuss possible reasons for any differences in the rankings of countries in your two lists. (All values in the table are for the year 2010.)

Country	Real GNI per Person	HDI
Australia	$38,692	0.937
China	7,258	0.663
Greece	27,580	0.855
Iran	11,764	0.702
Norway	58,810	0.938
Singapore	48,893	0.846
South Korea	29,518	0.877
United Arab Emirates	58,006	0.815
United States	47,094	0.902

Data from United Nations Development Programme, "The Human Development Index," (http://hdr.undp.org/en/statistics/hdi/).

2.10 **[Related to the** Making the Connection **on page 253]** Think about the increases since 2001 in spending for the Department of Homeland Security and the wars in Afghanistan and Iraq. These increases represent government expenditures that have increased GDP. Briefly explain whether you think that these increases in GDP have made the typical person better off.

8.3 **Real GDP versus Nominal GDP, pages 254–257**

LEARNING OBJECTIVE: Discuss the difference between real GDP and nominal GDP.

Summary

Nominal GDP is the value of final goods and services evaluated at current-year prices. **Real GDP** is the value of final goods and services evaluated at *base-year* prices. By keeping prices constant, we know that changes in real GDP represent changes in the quantity of goods and services produced in the economy. When the **price level**, the average prices of goods and services in the economy, is increasing, real GDP is greater than nominal GDP in years before the base year and less than nominal GDP for years after the base year. The **GDP deflator** is a measure of the price level and is calculated by dividing nominal GDP by real GDP and multiplying by 100.

 MyEconLab   Visit **www.myeconlab.com** to complete these exercises online and get instant feedback.

Review Questions

3.1 Why does inflation make nominal GDP a poor measure of the increase in total production from one year to the next?

How does the U.S. Bureau of Economic Analysis deal with the problem inflation causes with nominal GDP?

3.2 What is the GDP deflator, and how is it calculated?

3.3 Assuming that inflation has occurred over time, what is the relationship between nominal GDP and real GDP in each of the following situations?

a. In the years after the base year

b. In the base year

c. In the years before the base year

Problems and Applications

3.4 **[Related to** Solved Problem 8.3 **on page 254]** Suppose the information in the table on the next page is for a simple economy that produces only four goods and services: textbooks, hamburgers, shirts, and cotton. Assume that all the cotton is used in the production of shirts.

Product	2005 Quantity	2005 Price	2012 Quantity	2012 Price	2013 Quantity	2013 Price
Textbooks	90	$50.00	100	$60.00	100	$65.00
Hamburgers	75	2.00	100	2.00	120	2.25
Shirts	50	30.00	50	25.00	65	25.00
Cotton	100	0.80	800	0.60	120	0.70

    a. Use the information in the table to calculate real GDP for 2012 and 2013, assuming that the base year is 2005.

    b. What is the growth rate of real GDP during 2013?

3.5 Briefly explain whether you agree or disagree with the following statements.

    a. "If nominal GDP is less than real GDP, then the price level must have fallen during the year."

    b. "Whenever real GDP declines, nominal GDP must also decline."

    c. "If a recession is so severe that the price level declines, then we know that both real GDP and nominal GDP must decline."

    d. "Nominal GDP declined between 2008 and 2009, therefore the GDP deflator must also have declined."

3.6 The movie *Avatar* overtook *Titanic* as the highest-grossing movie of all time. An article on Forbes.com notes that "the average ticket price in 2008 (*Avatar* was released in 2009) was $7.18, up 56% from prices in 1997 when *Titanic* was in theaters." The article states that "A look at domestic grosses (box-office receipts) adjusted for inflation shows a more realistic view of *Avatar*'s performance."

    a. Why would adjusting for inflation show a more realistic view of *Avatar*'s performance at the box office?

    b. Which would be a more accurate measure of how well a movie has performed at the box office: The dollar value of tickets sold or the number of tickets sold? Why don't newspapers report the number of tickets sold rather than the dollar value of tickets sold? Would comparing the total number of tickets sold by all movies in 1939 with the total number of tickets sold by all movies in 2011 be a good way to measure how the relative importance of movies in the economy has changed over time? Briefly explain.

Based on Dorthy Pomerantz, "Is Avatar Really King of the Box Office?" Forbes.com, January 27, 2010.

3.7 Use the data in the following table to calculate the GDP deflator for each year (values are in billions of dollars):

Year	Nominal GDP	Real GDP
2006	$13,377	$12,959
2007	14,029	13,206
2008	14,292	13,162
2009	13,939	12,703
2010	14,527	13,088

Which year from 2007 to 2010 saw the largest percentage increase in the price level, as measured by changes in the GDP deflator? Briefly explain.

8.4   Other Measures of Total Production and Total Income, pages 257–259

LEARNING OBJECTIVE: Understand other measures of total production and total income.

Summary

The most important measure of total production and total income is gross domestic product (GDP). As we will see in later chapters, for some purposes, the other measures of total production and total income shown in Figure 8.4 are actually more useful than GDP. These measures are gross national product (GNP), national income, personal income, and disposable personal income.

 MyEconLab   Visit **www.myeconlab.com** to complete these exercises online and get instant feedback.

Review Questions

4.1 What is the difference between GDP and GNP? Briefly explain whether the difference is important for the United States.

4.2 What are the differences between national income, personal income, and disposable personal income?

4.3 What is gross domestic income? Which component of gross domestic income is the largest?

Problems and Applications

4.4 Suppose a country has many of its citizens temporarily working in other countries, and many of its firms have facilities in other countries. Furthermore, relatively few citizens of foreign countries are working in this country, and relatively few foreign firms have facilities in this country. In these circumstances, which would you expect to be larger for this country, GDP or GNP? Briefly explain.

4.5 Suppose the amount the federal government collects in personal income taxes increases, while the level of GDP remains the same. What will happen to the values of national income, personal income, and disposable personal income?

4.6 If you were attempting to forecast the level of consumption spending by households, which measure of total production or total income might be most helpful to you in making your forecast? Briefly explain.

4.7 Briefly discuss the accuracy of the following statement: "Corporate profits are much too high: Most corporations make profits equal to 50 percent of the price of the products they sell."

Chapter Outline and Learning Objectives

Bank of America Announces Plans to Lay Off 30,000 Employees

When we study macroeconomics, we are looking at the big picture: total production, total employment, and the price level. Of course, the big picture is made up of millions of consumers, workers, and firms. Few industries have had as many problems in recent years as financial services, which includes businesses such as banks and brokerages. In September 2011, Bank of America, the second largest bank in the United States, announced that it would be laying off 30,000 of its 288,000 employees. To some extent, the layoffs reflected the problems banks had been having since the financial crisis that began in 2008 and the particular problems that Bank of America had experienced.

But the layoffs also were an indication of how slowly the U.S. economy was recovering from the economic recession of 2007–2009. Although the recession had ended in June 2009, unemployment remained high more than two years later. Economists at the White House and the Federal Reserve were forecasting that unemployment would not return to more normal levels for at least another two years. Some economists were even more pessimistic and had begun speaking of the "new normal," in which unemployment might be stuck at high levels for many years.

In this chapter, we will focus on measuring changes in unemployment as well as changes in the price level, or inflation. Because both unemployment and inflation are major macroeconomic problems, it is important to understand how they are measured. In later chapters, we will analyze why unemployment remained so high in the years following the end of the 2007–2009 recession. Read **AN INSIDE LOOK** on **page 294** for a discussion of how the U.S. Postal Service considered layoffs, office closings, and termination of Saturday deliveries to deal with declining revenues and mounting debts.

Based on Dan Fitzpatrick, "BofA Readies the Knife," *Wall Street Journal*, September 13, 2011; and Frank Bruni, "The Fall This Summer," *New York Times*, August 27, 2011.

Economics in Your Life

Should You Change Your Career Plans if You Graduate during a Recession?

Suppose that you are a sophomore majoring in either economics or finance. You plan to find a job in the banking industry after graduation. The economy is now in a deep recession, and the unemployment rate is the highest in your lifetime, at over 9 percent. Sizable layoffs have occurred in the banking industry. Should you change your major? Should you still consider a job in the banking industry? As you read this chapter, see if you can answer these questions. You can check your answers against those we provide on **page 293** at the end of this chapter.

Unemployment and inflation are the macroeconomic problems that are most often discussed in the media and during political campaigns. For many people, the state of the economy can be summarized in just two measures: the unemployment rate and the inflation rate. In the 1960s, Arthur Okun, who was chairman of the Council of Economic Advisers during President Lyndon Johnson's administration, coined the term *misery index*, which adds together the inflation rate and the unemployment rate to give a rough measure of the state of the economy. As we will see in later chapters, although unemployment and inflation are important problems in the short run, the long-run success of an economy is best judged by its ability to generate high levels of real GDP per person. We devote this chapter to discussing how the government measures the unemployment and inflation rates. In particular, we will look closely at the statistics on unemployment and inflation that the federal government issues each month.

9.1 LEARNING OBJECTIVE

Define the unemployment rate, the labor force participation rate, and the employment–population ratio and understand how they are computed.

Measuring the Unemployment Rate, the Labor Force Participation Rate, and the Employment–Population Ratio

At 8:30 A.M. on a Friday early in each month, the U.S. Department of Labor reports its estimate of the previous month's unemployment rate. If the unemployment rate is higher or lower than expected, investors are likely to change their views on the health of the economy. The result is seen an hour later, when trading begins on the New York Stock Exchange. Good news about unemployment usually causes stock prices to rise, and bad news causes stock prices to fall. The unemployment rate can also have important political implications. In most presidential elections, the incumbent president is reelected if unemployment is falling early in the election year but is defeated if unemployment is rising. This relationship held true in 2004, when the unemployment rate was lower during the first six months of 2004 than it had been during the last six months of 2003, and incumbent George W. Bush was reelected.

The unemployment rate is a key macroeconomic statistic. But how does the Department of Labor prepare its estimates of the unemployment rate, and how accurate are these estimates? We will explore the answers to these questions in this section.

The Household Survey

Each month, the U.S. Bureau of the Census conducts the *Current Population Survey* (often referred to as the *household survey*) to collect data needed to compute the unemployment rate. The bureau interviews adults in a sample of 60,000 households, chosen to represent the U.S. population, about the employment status of everyone in the household 16 years of age and older. The Department of Labor's Bureau of Labor Statistics (BLS) uses these data to calculate the monthly unemployment rate. People are considered *employed* if they worked during the week before the survey or if they were temporarily away from their jobs because they were ill, on vacation, on strike, or for other reasons. People are considered *unemployed* if they did not work in the previous week but were available for work and had actively looked for work at some time during the previous four weeks. The **labor force** is the sum of the *employed* and the *unemployed*. The **unemployment rate** is the percentage of the labor force that is unemployed.

The BLS classifies people who do not have a job and who are not actively looking for a job as *not in the labor force*. People not in the labor force include retirees, homemakers, full-time students, and people on active military service, in prison, or in mental hospitals. Also not in the labor force are people who are available for work and who have actively looked for a job at some point during the previous 12 months but who have not looked during the previous four weeks. Some people have not actively looked for work during the previous four weeks for reasons such as transportation difficulties or

Labor force The sum of employed and unemployed workers in the economy.

Unemployment rate The percentage of the labor force that is unemployed.

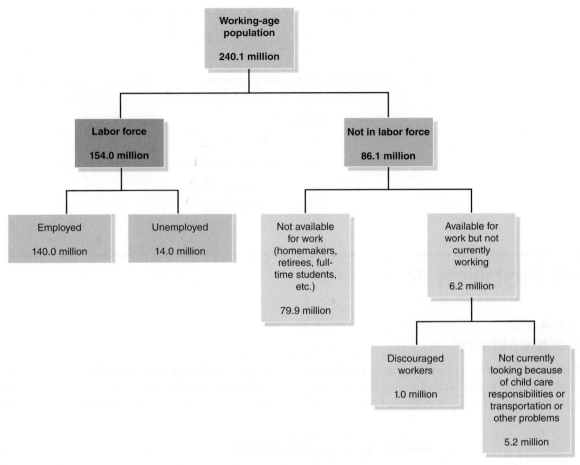

Figure 9.1 **The Employment Status of the Civilian Working-Age Population, September 2011**

In September 2011, the working-age population of the United States was 240.1 million. The working-age population is divided into those in the labor force (154.0 million) and those not in the labor force (86.1 million). The labor force is divided into the employed (140.0 million) and the unemployed (14.0 million). Those not in the labor force are divided into those not available for work (79.9 million) and those available for work but not currently working (6.2 million). Finally, those available for work but not in the labor force are divided into discouraged workers (1.0 million) and those not currently looking for work for other reasons (5.2 million). Data from U.S. Department of Labor, Bureau of Labor Statistics, *The Employment Situation—September 2011*, October 7, 2011.

childcare responsibilities. Other people who have not actively looked for work are called *discouraged workers.* **Discouraged workers** are available for work but have not looked for a job during the previous four weeks because they believe no jobs are available for them.

Figure 9.1 shows the employment status of the civilian working-age population in September 2011. We can use the information in the figure to calculate three important macroeconomic indicators:

> **Discouraged workers** People who are available for work but have not looked for a job during the previous four weeks because they believe no jobs are available for them.

- *The unemployment rate.* The unemployment rate measures the percentage of the labor force that is unemployed:

$$\frac{\text{Number of unemployed}}{\text{Labor force}} \times 100 = \text{Unemployment rate.}$$

Using the numbers from Figure 9.1, we can calculate the unemployment rate for September 2011:

$$\frac{14.0 \text{ million}}{154.0 \text{ million}} \times 100 = 9.1\%.$$

- *The labor force participation rate.* The **labor force participation rate** measures the percentage of the working-age population that is in the labor force:

$$\frac{\text{Labor force}}{\text{Working-age-population}} \times 100 = \text{Labor force participation rate.}$$

> **Labor force participation rate** The percentage of the working-age population in the labor force.

For September 2011, the labor force participation rate was

$$\frac{154.0 \text{ million}}{240.1 \text{ million}} \times 100 = 64.1\%.$$

- **The employment–population ratio.** The *employment–population ratio* measures the percentage of the working age population that is employed:

$$\frac{\text{Employment}}{\text{Working-age population}} \times 100 = \text{Employment–population ratio}.$$

For September 2011, the employment–population ratio was

$$\frac{140.0 \text{ million}}{240.1 \text{ million}} \times 100 = 58.3\%.$$

Solved Problem 9.1

What Happens if You Include the Military?

In the BLS household survey, people on active military service are not included in the totals for employment, the labor force, or the working-age population. Suppose people in the military were included in these categories. How would the unemployment rate, the labor force participation rate, and the employment–population ratio change?

Solving the Problem

Step 1: Review the chapter material. This problem is about calculating the unemployment rate and the labor force participation rate, so you may want to review the section "Measuring the Unemployment Rate, the Labor Force Participation Rate, and the Employment–Population Ratio," which begins on page 268.

Step 2: Show that including the military decreases the measured unemployment rate. The unemployment rate is calculated as

$$\frac{\text{Number of unemployed}}{\text{Labor force}} \times 100.$$

Including people in the military would increase the number of people counted as being in the labor force but would leave unchanged the number of people counted as unemployed. Therefore, the unemployment rate would decrease.

Step 3: Show that including the military increases both the measured labor force participation rate and the measured employment–population ratio. The labor force participation rate is calculated as

$$\frac{\text{Labor force}}{\text{Working-age population}} \times 100,$$

and the employment–population ratio is calculated as

$$\frac{\text{Employment}}{\text{Working-age population}} \times 100.$$

Including people in the military would increase the number of people in the labor force, the number of people employed, and the number of people in the working-age population all by the same amount. This change would increase the labor force participation rate and the employment–population ratio because adding the same number to both the numerator and the denominator of a fraction that is less than one increases the value of the fraction.

To see why this is true, consider the following simple example. Suppose that 100,000,000 people are in the working-age population and 50,000,000 are in the labor force, not counting people in the military. Suppose that 1,000,000 people are in the military. Then, the labor force participation rate excluding the military is

$$\frac{50{,}000{,}000}{100{,}000{,}000} \times 100 = 50\%,$$

and the labor force participation rate including the military is

$$\frac{51{,}000{,}000}{101{,}000{,}000} \times 100 = 50.5\%.$$

A similar calculation shows that including the military would increase the employment–population ratio.

Your Turn: For more practice, do related problem 1.9 on page 296 at the end of this chapter.

MyEconLab

Problems with Measuring the Unemployment Rate

Although the BLS reports the unemployment rate measured to the tenth of a percentage point, it is not a perfect measure of the current state of joblessness in the economy. One problem that the BLS confronts is distinguishing between the unemployed and people who are not in the labor force. During an economic recession, for example, an increase in discouraged workers usually occurs, as people who have had trouble finding a job stop actively looking. Because these workers are not counted as unemployed, the unemployment rate as measured by the BLS may understate the true degree of joblessness in the economy. The BLS also counts people as being employed if they hold part-time jobs even though they would prefer to hold full-time jobs. In a recession, counting as "employed" a part-time worker who wants to work full time tends to understate the degree of joblessness in the economy and make the employment situation appear better than it is.

Not counting discouraged workers as unemployed and counting people as employed who are working part time, although they would prefer to be working full time, has a substantial effect on the measured unemployment rate. In Figure 9.2, the red line shows the official measure of the unemployment rate and the blue line shows what the unemployment rate would be if the BLS had counted as unemployed all people who were available for work but not actively looking for jobs and all people who were in part-time jobs but wanted full-time jobs. The difference between the two measures of the unemployment rate is substantial and was particularly large during the 2007–2009 recession and the slow recovery that followed the recession. For example, in September 2011, using the broader definition of unemployment would have increased the measured unemployment rate from 9.1 percent to 16.5 percent.

Figure 9.2

The Official Unemployment Rate and a Broad Measure of the Unemployment Rate, 1994–2011

The red line shows the usual measure of the unemployment rate and the blue line shows what the unemployment rate would be if the BLS had counted as unemployed all people who were available for work but not actively looking for jobs and all people who were in part-time jobs but wanted full-time jobs. The difference between the measures was particularly large during the 2007–2009 recession and the weak recovery that followed. Shaded areas indicate months of recession.
Note: The usual measure is BLS series U-3 and the broader measure is BLS series U-6.
Data from U.S. Bureau of Labor Statistics.

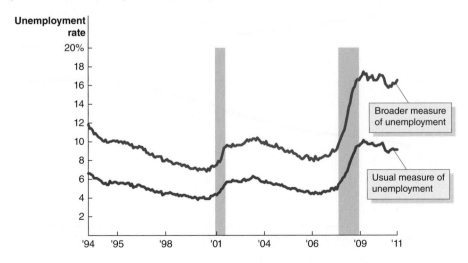

There are other measurement problems, however, that cause the measured unemployment rate to *overstate* the true extent of joblessness. These problems arise because the household survey does not verify the responses of people included in the survey. Some people who claim to be unemployed and actively looking for work may not be actively looking. A person might claim to be actively looking for a job to remain eligible for government payments to the unemployed. In this case, a person who is actually not in the labor force is counted as unemployed. Other people might be employed but engaged in illegal activity—such as drug dealing—or might want to conceal a legitimate job to avoid paying taxes. In these cases, individuals who are actually employed are counted as unemployed. These inaccurate responses to the survey bias the unemployment rate as measured by the BLS toward overstating the true extent of joblessness. We can conclude that, although the unemployment rate provides some useful information about the employment situation in the country, it is far from an exact measure of joblessness in the economy.

Trends in Labor Force Participation

The labor force participation rate is important because it determines the amount of labor that will be available to the economy from a given population. The higher the labor force participation rate, the more labor that will be available and the higher a country's levels of GDP and GDP per person. Figure 9.3 highlights two important trends in the labor force participation rates of adults aged 16 and over in the United States since 1948: the rising labor force participation rate of adult women and the falling labor force participation rate of adult men.

The labor force participation rate of adult males has fallen from 87 percent in 1948 to 71 percent in 2010. Most of this decline is due to older men retiring earlier and younger men remaining in school longer. There has also been a decline in labor force participation among males who are not in school but who are too young to retire. Over the longer term, this decline appears to be partly due to Congress having made it easier for people to receive cash payments under the Social Security Disability Insurance program. In the shorter term, the decline is due to the severity of the 2007–2009 recession and the weakness of the recovery following the recession.

The decline in labor force participation among adult men has been more than offset by a sharp increase in the labor force participation rate for adult women, which rose from 33 percent in 1948 to 59 percent in 2010. As a result, the overall labor force participation rate rose from 59 percent in 1948 to 65 percent in 2010. The increase in the

Figure 9.3

Trends in the Labor Force: Participation Rates of Adult Men and Women since 1948

The labor force participation rate of adult men has declined gradually since 1948, but the labor force participation rate of adult women has increased significantly, making the overall labor force participation rate higher today than it was in 1948.

Data from U.S. Bureau of Labor Statistics.

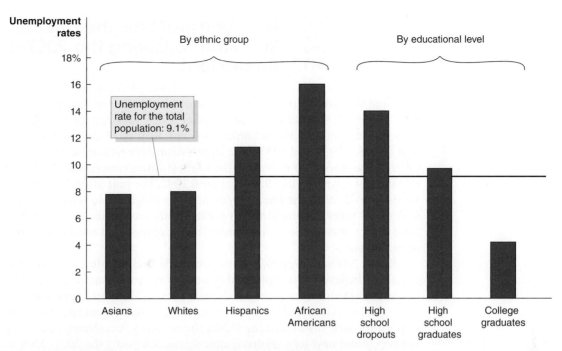

Figure 9.4 **Unemployment Rates in the United States, September 2011**

The unemployment rate of African Americans is the highest of the four ethnic groups shown, while the unemployment rate of Asians is the lowest. High school dropouts have an unemployment rate that is triple the unemployment rate for college graduates. *Notes:* The unemployment rates for ethnic groups apply to people 16 and older; the unemployment rates by educational attainment apply to people 25 and older. People identified as Hispanic may be of any race.

Data from U.S. Department of Labor, Bureau of Labor Statistics, *The Employment Situation—September 2011*, October 7, 2011.

labor force participation rate of women has several causes, including changing social attitudes due in part to the women's movement, federal legislation outlawing discrimination, increasing wages for women, and the typical family having fewer children.

Unemployment Rates for Different Groups

Different groups in the population can have very different unemployment rates. Figure 9.4 shows unemployment rates in September 2011 for different ethnic groups and for groups with different levels of educational attainment. While the overall unemployment rate was 9.1 percent, Asians had an unemployment rate of 7.8 percent, and African Americans had an unemployment rate of 16.0 percent. The unemployment rate for people over age 25 without a high school degree was 14.0 percent, while the unemployment rate for college graduates was only 4.2 percent.

How Long Are People Typically Unemployed?

The longer a person is unemployed, the greater the hardship. During the Great Depression of the 1930s, some people were unemployed for years at a time. In the modern U.S. economy, the typical unemployed person stays unemployed for a relatively brief period of time, although that time lengthens significantly during a severe recession. For example, in April 2007—which was during a period of economic expansion—82 percent of the people who were unemployed had been unemployed for less than six months. In September 2011, after the end of the 2007–2009 recession, but during a time when the economy was growing slowly, only 55 percent of the unemployed had been jobless for less than six months. The average period of unemployment was only 17 weeks in April 2007 but was 41 weeks in September 2011. The severity of unemployment during and after the 2007–2009 recession was a sharp break with the normal U.S. experience where the typical person who loses a job will find another one or be recalled to a previous job within a few months.

<table>
<tr><td>Making
the
Connection</td><td>

How Unusual Was the Unemployment Situation Following the 2007–2009 Recession?

</td></tr>
</table>

The Great Depression of the 1930s left its mark on nearly everyone who lived through it. The Depression began in August 1929, became worse after the stock market crash of October 1929, and reached its low point in 1933, following the collapse of the banking system. Real GDP declined by more than 25 percent between 1929 and 1933—the largest drop ever recorded. The unemployment rate in 1933 was above 20 percent—the highest rate ever recorded. The unemployment rate did not return to its 1929 level until 1942, the year after the United States entered World War II. With the unemployment rate so high for so long, many people were out of work for years. As one historian put it, "What was distinctive about the Great Depression, in fact, was … the *extraordinary lengths of time* that most jobless men and women remained out of work."

By the 2000s, many people in the United States, including most economists and policymakers, believed that prolonged periods of unemployment such as the U.S. economy had suffered from during the 1930s were very unlikely to happen again. Although the 1981–1982 recession had been severe and the unemployment rate had risen above 10 percent for the first time since the 1930s, the recovery was strong, and many unemployed workers found new jobs relatively quickly. So, following the 2007–2009 recession, most economists and policymakers were unprepared for how slowly the unemployment rate declined and for how much the average period of unemployment rose. During the 1981–1982 recession, the unemployment rate peaked at 10.8 percent in December 1982, but 23 months later, in November 1984, it had already declined to 7.2 percent. In contrast, after the recession of 2007–2009, the unemployment rate peaked at 10.1 percent in October 2009, while 23 months later, it had declined by only 1 percentage point, to 9.1 percent. The figure below shows that the average period of unemployment was twice as high following the 2007–2009 recession as following any other recession since the end of World War II.

Unemployment was so persistent and widespread that a survey taken by the Pew Research Center in the spring of 2011 found that more than half of all households had experienced at least one member losing his or her job during the previous year. Another Pew survey taken in June 2011 found that more than half of people with jobs expected to receive a pay cut or to lose their job during the next year.

As we have seen, one drawback to the unemployment data is that workers who drop out of the labor market stop being counted as unemployed. As a result, some economists focus on the employment–population ratio because it measures the fraction of the population that has jobs. The figure on the next page shows the employment–population ratio for the period 1948 to 2011. The overall upward trend of the ratio reflects the increased labor force participation rate of women. In each recession, the employment–population ratio falls as some workers lose their jobs. The fall of the employment–population ratio was particularly dramatic during the recession of 2007–2009, and the ratio actually continued to decline during the two years following the end of the recession. The fall of the employment–population ratio may give an even better indication than does the unemployment rate of how weak the U.S. labor market was during and after the 2007–2009 recession.

As we will see in later chapters, explaining the weakness of the U.S. labor market during and after the 2007–2009 recession had become a top priority of economists and policymakers.

Based on Alexander Keyssar, *Out of Work: The First Century of Unemployment in Massachusetts,* (New York: Cambridge University Press, 1986), p. 290; Federal Reserve Bank of St. Louis; U.S. Bureau of Labor Statistics; Pew Research Center, "The Recession, Economic Stress, and Optimism," May 4, 2011; and Pew Research Center, "Views of Personal Finances," June 23, 2011.

Your Turn: Test your understanding by doing related problem 1.11 on page 297 at the end of this chapter.   MyEconLab

---

The Establishment Survey: Another Measure of Employment

In addition to the household survey, the BLS uses the *establishment survey*, sometimes called the *payroll survey*, to measure total employment in the economy. This monthly survey samples about 300,000 business establishments (such as factories, stores, and offices). A small company typically operates only one establishment, but a large company may operate many establishments. The establishment survey provides information on the total number of persons who are employed *and on a company payroll*. The establishment survey has four drawbacks. First, the survey does not provide information on the number of self-employed persons because they are not on a company payroll. Second, the survey may fail to count some persons employed at newly opened firms that are not included in the survey. Third, the survey provides no information on unemployment. Fourth, the initial employment values for the establishment survey can be significantly revised as data from additional establishments become available. Despite these drawbacks, the establishment survey has the advantage of being determined by actual payrolls rather than by unverified answers, as is the case with the household survey. In recent years, some economists have come to rely more on establishment survey data than on household survey data in analyzing current labor market conditions. Some financial analysts who forecast the future state of the economy to help forecast stock prices have also begun to rely more on establishment survey data than on household survey data.

Table 9.1 shows household survey and establishment survey data for the months of August and September 2011. Notice that the household survey, because it includes the

Table 9.1 Household and Establishment Survey Data for August and September 2011

	Household Survey			Establishment Survey		
	August	September	Change	August	September	Change
Employed	139,627,000	140,025,000	398,000	131,231,000	131,334,000	103,000
Unemployed	13,967,000	13,992,000	25,000			
Labor force	153,594,000	154,017,000	423,000			
Unemployment rate	9.1%	9.1%	0%			

Note: The sum of employed and unemployed may not equal the labor force due to rounding.
Data from U.S. Department of Labor, Bureau of Labor Statistics, *The Employment Situation—September 2011*, October 7, 2011.

self-employed, gives a larger total for employment than does the establishment survey. The household survey provides information on the number of persons unemployed and on the number of persons in the labor force. This information is not available in the establishment survey. Between August and September 2011, employment rose by 398,000 in the household survey, while it rose by only 103,000 in the establishment survey. This substantial discrepancy is partly due to the slightly different groups covered by the two surveys and partly to inaccuracies in the surveys.

Revisions in the Establishment Survey Employment Data: How Bad Was the 2007–2009 Recession?

Economists and policymakers rely on government economic data, such as the employment data from the establishment survey, to understand the current state of the economy. Given the size of the U.S. economy, though, government agencies, such as the Bureau of Economic Analysis, the Bureau of Labor Statistics, and the Census Bureau, need considerable time to gather complete and accurate data on GDP, employment, and other macroeconomic variables. To avoid long waits in supplying data to policymakers and the general public, government agencies typically issue preliminary estimates that they revise as additional information becomes available. As we noted earlier, the data from the BLS on employment as gathered in the establishment survey can be subject to particularly large revisions over time.

Figure 9.5 shows for each month from December 2007 to December 2010 the difference between the value for the change in employment as initially reported in the establishment survey and the revised value available in September 2011. The green bars show months for which the BLS revised its preliminary estimates to show that fewer jobs were lost (or more jobs were created) than originally reported, and the red bars show months for which the BLS revised its preliminary estimates to show that more jobs were lost (or fewer jobs were created). For example, the BLS initially reported that employment

Figure 9.5

Revisions to Employment Changes, as Reported in the Establishment Survey

Over time, the BLS revises its preliminary estimates of changes in employment. During the 2007–2009 recession, many more jobs were lost than the preliminary estimates showed. The green bars show months for which the BLS revised its preliminary estimates to show fewer jobs lost (or more jobs created), and the red bars show months for which the BLS revised its preliminary estimates to show more jobs lost (or fewer jobs created).
Data from U.S. Bureau of Labor Statistics.

	Number of Establishments	Number of Jobs
Establishments Creating Jobs		
Existing establishments	1,447,000	5,609,000
New establishments	382,000	1,345,000
Establishments Eliminating Jobs		
Existing establishments	1,418,000	5,162,000
Closing establishments	352,000	1,229,000

Data from U.S. Bureau of Labor Statistics, *Business Employment Dynamics: Fourth Quarter 2010*, August 2, 2011.

Table 9.2

Establishments Creating and Eliminating Jobs, September–December 2010

declined by 159,000 jobs during September 2008. In fact, after additional data became available, the BLS revised its estimate to show that employment had declined by 434,000 jobs during the month—a difference of 275,000 more jobs lost. As the recession deepened between April 2008 and April 2009, the BLS's initial reports underestimated the number of jobs lost by 2.3 million. In other words, the recession of 2007–2009 turned out to be much more severe than economists and policymakers realized at the time.

Job Creation and Job Destruction over Time

One important fact about employment is not very well known: The U.S. economy creates and destroys millions of jobs every year. In 2010, for example, about 26.6 million jobs were created, and about 25.4 million jobs were destroyed. This degree of job creation and destruction is not surprising in a vibrant market system where new firms are constantly being started, some existing firms are expanding, some existing firms are contracting, and some firms are going out of business. The creation and destruction of jobs results from changes in consumer tastes, technological progress, and the successes and failures of entrepreneurs in responding to the opportunities and challenges of shifting consumer tastes and technological change. The large volume of job creation and job destruction helps explain why during most years, the typical person who loses a job is unemployed for a relatively brief period of time.

When the BLS announces each month the increases or decreases in the number of persons employed and unemployed, these are net figures. That is, the change in the number of persons employed is equal to the total number of jobs created minus the number of jobs eliminated. Take, for example, the months from September to December 2010. During that period, 6,954,000 jobs were created, and 6,391,000 were eliminated, for a net increase of 563,000 jobs. Because the net change is so much smaller than the total job increases and decreases, the net change doesn't fully represent how dynamic the U.S. job market really is.

The data in Table 9.2 reinforce the idea of how large the volume of job creation and job elimination is over a period as brief as three months. The table shows the number of establishments (that is, offices, factories, or stores) creating and eliminating jobs during the period from September through December 2010. About 382,000 new establishments opened, creating 1.35 million new jobs, and 352,000 establishments closed, eliminating 1.23 million jobs.

Types of Unemployment

Figure 9.6 illustrates that the unemployment rate follows the business cycle, rising during recessions and falling during expansions. Notice, though, that the unemployment rate never falls to zero. To understand why this is true, we need to discuss the three types of unemployment:

1. Frictional unemployment
2. Structural unemployment
3. Cyclical unemployment

Figure 9.6

The Annual Unemployment Rate in the United States, 1950–2010

The unemployment rate rises during recessions and falls during expansions. Shaded areas indicate recessions.
Data from U.S. Bureau of Labor Statistics.

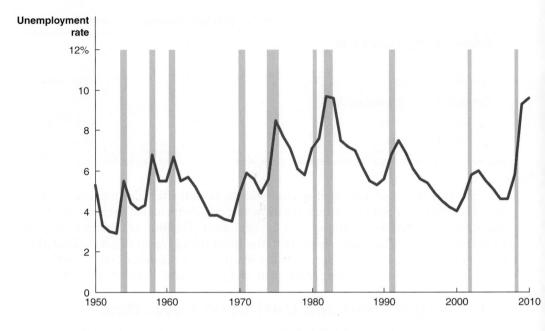

Frictional Unemployment and Job Search

Workers have different skills, interests, and abilities, and jobs have different skill requirements, working conditions, and pay levels. As a result, a new worker entering the labor force or a worker who has lost a job probably will not find an acceptable job right away. Most workers spend at least some time engaging in *job search*, just as most firms spend time searching for a new person to fill a job opening. **Frictional unemployment** is short-term unemployment that arises from the process of matching workers with jobs. Some frictional unemployment is unavoidable. As we have seen, the U.S. economy creates and destroys millions of jobs each year. The process of job search takes time, so there will always be some workers who are frictionally unemployed because they are between jobs and in the process of searching for new ones.

Some unemployment is due to seasonal factors, such as weather or fluctuations in demand for some products or services during different times of the year. For example, stores located in beach resort areas reduce their hiring during the winter, and ski resorts reduce their hiring during the summer. Department stores increase their hiring in November and December and reduce their hiring after New Year's Day. In agricultural areas, employment increases during harvest season and declines thereafter. Construction workers in many parts of the United States experience greater unemployment during the winter than during the summer. *Seasonal unemployment* refers to unemployment due to factors such as weather, variations in tourism, and other calendar-related events. Because seasonal unemployment can make the unemployment rate seem artificially high during some months and artificially low during other months, the BLS reports two unemployment rates each month—one that is *seasonally adjusted* and one that is not seasonally adjusted. The seasonally adjusted data eliminate the effects of seasonal unemployment. Economists and policymakers rely on the seasonally adjusted data as a more accurate measure of the current state of the labor market.

Would eliminating all frictional unemployment be good for the economy? No, because some frictional unemployment actually increases economic efficiency. Frictional unemployment occurs because workers and firms take the time necessary to ensure a good match between the attributes of workers and the characteristics of jobs. By devoting time to job search, workers end up with jobs they find satisfying and in which they can be productive. Of course, having more productive and better-satisfied workers is also in the best interest of firms.

Frictional unemployment Short-term unemployment that arises from the process of matching workers with jobs.

Structural Unemployment

By 2011, computer-generated three-dimensional animation, which was used in movies such as *Kung Fu Panda 2* and *Cars 2*, had become much more popular than traditional hand-drawn two-dimensional animation. Many people who were highly skilled in hand-drawn animation lost their jobs at Walt Disney Pictures, DreamWorks, and other movie studios. To become employed again, many of these people either became skilled in computer-generated animation or found new occupations. In the meantime, they were unemployed. Economists consider these animators *structurally unemployed*. **Structural unemployment** arises from a persistent mismatch between the job skills or attributes of workers and the requirements of jobs. While frictional unemployment is short term, structural unemployment can last for longer periods because workers need time to learn new skills. For example, employment by U.S. steel firms dropped by more than half between the early 1980s and the early 2000s as a result of competition from foreign producers and technological change that substituted machines for workers. Many steel-workers found new jobs in other industries only after lengthy periods of retraining.

Some workers lack even basic skills, such as literacy, or have addictions to alcohol or other drugs that make it difficult for them to perform adequately the duties of almost any job. These workers may remain structurally unemployed for years.

Structural unemployment
Unemployment that arises from a persistent mismatch between the skills and attributes of workers and the requirements of jobs.

Cyclical Unemployment

When the economy moves into recession, many firms find their sales falling and cut back on production. As production falls, firms start laying off workers. Workers who lose their jobs because of a recession are experiencing **cyclical unemployment**. For example, Ford laid off workers during the recession of 2007–2009. As the economy slowly recovered from the recession, Ford began rehiring those workers. The Ford workers who had been laid off from their jobs during the recession and then rehired during the following expansion had experienced cyclical unemployment.

Cyclical unemployment
Unemployment caused by a business cycle recession.

Full Employment

As the economy moves through the expansion phase of the business cycle, cyclical unemployment eventually drops to zero. The unemployment rate will not be zero, however, because of frictional and structural unemployment. As Figure 9.6 shows, the unemployment rate in the United States is rarely below 4 percent. When the only remaining unemployment is structural and frictional unemployment, the economy is said to be at *full employment*.

Economists consider frictional and structural unemployment as the normal underlying level of unemployment in the economy. The fluctuations around this normal level of unemployment that we see in Figure 9.6 are mainly due to the changes in the level of cyclical unemployment. This normal level of unemployment, which is the sum of frictional and structural unemployment, is called the **natural rate of unemployment**. Economists disagree on the exact value of the natural rate of unemployment, and there is good reason to believe it varies over time. Currently, most economists estimate the natural rate to be between 5 percent and 6 percent. The natural rate of unemployment is also sometimes called the *full-employment rate of unemployment*.

Natural rate of unemployment
The normal rate of unemployment, consisting of frictional unemployment plus structural unemployment.

Making the Connection	How Should We Categorize Unemployment at Bank of America?

We saw at the beginning of the chapter that in the fall of 2011, Bank of America, the second largest bank in the United States, announced that it would be laying off 30,000 of its 288,000 employees. Was the unemployment caused by the layoffs at Bank of America frictional unemployment, structural unemployment, or cyclical unemployment? In answering this question, we should acknowledge that categorizing unemployment as frictional, structural, or cyclical is useful in understanding the sources of unemployment, but it can be difficult to apply

The people who lost their jobs at Bank of America fit into more than one category of unemployment.

these categories in a particular case. The BLS, for instance, provides estimates of total unemployment but does not classify it as frictional, structural, or cyclical.

Despite these difficulties, we can roughly categorize the unemployment caused by Bank of America's announcement. We begin by considering the three basic reasons the layoffs occurred: the long-term decline in the commercial banking sector; the recession of 2007–2009 that temporarily reduced the demand for mortgages and other loans; and the particular problems that Bank of America was experiencing in 2011. Each reason corresponds to a category of unemployment. During the housing boom of the mid-2000s, the financial sector of the economy, including banks, expanded rapidly. The financial sector began to contract during the recession of 2007–2009 as the need for mortgages and other loans began to decline. Employment in the financial sector was still declining in the fall of 2011. Although some of this decline was related to the severity of the recession and the slowness of the recovery, many economists believed that employment in the financial sector was unlikely to return to the levels seen at the height of the housing boom in 2005 and 2006. Therefore, some of the employees laid off by Bank of America were unlikely to find new jobs without leaving the financial sector, so they had become structurally unemployed. Some of the decline in demand for loans and other banking and financial services was due to the effects of the 2007–2009 recession rather than to long-term problems in the financial sector. So, some of the workers Bank of America laid off were cyclically unemployed and could expect to find other jobs with financial firms after the economic recovery strengthened.

Finally, Bank of America was suffering from some problems that were not shared by all other banks. In 2008, after the recession had already begun, Bank of America purchased Countrywide Financial for over $4 billion. Countrywide had been the leading mortgage lender in the United States. Unfortunately, many of its loans had been made to borrowers with poor credit who defaulted on their loans once housing prices began to decline. Managers at Bank of America had underestimated the problems at Countrywide, which continued to suffer losses into 2011. In addition, some of Countrywide's lending practices were disputed in lawsuits that might cost Bank of America billions of dollars to settle. Bank of America would have laid off fewer workers if it had not been suffering from these problems. As a result, it was likely that some of these workers would be able to find jobs at competing banks after relatively brief job searches. These workers were frictionally unemployed.

Based on Dan Fitzpatrick, "BofA Readies the Knife," *Wall Street Journal*, September 13, 2011; "Bank Withdrawals," *Economist*, August 9, 2011; and Nelson D. Schwartz, "Bank of America Confirms Plan to Cut 30,000 Positions," *New York Times*, September 12, 2011.

MyEconLab **Your Turn:** Test your understanding by doing related problem 2.6 on page 297 at the end of this chapter.

9.3 LEARNING OBJECTIVE

Explain what factors determine the unemployment rate.

Explaining Unemployment

We have seen that some unemployment is a result of the business cycle. In later chapters, we will explore the causes of the business cycle, which will help us understand the causes of cyclical unemployment. In this section, we will look at the factors that determine the levels of frictional and structural unemployment.

Government Policies and the Unemployment Rate

Workers search for jobs by sending out resumes, registering with Internet job sites such as Monster.com, and getting job referrals from friends and relatives. Firms fill job openings by advertising in newspapers, listing openings online, participating in job fairs, and recruiting on college campuses. Government policy can aid these private efforts. Governments can help reduce the level of frictional unemployment by pursuing policies that help speed up the process of matching unemployed workers with unfilled jobs. Governments can help reduce structural unemployment by implementing policies that aid worker retraining. For example, the federal government's Trade Adjustment Assistance program offers training to workers whose firms laid them off as a result of competition from foreign firms.

Some government policies, however, can add to the level of frictional and structural unemployment. These government policies increase the unemployment rate either by increasing the time workers devote to searching for jobs, by providing disincentives for firms to hire workers, or by keeping wages above their market level.

Unemployment Insurance and Other Payments to the Unemployed Suppose you have been in the labor force for a few years but have just lost your job. You could probably find a low-wage job immediately if you needed to—perhaps at Wal-Mart or McDonald's. But you might decide to search for a better, higher-paying job by sending out resumes and responding to want ads and Internet job postings. Remember that the *opportunity cost* of any activity is the highest-valued alternative that you must give up to engage in that activity. In this case, the opportunity cost of continuing to search for a job is the salary you are giving up at the job you could have taken. The longer you search, the greater your chances of finding a better, higher-paying job, but the longer you search, the more salary you have given up by not working, so the greater the opportunity cost.

In the United States and most other industrial countries, the unemployed are eligible for *unemployment insurance payments* from the government. In the United States, these payments vary by state but are generally equal to about half the average wage. The unemployed spend more time searching for jobs because they receive these payments. This additional time spent searching raises the unemployment rate. Does this mean that the unemployment insurance program is a bad idea? Most economists would say no. Before Congress established the unemployment insurance program at the end of the 1930s, unemployed workers suffered very large declines in their incomes, which led them to greatly reduce their spending. This reduced spending contributed to the severity of recessions. Unemployment insurance helps the unemployed maintain their income and spending, which lessens the personal hardship of being unemployed and also helps reduce the severity of recessions.

In the United States, unemployed workers are generally eligible to receive unemployment insurance payments equal to about half their previous wage for only six months, although this period is typically extended during recessions, as happened during and after the recession of 2007–2009. After that, the opportunity cost of continuing to search for a job rises. In many other high-income countries, such as Canada and most of the countries of Western Europe, workers are eligible to receive unemployment payments for a year or more, and the payments may equal 70 percent to 80 percent of their previous wage. In addition, many of these countries have generous *social insurance programs* that allow unemployed adults to receive some government payments even after their eligibility for unemployment insurance has ended. In the United States, very few government programs make payments to healthy adults, with the exception of the Temporary Assistance for Needy Families program, which allows single parents to receive payments for up to five years. Although there are many reasons unemployment rates may differ across countries, most economists believe that because the opportunity cost of job search is lower in Canada and countries of Western Europe, unemployed workers in those countries search longer for jobs and, therefore, the unemployment rates in those countries tend to be higher than in the United States. During the 2007–2009 recession, however, unemployment rates were lower in Canada and Germany than in the United States.

Minimum Wage Laws In 1938, the federal government enacted a national minimum wage law. At first, the lowest legal wage firms could pay workers was $0.25 per hour. Over the years, Congress has gradually raised the minimum wage; in 2011, it was $7.25 per hour. Some states and cities also have minimum wage laws. For example, in 2011, the minimum wage in California was $8.00 per hour, and the minimum wage in

San Francisco was $9.92 per hour. If the minimum wage is set above the market wage determined by the demand and supply of labor, the quantity of labor supplied will be greater than the quantity of labor demanded. Some workers will be unemployed who would have been employed if there were no minimum wage. As a result, the unemployment rate will be higher than it would be without a minimum wage. Economists agree that the current minimum wage is above the market wage for some workers, but they disagree on the amount of unemployment that has resulted. Because teenagers generally have relatively few job-related skills, they are the group most likely to receive the minimum wage. Studies estimate that a 10 percent increase in the minimum wage reduces teenage employment by about 2 percent. Because teenagers and others receiving the minimum wage are a relatively small part of the labor force, most economists believe that, at its present level, the effect of the minimum wage on the unemployment rate in the United States is fairly small.

Labor Unions

Labor unions are organizations of workers that bargain with employers for higher wages and better working conditions for their members. In unionized industries, the wage is usually above what otherwise would be the market wage. This above-market wage results in employers in unionized industries hiring fewer workers, but does it also significantly increase the overall unemployment rate in the economy? Most economists would say the answer is "no" because only about 9 percent of workers outside the government sector are unionized. Although unions remain strong in a few industries, such as airlines, automobiles, steel, and telecommunications, most industries in the United States are not unionized. The result is that most workers who can't find jobs in unionized industries because the wage is above its market level can find jobs in other industries.

Efficiency Wages

Efficiency wage A higher-than-market wage that a firm pays to increase worker productivity.

Many firms pay higher-than-market wages not because the government requires them to or because they are unionized but because they believe doing so will increase their profits. This may seem like a paradox: Wages are the largest cost for many employers, so paying higher wages seems like a good way for firms to lower profits rather than to increase them. The key to understanding the paradox is that the level of wages can affect the level of worker productivity. Many studies have shown that workers are motivated by higher wages to work harder. An **efficiency wage** is a higher-than-market wage that a firm pays to motivate workers to be more productive. Can't firms ensure that workers work hard by supervising them? In some cases, they can. For example, a telemarketing firm can monitor workers electronically to ensure that they make the required number of phone calls per hour. In many business situations, however, it is much more difficult to monitor workers. Many firms must rely on workers being motivated enough to work hard. By paying a wage above the market wage, a firm raises the costs to workers of losing their jobs because many alternative jobs will pay only the market wage. The increase in productivity that results from paying the high wage can more than offset the extra cost of the wage, thereby lowering the firm's costs of production.

Because the efficiency wage is above the market wage, it results in the quantity of labor supplied being greater than the quantity of labor demanded, just as do minimum wage laws and unions. So, efficiency wages are another reason economies experience some unemployment even when cyclical unemployment is zero.

9.4 LEARNING OBJECTIVE

Define price level and inflation rate and understand how they are computed.

Measuring Inflation

One of the facts of economic life is that the prices of most goods and services rise over time. As a result, the cost of living continually rises. In 1914, Henry Ford began paying his workers a wage of $5 per day, which was more than twice as much as other automobile manufacturers were paying. Ford's $5-a-day wage provided his workers with a middle-class income because prices were so low. In 1914, Ford's Model T, the best-selling car in the country, sold for less than $600, the price of a man's suit was $15, the price of a ticket to a movie theater was $0.15, and the price of a box of Kellogg's Corn Flakes was $0.08. In 2011, with the cost of living being much higher than it was in 1914, the minimum wage law required firms to pay a wage of at least $7.25 per *hour*, more than Ford's highly paid workers earned in a day.

Knowing how the government compiles the employment and unemployment statistics is important in interpreting them. The same is true of the government's statistics on the cost of living. As we saw in Chapter 8, the **price level** measures the average prices of goods and services in the economy. The **inflation rate** is the percentage increase in the price level from one year to the next. In Chapter 8, we introduced the *GDP deflator* as a measure of the price level. The GDP deflator is the broadest measure we have of the price level because it includes the price of every final good and service. But for some purposes it is too broad. For example, if we want to know how inflation affects the typical household, the GDP price deflator may be misleading because it includes the prices of products such as large electric generators and machine tools that are included in the investment component of GDP but are not purchased by the typical household. In this chapter, we will focus on measuring the inflation rate by changes in the *consumer price index* because changes in this index come closest to measuring changes in the cost of living as experienced by the typical household. We will also briefly discuss a third measure of inflation: the *producer price index*.

Price level A measure of the average prices of goods and services in the economy.

Inflation rate The percentage increase in the price level from one year to the next.

The Consumer Price Index

To obtain prices of a representative group of goods and services, the BLS surveys 30,000 households nationwide on their spending habits. It uses the results of this survey to construct a *market basket* of 211 types of goods and services purchased by the typical urban family of four. Figure 9.7 shows the goods and services in the market basket, grouped into eight broad categories. Almost three-quarters of the market basket falls into the categories of housing, transportation, and food. Each month, hundreds of BLS employees visit 23,000 stores in 87 cities and record prices of the goods and services in the market basket. Each price in the consumer price index is given a weight equal to the fraction of the typical family's budget spent on that good or service. The **consumer price index (CPI)** is an average of the prices of the goods and services purchased by the typical urban family of four. One year is chosen as the base year, and the value of the CPI is set equal to 100 for that year. In any year other than the base year, the CPI is equal to the ratio of the dollar amount necessary to buy the market basket of goods in that year divided by the dollar amount necessary to buy the market basket of goods in

Consumer price index (CPI) An average of the prices of the goods and services purchased by the typical urban family of four.

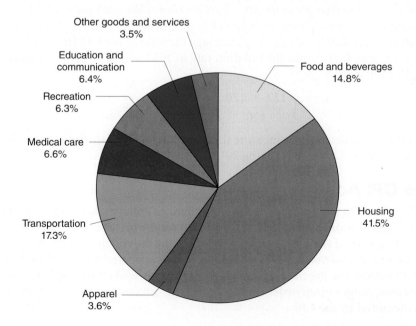

Other goods and services
3.5%

Education and communication
6.4%

Recreation
6.3%

Medical care
6.6%

Transportation
17.3%

Apparel
3.6%

Food and beverages
14.8%

Housing
41.5%

Figure 9.7

The CPI Market Basket, December 2010

The Bureau of Labor Statistics surveys 30,000 households on their spending habits. The results are used to construct a *market basket* of goods and services purchased by the typical urban family of four. The chart shows these goods and services, grouped into eight broad categories. The percentages represent the expenditure shares of the categories within the market basket. The categories of housing, transportation, and food make up about three-quarters of the market basket. Data from U.S. Bureau of Labor Statistics.

the base year, multiplied by 100. Because the CPI measures the cost to the typical family to buy a representative basket of goods and services, it is sometimes referred to as the *cost-of-living index*.

A simple example can clarify how the CPI is constructed. For purposes of this example, we assume that the market basket has only three products: eye examinations, pizzas, and books:

| Product | Base Year (1999) | | | 2012 | | 2013 | |
	Quantity	Price	Expenditures	Price	Expenditures (on base-year quantities)	Price	Expenditures (on base-year quantities)
Eye examinations	1	$50.00	$50.00	$100.00	$100.00	$85.00	$85.00
Pizzas	20	10.00	200.00	15.00	300.00	14.00	280.00
Books	20	25.00	500.00	25.00	500.00	27.50	550.00
TOTAL			$750.00		$900.00		$915.00

Suppose that during the base year, 1999, a survey determines that each month, the typical family purchases 1 eye examination, 20 pizzas, and 20 books. At 1999 prices, the typical family must spend $750.00 to purchase this market basket of goods and services. The CPI for every year after the base year is determined by dividing the amount necessary to purchase the market basket in that year by the amount required in the base year, then multiplying by 100. Notice that the quantities of the products purchased in 2012 and 2013 are irrelevant in calculating the CPI because *we are assuming that households buy the same market basket of products each month.* Using the numbers in the table, we can calculate the CPI for 2012 and 2013:

Formula	Applied to 2012	Applied to 2013
$\text{CPI} = \dfrac{\text{Expenditures in the current year}}{\text{Expenditures in the base year}} \times 100$	$\left(\dfrac{\$900}{\$750}\right) \times 100 = 120$	$\left(\dfrac{\$915}{\$750}\right) \times 100 = 122$

How do we interpret values such as 120 and 122? First, recognize that they are *index numbers*, which means they are not measured in dollars or any other units. *The CPI is intended to measure changes in the price level over time.* We can't use the CPI to tell us in an absolute sense how high the price level is—only how much it has changed over time. We measure the inflation rate as the percentage increase in the CPI from one year to the next. For our simple example, the inflation rate in 2013 would be the percentage change in the CPI from 2012 to 2013:

$$\left(\frac{122 - 120}{120}\right) \times 100 = 1.7\%.$$

Because the CPI is designed to measure the cost of living, we can also say that the cost of living increased by 1.7 percent during 2013.

Is the CPI Accurate?

The CPI is the most widely used measure of inflation. Policymakers use the CPI to track the state of the economy. Businesses use it to help set the prices of their products and the wages and salaries of their employees. Each year, the federal government increases the Social Security payments made to retired workers by a percentage equal to the increase in the CPI during the previous year. In setting alimony and child support payments in divorce cases, judges often order that the payments increase each year by the inflation rate, as measured by the CPI.

Don't Let This Happen to You

Don't Miscalculate the Inflation Rate

Suppose you are given the data in the following table and are asked to calculate the inflation rate for 2010:

Year	CPI
2009	216
2010	219

It is tempting to avoid any calculations and simply to report that the inflation rate in 2010 was 119 percent because 219 is a 119 percent increase from 100. But 119 percent would be the wrong answer. A value for the CPI of 219 in 2010 tells us that the price level in 2010 was 119 percent higher than in the base year, but the inflation rate is the percentage increase in the price level from the previous year, *not* the percentage increase from the base year. The correct calculation of the inflation rate for 2010 is:

$$\left(\frac{219 - 216}{216} \right) \times 100 = 1.4\%.$$

MyEconLab

Your Turn: Test your understanding by doing related problem 4.5 on page 298 at the end of this chapter.

It is important that the CPI be as accurate as possible, but there are four biases that cause changes in the CPI to overstate the true inflation rate:

- **Substitution bias.** In constructing the CPI, the BLS assumes that each month, consumers purchase the same amount of each product in the market basket. In fact, consumers are likely to buy fewer of those products that increase most in price and more of those products that increase least in price (or fall the most in price). For instance, if apple prices rise rapidly during the month while orange prices fall, consumers will reduce their apple purchases and increase their orange purchases. Therefore, the prices of the market basket consumers actually buy will rise less than the prices of the market basket the BLS uses to compute the CPI.

- **Increase in quality bias.** Over time, most products included in the CPI improve in quality: Automobiles become more durable and side air bags become standard equipment, computers become faster and have more memory, dishwashers use less water while getting dishes cleaner, and so on. Increases in the prices of these products partly reflect their improved quality and partly are pure inflation. The BLS attempts to make adjustments so that only the pure inflation part of price increases is included in the CPI. These adjustments are difficult to make, however, so the recorded price increases overstate the pure inflation in some products.

- **New product bias.** For many years, the BLS updated the market basket of goods used in computing the CPI only every 10 years. So, new products introduced between updates were not included in the market basket. For example, the 1987 update took place before cell phones were introduced. Although millions of American households used cell phones by the mid-1990s, they were not included in the CPI until the 1997 update. The prices of many products, such as cell phones, Blu-ray players, and LED televisions, decrease in the years immediately after they are introduced. If the market basket is not updated frequently, these price decreases are not included in the CPI.

- **Outlet bias.** During the mid-1990s, many consumers began to increase their purchases from discount stores such as Sam's Club and Costco. By the late 1990s, the Internet began to account for a significant fraction of sales of some products. Because the BLS continued to collect price statistics from traditional full-price retail stores, the CPI did not reflect the prices some consumers actually paid.

Most economists believe these biases cause changes in the CPI to overstate the true inflation rate by 0.5 percentage point to 1 percentage point. That is, if the CPI indicates that the inflation rate was 3 percent, it is probably between 2 percent and 2.5 percent. The BLS continues to take steps to reduce the size of the bias. For example, the BLS has reduced the size of the substitution and new product biases by updating the market basket every 2 years rather than every 10 years. The BLS has reduced the size of the outlet bias by conducting a point-of-purchase survey to track where consumers actually make their purchases. Finally, the BLS has used statistical methods to reduce the size of the quality bias. Prior to these changes, the size of the total bias in the CPI was probably greater than 1 percent.

The Producer Price Index

Producer price index (PPI) An average of the prices received by producers of goods and services at all stages of the production process.

In addition to the GDP deflator and the CPI, the government also computes the **producer price index (PPI)**. Like the CPI, the PPI tracks the prices of a market basket of goods. But, whereas the CPI tracks the prices of goods and services purchased by the typical household, the PPI tracks the prices firms receive for goods and services at all stages of production. The PPI includes the prices of intermediate goods, such as flour, cotton, yarn, steel, and lumber; and raw materials, such as raw cotton, coal, and crude petroleum. If the prices of these goods rise, the cost to firms of producing final goods and services will rise, which may lead firms to increase the prices of goods and services purchased by consumers. Changes in the PPI therefore can give an early warning of future movements in the CPI.

Using Price Indexes to Adjust for the Effects of Inflation

9.5 LEARNING OBJECTIVE

Use price indexes to adjust for the effects of inflation.

You are likely to receive a much higher salary after graduation than your parents did 25 or more years ago, but prices 25 years ago were, on average, much lower than prices today. Put another way, the purchasing power of a dollar was much higher 25 years ago because the prices of most goods and services were much lower. Price indexes such as the CPI give us a way of adjusting for the effects of inflation so that we can compare dollar values from different years. For example, suppose your mother received a salary of $20,000 in 1984. By using the CPI, we can calculate what $20,000 in 1984 was equivalent to in 2010. The consumer price index is 104 for 1984 and 219 for 2010. Because 219/104 = 2.1, we know that, on average, prices were about 2.1 times as high in 2010 as in 1984. We can use this result to inflate a salary of $20,000 received in 1984 to its value in terms of 2010 purchasing power:

$$\text{Value in 2010 dollars} = \text{Value in 1984 dollars} \times \left(\frac{\text{CPI in 2010}}{\text{CPI in 1984}} \right)$$

$$= \$20,000 \times \left(\frac{219}{104} \right) = \$42,115.$$

Our calculation shows that if you were paid a salary of $42,115 in 2010, you would be able to purchase roughly the same amount of goods and services that your mother could have purchased with a salary of $20,000 in 1984. Economic variables that are calculated in current-year prices are referred to as *nominal variables*. The calculation we have just made uses a price index to adjust a nominal variable—your mother's salary—for the effects of inflation.

For some purposes, we are interested in tracking changes in an economic variable over time rather than in seeing what its value would be in today's dollars. In that case, to correct for the effects of inflation, we can divide the nominal variable by a price index and multiply by 100 to obtain a *real variable*. The real variable will be measured in dollars of the base year for the price index. Currently, the base year for the CPI is the average of prices in the years 1982 to 1984.

Solved Problem **9.5**

Calculating Real Average Hourly Earnings

In addition to data on employment, the BLS establishment survey gathers data on average hourly earnings of production workers. Production workers are all workers, except for managers and professionals. Average hourly earnings are the wages or salaries earned by these workers per hour. Economists closely follow average hourly earnings because they are a broad measure of the typical worker's income. Use the information in the following table to calculate real average hourly earnings for each year. What was the percentage change in real average hourly earnings between 2009 and 2010?

Year	Nominal Average Hourly Earnings	CPI (1982–1984 = 100)
2008	$21.62	216.2
2009	22.21	215.9
2010	22.59	218.6

Solving the Problem

Step 1: **Review the chapter material.** This problem is about using price indexes to correct for inflation, so you may want to review the section "Using Price Indexes to Adjust for the Effects of Inflation" on page 286.

Step 2: **Calculate real average hourly earnings for each year.** To calculate real average hourly earnings for each year, divide nominal average hourly earnings by the CPI and multiply by 100. For example, real average hourly earnings for 2008 are equal to

$$\left(\frac{\$21.62}{216.2}\right) \times 100 = \$10.00.$$

These are the results for all three years:

Year	Nominal Average Hourly Earnings	CPI (1982–1984 = 100)	Real Average Hourly Earnings (1982–1984 dollars)
2008	$21.62	216.2	$10.00
2009	22.21	215.9	10.29
2010	22.59	218.6	10.33

Step 3: **Calculate the percentage change in real average earnings from 2009 to 2010.** This percentage change is equal to

$$\left(\frac{\$10.33 - \$10.29}{\$10.29}\right) \times 100 = 0.4\%.$$

We can conclude that real average hourly earnings increased slightly between 2009 and 2010.

Extra Credit: The values we computed for real average hourly earnings are in 1982–1984 dollars. Because this period is more than 25 years ago, the values are somewhat difficult to interpret. We can convert the earnings to 2010 dollars by using the method we used earlier to calculate your mother's salary. But notice that, for purposes of calculating the *change* in the value of real average hourly earnings over time, the base year of the price index doesn't matter. The change from 2009 to 2010 would have still been 0.4 percent, no matter what the base year of the price index was. If you don't see that this is true, test it by using the mother's salary method to calculate real average hourly earnings for 2009 and 2010 in 2010 dollars. Then calculate the percentage change. Unless you make an arithmetic error, you should find that the answer is still 0.4 percent.

MyEconLab **Your Turn:** For more practice, do related problems 5.3, 5.4, 5.5, and 5.6 on pages 299–300 at the end of this chapter.

9.6 LEARNING OBJECTIVE

Distinguish between the nominal interest rate and the real interest rate.

Nominal interest rate The stated interest rate on a loan.

Real interest rate The nominal interest rate minus the inflation rate.

Real versus Nominal Interest Rates

The difference between nominal and real values is important when money is being borrowed and lent. As we saw in Chapter 8, the *interest rate* is the cost of borrowing funds, expressed as a percentage of the amount borrowed. If you lend someone $1,000 for one year and charge an interest rate of 6 percent, the borrower will pay back $1,060, or 6 percent more than the amount you lent. But is $1,060 received one year from now really 6 percent more than $1,000 today? If prices rise during the year, you will not be able to buy as much with $1,060 one year from now as you could with that amount today. Your true return from lending the $1,000 is equal to the percentage change in your purchasing power after taking into account the effects of inflation.

The stated interest rate on a loan is the **nominal interest rate**. The **real interest rate** corrects the nominal interest rate for the effect of inflation on purchasing power. As a simple example, suppose that the only good you purchase is DVDs, and at the beginning of the year, the price of DVDs is $10.00. With $1,000, you can purchase 100 DVDs. If you lend the $1,000 out for one year at an interest rate of 6 percent, you will receive $1,060 at the end of the year. Suppose the inflation rate during the year is 2 percent, so that the price of DVDs has risen to $10.20 by the end of the year. How has your purchasing power increased as a result of making the loan? At the beginning of the year, your $1,000 could purchase 100 DVDs. At the end of the year, your $1,060 can purchase $1,060/$10.20 = 103.92 DVDs. In other words, you can purchase almost 4 percent more DVDs. So, in this case, the real interest rate you received from lending was a little less than 4 percent (actually, 3.92 percent). For low rates of inflation, a convenient approximation for the real interest rate is

$$\text{Real interest rate} = \text{Nominal interest rate} - \text{Inflation rate}.$$

In our example, we can calculate the real interest rate by using this formula as 6 percent − 2 percent = 4 percent, which is close to the actual value of 3.92 percent. If the inflation rate during the year was 4 percent, the real interest rate would be only 2 percent. Holding the nominal interest rate constant, the higher the inflation rate, the lower the real interest rate. Notice that if the inflation rate turns out to be higher than expected, borrowers pay and lenders receive a lower real interest rate than either of them expected. For example, if both you and the person to whom you lent the $1,000 expected the inflation rate to be 2 percent, you both expected the real interest rate on the loan to be 4 percent. If inflation actually turns out to be 4 percent, the real interest rate on the loan will be 2 percent: That's bad news for you but good news for your borrower.

For the economy as a whole, we can measure the nominal interest rate as the interest rate on three-month U.S. Treasury bills. U.S. Treasury bills are short-term loans investors make to the federal government. We can use inflation as measured by changes in the CPI to calculate the real interest rate on Treasury bills. Figure 9.8 shows the nominal and real interest rates for the years 1970 through 2010. Notice that when the inflation rate is low, as it has been during most years since the early 1990s, the gap between the nominal and real interest rates is small. When the inflation rate is high, as it was during the mid- to late 1970s, the gap between the nominal and real interest rates becomes large. In fact, a particular nominal interest rate can be associated in different periods with very different real interest rates. For example, during late 1975, the nominal interest rate was about 5.5 percent, but because the inflation rate was 7 percent,

Figure 9.8   Nominal and Real Interest Rates, 1970–2010

The real interest rate is equal to the nominal interest rate minus the inflation rate. The real interest rate provides a better measure of the true cost of borrowing and the true return on lending than does the nominal interest rate. The nominal interest rate in the figure is the interest rate on three-month U.S. Treasury bills.

The inflation rate is measured by the percentage change in the CPI from the same quarter during the previous year.
Data from Federal Reserve Bank of St. Louis.

the real interest rate was −1.5 percent. In early 1987, the nominal interest rate was also 5.5 percent, but because the inflation rate was only 2 percent, the real interest rate was 3.5 percent.

This example shows that it is impossible to know whether a particular nominal interest rate is "high" or "low." It all depends on the inflation rate. *The real interest rate provides a better measure of the true cost of borrowing and the true return from lending than does the nominal interest rate.* When firms are deciding whether to borrow the funds to buy an investment good, such as a new factory, they will look at the real interest rate because the real interest rate measures the true cost to the firm of borrowing.

Is it possible for the nominal interest rate to be less than the real interest rate? Yes, but only when the inflation rate is negative. A negative inflation rate is referred to as **deflation** and occurs on the rare occasions when the price level falls. During the years shown in Figure 9.8, the inflation rate as measured by changes in the CPI was only negative during the first nine months of 2009.

Deflation A decline in the price level.

Does Inflation Impose Costs on the Economy?

9.7 LEARNING OBJECTIVE

Discuss the problems that inflation causes.

Imagine waking up tomorrow morning and finding that every price in the economy has doubled. The prices of food, gasoline, DVDs, computers, houses, and haircuts have all doubled. But suppose that all wages and salaries have also doubled. Will this doubling of prices and wages matter? Think about walking into Best Buy, expecting to find an iPad selling for $499. Instead, you find it selling for $998. Will you turn around and walk out? Probably not, because your salary has also increased overnight from $45,000 per year to

$90,000 per year. So, the purchasing power of your salary has remained the same, and you are just as likely to buy the iPad today as you were yesterday.

This hypothetical situation makes an important point: Nominal incomes generally increase with inflation. Remember from Chapter 8 that we can think of the $499 price of an iPad as representing either the value of the product or the value of all the income generated in producing the product. The two amounts are the same, whether the iPad sells for $499 or $998. When the price of the iPad rises from $499 to $998, that extra $499 ends up as income that goes to the workers at Apple, the salespeople at Best Buy, or the stockholders of Apple, just as the first $499 did.

It's tempting to think that the problem with inflation is that, as prices rise, consumers can no longer afford to buy as many goods and services, but our example shows that this is a fallacy. An expected inflation rate of 10 percent will raise the average price of goods and services by 10 percent, but it will also raise average incomes by 10 percent. Goods and services will be as affordable to the average consumer as they would be if there were no inflation.

Inflation Affects the Distribution of Income

If inflation will not reduce the affordability of goods and services to the average consumer, why do people dislike inflation? One reason is that the argument in the previous section applies to the *average* person but not to every person. Some people will find their incomes rising faster than the rate of inflation, and so their purchasing power will rise. Other people will find their incomes rising more slowly than the rate of inflation—or not at all—and their purchasing power will fall. People on fixed incomes are particularly likely to be hurt by inflation. If a retired worker receives a pension fixed at $3,000 per month, over time, inflation will reduce the purchasing power of that payment. In that way, inflation can change the distribution of income in a manner that strikes many people as being unfair.

The extent to which inflation redistributes income depends in part on whether the inflation is *anticipated*—in which case consumers, workers, and firms can see it coming and can prepare for it—or *unanticipated*—in which case they do not see it coming and do not prepare for it.

The Problem with Anticipated Inflation

Like many of life's problems, inflation is easier to manage if you see it coming. Suppose that everyone knows that the inflation rate for the next 10 years will be 10 percent per year. Workers know that unless their wages go up by at least 10 percent per year, the real purchasing power of their wages will fall. Businesses will be willing to increase workers' wages enough to compensate for inflation because they know that the prices of the products they sell will increase. Lenders will realize that the loans they make will be paid back with dollars that are losing 10 percent of their value each year, so they will charge a higher interest rate to compensate. Borrowers will be willing to pay these higher interest rates because they also know they are paying back these loans with dollars that are losing value. So far, there don't seem to be costs to anticipated inflation.

Even when inflation is perfectly anticipated, however, some individuals will experience a cost. Inevitably, there will be a redistribution of income, as some people's incomes fall behind even an anticipated level of inflation. In addition, firms and consumers have to hold some paper money to facilitate their buying and selling. Anyone holding paper money will find its purchasing power decreasing each year by the rate of inflation. To avoid this cost, workers and firms will try to hold as little paper money as possible, but they will have to hold some. In addition, firms that print catalogs listing the prices of their products will have to reprint them more frequently. Supermarkets and other stores that mark prices on packages or on store shelves will have to devote more time and labor to changing the marked prices. The costs to firms of changing prices are called **menu costs**. At moderate levels of anticipated inflation, menu costs are relatively small, but at very high levels of inflation, such as those experienced in

Menu costs The costs to firms of changing prices.

some developing countries, menu costs and the costs due to paper money losing value can become substantial. Finally, even anticipated inflation acts to raise the taxes paid by investors and raises the cost of capital for business investment. These effects arise because investors are taxed on the nominal payments they receive rather than on the real payments.

The Problem with Unanticipated Inflation

In any high-income economy—such as the United States—households, workers, and firms routinely enter into contracts that commit them to make or receive certain payments for years in the future. For example, when firms sign wage contracts, they commit to paying a specified wage for the duration of the contract. When people buy homes, they usually borrow most of the amount they need from a bank. These loans, called *mortgage loans*, commit a borrower to make a fixed monthly payment for the length of the loan. Most mortgage loans are for long periods, often as long as 30 years.

To make these long-term commitments, households, workers, and firms must forecast the rate of inflation. If a firm believes the inflation rate over the next three years will be 6 percent per year, signing a three-year contract with a union that calls for wage increases of 8 percent per year may seem reasonable because the firm may be able to raise its prices by at least the rate of inflation each year. If the firm believes that the inflation rate will be only 2 percent over the next three years, paying wage increases of 8 percent may significantly reduce its profits or even force it out of business.

When people borrow money or banks lend money, they must forecast the inflation rate so they can calculate the real rate of interest on a loan. In 1980, banks were charging interest rates of 18 percent or more on mortgage loans. This rate seems very high compared to the less than 5 percent charged on such loans in 2011, but the inflation rate in 1980 was more than 13 percent and was expected to remain high. In fact, the inflation rate declined unexpectedly during the early 1980s. By 1983, the inflation rate was only about 3 percent. People who borrowed money for 30 years at the high interest rates of 1980 soon found that the real interest rate on their loans was much higher than they expected.

When the actual inflation rate turns out to be very different from the expected inflation rate, some people gain, and other people lose. This outcome seems unfair to most people because they are either winning or losing only because something unanticipated has happened. This apparently unfair redistribution is a key reason people dislike unanticipated inflation.

Making the Connection | What's So Bad about Falling Prices?

We have just discussed how inflation being higher than expected can cause problems for consumers, workers, and firms. But what if an economy begins to experience falling prices—*deflation*, rather than inflation? A falling price level might seem like good news for the economy. After all, falling prices should encourage consumers to increase their spending as goods and services become less expensive. In fact, though, deflation tends to have the opposite effect on consumers. Episodes of deflation are relatively rare, but we can draw some lessons from two important deflationary episodes: the United States during the 1930s and Japan during the 1990s. In both cases, many consumers reduced their spending in the face of falling prices, apparently because they were waiting for prices to go even lower. Waiting for falling prices to go even lower was also a problem for the U.S. housing market in the late 2000s. A large run-up in housing prices took place from 2002 to 2006. When prices began to decline, many potential buyers postponed purchases in the expectation that prices would continue to fall.

The figure on the next page shows annual changes in the consumer price index in the United States during the years between 1925 and 1940. The beginning of the Great Depression in 1929 caused the country to experience severe deflation.

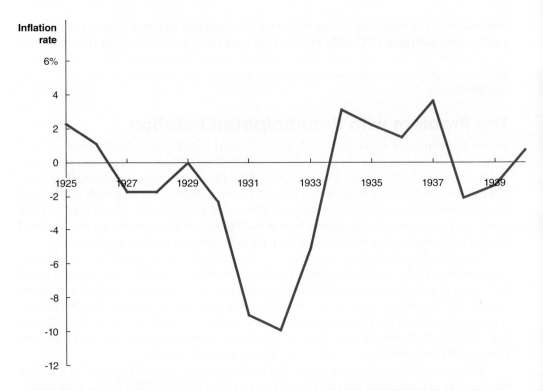

The deflation of the 1930s hurt the U.S. economy not just because it may have led some consumers to postpone purchases but also because it increased the burden on borrowers. For example, suppose that in 1929 you had borrowed money for five years at a nominal interest rate of 5 percent. What real interest rate would you have paid during those years? We have seen that to calculate the real interest rate, we need to subtract the inflation rate from the nominal interest rate. With deflation, the change in the price level is negative, so to calculate the real interest rate, we are in effect *adding* the change in the price level to the nominal interest rate. The following table uses the actual deflation rate in each year to calculate the resulting real interest rates on your loan:

	1929	1930	1931	1932	1933
Nominal interest rate	5%	5%	5%	5%	5%
Change in the consumer price index	0	−2.3	−9.0	−9.9	−5.1
Real interest rate	5	7.30	14.00	14.90	10.10

The bottom row of the table shows that although the nominal interest rate on your loan is only 5 percent, in three of the five years the real interest rate you pay is greater than 10 percent. In fact, high real interest rates inflicted serious losses on both household and business borrowers during the early 1930s and contributed to the severity of the Great Depression.

During the 2001 and 2007–2009 recessions, some policymakers and economists feared that the U.S. economy would experience deflation. Fortunately, significant deflation did not occur. If it had, those recessions would likely have been more severe than they were.

MyEconLab   **Your Turn:** Test your understanding by doing related problem 7.9 on page 301 at the end of this chapter.

Continued from page 641

Economics in Your Life

At the beginning of this chapter, we asked whether layoffs in the banking industry should cause you to change your major and give up your plans to pursue a career in banking. We have learned in this chapter that unemployment rates are higher and layoffs are more common in a recession than in an economic expansion. Because you are a sophomore, you will graduate a few years later, when the recession will likely have ended and the unemployment rate will have declined. You might also want to investigate whether the layoffs in the banking industry represent a permanent contraction in the size of the industry or whether they reflect a temporary decline due to the recession. If the reduction of banking jobs is more likely to be permanent, then you might consider a career in another industry. If the layoffs appear to be related to the current recession, then you probably do not need to change your career plans.

Conclusion

Inflation and unemployment are key macroeconomic problems. Presidential elections are often won and lost on the basis of which candidate is able to convince the public that he or she can best deal with these problems. Many economists, however, would argue that, in the long run, maintaining high rates of growth of real GDP per person is the most important macroeconomic concern. Only when real GDP per person is increasing will a country's standard of living increase. We turn in the next chapter to discussing the important issue of economic growth.

Read *An Inside Look* on the next page for a discussion of cost-cutting proposals by officials at the U.S. Postal Service for dealing with a loss of $8 billion in 2010.

Will Pink Slips Be in the Mail for Postal Workers?

ASSOCIATED PRESS

Postal Service Considers Cutting 120,000 Jobs

The financially strapped U.S. Postal Service is considering cutting as many as 120,000 jobs.

Facing a second year of losses totaling $8 billion or more, the agency also wants to pull its workers out of the retirement and health benefits plans covering federal workers and set up its own benefit systems.

Congressional approval would be needed for either step, and both could be expected to face severe opposition from postal unions which have contracts that ban layoffs.

The post office has cut 110,000 jobs over the last four years and is currently engaged in eliminating 7,500 administrative staff.

But the loss of mail to the Internet and the decline in advertising caused by the recession have rocked the agency.

Postal officials have said they will be unable to make a $5.5 billion payment to cover future employee health care costs due Sept. 30. It is the only federal agency required to make such a payment but, because of the complex way government finances are counted, eliminating it would make the federal budget deficit appear $5.5 billion larger.

If Congress doesn't act and current losses continue, the post office will be unable to make that payment at the end of September because it will have reached its borrowing limit and simply won't have the cash to do so, the agency said earlier.

In that event, Postmaster General Patrick Donahoe said, "Our intent is to continue to deliver the mail, pay our employees and pay our suppliers."

Postal officials have sought congressional assistance repeatedly over the last few years, including requests to be allowed to end Saturday mail delivery, and several bills have been proposed, but none has been acted on.

In addition the post office recently said it is considering closing 3,653 post offices, stations and other facilities, about one-10th of its offices around the country, in an effort to save money. Offices under consideration for closing are largely rural with little traffic.

And in June the post office suspended contributions to its employees' pension fund, which it said was overfunded.

In its 2010 annual report the post office reported a loss of more than $8 billion on revenues of $67 billion and expenses of $75 billion.

And even while total mail volume fell from 202 billion items to 170 billion from 2008 to 2010 the number of places the agency has to deliver mail increased by 1.7 million as Americans built new homes, offices and businesses.

The latest cutback plans were first reported by *The Washington Post*, which said a notice to employees informing them of its proposals stated: "Financial crisis calls for significant actions; we will be insolvent next month due to significant declines in mail volume and retiree health benefit prefunding costs imposed by Congress."

Key Points in the Article

In 2011, the U.S. Postal Service considered layoffs as a way to deal with a second consecutive year of heavy losses. Officials with the cash-strapped Postal Service stated that it would not be able to make a $5.5 billion payment to its health care plan without cutting its losses. In addition to layoffs, the agency has proposed cutting costs by restructuring its employee retirement and health care plans, eliminating Saturday delivery, and shutting down approximately one-tenth of its offices. Postal officials need congressional approval to move forward with any of these actions, and significant opposition was expected from postal unions and some members of Congress.

Analyzing the News

a The recession and a changing economy help explain the growing losses at the U.S. Postal Service. Many companies are sending fewer advertisements and catalogs to potential customers as a result of the recession. This reduction in through-the-mail advertising has had a direct effect on postal revenues. In addition to the decline in advertisements, the Postal Service has seen a continued decline in the use of first-class mail, with a growing number of customers using the Internet to send and pay bills and as a means of communication.

The postal system is just one area of the economy that is facing declining revenues and mounting debts. The economic recession that began in 2007 and its lingering effects have led to higher unemployment. The figure below shows the unemployment rates in different sectors of the economy during August 2011. The overall unemployment rate was 9.1 percent, much higher than the 4.6 percent in August 2007. The construction sector and the hospitality and leisure sector suffered the most in the economic downturn, with the unemployment rate in each above 10 percent. The health care and education, mining, financial, and government workers sectors were least affected; their unemployment rates were below 6.5 percent.

b Layoffs are not the only cost-cutting measure the Postal Service is considering. Over the past several years, postal officials have proposed ending Saturday delivery service and have recently suggested closing more than 3,600 post offices and other facilities. The Postal Service is a semi-independent federal agency, and its operating expenses are primarily paid for by those who use the service. However, the Postal Service must receive congressional approval to undertake actions such as employee layoffs, delivery schedule changes, and office closings. The need for congressional approval makes it much more difficult and time-consuming for the Postal

Service to proceed with cost-cutting measures than if the service were a private firm.

c The U.S. Postal Service reported a loss of $8 billion in 2010 and expected to lose that much or more in 2011. The recent losses resulted primarily from a drop in the volume of mail being sent, with 32 billion fewer items being mailed in 2010 than in 2008. In addition to this drop in volume, the postal system added an additional 1.7 million new addresses for mail delivery during this time, adding to its costs at a time of declining revenue.

Thinking Critically

1. The article indicates that much of the Postal Service's financial difficulties have arisen due to a decline in advertising and to a loss of mail to the Internet. Assuming that the Postal Service does eliminate 120,000 jobs, would it be best to think of these laid-off workers as being frictionally, structurally, or cyclically unemployed? Briefly explain.

2. The figure indicates that the unemployment rate in the construction sector in August 2011 was 13.5 percent, which was almost 50 percent greater than the overall unemployment rate. Beginning in 2006, housing construction entered a period of decline that some economists believed might last for several years. If housing construction had entered a long-lived period of decline, how should we characterize the unemployment in construction: frictional, structural, cyclical, or some combination of these types?

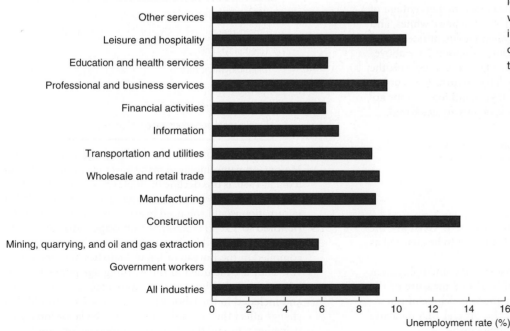

Unemployment rates vary widely across different sectors of the economy.

Chapter Summary and Problems

Key Terms

Consumer price index (CPI), p. 283

Cyclical unemployment, p. 279

Deflation, p. 289

Discouraged workers, p. 269

Efficiency wage, p. 282

Frictional unemployment, p. 278

Inflation rate, p. 283

Labor force, p. 268

Labor force participation rate, p. 269

Menu costs, p. 290

Natural rate of unemployment, p. 279

Nominal interest rate, p. 288

Price level, p. 283

Producer price index (PPI), p. 286

Real interest rate, p. 288

Structural unemployment, p. 279

Unemployment rate, p. 268

9.1 **Measuring the Unemployment Rate, the Labor Force Participation Rate, and the Employment–Population Ratio, pages 268–277**

LEARNING OBJECTIVE: Define the unemployment rate, the labor force participation rate, and the employment–population ratio and understand how they are computed.

Summary

The U.S. Bureau of Labor Statistics uses the results of the monthly household survey to calculate the *unemployment rate*, the *labor force participation rate*, and the *employment–population ratio*. The **labor force** is the total number of people who have jobs plus the number of people who do not have jobs but are actively looking for them. The **unemployment rate** is the percentage of the labor force that is unemployed. **Discouraged workers** are people who are available for work but who are not actively looking for a job because they believe no jobs are available for them. Discouraged workers are not counted as unemployed. The **labor force participation rate** is the percentage of the working-age population in the labor force. Since 1950, the labor force participation rate of women has been rising, while the labor force participation rate of men has been falling. The employment–population ratio measures the percentage of the working-age population that is employed. Asians, whites, and college graduates have below-average unemployment rates. African Americans, Hispanics, and high school dropouts have above-average unemployment rates. Except during severe recessions, the typical unemployed person finds a new job or returns to his or her previous job within a few months. Each year, millions of jobs are created in the United States, and millions of jobs are destroyed.

 Visit **www.myeconlab.com** to complete these exercises online and get instant feedback.

Review Questions

1.1 How is the unemployment rate measured? What are the three conditions someone needs to meet to be counted as unemployed?

1.2 What are the problems in measuring the unemployment rate? In what ways does the official BLS measure of the unemployment rate understate the true degree of unemployment? In what ways does the official BLS measure overstate the true degree of unemployment?

1.3 Which groups tend to have above-average unemployment rates, and which groups tend to have below-average unemployment rates?

1.4 What does the labor force participation rate measure? Since 1950, how have the labor force participation rates of men and women changed?

1.5 What does the employment-population ratio measure? How does an unemployed person dropping out of the labor force affect the unemployment rate? How does it affect the employment-population ratio?

1.6 What is the difference between the household survey and the establishment survey? Which survey do many economists prefer for measuring changes in employment? Why?

Problems and Applications

1.7 Fill in the missing values in the following table of data collected in the household survey for September 2011:

Working-age population	
Employment	140,025,000
Unemployment	
Unemployment rate	9.1%
Labor force	
Labor force participation rate	64.2%
Employment-population ratio	

1.8 **[Related to the** Chapter Opener **on page 641]** The Ford Motor Company employed many fewer people in 2011 than it did in 1980. Is this decline in employment frictional, structural, cyclical, or some combination of these factors? What information would you need to arrive at a definite answer?

1.9 **[Related to** Solved Problem 9.1 **on page 270]** Homemakers are not included in the employment or labor force totals compiled in the Bureau of Labor Statistics household survey. They are included in the working-age population totals. Suppose that homemakers were counted as employed and included in the labor force statistics. How would that change affect the unemployment rate, the labor force participation rate, and the employment–population ratio?

1.10 Look again at Table 9.1 on page 276. Between August and September 2011, the household survey shows that the total number of people employed increased by 398,000. Yet the unemployment rate remained the same. Shouldn't the unemployment rate fall when the number of people employed increases? Briefly explain.

1.11 **[Related to the** Making the Connection **on page 274]** An article published in the *New York Times* in July 2011 argued that: "For the second straight year, the recovery in the job market has essentially stalled. This chart, showing the share of adults with jobs, offers the best summary you'll find." The "share of adults with jobs" is known more formally as the employment-population ratio. Why might the employment-population ratio provide the "best summary" of the state of the job market rather than the unemployment rate?

Based on David Leonhardt, "Overly Optimistic, Once Again," *New York Times*, July 8, 2011.

1.12 Is it possible for the total number of people who are unemployed to increase while the unemployment rate decreases? Briefly explain.

1.13 In a speech delivered in the summer of 2011, President Barack Obama observed, "Even though the economy is growing, even though it's created more than two million jobs over the past 15 months, we still face some tough times." Is it likely that the U.S. economy created only about two million jobs during this time period? If not, what was President Obama referring to?

Based on Catherine Rampell, "Hiring in U.S. Slowed in May With 54,000 Jobs Added," *New York Times*, June 3, 2011.

9.2 **Types of Unemployment, pages 277–280**
LEARNING OBJECTIVE: Identify the three types of unemployment.

Summary

There are three types of unemployment: frictional, structural, and cyclical. **Frictional unemployment** is short-term unemployment that arises from the process of matching workers with jobs. One type of frictional unemployment is *seasonal unemployment*, which refers to unemployment due to factors such as weather, variations in tourism, and other calendar-related events. **Structural unemployment** arises from a persistent mismatch between the job skills or attributes of workers and the requirements of jobs. **Cyclical unemployment** is caused by a business cycle recession. The **natural rate of unemployment** is the normal rate of unemployment, consisting of structural unemployment and frictional unemployment. The natural rate of unemployment is also sometimes called the *full-employment rate of unemployment*.

 Visit **www.myeconlab.com** to complete these exercises online and get instant feedback.

Review Questions

2.1 What are the three types of unemployment?
2.2 What is the relationship between frictional unemployment and job search?
2.3 What is the natural rate of unemployment? What is the relationship between the natural rate of unemployment and full employment? Would it be better for economists

to define full employment as being an unemployment rate equal to zero?

Problems and Applications

2.4 Macroeconomic conditions affect the decisions firms and families make. Why, for example, might a student graduating from college enter the job market during an economic expansion but apply for graduate school during a recession?
2.5 A politician makes the following argument: "The economy would operate more efficiently if frictional unemployment were eliminated. Therefore, a goal of government policy should be to reduce the frictional rate of unemployment to the lowest possible level." Briefly explain whether you agree with this argument.
2.6 **[Related to the** Making the Connection **on page 279]** What advice for finding a job would you give someone who is frictionally unemployed? What advice would you give someone who is structurally unemployed? What advice would you give someone who is cyclically unemployed?
2.7 Recall from Chapter 3 the definitions of *normal goods* and *inferior goods*. During an economic expansion, would you rather be working in an industry that produces a normal good or in an industry that produces an inferior good? Why? During a recession, would you rather be working in an industry that produces a normal good or an inferior good? Why?

9.3 **Explaining Unemployment, pages 280–282**
LEARNING OBJECTIVE: Explain what factors determine the unemployment rate.

Summary

Government policies can reduce the level of frictional and structural unemployment by aiding the search for jobs and the retraining of workers. Some government policies, however, can add to the level of frictional and structural unemployment. Unemployment insurance payments can raise the unemployment rate by extending the time that unemployed workers search for jobs. Government policies have caused the unemployment rates in most other high-income countries typically to be higher than in the United

States. Wages above market levels can also increase unemployment. Wages may be above market levels because of the minimum wage, labor unions, and *efficiency wages*. An **efficiency wage** is a higher-than-market wage that a firm pays to increase worker productivity.

MyEconLab Visit **www.myeconlab.com** to complete these exercises online and get instant feedback.

Review Questions

3.1 What effect does the payment of government unemployment insurance have on the unemployment rate? On the severity of recessions?

3.2 Discuss the effect of each of the following on the unemployment rate.
 a. The federal minimum wage law
 b. Labor unions
 c. Efficiency wages

3.3 Why has the unemployment rate in the United States typically been lower than the unemployment rates in Canada and countries in Western Europe?

Problems and Applications

3.4 In 2007, Ségolène Royal, who was running unsuccessfully for president of France, proposed that workers who lost their jobs would receive unemployment payments equal to 90 percent of their previous wages during their first year of unemployment. If this proposal were enacted, what would likely be the effect on the unemployment rate in France? Briefly explain.

Based on Alessandra Galloni and David Gauthier-Villars, "France's Royal Introduces Platform Ahead of Election," *Wall Street Journal*, February 12, 2007.

3.5 If Congress eliminated the unemployment insurance system, what would be the effect on the level of frictional unemployment? What would be the effect on the level of real GDP? Would well-being in the economy be increased? Briefly explain.

3.6 Discuss the likely effect of each of the following on the unemployment rate:
 a. The length of time workers are eligible to receive unemployment insurance payments doubles.
 b. The minimum wage is abolished.
 c. Most U.S. workers join labor unions.
 d. More companies make information on job openings easily available on Internet job sites.

3.7 Why do you think the minimum wage was set at only $0.25 per hour in 1938? Wouldn't this wage have been well below the equilibrium wage?

3.8 An economic consultant studies the labor policies of a firm where it is difficult to monitor workers and prepares a report in which she recommends that the firm raise employee wages. At a meeting of the firm's managers to discuss the report, one manager makes the following argument: "I think the wages we are paying are fine. As long as enough people are willing to work here at the wages we are currently paying, why should we raise them?" What argument can the economic consultant make to justify her advice that the firm should increase its wages?

3.9 Costco typically pays its workers higher wages than does Wal-Mart. One analyst argues that Costco pays higher wages "because it requires higher-skilled workers to sell higher-cost products to more affluent customers." If this analyst is correct, can we conclude that Costco is paying efficiency wages and Wal-Mart is not? Briefly explain.

Based on Loti Montgomery, "Maverick Costco CEO Joins Push to Raise Minimum Wage," *Washington Post*, January 30, 2007.

9.4	**Measuring Inflation,** pages 282–286

LEARNING OBJECTIVE: Define price level and inflation rate and understand how they are computed.

Summary

The **price level** measures the average prices of goods and services. The **inflation rate** is equal to the percentage change in the price level from one year to the next. The federal government compiles statistics on three different measures of the price level: the consumer price index (CPI), the GDP price deflator, and the producer price index (PPI). The **consumer price index (CPI)** is an average of the prices of goods and services purchased by the typical urban family of four. Changes in the CPI are the best measure of changes in the cost of living as experienced by the typical household. Biases in the construction of the CPI cause changes in it to overstate the true inflation rate by 0.5 percentage point to 1 percentage point. The **producer price index (PPI)** is an average of prices received by producers of goods and services at all stages of production.

 Visit **www.myeconlab.com** to complete these exercises online and get instant feedback.

Review Questions

4.1 Briefly describe the three major measures of the price level.

4.2 Which price index does the government use to measure changes in the cost of living?

4.3 What potential biases exist in calculating the consumer price index? What steps has the Bureau of Labor Statistics taken to reduce the size of the biases?

4.4 What is the difference between the consumer price index and the producer price index?

Problems and Applications

4.5 [**Related to the** Don't Let This Happen to You **on page 285**] Briefly explain whether you agree or disagree with the following statement: "I don't believe the government price statistics. The CPI for 2010 was 218, but I know that the inflation rate couldn't have been as high as 118 percent in 2010."

4.6 In calculating the consumer price index for the year, why does the BLS use the quantities in the market basket, rather than the quantities purchased during the current year?

4.7 In October 2011, Apple introduced the iPhone 4S, which had new features, including an improved camera and voice control, but sold at the same price as the previous iPhone model. How was the consumer price index affected by the introduction of the iPhone 4S?

Based on Ian Sherr and Greg Bensinger, "New Apple iPhone Snared Big Sales on First Weekend," *Wall Street Journal*, October 18, 2011.

4.8 Consider a simple economy that produces only three products: haircuts, hamburgers, and DVDs. Use the information in the following table to calculate the inflation rate for 2010, as measured by the consumer price index.

Product	Base Year (1999) Quantity	Base Year (1999) Price	2011 Price	2012 Price
Haircuts	2	$10.00	$11.00	$16.20
Hamburgers	10	2.00	2.45	2.40
DVDs	6	15.00	15.00	14.00

4.9 The Standard & Poor's/Case-Shiller Home Price Index is one of the leading indicators of housing price trends in the

United States. The base year for the index is January 2000. The following table lists index numbers for July 2010 and July 2011 for five cities:

City	July 2010	July 2011
New York	173.8	167.2
Miami	147.5	140.7
Phoenix	109.51	99.8
Dallas	117.8	114.0
San Diego	162.6	152.9

a. Calculate the percentage change in housing prices from July 2010 to July 2011 for each of these five cities. In which city did housing prices change the most? The least?

b. Can you determine on the basis of these numbers which city had the most expensive homes in July 2011? Briefly explain.

Data from "S&P/Case-Shiller Home Price Indices," *Standard & Poor's Financial Services, LLC*, September 2011.

9.5 | Using Price Indexes to Adjust for the Effects of Inflation, pages 286–288

LEARNING OBJECTIVE: Use price indexes to adjust for the effects of inflation.

Summary

Price indexes are designed to measure changes in the price level over time, not the absolute level of prices. To correct for the effects of inflation, we can divide a *nominal variable* by a price index and multiply by 100 to obtain a *real variable*. The real variable will be measured in dollars of the base year for the price index.

 MyEconLab Visit **www.myeconlab.com** to complete these exercises online and get instant feedback.

Review Questions

5.1 What is the difference between a nominal variable and a real variable?

5.2 Briefly explain how you can use data on nominal wages for 2004 to 2011 and data on the consumer price index for the same years to calculate the real wage for these years.

Problems and Applications

5.3 **[Related to** Solved Problem 9.5 **on page 287]** In 1924, the famous novelist F. Scott Fitzgerald wrote an article for the *Saturday Evening Post* titled "How to Live on $36,000 a Year," in which he wondered how he and his wife had managed to spend all of that very high income without saving any of it. The CPI in 1924 was 17, and the CPI in 2010 was 218. What income would you have needed in 2010 to have had the same purchasing power that Fitzgerald's $36,000 had in 1924? Be sure to show your calculation.

From F. Scott Fitzgerald, "How to Live on $36,000 a Year," *Saturday Evening Post*, April 5, 1924.

5.4 **[Related to** Solved Problem 9.5 **on page 287]** Use the information in the following table to determine the percentage changes in the U.S. and French *real* minimum wages between 1957 and 2010. Does it matter for your answer that you have not been told the base year for the U.S. CPI or the French CPI? Was the percentage increase in the price level greater in the United States or in France during these years?

	United States		France	
Year	Minimum Wage (dollars per hour)	CPI	Minimum Wage (euros per hour)	CPI
1957	$1.00	27	€0.19	10
2010	7.25	215	8.86	128

Based on John M. Abowd, Francis Kramarz, Thomas Lemieux, and David N. Margolis, "Minimum Wages and Youth Employment in France and the United States," in D. Blanchflower and R. Freeman, eds., *Youth Employment and Joblessness in Advanced Countries*, (Chicago: University of Chicago Press, 1999), pp. 427–472 (the value for the minimum wage is given in francs; it was converted to euros at a conversion rate of 1 euro = 6.55957 francs); Insee online data bank, www.insee.fr; U.S. Department of Labor; and U.S. Bureau of Labor Statistics.

5.5 **[Related to** Solved Problem 9.5 **on page 287]** The Great Depression was the worst economic disaster in U.S. history in terms of declines in real GDP and increases in the unemployment rate. Use the data in the table on the next page to calculate the percentage decline in real GDP between 1929 and 1933:

Year	Nominal GDP (billions of dollars)	GDP Price Deflator 2005 = 100
1929	$103.6	10.6
1933	56.4	7.9

5.6 [Related to Solved Problem 9.5 **on page 287**] The following table shows the top 10 films of all time through October 2011, measured by box office receipts in the United States, as well as several other notable films farther down the list.

The CPI in 2010 was 218. Use this information and the data in the table to calculate the box office receipts for each film in 2010 dollars. Assume that each film generated all of its box office receipts during the year it was released. Use your results to prepare a new list of the top 10 films, based on their earnings in 2010 dollars. (Some of the films, such as the first *Star Wars* film, *Gone with the Wind*, and *Snow White and the Seven Dwarfs*, were re-released several times, so their receipts were actually earned during several different years, but we will ignore that complication.)

Data from The Internet Movie database, www.imdb.com.

Rank	Film	Total Box Office Receipts	Year Released	CPI
1	Avatar	$760,505,847	2009	215
2	Titanic	$600,779,824	1997	161
3	The Dark Knight	533,316,061	2008	215
4	Star Wars	460,935,655	1977	61
5	Shrek 2	436,471,036	2004	189
6	E.T.: The Extra-Terrestrial	434,949,459	1982	97
7	Star Wars: Episode I—The Phantom Menace	431,065,444	1999	167
8	Pirates of the Caribbean: Dead Man's Chest	423,032,628	2006	202
9	Toy Story 3	414,984,497	2010	218
10	Spider-Man	403,706,375	2002	180
56	Jaws	260,000,000	1975	54
115	Gone with the Wind	198,655,278	1939	14
130	Snow White and the Seven Dwarfs	184,925,485	1937	14
187	The Sound of Music	163,214,286	1965	32
212	One Hundred and One Dalmatians	153,000,000	1961	30

9.6 **Real versus Nominal Interest Rates,** pages 288–289

LEARNING OBJECTIVE: Distinguish between the nominal interest rate and the real interest rate.

Summary

The stated interest rate on a loan is the **nominal interest rate**. The **real interest rate** is the nominal interest rate minus the inflation rate. Because it is corrected for the effects of inflation, the real interest rate provides a better measure of the true cost of borrowing and the true return from lending than does the nominal interest rate. The nominal interest rate is always greater than the real interest rate unless the economy experiences *deflation*. **Deflation** is a decline in the price level.

MyEconLab Visit **www.myeconlab.com** to complete these exercises online and get instant feedback.

Review Questions

6.1 What is the difference between the nominal interest rate and the real interest rate?

6.2 If inflation is expected to increase, what will happen to the nominal interest rate? Briefly explain.

6.3 The chapter explains that it is impossible to know whether a particular nominal interest rate is "high" or "low." Briefly explain why.

6.4 If the economy is experiencing deflation, will the nominal interest rate be higher or lower than the real interest rate?

Problems and Applications

6.5 The following appeared in a newspaper article: "Inflation in the Lehigh Valley during the first quarter of [the year] was less than half the national rate. . . . So, unlike much of the nation, the fear here is deflation—when prices sink so low the CPI drops below zero." Do you agree with the reporter's definition of *deflation*? Briefly explain.

From Dan Shope, "Valley's Inflation Rate Slides," *Morning Call* (Allentown, PA), July 9, 1996.

6.6 Suppose you were borrowing money to buy a car. Which of these situations would you prefer: The interest rate on your car loan is 20 percent and the inflation rate is 19 percent or the interest rate on your car loan is 5 percent and the inflation rate is 2 percent? Briefly explain.

6.7 Describing the situation in England in 1920, the historian Robert Skidelsky wrote the following: "Who would not borrow at 4 percent a year, with prices going up 4 percent a *month*?" What was the real interest rate paid by borrowers in this situation? (*Hint:* What is the annual inflation rate, if the monthly inflation rate is 4 percent?)

Based on Robert Skidelsky, John Maynard Keynes: Volume 2, The Economist as Saviour 1920–1937, (New York: The Penguin Press), 1992, p. 39.

6.8 Suppose that the only good you purchase is hamburgers and that at the beginning of the year, the price of a hamburger is $2.00. Suppose you lend $1,000 for one year at an interest rate of 5 percent. At the end of the year, a hamburger costs $2.08. What is the real rate of interest you earned on your loan?

6.9 During the 1990s, Japan experienced periods of deflation and low nominal interest rates that approached zero percent. Why would lenders of funds agree to a nominal interest rate of almost zero percent? (Hint: Were real interest rates in Japan also low during this period?)

9.7 | Does Inflation Impose Costs on the Economy? pages 289–292

LEARNING OBJECTIVE: Discuss the problems that inflation causes.

Summary

Inflation does not reduce the affordability of goods and services to the average consumer, but it does impose costs on the economy. When inflation is anticipated, its main costs are that paper money loses some of its value and firms incur *menu costs*. **Menu costs** include the costs of changing prices on products and printing new catalogs. When inflation is unanticipated, the actual inflation rate can turn out to be different from the expected inflation rate. As a result, income is redistributed as some people gain and some people lose.

 MyEconLab Visit **www.myeconlab.com** to complete these exercises online and get instant feedback.

Review Questions

7.1 Why do nominal incomes generally increase with inflation? If nominal incomes increase with inflation, does inflation reduce the purchasing power of the average consumer? Briefly explain.

7.2 How can inflation affect the distribution of income?

7.3 Which is a greater problem: anticipated inflation or unanticipated inflation? Briefly explain.

7.4 What problems does deflation cause?

Problems and Applications

7.5 What are menu costs? What effect has the Internet had on the size of menu costs?

7.6 Suppose that the inflation rate turns out to be much higher than most people expected. In that case, would you rather have been a borrower or a lender? Briefly explain.

7.7 Suppose James and Frank both retire this year. For income from retirement, James will rely on a pension from his company that pays him a fixed $2,500 per month for as long as he lives. James hasn't saved anything for retirement. Frank has no pension but has saved a considerable amount, which he has invested in certificates of deposit (CDs) at his bank. Currently, Frank's CDs pay him interest of $2,300 per month.

a. Ten years from now, is James or Frank likely to have a higher real income? In your answer, be sure to define *real income*.

b. Now suppose that instead of being a constant amount, James's pension increases each year by the same percentage as the CPI. For example, if the CPI increases by 5 percent in the first year after James retires, then his pension in the second year equals $2,500 + ($2,500 × 0.05) = $2,625. In this case, 10 years from now, is James or Frank likely to have a higher real income?

7.8 Suppose that News Corporation, the owner of the *Wall Street Journal*, and the investors buying the firm's bonds both expect a 2 percent inflation rate for the year. Given this expectation, suppose the nominal interest rate on the bonds is 6 percent and the real interest rate is 4 percent. Suppose that a year after the investors purchase the bonds, the inflation rate turns out to be 6 percent, rather than the 2 percent that had been expected. Who gains and who loses from the unexpectedly high inflation rate?

7.9 [Related to the Making the Connection on page 291] During the late nineteenth century in the United States, many farmers borrowed heavily to buy land. During most of the period between 1870 and the mid-1890s, the United States experienced mild deflation: The price level declined each year. Many farmers engaged in political protests during these years, and deflation was often a subject of their protests. Explain why farmers would have felt burdened by deflation.

Economic Growth, the Financial System, and Business Cycles

Chapter Outline and Learning Objectives

Growth and the Business Cycle at Boeing

In December 1903, at Kitty Hawk, North Carolina, the Wright Flyer became the first human-piloted, machine-powered, heavier-than-air craft to fly—for all of 12 seconds and a distance of 120 feet. Roughly a century later, on November 10, 2005, the Boeing 777-200LR became the first commercial aircraft to fly nonstop more than halfway around the world—for 22 hours and 42 minutes, across 13,422 miles. This tremendous advance in aviation technology has been matched by technological progress in many other areas of the economy. In this chapter, we begin to explore how technological change has affected the standard of living in the United States and elsewhere around the world.

William Boeing established the Boeing Company in 1916. Today, Boeing is one of the world's largest manufacturers of commercial jetliners, military aircraft, satellites, missiles, and defense systems. The company employs more than 165,000 people in 70 countries. Boeing's experiences have often mirrored two key macroeconomic facts: In the long run, the U.S. economy has experienced economic growth, and in the short run, the economy has experienced a series of business cycles. Boeing has also experienced growth over the long run, while being affected by the business cycle.

In 2007, Boeing received a record 1,413 orders for new commercial jets, as the United States and much of the rest of the world was experiencing a period of strong economic growth. As the U.S. and world economies entered a recession in 2008, Boeing's orders fell to 662, and then plummeted to 142 in 2009. As the economy improved in 2010, Boeing's orders rebounded to 530. In 2011, Randy Tinseth, vice president for marketing at Boeing Commercial Airplanes, predicted that, despite the recent short-run swings in orders, long-run prospects for the airline industry were good: "Not only is there strong demand for air travel and new airplanes today, but the fundamental drivers of air travel—including economic growth, world trade and liberalization—all point to a healthy long-term demand."

In this chapter, we provide an overview of long-run growth and the business cycle and discuss their importance for firms, for consumers, and for the economy as a whole.

Read **AN INSIDE LOOK** on **page 330** for a discussion of how the International Air Transport Association uses projected global GDP numbers to forecast lower profits in the airline industry during 2012.

Based on David Pearson, "Boeing Sees Rising Aircraft Demand," *Wall Street Journal*, June 16, 2011; Julie Johnson, "Boeing Aircraft Orders Rebound in 2010," *Chicago Tribune*, January 6, 2011; and James Wallace, "Boeing 777 Stretches Its Wings, Record," *Seattle Post Intelligencer*, November 11, 2005.

Economics in Your Life

Do You Help the Economy More if You Spend or if You Save?

Suppose that you have received an income tax refund check from the U.S. government. You are not sure what to do with the money, so you ask your two roommates for advice. One roommate tells you that if you want to help the economy, you should save all the money because a country's economic growth depends on the amount of saving by households. The other roommate disagrees and advises you to spend all the money because consumer spending is a major component of gross domestic product (GDP), and your spending would help increase production and create more jobs. Which of your two roommates is right? As you read this chapter, see if you can answer this question. You can check your answer against the one we provide on **page 328** at the end of this chapter.

A successful economy is capable of increasing production of goods and services faster than the growth in population. Attaining this level of growth is the only way that the standard of living of the average person in a country can increase. Unfortunately, many economies around the world are not growing at all or are growing very slowly. Most people in those countries live on about the same levels of income as their ancestors did decades, or even centuries, ago. In the United States and other developed countries, however, incomes and living standards are much higher today than they were 50 years ago. An important macroeconomic topic is why some countries grow much faster than others.

As we will see, one determinant of economic growth is the ability of firms to expand their operations, buy additional equipment, train workers, and adopt new technologies. To carry out these activities, firms must acquire funds from households, either directly through financial markets—such as the stock and bond markets—or indirectly through financial intermediaries—such as banks. Financial markets and financial intermediaries together comprise the *financial system*. In this chapter, we present an overview of the financial system and see how funds flow from households to firms through the *market for loanable funds*.

Business cycle Alternating periods of economic expansion and economic recession.

Since at least the early nineteenth century, the U.S. economy has experienced periods of expanding production and employment followed by periods of recession during which production and employment decline. As we noted in Chapter 8, these alternating periods of expansion and recession are called the **business cycle**. The business cycle is not uniform: Each period of expansion is not the same length, nor is each period of recession, but every period of expansion in U.S. history has been followed by a period of recession, and every period of recession has been followed by a period of expansion.

In this chapter, we begin to explore two key aspects of macroeconomics: the long-run growth that has steadily raised living standards in the United States and the short-run fluctuations of the business cycle.

Long-Run Economic Growth

Most people in the United States, Western Europe, Japan, and other high-income countries expect that over time, their standard of living will improve. They expect that year after year, firms will introduce new and improved products, new prescription drugs and better surgical techniques will overcome more diseases, and their ability to afford these goods and services will increase. For most people, these are reasonable expectations.

In 1900, the United States was already enjoying the highest standard of living in the world. Yet in that year, only 3 percent of U.S. homes had electricity, only 15 percent had indoor flush toilets, and only 25 percent had running water. The lack of running water meant that before people could cook or bathe, they had to pump water from wells and haul it to their homes in buckets—on average about 10,000 gallons per year per family. Not surprisingly, water consumption averaged only about 5 gallons per person per day, compared with about 150 gallons today. The result was that people washed themselves and their clothing only infrequently. A majority of families living in cities had to use outdoor toilets, which they shared with other families. Diseases such as smallpox, typhus, dysentery, and cholera were still common. In 1900, 5,000 of the 45,000 children born in Chicago died before their first birthday. Life expectancy at birth was about 47 years, compared with 78 years in 2011. Few families had electric lights, relying instead on the limited illumination provided by burning candles or burning kerosene or coal oil in lamps. Many homes were heated in the winter by burning coal, which contributed to

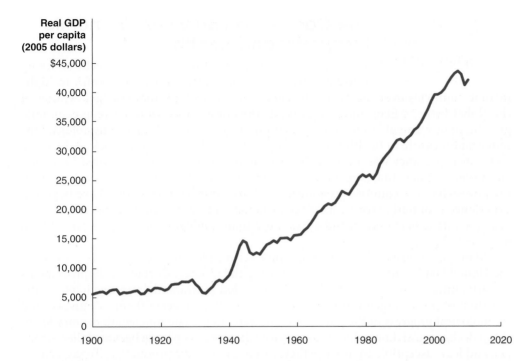

Figure 10.1

The Growth in Real GDP per Capita, 1900–2010

Measured in 2005 dollars, real GDP per capita in the United States grew from about $5,600 in 1900 to about $42,200 in 2010. The average American in the year 2010 could buy nearly eight times as many goods and services as the average American in the year 1900.

Data from Louis D. Johnston and Samuel H. Williamson, "What Was the U.S. GDP Then?" MeasuringWorth, 2011; and U.S. Bureau of Economic Analysis.

the severe pollution that fouled the air of most large cities. There were no modern appliances, and most women worked inside the home at least 80 hours per week. The typical American homemaker in 1900 baked a half-ton of bread per year.

The process of **long-run economic growth** brought the typical American from the standard of living of 1900 to the standard of living of today. The best measure of the standard of living is real GDP per person, which is usually referred to as *real GDP per capita*. So, we measure long-run economic growth by increases in real GDP per capita over long periods of time, generally decades or more. We use real GDP rather than nominal GDP to adjust for changes in the price level over time. Figure 10.1 shows the growth in real GDP per capita in the United States from 1900 to 2010. The figure shows that although real GDP per capita fluctuates because of the short-run effects of the business cycle, over the long run, the trend is strongly upward. It is the upward trend in real GDP per capita that we focus on when discussing long-run economic growth.

The values in Figure 10.1 are measured in prices of the year 2005, so they represent constant amounts of purchasing power. In 1900, real GDP per capita was about $5,600. Over a century later, in 2010, it had risen to about $42,200, which means that the average American in 2010 could purchase nearly eight times as many goods and services as the average American in 1900. Large as it is, this increase in real GDP per capita actually understates the true increase in the standard of living of Americans in 2010 compared with 1900. Many of today's goods and services were not available in 1900. For example, if you lived in 1900 and became ill with a serious infection, you would have been unable to purchase antibiotics to treat your illness—no matter how high your income. You might have died from an illness for which even a very poor person in today's society could receive effective medical treatment. Of course, the quantity of goods and services that a person can buy is not a perfect measure of how happy or contented that person may be. The level of education, life expectancy, crime, spiritual well-being, pollution, and many other factors ignored in calculating GDP contribute to a person's happiness. Nevertheless, economists rely heavily on comparisons of real GDP per capita because it is the best means of comparing the performance of one economy over time or the performance of different economies at any particular time.

Long-run economic growth The process by which rising productivity increases the average standard of living.

Making
the
Connection

The Connection between Economic Prosperity and Health

We can see the direct effect of economic growth on living standards by looking at improvements in health in high-income countries over the past 100 years. The research of Robert Fogel, winner of the Nobel Prize in Economics, highlights the close connection between economic growth, improvements in technology, and improvements in human physiology. One important measure of health is life expectancy at birth. As the graph below shows, in 1900, life expectancy was less than 50 years in the United States, the United Kingdom, and France. Today, life expectancy is about 80 years. Although life expectancies in the lowest-income countries remain very short, some countries that have begun to experience economic growth have seen dramatic increases in life expectancies. For example, life expectancy in India has more than doubled from 27 years in 1900 to 67 years today.

Many economists believe there is a link between health and economic growth. In the United States and Western Europe during the nineteenth century, improvements in agricultural technology and rising incomes led to dramatic improvements in the nutrition of the average person. The development of the germ theory of disease and technological progress in the purification of water in the late nineteenth century led to sharp declines in sickness due to waterborne diseases. As people became taller, stronger, and less susceptible to disease, they also became more productive. Today, economists studying economic development have put increasing emphasis on the need for low-income countries to reduce disease and increase nutrition if they are to experience economic growth.

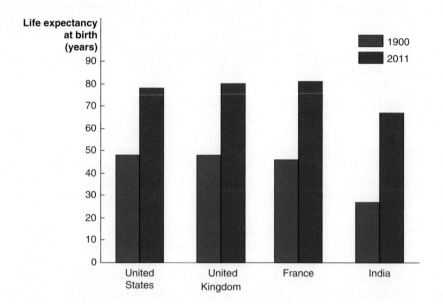

Many researchers believe that the state of human physiology will continue to improve as technology advances. In high-income countries, life expectancy at birth is expected to rise from about 80 years today to about 90 years by the middle of the twenty-first century. Technological advances will continue to reduce the average number of hours worked per day and the number of years the average person spends in the paid workforce. Individuals spend about 10 hours per day sleeping, eating, and bathing. Their remaining "discretionary hours" are divided between paid work and leisure. The graph on the next page is based on estimates by Robert Fogel that contrast how individuals in the United States will divide their time in 2040 compared with 1880 and 1995. Not only will technology and economic growth allow people in the near future to live longer lives, but a much smaller fraction of those lives will need to be spent at paid work.

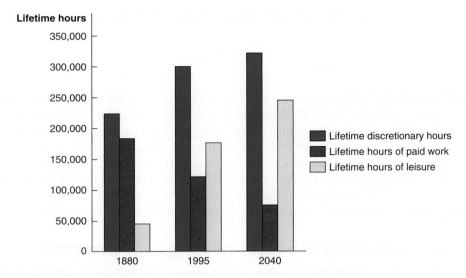

Based on Robert William Fogel, *The Escape from Hunger and Premature Death, 1700–2100*, (New York: Cambridge University Press, 2004); and U.S. Central Intelligence Agency, *The 2011 World Factbook*, online version.

Your Turn: Test your understanding by doing related problem 1.8 on page 332 at the end of this chapter.

MyEconLab

Calculating Growth Rates and the Rule of 70

The growth rate of real GDP or real GDP per capita during a particular year is equal to the percentage change from the previous year. For example, measured in prices of the year 2005, real GDP equaled $12,703 billion in 2009 and rose to $13,088 billion in 2010. We calculate the growth of real GDP in 2010 as:

$$\left(\frac{\$13,088 \text{ billion} - \$12,703 \text{ billion}}{\$12,703 \text{ billion}} \right) \times 100 = 3.0\%.$$

For longer periods of time, we can use the *average annual growth rate*. For example, real GDP in the United States was $2,004 billion in 1950 and $13,088 billion in 2010. To find the average annual growth rate during this 60-year period, we compute the annual growth rate that would result in $2,004 billion increasing to $13,088 billion over 60 years. In this case, the growth rate is 3.2 percent. That is, if $2,004 billion grows at an average rate of 3.2 percent per year, after 60 years, it will have grown to $13,088 billion.

For shorter periods of time, we get approximately the same answer by averaging the growth rate for each year. For example, real GDP in the United States *fell* by 0.3 percent in 2008, *fell* by 3.5 percent in 2009, and grew by 3.0 percent in 2010. So, the average annual growth rate of real GDP for the period 2008–2010 was −0.3 percent, which is the average of the three annual growth rates:

$$\frac{-0.3\% + (-3.5\%) + 3.0\%}{3} = -0.3\%$$

Note that during this period, the "growth" rate was actually negative because real GDP declined during the recession years of 2008 and 2009. Finally, when discussing long-run economic growth, we usually shorten "average annual growth rate" to "growth rate."

We can judge how rapidly an economic variable is growing by calculating the number of years it would take to double. For example, if real GDP per capita in a country doubles, say, every 20 years, most people in the country will experience significant increases in their standard of living over the course of their lives. If real GDP per capita doubles only every 100 years, increases in the standard of living will occur too slowly to notice. One easy way to calculate approximately how many years it will take real GDP per capita to double is to use the *rule of 70*. The formula for the rule of 70 is as follows:

$$\text{Number of years to double} = \frac{70}{\text{Growth rate}}.$$

For example, if real GDP per capita is growing at a rate of 5 percent per year, it will double in $70/5 = 14$ years. If real GDP per capita is growing at a rate of 2 percent per year, it will take $70/2 = 35$ years to double. These examples illustrate an important point that we will discuss further in Chapter 11: Small differences in growth rates can have large effects on how rapidly the standard of living in a country increases. Finally, notice that the rule of 70 applies not just to growth in real GDP per capita but to growth in any variable. For example, if you invest $1,000 in the stock market, and your investment grows at an average annual rate of 7 percent, your investment will double to $2,000 in 10 years.

What Determines the Rate of Long-Run Growth?

Labor productivity The quantity of goods and services that can be produced by one worker or by one hour of work.

In Chapter 11, we will explore the sources of economic growth in more detail and discuss why growth in the United States and other high-income countries has been so much faster than growth in low-income countries. For now, we will focus on the basic point that *increases in real GDP per capita depend on increases in labor productivity*. **Labor productivity** is the quantity of goods and services that can be produced by one worker or by one hour of work. In analyzing long-run growth, economists usually measure labor productivity as output per hour of work to avoid the effects of fluctuations in the length of the workday and in the fraction of the population employed. If the quantity of goods and services consumed by the average person is to increase, the quantity of goods and services produced per hour of work must also increase. Why in 2010 was the average American able to consume almost eight times as many goods and services as the average American in 1900? Because the average American worker in 2010 was eight times as productive as the average American worker in 1900.

If increases in labor productivity are the key to long-run economic growth, what causes labor productivity to increase? Economists believe two key factors determine labor productivity: the quantity of capital per hour worked and the level of technology. Therefore, economic growth occurs if the quantity of capital per hour worked increases and if technological change occurs.

Capital Manufactured goods that are used to produce other goods and services.

Increases in Capital per Hour Worked

Workers today in high-income countries such as the United States have more physical capital available than workers in low-income countries or workers in the high-income countries of 100 years ago. Recall that **capital** refers to manufactured goods that are used to produce other goods and services. Examples of capital are computers, factory buildings, machine tools, warehouses, and trucks. The total amount of physical capital available in a country is known as the country's *capital stock*.

As the capital stock per hour worked increases, worker productivity increases. A secretary who uses a personal computer can produce more documents per day than a secretary who uses only a typewriter. A worker who uses a backhoe can excavate more earth than a worker who uses only a shovel.

Human capital refers to the accumulated knowledge and skills workers acquire from education and training or from their life experiences. For example, workers with a college education generally have more skills and are more productive than workers who have only a high school degree. Increases in human capital are particularly important in stimulating economic growth.

Technological Change

Economic growth depends more on *technological change* than on increases in capital per hour worked. *Technology* refers to the processes a firm uses to turn inputs into outputs of goods and services. Technological change is an increase in the quantity of output firms can produce, using a given quantity of inputs. Technological change can come from many sources. For example, a firm's managers may rearrange a factory floor or the layout of a retail store to increase production and sales. Most technological change, however, is embodied in new machinery, equipment, or software.

A very important point is that just accumulating more inputs—such as labor, capital, and natural resources—will not ensure that an economy experiences economic growth unless technological change also occurs. For example, the Soviet Union failed to maintain a high rate of economic growth, even though it continued to increase the quantity of capital available per hour worked, because it experienced relatively little technological change.

In implementing technological change, *entrepreneurs* are of crucial importance. Recall from Chapter 2 that an entrepreneur is someone who operates a business, bringing together the factors of production—labor, capital, and natural resources—to produce goods and services. In a market economy, entrepreneurs make the crucial decisions about whether to introduce new technology to produce better or lower-cost products. Entrepreneurs also decide whether to allocate a firm's resources to research and development that can result in new technologies. One of the difficulties centrally planned economies have in sustaining economic growth is that managers employed by the government are usually much slower to develop and adopt new technologies than entrepreneurs in a market system.

Solved Problem 10.1

The Role of Technological Change in Growth

Between 1960 and 1995, real GDP per capita in Singapore grew at an average annual rate of 6.2 percent. This very rapid growth rate results in the level of real GDP per capita doubling about every 11.3 years. In 1995, Alwyn Young of the London School of Economics published an article in which he argued that Singapore's growth depended more on increases in capital per hour worked, increases in the labor force participation rate, and the transfer of workers from agricultural to nonagricultural jobs than on technological change. If Young's analysis was correct, predict what was likely to happen to Singapore's growth rate in the years after 1995.

Solving the Problem

Step 1: **Review the chapter material.** This problem is about what determines the rate of long-run growth, so you may want to review the section "What Determines the Rate of Long-Run Growth?" which begins on page 308.

Step 2: **Predict what happened to the growth rate in Singapore after 1995.** As countries begin to develop, they often experience an increase in the labor force participation rate, as workers who are not part of the paid labor force respond to rising wage rates. Many workers also leave the agricultural sector—where output per hour worked is often low—for the nonagricultural sector. These changes increase real GDP per capita, but they are "one-shot" changes that eventually come to an end, as the labor force participation rate and the fraction of the labor force outside agriculture both approach the levels found in high-income countries. Similarly, as we already noted, increases in capital per hour worked cannot sustain high rates of economic growth unless they are accompanied by technological change.

We can conclude that Singapore was unlikely to sustain its high growth rates in the years after 1995. In fact, from 1996 to 2010, the growth of real GDP per capita slowed to an average rate of 3.2 percent per year. Although this growth rate is comparable to rates experienced in high-income countries, such as the United States, it leads to a doubling of real GDP per capita only every 21.9 years rather than every 11.3 years.

Based on Alwyn Young, "The Tyranny of Numbers: Confronting the Statistical Realities of the East Asian Growth Experience," *Quarterly Journal of Economics*, Vol. 110, No. 3, August 1995, pp. 641–680; and International Monetary Fund, *World Economic Outlook Database*, September 2011.

Your Turn: For more practice, do related problem 1.12 on page 333 at the end of this chapter. MyEconLab

Finally, an additional requirement for economic growth is that the government must provide secure rights to private property. As we saw in Chapter 2, a market system cannot function unless rights to private property are secure. In addition, the government can help the market work and aid economic growth by establishing an independent court system that enforces contracts between private individuals. Many economists would also say that the government has a role in facilitating the development of an efficient financial system, as well as systems of education, transportation, and communication. Economist Richard Sylla of New York University has argued that every country that has experienced economic growth first experienced a "financial revolution." For example, before the United States was able to experience significant economic growth in the early nineteenth century, the country's banking and monetary systems were reformed under the guidance of Alexander Hamilton, who was appointed the country's first secretary of the Treasury in 1789. Without supportive government policies, long-run economic growth is unlikely to occur.

Making the Connection | What Explains Rapid Economic Growth in Botswana?

Economic growth in much of sub-Saharan Africa has been very slow. As desperately poor as most of these countries were in 1960, some are even poorer today. The growth rate in one country in this region stands out, however, as being exceptionally rapid. The graph below shows the average annual growth rate in real GDP per capita between 1960 and 2009 for Botswana and the six most populous sub-Saharan countries. Botswana's average annual growth rate over this 49-year period was three times as great as that of Tanzania and South Africa, which were the second and third-fastest-growing countries in the group. Botswana may seem an unlikely country to experience rapid growth because it has been hard hit by the HIV epidemic. Despite the disruptive effects of the epidemic, growth in real per capita GDP continued to be rapid, with the International Monetary Fund projecting increases in real GDP per capita of 5.9 percent in 2010 and 5.0 percent in 2011.

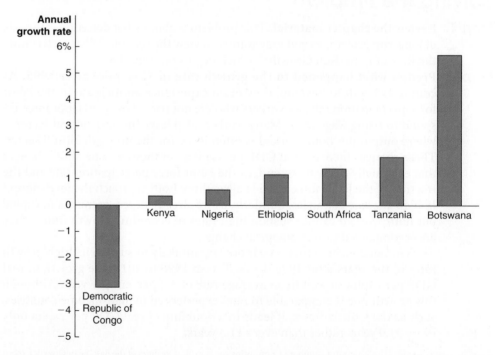

Note: Data for Democratic Republic of Congo are for 1970–2004.

Source: Authors' calculations from data in Alan Heston, Robert Summers, and Bettina Aten, *Penn World Table*, Version 7.0, Center for International Comparisons of Production, Income and Prices at the University of Pennsylvania, June 3, 2011.

What explains Botswana's rapid growth rate? Several factors have been important. Botswana avoided the civil wars that plagued other African countries during these years. The country also benefited from earnings from diamond exports. But many economists believe the pro-growth policies of Botswana's government are the most important reason for the country's success. Economists Shantayanan Devarajan of the World Bank, William Easterly of New York University, and Howard Pack of the University of Pennsylvania summarized these policies as follows:

> The government [of Botswana] made it clear it would protect private property rights. It was a "government of cattlemen" who were attuned to commercial interests. . . . The relative political stability and relatively low corruption also made Botswana a favorable location for investment. Botswana's relatively high level of press freedom and democracy (continuing a pre-colonial tradition that held chiefs responsible to tribal members) held the government responsible for any economic policy mistakes.

These policies—protecting private property, avoiding political instability and corruption, and allowing press freedom and democracy—may seem a straightforward recipe for providing an environment in which economic growth can occur. As we will see in Chapter 10, however, in practice, these are policies many countries have difficulty implementing successfully.

Based on International Monetary Fund, *World Economic Outlook Database*, September 2011; and Shantayanan Devarajan, William Easterly, and Howard Pack, "Low Investment Is Not the Constraint on African Development," *Economic Development and Cultural Change*, Vol. 51, No. 3, April 2003, pp. 547–571.

Your Turn: Test your understanding by doing related problem 1.14 on page 333 at the end of this chapter.

MyEconLab

Potential GDP

Because economists take a long-run perspective in discussing economic growth, the concept of *potential GDP* is useful. **Potential GDP** is the level of real GDP attained when all firms are producing at capacity. The capacity of a firm is *not* the maximum output the firm is capable of producing. A Boeing assembly plant could operate 24 hours per day for 52 weeks per year and would be at its maximum production level. The plant's capacity, however, is measured by its production when operating on normal hours, using a normal workforce. If all firms in the economy were operating at capacity, the level of total production of final goods and services would equal potential GDP. Potential GDP increases over time as the labor force grows, new factories and office buildings are built, new machinery and equipment are installed, and technological change takes place.

Growth in potential GDP in the United States is estimated to be about 3.3 percent per year. In other words, each year, the capacity of the economy to produce final goods and services expands by 3.3 percent. The *actual* level of real GDP may increase by more or less than 3.3 percent as the economy moves through the business cycle. Figure 10.2 shows movements in actual and potential GDP for the years since 1989. The smooth red line represents potential GDP, and the blue line represents actual real GDP. Notice that in each of the three recessions since 1989, actual real GDP has fallen below potential GDP. During the 2007–2009 recession, the gap between actual real GDP and potential GDP was particularly large, which is an indication of how severe the recession was.

Potential GDP The level of real GDP attained when all firms are producing at capacity.

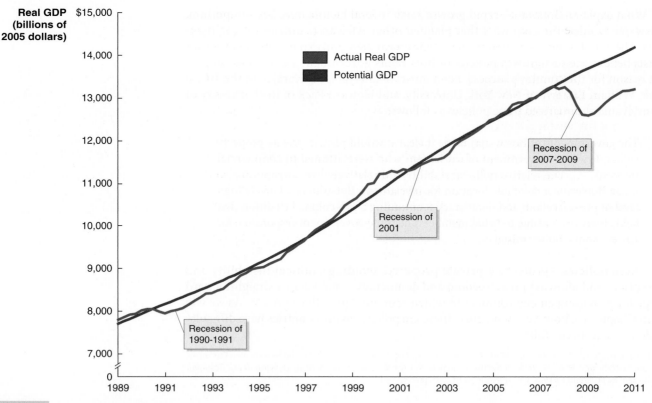

Figure 10.2 **Actual and Potential GDP**

Potential GDP increases every year as the labor force and the capital stock grow and technological change occurs. The smooth red line represents potential GDP, and the blue line represents actual real GDP. During the three recessions since 1989, actual real GDP has been less than potential GDP.

Data from Federal Reserve Bank of St. Louis.

10.2 LEARNING OBJECTIVE

Discuss the role of the financial system in facilitating long-run economic growth.

Saving, Investment, and the Financial System

The process of economic growth depends on the ability of firms to expand their operations, buy additional equipment, train workers, and adopt new technologies. Firms can finance some of these activities from *retained earnings*, which are profits that are reinvested in the firm rather than paid to the firm's owners. For many firms, retained earnings are not sufficient to finance the rapid expansion required in economies experiencing high rates of economic growth. Firms can acquire funds from households, either directly through financial markets—such as the stock and bond markets—or indirectly through financial intermediaries—such as banks. Financial markets and financial intermediaries together comprise the **financial system**. Without a well-functioning financial system, economic growth is impossible because firms will be unable to expand and adopt new technologies. As we noted earlier, no country without a well-developed financial system has been able to sustain high levels of economic growth.

Financial system The system of financial markets and financial intermediaries through which firms acquire funds from households.

An Overview of the Financial System

The financial system channels funds from savers to borrowers and channels returns on the borrowed funds back to savers. Recall from Chapter 6 that in **financial markets**, such as the stock market or the bond market, firms raise funds by selling financial securities directly to savers. A *financial security* is a document—sometimes in electronic form—that states the terms under which funds pass from the buyer of the security—who is providing funds—to the seller. *Stocks* are financial securities that represent partial

Financial markets Markets where financial securities, such as stocks and bonds, are bought and sold.

ownership of a firm. If you buy one share of stock in General Electric, you become one of millions of owners of that firm. *Bonds* are financial securities that represent promises to repay a fixed amount of funds. When General Electric sells a bond, the firm promises to pay the purchaser of the bond an interest payment each year for the term of the bond, as well as a final payment of the amount of the loan.

Financial intermediaries, such as banks, mutual funds, pension funds, and insurance companies, act as go-betweens for borrowers and lenders. In effect, financial intermediaries borrow funds from savers and lend them to borrowers. When you deposit funds in your checking account, you are lending your funds to the bank. The bank may lend your funds (together with the funds of other savers) to an entrepreneur who wants to start a business. Suppose Lena wants to open a laundry. Rather than you lending money directly to Lena's Laundry, the bank acts as a go-between for you and Lena. Intermediaries pool the funds of many small savers to lend to many individual borrowers. The intermediaries pay interest to savers in exchange for the use of savers' funds and earn a profit by lending money to borrowers and charging borrowers a higher rate of interest on the loans. For example, a bank might pay you as a depositor a 3 percent rate of interest, while it lends the money to Lena's Laundry at a 6 percent rate of interest.

> **Financial intermediaries** Firms, such as banks, mutual funds, pension funds, and insurance companies, that borrow funds from savers and lend them to borrowers.

Banks, mutual funds, pension funds, and insurance companies also make investments in stocks and bonds on behalf of savers. For example, *mutual funds* sell shares to savers and then use the funds to buy a portfolio of stocks, bonds, mortgages, and other financial securities. Large mutual fund companies, such as Fidelity, Vanguard, and Dreyfus, offer many stock and bond funds. Some funds hold a wide range of stocks or bonds; others specialize in securities issued by a particular industry or sector, such as technology; and others invest as index funds in fixed market baskets of securities, such as shares of the Standard & Poor's 500 firms. Over the past 30 years, the role of mutual funds in the financial system has increased dramatically. Today, competition among hundreds of mutual fund firms gives investors thousands of funds from which to choose.

In addition to matching households that have excess funds with firms that want to borrow funds, the financial system provides three key services for savers and borrowers: risk sharing, liquidity, and information. *Risk* is the chance that the value of a financial security will change relative to what you expect. For example, you may buy a share of stock in Google at a price of $450, only to have the price fall to $100. Most individual savers are not gamblers and seek a steady return on their savings rather than erratic swings between high and low earnings. The financial system provides risk sharing by allowing savers to spread their money among many financial investments. For example, you can divide your money among a bank certificate of deposit, individual bonds, and a mutual fund.

Liquidity is the ease with which a financial security can be exchanged for money. The financial system provides the service of liquidity by providing savers with markets in which they can sell their holdings of financial securities. For example, savers can easily sell their holdings of the stocks and bonds issued by large corporations on the major stock and bond markets.

A third service that the financial system provides savers is the collection and communication of *information*, or facts about borrowers and expectations about returns on financial securities. For example, Lena's Laundry may want to borrow $10,000 from you. Finding out what Lena intends to do with the funds and how likely she is to pay you back may be costly and time-consuming. By depositing $10,000 in the bank, you are, in effect, allowing the bank to gather this information for you. Because banks specialize in gathering information on borrowers, they are able to do it faster and at a lower cost than can individual savers. The financial system plays an important role in communicating information. If you read a news story announcing that an automobile firm has invented a car with an engine that runs on water, how would you determine the effect of that discovery on the firm's profits? Financial markets do the job for you by incorporating information into the prices of stocks, bonds, and other financial securities. In this example, the expectation of higher future profits would boost the prices of the automobile firm's stock and bonds.

The Macroeconomics of Saving and Investment

As we have seen, the funds available to firms through the financial system come from saving. When firms use funds to purchase machinery, factories, and office buildings, they are engaging in investment. In this section, we explore the macroeconomics of saving and investment. A key point we will develop is that *the total value of saving in the economy must equal the total value of investment.* We saw in Chapter 8 that *national income accounting* refers to the methods the Bureau of Economic Analysis uses to keep track of total production and total income in the economy. We can use some relationships from national income accounting to understand why total saving must equal total investment.

We begin with the relationship between GDP (Y) and its components, consumption (C), investment (I), government purchases (G), and net exports (NX):

$$Y = C + I + G + NX.$$

Remember that GDP is a measure of both total production in the economy and total income.

In an *open economy*, there is interaction with other economies in terms of both trading of goods and services and borrowing and lending. All economies today are open economies, although they vary significantly in the extent of their openness. In a *closed economy*, there is no trading or borrowing and lending with other economies. For simplicity, we will develop the relationship between saving and investment for a closed economy. This allows us to focus on the most important points in a simpler framework. We will consider the case of an open economy in Chapter 18.

In a closed economy, net exports are zero, so we can rewrite the relationship between GDP and its components as

$$Y = C + I + G.$$

If we rearrange this relationship, we have an expression for investment in terms of the other variables:

$$I = Y - C - G.$$

This expression tells us that in a closed economy, investment spending is equal to total income minus consumption spending and minus government purchases.

We can also derive an expression for total saving. *Private saving* is equal to what households retain of their income after purchasing goods and services (C) and paying taxes (T). Households receive income for supplying the factors of production to firms. This portion of household income is equal to Y. Households also receive income from government in the form of *transfer payments* (TR). Recall that transfer payments include Social Security payments and unemployment insurance payments. We can write an expression for private saving (S_{Private}):

$$S_{\text{Private}} = Y + TR - C - T.$$

The government also engages in saving. *Public saving* (S_{Public}) equals the amount of tax revenue the government retains after paying for government purchases and making transfer payments to households:

$$S_{\text{Public}} = T - G - TR.$$

So, total saving in the economy (S) is equal to the sum of private saving and public saving:

$$S = S_{\text{Private}} + S_{\text{Public}},$$

or:

$$S = (Y + TR - C - T) + (T - G - TR),$$

or:

$$S = Y - C - G.$$

The right side of this expression is identical to the expression we derived earlier for investment spending. So, we can conclude that total saving must equal total investment:

$$S = I.$$

When the government spends the same amount that it collects in taxes, there is a *balanced budget*. When the government spends more than it collects in taxes, there is a *budget deficit*. In the case of a deficit, T is less than $G + TR$, which means that public saving is negative. Negative saving is also known as *dissaving*. How can public saving be negative? When the federal government runs a budget deficit, the U.S. Department of the Treasury sells Treasury bonds to borrow the money necessary to fund the gap between taxes and spending. In this case, rather than adding to the total amount of saving available to be borrowed for investment spending, the government is subtracting from it. (Notice that if households borrow more than they save, the total amount of saving will also fall.) With less saving, investment must also be lower. We can conclude that, holding constant all other factors, there is a lower level of investment spending in the economy when there is a budget deficit than when there is a balanced budget.

When the government spends less than it collects in taxes, there is a *budget surplus*. A budget surplus increases public saving and the total level of saving in the economy. A higher level of saving results in a higher level of investment spending. Therefore, holding constant all other factors, there is a higher level of investment spending in the economy when there is a budget surplus than when there is a balanced budget.

The U.S. federal government has experienced dramatic swings in the state of its budget over the past 20 years. In 1992, the federal budget deficit was $297.4 billion. The federal budget had a surplus of $189.5 billion in 2000, but a dramatic decline in taxes and increase in government spending resulting from the recession of 2007–2009 led to record deficits of $1.4 trillion in 2009 and $1.5 trillion in 2010.

The Market for Loanable Funds

We have seen that the value of total saving must equal the value of total investment, but we have not yet discussed how this equality is actually brought about in the financial system. We can think of the financial system as being composed of many markets through which funds flow from lenders to borrowers: the market for certificates of deposit at banks, the market for stocks, the market for bonds, the market for mutual fund shares, and so on. For simplicity, we can combine these markets into a single market for *loanable funds*. In the model of the **market for loanable funds**, the interaction of borrowers and lenders determines the market interest rate and the quantity of loanable funds exchanged. As we will discuss in Chapter 18, firms can also borrow from savers in other countries. For the remainder of this chapter, we will assume that there are no interactions between households and firms in the United States and those in other countries.

Market for loanable funds The interaction of borrowers and lenders that determines the market interest rate and the quantity of loanable funds exchanged.

Demand and Supply in the Loanable Funds Market

The demand for loanable funds is determined by the willingness of firms to borrow money to engage in new investment projects, such as building new factories or carrying out research and development of new products. In determining whether to borrow funds, firms compare the return they expect to make on an investment with the interest rate they must pay to borrow the necessary funds. For example, if Home Depot is considering opening several new stores and expects to earn a return of 15 percent on its investment, the investment will be profitable if Home Depot can borrow the funds at an interest rate of 10 percent but will not be profitable if the interest rate is 20 percent. In Figure 10.3, the demand for loanable funds is downward sloping because the lower the interest rate, the more investment projects firms can profitably undertake, and the greater the quantity of loanable funds they will demand.

The supply of loanable funds is determined by the willingness of households to save and by the extent of government saving or dissaving. When households save, they reduce the amount of goods and services they can consume and enjoy today. The willingness

Figure 10.3

The Market for Loanable Funds

The demand for loanable funds is determined by the willingness of firms to borrow money to engage in new investment projects. The supply of loanable funds is determined by the willingness of households to save and by the extent of government saving or dissaving. Equilibrium in the market for loanable funds determines the real interest rate and the quantity of loanable funds exchanged.

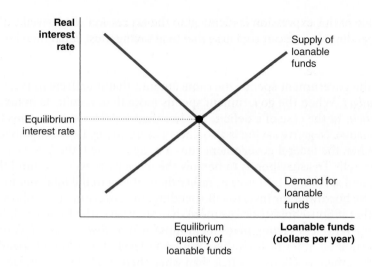

of households to save rather than consume their incomes today will be determined in part by the interest rate they receive when they lend their savings. The higher the interest rate, the greater the reward for saving and the larger the amount of funds households will save. Therefore, the supply curve for loanable funds in Figure 10.3 is upward sloping because the higher the interest rate, the greater the quantity of saving supplied.

In Chapter 9, we discussed the distinction between the *nominal interest rate* and the *real interest rate*. The nominal interest rate is the stated interest rate on a loan. The real interest rate corrects the nominal interest rate for the effect of inflation and is equal to the nominal interest rate minus the inflation rate. Because both borrowers and lenders are interested in the real interest rate they will receive or pay, equilibrium in the market for loanable funds determines the real interest rate rather than the nominal interest rate.

Making the Connection	Ebenezer Scrooge: Accidental Promoter of Economic Growth?

Ebenezer Scrooge's name has become synonymous with miserliness. Before his reform at the end of Charles Dickens's *A Christmas Carol*, Scrooge is extraordinarily reluctant to spend money. Although he earns a substantial income, he lives in a cold, dark house that he refuses to heat or light adequately, and he eats a meager diet of gruel because he refuses to buy more expensive food. Throughout most of the book, Dickens portrays Scrooge's behavior in an unfavorable way. Only at the end of the book, when the reformed Scrooge begins to spend lavishly on himself and others, does Dickens praise his behavior.

As economist Steven Landsburg of the University of Rochester points out, however, economically speaking, it may be the pre-reform Scrooge who is more worthy of praise:

> In this whole world, there is nobody more generous than the miser—the man who could deplete the world's resources but chooses not to. The only difference between miserliness and philanthropy is that the philanthropist serves a favored few while the miser spreads his largess far and wide.

Who was better for economic growth: Scrooge the saver or Scrooge the spender?

We can extend Landsburg's discussion to consider whether the actions of the pre-reform Scrooge or the actions of the post-reform Scrooge are more helpful to economic growth. Pre-reform Scrooge spends very little, investing most of his income in the financial markets. These funds became available for firms to borrow to build new factories and to carry out research and development. Post-reform Scrooge spends much more—and saves much less. Funds that he had previously saved are now spent on food for Bob Cratchit's family and on "making merry" at Christmas. In other words, the actions of post-reform Scrooge contribute to more consumption goods being produced and fewer investment goods. We can conclude that Scrooge's reform caused economic growth to slow down—if only by a little. The larger point is, of course, that savers provide the funds that are indispensable for the investment spending that economic growth requires, and the only way to save is to not consume.

From "What I Like About Scrooge," *Slate*, December 9, 2004.

Your Turn: Test your understanding by doing related problem 2.16 on page 334 at the end of this chapter.   MyEconLab

---

Explaining Movements in Saving, Investment, and Interest Rates

Equilibrium in the market for loanable funds determines the quantity of loanable funds that will flow from lenders to borrowers each period. It also determines the real interest rate that lenders will receive and that borrowers must pay. We draw the demand curve for loanable funds by holding constant all factors, other than the interest rate, that affect the willingness of borrowers to demand funds. We draw the supply curve by holding constant all factors, other than the interest rate, that affect the willingness of lenders to supply funds. A shift in either the demand curve or the supply curve will change the equilibrium interest rate and the equilibrium quantity of loanable funds.

If, for example, the profitability of new investment increases due to technological change, firms will increase their demand for loanable funds. Figure 10.4 shows the effect of an increase in demand in the market for loanable funds. As in the markets for goods and services we studied in Chapter 3, an increase in demand in the market for loanable funds shifts the demand curve to the right. In the new equilibrium, the interest rate increases from i_1 to i_2, and the equilibrium quantity of loanable funds increases from L_1 to L_2. Notice that an increase in the quantity of loanable funds means that both the quantity of saving by households and the quantity of investment by firms have increased.

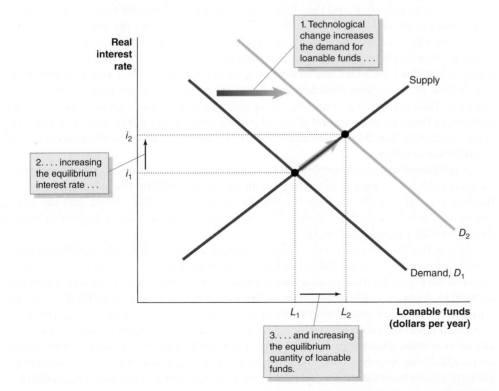

Figure 10.4

An Increase in the Demand for Loanable Funds

An increase in the demand for loanable funds increases the equilibrium interest rate from i_1 to i_2, and it increases the equilibrium quantity of loanable funds from L_1 to L_2. As a result, saving and investment both increase.

Figure 10.5

The Effect of a Budget Deficit on the Market for Loanable Funds

When the government begins running a budget deficit, the supply of loanable funds shifts to the left. The equilibrium interest rate increases from i_1 to i_2, and the equilibrium quantity of loanable funds falls from L_1 to L_2. As a result, saving and investment both decline.

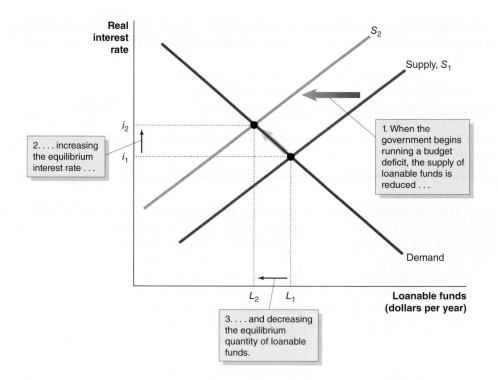

2. . . . increasing the equilibrium interest rate . . .

1. When the government begins running a budget deficit, the supply of loanable funds is reduced . . .

3. . . . and decreasing the equilibrium quantity of loanable funds.

Crowding out A decline in private expenditures as a result of an increase in government purchases.

Increasing investment increases the capital stock and the quantity of capital per hour worked, helping to increase economic growth.

We can also use the market for loanable funds to examine the effect of a government budget deficit. Putting aside the effects of foreign saving—which we will consider in Chapter 18—recall that if the government begins running a budget deficit, it reduces the total amount of saving in the economy. Suppose the government increases spending, which results in a budget deficit. We illustrate the effects of the budget deficit in Figure 10.5 by shifting the supply of loanable funds to the left. In the new equilibrium, the interest rate is higher, and the equilibrium quantity of loanable funds is lower. Running a deficit has reduced the level of total saving in the economy and, by increasing the interest rate, has also reduced the level of investment spending by firms. By borrowing to finance its budget deficit, the government will have *crowded out* some firms that would otherwise have been able to borrow to finance investment. **Crowding out** refers to a decline in investment spending as a result of an increase in government purchases. In Figure 10.5, the decline in investment spending due to crowding out is shown by the movement from L_1 to L_2 on the demand for loanable funds curve. Lower investment spending means that the capital stock and the quantity of capital per hour worked will not increase as much.

A government budget surplus has the opposite effect of a deficit: A budget surplus increases the total amount of saving in the economy, shifting the supply of loanable funds to the right. In the new equilibrium, the interest rate will be lower, and the quantity of loanable funds will be higher. We can conclude that a budget surplus increases the level of saving and investment.

In practice, however, the effect of government budget deficits and surpluses on the equilibrium interest rate is relatively small. (This finding reflects in part the importance of global saving in determining the interest rate.) For example, a recent study found that increasing government borrowing by an amount equal to 1 percent of GDP would increase the equilibrium real interest rate by only about 0.003 percentage point. However, this small effect on interest rates does not imply that we can ignore the effect of deficits on economic growth. Paying off government debt in the future may require higher taxes, which can depress economic growth. In 2011, many economists and policymakers were concerned that the large deficits projected for future years might be an obstacle to growth.

Solved Problem 10.2

How Would a Consumption Tax Affect Saving, Investment, the Interest Rate, and Economic Growth?

Some economists and policymakers have suggested that the federal government shift from relying on an income tax to relying on a *consumption tax*. Under the income tax, households pay taxes on all income earned. Under a consumption tax, households pay taxes only on the income they spend.

Households would pay taxes on saved income only if they spent the money at a later time. Use the market for loanable funds model to analyze the effect on saving, investment, the interest rate, and economic growth of switching from an income tax to a consumption tax.

Solving the Problem

Step 1: **Review the chapter material.** This problem is about applying the market for loanable funds model, so you may want to review the section "Explaining Movements in Saving, Investment, and Interest Rates," which begins on page 317.

Step 2: **Explain the effect of switching from an income tax to a consumption tax.** Households are interested in the return they receive from saving after they have paid their taxes. For example, consider someone who puts his savings in a certificate of deposit at an interest rate of 4 percent and whose tax rate is 25 percent. Under an income tax, this person's after-tax return to saving is 3 percent $[4 - (4 \times 0.25)]$. Under a consumption tax, income that is saved is not taxed, so the return rises to 4 percent. We can conclude that moving from an income tax to a consumption tax would increase the return to saving, causing the supply of loanable funds to increase.

Step 3: **Draw a graph of the market for loanable funds to illustrate your answer.** The supply curve for loanable funds will shift to the right as the after-tax return to saving increases under the consumption tax. The equilibrium interest rate will fall, and the levels of saving and investment will both increase. Because investment increases, the capital stock and the quantity of capital per hour worked will grow, and the rate of economic growth should increase. Note that the size of the fall in the interest rate and size of the increase in loanable funds shown in the graph are larger than the effects that most economists expect would actually result from the replacement of the income tax with a consumption tax.

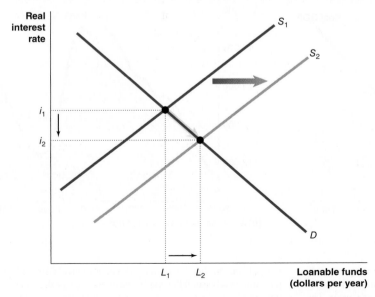

Your Turn: For more practice, do related problem 2.15 on page 334 at the end of this chapter.   MyEconLab

The Business Cycle

Figure 10.1 on page 305 illustrates the tremendous increase during the past 110 years in the standard of living of the average American. But close inspection of the figure reveals that real GDP per capita did not increase every year during this time. For example, during the first half of the 1930s, real GDP per capita *fell* for several years in a row. What accounts for these fluctuations in the long-run upward trend?

Some Basic Business Cycle Definitions

The fluctuations in real GDP *per capita* shown in Figure 10.1 reflect the underlying fluctuations in real GDP. Since at least the early nineteenth century, the U.S. economy has experienced business cycles that consist of alternating periods of expanding and contracting economic activity. Because real GDP is our best measure of economic activity, the business cycle is usually illustrated using movements in real GDP.

During the *expansion phase* of the business cycle, production, employment, and income are increasing. The period of expansion ends with a *business cycle peak*. Following the business cycle peak, production, employment, and income decline as the economy enters the *recession phase* of the cycle. The recession comes to an end with a *business cycle trough*, after which another period of expansion begins. Figure 10.6 illustrates the phases of the business cycle. Panel (a) shows an idealized business cycle, with real GDP increasing smoothly in an expansion to a business cycle peak and then decreasing smoothly in a recession to a business cycle trough, which is followed by another expansion. Panel (b) shows the somewhat messier reality of an actual business cycle by plotting fluctuations in real GDP during the period from 2005 to 2011. The figure shows that the expansion that began in 2001 continued until a business cycle peak was reached in December 2007. The following recession was the longest and the most severe since the Great Depression of the 1930s. The severity of the recession led some economists to refer to it as the "Great Recession." A business cycle trough was reached in June 2009, when the next expansion began. Although real GDP grew following the business cycle trough, the growth was slower than is typical at the beginning of a business cycle expansion.

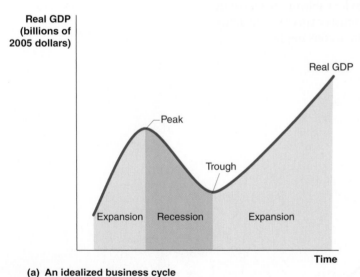

(a) An idealized business cycle

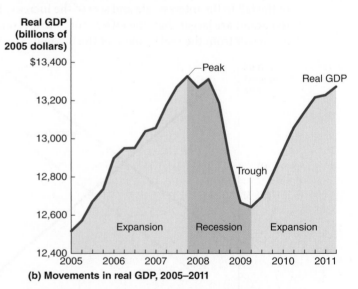

(b) Movements in real GDP, 2005–2011

Figure 10.6   **The Business Cycle**

Panel (a) shows an idealized business cycle, with real GDP increasing smoothly in an expansion to a business cycle peak and then decreasing smoothly in a recession to a business cycle trough, which is followed by another expansion. The periods of expansion are shown in green, and the period of recession is shown in red. Panel (b) shows the actual movements in real GDP for 2005 to 2011. The recession that began following the business cycle peak in December 2007 was the longest and the most severe since the Great Depression of the 1930s.

Table 10.1

The U.S. Business Cycle

Peak	Trough	Length of Recession
July 1953	May 1954	10 months
August 1957	April 1958	8 months
April 1960	February 1961	10 months
December 1969	November 1970	11 months
November 1973	March 1975	16 months
January 1980	July 1980	6 months
July 1981	November 1982	16 months
July 1990	March 1991	8 months
March 2001	November 2001	8 months
December 2007	June 2009	18 months

Data from National Bureau of Economic Research.

How Do We Know When the Economy Is in a Recession?

The federal government produces many statistics that make it possible to monitor the economy. But the federal government does not officially decide when a recession begins or when it ends. Instead, most economists accept the decisions of the Business Cycle Dating Committee of the National Bureau of Economic Research (NBER), a private research group located in Cambridge, Massachusetts. Although writers for newspapers and magazines often define a recession as two consecutive quarters of declining real GDP, the NBER has a broader definition: "A recession is a significant decline in activity spread across the economy, lasting more than a few months, visible in industrial production, employment, real income, and wholesale–retail trade."

The NBER is fairly slow in announcing business cycle dates because it takes time to gather and analyze economic statistics. Typically, the NBER will announce that the economy is in a recession only well after the recession has begun. For instance, the NBER did not announce that a recession had begun in December 2007 until 11 months later, at the end of November 2008. Table 10.1 lists the business cycle peaks and troughs identified by the NBER for the years since 1950. The length of each recession is the number of months from each peak to the following trough.

Making the Connection | Can a Recession Be a Good Time for a Business to Expand?

During a recession, business managers have to quickly make many decisions, such as whether to reduce production, cut prices, close stores or other facilities, or lay off workers. In addition to making decisions aimed at dealing with the immediate effects of the recession, managers also have to consider how to prepare for the expansion that will follow the recession. Managers know that every recession, even one as severe as the recession of 2007–2009, will be followed by an expansion during which demand for their products is likely to increase. But it can be difficult to commit resources to future expansion when current conditions are bleak and when the end of the recession is difficult to predict.

The payoff, though, to preparing for future growth can be very large. For example, at the end of World War II in 1945, many economists and business managers expected that the U.S. economy would enter a severe recession. Sears and Montgomery Ward were the two largest department store chains in the country. Sears CEO Robert Wood, expecting continuing prosperity, moved to open new stores across the country, while Sewell Avery, CEO of Montgomery Ward, expecting falling incomes and rising unemployment, refused to authorize any new stores and closed a number of existing ones. As a result, when strong economic growth occurred during the late 1940s, Sears rapidly gained market share at Montgomery Ward's expense.

Businesses such as Intel viewed the recession of 2007–2009 as an opportunity to expand operations.

Following the September 11, 2001, terrorist attacks, the managers of many hotels expected a prolonged period of reduced travel. They responded by laying off workers and postponing or canceling new construction. Isadore Sharp, the chairman and CEO of Four Seasons Hotels, decided that although the recession would severely hurt the hotel industry, the effects would be short-lived. He decided to push ahead with construction of 18 hotels and begin construction of 10 more. By his own account, "We maintained or enhanced our market share in most regions, contrary to the predictions of various industry experts." In a letter to his shareholders in March 2002, he wrote: "We are well positioned for the economic recovery expected later this year."

During the severe recession of 2007–2009, managers had similar decisions to make. Based in Greensboro, North Carolina, VF Corporation is the largest apparel maker in the world. While many firms, such as J.Crew, Anne Klein, and Liz Claiborne, were closing stores or postponing opening new ones, VF CEO Eric Wiseman pushed ahead, opening 89 stores in 2008 and 70 in 2009. One retail analyst was quoted as saying: "Unfortunately, many companies pull in the reins in a downturn, but these are often the best opportunities to grow." Similarly, Intel, the computer chip manufacturer, decided in early 2009 to proceed with a $7 billion expansion of its factories in the United States, while many rival firms were reducing their spending on new factories as computer sales declined. Intel's CEO Paul Otellini was quoted as saying, "I thought it was important for a company like Intel to stand up and say we have confidence." Heavy equipment manufacturer Caterpillar, Inc., announced that it would build several new facilities and expand some existing ones in order "to meet the expected increase in customer demand."

Through 2011, the recovery from the 2007–2009 recession was much slower than the typical recovery, which led some economists and analysts to wonder whether continued slow growth might make the decision by some businesses to expand less profitable than expected. So, how the decisions by VF, Intel, and Caterpillar will turn out remains to be seen, but, over the long run, for many firms, betting on the future of the U.S. economy has paid off.

Based on Robert Sobel, *When Giants Stumble*, (Paramus, NJ: Prentice Hall, 1999); Isadore Sharp, *Four Seasons: The Story of a Business Philosophy*, (New York: Portfolio, 2009); Bob Tita, "Caterpillar to Expand Kansas Plant," *Wall Street Journal*, August 18, 2011; Rachel Dodes, "VF Dresses Up Its Operations, Bucking Recession," *Wall Street Journal*, March 31, 2009; and Don Clark, "Intel to Invest $7 Billion in U.S. Plants," *Wall Street Journal*, February 10, 2009.

MyEconLab **Your Turn:** Test your understanding by doing related problem 3.7 on page 335 at the end of this chapter.

What Happens during the Business Cycle?

Each business cycle is different. The lengths of the expansion and recession phases and which sectors of the economy are most affected are rarely the same in any two cycles. But most business cycles share certain characteristics, which we will discuss in this section. As the economy nears the end of an expansion, interest rates are usually rising, and the wages of workers are usually rising faster than prices. As a result of rising interest rates and rising wages, the profits of firms will be falling. Typically, toward the end of an expansion, both households and firms will have substantially increased their debts. These debts are the result of the borrowing that firms and households undertake to help finance their spending during the expansion.

A recession will often begin with a decline in spending by firms on capital goods, such as machinery, equipment, new factories, and new office buildings, or by households on new houses and consumer durables, such as furniture and automobiles. As spending declines, firms selling capital goods and consumer durables will find their sales declining. As sales decline, firms cut back on production and begin to lay off workers. Rising unemployment and falling profits reduce income, which leads to further declines in spending.

As the recession continues, economic conditions gradually begin to improve. The declines in spending eventually come to an end; households and firms begin to reduce their debt, thereby increasing their ability to spend; and interest rates decline, making it more likely that households and firms will borrow to finance new spending. Firms begin to increase their spending on capital goods as they anticipate the need for additional production during the next expansion. Increased spending by households on consumer durables and by businesses on capital goods will finally bring the recession to an end and begin the next expansion.

The Effect of the Business Cycle on Boeing *Durables* are goods that are expected to last for three or more years. Consumer durables include furniture, appliances, and automobiles, and producer durables include machine tools, electric generators, and commercial airplanes. *Nondurables* are goods that are expected to last for fewer than three years. Consumer nondurables include goods such as food and clothing. Durables are affected more by the business cycle than are nondurables. During a recession, workers reduce spending if they lose their jobs, fear losing their jobs, or suffer wage cuts. Because people can often continue using their existing furniture, appliances, or automobiles, they are more likely to postpone spending on durables than spending on nondurables. Similarly, when firms experience declining sales and profits during a recession, they often cut back on purchases of producer durables.

We mentioned in our discussion of Boeing at the beginning of this chapter that the firm's sales are significantly affected by the business cycle. Panel (a) of Figure 10.7 shows movements in real GDP for each quarter from the beginning of 1990 through the end of 2010. We can see both the upward trend in real GDP over time and the effects of the recessions of 1990–1991, 2001, and 2007–2009. Panel (b) shows movements in the total

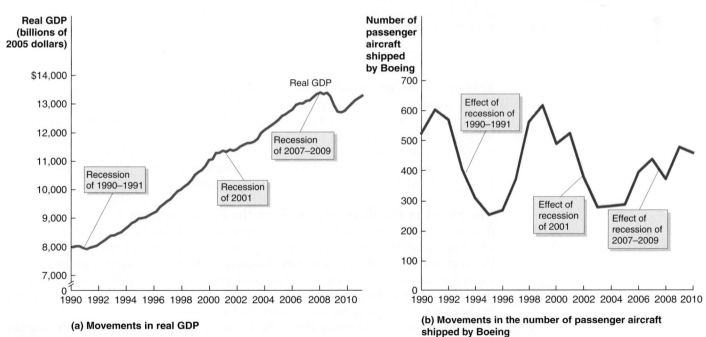

(a) Movements in real GDP

(b) Movements in the number of passenger aircraft shipped by Boeing

Figure 10.7   **The Effect of the Business Cycle on Boeing**

Panel (a) shows movements in real GDP for each quarter from the beginning of 1990 through the end of 2010. Panel (b) shows movements in the number of passenger aircraft shipped by Boeing for the same years. In panel (b), the effects of the recessions on Boeing are typically more dramatic than the effects on

the economy as a whole, although Boeing suffered a relatively mild decline in deliveries during the 2007–2009 recession.

Data from U.S. Bureau of Economic Analysis; and Boeing.

Figure 10.8 **The Effect of Recessions on the Inflation Rate**

Toward the end of a typical expansion, the inflation rate begins to rise. Recessions, marked by the shaded vertical bars, cause the inflation rate to fall. By the end of a recession, the inflation rate is significantly below what it had been at the beginning of the recession.

Note: The points on the figure represent the annual inflation rate measured by the percentage change in the consumer price index from the same month during the previous year. Data from U.S. Bureau of Labor Statistics.

number of passenger aircraft delivered by Boeing during the same years. The effects of the recessions on Boeing are typically more dramatic and long-lived than the effects on the economy as a whole, although Boeing suffered a relatively mild decline in deliveries during the 2007–2009 recession as increased demand from foreign airlines helped to offset declines in demand from U.S. airlines. In each of the recessions shown, U.S. airlines suffered declines in ticket sales and cut back on purchases of aircraft. As a result, Boeing suffered declines in sales during each recession.

The Effect of the Business Cycle on the Inflation Rate In Chapter 9, we saw that the *price level* measures the average prices of goods and services in the economy and that the *inflation rate* is the percentage increase in the price level from one year to the next. An important fact about the business cycle is that during economic expansions, the inflation rate usually increases, particularly near the end of the expansion, and during recessions, the inflation rate usually decreases. Figure 10.8 illustrates that this has been true of the three recessions since the late 1980s.

In every recession since 1950, the inflation rate has been lower during the 12 months after the recession ends than it was during the 12 months before the recession began. The average decline in the inflation rate has been about 2.5 percentage points. This result is not surprising. During a business cycle expansion, spending by businesses and households is strong, and producers of goods and services find it easier to raise prices. As spending declines during a recession, firms have a more difficult

Don't Let This Happen to You

Don't Confuse the Price Level and the Inflation Rate

Do you agree with the following statement: "The consumer price index is a widely used measure of the inflation rate"? This statement may sound plausible, but it is incorrect. As we saw in Chapter 9, the consumer price index is a measure of the *price level*, not of the inflation rate. We can measure the inflation rate as the *percentage change* in the consumer price index from one year to the next. In macroeconomics,

it is important not to confuse the level of a variable with the change in the variable. To give another example, real GDP does not measure economic growth. Economic growth is measured by the percentage change in real GDP from one year to the next.

MyEconLab

Your Turn: Test your understanding by doing related problem 3.6 on page 335 at the end of this chapter.

time selling their goods and services and are likely to increase prices less than they otherwise might have.

The Effect of the Business Cycle on the Unemployment Rate Recessions cause the inflation rate to fall, but they cause the unemployment rate to increase. As firms see their sales decline, they begin to reduce production and lay off workers. Figure 10.9

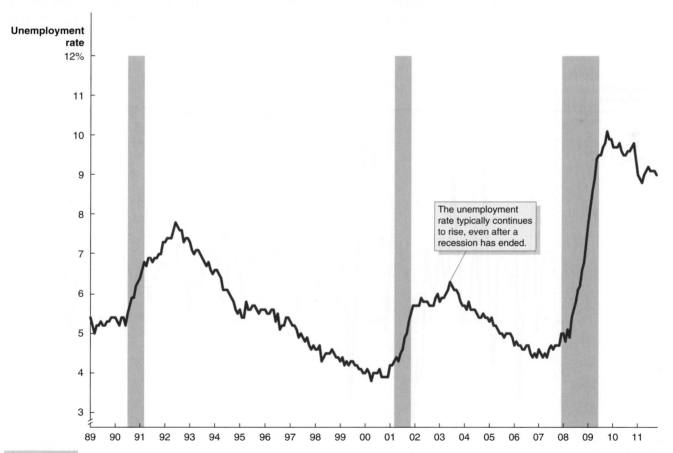

Figure 10.9 How Recessions Affect the Unemployment Rate

Unemployment rises during recessions and falls during expansions. The reluctance of firms to hire new employees during the early stages of a recovery means that the unemployment rate usually continues to rise even after the recession has ended.

Data from U.S. Bureau of Labor Statistics.

shows that this has been true of the three recessions since the late 1980s. Notice in the figure that the unemployment rate continued to rise even after the recessions of 1990–1991, 2001, and 2007–2009 had ended. This pattern, which is typical, is due to two factors. First, even though employment begins to increase as the recession ends, it may be increasing more slowly than the growth in the labor force resulting from population growth. If employment grows slowly enough relative to the growth in the labor force, it is possible for the unemployment rate to increase. Second, some firms continue to operate well below their capacity even after a recession has ended and production has begun to increase. As a result, at first, firms may not hire back all the workers they have laid off and may even continue for a while to lay off more workers.

During the recessions since 1950, the unemployment rate has risen on average by about 1.2 percentage points during the 12 months after a recession has begun. So, on average, more than 1 million more workers have been unemployed during the 12 months after a recession has begun than during the previous 12 months.

Is the "Great Moderation" Over? Figure 10.10, which shows the year-to-year percentage changes in real GDP since 1900, illustrates a striking change in fluctuations in real GDP beginning around 1950. Before 1950, real GDP went through much greater year-to-year fluctuations than it has since that time. Fluctuations since the mid-1980s have been particularly mild. By the early twenty-first century, some economists had begun referring to the absence of severe recessions in the United States as the "Great Moderation." However, economists began questioning this view with the recession that began in December 2007. This recession was the longest and most severe since the Great Depression of the 1930s and was referred to as the Great Contraction.

Figure 10.10   Fluctuations in Real GDP, 1900–2010

Fluctuations in real GDP were greater before 1950 than they have been since 1950.

Data from Louis D. Johnston and Samuel H. Williamson, "What Was the U.S. GDP Then?" Measuring Worth, 2011; and U.S. Bureau of Economic Analysis.

Period	Average Length of Expansions	Average Length of Recessions
1870–1900	26 months	26 months
1900–1950	25 months	19 months
1950–2009	61 months	11 months

Table 10.2

Until 2007, the Business Cycle Had Become Milder

Note: The World War I and World War II periods have been omitted from the computations in the table. The expansion that began in June 2009 is not included.
Data from National Bureau of Economic Research.

The percentage decline in real GDP during 2009 was the largest since 1932. Economists and policymakers were unsure whether the Great Moderation would return with the end of the Great Contraction.

The unusual severity of the 2007–2009 recession can be seen by comparing its length to the lengths of other recent recessions. Table 10.2 shows that in the late nineteenth century, the average length of recessions was the same as the average length of expansions. During the first half of the twentieth century, the average length of expansions decreased slightly, and the average length of recessions decreased significantly. As a result, expansions were about six months longer than recessions during these years. The most striking change came after 1950, when the length of expansions greatly increased and the length of recessions decreased. After 1950, expansions were more than five times as long as recessions. In other words, in the late nineteenth century, the U.S. economy spent as much time in recession as it did in expansion. After 1950, the U.S. economy experienced long expansions interrupted by relatively short recessions.

The recession of 2007–2009 is an exception to this experience of relatively short, mild recessions. The recession lasted 18 months, the longest of the post-1950 period. Does the length and depth of the 2007–2009 recession indicate that the United States is returning to an era of severe fluctuations in real GDP? A full answer to this question will not be possible for at least several years. But in the next section, we provide some perspective on the question by considering why the period from 1950 to 2007 was one of relative macroeconomic stability.

Will the U.S. Economy Return to Stability?

Shorter recessions, longer expansions, and less severe fluctuations in real GDP have resulted in a significant improvement in the economic well-being of Americans. Economists have offered several explanations for why the U.S. economy experienced a period of relative stability from 1950 to 2007:

- *The increasing importance of services and the declining importance of goods.* As services such as medical care or investment advice have become a much larger fraction of GDP, there has been a corresponding relative decline in the production of goods. For example, at one time, manufacturing production accounted for about 40 percent of GDP, but in 2010, it accounted for less than 12 percent. Manufacturing production, particularly production of durable goods such as automobiles, fluctuates more than the production of services. Because durable goods are usually more expensive than services, during a recession households will cut back more on purchases of durables than they will on purchases of services.

- *The establishment of unemployment insurance and other government transfer programs that provide funds to the unemployed.* Before the 1930s, programs such as unemployment insurance, which provides government payments to workers who lose their jobs, and Social Security, which provides government payments to retired and disabled workers, did not exist. These and other government programs make it possible for workers who lose their jobs during recessions to have higher incomes and, therefore, to spend more than they would otherwise. This additional spending may have helped to shorten recessions.

- *Active federal government policies to stabilize the economy.* Before the Great Depression of the 1930s, the federal government did not attempt to end recessions or prolong expansions. Because the Great Depression was so severe, with the unemployment rate rising to more than 20 percent of the labor force and real GDP declining by almost 30 percent, public opinion began favoring government attempts to stabilize the economy. In the years since World War II, the federal government has actively tried to use macroeconomic policy measures to end recessions and prolong expansions. Many economists believe that these government policies have played a key role in stabilizing the economy. Other economists, however, argue that active government policy has had little effect. The debate over the role of macroeconomic policy became particularly intense during and after the 2007–2009 recession. We will consider the debate over macroeconomic policy further in Chapters 15 and 16, when we discuss the federal government's *monetary* and *fiscal policies*.

- *The increased stability of the financial system.* The severity of the Great Depression of the 1930s was caused in part by instability in the financial system. More than 5,000 banks failed between 1929 and 1933, reducing the savings of many households and making it difficult for households and firms to obtain the credit needed to maintain their spending. In addition, a decline of more than 80 percent in stock prices greatly reduced the wealth of many households and made it difficult for firms to raise funds by selling stock. In Chapters 14 and 15, we will discuss some of the institutional changes that resulted in increased stability in the financial system during the years after the Great Depression. Most economists believe that the return of financial instability during the 2007–2009 recession is a key reason the recession was so severe. If the United States is to return to macroeconomic stability, stability will first have to return to the financial system.

Continued from page 303

Economics in Your Life

Do You Help the Economy More if You Spend or if You Save?

At the beginning of the chapter, we posed a question: Which of your two roommates is right: The one who argues that you would help the economy more by saving your tax refund check, or the one who argues that you should spend it? In this chapter, we have seen that consumption spending promotes the production of more consumption goods and services—such as jeans and haircuts—and fewer investment goods and services—such as physical capital and worker education. Saving—and, therefore, not consuming—is necessary to fund investment expenditure. So, saving your refund check will help the economy over the long run. But if the economy is in a recession, spending your refund check will spur more production of consumption goods. In a sense, then, both of your roommates are correct: Spending your check will help stimulate the economy during a recession, while saving it will help the economy grow over the long run.

Conclusion

The U.S. economy remains a remarkable engine for improving the well-being of Americans. The standard of living of Americans today is much higher than it was 100 years ago. But households and firms are still subject to the ups and downs of the business cycle. In the following chapters, we will continue our analysis of this basic fact of macroeconomics: Ever-increasing long-run prosperity is achieved in the context of short-run instability.

Read *An Inside Look* on the next page for a discussion of how the airline industry revises profit estimates based on global GDP projections.

RTTNEWS

IATA Lifts 2011 Airline Profit Forecast; Expects Fall in 2012

The International Air Transport Association or IATA on Tuesday lifted its airline industry profit forecast for fiscal 2011, citing better than expected passenger demand in most regions, even though cargo markets were weak. Meanwhile, it expects lower profit for the year 2012, with a very tough environment going ahead.

(a) For the year 2011, IATA currently expects industry profit to be $6.9 billion, compared to a previous projection of $4 billion. Meanwhile, the agency emphasized that profitability, with a net margin rate of 1.2 percent, is still exceptionally weak, despite the improvements, considering the industry's total revenues of $594 billion.

In an early June announcement, IATA, which represents around 230 airlines in over 115 countries, had slashed its profit outlook for the year from an earlier projection of $8.6 billion, citing high oil prices, natural disasters in Japan, and the political unrest in the Middle East and North Africa. The latest forecast is significantly lower than the $18 billion net profit recorded in 2010.

(b) For the year 2011, passenger numbers are expected to grow 5.9 percent, compared to a previous forecast of 4.4 percent growth, reflecting stronger than anticipated demand, despite the gloomy economic outlook. Total passenger numbers would now be 2.833 billion, up from the previous forecast of 2.793 billion.

Tighter supply and demand conditions in passenger markets over the first half is expected to offset the impact of a weaker second half.

Meanwhile, IATA slashed its forecast for air freight's full-year volume growth to 1.4 percent from 5.5 percent. Airlines are expected to carry 46.4 million tonnes of cargo in 2011, down from the previous forecast of 48.2 million. The agency does not expect a revival in air freight before 2012.

For the year, passenger revenues are now projected to be $464 billion, $7 billion higher than the June forecast, while freight revenue projections fell by $5 billion to $67 billion reflecting weaker freight markets.

IATA said its forecast is built around global projected GDP growth of 2.5 percent in 2011 falling to 2.4 percent in 2012.

IATA also lifted profit forecast for all regions, despite the ongoing impacts of the Japanese earthquake and tsunami in Asia and potential demand shocks associated with political instability in Middle East.

Meanwhile, IATA expects African carriers to break even, compared to previous loss forecast.

(c) Tony Tyler, IATA's Director General and CEO, stated that the airlines are competing in a very tough environment and that 2012 will be even more difficult.

For 2012, IATA projects profits to fall to $4.9 billion on revenues of $632 billion for a net margin of just 0.8 percent. Passenger markets are expected to grow 4.6 percent, and cargo markets by 4.2 percent.

IATA said the fourth quarter of 2011 and the first half of 2012 may well see the weakest point for air transport markets, with debt-burdened Western economies set for an extended period of weak economic activity.

Tyler stated, "Relatively stronger economic growth and some rebound in cargo will help Asia Pacific airlines to maintain their 2012 profits close to 2011 levels at $2.3 billion. The rest of the industry will see declining profitability. And the worst hit is expected to be Europe where the economic crisis means the industry is only expected to return a combined profit of $300 million. A long slow struggle lies ahead."

Key Points in the Article

An airline industry trade association, the International Air Transport Association (IATA), revised its profit forecast for the industry for 2011 to $6.9 billion in September, up from $4 billion in June. Profit forecasts were increased for all regions of the globe. The higher profits, which are still less than the $18 billion profit recorded in 2010, would mainly be the result of increased demand for passenger travel, with passenger numbers projected to increase by 5.9 percent for the year. Freight volume, however, is expected to grow only 1.4 percent for the year, down from the earlier estimate of 5.5 percent. For 2012, IATA projects industry profits to decline to $4.9 billion, despite expected growth in passengers and freight of 4.6 percent and 4.2 percent, respectively. IATA's revised profit forecasts are based on projected global GDP growth of 2.5 percent in 2011 and 2.4 percent in 2012.

Analyzing the News

(a) In 2010, the airline industry rebounded from the effects of the global economic recession, recording net profits of $18 billion.

However, the rebound was short-lived. An airline industry trade association, IATA, has twice lowered its forecast of profit for the industry for 2011. IATA reduced its original estimate of $8.6 billion to $4 billion in June and then increased that estimate to $6.9 billion in September. These 2011 profit estimates are considerably less than the $18 billion profit the industry earned in 2010. As IATA noted, the profit margin of 1.2 percent is very weak for an industry with total revenue of $594 billion.

(b) Despite the expected decline in profits from 2010 and a cautious economic outlook, passenger numbers are expected to increase in 2011 by 5.8 percent from the previous year, to a total of 2.833 billion. During the recession of 2007–2009, airlines decreased ticket prices and cut back on flights in response to decreasing demand. While the number of flights has remained lower than prior to the recession, ticket prices began to rise in 2010 as passenger demand increased. As we saw in Chapter 3, an increase in market demand causes an increase in the equilibrium market price and an increase in the equilibrium quantity, while a decrease in market supply causes an increase in the equilibrium price and a decrease in the equilibrium quantity. The graph below illustrates this point: The demand curve shifts to the right from D_1 to D_2, showing the increase in market demand for air travel, and the supply curve shifts to the left from S_1 to S_2, showing the decrease in market supply of air travel as airlines cut back on the number of flights they offered. Both the increase in demand and the decrease in supply cause the equilibrium price to increase. The increase in demand causes the equilibrium quantity to increase and the decrease in supply causes the equilibrium quantity to decrease. In the graph, the equilibrium quantity is shown to have remained constant at Q_1, because of shifts of equal magnitude of supply and demand.

(c) The IATA industry outlook for 2012 is not encouraging. Airline profits are projected to fall to $4.9 billion, with the profit margin decreasing to 0.8 percent. At the same time, revenues are projected to increase to $632 billion, with passenger travel up 4.6 percent and freight up 4.2 percent. The airline industry is expected to suffer a decline in profits despite an increase in passengers and freight and a rise in total revenue.

Thinking Critically

1. Suppose the U.S. government regulated U.S. airline ticket prices. How might such a policy affect the profitability of U.S. airlines during a weak economy?
2. Suppose the U.S. government decides to provide U.S. airlines with low-interest loans, regardless of their creditworthiness, in an attempt to help the airlines increase their profits. Would such a policy be likely to succeed? Briefly explain.

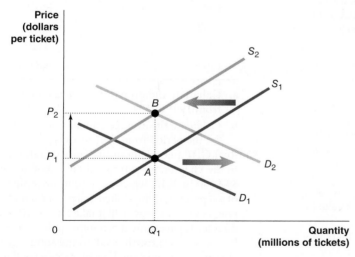

For air travel, higher demand and lower supply cause higher ticket prices.

Chapter Summary and Problems

Key Terms

Business cycle, p. 304

Capital, p. 308

Crowding out, p. 318

Financial intermediaries, p. 313

Financial markets, p. 312

Financial system, p. 312

Labor productivity, p. 308

Long-run economic growth, p. 305

Market for loanable funds, p. 315

Potential GDP, p. 311

 10.1 **Long-Run Economic Growth,** pages 304–312

LEARNING OBJECTIVE: Discuss the importance of long-run economic growth.

Summary

The U.S. economy has experienced both *long-run economic growth* and the *business cycle*. The **business cycle** refers to alternating periods of economic expansion and economic recession. **Long-run economic growth** is the process by which rising productivity increases the standard of living of the typical person. Because of economic growth, the typical American today can buy almost eight times as much as the typical American of 1900. Long-run growth is measured by increases in real GDP per capita. Increases in real GDP per capita depend on increases in labor productivity. **Labor productivity** is the quantity of goods and services that can be produced by one worker or by one hour of work. Economists believe two key factors determine labor productivity: the quantity of capital per hour worked and the level of technology. **Capital** refers to manufactured goods that are used to produce other goods and services. *Human capital* is the accumulated knowledge and skills workers acquire from education, training, or their life experiences. Economic growth occurs if the quantity of capital per hour worked increases and if technological change occurs. Economists often discuss economic growth in terms of growth in **potential GDP**, which is the level of GDP attained when all firms are producing at capacity.

MyEconLab Visit **www.myeconlab.com** to complete these exercises online and get instant feedback.

Review Questions

1.1 By how much did real GDP per capita increase in the United States between 1900 and 2010? Discuss whether the increase in real GDP per capita is likely to be greater or smaller than the true increase in living standards.

1.2 What is the rule of 70? If real GDP per capita grows at a rate of 7 percent per year, how many years will it take to double?

1.3 What is the most important factor in explaining increases in real GDP per capita in the long run?

1.4 What two key factors cause labor productivity to increase over time?

1.5 What is potential real GDP? Does potential real GDP remain constant over time?

Problems and Applications

1.6 Briefly discuss whether you would rather live in the United States of 1900 with an income of $1,000,000 per year or the United States of 2012 with an income of $50,000 per year. Assume that the incomes for both years are measured in 2012 dollars.

1.7 A question from Chapter 8 asked about the relationship between real GDP and the standard of living in a country. Based on what you read about economic growth in this chapter, elaborate on the importance of growth in GDP, particularly real GDP per capita, to the quality of life of a country's citizens.

1.8 [Related to the Making the Connection on page 306] Think about the relationship between economic prosperity and life expectancy. What implications does this relationship have for the size of the health care sector of the economy? In particular, is this sector likely to expand or contract in coming years?

1.9 Use the table to answer the following questions.

Year	Real GDP (billions of 2005 dollars)
1990	$8,034
1991	8,015
1992	8,287
1993	8,523
1994	8,871

a. Calculate the growth rate of real GDP for each year from 1991 to 1994.

b. Calculate the average annual growth rate of real GDP for the period from 1991 to 1994.

1.10 Real GDP per capita in the United States, as mentioned in the chapter, grew from about $5,600 in 1900 to about $42,200 in 2010, which represents an annual growth rate of 1.8 percent. If the United States continues to grow at this rate, how many years will it take for real GDP per capita to double? If government economic policies meant to stimulate economic growth result in the annual growth rate increasing to 2.0 percent, how many years will it take for real GDP per capita to double?

1.11 A study conducted by the Moscow-based management consulting firm Strategy Partners found that average labor productivity in Russia is only 17 percent of labor productivity in the United States. What factors would cause U.S. labor productivity to be nearly six times higher than Russian labor productivity?

Based on Jason Bush, "Why Is Russia's Productivity So Low?" *BusinessWeek*, May 8, 2009.

1.12 [Related to Solved Problem 10.1 **on page 309**] An article in the *Economist* magazine compares Panama to Singapore. It quotes Panama's president as saying: "We copy a lot from Singapore and we need to copy more." The article observes that: "Panama is not even one-fifth as rich as its Asian model on a per-person basis. But Singapore would envy its growth: from 2005 to 2010 its economy expanded by more than 8% a year, the fastest rate in the Americas." Judging from the experience of Singapore, if Panama is to maintain these high growth rates, what needs to be true about the sources of Panama's growth?

Based on "A Singapore for Central America?" *Economist*, July 14, 2011.

1.13 A newspaper article on labor productivity in the United States observes that, " . . . the best measure of productivity is probably output per hour, not output per person." Briefly explain whether you agree.

From David Leonhardt, "Even More Productive than Americans," *New York Times*, January 26, 2011.

1.14 [Related to the Making the Connection **on page 310**] If the keys to Botswana's rapid economic growth seem obvious, why have other countries in the region had so much difficulty following them?

10.2 Saving, Investment, and the Financial System, pages 312–319

LEARNING OBJECTIVE: Discuss the role of the financial system in facilitating long-run economic growth.

Summary

Financial markets and financial intermediaries together comprise the **financial system**. A well-functioning financial system is an important determinant of economic growth. Firms acquire funds from households, either directly through financial markets—such as the stock and bond markets—or indirectly through financial intermediaries—such as banks. The funds available to firms come from *saving*. There are two categories of saving in the economy: *private saving* by households and *public saving* by the government. The value of total saving in the economy is always equal to the value of total investment spending. In the model of the **market for loanable funds**, the interaction of borrowers and lenders determines the market interest rate and the quantity of loanable funds exchanged.

MyEconLab   Visit **www.myeconlab.com** to complete these exercises online and get instant feedback.

Review Questions

2.1 Why is the financial system of a country important for long-run economic growth? Why is it essential for economic growth that firms have access to adequate sources of funds?

2.2 How does the financial system—either financial markets or financial intermediaries—provide risk sharing, liquidity, and information for savers and borrowers?

2.3 Briefly explain why the total value of saving in the economy must equal the total value of investment.

2.4 What are loanable funds? Why do businesses demand loanable funds? Why do households supply loanable funds?

Problems and Applications

2.5 Suppose you can receive an interest rate of 3 percent on a certificate of deposit at a bank that is charging borrowers 7 percent on new car loans. Why might you be unwilling to loan money directly to someone who wants to borrow from you to buy a new car, even if that person offers to pay you an interest rate higher than 3 percent?

2.6 An International Monetary Fund Factsheet makes the following observation regarding stable financial systems: "A sound financial system is . . . essential for supporting economic growth." Do you agree with this observation? Briefly explain.

Based on "Financial System Soundness," *International Monetary Fund Factsheet*, April 2009.

2.7 Consider the following data for a closed economy:

$Y = \$11$ trillion

$C = \$8$ trillion

$I = \$2$ trillion

$TR = \$1$ trillion

$T = \$3$ trillion

Use these data to calculate the following:
a. Private saving
b. Public saving
c. Government purchases
d. The government budget deficit or budget surplus

2.8 Consider the following data for a closed economy:

$Y = \$12$ trillion

$C = \$8$ trillion

$G = \$2$ trillion

$S_{Public} = -\$0.5$ trillion

$T = \$2$ trillion

Use these data to calculate the following:
a. Private saving
b. Investment spending
c. Transfer payments
d. The government budget deficit or budget surplus

2.9 In problem 2.8, suppose that government purchases increase from $2 trillion to $2.5 trillion. If the values for Y and C are unchanged, what must happen to the values of S and I? Briefly explain.

2.10 Use the graph on the next page to answer the following questions:
a. Does the shift from S_1 to S_2 represent an increase or a decrease in the supply of loanable funds?
b. With the shift in supply, what happens to the equilibrium quantity of loanable funds?

c. With the change in the equilibrium quantity of loanable funds, what happens to the quantity of saving? What happens to the quantity of investment?

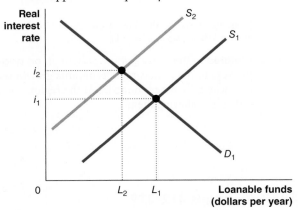

2.11 Use this graph to answer the following questions:

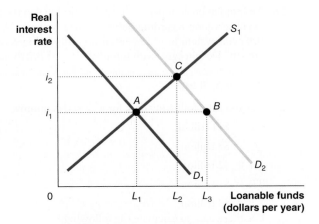

a. With the shift in the demand for loanable funds, what happens to the equilibrium real interest rate and the equilibrium quantity of loanable funds?

b. How can the equilibrium quantity of loanable funds increase when the real interest rate increases? Doesn't the quantity of loanable funds demanded decrease when the interest rate increases?

c. How much would the quantity of loanable funds demanded have increased if the interest rate had remained at i_1?

d. How much does the quantity of loanable funds supplied increase with the increase in the interest rate from i_1 to i_2?

2.12 Suppose that the economy is currently in a recession and that economic forecasts indicate that the economy will soon enter an expansion. What is the likely effect of the expansion on the expected profitability of new investment in plant and equipment? In the market for loanable funds, graph and explain the effect of the forecast of an economic expansion, assuming that borrowers and lenders believe the forecast is accurate. What happens to the equilibrium real interest rate and the quantity of loanable funds? What happens to the quantity of saving and investment?

2.13 Firms care about their after-tax rate of return on investment projects. In the market for loanable funds, graph and explain the effect of an increase in taxes on business profits. (For simplicity, assume no change in the federal budget deficit or budget surplus.) What happens to the equilibrium real interest rate and the quantity of loanable funds? What will be the effect on the quantity of investment by firms and the economy's capital stock in the future?

2.14 The federal government in the United States has been running very large budget deficits.

a. Use a market for loanable funds graph to illustrate the effect of the federal budget deficits. What happens to the equilibrium real interest rate and the quantity of loanable funds? What happens to the quantity of saving and investment?

b. Now suppose that households believe that deficits will be financed by higher taxes in the near future, and households increase their saving in anticipation of paying those higher taxes. Briefly explain how your analysis in part a will be affected.

2.15 **[Related to** Solved Problem 10.2 **on page 319]** Savers are taxed on the nominal interest payments they receive rather than the real interest payments. Suppose the government shifted from taxing nominal interest payments to taxing only real interest payments. (That is, savers could subtract the inflation rate from the nominal interest rate they received and only pay taxes on the resulting real interest rate.) Use a market for loanable funds graph to analyze the effects of this change in tax policy. What happens to the equilibrium real interest rate and the equilibrium quantity of loanable funds? What happens to the quantity of saving and investment?

2.16 **[Related to the** Making the Connection **on page 316]** The *Making the Connection* claims that Ebenezer Scrooge promoted economic growth more when he was a miser and saved most of his income than when he reformed and began spending freely. Suppose, though, that most of his spending after he reformed involved buying food for the Cratchits and other poor families. Many economists believe that there is a close connection between how much very poor people eat and how much they are able to work and how productive they are while working. Does this fact affect the conclusion about whether the pre-reform or post-reform Scrooge had a more positive impact on economic growth? Briefly explain.

10.3 **The Business Cycle, pages 320–328**

LEARNING OBJECTIVE: Explain what happens during the business cycle.

Summary

During the expansion phase of the business cycle, production, employment, and income are increasing. The period of expansion ends with a business cycle peak. Following the business cycle peak, production, employment, and income decline during the recession phase of the cycle. The recession comes to an end with a business cycle trough, after which another period of expansion begins. The inflation rate usually rises near the end of a business cycle expansion and then falls during a recession. The unemployment rate declines during the later part of an expansion and increases during a recession. The unemployment rate often continues to increase even after an expansion has begun. Economists have not found a method to predict when recessions will begin and end. Recessions are difficult to predict because they are due to more than one cause. Until the severe recession of 2007–2009, recessions had been milder and the economy had been more stable in the period since 1950.

MyEconLab   Visit **www.myeconlab.com** to complete these exercises online and get instant feedback.

Review Questions

3.1 What are the names of the following events that occur during a business cycle?
  a. The high point of economic activity
  b. The low point of economic activity
  c. The period between the high point of economic activity and the following low point
  d. The period between the low point of economic activity and the following high point

3.2 Briefly describe the effect of the business cycle on the inflation rate and the unemployment rate. Why might the unemployment rate continue to rise during the early stages of a recovery?

3.3 Briefly compare the severity of recessions before and after 1950. What explanations have economists offered for the period of relative macroeconomic stability from 1950 to 2007?

Problems and Applications

3.4 **[Related to the** Chapter Opener **on page 303]** Briefly explain whether production of each of the following goods is likely to fluctuate more or less than real GDP does during the business cycle:

  a. Ford F-150 trucks
  b. McDonald's Big Macs
  c. Kenmore refrigerators
  d. Huggies diapers
  e. Boeing passenger aircraft

3.5 The National Bureau of Economic Research, a private group, is responsible for declaring when recessions begin and end. Can you think of reasons the Bureau of Economic Analysis, part of the federal government, might not want to take on this responsibility?

3.6 **[Related to the** Don't Let This Happen to You **on page 325]** "Real GDP in 2010 was $13.1 trillion. This value is a large number. Therefore, economic growth must have been high during 2010." Briefly explain whether you agree with this statement.

3.7 **[Related to the** Making the Connection **on page 321]** As we have seen, some firms prosper by expanding during recessions. What risks do firms take when they pursue this strategy? Are there circumstances in particular industries under which a more cautious approach might be advisable? Briefly explain.

3.8 Imagine that you own a business and that during the next recession, you lay off 10 percent of your workforce. When economic activity picks up and your sales begin to increase, why might you not immediately start rehiring workers?

3.9 An article in the *Economist* magazine refers to "The Great Delusion of a Great Moderation. . . ." What is the Great Moderation? By 2011, why might some people have considered the Great Moderation to have been a delusion?

Based on "Lending a Hand," *Economist*, September 10, 2011.

Long-Run Economic Growth: Sources and Policies

Chapter Outline and Learning Objectives

Google's Dilemma in China

Google was founded in 1998 by Larry Page and Sergey Brin. By 2011, Google employed more than 28,000 people and had annual revenues exceeding $29 billion. But Google encountered problems when expanding into China in 2006. The Chinese government insisted on regulating how people in that country access the Internet. In setting up Google.cn, Google had to agree to block searches of sensitive topics, such as the 1989 pro-democracy demonstrations in Tiananmen Square.

In late 2009, hackers stole some of Google's most important intellectual property by breaking into its computer system. Company executives suspected that Chinese government officials were involved in the theft. In January 2010, Google decided it would no longer cooperate with the Chinese government to censor Internet searchers and moved its Chinese search service from the mainland to Hong Kong.

Google's problems highlight one of the paradoxes of China in recent years: very rapid economic growth occurring in the context of government regulations that can stifle that growth. From the time the Communist Party seized control of China in 1949 until the late 1970s, the government controlled production, and the country experienced very little economic growth. China moved away from a *centrally planned economy* in 1978, and real GDP per capita grew at a rate of 6.5 percent per year between 1979 and 1995; it grew at the white-hot rate of more than 9 percent per year between 1996 and 2010. These rapid growth rates have transformed the Chinese economy: Real GDP per capita today is 10 times higher than it was 50 years ago.

But, as the experience of Google has shown, China is not a democracy, and the Chinese government has failed to fully establish the rule of law, particularly with respect to the consistent enforcement of property rights. This is a problem for the long-term prospects of the Chinese economy because without the rule of law, entrepreneurs cannot fulfill their role in the market system of bringing together the factors of production—labor, capital, and natural resources—to produce goods and services.

Read **AN INSIDE LOOK** on **page 366** for a discussion of China's long-term plan to decrease its reliance on investment spending as a means of achieving sustainable economic growth.

Based on Steven Levy, "Inside Google's China Misfortune," *Fortune*, April 15, 2011; and Kathrin Hille, "China Renews Google's Website License," *Financial Times*, September 7, 2011.

Economics in Your Life

Would You Be Better Off without China?

Suppose that you could choose to live and work in a world with the Chinese economy growing very rapidly or in a world with the Chinese economy as it was before 1978—very poor and growing slowly. Which world would you choose to live in? How does the current high-growth, high-export Chinese economy affect you as a consumer? How does it affect you as someone about to start a career? As you read the chapter, see if you can answer these questions. You can check your answers against those we provide on **page 364** at the end of this chapter.

Economic growth is not inevitable. For most of human history, no sustained increases in output per capita occurred, and, in the words of the philosopher Thomas Hobbes, the lives of most people were "poor, nasty, brutish, and short." Sustained economic growth first began with the Industrial Revolution in England in the late eighteenth century. From there, economic growth spread to the United States, Canada, and the countries of Western Europe. Following World War II, rapid economic growth also began in Japan and, eventually, in several other Asian countries, but the economies of many other countries stagnated, leaving their people mired in poverty.

Real GDP per capita is the best measure of a country's standard of living because it represents the ability of the average person to buy goods and services. Economic growth occurs when real GDP per capita increases. Why have countries such as the United States and the United Kingdom, which had high standards of living at the beginning of the twentieth century, continued to grow rapidly? Why have countries such as Argentina, which at one time had relatively high standards of living, failed to keep pace? Why was the Soviet Union unable to sustain the rapid growth rates of its early years? Why are some countries that were very poor at the beginning of the twentieth century still very poor today? And why have some countries, such as South Korea and Japan, that once were very poor now become much richer? What explains China's very rapid recent growth rates? In this chapter, we will develop a *model of economic growth* that helps us answer these important questions.

Economic Growth over Time and around the World

You live in a world that is very different from the world when your grandparents were young. You can listen to music on an iPod that fits in your pocket; your grandparents played vinyl records on large stereo systems. You can pick up a cell phone or send a text message to someone in another city, state, or country; your grandparents mailed letters that took days or weeks to arrive. More importantly, you have access to health care and medicines that have prolonged life and improved its quality. In many poorer countries, however, people endure grinding poverty and have only the bare necessities of life, just as their great-grandparents did.

The difference between you and people in poor countries is that you live in a country that has experienced substantial economic growth. With economic growth, an economy produces both increasing quantities of goods and services and better goods and services. It is only through economic growth that living standards can increase, but through most of human history, no economic growth took place. Even today, billions of people are living in countries where economic growth is extremely slow.

Economic Growth from 1,000,000 B.C. to the Present

In 1,000,000 B.C., our ancestors survived by hunting animals and gathering edible plants. Farming was many years in the future, and production was limited to food, clothing, shelter, and simple tools. Bradford DeLong, an economist at the University of California, Berkeley, estimates that in those primitive circumstances, GDP per capita was about $140 per year in 2010 dollars, which was the minimum amount necessary to sustain life. DeLong estimates that real GDP per capita worldwide was still $140 in the year 1300 A.D. In other words, no sustained economic growth occurred between 1,000,000 B.C. and 1300 A.D. A peasant toiling on a farm in France in the year 1300 was no better off than his ancestors thousands of years before. In fact, for most of human existence, the typical person had only the bare minimum of food, clothing, and shelter necessary to sustain life. Few people survived beyond age 40, and most people suffered from debilitating illnesses.

Significant economic growth did not begin until the **Industrial Revolution**, which started in England around the year 1750. The production of cotton cloth in

Industrial Revolution The application of mechanical power to the production of goods, beginning in England around 1750.

factories using machinery powered by steam engines marked the beginning of the Industrial Revolution. Before that time, production of goods had relied almost exclusively on human or animal power. The use of mechanical power spread to the production of many other goods, greatly increasing the quantity of goods each worker could produce. First England and then other countries, such as the United States, France, and Germany, experienced *long-run economic growth*, with sustained increases in real GDP per capita that eventually raised living standards in those countries to the high levels of today.

Making the Connection | Why Did the Industrial Revolution Begin in England?

The Industrial Revolution was a key turning point in human history. Before the Industrial Revolution, economic growth was slow and halting. After the Industrial Revolution, economic growth became rapid and sustained in a number of countries. Although historians and economists agree on the importance of the Industrial Revolution, they have not reached a consensus on why it happened in the time and place that it did. Why the eighteenth century and not the sixteenth century or the twenty-first century? Why England and not China or India or Africa or Japan?

The British government's guarantee of property rights set the stage for the Industrial Revolution.

There is always a temptation to read history backward. We know when and where the Industrial Revolution occurred; therefore, it had to happen where it did and when it did. But what was so special about England in the eighteenth century? Nobel Laureate Douglass North, of Washington University in St. Louis, has argued that institutions in England differed significantly from those in other countries in ways that greatly aided economic growth. North believes that the Glorious Revolution of 1688 was a key turning point. After that date, the British Parliament, rather than the king, controlled the government. The British court system also became independent of the king. As a result, the British government was credible when it committed to upholding private property rights, protecting wealth, and eliminating arbitrary increases in taxes. These institutional changes gave entrepreneurs the incentive to make the investments necessary to use the important technological developments of the second half of the eighteenth century—particularly the spinning jenny and the water frame, which were used in the production of cotton textiles, and the steam engine, which was used in mining and in the manufacture of textiles and other products. Without the institutional changes, entrepreneurs would have been reluctant to risk their property or their wealth by starting new businesses.

Although not all economists agree with North's specific argument about the origins of the Industrial Revolution, we will see that most economists accept the idea that economic growth is not likely to occur unless a country's government provides the type of institutional framework North describes.

Based on Douglass C. North, *Understanding the Process of Economic Change*, (Princeton, NJ: Princeton University Press, 2005); and Douglass C. North and Barry R. Weingast, "Constitutions and Commitment: The Evolution of Institutions Governing Public Choice in Seventeenth-Century England," *Journal of Economic History*, Vol. 49, No. 4, December 1989.

Your Turn: Test your understanding by doing related problem 1.3 on page 368 at the end of this chapter.   MyEconLab

Figure 11.1 shows how growth rates of real GDP per capita for the entire world have changed over long periods. Prior to 1300 A.D., there were no sustained increases in real GDP per capita. Over the next 500 years, to 1800, there was very slow growth. Significant growth began in the nineteenth century, as a result of the Industrial Revolution. A further acceleration in growth occurred during the twentieth century, as the average growth rate increased from 1.3 percent per year to 2.3 percent per year.

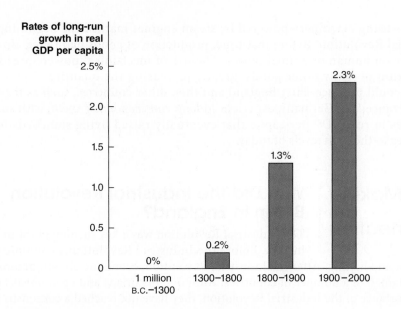

Figure 11.1

Average Annual Growth Rates for the World Economy

World economic growth was essentially zero in the years before 1300, and it was very slow—an average of only 0.2 percent per year—before 1800. The Industrial Revolution made possible the sustained increases in real GDP per capita that have allowed some countries to attain high standards of living. Data from J. Bradford DeLong, "Estimating World GDP, One Million B.C.–Present," working paper, University of California, Berkeley.

Small Differences in Growth Rates Are Important

The difference between 1.3 percent and 2.3 percent may seem trivial, but over long periods, small differences in growth rates can have a large effect. For example, suppose you have $100 in a savings account earning an interest rate of 1.3 percent, which means you will receive an interest payment of $1.30 this year. If the interest rate on the account is 2.3 percent, you will earn $2.30. The difference of an extra $1.00 interest payment seems insignificant. But if you leave the interest as well as the original $100 in your account for another year, the difference becomes greater because now the higher interest rate is applied to a larger amount—$102.30—and the lower interest rate is applied to a smaller amount—$101.30. This process, known as *compounding*, magnifies even small differences in interest rates over long periods of time. Over a period of 50 years, your $100 would grow to $312 at an interest rate of 2.3 percent but to only $191 at an interest rate of 1.3 percent.

The principle of compounding applies to economic growth rates as well as to interest rates. For example, in 1950, real GDP per capita in Argentina was $5,474 (measured in 2005 dollars), which was larger than Italy's real GDP per capita of $5,361. Over the next 60 years, the economic growth rate in Italy averaged 2.8 percent per year, while in Argentina, the growth rate was only 1.4 percent per year. Although this difference in growth rates of only 1.4 percentage points may seem small, in 2010, real GDP per capita in Italy had risen to $27,930, while real GDP per capita in Argentina was only $12,931. In other words, because of a relatively small difference in the growth rates of the two economies, the standard of living of the typical person in Italy went from being below that of the typical person in Argentina to being much higher. The important point to keep in mind is this: *In the long run, small differences in economic growth rates result in big differences in living standards.*

Why Do Growth Rates Matter?

Why should anyone care about growth rates? Growth rates matter because an economy that grows too slowly fails to raise living standards. In some countries in Africa and Asia, very little economic growth has occurred in the past 50 years, so many people remain in severe poverty. In high-income countries, only 4 out of every 1,000 babies die before they are they one year old. In the poorest countries, more than 100 out of every 1,000 babies die before they are one year old, and millions of children die annually from diseases that could be avoided by having access to clean water or that could be cured by using medicines that cost only a few dollars.

Although their problems are less dramatic, countries that experience slow growth have also missed opportunities to improve the lives of their citizens. For example, the failure of Argentina to grow as rapidly as the other countries that had similar levels of GDP per capita in 1950 has left many of its people in poverty. Life expectancy in Argentina is lower than in the United States and other high-income countries, and nearly twice as many babies in Argentina die before age one.

Don't Let This Happen to You

Don't Confuse the Average Annual Percentage Change with the Total Percentage Change

When economists talk about growth rates over a period of more than one year, the numbers are always *average annual percentage changes* and *not* total percentage changes. For example, in the United States, real GDP per capita was $13,213 in 1950 and $42,205 in 2010. The percentage change in real GDP per capita between these two years is

$$\left(\frac{\$42,205 - \$13,213}{\$13,213} \right) \times 100 = 219\%.$$

However, this is *not* the growth rate between the two years. The growth rate between these two years is the rate at which $13,213 in 1950 would have to grow on average *each year* to end up as $42,205 in 2010, which is 2.0 percent.

MyEconLab

Your Turn: Test your understanding by doing related problem 1.6 on page 369 at the end of this chapter.

"The Rich Get Richer and ..."

We can divide the world's economies into two groups: the *high-income countries*, sometimes also referred to as the *industrial countries*, and the poorer countries, or *developing countries*. The high-income countries include the countries of Western Europe, Australia, Canada, Japan, New Zealand, and the United States. The developing countries include most of the countries of Africa, Asia, and Latin America. In the 1980s and 1990s, a small group of countries, mostly East Asian countries such as Singapore, South Korea, and Taiwan, experienced high rates of growth and are sometimes referred to as the *newly industrializing countries*. Figure 11.2 shows the

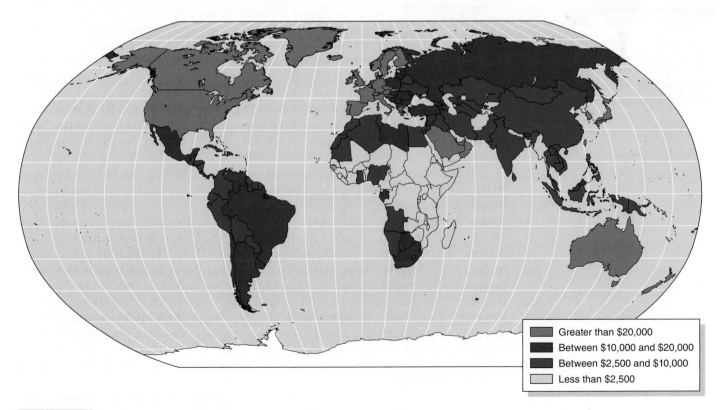

Greater than $20,000
Between $10,000 and $20,000
Between $2,500 and $10,000
Less than $2,500

Figure 11.2   GDP per Capita, 2010

GDP per capita is measured in U.S. dollars, corrected for differences across countries in the cost of living.

levels of GDP per capita around the world in 2010. GDP is measured in U.S. dollars, corrected for differences across countries in the cost of living. In 2010, GDP per capita ranged from a high of $82,600 in Luxembourg to a low of $300 in the African countries of Burundi and the Democratic Republic of the Congo. To understand why the gap between rich and poor countries exists, we need to look at what causes economies to grow.

<table>
<tr><td align="right">Making
the
Connection</td><td>

Is Income All That Matters?

</td></tr>
</table>

The more income you have, the more goods and services you can buy. When people are surviving on very low incomes of $2 per day or less, their ability to buy even minimal amounts of food, clothing, and housing is limited. So, most economists argue that unless the incomes of the very poor increase significantly, they will be unable to attain a higher standard of living. In some countries—primarily those colored yellow in Figure 11.2—the growth in average income has been very slow, or even negative, over a period of decades. Many economists and policymakers have concluded that the standard of living in these countries has been largely unchanged for many years.

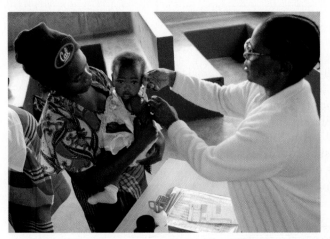

In sub-Saharan Africa and other parts of the world, increases in technology and knowledge are leading to improvements in health care and the standard of living.

Recently, however, some economists have argued that if we look beyond income to other measures of the standard of living, we can see that even the poorest countries have made significant progress in recent decades. For example, Charles Kenny, an economist with the World Bank, argues that "those countries with the lowest quality of life are making the fastest progress in improving it—across a range of measures including health, education, and civil and political liberties." For example, between 1960 and 2010, deaths among children declined, often by more than 50 percent, in nearly all countries, including most of those with the lowest incomes. Even in sub-Saharan Africa, where growth in incomes has been very slow, the percentage of children dying before age five has decreased by more than 30 percent over the past 50 years. Similarly, the percentage of people able to read and write has more than doubled in sub-Saharan Africa since 1970. Many more people now live in democracies where basic civil rights are respected than at any other time in world history. Although some countries, such as Somalia, the Democratic Republic of the Congo, and Afghanistan, have suffered from civil wars, political instability has also decreased in many countries in recent years, which has reduced the likelihood of dying from violence.

What explains these improvements in health, education, democracy, and political stability? William Easterly, an economist at New York University, has found that although at any given time, countries that have a higher income also have a higher standard of living, over time increases in income *within a particular country* typically have very little effect on the country's standard of living in terms of health, education, individual rights, political stability, and similar factors. Kenny's argument and Easterly's finding are connected: Some increases in living standards do not require significant increases in income. The key factors in raising living standards in low-income countries have been increases in technology and knowledge—such as the development of inexpensive vaccines that reduce epidemics or the use of mosquito-resistant netting that reduces prevalence of malaria—that are inexpensive enough to be widely available. Changes in attitudes, such as placing a greater value on education, particularly for girls, or increasing support for political freedoms, have also played a role in improving conditions in low-income countries.

There are limits, of course, to how much living standards can increase if incomes stagnate. Ultimately, much higher rates of economic growth will be necessary for low-income countries to significantly close the gap in living standards with high-income countries.

Based on Charles Kenny, *Getting Better*, (New York: Basic Books, 2011); Ursula Casabonne and Charles Kenny, "The Best Things in Life Are (Nearly) Free: Technology, Knowledge, and Global Health," *World Development*, forthcoming; and William Easterly, "Life during Growth," *Journal of Economic Growth*, Vol. 4, No. 3, September 1999, pp. 239–276.

Your Turn: Test your understanding by doing related problems 1.7 and 1.8 on page 369 at the end of this chapter.

MyEconLab

What Determines How Fast Economies Grow?

11.2 LEARNING OBJECTIVE

Use the economic growth model to explain why growth rates differ across countries.

To explain changes in economic growth rates over time within countries and differences in growth rates among countries, we need to develop an *economic growth model*. An **economic growth model** explains growth rates in real GDP per capita over the long run. As we noted in Chapter 10, the average person can buy more goods and services only if the average worker produces more goods and services. Recall that **labor productivity** is the quantity of goods and services that can be produced by one worker or by one hour of work. Because of the importance of labor productivity in explaining economic growth, the economic growth model focuses on the causes of long-run increases in labor productivity.

How can a country's workers become more productive? Economists believe two key factors determine labor productivity: the quantity of capital per hour worked and the level of technology. Therefore, the economic growth model focuses on technological change and changes over time in the quantity of capital available to workers in explaining changes in real GDP per capita. Recall that **technological change** is a change in the quantity of output firms can produce using a given quantity of inputs.

There are three main sources of technological change:

- **Better machinery and equipment.** Beginning with the steam engine during the Industrial Revolution, the invention of new machinery has been an important source of rising labor productivity. Today, continuing improvements in computers, factory machine tools, electric generators, and many other machines contribute to increases in labor productivity.

- **Increases in human capital.** Capital refers to *physical capital*, including computers, factory buildings, machine tools, warehouses, and trucks. The more physical capital workers have available, the more output they can produce. **Human capital** is the accumulated knowledge and skills that workers acquire from education and training or from their life experiences. As workers increase their human capital through education or on-the-job training, their productivity also increases. The more educated workers are, the greater is their human capital.

- **Better means of organizing and managing production.** Labor productivity increases if managers can do a better job of organizing production. For example, the *just-in-time system*, first developed by Toyota Motor Corporation, involves assembling goods from parts that arrive at the factory at exactly the time they are needed. With this system, Toyota needs fewer workers to store and keep track of parts in the factory, so the quantity of goods produced per hour worked increases.

Note that technological change is *not* the same thing as more physical capital. New capital can embody technological change, as when a faster computer chip is embodied in a new computer. But simply adding more capital that is the same as existing capital is not technological change. To summarize, we can say that a country's standard of living will be higher the more capital workers have available on their jobs, the better the capital, the more human capital workers have, and the better the job business managers do in organizing production.

Economic growth model A model that explains growth rates in real GDP per capita over the long run.

Labor productivity The quantity of goods and services that can be produced by one worker or by one hour of work.

Technological change A change in the quantity of output a firm can produce using a given quantity of inputs.

Human capital The accumulated knowledge and skills that workers acquire from education and training or from their life experiences.

The Per-Worker Production Function

The economic growth model explains increases in real GDP per capita over time as resulting from increases in just two factors: the quantity of physical capital available to workers and technological change. Often when analyzing economic growth, we look at increases in real GDP *per hour worked* and increases in capital *per hour worked*. We use measures of GDP per hour and capital per hour rather than per person so we can analyze changes in the underlying ability of an economy to produce more goods with a given amount of labor without having to worry about changes in the fraction of the population working or in the length of the workday. We can illustrate the economic growth model using the **per-worker production function**, which is the relationship between real GDP per hour worked and capital per hour worked, *holding the level of technology constant*. Figure 11.3 shows the per-worker production function as a graph. In the figure, we measure capital per hour worked along the horizontal axis and real GDP per hour worked along the vertical axis. Letting *K* stand for capital, *L* stand for labor, and *Y* stand for real GDP, real GDP per hour worked is *Y/L*, and capital per hour worked is *K/L*. The curve represents the production function. Notice that we do not explicitly show technological change in the figure. We assume that as we move along the production function, the level of technology remains constant. As we will see, we can illustrate technological change using this graph by *shifting up* the curve representing the production function.

The figure shows that increases in the quantity of capital per hour worked result in movements up the per-worker production function, increasing the quantity of output each worker produces. When *holding technology constant*, however, equal increases in the amount of capital per hour worked lead to *diminishing* increases in output per hour worked. For example, increasing capital per hour worked from $20,000 to $30,000 increases real GDP per hour worked from $200 to $350, an increase of $150. Another $10,000 increase in capital per hour worked, from $30,000 to $40,000, increases real GDP per hour worked from $350 to $475, an increase of only $125. Each additional $10,000 increase in capital per hour worked results in progressively smaller increases in real GDP per hour worked. In fact, at very high levels of capital per hour worked, further increases in capital per hour worked will not result in any increase in real GDP per hour worked. This effect results from the *law of diminishing returns*, which states that as we add more of one input—in this case, capital—to a fixed quantity of another input—in this case, labor—output increases by smaller additional amounts.

Why are there diminishing returns to capital? Consider a simple example in which you own a copy store. At first you have 10 employees but only 1 copy machine, so each of your workers is able to produce relatively few copies per day. When you buy a second copy

Per-worker production function
The relationship between real GDP per hour worked and capital per hour worked, holding the level of technology constant.

Figure 11.3

The Per-Worker Production Function

The per-worker production function shows the relationship between capital per hour worked and real GDP per hour worked, holding technology constant. Increases in capital per hour worked increase output per hour worked but at a diminishing rate. For example, an increase in capital per hour worked from $20,000 to $30,000 increases real GDP per hour worked from $200 to $350. An increase in capital per hour worked from $30,000 to $40,000 increases real GDP per hour worked only from $350 to $475. Each additional $10,000 increase in capital per hour worked results in a progressively smaller increase in output per hour worked.

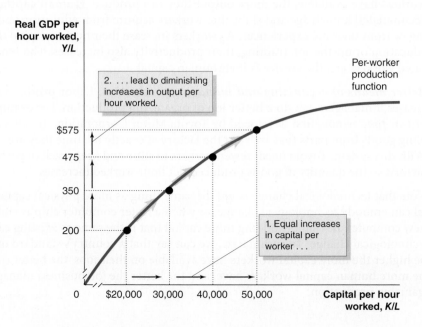

machine, your employees will be able to produce more copies. Adding additional copy machines will continue to increase your output—but by increasingly smaller amounts. For example, adding a twentieth copy machine to the 19 you already have will not increase the copies each worker is able to make by nearly as much as adding a second copy machine did. Eventually, adding additional copying machines will not increase your output at all.

Which Is More Important for Economic Growth: More Capital or Technological Change?

Technological change helps economies avoid diminishing returns to capital. Let's consider two simple examples of the effects of technological change. First, suppose you have 10 copy machines in your copy store. Each copy machine can produce 10 copies per minute. You don't believe that adding an eleventh machine identical to the 10 you already have will significantly increase the number of copies your employees can produce in a day. Then you find out that a new copy machine has become available that produces 20 copies per minute. If you replace your existing machines with the new machines, the productivity of your workers will increase. The replacement of existing capital with more productive capital is an example of technological change.

Or suppose you realize that the layout of your store could be improved. Maybe the paper for the machines is on shelves at the back of the store, which requires your workers to spend time walking back and forth whenever the machines run out of paper. By placing the paper closer to the copy machines, you can improve the productivity of your workers. Reorganizing how production takes place so as to increase output is also an example of technological change.

Technological Change: The Key to Sustaining Economic Growth

Figure 11.4 shows the effect of technological change on the per-worker production function. Technological change shifts up the per-worker production function and allows an economy to produce more real GDP per hour worked with the same quantity of capital per hour worked. For example, if the current level of technology puts the economy on production function$_1$, then when capital per hour worked is $50,000, real GDP per hour worked is $575. Technological change that shifts the economy to production function$_2$

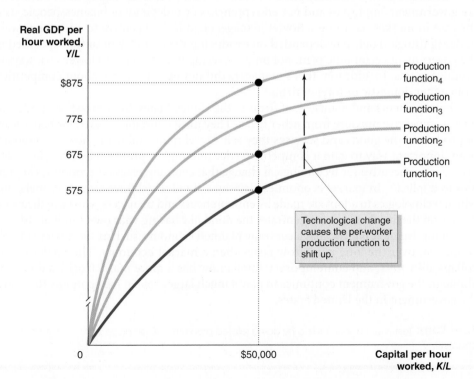

Figure 11.4

Technological Change Increases Output per Hour Worked

Technological change shifts up the production function and allows more output per hour worked with the same amount of capital per hour worked. For example, along Production function$_1$ with $50,000 in capital per hour worked, the economy can produce $575 in real GDP per hour worked. However, an increase in technology that shifts the economy to Production function$_2$ makes it possible to produce $675 in real GDP per hour worked with the same level of capital per hour worked.

makes it possible to produce $675 in goods and services per hour worked with the same level of capital per hour worked. Further increases in technology that shift the economy to higher production functions result in further increases in real GDP per hour worked. Because of diminishing returns to capital, continuing increases in real GDP per hour worked can be sustained only if there is technological change. Remember that a country will experience increases in its standard of living only if it experiences increases in real GDP per hour worked. Therefore, we can draw the following important conclusion: *In the long run, a country will experience an increasing standard of living only if it experiences continuing technological change.*

The fall of the Berlin Wall in 1989 symbolized the failure of Communism.

Making the Connection | What Explains the Economic Failure of the Soviet Union?

The economic growth model can help explain one of the most striking events of the twentieth century: the economic collapse of the Soviet Union. The Soviet Union was formed from the old Russian Empire following the Communist revolution of 1917. Under Communism, the Soviet Union was a centrally planned economy where the government owned nearly every business and made all production and pricing decisions. In 1960, Nikita Khrushchev, the leader of the Soviet Union, addressed the United Nations in New York City. He declared to the United States and the other democracies, "We will bury you. Your grandchildren will live under Communism."

Many people at the time took Khrushchev's boast seriously. Capital per hour worked grew rapidly in the Soviet Union from 1950 through the 1980s. At first, these increases in capital per hour worked also produced rapid increases in real GDP per hour worked. Rapid increases in real GDP per hour worked during the 1950s caused some economists in the United States to predict incorrectly that the Soviet Union would someday surpass the United States economically. In fact, diminishing returns to capital meant that the additional factories the Soviet Union was building resulted in smaller and smaller increases in real GDP per hour worked.

The Soviet Union did experience some technological change—but at a rate much slower than in the United States and other high-income countries. Why did the Soviet Union fail the crucial requirement for growth: implementing new technologies? The key reason is that in a centrally planned economy, the people managing most businesses are government employees and not entrepreneurs or independent businesspeople, as is the case in market economies. Soviet managers had little incentive to adopt new ways of doing things. Their pay depended on producing the quantity of output specified in the government's economic plan, not on discovering new, better, and lower-cost ways to produce goods. In addition, these managers did not have to worry about competition from either domestic or foreign firms.

Entrepreneurs and managers of firms in the United States, by contrast, are under intense competitive pressure from other firms. They must constantly search for better ways of producing the goods and services they sell. Developing and using new technologies is an important way to gain a competitive edge and higher profits. The drive for profit provides an incentive for technological change that centrally planned economies are unable to duplicate. In market economies, decisions about which investments to make and which technologies to adopt are made by entrepreneurs and managers who have their own money on the line. Nothing concentrates the mind like having your own funds at risk.

In hindsight, it is clear that a centrally planned economy, such as the Soviet Union's, could not, over the long run, grow faster than a market economy. The Soviet Union collapsed in 1991, and contemporary Russia now has a more market-oriented system, although the government continues to play a much larger role in the economy than does the government in the United States.

MyEconLab **Your Turn:** Test your understanding by doing related problem 2.10 on page 370 at the end of this chapter.

Solved Problem 11.2

Using the Economic Growth Model to Analyze the Failure of the Soviet Economy

Use the economic growth model and the information in the *Making the Connection* on page 346 to analyze the economic problems the Soviet Union encountered.

Solving the Problem

Step 1: Review the chapter material. This problem is about using the economic growth model to explain the failure of the Soviet economy, so you may want to review the *Making the Connection* on page 346.

Step 2: Draw a graph like Figure 11.3 on page 344 to illustrate the economic problems of the Soviet Union. For simplicity, assume that the Soviet Union experienced no technological change.

The Soviet Union experienced rapid increases in capital per hour worked from 1950 through the 1980s, but its failure to implement new technology meant that output per hour worked grew at a slower and slower rate.

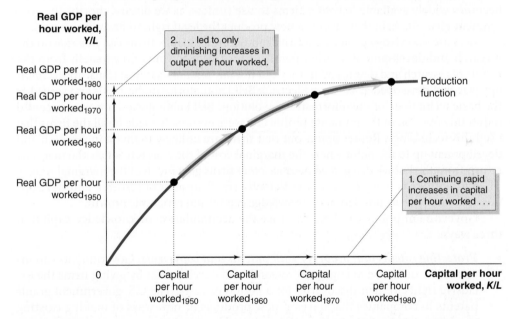

Extra Credit: The Soviet Union hoped to raise the standard of living of its citizens above that enjoyed in the United States and other high-income countries. Its strategy was to make continuous increases in the quantity of capital available to its workers. The economic growth model helps us understand the flaws in this policy for achieving economic growth.

Your Turn: For more practice, do related problems 2.7 and 2.8 on page 370 at the end of this chapter.   MyEconLab

New Growth Theory

The economic growth model we have been using was first developed in the 1950s by Nobel Laureate Robert Solow of MIT. According to this model, productivity growth is the key factor in explaining long-run growth in real GDP per capita. In recent years, some economists have become dissatisfied with this model because it does not

New growth theory A model of long-run economic growth that emphasizes that technological change is influenced by economic incentives and so is determined by the working of the market system.

explain the factors that determine productivity growth. What has become known as the **new growth theory** was developed by Paul Romer, an economist at Stanford University, to provide a better explanation of the sources of productivity change. Romer argues that the rate of technological change is influenced by how individuals and firms respond to economic incentives. Earlier accounts of economic growth did not explain technological change or attributed it to factors such as chance scientific discoveries.

Romer argues that the accumulation of *knowledge capital* is a key determinant of economic growth. Firms add to an economy's stock of knowledge capital when they engage in research and development or otherwise contribute to technological change. We have seen that accumulation of physical capital is subject to diminishing returns: Increases in capital per hour worked lead to increases in real GDP per hour worked but at a decreasing rate. Romer argues that the same is true of knowledge capital *at the firm level*. As firms add to their stock of knowledge capital, they increase their output but at a decreasing rate. At the level of the entire economy rather than just individual firms, however, Romer argues that knowledge capital is subject to *increasing returns*. Increasing returns can exist because knowledge, once discovered, becomes available to everyone. The use of physical capital, such as a computer or machine tool, is *rival* because if one firm uses it, other firms cannot, and it is *excludable* because the firm that owns the capital can keep other firms from using it. The use of knowledge capital, such as the chemical formula for a drug that cures cancer, is nonrival, however, because one firm's using that knowledge does not prevent another firm from using it. Knowledge capital is also nonexcludable because once something like a chemical formula becomes known, it becomes widely available for other firms to use (unless, as we discuss shortly, the government gives the firm that invents a new product the legal right to its exclusive use).

Because knowledge capital is nonrival and nonexcludable, firms can *free ride* on the research and development of other firms. Firms free ride when they benefit from the results of research and development they did not pay for. For example, transistor technology was first developed at Western Electric's Bell Laboratories in the 1950s and served as the basic technology of the information revolution. Bell Laboratories, however, received only a tiny fraction of the immense profits that were eventually made by all the firms that used this technology. Romer points out that firms are unlikely to invest in research and development up to the point where the marginal cost of the research equals the marginal return from the knowledge gained because *other* firms gain much of the marginal return. Therefore, there is likely to be an inefficiently small amount of research and development, slowing the accumulation of knowledge capital and economic growth.

Government policy can help increase the accumulation of knowledge capital in three ways:

Patent The exclusive right to produce a product for a period of 20 years from the date the patent is applied for.

- *Protecting intellectual property with patents and copyrights.* Governments can increase the incentive to engage in research and development by giving firms the exclusive rights to their discoveries for a period of years. The U.S. government grants patents to companies that develop new products or new ways of making existing products. A **patent** gives a firm the exclusive legal right to a new product for a period of 20 years from the date a patent on the product is applied for. For example, a pharmaceutical firm that develops a drug that cures cancer can secure a patent on the drug, keeping other firms from manufacturing the drug without permission. The profits earned during the period the patent is in force provide firms with an incentive for undertaking the research and development. The patent system has drawbacks, however. In filing for a patent, a firm must disclose information about the product or process. This information enters the public record and may help competing firms develop products or processes that are similar but that do not infringe on the patent. To avoid this problem, a firm may try to keep the results of its research a *trade secret*, without patenting it. (A famous example of a trade secret is the formula for Coca-Cola.) Tension also arises between the government's objectives of providing patent protection that gives firms the incentive to engage in research and development and making sure that the knowledge gained through the research is widely available, which increases the positive effect of the knowledge on the economy. Economists debate the features of an ideal patent system.

Just as a new product or a new method of making a product receives patent protection, books, films, and other artistic works receive *copyright* protection. Under U.S. law, the creator of a book, a film, or other artistic work has the exclusive right to use the creation during the creator's lifetime. The creator's heirs retain this exclusive right for 70 years after the creator's death.

- *Subsidizing research and development.* The government can use subsidies to increase the quantity of research and development that takes place. In the United States, the federal government conducts some research directly. For example, the National Institutes of Health conducts medical research. The government also subsidizes research by providing grants to researchers in universities through the National Science Foundation and other agencies. Finally, the government provides tax benefits to firms that invest in research and development.

- *Subsidizing education.* People with technical training carry out research and development. If firms are unable to capture all the profits from research and development, they will pay lower wages and salaries to technical workers. These lower wages and salaries reduce the incentive to workers to receive this training. If the government subsidizes education, it can increase the number of workers who have technical training. In the United States, the government subsidizes education by directly providing free education from grades kindergarten through 12 and by providing support for public colleges and universities. The government also provides student loans at reduced interest rates.

These government policies can bring the accumulation of knowledge capital closer to the optimal level.

Joseph Schumpeter and Creative Destruction

The new growth theory has revived interest in the ideas of Joseph Schumpeter. Born in Austria in 1883, Schumpeter served briefly as that country's finance minister. In 1932, he became an economics professor at Harvard. Schumpeter developed a model of growth that emphasized his view that new products unleash a "gale of creative destruction" that drives older products—and, often, the firms that produced them—out of the market. According to Schumpeter, the key to rising living standards is not small changes to existing products but, rather, new products that meet consumer wants in qualitatively better ways. For example, in the early twentieth century, the automobile displaced the horse-drawn carriage by meeting consumer demand for personal transportation in a way that was qualitatively better. In the early twenty-first century, the DVD and the DVD player displaced the VHS tape and the VCR by better meeting consumer demand for watching films at home. Downloading or streaming movies from the Internet may be in the process of displacing the DVD just as the DVD displaced the VHS tape.

To Schumpeter, the entrepreneur is central to economic growth: "The function of entrepreneurs is to reform or revolutionize the pattern of production by exploiting an invention or, more generally, an untried technological possibility for producing new commodities or producing an old one in a new way."

The profits an entrepreneur hopes to earn provide the incentive for bringing together the factors of production—labor, capital, and natural resources—to start new firms and introduce new goods and services. Successful entrepreneurs can use their profits to finance the development of new products and are better able to attract funds from investors.

Economic Growth in the United States

The economic growth model can help us understand the record of growth in the United States. Figure 11.5 shows average annual growth rates in real GDP per hour worked since 1800. As the United States experienced the Industrial Revolution during the nineteenth century, U.S. firms increased the quantities of capital per hour worked. New technologies

11.3 LEARNING OBJECTIVE

Discuss fluctuations in productivity growth in the United States.

Figure 11.5

Average Annual Growth Rates in Real GDP per Hour Worked in the United States

The growth rate in the United States increased from 1800 through the mid-1970s. Then, for more than 20 years, growth slowed before increasing again in the mid-1990s. Note: The values for 1800–1900 are real GDP per worker. The values for 1900–2010 are real GDP per hour worked and are the authors' calculations, based on the methods used in Neville Francis and Valerie A. Ramey, "The Source of Historical Economic Fluctuations: An Analysis Using Long-Run Restrictions," in Jeffrey Frankel, Richard Clarida, and Francesco Giavazzi, eds., *International Seminar in Macroeconomics*, (Chicago: University of Chicago Press, 2005); the authors thank Neville Francis for kindly providing data through 2004.

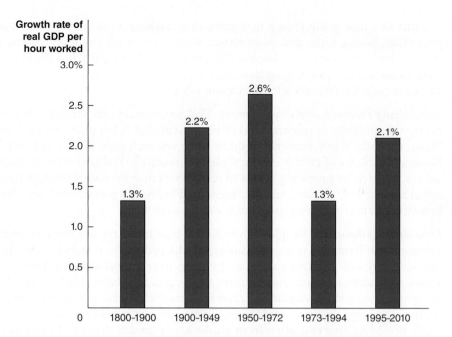

such as the steam engine, the railroad, and the telegraph also became available. Together, these factors resulted in an average annual growth rate of real GDP per worker of 1.3 percent from 1800 to 1900. Real GDP per capita grew at the slower rate of 1.1 percent during this period. At this growth rate, real GDP *per capita* would double about every 63 years, which means that living standards were growing steadily but relatively slowly.

By the twentieth century, technological change had been institutionalized. Many large corporations began to set up research and development facilities to improve the quality of their products and the efficiency with which they produced them. Universities also began to conduct research that had business applications. After World War II, many corporations began to provide significant funds to universities to help pay for research. In 1950, the federal government created the National Science Foundation, whose main goal is to support university researchers. The accelerating rate of technological change led to more rapid growth rates.

Economic Growth in the United States since 1950

Continuing technological change allowed the U.S. economy to avoid the diminishing returns to capital that stifled growth in the Soviet economy. In fact, until the 1970s, the growth rate of the U.S. economy accelerated over time. As Figure 11.5 shows, growth in the first half of the twentieth century was faster than growth during the nineteenth century, and growth in the immediate post–World War II period from 1950 to 1972 was faster yet. Then the unexpected happened: For more than 20 years, from 1973 to 1994, the growth rate of real GDP per hour worked slowed. The growth rate during these years was more than 1 percentage point per year lower than during the 1950–1972 period. Beginning in the mid-1990s, the growth rate picked up again, although it remained below the levels of the immediate post–World War II period.

What Caused the Productivity Slowdown of 1973–1994?

Several explanations have been offered for the productivity slowdown of the mid-1970s to mid-1990s, but none is completely satisfying. Some economists argue that productivity really didn't slow down; it only *appears* to have slowed down because of problems in measuring productivity accurately. After 1970, services—such as haircuts and financial advice—became a larger fraction of GDP, and goods—such as automobiles and hamburgers—became a smaller fraction. It is more difficult to measure increases in the output of services than to measure increases in the output of goods. For example, before banks began using automated teller machines (ATMs) in the 1980s, you could withdraw money only by going to a bank before closing time—which was usually 3:00 P.M. Once ATMs became available, you could withdraw money at any time of the day or night at a variety of locations. This increased convenience from ATMs does not show up in GDP. If it did, measured output per hour worked would have grown more rapidly.

There may also be a measurement problem in accounting for improvements in the environment and in health and safety. During these years, new laws required firms to spend billions of dollars reducing pollution, improving workplace safety, and redesigning products to improve their safety. This spending did not result in additional output that would be included in GDP—although it may have increased overall well-being. If these increases in well-being had been included in GDP, measured output per hour worked would have grown more rapidly.

In the early 1980s, many economists thought the rapid oil price increases that occurred between 1974 and 1979 explained the productivity slowdown, but the productivity slowdown continued after U.S. firms had fully adjusted to high oil prices. In fact, it continued into the late 1980s and early 1990s, when oil prices declined.

Some economists argue that deterioration in the U.S. educational system may have contributed to the slowdown in growth from the mid-1970s to mid-1990s. Scores on some standardized tests began to decline in the 1970s, which may indicate that workers entering the labor force were less well educated and less productive than in earlier decades. Another possibility is that the skills required to perform many jobs increased during the 1970s and 1980s, while the preparation that workers had received in school did not keep pace.

The United States was not alone in experiencing the slowdown in productivity. All the high-income countries experienced a growth slowdown between the mid-1970s and the mid-1990s. Because all the high-income economies began producing more services and fewer goods and enacted stricter environmental regulations at about the same time, explanations of the productivity slowdown that emphasize measurement problems become more plausible. In the end, though, economists are still debating why the productivity slowdown took place.

Can the United States Maintain High Rates of Productivity Growth?

As Figure 11.5 shows, productivity growth, as measured by increases in real GDP per hour worked, increased between 1995 and 2010 compared to the previous 20-year period. Some economists argue that the development of a "new economy" based on information technology caused the higher productivity growth that began in the mid-1990s. The spread of ever-faster and increasingly less expensive computers has made communication and data processing easier and faster than ever before. Today, a single desktop computer has more computing power than all the mainframe computers NASA used to control the *Apollo* spacecrafts that landed on the moon in the late 1960s and early 1970s.

Faster data processing has had a major effect on nearly every firm. Business record keeping, once done laboriously by hand, is now done more quickly and accurately by computer. The increase in Internet use during the 1990s brought changes to the ways firms sell to consumers and to each other. Cell phones, laptop computers, and wireless Internet access allow people to work away from the office, both at home and while traveling. These developments have significantly increased labor productivity.

Many economists are optimistic that the increases in productivity that began in the mid-1990s will continue. The use of computers, as well as information and communications technology in general, increases as prices continue to fall. By 2011, well-equipped desktop computers could be purchased for less than $300. Further innovations in information and communications technology may continue to contribute to strong productivity growth. Some economists are skeptical, however, about the ability of the economy to continue to sustain high rates of productivity growth. These economists argue that in the 1990s, innovations in information and communications technology—such as the development of the World Wide Web, Windows 95, and computerized inventory control systems—raised labor productivity by having a substantial effect on how businesses operated. By the early 2000s, these economists argue, innovations in information and communications technology were having a greater effect on consumer products, such as cell phones, than on labor productivity. If the increases in output per hour worked that began in the mid-1990s do continue, this trend will be good news for increases in living standards in the United States.

11.4 LEARNING OBJECTIVE

Explain economic catch-up and discuss why many poor countries have not experienced rapid economic growth.

Why Isn't the Whole World Rich?

The economic growth model tells us that economies grow when the quantity of capital per hour worked increases and when technological change takes place. This model seems to provide a good blueprint for developing countries to become rich: (1) Increase the quantity of capital per hour worked and (2) use the best available technology. There are economic incentives for both of these things to happen in poor countries. The profitability of using additional capital or better technology is generally greater in a developing country than in a high-income country. For example, replacing an existing computer with a new, faster computer will generally have a relatively small payoff for a firm in the United States. In contrast, installing a new computer in a Zambian firm where records have been kept by hand is likely to have an enormous payoff.

This observation leads to an important conclusion: *The economic growth model predicts that poor countries will grow faster than rich countries.* If this prediction is correct, we should observe poor countries catching up to rich countries in levels of GDP per capita (or income per capita). Has this **catch-up**—or *convergence*—actually occurred? Here we come to a paradox: If we look only at the countries that currently have high incomes, we see that the lower-income countries have been catching up to the higher-income countries, but the developing countries as a group have not been catching up to the high-income countries as a group.

Catch-up The prediction that the level of GDP per capita (or income per capita) in poor countries will grow faster than in rich countries.

Catch-up: Sometimes but Not Always

We can construct a graph that makes it easier to see whether catch-up is happening. In Figure 11.6, the horizontal axis shows the initial level of real GDP per capita, and the vertical axis shows the rate at which real GDP per capita is growing. We can then plot points on the graph for rich and poor countries. Each point represents the combination

Figure 11.6

The Catch-up Predicted by the Economic Growth Model

According to the economic growth model, countries that start with lower levels of real GDP per capita should grow faster (points near the top of the line) than countries that start with higher levels of real GDP per capita (points near the bottom of the line).

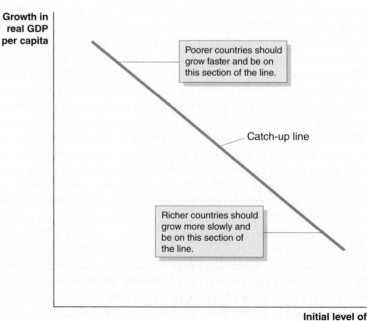

of a country's initial level of real GDP per capita and its growth rate over the following years. Low-income countries should be in the upper-left part of the graph because they would have low initial levels of real GDP per capita but fast growth rates. High-income countries should be in the lower-right part of the graph because they would have high initial levels of real GDP per capita but slow growth rates.

Catch-up among the High-Income Countries If we look at only the countries that currently have high incomes, we can see the catch-up predicted by the economic growth model. Figure 11.7 shows that the high-income countries that had the lowest incomes in 1960, such as Taiwan, Korea, and Singapore, grew the fastest between 1960 and 2009. Countries that had the highest incomes in 1960, such as Switzerland and the United States, grew the slowest.

Are the Developing Countries Catching Up to the High-Income Countries? If we expand our analysis to include every country for which statistics are available, it becomes more difficult to find the catch-up predicted by the economic growth model. Figure 11.8 does not show a consistent relationship between the level of real GDP in 1960 and growth from 1960 to 2009. Some countries that had low levels of real GDP per capita in 1960, such as Niger, Madagascar, and the Democratic Republic of the Congo, actually experienced *negative* economic growth: They had *lower* levels of real GDP per capita in 2009 than in 1960. Other countries that started with low levels of real GDP per capita, such as Malaysia and South Korea, grew rapidly. Some middle-income countries in 1960, such as Venezuela, hardly grew between 1960 and 2009, while others, such as Israel, experienced significant growth.

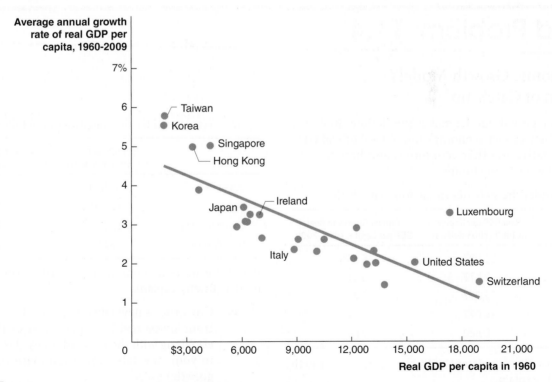

Figure 11.7   **There Has Been Catch-up among High-Income Countries**

If we look only at countries that currently have high incomes, we see that countries such as Taiwan, Korea, and Singapore that had the lowest incomes in 1960 grew the fastest between 1960 and 2009. Countries such as Switzerland and the United States that had the highest incomes in 1960 grew the slowest.

Note: Data are real GDP per capita in 2005 dollars. Each point in the figure represents one high-income country.

Authors' calculations from data in Alan Heston, Robert Summers, and Bettina Aten, *Penn World Table Version 7.0*, Center for International Comparisons of Production, Income and Prices at the University of Pennsylvania, June 3, 2011.

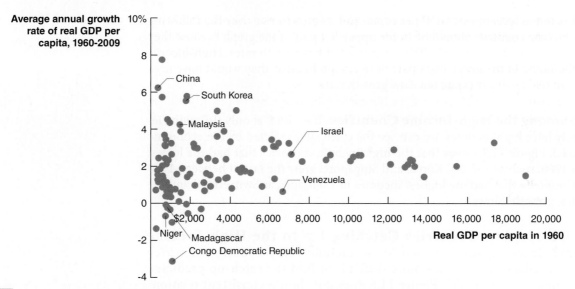

Figure 11.8 **Most of the World Hasn't Been Catching Up**

If we look at all countries for which statistics are available, we do not see the catch-up predicted by the economic growth model. Some countries that had low levels of real GDP per capita in 1960, such as Niger, Madagascar, and the Democratic Republic of the Congo, actually experienced *negative* economic growth. Other countries that started with low levels of real GDP per capita, such as Malaysia and South Korea, grew rapidly. Some middle-income countries in 1960, such as Venezuela, hardly grew between 1960 and 2009, while others, such as Israel, experienced significant growth.

Note: Data are real GDP per capita in 2005 dollars. Each point in the figure represents one country.

Authors' calculations from data in Alan Heston, Robert Summers, and Bettina Aten, *Penn World Table Version 7.0*, Center for International Comparisons of Production, Income and Prices at the University of Pennsylvania, June 3, 2011.

Solved Problem 11.4

The Economic Growth Model's Prediction of Catch-up

The economic growth model makes predictions about the relationship between an economy's initial level of real GDP per capita relative to other economies and how fast the economy will grow in the future.

a. Consider the statistics in the following table:

Country	Real GDP per Capita in 1960 (2005 dollars)	Annual Growth in Real GDP per Capita, 1960–2009
Taiwan	$1,826	5.78%
Panama	2,171	3.21
Brazil	2,877	2.43
Algeria	4,077	0.81
Venezuela	6,662	0.64

Are these statistics consistent with the economic growth model? Briefly explain.

b. Now consider the statistics in the following table:

Country	Real GDP per Capita in 1960 (2005 dollars)	Annual Growth in Real GDP per Capita, 1960–2009
Japan	$6,094	3.44%
Belgium	10,241	2.52
United Kingdom	12,842	1.97
New Zealand	13,803	1.44

Are these statistics consistent with the economic growth model? Briefly explain.

c. Construct a new table that lists all nine countries, from lowest real GDP per capita in 1960 to highest, along with their growth rates. Are the statistics in your new table consistent with the economic growth model?

Solving the Problem

Step 1: **Review the chapter material.** This problem is about catch-up in the economic growth model, so you may want to review the section "Why Isn't the Whole World Rich?" which begins on page 352.

Step 2: **Explain whether the statistics in the table in part a are consistent with the economic growth model.** These statistics are consistent with the economic growth model. The countries with the lowest levels of real GDP per capita in 1960 had the fastest growth rates between 1960 and 2009, and the countries with the highest levels of real GDP per capita had the slowest growth rates.

Step 3: **Explain whether the statistics in the table in part b are consistent with the economic growth model.** These statistics are also consistent with the economic growth model. Once again, the countries with the lowest levels of real GDP per capita in 1960 had the fastest growth rates between 1960 and 2009, and the countries with the highest levels of real GDP per capita had the slowest growth rates.

Step 4: **Construct a table that includes all nine countries from the tables in parts a and b and discuss the results.**

Country	Real GDP per Capita in 1960 (2005 dollars)	Annual Growth in Real GDP per Capita, 1960–2009
Taiwan	$1,826	5.78%
Panama	2,171	3.21
Brazil	2,877	2.43
Algeria	4,077	0.81
Japan	6,094	3.44
Venezuela	6,662	0.64
Belgium	10,241	2.52
United Kingdom	12,842	1.97
New Zealand	13,803	1.44

The statistics in the new table are not consistent with the predictions of the economic growth model. For example, New Zealand and the United Kingdom had higher levels of real GDP per capita in 1960 than did Algeria and Venezuela. The economic growth model predicts that New Zealand and the United Kingdom should, therefore, have grown more slowly than Algeria and Venezuela. The data in the table show, however, that New Zealand and the United Kingdom grew faster. Similarly, Belgium grew faster than Brazil, even though its real GDP per capita was already much higher than Brazil's in 1960.

Extra Credit: The statistics in these tables confirm what we saw in Figures 11.7 and 11.8 on pages 353–354: There has been catch-up among the high-income countries, but there has not been catch-up if we include in the analysis all the countries of the world.

Your Turn: For more practice, do problems 4.5 and 4.6 on page 372 at the end of this chapter.   MyEconLab

Why Haven't Most Western European Countries, Canada, and Japan Caught Up to the United States?

Figure 11.7 indicates that there has been catch-up among the high-income countries over the past 50 years. If we look at the catch-up of other high-income countries to the United States, we discover a surprising fact: Over the past 20 years, other high-income countries have actually fallen further behind the United States rather than catching up to it. Figure 11.9 shows real GDP per capita in Canada, Japan, and the five largest economies in Western Europe relative to real GDP per capita in the United States. The blue bars show real GDP per capita in 1990 relative to the United States, and the red bars show real GDP per capita in 2010 relative to the United States. In each case, relative levels of real GDP per capita were lower in 2010 than they were in 1990. Each of these countries experienced significant catch-up to the United States between 1960 and 1990, but they have experienced no catch-up since 1990.

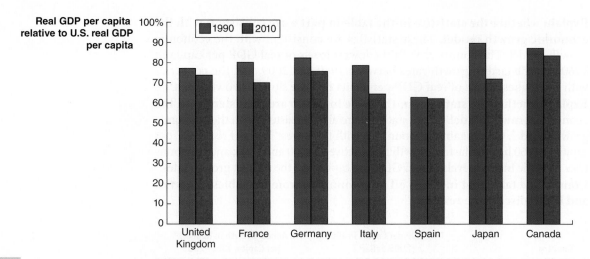

Figure 11.9 **Other High-Income Countries Have Stopped Catching Up to the United States**

The blue bars show real GDP per capita in 1990 relative to the United States, and the red bars show real GDP per capita in 2010 relative to the United States. In each case, relative levels of real GDP per capita are lower in 2010 than they were in 1990, which means that these countries have ceased catching up to the United States.

Data from Alan Heston, Robert Summers, and Bettina Aten, *Penn World Table Version 7.0*, Center for International Comparisons of Production, Income and Prices at the University of Pennsylvania, June 3, 2011; and U.S. Central Intelligence Agency, *The World Factbook*, online version, www.cia.gov/library/publications/the-world-factbook.

Why have other high-income countries had trouble completely closing the gap in real GDP per capita with the United States? Many economists believe there are two main explanations: the greater flexibility of U.S. labor markets and the greater efficiency of the U.S. financial system. U.S. labor markets are more flexible than labor markets in other countries for several reasons. In many European countries, government regulations make it difficult for firms to fire workers and thereby make firms reluctant to hire workers in the first place. As a result, many younger workers have difficulty finding jobs, and once a job is found, a worker tends to remain in it even if his or her skills and preferences are not a good match for the characteristics of the job. In the United States, by contrast, government regulations are less restrictive, workers have an easier time finding jobs, and workers change jobs fairly frequently. This high rate of job mobility ensures a better match between workers' skills and preferences and the characteristics of jobs, which increases labor productivity. Many European countries also have restrictive work rules that limit the flexibility of firms to implement new technologies. These rules restrict the tasks firms can ask workers to perform and the number of hours they work. So, the rules reduce the ability of firms to use new technologies that may require workers to learn new skills, perform new tasks, or work during the night or early mornings.

Workers in the United States tend to enter the labor force earlier, retire later, and experience fewer long spells of unemployment than do workers in Europe. As we noted in Chapter 9, unemployed workers in the United States typically receive smaller government payments for a shorter period of time than do unemployed workers in Canada and most of the countries of Western Europe. Because the opportunity cost of being unemployed is lower in those countries, the unemployment rate tends to be higher, and the fraction of the labor force that is unemployed for more than one year also tends to be higher. Studies have shown that workers who are employed for longer periods tend to have greater skills, greater productivity, and higher wages. Many economists believe that the design of the U.S. unemployment insurance program has contributed to the greater flexibility of U.S. labor markets and to higher rates of growth in labor productivity and real GDP per capita.

As we have seen, technological change is essential for rapid productivity growth. To obtain the funds needed to implement new technologies, firms turn to the financial system. It is important that funds for investment be not only available but also allocated efficiently. We saw in Chapter 6 that large corporations can raise funds by selling stocks and bonds in financial markets. U.S. corporations benefit from the efficiency of U.S. financial markets. The level of legal protection of investors is relatively high in

U.S. financial markets, which encourages both U.S. and foreign investors to buy stocks and bonds issued by U.S. firms. The volume of trading in U.S. financial markets also ensures that investors will be able to quickly sell the stocks and bonds they buy. This *liquidity* serves to attract investors to U.S. markets.

Smaller firms that are unable to issue stocks and bonds often obtain funding from banks. Entrepreneurs founding new firms—"start-ups"—particularly firms that are based on new technologies, generally find that investors are unwilling to buy their stocks and bonds because the firms lack records of profitability. Banks are also reluctant to lend to new firms founded to introduce new and unfamiliar technologies. However, some technology start-ups obtain funds from *venture capital firms*. Venture capital firms raise funds from institutional investors, such as pension funds, and from wealthy individuals. The owners of venture capital firms closely examine the business plans of start-up firms, looking for those that appear most likely to succeed. In exchange for providing funding, a venture capital firm often becomes part owner of the start-up and may even play a role in managing the firm. A successful venture capital firm is able to attract investors who would not otherwise be willing to provide funds to start-ups because the investors would lack enough information on the start-up. A number of well-known U.S. high-technology firms, such as Google, relied on venture capitals firms to fund their early expansion. The ability of venture capital firms to finance technology-driven start-up firms may be giving the United States an advantage in bringing new products and new processes to market.

The U.S. financial system suffered severe problems between 2007 and 2009. But, over the long run, it has succeeded in efficiently allocating investment funds.

Why Don't More Low-Income Countries Experience Rapid Growth?

The economic growth model predicts that the countries that were very poor in 1960 should have grown rapidly over the next 50 years. As we have just seen, a few did, but most did not. Why are many low-income countries growing so slowly? There is no single answer, but most economists point to four key factors:

- Failure to enforce the rule of law

- Wars and revolutions

- Poor public education and health

- Low rates of saving and investment

Failure to Enforce the Rule of Law In the years since 1960, increasing numbers of developing countries, including China, have abandoned centrally planned economies in favor of more market-oriented economies. For entrepreneurs in a market economy to succeed, however, the government must guarantee private **property rights** and enforce contracts. Unless entrepreneurs feel secure in their property, they will not risk starting a business. It is also difficult for businesses to operate successfully in a market economy unless they can use an independent court system to enforce contracts. The **rule of law** refers to the ability of a government to enforce the laws of the country, particularly with respect to protecting private property and enforcing contracts. The failure of many developing countries to guarantee private property rights and to enforce contracts has hindered their economic growth.

Consider, for example, the production of shoes in a developing country. Suppose the owner of a shoe factory signs a contract with a leather tannery to deliver a specific quantity of leather on a particular date for a particular price. On the basis of this contract, the owner of the shoe factory signs a contract to deliver a specific quantity of shoes to a shoe wholesaler. This contract specifies the quantity of shoes to be delivered, the quality of the shoes, the delivery date, and the price. The owner of the leather tannery uses the contract with the shoe factory to enter into a contract with cattle ranchers

Property rights The rights individuals or firms have to the exclusive use of their property, including the right to buy or sell it.

Rule of law The ability of a government to enforce the laws of the country, particularly with respect to protecting private property and enforcing contracts.

for the delivery of hides. The shoe wholesaler enters into contracts to deliver shoes to retail stores, where they are sold to consumers. For the flow of goods from cattle ranchers to shoe customers to operate efficiently, each business must carry out the terms of the contract it has signed. In developed countries, such as the United States, businesses know that if they fail to carry out a contract, they may be sued in court and forced to compensate the other party for any economic damages.

Many developing countries do not have functioning, independent court systems. Even if a court system does exist, a case may not be heard for many years. In some countries, bribery of judges and political favoritism in court rulings are common. If firms cannot enforce contracts through the court system, they will insist on carrying out only face-to-face cash transactions. For example, the shoe manufacturer will wait until the leather producer brings the hides to the factory and will then buy them for cash. The wholesaler will wait until the shoes have been produced before making plans for sales to retail stores. Production still takes place, but it is carried out more slowly and inefficiently. With slow and inefficient production, firms have difficulty finding investors willing to provide them with the funds they need to expand.

| Making the Connection | What Do Parking Tickets in New York City Tell Us about Poverty in the Developing World? |

In many developing countries, government officials insist on receiving bribes to process most transactions. For example, someone may need to pay an official before being allowed to open a shoe store or to purchase farm land. This corruption represents a breakdown in the rule of law. Generally, the more corrupt a country's government, the lower the country's growth rate. Economists at the World Bank have developed an index that ranks the countries of the world from most corrupt to least corrupt. The figure below compares GDP per capita in the 20 most corrupt and the 20 least corrupt countries. GDP per capita is more than 10 times higher in the least corrupt countries than in the most corrupt countries.

But does corruption cause countries to be poor, or does a country's being poor lead to its being corrupt? Some economists have made the controversial argument that corruption may be the result of culture. If a culture of corruption exists in a country, then the country may have great difficulty establishing an honest government that is willing to enforce the rule of law. Economists Raymond Fisman of the Columbia Business School and Edward Miguel of the University of California, Berkeley, came up with an ingenious method of testing whether a culture of corruption exists in some countries. Every country in the world sends delegates to the United Nations in New York City. Under international law, these delegates cannot be prosecuted for violating U.S. laws, including parking regulations. So, a delegate to the United Nations can double park or park next to a fire hydrant and ignore any parking ticket he or she would receive.

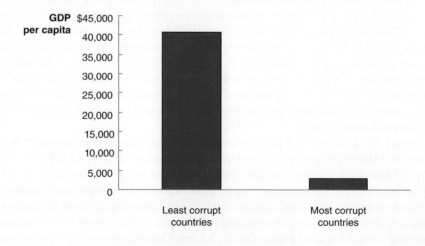

Fisman and Miguel argue that if a culture of corruption exists in some countries, the delegates from these countries will be more likely to ignore parking tickets than will the delegates from countries without a culture of corruption. Fisman and Miguel gathered statistics on the number of parking violations per delegate and compared the statistics to the World Bank's index of corruption. They found that as the level of corruption in a country increases, so does the number of parking violations by the country's United Nations delegates. For example, the figure below shows that the 15 percent of countries that are most corrupt had more than 10 times as many parking violations as the 15 percent of countries that are least corrupt.

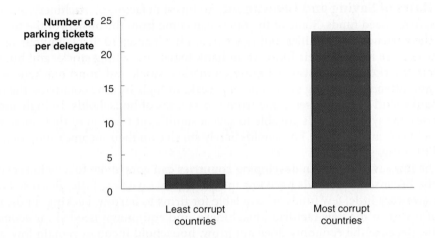

Of course, ignoring parking regulations is a relatively minor form of corruption. But if Fisman and Miguel are correct, and a culture of corruption has taken hold in some developing countries, then it may be a difficult task to reform their governments enough to establish the rule of law.

Based on Raymond Fisman and Edward Miguel, *Economic Gangsters*, (Princeton, NJ: Princeton University Press, 2008), Chapter 4; Daniel Kaufmann, Aart Kraay, and Massimo Mastruzzi, *Governance Matters V: Aggregate Governance Indicators, 1996–2007*, World Bank working paper; and International Monetary Fund, *World Economic Outlook Database*, April 2009.

Your Turn: Test your understanding by doing related problem 4.8 on page 372 at the end of this chapter.   MyEconLab

Wars and Revolutions Many of the countries that were very poor in 1960 have experienced extended periods of war or violent changes of government during the years since. These wars have made it impossible for countries such as Afghanistan, Angola, Ethiopia, the Central African Republic, and the Congo to accumulate capital or adopt new technologies. In fact, conducting any kind of business has been very difficult. The positive effect on growth of ending war was shown in Mozambique, which suffered through almost two decades of civil war and declining real GDP per capita. With the end of civil war, Mozambique experienced a strong annual growth rate of 3.7 percent in real GDP per capita from 1990 to 2009.

Poor Public Education and Health We have seen that human capital is one of the determinants of labor productivity. Many low-income countries have weak public school systems, so many workers are unable to read and write. Few workers acquire the skills necessary to use the latest technology.

Many low-income countries suffer from diseases that are either nonexistent or treated readily in high-income countries. For example, few people in developed countries suffer from malaria, but more than 1 million Africans die from it each year.

Treatments for AIDS have greatly reduced deaths from this disease in the United States and Europe. But millions of people in low-income countries continue to die from AIDS. These countries often lack the resources, and their governments are often too ineffective, to provide even routine medical care, such as childhood vaccinations.

People who are sick work less and are less productive when they do work. Poor nutrition or exposure to certain diseases in childhood can leave people permanently weakened and can affect their intelligence as adults. Poor health has a significant negative effect on the human capital of workers in developing countries.

Low Rates of Saving and Investment To invest in factories, machinery, and computers, firms need funds. Some of the funds can come from the owners of the firm and from their friends and families, but as we noted in Chapter 10, firms in high-income countries raise most of their funds from bank loans and selling stocks and bonds in financial markets. In most developing countries, stock and bond markets do not exist, and often the banking system is very weak. In high-income countries, the funds that banks lend to businesses come from the savings of households. In high-income countries, many households are able to save a significant fraction of their income. In developing countries, many households barely survive on their incomes and, therefore, have little or no savings.

The low savings rates in developing countries can contribute to a vicious cycle of poverty. Because households have low incomes, they save very little. Because households save very little, few funds are available for firms to borrow. Lacking funds, firms do not invest in the new factories, machinery, and equipment needed for economic growth. Because the economy does not grow, household incomes remain low, as do their savings, and so on.

The Benefits of Globalization

Foreign direct investment (FDI) The purchase or building by a corporation of a facility in a foreign country.

Foreign portfolio investment The purchase by an individual or a firm of stocks or bonds issued in another country.

One way for a developing country to break out of the vicious cycle of low saving and investment and low growth is through foreign investment. **Foreign direct investment (FDI)** occurs when corporations build or purchase facilities in foreign countries. **Foreign portfolio investment** occurs when an individual or a firm buys stocks or bonds issued in another country. Foreign direct investment and foreign portfolio investment can give a low-income country access to funds and technology that otherwise would not be available. Until recently, many developing countries were reluctant to take advantage of this opportunity.

From the 1940s through the 1970s, many developing countries closed themselves off from the global economy. They did this for several reasons. During the 1930s and early 1940s, the global trading and financial system collapsed as a result of the Great Depression and World War II. Developing countries that relied on exporting to the high-income countries were hurt economically. Also, many countries in Africa and Asia achieved independence from the colonial powers of Europe during the 1950s and 1960s and were afraid of being dominated by them economically. As a result, many developing countries imposed high tariffs on foreign imports and strongly discouraged or even prohibited foreign investment. This made it difficult to break out of the vicious cycle of poverty.

Globalization The process of countries becoming more open to foreign trade and investment.

The policies of high tariff barriers and avoiding foreign investment failed to produce much growth, so by the 1980s, many developing countries began to change policies. The result was **globalization**, which refers to the process of countries becoming more open to foreign trade and investment.

If we measure globalization by the fraction of a country's GDP accounted for by exports, we see that globalization and growth are strongly positively associated. Figure 11.10 shows that developing countries that were more globalized grew faster during the 1990s than developing countries that were less globalized. Globalization has benefited developing countries by making it easier for them to get investment funds and technology.

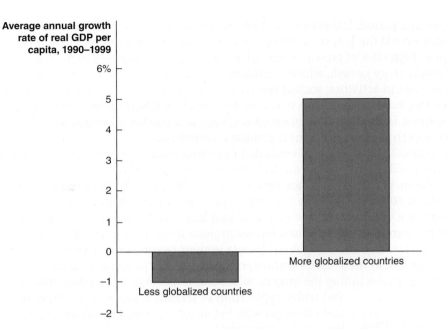

Average annual growth rate of real GDP per capita, 1990–1999

Less globalized countries

More globalized countries

Figure 11.10

Globalization and Growth

Developing countries that were more open to foreign trade and investment grew much faster during the 1990s than developing countries that were less open.

Data from David Dollar, "Globalization, Inequality, and Poverty since 1980," *World Bank Research Observer*, Vol. 20, No. 2, Fall 2005, pp. 145–175.

Growth Policies

What can governments do to promote long-run economic growth? We have seen that even small differences in growth rates compounded over the years can lead to major differences in standards of living. Therefore, there is potentially a very high payoff to government policies that increase growth rates. We have already discussed some of these policies in this chapter. In this section, we explore additional policies.

Enhancing Property Rights and the Rule of Law

A market system cannot work well unless property rights are enforced. Entrepreneurs are unlikely to risk their own funds, and investors are unlikely to lend their funds to entrepreneurs, unless property is safe from being arbitrarily seized. We have seen that in many developing countries, the rule of law and property rights are undermined by government *corruption*. In some developing countries, it is impossible for an entrepreneur to obtain a permit to start a business without paying bribes, often to several different government officials. Is it possible for a country to reform a corrupt government bureaucracy?

Although today the United States ranks among the least corrupt countries, recent research by economists Edward Glaeser and Claudia Goldin of Harvard University has shown that in the late nineteenth and early twentieth centuries, corruption was a significant problem in the United States. The fact that political reform movements and crusading newspapers helped to reduce corruption in the United States to relatively low levels by the 1920s provides some hope for reform movements that aim to reduce corruption in developing countries today.

Property rights are unlikely to be secure in countries that are afflicted by wars and civil strife. For a number of countries, increased political stability is a necessary prerequisite to economic growth.

11.5 LEARNING OBJECTIVE

Discuss government policies that foster economic growth.

Making the Connection | **Will China's Standard of Living Ever Exceed That of the United States?**

In 2010, GDP per capita in the United States was more than six times higher than GDP per capita in China. However, the growth rate of real GDP per capita in the United States has averaged only 1.9 percent per year since 1980, compared to China's average rate of 8.9 percent per year over the same time period. If these growth rates were to continue, then China's standard of living would exceed the U.S. standard of living in the year 2038. However, for China to maintain its high rates of growth in real GDP per capita, it would have to maintain high rates of productivity growth, which is unlikely for several reasons. First, the United States invests more in activities, such as research and development, that result in new technologies and increases in productivity. Second, much of China's growth is likely due to the transition from a centrally planned economy to a market economy, so China's growth rate is likely to decrease as the transition is completed.

Another looming problem is demographic. Because of China's low birthrate, the country will soon experience a decline in its labor force. Over the next two decades, the population of men and women between 15 and 29 years will fall by roughly 100 million, or about 30 percent. China will also experience a large increase in older workers, a group that will likely be less educated and less healthy than younger workers. Given current trends, the U.S. Census Bureau projects fewer people under age 50 in China in 2030 than today, including fewer people in their twenties and early thirties and many more people in their sixties and older. China still has potential sources for enhancing productivity, including the migration of rural workers to more productive urban jobs

Some economists argue that China may have overinvested in physical capital, such as bullet trains.

and wider application of technical know-how. These factors can fuel future growth, but at some point, China's demographic problems could slow growth.

Perhaps most troubling for China is the fact that, as we saw in the chapter opener, the country remains autocratic, with the Communist Party refusing to allow meaningful elections and continuing to limit freedom of expression. Secure property rights and the rule of law have never been fully established in China. Some observers believe that the lack of political freedom in China may ultimately lead to civil unrest, which could slow growth rates. Whether or not civil unrest eventually develops, the lack of democracy in China may already be resulting in problems that could slow growth in the near future. Nouriel Roubini, an economist at New York University, argues that China's Communist Party may be repeating some of the mistakes committed by the Soviet Communist Party decades ago. He argues that by employing policies that have resulted in investment being 50 percent of GDP, the government may have boosted short-term growth at the expense of the health of the economy in the long term. He notes that:

> China is rife with overinvestment in physical capital, infrastructure, and property. To a visitor, this is evident in sleek but empty airports and bullet trains . . . highways to nowhere, thousands of colossal new central and provincial government buildings, ghost towns, and brand-new aluminum smelters kept closed to prevent global prices from plunging.

China has been engaged in an economic experiment: Can a country maintain high rates of economic growth in the long run while denying its citizens basic political rights?

Based on Nicholas Eberstadt, "The Demographic Future," *Foreign Affairs*, Vol. 89, No. 6, November/December 2010, pp. 54–64; and Nouriel Roubini, "Beijing's Empty Bullet Trains," *Slate*, April 14, 2011.

MyEconLab **Your Turn:** Test your understanding by doing related problem 5.4 on page 373 at the end of this chapter.

Improving Health and Education

Recently, many economists have become convinced that poor health is a major impediment to growth in some countries. As we saw in Chapter 10, the research of Nobel Laureate Robert Fogel emphasizes the important interaction between health and economic growth. As people's health improves and they become stronger and less susceptible to disease, they also become more productive. Recent initiatives in developing countries to increase vaccinations against infectious diseases, to improve access to treated water, and to improve sanitation have begun to reduce rates of illness and death.

We discussed earlier in this chapter Paul Romer's argument that there are increasing returns to knowledge capital. Nobel Laureate Robert Lucas of the University of Chicago similarly argues that there are increasing returns to *human* capital. Lucas argues that productivity increases as the total stock of human capital increases but that these productivity increases are not completely captured by individuals as they decide how much education to purchase. Therefore, the market may produce an inefficiently low level of education and training unless education is supported by the government. Some researchers have been unable to find evidence of increasing returns to human capital, but many economists believe that government subsidies for education have played an important role in promoting economic growth.

The rising incomes that result from economic growth can help developing countries deal with the brain drain. The *brain drain* refers to highly educated and successful individuals leaving developing countries for high-income countries. This migration occurs when successful individuals believe that economic opportunities are very limited in the domestic economy. Rapid economic growth in India and China in recent years has resulted in more entrepreneurs, engineers, and scientists deciding to remain in those countries rather than leave for the United States or other high-income countries.

Policies That Promote Technological Change

One of the lessons from the economic growth model is that technological change is more important than increases in capital in explaining long-run growth. Government policies that facilitate access to technology are crucial for low-income countries. The easiest way for developing countries to gain access to technology is through foreign direct investment, where foreign firms are allowed to build new facilities or to buy domestic firms. Recent economic growth in India has been greatly aided by the Indian government's relaxation of regulations on foreign investment. Relaxing these regulations made it possible for India to gain access to the technology of Dell, Microsoft, and other multinational corporations.

In high-income countries, government policies can aid the growth of technology by subsidizing research and development. As we noted previously, in the United States, the federal government conducts some research and development on its own and also provides grants to researchers in universities. Tax breaks to firms undertaking research and development also facilitate technological change.

Policies That Promote Saving and Investment

We noted in Chapter 10 that firms turn to the loanable funds market to finance expansion and research and development. Policies that increase the incentives to save and invest will increase the equilibrium level of loanable funds and may increase the level of real GDP per capita. As we also discussed in Chapter 10, tax incentives can lead to increased savings. In the United States, many workers are able to save for retirement by placing funds in 401(k) or 403(b) plans or in Individual Retirement Accounts (IRAs). Income placed in these accounts is not taxed until it is withdrawn during retirement. Because the funds are allowed to accumulate tax free, the return is increased, which raises the incentive to save.

Governments also increase incentives for firms to engage in investment in physical capital by using *investment tax credits*. Investment tax credits allow firms to deduct from their taxes some fraction of the funds they have spent on investment. Reductions in the taxes firms pay on their profits also increase the after-tax return on investments.

Is Economic Growth Good or Bad?

Although we didn't state so explicitly, in this chapter we have assumed that economic growth is desirable and that governments should undertake policies that will increase growth rates. It seems undeniable that increasing the growth rates of very low-income countries would help relieve the daily suffering that many people in those countries endure. But some people are unconvinced that, at least in the high-income countries, further economic growth is desirable.

The arguments against further economic growth tend to be motivated either by concern about the effects of growth on the environment or by concern about the effects of the globalization process that has accompanied economic growth in recent years. In 1973, the Club of Rome published a controversial book titled *The Limits to Growth*, which predicted that economic growth would likely grind to a halt in the United States and other high-income countries because of increasing pollution and the depletion of natural resources, such as oil. Although these dire predictions have not yet come to pass, many people remain concerned that economic growth may be contributing to global warming, deforestation, and other environmental problems.

In Chapter 7, we discussed the opposition to globalization. We noted that some people believe that globalization has undermined the distinctive cultures of many countries, as imports of food, clothing, movies, and other goods have displaced domestically produced goods. We have seen that allowing foreign direct investment is an important way in which low-income countries can gain access to the latest technology. Some people, however, see multinational firms that locate in low-income countries as unethical because they claim the firms are paying very low wages and are failing to follow the same safety and environmental regulations they are required to follow in high-income countries.

As with many other normative questions, economic analysis can contribute to the ongoing political debate over the consequences of economic growth, but it cannot settle the issue.

Continued from page 337

Economics in Your Life

Would You Be Better Off without China?

At the beginning of the chapter, we asked you to imagine that you could choose to live and work in a world with the Chinese economy growing very rapidly or in a world with the Chinese economy as it was before 1978—very poor and growing slowly. Which world would you choose to live in? How does the current high-growth, high-export Chinese economy affect you as a consumer? How does it affect you as someone about to start a career?

It's impossible to walk into stores in the United States without seeing products imported from China. Many of these products were at one time made in the United States. Imports from China replace domestically produced goods when the imports are either less expensive or of higher quality than the domestic goods they replace. Therefore, the rapid economic growth that has enabled Chinese firms to be competitive with firms in the United States has benefited you as a consumer: You have lower-priced goods and better goods available for purchase than you would if China had remained very poor. As you begin your career, there are some U.S. industries that, because of competition from Chinese firms, will have fewer jobs to offer. But, as we saw when discussing international trade in Chapter 7, expanding trade changes the types of products each country makes, and, therefore, the types of jobs available, but it does not affect the total number of jobs. So, the economic rise of China will affect the mix of jobs available to you in the United States but will not make finding a job any more difficult.

Conclusion

For much of human history, most people have had to struggle to survive. Even today, two-thirds of the world's population lives in extreme poverty. The differences in living standards among countries today are a result of many decades of sharply different rates of economic growth. According to the economic growth model, increases in the quantity of capital per hour worked and increases in technology determine how rapidly increases will occur in real GDP per hour worked and a country's standard of living. The keys to higher living standards seem straightforward: Establish the rule of law, provide basic education and health care for the population, increase the amount of capital per hour worked, adopt the best technology, and participate in the global economy. However, for many countries, these policies have proved very difficult to implement.

Having discussed what determines the growth rate of economies, we will turn in the following chapters to the question of why economies experience short-run fluctuations in output, employment, and inflation. First, read *An Inside Look at Policy* on the next page for a discussion of the Chinese government's attempts to become less dependent on investment spending for economic growth.

Despite a Plan for Change, Investment Still Spurs China's Growth

REUTERS

Analysis: China Unlikely to Cool Investment as Its Growth Engine

China's long-term plan to cut reliance on investment as a growth engine is clashing with its short-term need for protection against a worsening global outlook.

Beijing has made it clear that consumption, not investment, must eventually do more of the work to drive the world's No. 2 economy.

But with debt troubles in the United States and Europe casting doubt on worldwide demand, it's likely China will keep investing by the billions for now, even if that takes Beijing further from its ultimate goal.

(a) Chinese consumers are a long way from becoming big spenders, so massive investment is still the fastest and easiest way for China to prop up its economy if push comes to shove. . . .

Without doubt, having heavy investment carries a price. Analysts say it generates waste and excess capacity, fuels inflation and produces diminishing economic returns. State investment is like an unsustainable life-support system that China needs to wean itself off.

In 2009—the last year for which figures are available—investment made up 65 percent of China's gross domestic product, a far higher share than in other major or Asian economies. Household consumption, however, accounted for just 35 percent, compared with 70 percent in the United States.

(b) Unstable, Unbalanced, Uncoordinated

In the words of China Premier Wen Jiabao, the Chinese growth model is on all counts unstable, unbalanced, uncoordinated and ultimately unsustainable.

Some of the more bearish economists argue that wasteful investment is inflating a property price bubble and saddling banks with bad loans, sowing the seeds of a future crisis.

An example of healthier investment, economists say, would be companies stepping up capital expenditures on improving China's manufacturing technologies. . . .

Rebalancing, Some Day

On the surface, China seems serious about following through on promises to invest less to rebalance its economy, and it has good reasons to be wary of repeating its 2008 spending spree.

Some of the 4 trillion yuan ($626 billion) stimulus package announced in 2008 was squandered on ill-advised projects and economists now worry that a sizable fraction of loans to local governments won't be repaid.

Banks may be wary of extending more large loans, making it difficult for local governments to invest their way to growth in the future. . . .

Homes Priced Out of Reach

Soaring property prices have put homes out of reach for many ordinary Chinese, and that has become a source of public ire. Keenly aware of that, Beijing wants to build more public homes to keep them affordable.

And with the real estate market accounting for a quarter of total investment in the first half of this year, China could get decent bang for its buck if it ramps up spending in the sector. . . .

To be sure, Beijing says it wants to cure China of its penchant for investment-driven growth. Under its broad five-year economic plan starting from 2011, it envisions a fairer Chinese economy where consumption climbs on rising incomes. . . .

(c) Few Big Spenders

Many analysts have said that Chinese consumers cannot pull their weight as big spenders because the bulk of national income goes to the state instead of workers. A flimsy social safety net encourages high saving rates.

For younger workers, consumption tends to be higher, but between expensive housing and strong cultural pressure to support aging parents and grandparents, they too face limits on how much they can spend.

In a paper published last month, the International Monetary Fund outlined key reforms China should implement to empower its consumers.

It called for a liberalization of financial markets; a reduction in personal income taxes; better healthcare services; increasing the cost of land, energy and pollution; raising dividend payouts from state firms, and improving labor mobility.

However, it would be years before these reforms take effect. . . .

Key Points in the Article

The Chinese economy has been growing at a rapid pace over the past decade, due in large part to high levels of investment. However, the Chinese government has stated that its recent growth will be unsustainable without a shift away from investment spending. The government has established a five-year economic plan that calls for greater reliance on consumption as a means to sustain economic growth. Many analysts believe that achieving this goal will not happen anytime soon because (1) a majority of national income goes to the government instead of workers, and (2) other reforms are needed before Chinese consumers have the willingness and the financial ability to significantly increase consumption.

Analyzing the News

a As you read in the chapter, the quantity of capital available to workers is a source of long-run economic growth. From 1996 to 2010, China experienced an annual growth rate of real GDP per capita of more than 9 percent. Much of this growth came from investment in capital goods. In 2009, investment spending accounted for 65 percent of Chinese GDP, a far higher percentage than in other major economies, and consumption was only 35 percent. In contrast, consumption spending is 70 percent of GDP in the United States. Relying on investment as a means of economic growth is

not a long-run solution, though, as eventually an economy encounters diminishing returns to capital. Because of diminishing returns to capital, further increases in the quantity of capital would result in even smaller increases in real GDP per worker. The production function in the figure below illustrates this point: An increase in capital per hour worked from $(K/L)_{2010}$ to $(K/L)_{2011}$ leads to an increase in output per hour worked from $(Y/L)_{2010}$ to $(Y/L)_{2011}$. This increase in output per hour is much smaller than the increase resulting from the same size increase in capital per hour worked from $(K/L)_{2001}$ to $(K/L)_{2002}$, when the level of capital per hour worked was much smaller.

b Chinese Premier Wen Jiabao understands that the country's current economic growth model is unsustainable in the long run, yet China has continued on the path of high rates of investment. A main reason for this strategy has been a decrease in worldwide demand caused by the global economic downturn. While this investment strategy is not sustainable in the long run, some economists have suggested that increasing government expenditures on research and development in an effort to improve China's manufacturing technologies would be a good option for the Chinese economy.

c A primary reason that China has yet to succeed in increasing consumption is because Chinese consumers have low incomes and high savings rates. A large

portion of Chinese national income currently goes to the government rather than to workers, although China has announced its desire to increase income levels to encourage more consumption. Increasing consumption may take time, though, as the following reforms may be needed to encourage consumers to increase spending: reduced personal income taxes, liberalized financial markets, and improved labor mobility.

Thinking Critically About Policy

1. What policies can the Chinese government pursue to raise the country's long-run economic growth without further increases in investment spending? How would these policies affect China's per-worker production function?

2. According to the article, consumption in China has not grown significantly because a "flimsy social safety net encourages high saving rates." Explain what the article means by "flimsy social safety net." Why would a flimsy social safety net lead to high saving rates and low rates of consumption? Briefly explain.

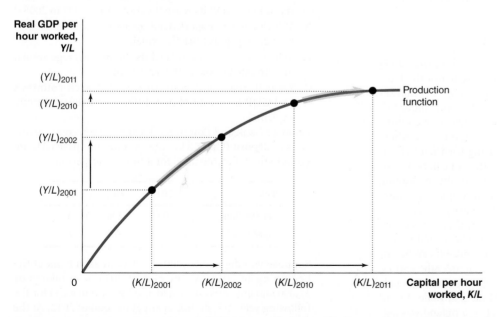

Continuous increases in capital per hour worked lead to smaller and smaller increases in output per hour worked.

Chapter Summary and Problems

Key Terms

Catch-up, p. 352

Economic growth model, p. 343

Foreign direct investment (FDI), p. 360

Foreign portfolio investment, p. 360

Globalization, p. 360

Human capital, p. 343

Industrial Revolution, p. 338

Labor productivity, p. 343

New growth theory, p. 348

Patent, p. 348

Per-worker production function, p. 344

Property rights, p. 357

Rule of law, p. 357

Technological change, p. 343

11.1 **Economic Growth over Time and around the World, pages 338–343**
LEARNING OBJECTIVE: Define economic growth, calculate economic growth rates, and describe global trends in economic growth.

Summary

Until around 1300 A.D., most people survived with barely enough food. Living standards began to rise significantly only after the **Industrial Revolution** began in England in the 1700s, with the application of mechanical power to the production of goods. The best measure of a country's standard of living is its level of real GDP per capita. Economic growth occurs when real GDP per capita increases, thereby increasing the country's standard of living.

 Visit **www.myeconlab.com** to complete these exercises online and get instant feedback.

Review Questions

1.1 Why does a country's rate of economic growth matter?
1.2 Explain the difference between the total percentage increase in real GDP between 1999 and 2009 and the average annual growth rate in real GDP between the same years.

Problems and Applications

1.3 **[Related to the** Making the Connection **on page 339]**
Economists Carol Shiue and Wolfgang Keller of the University of Texas at Austin published a study of "market efficiency" in the eighteenth century in England, other European countries, and China. If the markets in a country are efficient, a product should have the same price wherever in the country it is sold, allowing for the effect of transportation costs. If prices are not the same in two areas within a country, it is possible to make profits by buying the product where its price is low and reselling it where its price is high. This trading will drive prices to equality. Trade is most likely to occur, however, if entrepreneurs feel confident that their gains will not be seized by the government and that contracts to buy and sell can be enforced in the courts. Therefore, in the eighteenth century, the more efficient a country's markets, the more its institutions favored long-run growth. Shiue and Keller found that in 1770, the efficiency of markets in England was significantly greater than the efficiency of markets elsewhere in Europe and in China. How does this finding relate to

Douglas North's argument concerning why the Industrial Revolution occurred in England?
Based on Carol H. Shiue and Wolfgang Keller, "Markets in China and Europe on the Eve of the Industrial Revolution," *American Economic Review*, Vol. 97, No. 4, September 2007, pp. 1189–1216.

1.4 Use the data on real GDP in this table to answer the following questions.

Country	2007	2008	2009	2010
Brazil	1,295.7	1,362.6	1,353.8	1,455.2
Mexico	8,806.7	8,911.4	8,362.4	8,815.3
Thailand	4,259.5	4,368.4	4,265.1	4,597.0

Note: All values are in billions of units of domestic currency at constant prices.
Data from International Monetary Fund.

a. Which country experienced the highest rate of economic growth during 2008 (that is, for which country did real GDP increase the most from 2007 to 2008)?
b. Which country experienced the worst economic recession during 2009? Briefly explain.
c. Which country experienced the highest average annual growth rate between 2008 and 2010?
d. Does it matter for your answer that each country's real GDP is measured in a different currency? Briefly explain.

1.5 Andover Bank and Lowell Bank each sell one-year certificates of deposit (CDs). The interest rates on these CDs are given in the following table for a three-year period:

Bank	2011	2012	2013
Andover Bank	5%	5%	5%
Lowell Bank	2	6	7

Suppose you deposit $1,000 in a CD in each bank at the beginning of 2011. At the end of 2011, you take your $1,000 and any interest earned and invest it in a CD for the following year. You do this again at the end of 2012. At the end of 2013, will you have earned more on your Andover Bank CDs or on your Lowell Bank CDs? Briefly explain.

1.6 [Related to the Don't Let This Happen to You **on page 341]** Use the data for the United States in this table to answer the following questions:

Year	Real GDP per Capita (2005 prices)
2006	$ 43,332
2007	43,726
2008	43,178
2009	41,313
2010	42,205

a. What was the percentage change in real GDP per capita between 2006 and 2010?

b. What was the average annual growth rate in real GDP per capita between 2006 and 2010? (*Hint:* Remember from Chapter 10 that the average annual growth rate for relatively short periods can be approximated by averaging the growth rates for each year during the period.)

1.7 [Related to the Making the Connection **on page 342]** In his book *The White Man's Burden*, William Easterly reports that

A vaccination campaign in southern Africa virtually eliminated measles as a killer of children. Routine childhood immunization combined with measles vaccination in seven southern Africa nations starting in 1996 virtually eliminated measles in those countries by 2000. A national campaign in Egypt to make parents aware of the use of oral rehydration therapy from 1982 to 1989 cut childhood deaths from diarrhea by 82 percent over that period.

a. Is it likely that real GDP per capita increased significantly in southern Africa and Egypt as a result of the near elimination of measles and the large decrease in childhood deaths from diarrhea? If these events did not increase real GDP per capita, is it still possible that they increased the standard of living in southern Africa and Egypt? Briefly explain.

b. Which seems more achievable for a developing country: the elimination of measles and childhood deaths from diarrhea or sustained increases in real GDP per capita? Briefly explain.

From William Easterly, *The White Man's Burden: Why the West's Efforts to Aid the Rest Have Done So Much Ill and So Little Good*, (New York: The Penguin Press, 2006), p. 241.

1.8 [Related to the Making the Connection **on page 342]** Economist Charles Kenny of the World Bank has argued that:

The process technologies—institutions like laws and inventory management systems—that appear central to raising incomes per capita flow less like water and more like bricks. But ideas and inventions—the importance of ABCs and vaccines for DPT—really might flow more easily across borders and over distances.

If Kenny is correct, what are the implications of these facts for the ability of low-income countries to rapidly increase their rates of growth of real GDP per capita in the decades ahead? What are the implications for the ability of these countries to increase their standards of living? Briefly explain.

From Charles Kenny, *Getting Better*, (New York: Basic Books, 2011), p. 117.

11.2 What Determines How Fast Economies Grow? pages 343–349

LEARNING OBJECTIVE: Use the economic growth model to explain why growth rates differ across countries.

Summary

An **economic growth model** explains changes in real GDP per capita in the long run. **Labor productivity** is the quantity of goods and services that can be produced by one worker or by one hour of work. Economic growth depends on increases in labor productivity. Labor productivity will increase if there is an increase in the amount of *capital* available to each worker or if there is an improvement in *technology*. **Technological change** is a change in the ability of a firm to produce a given level of output with a given quantity of inputs. There are three main sources of technological change: better machinery and equipment, increases in human capital, and better means of organizing and managing production. **Human capital** is the accumulated knowledge and skills that workers acquire from education and training or from their life experiences. We can say that an economy will have a higher standard of living the more capital it has per hour worked, the more human capital its workers have, the better its capital, and the better the job its business managers do in organizing production.

The **per-worker production function** shows the relationship between capital per hour worked and output per hour worked, holding technology constant. *Diminishing returns to capital* means that increases in the quantity of capital per hour worked will result in diminishing increases in output per hour worked. Technological change shifts up the per-worker production function, resulting in more output per hour worked at every level of capital per hour worked. The economic growth model stresses the importance of changes in capital per hour worked and technological change in explaining growth in output per hour worked. **New growth theory** is a model of long-run economic growth that emphasizes that technological change is influenced by how individuals and firms respond to economic incentives.

One way governments can promote technological change is by granting **patents**, which are exclusive rights to a product for a period of 20 years from the date the patent is applied for. To Joseph Schumpeter, the entrepreneur is central to the "creative destruction" by which the standard of living increases as qualitatively better products replace existing products.

MyEconLab Visit **www.myeconlab.com** to complete these exercises online and get instant feedback.

Review Questions

2.1 Using the per-worker production function graph from Figures 11.3 and 11.4 on pages 344–345, show the effect on real GDP per hour worked of an increase in capital per hour worked, holding technology constant. Now, again using the per-worker production function graph, show the effect on real GDP per hour worked of an increase in technology, holding constant the quantity of capital per hour worked.

2.2 What are the consequences for growth of diminishing returns to capital? How are some economies able to maintain high growth rates despite diminishing returns to capital?

2.3 Why are firms likely to underinvest in research and development, which slows the accumulation of knowledge capital, slowing economic growth? Briefly discuss three ways in which government policy can increase the accumulation of knowledge capital.

2.4 What is the *new growth theory*? How does the new growth theory differ from the growth theory developed by Robert Solow?

Problems and Applications

2.5 According to a study by an economist at the Federal Reserve Bank of Minneapolis, during the mid-1980s, managers at iron mines in Canada and the United States increased output per hour worked by 100 percent through changes in work rules that increased workers' effort per hour worked and increased the efficiency of workers' effort. Briefly explain whether this increase in output per hour worked is an example of an improvement in technology.

Based on James A. Schmitz, Jr., "What Determines Labor Productivity? Lessons from the Dramatic Recovery of the U.S. and Canadian Iron-Ore Industries Following Their Early 1980s Crisis," Federal Reserve Bank of Minneapolis Research Department Staff Report 286, February 2005.

2.6 Which of the following will result in a movement along China's per-worker production function, and which will result in a shift of China's per-worker production function? Briefly explain.

    a. Capital per hour worked increases from 5 million yuan per hour worked to 6 million yuan per hour worked.

    b. The Chinese government doubles its spending on support for university research.

    c. A reform of the Chinese school system results in more highly trained Chinese workers.

2.7 **[Related to** Solved Problem 11.2 **on page 347]** Use the graph at the top of the next column. to answer the following questions.

    a. True or false: The movement from point *A* to point *B* shows the effects of technological change.

    b. True or false: The economy can move from point *B* to point *C* only if there are no diminishing returns to capital.

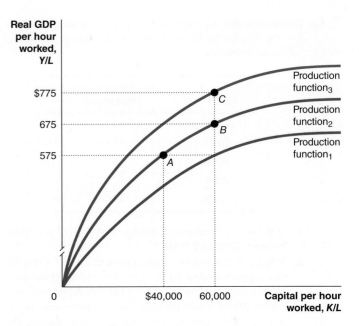

    c. True or false: To move from point *A* to point *C*, the economy must increase the amount of capital per hour worked and experience technological change.

2.8 **[Related to** Solved Problem 11.2 **on page 347]** Shortly before the fall of the Soviet Union, the economist Gur Ofer of Hebrew University of Jerusalem, wrote this: "The most outstanding characteristic of Soviet growth strategy is its consistent policy of very high rates of investment, leading to a rapid growth rate of [the] capital stock." Explain why this turned out to be a very poor growth strategy.

From Gur Ofer, "Soviet Economic Growth, 1928–1985," *Journal of Economic Literature*, Vol. 25, No. 4, December 1987, p. 1,784.

2.9 Why is the role of the entrepreneur much more important in the new growth theory than in the traditional economic growth model?

2.10 **[Related to the** Making the Connection **on page 346]** The *Making the Connection* argues that a key difference between market economies and centrally planned economies, like that of the former Soviet Union, is as follows:

> In market economies, decisions about which investments to make and which technologies to adopt are made by entrepreneurs and managers with their own money on the line. In the Soviet system, these decisions were usually made by salaried bureaucrats trying to fulfill a plan formulated in Moscow.

But in large corporations, investment decisions are often made by salaried managers who do not have their own money on the line. These managers are spending the money of the firm's shareholders rather than their own money. Why, then, do the investment decisions of salaried managers in the United States tend to be better for the long-term growth of the economy than were the decisions of salaried bureaucrats in the Soviet Union?

11.3 **Economic Growth in the United States,** pages 349–352

LEARNING OBJECTIVE: Discuss fluctuations in productivity growth in the United States.

Summary

Productivity in the United States grew rapidly from the end of World War II until the mid-1970s. Growth then slowed down for 20 years before increasing again after 1995. Economists continue to debate the reasons for the growth slowdown of the mid-1970s to mid-1990s. Leading explanations for the productivity slowdown are measurement problems, high oil prices, and a decline in labor quality. Because Western Europe and Japan experienced a productivity slowdown at the same time as the United States, explanations that focus on factors affecting only the United States are unlikely to be correct. Some economists argue that the development of a "new economy" based on information technology caused the higher productivity growth that began in the mid-1990s. Economists debate whether the higher productivity growth that began in the mid-1990s will continue.

 MyEconLab Visit **www.myeconlab.com** to complete these exercises online and get instant feedback.

Review Questions

3.1 Describe the record of productivity growth in the United States from 1800 to the present. What explains the slowdown in productivity growth from the mid-1970s to the mid-1990s? Why did productivity growth increase beginning in 1995?

3.2 Why do some economists believe that the higher productivity growth rates that began in the mid-1990s can be sustained?

Problems and Applications

3.3 Figure 11.5 on page 350 shows growth rates in real GDP per hour worked in the United States for various periods from 1900 onward. How might the growth rates in the figure be different if they were calculated for real GDP *per capita* instead of per hour worked? (*Hint:* How do you think the number of hours worked per person has changed in the United States since 1900?)

3.4 An article in the *Wall Street Journal* observes: "For 2008, productivity grew an astounding 2.8% from 2007 even as the economy suffered through its worst recession in decades." How is it possible for labor productivity—output per hour worked—to increase if output—real GDP—is falling?

From Brian Blackstone, "Productivity Proves Resilient," *Wall Street Journal*, April 29, 2009.

3.5 Economist Robert Gordon of Northwestern University has argued that:

> My interpretation of the [information] revolution is that it is increasingly burdened by diminishing returns. The push to ever smaller devices runs up against the fixed size of the human finger that must enter information on the device. Most of the innovations since 2000 have been directed to consumer enjoyment rather than business productivity, including video games, DVD players, and iPods. iPhones are nice, but the ability to reschedule business meetings and look up corporate documents while on the road already existed by 2003.

If Gordon's observations about the information revolution are correct, what are the implications for future labor productivity growth rates in the United States?

From Robert J. Gordon, "Revisiting U.S. Productivity Growth over the Past Century with a View of the Future," National Bureau of Economic Research Working Paper 15834, March 2010.

11.4 **Why Isn't the Whole World Rich?** pages 352–361

LEARNING OBJECTIVE: Explain economic catch-up and discuss why many poor countries have not experienced rapid economic growth.

Summary

The economic growth model predicts that poor countries will grow faster than rich countries, resulting in **catch-up**. In recent decades, some poor countries have grown faster than rich countries, but many have not. Some poor countries do not experience rapid growth for four main reasons: wars and revolutions, poor public education and health, failure to enforce the rule of law, and low rates of saving and investment. The **rule of law** refers to the ability of a government to enforce the laws of the country, particularly with respect to protecting private property and enforcing contracts. **Globalization** has aided countries that have opened their economies to foreign trade and investment. **Foreign direct investment (FDI)** is the purchase or building by a corporation of a facility in a foreign country. **Foreign portfolio investment** is the purchase by an individual or firm of stocks or bonds issued in another country.

 MyEconLab Visit **www.myeconlab.com** to complete these exercises online and get instant feedback.

Review Questions

4.1 Why does the economic growth model predict that poor countries should catch up to rich countries in income per capita? Have poor countries been catching up to rich countries?

4.2 In what ways does the United States have greater flexibility in its labor markets and greater efficiency in its financial system than other higher income countries such as those in Europe? How might this greater flexibility in labor markets and greater efficiency in financial markets lead to higher growth rates in real GDP per capita?

4.3 What are the main reasons many poor countries have experienced slow growth?

4.4 What does *globalization* mean? How have developing countries benefited from globalization?

Problems and Applications

4.5 [Related to Solved Problem 11.4 **on page 354**] Briefly explain whether the statistics in the following table are consistent with the economic growth model's predictions of catch-up.

Country	Real GDP per Capita in 1960	Growth in Real GDP per Capita, 1960–2009
China	$363	6.23%
Uganda	655	1.16
Madagascar	1,268	–0.23
Ireland	6,971	3.25
United States	15,438	2.02

Authors' calculations from data in Alan Heston, Robert Summers, and Bettina Aten, *Penn World Table Version 7.0*, Center for International Comparisons of Production, Income and Prices at the University of Pennsylvania, June 3, 2011.

4.6 [Related to Solved Problem 11.4 **on page 354**] In the following figure, each dot represents a country, with its initial real GDP per capita and its growth rate of real GDP per capita.

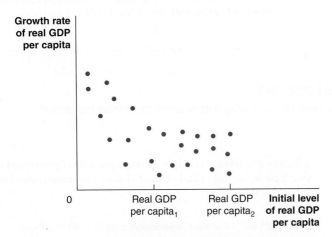

a. For the range of initial GDP per capita from 0 to Real GDP per capita₂, does the figure support the economic growth model's prediction of catch-up? Briefly explain.

b. For the range of initial GDP per capita from 0 to Real GDP per capita₁, does the figure support the catch-up prediction? Briefly explain.

c. For the range from initial Real GDP per capita₁ to Real GDP per capita₂, does the figure support the catch-up prediction? Briefly explain.

4.7 An opinion column in the *Economist* argued, "Globalisation, far from being the greatest cause of poverty, is its only feasible cure." What does globalization have to do with reducing poverty?

From Clive Crook, "Globalisation and Its Critics," *Economist*, September 27, 2001.

4.8 [Related to the Making the Connection **on page 358**] The relationship that Raymond Fisman and Edward Miguel found between the extent of corruption in a country and the number of parking violations committed by the country's United Nations delegates in New York isn't perfect. For example, "Ecuador and Colombia both have perfectly clean parking slates, despite the experts' view of them as fairly corrupt places." Does this observation invalidate Fisman and Miguel's conclusions about whether the parking violations data provide evidence in favor of there being a culture of corruption in some countries? Briefly explain.

Based on Raymond Fisman and Edward Miguel, *Economic Gangsters*, (Princeton, NJ: Princeton University Press, 2009), p. 89.

4.9 In a speech in 2009, President Barack Obama made the following observations: "I know that for many, the face of globalization is contradictory. . . . Trade can bring new wealth and opportunities, but also huge disruptions and change in communities." How does trade bring "new wealth and opportunities"? How does trade bring "huge disruptions and change"?

From "Obama's Speech in Cairo," *Wall Street Journal*, June 4, 2009.

4.10 A columnist in the *New York Times* observes that, "many analysts agree that economic reform, of which integration into the global economy was a key element, has lifted millions of people out of poverty in India. What does "integration into the global economy" mean? How might integration into the global economy reduce poverty in India?

From Vivek Dehejia, "Has Globalization Helped India's Poor?" *New York Times*, October 7, 2011.

4.11 The Roman Empire lasted from 27 B.C. to 476 A.D. The empire was wealthy enough to build such monuments as the Roman Coliseum. Roman engineering skill was at a level high enough that aqueducts built during the empire to carry water long distances remained in use for hundreds of years. Yet the empire's growth rate of real GDP per capita was very low, perhaps zero. Why didn't the Roman Empire experience sustained economic growth? What would the world be like today if it had? (*Note:* There are no definite answers to this question; it is intended to get you to think about the preconditions for economic growth.)

11.5 Growth Policies, pages 361–364

LEARNING OBJECTIVE: Discuss government policies that foster economic growth.

Summary

Governments can attempt to increase economic growth through policies that enhance property rights and the rule of law, improve health and education, subsidize research and development, and provide incentives for savings and investment. Whether continued economic growth is desirable is a normative question that cannot be settled by economic analysis.

MyEconLab   Visit **www.myeconlab.com** to complete these exercises online and get instant feedback.

Review Questions

5.1 Briefly describe three government policies that can increase economic growth.

5.2 Can economics arrive at the conclusion that economic growth will always improve economic well-being? Briefly explain.

Problems and Applications

5.3 **[Related to the** Chapter Opener **on page 337]** In discussing the future of China, the *Economist* magazine observed:

> And there are ... clear limits to the march of freedom in China; although personal and economic freedoms have multiplied, political freedoms have been disappointingly constrained since Hu Jintao became president in 2003.

Briefly discuss whether the limits on political freedom in China are likely to eventually become an obstacle to its continued rapid economic growth.

From "China's Dash for Freedom," *Economist*, July 31, 2008.

5.4 **[Related to the** Making the Connection **on page 361]** In China, why may a lower birthrate lead to slower growth in real GDP per capita? Why might high levels of spending on investment in China lead to high rates of growth in the short run, but not in the long run?

5.5 Is it likely to be easier for the typical developing country to improve the state of public health or to improve the average level of education? Briefly explain.

5.6 Briefly explain which of the following policies are likely to increase the rate of economic growth in the United States.

a. Congress passes an investment tax credit, which reduces a firm's taxes if it installs new machinery and equipment.

b. Congress passes a law that allows taxpayers to reduce their income taxes by the amount of state sales taxes they pay.

c. Congress provides more funds for low-interest loans to college students.

5.7 Economist George Ayittey, in an interview on PBS about economic development in Africa, stated that of the 54 African countries, only 8 had a free press. For Africa's economic development, Ayittey argued strongly for the establishment of a free press. Why would a free press be vital for the enhancement of property rights and the rule of law? How could a free press help reduce corruption?

From George Ayittey, *Border Jumpers*, Anchor Interview Transcript, WideAngle, PBS.org, July 24, 2005.

5.8 More people in high-income countries than in low-income countries tend to believe that rapid rates of economic growth are not desirable. Recall the concept of a "normal good" from Chapter 3. Does this concept provide insight into why some people in high-income countries might be more concerned with certain consequences of rapid economic growth than are people in low-income countries?

Chapter Outline and Learning Objectives

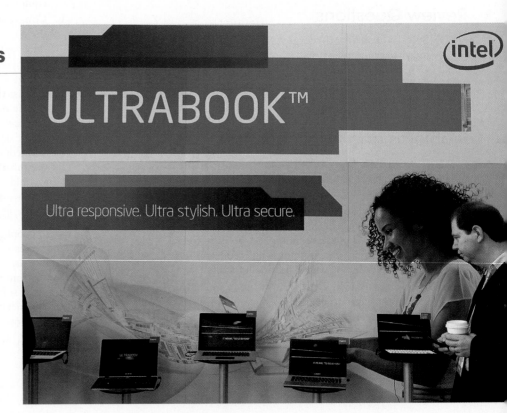

intel

ULTRABOOK™

Ultra responsive. Ultra stylish. Ultra secure.

Fluctuating Demand Helps— and Hurts—Intel and Other Firms

Intel is the world's largest semiconductor manufacturer and a major supplier of the microprocessors and memory chips found in most personal computers. Robert Noyce and Gordon Moore founded the firm in 1968. The performance of computers has improved very rapidly over the past 40 years, making possible the information revolution, in which Intel has been a key participant. By 2010, Intel had more than 82,000 employees and annual revenues of over $43 billion. Because of its dependence on computer sales, Intel is vulnerable to the swings of the business cycle. During the 2001 recession, for example, Intel's revenue fell 21 percent, and the firm laid off 5,000 workers. Intel was also hurt by the 2007–2009 recession. During the last quarter of 2008, its revenues fell 90 percent, and it laid off 6,000 workers.

But Intel bounced back in 2010, as the U.S. economy recovered from the recession. Real GDP grew by 3.0 percent in 2010. Increased demand for computers and other technology-based products, especially in China and other emerging markets, increased the demand for the parts Intel sells to computer manufacturers. Intel's revenue continued to grow through the first half of 2011, although analysts cautioned that a slowdown in real GDP growth—only 0.4 percent in the first quarter of 2011 and

1.3 percent in the second quarter—could eventually reduce Intel's sales.

Other firms also suffered from the slow economic growth in 2011. Cisco Systems, a manufacturer of computer networking equipment, announced that it would lay off 6,500 employees. Lockheed Martin, supplier of weapons to the Department of Defense, also announced plans to lay off 6,500 employees. Layoffs were not limited to technology firms. Cracker Barrel Old Country Store joined the list of firms cutting workers. Steven Ricchiuto, chief economist at Mizuho Securities, explained, "They're looking to reduce staff [and this] means they don't see a pickup in demand going forward."

These firms were cutting production and employment as a result of the sluggish growth of total spending, or *aggregate expenditure*. In this chapter, we will explore how changes in aggregate expenditure affect the level of total production in the economy.

AN INSIDE LOOK on **page 408** discusses the expected rebound in sales in the restaurant industry following the recession of 2007–2009.

Based on Conor Dougherty, "Layoffs Deepen Gloom," *The Wall Street Journal*, July 21, 2011; and Kathryn Glass, "Intel's Quarterly Results Beat Expectations, *FOXBusiness.com*," July 20, 2011.

Economics in Your Life

When Consumer Confidence Falls, Is Your Job at Risk?

Suppose that while attending college, you work part time, assembling desktop computers for a large computer company. One morning, you read in the local newspaper that consumer confidence in the economy has fallen and, consequently, many households expect their future income to be dramatically less than their current income. Should you be concerned about losing your job? What factors should you consider in deciding how likely your company is to lay you off? As you read the chapter, see if you can answer these questions. You can check your answers against those we provide on **page 407** at the end of this chapter.

Aggregate expenditure (AE) Total spending in the economy: the sum of consumption, planned investment, government purchases, and net exports.

In Chapter 11, we analyzed the determinants of long-run growth in the economy. In the short run, as we saw in Chapter 10, the economy experiences a business cycle around the long-run upward trend in real GDP. In this chapter, we begin exploring the causes of the business cycle by examining the effect of changes in total spending on real GDP.

During some years, total spending in the economy, or **aggregate expenditure (AE)**, and total production of goods and services increase by the same amount. If this happens, most firms will sell about what they expected to sell, and they probably will not increase or decrease production or the number of workers they hire. During other years, total spending in the economy increases more than the production of goods and services. In those years, firms will increase production and hire more workers. But at other times, such as during 2008 and early 2009, total spending does not increase as much as total production. As a result, firms cut back on production and lay off workers, and the economy moves into a recession. In this chapter, we will explore why changes in total spending play such an important role in the economy.

Understand how macroeconomic equilibrium is determined in the aggregate expenditure model.

Aggregate expenditure model A macroeconomic model that focuses on the short-run relationship between total spending and real GDP, assuming that the price level is constant.

The Aggregate Expenditure Model

The business cycle involves the interaction of many economic variables. A simple model called the *aggregate expenditure model* can help us begin to understand the relationships among some of these variables. Recall from Chapter 8 that GDP is the value of all the final goods and services produced in an economy during a particular year. Real GDP corrects nominal GDP for the effects of inflation. The **aggregate expenditure model** focuses on the short-run relationship between total spending and real GDP. An important assumption of the model is that the price level is constant. In Chapter 13, we will develop a more complete model of the business cycle that relaxes the assumption of constant prices.

The key idea of the aggregate expenditure model is that *in any particular year, the level of GDP is determined mainly by the level of aggregate expenditure*. To understand the relationship between aggregate expenditure and real GDP, we need to look more closely at the components of aggregate expenditure.

Aggregate Expenditure

Economists first began to study the relationship between changes in aggregate expenditure and changes in GDP during the Great Depression of the 1930s. The United States, the United Kingdom, and other industrial countries suffered declines in real GDP of 20 percent or more during the early 1930s. In 1936, the English economist John Maynard Keynes published a book, *The General Theory of Employment, Interest, and Money*, that systematically analyzed the relationship between changes in aggregate expenditure and changes in GDP. Keynes identified four components of aggregate expenditure that together equal GDP (these are the same four components we discussed in Chapter 8):

- *Consumption (C).* This is spending by households on goods and services, such as automobiles and haircuts.

- *Planned investment (I).* This is planned spending by firms on capital goods, such as factories, office buildings, and machine tools, and by households on new homes.

- *Government purchases (G).* This is spending by local, state, and federal governments on goods and services, such as aircraft carriers, bridges, and the salaries of FBI agents.

- *Net exports (NX).* This is spending by foreign firms and households on goods and services produced in the United States minus spending by U.S. firms and households on goods and services produced in other countries.

So, we can write

$$\text{Aggregate expenditure} = \text{Consumption} + \text{Planned investment} \\ + \text{Government purchases} + \text{Net exports,}$$

or

$$AE = C + I + G + NX.$$

Governments around the world gather statistics on aggregate expenditure on the basis of these four components. And economists and business analysts usually explain changes in GDP in terms of changes in these four components of spending.

The Difference between Planned Investment and Actual Investment

Before considering further the relationship between aggregate expenditure and GDP, we need to consider an important distinction: Notice that *planned* investment spending, rather than actual investment spending, is a component of aggregate expenditure. You might wonder how the amount that businesses plan to spend on investment can be different from the amount they actually spend. We can begin resolving this puzzle by remembering that goods that have been produced but have not yet been sold are referred to as **inventories**. Changes in inventories are included as part of investment spending, along with spending on machinery, equipment, office buildings, and factories. We assume that the amount businesses plan to spend on machinery and office buildings is equal to the amount they actually spend, but the amount businesses plan to spend on inventories may be different from the amount they actually spend.

Inventories Goods that have been produced but not yet sold.

For example, Doubleday Publishing may print 1.5 million copies of the latest John Grisham novel, expecting to sell them all. If Doubleday does sell all 1.5 million, its inventories will be unchanged, but if it sells only 1.2 million, it will have an unplanned increase in inventories. In other words, changes in inventories depend on sales of goods, which firms cannot always forecast with perfect accuracy.

For the economy as a whole, we can say that actual investment spending will be greater than planned investment spending when there is an unplanned increase in inventories. Actual investment spending will be less than planned investment spending when there is an unplanned decrease in inventories. *Therefore, actual investment will equal planned investment only when there is no unplanned change in inventories.* In this chapter, we will use I to represent planned investment. We will also assume that the government data on investment spending compiled by the U.S. Bureau of Economic Analysis represents planned investment spending. This is a simplification, however, because the government collects data on actual investment spending, which equals planned investment spending only when unplanned changes in inventories are zero.

Macroeconomic Equilibrium

Macroeconomic equilibrium is similar to microeconomic equilibrium. In microeconomics, equilibrium in the apple market occurs at the point at which the quantity of apples demanded equals the quantity of apples supplied. When we have equilibrium in the apple market, the quantity of apples produced and sold will not change unless the demand for apples or the supply of apples changes. For the economy as a whole, macroeconomic equilibrium occurs where total spending, or aggregate expenditure, equals total production, or GDP:

$$\text{Aggregate expenditure} = \text{GDP.}$$

As we saw in Chapter 11, over the long run, real GDP in the United States grows, and the standard of living rises. In this chapter, we are interested in understanding why GDP fluctuates in the short run. To simplify the analysis of macroeconomic equilibrium, we assume that the economy is not growing. In the next chapter, we discuss the more realistic case of macroeconomic equilibrium in a growing economy. If we assume that the economy is not growing, then equilibrium GDP will not change unless aggregate expenditure changes.

Adjustments to Macroeconomic Equilibrium

The apple market isn't always in equilibrium because sometimes the quantity of apples demanded is greater than the quantity supplied, and sometimes the quantity supplied is greater than the quantity demanded. The same outcome holds for the economy as a whole. Sometimes the economy is in macroeconomic equilibrium, and sometimes it isn't. When aggregate expenditure is greater than GDP, the total amount of spending in the economy is greater than the total amount of production. With spending being greater than production, many businesses will sell more goods and services than they had expected to sell. For example, the manager of a Home Depot store might like to keep 50 refrigerators in stock to give customers the opportunity to see a variety of different sizes and models. If sales are unexpectedly high, the store may end up with only 20 refrigerators. In that case, the store will have an unplanned decrease in inventories: Its inventory of refrigerators will decline by 30.

How will the store manager react when more refrigerators are sold than expected? The manager is likely to order more refrigerators. If other stores selling refrigerators are experiencing similar sales increases and are also increasing their orders, then General Electric, Whirlpool, and other refrigerator manufacturers will significantly increase their production. These manufacturers may also increase the number of workers they hire. If the increase in sales is affecting not just refrigerators but also other appliances, automobiles, furniture, computers, and other goods and services, then GDP and total employment will begin to increase. In summary, *when aggregate expenditure is greater than GDP, inventories will decline, and GDP and total employment will increase.*

Now suppose that aggregate expenditure is less than GDP. With spending being less than production, many businesses will sell fewer goods and services than they had expected to sell, so their inventories will increase. For example, the manager of the Home Depot store who wants 50 refrigerators in stock may find that because of slow sales, the store has 75 refrigerators, so the store manager will cut back on orders for new refrigerators. If other stores also cut back on their orders, General Electric and Whirlpool will reduce production and lay off workers.

If the decrease in sales is affecting not just refrigerators but also many other goods and services, GDP and total employment will begin to decrease. These events happened at many firms during 2008. In summary, *when aggregate expenditure is less than GDP, inventories will increase, and GDP and total employment will decrease.*

Only when aggregate expenditure equals GDP will firms sell what they expected to sell. In that case, their inventories will be unchanged, and they will not have an incentive to increase or decrease production. The economy will be in macroeconomic equilibrium. Table 12.1 summarizes the relationship between aggregate expenditure and GDP.

Table 12.1

The Relationship between Aggregate Expenditure and GDP

If . . .	then . . .	and . . .
aggregate expenditure is *equal* to GDP	inventories are *unchanged*	the economy is in *macroeconomic equilibrium.*
aggregate expenditure is *less* than GDP	inventories *rise*	GDP and employment *decrease.*
aggregate expenditure is *greater* than GDP	inventories *fall*	GDP and employment *increase.*

Increases and decreases in aggregate expenditure cause the year-to-year changes we see in GDP. Economists devote considerable time and energy to forecasting what will happen to each component of aggregate expenditure. If economists forecast that aggregate expenditure will decline in the future, that is equivalent to forecasting that GDP will decline and that the economy will enter a recession. Individuals and firms closely watch these forecasts because changes in GDP can have dramatic consequences. When GDP is increasing, so are wages, profits, and job opportunities. Declining GDP can be bad news for workers, firms, and job seekers.

When economists forecast that aggregate expenditure is likely to decline and that the economy is headed for a recession, the federal government may implement *macroeconomic policies* in an attempt to head off the decrease in expenditure and keep the economy from falling into recession. We discuss these macroeconomic policies in Chapters 15 and 16.

Determining the Level of Aggregate Expenditure in the Economy

To better understand how macroeconomic equilibrium is determined in the aggregate expenditure model, we look more closely at the components of aggregate expenditure. Table 12.2 lists the four components of aggregate expenditure for the year 2010. Each component is measured in *real* terms, meaning that it is corrected for inflation by being measured in billions of 2005 dollars. Consumption is clearly the largest component of aggregate expenditure. Investment and government purchases are of roughly similar size. Net exports were negative because in 2010, as in most years since the early 1970s, the United States imported more goods and services than it exported. Next, we consider the variables that determine each of the four components of aggregate expenditure.

Consumption

Figure 12.1 shows movements in real consumption from 1979 through the second quarter of 2011. Notice that consumption follows a smooth, upward trend. Only during periods of recession does the growth in consumption decline.

The following are the five most important variables that determine the level of consumption:

- Current disposable income

- Household wealth

- Expected future income

- The price level

- The interest rate

We now discuss how changes in each of these variables affect consumption.

> **12.2 LEARNING** OBJECTIVE
>
> Discuss the determinants of the four components of aggregate expenditure and define marginal propensity to consume and marginal propensity to save.

Expenditure Category	Real Expenditure (billions of 2005 dollars)
Consumption	$9,221
Planned investment	1,715
Government purchases	2,557
Net exports	−422

Data from U.S. Bureau of Economic Analysis.

> **Table 12.2**
>
> **Components of Real Aggregate Expenditure, 2010**

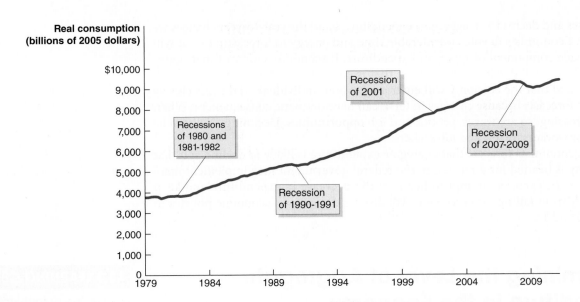

Figure 12.1 **Real Consumption**

Consumption follows a smooth, upward trend, interrupted only infrequently by brief recessions.

Note: The values are quarterly data seasonally adjusted at an annual rate. Data from U.S. Bureau of Economic Analysis.

Current Disposable Income The most important determinant of consumption is the current disposable income of households. Recall from Chapter 8 that disposable income is the income remaining to households after they have paid the personal income tax and received government *transfer payments*, such as Social Security payments. For most households, the higher their disposable income, the more they spend, and the lower their income, the less they spend. Macroeconomic consumption is the total of all the consumption of U.S. households. So, we would expect consumption to increase when the current disposable income of households increases and to decrease when the current disposable income of households decreases. As we discussed in Chapter 8, total income in the United States expands during most years. Only during recessions, which happen infrequently, does total income decline. The main reason for the general upward trend in consumption shown in Figure 12.1 is that disposable income has followed a similar upward trend.

Household Wealth Consumption depends in part on the wealth of households. A household's *wealth* is the value of its *assets* minus the value of its *liabilities*. Recall from Chapter 6 that an asset is anything of value owned by a person or a firm, and a liability is anything owed by a person or a firm. A household's assets include its home, stock and bond holdings, and bank accounts. A household's liabilities include any loans that it owes. A household with $10 million in wealth is likely to spend more than a household with $10,000 in wealth, even if both households have the same disposable income. Therefore, when the wealth of households increases, consumption should increase, and when the wealth of households decreases, consumption should decrease. Shares of stock are an important category of household wealth. When stock prices increase, household wealth will increase, and so should consumption. For example, a family whose stock holdings increase in value from $50,000 to $100,000 may be willing to spend a larger fraction of its income because it is less concerned with adding to its savings. A decline in stock prices should lead to a decline in consumption. Economists who have studied the determinants of consumption have concluded that permanent increases in wealth have a larger impact than temporary increases. A recent estimate of the effect of changes in wealth on consumption spending indicates that, for every permanent $1 increase in household wealth, consumption spending will increase by between 4 and 5 cents per year.

Making the Connection

Do Changes in Housing Wealth Affect Consumption Spending?

From 2000 to 2006, housing prices increased sharply in many parts of the United States. The figure below shows the S&P/ Case-Shiller index of housing prices, which represents changes in the prices of single-family homes. As measured by this index, housing prices increased nearly 90 percent between the beginning of 2000 and the beginning of 2006. Housing prices then declined over 30 percent between the beginning of 2006 and the beginning of 2009. *Housing wealth* equals the market value of houses minus the value of loans people have taken out to pay for the houses. For example, someone who owns a house with a market price of $200,000 and who has a mortgage of $150,000 would have housing wealth of $50,000. Between 2000 and 2005, total housing wealth increased by about $5.5 trillion before falling by $7.0 trillion through mid-2011.

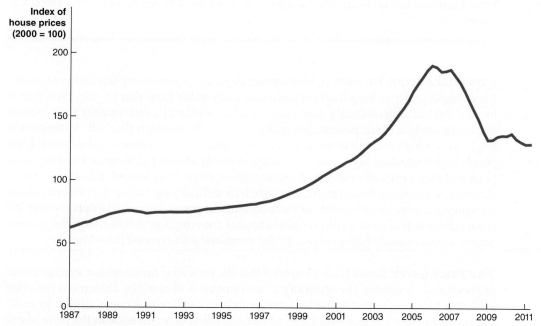

Data from S&P/Case-Shiller, standardandpoors.com.

Did these big swings in housing wealth affect consumption spending? Economists are divided in their opinions. Charles Calomiris of Columbia University, Stanley Longhofer of the Barton School of Business, and William Miles of Wichita State University argue that changes in housing wealth have little or no effect on consumption. They argue that consumers do not consider houses to be assets similar to their holdings of stocks and bonds because they own houses primarily so they can consume the housing services a home provides. Only consumers who intend to sell their current house and buy a smaller one—for example, "empty nesters" whose children have left home—will benefit from an increase in housing prices. But taking the population as a whole, the number of empty nesters may be smaller than the number of first-time home buyers plus the number of homeowners who want to buy larger houses. These two groups are hurt by rising home prices. Although it appears that consumption increases when housing prices increase, in fact, increases in income are responsible for both the increases in housing prices and the increases in consumption; increases in housing prices have no independent effect on consumption. (This is an example of the omitted variable problem discussed on page 32 of the appendix to Chapter 1.)

Atif Mian and Amir Sufi, both of the University of Chicago, strongly disagree with Calomiris, Longhofer, and Miles. Mian and Sufi tracked a sample of 70,000 consumers from 1998 to 2008 and found that consumers living in cities that experienced dramatic increases in housing prices borrowed heavily as their housing wealth increased. Consumers used these borrowed funds to increase their spending on goods and services.

Mian and Sufi believe that the sharp decline in consumption spending in 2008—the largest since 1980—occurred because falling housing prices resulted in lower housing wealth and lower consumer borrowing to finance spending.

The debate over the effect of changes in housing wealth on consumption spending illustrates an important fact about macroeconomics: Many macroeconomic variables, such as GDP, housing prices, consumption spending, and investment spending, rise and fall at about the same time during the business cycle. Because many macroeconomic variables move together, economists sometimes have difficulty determining whether movements in one variable are causing movements in another variable.

Based on Atif R. Mian and Amir Sufi, "House Prices, Home Equity–Based Borrowing, and the U.S. Household Leverage Crisis," *American Economic Review*, Vol. 101, No. 5, August 2011, pp. 2132–2156; Atif Mian and Amir Sufi, "Housing Bubble Fueled Consumer Spending," *Wall Street Journal*, June 25, 2009; Charles W. Calomiris, Stanley D. Longhofer, and William Miles, "The (Mythical?) Housing Wealth Effect," National Bureau of Economic Research Working Paper 15075, June 2009; and Charles W. Calomiris, Stanley D. Longhofer, and William Miles, "The (Mythical?) Housing Wealth Effect," *Wall Street Journal*, June 22, 2009.

MyEconLab **Your Turn:** Test your understanding by doing related problem 2.11 on page 411 at the end of this chapter.

Expected Future Income Consumption depends in part on expected future income. Most people prefer to keep their consumption fairly stable from year to year, even if their income fluctuates significantly. Some salespeople, for example, earn most of their income from commissions (fixed percentages of the price) on the products they sell. A salesperson might have a high income in some years and a much lower income in other years. Most people in this situation keep their consumption steady and do not increase it during good years and then drastically cut it back during slower years. If we looked only at the current income of someone in this situation, we might have difficulty estimating the person's current consumption. Instead, we need to take into account the person's expected future income. We can conclude that current income explains current consumption well *but only when current income is not unusually high or unusually low compared with expected future income.*

The Price Level Recall from Chapter 9 that the *price level* measures the average prices of goods and services in the economy. Consumption is affected by changes in the price level. It is tempting to think that an increase in prices will reduce consumption by making goods and services less affordable. In fact, the effect of an increase in the price of *one* product on the quantity demanded of that product is different from the effect of an increase in the price level on *total* spending by households on goods and services. Changes in the price level affect consumption mainly through their effect on household wealth. An increase in the price level will result in a decrease in the *real* value of household wealth. For example, if you have $2,000 in a checking account, the higher the price level, the fewer goods and services you can buy with your money. If the price level falls, the real value of your $2,000 increases. Therefore, as the price level rises, the real value of your wealth declines, and so will your consumption, at least a little. Conversely, if the price level falls—which happens very rarely in the United States—your consumption will increase.

The Interest Rate Finally, consumption depends on the interest rate. When the interest rate is high, the reward for saving is increased, and households are likely to save more and spend less. In Chapter 9, we discussed the distinction between the *nominal interest rate* and the *real interest rate*. The nominal interest rate is the stated interest rate on a loan or a financial investment such as a bond. The real interest rate corrects the nominal interest rate for the effect of inflation and is equal to the nominal interest rate minus the inflation rate. Because households are concerned with the payments they will make or receive after the effects of inflation are taken into account, consumption spending depends on the real interest rate.

We saw in Chapter 8 that consumption spending is divided into three categories: spending on *services*, such as medical care, education, and haircuts; spending on *nondurable goods*, such as food and clothing; and spending on *durable goods*, such as automobiles and furniture. Spending on durable goods is most likely to be affected by changes in the interest rate because a high real interest rate increases the cost of spending financed by borrowing. The monthly payment on a four-year car loan will be higher if the real interest rate on the loan is 4 percent than if the real interest rate is 2 percent.

The Consumption Function Panel (a) in Figure 12.2 illustrates the relationship between consumption and disposable income during the years 1960 to 2010. In panel (b), we draw a straight line through the points representing consumption and disposable income. The fact that most of the points lie almost on the line shows the close relationship between consumption and disposable income. Because changes in consumption depend on changes in disposable income, we can say that *consumption is a function of disposable income*. The relationship between consumption spending and disposable income illustrated in panel (b) of Figure 12.2 is called the **consumption function**.

The slope of the consumption function, which is equal to the change in consumption divided by the change in disposable income, is referred to as the **marginal propensity to consume (*MPC*)**. Using the Greek letter delta, Δ, to represent "change in," C to represent consumption spending, and YD to represent disposable income, we can write the expression for the *MPC* as follows:

$$MPC = \frac{\text{Change in consumption}}{\text{Change in disposable income}} = \frac{\Delta C}{\Delta YD}.$$

For example, between 2006 and 2007, consumption spending increased by $208 billion, while disposable income increased by $228 billion. The marginal propensity to consume was, therefore:

$$\frac{\Delta C}{\Delta YD} = \frac{\$208 \text{ billion}}{\$228 \text{ billion}} = 0.91.$$

The value for the *MPC* tells us that households in 2007 spent 91 percent of the increase in their household income.

Consumption function The relationship between consumption spending and disposable income.

Marginal propensity to consume (*MPC*) The slope of the consumption function: The amount by which consumption spending changes when disposable income changes.

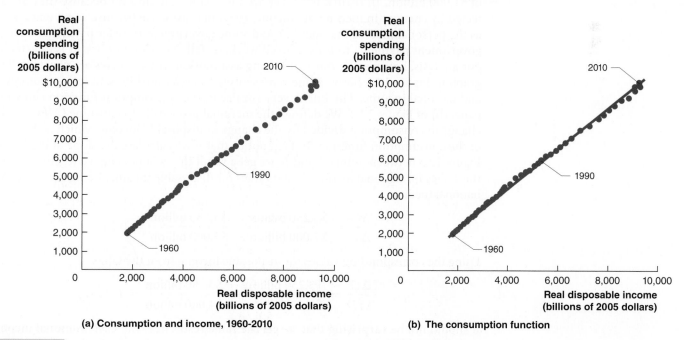

(a) Consumption and income, 1960-2010

(b) The consumption function

Figure 12.2 **The Relationship between Consumption and Income, 1960–2010**

Panel (a) shows the relationship between consumption and income. The points represent combinations of real consumption spending and real disposable income for the years 1960 to 2010. In panel (b), we draw a straight line through the points from panel (a). The line, which represents the relationship between

consumption and disposable income, is called the *consumption function*. The slope of the consumption function is the marginal propensity to consume. Data from U.S. Bureau of Economic Analysis.

We can also use the *MPC* to determine how much consumption will change as income changes. To see this relationship, we rewrite the expression for the *MPC*:

Change in consumption = Change in disposable income × *MPC*.

For example, with an *MPC* of 0.91, a $10 billion increase in disposable income will increase consumption by $10 billion × 0.91, or $9.1 billion.

The Relationship between Consumption and National Income

We have seen that consumption spending by households depends on disposable income. We now shift our focus slightly to the similar relationship that exists between consumption spending and GDP. We make this shift because we are interested in using the aggregate expenditure model to explain changes in real GDP rather than changes in disposable income. The first step in examining the relationship between consumption and GDP is to recall from Chapter 8 that the differences between GDP and national income are small and can be ignored without affecting our analysis. In fact, in this and the following chapters, we will use the terms *GDP* and *national income* interchangeably. Also recall that disposable income is equal to national income plus government transfer payments minus taxes. Taxes minus government transfer payments are referred to as *net taxes*. So, we can write the following:

Disposable income = National income − Net taxes.

We can rearrange the equation like this:

National income = GDP = Disposable income + Net taxes.

The table in Figure 12.3 shows hypothetical values for national income (or GDP), net taxes, disposable income, and consumption spending. Notice that national income and disposable income differ by a constant amount, which is equal to net taxes of $1,000 billion. In reality, net taxes are not a constant amount because they are affected by changes in income. As income rises, net taxes rise because some taxes, such as the personal income tax, increase and some government transfer payments, such as government payments to unemployed workers, fall. Nothing important is affected in our analysis, however, by our simplifying assumption that net taxes are constant. The graph in Figure 12.3 shows a line representing the relationship between consumption and national income. The line is very similar to the consumption function shown in panel (b) of Figure 12.2. We defined the marginal propensity to consume (*MPC*) as the change in consumption divided by the change in disposable income, which is the slope of the consumption function. In fact, notice that if we calculate the slope of the line in Figure 12.3 between points *A* and *B*, we get a result that will not change whether we use the values for national income or the values for disposable income. Using the values for national income:

$$\frac{\Delta C}{\Delta Y} = \frac{\$5,250 \text{ billion} - \$3,750 \text{ billion}}{\$7,000 \text{ billion} - \$5,000 \text{ billion}} = 0.75.$$

Using the corresponding values for disposable income from the table:

$$\frac{\Delta C}{\Delta YD} = \frac{\$5,250 \text{ billion} - \$3,750 \text{ billion}}{\$6,000 \text{ billion} - \$4,000 \text{ billion}} = 0.75.$$

It should not be surprising that we get the same result in either case. National income and disposable income differ by a constant amount, so changes in the two numbers always give us the same value, as shown in the last two columns of the table in Figure 12.3. Therefore, we can graph the consumption function using national income rather than using disposable income. We can also calculate the *MPC* using either the change in national income or the change in disposable income and always get the same value.

National Income or GDP (billions of dollars)	Net Taxes (billions of dollars)	Disposable Income (billions of dollars)	Consumption (billions of dollars)	Change in National Income (billions of dollars)	Change in Disposable Income (billions of dollars)
$1,000	$1,000	$0	$750	–	–
3,000	1,000	2,000	2,250	$2,000	$2,000
5,000	1,000	4,000	3,750	2,000	2,000
7,000	1,000	6,000	5,250	2,000	2,000
9,000	1,000	8,000	6,750	2,000	2,000
11,000	1,000	10,000	8,250	2,000	2,000
13,000	1,000	12,000	9,750	2,000	2,000

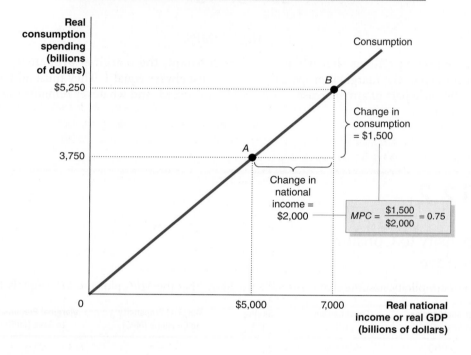

Figure 12.3

The Relationship between Consumption and National Income

Because national income differs from disposable income only by net taxes—which, for simplicity, we assume are constant—we can graph the consumption function using national income rather than disposable income. We can also calculate the *MPC*, which is the slope of the consumption function, using either the change in national income or the change in disposable income and always get the same value. The slope of the consumption function between point *A* and point *B* is equal to the change in consumption—$1,500 billion—divided by the change in national income—$2,000 billion—or 0.75.

Income, Consumption, and Saving

To complete our discussion of consumption, we can look briefly at the relationships among income, consumption, and saving. Households either spend their income, save it, or use it to pay taxes. For the economy as a whole, we can write the following:

$$\text{National income} = \text{Consumption} + \text{Saving} + \text{Taxes}.$$

When national income increases, there must be some combination of an increase in consumption, an increase in saving, and an increase in taxes:

$$\text{Change in national income} = \text{Change in consumption} + \text{Change in saving} + \text{Change in taxes}.$$

Using symbols, where Y represents national income (and GDP), C represents consumption, S represents saving, and T represents taxes, we can write the following:

$$Y = C + S + T$$

and

$$\Delta Y = \Delta C + \Delta S + \Delta T.$$

To simplify, we can assume that taxes are always a constant amount, in which case $\Delta T = 0$ so the following is also true:

$$\Delta Y = \Delta C + \Delta S.$$

Marginal propensity to save (MPS)
The amount by which saving changes when disposable income changes.

We have already seen that the marginal propensity to consume equals the change in consumption divided by the change in income. We can define the **marginal propensity to save (MPS)** as the amount by which saving increases when disposable income increases. We can measure the MPS as the change in saving divided by the change in disposable income. In calculating the MPS, as in calculating the MPC, we can safely ignore the difference between national income and disposable income.

If we divide the last equation on the previous page by the change in income, ΔY, we get an equation that shows the relationship between the marginal propensity to consume and the marginal propensity to save:

$$\frac{\Delta Y}{\Delta Y} = \frac{\Delta C}{\Delta Y} + \frac{\Delta S}{\Delta Y}$$

or

$$1 = MPC + MPS.$$

This equation tells us that when taxes are constant, the marginal propensity to consume plus the marginal propensity to save must always equal 1. They must add up to 1 because part of any increase in income is consumed, and whatever remains must be saved.

Solved Problem 12.2

Calculating the Marginal Propensity to Consume and the Marginal Propensity to Save

Fill in the blanks in the following table. For simplicity, assume that taxes are zero. Show that the MPC plus the MPS equals 1.

National Income and Real GDP (Y)	Consumption (C)	Saving (S)	Marginal Propensity to Consume (MPC)	Marginal Propensity to Save (MPS)
$9,000	$8,000		—	—
10,000	8,600			
11,000	9,200			
12,000	9,800			
13,000	10,400			

Solving the Problem

Step 1: **Review the chapter material.** This problem is about the relationship among income, consumption, and saving, so you may want to review the section "Income, Consumption, and Saving," which begins on page 385.

Step 2: **Fill in the table.** We know that $Y = C + S + T$. With taxes equal to zero, this equation becomes $Y = C + S$. We can use this equation to fill in the "Saving" column. We can use the equations for the MPC and the MPS to fill in the other two columns:

$$MPC = \frac{\Delta C}{\Delta Y}$$

$$MPS = \frac{\Delta S}{\Delta Y}$$

For example, to calculate the value of the MPC in the second row, we have:

$$MPC = \frac{\Delta C}{\Delta Y} = \frac{\$8,600 - \$8,000}{\$10,000 - \$9,000} = \frac{\$600}{\$1,000} = 0.6.$$

To calculate the value of the *MPS* in the second row, we have:

$$MPS = \frac{\Delta S}{\Delta Y} = \frac{\$1,400 - \$1,000}{\$10,000 - \$9,000} = \frac{\$400}{\$1,000} = 0.4.$$

National Income and Real GDP (*Y*)	Consumption (*C*)	Saving (*S*)	Marginal Propensity to Consume (*MPC*)	Marginal Propensity to Save (*MPS*)
$9,000	$8,000	$1,000	—	—
10,000	8,600	1,400	0.6	0.4
11,000	9,200	1,800	0.6	0.4
12,000	9,800	2,200	0.6	0.4
13,000	10,400	2,600	0.6	0.4

Step 3: Show that the *MPC* plus the *MPS* equals 1. At every level of national income, the *MPC* is 0.6 and the *MPS* is 0.4. Therefore, the *MPC* plus the *MPS* is always equal to 1.

Your Turn: For more practice, do related problem 2.13 on page 411 at the end of this chapter.   MyEconLab

Planned Investment

Figure 12.4 shows movements in real investment spending from 1979 through the second quarter of 2011. Notice that, unlike consumption, investment does not follow a smooth, upward trend. Investment declined significantly during the recessions of 1980, 1981–1982, 1990–1991, 2001, and 2007–2009.

The four most important variables that determine the level of investment are:

- Expectations of future profitability

- Interest rate

- Taxes

- Cash flow

Expectations of Future Profitability Investment goods, such as factories, office buildings, and machinery and equipment, are long lived. A firm is unlikely to build a new factory unless it is optimistic that the demand for its product will remain strong for at least several years. When the economy moves into a recession, many firms postpone

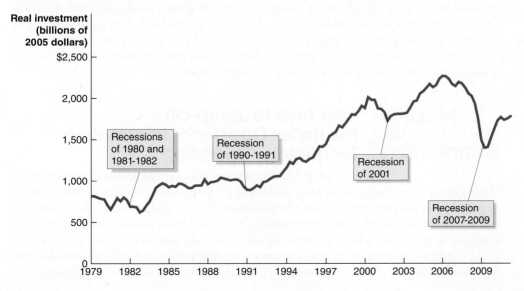

Figure 12.4

Real Investment

Investment is subject to larger changes than is consumption. Investment declined significantly during the recessions of 1980, 1981–1982, 1990–1991, 2001, and 2007–2009.

Note: The values are quarterly data, seasonally adjusted at an annual rate.

Data from U.S. Bureau of Economic Analysis.

buying investment goods even if the demand for their own product is strong because they are afraid that the recession may become worse. During an expansion, some firms may become optimistic and begin to increase spending on investment goods even before the demand for their own product has increased. The key point is this: *The optimism or pessimism of firms is an important determinant of investment spending.*

Residential construction is included in investment spending. Since 1990, residential construction has averaged about 30 percent of total investment spending. But the swings in residential construction have been quite substantial, ranging from 36 percent of investment spending at the height of the housing boom in 2005, down to 18 percent in 2011. The sharp decline in spending on residential construction beginning in 2006 helped to bring on the 2007–2009 recession and contributed to the recession's severity.

Interest Rate Some business investment is financed by borrowing, which takes the form of issuing corporate bonds or receiving loans from banks. Households also borrow to finance most of their spending on new homes. The higher the interest rate, the more expensive it is for firms and households to borrow. Because households and firms are interested in the cost of borrowing after taking into account the effects of inflation, investment spending depends on the real interest rate. Therefore, holding the other factors that affect investment spending constant, there is an inverse relationship between the real interest rate and investment spending: *A higher real interest rate results in less investment spending, and a lower real interest rate results in more investment spending.* As we will discuss further in Chapter 15, the ability of households to borrow money at very low real interest rates helps explain the rapid increase in spending on residential construction from 2002 to 2006.

Taxes Taxes affect the level of investment spending. Firms focus on the profits that remain after they have paid taxes. The federal government imposes a *corporate income tax* on the profits corporations earn, including profits from the new buildings, equipment, and other investment goods they purchase. A reduction in the corporate income tax increases the after-tax profitability of investment spending. An increase in the corporate income tax decreases the after-tax profitability of investment spending. *Investment tax incentives* also increase investment spending. An investment tax incentive provides firms with a tax reduction when they spend on new investment goods.

Cash flow The difference between the cash revenues received by a firm and the cash spending by the firm.

Cash Flow Most firms do not borrow to finance spending on new factories, machinery, and equipment. Instead, they use their own funds. **Cash flow** is the difference between the cash revenues received by a firm and the cash spending by the firm. Neither noncash receipts nor noncash spending is included in cash flow. For example, tax laws allow firms to count depreciation to replace worn out or obsolete machinery and equipment as a cost, even if new machinery and equipment have not actually been purchased. Because this is noncash spending, it is not included when calculating cash flow. The largest contributor to cash flow is profit. The more profitable a firm is, the greater its cash flow and the greater its ability to finance investment. During periods of recession, many firms experience reduced profits, which in turn reduces their ability to finance spending on new factories or machinery and equipment.

Making the Connection | Intel Tries to Jump Off the Roller Coaster of Information Technology Spending

We saw in the chapter opener that continued improvement in Intel's microprocessors has been a key reason the performance of computers has increased so rapidly over the past 40 years. But computers are durable goods, and spending on them follows the business cycle. During recessions, firms and households reduce spending on computers, getting by with their existing machines and software. As the graph on the next page shows, purchases of information processing equipment and software declined 8 percent during the 2001 recession and 9 percent during the 2007–2009 recession.

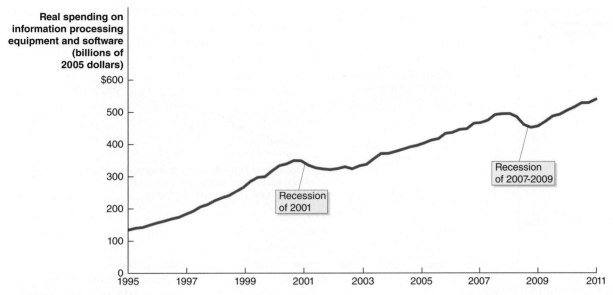

Data from U.S. Bureau of Economic Analysis.

We saw in Chapter 10 that Intel CEO Paul Otellini remained optimistic about the future demand for computers and pressed ahead in 2009 with a $7 billion expansion of Intel factories in the United States. But Otellini was also concerned that its dependence on sales of microprocessors to Apple, Dell, and other computer firms made it vulnerable to sharp declines in sales during recessions. To help deal with this vulnerability, Intel began to develop memory chips that could be used in portable consumer electronic devices, such as Apple's iPod, and in cell phones. Intel made progress toward this goal when it came to an agreement with Nokia, which manufactures about 40 percent of cell phones sold worldwide, to collaborate on the development of new portable devices.

The cell phone market was particularly attractive to Intel because more than 1 billion cell phones are sold each year, as opposed to several hundred million computers. Sales of cell phones also declined much less during the recession of 2007–2009 than did sales of personal computers. Otellini believed Intel's experience with computer chips would allow the company to expand into making chips for other devices because, he argued, "All consumer electronics—and I mean all—are aimed at bringing the Internet into devices." By 2011, the new factories the firm started building in 2009 had begun to develop results, including production of the Atom chip that it adapted for use in cell phones. But Intel faced stiff competition from existing chip suppliers, such as Qualcomm, Texas Instruments, and NVIDIA, and whether it would succeed in becoming less dependent on sales of personal computers remained to be seen.

Based on Tiernan Ray, "ARM Elbows Out Intel in the Post-PC World," *Barron's*, September 17, 2011; Ashlee Vance, "Intel's Bet on Innovation Pays Off in Faster Chips," *New York Times*, January 14, 2010; Don Clark, "Intel Makes Another Run at Phones with Nokia," *Wall Street Journal*, June 24, 2009; and Michael V. Copeland, "Intel's Secret Plan," cnnmoney.com, May 13, 2009.

Your Turn: Test your understanding by doing related problem 2.14 on page 411 at the end of this   MyEconLab
chapter.

Government Purchases

Total government purchases include all spending by federal, local, and state governments for goods and services. Recall from Chapter 8 that government purchases do not include transfer payments, such as Social Security payments by the federal government or pension payments by local governments to retired police officers and firefighters because the government does not receive a good or service in return.

Figure 12.5 shows levels of real government purchases from 1979 through the second quarter of 2011. Government purchases grew steadily for most of this period, with

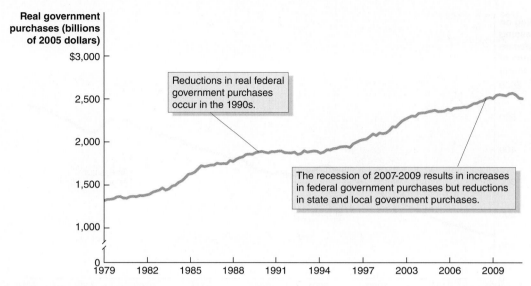

Figure 12.5 **Real Government Purchases**

Government purchases grew steadily for most of the 1979–2011 period, with the exception of the early 1990s, when concern about the federal budget deficit caused real government purchases to fall for three years, beginning in 1992.

Note: The values are quarterly data, seasonally adjusted at an annual rate. Data from U.S. Bureau of Economic Analysis.

the exception of the early 1990s, when Congress and Presidents George H. W. Bush and Bill Clinton enacted a series of spending reductions after they became concerned that spending by the federal government was growing much faster than tax receipts. As a result, real government purchases declined for three years, beginning in 1992. Contributing to the slow growth of government purchases during the 1990s was the end of the Cold War between the United States and the Soviet Union in 1989. Real federal government spending on national defense declined by 24 percent from 1990 to 1998, before rising by 60 percent between 1998 and 2011, in response to the war on terrorism and the wars in Iraq and Afghanistan. As we will discuss further in Chapter 16, total federal government purchases increased sharply beginning in 2009, as President Barack Obama and Congress attempted to offset declining consumption and investment spending during the recession. Increased federal government purchases were partially offset, however, by lower state and local government purchases.

Net Exports

Net exports equal exports minus imports. We can calculate net exports by taking the value of spending by foreign firms and households on goods and services produced in the United States and *subtracting* the value of spending by U.S. firms and households on goods and services produced in other countries. Figure 12.6 illustrates movements in real net exports from 1979 through the second quarter of 2011. During nearly all these years, the United States imported more goods and services than it exported, so net exports were negative. Net exports usually increase when the U.S. economy is in recession—although this happened to only a minor extent during the 2001 recession—and fall when the U.S. economy is expanding. We will explore the behavior of net exports further in Chapter 18.

The following are the three most important variables that determine the level of net exports:

- The price level in the United States relative to the price levels in other countries

- The growth rate of GDP in the United States relative to the growth rates of GDP in other countries

- The exchange rate between the dollar and other currencies

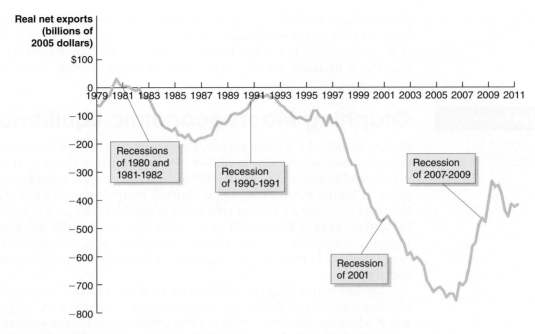

Figure 12.6   Real Net Exports

Net exports were negative in most years between 1979 and 2011. Net exports have usually increased when the U.S. economy is in recession and decreased when the U.S. economy is expanding, although they fell during most of the 2001 recession.

Note: The values are quarterly data, seasonally adjusted at an annual rate. Data from U.S. Bureau of Economic Analysis.

The Price Level in the United States Relative to the Price Levels in Other Countries If inflation in the United States is lower than inflation in other countries, prices of U.S. products increase more slowly than the prices of products of other countries. This slower increase in the U.S. price level increases the demand for U.S. products relative to the demand for foreign products. So, U.S. exports increase and U.S. imports decrease, which increases net exports. The reverse happens during periods when the inflation rate in the United States is higher than the inflation rates in other countries: U.S. exports decrease and U.S. imports increase, which decreases net exports.

The Growth Rate of GDP in the United States Relative to the Growth Rates of GDP in Other Countries As GDP increases in the United States, the incomes of households rise, leading them to increase their purchases of goods and services. Some of the additional goods and services purchased with rising incomes are produced in the United States, but some are imported. When incomes rise faster in the United States than in other countries, U.S. consumers' purchases of foreign goods and services increase faster than foreign consumers' purchases of U.S. goods and services. As a result, net exports fall. When incomes in the United States rise more slowly than incomes in other countries, net exports rise.

The Exchange Rate between the Dollar and Other Currencies As the value of the U.S. dollar rises, the foreign currency price of U.S. products sold in other countries rises, and the dollar price of foreign products sold in the United States falls. For example, suppose that the exchange rate between the Japanese yen and the U.S. dollar is 100 Japanese yen for one U.S. dollar, or ¥100 = $1. At this exchange rate, someone in the United States could buy ¥100 for $1, or someone in Japan could buy $1 for ¥100. Leaving aside transportation costs, at this exchange rate, a U.S. product that sells for $1 in the United States will sell for ¥100 in Japan, and a Japanese product that sells for ¥100 in Japan will sell for $1 in the United States. If the exchange rate changes to ¥150 = $1, then the value of the dollar will have risen because it takes more yen to buy $1. At the new exchange rate, the U.S. product that still sells for $1 in the United States will now sell for ¥150 in Japan, reducing the quantity demanded by Japanese consumers. The Japanese product that still sells for ¥100 in Japan will now sell for only $0.67 in the United States, increasing the quantity demanded by U.S. consumers. An increase in the value of the dollar will reduce exports and increase imports, so net exports will fall. A decrease in the value of the dollar will increase exports and reduce imports, so net exports will rise.

Graphing Macroeconomic Equilibrium

Having examined the components of aggregate expenditure, we can now look more closely at macroeconomic equilibrium. We saw earlier in the chapter that macroeconomic equilibrium occurs when GDP is equal to aggregate expenditure. We can use a graph called the *45°-line diagram* to illustrate macroeconomic equilibrium. (The 45°-line diagram is also sometimes referred to as the *Keynesian cross* because it is based on the analysis of John Maynard Keynes.) To become familiar with this diagram, consider Figure 12.7, which is a 45°-line diagram that shows the relationship between the quantity of Pepsi sold (on the vertical axis) and the quantity of Pepsi produced (on the horizontal axis).

The line on the diagram forms an angle of 45° with the horizontal axis. The line represents all the points that are equal distances from both axes. So, points such as *A* and *B*, where the number of bottles of Pepsi produced equals the number of bottles sold, are on the 45° line. Points such as *C*, where the quantity sold is greater than the quantity produced, lie above the line. Points such as *D*, where the quantity sold is less than the quantity produced, lie below the line.

Figure 12.8 is similar to Figure 12.7 except that it measures real national income, or real GDP (Y), on the horizontal axis and planned real aggregate expenditure (AE) on the vertical axis. Because macroeconomic equilibrium occurs where planned aggregate expenditure equals GDP, *we know that all points of macroeconomic equilibrium must lie along the 45° line.* For all points above the 45° line, planned aggregate expenditure will be greater than GDP. For all points below the 45° line, planned aggregate expenditure will be less than GDP.

The 45° line shows many potential points of macroeconomic equilibrium. During any particular year, only one of these points will represent the actual level of equilibrium

Figure 12.7

An Example of a 45°-Line Diagram

The 45° line shows all the points that are equal distances from both axes. Points such as *A* and *B*, at which the quantity produced equals the quantity sold, are on the 45° line. Points such as *C*, at which the quantity sold is greater than the quantity produced, lie above the line. Points such as *D*, at which the quantity sold is less than the quantity produced, lie below the line.

Figure 12.8

The Relationship between Planned Aggregate Expenditure and GDP on a 45°-Line Diagram

Every point of macroeconomic equilibrium is on the 45° line, where planned aggregate expenditure equals GDP. At points above the line, planned aggregate expenditure is greater than GDP. At points below the line, planned aggregate expenditure is less than GDP.

real GDP, given the actual level of planned real expenditure. To determine this point, we need to draw a line on the graph to show the *aggregate expenditure function*. The aggregate expenditure function shows us the amount of planned aggregate expenditure that will occur at every level of national income, or GDP.

Changes in GDP have a much greater effect on consumption than on planned investment, government purchases, or net exports. We assume for simplicity that the variables that determine planned investment, government purchases, and net exports all remain constant, as do the variables other than GDP that affect consumption. For example, we assume that a firm's level of planned investment at the beginning of the year will not change during the year, even if the level of GDP changes.

Figure 12.9 shows the aggregate expenditure function on the 45°-line diagram. The lowest upward-sloping line, *C*, represents the consumption function, as shown in Figure 12.2, panel (b), on page 383. The quantities of planned investment, government purchases, and net exports are constant because we assumed that the variables they depend on are constant. So, the level of planned aggregate expenditure at any level of GDP is the amount of consumption spending at that level of GDP plus the sum of the constant amounts of planned investment, government purchases, and net exports. In Figure 12.9, we add each component of spending successively to the consumption function line to arrive at the line representing planned aggregate expenditure (*AE*). The *C* + *I* line is higher than the *C* line by the constant amount of planned investment; the *C* + *I* + *G* line is higher than the *C* + *I* line by the constant amount of government purchases; and the *C* + *I* + *G* + *NX* line is higher than the *C* + *I* + *G* line by the constant amount of *NX*. (In many years, however, *NX* is negative, which would cause the *C* + *I* + *G* + *NX* line to be *below* the *C* + *I* + *G* line.) The *C* + *I* + *G* + *NX* line shows all four components of expenditure and is the aggregate expenditure (*AE*) function. At the point where the *AE* line crosses the 45° line, planned aggregate expenditure is equal to GDP, and the economy is in macroeconomic equilibrium.

Figure 12.10 makes the relationship between planned aggregate expenditure and GDP clearer by showing only the 45° line and the *AE* line. The figure shows that the *AE* line intersects the 45° line at a level of real GDP of $10 trillion. Therefore, $10 trillion represents the equilibrium level of real GDP. To see why this is true, consider the situation if real GDP were only $8 trillion. By moving vertically from $8 trillion on the

Figure 12.9

Macroeconomic Equilibrium on the 45°-Line Diagram

Macroeconomic equilibrium occurs where the aggregate expenditure (*AE*) line crosses the 45° line. The lowest upward-sloping line, *C*, represents the consumption function. The quantities of planned investment, government purchases, and net exports are constant because we assumed that the variables they depend on are constant. So, the total of planned aggregate expenditure at any level of GDP is the amount of consumption at that level of GDP plus the sum of the constant amounts of planned investment, government purchases, and net exports. We successively add each component of spending to the consumption function line to arrive at the line representing aggregate expenditure.

horizontal axis up to the *AE* line, we see that planned aggregate expenditure will be greater than $8 trillion at this level of real GDP. Whenever total spending is greater than total production, firms' inventories will fall. The fall in inventories is equal to the vertical distance between the *AE* line, which shows the level of total spending, and the 45° line, which shows the $8 trillion of total production. Unplanned declines in inventories lead firms to increase their production. As real GDP increases from $8 trillion, so will total income and, therefore, consumption. The economy will move up the *AE* line as consumption increases. The gap between total spending and total production will fall, but as long as the *AE* line is above the 45° line, inventories will continue to decline, and firms will continue to expand production. When real GDP rises to $10 trillion, inventories stop falling, and the economy will be in macroeconomic equilibrium.

As Figure 12.10 shows, if GDP is initially $12 trillion, planned aggregate expenditure will be less than GDP, and firms will experience an unplanned increase in inventories. Rising inventories lead firms to decrease production. As GDP falls from $12 trillion, consumption will also fall, which causes the economy to move down the *AE* line. The gap between planned aggregate expenditure and GDP will fall, but as long as the *AE* line is below the 45° line, inventories will continue to rise, and firms will continue to cut production. When GDP falls to $10 trillion, inventories will stop rising, and the economy will be in macroeconomic equilibrium.

Showing a Recession on the 45°-Line Diagram

Notice that *macroeconomic equilibrium can occur at any point on the 45° line*. Ideally, we would like equilibrium to occur at *potential GDP*. At potential GDP, firms will be operating at their normal level of capacity, and the economy will be at the *natural rate of unemployment*. As we saw in Chapter 9, at the natural rate of unemployment, the economy will be at *full employment*: Everyone in the labor force who wants a job will have one, except the structurally and frictionally unemployed. However, for equilibrium to occur

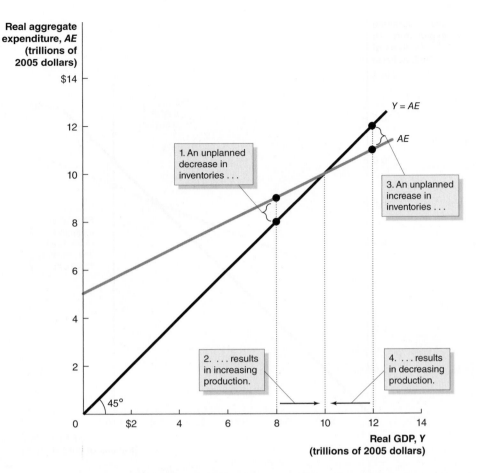

Figure 12.10

Macroeconomic Equilibrium

Macroeconomic equilibrium occurs where the *AE* line crosses the 45° line. In this case, that occurs at GDP of $10 trillion. If GDP is less than $10 trillion, the corresponding point on the *AE* line is above the 45° line, planned aggregate expenditure is greater than total production, firms will experience an unplanned decrease in inventories, and GDP will increase. If GDP is greater than $10 trillion, the corresponding point on the *AE* line is below the 45° line, planned aggregate expenditure is less than total production, firms will experience an unplanned increase in inventories, and GDP will decrease.

at the level of potential GDP, planned aggregate expenditure must be high enough. As Figure 12.11 shows, if there is insufficient total spending, equilibrium will occur at a lower level of real GDP. Many firms will be operating below their normal capacity, and the unemployment rate will be above the natural rate of unemployment.

Suppose that the level of potential GDP is $10 trillion. As Figure 12.11 shows, when GDP is $10 trillion, planned aggregate expenditure is below $10 trillion, perhaps because business firms have become pessimistic about their future profitability and have reduced their investment spending. The shortfall in planned aggregate expenditure that leads to the recession can be measured as the vertical distance between the *AE* line and the 45° line at the level of potential GDP. The shortfall in planned aggregate expenditure is exactly equal to the unplanned increase in inventories that would occur if the economy were initially at a level of GDP of $10 trillion. The unplanned increase in inventories measures the amount by which current planned aggregate expenditure is too low for the current level of production to be the equilibrium level. Or, put another way, if any of the four components of aggregate expenditure increased by this amount, the *AE* line would shift upward and intersect the 45° line at GDP of $10 trillion, and the economy would be in macroeconomic equilibrium at full employment.

Figure 12.11 shows that macroeconomic equilibrium will occur when real GDP is $9.8 trillion. Because this is 2 percent below the potential level of real GDP of $10 trillion, many firms will be operating below their normal capacity, and the unemployment rate will be well above the natural rate of unemployment. The economy will remain at this level of real GDP until there is an increase in one or more of the components of aggregate expenditure.

The Important Role of Inventories

Whenever planned aggregate expenditure is less than real GDP, some firms will experience unplanned increases in inventories. If firms do not cut back their production promptly when spending declines, they will accumulate inventories. If firms accumulate

Figure 12.11

Showing a Recession on the 45°-Line Diagram

When the aggregate expenditure line intersects the 45° line at a level of GDP below potential GDP, the economy is in recession. The figure shows that potential GDP is $10 trillion, but because planned aggregate expenditure is too low, the equilibrium level of GDP is only $9.8 trillion, where the AE line intersects the 45° line. As a result, some firms will be operating below their normal capacity, and unemployment will be above the natural rate of unemployment. We can measure the shortfall in planned aggregate expenditure as the vertical distance between the AE line and the 45° line at the level of potential GDP.

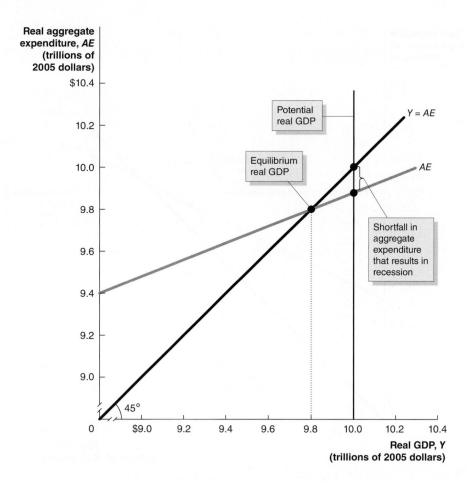

excess inventories, then even if spending quickly returns to its normal levels, firms will have to sell their excess inventories before they can return to producing at normal levels. For example, almost half of the sharp 6.7 percent annual rate of decline in real GDP during the first quarter of 2009 resulted from firms cutting production as they sold off unintended accumulations of inventories.

A Numerical Example of Macroeconomic Equilibrium

In forecasting real GDP, economists rely on quantitative models of the economy. We can increase our understanding of the causes of changes in real GDP by considering a simple numerical example of macroeconomic equilibrium. Although simplified, this example captures some of the key features contained in the quantitative models that economic forecasters use. Table 12.3 shows several hypothetical combinations of real

Table 12.3 Macroeconomic Equilibrium

Real GDP (Y)	Consumption (C)	Planned Investment (I)	Government Purchases (G)	Net Exports (NX)	Planned Aggregate Expenditure (AE)	Unplanned Change in Inventories	Real GDP Will . . .
$8,000	$6,200	$1,500	$1,500	−$500	$8,700	−$700	increase
9,000	6,850	1,500	1,500	−500	9,350	−350	increase
10,000	7,500	1,500	1,500	−500	10,000	0	be in equilibrium
11,000	8,150	1,500	1,500	−500	10,650	+350	decrease
12,000	8,800	1,500	1,500	−500	11,300	+700	decrease

Note: The values are in billions of 2005 dollars.

GDP and planned aggregate expenditure. The first column lists real GDP. The next four columns list levels of the four components of planned aggregate expenditure that occur at the corresponding level of real GDP. We assume that planned investment, government purchases, and net exports do not change as GDP changes. Because consumption depends on GDP, it increases as GDP increases.

In the first row, GDP of $8,000 billion (or $8 trillion) results in consumption of $6,200 billion. Adding consumption, planned investment, government purchases, and net exports across the row gives planned aggregate expenditure of $8,700 billion, which is shown in the sixth column. Because planned aggregate expenditure is greater than GDP, inventories will fall by $700 billion. This unplanned decline in inventories will lead firms to increase production, and GDP will increase. GDP will continue to increase until it reaches $10,000 billion. At that level of GDP, planned aggregate expenditure is also $10,000 billion, unplanned changes in inventories are zero, and the economy is in macroeconomic equilibrium.

In the last row of Table 12.3, GDP of $12,000 billion results in consumption of $8,800 billion and planned aggregate expenditure of $11,300 billion. Because planned aggregate expenditure is less than GDP, inventories will increase by $700 billion. This unplanned increase in inventories will lead firms to decrease production, and GDP will decrease. GDP will continue to decrease until it reaches $10,000 billion, unplanned changes in inventories are zero, and the economy is in macroeconomic equilibrium.

Only when real GDP equals $10,000 billion will the economy be in macroeconomic equilibrium. At other levels of real GDP, planned aggregate expenditure will be higher or lower than GDP, and the economy will be expanding or contracting.

Don't Let This Happen to You

Don't Confuse Aggregate Expenditure with Consumption Spending

Macroeconomic equilibrium occurs where planned aggregate expenditure equals GDP. But, remember that planned aggregate expenditure equals the sum of consumption spending, planned investment spending, government purchases, and net exports, *not* consumption spending by itself. If GDP were equal to consumption, the economy would not be in equilibrium. Planned investment plus government purchases plus net exports will always be a positive number. Therefore, if consumption were equal to GDP, aggregate expenditure would have to be greater than GDP. In that case, inventories would be decreasing, and GDP would be *increasing*; GDP would not be in equilibrium.

Test your understanding of macroeconomic equilibrium with this problem:

Question: Do you agree with the following argument?

The chapter says macroeconomic equilibrium occurs where planned aggregate expenditure equals GDP. GDP is equal to national income. So, at equilibrium, planned aggregate expenditure must equal national income. But, we know that consumers do not spend all of their income: They save at least some and use some to pay taxes. Therefore, aggregate expenditure will never equal national income, and the basic macroeconomic story is incorrect.

Answer: As discussed in Chapter 8, national income equals GDP (disregarding depreciation, as we have throughout this chapter). So, it is correct to say that in macroeconomic equilibrium, planned aggregate expenditure must equal national income. But the last sentence of the argument is incorrect because it assumes that aggregate expenditure is the same as consumption spending. Because of saving and taxes, consumption spending is always much less than national income, but in equilibrium, the sum of consumption spending, planned investment spending, government purchases, and net exports does, in fact, equal GDP and national income. So, the argument is incorrect because it confuses consumption spending with aggregate expenditure.

MyEconLab

Your Turn: Test your understanding by doing related problem 3.11 on page 412 at the end of this chapter.

Solved Problem 12.3

Determining Macroeconomic Equilibrium

Fill in the blanks in the following table and determine the equilibrium level of real GDP.

Real GDP (Y)	Consumption (C)	Planned Investment (I)	Government Purchases (G)	Net Exports (NX)	Planned Aggregate Expenditure (AE)	Unplanned Change in Inventories
$8,000	$6,200	$1,675	$1,675	−$500		
9,000	6,850	1,675	1,675	−500		
10,000	7,500	1,675	1,675	−500		
11,000	8,150	1,675	1,675	−500		
12,000	8,800	1,675	1,675	−500		

Note: The values are in billions of 2005 dollars.

Solving the Problem

Step 1: **Review the chapter material.** This problem is about determining macroeconomic equilibrium, so you may want to review the section "A Numerical Example of Macroeconomic Equilibrium," which begins on page 396.

Step 2: **Fill in the missing values in the table.** We can calculate the missing values in the last two columns by using two equations:

Planned aggregate expenditure (AE) = Consumption (C)
+ Planned investment (I) + Government purchases (G)
+ Net exports (NX)

and

Unplanned change in inventories = Real GDP (Y)
−Planned aggregate expenditure (AE).

For example, to fill in the first row, we have AE = $6,200 billion + $1,675 billion + $1,675 billion + (−$500 billion) = $9,050 billion; and unplanned change in inventories = $8,000 billion − $9,050 billion = −$1,050 billion.

Real GDP (Y)	Consumption (C)	Planned Investment (I)	Government Purchases (G)	Net Exports (NX)	Planned Aggregate Expenditure (AE)	Unplanned Change in Inventories
$8,000	$6,200	$1,675	$1,675	−$500	$9,050	−$1,050
9,000	6,850	1,675	1,675	−500	9,700	−700
10,000	7,500	1,675	1,675	−500	10,350	−350
11,000	8,150	1,675	1,675	−500	11,000	0
12,000	8,800	1,675	1,675	−500	11,650	350

Step 3: **Determine the equilibrium level of real GDP.** Once you fill in the table, you should see that equilibrium real GDP must be $11,000 billion because only at that level is real GDP equal to planned aggregate expenditure.

MyEconLab **Your Turn:** For more practice, do related problem 3.12 on page 413 at the end of this chapter.

The Multiplier Effect

To this point, we have seen that aggregate expenditure determines real GDP in the short run and we have seen how the economy adjusts if it is not in equilibrium. We have also seen that whenever aggregate expenditure changes, there will be a new level of equilibrium real GDP. In this section, we will look more closely at the effects of a change in aggregate expenditure on equilibrium real GDP. We begin the discussion with Figure 12.12, which illustrates the effects of an increase in planned investment spending. We assume that the economy starts in equilibrium at point A, at which real GDP is $9.6 trillion. Firms then become more optimistic about their future profitability and increase spending on factories, machinery, and equipment by $100 billion. This increase in investment spending shifts the AE line up by $100 billion, from the dark tan line (AE_1) to the light tan line (AE_2). The new equilibrium occurs at point B, at which real GDP is $10.0 trillion, which equals potential real GDP.

Notice that the initial $100 billion increase in planned investment spending results in a $400 billion increase in equilibrium real GDP. The increase in planned investment spending has had a *multiplied effect* on equilibrium real GDP. It is not only investment spending that will have this multiplied effect; any increase in *autonomous expenditure* will shift up the aggregate expenditure function and lead to a multiplied increase in equilibrium GDP. **Autonomous expenditure** does not depend on the level of GDP. In the aggregate expenditure model we have been using, planned investment spending, government spending, and net exports are all autonomous expenditures. Consumption actually has both an autonomous component, which does not depend on the level of GDP, and a nonautonomous—or *induced*—component that does depend on the level of GDP. For example, if households decide to spend more of their incomes—and save less—at every level of income, there will be an autonomous increase in consumption spending, and the aggregate expenditure function will shift up. If, however, real GDP increases and households increase their consumption spending, as indicated by the consumption function, the economy will move up along the aggregate expenditure function, and the increase in consumption spending will be nonautonomous.

The ratio of the increase in equilibrium real GDP to the increase in autonomous expenditure is called the **multiplier**. The series of induced increases in consumption spending that results from an initial increase in autonomous expenditure is called the **multiplier effect**. The multiplier effect occurs because an initial increase in autonomous expenditure sets off a series of increases in real GDP.

12.4 LEARNING OBJECTIVE

Describe the multiplier effect and use the multiplier formula to calculate changes in equilibrium GDP.

Autonomous expenditure An expenditure that does not depend on the level of GDP.

Multiplier The increase in equilibrium real GDP divided by the increase in autonomous expenditure.

Multiplier effect The process by which an increase in autonomous expenditure leads to a larger increase in real GDP.

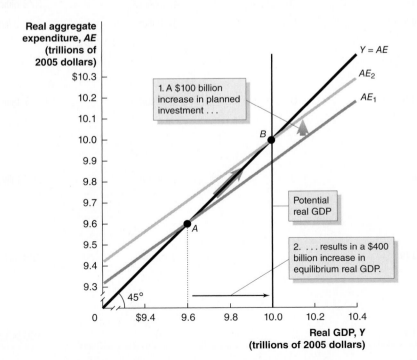

Figure 12.12

The Multiplier Effect

The economy begins at point A, at which equilibrium real GDP is $9.6 trillion. A $100 billion increase in planned investment shifts up aggregate expenditure from AE_1 to AE_2. The new equilibrium is at point B, where real GDP is $10.0 trillion, which is potential real GDP. Because of the multiplier effect, a $100 billion increase in investment results in a $400 billion increase in equilibrium real GDP.

We can look more closely at the multiplier effect shown in Figure 12.12. Suppose the whole $100 billion increase in investment spending shown in the figure consists of firms building additional factories and office buildings. Initially, this additional spending will cause the construction of factories and office buildings to increase by $100 billion, so GDP will also increase by $100 billion. Remember that increases in production result in equal increases in national income. So, this increase in real GDP of $100 billion is also an increase in national income of $100 billion. In this example, the income is received as wages and salaries by the employees of the construction firms, as profits by the owners of the firms, and so on. After receiving this additional income, these workers, managers, and owners will increase their consumption of cars, appliances, furniture, and many other products. If the marginal propensity to consume (*MPC*) is 0.75, we know the increase in consumption spending will be $75 billion. This additional $75 billion in spending will cause the firms making the cars, appliances, and other products to increase production by $75 billion, so GDP will rise by $75 billion. This increase in GDP means national income has also increased by another $75 billion. This increased income will be received by the owners and employees of the firms producing the cars, appliances, and other products. These workers, managers, and owners in turn will increase their consumption spending, and the process of increasing production, income, and consumption will continue.

Eventually, the total increase in consumption will be $300 billion (we will soon show how we know this is true). This $300 billion increase in consumption combined with the initial $100 billion increase in investment spending will result in a total change in equilibrium GDP of $400 billion. Table 12.4 summarizes how changes in GDP and spending caused by the initial $100 billion increase in investment will result in equilibrium GDP rising by $400 billion. We can think of the multiplier effect occurring in rounds of spending. In round 1, there is an increase of $100 billion in autonomous

Table 12.4

The Multiplier Effect in Action

	Additional Autonomous Expenditure (investment)	Additional Induced Expenditure (consumption)	Total Additional Expenditure = Total Additional GDP
Round 1	$100 billion	$0	$100 billion
Round 2	0	75 billion	175 billion
Round 3	0	56 billion	231 billion
Round 4	0	42 billion	273 billion
Round 5	0	32 billion	305 billion
.	.	.	.
.	.	.	.
.	.	.	.
Round 10	0	8 billion	377 billion
.	.	.	.
.	.	.	.
Round 15	0	2 billion	395 billion
.	.	.	.
.	.	.	.
Round 19	0	1 billion	398 billion
.	.	.	.
.	.	.	.
Round *n*	0	0	400 billion

expenditure—the $100 billion in planned investment spending in our example—which causes GDP to rise by $100 billion. In round 2, induced expenditure rises by $75 billion (which equals the $100 billion increase in real GDP in round 1 multiplied by the *MPC*). The $75 billion in induced expenditure in round 2 causes a $75 billion increase in real GDP, which leads to a $56 billion increase in induced expenditure in round 3, and so on. The final column sums up the total increases in expenditure, which equal the total increase in GDP. In each round, the additional induced expenditure becomes smaller because the *MPC* is less than 1. By round 10, additional induced expenditure is only $8 billion, and the total increase in GDP from the beginning of the process is $377 billion. By round 19, the process is almost complete: Additional induced expenditure is only about $1 billion, and the total increase in GDP is $398 billion. Eventually, the process will be finished, although we cannot say precisely how many spending rounds it will take, so we simply label the last round *n* rather than give it a specific number.

We can calculate the value of the multiplier in our example by dividing the increase in equilibrium real GDP by the increase in autonomous expenditure:

$$\frac{\Delta Y}{\Delta I} = \frac{\text{Change in real GDP}}{\text{Change in investment spending}} = \frac{\$400 \text{ billion}}{\$100 \text{ billion}} = 4.$$

With a multiplier of 4, each increase in autonomous expenditure of $1 will result in an increase in equilibrium GDP of $4.

Making the Connection | The Multiplier in Reverse: The Great Depression of the 1930s

An increase in autonomous expenditure causes an increase in equilibrium real GDP, but the reverse is also true: A decrease in autonomous expenditure causes a decrease in real GDP. Many Americans became aware of this fact in the 1930s, when reductions in autonomous expenditure were magnified by the multiplier into the largest decline in real GDP in U.S. history.

In August 1929, the economy reached a business cycle peak, and a downturn in production began. In October, the stock market crashed, destroying billions of dollars of wealth and increasing pessimism among households and firms. Both consumption spending and planned investment spending declined. The passage by the U.S. Congress of the Smoot–Hawley Tariff Act in June 1930 helped set off a trade war that reduced net exports. A series of banking crises that began in fall 1930 limited the ability of households and firms to finance consumption and investment. As aggregate expenditure declined, many firms experienced declining sales and began to lay off workers. Falling levels of production and income induced further declines in consumption spending, which led to further cutbacks in production and employment, leading to further declines in income, and so on, in a downward spiral. The following table shows the severity of the economic downturn by contrasting the business cycle peak of 1929 with the business cycle trough of 1933:

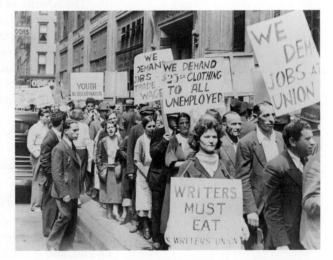

The multiplier effect contributed to the very high levels of unemployment during the Great Depression.

Year	Consumption	Investment	Net Exports	Real GDP	Unemployment Rate
1929	$737 billion	$102 billion	−$11 billion	$977 billion	3.2%
1933	$601 billion	$19 billion	−$12 billion	$716 billion	24.9%

Note: The values are in 2005 dollars.
Data from U.S. Bureau of Economic Analysis; and U.S. Bureau of Labor Statistics.

We can use a 45°-line diagram to illustrate the multiplier effect working in reverse during these years. The economy was at potential real GDP in 1929, before the declines in aggregate expenditure began. Declining consumption, planned investment, and net exports shifted the aggregate expenditure function down from AE_{1929} to AE_{1933}, reducing equilibrium real GDP from \$977 billion in 1929 to \$716 billion in 1933. The depth and length of this economic downturn led to its being labeled the Great Depression.

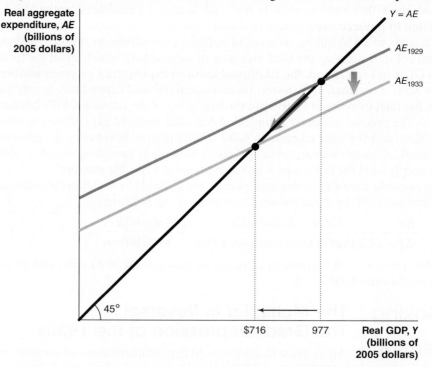

The severity of the Great Depression forced thousands of firms to declare bankruptcy. Even firms that survived experienced sharp declines in sales. By 1933, production at U.S. Steel had declined 90 percent, and production at General Motors had declined more than 75 percent. High rates of unemployment forced many families into poverty and a daily struggle for survival. Recovery from the business cycle trough in 1933 was slow. Real GDP did not regain its 1929 level until 1936, and a growing labor force meant that the unemployment rate did not fall below 10 percent until the United States entered World War II in 1941.

MyEconLab **Your Turn:** Test your understanding by doing related problem 4.4 on page 413 at the end of this chapter.

A Formula for the Multiplier

Table 12.4 shows that during the multiplier process, each round of increases in consumption is smaller than in the previous round, so eventually, the increases will come to an end, and we will have a new macroeconomic equilibrium. But how do we know that when we add all the increases in GDP, the total will be \$400 billion? We can show that this is true by first writing out the total change in equilibrium GDP:

The total change in equilibrium real GDP equals the initial increase in planned investment spending = \$100 billion

Plus the first induced increase in consumption = $MPC \times \$100$ billion

Plus the second induced increase in consumption = $MPC \times (MPC \times \$100$ billion)
$$= MPC^2 \times \$100 \text{ billion}$$

Plus the third induced increase in consumption = $MPC \times (MPC^2 \times \$100$ billion)
$$= MPC^3 \times \$100 \text{ billion}$$

Plus the fourth induced increase in consumption = $MPC \times (MPC^3 \times \$100$ billion)
$$= MPC^4 \times \$100 \text{ billion}$$

And so on . . .

Or:

$$\text{Total change in GDP} = \$100 \text{ billion} + MPC \times \$100 \text{ billion} + MPC^2$$
$$\times \$100 \text{ billion} + MPC^3 \times \$100 \text{ billion} + MPC^4 \times \$100 \text{ billion} + \ldots)$$

where the ellipsis (...) indicates that the expression contains an infinite number of similar terms.

If we factor out the $100 billion from each expression, we have:

$$\text{Total change in GDP} = \$100 \text{ billion} \times (1 + MPC + MPC^2 + MPC^3$$
$$+ MPC^4 + \ldots)$$

Mathematicians have shown that an expression like the one in the parentheses sums to

$$\frac{1}{1 - MPC}.$$

In this case, the MPC is equal to 0.75. So, we can now calculate that the change in equilibrium GDP = 1 billion $\times [1/(1 - 0.75)] = 100$ billion $\times 4 = 400$ billion. We have also derived a general formula for the multiplier:

$$\text{Multiplier} = \frac{\text{Change in equilibrium real GDP}}{\text{Change in autonomous expenditure}} = \frac{1}{1 - MPC}.$$

In this case, the multiplier is $1/(1 - 0.75)$, or 4, which means that for each additional $1 of autonomous spending, equilibrium GDP will increase by $4. A $100 billion increase in planned investment spending results in a $400 billion increase in equilibrium GDP. Notice that the value of the multiplier depends on the value of the MPC. In particular, the larger the value of the MPC, the larger the value of the multiplier. For example, if the MPC were 0.9 instead of 0.75, the value of the multiplier would increase from 4 to $1/(1 - 0.9) = 10$.

Summarizing the Multiplier Effect

You should note four key points about the multiplier effect:

1. The multiplier effect occurs both when autonomous expenditure increases and when it decreases. For example, with an MPC of 0.75, a *decrease* in planned investment of $100 billion will lead to a *decrease* in equilibrium income of $400 billion.
2. The multiplier effect makes the economy more sensitive to changes in autonomous expenditure than it would otherwise be. Between the fourth quarter of 2005 and the first quarter of 2009, spending on residential construction declined more than 50 percent. This decline in spending set off a series of declines in production, income, and spending, so that firms such as automobile dealerships and clothing stores, which are far removed from the housing industry, also experienced sales declines. Because of the multiplier effect, a decline in spending and production in one sector of the economy can lead to declines in spending and production in many other sectors of the economy.
3. The larger the MPC, the larger the value of the multiplier. With an MPC of 0.75, the multiplier is 4, but with an MPC of 0.50, the multiplier is only 2. This direct relationship between the value of the MPC and the value of the multiplier holds true because the larger the MPC, the more additional consumption takes place after each rise in income during the multiplier process.
4. The formula for the multiplier, $1/(1 - MPC)$, is oversimplified because it ignores some real-world complications, such as the effect that increases in GDP have on imports, inflation, interest rates, and individual income taxes. These effects combine to cause the simple formula to overstate the true value of the multiplier. Beginning in Chapter 13, we will start to take into account these real-world complications.

Solved Problem 12.4

Using the Multiplier Formula

Use the information in the table to answer the following questions:

Real GDP (Y)	Consumption (C)	Planned Investment (I)	Government Purchases (G)	Net Exports (NX)
$8,000	$6,900	$1,000	$1,000	−$500
9,000	7,700	1,000	1,000	−500
10,000	8,500	1,000	1,000	−500
11,000	9,300	1,000	1,000	−500
12,000	10,100	1,000	1,000	−500

Note: The values are in billions of 2005 dollars.

a. What is the equilibrium level of real GDP?

b. What is the *MPC*?

c. Suppose government purchases increase by $200 billion. What will be the new equilibrium level of real GDP? Use the multiplier formula to determine your answer.

Solving the Problem

Step 1: **Review the chapter material.** This problem is about the multiplier process, so you may want to review the section "The Multiplier Effect," which begins on page 399.

Step 2: **Determine equilibrium real GDP.** Just as in Solved Problem 12.2 on page 386, we can find macroeconomic equilibrium by calculating the level of planned aggregate expenditure for each level of real GDP.

Real GDP (Y)	Consumption (C)	Planned Investment (I)	Government Purchases (G)	Net Exports (NX)	Planned Aggregate Expenditure (AE)
$8,000	$6,900	$1,000	$1,000	−$500	$8,400
9,000	7,700	1,000	1,000	−500	9,200
10,000	8,500	1,000	1,000	−500	10,000
11,000	9,300	1,000	1,000	−500	10,800
12,000	10,100	1,000	1,000	−500	11,600

We can see that macroeconomic equilibrium will occur when real GDP equals $10,000 billion.

Step 3: **Calculate the *MPC*.**

$$MC = \frac{\Delta C}{\Delta Y}.$$

In this case:

$$MPC = \frac{\$800 \text{ billion}}{\$1,000 \text{ billion}} = 0.8.$$

Step 4: **Use the multiplier formula to calculate the new equilibrium level of real GDP.** We could find the new level of equilibrium real GDP by constructing a new table with government purchases increased from $1,000 to $1,200. But the multiplier allows us to calculate the answer directly. In this case:

$$\text{Multiplier} = \frac{1}{1 - MPC} = \frac{1}{1 - 0.8} = 5.$$

So:

Change in equilibrium real GDP = Change in autonomous expenditure $\times$ 5.

Or:

Change in equilibrium real GDP = $200 billion × 5 = $1,000 billion.

Therefore:

New level of equilibrium GDP = $10,000 billion + $1,000 billion

= $11,000 billion.

Your Turn: For more practice, do related problem 4.5 on page 413 at the end of this chapter.   MyEconLab

The Paradox of Thrift

We saw in Chapters 10 and 11 that an increase in savings can increase the rate of economic growth in the long run by providing funds for investment. But in the short run, if households save more of their income and spend less of it, aggregate expenditure and real GDP will decline. In discussing the aggregate expenditure model, John Maynard Keynes argued that if many households decide at the same time to increase their saving and reduce their spending, they may make themselves worse off by causing aggregate expenditure to fall, thereby pushing the economy into a recession. The lower incomes in the recession might mean that total saving does not increase, despite the attempts by many individuals to increase their own saving. Keynes referred to this outcome as the *paradox of thrift* because what appears to be something favorable to the long-run performance of the economy might be counterproductive in the short run.

As we mentioned in Chapter 8, households had been saving very little of their income in the mid-2000s but increased their saving markedly in late 2008 and 2009. The personal saving rate is saving by households as a percentage of disposable personal income. By mid-2009, the personal saving rate had increased to 6 percent. Some economists argued that this increase in saving contributed to the recession by reducing consumption spending. Other economists were more skeptical of the reasoning behind the paradox of thrift. As we saw in Chapter 10, an increase in saving, by increasing the supply of loanable funds, should lower the real interest rate and increase the level of investment spending. This increase in investment spending might offset some or all of the decline in consumption spending attributable to increased saving. Economists continue to debate the short-run effects of an increase in saving.

The Aggregate Demand Curve

12.5 LEARNING OBJECTIVE

Understand the relationship between the aggregate demand curve and aggregate expenditure.

When demand for a product increases, firms usually respond by increasing production, but they are also likely to increase prices. Similarly, when demand falls, production falls, but often, prices also fall. We would expect, then, that an increase or a decrease in aggregate expenditure would affect not just real GDP but also the *price level*. Will a change in the price level, in turn, affect the components of aggregate expenditure? In fact, as we will see, increases in the price level cause aggregate expenditure to fall, and decreases in the price level cause aggregate expenditure to rise. There are three main reasons for this inverse relationship between changes in the price level and changes in aggregate expenditure. We discussed the first two reasons earlier in this chapter, when considering the factors that determine consumption and net exports:

- A rising price level decreases consumption by decreasing the real value of household wealth; a falling price level has the reverse effect.

- If the price level in the United States rises relative to the price levels in other countries, U.S. exports will become relatively more expensive, and foreign imports will become relatively less expensive, causing net exports to fall. A falling price level in the United States has the reverse effect.

- When prices rise, firms and households need more money to finance buying and selling. If the central bank (the Federal Reserve in the United States) does not increase the money supply, the result will be an increase in the interest rate. In Chapter 14, we will analyze in more detail why this happens. As we discussed earlier in this chapter, at a higher interest rate, investment spending falls as firms borrow less money to build new factories or to install new machinery and equipment and households borrow less money to buy new houses. A falling price level has the reverse effect: Other things being equal, interest rates will fall, and investment spending will rise.

We can now incorporate the effect of a change in the price level into the basic aggregate expenditure model, in which equilibrium real GDP is determined by the intersection of the aggregate expenditure (AE) line and the 45° line. Remember that we measure the price level as an index number with a value of 100 in the base year. If the price level rises from, say, 100 to 103, consumption, planned investment, and net exports will all fall, causing the AE line to shift down on the 45°-line diagram. The AE line shifts down because with higher prices, less spending will occur in the economy at every level of GDP. Panel (a) of Figure 12.13 shows that the downward shift of the AE line results in a lower level of equilibrium real GDP.

If the price level falls from, say, 100 to 97, then investment, consumption, and net exports will all rise. As panel (b) of Figure 12.13 shows, the AE line will shift up, which will cause equilibrium real GDP to increase.

Figure 12.14 summarizes the effect of changes in the price level on real GDP. The table shows the combinations of price level and real GDP from Figure 12.13. The graph plots the numbers from the table. In the graph, the price level is measured on the vertical axis, and real GDP is measured on the horizontal axis. The relationship shown in Figure 12.14 between the price level and the level of planned aggregate expenditure is known as the **aggregate demand (AD) curve**.

Aggregate demand (AD) curve
A curve that shows the relationship between the price level and the level of planned aggregate expenditure in the economy, holding constant all other factors that affect aggregate expenditure.

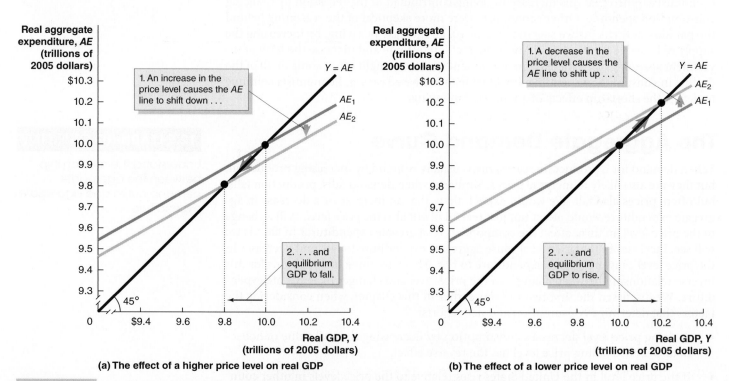

(a) The effect of a higher price level on real GDP   **(b) The effect of a lower price level on real GDP**

Figure 12.13   **The Effect of a Change in the Price Level on Real GDP**

In panel (a), an increase in the price level results in declining consumption, planned investment, and net exports and causes the aggregate expenditure line to shift down from AE_1 to AE_2. As a result, equilibrium real GDP declines from $10.0 trillion to $9.8 trillion. In panel (b), a decrease in the price level results in rising consumption, planned investment, and net exports and causes the aggregate expenditure line to shift up from AE_1 to AE_2. As a result, equilibrium real GDP increases from $10.0 trillion to $10.2 trillion.

Price level	Equilibrium real GDP
97	$10.2 trillion
100	10.0 trillion
103	9.8 trillion

Figure 12.14

The Aggregate Demand Curve

The aggregate demand (*AD*) curve shows the relationship between the price level and the level of planned aggregate expenditure in the economy. When the price level is 97, real GDP is $10.2 trillion. An increase in the price level to 100 causes consumption, investment, and net exports to fall, which reduces real GDP to $10.0 trillion.

Continued from page 375

Economics in Your Life

When Consumer Confidence Falls, Is Your Job at Risk?

At the beginning of this chapter, we asked you to suppose that you work part time assembling desktop computers for a large computer company. You have learned that consumer confidence in the economy has fallen and that many households expect their future income to be dramatically less than their current income. Should you be concerned about losing your job? We have seen in this chapter that if consumers expect their future incomes to decline, they will cut their consumption spending, and consumption spending is more than two-thirds of aggregate expenditure. So, if the decline in consumer confidence is correctly forecasting a decline in consumption spending, then aggregate expenditures and GDP will also likely decline. If the economy moves into a recession, spending on computers by households and firms is likely to fall, which could reduce your firm's sales and possibly cost you a job. Before you panic, though, keep in mind that surveys of consumer confidence do not have a good track record in predicting recessions, so you may not have to move back in with your parents after all.

Conclusion

In this chapter, we examined a key macroeconomic idea: In the short run, the level of GDP is determined mainly by the level of aggregate expenditure. When economists forecast changes in GDP, they do so by forecasting changes in the four components of aggregate expenditure. We constructed an aggregate demand curve by taking into account how changes in the price level affect aggregate expenditure.

But our story is incomplete. In Chapter 13, we will analyze the *aggregate supply curve*. Then, we will use the aggregate demand curve and the aggregate supply curve to show how equilibrium real GDP and the equilibrium price level are simultaneously determined.

We also need to discuss the roles that the financial system and government policy play in determining real GDP and the price level in the short run. We will cover these important topics in the next three chapters. Before moving on, read *An Inside Look* on the next page, for a discussion of how a rebound in sales in the restaurant industry affects aggregate expenditure in the economy.

Turnaround Projected for the Restaurant Industry

NATIONAL RESTAURANT ASSOCIATION

Restaurant Industry Sales Turn Positive in 2011 after Three Tough Years

Restaurant industry sales are expected to reach a record $604 billion and post positive growth in 2011 after a three-year period of negative real sales growth, according to National Restaurant Association research released today. The Association's 2011 *Restaurant Industry Forecast* projects an industry sales increase of 3.6 percent over 2010 sales, which equals 1.1 percent in real (inflation-adjusted) terms.

(a) The nation's 960,000 restaurants will continue to be strong contributors to the recovery of the nation's economy, with industry sales representing 4 percent of the U.S. gross domestic product and employees comprising nearly 10 percent of the U.S. workforce. Its total economic impact exceeds $1.7 trillion, as every dollar spent in restaurants generates $2.05 spent in the overall economy. Restaurants are the nation's second-largest private sector employer with 12.8 million employees.

"As the national economy is slowly improving, the restaurant industry is climbing out of its most challenging period in decades to post positive real sales growth in 2011," said Hudson Riehle, senior vice president of the Research and Knowledge Group for the National Restaurant Association. "As in 2010, restaurant industry job growth is expected to outpace the national economy this year, emphasizing the importance of the industry to the nation's economy."

"The U.S. restaurant industry is an economic juggernaut whose annual sales are larger than 90 percent of the world's economies—if it were a country, it would rank as the 18th largest economy in the world. While pockets of challenges remain, we are looking forward to a brighter future in 2011," he added.

Industry Segment Growth

(b) Continuing the trend from last year, the quick-service restaurant segment is expected to post slightly stronger sales growth than the full-service segment. Quick-service restaurants are projected to post sales of $167.7 billion this year, a gain of 3.3 percent over 2010. Sales at full-service restaurants are projected to reach $194.6 billion in 2011, an increase of 3.1 percent in current dollars over 2010. . . .

State and Regional Sales Growth

Among the 50 states, North Carolina is expected to post the strongest sales growth in 2011 at 4.2 percent (industry sales are projected at $14.1 billion), followed by Idaho ($1.8 billion) and Virginia ($12.8 billion) at 4.0 percent. Forecast to post growth at 3.9 percent: Colorado ($8.6 billion), Florida ($30.1 billion), Maryland ($9.4 billion) and Texas ($36.7 billion).

Of the nine U.S. Census regions, the South Atlantic is expected to post the strongest restaurant sales growth at 3.9 percent, totaling $93.9 billion among its eight states (Delaware, Florida, Georgia, Maryland, North Carolina, South Carolina, Virginia and West Virginia) and the District of Columbia.

Workforce Outlook

(c) The restaurant industry posted modest job growth last year, and that growth is expected to accelerate in 2011. This year, the industry will add jobs at a rate of 2.4 percent, compared with the 1.8 percent expected for the national economy. In the next decade, the industry will add 1.3 million positions.

In the states, the restaurant industries in Texas and Florida will show the strongest job growth over the next 10 years at roughly 17 percent, followed by Arizona and Alabama at roughly 16 percent.

Consumer and Menu Trends

According to the National Restaurant Association's 2011 *Restaurant Industry Forecast*, consumers today spend 49 percent of their food budget in the restaurant community, compared with only 25 percent in 1955. The economic downturn has created a substantial pent-up demand for restaurant services—more than two out of five consumers say they are not dining out or using takeout as often as they would like—which positions the restaurant industry for growth in 2011. . . .

Key Points in the Article

The National Restaurant Association expected industry sales to reach $604 billion in 2011, up 3.6 percent from 2010. Both the quick-service and full-service segments of the market were expected to grow. The strongest growth was expected in the South Atlantic region, with an annual increase in sales of 3.9 percent and total sales exceeding $93 billion. Employment for the industry was also expected to increase by 2.4 percent in 2011, higher than the 1.8 percent expected growth in employment for the economy as a whole. Over the next decade, the restaurant industry is expected to add 1.3 million jobs, with Texas and Florida leading the way.

Analyzing the News

(a) The National Restaurant Association's 2011 industry forecast projects growth in an industry that has been on the decline for the previous three years. For 2011, sales at the 960,000 restaurants in the United States are expected to account for 4 percent of U.S. GDP, and the 12.8 million employees at these restaurants will account for almost 10 percent of the nation's labor force. The association states that the industry has an economic effect of more than $1.7 trillion, with every dollar spent in restaurants generating an estimated total of $2.05 in spending in the economy.

(b) Sales in both the quick-service and full-service segments of the restaurant industry were expected to grow in 2011. Quick-service restaurant sales, a segment comprising primarily of fast-food outlets, are expected to be $167.7 billion, a 3.3 percent increase for the year. Full-service sales, or sales at restaurants that offer table service, are projected at $194.6 billion, representing an increase of 3.1 percent. Consumer purchases of restaurant meals would be counted as part of consumption spending. The figure below illustrates the effect of an increase in real aggregate expenditure on real GDP. The economy begins at equilibrium at point A, and real GDP is Y_1. As a result of an increase in consumption spending, aggregate expenditure shifts up from AE_1 to AE_2, and the new equilibrium moves from point A to point B. In this case, real GDP increases from Y_1 to Y_2.

(c) The expected increase in sales in the restaurant industry is expected to result in an increase in industry employment during 2011. Following job losses in 2008 and 2009, the industry did experience slight job growth in 2010, and employment growth is expected to be 2.4 percent in 2011. This growth rate outpaces the expected job growth rate for the national economy by 33 percent. The restaurant industry employs nearly 10 percent of the nation's workforce, so an increase in job growth in this industry can be quite significant for the economy. As employment increases, the level of aggregate expenditure should also increase because the increase in employment will result in additional consumer spending in the economy. In the figure below, an increase in aggregate expenditure from AE_1 to AE_2, first causes the amount of planned aggregate expenditure to be greater than real GDP at point A. Firms then respond to the increase in sales by increasing production and employment until the economy reaches equilibrium at point B and real GDP eventually increases from Y_1 to Y_2.

Thinking Critically

1. The article states that $1 spent in restaurants results in $2.05 spent in the entire economy. Suppose the U.S. government issues to each citizen $500 in vouchers that can only be spent in restaurants. How would this program affect aggregate expenditure and equilibrium real GDP?

2. Suppose that in an effort to aid the economy, the federal government enacts a law that prohibits any imported food products to be used in restaurants. How would this law affect aggregate expenditure and equilibrium real GDP in the United States? Does your answer depend on how the governments of other countries react to the law? Briefly explain.

An increase in aggregate expenditure results in an increase in real GDP.

Chapter Summary and Problems

Key Terms

Aggregate demand (*AD*) curve, p. 406

Aggregate expenditure (*AE*), p. 376

Aggregate expenditure model, p. 376

Autonomous expenditure, p. 399

Cash flow, p. 388

Consumption function, p. 383

Inventories, p. 377

Marginal propensity to consume (*MPC*), p. 383

Marginal propensity to save (*MPS*), p. 386

Multiplier, p. 399

Multiplier effect, p. 399

 12.1 **The Aggregate Expenditure Model,** pages 376–379

LEARNING OBJECTIVE: Understand how macroeconomic equilibrium is determined in the aggregate expenditure model.

Summary

Aggregate expenditure (*AE*) is the total amount of spending in the economy. The **aggregate expenditure model** focuses on the relationship between total spending and real GDP in the short run, assuming that the price level is constant. In any particular year, the level of GDP is determined by the level of total spending, or aggregate expenditure, in the economy. The four components of aggregate expenditure are consumption (*C*), planned investment (*I*), government purchases (*G*), and net exports (*NX*). When aggregate expenditure is greater than GDP, there is an unplanned decrease in **inventories**, which are goods that have been produced but not yet sold, and GDP and total employment will increase. When aggregate expenditure is less than GDP, there is an unplanned increase in inventories, and GDP and total employment will decline. When aggregate expenditure is equal to GDP, firms will sell what they expected to sell, production and employment will be unchanged, and the economy will be in macroeconomic equilibrium.

MyEconLab   Visit www.myeconlab.com to complete these exercises online and get instant feedback.

Review Questions

1.1 What is the key idea in the aggregate expenditure macroeconomic model?

1.2 What is the main reason for changes in GDP in the short run?

1.3 What are inventories? What usually happens to inventories at the beginning of a recession? At the beginning of an expansion?

1.4 Which of the following does the aggregate expenditure model seek to explain: long-run economic growth, the business cycle, inflation, and cyclical unemployment?

Problems and Applications

1.5 Into which category of aggregate expenditure would each of the following transactions fall?
   a. The Jones family buys a new car.
   b. The San Diego Unified School District buys 12 new school buses.
   c. The Jones family buys a newly constructed house from the Garcia Construction Co.
   d. A consumer in Japan orders a computer online from Dell.
   e. Prudential insurance company purchases 250 new computers from Dell.

1.6 Suppose Apple plans to produce 20.2 million iPhones this year. The company expects to sell 20.1 million and add 100,000 to the inventories in its stores.
   a. Suppose that at the end of the year, Apple has sold 19.9 million iPhones. What was Apple's planned investment? What was Apple's actual investment?
   b. Now suppose that at the end of the year, Apple has sold 20.3 million iPhones. What was Apple's planned investment? What was Apple's actual investment?

1.7 In the first quarter of 2011, business inventories increased by $49.1 billion. Can we tell from this information whether aggregate expenditure was higher or lower than GDP during the first quarter of 2011? If not, what other information do we need?

Data from Bureau of Economic Analysis.

1.8 A survey conducted by the Institute for Supply Management in June 2011 showed a significant increase in inventories in manufacturing. An analyst for the investment bank Goldman Sachs commented that the increase in inventories was "a negative for future activity." Why might an increase in inventories be considered bad news for future production in manufacturing?

Based on Kelly Evans, "Factories Offer a Clue to Second-Half Hopes," *Wall Street Journal*, July 15, 2011.

 12.2 **Determining the Level of Aggregate Expenditure in the Economy,** pages 379–392

LEARNING OBJECTIVE: Discuss the determinants of the four components of aggregate expenditure and define marginal propensity to consume and marginal propensity to save.

Summary

The five determinants of consumption are current disposable income, household wealth, expected future income, the price level, and the interest rate. The **consumption function** is the relationship between consumption and disposable income. The **marginal propensity to consume** (*MPC*) is the change in consumption divided by the change in disposable income. The **marginal**

propensity to save (*MPS*) is the change in saving divided by the change in disposable income. The determinants of planned investment are expectations of future profitability, real interest rate, taxes, and **cash flow**, which is the difference between the cash revenues received by a firm and the cash spending by the firm. Government purchases include spending by the federal government and by local and state governments for goods and services. Government purchases do not include *transfer payments*, such as Social Security payments by the federal government or pension payments by local governments to retired police officers and firefighters. The three determinants of net exports are changes in the price level in the United States relative to changes in the price levels in other countries, the growth rate of GDP in the United States relative to the growth rates of GDP in other countries, and the exchange rate between the dollar and other currencies.

MyEconLab   Visit **www.myeconlab.com** to complete these exercises online and get instant feedback.

Review Questions

2.1 In the aggregate expenditure model, why is it important to know the factors that determine consumption spending, investment spending, government purchases, and net exports?

2.2 Give an example of each of the four categories of aggregate expenditure.

2.3 What are the five main determinants of consumption spending? Which of these is the most important? How would a rise in stock prices or housing prices affect consumption spending?

2.4 Compare what happened to real investment between 1979 and the second quarter of 2011 with what happened to real consumption during that period.

2.5 What are the four main determinants of investment? How would a change in interest rates affect investment?

2.6 What are the three main determinants of net exports? How would an increase in the growth rate of GDP in the BRIC nations (Brazil, Russia, India, and China) affect U.S. net exports?

Problems and Applications

2.7 **[Related to the** Chapter Opener **on page 375]** Suppose a major U.S. furniture manufacturer is forecasting demand for its products during the next year. How will the forecast be affected by each of the following?
  a. A survey shows a sharp rise in consumer confidence that income growth will be increasing
  b. Real interest rates are expected to increase
  c. The exchange rate value of the U.S. dollar is expected to increase
  d. Planned investment spending in the economy is expected to decrease

2.8 Draw the consumption function and label each axis. Show the effect of an increase in income on consumption spending. Does the change in income cause a movement along the consumption function or a shift of the consumption function? How would an increase in expected future income or an increase in household wealth affect the consumption function? Would these increases cause a movement along the consumption function or a shift of the consumption function?

2.9 Many people have difficulty borrowing as much money as they want to, even if they are confident that their incomes in the future will be high enough to easily pay back the borrowed funds. For example, many students in medical school will earn high incomes after they graduate and become physicians. If they could, they would probably borrow now in order to live more comfortably while in medical school and pay the loans back out of their higher future income. Unfortunately, banks are usually reluctant to make loans to people who currently have low incomes, even if there is a good chance that their incomes will be much higher in the future. If people could always borrow as much as they want to, would you expect consumption to become more or less sensitive to current income? Briefly explain.

2.10 An economics student raises the following objection: "The textbook said that a higher interest rate lowers investment, but this doesn't make sense. I know that if I can get a higher interest rate, I am certainly going to invest more in my savings account." Do you agree with this reasoning?

2.11 **[Related to the** Making the Connection **on page 381]** Writing about the state of the British economy, an article in the *Economist* argued: "Spending will be hit . . . by weak stock-markets and shrinking housing wealth." Would Calomiris, Longhofer, and Miles agree with this argument? Would Mian and Sufi? Briefly explain.
  Based on "Combating the Recession," *Economist*, January 8, 2009.

2.12 Unemployed workers receive unemployment insurance payments from the government. Does the existence of unemployment insurance make it likely that consumption will fluctuate more or fluctuate less over the business cycle than it would in the absence of unemployment insurance? Briefly explain.

2.13 **[Related to** Solved Problem 12.2 **on page 386]** Fill in the blanks in the following table. Assume for simplicity that taxes are zero. Also assume that the values represent billions of 2005 dollars.

National Income and Real GDP (Y)	Consumption (C)	Saving (S)	Marginal Propensity to Consume (MPC)	Marginal Propensity to Save (MPS)
$9,000	$8,000		—	—
10,000	8,750			
11,000	9,500			
12,000	10,250			
13,000	11,000			

2.14 **[Related to the** Making the Connection **on page 388]** We saw that Intel hopes to increase sales of microprocessors used in cell phones and other small consumer electronics products. During a recession, why would spending on these products be more stable than spending on computers?

Graphing Macroeconomic Equilibrium, pages 392–398
LEARNING OBJECTIVE: Use a 45°-line diagram to illustrate macroeconomic equilibrium.

Summary

The 45°-line diagram shows all the points where aggregate expenditure equals real GDP. On the 45°-line diagram, macroeconomic equilibrium occurs where the line representing the aggregate expenditure function crosses the 45° line. The economy is in recession when the aggregate expenditure line intersects the 45° line at a level of GDP that is below potential GDP. Numerically, macroeconomic equilibrium occurs when:

Consumption + Planned investment +

Government purchases + Net exports = GDP.

 Visit **www.myeconlab.com** to complete these exercises online and get instant feedback.

Review Questions

3.1 What is the meaning of the 45° line in the 45°-line diagram?

3.2 Use a 45°-line diagram to illustrate macroeconomic equilibrium. Make sure your diagram shows the aggregate expenditure function and the level of equilibrium real GDP and that your axes are properly labeled.

3.3 What does the slope of the aggregate expenditure line equal? How is the slope of the aggregate expenditure line related to the slope of the consumption function?

3.4 What is the macroeconomic consequence if firms accumulate large amounts of unplanned inventory at the beginning of a recession?

3.5 What is the difference between aggregate expenditure and consumption spending?

Problems and Applications

3.6 At point A in the following graph, is planned aggregate expenditure greater than, equal to, or less than GDP? What about at point B? At point C? For points A and C, indicate the vertical distance that measures the unintended change in inventories.

3.7 Suppose we drop the assumption that net exports do not depend on real GDP. Draw a graph with the value of net exports on the vertical axis and the value of real GDP on

the horizontal axis. Now, add a line representing the relationship between net exports and real GDP. Does your net exports line have a positive or negative slope? Briefly explain.

3.8 A Federal Reserve Board publication makes the following observation: "The impact of inventory increases on the business cycle depends upon whether [the increases] are planned or unplanned." Do you agree? Briefly explain.

3.9 Jack Lavery, former chief economist at Merrill Lynch, made the following observation about the U.S. economy in April 2009: "I expect inventory drawdown to be even more pronounced in the second quarter, which will contribute to the fourth successive quarterly decline in real GDP." What does Lavery mean by "inventory drawdown"? What component of aggregate expenditure would be affected by an inventory drawdown? Why would this contribute to GDP decline?

Based on Jack Lavery, "Real GDP Declines Far More Than Predicted," minyanville.com, April 29, 2009.

3.10 Consider the following table, which shows the change in inventories for each quarter from 2007:I to 2011:II measured in billions of 2005 dollars. Provide a macroeconomic explanation for this pattern. (Hint: When did the recession during this period begin and end?)

Year	Quarter	Change in Inventories
2007	I	$17.3
	II	44.9
	III	36.1
	IV	12.6
2008	I	−12.5
	II	−14.2
	III	−38.1
	IV	−80.3
2009	I	−161.6
	II	−183.0
	III	−178.7
	IV	−56.5
2010	I	39.9
	II	64.6
	III	92.3
	IV	38.3
2011	I	49.1
	II	39.1

3.11 **[Related to the** Don't Let This Happen to You **on page 397]** Briefly explain whether you agree with the following argument: "The equilibrium level of GDP is determined by the level of aggregate expenditure. Therefore, GDP will decline only if households decide to spend less on goods and services."

3.12 **[Related to** Solved Problem 12.3 **on page 398]** Fill in the missing values in the following table. Assume that the value of the *MPC* does not change as real GDP changes. Also assume that the values represent billions of 2005 dollars.

Real GDP (Y)	Consumption (C)	Planned Investment (I)	Government Purchases (G)	Net Exports (NX)	Planned Aggregate Expenditure (AE)	Unplanned Change in Inventories
$9,000	$7,600	$1,200	$1,200	−$400		
10,000	8,400	1,200	1,200	−400		
11,000		1,200	1,200	−400		
12,000		1,200	1,200	−400		
13,000		1,200	1,200	−400		

a. What is the value of the *MPC*?
b. What is the value of equilibrium real GDP?

 The Multiplier Effect, pages 399–405

LEARNING OBJECTIVE: Describe the multiplier effect and use the multiplier formula to calculate changes in equilibrium GDP.

Summary

Autonomous expenditure is expenditure that does not depend on the level of GDP. An autonomous change is a change in expenditure not caused by a change in income. An *induced change* is a change in aggregate expenditure caused by a change in income. An autonomous change in expenditure will cause rounds of induced changes in expenditure. Therefore, an autonomous change in expenditure will have a *multiplier effect* on equilibrium GDP. The **multiplier effect** is the process by which an increase in autonomous expenditure leads to a larger increase in real GDP. The **multiplier** is the ratio of the change in equilibrium GDP to the change in autonomous expenditure. The formula for the multiplier is

$$\frac{1}{1 - MPC}.$$

Because of the paradox of thrift, an attempt by many individuals to increase their saving may lead to a reduction in aggregate expenditure and a recession.

MyEconLab   Visit **www.myeconlab.com** to complete these exercises online and get instant feedback.

Review Questions

4.1 What is the multiplier effect? Use a 45°-line diagram to illustrate the multiplier effect of a decrease in government purchases.

4.2 What is the formula for the multiplier? Explain why this formula is considered to be too simple.

Problems and Applications

4.3 In Figure 12.12 on page 399, the economy is initially in equilibrium at point *A*. Aggregate expenditure and real

GDP both equal $9.6 trillion. The increase in investment of $100 billion increases aggregate expenditure to $9.7 trillion. If real GDP increases to $9.7 trillion, will the economy be in equilibrium? Briefly explain. What happens to aggregate expenditure when real GDP increases to $9.7 trillion?

4.4 **[Related to the** Making the Connection **on page 401.]** If the multiplier had a value of 4 in 1929, how large must the change in autonomous expenditure have been to cause the decline in real GDP between 1929 and 1933 shown in the table on page 401? If the multiplier had a value of 2, how large must the change in autonomous expenditure have been?

4.5 **[Related to** Solved Problem 12.4 **on page 404.]** Use the information in the following table to answer the following questions. Assume that the values represent billions of 2005 dollars.

Real GDP (Y)	Consumption (C)	Planned Investment (I)	Government Purchases (G)	Net Exports (NX)
$8,000	$7,300	$1,000	$1,000	−$500
9,000	7,900	1,000	1,000	−500
10,000	8,500	1,000	1,000	−500
11,000	9,100	1,000	1,000	−500
12,000	9,700	1,000	1,000	−500

a. What is the equilibrium level of real GDP?
b. What is the *MPC*?
c. Suppose net exports increase by $400 billion. What will be the new equilibrium level of real GDP? Use the multiplier formula to determine your answer.

4.6 If the marginal propensity to consume is 0.75, by how much will an increase in planned investment spending of $400 billion shift up the aggregate expenditure line? By how much will it increase equilibrium real GDP?

4.7 Explain whether each of the following would cause the value of the multiplier to be larger or smaller.
  a. An increase in real GDP increases imports.
  b. An increase in real GDP increases interest rates.
  c. An increase in in real GDP increases the marginal propensity to consume.
  d. An increase in real GDP causes the average tax rate paid by households to decrease.
  e. An increase in real GDP increases the price level.

4.8 Explain whether you agree with the following statement:

> Some economists claim that the recession of 2007–2009 was caused by a decline in spending on residential construction. This can't be true. If there had just been a decline in spending on residential construction, the only firms hurt would have been home builders and firms selling lumber and other goods used in building houses. In fact, many firms experienced falling sales during that recession, including automobile, appliance, and furniture firms.

4.9 Suppose booming economies in the BRIC nations (Brazil, Russia, India, and China) causes net exports to rise by $75 billion in the United States. If the *MPC* is 0.8, what will be the change in equilibrium GDP?

4.10 Would a larger multiplier lead to longer and more severe recessions or shorter and less severe recessions? Briefly explain.

4.11 Use the following graph to answer the questions.

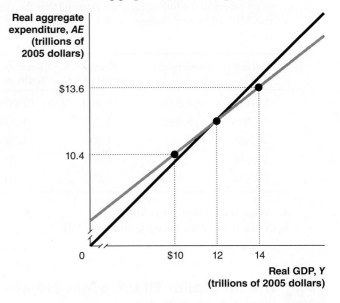

a. What is the value of equilibrium real GDP?
b. What is the value of the *MPC*?
c. What is the value of the multiplier?
d. What is the value of unplanned changes in inventories when real GDP has each of the following values?
  • $10 trillion
  • $12 trillion
  • $14 trillion

12.5 **The Aggregate Demand Curve, pages 405–407**
LEARNING OBJECTIVE: Understand the relationship between the aggregate demand curve and aggregate expenditure.

Summary

Increases in the price level cause a reduction in consumption, investment, and net exports. This causes the aggregate expenditure function to shift down on the 45°-line diagram, leading to a lower equilibrium real GDP. A decrease in the price level leads to a higher equilibrium real GDP. The **aggregate demand curve** shows the relationship between the price level and the level of aggregate expenditure, holding constant all factors other than the price level that affect aggregate expenditure.

 MyEconLab Visit www.myeconlab.com to complete these exercises online and get instant feedback.

Review Questions

5.1 Briefly explain the difference between aggregate expenditure and aggregate demand.
5.2 Briefly explain which components of aggregate expenditure are affected by a change in the price level.

5.3 Does a change in the price level cause a movement along the aggregate expenditure line or a shift of the aggregate expenditure line? Does a change in the price level cause a movement along the aggregate demand curve or a shift of the aggregate demand curve?

Problems and Applications

5.4 Briefly explain why the aggregate expenditure line is upward sloping, while the aggregate demand curve is downward sloping.
5.5 Briefly explain whether you agree with the following statement: "The reason the aggregate demand curve slopes downward is that when the price level is higher, people cannot afford to buy as many goods and services."
5.6 Suppose that exports become more sensitive to changes in the price level in the United States. That is, when the price level in the United States rises, exports decline by more than they previously did. Will this change make the aggregate demand curve steeper or less steep? Briefly explain.

Appendix

The Algebra of Macroeconomic Equilibrium

LEARNING OBJECTIVE

Apply the algebra of macroeconomic equilibrium.

In this chapter, we relied primarily on graphs and tables to illustrate the aggregate expenditure model of short-run real GDP. Graphs help us understand economic change *qualitatively*. When we write an economic model using equations, we make it easier to make *quantitative estimates*. When economists forecast future movements in GDP, they often rely on *econometric models*. An econometric model is an economic model written in the form of equations, where each equation has been statistically estimated, using methods similar to the methods used in estimating demand curves that we briefly described in Chapter 3. We can use equations to represent the aggregate expenditure model described in this chapter.

The following equations are based on the example shown in Table 12.3 on page 396. Y stands for real GDP, and the numbers (with the exception of the MPC) represent billions of dollars.

1. $C = 1,000 + 0.65\,Y$ Consumption function
2. $I = 1,500$ Planned investment function
3. $G = 1,500$ Government spending function
4. $NX = -500$ Net export function
5. $Y = C + I + G + NX$ Equilibrium condition

The first equation is the consumption function. The MPC is 0.65, and 1,000 is autonomous consumption, which is the level of consumption that does not depend on income. If we think of the consumption function as a line on the 45°-line diagram, 1,000 would be the intercept, and 0.65 would be the slope. The "functions" for the other three components of planned aggregate expenditure are very simple because we have assumed that these components are not affected by GDP and, therefore, are constant. Economists who use this type of model to forecast GDP would, of course, use more realistic investment, government, and net export functions. The *parameters* of the functions—such as the value of autonomous consumption and the value of the MPC in the consumption function—would be estimated statistically, using data on the values of each variable over a period of years.

In this model, GDP is in equilibrium when it equals planned aggregate expenditure. Equation 5—the equilibrium condition—shows us how to calculate equilibrium in the model: We need to substitute equations 1 through 4 into equation 5. Doing so gives us the following:

$$Y = 1,000 + 0.65Y + 1,500 + 1,500 - 500.$$

We need to solve this expression for Y to find equilibrium GDP. The first step is to subtract $0.65Y$ from both sides of the equation:

$$Y - 0.65Y = 1,000 + 1,500 + 1,500 - 500.$$

Then, we solve for Y:

$$0.35Y = 3,500.$$

Or:

$$Y = \frac{3,500}{0.35} = 10,000.$$

To make this result more general, we can replace particular values with general values represented by letters:

1. $C = \overline{C} + MPC(Y)$ Consumption function
2. $I = \overline{I}$ Planned investment function
3. $G = \overline{G}$ Government spending function
4. $NX = \overline{NX}$ Net export function
5. $Y = C + I + G + NX$ Equilibrium condition

The letters with bars over them represent fixed, or autonomous, values. So, for example, $\overline{C}$ represents autonomous consumption, which had a value of 1,000 in our original example. Now, solving for equilibrium, we get

$$Y = \overline{C} + MPC(Y) + \overline{I} + \overline{G} + \overline{NX},$$

or

$$Y - MPC(Y) = \overline{C} + \overline{I} + \overline{G} + \overline{NX},$$

or

$$Y(1 - MPC) = \overline{C} + \overline{I} + \overline{G} + \overline{NX},$$

or

$$Y = \frac{\overline{C} + \overline{I} + \overline{G} + \overline{NX}}{1 - MPC}.$$

Remember that $1/(1 - MPC)$ is the multiplier, and all four variables in the numerator of the equation represent autonomous expenditure. Therefore, an alternative expression for equilibrium GDP is:

Equilibrium GDP = Autonomous expenditure × Multiplier.

12A **The Algebra of Macroeconomic Equilibrium, pages 415–416**

LEARNING OBJECTIVE: Apply the algebra of macroeconomic equilibrium.

 Visit **www.myeconlab.com** to complete these exercises online and get instant feedback.

Review Questions

12A.1 Write a general expression for the aggregate expenditure function. If you think of the aggregate expenditure function as a line on the 45°-line diagram, what would be the intercept and what would be the slope, using the general values represented by letters?

12A.2 Find equilibrium GDP using the following macroeconomic model (where the numbers, with the exception of the *MPC*, represent billions of dollars).

1. $C = 1,500 + 0.75\,Y$ Consumption function
2. $I = 1,250$ Planned investment function

3. $G = 1,250$ Government spending function
4. $NX = 2500$ Net export function
5. $Y = C + I + G + NX$ Equilibrium condition

12A.3 For the macroeconomic model in problem 12A.2, write the aggregate expenditure function. For GDP of $16,000, what is the value of aggregate expenditure, and what is the value of the unintended change in inventories? For GDP of $12,000, what is the value of aggregate expenditure, and what is the value of the unintended change in inventories?

12A.4 Suppose that autonomous consumption is 500, government purchases are 1,000, planned investment spending is 1,250, net exports are −250, and the *MPC* is 0.8. What is equilibrium GDP?

Aggregate Demand and Aggregate Supply Analysis

Chapter Outline and Learning Objectives

The Fortunes of FedEx Follow the Business Cycle

FedEx plays a large role in moving packages around the United States and around the world. The value of packages handled by FedEx is about 4 percent of U.S. GDP and 1.5 percent of global GDP. Some Wall Street analysts use a "FedEx indicator" to guage the state of the economy because there is usually a close relationship between fluctuations in FedEx's business and fluctuations in GDP.

Fred Smith came up with the idea for the company in 1965, in an undergraduate term paper. He proposed an entirely new system of delivering packages: One firm would control shipping freight, from pickup to delivery. The firm would operate its own planes on a "hub-and-spoke" system: Packages would be collected and flown to a central hub, where they would be sorted and then flown to their destination for final delivery by truck.

Despite FedEx's tremendous success over the past 40 years, the business cycle has always affected the company's business. For example, as the U.S. entered a recession in December 2007, businesses and individuals cut back on shipping packages. In the first quarter of 2008, FedEx reported its first loss, after 11 straight years of profits. As the 2007–2009 recession dragged on, FedEx announced in March 2009 that it was laying off 1,000 employees and was imposing a 5 to 20 percent pay cut on its remaining employees. By September 2009, economic conditions had begun to improve, and FedEx announced that its profits for the three months ending on August 31 were 35 percent higher than its executives had expected. But as U.S. GDP growth slowed in 2011, so did FedEx's fortunes. Weak consumer demand and half-empty cargo planes led FedEx to announce in September that it was lowering its forecast for end-of-the-year profits. Fred Smith explained: "We expect sluggish economic growth will continue. . . . The consumer just doesn't have an appetite" for increased spending.

To understand how the business cycle affects FedEx and other firms, we need to explore the effects that recessions and expansions have on production, employment, and prices.

AN INSIDE LOOK on **page 444** discusses why a slowdown in cargo shipments signals problems in the wider economy.

Based on Lynn Adler, "FedEx Pares 2012 Outlook, Shares Hit 2-Year Low," *Reuters*, September 22, 2011; Hal Weiztman, "FedEx to Cut Costs by $1 Bn," *Financial Times*, March 19, 2009; "FedEx Confirms 1,000 Layoffs, 500 in Memphis," *Memphis Business Journal*, April 3, 2009; Bob Sechler, "FedEx Boosts Outlook," *Wall Street Journal*, September 11, 2009; and David Gaffen, "The FedEx Indicator," *Wall Street Journal*, February 20, 2007.

Economics in Your Life

Is an Employer Likely to Cut Your Pay during a Recession?

Suppose that you have worked as a barista for a local coffeehouse for two years. From on-the-job training and experience, you have honed your coffee-making skills and mastered the perfect latte. Then the economy moves into a recession, and sales at the coffeehouse decline. Is the owner of the coffeehouse likely to cut the prices of lattes and other drinks? Suppose the owner asks to meet with you to discuss your wages for next year. Is the owner likely to cut your pay? As you read the chapter, see if you can answer these questions. You can check your answers against those we provide on **page 443** at the end of this chapter.

W e saw in Chapter 10 that the U.S. economy has experienced a long-run upward trend in real GDP. This upward trend has resulted in the standard of living in the United States being much higher today than it was 50 years ago. In the short run, however, real GDP fluctuates around this long-run upward trend because of the business cycle. Fluctuations in GDP lead to fluctuations in employment. These fluctuations in real GDP and employment are the most visible and dramatic part of the business cycle. During recessions, we are more likely to see factories close, small businesses declare bankruptcy, and workers lose their jobs. During expansions, we are more likely to see new businesses open and new jobs created. In addition to these changes in output and employment, the business cycle causes changes in wages and prices. Some firms react to a decline in sales by cutting back on production, but they may also cut the prices they charge and the wages they pay. Other firms respond to a recession by raising prices and workers' wages by less than they otherwise would have.

In this chapter, we expand our story of the business cycle by developing the aggregate demand and aggregate supply model. This model will help us analyze the effects of recessions and expansions on production, employment, and prices.

13.1 LEARNING OBJECTIVE

Identify the determinants of aggregate demand and distinguish between a movement along the aggregate demand curve and a shift of the curve.

Aggregate demand and aggregate supply model A model that explains short-run fluctuations in real GDP and the price level.

Aggregate demand (*AD*) curve A curve that shows the relationship between the price level and the quantity of real GDP demanded by households, firms, and the government.

Short-run aggregate supply (*SRAS*) curve A curve that shows the relationship in the short run between the price level and the quantity of real GDP supplied by firms.

Aggregate Demand

To understand what happens during the business cycle, we need an explanation of why real GDP, the unemployment rate, and the inflation rate fluctuate. We have already seen that fluctuations in the unemployment rate are caused mainly by fluctuations in real GDP. In this chapter, we use the **aggregate demand and aggregate supply model** to explain short-run fluctuations in real GDP and the price level. As Figure 13.1 shows, real GDP and the price level in this model are determined in the short run by the intersection of the *aggregate demand curve* and the *aggregate supply curve*. Fluctuations in real GDP and the price level are caused by shifts in the aggregate demand curve or in the aggregate supply curve.

The **aggregate demand (*AD*) curve** shows the relationship between the price level and the quantity of real GDP demanded by households, firms, and the government. The **short-run aggregate supply (*SRAS*) curve** shows the relationship in the short run between the price level and the quantity of real GDP supplied by firms. The aggregate demand and short-run aggregate supply curves in Figure 13.1 look similar to the individual market demand and supply curves we studied in Chapter 3. However, because these curves apply to the whole economy, rather than to just a single market, the aggregate demand and aggregate supply model is very different from the model of demand and supply in individual markets. Because we are dealing with the economy as a whole, we need

Figure 13.1

Aggregate Demand and Aggregate Supply

In the short run, real GDP and the price level are determined by the intersection of the aggregate demand curve and the short-run aggregate supply curve. In the figure, real GDP is measured on the horizontal axis, and the price level is measured on the vertical axis by the GDP deflator. In this example, the equilibrium real GDP is $14.0 trillion, and the equilibrium price level is 100.

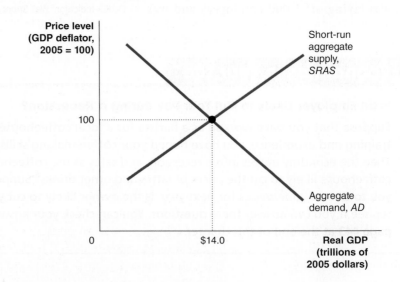

macroeconomic explanations of why the aggregate demand curve is downward sloping, why the short-run aggregate supply curve is upward sloping, and why the curves shift. We begin by explaining why the aggregate demand curve is downward sloping.

Why Is the Aggregate Demand Curve Downward Sloping?

We saw in Chapter 8 that GDP has four components: consumption (C), investment (I), government purchases (G), and net exports (NX). If we let Y stand for GDP, we have the following relationship:

$$Y = C + I + G + NX.$$

The aggregate demand curve is downward sloping because a fall in the price level increases the quantity of real GDP demanded. To understand why this is true, we need to look at how changes in the price level affect each component of aggregate demand. We begin with the assumption that government purchases are determined by the policy decisions of lawmakers and are not affected by changes in the price level. We can then consider the effect of changes in the price level on the three other components: consumption, investment, and net exports.

The Wealth Effect: How a Change in the Price Level Affects Consumption

Current income is the most important variable determining the consumption of households. As income rises, consumption will rise, and as income falls, consumption will fall. But consumption also depends on household wealth. A household's wealth is the difference between the value of its assets and the value of its debts. Consider two households, both with incomes of $80,000 per year. The first household has wealth of $5 million, and the second household has wealth of $50,000. The first household is likely to spend more of its income than the second household. So, as total household wealth rises, consumption will rise. Some household wealth is held in cash or other *nominal assets* that lose value as the price level rises and gain value as the price level falls. For instance, if you have $10,000 in cash, a 10 percent increase in the price level will reduce the purchasing power of that cash by 10 percent. When the price level rises, the *real value* of household wealth declines, and so will consumption, thereby reducing the demand for goods and services. When the price level falls, the real value of household wealth rises, and so will consumption and the demand for goods and services. This effect of the price level on consumption is called the *wealth effect*, and it is one reason the aggregate demand curve is downward sloping.

The Interest-Rate Effect: How a Change in the Price Level Affects Investment

When prices rise, households and firms need more money to finance buying and selling. Therefore, when the price level rises, households and firms will try to increase the amount of money they hold by withdrawing funds from banks, borrowing from banks, or selling financial assets, such as bonds. These actions tend to drive up the interest rate charged on bank loans and the interest rate on bonds. (In Chapter 15, we analyze in more detail the relationship between money and interest rates.) A higher interest rate raises the cost of borrowing for firms and households. As a result, firms will borrow less to build new factories or to install new machinery and equipment, and households will borrow less to buy new houses. To a smaller extent, consumption will also fall as households borrow less to finance spending on automobiles, furniture, and other durable goods. So, because a higher price level increases the interest rate and reduces investment spending, it also reduces the quantity of goods and services demanded. A lower price level will decrease the interest rate and increase investment spending, thereby increasing the quantity of goods and services demanded. This effect of the price level on investment is known as the *interest-rate effect*, and it is a second reason the aggregate demand curve is downward sloping.

The International-Trade Effect: How a Change in the Price Level Affects Net Exports

Net exports equal spending by foreign households and firms on goods and services produced in the United States minus spending by U.S. households and firms on goods and services produced in other countries. If the price level in the United States rises relative to the price levels in other countries, U.S. exports will become relatively more expensive, and foreign imports will become relatively less expensive. Some consumers in foreign countries will shift from buying U.S. products to buying domestic products, and some U.S. consumers will also shift from buying U.S. products to buying imported products. U.S. exports will fall, and U.S. imports will rise, causing net exports to fall, thereby reducing the quantity of goods and services demanded. A lower price level in the United States relative to other countries has the reverse effect, causing net exports to rise, increasing the quantity of goods and services demanded. This effect of the price level on net exports is known as the *international-trade effect,* and it is a third reason the aggregate demand curve is downward sloping.

Shifts of the Aggregate Demand Curve versus Movements along It

An important point to remember is that the aggregate demand curve tells us the relationship between the price level and the quantity of real GDP demanded, *holding everything else constant.* If the price level changes but other variables that affect the willingness of households, firms, and the government to spend are unchanged, the economy will move up or down a stationary aggregate demand curve. If any variable other than the price level changes, the aggregate demand curve will shift. For example, if government purchases increase and the price level remains unchanged, the aggregate demand curve will shift to the right at every price level. Or, if firms become pessimistic about the future profitability of investment and cut back spending on factories and machinery, the aggregate demand curve will shift to the left.

The Variables That Shift the Aggregate Demand Curve

The variables that cause the aggregate demand curve to shift fall into three categories:

- Changes in government policies
- Changes in the expectations of households and firms
- Changes in foreign variables

Monetary policy The actions the Federal Reserve takes to manage the money supply and interest rates to pursue macroeconomic policy objectives.

Fiscal policy Changes in federal taxes and purchases that are intended to achieve macroeconomic policy objectives.

Changes in Government Policies As we will discuss further in Chapters 15 and 16, the federal government uses monetary policy and fiscal policy to shift the aggregate demand curve. **Monetary policy** involves actions the Federal Reserve—the nation's central bank—takes to manage the money supply and interest rates and to ensure the flow of funds from lenders to borrowers. The Federal Reserve takes these actions to attain macroeconomic policy objectives, such as high employment, price stability, and high rates of economic growth. For example, by lowering interest rates, the Federal Reserve can lower the cost to firms and households of borrowing. Lowering borrowing costs increases consumption and investment spending, which shifts the aggregate demand curve to the right. Higher interest rates shift the aggregate demand curve to the left. **Fiscal policy** involves changes in federal taxes and purchases that are intended to achieve macroeconomic policy objectives. Because government purchases are one component of aggregate demand, an increase in government purchases shifts the aggregate demand curve to the right, and a decrease in government purchases shifts the aggregate demand curve to the left. An increase in personal income taxes reduces the amount of spendable income available to households. Higher personal income taxes reduce consumption spending and shift the aggregate demand curve to the left. Lower personal income taxes shift the aggregate demand curve to the right. Increases in business taxes reduce the profitability of investment spending and shift the aggregate demand curve to the left. Decreases in business taxes shift the aggregate demand curve to the right.

Changes in the Expectations of Households and Firms If households become more optimistic about their future incomes, they are likely to increase their current

Don't Let This Happen to You

Understand Why the Aggregate Demand Curve Is Downward Sloping

The aggregate demand curve and the demand curve for a single product are both downward sloping—but for different reasons. When we draw a demand curve for a single product, such as apples, we know that it will slope downward because as the price of apples rises, apples become more expensive relative to other products—such as oranges—and consumers will buy fewer apples and more of the other products. In other words, consumers substitute other products for apples. When the overall price level rises, the prices of all domestically produced goods and services are rising, so consumers have no other domestic products to which they can switch. The aggregate demand curve slopes downward for the reasons given on pages 421–422: A lower price level raises the real value of household wealth (which increases consumption), lowers interest rates (which increases investment and consumption), and makes U.S. exports less expensive and foreign imports more expensive (which increases net exports).

MyEconLab

Your Turn: Test your understanding by doing related problem 1.6 on page 446 at the end of this chapter.

consumption. This increased consumption will shift the aggregate demand curve to the right. If households become more pessimistic about their future incomes, the aggregate demand curve will shift to the left. Similarly, if firms become more optimistic about the future profitability of investment spending, the aggregate demand curve will shift to the right. If firms become more pessimistic, the aggregate demand curve will shift to the left.

Changes in Foreign Variables If firms and households in other countries buy fewer U.S. goods or if firms and households in the United States buy more foreign goods, net exports will fall, and the aggregate demand curve will shift to the left. As we saw in Chapter 8, when real GDP increases, so does the income available for consumers to spend. If real GDP in the United States increases faster than real GDP in other countries, U.S. imports will increase faster than U.S. exports, and net exports will fall. Net exports will also fall if the *exchange rate* between the dollar and foreign currencies rises because the price in foreign currency of U.S. products sold in other countries will rise, and the dollar price of foreign products sold in the United States will fall. For example, if the current exchange rate between the dollar and the euro is $1 = €1 then a $500 iPad exported from the United States to France will cost €500 in France, and a €50 bottle of French wine will cost $50 in the United States. But if the exchange rate rises to $1 = €1.50, the iPad's price will rise to €750 in France, causing its sales to decline, and the price of the French wine will fall to $33.33 per bottle in the United States, causing its sales to increase. U.S. exports will fall, U.S. imports will rise, and the aggregate demand curve will shift to the left.

An increase in net exports at every price level will shift the aggregate demand curve to the right. Net exports will increase if real GDP grows more slowly in the United States than in other countries or if the value of the dollar falls against other currencies. A change in net exports that results from a change in the price level in the United States will result in a movement along the aggregate demand curve, *not* a shift of the aggregate demand curve.

Solved Problem 13.1

Movements along the Aggregate Demand Curve versus Shifts of the Aggregate Demand Curve

Suppose the current price level is 110, and the current level of real GDP is $14.2 trillion. Illustrate each of the following situations on a graph.

a. The price level rises to 115, while all other variables remain constant.

b. Firms become pessimistic and reduce their investment. Assume that the price level remains constant.

Solving the Problem

Step 1: **Review the chapter material.** This problem is about understanding the difference between movements along an aggregate demand curve and shifts of an aggregate demand curve, so you may want to review the section "Shifts of the Aggregate Demand Curve versus Movements along It," on page 422.

Step 2: **To answer part a. draw a graph that shows a movement along the aggregate demand curve.** Because there will be a movement along the aggregate demand curve but no shift of the aggregate demand curve, your graph should look like this:

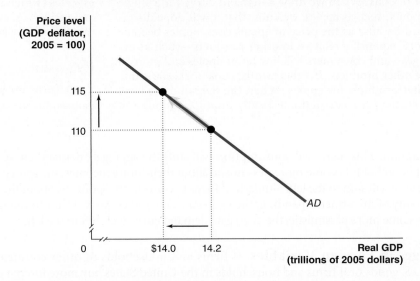

We don't have enough information to be certain what the new level of real GDP demanded will be. We only know that it will be less than the initial level of $14.2 trillion; the graph shows the value as $14.0 trillion.

Step 3: **To answer part b. draw a graph that shows a shift of the aggregate demand curve.** We know that the aggregate demand curve will shift to the left, but we don't have enough information to know how far to the left it will shift. Let's assume that the shift is $300 billion (or $0.3 trillion). In that case, your graph should look like this:

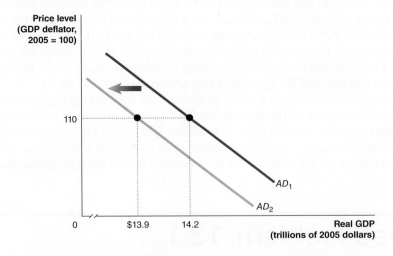

The graph shows a parallel shift in the aggregate demand curve so that at every price level, the quantity of real GDP demanded declines by $300 billion. For example, at a price level of 110, the quantity of real GDP demanded declines from $14.2 trillion to $13.9 trillion.

MyEconLab **Your Turn:** For more practice, do related problem 1.7 on page 447 at the end of this chapter.

Table 13.1 summarizes the most important variables that cause the aggregate demand curve to shift. The table shows the shift in the aggregate demand curve that results from an increase in each of the variables. A *decrease* in these variables would cause the aggregate demand curve to shift in the opposite direction.

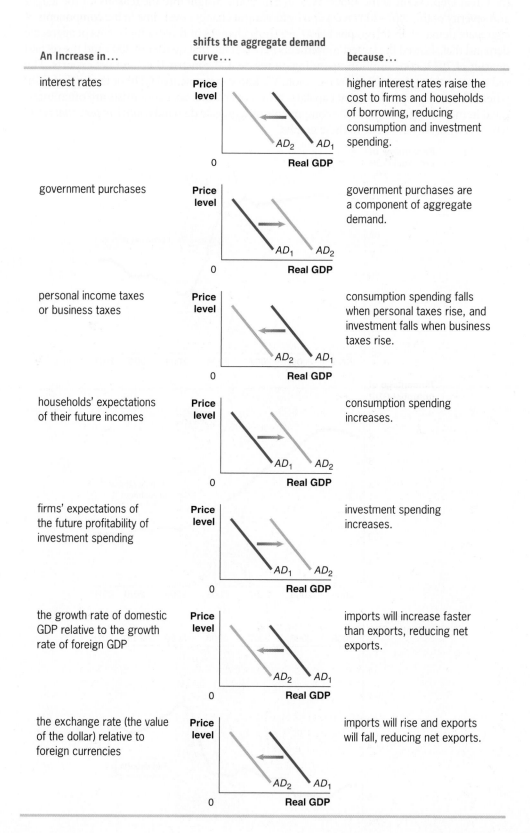

An Increase in...	shifts the aggregate demand curve...	because...
interest rates		higher interest rates raise the cost to firms and households of borrowing, reducing consumption and investment spending.
government purchases		government purchases are a component of aggregate demand.
personal income taxes or business taxes		consumption spending falls when personal taxes rise, and investment falls when business taxes rise.
households' expectations of their future incomes		consumption spending increases.
firms' expectations of the future profitability of investment spending		investment spending increases.
the growth rate of domestic GDP relative to the growth rate of foreign GDP		imports will increase faster than exports, reducing net exports.
the exchange rate (the value of the dollar) relative to foreign currencies		imports will rise and exports will fall, reducing net exports.

Table 13.1

Variables That Shift the Aggregate Demand Curve

Making
the
Connection

Which Components of Aggregate Demand Changed the Most during the 2007–2009 Recession?

The recession of 2007–2009 was the longest and most severe since the Great Depression of the 1930s. We can gain some insight into the reasons for the length and severity of the 2007–2009 recession by looking at changes over time in the components of aggregate demand. In the graphs below, we show changes in three components of aggregate demand that showed the largest movements between the first quarter of 2005 and the second quarter of 2011: consumption, spending on residential construction, and net exports. The red bars represent the 2007–2009 recession. We know that potential GDP, or the level of GDP when all firms are producing at capacity, grows over time. So, economists are often interested in measuring changes in the components of aggregate demand *relative to potential GDP*, which is what we have done in these graphs.

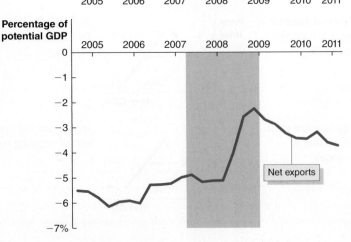

The figure allows us to note a number of facts about the 2007–2009 recession:

- In the two years before the beginning of the recession, spending on residential construction had already declined significantly relative to potential GDP.

- For more than two years following the end of the recession, spending on residential construction did not increase relative to potential GDP.

- Consumption, which usually remains relatively stable during a recession, declined significantly relative to potential GDP during the recession and remained low for more than two years after the recession had ended.

- Net exports increased just before, during, and after the recession. (Because net exports were negative throughout this period, it increased by becoming a smaller negative number.)

Although not shown in the graphs, business fixed investment and changes in business inventories—the nonresidential construction components of investment spending—actually rose relative to potential GDP during the recession. Government purchases remained fairly stable relative to potential GDP throughout the recession, before declining in late 2010 and the first half of 2011. Federal government purchases surged during the recession, but state and local governments reduced their spending as falling household incomes and falling business profits reduced state and local tax revenues.

We can briefly account for these facts. The housing sector underwent a boom from 2002 to 2005, with rapid increases in both housing prices and spending on new housing. The housing boom, though, turned into a housing bust beginning in 2006, which explains the sharp decline in spending on residential construction. The continued low levels of spending on residential construction helps explain why the recession was the longest since the Great Depression and why the economic expansion that began in June 2009 was relatively weak. As one newspaper article noted in late 2011: "Americans aren't spending because their home values are declining and employment prospects are dimming, and housing and employment is struggling because Americans won't spend."

High levels of unemployment reduced household incomes and led to declines in consumption spending. In addition, many households increased their saving and paid off debts, further reducing consumption spending. The continuing low levels of consumption spending also contributed to the severity of the recession and the weakness of the following expansion. Finally, efforts by the Federal Reserve to reduce interest rates helped to lower the value of the U.S. dollar, thereby reducing the prices of U.S. exports and increasing the prices of foreign imports. The result was an increase in net exports. (We will discuss further the effect of Federal Reserve policy on net exports in Chapters 15 and 18.)

Based on U.S. Bureau of Economic Analysis; Congressional Budget Office; and S. Mitra Kalita, "Housing's Job Engine Falters," *Wall Street Journal*, October 5, 2011.

Your Turn: Test your understanding by doing related problem 1.8 on page 447 at the end of this chapter.   MyEconLab

Aggregate Supply

The aggregate demand curve is one component of the aggregate demand and aggregate supply model. Now we turn to aggregate supply, which shows the effect of changes in the price level on the quantity of goods and services that firms are willing and able to supply. Because the effect of changes in the price level on aggregate supply is very different in the short run from what it is in the long run, we use two aggregate supply curves: one for the short run and one for the long run. We start by considering the *long-run aggregate supply curve*.

The Long-Run Aggregate Supply Curve

In Chapter 11, we saw that in the long run, the level of real GDP is determined by the number of workers, the *capital stock*—including factories, office buildings, and machinery and equipment—and the available technology. Because changes in the price level

13.2 LEARNING OBJECTIVE

Identify the determinants of aggregate supply and distinguish between a movement along the short-run aggregate supply curve and a shift of the curve.

The Long-Run Aggregate Supply Curve

Changes in the price level do not affect the level of aggregate supply in the long run. Therefore, the long-run aggregate supply (*LRAS*) curve is a vertical line at the potential level of real GDP. For instance, the price level was 113 in 2011, and potential real GDP was $14.3 trillion. If the price level had been 123, or if it had been 103, long-run aggregate supply would still have been a constant $14.3 trillion. Each year, the long-run aggregate supply curve shifts to the right, as the number of workers in the economy increases, more machinery and equipment are accumulated, and technological change occurs.

Long-run aggregate supply (*LRAS*) curve A curve that shows the relationship in the long run between the price level and the quantity of real GDP supplied.

do not affect the number of workers, the capital stock, or technology, *in the long run, changes in the price level do not affect the level of real GDP*. Remember that the level of real GDP in the long run is called *potential GDP*, or *full-employment GDP*. At potential GDP, firms will operate at their normal level of capacity, and everyone who wants a job will have one, except the structurally and frictionally unemployed. There is no reason for this normal level of capacity to change just because the price level has changed. The **long-run aggregate supply (*LRAS*) curve** shows the relationship in the long run between the price level and the quantity of real GDP supplied. As Figure 13.2 shows, in 2011, the price level was 113, and potential real GDP was $14.3 trillion. If the price level had been 123, or if it had been 103, long-run aggregate supply would still have been a constant $14.3 trillion. Therefore, the *LRAS* curve is a vertical line.

Figure 13.2 also shows that the long-run aggregate supply curve shifts to the right each year. This shift occurs because potential real GDP increases each year, as the number of workers in the economy increases, the economy accumulates more machinery and equipment, and technological change occurs. Figure 13.2 shows potential real GDP increasing from $14.3 trillion in 2011 to $14.6 trillion in 2012 and to $14.9 trillion in 2013.

The Short-Run Aggregate Supply Curve

While the *LRAS* curve is vertical, the *SRAS* curve is upward sloping. The *SRAS* curve is upward sloping because, over the short run, as the price level increases, the quantity of goods and services firms are willing to supply will increase. The main reason firms behave this way is that, *as prices of final goods and services rise, prices of inputs—such as the wages of workers or the price of natural resources—rise more slowly*. Profits rise when the prices of the goods and services firms sell rise more rapidly than the prices they pay for inputs. Therefore, a higher price level leads to higher profits and increases the willingness of firms to supply more goods and services. A secondary reason the *SRAS* curve slopes upward is that, as the price level rises or falls, some firms are slow to adjust their prices. A firm that is slow to raise its prices when the price level is increasing may find its sales increasing and, therefore, will increase production. A firm that is slow to reduce its prices when the price level is decreasing may find its sales falling and, therefore, will decrease production.

Why do some firms adjust prices more slowly than others, and why might the wages of workers and the prices of other inputs change more slowly than the prices of final goods and services? Most economists believe the explanation is that *some firms and workers fail to accurately predict changes in the price level*. If firms and workers could predict the future price level exactly, the short-run aggregate supply curve would be the same as the long-run aggregate supply curve.

But how does the failure of workers and firms to predict the price level accurately result in an upward-sloping *SRAS* curve? Economists are not in complete agreement on this point, but we can briefly discuss the three most common explanations:

1. Contracts make some wages and prices "sticky."
2. Firms are often slow to adjust wages.
3. Menu costs make some prices sticky.

Contracts Make Some Wages and Prices "Sticky" Prices or wages are said to be "sticky" when they do not respond quickly to changes in demand or supply. Contracts can make wages or prices sticky. For example, suppose United Parcel Service (UPS) negotiates a three-year contract with the Independent Pilots Association, the union for the pilots who fly the company's cargo planes, during a time when the economy is in recession and the volume of packages being shipped is falling. Suppose that after the union signs the contract, the economy begins to expand rapidly, and the volume of packages shipped increases, so that UPS can raise the rates it charges. UPS will find that shipping more packages will be profitable because the prices it charges are rising, while the wages it pays its pilots are fixed by contract. Or a steel mill might have signed a multiyear contract to buy coal, which is used in making steel, at a time when the demand for steel was stagnant. If steel demand and steel prices begin to rise rapidly, producing additional steel will be profitable because coal prices will remain fixed by contract. In both of these cases, rising prices lead to higher output. If these examples are representative of enough firms in the economy, a rising price level should lead to a greater quantity of goods and services supplied. In other words, the short-run aggregate supply curve will be upward sloping.

Notice, though, that if the pilots at UPS or the managers of the coal companies had accurately predicted what would happen to prices, this prediction would have been reflected in the contracts, and UPS and the steel mill would not have earned greater profits when prices rose. In that case, rising prices would not have led to higher output.

Firms Are Often Slow to Adjust Wages We just noted that the wages of many union workers remain fixed by contract for several years. Many nonunion workers also have their wages or salaries adjusted only once a year. For instance, suppose you accept a job at a management consulting firm in June, at a salary of $45,000 per year. The firm probably will not adjust your salary until the following June, even if the prices it can charge for its services later in the year are higher or lower than the firm had expected them to be when they hired you. If firms are slow to adjust wages, a rise in the price level will increase the profitability of hiring more workers and producing more output. A fall in the price level will decrease the profitability of hiring more workers and producing more output. Once again, we have an explanation for why the short-run aggregate supply curve slopes upward.

It is worth noting that firms are often slower to *cut* wages than to increase them. Cutting wages can have a negative effect on the morale and productivity of workers and can also cause some of a firm's best workers to quit and look for jobs elsewhere.

Menu Costs Make Some Prices Sticky Firms base their prices today partly on what they expect future prices to be. For instance, before it prints menus, a restaurant has to decide the prices it will charge for meals. Many firms print catalogs that list the prices of their products. If demand for their products is higher or lower than the firms had expected, they may want to charge prices that are different from the ones printed in their menus or catalogs. Changing prices would be costly, however, because it would involve printing new menus or catalogs. The costs to firms of changing prices are called **menu costs**. To see why menu costs can lead to an upward-sloping short-run aggregate supply curve, consider the effect of an unexpected increase in the price level. In this case, firms will want to increase the prices they charge. Some firms, however, may not be willing to increase prices because of menu costs. Because of their relatively low prices, these firms will find their sales increasing, which will cause them to increase output. Once again, we have an explanation for a higher price level leading to a larger quantity of goods and services supplied.

Menu costs The costs to firms of changing prices.

Shifts of the Short-Run Aggregate Supply Curve versus Movements along It

It is important to remember the difference between a shift in a curve and a movement along a curve. The short-run aggregate supply curve tells us the short-run relationship between the price level and the quantity of goods and services firms are willing to supply, *holding constant all other variables that affect the willingness of firms to supply goods and services*. If the price level changes but other variables are unchanged, the economy will move up or down a stationary aggregate supply curve. If any variable other than the price level changes, the aggregate supply curve will shift.

Variables That Shift the Short-Run Aggregate Supply Curve

We now briefly discuss the five most important variables that cause the short-run aggregate supply curve to shift.

Increases in the Labor Force and in the Capital Stock A firm will supply more output at every price if it has more workers and more physical capital. The same is true of the economy as a whole. So, as the labor force and the capital stock grow, firms will supply more output at every price level, and the short-run aggregate supply curve will shift to the right. In Japan, the population is aging, and the labor force is decreasing. Holding other variables constant, this decrease in the labor force causes the short-run aggregate supply curve in Japan to shift to the left.

Technological Change As positive technological change takes place, the productivity of workers and machinery increases, which means firms can produce more goods and services with the same amount of labor and machinery. This increase in productivity reduces the firms' costs of production and, therefore, allows them to produce more output at every price level. As a result, the short-run aggregate supply curve shifts to the right.

Expected Changes in the Future Price Level If workers and firms believe that the price level is going to increase by 3 percent during the next year, they will try to adjust their wages and prices accordingly. For instance, if a labor union believes there will be 3 percent inflation next year, it knows that wages must rise 3 percent to preserve the purchasing power of those wages. Similar adjustments by other workers and firms will result in costs increasing throughout the economy by 3 percent. The result, shown in Figure 13.3, is that the short-run aggregate supply curve will shift to the left, so that any

Figure 13.3

How Expectations of the Future Price Level Affect the Short-Run Aggregate Supply Curve

The *SRAS* curve shifts to reflect worker and firm expectations of future prices.

1. If workers and firms expect that the price level will rise by 3 percent, from 100 to 103, they will adjust their wages and prices by that amount.
2. Holding constant all other variables that affect aggregate supply, the short-run aggregate supply curve will shift to the left.

If workers and firms expect that the price level will be lower in the future, the short-run aggregate supply curve will shift to the right.

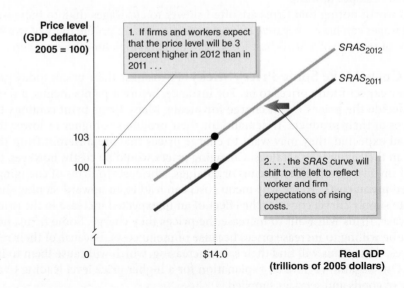

level of real GDP is now associated with a price level that is 3 percent higher. In general, *if workers and firms expect the price level to increase by a certain percentage, the* SRAS *curve will shift by an equivalent amount*, holding constant all other variables that affect the SRAS curve.

Adjustments of Workers and Firms to Errors in Past Expectations about the Price Level Workers and firms sometimes make incorrect predictions about the price level. As time passes, they will attempt to compensate for these errors. Suppose, for example, that the Independent Pilots Association signs a contract with UPS that provides for only small wage increases because the company and the union both expect only small increases in the price level. If increases in the price level turn out to be unexpectedly large, the union will take this into account when negotiating the next contract. The higher wages UPS pilots receive under the new contract will increase UPS's costs and result in UPS needing to receive higher prices to produce the same level of output. If workers and firms across the economy are adjusting to the price level being higher than expected, the SRAS curve will shift to the left. If they are adjusting to the price level being lower than expected, the SRAS curve will shift to the right.

Unexpected Changes in the Price of an Important Natural Resource An unexpected event that causes the short-run aggregate supply curve to shift is known as a **supply shock**. Supply shocks are often caused by unexpected increases or decreases in the prices of important natural resources that can cause firms' costs to be different from what they had expected. Oil prices can be particularly volatile. Some firms use oil in the production process. Other firms use products, such as plastics, that are made from oil. If oil prices rise unexpectedly, the costs of production will rise for these firms. Some utilities also burn oil to generate electricity, so electricity prices will rise. Rising oil prices lead to rising gasoline prices, which raise transportation costs for many firms. Because firms face rising costs, they will supply the same level of output only if they receive higher prices, and the short-run aggregate supply curve will shift to the left.

> **Supply shock** An unexpected event that causes the short-run aggregate supply curve to shift.

Because the U.S. economy has experienced at least some inflation every year since the 1930s, workers and firms always expect next year's price level to be higher than this year's price level. Holding everything else constant, expectations of a higher price level will cause the SRAS curve to shift to the left. But everything else is not constant because every year, the U.S. labor force and the U.S. capital stock expand, and changes in technology occur, which cause the SRAS curve to shift to the right. Whether in any particular year the SRAS curve shifts to the left or to the right depends on how large an impact these variables have during that year.

Table 13.2 summarizes the most important variables that cause the SRAS curve to shift. The table shows the shift in the SRAS curve that results from an *increase* in each of the variables. A *decrease* in these variables would cause the SRAS curve to shift in the opposite direction.

Macroeconomic Equilibrium in the Long Run and the Short Run

13.3 LEARNING OBJECTIVE

Use the aggregate demand and aggregate supply model to illustrate the difference between short-run and long-run macroeconomic equilibrium.

Now that we have discussed the components of the aggregate demand and aggregate supply model, we can use it to analyze changes in real GDP and the price level. In Figure 13.4, we bring the aggregate demand curve, the short-run aggregate supply curve, and the long-run aggregate supply curve together in one graph, to show the *long-run macroeconomic equilibrium* for the economy. In the figure, equilibrium occurs at real GDP of $14.0 trillion and a price level of 100. Notice that in long-run equilibrium, the short-run aggregate supply curve and the aggregate demand curve intersect at a point on the long-run aggregate supply curve. Because equilibrium occurs at a point along the long-run aggregate supply curve, we know the economy is at potential real GDP: Firms will be

Table 13.2

Variables That Shift the Short-Run Aggregate Supply Curve

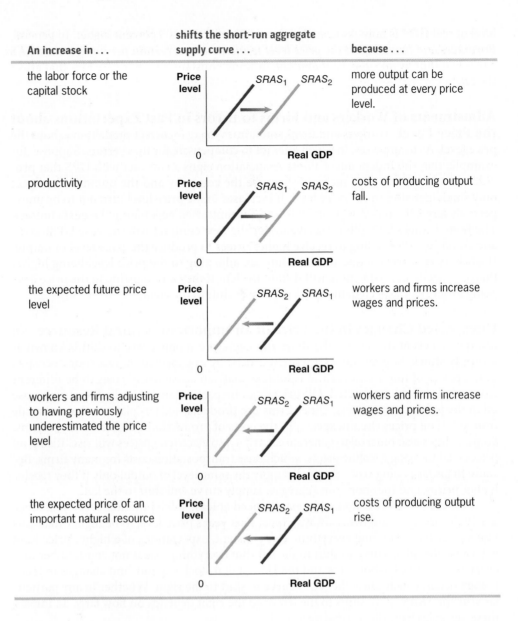

An increase in . . .	shifts the short-run aggregate supply curve . . .	because . . .
the labor force or the capital stock		more output can be produced at every price level.
productivity		costs of producing output fall.
the expected future price level		workers and firms increase wages and prices.
workers and firms adjusting to having previously underestimated the price level		workers and firms increase wages and prices.
the expected price of an important natural resource		costs of producing output rise.

Figure 13.4

Long-Run Macroeconomic Equilibrium

In long-run macroeconomic equilibrium, the *AD* and *SRAS* curves intersect at a point on the *LRAS* curve. In this case, equilibrium occurs at real GDP of $14.0 trillion and a price level of 100.

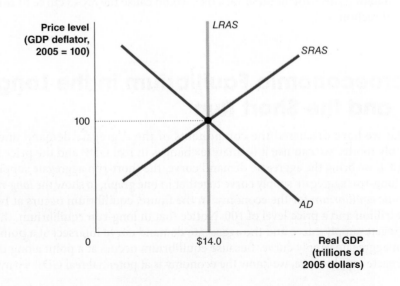

operating at their normal level of capacity, and everyone who wants a job will have one, except the structurally and frictionally unemployed. We know, however, that the economy is often not in long-run macroeconomic equilibrium. In the following section, we discuss the economic forces that can push the economy away from long-run equilibrium.

Recessions, Expansions, and Supply Shocks

Because the full analysis of the aggregate demand and aggregate supply model can be complicated, we begin with a simplified case, using two assumptions:

1. The economy has not been experiencing any inflation. The price level is currently 100, and workers and firms expect it to remain at 100 in the future.
2. The economy is not experiencing any long-run growth. Potential real GDP is $14.0 trillion and will remain at that level in the future.

These assumptions are simplifications because in reality, the U.S. economy has experienced at least some inflation every year since the 1930s, and the potential real GDP also increases every year. However, the assumptions allow us to understand more easily the key ideas of the aggregate demand and aggregate supply model. In this section, we examine the short-run and long-run effects of recessions, expansions, and supply shocks.

Recession

The Short-Run Effect of a Decline in Aggregate Demand Suppose that rising interest rates cause firms to reduce spending on factories and equipment and cause households to reduce spending on new homes. The decline in investment that results will shift the aggregate demand curve to the left, from AD_1 to AD_2, as shown in Figure 13.5. The economy moves from point A to a new *short-run macroeconomic equilibrium*, where the AD_2 curve intersects the $SRAS_1$ curve at point B. In the new short-run equilibrium, real GDP has declined from $14.0 trillion to $13.8 trillion and is below its potential level. This lower level of GDP will result in declining profitability for many firms and layoffs for some workers: the economy will be in recession.

Adjustment Back to Potential GDP in the Long Run We know that a recession will eventually end because there are forces at work that push the economy back to potential GDP in the long run. Figure 13.5 shows how the economy moves from recession back to potential GDP. The shift from AD_1 to AD_2 initially leads to a short-run equilibrium, with the price level having fallen from 100 to 98 (point B). Workers and firms will

Figure 13.5

The Short-Run and Long-Run Effects of a Decrease in Aggregate Demand

In the short run, a decrease in aggregate demand causes a recession. In the long run, it causes only a decrease in the price level.

begin to adjust to the price level being lower than they had expected it to be. Workers will be willing to accept lower wages—because each dollar of wages is able to buy more goods and services—and firms will be willing to accept lower prices. In addition, the unemployment resulting from the recession will make workers more willing to accept lower wages, and the decline in demand will make firms more willing to accept lower prices. As a result, the *SRAS* curve will shift to the right, from $SRAS_1$ to $SRAS_2$. At this point, the economy will be back in long-run equilibrium (point *C*). The shift from $SRAS_1$ to $SRAS_2$ will not happen instantly. It may take the economy several years to return to potential GDP. The important conclusion is that a decline in aggregate demand causes a recession in the short run, but in the long run it causes only a decline in the price level.

Economists refer to the process of adjustment back to potential GDP just described as an *automatic mechanism* because it occurs without any actions by the government. An alternative to waiting for the automatic mechanism to end a recession is for the government to use monetary and fiscal policy to shift the *AD* curve to the right and restore potential GDP more quickly. We will discuss monetary and fiscal policy in Chapters 15 and 16. Economists debate whether it is better to wait for the automatic mechanism to end recessions or whether it is better to use monetary and fiscal policy.

| Making the Connection | **Does It Matter What Causes a Decline in Aggregate Demand?** |

We have seen that GDP has four components and that a decrease in any of the four components can cause the aggregate demand curve to shift to the left, bringing on a recession. In practice, though, most recessions in the United States since World War II have begun with a decline in residential construction. Edward Leamer of the University of California, Los Angeles has gone so far as to argue that "housing *is* the business cycle," meaning that declines in residential construction are the most important reason for the declines in aggregate demand that lead to recessions. The shaded periods in the graph below represent recessions. The graph shows that spending on residential construction has declined prior to every recession since 1955.

The figure shows again a fact that we noted earlier in the chapter: The decline in residential construction during the 2007–2009

The collapse in spending on housing added to the severity of the 2007–2009 recession.

Data from U.S. Bureau of Economic Analysis.

recession was particularly severe. Spending on residential construction declined by almost 60 percent from the fourth quarter of 2005 to the second quarter of 2010. Largely because of these problems in the housing sector, the decline in real GDP during the recession of 2007–2009 was larger than during any other recession since the Great Depression of the 1930s.

What causes declines in spending on residential construction, and why was the decline that preceded the 2007–2009 recession so severe? As we discussed in Chapter 10, late in a business cycle expansion, the inflation rate and interest rates start to increase. As we will discuss in Chapter 15, higher interest rates often result from monetary policy actions as the Federal Reserve tries to slow down the economy and reduce the rate of inflation. Higher interest rates reduce consumer demand for new houses by increasing the cost of loans.

But the collapse in residential construction prior to and during the recession of 2007–2009 was due more to the deflating of the "housing bubble" of 2002–2005 and to the financial crisis that began in 2007 than to higher interest rates. We will discuss both the housing bubble and the financial crisis later in this chapter. At this point, we can note that research by Carmen M. Reinhart of the University of Maryland and Kenneth S. Rogoff of Harvard University shows that declines in aggregate demand that result from financial crises tend to be larger and more long lasting than declines due to other factors. So, the experience of 2007–2009 indicates that, in fact, the source of the decline in aggregate demand can be important in determining the severity of a recession.

Based on Edward E. Leamer, "Housing Is the Business Cycle," in *Housing, Housing Finance, and Monetay Policy*, Federal Reserve Bank of Kansas City, August 2007; and Carmen M. Reinhart and Kenneth S. Rogoff, "The Aftermath of Financial Crises," *American Economic Review*, Vol. 99, No. 2, May 2009, pp. 466–472.

Your Turn: Test your understanding by doing related problem 3.6 on page 448 at the end of this chapter.   MyEconLab

---

Expansion

The Short-Run Effect of an Increase in Aggregate Demand Suppose that instead of becoming pessimistic, many firms become optimistic about the future profitability of new investment, as happened during the information technology and telecommunications booms of the late 1990s. The resulting increase in investment will shift the *AD* curve to the right, as shown in Figure 13.6. Equilibrium moves from point *A* to point *B*. Real GDP rises from $14.0 trillion to $14.3 trillion, and the price level rises from 100 to 103. The economy will be above potential real GDP: Firms are operating

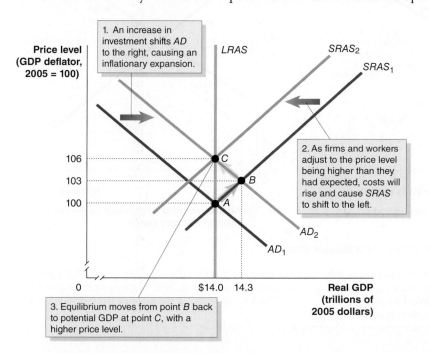

Figure 13.6

The Short-Run and Long-Run Effects of an Increase in Aggregate Demand

In the short run, an increase in aggregate demand causes an increase in real GDP. In the long run, it causes only an increase in the price level.

beyond their normal level of capacity, and some workers who would ordinarily be structurally or frictionally unemployed or who would not be in the labor force are employed.

Adjustment Back to Potential GDP in the Long Run Just as an automatic mechanism brings the economy back to potential GDP from a recession, an automatic mechanism brings the economy back from a short-run equilibrium beyond potential GDP. Figure 13.6 illustrates this mechanism. The shift from AD_1 to AD_2 initially leads to a short-run equilibrium, with the price level rising from 100 to 103 (point B). Workers and firms will begin to adjust to the price level being higher than they had expected. Workers will push for higher wages—because each dollar of wages is able to buy fewer goods and services—and firms will charge higher prices. In addition, the low levels of unemployment resulting from the expansion will make it easier for workers to negotiate for higher wages, and the increase in demand will make it easier for firms to receive higher prices. As a result, the $SRAS$ curve will shift to the left, from $SRAS_1$ to $SRAS_2$. At this point, the economy will be back in long-run equilibrium. Once again, the shift from $SRAS_1$ to $SRAS_2$ will not happen instantly. The process of returning to potential GDP may stretch out for more than a year.

Supply Shock

The Short-Run Effect of a Supply Shock Suppose oil prices increase substantially. This supply shock will increase many firms' costs and cause the $SRAS$ curve to shift to the left, as shown in panel (a) of Figure 13.7. Notice that the price level is higher in the new short-run equilibrium (102 rather than 100), but real GDP is lower ($13.7 trillion rather than $14 trillion). This unpleasant combination of inflation and recession is called **stagflation**.

Stagflation A combination of inflation and recession, usually resulting from a supply shock.

Adjustment Back to Potential GDP in the Long Run The recession caused by a supply shock increases unemployment and reduces output. This eventually results in workers being willing to accept lower wages and firms being willing to accept lower

(a) A recession with a rising price level—the short-run effect of a supply shock

(b) Adjustment back to potential GDP—the long-run effect of a supply shock

Figure 13.7 The Short-Run and Long-Run Effects of a Supply Shock

Panel (a) shows that a supply shock, such as a large increase in oil prices, will cause a recession and a higher price level in the short run. The recession caused by the supply shock increases unemployment and reduces output. In panel (b), rising unemployment and falling output result in workers being willing to

accept lower wages and firms being willing to accept lower prices. The short-run aggregate supply curve shifts from $SRAS_2$ to $SRAS_1$. Equilibrium moves from point B back to potential GDP and the original price level at point A.

prices. In panel (b) of Figure 13.7, the short-run aggregate supply curve shifts from $SRAS_2$ to $SRAS_1$, moving the economy from point *B* back to point *A*. The economy is back to potential GDP at the original price level. It may take several years for this process to be completed. An alternative would be to use monetary and fiscal policy to shift the aggregate demand to the right. Using policy in this way would bring the economy back to potential GDP more quickly but would result in a permanently higher price level.

Making the Connection | How Long Does It Take to Return to Potential GDP? Economic Forecasts Following the Recession of 2007–2009

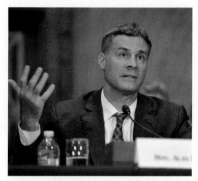

Alan Krueger, the chair of the Council of Economic Advisers in the Obama administration, provided an estimate of how long the economy would take to return to potential GDP.

Making accurate macroeconomic forecasts is difficult. As we have seen, many factors can cause aggregate demand or aggregate supply to shift. Because it is challenging to predict how much aggregate demand and aggregate supply will shift, economists often have difficulty predicting the beginning and end of a recession. The Federal Reserve, foreign central banks, other government agencies, large banks, forecasting firms, and academic economists use a variety of forecasting models to predict changes in GDP. Most forecasting models consist of equations that represent the macroeconomic relationships—such as the relationship between disposable income and consumption spending—that underlie the aggregate demand and aggregate supply model. After economists have statistically estimated the equations using economic data, they can use the models to forecast values for GDP and the price level.

Most economists agree that an automatic mechanism brings the economy back to potential GDP in the long run. But how long is the long run? When the recession of 2007–2009 ended in June 2009, the economy was far from potential GDP. Even two years later, in mid-2011, real GDP remained more than 7 percent below potential GDP. How long would it take for the economy to finally return to potential GDP? The figure below shows the Congressional Budget Office's estimates of potential GDP along with three forecasts of real GDP made in 2011 by the following:

- Economists on the president's staff at the White House
- Officials at the Federal Reserve
- Economists at the Congressional Budget Office (CBO)

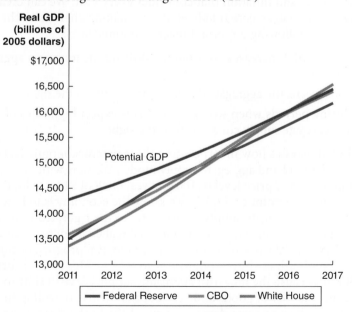

The forecasts of the White House and the CBO agreed that real GDP would not return to potential GDP until 2016. The projections of the Federal Reserve were even more pessimistic, with real GDP remaining below potential GDP in 2017. These forecasts indicate how severe the 2007–2009 recession was in that real GDP was not expected to return to potential GDP until nearly seven years after the end of the recession. Prior to the

2007–2009 recession, the recession of 1981–1982 had been the most severe since the Great Depression. Yet it took less than three years after the end of that recession for real GDP to return to potential GDP.

These macroeconomic forecasts played an important role in the policy debates of 2011 and 2012. As we will discuss in Chapters 16 and 17, economists and policymakers disagreed about why the U.S. economy would take so long to return to potential GDP and about what measures the federal government might take to shorten the time.

Note: The Federal Reserve's forecast uses averages of the forecasts of the individual members of the Federal Open Market Committee.

Based on Board of Governors of the Federal Reserve System, "Economic Projections of Federal Reserve Board Members and Federal Reserve Bank Presidents, April 2011," April 27, 2011; Congressional Budget Office, "Data Underlying Selected Economic Figures, Real Gross Domestic Product, 1980–2021," January 27, 2011; and Office of Management and Budget, "Budget of the U.S. Government, Fiscal Year 2012, Mid-Session Review," September 1, 2011.

MyEconLab **Your Turn:** Test your understanding by doing related problem 3.9 on page 449 at the end of this chapter.

13.4 LEARNING OBJECTIVE

Use the dynamic aggregate demand and aggregate supply model to analyze macroeconomic conditions.

A Dynamic Aggregate Demand and Aggregate Supply Model[*]

The basic aggregate demand and aggregate supply model used so far in this chapter provides important insights into how short-run macroeconomic equilibrium is determined. Unfortunately, the model also provides some misleading results. For instance, it incorrectly predicts that a recession caused by the aggregate demand curve shifting to the left will cause the price level to fall, which has not happened for an entire year since the 1930s. The difficulty with the basic model arises from the following two assumptions we made: (1) The economy does not experience continuing inflation, and (2) the economy does not experience long-run growth. We can develop a more useful aggregate demand and aggregate supply model by dropping these assumptions. The result will be a model that takes into account that the economy is not *static*, with an unchanging level of potential real GDP and no continuing inflation, but *dynamic*, with potential real GDP that grows over time and inflation that continues every year. We can create a *dynamic aggregate demand and aggregate supply model* by making changes to the basic model that incorporate the following important macroeconomic facts:

- Potential real GDP increases continually, shifting the long-run aggregate supply curve to the right.

- During most years, the aggregate demand curve shifts to the right.

- Except during periods when workers and firms expect high rates of inflation, the short-run aggregate supply curve shifts to the right.

Figure 13.8 illustrates how incorporating these macroeconomic facts changes the basic aggregate demand and aggregate supply model. We start with $SRAS_1$ and AD_1 intersecting at point A, at a price level of 100 and real GDP of $14.0 trillion. Because this intersection occurs at a point on $LRAS_1$, we know the economy is in long-run equilibrium. The long-run aggregate supply curve shifts to the right, from $LRAS_1$ to $LRAS_2$. This shift occurs because during the year, potential real GDP increases as the U.S. labor force and the U.S. capital stock increase and technological progress occurs. The short-run aggregate supply curve shifts from $SRAS_1$ to $SRAS_2$. This shift occurs because the same variables that cause the long-run aggregate supply curve to shift to the right will also increase the quantity of goods and services that firms are willing to supply in the short run. Finally, the aggregate demand curve shifts to the right, from AD_1 to AD_2. The aggregate demand curve shifts for several reasons: As the population grows and incomes rise, consumption will increase over time. As the economy grows, firms will expand capacity, and new firms will be formed, increasing investment. An expanding

[*]This section may be omitted without loss of continuity.

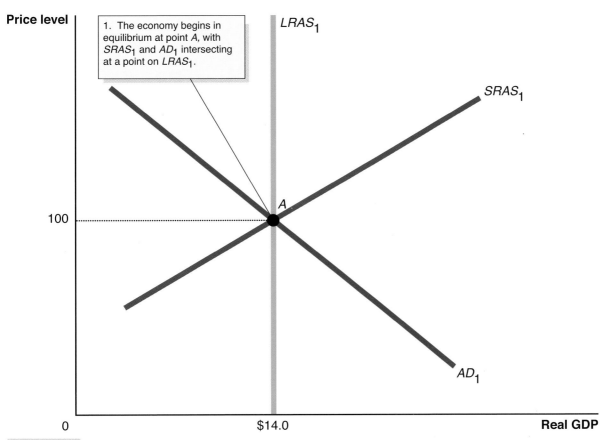

Figure 13.8   **A Dynamic Aggregate Demand and Aggregate Supply Model**

We start with the basic aggregate demand and aggregate supply model.

population and an expanding economy require increased government services, such as more police officers and teachers, so government purchases will increase.

The new equilibrium in Figure 13.8 occurs at point B, where AD_2 intersects $SRAS_2$ on $LRAS_2$. In the new equilibrium, the price level remains at 100, while real GDP increases to $14.3 trillion. Notice that there has been no inflation because the price level is unchanged, at 100. There has been no inflation because aggregate demand and aggregate supply shifted to the right by exactly as much as long-run aggregate supply. We would not expect this to be the typical situation for two reasons. First, the $SRAS$ curve is also affected by workers' and firms' expectations of future changes in the price level and by supply shocks. These variables can partially or completely offset the normal tendency of the $SRAS$ curve to shift to the right over the course of a year. Second, we know that consumers, firms, and the government may cut back on expenditures. This reduced spending will result in the aggregate demand curve shifting to the right less than it normally would or, possibly, shifting to the left. In fact, as we will see shortly, *changes in the price level and in real GDP in the short run are determined by shifts in the* SRAS *and* AD *curves*.

What Is the Usual Cause of Inflation?

The dynamic aggregate demand and aggregate supply model provides a more accurate explanation than the basic model of the source of most inflation. If total spending in the economy grows faster than total production, prices rise. Figure 13.9 illustrates this point by showing that if the AD curve shifts to the right by more than the $LRAS$ curve, inflation results because equilibrium occurs at a higher price level, point B. In the new equilibrium, the $SRAS$ curve has shifted to the right by less than the $LRAS$ curve because the anticipated increase in prices offsets some of the technological change and increases in the labor force and capital stock that occur during the year. Although inflation generally

Figure 13.9

Using Dynamic Aggregate Demand and Aggregate Supply to Understand Inflation

The most common cause of inflation is total spending increasing faster than total production.

1. The economy begins at point A, with real GDP of $14.0 trillion and a price level of 100. An increase in full-employment real GDP from $14.0 trillion to $14.3 trillion causes long-run aggregate supply to shift from $LRAS_1$ to $LRAS_2$. Aggregate demand shifts from AD_1 to AD_2.

2. Because AD shifts to the right by more than the $LRAS$ curve, the price level in the new equilibrium rises from 100 to 104.

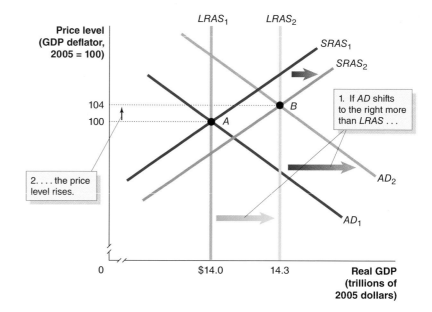

results from total spending growing faster than total production, a shift to the left of the short-run aggregate supply curve can also cause an increase in the price level, as we saw earlier, in the discussion of supply shocks.

As we saw in Figure 13.8, if aggregate demand increases by the same amount as short-run and long-run aggregate supply, the price level will not change. In this case, the economy experiences economic growth without inflation.

The Recession of 2007–2009

We can use the dynamic aggregate demand and aggregate supply model to analyze the recession of 2007–2009. The recession began in December 2007, with the end of the economic expansion that had begun in November 2001. Several factors combined to bring on the recession:

- *The end of the housing bubble.* The figure in the *Making the Connection* on page 434 shows that spending on residential construction increased rapidly from 2002 to 2005, before declining more than 60 percent between the end of 2005 and the beginning of 2010. The increase in spending on housing was partly the result of actions the Federal Reserve had taken to lower interest rates during and after the recession of 2001. As interest rates on mortgage loans declined, more consumers began to buy new homes. But by 2005, it was clear that a speculative bubble was partly responsible for the rapidly rising prices of both newly built and existing homes. A bubble occurs when people become less concerned with the underlying value of an asset—either a physical asset, such as a house, or a financial asset, such as a stock—and focus instead on expectations of the price of the asset increasing. In some areas of the country, such as California, Arizona, and Florida, many homes were purchased by investors who intended to resell them for higher prices than they paid for them and did not intend to live in them. Some popular television programs explored ways that people could "flip" houses by buying and quickly reselling them. Speculative bubbles eventually end, and the housing bubble started to deflate in 2006. Both new home sales and housing prices began to decline. The growth of aggregate demand slowed as spending on residential construction—a component of investment spending—fell. We will discuss the housing bubble further in Chapter 15.

- *The financial crisis.* Problems in the housing market were bad news for workers and firms involved with residential construction. In addition, falling housing prices led to an increased number of borrowers defaulting on their mortgage loans. These defaults caused banks and some other financial institutions to suffer heavy losses. Beginning in the spring of 2008, the U.S. Department of the Treasury and the Federal Reserve intervened to save several large financial institutions from bankruptcy. We will look at the details of the financial crisis in Chapters 14 and 15. For now we can note that the financial crisis led to a "credit crunch" that made it difficult for many households and firms to obtain the loans they needed to finance their spending. This drying up of credit contributed to declines in consumption spending and investment spending.

- ***The rapid increase in oil prices during 2008.*** Oil prices, which had been as low as $34 per barrel in 2004, had risen to $140 per barrel by mid-2008. The increase in the price of oil appeared to be caused by increased demand in rapidly growing economies, particularly India and China, and by the difficulty in developing new supplies of oil in the short run. With the deepening of the recession, worldwide demand for oil declined, and oil prices fell to about $40 per barrel in early 2009. As we have seen in this chapter, rising oil prices can result in a *supply shock* that causes the short-run aggregate supply curve to shift to the left. Although rising oil prices contributed to the severity of the recession, they had less impact than some economists had predicted. The U.S. economy appears to have become less vulnerable to increases in oil prices. Increases in the price of oil during the 1970s and early 1980s led many firms to switch to less-oil-dependent production processes. For example, FedEx and other firms used more fuel-efficient jets and trucks. As a result, the U.S. economy was consuming almost 60 percent less oil per dollar of GDP than it had in the mid-1970s. During 2008, oil price increases did not shift the short-run aggregate supply curve as far to the left as similar increases had 30 years earlier.

Figure 13.10 illustrates the beginning of the recession by showing the economy's short-run macroeconomic equilibrium in 2007 and 2008. In the figure, short-run equilibrium for 2007 occurs where AD_{2007} intersects $SRAS_{2007}$ at real GDP of $13.21 trillion and a price level of 106.2. Real GDP in 2007 was slightly above potential real GDP of $13.20 trillion, shown by $LRAS_{2007}$. During 2008, aggregate demand shifted to the right, from AD_{2007} to AD_{2008}. Aggregate demand increased by less than potential GDP because of the negative effects of the bursting of the housing bubble and the financial crisis on consumption spending and investment spending. The supply shock from higher oil prices caused short-run aggregate supply to shift to the left, from $SRAS_{2007}$ to $SRAS_{2008}$. Short-run equilibrium for 2008 occurred at real GDP of $13.16 trillion and a price level of 108.6. A large gap opened between short-run equilibrium real GDP and potential GDP. Not surprisingly, unemployment rose from 4.6 percent in 2007 to 5.8 percent in 2008. The price level increased only from 106.2 to 108.6, so the inflation rate was a low 2.3 percent.

The recession persisted into 2009, as potential real GDP increased to $13.78 trillion, while real GDP fell to $12.70 trillion. This increased gap between real GDP and potential GDP caused the unemployment rate to soar to 9.3 percent—the highest unemployment

Figure 13.10

The Beginning of the Recession of 2007–2009

Between 2007 and 2008, the *AD* curve shifted to the right, but not by nearly enough to offset the shift to the right of the *LRAS* curve, which represented the increase in potential real GDP from $13.20 trillion to $13.51 trillion. Because of a sharp increase in oil prices, short-run aggregate supply shifted to the left, from $SRAS_{2007}$ to $SRAS_{2008}$. Real GDP decreased from $13.21 trillion in 2007 to $13.16 trillion in 2008, which was far below the potential real GDP, shown by $LRAS_{2008}$. As a result, the unemployment rate rose from 4.6 percent in 2007 to 5.8 percent in 2008. Because the increase in aggregate demand was small, the price level increased only from 106.2 in 2007 to 108.6 in 2008, so the inflation rate for 2008 was only 2.3 percent.

rate since the recession of 1981–1982 and the second highest since the Great Depression of the 1930s. Although the recession ended in June 2009, real GDP grew only slowly during 2010 and 2011, leaving the unemployment rate above 9 percent.

The severity of the recession of 2007–2009 resulted in some of the most dramatic changes in government economic policy since the Great Depression. We will explore these new policies in Chapters 15 and 16.

Solved Problem 13.4

Showing the Oil Shock of 1974–1975 on a Dynamic Aggregate Demand and Aggregate Supply Graph

The 1974–1975 recession clearly illustrates how a supply shock affects the economy. Following the Arab–Israeli War of 1973, the Organization of the Petroleum Exporting Countries (OPEC) increased the price of a barrel of oil from less than $3 to more than $10. Use this information and the statistics in the following table to draw a dynamic aggregate demand and aggregate supply graph showing macroeconomic equilibrium for 1974 and 1975. Assume that the aggregate demand curve did not shift between 1974 and 1975. Provide a brief explanation of your graph.

	Actual Real GDP	Potential Real GDP	Price Level
1974	$4.89 trillion	$4.92 trillion	30.7
1975	$4.88 trillion	$5.09 trillion	33.6

Data from U.S. Bureau of Economic Analysis; and Congressional Budget Office.

Solving the Problem

Step 1: **Review the chapter material.** This problem is about using the dynamic aggregate demand and aggregate supply model, so you may want to review the section "A Dynamic Aggregate Demand and Aggregate Supply Model," which begins on page 438.

Step 2: **Use the information in the table to draw the graph.** You need to draw five curves: *SRAS* and *LRAS* for both 1974 and 1975 and *AD*, which is the same for both years. You know that the two *LRAS* curves will be vertical lines at the values given for potential GDP in the table. Because of the large supply shock, you know that the *SRAS* curve shifted to the left. You are instructed to assume that the *AD* curve did not shift. Your graph should look like this:

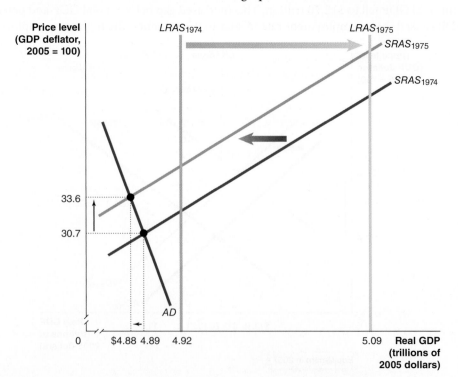

Step 3: **Explain your graph.** $LRAS_{1974}$ and $LRAS_{1975}$ are at the levels of potential real GDP for each year. Macroeconomic equilibrium for 1974 occurs where the AD curve intersects the $SRAS_{1974}$ curve, with real GDP of $4.89 trillion and a price level of 30.7. Macroeconomic equilibrium for 1975 occurs where the AD curve intersects the $SRAS_{1975}$ curve, with real GDP of $4.88 trillion and a price level of 33.6.

Extra Credit: As a result of the supply shock, the economy moved from an equilibrium output just below potential GDP in 1974 (the recession actually began right at the end of 1973) to an equilibrium well below potential GDP in 1975. With real GDP in 1975 about 4.1 percent below its potential level, the unemployment rate soared from 5.6 percent in 1974 to 8.5 percent in 1975.

Your Turn: For more practice, do related problems 4.5 and 4.6 on pages 449–450 at the end of this chapter.

MyEconLab

Continued from page 419

Economics in Your Life

Is an Employer Likely to Cut Your Pay during a Recession?

At the beginning of this chapter, we asked you to consider whether during a recession your employer is likely to reduce your pay and cut the prices of the products he or she sells. In this chapter, we saw that even during a recession, the price level rarely falls. In fact, in the United States, the GDP deflator has not fallen for an entire year since the 1930s. Although some firms reduced prices during the recession of 2007–2009, most firms did not. So, the owner of the coffeehouse where you work will probably not cut the price of lattes unless sales have declined drastically. We also saw that most firms are more reluctant to cut wages than to increase them because wage cuts can have a negative effect on worker morale and productivity. Because the recession of 2007–2009 was particularly severe, some firms did cut wages. But given that you are a highly skilled barista, your employer is unlikely to cut your wages for fear that you might quit and work for a competitor.

Conclusion

Chapter 3 demonstrated the power of the microeconomic model of demand and supply in explaining how the prices and quantities of individual products are determined. This chapter showed that we need a different model to explain the behavior of the whole economy. We saw that the macroeconomic model of aggregate demand and aggregate supply explains fluctuations in real GDP and the price level.

Fluctuations in real GDP, employment, and the price level have led the federal government to implement macroeconomic policies. We will explore these policies in Chapters 15 and 16, but first, in Chapter 14, we consider the role money plays in the economy.

Read *An Inside Look* on the next page for a discussion of how a decline in air cargo shipments caused the airline industry to be concerned about the health of the economy.

Smaller Freight Volumes Signal Continued Economic Troubles

BLOOMBERG

Air Cargo Down as Comerica Mulls Recession Risk: Freight Markets

(a) Sagging cargo shipments in the belly of passenger jets at carriers such as United Continental Holdings Inc. (UAL) and Delta Air Lines Inc. (DAL) are stoking concern that the U.S. economy risks a double-dip recession.

United's cargo traffic plunged 17 percent in August for the fourth straight drop that exceeded 10 percent, while Delta's cargo was little changed for three months in a row and American Airlines extended a streak of decreases that began in May.

"We have a lot of consumer nervousness over the economy," Delta Chief Cargo Officer Neel Shah said in a telephone interview. "One day people feel good, and the next day they feel bad, and it's that volatility that's the problem."

(b) Cargo is a bellwether for the carriers' main business of flying people, said Hunter Keay, a Wolfe Trahan & Co. analyst. While cargo is less than 4 percent of sales at the biggest U.S. airlines, their monthly reports offer more-timely soundings on the $60 billion global air-freight market than quarterly results from FedEx Corp. (FDX) and United Parcel Service Inc. (UPS).

Frequent flights and broad networks help airlines win business for everything from U.S. mail to electronics, along with niche shipments such as sushi-grade seafood, baby chicks for poultry farms and caskets containing human remains.

"The decline in air cargo is yet another indicator among so many that suggests the economy continues to be weak and may be inching closer to recession," said Robert Dye, Comerica Inc. (CMA)'s chief economist. . . .

The slide in air-carrier cargo correlates with "consumer confidence falling off a cliff" in August, Dye said in an interview from Dallas. The Bloomberg Consumer Comfort Index slid to minus 49.3 in the week ended Sept. 4, 2011's second-worst reading, and stayed at that level last week.

Dye rates the risk of a recession at 45 percent. Mark Vitner, senior economist at Wells Fargo Securities LLC in Charlotte, North Carolina, put the chances at one in three. The cargo drop "flies in the face" of assertions that shipping disruptions from Japan's earthquake had been resolved, he said.

"I don't think it's unreasonable to look at these cargo numbers and grow a little suspicious on what it means for passenger trends," Keay, who is based in New York, said in an interview.

Analysts and investors have been watching for signs of a return to recession because unemployment has hovered at about 9 percent or more for two years, damping consumer confidence and spending. . . .

The airline-cargo slowdown began in May, following Japan's March 11 earthquake and tsunami. Carriers also cited tougher comparisons with a year earlier when many businesses replenished inventory as the economy improved.

At Atlanta-based Delta, cargo traffic had been growing by 15 percent in March and April before cooling to a 2.1 percent pace for May. Traffic has been little changed since then. Exports are down from China and Japan, and domestic U.S. loads are shrinking, Shah said. . . .

(c) "Historically, cargo has been a pretty good leading indicator for business and premium traffic by about three to six months," Michael Linenberg, a Deutsche Bank AG analyst in New York, said in a note last month. "Business and premium traffic tends to lead leisure travel by a similar time frame."

Even as industry executives such as Delta President Ed Bastian said this week at a conference hosted by Linenberg that travel demand was firm, some also signaled their concern with steps to shrink passenger capacity.

Delta said it would trim 2012 flying by 2 percent to 3 percent, while American said it would pare available seats next quarter by 0.5 percent and said its plans for next year are under review. United and Delta previously scaled back on seating for the end of this year.

"Cargo is usually the canary in the mine shaft," Delta's Shah said. "I don't know if we're going to face that sort of situation this time. Passenger demand is holding up quite well, yet everyone is being very cautious with costs and capacity."

Source: "Air Cargo Down as Comerica Mulls Recession Risk: Freight Markets," by Mary Jane Credeur from *Bloomberg*, September 15, 2011.Copyright © 2011 by Bloomberg. Reprinted by permission of the YGS Group.

Key Points in the Article

Although cargo shipments account for only a small percentage of total business for the major airlines, they have historically been good indicators of future passenger travel. A decline in shipments has some industry analysts concerned that passenger air travel may also experience declines in the next 6 to 12 months. Airlines have reacted with planned cuts in passenger service. The air cargo slowdown began in May 2011, occurring alongside a drop in consumer confidence tied to an unemployment rate that continued to exceed 9 percent. Some analysts view the decline in cargo shipments and the airlines' actions to scale back passenger service as an indication that an already-sluggish economy may be slipping even further.

Analyzing the News

a Three major U.S. airlines indicated in August 2011 that air cargo shipments remained sluggish or had declined since May. While shipments with Delta Air Lines were little changed, those at American Airlines and United Air Lines fell for the fourth consecutive month, with the percentage of United's shipments falling by double digits each month.

b Air cargo shipments are viewed as an indicator of the future volume of passenger travel and also the state of the economy in general. Cargo accounts for less than 4 percent of sales at the nation's largest airlines, but trends in the cargo segment often precede similar trends in the passenger segment. With their extensive networks and large number of daily flights, airlines have attracted a vast array of cargo customers, so the decline in cargo reflects the lower volume of shipments occurring in a number of industries across the country. According to Robert Dye, the chief economist at Comerica, this "is yet another indicator among so many that suggests the economy continues to be weak and may be inching closer to recession." We can use the aggregate demand and aggregate supply model to analyze what happened to the U.S. economy during the 2007–2009 recession. The figure below shows that the economy during the fourth quarter of 2007 was in long-run equilibrium. Real GDP in 2005 dollars was $13.4 trillion, and the price level was 107.4. Declines in consumption and investment spending caused the aggregate demand curve to shift to the left, from $AD_{Q4,2007}$ to $AD_{Q1,2009}$. Meanwhile, aggregate supply also decreased, partly as a result of lower capital investment and increases in oil and commodity prices in 2008. The short-run aggregate supply curve shifts to the left, from $SRAS_{Q4,2007}$ to $SRAS_{Q1,2009}$, but the decline in aggregate supply is greater than the decline in aggregate demand. As a result, short-run real

GDP fell to $12.7 trillion in the first quarter of 2009, and the price level rose to 108.6. Since the end of the recession, the economy has improved slightly, but real GDP had grown to only $13.3 trillion by the second quarter of 2011, still less than it was at the beginning of the recession, and the price level had increased to 116.0.

c Because the trends in cargo shipments often indicate future trends in passenger air travel, airlines initiated plans to reduce passenger capacity for late 2011 and 2012. This is yet another indication of a fear that the economy may be slowing down and could be moving toward another recession.

Thinking Critically

1. Between the fourth quarter of 2007 and the first quarter of 2009, the U.S. unemployment rate rose from 4.8 percent to 8.5 percent. In the aggregate demand and aggregate supply graph shown, where would the long-run aggregate supply curve have been in 2009? Briefly explain.

2. For the second quarter of 2011, real GDP in 2005 dollars was $13.3 trillion and the price level was 116.0. Use an aggregate demand and aggregate supply graph to illustrate the changes from the first quarter of 2009 to the second quarter of 2011 and explain what happened to aggregate demand and aggregate supply to result in these changes.

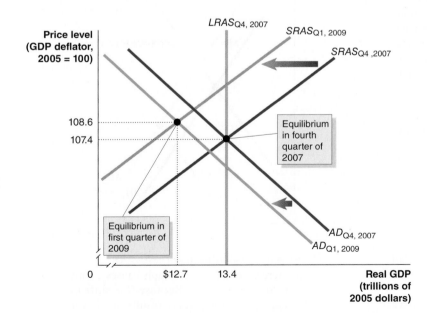

Real GDP declined between the fourth quarter of 2007 and the first quarter of 2009.

Chapter Summary and Problems

Key Terms

Aggregate demand and aggregate supply model, p. 420

Aggregate demand (AD) curve, p. 420

Fiscal policy, p. 422

Long-run aggregate supply (LRAS) curve, p. 428

Menu costs, p. 429

Monetary policy, p. 422

Short-run aggregate supply (SRAS) curve, p. 420

Stagflation, p. 436

Supply shock, p. 431

 13.1 **Aggregate Demand,** pages 420–427

LEARNING OBJECTIVE: Identify the determinants of aggregate demand and distinguish between a movement along the aggregate demand curve and a shift of the curve.

Summary

The **aggregate demand and aggregate supply model** enables us to explain short-run fluctuations in real GDP and price level. The **aggregate demand curve** shows the relationship between the price level and the level of planned aggregate expenditures by households, firms, and the government. The **short-run aggregate supply curve** shows the relationship in the short run between the price level and the quantity of real GDP supplied by firms. The **long-run aggregate supply curve** shows the relationship in the long run between the price level and the quantity of real GDP supplied. The four components of aggregate demand are consumption (C), investment (I), government purchases (G), and net exports (NX). The aggregate demand curve is downward sloping because a decline in the price level causes consumption, investment, and net exports to increase. If the price level changes but all else remains constant, the economy will move up or down a stationary aggregate demand curve. If any variable other than the price level changes, the aggregate demand curve will shift. The variables that cause the aggregate demand curve to shift are divided into three categories: changes in government policies, changes in the expectations of households and firms, and changes in foreign variables. For example, **monetary policy** involves the actions the Federal Reserve takes to manage the money supply and interest rates to pursue macroeconomic policy objectives. When the Federal Reserve takes actions to change interest rates, consumption and investment spending will change, shifting the aggregate demand curve. **Fiscal policy** involves changes in federal taxes and purchases that are intended to achieve macroeconomic policy objectives. Changes in federal taxes and purchases shift the aggregate demand curve.

MyEconLab Visit **www.myeconlab.com** to complete these exercises online and get instant feedback.

Review Questions

1.1 What relationship is shown by the aggregate demand curve? What relationship is shown by the aggregate supply curve?

1.2 Explain the three reasons the aggregate demand curve slopes downward.

1.3 What are the differences between the AD curve and the demand curve for an individual product, such as apples?

1.4 What variables cause the AD curve to shift? For each variable, identify whether an increase in that variable will cause the AD curve to shift to the right or to the left.

Problems and Applications

1.5 Explain how each of the following events would affect the aggregate demand curve.
   a. An increase in the price level
   b. An increase in government purchases
   c. Higher state income taxes
   d. Higher interest rates
   e. Faster income growth in other countries

1.6 [Related to the Don't Let This Happen to You **on page 423]** A student was asked to draw an aggregate demand and aggregate supply graph to illustrate the effect of an increase in aggregate supply. The student drew the following graph:

The student explains the graph as follows:

   An increase in aggregate supply causes a shift from $SRAS_1$ to $SRAS_2$. Because this shift in the aggregate supply curve results in a lower price level, consumption, investment, and net exports will increase. This change causes the aggregate demand curve to shift to the right, from AD_1 to AD_2. We know that real GDP will increase, but we can't be sure whether the price level will rise or fall because that depends on whether the aggregate supply curve or the aggregate demand curve has shifted farther to the right. I assume that aggregate supply shifts out farther than aggregate demand, so I show the final price level, P_3, as being lower than the initial price level, P_1.

Explain whether you agree with the student's analysis. Be careful to explain exactly what—if anything—you find wrong with this analysis.

1.7 [Related to Solved Problem 13.1 **on page 423**] Explain whether each of the following will cause a shift of the AD curve or a movement along the AD curve.
   a. Firms become more optimistic and increase their spending on machinery and equipment.
   b. The federal government increases taxes in an attempt to reduce a budget deficit.
   c. The U.S. economy experiences 4 percent inflation.

1.8 [Related to the Making the Connection **on page 426**] If real GDP in the United States declined by more during the 2007–2009 recession than did real GDP in Canada, China, and other trading partners of the United States, would the effect be to increase or decrease U.S. net exports? Briefly explain.

13.2 Aggregate Supply, pages 427–431

LEARNING OBJECTIVE: Identify the determinants of aggregate supply and distinguish between a movement along the short-run aggregate supply curve and a shift of the curve.

Summary

The **long-run aggregate supply curve** is a vertical line because in the long run, real GDP is always at its potential level and is unaffected by the price level. The short-run aggregate supply curve slopes upward because workers and firms fail to predict accurately the future price level. The three main explanations of why this failure results in an upward-sloping aggregate supply curve are that (1) contracts make wages and prices "sticky;" (2) businesses often adjust wages slowly; and (3) menu costs make some prices sticky. **Menu costs** are the costs to firms of changing prices on menus or in catalogs. If the price level changes but all else remains constant, the economy will move up or down a stationary aggregate supply curve. If any variable other than the price level changes, the aggregate supply curve will shift. The aggregate supply curve shifts as a result of increases in the labor force and capital stock, technological change, expected increases or decreases in the future price level, adjustments of workers and firms to errors in past expectations about the price level, and unexpected increases or decreases in the price of an important raw material. A **supply shock** is an unexpected event that causes the short-run aggregate supply curve to shift.

 MyEconLab   Visit **www.myeconlab.com** to complete these exercises online and get instant feedback.

Review Questions

2.1 Explain why the long-run aggregate supply curve is vertical.

2.2 What variables cause the long-run aggregate supply curve to shift? For each variable, identify whether an increase in that variable will cause the long-run aggregate supply curve to shift to the right or to the left.

2.3 Why does the short-run aggregate supply curve slope upward?

2.4 What variables cause the short-run aggregate supply curve to shift? For each variable, identify whether an increase in that variable will cause the short-run aggregate supply curve to shift to the right or to the left.

Problems and Applications

2.5 Explain how each of the following events would affect the long-run aggregate supply curve.
   a. A higher price level
   b. An increase in the labor force
   c. An increase in the quantity of capital goods
   d. Technological change

2.6 An article in the *Economist* magazine noted that "the economy's potential to supply goods and services [is] determined by such things as the labour force and capital stock, as well as inflation expectations." Do you agree with this list of the determinants of potential GDP? Briefly explain.
Based on "Money's Muddled Message," *Economist*, May 19, 2009.

2.7 Explain how each of the following events would affect the short-run aggregate supply curve.
   a. An increase in the price level
   b. An increase in what the price level is expected to be in the future
   c. A price level that is currently higher than expected
   d. An unexpected increase in the price of an important raw material
   e. An increase in the labor force participation rate

2.8 Suppose that workers and firms could always predict next year's price level with perfect accuracy. Briefly explain whether in these circumstances the *SRAS* curve would still slope upward.

2.9 Workers and firms often enter into contracts that fix prices or wages, sometimes for years at a time. If the price level turns out to be higher or lower than was expected when the contract was signed, one party to the contract will lose out. Briefly explain why, despite knowing this, workers and firms still sign long-term contracts.

2.10 What are menu costs? How has the widespread use of computers and the Internet affected menu costs? If menu costs were eliminated, would the short-run aggregate supply curve be a vertical line? Briefly explain.

13.3 Macroeconomic Equilibrium in the Long Run and the Short Run, pages 431–438

LEARNING OBJECTIVE: Use the aggregate demand and aggregate supply model to illustrate the difference between short-run and long-run macroeconomic equilibrium.

Summary

In long-run macroeconomic equilibrium, the aggregate demand and short-run aggregate supply curves intersect at a point *on* the long-run aggregate supply curve. In short-run macroeconomic equilibrium, the aggregate demand and short-run aggregate supply curves often intersect at a point *off* the long-run aggregate supply curve. An automatic mechanism drives the economy to long-run equilibrium. If short-run equilibrium occurs at a point below potential real GDP, wages and prices will fall, and the short-run aggregate supply curve will shift to the right until potential GDP is restored. If short-run equilibrium occurs at a point beyond potential real GDP, wages and prices will rise, and the short-run aggregate supply curve will shift to the left until potential GDP is restored. Real GDP can be temporarily above or below its potential level, either because of shifts in the aggregate demand curve or because supply shocks lead to shifts in the aggregate supply curve. **Stagflation** is a combination of inflation and recession, usually resulting from a supply shock.

MyEconLab   Visit www.myeconlab.com to complete these exercises online and get instant feedback.

Review Questions

3.1 What is the relationship among the *AD*, *SRAS*, and *LRAS* curves when the economy is in long-run macroeconomic equilibrium?

3.2 Why might a supply shock lead to stagflation?

3.3 Why are the long-run effects of an increase in aggregate demand on price and output different from the short-run effects?

Problems and Applications

3.4 Draw a basic aggregate demand and aggregate supply graph (with *LRAS* constant) that shows the economy in long-run equilibrium.

  a. Assume that there is a large increase in demand for U.S. exports. Show the resulting short-run equilibrium on your graph. In this short-run equilibrium, is the unemployment rate likely to be higher or lower than it was before the increase in exports? Briefly explain. Explain how the economy adjusts back to long-run equilibrium. When the economy has adjusted back to long-run equilibrium, how have the values of each of the following changed relative to what they were before the increase in exports:
   i   Real GDP
   ii   The price level
   iii The unemployment rate

  b. Assume that there is an unexpected increase in the price of oil. Show the resulting short-run equilibrium on your graph. Explain how the economy adjusts back to long-run equilibrium. In this short-run equilibrium, is the unemployment rate likely to be higher or lower than it was before the increase in the price of oil?

Briefly explain. When the economy has adjusted back to long-run equilibrium, how have the values of each of the following changed relative to what they were before the increase in the price of oil:
   i   Real GDP
   ii   The price level
   iii The unemployment rate

3.5 List four variables that would cause a decrease in real GDP (if large enough, a recession). Indicate whether changes in each variable increase or decrease aggregate demand or short-run aggregate supply. Next, state four variables that would cause an increase in the price level (short-run inflation). Indicate whether changes in the variable increase or decrease aggregate demand or short-run aggregate supply.

3.6 **[Related to the** Making the Connection **on page 434]** Edward Leamer of the University of California, Los Angeles, has argued that "housing *is* the business cycle." Why would spending on housing be likely to fluctuate more than spending by households on consumer durables, such as automobiles or furniture, or spending by firms on plant and equipment?

Based on Edward E. Leamer, "Housing Is the Business Cycle," *Housing, Housing Finance, and Monetary Policy*, Federal Reserve Bank of Kansas City, August 2007.

3.7 Consider the data in the following table for the years 1969 and 1970 (where the values for real GDP and potential GDP are in 2005 dollars):

Year	Actual Real GDP	Potential GDP	Unemployment Rate
1969	$4.26 trillion	$4.19 trillion	3.5%
1970	$4.27 trillion	$4.34 trillion	4.9%

Data from U.S. Bureau of Labor Statistics; and U.S. Bureau of Economic Analysis.

  a. In 1969, actual real GDP was greater than potential real GDP. Explain how this is possible.

  b. Even though real GDP in 1970 was slightly greater than real GDP in 1969, the unemployment rate increased substantially from 1969 to 1970. Why did this increase in unemployment occur?

  c. Was the inflation rate in 1970 likely to have been higher or lower than the inflation rate in 1969? Does your answer depend on whether the recession that began in December 1969 was caused by a change in a component of aggregate demand or by a supply shock?

3.8 Use the graph on the next page to answer the following questions:

  a. Which of the points *A*, *B*, *C*, or *D* can represent a long-run equilibrium?

  b. Suppose that initially the economy is at point *A*. If aggregate demand increases from AD_1 to AD_2, which point represents the economy's short-run equilibrium? Which point represents the eventual long-run equilibrium? Briefly explain how the economy adjusts from the short-run equilibrium to the long-run equilibrium.

3.9 [Related to the Making the Connection **on page 437**]
In early 2009, Christina Romer, who was then chair of the
Council of Economic Advisers, and Jared Bernstein, who was
then an economic adviser to Vice President Joseph Biden,

forecast how long they expected it would take for real GDP
to return to potential GDP, assuming that Congress passed
fiscal policy legislation proposed by President Obama:

It should be understood that all of the estimates presented in this memo are subject to
significant margins of error. There is the obvious uncertainty that comes from modeling
a hypothetical package rather than the final
legislation passed by the Congress. But, there is
the more fundamental uncertainty that comes
with any estimate of the effects of a program.
Our estimates of economic relationships . . .
are derived from historical experience and so
will not apply exactly in any given episode.
Furthermore, the uncertainty is surely higher
than normal now because the current recession is unusual both in its fundamental causes
and its severity.

Why would the causes of a recession and its severity affect
the accuracy of forecasts of when the economy would return to potential GDP?

From Christina Romer and Jared Bernstein, *The Job Impact of the
American Recovery and Reinvestment Plan*, January 9, 2009, p. 2.

13.4 | **A Dynamic Aggregate Demand and Aggregate Supply Model,** pages 438–443
LEARNING OBJECTIVE: Use the dynamic aggregate demand and aggregate supply model to analyze
macroeconomic conditions.

Summary

To make the aggregate demand and aggregate supply model
more realistic, we need to make it *dynamic* by incorporating
three facts that were left out of the basic model: (1) Potential
real GDP increases continually, shifting the long-run aggregate
supply curve to the right; (2) during most years, aggregate demand shifts to the right; and (3) except during periods when
workers and firms expect high rates of inflation, the aggregate
supply curve shifts to the right. The dynamic aggregate demand
and aggregate supply model allows us to analyze macroeconomic conditions, including the beginning of the 2007–2009
recession.

MyEconLab Visit **www.myeconlab.com** to complete these
exercises online and get instant feedback.

Review Questions

4.1 What are the key differences between the basic aggregate
demand and aggregate supply model and the dynamic aggregate demand and aggregate supply model?

4.2 In the dynamic aggregate demand and aggregate supply
model, what is the result of aggregate demand increasing
more quickly than potential real GDP? What is the result
of aggregate demand increasing more slowly than potential
real GDP?

4.3 Briefly discuss the factors that brought on the recession of
2007–2009.

Problems and Applications

4.4 Draw a dynamic aggregate demand and aggregate supply
graph showing the economy moving from potential GDP
in 2013 to potential GDP in 2014 , with no inflation. Your
graph should contain the *AD*, *SRAS*, and *LRAS* curves for
both 2013 and 2014 and should indicate the short-run
macroeconomic equilibrium for each year and the directions in which the curves have shifted. Identify what must
happen to have growth during 2014 without inflation.

4.5 [Related to Solved Problem 13.4 **on page 442**] Consider
the information in the following table for the first two
years of the Great Depression (where the values for real
GDP and potential GDP are in 2005 dollars):

Year	Actual Real GDP	Potential GDP	Price Level
1929	$977.0 billion	$977.7 billion	10.6
1930	$892.8 billion	$1,011.4 billion	10.2

Data from U.S. Bureau of Labor Statistics; and U.S. Bureau of Economic
Analysis.

a. The table shows that something happened during
1929–1930 that has not happened during the recessions
of the past 50 years. What is it?

b. Draw a dynamic aggregate demand and aggregate supply graph to illustrate what happened during these years.
Your graph should contain the *AD*, *SRAS*, and *LRAS*
curves for both 1929 and 1930 and should indicate the

short-run macroeconomic equilibrium for each year and the directions in which the curves shifted.

4.6 **[Related to** Solved Problem 13.4 **on page 442]** Look at the table in Solved Problem 13.4. The price level for 1974 is given as 30.7, and the price level for 1975 is given as 33.6. The values for the price level are well below 100. Does this indicate that inflation must have been low during these years? Briefly explain.

4.7 In the graph below, suppose that the economy moves from point *A* in year 1 to point *B* in year 2. Using the graph, briefly explain your answer to each of the questions.
   a. What is the growth rate in potential real GDP from year 1 to year 2?
   b. Is the unemployment rate in year 2 higher or lower than in year 1?
   c. What is the inflation rate in year 2?
   d. What is the growth rate of real GDP in year 2?

4.8 Explain whether you agree with the following statement:
   The dynamic aggregate demand and aggregate supply model predicts that a recession caused by a decline in *AD* will cause the inflation rate to fall. I know that the 2007–2009 recession was caused by a fall in *AD*, but the inflation rate was not lower as a result of the recession. The prices of most products were definitely higher in 2008 than they were in 2007, so the inflation rate could not have fallen.

4.9 In a speech in late 2011, President Barack Obama argued that: "Probably the single greatest cause of the financial crisis and this brutal recession has been the housing bubble that burst four years ago." What did President Obama mean by the "housing bubble"? How can a housing bubble bring on a recession?

   From Laura Meckler, "Obama Says Plan Will Cut Mortgage Payments for Millions," *Wall Street Journal*, October 24, 2011.

4.10 **[Related to the** Chapter Opener **on page 419]** An article in the *Wall Street Journal* in late 2011 notes that "FedEx Corp.'s forecast for record holiday shipping this year shows that U.S. customers are buying more things on-line. But retailers still anticipate a soft holiday season, with the growth in shipping volume largely expected to come from shoppers scouring the Web for cheap deals." What are the implications of this information for the usefulness of the "FedEx indicator" discussed in the chapter opener?

   Based on Bob Sechler and Jennifer Levitz, "More Boxes for FedEx," *Wall Street Journal*, October 25, 2011.

Appendix

Macroeconomic Schools of Thought

LEARNING OBJECTIVE

Understand macroeconomic schools of thought.

Macroeconomics became a separate field of economics in 1936, with the publication of John Maynard Keynes's book *The General Theory of Employment, Interest, and Money*. Keynes, an economist at the University of Cambridge in England, was attempting to explain the devastating Great Depression of the 1930s. As we discussed in Chapter 12, real GDP in the United States declined more than 25 percent between 1929 and 1933 and did not return to its potential level until the United States entered World War II in 1941. The unemployment rate soared to 25 percent by 1933 and did not return to its 1929 level until 1942. Keynes developed a version of the aggregate demand and aggregate supply model to explain these facts. The widespread acceptance during the 1930s and 1940s of Keynes's model became known as the **Keynesian revolution**.

In fact, using the aggregate demand and aggregate supply model remains the most widely accepted approach to analyzing macroeconomic issues. Because the model has been modified significantly from Keynes's day, many economists who use the model today refer to themselves as *new Keynesians*. The new Keynesians emphasize the importance of the stickiness of wages and prices in explaining fluctuations in real GDP. A significant number of economists, however, dispute whether using the aggregate demand and aggregate supply model, as we have discussed it in this chapter, is the best way to analyze macroeconomic issues. These alternative *schools of thought* use models that differ significantly from the standard aggregate demand and aggregate supply model. We can briefly consider each of the three major alternative models:

Keynesian revolution The name given to the widespread acceptance during the 1930s and 1940s of John Maynard Keynes's macroeconomic model.

1. The monetarist model

2. The new classical model

3. The real business cycle model

The Monetarist Model

The monetarist model—also known as the neo-Quantity Theory of Money model—was developed beginning in the 1940s by Milton Friedman, an economist at the University of Chicago who was awarded the Nobel Prize in Economics in 1976. Friedman argued that the Keynesian approach overstates the amount of macroeconomic instability in the economy. In particular, he argued that the economy will ordinarily be at potential real GDP. In the book *A Monetary History of the United States: 1867–1960*, written with Anna Jacobson Schwartz, Friedman argued that most fluctuations in real output were caused by fluctuations in the money supply rather than by fluctuations in consumption spending or investment spending. Friedman and Schwartz argued that the severity of the Great Depression was caused by the Federal Reserve's allowing the quantity of money in the economy to fall by more than 25 percent between 1929 and 1933.

In the United States, the Federal Reserve is responsible for managing the quantity of money. As we will discuss further in Chapter 15, the Federal Reserve has typically focused more on controlling interest rates than on controlling the money supply. Friedman has argued that the Federal Reserve should change its practices and adopt a **monetary growth rule**, which is a plan for increasing the quantity of money at a fixed rate. Friedman believed that adopting a monetary growth rule would reduce fluctuations in real GDP, employment, and inflation.

Friedman's ideas, which are referred to as **monetarism**, attracted significant support during the 1970s and early 1980s, when the economy experienced high rates of unemployment and inflation. The support for monetarism declined during the late 1980s and 1990s, when the unemployment and inflation rates were relatively low. In Chapter 14, we will discuss the *quantity theory of money*, which underlies the monetarist model.

Monetary growth rule A plan for increasing the quantity of money at a fixed rate that does not respond to changes in economic conditions.

Monetarism The macroeconomic theories of Milton Friedman and his followers, particularly the idea that the quantity of money should be increased at a constant rate.

The New Classical Model

The new classical model was developed in the mid-1970s by a group of economists including Nobel Laureate Robert Lucas of the University of Chicago, Nobel Laureate Thomas Sargent of New York University, and Robert Barro of Harvard University. Some of the views held by the new classical macroeconomists are similar to those held by economists before the Great Depression. Keynes referred to the economists before the Great Depression as "classical economists." Like the classical economists, the new classical macroeconomists believe that the economy normally will be at potential real GDP. They also believe that wages and prices adjust quickly to changes in demand and supply. Put another way, they believe the stickiness in wages and prices emphasized by the new Keynesians is unimportant.

Lucas argues that workers and firms have *rational expectations*, meaning that they form their expectations of the future values of economic variables, such as the inflation rate, by making use of all available information, including information on variables—such as changes in the quantity of money—that might affect aggregate demand. If the actual inflation rate is lower than the expected inflation rate, the actual real wage will be higher than the expected real wage. These higher real wages will lead to a recession because they will cause firms to hire fewer workers and cut back on production. As workers and firms adjust their expectations to the lower inflation rate, the real wage will decline, and employment and production will expand, bringing the economy out of recession. The ideas of Lucas and his followers are referred to as the **new classical macroeconomics**. Supporters of the new classical model agree with supporters of the monetarist model that the Federal Reserve should adopt a monetary growth rule. They argue that a monetary growth rule will make it easier for workers and firms to accurately forecast the price level, thereby reducing fluctuations in real GDP.

New classical macroeconomics The macroeconomic theories of Robert Lucas and others, particularly the idea that workers and firms have rational expectations.

The Real Business Cycle Model

Beginning in the 1980s, some economists, including Nobel Laureates Finn Kydland of Carnegie Mellon University and Edward Prescott of Arizona State University, began to argue that Lucas was correct in assuming that workers and firms formed their expectations rationally and that wages and prices adjust quickly to supply and demand but was wrong about the source of fluctuations in real GDP. They argue that fluctuations in real GDP are caused by temporary shocks to productivity. These shocks can be negative, such as a decline in the availability of oil or other raw materials, or positive, such as technological change that makes it possible to produce more output with the same quantity of inputs.

According to this school of thought, shifts in the aggregate demand curve have no impact on real GDP because the short-run aggregate supply curve is vertical. Other schools of thought believe that the short-run aggregate supply curve is upward sloping and that only the *long-run* aggregate supply curve is vertical. Fluctuations in real GDP occur when a negative productivity shock causes the short-run aggregate supply curve to shift to the left—reducing real GDP—or a positive productivity shock causes the short-run aggregate supply curve to shift to the right—increasing real GDP. Because this model focuses on "real" factors—productivity shocks—rather than changes in the quantity of money to explain fluctuations in real GDP, it is known as the **real business cycle model**.

Real business cycle model A macroeconomic model that focuses on real, rather than monetary, causes of the business cycle.

Making
the
Connection | **Karl Marx: Capitalism's Severest Critic**

The schools of macroeconomic thought we have discussed in this appendix are considered part of mainstream economic theory because of their acceptance of the market system as the best means of raising living standards in the long run. One quite influential critic of mainstream economic theory was Karl Marx. Marx was born in Trier, Germany, in 1818. After graduating from the University of Berlin in 1841, he began a career as a political journalist and agitator. His political activities caused him to be expelled first from Germany and then from France and Belgium. In 1849, he moved to London, where he spent the remainder of his life.

In 1867, Marx published the first volume of his greatest work, *Das Kapital*. Marx read closely the most prominent mainstream economists, including Adam Smith, David Ricardo, and John Stuart Mill. But Marx believed that he understood how market systems would evolve in the long run much better than those earlier authors. Marx argued that the market system would eventually be replaced by a Communist economy, in which the workers would control production. He believed in the *labor theory of value*, which attributed all of the value of a good or service to the labor embodied in it. According to Marx, the owners of businesses—capitalists—did not earn profits by contributing anything of value to the production of goods or services. Instead, capitalists earned profits because their "monopoly of the means of production"—their ownership of factories and machinery—allowed them to exploit workers by paying them wages that were much lower than the value of workers' contribution to production.

Marx argued that the wages of workers would be driven to levels that allowed only bare survival. He also argued that small firms would eventually be driven out of business by larger firms, forcing owners of small firms into the working class. Control of production would ultimately be concentrated in the hands of a few firms, which would have difficulty selling the goods they produced to the impoverished masses. A final economic crisis would lead the working classes to rise up, seize control of the economy, and establish Communism. Marx died in 1883, without having provided a detailed explanation of how the Communist economy would operate.

Marx had relatively little influence on mainstream thinking in the United States, but several political parties in Europe were guided by his ideas. In 1917, the Bolshevik party seized control of Russia and established the Soviet Union, the first Communist state. Although the Soviet Union was a vicious dictatorship under Vladimir Lenin and his successor, Joseph Stalin, its prestige rose when it avoided the macroeconomic difficulties that plagued the market economies during the 1930s. By the late 1940s, Communist parties had also come to power in China and the countries of Eastern Europe. Poor economic performance contributed to the eventual collapse of the Soviet Union and its replacement by a market system, although one in which government intervention is still widespread. The Communist Party remains in power in China, but the economy is evolving toward a market system. Today, only North Korea and Cuba have economies that claim to be based on the ideas of Karl Marx.

Karl Marx predicted that a final economic crisis would lead to the collapse of the market system.

Key Terms

Keynesian revolution, p. 451

Monetarism, p. 451

Monetary growth rule, p. 451

New classical macroeconomics, p. 452

Real business cycle model, p. 452

Money, Banks, and the Federal Reserve System

Chapter Outline and Learning Objectives

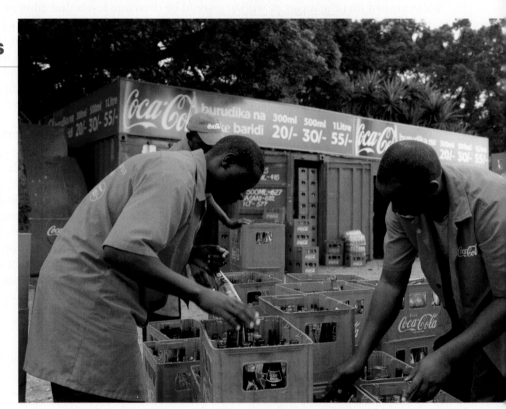

Coca-Cola Dries Up as Money Floods Zimbabwe

People in Africa buy 36 billion bottles of Coca-Cola a year. In 2008, Zimbabwe, a country in southern Africa, ran out of locally produced Coke for the first time in at least 40 years. Because they could not obtain U.S. dollars, local Coke bottlers were not able to import from the United States the concentrated syrup used to make the soft drink. A meager amount of Coke was imported from South Africa, but a single bottle sold for around 15 billion Zimbabwean dollars! Zimbabwe was suffering the effects of an inflation rate so high that it is called a *hyperinflation*. Zimbabwe's hyperinflation was of epic proportions, perhaps the worst in world history. When it was first introduced in 1980, 1 Zimbabwean dollar was worth 1.47 U.S. dollars. By the end of 2008, the exchange rate was 1 U.S. dollar to 2 *billion* Zimbabwean dollars, and prices for some large transactions in Zimbabwe were calculated in quadrillions (15 zeros) and quintillions (18 zeros).

In addition to the Coke shortage, Zimbabweans were suffering shortages of fuel, food, and other basic goods. As the value of the Zimbabwean currency fell against other currencies, it was difficult for local businesses such as the Coke bottlers to find anyone willing to exchange U.S. dollars for Zimbabwean dollars. What made Zimbabwe's currency almost worthless? The government of Zimbabwe had decided to pay for all of its expenses by printing more and more money. The faster the government printed money, the faster prices rose. Eventually, both foreigners and local residents refused to accept the Zimbabwean dollar in exchange for goods and services, and the country's economy plunged into a devastating recession, with real GDP falling more than 12 percent during 2008. In early 2009, the government issued 100 trillion dollar bills, not enough for a bus ticket in Harare, Zimbabwe's capital city. Eventually, in 2009, a new Zimbabwean government took the drastic step of abandoning its own currency and making the U.S. dollar the country's official currency.

AN INSIDE LOOK AT POLICY on **page 482** discusses how banks in 2011 increased their loans to both consumers and businesses and how that affected the recovery from the recession of 2007–2009.

Based on Angus Shaw, "Coca Cola Dries Up in Zimbabwe," newzimbabwe.com, December 1, 2008; Patrick McGroarty and Farai Mutsaka, "How to Turn 100 Trillion Dollars into Five and Feel Good About It," *Wall Street Journal*, May 11, 2011; Marcus Walker and Andrew Higgins, "Zimbabwe Can't Paper Over Its Million-Percent Inflation Anymore," *Wall Street Journal*, July 2, 2008; and "Wait and See," *Economist*, February 5, 2009.

Economics in Your Life

What if Money Became Increasingly Valuable?

Most people are used to the fact that as prices rise each year, the purchasing power of money falls. You will be able to buy fewer goods and services with $1,000 one year from now than you can buy today, and you will be able to buy even fewer goods and services the year after that. In fact, with an inflation rate of just 3 percent, in 25 years, $1,000 will buy only what $475 can buy today. Suppose, though, that you could live in an economy where the purchasing power of money rose each year? What would be the advantages and disadvantages of living in such an economy? As you read the chapter, see if you can answer these questions. You can check your answers against those we provide on **page 480** at the end of this chapter.

In this chapter, we will explore the role of money in the economy. We will see how the banking system creates money and what policy tools the Federal Reserve uses to manage the quantity of money. We will also look at the crisis in the banking system during the past few years. At the end of the chapter, we will explore the link between changes in the quantity of money and changes in the price level. What you learn in this chapter will serve as an important foundation for understanding monetary policy and fiscal policy, which we study in the next three chapters.

14.1 LEARNING OBJECTIVE

Define money and discuss the four functions of money.

Money Assets that people are generally willing to accept in exchange for goods and services or for payment of debts.

Asset Anything of value owned by a person or a firm.

What Is Money, and Why Do We Need It?

Could an economy function without money? We know the answer to this question is "yes" because there are many historical examples of economies in which people traded goods for other goods rather than using money. For example, a farmer on the American frontier during colonial times might have traded a cow for a plow. Most economies, though, use money. What is money? The economic definition of **money** is any asset that people are generally willing to accept in exchange for goods and services or for payment of debts. Recall from Chapter 6 that an **asset** is anything of value owned by a person or a firm. There are many possible kinds of money: In West Africa, at one time, cowrie shells served as money. During World War II, prisoners of war used cigarettes as money.

Barter and the Invention of Money

To understand the importance of money, let's consider further the situation in economies that do not use money. These economies, where goods and services are traded directly for other goods and services, are called *barter economies*. Barter economies have a major shortcoming. To illustrate this shortcoming, consider a farmer on the American frontier in colonial days. Suppose the farmer needed another cow and proposed trading a spare plow to a neighbor for one of the neighbor's cows. If the neighbor did not want the plow, the trade would not happen. For a barter trade to take place between two people, each person must want what the other one has. Economists refer to this requirement as a *double coincidence of wants*. The farmer who wants the cow might eventually be able to obtain one if he first trades with some other neighbor for something the neighbor with the cow wants. However, it may take several trades before the farmer is ultimately able to trade for what the neighbor with the cow wants. Locating several trading partners and making several intermediate trades can take considerable time and energy.

The problems with barter give societies an incentive to identify a product that most people will accept in exchange for what they have to trade. For example, in colonial times, animal skins were very useful in making clothing. The first governor of Tennessee actually received a salary of 1,000 deerskins per year, and the secretary of the Treasury received 450 otter skins per year. A good used as money that also has value independent of its use as money is called a **commodity money**. Historically, once a good became widely accepted as money, people who did not have an immediate use for it would be willing to accept it. A colonial farmer—or the governor of Tennessee—might not want a deerskin, but as long as he knew he could use the deerskin to buy other goods and services, he would be willing to accept it in exchange for what he had to sell.

Commodity money A good used as money that also has value independent of its use as money.

Trading goods and services is much easier when money becomes available. People only need to sell what they have for money and then use the money to buy what they want. If the colonial family could find someone to buy their plow, they could use the money to buy the cow they wanted. The family with the cow would accept the money because they knew they could use it to buy what they wanted. When money is available, families are less likely to produce everything or nearly everything they need themselves and more likely to specialize.

Most people in modern economies are highly specialized. They do only one thing—work as a nurse, an accountant, or an engineer—and use the money they earn to buy everything else they need. As we discussed in Chapter 2, people become much more productive by specializing because they can pursue their *comparative advantage*. The high income levels in modern economies are based on the specialization that money makes possible. We can now answer the question, "Why do we need money?" *By making exchange easier, money allows people to specialize and become more productive.*

The Functions of Money

Anything used as money—whether a deerskin, a cowrie seashell, cigarettes, or a dollar bill—should fulfill the following four functions:

- Medium of exchange

- Unit of account

- Store of value

- Standard of deferred payment

Medium of Exchange   Money serves as a medium of exchange when sellers are willing to accept it in exchange for goods or services. When the local supermarket accepts your $5 bill in exchange for bread and milk, the $5 bill is serving as a medium of exchange. With a medium of exchange, people can sell goods and services for money and use the money to buy what they want. An economy is more efficient when a single good is recognized as a medium of exchange.

Unit of Account   In a barter system, each good has many prices. A cow may be worth two plows, 20 bushels of wheat, or six axes. Once a single good is used as money, each good has a single price rather than many prices. This function of money gives buyers and sellers a *unit of account*, a way of measuring value in the economy in terms of money. Because the U.S. economy uses dollars as money, each good has a price in terms of dollars.

Store of Value   Money allows value to be stored easily: If you do not use all your dollars to buy goods and services today, you can hold the rest to use in the future. Money is not the only store of value, however. Any asset—shares of Coca-Cola stock, Treasury bonds, real estate, or Renoir paintings, for example—represents a store of value. Financial assets, such as stocks and bonds, offer an important benefit relative to holding money because they pay a higher rate of interest or may increase in value in the future. Other assets also have advantages relative to money because they provide services. A house, for example, offers you a place to sleep.

Why, then, do people hold any money? The answer has to do with *liquidity*, or the ease with which an asset can be converted into the medium of exchange. Because money is the medium of exchange, it is the most liquid asset. If you want to buy something and you need to sell an asset to do so, you are likely to incur a cost. For example, if you want to buy a car and need to sell bonds or stocks in order to do so, you will need to pay a commission to your broker. To avoid such costs, people are willing to hold some of their wealth in the form of money, even though other assets offer a greater return as a store of value.

Standard of Deferred Payment   Money is useful because it can serve as a standard of deferred payment in borrowing and lending. Money can facilitate exchange at a *given point in time* by providing a medium of exchange and unit of account. Money can facilitate exchange *over time* by providing a store of value and a standard of deferred payment. For example, a computer manufacturer may buy hard drives from another firm in exchange for the promise of making payment in 60 days.

How important is it that money be a reliable store of value and standard of deferred payment? People care about how much food, clothing, and other goods and services their dollars will buy. The value of money depends on its purchasing power, which refers to its ability to buy goods and services. Inflation causes a decline in purchasing power because with rising prices, a given amount of money can purchase fewer goods and services. When inflation reaches the levels seen in Zimbabwe, money is no longer a reliable store of value or standard of deferred payment.

What Can Serve as Money?

Having a medium of exchange helps to make transactions easier, allowing the economy to work more efficiently. The next logical question is this: What can serve as money? That is, which assets should be used as the medium of exchange? We saw earlier that an asset must, at a minimum, be generally accepted as payment to serve as money. In practical terms, however, it must be even more.

Five criteria make a good suitable for use as a medium of exchange:

1. The good must be *acceptable* to (that is, usable by) most people.
2. It should be of *standardized quality* so that any two units are identical.
3. It should be *durable* so that value is not lost by spoilage.
4. It should be *valuable* relative to its weight so that amounts large enough to be useful in trade can be easily transported.
5. The medium of exchange should be *divisible* because different goods are valued differently.

Dollar bills meet all these criteria. What determines the acceptability of dollar bills as a medium of exchange? Basically, it is through self-fulfilling expectations: You value something as money only if you believe that others will accept it from you as payment. A society's willingness to use paper dollars as money makes dollars an acceptable medium of exchange.

Commodity Money Commodity money has value independent of its use as money. Gold, for example, was a common form of money in the nineteenth century because it was a medium of exchange, a unit of account, a store of value, and a standard of deferred payment. But commodity money has a significant problem: Its value depends on its purity. Therefore, someone who wanted to cheat could mix impure metals with a precious metal. Another problem with using gold as money was that the money supply was difficult to control because it depended partly on unpredictable discoveries of new gold fields.

Federal Reserve The central bank of the United States.

Fiat money Money, such as paper currency, that is authorized by a central bank or governmental body and that does not have to be exchanged by the central bank for gold or some other commodity money.

Fiat Money It can be inefficient for an economy to rely on only gold or other precious metals for its money supply. What if you had to transport bars of gold to settle your transactions? Not only would doing so be difficult and costly, but you would run the risk of being robbed. To get around this problem, private institutions or governments began to store gold and issue paper certificates that could be redeemed for gold. In modern economies, paper currency is generally issued by a *central bank*, which is an agency of the government that regulates the money supply. The **Federal Reserve** is the central bank of the United States. Today, no government in the world issues paper currency that can be redeemed for gold. Paper currency has no value unless it is used as money, and it is therefore not a commodity money. Instead, paper currency is a **fiat money**, which has no value except as money. If paper currency has no value except as money, why do consumers and firms use it?

If you look at the top of a U.S. dollar bill, you will see that it is actually a *Federal Reserve Note*, issued by the Federal Reserve. Because U.S. dollars are fiat money, the Federal Reserve is not required to give you gold or silver for your dollar bills. Federal Reserve currency is *legal tender* in the United States, which means the federal government requires that it be accepted in payment of debts and requires that cash or checks denominated in dollars be used in payment of taxes. Despite being legal tender, dollar bills would not be a good medium of exchange and could not serve as money if they weren't widely accepted by people. The key to this acceptance is that *households and firms have confidence that if they accept paper dollars in exchange for goods and services, the dollars will not lose much value during the time they hold them.* Without this confidence, dollar bills would not serve as a medium of exchange.

Making the Connection

Apple Didn't Want My Cash!

If Federal Reserve Notes are legal tender, doesn't that mean that everyone in the United States, including every business, has to accept paper money? The answer to this question is "no," as a woman in California found out when she went to an Apple store in Palo Alto and tried to buy an iPad using $600 in currency. At that point, the iPad had just been released, and Apple did not want to sell large numbers to people who were buying them to resell on eBay, Craigslist, or elsewhere. So, a customer wanting to buy an iPad had to pay either with a credit card or a debit card, which would make it easier for Apple to keep track of anyone attempting to buy more than the limit of two per customer.

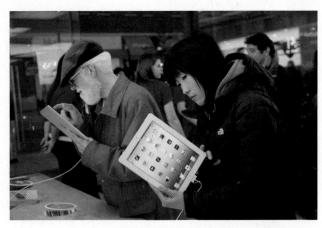

The law doesn't require Apple to accept paper money from these customers.

Because Federal Reserve Notes are legal tender, creditors must accept them in payment of debts, and the government will accept them in payment of taxes. However, as this incident makes clear, firms do not have to accept cash as payment for goods and services. As the U.S. Treasury Department explains on its Web site:

> There is . . . no Federal statute mandating that a private business, a person or an organization must accept currency or coins as payment for goods and/or services. . . . For example, a bus line may prohibit payment of fares in pennies or dollar bills. In addition, movie theaters, convenience stores and gas stations may refuse to accept large denomination currency (usually notes above $20) as a matter of policy.

The woman who tried to buy an iPad for cash was disabled and on a limited income, so the incident led to bad publicity for Apple. As a result, Apple decided to lift its ban on paying for iPads with cash, provided that the customer was willing to set up an Apple account at the time of purchase. In addition, Apple presented a free iPad to the customer who was originally turned down when she tried to pay with cash.

Based on Michael Winter, "Apple Ends No-Cash Policy and California Woman Gets Free iPad," www.usatoday.com, May 20, 2010; and U.S. Treasury, "FAQs: Currency," http://www.treasury.gov/resource-center/faqs/Currency/Pages/edu_faq_currency_index2.aspx.

Your Turn: Test your understanding by doing related problem 1.9 on page 485 at the end of this chapter.

MyEconLab

How Is Money Measured in the United States Today?

14.2 LEARNING OBJECTIVE

Discuss the definitions of the money supply used in the United States today.

A narrow definition of money would include only those assets that obviously function as a medium of exchange: currency, checking account deposits, and traveler's checks. These assets can easily be used to buy goods and services and thus act as a medium of exchange. This strict interpretation is too narrow, however, as a measure of the money supply in the real world. Many other assets can fill the role of a medium of exchange, although they are not as liquid as checking account deposits or cash. For example, you can convert your savings account at a bank to cash.

In the United States, the Federal Reserve has conducted several studies of the appropriate definition of *money*. The job of defining the money supply has become more difficult during the past two decades, as innovation in financial markets and institutions has created new substitutes for traditional checking accounts. Outside the United States, other central banks use similar measures. Next, we will look more closely at the Fed's definitions of the money supply.

M1 The narrowest definition of the money supply: The sum of currency in circulation, checking account deposits in banks, and holdings of traveler's checks.

M1: The Narrowest Definition of the Money Supply

Figure 14.1 illustrates the definitions of the money supply. The narrowest definition is called **M1**. It includes:

1. *Currency*, which is all the paper money and coins that are in circulation, where "in circulation" means not held by banks or the government
2. The value of all checking account deposits at banks
3. The value of traveler's checks (Because this last category is so small—about $4.4 billion in August 2011—relative to the other two categories, we will ignore it in our discussion of the money supply.)

Although currency has a larger value than checking account deposits, checking account deposits are used much more often than currency to make payments. More than 80 percent of all expenditures on goods and services are made with checks rather than with currency. In fact, the total amount of currency in circulation—$977 billion in August 2011—is a misleading number. This amount is more than $2,800 per person—adult or child—in the United States. If this sounds like an unrealistically large amount of currency to be held per person, it is. Economists estimate that more than 60 percent of U.S. currency is actually outside the borders of the United States.

Who holds these dollars outside the United States? Foreign banks and foreign governments hold some dollars, but most are held by households and firms in countries where there is not much confidence in the local currency. When inflation rates are very high, many households and firms do not want to hold their domestic currency because it is losing its value too rapidly. The value of the U.S. dollar will be much more stable than their domestic currency. If enough people are willing to accept dollars as well as—or instead of—domestic currency, dollars become a second currency for the country. As we saw in the chapter opener, when inflation soared in Zimbabwe, the government was led to adopt the U.S. dollar as the country's official currency.

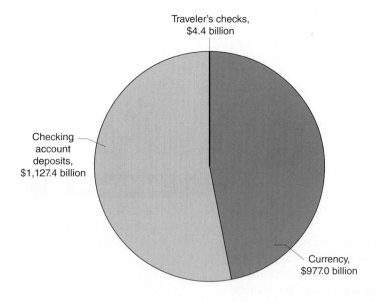

(a) M1 = $2,108.8 billion

(b) M2 = $9,544.9 billion

Figure 14.1   **Measuring the Money Supply, August 2011**

The Federal Reserve uses two different measures of the money supply: M1 and M2. M2 includes all the assets in M1, as well as the additional assets shown in panel (b).

Data from Board of Governors of the Federal Reserve System, "Federal Reserve Statistical Release, H6," September 29, 2011.

Making the Connection	## Do We Still Need the Penny?

We have seen that fiat money has no value except as money. Governments actually make a profit from issuing fiat money because fiat money is usually produced using paper or low-value metals that cost far less than the face value of the money. For example, it costs only about 4 cents for the federal Bureau of Engraving and Printing to manufacture a $20 bill. The government's profit from issuing fiat money—which is equal to the difference between the face value of the money and its production cost—is called *seigniorage*.

With small-denomination coins—like pennies or nickels—there is a possibility that the coins will cost more to produce than their face value. This was true in the early 1980s, when the rising price of copper meant the federal government was spending more than 1 cent to produce a penny. That led the government to switch from making pennies from copper to making them from zinc. Unfortunately, by 2007, the rising price of zinc meant that once again, the penny cost more than 1 cent to produce. Although the price of zinc later declined, many economists began to ask whether the penny should simply be abolished. Not only does it sometimes cost more to produce than it is worth, but inflation has eroded its purchasing power to such an extent that some people just find the penny to be a nuisance. Many people will not bother to pick up a penny from the sidewalk. In fact, several other countries, including Great Britain, Australia, and the European countries that use the euro, have eliminated their lowest-denomination coins; Canada is also considering doing so.

Some economists, though, have argued that eliminating the penny would subject consumers to a "rounding tax." For example, a good that had been priced at $2.99 will cost $3.00 if the penny is eliminated. Some estimates have put the cost to consumers of the rounding tax as high as $600 million. But Robert Whaples, an economist at Wake Forest University, after analyzing almost 200,000 transactions from a convenience store chain, concludes that "the 'rounding tax' is a myth. In reality, the number of times consumers' bills would be rounded upward is almost exactly equal to the number of times they would be rounded downward."

François Velde, an economist at the Federal Reserve Bank of Chicago, has come up with perhaps the most ingenious solution to the problem of the penny: The federal government would simply declare that Lincoln pennies are now worth 5 cents. There would then be two 5-cent coins in circulation—the current Jefferson nickels and the current Lincoln pennies—and no 1-cent coins. In the future, only the Lincoln coins—now worth 5 cents—would be minted. This would solve the problem of consumers and retail stores having to deal with pennies, it would make the face value of the Lincoln 5-cent coin greater than its cost of production, and it would also deal with the problem that the current Jefferson nickel frequently costs more than 5 cents to produce. But will Lincoln pennies actually be accepted as being worth 5 cents simply because the government says so? The answer is "yes" because as long as the government is willing to exchange 20 Lincoln coins for a paper dollar, everyone else will be willing to do so as well. Of course, if this plan were adopted, anyone with a hoard of pennies would find that their money would be worth five times as much overnight!

Whether or not pennies get turned into nickels, it seems very likely that one way or another, the penny will eventually disappear from the U.S. money supply.

Unfortunately, these cost the government more than a penny to produce.

Based on Robert Whaples, "Why Keeping the Penny No Longer Makes Sense," *USA Today*, July 12, 2006; Austan Goolsbee, "Now That a Penny Isn't Worth Much, It's Time to Make It Worth 5 Cents," *New York Times*, February 1, 2007; François Velde, "What's a Penny (or a Nickel) Really Worth?" Federal Reserve Bank of Chicago, Chicago Fed Letter, No. 235a, February 2007; and Nicholas Kohler, "A Penny Dropped," macleans.ca, January 14, 2011.

Your Turn: Test your understanding by doing related problems 2.10 and 2.11 on page 485 at the end of this chapter.　　MyEconLab

M2: A Broader Definition of Money

Before 1980, U.S. law prohibited banks from paying interest on checking account deposits. Households and firms held checking account deposits primarily to buy goods and services. M1 was, therefore, very close to the function of money as a medium of exchange. Almost all currency, checking account deposits, and traveler's checks were held with the intention of buying and selling, not with the intention of storing value. In 1980, the law was changed to allow banks to pay interest on certain types of checking accounts. This change reduced the difference between checking accounts and savings accounts, although people are still not allowed to write checks against their savings account balances.

M2 A broader definition of the money supply: It includes M1 plus savings account balances, small-denomination time deposits, balances in money market deposit accounts in banks, and noninstitutional money market fund shares.

After 1980, economists began to pay closer attention to a broader definition of the money supply, **M2**. As panel (b) of Figure 14.1 shows, M2 includes everything that is in M1, plus savings account deposits, small-denomination time deposits—such as certificates of deposit (CDs)—balances in money market deposit accounts in banks, and noninstitutional money market fund shares. Small-denomination time deposits are similar to savings accounts, but the deposits are for a fixed period of time—usually from six months to several years—and withdrawals before that time are subject to a penalty. Mutual fund companies sell shares to investors and use the funds raised to buy financial assets such as stocks and bonds. Some of these mutual funds, such as Vanguard's Treasury Money Market Fund or Fidelity's Cash Reserves Fund, are called *money market mutual funds* because they invest in very short-term bonds, such as U.S. Treasury bills. The balances in these funds are included in M2. Each week, the Federal Reserve publishes statistics on M1 and M2. In the discussion that follows, we will use the M1 definition of the money supply because it corresponds most closely to money as a medium of exchange.

There are two key points to keep in mind about the money supply:

1. The money supply consists of *both* currency and checking account deposits.

2. Because balances in checking account deposits are included in the money supply, banks play an important role in the way the money supply increases and decreases. We will discuss this second point further in the next section.

Don't Let This Happen to You

Don't Confuse Money with Income or Wealth

According to *Forbes* magazine, Bill Gates's wealth of $56 billion makes him the second-richest person in the world. He also has a very large income, but how much money does he have? Your *wealth* is equal to the value of your assets minus the value of any debts you have. Your *income* is equal to your earnings during the year. Bill Gates's earnings as chairman of Microsoft and from his investments are very large. But his *money* is just equal to what he has in currency and in checking accounts. Only a small proportion of Gates's $56 billion in wealth is likely to be in currency or checking accounts. Most of his wealth is invested in stocks and bonds and other financial assets that are not included in the definition of money.

In everyday conversation, we often describe someone who is wealthy or who has a high income as "having a lot of money." But when economists use the word *money*, they are usually referring to currency plus checking account deposits. It is important to keep straight the differences between wealth, income, and money.

Just as money and income are not the same for a person, they are not the same for the whole economy. National income in the United States was equal to $12.8 trillion in 2010. The money supply in 2010 was $1.8 trillion (using the M1 measure). There is no reason national income in a country should be equal to the country's money supply, nor will an increase in a country's money supply necessarily increase the country's national income.

Based on "The World's Billionaires," *Forbes*, March 19, 2011.

MyEconLab

Your Turn: Test your understanding by doing related problems 2.7 and 2.8 on page 485 at the end of this chapter.

Solved Problem 14.2

The Definitions of M1 and M2

Suppose you decide to withdraw $2,000 from your checking account and use the money to buy a bank certificate of deposit (CD). Briefly explain how this will affect M1 and M2.

Solving the Problem

Step 1: **Review the chapter material.** This problem is about the definitions of the money supply, so you may want to review the section "How Is Money Measured in the United States Today?" which begins on page 459.

Step 2: **Use the definitions of M1 and M2 to answer the problem.** Funds in checking accounts are included in both M1 and M2. Funds in CDs are included only in M2. It is tempting to answer this problem by saying that shifting $2,000 from a checking account to a CD reduces M1 by $2,000 and increases M2 by $2,000, but the $2,000 in your checking account was already counted in M2. So, the correct answer is that your action reduces M1 by $2,000 but leaves M2 unchanged.

Your Turn: For more practice, do related problems 2.5 and 2.6 on page 485 at the end of this chapter. MyEconLab

What about Credit Cards and Debit Cards?

Many people buy goods and services with credit cards, yet credit cards are not included in definitions of the money supply. The reason is that when you buy something with a credit card, you are in effect taking out a loan from the bank that issued the credit card. Only when you pay your credit card bill at the end of the month—often with a check or an electronic transfer from your checking account—is the transaction complete. In contrast, with a debit card, the funds to make the purchase are taken directly from your checking account. In either case, the cards themselves do not represent money.

How Do Banks Create Money?

14.3 LEARNING OBJECTIVE

Explain how banks create money.

We have seen that the most important component of the money supply is checking accounts in banks. To understand the role money plays in the economy, we need to look more closely at how banks operate. Banks are profit-making private businesses, just like bookstores and supermarkets. Some banks are quite small, with just a few branches, and they do business in a limited area. Others are among the largest corporations in the United States, with hundreds of branches spread across many states. The key role that banks play in the economy is to accept deposits and make loans. By doing this, they create checking account deposits.

Bank Balance Sheets

To understand how banks create money, we need to briefly examine a typical bank balance sheet. Recall from Chapter 6 that on a balance sheet, a firm's assets are listed on the left, and its liabilities and stockholders' equity are listed on the right. Assets are the value of anything owned by the firm, liabilities are the value of anything the firm owes, and stockholders' equity is the difference between the total value of assets and the total value of liabilities. Stockholders' equity represents the value of the firm if it had to be closed, all its assets were sold, and all its liabilities were paid off. A corporation's stockholders' equity is also referred to as its *net worth*.

Figure 14.2 shows the actual balance sheet of a large bank. The key assets on a bank's balance sheet are its *reserves*, loans, and holdings of securities, such as U.S. Treasury bills.

Figure 14.2

Balance Sheet for a Large Bank, December 31, 2010

The items on a bank's balance sheet of greatest economic importance are its reserves, loans, and deposits. Notice that the difference between the value of this bank's total assets and its total liabilities is equal to its stockholders' equity. As a consequence, the left side of the balance sheet always equals the right side.

Note: Some entries have been combined to simplify the balance sheet.

Assets (in millions)		Liabilities and Stockholders' Equity (in millions)	
Reserves	$108,427	Deposits	$1,010,430
Loans	898,555	Short-term borrowing	394,572
Securities	896,097	Long-term debt	359,180
Buildings and equipment	14,306	Other liabilities	272,479
Other assets	347,524	Total liabilities	$2,036,661
		Stockholders' equity	228,248
Total assets	$2,264,909	Total liabilities and stockholders' equity	$2,264,909

Reserves Deposits that a bank keeps as cash in its vault or on deposit with the Federal Reserve.

Required reserves Reserves that a bank is legally required to hold, based on its checking account deposits.

Required reserve ratio The minimum fraction of deposits banks are required by law to keep as reserves.

Excess reserves Reserves that banks hold over and above the legal requirement.

Reserves are deposits that a bank has retained rather than loaned out or invested. Banks keep reserves either physically within the bank, as *vault cash*, or on deposit with the Federal Reserve. Banks are required by law to keep as reserves 10 percent of their checking account deposits above a threshold level, which in 2011 was $58.8 million. These reserves are called **required reserves**. The minimum fraction of deposits that banks are required to keep as reserves is called the **required reserve ratio**. We can abbreviate the required reserve ratio as *RR*. Any reserves that banks hold over and above the legal requirement are called **excess reserves**. The balance sheet in Figure 14.2 shows that loans are this bank's largest asset, which is true of most banks.

Banks make *consumer loans* to households and *commercial loans* to businesses. A loan is an asset to a bank because it represents a promise by the person taking out the loan to make certain specified payments to the bank. A bank's reserves and its holdings of securities are also assets because they are things of value owned by the bank.

As with most banks, this bank's largest liability is its deposits. Deposits include checking accounts, savings accounts, and certificates of deposit. Deposits are liabilities to banks because they are owed to the households or firms that have deposited the funds. If you deposit $100 in your checking account, the bank owes you the $100, and you can ask for it back at any time. So, your checking account is an asset to you, and it is a liability to the bank.

Using T-Accounts to Show How a Bank Can Create Money

It is easier to show how banks create money by using a T-account than by using a balance sheet. A T-account is a stripped-down version of a balance sheet that shows only how a transaction *changes* a bank's balance sheet. For example, suppose you deposit $1,000 in currency into an account at Bank of America. This transaction raises the total deposits at Bank of America by $1,000 and also raises its reserves by $1,000. We show this on the following T-account:

Assets		**Liabilities**	
Reserves	+$1,000	Deposits	+$1,000

Your deposit of $1,000 into your checking account increases Bank of America's assets and liabilities by the same amount.

Remember that because the total value of all the entries on the right side of a balance sheet must always be equal to the total value of all the entries on the left side of a balance sheet, any transaction that increases (or decreases) one side of the balance sheet must also increase (or decrease) the other side of the balance sheet. In this case, the T-account shows that we increased both sides of the balance sheet by $1,000.

Initially, this transaction does not increase the money supply. The currency component of the money supply declines by $1,000 because the $1,000 you deposited is no longer in circulation and, therefore, is not counted in the money supply. But the decrease in currency is offset by a $1,000 increase in the checking account deposit component of the money supply.

This initial change is not the end of the story, however. Banks are required to keep 10 percent of deposits as reserves. Because the Federal Reserve pays banks only a low rate of interest on their reserves, banks have an incentive to loan out or buy securities with the other 90 percent. In this case, Bank of America can keep $100 as required reserves and loan out the other $900, which represents excess reserves. Suppose Bank of America loans out the $900 to someone to buy a very inexpensive used car. Bank of America could give the $900 to the borrower in currency, but usually banks make loans by increasing the borrower's checking account. We can show this with another T-account:

Assets		Liabilities	
Reserves	+$1,000	Deposits	+$1,000
Loans	+$900	Deposits	+$900

1. By loaning out $900 in excess reserves . . .

2. . . . Bank of America has increased the money supply by $900.

A key point to recognize is that *by making this $900 loan, Bank of America has increased the money supply by $900.* The initial $1,000 in currency you deposited into your checking account has been turned into $1,900 in checking account deposits—a net increase in the money supply of $900.

But the story does not end here. The person who took out the $900 loan did so to buy a used car. To keep things simple, let's suppose he buys the car for exactly $900 and pays by writing a check on his account at Bank of America. The seller of the used car will now deposit the check in her bank. That bank may also be a branch of Bank of America, but in most cities, there are many banks, so let's assume that the seller of the car has her account at a branch of PNC Bank. Once she deposits the check, PNC Bank will send it to Bank of America to *clear* the check and collect the $900. We show the result in the following T-accounts:

Bank of America

Assets		Liabilities	
Reserves	+$100	Deposits	+$1,000
Loans	+$900		

1. When the $900 check that was deposited in a PNC account arrives to be cleared, the increase in Bank of America's reserves (shown in the previous T-account) falls by $900, to $100 . . .

2. . . . and the increase in Bank of America's deposits falls by $900, to $1,000.

PNC Bank

Assets		Liabilities	
Reserves	+$900	Deposits	+$900

After the check drawn on the account at Bank of America clears, PNC's reserves and deposits both increase by $900.

After the car buyer's check clears, Bank of America has lost $900 in deposits—the amount loaned to the car buyer—and $900 in reserves—the amount it had to pay PNC when PNC sent Bank of America the car buyer's check. PNC has an increase in checking account deposits of $900—the deposit of the car seller—and an increase in reserves of $900—the amount it received from Bank of America.

PNC has 100 percent reserves against this new $900 deposit, when it needs only 10 percent reserves. The bank has an incentive to keep $90 as reserves and to loan out the other $810, which are excess reserves. If PNC does this, we can show the change in its balance sheet by using another T-account:

PNC Bank

Assets		Liabilities	
Reserves	+$900	Deposits	+$900
Loans	+$810	Deposits	+$810

By making an $810 loan, PNC has increased both its loans and its deposits by $810.

In loaning out the $810 in excess reserves, PNC creates a new checking account deposit of $810. The initial deposit of $1,000 in currency into Bank of America has now resulted in the creation of $1,000 + $900 + $810 = $2,710 in checking account deposits. The money supply has increased by $2,710 − $1,000 = $1,710.

The process is still not finished. The person who borrows the $810 will spend it by writing a check against his account. Whoever receives the $810 will deposit it in her bank, which could be a Bank of America branch or a PNC branch or a branch of some other bank. That new bank—if it's not PNC—will send the check to PNC and will receive $810 in new reserves. That new bank will have an incentive to loan out 90 percent of these reserves—keeping 10 percent to meet the legal requirement—and the process will go on. At each stage, the additional loans being made and the additional deposits being created are shrinking by 10 percent, as each bank has to withhold that amount as required reserves. We can use a table to show the total increase in checking account deposits set off by your initial deposit of $1,000. The dots in the table represent additional rounds in the money creation process:

Bank	Increase in Checking Account Deposits	
Bank of America	$1,000	
PNC	+ 900	(= 0.9 × $1,000)
Third Bank	+ 810	(= 0.9 × $900)
Fourth Bank	+ 729	(= 0.9 × $810)
•	+ •	
•	+ •	
•	+ •	
Total change in checking account deposits	= $10,000	

The Simple Deposit Multiplier

Your initial deposit of $1,000 increased the reserves of the banking system by $1,000 and led to a total increase in checking account deposits of $10,000. The ratio of the amount of deposits created by banks to the amount of new reserves is called the **simple deposit multiplier**. In this case, the simple deposit multiplier is equal to $10,000/$1,000 = 10. Why 10? How do we know that your initial $1,000 deposit ultimately leads to a total increase in deposits of $10,000?

There are two ways to answer this question. First, each bank in the process is keeping reserves equal to 10 percent of its deposits. For the banking system as a whole, the total increase in reserves is $1,000—the amount of your original currency deposit. Therefore, the system as a whole will end up with $10,000 in deposits because $1,000 is 10 percent of $10,000.

Simple deposit multiplier The ratio of the amount of deposits created by banks to the amount of new reserves.

A second way to answer the question is by deriving an expression for the simple deposit multiplier. The total increase in deposits equals:

$$\$1,000 + [0.9 \times \$1,000] + [(0.9 \times 0.9) \times \$1,000] + [(0.9 \times 0.9 \times 0.9) \times \$1,000] + \ldots$$

or

$$\$1,000 + [0.9 \times \$1,000] + [0.9^2 \times \$1,000] + [0.9^3 \times \$1,000] + \ldots$$

or

$$\$1,000 + (1 + 0.9 + 0.9^2 + 0.9^3 + \ldots).$$

The rules of algebra tell us that an expression like the one in the parentheses sums to:

$$\frac{1}{1 - 0.9}.$$

Simplifying further, we have

$$\frac{1}{0.10} = 10.$$

So

$$\text{Total increase in deposit} = \$1,000 \times 10 = \$10,000.$$

Note that 10 is equal to 1 divided by the required reserve ratio, *RR*, which in this case is 10 percent, or 0.10. This gives us another way of expressing the simple deposit multiplier:

$$\text{Simple deposit multiplier} = \frac{1}{RR}.$$

This formula makes it clear that the higher the required reserve ratio, the smaller the simple deposit multiplier. With a required reserve ratio of 10 percent, the simple deposit multiplier is 10. If the required reserve ratio were 20 percent, the simple deposit multiplier would fall to 1/0.20, or 5. We can use this formula to calculate the total increase in checking account deposits from an increase in bank reserves due to, for instance, currency being deposited in a bank:

$$\text{Change in checking account deposits} = \text{Change in bank reserves} \times \frac{1}{RR}.$$

For example, if $100,000 in currency is deposited in a bank and the required reserve ratio is 10 percent, then

$$\text{Change in checking account deposits} = \$100,000 \times \frac{1}{0.10}$$

$$= \$100,000 \times 10 = \$1,000,000.$$

Don't Let This Happen to You

Don't Confuse Assets and Liabilities

Consider the following reasoning: "How can checking account deposits be a liability to a bank? After all, they are something of value that is in the bank. Therefore, checking account deposits should be counted as a bank *asset* rather than as a bank liability."

This statement is incorrect. The balance in a checking account represents something the bank *owes* to the owner of the account. Therefore, it is a liability to the bank, although it is an asset to the owner of the account. Similarly, your car loan is a liability to you—because it is a debt you owe to the bank—but it is an asset to the bank.

MyEconLab

Your Turn: Test your understanding by doing related problem 3.12 on page 486 at the end of this chapter.

Solved Problem 14.3

Showing How Banks Create Money

Suppose you deposit $5,000 in currency into your checking account at a branch of PNC Bank, which we will assume has no excess reserves at the time you make your deposit. Also assume that the required reserve ratio is 0.10.

a. Use a T-account to show the initial effect of this transaction on PNC's balance sheet.

b. Suppose that PNC makes the maximum loan it can from the funds you deposited. Use a T-account to show the initial effect on PNC's balance sheet from granting the loan. Also include in this T-account the transaction from question a.

c. Now suppose that whoever took out the loan in question b. writes a check for this amount and

that the person receiving the check deposits it in Bank of America. Show the effect of these transactions on the balance sheets of PNC Bank and Bank of America *after the check has cleared*. On the T-account for PNC Bank, include the transactions from questions a. and b.

d. What is the maximum increase in checking account deposits that can result from your $5,000 deposit? What is the maximum increase in the money supply that can result from your deposit? Explain.

Solving the Problem

Step 1: **Review the chapter material.** This problem is about how banks create checking account deposits, so you may want to review the section "Using T-Accounts to Show How a Bank Can Create Money," which begins on page 464.

Step 2: **Answer part a. by using a T-account to show the effect of the deposit.** Keeping in mind that T-accounts show only the changes in a balance sheet that result from the relevant transaction and that assets are on the left side of the account and liabilities are on the right side, we have:

PNC Bank

Assets		Liabilities	
Reserves	+$5,000	Deposits	+$5,000

Because the bank now has your $5,000 in currency in its vault, its reserves (and, therefore, its assets) have risen by $5,000. But this transaction also increases your checking account balance by $5,000. Because the bank owes you this money, the bank's liabilities have also risen by $5,000.

Step 3: **Answer part b. by using a T-account to show the effect of the loan.** The problem tells you to assume that PNC Bank currently has no excess reserves and that the required reserve ratio is 10 percent. This requirement means that if the bank's checking account deposits go up by $5,000, the bank must keep $500 as reserves and can loan out the remaining $4,500. Remembering that new loans usually take the form of setting up, or increasing, a checking account for the borrower, we have:

PNC Bank

Assets		Liabilities	
Reserves	+$5,000	Deposits	+$5,000
Loans	+$4,500	Deposits	+$4,500

The first line of the T-account shows the transaction from question a. The second line shows that PNC has loaned out $4,500 by increasing the checking account of the borrower by $4,500. The loan is an asset to PNC because it represents a promise by the borrower to make certain payments spelled out in the loan agreement.

Step 4: **Answer part c. by using T-accounts for PNC and Bank of America to show the effect of the check clearing.** We now show the effect of the borrower having spent the $4,500 he received as a loan from PNC. The person who received the $4,500 check deposits it in her account at Bank of America. We need two T-accounts to show this activity:

PNC Bank

Assets		Liabilities	
Reserves	+$500	Deposits	+$5,000
Loans	+$4,500		

Bank of America

Assets		Liabilities	
Reserves	+$4,500	Deposits	+$4,500

Look first at the T-account for PNC. Once Bank of America sends the check written by the borrower to PNC, PNC loses $4,500 in reserves, and Bank of America gains $4,500 in reserves. The $4,500 is also deducted from the account of the borrower. PNC is now satisfied with the result. It received a $5,000 deposit in currency from you. When that money was sitting in the bank vault, it wasn't earning any interest for PNC. Now $4,500 of the $5,000 has been loaned out and is earning interest. These interest payments allow PNC to cover its costs and earn a profit, which it has to do to remain in business.

Bank of America now has an increase in deposits of $4,500, resulting from the check being deposited, and an increase in reserves of $4,500. Bank of America is in the same situation as PNC was in question a: It has excess reserves as a result of this transaction and a strong incentive to lend them out.

Step 5: **Answer part d. by using the simple deposit multiplier formula to calculate the maximum increase in checking account deposits and the maximum increase in the money supply.** The simple deposit multiplier expression is (remember that RR is the required reserve ratio)

$$\text{Change in checking account deposits} = \text{Change in bank reserves} \times \frac{1}{RR}.$$

In this case, bank reserves rose by $5,000 as a result of your initial deposit, and the required reserve ratio is 0.10, so:

$$\text{Change in checking account deposits} = \$5,000 \times \frac{1}{0.10}$$

$$= \$5,000 \times 10 = \$50,000.$$

Because checking account deposits are part of the money supply, it is tempting to say that the money supply has also increased by $50,000. Remember, though, that your $5,000 in currency was counted as part of the money supply while you had it, but it is not included when it is sitting in a bank vault. Therefore:

Increase in checking account deposits − Decline in currency in
circulation = Change in the money supply

or

$$\$50,000 - \$5,000 = \$45,000.$$

MyEconLab **Your Turn:** For more practice, do related problem 3.10 on page 486 at the end of the chapter.

The Simple Deposit Multiplier versus the Real-World Deposit Multiplier

The story we have told about the way an increase in reserves in the banking system leads to the creation of new deposits and, therefore, an increase in the money supply has been simplified in two ways. First, we assumed that banks do not keep any excess reserves. That is, we assumed that when you deposited $1,000 in currency into your checking account at Bank of America, it loaned out $900, keeping only the $100 in required reserves. In fact, banks often keep some excess reserves to guard against the possibility that many depositors may simultaneously make withdrawals from their accounts. During the financial crisis that began in 2007, banks kept substantial excess reserves. The more excess reserves banks keep, the smaller the deposit multiplier. Imagine an extreme case in which Bank of America keeps your entire $1,000 as reserves. If Bank of America does not loan out any of your deposit, the process described earlier—loans leading to the creation of new deposits, leading to the making of additional loans, and so on—will not take place. The $1,000 increase in reserves will lead to a total increase of $1,000 in deposits, and the deposit multiplier will be only 1, not 10.

Second, we assumed that the whole amount of every check is deposited in a bank; no one takes any of it out as currency. In reality, households and firms keep roughly constant the amount of currency they hold relative to the value of their checking account balances. So, we would expect to see people increasing the amount of currency they hold as the balances in their checking accounts rise. Once again, think of the extreme case. Suppose that when Bank of America makes the initial $900 loan to the borrower who wants to buy a used car, the seller of the car cashes the check instead of depositing it. In that case, PNC does not receive any new reserves and does not make any new loans. Once again, the $1,000 increase in your checking account at Bank of America is the only increase in deposits, and the deposit multiplier is 1.

The effect of these two factors is to reduce the real-world deposit multiplier to about 2.5 during normal times. This means that a $1 increase in the reserves of the banking system results in about a $2.50 increase in deposits. During the financial crisis of 2007–2009, the surge in bank holdings of excess reserves reduced the multiplier to about 1.

Although the story of the deposit multiplier can be complicated, the key point to bear in mind is that the most important part of the money supply is the checking account balance component. When banks make loans, they increase checking account balances, and the money supply expands. Banks make new loans whenever they gain reserves. The whole process can also work in reverse: If banks lose reserves, they reduce their outstanding loans and deposits, and the money supply contracts.

We can summarize these important conclusions:

1. When banks gain reserves, they make new loans, and the money supply expands.
2. When banks lose reserves, they reduce their loans, and the money supply contracts.

The Federal Reserve System

Many people are surprised to learn that banks do not keep locked away in their vaults all the funds that are deposited in checking accounts. The United States, like nearly all other countries, has a **fractional reserve banking system**, which means that banks keep less than 100 percent of deposits as reserves. When people deposit money in a bank, the bank loans most of the money to someone else. What happens, though, if depositors want their money back? This would seem to be a problem because banks have loaned out most of the money and can't easily get it back.

In practice, though, withdrawals are usually not a problem for banks. On a typical day, about as much money is deposited as is withdrawn. If a small amount more is withdrawn than deposited, banks can cover the difference from their excess reserves or by borrowing from other banks. Sometimes depositors lose confidence in a bank when they question the value of the bank's underlying assets, particularly its loans. Often, the reason for a loss of confidence is bad news, whether true or false. When many depositors simultaneously decide to withdraw their money from a bank, there is a **bank run**. If many banks experience runs at the same time, the result is a **bank panic**. It is possible for one bank to handle a run by borrowing from other banks, but if many banks simultaneously experience runs, the banking system may be in trouble.

A *central bank*, like the Federal Reserve in the United States, can help stop a bank panic by acting as a *lender of last resort*. In acting as a lender of last resort, a central bank makes loans to banks that cannot borrow funds elsewhere. The banks can use these loans to pay off depositors. When the panic ends and the depositors put their money back in their accounts, the banks can repay the loans to the central bank.

The Establishment of the Federal Reserve System

Bank panics lead to severe disruptions in business activity because households and firms have trouble gaining access to their accounts and may be unable to borrow money. Not surprisingly, in the United States, each bank panic in the late nineteenth and early twentieth centuries was accompanied by a recession. With the intention of putting an end to bank panics, in 1913, Congress passed the Federal Reserve Act, setting up the Federal Reserve System—often referred to as "the Fed." The system began operation in 1914, with the authority to make loans to banks. The loans the Fed makes to banks are called **discount loans**, and the interest rate it charges on the loans is called the **discount rate**. When a bank receives a loan from the Fed, its reserves increase by the amount of the loan.

The Fed's first test as a lender of last resort came in the early years of the Great Depression of the 1930s, when many banks were hit by bank runs as depositors pulled funds out of checking and savings accounts. Although the Fed had been established to act as a lender of last resort, Fed officials declined to make loans to many banks because the officials were worried that banks experiencing runs had made bad loans and other investments. The Fed believed that making loans to banks that were in financial trouble because of bad investments might reduce the incentive bank managers had to be careful in their investment decisions. Partly due to the Fed's unwillingness to act as a lender of last resort, more than 5,000 banks failed during the early 1930s. Today, many economists are critical of the Fed's decisions in the early 1930s because they believe these decisions increased the severity of the Great Depression. In 1934, Congress established the Federal Deposit Insurance Corporation (FDIC) to insure deposits in most banks up to a limit, which is currently $250,000 per deposit. Deposit insurance has greatly reduced bank runs because it has reassured all but the largest depositors that their deposits are safe, even if their bank goes out of business. During the financial crisis of 2007–2009, some banks experienced runs when depositors with funds exceeding the deposit insurance limit feared that they would suffer losses if their banks failed.

To aid the Fed in carrying out its responsibilities, in 1913 Congress divided the country into 12 Federal Reserve districts, as shown in Figure 14.3. Each district has its

Fractional reserve banking system A banking system in which banks keep less than 100 percent of deposits as reserves.

Bank run A situation in which many depositors simultaneously decide to withdraw money from a bank.

Bank panic A situation in which many banks experience runs at the same time.

Discount loans Loans the Federal Reserve makes to banks.

Discount rate The interest rate the Federal Reserve charges on discount loans.

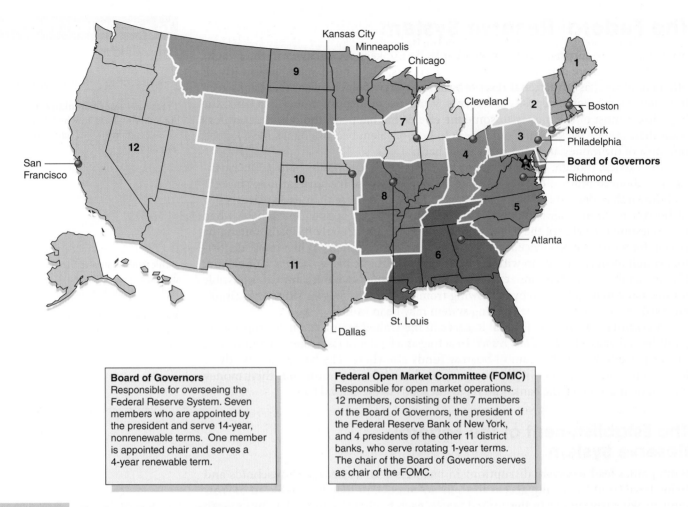

Board of Governors
Responsible for overseeing the
Federal Reserve System. Seven
members who are appointed by
the president and serve 14-year,
nonrenewable terms. One member
is appointed chair and serves a
4-year renewable term.

Federal Open Market Committee (FOMC)
Responsible for open market operations.
12 members, consisting of the 7 members
of the Board of Governors, the president of
the Federal Reserve Bank of New York,
and 4 presidents of the other 11 district
banks, who serve rotating 1-year terms.
The chair of the Board of Governors serves
as chair of the FOMC.

Figure 14.3 **The Federal Reserve System**

The United States is divided into 12 Federal Reserve districts, each of which
has a Federal Reserve bank. The real power within the Federal Reserve System,
however, lies in Washington, DC, with the Board of Governors, which consists
of 7 members appointed by the president. Monetary policy is carried out by the
14-member Federal Open Market Committee.

Data from Board of Governors of the Federal Reserve System.

own Federal Reserve bank, which provides services to banks in that district. The real
power of the Fed, however, lies in Washington, DC, with the Board of Governors. The
seven members of the Board of Governors are appointed by the president of the United
States to 14-year, nonrenewable terms. One member of the Board of Governors is chosen to be chair and serves a 4-year, renewable term. In 2012, the chair of the Board of
Governors was Ben Bernanke. In addition to acting as a lender of last resort to banks,
the Fed acts as a bankers' bank, providing services such as check clearing to banks, and
also has the responsibility of managing the nation's money supply.

How the Federal Reserve Manages the Money Supply

Although Congress established the Fed primarily to stop bank panics by acting as a
lender of last resort, today the Fed is also responsible for managing the money supply.
As we will discuss in more detail in Chapter 15, managing the money supply is part of
monetary policy, which the Fed undertakes to pursue macroeconomic objectives. To
manage the money supply, the Fed uses three *monetary policy tools*:

Monetary policy The actions the
Federal Reserve takes to manage
the money supply and interest rates
to pursue macroeconomic policy
objectives.

1. Open market operations
2. Discount policy
3. Reserve requirements

Remember that the most important component of the money supply is checking account deposits. Not surprisingly, all three of the Fed's policy tools are aimed at affecting the reserves of banks as a means of changing the volume of checking account deposits.

Open Market Operations

Eight times per year, the **Federal Open Market Committee (FOMC)** meets in Washington, DC, to discuss monetary policy. The committee has 12 voting members: the 7 members of the Federal Reserve's Board of Governors, the president of the Federal Reserve Bank of New York, and 4 presidents from the other 11 Federal Reserve banks. These 4 presidents serve one-year rotating terms on the FOMC. The chair of the Board of Governors also serves as the chair of the FOMC.

The U.S. Treasury borrows money by selling bills, notes, and bonds. Remember that the *maturity* of a financial asset is the period of time until the purchaser receives payment of the face value or principal. Usually, bonds have face values of $1,000. Treasury bills have maturities of 1 year or less, Treasury notes have maturities of 2 years to 10 years, and Treasury bonds have maturities of 30 years. To increase the money supply, the FOMC directs the *trading desk*, located at the Federal Reserve Bank of New York, to *buy* U.S. Treasury securities—most frequently bills, but sometimes notes or bonds—from the public. When the sellers of the Treasury securities deposit the funds in their banks, the reserves of banks rise. This increase in reserves starts the process of increasing loans and checking account deposits that increases the money supply. To decrease the money supply, the FOMC directs the trading desk to *sell* Treasury securities. When the buyers of the Treasury securities pay for them with checks, the reserves of their banks fall. This decrease in reserves starts a contraction of loans and checking account deposits that reduces the money supply. The buying and selling of Treasury securities is called **open market operations**.

There are three reasons the Fed conducts monetary policy principally through open market operations. First, because the Fed initiates open market operations, it completely controls their volume. Second, the Fed can make both large and small open market operations. Third, the Fed can implement its open market operations quickly, with no administrative delay or required changes in regulations. Many other central banks, including the European Central Bank and the Bank of Japan, also use open market operations to conduct monetary policy.

The Federal Reserve is responsible for putting the paper currency of the United States into circulation. Recall that if you look at the top of a dollar bill, you see the words "Federal Reserve Note." When the Fed takes actions to increase the money supply, commentators sometimes say that it is "printing more money." The main way the Fed increases the money supply, however, is not by printing more currency but by buying Treasury securities. Similarly, to reduce the money supply, the Fed does not set fire to stacks of paper currency. Instead, it sells Treasury securities. We will spend more time discussing how and why the Fed manages the money supply in Chapter 15, when we discuss monetary policy.

Discount Policy

As we have seen, when a bank borrows money from the Fed by taking out a discount loan, the interest rate the bank pays is known as the discount rate. By lowering the discount rate, the Fed can encourage banks to take additional loans and thereby increase their reserves. With more reserves, banks will make more loans to households and firms, which will increase checking account deposits and the money supply. Raising the discount rate will have the reverse effect.

Reserve Requirements

When the Fed reduces the required reserve ratio, it converts required reserves into excess reserves. For example, suppose a bank has $100 million in checking account deposits, and the required reserve ratio is 10 percent. The bank will be required to hold $10 million as reserves. If the Fed reduces the required reserve ratio to 8 percent, the bank will need to hold only $8 million as reserves. The Fed can thereby convert $2 million worth of reserves from required reserves to excess reserves. This $2 million is then available for the bank to lend out. If the Fed *raises* the required reserve ratio from 10 percent to 12 percent, it will have the reverse effect.

Federal Open Market Committee (FOMC) The Federal Reserve committee responsible for open market operations and managing the money supply in the United States.

Open market operations The buying and selling of Treasury securities by the Federal Reserve in order to control the money supply.

The Fed changes reserve requirements much more rarely than it conducts open market operations or changes the discount rate. Because changes in reserve requirements require significant alterations in banks' holdings of loans and securities, frequent changes would be disruptive. Also, because the Fed pays banks only a low interest rate on reserves, the use of reserve requirements to manage the money supply effectively places a tax on banks' deposit-taking and lending activities, which can be costly for the economy.

The "Shadow Banking System" and the Financial Crisis of 2007–2009

The banks we have been discussing in this chapter are *commercial banks*, whose most important economic role is to accept funds from depositors and lend those funds to borrowers. In Chapter 6, we noted that large firms can sell stocks and bonds on financial markets but that investors are typically unwilling to buy stocks and bonds from small and medium-sized firms because they lack sufficient information on the financial health of smaller firms. So, smaller firms—and households—have traditionally relied on bank loans for their credit needs. In the past 20 years, however, two important developments have occurred in the financial system: (1) Banks have begun to resell many of their loans rather than keep them until they are paid off, and (2) financial firms other than commercial banks have become sources of credit to businesses.

Securitization Comes to Banking Traditionally, when a bank made a *residential mortgage loan* to a household to buy a home or made a commercial loan to a business, the bank would keep the loan and collect the payments until the loan was paid off. A financial asset—such as a loan or a stock or a bond—is considered a **security** if it can be bought and sold in a *financial market* as, for instance, shares of stock issued by the Coca-Cola Company can be bought and sold on the New York Stock Exchange. When a financial asset is first sold, the sale takes place in the *primary market*. Subsequent sales take place in the *secondary market*. Prior to 1970, most loans were not securities because they could not be resold—there was no secondary market for them. First, residential mortgages and then other loans, including car loans and commercial loans, began to be *securitized*. The process of **securitization** involves creating a secondary market in which loans that have been bundled together can be bought and sold in financial markets, just as corporate or government bonds are. Figure 14.4 outlines the securitization process.

Security A financial asset—such as a stock or a bond—that can be bought and sold in a financial market.

Securitization The process of transforming loans or other financial assets into securities.

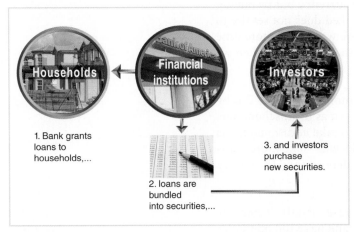

1. Bank grants loans to households,...

2. loans are bundled into securities,...

3. and investors purchase new securities.

(a) Securitizing a loan

1. Banks collect loan payments from households,...

2. collect a fee for processing the payments ...

3. and send the payments to investors.

(b) The flow of payments on a securitized loan

Figure 14.4 **The Process of Securitization**

Panel (a) shows how in the securitization process banks grant loans to households and bundle the loans into securities that are then sold to investors. Panel (b) shows that banks collect payments on the original loans and, after taking a fee, send the payments to the investors who bought the securities.

We will discuss the process of securitization further in Chapter 15, when we discuss monetary policy.

The Shadow Banking System In addition to the changes resulting from securitization, the financial system was transformed in the 1990s and 2000s by the increasing importance of nonbank financial firms. Investment banks, such as Goldman Sachs and Morgan Stanley, differ from commercial banks in that they do not accept deposits, and they rarely lend directly to households. Instead, investment banks traditionally concentrated on providing advice to firms issuing stocks and bonds or considering mergers with other firms. In the late 1990s, investment banks expanded their buying of mortgages, bundling large numbers of them together as bonds known as *mortgage-backed securities*, and reselling them to investors. Mortgage-backed securities proved very popular with investors because they often paid higher interest rates than other securities with comparable default risk.

Money market mutual funds have also increased their importance in the financial system over time. These funds sell shares to investors and use the money to buy short-term securities such as Treasury bills and commercial paper issued by corporations. Commercial paper represents short-term borrowing corporations use to fund their day-to-day operations. Many corporations that previously met such needs by borrowing from banks began instead to sell commercial paper to money market mutual funds.

Hedge funds raise money from wealthy investors and use sophisticated investment strategies that often involve significant risk. By 2005, hedge funds had become an important source of demand for securitized loans and an important source of loans to other financial firms.

In 2008, Timothy Geithner, who became Treasury secretary in the Obama administration, referred to investment banks, money market mutual funds, hedge funds, and other financial firms engaged in similar activities as the "shadow banking system." By raising money from individual investors and providing it directly or indirectly to firms and households, these firms were carrying out a function that at one time was almost exclusively the domain of commercial banks.

The Financial Crisis of 2007–2009 The firms in the shadow banking system differed from commercial banks in two important ways: First, the government agencies—including the Federal Reserve—that regulated the commercial banking system did not regulate these firms. Second, these firms were more highly *leveraged*—that is, they relied more heavily on borrowed money to finance their operations—than were commercial banks. If a firm uses a small amount of its own money and a lot of borrowed money to make an investment, both the firm's potential profits and its potential losses are increased. For example, suppose a firm invests $100 of its own money. If the investment earns a return of $3, the firm has earned 3 percent ($3/$100) on its funds. But if the firm's investment consists of $10 of its own money and $90 it has borrowed, a return of $3 becomes a return of 30 percent ($3/$10) on the firm's $10 investment. If the investment loses $2, however, the firm's return is −20 percent (−$2/$10). Leveraged investments have a potential for both large gains and large losses.

As mentioned earlier, commercial banks have rarely experienced runs since Congress established federal deposit insurance in the 1930s. However, beginning in 2007, firms in the shadow banking system were quite vulnerable to runs. As we will discuss further in Chapter 15, the underlying cause of the financial crisis of 2007–2009 was problems in the U.S. housing market. As housing prices began to fall, a significant number of borrowers began to default on their mortgages, which caused mortgage-backed securities to lose value. Financial firms, including both commercial banks and many firms in the shadow banking system, that had invested in these securities suffered heavy losses. The more leveraged the firm, the larger the losses. Although deposit insurance helped commercial banks avoid runs, investment banks and other financial firms that had borrowed short term and invested the funds long term were in trouble. As lenders refused to renew their short-term loans, many of these firms had to sell their holdings of securities in an attempt to raise cash. But as the prices of these securities continued to fall, the losses to these firms increased.

In the spring of 2008, the investment bank Bear Stearns was saved from bankruptcy only when the Federal Reserve arranged for it to be acquired by JPMorgan Chase. In the fall of 2008, the Federal Reserve and the U.S. Treasury decided not to take action to save the investment bank Lehman Brothers, which failed. The failure of Lehman Brothers reverberated throughout the financial system, setting off a panic. The process of securitization—apart from government-guaranteed residential mortgages—ground to a halt. The well-publicized difficulties of a money market mutual fund that had suffered losses on loans to Lehman Brothers led to a wave of withdrawals from these funds. In turn, the funds were no longer able to fulfill their role as buyers of corporate commercial paper. As banks and other financial firms sold assets and cut back on lending to shore up their financial positions, the flow of funds from savers to borrowers was disrupted. The resulting credit crunch significantly worsened the recession that had begun in December 2007.

The Fed's Response The Fed, in combination with the U.S. Treasury, took vigorous action to deal with the financial panic. We will discuss the Fed's actions further in Chapter 15, but for now, we can mention several particularly important policy actions. First, in the fall of 2008, under the Troubled Asset Relief Program (TARP), the Fed and Treasury began attempting to stabilize the commercial banking system by providing funds to banks in exchange for stock. Taking partial ownership of private commercial banks was an unprecedented move by the federal government. The Fed also modified its discount policy by setting up several new "lending facilities." These lending facilities made it possible for the Fed to grant discount loans to financial firms—such as investment banks—that had not previously been eligible. In addition, the Fed addressed problems in the commercial paper market by directly buying commercial paper for the first time since the 1930s.

Although the recession continued into 2009, the extraordinary actions of the Treasury and Fed appeared to have stabilized the financial system. Still, even by late 2011, the flow of funds from savers to borrowers had not yet returned to normal levels, and economists and policymakers were debating the wisdom of some of the Fed's actions. We will return to the Fed's response to the recession of 2007–2009 in Chapter 14.

14.5 LEARNING OBJECTIVE

Explain the quantity theory of money and use it to explain how high rates of inflation occur.

The Quantity Theory of Money

People have been aware of the connection between increases in the money supply and inflation for centuries. In the sixteenth century, the Spanish conquered Mexico and Peru and shipped large quantities of gold and silver from those countries back to Spain. The gold and silver were minted into coins and spent across Europe to further the political ambitions of the Spanish kings. Prices in Europe rose steadily during these years, and many observers discussed the relationship between this inflation and the flow of gold and silver into Europe from the Americas.

Connecting Money and Prices: The Quantity Equation

In the early twentieth century, Irving Fisher, an economist at Yale, formalized the connection between money and prices by using the *quantity equation*:

$$M \times V = P \times Y.$$

The quantity equation states that the money supply (M) multiplied by the *velocity of money* (V) equals the price level (P) multiplied by real output (Y). Fisher defined the

velocity of money, often referred to simply as "velocity," as the average number of times each dollar of the money supply is used to purchase goods and services included in GDP. Rewriting the original equation by dividing both sides by M, we have the equation for velocity:

$$V = \frac{P \times Y}{M}.$$

If we use M1 to measure the money supply, the GDP price deflator to measure the price level, and real GDP to measure real output, the value for velocity for 2010 was

$$V = \frac{1.11 \times \$13,088 \text{ billion}}{\$1,832 \text{ billion}} = 7.9.$$

This result tells us that, on average during 2010, each dollar of M1 was spent about eight times on goods or services included in GDP.

Because velocity is defined to be equal to $(P \times Y)/M$, we know that the quantity equation must always hold true: The left side *must* be equal to the right side. A theory is a statement about the world that might possibly be false. Therefore, the quantity equation is not a theory. Irving Fisher turned the quantity equation into the **quantity theory of money** by asserting that velocity was constant. He argued that the average number of times a dollar is spent depends on how often people get paid, how often they do their grocery shopping, how often businesses mail bills, and other factors that do not change very often. Because this assertion may be true or false, the quantity theory of money is, in fact, a theory.

Velocity of money The average number of times each dollar in the money supply is used to purchase goods and services included in GDP.

Quantity theory of money A theory about the connection between money and prices that assumes that the velocity of money is constant.

The Quantity Theory Explanation of Inflation

The quantity equation gives us a way of showing the relationship between changes in the money supply and changes in the price level, or inflation. To see this relationship more clearly, we can use a handy mathematical rule that states that an equation where variables are multiplied together is equal to an equation where the *growth rates* of these variables are *added* together. So, we can transform the quantity equation from

$$M \times V = P \times Y$$

to

Growth rate of the money supply $+$ Growth rate of velocity $=$
Growth rate of the price level (or inflation rate) $+$ Growth rate of real output.

This way of writing the quantity equation is more useful for investigating the effect of changes in the money supply on the inflation rate. Remember that the growth rate for any variable is the percentage change in the variable from one year to the next. The growth rate of the price level is the inflation rate, so we can rewrite the quantity equation to help understand the factors that determine inflation:

Inflation rate $=$ Growth rate of the money supply $+$
Growth rate of velocity $-$ Growth rate of real output.

If Irving Fisher was correct that velocity is constant, then the growth rate of velocity will be zero. That is, if velocity is, say, always eight, then its percentage change from one year to the next will always be zero. This assumption allows us to rewrite the equation one last time:

Inflation rate $=$ Growth rate of the money supply $-$ Growth rate of real output.

This equation leads to the following predictions:

1. If the money supply grows at a faster rate than real GDP, there will be inflation.
2. If the money supply grows at a slower rate than real GDP, there will be deflation. (Recall that *deflation* is a decline in the price level.)
3. If the money supply grows at the same rate as real GDP, the price level will be stable, and there will be neither inflation nor deflation.

It turns out that Irving Fisher was wrong in asserting that the velocity of money is constant. From year to year, there can be significant fluctuations in velocity. As a result, the predictions of the quantity theory of money do not hold every year, but most economists agree that the quantity theory provides useful insight into the long-run relationship between the money supply and inflation: *In the long run, inflation results from the money supply growing at a faster rate than real GDP.*

How Accurate Are Estimates of Inflation Based on the Quantity Theory?

Note that the accuracy of the quantity theory depends on whether the key assumption that velocity is constant is correct. If velocity is not constant, then there may not be a tight link between increases in the money supply and increases in the price level. For example, an increase in the quantity of money might be offset by a decline in velocity, leaving the price level unaffected. Because velocity can move erratically in the short run, we would not expect the quantity equation to provide good forecasts of inflation in the short run. Over the long run, however, there is a strong link between changes in the money supply and inflation. Panel (a) of Figure 14.5 shows the relationship between the growth of the M2 measure of the money supply and the inflation rate by decade in the United States. (We use M2 here because data on M2 are available for a longer period of time than for M1.) Because of variations in the rate of growth of real GDP and in velocity, there is not an exact relationship between the growth rate of M2 and the inflation rate. But there is a clear pattern that decades with higher growth rates in the money supply were also decades with higher inflation rates. In other words, most of the variation in inflation rates across decades can be explained by variation in the rates of growth of the money supply.

Panel (b) provides further evidence consistent with the quantity theory by looking at rates of growth of the money supply and rates of inflation across countries for the decade from 1999 to 2008. Although there is not an exact relationship between rates

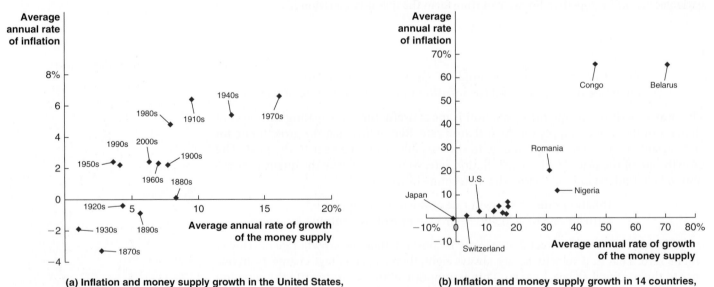

(a) Inflation and money supply growth in the United States, 1870s–2000s

(b) Inflation and money supply growth in 14 countries, 1999–2008

Figure 14.5 **The Relationship between Money Growth and Inflation over Time and around the World**

Panel (a) shows that, by and large, in the United States, the rate of inflation has been highest during the decades in which the money supply has increased most rapidly, and the rate of inflation has been lowest during the decades in which the money supply has increased least rapidly. Panel (b) shows that for the decade from 1999 to 2008, there is not an exact relationship between money supply growth and inflation, but in countries such as the United States, Japan, and Switzerland, both the growth rate of the money supply and the rate of inflation

were low, while countries such as Belarus, the Congo, and Romania had both high rates of growth of the money supply and high rates of inflation.

Data from: Panel (a): for 1870s to 1960s, Milton Friedman and Anna J. Schwartz, *Monetary Trends in the United States and United Kingdom: Their Relation to Income, Prices, and Interest Rates, 1867–1975*, (Chicago: University of Chicago Press, 1982), Table 4.8; and for the 1970s to 2000s: Federal Reserve Board of Governors and U.S. Bureau of Economic Analysis; Panel (b): World Bank.

of growth of the money supply and rates of inflation across countries, panel (b) shows that countries where the money supply grew rapidly tended to have high inflation rates, while countries where the money supply grew more slowly tended to have much lower inflation rates. Not included in panel (b) are data for the African country of Zimbabwe, which we mentioned at the beginning of the chapter. Over this decade, the money supply in Zimbabwe grew by more than 7,500 percent per year. The result was an accelerating rate of inflation that eventually reached 15 billion percent during 2008. Zimbabwe was suffering from hyperinflation—that is, a rate of inflation that exceeds 100 percent per year.

High Rates of Inflation

Why do governments allow high rates of inflation? The quantity theory can help us to understand the reasons for high rates of inflation, such as that experienced by Zimbabwe. Very high rates of inflation—in excess of 100 percent per year—are known as *hyperinflation*. Hyperinflation is caused by central banks increasing the money supply at a rate far in excess of the growth rate of real GDP. A high rate of inflation causes money to lose its value so rapidly that households and firms avoid holding it. If, as happened in Zimbabwe, the inflation becomes severe enough, people stop using paper currency, so it no longer serves the important functions of money discussed earlier in this chapter. Economies suffering from high inflation usually also suffer from very slow growth, if not severe recession.

Given the dire consequences that follow from high inflation, why do governments cause it by expanding the money supply so rapidly? The main reason is that governments often want to spend more than they are able to raise through taxes. Developed countries, such as the United States, can usually bridge gaps between spending and taxes by borrowing through selling bonds to the public. Developing countries, such as Zimbabwe, often have difficulty selling bonds because investors are skeptical of their ability to pay back the money. If they are unable to sell bonds to the public, governments in developing countries will force their central banks to purchase them. As we discussed previously, when a central bank buys bonds, the money supply will increase.

Making the Connection	The German Hyperinflation of the Early 1920s

When Germany lost World War I, a revolution broke out that overthrew Kaiser Wilhelm II and installed a new government known as the Weimar Republic. In the peace treaty of 1919, the Allies—the United States, Great Britain, France, and Italy—imposed payments called *reparations* on the new German government. The reparations were meant as compensation to the Allies for the damage Germany had caused during the war. It was very difficult for the German government to use tax revenue to cover both its normal spending and the reparations.

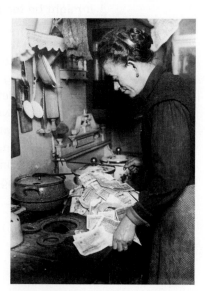

The German government decided to pay for the difference between its spending and its tax revenues by selling bonds to the central bank, the Reichsbank. After a few years, the German government fell far behind in its reparations payments. In January 1923, the French government sent troops into the German industrial area known as the Ruhr to try to collect the payments directly. German workers in the Ruhr went on strike, and the German government decided to support them by paying their salaries. Raising the funds to do so was financed by an inflationary monetary policy: The German government sold bonds to the Reichsbank, thereby increasing the money supply.

The inflationary increase in the money supply was very large: The total number of marks—the German currency—in circulation rose from 115 million in January 1922 to 1.3 billion in January 1923 and then to 497 billion *billion*, or 497,000,000,000,000,000,000, in December 1923. Just as the quantity theory predicts, the result was a staggeringly high rate of inflation. The German price index that stood at 100 in 1914 and 1,440 in January 1922 had risen to 126,160,000,000,000 in December 1923. The German mark

During the hyperinflation of the 1920s, people in Germany used paper currency to light their stoves.

became worthless. The German government ended the hyperinflation by (1) negotiating a new agreement with the Allies that reduced its reparations payments, (2) reducing other government expenditures and raising taxes to balance its budget, and (3) replacing the existing mark with a new mark. Each new mark was worth 1 trillion old marks. The German central bank was also limited to issuing a total of 3.2 billion new marks.

These steps were enough to bring the hyperinflation to an end—but not before the savings of anyone holding the old marks had been wiped out. Most middle-income Germans were extremely resentful of this outcome. Many historians believe that the hyperinflation greatly reduced the allegiance of many Germans to the Weimar Republic and may have helped pave the way for Adolph Hitler and the Nazis to seize power 10 years later.

Based on Thomas Sargent, "The End of Four Big Hyperinflations," *Rational Expectations and Inflation*, (New York: Harper & Row, 1986).

MyEconLab   **Your Turn:** Test your understanding by doing related problem 5.10 on page 488 at the end of this chapter.

Continued from page 455

Economics in Your Life

What if Money Became Increasingly Valuable?

At the beginning of the chapter, we asked you to consider whether you would like to live in an economy in which the purchasing power of money rises every year. The first thing to consider when thinking about the advantages and disadvantages of this situation is that the only way for the purchasing power of money to increase is for the price level to fall; in other words, *deflation* must occur. Because the price level in the United States hasn't fallen for an entire year since the 1930s, most people alive today have experienced only rising price levels—and declining purchasing power of money. Would replacing rising prices with falling prices necessarily be a good thing? It might be tempting to say "yes," because if you have a job, your salary will buy more goods and services each year. But, in fact, just as a rising price level results in most wages and salaries rising each year, a falling price level is likely to mean falling wages and salaries each year. So, it is likely that, on average, people would not see the purchasing power of their incomes increase, even if the purchasing power of any currency they hold would increase. There can also be a significant downside to deflation, particularly if the transition from inflation to deflation happens suddenly. In Chapter 9, we defined the real interest rate as being equal to the nominal interest rate minus the inflation rate. If an economy experiences deflation, then the real interest rate will be greater than the nominal interest rate. A rising real interest rate can be bad news for anyone who has borrowed, including homeowners who may have substantial mortgage loans. So, you are probably better off living in an economy experiencing mild inflation than one experiencing deflation.

Conclusion

Money plays a key role in the functioning of an economy by facilitating trade in goods and services and by making specialization possible. Without specialization, no advanced economy can prosper. Households and firms, banks, and the central bank (the Federal Reserve in the United States) are participants in the process of creating the money supply. In Chapter 15, we will explore how the Federal Reserve uses monetary policy to promote its economic objectives.

An Inside Look at Policy on the next page discusses how an increase in bank lending to consumers and businesses is a positive signal for the economy.

Increased Lending Boosts Money Supply Growth

FISCAL TIMES

Bank Lending Signals a Strengthening Economy

The financial crisis of 2008 rocked the foundation of the U.S. banking sector. The shock left banks short of capital and hesitant to lend, even as the recession cut deeply into loan demand. The Federal Reserve has pumped in an ocean of lendable funds, trying to prime the process of bringing banks and borrowers together. But many still wonder when, if ever, bank lending will return to normal.

We're not there yet, but recent signs have been encouraging. Despite the sluggish economy, loan growth is finally beginning to pick up in key areas, reflecting both greater willingness to lend and increased desire to borrow. Loan volume of U.S. commercial banks rose at a one percent annual rate in June as expansion in business loans and non-mortgage consumer lending more than offset the ongoing contraction in real estate financing. It was the third consecutive monthly increase after steady declines for more than two years. . . .

(a) Lending to businesses is leading the credit upswing. The volume of commercial and industrial (C&I) loans in the second quarter rose at a 9.6 percent annual rate, the largest increase in 2½ years. Banks have progressively eased lending standards for C&I loans to large and medium-sized companies for the past six quarters. Small companies have seen easier terms and conditions in each of the past four quarters. Economists expect to see signs that this loosening in standards is continuing when the Fed issues it third-quarter report from bank senior loan officers in mid-August.

More credit is starting to flow to small businesses, as well. That's important, because small firms account for about half of U.S. job creation, and depend greatly on banks for credit, unlike large corporations that have the option to raise funds in the capital markets by issuing bonds. In the second quarter, the balance of banks reporting stronger vs. weaker demand for commercial and industrial (C&I) loans by small businesses was positive for the first time in five years, according to the latest Fed survey. Another positive sign is the gradual rise in C&I loans made by small banks, whose customers tend to be small local companies. Small-bank C&I loan volume has been rising gradually in 2011 after hitting bottom late last year.

Despite increased attention by policymakers over the past year to the dearth of small business lending, the problem has been not so much banks' unwillingness to lend but simply a lack of loan demand, reflecting weak sales. Although the percentage of small companies saying credit is harder to get is still somewhat higher than before the recession, it has fallen steadily over the past two years, from a peak of 16 percent, to 9 percent in June, according to the National Federation of Independent Business.

(b) Banks are also warming to consumer loans. Despite sluggish job markets, households have made great progress in getting their financial obligations under control, allowing qualified borrowers to take on more debt. So far this year, monthly financial obligations of households have fallen to only 16.4 percent of household income, the lowest since 1994. In the second quarter, the percentage of banks reporting increased demand for auto loans was the highest since 2003.

Banks began easing lending standards for auto loans, credit cards, and other borrowing this time last year. In the 2011 second quarter the percentage of loan officers saying they were more willing to make consumer loans rose to the highest level in 17 years. . . .

(c) The ebb and flow of bank lending during recessions and recoveries exerts a powerful force on any business cycle. Aside from this cycle's problems in mortgage lending, banks are finally beginning to behave as they usually do in a recovery. Barring some new shock, especially from the debt troubles in Washington or Europe, evidence that loan growth is beginning to expand in response to easier lending standards and stronger loan demand is a key sign that the recovery has staying power.

Key Points in the Article

The financial crisis of 2007–2009 resulted in decreases in both the supply of funds available to lend and in the demand for those funds. Despite the Federal Reserve's infusion of large amounts of funds into the economy, bank lending continued to decline for more than two years. In April 2011, loan volumes finally began to increase. The largest increase occurred in business lending, with the volume of commercial and industrial (C&I) loans rising at an annual rate of 9.6 percent for the second quarter of 2011, which was the largest increase in over two years. The increase in small business lending was particularly encouraging, with banks in the second quarter reporting increased demand for small business loans for the first time in five years. The market for consumer loans was improving as well. As consumer debt as a percentage of income fell to its lowest level since 1994, banks became more willing to make consumer loans. The expansion of loan growth was a positive sign for the economy during what had been a sluggish recovery from the recession.

Analyzing the News

a As we saw in Chapter 10, banks help channel funds from savers to borrowers by making loans to individuals and businesses. Rising defaults on home loans after the housing bubble burst led to the collapse of a number of financial intermediaries in 2008, and loan volume declined for more than two years. Growth in the market for loans reemerged in the second quarter of 2011, with business loans leading the upswing. Commercial and industrial loans rose at an annual rate of 9.6 percent as banks continued to loosen lending requirements for small, medium, and large companies. As Figure 1 below shows, the percentage change in commercial and industrial bank loans turned positive toward the end of 2010, and it accelerated for much of the second quarter of 2011.

b Loans to consumers began to increase in mid-2011. Following the collapse of financial markets in 2008, banks were much less willing to make consumer loans, increasing their lending standards as households' financial obligations grew. The decrease in the supply of funds available to households was met with a decrease in the demand for these funds as households worked to reduce their debts. As household debts became more manageable, banks became increasingly willing to make consumer loans, as shown in Figure 2 below.

c As you read in this chapter, banks create money by loaning out excess reserves. Because of the money multiplier process, a given amount of new reserves results in a multiple increase in bank deposits. In an attempt to bring lenders and borrowers together following the financial crisis of 2008, the Federal Reserve made a large amount of new funds available to financial markets. These extra funds had the potential to affect the economy as banks, responding to an increase in demand, finally began to see an increase in loans in 2011. The increases in excess reserves, bank deposits, and loan volume are indications that the economy was in the expansion phase of the business cycle and were positive signs for continued economic recovery.

Thinking Critically About Policy

1. During the financial crisis of 2007–2009, the Fed attempted to stimulate the economy by taking actions to increase the money supply. How effective would these actions be if banks remained reluctant to make consumer loans while households remained reluctant to obtain loans? Briefly explain.

2. The quantity theory of money predicts that a large increase in the money supply will result in inflation. Why, then, even though the money supply increased rapidly was inflation relatively low during the recession of 2007–2009 and its immediate aftermath?

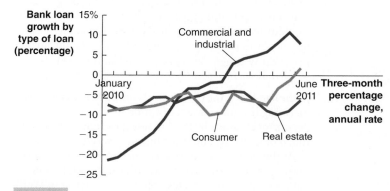

Figure 1

Loans to businesses and consumers are growing, but real estate loans keep falling.

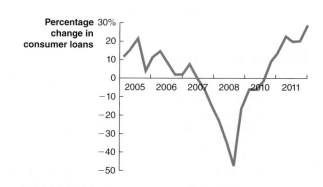

Figure 2

More banks say they are willing to make consumer loans.

Chapter Summary and Problems

Key Terms

14.1	**What Is Money, and Why Do We Need It?** pages 456–459
	LEARNING OBJECTIVE: Define money and discuss the four functions of money.

Summary

A *barter economy* is an economy that does not use money and in which people trade goods and services directly for other goods and services. Barter trade occurs only if there is a *double coincidence of wants*, where both parties to the trade want what the other one has. Because barter is inefficient, there is strong incentive to use **money**, which is any **asset** that people are generally willing to accept in exchange for goods or services or in payment of debts. An *asset* is anything of value owned by a person or a firm. A **commodity money** is a good used as money that also has value independent of its use as money. Money has four functions: It is a medium of exchange, a unit of account, a store of value, and a standard of deferred payment. The *gold standard* was a monetary system under which the government produced gold coins and paper currency that were convertible into gold. The gold standard collapsed in the early 1930s. Today, no government in the world issues paper currency that can be redeemed for gold. Instead, paper currency is **fiat money**, which has no value except as money.

MyEconLab   Visit **www.myeconlab.com** to complete these exercises online and get instant feedback.

Review Questions

1.1 A baseball fan with an Albert Pujols baseball card wants to trade it for a Derek Jeter baseball card, but everyone the fan knows who has a Jeter card doesn't want a Pujols card. What do economists call the problem this fan is having?

1.2 What is the difference between commodity money and fiat money?

1.3 What are the four functions of money? Can something be considered money if it does not fulfill all four functions?

1.4 Why do businesses accept paper currency when they know that, unlike a gold coin, the paper the currency is printed on is worth very little?

Problems and Applications

1.5 The English economist William Stanley Jevons described a world tour during the 1880s by a French singer, Mademoiselle Zélie. One stop on the tour was a theater in the Society Islands, part of French Polynesia in the South Pacific. She performed for her usual fee, which was one-third of the receipts. This turned out to be three pigs, 23 turkeys, 44 chickens, 5,000 coconuts, and "considerable quantities of bananas, lemons, and oranges." She estimated that all of this would have had a value in France of 4,000 francs. According to Jevons, "as Mademoiselle could not consume any considerable portion of the receipts herself, it became necessary in the meantime to feed the pigs and poultry with the fruit." Do the goods Mademoiselle Zélie received as payment fulfill the four functions of money described in the chapter? Briefly explain.

Based on W. Stanley Jevons, *Money and the Mechanism of Exchange*, (New York: D. Appleton and Company, 1889), pp. 1–2.

1.6 **[Related to the** Chapter Opener **on page 455]** An article in the New York Times provides the following description of a hospital in Zimbabwe: "People lined up on the veranda of the American mission hospital here from miles around to barter for doctor visits and medicines, clutching scrawny chickens, squirming goats and buckets of maize." Why wouldn't the people buying medical services at this hospital use money to pay for the medical services they are buying?

From Celia W. Dugger, "Zimbabwe Health Care, Paid With Peanuts," *New York Times*, December 18, 2011.

1.7 In the late 1940s, the Communists under Mao Zedong were defeating the government of China in a civil war. The paper currency issued by the Chinese government was losing much of its value, and most businesses refused to accept it. At the same time, there was a paper shortage in Japan. During these years, Japan was still under military occupation by the United States, following its defeat in World War II. Some of the U.S. troops in Japan realized that they could use dollars to buy up vast amounts of paper currency in China, ship it to Japan to be recycled into paper, and make a substantial profit. Under these circumstances, was the Chinese paper currency a commodity money or a fiat money? Briefly explain.

1.8 According to Peter Heather, a historian at the University of Oxford, during the Roman Empire, the German tribes east of the Rhine River produced no coins of their own but used Roman coins instead:

> Although no coinage was produced in Germania, Roman coins were in plentiful circulation and could easily have provided a medium of exchange (already in the first century, Tacitus tells us, Germani of the Rhine region were using good-quality Roman silver coins for this purpose).

a. What is a medium of exchange?

b. What does the author mean when he writes that Roman coins could have provided the German tribes with a medium of exchange?

c. Why would any member of a German tribe have been willing to accept a Roman coin from another member of the tribe in exchange for goods or services when the tribes were not part of the Roman Empire and were not governed by Roman law?

Based on Peter Heather, *The Fall of the Roman Empire: A New History of Rome and the Barbarians*, (New York: Oxford University Press, 2006), p. 89.

1.9 **[Related to the** Making the Connection **on page 459]** Suppose that Congress changes the law to require all firms to accept paper currency in exchange for whatever they are selling. Briefly discuss who would gain and who would lose from this legislation.

14.2 How Is Money Measured in the United States Today? pages 459–463

LEARNING OBJECTIVE: Discuss the definitions of the money supply used in the United States today.

Summary

The narrowest definition of the money supply in the United States today is **M1**, which includes currency, checking account balances, and traveler's checks. A broader definition of the money supply is **M2**, which includes everything that is in M1, plus savings accounts, small-denomination time deposits (such as certificates of deposit [CDs]), money market deposit accounts in banks, and noninstitutional money market fund shares.

 MyEconLab Visit www.myeconlab.com to complete these exercises online and get instant feedback.

Review Questions

2.1 What is the main difference between the M1 and M2 definitions of the money supply?

2.2 Why does the Federal Reserve use two definitions of the money supply rather than one?

2.3 Distinguish among money, income, and wealth. Which one of the three does the central bank of a country control?

Problems and Applications

2.4 Briefly explain whether each of the following is counted in M1.
a. The coins in your pocket
b. The funds in your checking account
c. The funds in your savings account
d. The traveler's checks that you have left over from a trip
e. Your Citibank Platinum MasterCard

2.5 **[Related to** Solved Problem 14.2 **on page 463]** Suppose you have $2,000 in currency in a shoebox in your closet. One day, you decide to deposit the money in a checking account. Briefly explain how this will affect M1 and M2.

2.6 **[Related to** Solved Problem 14.2 **on page 463]** Suppose you decide to withdraw $100 in currency from your checking account. What is the effect on M1? Ignore any actions the bank may take as a result of your having withdrawn the $100.

2.7 **[Related to the** Don't Let This Happen to You **on page 462]** Briefly explain whether you agree with the following statement: "I recently read that more than half of the money issued by the government is actually held by people in foreign countries. If that's true, then the United States is less than half as wealthy as government statistics indicate."

2.8 **[Related to the** Don't Let This Happen to You **on page 462]** A newspaper article contains the statement: "Income is only one way of measuring wealth." Do you agree that income is a way of measuring wealth?

From Sam Roberts, "As the Data Show, There's a Reason the Wall Street Protesters Chose New York," *New York Times*, October 25, 2011.

2.9 The paper currency of the United States is technically called "Federal Reserve Notes." The following excerpt is from the Federal Reserve Act: "Federal Reserve Notes . . . shall be redeemed in lawful money on demand at the Treasury Department of the United States, in the city of Washington, District of Columbia, or at any Federal Reserve bank." If you took a $20 bill to the Treasury Department or a Federal Reserve bank, with what type of "lawful money" is the government likely to redeem it?

2.10 **[Related to the** Making the Connection **on page 461]** In the nineteenth century, the Canadian government had difficulty getting banks and the public to accept the penny, which had been introduced a few years before. As a result, the government offered pennies for sale at a 20 percent discount. One account of this episode describes what the Canadian government did as "negative seigniorage." What is seigniorage? Why might the Canadian government's selling pennies at a 20 percent discount be considered "negative seigniorage"?

Based on Nicholas Kohler, "A Penny Dropped," macleans.ca, January 14, 2011.

2.11 **[Related to the** Making the Connection **on page 461]** There are currently about 1.4 billion pennies in circulation. Suppose the proposal of economist François Velde to make the current penny worth 5 cents were adopted. What would be the effect on the value of M1? Is this change likely to have much impact on the economy? (*Hint:* According to the information given in this chapter, what is the current value of M1?)

Based on Austan Goolsbee, "Now That a Penny Isn't Worth Much, It's Time to Make It Worth 5 Cents," *New York Times*, February 1, 2007.

14.3 **How Do Banks Create Money?** pages 463–470
LEARNING OBJECTIVE: Explain how banks create money.

Summary

On a bank's balance sheet, *reserves* and loans are assets, and deposits are liabilities. **Reserves** are deposits that the bank has retained rather than loaned out or invested. **Required reserves** are reserves that banks are legally required to hold. The fraction of deposits that banks are required to keep as reserves is called the **required reserve ratio**. Any reserves banks hold over and above the legal requirement are called **excess reserves**. When a bank accepts a deposit, it keeps only a fraction of the funds as reserves and loans out the remainder. In making a loan, a bank increases the checking account balance of the borrower. When the borrower uses a check to buy something with the funds the bank has loaned, the seller deposits the check in his bank. The seller's bank keeps part of the deposit as reserves and loans out the remainder. This process continues until no banks have excess reserves. In this way, the process of banks making new loans increases the volume of checking account balances and the money supply. This money creation process can be illustrated with T-accounts, which are stripped-down versions of balance sheets that show only how a transaction changes a bank's balance sheet. The **simple deposit multiplier** is the ratio of the amount of deposits created by banks to the amount of new reserves. An expression for the simple deposit multiplier is $1/RR$.

MyEconLab   Visit **www.myeconlab.com** to complete these exercises online and get instant feedback.

Review Questions

3.1 What are the largest asset and the largest liability of a typical bank?

3.2 Suppose you decide to withdraw $100 in cash from your checking account. Draw a T-account showing the effect of this transaction on your bank's balance sheet.

3.3 What does it mean to say that banks "create money"?

3.4 Give the formula for the simple deposit multiplier. If the required reserve ratio is 20 percent, what is the maximum increase in checking account deposits that will result from an increase in bank reserves of $20,000?

3.5 What causes the real-world money multiplier to be smaller than the simple deposit multiplier?

Problems and Applications

3.6 An article on The Motley Fool Web site states:

> Deposits are the lifeblood of banks. Bank of America for example, had nearly $1 trillion in deposits at the end of March, representing nearly half of its total liabilities. Citigroup and Wells Fargo held around $800 billion each in deposits at the end of the first quarter.

Briefly explain the statement "deposits are the life-blood of banks."

"Should Your Bank Deposits Be at Risk?" by Matt Koppenheffer from www.fool.com, May 21, 2009. Copyright © 2009 by The Motley Fool. Reprinted by permission.

3.7 The following is from an article on community banks: "Their commercial-lending businesses, funded by their stable deposit bases, make them steady earners." What is commercial lending? In what sense are loans "funded" by deposits?
From Karen Richardson, "Clean Books Bolster Traditional Lenders," *Wall Street Journal*, April 30, 2007.

3.8 "Most of the money supply of the United States is created by banks making loans." Briefly explain whether you agree with this statement.

3.9 Would a series of bank runs in a country decrease the total quantity of M1? Wouldn't a bank run simply move funds in a checking account to currency in circulation? How could that movement of funds decrease the quantity of money?

3.10 [Related to Solved Problem 14.3 **on page 468**] Suppose you deposit $2,000 in currency into your checking account at a branch of Bank of America, which we will assume has no excess reserves at the time you make your deposit. Also assume that the required reserve ratio is 0.20, or 20 percent.
   a. Use a T-account to show the initial impact of this transaction on Bank of America's balance sheet.
   b. Suppose that Bank of America makes the maximum loan it can from the funds you deposited. Using a T-account, show the initial impact of granting the loan on Bank of America's balance sheet. Also include on this T-account the transaction from part a.
   c. Now suppose that whoever took out the loan in part b writes a check for this amount and that the person receiving the check deposits it in a branch of Citibank. Show the effect of these transactions on the balance sheets of Bank of America and Citibank *after the check has been cleared*. (On the T-account for Bank of America, include the transactions from parts a and b.)
   d. What is the maximum increase in checking account deposits that can result from your $2,000 deposit? What is the maximum increase in the money supply? Explain.

3.11 Consider the following simplified balance sheet for a bank:

Assets		Liabilities	
Reserves	$10,000	Deposits	$70,000
Loans	$66,000	Stockholders' equity	$6,000

   a. If the required reserve ratio is 0.10, or 10 percent, how much in excess reserves does the bank hold?
   b. What is the maximum amount by which the bank can expand its loans?
   c. If the bank makes the loans in part b, show the *immediate* impact on the bank's balance sheet.

3.12 [Related to the Don't Let This Happen to You **on page 467**] Briefly explain whether you agree with the following statement: "Assets are things of value that people own. Liabilities are debts. Therefore, a bank will always consider a checking account deposit to be an asset and a car loan to be a liability."

14.4 **The Federal Reserve System**, pages 471–476

LEARNING OBJECTIVE: Discuss the three policy tools the Federal Reserve uses to manage the money supply.

Summary

The United States has a **fractional reserve banking system** in which banks keep less than 100 percent of deposits as reserves. In a **bank run**, many depositors decide simultaneously to withdraw money from a bank. In a **bank panic**, many banks experience runs at the same time. The **Federal Reserve System** ("the Fed") is the central bank of the United States. It was originally established in 1913 to stop bank panics. The recession of 2007–2009 put renewed emphasis on the Fed's goal of financial market stability. **Monetary policy** refers to the actions the Federal Reserve takes to manage the money supply and interest rates to pursue macroeconomic policy objectives. The Fed's three monetary policy tools are open market operations, discount policy, and reserve requirements. **Open market operations** are the buying and selling of Treasury securities by the Federal Reserve. The loans the Fed makes to banks are called **discount loans**, and the interest rate the Fed charges on discount loans is the **discount rate**. The **Federal Open Market Committee (FOMC)** meets in Washington, DC, eight times per year to discuss monetary policy. In the past 20 years, a "shadow banking system" has developed. During the financial crisis of 2007–2009, the existence of the shadow banking system complicated the Fed's policy response. A **security** is a financial asset—such as a stock or a bond—that can be bought and sold in a financial market. The process of **securitization** involves creating a secondary market in which loans that have been bundled together can be bought and sold in financial markets just as corporate or government bonds are.

MyEconLab   Visit **www.myeconlab.com** to complete these exercises online and get instant feedback.

Review Questions

4.1 Why did Congress decide to set up the Federal Reserve System in 1913?

4.2 What policy tools does the Fed use to control the money supply? Which tool is the most important?

4.3 Why does an open market purchase of Treasury securities by the Federal Reserve increase bank reserves? Why does an open market sale of Treasury securities by the Federal Reserve decrease bank reserves?

4.4 What is the "shadow banking system"? Why were the financial firms of the shadow banking system more vulnerable than commercial banks to bank runs?

Problems and Applications

4.5 The text explains that the United States has a "fractional reserve banking system." Why do most depositors seem to be unworried that banks loan out most of the deposits they receive?

4.6 Suppose that you are a bank manager, and the Federal Reserve raises the required reserve ratio from 10 percent to 12 percent. What actions would you need to take? How would your actions and those of other bank managers end up affecting the money supply?

4.7 Suppose that the Federal Reserve makes a $10 million discount loan to First National Bank (FNB) by increasing FNB's account at the Fed.

a. Use a T-account to show the impact of this transaction on FNB's balance sheet. Remember that the funds a bank has on deposit at the Fed count as part of its reserves.

b. Assume that before receiving the discount loan, FNB has no excess reserves. What is the maximum amount of this $10 million that FNB can lend out?

c. What is the maximum total increase in the money supply that can result from the Fed's discount loan? Assume that the required reserve ratio is 10 percent.

4.8 In a speech delivered in June 2008, Timothy Geithner, then president of the Federal Reserve Bank of New York and later U.S. Treasury secretary, said:

> The structure of the financial system changed fundamentally during the boom. . . . [The] non-bank financial system grew to be very large. . . . [The] institutions in this parallel financial system [are] vulnerable to a classic type of run, but without the protections such as deposit insurance that the banking system has in place to reduce such risks.

a. What did Geithner mean by the "non-bank financial system"?

b. What is a "classic type of run," and why were institutions in the nonbank financial system vulnerable to it?

c. Why would deposit insurance provide the banking system with protection against runs?

From Timothy F. Geithner, "Reducing Systemic Risk in a Dynamic Financial System," remarks at the Economics Club of New York, June 9, 2008.

4.9 When the Federal Reserve steps in as the lender of last resort to prevent a bank panic, does this constitute a "bail out of the banks"? Briefly explain.

The Quantity Theory of Money, pages 476–481

14.5

LEARNING OBJECTIVE: Explain the quantity theory of money and use it to explain how high rates of inflation occur.

Summary

The *quantity equation*, which relates the money supply to the price level, is $M \times V = P \times Y$ where M is the money supply, V is the *velocity of money*, P is the price level, and Y is real output. The **velocity of money** is the average number of times each dollar in the money supply is spent during the year. Economist Irving Fisher developed the **quantity theory of money**, which assumes that the velocity of money is constant. If the quantity theory of money is correct, the inflation rate should equal the rate of growth of the money supply minus the rate of growth of real output. Although the quantity theory of money is not literally correct because the velocity of money is not constant, it is true that in the long run, inflation results from the money supply growing faster than real GDP. When governments attempt to raise revenue by selling large quantities of bonds to the central bank, the money supply will increase rapidly, resulting in a high rate of inflation.

MyEconLab   Visit **www.myeconlab.com** to complete these exercises online and get instant feedback.

Review Questions

5.1 What is the quantity theory of money? What explanation does the quantity theory provide for inflation?

5.2 Is the quantity theory of money better able to explain the inflation rate in the long run or in the short run? Briefly explain.

5.3 What is hyperinflation? Why do governments sometimes allow it to occur?

Problems and Applications

5.4 If the money supply is growing at a rate of 6 percent per year, real GDP is growing at a rate of 3 percent per year, and velocity is constant, what will the inflation rate be? If velocity is increasing 1 percent per year instead of remaining constant, what will the inflation rate be?

5.5 Suppose that during one period, the velocity of money is constant and during another period, it undergoes large fluctuations. During which period will the quantity theory of money be more useful in explaining changes in the inflation rate? Briefly explain.

5.6 In an article titled "We Should Celebrate Price Deflation" in the *American Free Press*, Professor Peter Spencer of York University in England is quoted as saying: "This printing of money 'will keep the [deflation] wolf from the door.'" In the same article, Ambrose Evans-Pritchard, a writer for the London-based newspaper *The Telegraph*, is quoted as saying: "Deflation has . . . insidious traits. It causes shoppers to hold back. Once this psychology gains a grip, it can gradually set off a self-feeding spiral that is hard to stop."

a. What is price deflation?

b. What does Professor Spencer mean by the statement, "This printing of money 'will keep the [deflation] wolf from the door'"?

c. Why would deflation cause "shoppers to hold back," and what does Evans-Pritchard mean when he says, "Once this psychology gains a grip, it can gradually set off a self-feeding spiral that is hard to stop"?

Based on Doug French, "We Should Celebrate Price Deflation," *American Free Press*, November 17, 2008.

5.7 During the Civil War, the Confederate States of America printed lots of its own currency—Confederate dollars—to fund the war. By the end of the war, the Confederate government had printed nearly 1.5 billion paper dollars. How would such a large quantity of Confederate dollars have affected the value of the Confederate currency? With the war drawing to an end, would Southerners have been as willing to use and accept Confederate dollars? How else could they have made exchanges?

Based on Federal Reserve Bank of Richmond, "Textual Transcript of Confederate Currency."

5.8 [Related to the Chapter Opener **on page 455]** In April 2009, the African nation of Zimbabwe suspended the use of its own currency, the Zimbabwean dollar. According to an article from the Voice of America, "Hyperinflation in 2007 and 2008 made Zimbabwe's currency virtually worthless despite the introduction of bigger and bigger notes, including a 10 trillion dollar bill." Zimbabwe's Economic Planning Minister, Elton Mangoma, was quoted as saying the Zimbabwean dollar "will be out for at least a year," and in January 2009, the government of Zimbabwe made the U.S. dollar the country's official currency. Why would hyperinflation make a currency "virtually worthless"? How might using the U.S. dollar as its currency help to stabilize Zimbabwe's economy?

From Voice of America News, "Zimbabwe Suspends Use of Own Currency," voanews.com, April 12, 2009.

5.9 [Related to the Chapter Opener **on page 455]** A *New York Times* article on Zimbabwe describes conditions in summer 2008 as follows: "Official inflation soared to 2.2 million percent in Zimbabwe—by far the highest in the world . . . [and] unemployment has reached 80 percent." Is there a connection between the very high inflation rate and the very high rate of unemployment? Briefly explain.

From "Inflation Soars to 2 Million Percent in Zimbabwe," *New York Times*, July 17, 2008.

5.10 [Related to the Making the Connection **on page 479]** During the German hyperinflation of the 1920s, many households and firms in Germany were hurt economically. Do you think any groups in Germany benefited from the hyperinflation? Briefly explain.

Monetary Policy

Chapter Outline and Learning Objectives

Monetary Policy, Toll Brothers, and the Housing Market

If you lose your job or are afraid that you might, you are not likely to buy a new house. It's not surprising, then, that residential construction tends to fall during a recession. In addition, recessions often begin after the Federal Reserve increases interest rates to slow the growth in aggregate demand in order to reduce the inflation rate. Higher interest rates increase the cost of buying houses, further reducing demand for them. Not surprisingly, firms that build homes usually don't do well during recessions. For example, during the recessions of 1974–1975 and 1981–1982, residential construction declined by more than 30 percent.

The recession of 2001 was different, however. In early 2001, the members of the Federal Reserve's Federal Open Market Committee (FOMC) concluded that a recession was about to begin and took action to drive down interest rates. This action succeeded in heading off what some economists had predicted would be a prolonged and severe recession. In fact, the Fed's strategy resulted in spending on residential construction actually rising by 5 percent during the 2001 recession.

Toll Brothers is a homebuilder headquartered in Huntingdon Valley, Pennsylvania. Toll Brothers' profit actually increased during 2001. However, the recession of 2007–2009 was a different story. Toll Brothers suffered a record loss of more than $750 million— and it wasn't alone. Nearly all homebuilders suffered severe declines in sales, and many went bankrupt. The key problem was that by 2005, the housing market boom had turned into a "bubble." In a bubble, prices soar to levels that are not sustainable. When the housing bubble finally burst in 2006, sales of new homes and prices of existing homes began a sharp decline. By 2007, the economy had entered a recession. This time, unfortunately, the Fed found that cutting interest rates was not enough to revive the housing market or the general economy. Beginning in 2008, the Fed was forced to turn to new policies to try to pull the economy out of recession.

In this chapter, we will study how monetary policy affects economic activity. Read **AN INSIDE LOOK AT POLICY** on **page 522** for a discussion of "Operation Twist," the Federal Reserve's attempt to boost the economy in late 2011.

Based on Toll Brothers, *Annual Report*, 2010.

Economics in Your Life

Should You Buy a House during a Recession?

If you are like most college students, buying a house is one of the farthest things from your mind. But suppose you think forward a few years to when you might be married and maybe even (gasp!) have children. Leaving behind years of renting apartments, you are considering buying a house. But, suppose that according to an article in the *Wall Street Journal*, a majority of economists are predicting that a recession is likely to begin soon. What should you do? Would this be a good time or a bad time to buy a house? As you read the chapter, see if you can answer these questions. You can check your answers against those we provide on **page 521** at the end of this chapter.

I n Chapter 14, we saw that banks play an important role in providing credit to households and firms, and in creating the money supply. We also saw that Congress established the Federal Reserve to stabilize the financial system and that the Fed is responsible for managing the money supply. In this chapter, we will discuss the Fed's four main policy goals: (1) price stability, (2) high employment, (3) stability of financial markets and institutions, and (4) economic growth. We will explore how the Federal Reserve decides which *monetary policy* actions to take to achieve its goals.

Define monetary policy and describe the Federal Reserve's monetary policy goals.

Monetary policy The actions the Federal Reserve takes to manage the money supply and interest rates to pursue macroeconomic policy goals.

What Is Monetary Policy?

In 1913, Congress passed the Federal Reserve Act, creating the Federal Reserve System ("the Fed"). The main responsibility of the Fed was to make discount loans to banks to prevent the bank panics we discussed in Chapter 14. As a result of the Great Depression of the 1930s, Congress amended the Federal Reserve Act to give the Federal Reserve's Board of Governors broader responsibility to act "so as to promote effectively the goals of maximum employment, stable prices, and moderate long-term interest rates."

Since World War II, the Federal Reserve has carried out an active *monetary policy*. **Monetary policy** refers to the actions the Fed takes to manage the money supply and interest rates to pursue its macroeconomic policy goals.

The Goals of Monetary Policy

The Fed has four main *monetary policy goals* that are intended to promote a well-functioning economy:

1. Price stability
2. High employment
3. Stability of financial markets and institutions
4. Economic growth

We briefly consider each of these goals.

Price Stability   As we have seen in previous chapters, rising prices erode the value of money as a medium of exchange and a store of value. Especially after inflation rose dramatically and unexpectedly during the 1970s, policymakers in most industrial countries have had price stability as a policy goal. Figure 15.1 shows that from the early 1950s until 1968, the inflation rate remained below 4 percent per year. Inflation was above

Figure 15.1

The Inflation Rate, January 1952–August 2011

For most of the 1950s and 1960s, the inflation rate in the United States was 4 percent or less. During the 1970s, the inflation rate increased, peaking during 1979–1981, when it averaged more than 10 percent. After 1992, the inflation rate was usually less than 4 percent, until increases in oil prices pushed it above 5 percent during summer 2008. The effects of the recession caused several months of deflation—a falling price level—during early 2009.
Note: The inflation rate is measured as the percentage change in the consumer price index (CPI) from the same month in the previous year.

4 percent for most of the 1970s. In early 1979, the inflation rate increased to more than 10 percent, where it remained until late 1981, when it began to rapidly fall back to the 4 percent range. After 1992, the inflation rate was usually below 4 percent, until rapid increases in gasoline prices helped push it above 5 percent in summer 2008. The effects of the recession caused several months of deflation—a falling price level—during early 2009.

The inflation rates during the years 1979–1981 were the highest the United States has ever experienced during peacetime. When Paul Volcker became chairman of the Federal Reserve's Board of Governors in August 1979, he made fighting inflation his top policy goal. Alan Greenspan, who succeeded Volcker in August 1987, and Ben Bernanke, who succeeded Greenspan in January 2006, continued to focus on inflation. Volcker, Greenspan, and Bernanke argued that if inflation is low over the long run, the Fed will have the flexibility it needs to lessen the impact of recessions. Although the severity of the 2007–2009 recession led the Fed to adopt extraordinary policy measures that we will discuss later in this chapter, price stability remains a key policy goal of the Fed.

High Employment In addition to price stability, high employment, or a low rate of unemployment, is an important monetary policy goal. Unemployed workers and underused factories and office buildings reduce GDP below its potential level. Unemployment causes financial distress and decreases the self-esteem of workers who lack jobs. The goal of high employment extends beyond the Fed to other branches of the federal government. At the end of World War II, Congress passed the Employment Act of 1946, which stated that it was the "responsibility of the Federal Government ... to foster and promote ... conditions under which there will be afforded useful employment, for those able, willing, and seeking to work, and to promote maximum employment, production, and purchasing power." Because price stability and high employment are explicitly mentioned in the Employment Act, it is sometimes said that the Fed has a *dual mandate* to attain these two goals.

Stability of Financial Markets and Institutions Resources are lost when financial markets and institutions are not efficient in matching savers and borrowers. Firms with the potential to produce goods and services that consumers value cannot obtain the financing they need to design, develop, and market those products. Savers waste resources looking for satisfactory investments. The Fed promotes the stability of financial markets and institutions so that an efficient flow of funds from savers to borrowers will occur. As we saw in Chapter 14, the financial crisis of 2007–2009 brought the issue of stability in financial markets to the forefront.

The financial crisis of 2007–2009 was similar to the banking crises that led Congress to create the Federal Reserve System in 1913. A key difference is that while earlier banking crises affected commercial banks, the events of 2007–2009 also affected investment banks. Investment banks can be subject to *liquidity problems* because they often borrow short term—sometimes as short as overnight—and invest the funds in longer-term investments. Commercial banks borrow from households and firms in the form of checking and savings deposits, while investment banks borrow primarily from other financial firms, such as other investment banks, mutual funds, or hedge funds, which are similar to mutual funds but typically engage in more complex—and risky—investment strategies. Just as commercial banks can experience crises if depositors begin to withdraw funds, investment banks can experience crises if other financial firms stop offering them short-term loans. In 2008, the Fed decided to ease the liquidity problems facing investment banks by temporarily allowing them to receive discount loans, which had previously been available only to commercial banks. Later in this chapter, we will discuss in more detail the new policies the Fed enacted to help deal with the financial crisis.

Economic Growth We discussed in Chapters 10 and 11 the importance of economic growth to raising living standards. Policymakers aim to encourage *stable* economic growth because it allows households and firms to plan accurately and encourages the long-run investment that is needed to sustain growth. Policy can spur economic growth by providing incentives for saving to ensure a large pool of investment funds, as well as by providing direct incentives for business investment. Congress and the president, however, may be better able to increase saving and investment than is the Fed. For example, Congress and the president can change the tax laws to increase the return to saving and investing. In fact, some economists question whether the Fed can play a role in promoting economic growth beyond attempting to meet its goals of price stability, high employment, and financial stability.

In the next section, we will look at how the Fed attempts to attain its monetary policy goals. Although the Fed has multiple monetary policy goals, during most periods, its most important goals have been price stability and high employment. But the turmoil in financial markets that began in 2007 led the Fed to put new emphasis on the goal of financial market stability.

15.2 LEARNING OBJECTIVE

Describe the Federal Reserve's monetary policy targets and explain how expansionary and contractionary monetary policies affect the interest rate.

The Money Market and the Fed's Choice of Monetary Policy Targets

The Fed aims to use its policy tools to achieve its monetary policy goals. Recall from Chapter 14 that the Fed's policy tools are open market operations, discount policy, and reserve requirements. At times, the Fed encounters conflicts between its policy goals. For example, as we will discuss later in this chapter, the Fed can raise interest rates to reduce the inflation rate. But, as we saw in Chapter 13, higher interest rates typically reduce household and firm spending, which may result in slower growth and higher unemployment. So, a policy that is intended to achieve one monetary policy goal, such as reducing inflation, may have an adverse effect on another policy goal, such as high employment.

Monetary Policy Targets

The Fed tries to keep both the unemployment and inflation rates low, but it can't affect either of these economic variables directly. The Fed cannot tell firms how many people to employ or what prices to charge for their products. Instead, the Fed uses variables, called *monetary policy targets*, that it can affect directly and that, in turn, affect variables, such as real GDP, employment, and the price level, that are closely related to the Fed's policy goals. The two main monetary policy targets are the money supply and the interest rate. As we will see, the Fed typically uses the interest rate as its policy target.

It's important to bear in mind that while the Fed has typically used the money supply and the interest rate as its targets, these targets were not central to the Fed's policy decisions during the recession of 2007–2009. As we will discuss later in this chapter, because U.S. financial markets suffered a degree of disruption not seen since the Great Depression of the 1930s, the Fed was forced to develop new policy tools. However, it is still important to have a good grasp of how the Fed carries out policy during normal times.

The Demand for Money

The Fed's two monetary policy targets are related in an important way. To see this relationship, we first need to examine the demand and supply for money. Figure 15.2 shows the demand curve for money. The interest rate is on the vertical axis, and the quantity of money is on the horizontal axis. Here we are using the M1 definition of money, which equals currency in circulation plus checking account deposits. Notice that the demand curve for money is downward sloping.

To understand why the demand curve for money is downward sloping, consider that households and firms have a choice between holding money and holding other financial assets, such as U.S. Treasury bills. Money has one particularly desirable characteristic: You can use it to buy goods, services, or financial assets. Money also has one undesirable characteristic: It earns either no interest or a very low rate of interest. The currency in your wallet earns no interest, and the money in your checking account earns

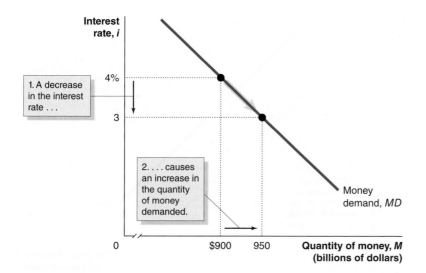

Figure 15.2

The Demand for Money

The money demand curve slopes downward because lower interest rates cause households and firms to switch from financial assets such as U.S. Treasury bills to money. All other things being equal, a fall in the interest rate from 4 percent to 3 percent will increase the quantity of money demanded from $900 billion to $950 billion. An increase in the interest rate will decrease the quantity of money demanded.

either no interest or very little interest. Alternatives to money, such as U.S. Treasury bills, pay interest but have to be sold if you want to use the funds to buy something. When interest rates rise on financial assets such as U.S. Treasury bills, the amount of interest that households and firms lose by holding money increases. When interest rates fall, the amount of interest households and firms lose by holding money decreases. Remember that *opportunity cost* is what you have to forgo to engage in an activity. The interest rate is the opportunity cost of holding money.

We now have an explanation of why the demand curve for money slopes downward: When interest rates on Treasury bills and other financial assets are low, the opportunity cost of holding money is low, so the quantity of money demanded by households and firms will be high; when interest rates are high, the opportunity cost of holding money will be high, so the quantity of money demanded will be low. In Figure 15.2, a decrease in interest rates from 4 percent to 3 percent causes the quantity of money demanded by households and firms to rise from $900 billion to $950 billion.

Shifts in the Money Demand Curve

We saw in Chapter 3 that the demand curve for a good is drawn holding constant all variables, other than the price, that affect the willingness of consumers to buy the good. Changes in variables other than the price cause the demand curve to shift. Similarly, the demand curve for money is drawn holding constant all variables, other than the interest rate, that affect the willingness of households and firms to hold money. Changes in variables other than the interest rate cause the demand curve to shift. The two most important variables that cause the money demand curve to shift are real GDP and the price level.

An increase in real GDP means that the amount of buying and selling of goods and services will increase. This additional buying and selling increases the demand for money as a medium of exchange, so the quantity of money households and firms want to hold increases at each interest rate, shifting the money demand curve to the right. A decrease in real GDP decreases the quantity of money demanded at each interest rate, shifting the money demand curve to the left. A higher price level increases the quantity of money required for a given amount of buying and selling. Eighty years ago, for example, when the price level was much lower and someone could purchase a new car for $500 and a salary of $30 per week put you in the middle class, the quantity of money demanded by households and firms was much lower than today, even adjusting for the effect of the lower real GDP and smaller population of those years. An increase in the price level increases the quantity of money demanded at each interest rate, shifting the money demand curve to the right. A decrease in the price level decreases the quantity of money demanded at each interest rate, shifting the money demand curve to the left. Figure 15.3 illustrates shifts in the money demand curve.

Figure 15.3

Shifts in the Money Demand Curve

Changes in real GDP or the price level cause the money demand curve to shift. An increase in real GDP or an increase in the price level will cause the money demand curve to shift from MD_1 to MD_2. A decrease in real GDP or a decrease in the price level will cause the money demand curve to shift from MD_1 to MD_3.

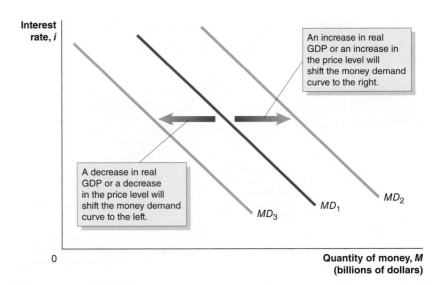

How the Fed Manages the Money Supply: A Quick Review

Having discussed money demand, we now turn to money supply. In Chapter 14, we saw how the Federal Reserve manages the money supply. Eight times per year, the Federal Open Market Committee (FOMC) meets in Washington, DC. If the FOMC decides to increase the money supply, it orders the trading desk at the Federal Reserve Bank of New York to purchase U.S. Treasury securities. The sellers of these Treasury securities deposit the funds they receive from the Fed in banks, which increases the banks' reserves. Typically, the banks loan out most of these reserves, which creates new checking account deposits and expands the money supply. If the FOMC decides to decrease the money supply, it orders the trading desk to sell Treasury securities, which decreases banks' reserves and contracts the money supply.

Equilibrium in the Money Market

In Figure 15.4, we include both the money demand and money supply curves. We can use this figure to see how the Fed affects both the money supply and the interest rate. For simplicity, we assume that the Federal Reserve is able to completely control the money supply. Therefore, the money supply curve is a vertical line, and changes

Figure 15.4

The Effect on the Interest Rate When the Fed Increases the Money Supply

When the Fed increases the money supply, households and firms will initially hold more money than they want, relative to other financial assets. Households and firms use the money they don't want to hold to buy Treasury bills and make deposits in interest-paying bank accounts. This increase in demand allows banks and sellers of Treasury bills and similar securities to offer lower interest rates. Eventually, interest rates will fall enough that households and firms will be willing to hold the additional money the Fed has created. In the figure, an increase in the money supply from $900 billion to $950 billion causes the money supply curve to shift to the right, from MS_1 to MS_2, and causes the equilibrium interest rate to fall from 4 percent to 3 percent.

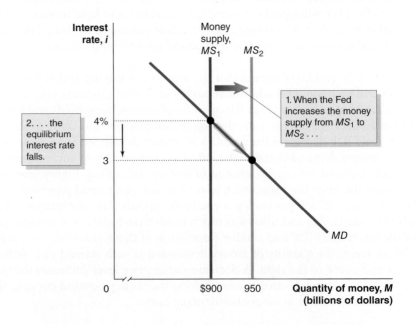

in the interest rate have no effect on the quantity of money supplied. Just as with other markets, equilibrium in the *money market* occurs where the money demand curve crosses the money supply curve. If the Fed increases the money supply, the money supply curve will shift to the right, and the equilibrium interest rate will fall. In Figure 15.4, when the Fed increases the money supply from $900 billion to $950 billion, the money supply curve shifts from MS_1 to MS_2, and the equilibrium interest rate falls from 4 percent to 3 percent.

In the money market, the adjustment from one equilibrium to another equilibrium is a little different from the adjustment in the market for a good. In Figure 15.4, the money market is initially in equilibrium, with an interest rate of 4 percent and a money supply of $900 billion. When the Fed increases the money supply by $50 billion, households and firms have more money than they want to hold at an interest rate of 4 percent. What do households and firms do with the extra $50 billion? They are most likely to use the money to buy short-term financial assets, such as Treasury bills, or to deposit the money in interest-paying bank accounts, such as certificates of deposit. This increase in demand for interest-paying bank accounts and short-term financial assets allows banks to offer lower interest rates on certificates of deposit, and it allows sellers of Treasury bills and similar assets to also offer lower interest rates. As the interest rates on certificates of deposit, Treasury bills, and other short-term assets fall, the opportunity cost of holding money also falls. Households and firms move down the money demand curve. Eventually the interest rate will have fallen enough that households and firms are willing to hold the additional $50 billion worth of money the Fed has created, and the money market will be back in equilibrium. To summarize: *When the Fed increases the money supply, the short-term interest rate must fall until it reaches a level at which households and firms are willing to hold the additional money.*

Figure 15.5 shows what happens when the Fed decreases the money supply. The money market is initially in equilibrium, at an interest rate of 4 percent and a money supply of $900 billion. If the Fed decreases the money supply to $850 billion, households and firms will be holding less money than they would like, relative to other financial assets, at an interest rate of 4 percent. To increase their money holdings, they will sell Treasury bills and other short-term financial assets and withdraw funds from certificates of deposit and other interest-paying bank accounts. Banks will have to offer higher interest rates in order to retain depositors, and sellers of Treasury bills and similar securities will have to offer higher interest rates in order to find buyers. Rising short-term interest rates increase the opportunity cost of holding money, causing households and firms to move up the money demand curve. Equilibrium is finally restored at an interest rate of 5 percent.

Figure 15.5

The Effect on Interest Rates When the Fed Decreases the Money Supply

When the Fed decreases the money supply, households and firms will initially hold less money than they want, relative to other financial assets. Households and firms will sell Treasury bills and other financial assets and withdraw money from interest-paying bank accounts. These actions will increase interest rates. Eventually, interest rates will rise to the point at which households and firms will be willing to hold the smaller amount of money that results from the Fed's actions. In the figure, a reduction in the money supply from $900 billion to $850 billion causes the money supply curve to shift to the left, from MS_1 to MS_2, and causes the equilibrium interest rate to rise from 4 percent to 5 percent.

A Tale of Two Interest Rates

In Chapter 10, we discussed the loanable funds model of the interest rate. In that model, the equilibrium interest rate is determined by the demand and supply for loanable funds. Why do we need two models of the interest rate? The answer is that the loanable funds model is concerned with the *long-term real rate of interest*, and the money market model is concerned with the *short-term nominal rate of interest*. The long-term real rate of interest is the interest rate that is most relevant when savers consider purchasing a long-term financial investment such as a corporate bond. It is also the rate of interest that is most relevant to firms that are borrowing to finance long-term investment projects such as new factories or office buildings, or to households that are taking out mortgage loans to buy new homes.

When conducting monetary policy, however, the short-term nominal interest rate is the most relevant interest rate because it is the interest rate most affected by increases and decreases in the money supply. Often—but not always—there is a close connection between movements in the short-term nominal interest rate and movements in the long-term real interest rate. So, when the Fed takes actions to increase the short-term nominal interest rate, usually the long-term real interest rate also increases. In other words, as we will discuss in the next section, when the interest rate on Treasury bills rises, the real interest rate on mortgage loans usually also rises, although sometimes only after a delay.

Choosing a Monetary Policy Target

As we have seen, the Fed uses monetary policy targets to affect economic variables such as real GDP or the price level, that are closely related to the Fed's policy goals. The Fed can use either the money supply or the interest rate as its monetary policy target. As Figure 15.5 shows, the Fed is capable of affecting both. The Fed has generally focused more on the interest rate than on the money supply. Since 1980, deregulation and financial innovations, including paying interest on checking accounts and the introduction of money market mutual funds, have made M1 less relevant as a measure of the medium of exchange. For a time, these developments led the Fed to rely on M2, a broader measure of the money supply that had a more stable historical relationship to economic growth. Even this relationship broke down in the early 1990s. In July 1993, then Fed Chairman Alan Greenspan informed the U.S. Congress that the Fed would cease using M1 or M2 targets to guide the conduct of monetary policy. The Fed has correspondingly increased its reliance on interest rate targets.

There are many different interest rates in the economy. For purposes of monetary policy, the Fed has targeted the interest rate known as the *federal funds rate*. In the next section, we discuss the federal funds rate before examining how targeting the interest rate can help the Fed achieve its monetary policy goals.

The Importance of the Federal Funds Rate

Recall from Chapter 14 that every bank must keep 10 percent of its checking account deposits above a certain threshold amount as reserves, either as currency held in the bank or as deposits with the Fed. The Fed pays banks a low interest rate on their reserve deposits, so banks normally have an incentive to invest reserves above the 10 percent minimum. As the financial crisis that began in 2007 deepened during 2008, bank reserves soared as banks attempted to meet an increase in deposit withdrawals and as they became reluctant to lend to any borrowers except those with the most flawless credit histories. These conditions were very unusual, however. In normal times, banks keep few excess reserves, and when they need additional reserves, they borrow in the *federal funds market* from banks that have reserves available. The **federal funds rate** is the interest rate banks charge each other on loans in the federal funds market. The loans in that market are usually very short term, often just overnight.

Federal funds rate The interest rate banks charge each other for overnight loans.

Despite the name, the Fed does not legally set the federal funds rate. Instead, the rate is determined by the supply of reserves relative to the demand for them. Because the Fed can increase and decrease the supply of bank reserves through open

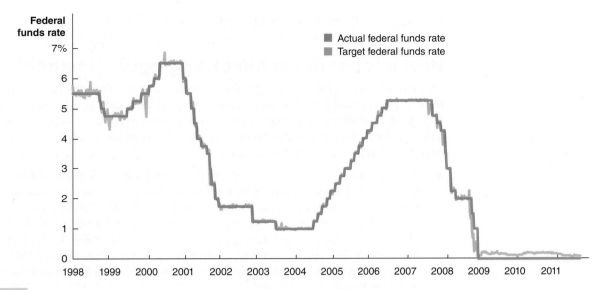

Figure 15.6 Federal Funds Rate Targeting, January 1998–September 2011

The Fed does not set the federal funds rate, but its ability to increase or decrease bank reserves quickly through open market operations keeps the actual federal funds rate close to the Fed's target rate. The orange line is the Fed's target for the federal funds rate, and the jagged green line represents the actual value for the federal funds rate on a weekly basis.

Note: The federal funds target for the period after December 2008 was 0 to 0.25 percent.
Data from Board of Governers of the Federal Reserve System.

market operations, it can set a *target* for the federal funds rate and usually come very close to hitting it. The FOMC announces a target for the federal funds rate after each meeting. In Figure 15.6, the orange line shows the Fed's targets for the federal funds rate since 1998. The jagged green line represents the actual federal funds rate on a weekly basis. The figure shows the rapid declines in the target for the federal funds rate beginning in September 2007, as the Fed responded to the start of the financial crisis. In December 2008, the Fed announced a range of 0 to 0.25 percent as its target. The actual federal funds rate fluctuated between 0.06 and 0.23 percent. These very low federal funds rates reflect the severity of the financial crisis.

The federal funds rate is not directly relevant for households and firms. Only banks can borrow or lend in the federal funds market. However, changes in the federal funds rate usually result in changes in interest rates on other short-term financial assets, such as Treasury bills, and changes in interest rates on long-term financial assets, such as corporate bonds and mortgages. A change in the federal funds rate has a greater effect on short-term interest rates than on long-term interest rates, and its effect on long-term interest rates may occur only after a lag in time. Although a majority of economists support the Fed's choice of the interest rate as its monetary policy target, some economists believe the Fed should concentrate on the money supply instead. We will discuss the views of these economists later in this chapter.

Monetary Policy and Economic Activity

Remember that the Fed uses the federal funds rate as a monetary policy target because it has good control of the federal funds rate through open market operations and because it believes that changes in the federal funds rate will ultimately affect economic variables that are related to its monetary policy goals. It is important to consider again the distinction between the nominal interest rate and the real interest rate. Recall that we calculate the real interest rate by subtracting the inflation rate from the nominal interest rate. Ultimately, the ability of the Fed to use monetary policy to affect economic variables such as real GDP depends on its ability to affect real interest rates, such as the real interest rates on mortgages and corporate bonds. Because the federal funds rate is a short-term nominal interest rate, the Fed sometimes has difficulty affecting long-term

15.3 LEARNING OBJECTIVE

Use aggregate demand and aggregate supply graphs to show the effects of monetary policy on real GDP and the price level.

real interest rates. Nevertheless, for purposes of the following discussion, we will assume that the Fed is able to use open market operations to affect long-term real interest rates.

How Interest Rates Affect Aggregate Demand

Changes in interest rates affect *aggregate demand*, which is the total level of spending in the economy. Recall from Chapter 13 that aggregate demand has four components: consumption, investment, government purchases, and net exports. Changes in interest rates will not affect government purchases, but they will affect the other three components of aggregate demand in the following ways:

- *Consumption.* Many households finance purchases of consumer durables, such as automobiles and furniture, by borrowing. Lower interest rates lead to increased spending on durables because they lower the total cost of these goods to consumers by lowering the interest payments on loans. Higher interest rates raise the cost of consumer durables, and households will buy fewer of them. Lower interest rates also reduce the return to saving, leading households to save less and spend more. Higher interest rates increase the return to saving, leading households to save more and spend less.

- *Investment.* Firms finance most of their spending on machinery, equipment, and factories out of their profits or by borrowing. Firms borrow either from the financial markets by issuing corporate bonds or from banks. Higher interest rates on corporate bonds or on bank loans make it more expensive for firms to borrow, so they will undertake fewer investment projects. Lower interest rates make it less expensive for firms to borrow, so they will undertake more investment projects. Lower interest rates can also increase investment through their effect on stock prices. As interest rates decline, stocks become a more attractive investment relative to bonds. The increase in demand for stocks raises their price. An increase in stock prices sends a signal to firms that the future profitability of investment projects has increased. By issuing additional shares of stocks, firms can acquire the funds they need to buy new factories and equipment, thereby increasing investment.

   Finally, spending by households on new homes is also part of investment. When interest rates on mortgage loans rise, the cost of buying new homes rises, and fewer new homes will be purchased. When interest rates on mortgage loans fall, more new homes will be purchased.

- *Net exports.* Recall that net exports are equal to spending by foreign households and firms on goods and services produced in the United States minus spending by U.S. households and firms on goods and services produced in other countries. The value of net exports depends partly on the exchange rate between the dollar and foreign currencies. When the value of the dollar rises, households and firms in other countries will pay more for goods and services produced in the United States, but U.S. households and firms will pay less for goods and services produced in other countries. As a result, the United States will export less and import more, so net exports fall. When the value of the dollar falls, net exports will rise. If interest rates in the United States rise relative to interest rates in other countries, investing in U.S. financial assets will become more desirable, causing foreign investors to increase their demand for dollars, which will increase the value of the dollar. As the value of the dollar increases, net exports will fall. If interest rates in the United States decline relative to interest rates in other countries, the value of the dollar will fall, and net exports will rise.

The Effects of Monetary Policy on Real GDP and the Price Level

In Chapter 13, we developed the *aggregate demand and aggregate supply model* to explain fluctuations in real GDP and the price level. In the basic version of the model, we assume that there is no economic growth, so the long-run aggregate supply curve

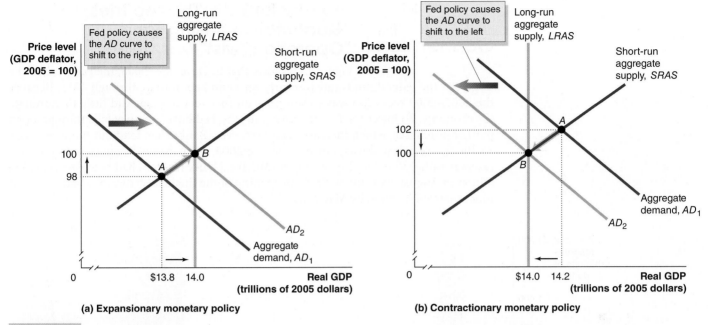

(a) Expansionary monetary policy

(b) Contractionary monetary policy

Figure 15.7 Monetary Policy

In panel (a), the economy begins in a recession at point A, with real GDP of $13.8 trillion and a price level of 98. An expansionary monetary policy causes aggregate demand to shift to the right, from AD_1 to AD_2, increasing real GDP from $13.8 trillion to $14.0 trillion and the price level from 98 to 100 (point B). With real GDP back at its potential level, the Fed can meet its goal of high employment.

In panel (b), the economy begins at point A, with real GDP at $14.2 trillion and the price level at 102. Because real GDP is greater than potential GDP, the economy experiences rising wages and prices. A contractionary monetary policy causes aggregate demand to shift to the left, from AD_1 to AD_2, decreasing real GDP from $14.2 trillion to $14.0 trillion and the price level from 102 to 100 (point B). With real GDP back at its potential level, the Fed can meet its goal of price stability.

does not shift. In panel (a) of Figure 15.7, we assume that the economy is in short-run equilibrium at point A, where the aggregate demand (AD_1) curve intersects the short-run aggregate supply ($SRAS$) curve. Real GDP is below potential real GDP, as shown by the $LRAS$ curve, so the economy is in a recession, with some firms operating below normal capacity and some workers having been laid off. To reach its goal of high employment, the Fed needs to carry out an **expansionary monetary policy** by increasing the money supply and decreasing interest rates. Lower interest rates cause an increase in consumption, investment, and net exports, which shifts the aggregate demand curve to the right, from AD_1 to AD_2. Real GDP increases from $13.8 trillion to potential GDP of $14.0 trillion, and the price level rises from 98 to 100 (point B). The policy successfully returns real GDP to its potential level. Rising production leads to increasing employment, allowing the Fed to achieve its goal of high employment.

In panel (b) of Figure 15.7, the economy is in short-run equilibrium at point A, with real GDP of $14.2 trillion, which is above potential real GDP of $14.0 trillion. With some firms producing beyond their normal capacity and the unemployment rate very low, wages and prices are increasing. To reach its goal of price stability, the Fed needs to carry out a **contractionary monetary policy** by decreasing the money supply and increasing interest rates. Higher interest rates cause a decrease in consumption, investment, and net exports, which shifts the aggregate demand curve from AD_1 to AD_2. Real GDP decreases from $14.2 trillion to $14.0 trillion, and the price level falls from 102 to 100 (point B). Why would the Fed want to intentionally cause real GDP to decline? Because in the long run, real GDP cannot continue to remain above potential GDP. Attempting to keep real GDP above potential GDP would result in rising inflation. As aggregate demand declines and real GDP returns to its potential level, upward pressure on wages and prices will be reduced, allowing the Fed to achieve its goal of price stability.

We can conclude that the Fed can use monetary policy to affect the price level and, in the short run, the level of real GDP, allowing it to attain its policy goals of high employment and price stability.

Expansionary monetary policy The Federal Reserve's decreasing interest rates to increase real GDP.

Contractionary monetary policy The Federal Reserve's increasing interest rates to reduce inflation.

Making
the
Connection

Too Low for Zero: The Fed Tries "Quantitative Easing" and "Operation Twist"

Figure 15.6 shows that in December 2008, the Fed pushed the target for the federal funds rate to nearly zero and kept it there through 2011. Because the 2007–2009 recession was so severe, even this very low rate did little to stimulate the economy. To lower the federal funds rate, the Fed buys Treasury bills through open market purchases, which increases bank reserves. Banks then lend out these reserves. As the figure below shows, however, in late 2008, many banks began piling up excess reserves rather than lending the funds out. Total bank reserves had been less than $50 billion in August 2008, but with the deepening of the financial crisis, they had soared to more than $900 billion by May 2009.

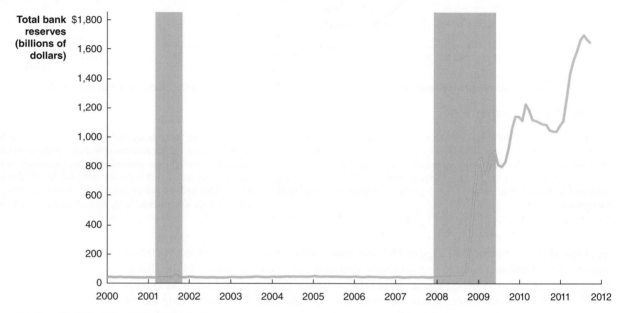

Data from The Federal Reserve Bank of St. Louis.

The increase in bank reserves was partly due to the Fed's decision in October 2008 to start paying interest of 0.25 percent on bank reserves held as deposits at the Fed. Primarily, though, the increase in reserves occurred because banks were reluctant to make loans at low interest rates to households and firms whose financial positions had been damaged by the recession. Some economists believed the Fed was facing a situation known as a *liquidity trap*, in which short-term interest rates are pushed to zero, leaving the central bank unable to lower them further. Some economists believe that liquidity traps occurred in the United States during the 1930s and in Japan during the 1990s.

Not being able to push the target for the federal funds rate below zero was a problem for the Fed. Glenn Rudebusch, an economist at the Federal Reserve Bank of San Francisco, calculated that given how high the unemployment rate was, the appropriate target for the federal funds rate was –5 percent. Because the federal funds rate cannot be negative, the Fed turned to other policies. In particular, the Fed decided to embark on a policy of *quantitative easing*, which involves buying securities beyond the short-term Treasury securities that are usually involved in open market operations. The Fed began purchasing 10-year Treasury notes to keep their interest rates from rising. Interest rates on home mortgage loans typically move closely with interest rates on 10-year Treasury notes. The Fed also purchased certain *mortgage-backed securities*. The Fed's objective was to keep interest rates on mortgages low and to keep funds flowing into the mortgage market in order to help stimulate demand for housing.

The Fed's first round of quantitative easing began in November 2008 and ended in June 2010. With the economy recovering only slowly, in November 2010, the Fed announced a second round of quantitative easing (dubbed QE2). With QE2, the Fed bought an additional $600 billion in long-term Treasury securities through June 2011. In September 2011, with the economic recovery remaining weak, the Fed announced a new program under which it would purchase $400 billion in long-term Treasury securities while selling an equal amount of shorter-term Treasury securities. This program, which some people in financial markets called "Operation Twist," had the same objective as quantitative easing: to reduce interest rates on long-term Treasury securities in order to increase aggregate demand.

Later in this chapter, we will consider other new programs the Fed put in place to deal with the recession of 2007–2009 and the slow recovery that followed, as its traditional focus on lowering the federal funds rate to stimulate the economy proved ineffective.

Based on Glenn Rudebusch, "The Fed's Monetary Policy Response to the Current Crisis," FRBSF Economic Letter, May 22, 2009.

The Fed pushed interest rates to very low levels during 2008 and 2009.

Your Turn: Test your understanding by doing related problems 3.11 and 3.12 on page 526 at the end of this chapter.

MyEconLab

Can the Fed Eliminate Recessions?

Panel (a) of Figure 15.7 on page 501 shows an expansionary monetary policy that performs perfectly by shifting the *AD* curve to bring the economy back to potential GDP. In fact, however, this ideal is very difficult for the Fed to achieve, as the length and severity of the 2007–2009 recession indicates. In practice, the best the Fed can do is keep recessions shorter and milder than they would otherwise be.

If the Fed is to be successful in offsetting the effects of the business cycle, it needs to quickly recognize the need for a change in monetary policy. If the Fed is late in recognizing that a recession has begun or that the inflation rate is increasing, it may not be able to implement a new policy soon enough to do much good. In fact, implementing a policy too late may actually destabilize the economy. To see how this can happen, consider Figure 15.8. The straight line represents the long-run growth trend in real GDP in the United States. On average, real GDP grows about 3.3 percent per year. The actual path of real GDP differs from the underlying trend because of the business cycle, which is shown by the red curved line. As we saw in Chapter 10, the actual business cycle is more irregular than the stylized cycle shown here.

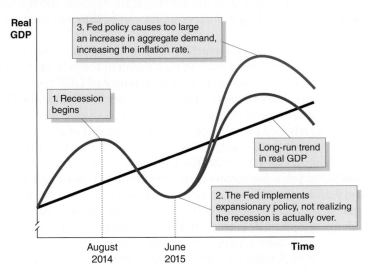

Figure 15.8

The Effect of a Poorly Timed Monetary Policy on the Economy

The upward-sloping straight line represents the long-run growth trend in real GDP. The curved red line represents the path real GDP takes because of the business cycle. If the Fed is too late in implementing a change in monetary policy, real GDP will follow the curved blue line. The Fed's expansionary monetary policy results in too great an increase in aggregate demand during the next expansion, which causes an increase in the inflation rate.

Suppose that a recession begins in August 2014. Because it takes months for economic statistics to be gathered by the Commerce Department, the Census Bureau, the Bureau of Labor Statistics, and the Fed itself, there is a *lag*, or delay, before the Fed recognizes that a recession has begun. Then it takes time for the Fed's economists to analyze the data. Finally, in June 2015, the FOMC concludes that the economy is in recession and begins an expansionary monetary policy. As it turns out, June 2015 is actually the trough of the recession, meaning that the recession has already ended, and an expansion has begun. In these circumstances, the Fed's expansionary policy is not needed to end the recession. The increase in aggregate demand caused by the Fed's lowering interest rates is likely to push the economy beyond potential real GDP and cause a significant acceleration in inflation. Real GDP ends up following the path indicated by the blue curved line. The Fed has inadvertently engaged in a *procyclical policy*, which increases the severity of the business cycle, as opposed to a *countercyclical policy*, which is meant to reduce the severity of the business cycle, and which is what the Fed intends to use. As we saw in Chapter 10, the typical recession since 1950 has lasted less than one year, which increases the likelihood that the Fed may accidentally engage in a procyclical policy. Making this mistake is, of course, less likely in a long and severe recession such as the recession of 2007–2009.

It is not unusual for employment or manufacturing production to decline for a month or two in the middle of an expansion. Distinguishing these minor ups and downs from the beginning of a recession is difficult. The National Bureau of Economic Research (NBER) announces dates for the beginning and end of recessions that most economists generally accept. An indication of how difficult it is to determine when recessions begin and end is that the NBER generally makes its announcements only after a considerable delay. The NBER did not announce that a recession had begun in March 2001 until November 2001, which is the same month it later determined that the recession had ended. The NBER did not announce that a recession had begun in December 2007 until December 2008. Failing to react until well after a recession has begun (or ended) can be a serious problem for the Fed. In the case of the 2007–2009 recession, however, the Fed did promptly cut the federal funds rate in September 2007, in response to the beginning of the financial crisis, even though the recession did not actually begin until two months later.

Making the Connection | Trying to Hit a Moving Target: Making Policy with "Real-Time Data"

The Fed relies on macroeconomic data to formulate monetary policy. One key piece of economic data is GDP, which is calculated quarterly by the Bureau of Economic Analysis (BEA). Unfortunately for Fed policymakers, the GDP data the BEA provides are frequently revised, and the revisions can be large enough that the actual state of the economy can be different from what it at first appeared to be.

The BEA's *advance estimate* of a quarter's GDP is not released until about a month after the quarter has ended. This delay can be a problem for policymakers because it means that, for instance, they will not receive an estimate of GDP for the period from January through March until the end of April. Presenting even more difficulty is the fact that the advance estimate will be subject to a number of revisions. The second estimate of a quarter's GDP is released about two months after the end of the quarter. The third estimate is released about three months after the end of the quarter. Although the BEA used to refer to the third estimate as the "final estimate," in fact, it continues to revise its estimates through the years. For instance, the BEA releases first annual, second annual, and third annual estimates one, two, and three years after the third estimate. Nor is that the end, because benchmark revisions of the estimates will occur in later years.

Why so many estimates? Because GDP is such a comprehensive measure of output in the economy, it is very time-consuming to collect the necessary data. To provide the advance estimate, the BEA relies on surveys conducted by the Commerce Department of retail sales and manufacturing shipments, as well as data from trade organizations, estimates of government spending, and so on. As time passes, these organizations gather additional data, and the BEA is able to refine its estimates.

Do these revisions to the GDP estimates matter? Sometimes they do, as the following example indicates. At the beginning of 2001, there were some indications that the U.S. economy might be headed for recession. The dot-com stock market bubble had burst the previous spring, wiping out trillions of dollars in stockholder wealth. Overbuilding of fiber-optic cable networks and other information technology also weighed on the economy. The advance estimate of the first quarter's GDP, though, showed a reasonably healthy increase in real GDP of 2.0% at an annual rate. It seemed as if there was nothing for government policymakers to be worried about. But, as the graph below shows, that estimate of 2.0% was revised a number of times over the years, mostly downward. Currently, BEA data indicate that real GDP actually declined by 1.3% at an annual rate during the first quarter of 2001. This swing of more than 3 percentage points is a large difference—a difference that changes the picture of what happened during the first quarter of 2001 from one of an economy experiencing moderate growth to one of an economy suffering a significant decline. The National Bureau of Economic Research dates the recession of 2001 as having begun in March, but some economists believe it actually began at the end of 2000. The current BEA estimates of GDP provide some support for this view.

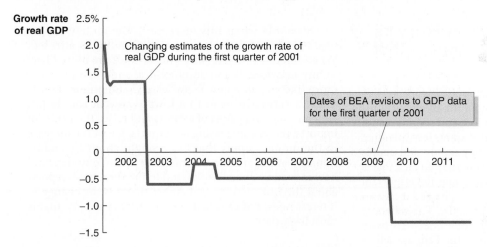

This example shows that in addition to the other problems the Federal Reserve encounters in successfully conducting monetary policy, it must make decisions using data that may be subject to substantial revisions.

Based on Federal Reserve Bank of Philadelphia, "Historical Data Files for the Real-Time Data Set," August 24, 2010; and Bruce T. Grimm and Teresa Weadock, "Gross Domestic Product: Revisions and Source Data," *Survey of Current Business*, Vol. 86, No. 2, February 2006, pp. 11–15.

Your Turn: Test your understanding by doing related problems 3.13 and 3.14 on pages 526 and 527 at the end of this chapter.   MyEconLab

---

A Summary of How Monetary Policy Works

Table 15.1 compares the steps involved in expansionary and contractionary monetary policies. We need to note an important qualification to this summary. At every point, we should add the phrase "relative to what would have happened without the policy." Table 15.1 isolates the impact of monetary policy, *holding constant all other factors affecting the variables involved*. In other words, we are invoking the *ceteris paribus* condition, discussed in Chapter 3. This point is important because, for example, a contractionary monetary policy does not cause the price level to fall; rather, a contractionary monetary policy causes the price level *to rise by less than it would have risen without the policy*. One final note on terminology: An expansionary monetary policy is sometimes referred to as a *loose* policy, or an *easy* policy. A contractionary monetary policy is sometimes referred to as a *tight* policy.

Table 15.1 Expansionary and Contractionary Monetary Policies

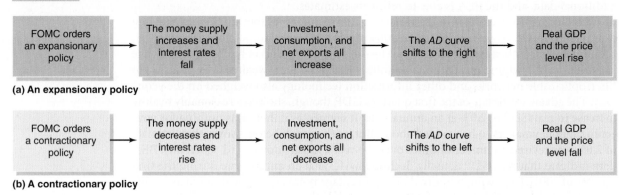

| FOMC orders an expansionary policy | → | The money supply increases and interest rates fall | → | Investment, consumption, and net exports all increase | → | The *AD* curve shifts to the right | → | Real GDP and the price level rise |

(a) An expansionary policy

| FOMC orders a contractionary policy | → | The money supply decreases and interest rates rise | → | Investment, consumption, and net exports all decrease | → | The *AD* curve shifts to the left | → | Real GDP and the price level fall |

(b) A contractionary policy

Don't Let This Happen to You

Remember That with Monetary Policy, It's the Interest Rates—Not the Money—That Counts

It is tempting to think of monetary policy working like this: If the Fed wants more spending in the economy, it increases the money supply, and people spend more because they now have more money. If the Fed wants less spending in the economy, it decreases the money supply, and people spend less because they now have less money. In fact, that is *not* how monetary policy works. Remember the important difference between money and income: The Fed increases the money supply by buying Treasury bills. The sellers of the Treasury bills have just exchanged one asset—Treasury bills—for another asset—a check from the Fed; the sellers have *not* increased their income. Even though the money supply is now larger, no one's income has increased, so no one's spending should be affected.

It is only when this increase in the money supply results in lower interest rates that spending is affected. When interest rates are lower, households are more likely to buy new homes and automobiles, and businesses are more likely to buy new factories and computers. Lower interest rates also lead to a lower value of the dollar, which lowers the prices of exports and raises the prices of imports, thereby increasing net exports. It isn't the increase in the money supply that has brought about this additional spending; *it's the lower interest rates*. To understand how monetary policy works, and to interpret news reports about the Fed's actions, remember that it is the change in interest rates, not the change in the money supply, that is most important.

MyEconLab

Your Turn: Test your understanding by doing related problem 3.15 on page 527 at the end of this chapter.

15.4 LEARNING OBJECTIVE

Use the dynamic aggregate demand and aggregate supply model to analyze monetary policy.

Monetary Policy in the Dynamic Aggregate Demand and Aggregate Supply Model*

The overview of monetary policy we just finished contains a key idea: The Fed can use monetary policy to affect aggregate demand, thereby changing the price level and the level of real GDP. The discussion of monetary policy illustrated by Figure 15.7 on page 501 is simplified, however, because it ignores two important facts about the economy: (1) The economy experiences continuing inflation, with the price level rising every year, and (2) the economy experiences long-run growth, with the *LRAS* curve shifting to the right every year. In Chapter 13, we developed a *dynamic aggregate demand and aggregate supply model* that takes into account these two facts. In this section, we use the dynamic model to gain a more complete understanding of monetary policy. Let's briefly review the dynamic model. Recall from Chapter 13 that over time, the U.S. labor force and U.S. capital stock will increase. Technological change will also occur. The result will be an increase in potential real GDP, which we show by the long-run aggregate supply

---

* This section may be omitted without loss of continuity.

curve shifting to the right. These factors will also result in firms supplying more goods and services at any given price level in the short run, which we show by the short-run aggregate supply curve shifting to the right. During most years, the aggregate demand curve will also shift to the right, indicating that aggregate expenditure will be higher at every price level. There are several reasons aggregate expenditure usually increases: As population grows and incomes rise, consumption will increase over time. Also, as the economy grows, firms expand capacity, and new firms are established, increasing investment spending. Finally, an expanding population and an expanding economy require increased government services, such as more police officers and teachers, so government purchases will expand.

The Effects of Monetary Policy on Real GDP and the Price Level: A More Complete Account

During certain periods, AD does not increase enough during the year to keep the economy at potential GDP. This slow growth in aggregate demand may be due to households and firms becoming pessimistic about the future state of the economy, leading them to cut back their spending on consumer durables, houses, and factories. As we have seen, the collapse of the housing bubble and the resulting financial crisis had a negative effect on aggregate demand during the 2007–2009 recession. Other possibilities exist as well: The federal government might decide to balance the budget by cutting back its purchases, or recessions in other countries might cause a decline in U.S. exports. In the hypothetical situation shown in Figure 15.9, in the first year, the economy is in equilibrium, at potential real GDP of $14.0 trillion and a price level of 100 (point A). In the second year, $LRAS$ increases to $14.4 trillion, but AD increases only to $AD_{2(\text{without policy})}$, which is not enough to keep the economy in macroeconomic equilibrium at potential GDP. If the Fed does not intervene, the short-run equilibrium will occur at $14.3 trillion (point B). The $100 billion gap between this level of real GDP and potential real GDP at $LRAS_2$ means that some firms are operating at less than their normal capacity. Incomes and profits will fall, firms will begin to lay off workers, and the unemployment rate will rise.

Economists at the Federal Reserve closely monitor the economy and continually update forecasts of future levels of real GDP and prices. When these economists anticipate that aggregate demand is not growing fast enough to allow the economy to remain at full employment, they present their findings to the FOMC, which decides

Figure 15.9

An Expansionary Monetary Policy

The economy begins in equilibrium at point A, with real GDP of $14.0 trillion and a price level of 100. Without monetary policy, aggregate demand will shift from AD_1 to $AD_{2(\text{without policy})}$, which is not enough to keep the economy at full employment because long-run aggregate supply has shifted from $LRAS_1$ to $LRAS_2$. The economy will be in short-run equilibrium at point B, with real GDP of $14.3 trillion and a price level of 102. By lowering interest rates, the Fed increases investment, consumption, and net exports sufficiently to shift aggregate demand to $AD_{2(\text{with policy})}$. The economy will be in equilibrium at point C, with real GDP of $14.4 trillion, which is its full employment level, and a price level of 103. The price level is higher than it would have been if the Fed had not acted to increase spending in the economy.

whether circumstances require a change in monetary policy. For example, suppose that the FOMC meets and considers a forecast from the staff indicating that during the following year, a gap of $100 billion will open between equilibrium real GDP and potential real GDP. In other words, the macroeconomic equilibrium illustrated by point *B* in Figure 15.9 will occur. The FOMC may then decide to carry out an expansionary monetary policy to lower interest rates to stimulate aggregate demand. The figure shows the results of a successful attempt to do this: *AD* has shifted to the right, and equilibrium occurs at potential GDP (point *C*). The Fed will have successfully headed off the falling incomes and rising unemployment that otherwise would have occurred. Bear in mind that we are illustrating a perfectly executed monetary policy that keeps the economy at potential GDP, which is difficult to achieve in practice for reasons already discussed.

Notice in Figure 15.9 that the expansionary monetary policy caused the inflation rate to be higher than it would have been. Without the expansionary policy, the price level would have risen from 100 to 102, so the inflation rate for the year would have been 2 percent. By shifting the aggregate demand curve, the expansionary policy caused the price level to increase from 102 to 103, raising the inflation rate from 2 percent to 3 percent.

Using Monetary Policy to Fight Inflation

In addition to using an expansionary monetary policy to reduce the severity of recessions, the Fed can also use a contractionary monetary policy to keep aggregate demand from expanding so rapidly that the inflation rate begins to increase. Figure 15.10 shows the situation during 2005 and 2006, when the Fed faced this possibility. During 2005, the economy was at equilibrium at potential GDP, but Fed Chair Alan Greenspan and other members of the FOMC were concerned that the continuing boom in the housing market might lead aggregate demand to increase so rapidly that the inflation rate would begin to accelerate. The Fed had been gradually increasing the target for the federal funds rate since mid-2004.

When Ben Bernanke assumed office as Fed chair in early 2006, he advocated continued increases in the target for the federal funds rate to slow the growth in aggregate demand. By June 2006, the target for the federal funds rate had been raised

Figure 15.10

A Contractionary Monetary Policy in 2006

The economy began 2005 in equilibrium at point *A*, with real GDP equal to potential GDP of $12.6 trillion and a price level of 100.0. From 2005 to 2006, potential GDP increased from $12.6 trillion to $12.9 trillion, as long-run aggregate supply increased from *LRAS*₂₀₀₅ to *LRAS*₂₀₀₆. The Fed raised interest rates because it believed the housing boom was causing aggregate demand to increase too rapidly. Without the increase in interest rates, aggregate demand would have shifted from *AD*₂₀₀₅ to *AD*₂₀₀₆(without policy), and the new short-run equilibrium would have occurred at point *B*. Real GDP would have been $13.2 trillion—$300 billion greater than potential GDP—and the price level would have been 104.5. The increase in interest rates resulted in aggregate demand increasing only to *AD*₂₀₀₆(with policy). Equilibrium occurred at point *C*, with real GDP of $13.0 trillion being only $100 billion greater than potential GDP and the price level rising only to 103.2.

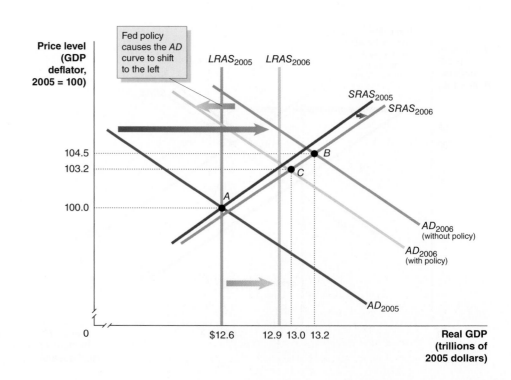

to 5.25 percent, from the low rate of 1 percent that had prevailed from June 2003 to May 2004. The FOMC issues a statement after each meeting that summarizes the committee's views on the current state of the economy and gives some indication of how monetary policy might change in the near future. After its meeting on June 29, 2006, the FOMC included the following remarks in its statement:

> The Federal Open Market Committee decided today to raise its target for the federal funds rate ... to 5-1/4 percent. Recent indicators suggest that economic growth is moderating from its quite strong pace earlier this year, partly reflecting a gradual cooling of the housing market and the lagged effects of increases in ... interest rates.... Although the moderation in the growth of aggregate demand should help to limit inflation pressures over time, the Committee judges that some inflation risks remain.

The committee kept the target for the federal funds rate constant at 5.25 percent until September 2007, when concern about difficulties in financial markets led it to cut the target to 4.75 percent. Although it is impossible to know exactly what would have happened during 2006 without the Fed's policy change, Figure 15.10 presents a plausible scenario. The figure shows that without the Fed's actions to increase interest rates, aggregate demand would have shifted farther to the right, and equilibrium would have occurred at a level of real GDP that was beyond the potential level. The price level would have risen from 100.0 in 2005 to 104.5 in 2006, meaning that the inflation rate would have been 4.5 percent. Because the Fed kept aggregate demand from increasing as much as it otherwise would have, equilibrium occurred at potential real GDP, and the price level in 2006 rose to only 103.2, keeping the inflation rate at 3.2 percent.

Solved Problem 15.4

The Effects of Monetary Policy

The hypothetical information in the following table shows what the values for real GDP and the price level will be in 2015 if the Fed does *not* use monetary policy:

Year	Potential GDP	Real GDP	Price Level
2014	$15.2 trillion	$15.2 trillion	114
2015	15.6 trillion	15.4 trillion	116

a. If the Fed wants to keep real GDP at its potential level in 2015, should it use an expansionary policy or a contractionary policy? Should the trading desk buy Treasury bills or sell them?

b. Suppose the Fed's policy is successful in keeping real GDP at its potential level in 2015. State whether each of the following will be higher or lower than if the Fed had taken no action:
    i   Real GDP
    ii Potential real GDP
    iii The inflation rate
    iv The unemployment rate

c. Draw an aggregate demand and aggregate supply graph to illustrate your answer. Be sure that your graph contains *LRAS* curves for 2014 and 2015; *SRAS* curves for 2014 and 2015; *AD* curve for 2014 and 2015, with and without monetary policy action; and equilibrium real GDP and the price level in 2015, with and without policy.

Solving the Problem

Step 1: **Review the chapter material**. This problem is about the effects of monetary policy on real GDP and the price level, so you may want to review the section "The Effects of Monetary Policy on Real GDP and the Price Level: A More Complete Account," which begins on page 507.

Step 2: **Answer the questions in part a. by explaining how the Fed can keep real GDP at its potential level.** The information in the table tells us that without monetary policy, the economy will be below potential real GDP in 2015. To keep real GDP at its potential level, the Fed must undertake an expansionary policy. To carry out an expansionary policy, the trading desk needs to buy Treasury bills. Buying Treasury bills will increase reserves in the banking system. Banks will increase their loans, which will increase the money supply and lower the interest rate.

Step 3: **Answer part b. by explaining the effect of the Fed's policy.** If the Fed's policy is successful, real GDP in 2015 will increase from $15.4 trillion, as given in the table, to its potential level of $15.6 trillion. Potential real GDP is not affected by monetary policy, so its value will not change. Because the level of real GDP will be higher, the unemployment rate will be lower than it would have been without policy. The expansionary monetary policy shifts the AD curve to the right, so short-run equilibrium will move up the short-run aggregate supply (SRAS) curve, and the price level will be higher.

Step 4: **Answer part c. by drawing the graph.** Your graph should look similar to Figure 15.9.

The economy starts in equilibrium in 2014 at point A, with the AD and SRAS curves intersecting along the LRAS curve. Real GDP is at its potential level of $15.2 trillion, and the price level is 114. Without monetary policy, the AD curve shifts to $AD_{2015(\text{without policy})}$, and the economy is in short-run equilibrium at point B. Because potential real GDP has increased from $15.2 trillion to $15.6 trillion, short-run equilibrium real GDP of $15.4 trillion is below the potential level. The price level has increased from 114 to 116. With policy, the AD curve shifts to $AD_{2015(\text{with policy})}$, and the economy is in equilibrium at point C. Real GDP is at its potential level of $15.6 trillion. We don't have enough information to be sure of the new equilibrium price level. We do know that it will be higher than 116. The graph shows the price level rising to 118. Therefore, without the Fed's expansionary policy, the inflation rate in 2015 would have been about 1.8 percent. With policy, it will be about 3.5 percent.

Extra Credit: Bear in mind that in reality, the Fed is unable to use monetary policy to keep real GDP exactly at its potential level, as this problem suggests.

MyEconLab **Your Turn:** For more practice, do related problems 4.4 and 4.5 on pages 527–528 at the end of this chapter.

A Closer Look at the Fed's Setting of Monetary Policy Targets

15.5 LEARNING OBJECTIVE

Discuss the Fed's setting of monetary policy targets.

We have seen that in carrying out monetary policy, the Fed changes its target for the federal funds rate, depending on the state of the economy. During times when the economy is not experiencing a financial crisis, is using the federal funds rate as a target the best way to conduct monetary policy? If the Fed targets the federal funds rate, how should it decide what the target level should be? In this section, we consider some important issues concerning the Fed's targeting policy.

Should the Fed Target the Money Supply?

Some economists have argued that rather than use an interest rate as its monetary policy target, the Fed should use the money supply. Many of the economists who make this argument belong to a school of thought known as *monetarism*. The leader of the monetarist school was Nobel Laureate Milton Friedman, who was skeptical that the Fed would be able to correctly time changes in monetary policy.

Friedman and his followers favored replacing *monetary policy* with a *monetary growth rule*. Ordinarily, we expect monetary policy to respond to changing economic conditions: When the economy is in recession, the Fed reduces interest rates, and when inflation is increasing, the Fed raises interest rates. A monetary growth rule, in contrast, is a plan for increasing the money supply at a constant rate that does not change in response to economic conditions. Friedman and his followers proposed a monetary growth rule of increasing the money supply every year at a rate equal to the long-run growth rate of real GDP, which is about 3.3 percent. If the Fed adopted this monetary growth rule, it would stick to it through changing economic conditions.

But what happens under a monetary growth rule if the economy moves into recession? Shouldn't the Fed abandon the rule to drive down interest rates? Friedman argued that the Fed should stick to the rule even during recessions because, he believed, active monetary policy destabilizes the economy, increasing the number of recessions and their severity. By keeping the money supply growing at a constant rate, Friedman argued, the Fed would greatly increase economic stability.

Although during the 1970s some economists and politicians pressured the Federal Reserve to adopt a monetary growth rule, most of that pressure has disappeared in recent years. A key reason is that the fairly close relationship between movements in the money supply and movements in real GDP and the price level that existed before 1980 has become much weaker. Since 1980, the growth rate of M1 has been unstable. In some years, M1 has grown more than 10 percent, while in other years, it has actually fallen. Yet despite these wide fluctuations in the growth of M1, growth in real GDP has been fairly stable, and inflation has remained low during most years.

Why Doesn't the Fed Target Both the Money Supply and the Interest Rate?

Most economists believe that an interest rate is the best monetary policy target, but, as we have just seen, other economists believe the Fed should target the money supply. Why doesn't the Fed satisfy both groups by targeting both the money supply and an interest rate? The simple answer to this question is that the Fed can't target both at the same time. To see why, look at Figure 15.11, which shows the money market.

Remember that the Fed controls the money supply, but it does not control money demand. Money demand is determined by decisions of households and firms as they weigh the trade-off between the convenience of money and its low interest rate compared with other financial assets. Suppose the Fed is targeting the interest rate and decides, given conditions in the economy, that the interest rate should be 5 percent.

The Fed Can't Target Both the Money Supply and the Interest Rate

The Fed is forced to choose between using either an interest rate or the money supply as its monetary policy target. In this figure, the Fed can set a target of $900 billion for the money supply or a target of 5 percent for the interest rate, but the Fed can't hit both targets because it can achieve only combinations of the interest rate and the money supply that represent equilibrium in the money market.

Taylor rule A rule developed by John Taylor that links the Fed's target for the federal funds rate to economic variables.

Or, suppose the Fed is targeting the money supply and decides that the money supply should be $900 billion. Figure 15.11 shows that the Fed can bring about an interest rate of 5 percent or a money supply of $900 billion, but it can't bring about both. The point representing an interest rate of 5 percent and a money supply of $900 billion is not on the money demand curve, so it can't represent an equilibrium in the money market. Only combinations of the interest rate and the money supply that represent equilibrium in the money market are possible.

The Fed has to choose between targeting an interest rate and targeting the money supply. For most of the period since World War II, the Fed has chosen an interest rate target.

The Taylor Rule

How does the Fed choose a target for the federal funds rate? The discussions at the meetings of the FOMC can be complex, and they take into account many economic variables. John Taylor of Stanford University has analyzed the factors involved in Fed decision making and developed the **Taylor rule** to explain federal funds rate targeting. The Taylor rule begins with an estimate of the value of the equilibrium real federal funds rate, which is the federal funds rate—adjusted for inflation—that would be consistent with real GDP being equal to potential real GDP in the long run. According to the Taylor rule, the Fed should set the target for the federal funds rate so that it is equal to the sum of the inflation rate, the equilibrium real federal funds rate, and two additional terms. The first of these additional terms is the *inflation gap*—the difference between current inflation and a target rate; the second is the *output gap*—the percentage difference between real GDP and potential real GDP. The inflation gap and output gap are each given "weights" that reflect their influence on the federal funds target rate. With weights of 1/2 for both gaps, we have the following Taylor rule:

Federal funds target rate = Current inflation rate + Real equilibrium federal funds rate
+ ((1/2) × Inflation gap) + ((1/2) × Output gap).

The Taylor rule includes expressions for the inflation gap and the output gap because the Fed is concerned about both inflation and fluctuations in real GDP. Taylor demonstrated that if the equilibrium real federal funds rate is 2 percent and the target rate of inflation is 2 percent, the preceding expression does a good job of explaining changes in the Fed's target for the federal funds rate during most years. Consider an example in which the current inflation rate is 1 percent, and real GDP is 1 percent below potential real GDP. In that case, the inflation gap is 1 percent −2 percent = −1 percent and the output gap is also −1 percent. Inserting these values in the Taylor rule, we can calculate the predicted value for the federal funds target rate:

Federal funds target rate = 1% + 2% + ((1/2) × −1%) + ((1/2) × −1%) = 2%.

The Taylor rule accurately predicted changes in the federal funds target during the period of Alan Greenspan's leadership of the Federal Reserve. For the period of the late 1970s and early 1980s, when Paul Volcker was chairman of the Federal Reserve, the Taylor rule predicts a federal funds rate target *lower* than the actual target the Fed used. This indicates that Chairman Volcker kept the federal funds rate at an unusually high level to bring down the very high inflation rates plaguing the economy in the late 1970s and early 1980s. In contrast, using data from the chairmanship of Arthur Burns from 1970 to 1978, the Taylor rule predicts a federal funds rate target *higher* than the actual target. This indicates that Chairman Burns kept the federal funds rate at an unusually low level during these years, which helps to explain why the inflation rate grew worse. During the mid-2000s the actual federal funds rate was also lower than the predicted federal funds rate. Some economists, including Taylor, argue that these low targets for the federal funds rate contributed to the excessive increase in spending on housing that we will discuss in the next section.

Although the Taylor rule does not account for changes in the target inflation rate or the equilibrium interest rate, many economists view the rule as a convenient tool for analyzing the federal funds target.

Should the Fed Target Inflation?

Over the past decade, many economists and central bankers, including the current Fed chair, Ben Bernanke, have proposed using *inflation targeting* as a framework for conducting monetary policy. With **inflation targeting**, the central bank commits to achieving a publicly announced inflation target of, for example, 2 percent. Inflation targeting does not impose an inflexible rule on the central bank. The central bank would still be free, for example, to take action in case of a severe recession. Nevertheless, monetary policy goals and operations would focus on inflation and inflation forecasts. Inflation targeting has been adopted by the central banks of New Zealand (1989), Canada (1991), the United Kingdom (1992), Finland (1993), Sweden (1993), and Spain (1994), and by the European Central Bank. Inflation targeting has also been used in some newly industrializing countries, such as Chile, South Korea, Mexico, and South Africa, as well as in some transition economies in Eastern Europe, such as the Czech Republic, Hungary, and Poland. Experience with inflation targeting has varied, but typically the move to inflation targeting has been accompanied by lower inflation (sometimes at the cost of temporarily higher unemployment).

Inflation targeting Conducting monetary policy so as to commit the central bank to achieving a publicly announced level of inflation.

Should the Fed adopt an inflation target? Arguments in favor of inflation targeting focus on four points. First, as we have already discussed, in the long run, real GDP returns to its potential level, and potential real GDP is not affected by monetary policy. Therefore, in the long run, the Fed can affect inflation but not real GDP. Having an explicit inflation target would draw the public's attention to this fact. Second, by announcing an inflation target, the Fed would make it easier for households and firms to form accurate expectations of future inflation, improving their planning and the efficiency of the economy. Third, an announced inflation target would help institutionalize good U.S. monetary policy. An inflation target would reduce the chances of abrupt changes in policy occurring as members join and leave the FOMC. Finally, an inflation target would promote accountability for the Fed by providing a yardstick against which Congress and the public could measure the Fed's performance.

Inflation targeting also has opponents, who typically raise three points. First, having a numeric target for inflation reduces the flexibility of monetary policy to address other policy goals. Second, inflation targeting assumes that the Fed can accurately forecast future inflation rates, which is not always the case. Finally, holding the Fed accountable only for an inflation goal may make it less likely that the Fed will achieve other important policy goals.

Although Ben Bernanke becoming chair of the Fed in January 2006 appeared to increase the chances that the Fed would adopt a policy of inflation targeting, the necessity of dealing with the recession of 2007–2009 at least temporarily pushed the issue off the Fed's agenda.

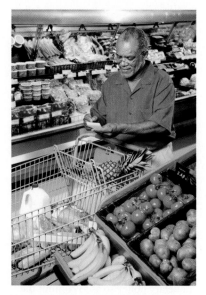

The Fed excludes food and energy prices from its main measure of inflation.

Making the Connection | How Does the Fed Measure Inflation?

To attain its goal of price stability, the Fed has to consider carefully the best way to measure the inflation rate. As we saw in Chapter 9, the consumer price index (CPI) is the most widely used measure of inflation. But we also saw that the CPI suffers from biases that cause it to overstate the true underlying rate of inflation. An alternative measure of changes in consumer prices can be constructed from the data gathered to calculate GDP. We saw in Chapter 8 that the GDP deflator is a broad measure of the price level that includes the price of every good or service that is in GDP. Changes in the GDP deflator are not a good measure of inflation experienced by the typical consumer, worker, or firm, however, because the deflator includes prices of goods, such as industrial equipment, that are not widely purchased. The *personal consumption expenditures price index (PCE)* is a measure of the price level that is similar to the GDP deflator, except it includes only the prices of goods from the consumption category of GDP.

In 2000, the Fed announced that it would rely more on the PCE than on the CPI in tracking inflation. The Fed noted three advantages that the PCE has over the CPI:

1. The PCE is a so-called chain-type price index, as opposed to the market-basket approach used in constructing the CPI. As we saw in Chapter 9, because consumers shift the mix of products they buy each year, the market-basket approach causes the CPI to overstate actual inflation. A chain-type price index allows the mix of products to change each year.

2. The PCE includes the prices of more goods and services than the CPI, so it is a broader measure of inflation.

3. Past values of the PCE can be recalculated as better ways of computing price indexes are developed and as new data become available. This allows the Fed to better track historical trends in the inflation rate.

In 2004, the Fed announced that it would begin to rely on a subcategory of the PCE: the so-called core PCE, which excludes food and energy prices. Prices of food and energy tend to fluctuate up and down for reasons that may not be related to the causes of general inflation and that cannot easily be controlled by monetary policy. Oil prices, in particular, have moved dramatically up and down in recent years. Therefore, a price index that includes food and energy prices may not give a clear view of underlying trends in inflation. The following graph shows movements in the CPI, the PCE, and the core PCE from January 1999 through September 2011. Although the three measures of inflation move roughly together, the core PCE has been more stable than the others. Note in particular that in early 2009, when the CPI and the PCE were indicating that the economy was experiencing deflation, the core PCE was still showing moderate inflation rates of about 1.5 percent.

If you want to know what the Fed thinks the current inflation rate is, the best idea is to look at data on the core PCE. These data are published monthly by the Bureau of Economic Analysis.

Data from U.S. Bureau of Economic Analysis; and U.S. Bureau of Labor Statistics.

Your Turn: Test your understanding by doing related problem 5.8 on page 528 at the end of this chapter.   MyEconLab

Fed Policies during the 2007–2009 Recession

15.6 LEARNING OBJECTIVE

Discuss the policies the Federal Reserve used during the 2007–2009 recession.

As we have seen, the Fed's traditional response to a recession is to lower the target for the federal funds rate. The severity of the recession of 2007–2009, particularly the problems in financial markets during those years, complicated the Fed's job. By December 2008, the Fed had effectively lowered the target for the federal funds rate to zero, but the zero interest rate alone did not achieve the Fed's desired expansionary effect on the economy. In this section, we will discuss some of the additional policy measures the Fed took during the 2007–2009 recession. Some of these measures were used for the first time in the Fed's history.

The Inflation and Deflation of the Housing Market Bubble

To understand the 2007–2009 recession and the difficulties in financial markets that occurred during it, we need to start by considering the housing market. As we mentioned in the chapter opener, the Fed lowered the target for the federal funds rate during the 2001 recession to stimulate demand for housing. The policy was successful, and most builders, such as Toll Brothers, experienced several years of high demand. By 2005, however, many economists argued that a "bubble" had formed in the housing market. As we discussed in Chapter 6, the price of any asset reflects the returns the owner of the asset expects to receive. For example, the price of a share of stock reflects the profitability of the firm issuing the stock because the owner of a share of stock has a claim on the firm's profits and assets. Many economists believe, however, that sometimes a *stock market bubble* can form when the prices of stocks rise above levels that can be justified by the profitability of the firms issuing the stock. Stock market bubbles end when enough investors decide stocks are overvalued and begin to sell. Why would an investor be willing to pay more for a share of stock than would be justified by its underlying value? There are two main explanations: The investor may be caught up in the enthusiasm of the moment and, by failing to gather sufficient information, may overestimate the true value of the stock; or the investor may expect to profit from buying stock at inflated prices if the investor can sell the stock at an even higher price before the bubble bursts.

The price of a house should reflect the value of the housing services the house provides. We can use the rents charged for comparable houses in an area to measure the value of housing services. By 2005, in some cities, the prices of houses had risen so much that monthly mortgage payments were far above the monthly rent on comparable houses. In addition, in some cities, there was an increase in the number of buyers who did not intend to live in the houses they purchased but were using them as investments. Like stock investors during a stock market bubble, these housing investors were expecting to make a profit by selling houses at higher prices than they had paid for them, and they were not concerned about whether the prices of the houses were above the value of the housing services provided.

During 2006 and 2007, it became clear that the air was rapidly escaping from the housing bubble. Figure 15.12 shows new home sales for each month from January 2000 through August 2011. New home sales rose by 60 percent between January 2000 and July 2005 and then fell by 80 percent between July 2005 and May 2010; sales remained at low levels during the following year. Sales of existing homes followed a similar pattern. Prices of new and existing homes in most markets also began to decline beginning in 2006, and the inventory of unsold homes offered for sale soared. Some homebuyers began having trouble making their loan payments. When lenders foreclosed on some of these loans, the lenders sold the homes, causing housing prices to decline further. *Subprime loans* are loans granted to borrowers with flawed credit histories. Some mortgage lenders that had concentrated on making subprime loans suffered heavy losses and

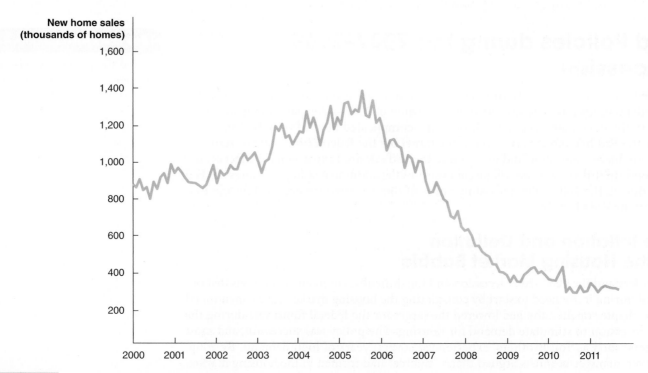

Figure 15.12 **The Housing Bubble**

Sales of new homes in the United States went on a roller-coaster ride, rising by 60 percent between January 2000 and July 2005, before falling by 80 percent between July 2005 and May 2010.

Note: The data are seasonally adjusted at an annual rate.
Data from U.S. Bureau of the Census.

went out of business, and most banks and other lenders tightened the requirements for borrowers. This *credit crunch* made it more difficult for potential homebuyers to obtain mortgages, further depressing the market.

The decline in the housing market affected other markets as well. For example, with home prices falling, consumption spending on furniture, appliances, and home improvements declined as many households found it more difficult to borrow against the value of their homes.

Was the housing bubble the result of overly optimistic expectations by homebuyers and builders who believed that new residential construction and housing prices would continue to rise at rapid rates indefinitely? While overly optimistic expectations may have played some role in the housing bubble, many economists believe that changes in the market for mortgages may have played a bigger role.

The Changing Mortgage Market

Until the 1970s, the commercial banks and savings and loans that granted mortgages kept the loans until the borrowers paid them off. As we saw in Chapter 14, a financial asset such as a mortgage is a security only if it can be resold in a secondary market. Many members of Congress believed that home ownership could be increased by creating a secondary market in mortgages. If banks and savings and loans could resell mortgages, then, in effect, individual investors would be able to provide funds for mortgages. The process would work like this: If a bank or savings and loan granted a mortgage and then resold the mortgage to an investor, the bank could use the funds received from the investor to grant another mortgage. In this way, banks and savings and loans could grant more mortgage loans because they would no longer depend only on deposits for the funds needed to make the loans. One barrier to creating a secondary market in mortgages was that most investors were unwilling to buy mortgages because they were afraid of losing money if the borrower stopped making payments, or *defaulted*, on the loan.

To reassure investors, Congress used two *government-sponsored enterprises (GSEs)*: the Federal National Mortgage Association ("Fannie Mae") and the Federal Home Loan Mortgage Corporation ("Freddie Mac"). These two institutions stand between investors and banks that grant mortgages. Fannie Mae and Freddie Mac sell bonds to investors and use the funds to purchase mortgages from banks. By the 1990s, a large secondary market existed in mortgages, with funds flowing from investors through Fannie Mae and Freddie Mac to banks and, ultimately, to individuals and families borrowing money to buy houses.

The Role of Investment Banks

By the 2000s, further changes had taken place in the mortgage market. First, investment banks became significant participants in the secondary market for mortgages. As we have seen, investment banks, such as Goldman Sachs and Morgan Stanley, differ from commercial banks in that they do not take in deposits and rarely lend directly to households. Instead, investment banks concentrate on providing advice to firms issuing stocks and bonds or considering mergers with other firms. Investment banks began buying mortgages, bundling large numbers of them together as bonds known as *mortgage-backed securities*, and reselling them to investors. Mortgage-backed securities proved very popular with investors because they often paid higher interest rates than other securities with comparable default risk.

Second, by the height of the housing bubble in 2005 and early 2006, lenders had greatly loosened the standards for obtaining a mortgage loan. Traditionally, only borrowers with good credit histories and who were willing to make a down payment equal to at least 20 percent of the value of the house they were buying would be able to receive a mortgage. By 2005, however, lenders were issuing many mortgages to subprime borrowers with flawed credit histories. In addition, "Alt-A" borrowers who stated—but did not document—their incomes and borrowers who made very small down payments found it easier to take out loans. Lenders also created new types of *adjustable-rate mortgages* that allowed borrowers to pay a very low interest rate for the first few years of the mortgage and then pay a higher rate in later years. The chance that the borrowers using these nontraditional mortgages would default was higher than for borrowers using traditional mortgages. Why would borrowers take out mortgages if they doubted that they could make the payments, and why would lenders grant these mortgages? The answer seems to be that both borrowers and lenders were anticipating that housing prices would continue to rise, which would reduce the chance that borrowers would default on the mortgages and would also make it easier for borrowers to convert to more traditional mortgages in the future.

Unfortunately, the decline in housing prices led to rising defaults among subprime and Alt-A borrowers, borrowers with adjustable-rate mortgages, and borrowers who had made only small down payments. When borrowers began defaulting on mortgages, the value of many mortgage-backed securities declined sharply. Investors feared that if they purchased these securities, they would not receive the promised payments because the payments on the securities depended on borrowers making their mortgage payments, which an increasing number were failing to do. Many commercial and investment banks owned these mortgage-backed securities, so the decline in the value of the securities caused these banks to suffer heavy losses. By mid-2007, the decline in the value of mortgage-backed securities and the large losses suffered by commercial and investment banks began to cause turmoil in the financial system. Many investors refused to buy mortgage-backed securities, and some investors would buy only bonds issued by the U.S. Treasury.

Making	
the	
Connection	

The Wonderful World of Leverage

Traditionally, most people taking out a mortgage make a down payment equal to 20 percent of the price of the house and borrow the remaining 80 percent. During the housing boom, however, many people purchased houses with down payments of 5 percent or less. In this sense, borrowers were highly *leveraged*, which means that their investment in their house was made mostly with borrowed money.

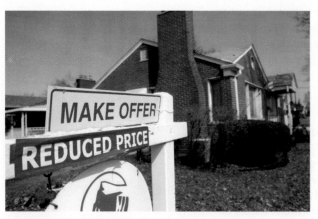

To see how leverage works in the housing market, consider the following example: Suppose you buy a $200,000 house on January 1, 2014. On January 1, 2015, the price of the house—if you decide to sell it—has risen to $220,000. What return have you earned on your investment in the house? The answer depends on how much you invested when you bought the house. For example, if you paid $200,000 in cash for the house, your return on that $200,000 investment is the $20,000 increase in the price of the house divided by your $200,000 investment, or 10 percent. Suppose that rather than paying cash, you made a down payment of 20 percent, or $40,000, and borrowed the rest by taking out a mortgage loan of $160,000. Now the return on your investment in the house is the $20,000 increase in the price of the house divided by your $40,000 investment, or 50 percent. If the down payment is less than 20 percent, your return on investment will be higher.

Making a very small down payment on a home mortgage leaves a buyer vulnerable to falling house prices.

The second column in the table below shows how the return on your investment increases as your down payment decreases:

	Return on your investment from . . .	
Down Payment	A 10 Percent Increase in the Price of Your House	A 10 Percent Decrease in the Price of Your House
100%	10%	−10%
20	50	−50
10	100	−100
5	200	−200

An investment financed at least partly by borrowing is called a *leveraged investment*. As this example shows, the larger the fraction of an investment financed by borrowing, the greater the degree of leverage in the investment, and the greater the potential return. But as the third column in the table shows, the reverse is also true: The greater the leverage, the greater the potential loss. To see why, consider once again that you buy a house for $200,000, except that in this case, after one year the price of the house falls to $180,000. If you paid $200,000 in cash for the house—so your leverage was zero—the $20,000 decline in the price of the house represents a loss of 10 percent of your investment. But if you made a down payment of only $10,000 and borrowed the remaining $190,000, then the $20,000 decline in the price of the house represents a loss of 200 percent of your investment. In fact, the house is now worth $10,000 less than the amount of your mortgage loan. The *equity* in your house is the difference between the market price of the house and the amount you owe on a loan. If the amount you owe is greater than the price of the house, you have *negative equity*. A home owner who has negative equity is also said to be "upside down" on his or her mortgage.

When the housing bubble burst and housing prices started to fall, many people found that they had negative equity. In that situation, some people defaulted on their loans, sometimes by simply moving out and abandoning their homes. Leverage had contributed to the housing boom and bust and the severity of the 2007–2009 recession.

Your Turn: Test your understanding by doing related problem 6.8 on page 529 at the end of this chapter.

MyEconLab

The Fed and the Treasury Department Respond

Because the problems in financial markets resulting from the bursting of the housing bubble were so profound, the Fed entered into an unusual partnership with the U.S. Treasury Department to develop suitable policies. Fed Chairman Ben Bernanke and U.S. Treasury Secretaries Henry Paulson (in the Bush administration) and Timothy Geithner (in the Obama administration) responded to the crisis by intervening in financial markets in unprecedented ways.

Initial Fed and Treasury Actions The financial crisis significantly worsened following the bankruptcy of the investment bank Lehman Brothers on September 15, 2008. So it is useful to look at the actions taken by the Fed and Treasury before and after that date. First, although the Fed traditionally made loans only to commercial banks, in March 2008, it announced it would temporarily make discount loans to *primary dealers*—firms that participate in regular open market transactions with the Fed. This change was intended to provide short-term funds to these dealers, some of which are investment banks. Second, also in March, the Fed announced that it would loan up to $200 billion of Treasury securities in exchange for mortgage-backed securities. This temporary program made it possible for primary dealers that owned mortgage-backed securities that were difficult or impossible to sell, to have access to Treasury securities that they could use as collateral for short-term loans. Third, once again in March, the Fed and the Treasury helped JPMorgan Chase acquire the investment bank Bear Stearns, which was on the edge of failing. The Fed agreed that if JPMorgan Chase would acquire Bear Stearns, the Fed would guarantee any losses JPMorgan Chase suffered on Bear Stearns's holdings of mortgage-backed securities, up to a limit of $29 billion. The Fed and Treasury were convinced that the failure of Bear Stearns had the potential of causing a financial panic, as many investors and financial firms would have stopped making short-term loans to other investment banks. Finally, in early September, the Treasury moved to have the federal government take control of Fannie Mae and Freddie Mac. Although Fannie Mae and Freddie Mac had been sponsored by the federal government, they were actually private businesses whose stock was bought and sold on the New York Stock Exchange. Under the Treasury's plan, Fannie Mae and Freddie Mac were each provided with up to $100 billion in exchange for 80 percent ownership of the firms. The firms were placed under the supervision of the Federal Housing Finance Agency. The Treasury believed that the bankruptcy of Fannie Mae and Freddie Mac would have caused a collapse in confidence in mortgage-backed securities, further devastating this already weak housing market.

Responses to the Failure of Lehman Brothers Some economists and policymakers criticized the decision by the Fed and the Treasury to help arrange the sale of Bear Stearns to JPMorgan Chase. Their main concern was with what is known as the *moral hazard problem*, which is the possibility that managers of financial firms such as Bear Stearns might make riskier investments if they believe that the federal government will save them from bankruptcy. The Treasury and Fed acted to save Bear Stearns because they believed that the failure of a large financial firm could have wider economic repercussions. As we discussed in Chapter 14, when a financial firm sells off its holdings of bonds and other assets, it causes their prices to fall, which in turn can undermine the financial position of other firms that also own these assets. In September 2008, when the investment bank Lehman Brothers was near bankruptcy, the Fed and the Treasury had to weigh the moral hazard problem against the possibility that the failure of Lehman Brothers would lead to further declines in asset prices and endanger the financial positions of other firms.

The Fed and the Treasury decided to allow Lehman Brothers to go bankrupt, which it did on September 15. The adverse reaction in financial markets was stronger than the Fed and Treasury had expected, which led them to reverse course two days later, when the Fed agreed to provide an $85 billion loan to the American International Group (AIG)—the largest insurance company in the United States—in exchange for an 80 percent ownership stake, effectively giving the federal government control of the company. One important result of the failure of Lehman Brothers was the heavy losses suffered by Reserve Primary Fund, a money market mutual fund that had invested in loans to Lehman Brothers. The problems at Reserve led many investors to withdraw their funds from it and other money market funds. These withdrawals reduced the ability of the money market funds to purchase commercial paper from corporations. Because in recent years corporations had become dependent on selling commercial paper to finance their operations, the Treasury and the Fed moved to stabilize this market and ensure that the flow of funds from investors to corporations continued. The Treasury announced a plan to provide insurance for deposits in money market mutual funds, similar to the existing insurance on bank deposits. The Fed announced that for a limited time it would lend directly to corporations by purchasing three-month commercial paper issued by non-financial corporations.

Finally, in October 2008, Congress passed the *Troubled Asset Relief Program (TARP)*, under which the Treasury attempted to stabilize the commercial banking system by providing funds to banks in exchange for stock. Taking partial ownership positions in private commercial banks was an unprecedented action for the federal government.

Clearly, the recession of 2007–2009 and the accompanying financial crisis had led the Fed and the Treasury to implement new approaches to policy. Many of these new approaches were controversial because they involved partial government ownership of financial firms, implicit guarantees to large financial firms that they would not be allowed to go bankrupt, and unprecedented intervention in financial markets. Although the approaches were new, they were intended to achieve the traditional macroeconomic policy goals of high employment, price stability, and stability of financial markets. What remains to be seen is whether these new approaches represent a permanent increase in federal government involvement in U.S. financial markets or whether the end of the recession will see policy return to more traditional approaches.

Continued from page 491

Economics in Your Life

Should You Buy a House during a Recession?

At the beginning of this chapter, we asked whether buying a house during a recession is a good idea. Clearly, there are many considerations to keep in mind when buying a house, which is the largest purchase you are likely to make in your lifetime. Included among these considerations are the price of the house relative to other comparable houses in the neighborhood, whether house prices in the neighborhood have been rising or falling, and the location of the house relative to stores, work, and good schools. Also important is the interest rate you will have to pay on the mortgage loan you would need in order to buy the house. As we have seen in this chapter, during a recession the Fed often takes actions to lower interest rates. So, mortgage rates are typically lower during a recession than at other times. You may want to take advantage of low interest rates to buy a house during a recession. But, recessions are also times of rising unemployment, and you would not want to make a commitment to borrow a lot of money for 15 or more years if you were in significant danger of losing your job. We can conclude, then, that if your job seems secure, buying a house during a recession may be a good idea.

Conclusion

Monetary policy is one way governments pursue goals for inflation, employment, and financial stability. Many journalists and politicians refer to the chairman of the Federal Reserve as second only to the president of the United States in his ability to affect the U.S. economy. Congress and the president, however, also use their power over spending and taxes to try to stabilize the economy. In Chapter 16, we discuss how *fiscal policy*—changes in government spending and taxes—affect the economy.

Read *An Inside Look at Policy* on the next page for a discussion of the Federal Reserve's new policies designed to reenergize the sluggish U.S. housing market.

Fed Attempts to Stimulate Housing Market . . . Again

ATLANTIC

Will the Fed's New Policies Revitalize the Housing Market?

Congress is gridlocked, consumers are pessimistic, and firms are barely hiring. To speed this recovery up—or to prevent a double dip—it might be up to the Federal Reserve. Last week it announced its latest attempt to revitalize the economy. Its chief target appears to be the still anemic housing market. Will the new policies work?

The Fed's Plan

The central bank will take two different actions meant to jumpstart the economy. First, there's "Operation Twist." The Fed will attempt to push down long-term interest rates by purchasing $400 billion in Treasury securities with six to 30 year terms. The program will last for nine months—through June 2012.

But here's the clever part: the Fed will sell shorter-dated Treasuries in exchange for bank reserves. This will prevent the Fed from having to expand its balance sheet to purchase longer-term Treasury securities. The relative increase in short term rates should be small, since short-term Treasuries are in high demand. . . .

The Fed announced another policy change as well. It has been reinvesting its maturing principal in additional Treasury securities. The central bank will refine that approach by investing maturing principal from its agency bonds and mortgage-backed securities in additional agency mortgage-backed securities. In this way, it will keep the size of its mortgage securities exposure level. But more importantly, this action will also increase the demand for mortgage-backed securities, which should push down mortgage interest rates.

The Medicine the Housing Market Needs?

In fact, the major target for all of the Fed's new action appears to be the U.S. housing market. Both Operation Twist and the new MBS reinvestment policy should help to push down mortgage interest rates. And they're low already: this week Freddie Mac reports the average 30-year mortgage interest rate at just 4.09%. Through the Fed's new policy, rates should easily dip below 4%.

Operation Twist could also help the reinvestment policy to have a more dramatic effect: as mortgage interest rates begin to decline, we should see mortgage refinancing soar. That means more maturing principal, which will provide even more capital for the Fed to reinvest in MBS to push down mortgage interest rates even further. . . .

But Will It Boost the Economy?

If mortgage interest rates decline significantly, then we'll almost certainly see more refinancing occur. That will provide a little bit of stimulus. Some Americans will lower their monthly mortgage payment. The impact that this has on the economy depends on how much these payments are lowered and how many people take advantage of the opportunity. That additional money they'll have can then be spent to stimulate the economy.

What's less clear, however, is whether or not the very low mortgage interest rates will lead to more home sales. Over the past year, even though interest rates were extremely low, they weren't enough to push more buyers into the market. Will even lower rates do the trick?

If home sales do increase, then prices may begin to stabilize—at least for a time. If the market isn't near the bottom, then once interest rates begin rising again, sales could decline and prices could begin to drop again. This is what we saw when the home buyer credit created a temporary burst of demand.

What we probably won't see is a significant increase in construction. The market still has plenty of existing inventory to work through before more homes are needed. So unless home demand truly explodes, we shouldn't expect a tidal wave of construction jobs.

As always, the effectiveness of the Fed's policy relies on the willingness of consumers, banks, and businesses to play along. First, Americans will need to seek refinancing and home purchases. Then, the banks must be willing to provide the credit for those new loans. If that encourages more spending due to consumers having more money in their pockets, then firms could begin hiring more aggressively. That's the plan—we'll see if it works.

Source: Daniel Indiviglio, "Will the Fed's New Policies Revitalize the Housing Market?" *The Atlantic,* September 24, 2011. Reprinted by permission of The Atlantic Monthly Group. All rights reserved.

Key Points in the Article

In late 2011, the Federal Reserve announced two new policies to stimulate the economy. One policy, referred to as "Operation Twist," has the Fed purchasing longer-term Treasury securities in an attempt to lower long-term interest rates. With the second policy, the Fed will invest maturing principal from its mortgage-backed securities and agency bonds in additional mortgage-backed securities, a move the Fed hopes will lower interest rates on mortgages. The primary focus of both policies is aiding the still-sluggish U.S. housing market. A decline in mortgage rates should encourage refinancing, leading to lower monthly mortgage payments and, therefore, more income to spend on other goods and services. Lower mortgage rates might also boost home sales, and this increase in demand may help stabilize housing prices. Whether these new Fed policies will be effective in boosting the economy by stimulating the housing market depends both on the willingness of banks to provide new mortgage loans and on the willingness of consumers to take advantage of the lower mortgage rates to either refinance existing loans or to purchase new homes.

Analyzing the News

(a) In December 2008, the Fed pushed the target for the federal funds rate to nearly zero, where it remained through 2011. Due to the severity of the 2007–2009 recession, this very low rate still did little to stimulate the economy. Because the federal funds rate cannot go below zero, the Fed embarked on a policy of quantitative easing: purchasing longer-term securities such as 10-year Treasury notes and certain mortgage-backed securities in an effort to keep mortgage rates low and help increase the demand for housing. With the economy remaining weak and the housing market still lethargic, the Fed announced its intention of implementing two new policies to attempt to boost the economy by increasing the demand for housing. With Operation Twist, the Fed will attempt to lower long-term interest rates by selling shorter-term Treasury securities and using the proceeds to buy Treasury securities with 6- to 30-year terms. The Fed will also invest the maturing principal from its mortgage-backed securities in additional mortgage-backed securities, which should reduce mortgage interest rates by increasing the demand for these securities.

(b) The Fed hopes that a significant decrease in mortgage rates will encourage current homeowners to refinance their mortgages to lower their monthly payments. Lower mortgage payments will provide these homeowners with additional funds that can be spent on more goods and services, helping to stimulate the economy.

(c) The figure below shows the average annual interest rates for federal funds, 30-year mortgages, and 10- and 30-year Treasury securities from 2001 through September 2011. By attempting to decrease the rates on these longer-term Treasury securities, the Fed hopes to reduce mortgage rates and increase home sales. An increase in home sales should help to stabilize home prices and boost the economy.

Thinking Critically About Policy

1. More than 80 percent of mortgages in the United States involve fixed interest rates rather than adjustable interest rates. How would the effect of monetary policy on aggregate demand change if there were more adjustable-rate mortgages than fixed-rate mortgages?

2. According to the figure, the federal funds rate began to increase dramatically in 2004, reaching a level closest to the 30-year fixed mortgage rate in 2007 before rapidly falling from 2007 to 2009. Explain how this rate change corresponds to the bursting of the U.S. housing bubble in 2005 and what the change in the federal funds rate indicates about the monetary policy employed by the Fed beginning in 2004.

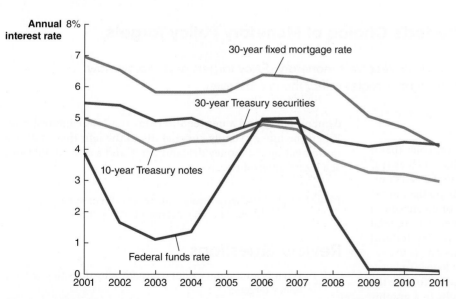

The average annual rates for federal funds, 30-year mortgages, and 10- and 30-year Treasury securities from 2001 through September 2011.

Chapter Summary and Problems

Key Terms

Contractionary monetary policy, p. 501

Expansionary monetary policy, p. 501

Federal funds rate, p. 498

Inflation targeting, p. 513

Monetary policy, p. 492

Taylor rule, p. 512

  What Is Monetary Policy? pages 492–494

LEARNING OBJECTIVE: Define monetary policy and describe the Federal Reserve's monetary policy goals.

Summary

Monetary policy is the actions the Fed takes to manage the money supply and interest rates to pursue its macroeconomic policy goals. The Fed has four *monetary policy goals* that are intended to promote a well-functioning economy: price stability, high employment, stability of financial markets and institutions, and economic growth.

MyEconLab Visit **www.myeconlab.com** to complete these exercises online and get instant feedback.

Review Questions

1.1 When Congress established the Federal Reserve in 1913, what was its main responsibility? When did Congress broaden the Fed's responsibilities?

1.2 What are the Fed's four monetary policy goals?

1.3 Why is the Fed sometimes said to have a "dual mandate"?

1.4 How can investment banks be subject to liquidity problems?

Problems and Applications

1.5 What is a bank panic? What role did bank panics play in the decision by Congress to establish the Federal Reserve?

1.6 Why is price stability one of the Fed's monetary policy goals? What problems can high inflation rates cause for the economy?

1.7 A former Federal Reserve official argued that at the Fed, "the objectives of price stability and low long-term interest rates are essentially the same objective." Briefly explain his reasoning.

From William Poole, "Understanding the Fed," Federal Reserve Bank of St. Louis Review, Vol. 89, No. 1, January/February 2007, p. 4.

1.8 Stock prices rose rapidly in 2005, as did housing prices in many parts of the country. By 2008, both stock prices and housing prices were declining sharply. Some economists have argued that rapid increases and decreases in the prices of assets such as shares of stock or houses can damage the economy. Currently, stabilizing asset prices is not one of the Federal Reserve's policy goals. In what ways would a goal of stabilizing asset prices be different from the four goals listed on page 492? Do you believe that stabilizing asset prices should be added to the list of the Fed's policy goals? Briefly explain.

  The Money Market and the Fed's Choice of Monetary Policy Targets, pages 494–499

LEARNING OBJECTIVE: Describe the Federal Reserve's monetary policy targets and explain how expansionary and contractionary monetary policies affect the interest rate.

Summary

The Fed's *monetary policy targets* are economic variables that it can affect directly and that in turn affect variables such as real GDP and the price level that are closely related to the Fed's policy goals. The two main monetary policy targets are the money supply and the interest rate. The Fed has most often chosen to use the interest rate as its monetary policy target. The Federal Open Market Committee announces a target for the **federal funds rate** after each meeting. The federal funds rate is the interest rate banks charge each other for overnight loans. To lower the interest rate, the Fed increases the money supply. To raise the interest rate, the Fed decreases the money supply. In a graphical analysis of the money market, when the money supply curve shifts to the right, the result is a movement down the money demand curve and a new equilibrium at a lower interest rate. When the money supply curve shifts to the left, the result is a movement up the money demand curve and a new equilibrium at a higher interest rate.

MyEconLab Visit **www.myeconlab.com** to complete these exercises online and get instant feedback.

Review Questions

2.1 What is a monetary policy target? Why does the Fed use policy targets?

2.2 What do economists mean by the demand for money? What is the advantage of holding money? What is the disadvantage?

2.3 Draw a demand and supply graph showing equilibrium in the money market. Suppose the Fed wants to lower the equilibrium interest rate. Show on the graph how the Fed would accomplish this objective.

2.4 What is the federal funds rate? What role does it play in monetary policy?

Problems and Applications

2.5 In the graph of the money market below, what could cause the money supply curve to shift from MS_1 to MS_2? What could cause the money demand curve to shift from MD_1 to MD_2?

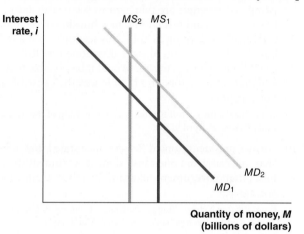

2.6 The following is from a December 2008 article in the *Wall Street Journal*:

> The Federal Reserve cut its target interest rate Tuesday to historic lows between zero and a quarter percentage point. . . . After two days of discussion among Fed officials, the central bank said it would use every weapon from its arsenal to lift the U.S. from recession. . . . Another Fed lending rate, the discount rate, will go to half a percentage point, a level last seen in the 1940s.

   a. What is the name of the "target interest rate" mentioned in this article?

   b. Briefly explain who borrows money and who lends money at this "target interest rate."

   c. What is the discount rate, and how is it different from the "target interest rate" mentioned in the article?

From "Fed Cuts Rates Near Zero to Battle Slump," *Wall Street Journal*, December 17, 2008.

2.7 If the Federal Reserve purchases $100 million worth of U.S. Treasury bills from the public, predict what will happen to the money supply. Explain your reasoning.

2.8 In response to problems in financial markets and a slowing economy, the Federal Open Market Committee (FOMC) began lowering its target for the federal funds rate from 5.25 percent in September 2007. Over the next year, the FOMC cut its federal funds rate target in a series of steps. Writing in the *New York Times*, economist Steven Levitt observed, "The Fed has been pouring more money into the banking system by cutting the target federal funds rate to 0 to 0.25 percent in December 2008." What is the relationship between the federal funds rate falling and the money supply increasing? How does lowering the target for the federal funds rate "pour money" into the banking system?

From Steven D. Levitt, "The Financial Meltdown Now and Then," *New York Times*, May 12, 2009.

2.9 In a column in the *Wall Street Journal*, two economists at the Council on Foreign Relations argue: "Simply put, the Fed must choose between managing the level of reserves and managing rates. It cannot do both." Do you agree? Briefly explain.

From Benn Steil and Paul Swartz, "Bye-Bye to the Fed-Funds Rate," *Wall Street Journal*, August 19, 2010.

15.3 **Monetary Policy and Economic Activity, pages 499–506**

LEARNING OBJECTIVE: Use aggregate demand and aggregate supply graphs to show the effects of monetary policy on real GDP and the price level.

Summary

An **expansionary monetary policy** lowers interest rates to increase consumption, investment, and net exports. This increased spending causes the aggregate demand (*AD*) curve to shift out more than it otherwise would, raising the level of real GDP and the price level. An expansionary monetary policy can help the Fed achieve its goal of high employment. A **contractionary monetary policy** raises interest rates to decrease consumption, investment, and net exports. This decreased spending causes the aggregate demand curve to shift out less than it otherwise would, reducing both the level of real GDP and the inflation rate below what they would be in the absence of policy. A contractionary monetary policy can help the Fed achieve its goal of price stability.

 Visit **www.myeconlab.com** to complete these exercises online and get instant feedback.

Review Questions

3.1 How does an increase in interest rates affect aggregate demand? Briefly discuss how each component of aggregate demand is affected.

3.2 If the Fed believes the economy is about to fall into recession, what actions should it take? If the Fed believes the inflation rate is about to increase, what actions should it take?

3.3 What were "quantitative easing" and "Operation Twist" and what was the Fed's objective in using them?

Problems and Applications

3.4 **[Related to the** Chapter Opener **on page 491]** An article in the *New York Times* in March 2002 reported that the housing market had been surprisingly strong during the previous year. According to the article, "In trying to explain the resilience of the housing market in the face of rising unemployment, shrinking stock portfolios and a soft economy, economists start with the Federal Reserve." Why start with the Federal Reserve in trying to explain the strength of the housing market during the 2001 recession?

From Daniel Altman, "Economy's Rock: Homes, Homes, Homes," *New York Times*, March 30, 2002.

3.5 In explaining why monetary policy did not pull Japan out of a recession in the early 2000s, an official at the Bank of Japan was quoted as saying that despite "major increases in the money supply," the money "stay[ed] in banks." Explain what the official meant by saying that the money stayed in banks. Why would that be a problem? Where does the money go if an expansionary monetary policy is successful?

Based on James Brooke, "Critics Say Koizumi's Economic Medicine Is a Weak Tea," *New York Times*, February 27, 2002.

3.6 According to an article in the *Wall Street Journal*:

In February... [Japan's] gauge of core consumer prices slipped 0.1% from a year earlier.... The Bank of Japan said last year it would regard prices as stable if they rose from zero to 2% a year.... The Bank of Japan's target for short-term interest rates is just 0.5%.... "It will be very difficult for the BOJ [Bank of Japan] to raise interest rates when prices are below the range it defines as stable," says Teizo Taya, special counselor for the Daiwa Institute of Research and a former BOJ policy board member.

a. What is the term for a falling price level?

b. Why would the Bank of Japan, the Japanese central bank, be reluctant to raise its target for short-term interest rates if the price level is falling?

c. Why would a country's central bank consider a falling price level to be undesirable?

"Japan's Consumer Prices May Threaten Economy," by Yuka Hayashi from *Wall Street Journal*, April 25, 2007. Copyright © 2011 by Dow Jones & Company, Inc. Reproduced with permission of Dow Jones & Company, Inc.

3.7 An article by three economists at the Federal Reserve Bank of Richmond notes that by the fall of 2011, many unemployed people in the United States had been out of work for more than six months. The economists argue that: "After a long period of unemployment, affected workers may become effectively unemployable." They conclude that: "Policy options [such as providing additional training] that increase the ability of unemployed workers to find work ... may be more effective at reducing unemployment than additional monetary stimulus."

a. What is a policy of monetary stimulus?

b. If many unemployed people have been out of work for a long time, why might policies that increase their ability to find jobs be more effective in reducing unemployment than a policy of monetary stimulus?

From Andreas Hornstein, Thomas A. Lubik, and Jessie Romero, "Potential Causes and Implications of the Rise in Long-Term Unemployment," Federal Reserve Bank of Richmond, Economic Brief, September 2011.

3.8 William McChesney Martin, who was Federal Reserve chairman from 1951 to 1970, was once quoted as saying, "The role of the Federal Reserve is to remove the punchbowl just as the party gets going." What did he mean?

3.9 **[Related to the** Chapter Opener **on page 491]** At the beginning of 2005, Robert Toll, CEO of Toll Brothers, argued that the United States was not experiencing a housing bubble. Instead, he argued that higher house prices reflected restrictions imposed by local governments on building new houses. He argued that the restrictions resulted from "NIMBY"—"Not in My Back Yard"—politics. Many existing homeowners are reluctant to see nearby farms and undeveloped land turned into new housing developments. As a result, according to Toll, "Towns don't want anything built." Why would the factors mentioned by Robert Toll cause housing prices to rise? Would it be possible to decide whether these factors or a bubble was the cause of rising housing prices?

From Shawn Tully, "Toll Brothers: The New King of the Real Estate Boom," *Fortune*, April 5, 2005.

3.10 Former president Ronald Reagan once stated that inflation "has one cause and one cause alone: government spending more than government takes in." Briefly explain whether you agree.

From Edward Nelson, "Budget Deficits and Interest Rates," *Monetary Trends*, Federal Reserve Bank of St. Louis, March 2004.

3.11 **[Related to the** Making the Connection **on page 502]** John Maynard Keynes is said to have remarked that using an expansionary monetary policy to pull an economy out of a deep recession can be like "pushing on a string." Briefly explain what Keynes is likely to have meant.

3.12 **[Related to the** Making the Connection **on page 502]** Martin Feldstein, an economist at Harvard University, has argued that QE2 led consumers to decrease saving and increase spending: "A likely reason for the fall in the saving rate and the resulting rise in consumer spending was the sharp increase in the stock market, which rose by 15% between August [2010] and the end of the year. That, of course, is what the Fed had been hoping for."

a. Why might QE2, which resulted in a decline in interest rates on long-term Treasury securities, have resulted in an increase in stock prices?

b. Why was the Fed hoping for consumers to increase their spending in late 2010?

From Martin Feldstein, "Quantitative Easing and America's Economic Rebound," www.project-syndicate.org, February 24, 2011.

3.13 **[Related to the** Making the Connection **on page 504]** The following is from a Federal Reserve publication:

In practice, monetary policymakers do not have up-to-the-minute, reliable information about the state of the economy and prices. Information is limited because of lags in the publication of data. Also, policymakers have less-than-perfect understanding of the way the economy works, including the knowledge of when and to what extent policy actions will affect aggregate demand. The operation of the economy changes over time, and with it the response of the economy to policy measures. These limitations add to uncertainties in the policy process and make determining the appropriate setting of monetary policy… more difficult.

If the Fed itself admits that there are many obstacles in the way of effective monetary policy, why does the Fed still engage in active monetary policy rather than use a monetary growth rule, as suggested by Milton Friedman and his followers?

From Board of Governors of the Federal Reserve System, *The Federal Reserve System: Purposes and Functions*, Washington, DC, 1994.

3.14 **[Related to the** Making the Connection **on page 504]** If policymakers at the Fed are aware that GDP data are sometimes subject to large revisions, how might this affect their views about how best to conduct policy?

3.15 **[Related to the** Don't Let This Happen to You **on page 506]** Briefly explain whether you agree with the following statement: "The Fed has an easy job. Say it wants to increase real GDP by $200 billion. All it has to do is increase the money supply by that amount."

15.4 Monetary Policy in the Dynamic Aggregate Demand and Aggregate Supply Model, pages 506–510

LEARNING OBJECTIVE: Use the dynamic aggregate demand and aggregate supply model to analyze monetary policy.

Summary

We can use the *dynamic aggregate demand and aggregate supply model* introduced in Chapter 13 to look more closely at expansionary and contractionary monetary policies. The dynamic aggregate demand and aggregate supply model takes into account that (1) the economy experiences continuing inflation, with the price level rising every year, and (2) the economy experiences long-run growth, with the *LRAS* curve shifting to the right every year. In the dynamic model, an expansionary monetary policy tries to ensure that the aggregate demand curve will shift far enough to the right to bring about macroeconomic equilibrium with real GDP equal to potential GDP. A contractionary monetary policy attempts to offset movements in aggregate demand that would cause macroeconomic equilibrium to occur at a level of real GDP that is greater than potential real GDP.

 Visit **www.myeconlab.com** to complete these exercises online and get instant feedback.

Review Questions

4.1 What are the key differences between how we illustrate an expansionary monetary policy in the basic aggregate demand and aggregate supply model and in the dynamic aggregate demand and aggregate supply model?

4.2 What are the key differences between how we illustrate a contractionary monetary policy in the basic aggregate demand and aggregate supply model and in the dynamic aggregate demand and aggregate supply model?

Problems and Applications

4.3 Explain whether you agree with this argument:

If the Fed actually ever carried out a contractionary monetary policy, the price level would fall. Because the price level has not fallen in the United States over an entire year since the 1930s, we can conclude that the Fed has not carried out a contractionary policy since the 1930s.

4.4 **[Related to** Solved Problem 15.4 **on page 509]** Use this graph to answer the following questions.

a. If the Fed does not take any policy action, what will be the level of real GDP and the price level in 2015?

b. If the Fed wants to keep real GDP at its potential level in 2015, should it use an expansionary policy or a contractionary policy? Should the trading desk be buying Treasury bills or selling them?

c. If the Fed takes no policy action, what will be the inflation rate in 2015? If the Fed uses monetary policy to keep real GDP at its full-employment level, what will be the inflation rate in 2015?

4.5 **[Related to** Solved Problem 15.4 **on page 509]** The hypothetical information in the following table shows what the situation will be in 2015 if the Fed does *not* use monetary policy.

Year	Potential GDP	Real GDP	Price Level
2014	$15.2 trillion	$15.2 trillion	110.0
2015	15.6 trillion	15.8 trillion	115.5

a. If the Fed wants to keep real GDP at its potential level in 2015, should it use an expansionary policy or a contractionary policy? Should the trading desk be buying T-bills or selling them?

b. If the Fed's policy is successful in keeping real GDP at its potential level in 2015, state whether each of the following will be higher, lower, or the same as it would have been if the Fed had taken no action:

   i. Real GDP

   ii. Potential real GDP

   iii. The inflation rate

   iv. The unemployment rate

c. Draw an aggregate demand and aggregate supply graph to illustrate the effects of the Fed's policy. Be sure that your graph contains *LRAS* curves for 2014 and 2015; *SRAS* curves for 2014 and 2015; *AD* curves for 2014 and 2015, with and without monetary policy action; and equilibrium real GDP and the price level in 2015, with and without policy.

15.5 **A Closer Look at the Fed's Setting of Monetary Policy Targets,** pages 511–515

LEARNING OBJECTIVE: Discuss the Fed's setting of monetary policy targets.

Summary

Some economists have argued that the Fed should use the money supply, rather than an interest rate, as its monetary policy target. Milton Friedman and other monetarists argued that the Fed should adopt a monetary growth rule of increasing the money supply every year at a fixed rate. Support for this proposal declined after 1980 because the relationship between movements in the money supply and movements in real GDP and the price level weakened. John Taylor analyzed the factors involved in Fed decision making and developed the **Taylor rule** for federal funds targeting. The Taylor rule links the Fed's target for the federal funds rate to economic variables. Over the past decade, many economists and central bankers have expressed significant interest in using **inflation targeting**, under which monetary policy is conducted to commit the central bank to achieving a publicly announced inflation target. A number of foreign central banks have adopted inflation targeting, but the Fed has not. The Fed's performance in the 1980s, 1990s, and early 2000s generally received high marks from economists, even without formal inflation targeting.

MyEconLab   Visit **www.myeconlab.com** to complete these exercises online and get instant feedback.

Review Questions

5.1 What is a monetary rule, as opposed to a monetary policy? What monetary rule would Milton Friedman have liked the Fed to follow? Why has support for a monetary rule of the kind advocated by Friedman declined since 1980?

5.2 For more than 20 years, the Fed has used the federal funds rate as its monetary policy target. Why doesn't the Fed target the money supply at the same time?

5.3 What is the Taylor rule? What is its purpose?

Problems and Applications

5.4 Suppose that the equilibrium real federal funds rate is 2 percent and the target rate of inflation is 2 percent. Use the following information and the Taylor rule to calculate the federal funds rate target:

   Current inflation rate = 4 percent
   Potential real GDP = $14.0 trillion
   Real GDP = $14.14 trillion

5.5 According to an article in the *Economist*:

> Calculations by David Mackie, of J.P. Morgan, show that virtually throughout the past six years, interest rates in the euro area have been lower than a Taylor rule would have prescribed, refuting the popular wisdom that the [European Central Bank] cares less about growth than does the Fed.

Why would keeping interest rates "lower than a Taylor rule would have prescribed" be an indication that the European Central Bank cared more about growth than popular wisdom held?

From "The European Central Bank: Haughty Indifference, or Masterly Inactivity?" *Economist*, July 14, 2005.

5.6 Glenn Rudebusch, an economist at the Federal Reserve Bank of San Francisco, argues that if the Fed had followed the Taylor rule during the recession of 2007–2009, then by the end of 2009 the target for the federal funds rate would have been −5 percent. Provide values for the Taylor rule equation given on page 512 that would result in a negative target for the federal funds rate. Is it possible for the federal funds rate to be negative?

Based on Glenn Rudebusch, "The Fed's Monetary Policy Response to the Current Crisis," *FRBSF Economic Letter*, May 22, 2009.

5.7 While serving as the president of the Federal Reserve Bank of St. Louis, William Poole stated, "Although my own preference is for zero inflation properly managed, I believe that a central bank consensus on some other numerical goal of reasonably low inflation is more important than the exact number." Briefly explain why the economy might gain the benefits of an explicit inflation target even if the target chosen is not a zero rate of inflation.

From William Poole, "Understanding the Fed," *Federal Reserve Bank of St. Louis Review*, Vol. 89, No. 1, January/February 2007, p. 4.

5.8 **[Related to the** Making the Connection **on page 514]** If the core PCE is a better measure of the inflation rate than is the CPI, why is the CPI more widely used? In particular, can you think of reasons the federal government uses the CPI when deciding how much to increase Social Security payments to retired workers to keep the purchasing power of the payments from declining?

15.6 **Fed Policies during the 2007-2009 Recession, pages 515-520**

LEARNING OBJECTIVE: Discuss the policies the Federal Reserve used during the 2007-2009 recession.

Summary

A housing bubble that began to deflate in 2006 led to the recession of 2007-2009 and an accompanying financial crisis. In response, the Federal Reserve instituted a variety of policy actions. In a series of steps, it cut the target for the federal funds rate from 5.25 percent in September 2007 to effectively zero in December 2008. The decline in the housing market caused wider problems in the financial system, as defaults on home mortgages rose and the value of mortgage-backed securities declined. The Fed and the U.S. Treasury Department implemented a series of new policies to provide liquidity and restore confidence. The Fed expanded the types of firms eligible for discount loans and began lending directly to corporations by purchasing commercial paper. Under the *Troubled Asset Relief Program*, the Treasury provided financial support to banks and other financial firms in exchange for part ownership. The Treasury also moved to have the federal government take control of Fannie Mae and Freddie Mac, government-sponsored firms that play a central role in the mortgage market. The failure of the investment bank Lehman Brothers in September 2008 led to a deepening of the financial crisis and provided the motivation for some of the new policies. Ultimately, the new policies stabilized the financial system, but their long-term effects remain the subject of debate.

MyEconLab Visit **www.myeconlab.com** to complete these exercises online and get instant feedback.

Review Questions

6.1 What is a mortgage? What were the important developments in the mortgage market during the years after 1970?

6.2 Beginning in 2008, the Federal Reserve and the U.S. Treasury Department responded to the financial crisis by intervening in financial markets in unprecedented ways. Briefly summarize the actions of the Fed and Treasury.

Problems and Applications

6.3 Some economists argue that one cause of the financial problems resulting from the housing crisis was the fact that lenders who grant mortgages no longer typically hold the mortgages until they are paid off. Instead, lenders usually resell their mortgages in secondary markets. How might a lender intending to resell a mortgage act differently than a lender intending to hold a mortgage?

6.4 An article in a Federal Reserve publication observes that "20 or 30 years ago, local financial institutions were the only option for some borrowers. Today, borrowers have access to national (and even international) sources of mortgage finance." What caused this change in the sources of mortgage finance? What would be the likely consequence of this change for the interest rates borrowers have to pay on mortgages? Briefly explain.

From Daniel J. McDonald and Daniel L. Thornton, "A Primer on the Mortgage Market and Mortgage Finance," *Federal Reserve Bank of St. Louis Review*, January/February 2008.

6.5 Charles Calomiris, an economist at Columbia University, was quoted as saying the following of the initiatives of the Treasury and Fed during the financial crisis of 2007-2009: "It has been a really head-spinning range of unprecedented and bold actions. . . . That is exactly as it should be. But I'm not saying that it's without some cost and without some risk." What was unprecedented about the Treasury and Fed's actions? What risks did these actions involve?

From Steven R. Weisman, "With Bold Steps, Fed Chief Quiets Some Criticism," *New York Times*, May 28, 2008.

6.6 Recall that "securitization" is the process of turning a loan, such as a mortgage, into a bond that can be bought and sold in secondary markets. An article in the *Economist* notes:

> That securitization caused more subprime mortgages to be written is not in doubt. By offering access to a much deeper pool of capital, securitization helped to bring down the cost of mortgages and made home-ownership more affordable for borrowers with poor credit histories.

What is a "subprime mortgage"? What is a "deeper pool of capital"? Why would securitization give mortgage borrowers access to a deeper pool of capital? Would a subprime borrower be likely to pay a higher or a lower interest rate than a borrower with a better credit history? Under what circumstances might a lender prefer to loan money to a borrower with a poor credit history rather than to a borrower with a good credit history? Briefly explain.

From "Ruptured Credit," *Economist*, May 15, 2008.

6.7 In the fall of 2011, investors began to fear that some European governments, particularly Greece and Italy, might default on the bonds they had issued, making the prices of the bonds fall sharply. Many European banks owned these bonds, and some investors worried that these banks might also be in financial trouble. An article in the *Economist* magazine referred to the "prospect of another Lehman moment." The article noted that, "Governments are once again having to step in to support their banks." What did the article mean by another "Lehman moment"? Why might European governments have felt the need to support their banks in order to avoid another Lehman moment?

From "Here We Go Again," *Economist*, October 8, 2011.

6.8 **[Related to the** Making the Connection **on page 518]** Suppose you buy a house for $150,000. One year later, the market price of the house has risen to $165,000. What is the return on your investment in the house if you made a down payment of 20 percent and took out a mortgage loan for the other 80 percent? What if you made a down payment of 5 percent and borrowed the other 95 percent? Be sure to show your calculations in your answer.

Chapter Outline and Learning Objectives

Does Government Spending Create Jobs?

Tutor-Saliba was founded in Southern California in 1949 and is today one of the largest heavy construction firms in the United States. In the fall of 2011, workers employed by Tutor-Saliba were hard at work on the Caldecott Tunnel in Northern California. The project would expand the tunnel through the Berkeley Hills from six lanes to eight in order to ease congestion between the cities of Orinda and Oakland. Part of the funding for the project came from the American Recovery and Reinvestment Act (ARRA, often referred to as the "stimulus bill"), which President Barack Obama and Congress had enacted in early 2009, in an attempt to increase aggregate demand during the recession of 2007–2009. Without this funding, the state of California would not have gone ahead with the project. The ARRA is an example of *discretionary fiscal policy* aimed at increasing real GDP and employment. To carry out the Caldecott Tunnel project, Tutor-Saliba hired an additional 106 workers. A spokesperson for the state agency in charge of the project argued that the increased employment effects from the project were even larger: "There is a ripple effect. There's truckers and equipment builders, and the deli in Orinda has never been as busy before."

The project to expand the Caldecott Tunnel is an example of increased government spending leading to increased employment. Or is it? A majority of economists agree that increased government spending leads to increased employment. But some economists argue that government spending shifts employment from one group of workers to another but doesn't increase *total* employment. Casey Mulligan, an economist at the University of Chicago, compares the effect of increases in government spending on projects like the Caldecott Tunnel to the effect of the New York Yankees building a new Yankee Stadium on the north side of East 161st Street in New York, across the street from the old Yankee Stadium on the south side of East 161st Street: "Not surprisingly, . . . spending by consumers, news organizations and entertainment businesses, among others, on the north side of East 161st Street was a lot more than it had been in years past. . . . [But] much of what happened north of East 161st Street was just a displacement of activity from the south side, rather than a creation of new activity."

The debate over the effects of government spending were particularly important during 2011 because the economy was recovering slowly from the 2007–2009 recession, with the unemployment rate remaining above 9 percent. In this chapter, we will examine discretionary fiscal policy and the debate over its effects. **AN INSIDE LOOK AT POLICY** on **page 562** discusses whether government-sponsored infrastructure spending is an effective means to create jobs in a slow-growing U.S. economy.

Based on Zusha Elinson, "Caldecott Tunnel Edges Forward, Tribute to Stimulus Bill," *New York Times*, September 10, 2011; and Casey B. Mulligan, "Local and National Stimulus," *New York Times*, August 24, 2011.

Economics in Your Life

What Would You Do with $500?

Suppose that the federal government announces that it will immediately mail you, and everyone else in the economy, a $500 tax rebate. In addition, you expect that in future years, your taxes will also be $500 less than they would otherwise have been. How will you respond to this increase in your disposable income? What effect will this tax rebate likely have on equilibrium real GDP in the short run? As you read the chapter, see if you can answer these questions. You can check your answers against those we provide on **page 561** at the end of this chapter.

I n Chapter 15, we discussed how the Federal Reserve uses monetary policy to pursue macroeconomic policy goals, including price stability and high employment. In this chapter, we will explore how the government uses *fiscal policy*, which involves changes in taxes and government purchases, to achieve similar policy goals. As we have seen, in the short run, the price level and the levels of real GDP and total employment in the economy depend on aggregate demand and short-run aggregate supply. The government can affect the levels of both aggregate demand and aggregate supply through fiscal policy. We will explore how Congress and the president decide which fiscal policy actions to take to achieve their goals. We will also discuss the debates among economists and policymakers over the effectiveness of fiscal policy.

Define fiscal policy.

Fiscal policy Changes in federal taxes and purchases that are intended to achieve macroeconomic policy objectives.

What Is Fiscal Policy?

Since the end of World War II, the federal government has been committed under the Employment Act of 1946 to intervening in the economy "to promote maximum employment, production, and purchasing power." As we saw in Chapter 15, the Federal Reserve closely monitors the economy, and the Federal Open Market Committee meets eight times per year to decide whether to change monetary policy. Less frequently, Congress and the president also make changes in taxes and government purchases to achieve macroeconomic policy objectives, such as high employment, price stability, and high rates of economic growth. Changes in federal taxes and spending that are intended to achieve macroeconomic policy objectives are called **fiscal policy**.

What Fiscal Policy Is and What It Isn't

In the United States, federal, state, and local governments all have responsibility for taxing and spending. Economists typically use the term *fiscal policy* to refer only to the actions of the federal government. State and local governments sometimes change their taxing and spending policies to aid their local economies, but these are not fiscal policy actions because they are not intended to affect the national economy. The federal government makes many decisions about taxes and spending, but not all of these decisions are fiscal policy actions because they are not intended to achieve macroeconomic policy goals. For example, a decision to cut the taxes of people who buy hybrid cars is an environmental policy action, not a fiscal policy action. Similarly, the spending increases to fund the war on terrorism and the wars in Iraq and Afghanistan were part of defense and homeland security policy, not fiscal policy.

Automatic Stabilizers versus Discretionary Fiscal Policy

Automatic stabilizers Government spending and taxes that automatically increase or decrease along with the business cycle.

There is an important distinction between *automatic stabilizers* and *discretionary fiscal policy*. Some types of government spending and taxes, which automatically increase and decrease along with the business cycle, are referred to as **automatic stabilizers**. The word *automatic* in this case refers to the fact that changes in these types of spending and taxes happen without actions by the government. For example, when the economy is expanding and employment is increasing, government spending on unemployment insurance payments to workers who have lost their jobs will automatically decrease. During a recession, as employment declines, this type of spending will automatically increase. Similarly, when the economy is expanding and incomes are rising, the amount the government collects in taxes will increase as people pay additional taxes on their higher incomes. When the economy is in recession, the amount the government collects in taxes will fall.

With discretionary fiscal policy, the government takes actions to change spending or taxes. The tax cuts Congress passed in 2008, 2009, and 2010 are examples of discretionary fiscal policy actions.

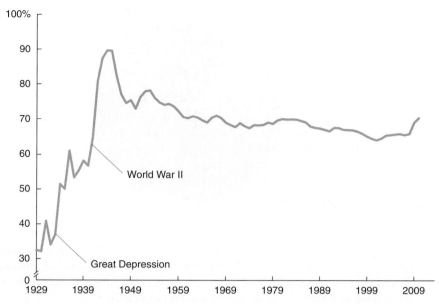

Figure 16.1

The Federal Government's Share of Total Government Expenditures, 1929–2010

Until the Great Depression of the 1930s, the majority of government spending in the United States occurred at the state and local levels. Since World War II, the federal government's share of total government expenditures has been between two-thirds and three-quarters. Data from U.S. Bureau of Economic Analysis.

An Overview of Government Spending and Taxes

To provide a context for understanding fiscal policy, it is important to understand the big picture of government taxing and spending. Before the Great Depression of the 1930s, the majority of government spending took place at the state and local levels. As Figure 16.1 shows, the size of the federal government expanded significantly during the crisis of the Great Depression. Since World War II, the federal government's share of total government expenditures has been between two-thirds and three-quarters.

Economists often measure government spending relative to the size of the economy by calculating government spending as a percentage of GDP. Remember that there is a difference between federal government *purchases* and federal government *expenditures*. When the federal government purchases an aircraft carrier or the services of an FBI agent, it receives a good or service in return. Federal government expenditures include purchases plus all other federal government spending. As Figure 16.2 shows, federal government *purchases* as a percentage of GDP have actually been falling since the end of the Korean War in the early 1950s. Total federal *expenditures* as a percentage of GDP rose from 1950 to the early 1990s and then fell from 1992 to 2001, before rising again. The decline in expenditures between 1992 and 2001 was partly the result of the end of the Cold War between the Soviet Union and the United States, which allowed for a substantial reduction in defense spending. Real federal government spending on national defense declined by almost 25 percent between 1990 and 1998, before rising by more

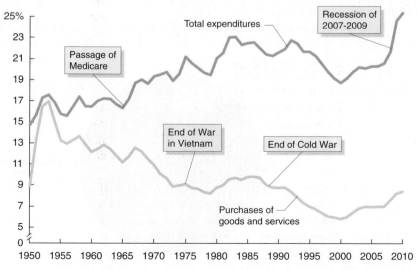

Figure 16.2

Federal Purchases and Federal Expenditures as a Percentage of GDP, 1950–2010

As a fraction of GDP, the federal government's *purchases* of goods and services have been declining since the Korean War in the early 1950s. Total *expenditures* by the federal government—including transfer payments—as a fraction of GDP slowly rose from 1950 through the early 1990s and fell from 1992 to 2001, before rising again. The recession of 2007–2009 and the slow recovery that followed led to a surge in federal government expenditures causing them to rise to their highest level as a percentage of GDP since World War II. Data from U.S. Bureau of Economic Analysis.

Figure 16.3

Federal Government Expenditures, 2010

Federal government *purchases* can be divided into defense spending—which makes up 22.1 percent of the federal budget—and spending on everything else the federal government does—from paying the salaries of FBI agents, to operating the national parks, to supporting scientific research—which makes up 9.4 percent of the budget. In addition to purchases, there are three other categories of federal government *expenditures*: interest on the national debt, grants to state and local governments, and transfer payments. Transfer payments rose from about 25 percent of federal government expenditures in the 1960s to nearly 46.6 percent in 2010.
Data from U.S. Bureau of Economic Analysis.

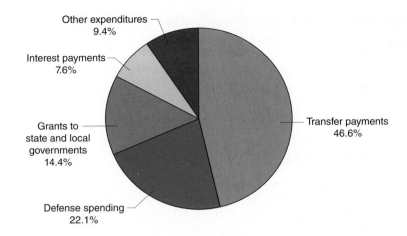

than 60 percent between 1998 and 2010 in response to the war on terrorism and the wars in Iraq and Afghanistan. The recession of 2007–2009 and the slow recovery that followed led to a surge in federal government expenditures causing them to rise to their highest level as a percentage of GDP since World War II.

In addition to purchases, there are three other categories of federal government expenditures: *interest on the national debt, grants to state and local governments*, and *transfer payments*. Interest on the national debt represents payments to holders of the bonds the federal government has issued to borrow money. Grants to state and local governments are payments made by the federal government to support government activity at the state and local levels. For example, to help reduce crime, Congress implemented a program of grants to local governments to hire more police officers. The largest and fastest-growing category of federal expenditures is transfer payments. Some of these programs, such as Social Security and unemployment insurance, began in the 1930s. Others, such as Medicare, which finances health care for the elderly, or the food stamps and Temporary Assistance for Needy Families programs, which are intended to aid the poor, began in the 1960s or later.

Figure 16.3 shows that in 2010, transfer payments were 46.6 percent of federal government expenditures. In the 1960s, transfer payments were only about 25 percent of federal government expenditures. As the U.S. population ages and medical costs continue to increase, federal government spending on the Social Security and Medicare programs will continue to increase, causing transfer payments to consume an increasing share of federal expenditures. Figure 16.3 shows that spending on most of the federal government's day-to-day activities—including running federal agencies such as the Environmental Protection Agency, the Federal Bureau of Investigation, the National Park Service, and the Immigration and Naturalization Service—makes up only 9.4 percent of federal government expenditures.

Figure 16.4 shows that in 2010, the federal government raised 36.9 percent of its revenue from individual income taxes. Payroll taxes to fund the Social Security and

Figure 16.4

Federal Government Revenue, 2010

In 2010, individual income taxes raised 36.9 percent of the federal government's revenues. Corporate income taxes raised 13.6 percent of revenue. Payroll taxes to fund the Social Security and Medicare programs rose from less than 10 percent of federal government revenues in 1950 to 40.0 percent in 2010. The remaining 9.6 percent of revenues were raised from excise taxes, tariffs on imports, and other sources.
Data from U.S. Bureau of Economic Analysis.

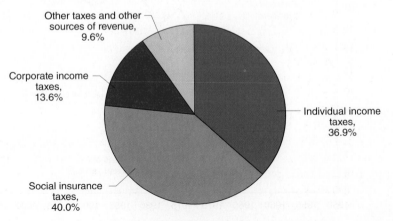

Medicare programs raised 40 percent of federal revenues. The tax on corporate profits raised 13.6 percent of federal revenues. The remaining 9.6 percent of federal revenues were raised from excise taxes on certain products, such as cigarettes and gasoline, from tariffs on goods imported from other countries, and from other sources, such as payments by companies that cut timber on federal lands.

Making the Connection | Is Spending on Social Security and Medicare a Fiscal Time Bomb?

Social Security, established in 1935 to provide payments to retired workers, began as a "pay-as-you-go" system, meaning that payments to current retirees were paid from taxes collected from current workers. In the early years of the program, many workers were paying into the system, and there were relatively few retirees. For example, in 1940, more than 35 million workers were paying into the system, and only 222,000 people were receiving benefits—a ratio of more than 150 workers to each beneficiary. In those early years, most retirees received far more in benefits than they had paid in taxes. For example, the first beneficiary was a legal secretary named Ida May Fuller. She worked for three years while the program was in place and paid total taxes of only $24.75. During her retirement, she collected $22,888.92 in benefits.

Will the federal government be able to keep the promises made by the Social Security and Medicare programs?

The Social Security and Medicare programs have been very successful in reducing poverty among elderly Americans, but in recent years, the ability of the federal government to finance current promises has been called into doubt. After World War II, the United States experienced a "baby boom," as birthrates rose and remained high through the early 1960s. Falling birthrates after 1965 have meant long-run problems for the Social Security system, as the number of workers per retiree has continually declined. Currently, there are only about three workers per retiree, and that ratio is expected to decline to two workers per retiree by 2035. Congress has attempted to deal with this problem by raising the age to receive full benefits from 65 to 67 and by increasing payroll taxes. In 1940, the combined payroll tax paid by workers and firms was 2 percent; in 2011, it was 15.3 percent (although a tax cut temporarily reduced it to 13.3 percent for that year).

Under the Medicare program, which was established in 1965, the federal government provides health care coverage to people age 65 and over. The long-term financial situation for Medicare is an even greater cause for concern than is Social Security. As Americans live longer and as new—and expensive—medical procedures are developed, the projected expenditures under the Medicare program will eventually far outstrip projected tax revenues. The federal government also faces increasing expenditures under the Medicaid program, which is administered by state governments and provides health care coverage to low-income people. In 2010, federal spending on Social Security, Medicare, and Medicaid equaled 10.4 percent of GDP. Spending on these three programs was less than 3 percent of GDP in 1962. The Congressional Budget Office (CBO) indicates that spending on these three programs will rise to 15.2 percent of GDP in 2030, 18.9 percent by 2050, and 25.8 percent by 2085. The graph on the next page illustrates these forecasts. Over the past 40 years, the federal government has spent an average of about 18.5 percent of GDP on *all programs* combined—from buying aircraft carriers to paying the salaries of FBI agents. So, if current trends continue, the federal government will eventually be spending, as a fraction of GDP, more on these three programs than it currently does on all programs combined. Over the coming decades, the gap between the benefits projected to be paid under the Social Security and Medicare programs and projected tax revenues is a staggering $72 *trillion*, or nearly five times the value of GDP in 2011. If current projections are accurate, policymakers are faced with the choice of significantly restraining spending on these programs, greatly increasing taxes on households and firms, or implementing some combination of spending restraints and tax increases. The alternatives will all clearly involve considerable pain. A report from the Congressional Budget Office concluded, "Even if taxation reached levels that were unprecedented in the United States, current spending policies could become financially unsustainable."

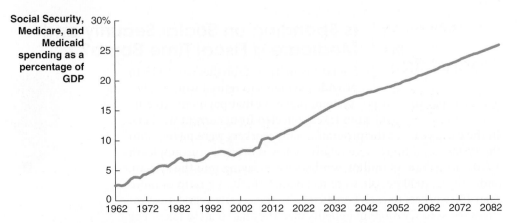

Note: The graph gives the Congressional Budget Office's "alternative fiscal scenario" of future spending.

A lively political debate has taken place over the future of the Social Security and Medicare programs. Some policymakers have proposed increasing taxes to fund future benefit payments. The tax increases needed, however, could be as much as 50 percent higher than current rates, and tax increases of that magnitude could discourage work effort, entrepreneurship, and investment, thereby slowing economic growth. There have also been proposals to slow the rate of growth of future benefits, while guaranteeing benefits to current recipients. While this strategy would avoid the need to raise taxes significantly, it would also require younger workers to save more for their retirement. Some economists and policymakers have argued for slower benefit growth for higher-income workers while leaving future benefits unchanged for lower-income workers. Whatever changes are ultimately made in the Medicare and Social Security programs, this policy debate is one of the most important for young people.

Based on Congressional Budget Office, The Long-Term Budget Outlook, June 2011; Congressional Budget Office, *Baseline Projections of Mandatory Outlays*, January 2009; 112th Congress, 1st Session, "The 2011 Annual Report of the Board of Trustees of the Federal Old-Age and Survivors Insurance and Disability Insurance Trust Funds," House Document 112–23, May 13, 2011; and the Social Security Administration Web site (www.ssa.gov).

MyEconLab **Your Turn:** Test your understanding by doing related problems 1.6 and 1.7 on page 564 at the end of this chapter.

16.2 LEARNING OBJECTIVE

Explain how fiscal policy affects aggregate demand and how the government can use fiscal policy to stabilize the economy.

The Effects of Fiscal Policy on Real GDP and the Price Level

The federal government uses macroeconomic policies to offset the effects of the business cycle on the economy. We saw in Chapter 15 that the Federal Reserve carries out monetary policy through changes in the money supply and interest rates. Congress and the president carry out fiscal policy through changes in government purchases and taxes. Because changes in government purchases and taxes lead to changes in aggregate demand, they can affect the level of real GDP, employment, and the price level. When the economy is in a recession, *increases* in government purchases or *decreases* in taxes will increase aggregate demand. As we saw in Chapter 13, the inflation rate may increase when real GDP is beyond potential GDP. Decreasing government purchases or raising taxes can slow the growth of aggregate demand and reduce the inflation rate.

Expansionary and Contractionary Fiscal Policy

Expansionary fiscal policy involves increasing government purchases or decreasing taxes. An increase in government purchases will increase aggregate demand directly because government purchases are a component of aggregate demand. A cut in taxes has an indirect effect on aggregate demand. Remember from Chapter 8 that the income households have available to spend after they have paid their taxes is called *disposable income.* Cutting the individual income tax will increase household disposable income and consumption spending. Cutting taxes on business income can increase aggregate demand by increasing business investment.

Figure 16.5 shows the results of an expansionary fiscal policy, using the basic version of the aggregate demand and aggregate supply model. In this model, there is no economic growth, so the long-run aggregate supply (*LRAS*) curve does not shift. Notice that this figure is very similar to Figure 15.7 on page 501, which shows the effects of an expansionary monetary policy. The goal of both expansionary monetary policy and expansionary fiscal policy is to increase aggregate demand relative to what it would have been without the policy.

In panel (a) of Figure 16.5, we assume that the economy is in short-run equilibrium at point *A*, where the aggregate demand (*AD₁*) curve intersects the short-run aggregate supply (*SRAS*) curve. Real GDP is below potential real GDP, so the economy is in recession, with some firms operating below normal capacity and some workers having been laid off. To bring real GDP back to potential GDP, Congress and the president increase government purchases or cut taxes, which will shift the aggregate demand curve to the right, from *AD₁* to *AD₂*. Real GDP increases from $14.2 trillion to potential GDP of $14.4 trillion, and the price level rises from 98 to 100 (point *B*). The policy has successfully returned real GDP to its potential level. Rising production will lead to increasing employment, reducing the unemployment rate.

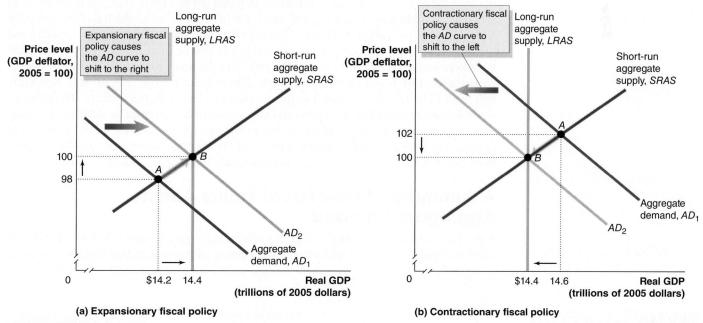

(a) Expansionary fiscal policy   **(b) Contractionary fiscal policy**

Figure 16.5 **Fiscal Policy**

In panel (a), the economy begins in recession at point *A*, with real GDP of $14.2 trillion and a price level of 98. An expansionary fiscal policy will cause aggregate demand to shift to the right, from *AD₁* to *AD₂*, increasing real GDP from $14.2 trillion to $14.4 trillion and the price level from 98 to 100 (point *B*). In panel (b), the economy begins at point *A*, with real GDP at $14.6 trillion and the price level at 102. Because real GDP is greater than potential GDP, the economy will experience rising wages and prices. A contractionary fiscal policy will cause aggregate demand to shift to the left, from *AD₁* to *AD₂*, decreasing real GDP from $14.6 trillion to $14.4 trillion and the price level from 102 to 100 (point *B*).

Don't Let This Happen to You

Don't Confuse Fiscal Policy and Monetary Policy

If you keep in mind the definitions of *money*, *income*, and *spending*, the difference between monetary policy and fiscal policy will be clearer. Students often make these two related mistakes: (1) They think of monetary policy as the Fed fighting recessions by increasing the money supply so people will have more money to spend; and (2) they think of fiscal policy as Congress and the president fighting recessions by spending more money. In this view, the only difference between fiscal policy and monetary policy is the source of the money.

To understand what's wrong with the descriptions of fiscal policy and monetary policy just given, first remember that the problem during a recession is not that there is too little *money*—currency plus checking account deposits—but too little *spending*. There may be too little spending for a number of reasons. For example, households may cut back on their spending on cars and houses because they are pessimistic about the future. Firms may cut back their spending because they have lowered their estimates of the future profitability of new machinery and factories.

Or the major trading partners of the United States—such as Japan and Canada—may be suffering from recessions, which cause households and firms in those countries to cut back their spending on U.S. products.

The purpose of expansionary monetary policy is to lower interest rates, which in turn increases aggregate demand. When interest rates fall, households and firms are willing to borrow more to buy cars, houses, and factories. The purpose of expansionary fiscal policy is to increase aggregate demand either by having the government directly increase its own purchases or by cutting taxes to increase household disposable income and, therefore, consumption spending.

Just as increasing or decreasing the money supply does not have a direct effect on government spending or taxes, increasing or decreasing government spending or taxes does not have a direct effect on the money supply. Fiscal policy and monetary policy have the same goals, but they have different effects on the economy.

MyEconLab

Your Turn: Test your understanding by doing related problem 2.6 on page 565 at the end of this chapter.

Contractionary fiscal policy involves decreasing government purchases or increasing taxes. Policymakers use contractionary fiscal policy to reduce increases in aggregate demand that seem likely to lead to inflation. In panel (b) of Figure 16.5, the economy is in short-run equilibrium at point *A*, with real GDP of $14.6 trillion, which is above potential real GDP of $14.4 trillion. With some firms producing beyond their normal capacity and the unemployment rate very low, wages and prices will be increasing. To bring real GDP back to potential GDP, Congress and the president decrease government purchases or increase taxes, which will shift the aggregate demand curve from AD_1 to AD_2. Real GDP falls from $14.6 trillion to $14.4 trillion, and the price level falls from 102 to 100 (point *B*).

We can conclude that Congress and the president can attempt to stabilize the economy by using fiscal policy to affect the price level and the level of real GDP. Of course, in practice it is extremely difficult for Congress and the president to use fiscal policy to eliminate the effects of the business cycle and keep real GDP always equal to potential GDP.

A Summary of How Fiscal Policy Affects Aggregate Demand

Table 16.1 summarizes how fiscal policy affects aggregate demand. Just as we did with monetary policy, we must add a very important qualification to this summary of fiscal policy: The table isolates the effect of fiscal policy *by holding constant monetary policy*

Table 16.1

Countercyclical Fiscal Policy

Problem	Type of Policy	Actions by Congress and the President	Result
Recession	Expansionary	Increase government spending or cut taxes	Real GDP and the price level rise.
Rising inflation	Contractionary	Decrease government spending or raise taxes	Real GDP and the price level fall.

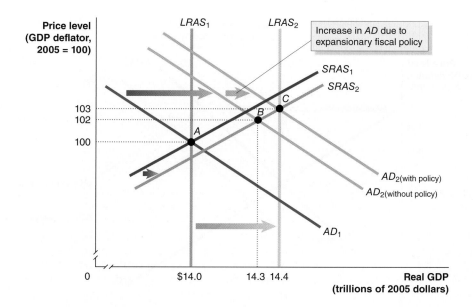

Figure 16.6

An Expansionary Fiscal Policy in the Dynamic Model

The economy begins in equilibrium at point A, at potential real GDP of \$14.0 trillion and a price level of 100. Without an expansionary policy, aggregate demand will shift from AD_1 to $AD_{2(\text{without policy})}$, which is not enough to keep the economy at potential GDP because long-run aggregate supply has shifted from $LRAS_1$ to $LRAS_2$. The economy will be in short-run equilibrium at point B, with real GDP of \$14.3 trillion and a price level of 102. Increasing government purchases or cutting taxes will shift aggregate demand to $AD_{2(\text{with policy})}$. The economy will be in equilibrium at point C, with real GDP of \$14.4 trillion, which is its potential level, and a price level of 103. The price level is higher than it would have been without an expansionary fiscal policy.

and all other factors affecting the variables involved. In other words, we are again invoking the *ceteris paribus* condition we discussed in Chapter 3. This point is important because, for example, a contractionary fiscal policy does not cause the price level to fall. A contractionary fiscal policy causes the price level *to rise by less than it would have without the policy.*

Fiscal Policy in the Dynamic Aggregate Demand and Aggregate Supply Model*

16.3 LEARNING OBJECTIVE

Use the dynamic aggregate demand and aggregate supply model to analyze fiscal policy.

The overview of fiscal policy we just finished contains a key idea: Congress and the president can use fiscal policy to affect aggregate demand, thereby changing the price level and the level of real GDP. The discussion of expansionary and contractionary fiscal policy illustrated by Figure 16.5 on page 537 is simplified, however, because it ignores two important facts about the economy: (1) The economy experiences continuing inflation, with the price level rising every year, and (2) the economy experiences long-run growth, with the *LRAS* curve shifting to the right every year. In Chapter 13, we developed a *dynamic aggregate demand and aggregate supply model* that took these two facts into account. In this section, we use the dynamic model to gain a more complete understanding of fiscal policy.

To briefly review the dynamic model, recall that over time, potential real GDP increases, which we show by the long-run aggregate supply curve shifting to the right. The factors that cause the *LRAS* curve to shift also cause firms to supply more goods and services at any given price level in the short run, which we show by the short-run aggregate supply curve shifting to the right. Finally, during most years, the aggregate demand curve also shifts to the right, indicating that aggregate expenditure is higher at every price level.

Figure 16.6 shows the results of an expansionary fiscal policy using the dynamic aggregate demand and aggregate supply model. Notice that this figure is very similar to Figure 15.9 on page 507, which showed the effects of an expansionary monetary policy. The goal of both expansionary monetary policy and expansionary fiscal policy is to increase aggregate demand relative to what it would have been without the policy.

In the hypothetical situation shown in Figure 16.6, the economy begins in equilibrium at potential real GDP of \$14.0 trillion and a price level of 100 (point A). In the second year, *LRAS* increases to \$14.4 trillion, but *AD* increases only to $AD_{2(\text{without policy})}$,

*This section may be omitted without loss of continuity.

Figure 16.7

A Contractionary Fiscal Policy in the Dynamic Model

The economy begins in equilibrium at point *A*, with real GDP of $14.0 trillion and a price level of 100. Without a contractionary policy, aggregate demand will shift from AD_1 to $AD_{2(\text{without policy})}$, which results in a short-run equilibrium beyond potential GDP at point *B*, with real GDP of $14.5 trillion and a price level of 105. Decreasing government purchases or increasing taxes can shift aggregate demand to $AD_{2(\text{with policy})}$. The economy will be in equilibrium at point *C*, with real GDP of $14.4 trillion, which is its potential level, and a price level of 103. The inflation rate will be 3 percent, as opposed to the 5 percent it would have been without the contractionary fiscal policy.

which is not enough to keep the economy in macroeconomic equilibrium at potential GDP. Let's assume that the Fed does not react to the situation with an expansionary monetary policy. In that case, without an expansionary fiscal policy of spending increases or tax reductions, the short-run equilibrium will occur at $14.3 trillion (point *B*). The $100 billion gap between this level of real GDP and the potential level means that some firms are operating at less than their full capacity. Incomes and profits will be falling, firms will begin to lay off workers, and the unemployment rate will rise.

Increasing government purchases or cutting taxes can shift aggregate demand to $AD_{2(\text{with policy})}$. The economy will be in equilibrium at point *C*, with real GDP of $14.4 trillion, which is its potential level, and a price level of 103. The price level is higher than it would have been without an expansionary fiscal policy.

Contractionary fiscal policy involves decreasing government purchases or increasing taxes. Policymakers use contractionary fiscal policy to reduce increases in aggregate demand that seem likely to lead to inflation. In Figure 16.7, the economy again begins at potential real GDP of $14.0 trillion and a price level of 100 (point *A*). Once again, *LRAS* increases to $14.4 trillion in the second year. In this scenario, the shift in aggregate demand to $AD_{2(\text{without policy})}$ results in a short-run macroeconomic equilibrium beyond potential GDP (point *B*). If we assume that the Fed does not respond to the situation with a contractionary monetary policy, the economy will experience a rising inflation rate. Decreasing government purchases or increasing taxes can keep real GDP from moving beyond its potential level. The result, shown in Figure 16.7, is that in the new equilibrium at point *C*, the inflation rate is 3 percent rather than 5 percent.

16.4 LEARNING OBJECTIVE

Explain how the government purchases and tax multipliers work.

The Government Purchases and Tax Multipliers

We saw in the chapter opener that in 2009, Congress and the president authorized spending to widen the Caldecott Tunnel in Northern California, in an attempt to increase aggregate demand during the recession of 2007–2009. Suppose that Congress and the president decide to spend $100 billion on expanding the Caldecott Tunnel and similar projects. (The total increase in federal spending under the ARRA was actually about $500 billion, including the $180 million spent to widen the Caldecott Tunnel.) How much will equilibrium real GDP increase as a result of this increase in government purchases? We might expect that the answer is greater than $100 billion because the initial increase in aggregate demand should lead to additional increases in income and spending. For example, to expand the Caldecott Tunnel, the California state government hired Tutor-Saliba, a private construction firm. Tutor-Saliba and the subcontractors it used hired workers to carry out the project. The firms that carried out the many other projects authorized under the ARRA also hired new workers. Newly hired workers are likely to increase their spending on cars, furniture, appliances, and other products. Sellers of these products will increase their production and hire more workers, and so on. At each step, real GDP and income will rise, thereby increasing consumption spending and aggregate demand. These additional waves of hiring are what the spokesperson for the state agency in charge of the Caldecott Tunnel project referred to in the chapter opener as a "ripple effect" from the project.

Economists refer to the initial increase in government purchases as *autonomous* because it is a result of a decision by the government and is not directly caused by changes in the level of real GDP. The increases in consumption spending that result from the initial autonomous increase in government purchases are *induced* because they are caused by the initial increase in autonomous spending. Economists refer to the series of induced increases in consumption spending that result from an initial increase in autonomous expenditures as the **multiplier effect**.

Figure 16.8 illustrates how an increase in government purchases affects the aggregate demand curve. The initial increase in government purchases causes the aggregate demand curve to shift to the right because total spending in the economy is now higher at every price level. The shift to the right from AD_1 to the dashed AD curve represents the effect of the initial increase of $100 billion in government purchases. Because this initial increase in government purchases raises incomes and leads to further increases in consumption spending, the aggregate demand curve will ultimately shift from AD_1 all the way to AD_2.

To better understand the multiplier effect, let's start with a simplified analysis in which we assume that the price level is constant. In other words, initially we will ignore the effect of an upward-sloping *SRAS*. Figure 16.9 shows how spending and real GDP increase over a number of periods, beginning with the initial increase in government purchases in the first period. The initial spending in the first period raises real GDP and total income in the economy by $100 billion. How much additional consumption spending will result from $100 billion in additional income? We know that in addition to increasing their consumption spending on domestically produced goods, households will save some of the increase in income, use some to pay income taxes, and use some to purchase imported goods, which will have no direct effect on spending and production in the U.S. economy. In Figure 16.9, we assume that in the second period, households increase their consumption spending by

Multiplier effect The series of induced increases in consumption spending that results from an initial increase in autonomous expenditures.

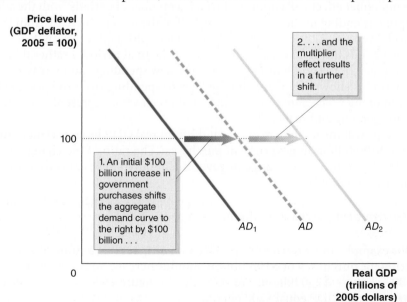

Price level
(GDP deflator,
2005 = 100)

2. . . . and the multiplier effect results in a further shift.

100

1. An initial $100 billion increase in government purchases shifts the aggregate demand curve to the right by $100 billion . . .

AD_1 AD AD_2

0

Real GDP
(trillions of
2005 dollars)

Figure 16.8

The Multiplier Effect and Aggregate Demand

An initial increase in government purchases of $100 billion causes the aggregate demand curve to shift to the right, from AD_1 to the dashed AD curve, and represents the effect of the initial increase of $100 billion in government purchases. Because this initial increase raises incomes and leads to further increases in consumption spending, the aggregate demand curve will ultimately shift further to the right, to AD_2.

Period	Additional Spending This Period	Cumulative Increase in Spending and Real GDP
1	$100 billion in government purchases	$100 billion
2	$50 billion in consumption spending	$150 billion
3	$25 billion in consumption spending	$175 billion
4	$12.5 billion in consumption spending	$187.5 billion
5	$6.25 billion in consumption spending	$193.75 billion
6	$3.125 billion in consumption spending	$196.875 billion
⋮	⋮	⋮
n	0	$200 billion

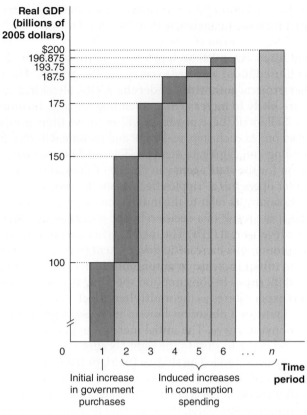

Figure 16.9 The Multiplier Effect of an Increase in Government Purchases

Following an initial increase in government purchases, spending and real GDP increase over a number of periods due to the multiplier effect. The new spending and increased real GDP in each period is shown in green, and the level of spending from the previous period is shown in orange. The sum of the orange and green areas represents the cumulative increase in spending and real GDP. In total, equilibrium real GDP will increase by $200 billion as a result of an initial increase of $100 billion in government purchases.

one-half of the increase in income from the first period—or by $50 billion. This spending in the second period will, in turn, increase real GDP and income by an additional $50 billion. In the third period, consumption spending will increase by $25 billion, or one-half of the $50 billion increase in income from the second period.

The multiplier effect will continue through a number of periods, with the additional consumption spending in each period being half of the income increase from the previous period. Eventually, the process will be complete, although we cannot say precisely how many periods it will take, so we simply label the final period n rather than give it a specific number. In the graph in Figure 16.9, the new spending and increased real GDP in each period is shown in green, and the level of spending from the previous period is shown in orange. The sum of the orange and green areas represents the cumulative increase in spending and real GDP.

How large will the total increase in equilibrium real GDP be as a result of the initial increase of $100 billion in government purchases? The ratio of the change in equilibrium real GDP to the initial change in government purchases is known as the *government purchases multiplier*:

$$\text{Government purchases multiplier} = \frac{\text{Change in equilibrium real GDP}}{\text{Change in government purchases}}.$$

If, for example, the government purchases multiplier has a value of 2, an increase in government purchases of $100 billion should increase equilibrium real GDP by $2 \times \$100 \text{ billion} = \$200 \text{ billion}$. We show this in Figure 16.9 by having the cumulative increase in real GDP equal $200 billion.

Tax cuts also have a multiplier effect. Cutting taxes increases the disposable income of households. When household disposable income rises, so will consumption spending. These increases in consumption spending will set off further increases in real GDP and income, just as increases in government purchases do. Suppose we consider a change in taxes of a specific amount—say, a tax cut of $100 billion—with the tax *rate* remaining unchanged. The expression for this tax multiplier is

$$\text{Tax multiplier} = \frac{\text{Change in equilibrium real GDP}}{\text{Change in taxes}}.$$

The tax multiplier is a negative number because changes in taxes and changes in real GDP move in opposite directions: An increase in taxes reduces disposable income, consumption, and real GDP, and a decrease in taxes raises disposable income, consumption, and real GDP. For example, if the tax multiplier is −1.6, a $100 billion *cut* in taxes will increase real GDP by −1.6 × −$100 billion = $160 billion. We would expect the tax multiplier to be smaller in absolute value than the government purchases multiplier. To see why, think about the difference between a $100 billion increase in government purchases and a $100 billion decrease in taxes. The whole of the $100 billion in government purchases results in an increase in aggregate demand. But households will save rather than spend some portion of a $100 billion decrease in taxes, and they will spend some portion on imported goods. The fraction of the tax cut that households save or spend on imports will not increase aggregate demand. Therefore, the first period of the multiplier process will see a smaller increase in aggregate demand than occurs when there is an increase in government purchases, and the total increase in equilibrium real GDP will be smaller.

The Effect of Changes in Tax Rates

A change in tax *rates* has a more complicated effect on equilibrium real GDP than does a tax cut of a fixed amount. To begin with, the value of the tax rate affects the size of the multiplier effect. The higher the tax rate, the smaller the multiplier effect. To see why, think about the size of the additional spending increases that take place in each period following an increase in government purchases. The higher the tax rate, the smaller the amount of any increase in income that households have available to spend, which reduces the size of the multiplier effect. So, a cut in tax rates affects equilibrium real GDP through two channels: (1) A cut in tax rates increases the disposable income of households, which leads them to increase their consumption spending, and (2) a cut in tax rates increases the size of the multiplier effect.

Taking into Account the Effects of Aggregate Supply

To this point, as we discussed the multiplier effect, we assumed that the price level was constant. We know, though, that because the *SRAS* curve is upward sloping, when the *AD* curve shifts to the right, the price level will rise. As a result of the rise in the price level, equilibrium real GDP will not increase by the full amount that the multiplier effect indicates. Figure 16.10 illustrates how an upward-sloping *SRAS* curve affects the size of the multiplier. To keep the graph relatively simple, we assume that the *SRAS* and *LRAS* curves do not shift. The economy starts at point *A*, with real GDP below its potential level. An increase in government purchases shifts the aggregate demand curve from AD_1 to the dashed *AD* curve. Just as in Figure 16.8, the multiplier effect causes a further shift in aggregate demand to AD_2. If the price level remained constant, real GDP would increase from $13.0 trillion at point *A* to $14.2 trillion at point *B*. However, because the *SRAS* curve is upward sloping, the price level rises from 100 to 103, reducing the total quantity of goods and services demanded in the economy. The new equilibrium occurs at point *C*, with real GDP having risen to $14.0 trillion, or by $200 billion less than if the price level had remained unchanged. We can conclude that the actual change in real GDP resulting from an increase in government purchases or a cut in taxes will be less than indicated by the simple multiplier effect with a constant price level.

Figure 16.10

**The Multiplier Effect and
Aggregate Supply**

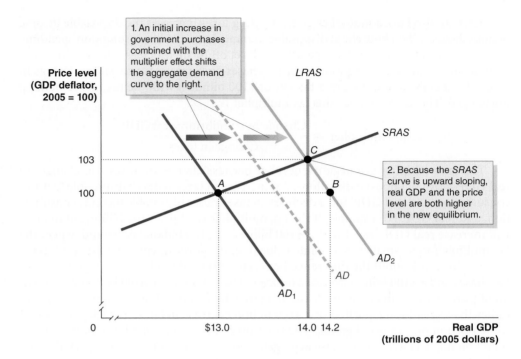

The economy is initially at point *A*. An increase in government purchases causes the aggregate demand curve to shift to the right, from AD_1 to the dashed *AD* curve. The multiplier effect results in the aggregate demand curve shifting further to the right, to AD_2 (point *B*). Because of the upward-sloping supply curve, the shift in aggregate demand results in a higher price level. In the new equilibrium at point *C*, both real GDP and the price level have increased. The increase in real GDP is less than indicated by the multiplier effect with a constant price level.

The Multipliers Work in Both Directions

Increases in government purchases and cuts in taxes have a positive multiplier effect on equilibrium real GDP. Decreases in government purchases and increases in taxes also have a multiplier effect on equilibrium real GDP, but in this case, the effect is negative. For example, an increase in taxes will reduce household disposable income and consumption spending. As households buy fewer cars, furniture, refrigerators, and other products, the firms that sell these products will cut back on production and begin laying off workers. Falling incomes will lead to further reductions in consumption spending. A reduction in government spending on defense would set off a similar process of decreases in real GDP and income. The cutback would be felt first by defense contractors selling directly to the government, and then it would spread to other firms.

We look more closely at the government purchases multiplier and the tax multiplier in the appendix to this chapter.

Solved Problem 16.4

Fiscal Policy Multipliers

Briefly explain whether you agree with the following statement: "Real GDP is currently $14.2 trillion, and potential real GDP is $14.4 trillion. If Congress and the president would increase government purchases by $200 billion or cut taxes by $200 billion, the economy could be brought to equilibrium at potential GDP."

Solving the Problem

Step 1: **Review the chapter material.** This problem is about the multiplier process, so you may want to review the section "The Government Purchases and Tax Multipliers," which begins on page 540.

Step 2: **Explain how the necessary increase in purchases or cut in taxes is less than $200 billion because of the multiplier effect.** The statement is incorrect because it does not consider the multiplier effect. Because of the multiplier effect, an increase in government purchases or a decrease in taxes of less than $200 billion is necessary to increase equilibrium real GDP by $200 billion. For instance, assume that the government purchases multiplier is 2 and the tax multiplier is −1.6. We can then calculate the necessary increase in government purchases as follows:

$$\text{Government purchases multiplier} = \frac{\text{Change in equilibrium real GDP}}{\text{Change in government purchases}}$$

$$2 = \frac{\$200 \text{ billion}}{\text{Change in government purchases}}$$

$$\text{Change in government purchases} = \frac{\$200 \text{ billion}}{2} = \$100 \text{ billion}.$$

And the necessary change in taxes:

$$\text{Tax multiplier} = \frac{\text{Change in equilibrium real GDP}}{\text{Change in taxes}}$$

$$-1.6 = \frac{\$200 \text{ billion}}{\text{Change in taxes}}$$

$$\text{Change in taxes} = \frac{\$200 \text{ billion}}{-1.6} = -\$125 \text{ billion}.$$

Your Turn: For more practice, do related problem 4.6 on page 566 at the end of this chapter. MyEconLab

The Limits of Using Fiscal Policy to Stabilize the Economy

16.5 LEARNING OBJECTIVE

Discuss the difficulties that can arise in implementing fiscal policy.

Poorly timed fiscal policy, like poorly timed monetary policy, can do more harm than good. As we discussed in Chapter 15, it takes time for policymakers to collect statistics and identify changes in the economy. If the government decides to increase spending or cut taxes to fight a recession that is about to end, the effect may be to increase the inflation rate. Similarly, cutting spending or raising taxes to slow down an economy that has actually already moved into recession can increase the length and depth of the recession.

Getting the timing right can be more difficult with fiscal policy than with monetary policy for two main reasons. Control over monetary policy is concentrated in the hands of the Federal Open Market Committee, which can change monetary policy at any of its meetings. By contrast, the president and a majority of the 535 members of Congress have to agree on changes in fiscal policy. The delays caused by the legislative process can be very long. For example, in 1962, President John F. Kennedy concluded that the U.S. economy was operating below potential GDP and proposed a tax cut to stimulate aggregate demand. Congress eventually agreed to the tax cut—but not until 1964. The events of 2001 and 2009 show, though, that it is sometimes possible to authorize changes in fiscal policy relatively quickly. When George W. Bush came into office in January 2001, the economy was on the verge of recession, and he immediately proposed a tax cut. Congress passed the tax cut, and the president signed it into law in early June 2001. Similarly, Barack Obama proposed a stimulus package as soon as he came into office in January 2009, and Congress had passed the proposal by February.

Even after a change in fiscal policy has been approved, it takes time to implement the policy. Suppose Congress and the president agree to increase aggregate demand by spending $30 billion more on constructing subway systems in several cities. It will probably take at least several months to prepare detailed plans for the construction. Local governments will then ask for bids from private construction companies. Once the winning bidders have been selected, they will usually need several months to begin the project. Only then will significant amounts of spending actually take place. This delay may push the spending beyond the end of the recession that the spending was intended to fight. Delays of this type are less of a concern during long and severe recessions, such as that of 2007–2009.

Does Government Spending Reduce Private Spending?

In addition to the timing problem, using increases in government purchases to increase aggregate demand presents another potential problem. We have been assuming that when the federal government increases its purchases by $30 billion, the multiplier effect will cause the increase in aggregate demand to be greater than $30 billion. However, the size of the multiplier effect may be limited if the increase in government purchases causes one of the nongovernment, or private, components of aggregate expenditures—consumption, investment, or net exports—to fall. A decline in private expenditures as a result of an increase in government purchases is called **crowding out**.

Crowding out A decline in private expenditures as a result of an increase in government purchases.

Crowding Out in the Short Run

Consider the case of a temporary increase in government purchases. Suppose the federal government decides to fight a recession by spending $30 billion more this year on subway construction. When the $30 billion has been spent, the program will end, and government spending will drop back to its previous level. As the spending takes place, income and real GDP will increase. These increases in income and real GDP will cause households and firms to increase their demand for currency and checking account balances to accommodate the increased buying and selling. Figure 16.11 shows the result, using the money market graph introduced in Chapter 15.

At higher levels of real GDP and income, households and firms demand more money at every interest rate. When the demand for money increases, the equilibrium interest rate will rise. Higher interest rates will result in a decline in each component of private expenditures. Consumption spending and investment spending will decline because households will borrow less to buy houses, cars, furniture, and appliances, and firms will borrow less to buy factories, computers, and machine tools. Net exports will

Figure 16.11

An Expansionary Fiscal Policy Increases Interest Rates

If the federal government increases spending, the demand for money will increase from Money demand$_1$ to Money demand$_2$ as real GDP and income rise. With the supply of money constant, at $950 billion, the result is an increase in the equilibrium interest rate from 3 percent to 5 percent, which crowds out some consumption, investment, and net exports.

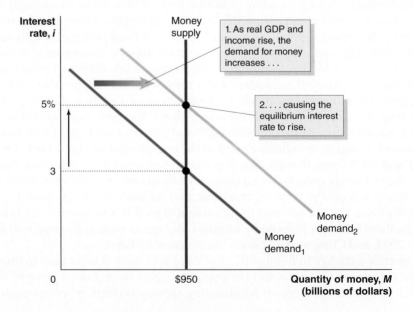

also decline because higher interest rates in the United States will attract foreign investors. German, Japanese, and Canadian investors will want to exchange the currencies of
their countries for U.S. dollars to invest in U.S. Treasury bills and other U.S. financial
assets. This increased demand for U.S. dollars will cause an increase in the exchange rate
between the dollar and other currencies. When the dollar increases in value, the prices
of U.S. products in foreign countries rise—causing a reduction in U.S. exports—and the
prices of foreign products in the United States fall—causing an increase in U.S. imports.
Falling exports and rising imports mean that net exports are falling.

The greater the sensitivity of consumption, investment, and net exports to changes
in interest rates, the more crowding out will occur. In a deep recession, many firms may
be so pessimistic about the future and have so much excess capacity that investment
spending will fall to very low levels and will be unlikely to fall much further, even if interest rates rise. In this case, crowding out is unlikely to be a problem. If the economy is
close to potential GDP, however, and firms are optimistic about the future, an increase
in interest rates may result in a significant decline in investment spending.

Figure 16.12 shows that crowding out may reduce the effectiveness of an expansionary fiscal policy. The economy begins in short-run equilibrium at point A, with real
GDP at $14.2 trillion. Real GDP is below potential GDP, so the economy is in recession.
Suppose that Congress and the president decide to increase government purchases to
bring the economy back to potential GDP. In the absence of crowding out, the increase
in government purchases will shift aggregate demand to $AD_{2(\text{no crowding out})}$ and bring
the economy to equilibrium at real GDP of $14.4 trillion, which is the potential level
of GDP (point B). But the higher interest rate resulting from the increased government
purchases will reduce consumption, investment, and net exports, causing aggregate
demand to shift back to $AD_{2(\text{crowding out})}$. The result is a new short-run equilibrium at
point C, with real GDP of $14.3 trillion, which is $100 billion short of potential GDP.

Crowding Out in the Long Run

Most economists agree that in the short run, an increase in government spending results
in partial, but not complete, crowding out. What is the long-run effect of a *permanent*
increase in government spending? In this case, most economists agree that the result is
complete crowding out. In the long run, the decline in investment, consumption, and
net exports exactly offsets the increase in government purchases, and aggregate demand
remains unchanged. To understand crowding out in the long run, recall from Chapter 13
that *in the long run, the economy returns to potential GDP*. Suppose that the economy is
currently at potential GDP and that government purchases are 35 percent of GDP. In

Figure 16.12

**The Effect of Crowding Out
in the Short Run**

The economy begins in a recession, with real
GDP of $14.2 trillion (point A). In the absence
of crowding out, an increase in government
purchases will shift aggregate demand to
$AD_{2(\text{no crowding out})}$ and bring the economy
to equilibrium at potential real GDP of $14.4
trillion (point B). But the higher interest rate
resulting from the increased government purchases will reduce consumption, investment,
and net exports, causing aggregate demand to
shift to $AD_{2(\text{crowding out})}$. The result is a new
short-run equilibrium at point C, with real
GDP of $14.3 trillion, which is $100 billion
short of potential real GDP.

that case, private expenditures—the sum of consumption, investment, and net exports—will make up the other 65 percent of GDP. If government purchases are increased permanently to 37 percent of GDP, in the long run, private expenditures must fall to 63 percent of GDP. There has been complete crowding out: Private expenditures have fallen by the same amount that government purchases have increased. If government spending is taking a larger share of GDP, then private spending must take a smaller share.

An expansionary fiscal policy does not have to cause complete crowding out in the short run. If the economy is below potential real GDP, it is possible for both government purchases and private expenditures to increase. But in the long run, any permanent increase in government purchases must come at the expense of private expenditures. Keep in mind, however, that it may take several—possibly many—years to arrive at this long-run outcome.

Fiscal Policy in Action: Did the Stimulus Package of 2009 Work?

As we have seen, Congress and the president can increase government purchases and cut taxes to increase aggregate demand either to avoid a recession or to shorten the length or severity of a recession that is already under way. The recession of 2007–2009 occurred during the end of the presidency of George W. Bush and the beginning of the presidency of Barack Obama. Both presidents used fiscal policy to fight the recession.

In early 2008, economists advising President Bush believed that the housing crisis, the resulting credit crunch, and rising oil prices were pushing the economy into a recession. (As we now know, a recession had actually already begun in December 2007.) These economists proposed cutting taxes to increase household disposable income, which would increase consumption spending and aggregate demand. Congress enacted a tax cut that took the form of *rebates* of taxes already paid. Rebate checks totaling $95 billion were sent to taxpayers between April and July 2008.

How effective were the rebates in increasing consumption spending? While economists are still studying the issue, economic analysis can give us some insight. Many economists believe that consumers base their spending on their *permanent income* rather than just on their *current income*. A consumer's permanent income reflects the consumer's expected future income. By basing spending on permanent income, a consumer can smooth out consumption over a period of years. For example, a medical student may have very low current income but a high expected future income. The student may borrow against this high expected future income rather than having to consume at a very low level in the present. Some people, however, have difficulty borrowing against their future income because banks or other lenders may not be convinced that a borrower's future income really will be significantly higher than his or her current income. One-time tax rebates, such as the one in 2008, increase consumers' current income but not their permanent income. Only a permanent decrease in taxes increases consumers' permanent income. Therefore, a tax rebate is likely to increase consumption spending less than would a permanent tax cut.

Some estimates of the effect of the 2008 tax rebate, including studies by Christian Broda of the University of Chicago and Jonathan Parker of Northwestern University, and by economists at the Congressional Budget Office, indicate that taxpayers spent between 33 and 40 percent of the rebates they received. Taxpayers who have difficulty borrowing against their future income increased their consumption the most. The 2008 tax rebates totaled $95 billion, so consumers may have increased their spending by about $35 billion as a result of the rebate.

American Recovery and Reinvestment Act of 2009 Although the tax rebates helped to increase aggregate demand, we saw in Chapter 15 that the recession worsened in September 2008, following the bankruptcy of the Lehman Brothers investment bank and the deepening of the financial crisis. President Obama took office in January 2009, pledging to pursue an expansionary fiscal policy. Congress responded in February by passing the American Recovery and Reinvestment Act of 2009, a $825 billion package of spending increases and tax cuts that was by far the largest fiscal policy action in U.S. history. The complexity of the "stimulus package," as it came to be known, makes its provisions difficult to summarize, but Figure 16.13 provides some highlights.

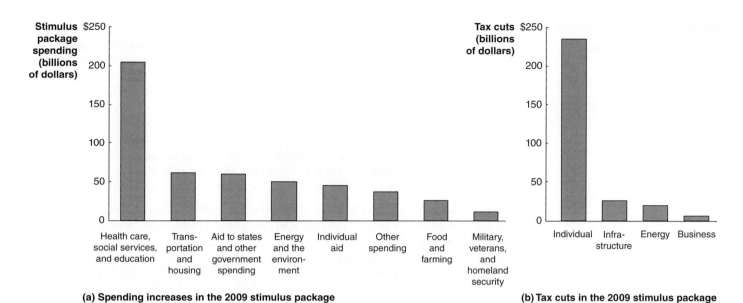

(a) Spending increases in the 2009 stimulus package

(b) Tax cuts in the 2009 stimulus package

Figure 16.13 The 2009 Stimulus Package

Congress and President Obama intended the spending increases and tax cuts in the stimulus package to increase aggregate demand and help pull the economy out of the 2007–2009 recession. Panel (a) shows how the increases in spending were distributed, and panel (b) shows how the tax cuts were distributed. Data from Congressional Budget Office.

About two-thirds of the stimulus package took the form of increases in government expenditures, and one-third took the form of tax cuts. Panel (a) shows the major categories of spending increases. The largest category—health care, social services, and education—included funds for biomedical research and grants to state governments to help fund Medicare spending, as well as funds for many other programs. The energy category included funding for research into alternative energy sources as well as modernization of the electric grid. Transportation and housing included substantial spending on infrastructure projects, such as repairing and expanding highways, bridges, and airports. Individual aid included spending on extended unemployment insurance payments. Panel (b) shows the major categories of tax cuts. The largest category was individual tax cuts, which included a $400 reduction in payroll taxes for workers earning up to $75,000 per year and a tax credit of up to $2,500 for tuition and other college expenses.

How Can We Measure the Effectiveness of the Stimulus Package? How effective was the Obama administration's stimulus package? At the time the package was passed, economists working for the administration estimated that the increase in aggregate demand resulting from the package would increase real GDP by 3.5 percent by the end of 2010 and increase employment by 3.5 million. In fact, between the beginning of 2009 and the end of 2010, real GDP increased by 4.4 percent, while employment declined by 3.3 million. Do these results indicate that the stimulus package was successful in increasing GDP, but not employment? We have to be careful in drawing that conclusion. To judge the effectiveness of the stimulus package, we have to measure its effects on real GDP and employment, *holding constant all other factors affecting real GDP and employment*. In other words, the actual movements in real GDP and employment are a mixture of the effects of the stimulus package and the effects of other factors, such as the Federal Reserve's monetary policy, other fiscal policy actions, and the typical changes in real GDP and employment during a business cycle that occur independently of government policy. Isolating the effects of the stimulus package from the effects of these other factors is very difficult and explains why economists differ in their views about how effective the stimulus package was.

Economists at the Congressional Budget Office (CBO) have provided estimates of the effectiveness of the stimulus package. The CBO is a nonpartisan organization, and many economists believe its estimates are reasonable. But because the estimates depend

Table 16.2				
CBO Estimates of the Effects of the Stimulus Package	Year	Change in Real GDP	Change in the Unemployment Rate	Change in Employment (millions of people)
	2009	0.9% to 1.9%	−0.3% to −0.5%	0.5 to 0.9
	2010	1.5% to 4.2%	−0.7% to −1.8%	1.3 to 3.3
	2011	0.8% to 2.3%	−0.5% to −1.4%	0.9 to 2.7
	2012	0.3% to 0.8%	−0.2% to −0.6%	0.4 to 1.1

Data from Congressional Budget Office, "Estimated Impact of the American Recovery and Reinvestment Act on Employment and Economic Output from April 2011 Through June 2011," August 2011.

on particular assumptions about the size of the government purchases and tax multipliers, some economists believe that the CBO estimates are too high, while other economists believe the estimates are too low. Table 16.2 presents the CBO's estimates of the effects of the stimulus package. To reflect the uncertainty in its calculation, the CBO provides a range of estimates. For example, in the absence of the stimulus package, the CBO estimates that employment in 2010 would have been between 1.3 million and 3.3 million less than it actually was and the unemployment rate would have been between 0.7 percent and 1.8 percent higher than it actually was.

If the CBO's estimates of the effects of the stimulus package are accurate, then this fiscal policy action significantly reduced the severity of the recession of 2007–2009 and its aftermath. However, relative to the severity of the recession, the effect of the package was comparatively small. For example, in 2010, the unemployment rate was 9.6 percent, which was far above the unemployment rate of 4.6 percent in 2007. According to the CBO, without the stimulus package, the unemployment rate would have been somewhere between 10.3 percent and 11.4 percent. So, the stimulus package reduced the increase in the unemployment rate that might otherwise have occurred, but did not come close to bringing the economy back to full employment.

Making the Connection | Why Was the Recession of 2007–2009 So Severe?

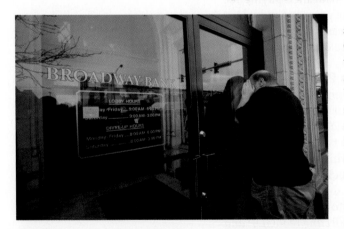

The financial crisis made the recession of 2007–2009 more severe and long-lasting than many other recessions.

The CBO estimates of the effects of the stimulus package indicate that even $825 billion in increased government spending and tax cuts left the economy with real GDP far from potential GDP and the unemployment rate above 9 percent. Why was the recession of 2007–2009 so severe? As we saw in Chapters 14 and 15, the recession was accompanied by a financial crisis. The U.S. economy had not experienced a significant financial crisis since the Great Depression of the 1930s. Both the Great Depression and the recession of 2007–2009 were severe. Was their severity the result of the accompanying financial crises? More generally, do recessions accompanied by financial crises tend to be more severe than recessions that do not involve bank crises?

Carmen Reinhart of the University of Maryland and Kenneth Rogoff of Harvard have gathered data on recessions and financial crises in a number of countries, in an attempt to answer this question. The table on the next page shows the average change in key economic variables during the period following a financial crisis for a number of countries, including the United States during the Great Depression and European and Asian countries in the post–World War II era. The table shows that for these countries, on average, the recessions following financial crises were quite severe. Unemployment rates increased by 7 percentage points—for example, from 5 percent to 12 percent—and continued increasing for nearly five years after a crisis had begun. Real GDP per capita also declined sharply, and the average length of a recession following a financial crisis has been nearly two years. Adjusted for inflation, stock prices dropped by more than half, and housing prices dropped by more than one-third. Government debt soared by 86 percent. The increased government debt was partly the result of increased government spending, including spending to bail out failed financial institutions. But most of the increased debt was the result of government budget deficits resulting from sharp declines in tax revenues as incomes and profits fell as a result of the recession. (We discuss government budget deficits and government debt in the next section.)

Economic Variable	Average Change	Average Duration of Change	Number of Countries
Unemployment rate	+7 percentage points	4.8 years	14
Real GDP per capita	−9.3%	1.9 years	14
Real stock prices	−55.9%	3.4 years	22
Real house prices	−35.5%	6 years	21
Real government debt	+86%	3 years	13

The table above does not include data for the United States during the 2007–2009 recession because that recession was still under way when Reinhart and Rogoff were compiling their data. The table below shows some key indicators for the 2007–2009 U.S. recession compared with other U.S. recessions of the post–World War II period:

	Duration	Decline in Real GDP	Peak Unemployment Rate
Average for postwar recessions	10.4 months	−1.7%	7.6%
Recession of 2007–2009	18 months	−4.1%	10.1%

Consistent with Reinhart and Rogoff's findings that recessions following financial panics tend to be unusually severe, the 2007–2009 recession was the worst in the United States since the Great Depression of the 1930s. The recession lasted nearly twice as long as the average of earlier postwar recessions, GDP declined by more than twice the average, and the peak unemployment rate was about one-third higher than the average.

Because most people did not see the financial crisis coming, they also failed to anticipate the severity of the 2007–2009 recession.

Note: In the second table, the duration of recessions is based on National Bureau of Economic Research business cycle dates, the decline in real GDP is measured as the simple percentage change from the quarter of the cyclical peak to the quarter of the cyclical trough, and the peak unemployment rate is the highest unemployment rate in any month following the cyclical peak.

Data from Carmen M. Reinhart and Kenneth S. Rogoff, *This Time Is Different: Eight Centuries of Financial Folly*, (Princeton, NJ: Princeton University Press, 2009), Figures 14.1–14.5; and the U.S. Bureau of Economic Analysis and National Bureau of Economic Research.

Your Turn: Test your understanding by doing related problem 5.6 on page 567 at the end of this chapter.

MyEconLab

The Size of the Multiplier: A Key to Estimating the Effects of Fiscal Policy

In preparing the values shown in Table 16.2, the CBO relied on estimates of the government purchases and tax multipliers. Economists have been debating the size of these multipliers for many years. When British economist John Maynard Keynes and his followers first developed the idea of spending and tax multipliers in the 1930s, they argued that the government purchases multiplier might be as large as 10. In that case, a $1 billion increase in government purchases would increase real GDP by $10 billion. Later research by economists indicated that the government purchases multiplier was much smaller, perhaps less than 2.

Estimating an exact number for the multiplier is difficult because over time, several factors can cause the aggregate demand and short-run aggregate supply curves to shift, leading to a change in equilibrium real GDP. It can be challenging to isolate the effect of an increase in government purchases on equilibrium GDP. In preparing their estimates of the effect of the stimulus package on GDP, Obama administration economists used an average of multiplier estimates from the Federal Reserve and from a private macro-economic forecasting firm. Their estimate of a government purchases multiplier of 1.57 indicates that a $1 billion increase in government purchases would increase equilibrium real GDP by $1.57 billion.

Because of the difficulty of estimating the size of the multiplier, some economists argue that the value used by the Obama administration's economists was too high, while others argued that it was too low. Robert Barro of Harvard University argues that increases in government spending during wartime are so large relative to other changes in aggregate demand that data from periods of war are best suited to estimating the size of the multiplier. Using such data, Barro estimated that the government purchases multiplier is only 0.8. Lawrence Christiano, Martin Eichenbaum, and Sergio Rebelo of Northwestern University argued, on the other hand, that the multiplier is likely to be larger when, as during 2009, short-term interest rates are near zero. They estimated that for these periods, the government purchases multiplier could be as large as 3.7.

As Table 16.3 shows, estimates of the size of the multiplier vary widely. The uncertainty about the size of the multiplier indicates the difficulty that economists have in arriving at a firm estimate of the effects of fiscal policy.

Table 16.3 **Estimates of the Size of the Multiplier**

Economist	Type of Multiplier	Size of Multiplier
Congressional Budget Office	Government purchases	1.0–2.5
Lawrence Christiano, Martin Eichenbaum, and Sergio Rebelo	Government purchases	1.05 (when short-term interest rates are not zero); 3.7 (when short-term interest rates are expected to be zero for at least five quarters)
Tommaso Monacelli, Roberto Perotti, and Antonella Trigari, Universita Bocconi	Government purchases	1.2 (after one year) and 1.5 (after two years)
Ethan Ilzetzki, London School of Economics, Enrique G. Mendoza, and Carlos A. Vegh, University of Maryland	Government purchases	0.8
Valerie Ramey, University of California, San Diego	Military expenditure	0.6–1.1
Robert J. Barro, Harvard University, and Charles J. Redlick, Bain Capital, LLC	Military expenditure	0.4–0.5 (after one year) and 0.6–0.7 (after two years)
John Cogan and John Taylor, Stanford University, and Tobias Cwik and Volker Wieland, Gothe University	A permanent increase in government expenditures	0.4
Christina Romer, University of California, Berkeley, and Jared Bernstein, chief economist and economic policy adviser to Vice President Joseph Biden	A permanent increase in government expenditures	1.6
Christina Romer (prior to serving as chair of the Council of Economic Advisers) and David Romer, University of California, Berkeley	Tax	2–3
Congressional Budget Office	Tax	0.6–1.5 (two-year tax cut for lower- and middle-income people) and 0.2–0.6 (one-year tax cut for higher-income people)
Robert J. Barro, Harvard University, and Charles J. Redlick, Bain Capital, LLC	Tax	1.1

Based on Tommaso Monacelli, Roberto Perotti, and Antonella Trigari, "Unemployment Fiscal Multipliers," *Journal of Monetary Economics*, Vol. 57, No. 5, July 2010, pp. 531–553; Ethan Ilzetzki, Enrique G. Mendoza, and Carlos A. Vegh, "How Big (Small?) Are Fiscal Multipliers?" National Bureau of Economic Research Working Paper No. 16479, December 2010; Robert J. Barro and Charles J. Redlick, "Macroeconomic Effects from Government Purchases and Taxes," National Bureau of Economic Research Working Paper 15369, September 2009; Lawrence Christiano, Martin Eichenbaum, and Sergio Rebelo, "When Is the Government Spending Multiplier Large?" *Journal of Political Economy*, Vol. 119, No. 1, February 2011, pp. 78–121; Jared Bernstein and Christina Romer, "The Job Impact of the American Reinvestment and Recovery Plan," January 9, 2009; John Cogan, Tobias Cwik, John Taylor, and Volker Wieland, "New Keynesian Versus Old Keynesian Government Spending Multipliers," *Journal of Economic Dynamics and Control*, Vol. 34, No. 3, March 2010, pp. 281–295; Valerie Ramey, "Identifying Government Spending Shocks: It's All in the Timing," *Quarterly Journal of Economics*, Vol. 126, No. 1, February 2011, pp. 1–50; Christina Romer and David Romer, "The Macroeconomic Effects of Tax Changes: Estimates Based on a New Measure of Fiscal Shocks," *American Economic Review*, Vol. 100, No. 3, June 2010, pp. 763–801; and U.S. Congressional Budget Office, "Estimated Impact of the American Recovery and Reinvestment Act on Employment and Economic Output from April 2011 through June 2011," August 2011.

Deficits, Surpluses, and Federal Government Debt

16.6 LEARNING OBJECTIVE

Define federal budget deficit and federal government debt and explain how the federal budget can serve as an automatic stabilizer.

The federal government's budget shows the relationship between its expenditures and its tax revenue. If the federal government's expenditures are greater than its tax revenue, a **budget deficit** results. If the federal government's expenditures are less than its tax revenue, a **budget surplus** results. As with many other macroeconomic variables, it is useful to consider the size of the surplus or deficit relative to the size of the overall economy. Figure 16.14 shows that, as a percentage of GDP, the largest deficits of the twentieth century came during World Wars I and II. During major wars, higher taxes only partially offset massive increases in government expenditures, leaving large budget deficits. Figure 16.14 also shows that during recessions government spending increases and tax revenues fall, increasing the budget deficit. In 1970, the federal government entered a long period of continuous budget deficits. From 1970 through 1997, the federal government's budget was in deficit every year. From 1998 through 2001, there were four years of budget surpluses. The recessions of 2001 and 2007–2009, tax cuts, and increased government spending on homeland security and the wars in Iraq and Afghanistan helped keep the budget in deficit in the years after 2001.

Figure 16.14 also shows the effects on the federal budget deficit of the Obama administration's $825 billion stimulus package and the severity of the 2007–2009 recession. From 2009 through 2011, the federal budget deficit was greater than 8 percent of GDP, which was the first time the deficit had been this large except during major wars in the history of the country.

Budget deficit The situation in which the government's expenditures are greater than its tax revenue.

Budget surplus The situation in which the government's expenditures are less than its tax revenue.

How the Federal Budget Can Serve as an Automatic Stabilizer

Discretionary fiscal policy can increase the federal budget deficit during recessions by increasing spending or cutting taxes to increase aggregate demand. For example, as we have just seen, the Obama administration's spending increases and tax cuts caused the federal budget deficit to soar during 2009. In many milder recessions, though, no significant fiscal policy actions are taken. In fact, most of the increase in the federal budget deficit during a typical recession takes place without Congress and the president taking

Figure 16.14 The Federal Budget Deficit, 1901–2011

During wars, government spending increases far more than tax revenues, increasing the budget deficit. The budget deficit also increases during recessions, as government spending increases and tax revenues fall.

Note: The value for 2011 is an estimate prepared by the Congressional Budget Office in June 2011.

Data from *Budget of the United States Government, Fiscal Year 2003, Historical Tables,* Washington, DC: U.S. Government Printing Office, 2002; U.S. Bureau of Economic Analysis; and Congressional Budget Office.

any action, but is instead due to the effects of the *automatic stabilizers* we mentioned earlier in this chapter.

Deficits occur automatically during recessions for two reasons: First, during a recession, wages and profits fall, causing government tax revenues to fall. Second, the government automatically increases its spending on transfer payments when the economy moves into recession. The government's contribution to the unemployment insurance program will increase as unemployment rises. Spending will also increase on programs to aid low-income people, such as the food stamps, Temporary Assistance for Needy Families, and Medicaid programs. These spending increases take place without Congress and the president taking any action. Existing laws already specify who is eligible for unemployment insurance and these other programs. As the number of eligible persons increases during a recession, so does government spending on these programs.

Because budget deficits automatically increase during recessions and decrease during expansions, economists often look at the *cyclically adjusted budget deficit or surplus*, which can provide a more accurate measure of the effects on the economy of the government's spending and tax policies than can the actual budget deficit or surplus. The **cyclically adjusted budget deficit or surplus** measures what the deficit or surplus would be if the economy were at potential GDP. In late 2011, the CBO projected that the deficit for 2012 would be about 6.2 percent of GDP. The CBO estimated that if real GDP were at its potential level, the deficit would be about 4.0 percent of GDP. The difference represented the effects of expansionary fiscal policy. If the federal government were to run a contractionary fiscal policy, the result would be a cyclically adjusted budget surplus.

Automatic budget surpluses and deficits can help to stabilize the economy. When the economy moves into a recession, wages and profits fall, which reduces the taxes that households and firms owe the government. In effect, households and firms have received an automatic tax cut, which keeps their spending higher than it otherwise would have been. In a recession, workers who have been laid off receive unemployment insurance payments, and households whose incomes have dropped below a certain level become eligible for food stamps and other government transfer programs. By receiving this extra income, households are able to spend more than they otherwise would have spent. This extra spending helps reduce the length and severity of the recession. Many economists argue that the lack of an unemployment insurance system and other government transfer programs contributed to the severity of the Great Depression. During the Great Depression, workers who lost their jobs saw their wage incomes drop to zero and had to rely on their savings, what they could borrow, or what they received from private charities. As a result, many unemployed workers cut back drastically on their spending, which made the downturn worse.

When GDP increases above its potential level, households and firms have to pay more taxes to the federal government, and the federal government makes fewer transfer payments. Higher taxes and lower transfer payments cause total spending to rise by less than it otherwise would have, which helps reduce the chance that the economy will experience higher inflation.

Cyclically adjusted budget deficit or surplus The deficit or surplus in the federal government's budget if the economy were at potential GDP.

Although government spending increased during the Great Depression, the cyclically adjusted budget was in surplus most years.

Making the Connection | Did Fiscal Policy Fail during the Great Depression?

Modern macroeconomic analysis began during the 1930s, with the publication of *The General Theory of Employment, Interest, and Money* by John Maynard Keynes. One conclusion many economists drew from Keynes's book was that an expansionary fiscal policy would be necessary to pull the United States out of the Great Depression. When Franklin D. Roosevelt became president in 1933, federal government expenditures increased as part of his New Deal program, and there was a federal budget deficit during each remaining year of the decade, except for 1937. The U.S. economy recovered very slowly, however, and did not reach potential GDP again until the outbreak of World War II in 1941.

Some economists and policymakers at the time argued that because the economy recovered slowly despite increases in government spending, fiscal policy had been ineffective. During the debate over President Obama's stimulus package, the argument that fiscal policy had failed during the New Deal was raised again. Economic historians have argued, however, that despite the increases in government spending, Congress and the president had not, in fact, implemented an expansionary fiscal policy during the 1930s. In separate studies, economists E. Cary Brown of MIT and Larry Peppers of Washington and Lee University argued that there was a cyclically adjusted budget deficit during only one year of the 1930s, and that one deficit was small. The following table provides data supporting their arguments. (All variables in the table are nominal rather than real.) The second column shows federal government expenditures increasing from 1933 to 1936, falling in 1937, and then increasing in 1938 and 1939. The third column shows a similar pattern, with the federal budget being in deficit each year after 1933 except for 1937. The fourth column, however, shows that in each year after 1933, the federal government ran a cyclically adjusted budget *surplus*. Because the level of income was so low and the unemployment rate was so high during these years, tax collections were far below what they would have been if the economy had been at potential GDP. As the fifth column shows, in 1933 and again in 1937 to 1939, the cyclically adjusted surpluses were large relative to GDP.

Year	Federal Government Expenditures (billions of dollars)	Actual Federal Budget Deficit or Surplus (billions of dollars)	Cyclically Adjusted Budget Deficit or Surplus (billions of dollars)	Cyclically Adjusted Budget Deficit or Surplus as a Percentage of GDP
1929	$2.6	$1.0	$1.24	1.20%
1930	2.7	0.2	0.81	0.89
1931	4.0	−2.1	−0.41	−0.54
1932	3.0	−1.3	0.50	0.85
1933	3.4	−0.9	1.06	1.88
1934	5.5	−2.2	0.09	0.14
1935	5.6	−1.9	0.54	0.74
1936	7.8	−3.2	0.47	0.56
1937	6.4	0.2	2.55	2.77
1938	7.3	−1.3	2.47	2.87
1939	8.4	−2.1	2.00	2.17

Although President Roosevelt proposed many new government spending programs, he had also promised during the 1932 presidential election campaign to balance the federal budget. He achieved a balanced budget only in 1937, but his reluctance to allow the actual budget deficit to grow too large helps explain why the cyclically adjusted budget remained in surplus. Many economists today would agree with E. Cary Brown's conclusion: "Fiscal policy, then, seems to have been an unsuccessful recovery device in the 'thirties—not because it did not work, but because it was not tried."

Based on E. Cary Brown, "Fiscal Policy in the "Thirties: A Reappraisal," *American Economic Review*, Vol. 46, No. 5, December 1956, pp. 857–879; Larry Peppers, "Full Employment Surplus Analysis and Structural Changes," *Explorations in Economic History*, Vol. 10, Winter 1973, pp. 197–210; and U.S. Bureau of Economic Analysis.

Your Turn: Test your understanding by doing related problem 6.8 on page 568 at the end of this chapter.   MyEconLab

Solved Problem 16.6

The Effect of Economic Fluctuations on the Budget Deficit

The federal government's budget deficit was $207.8 billion in 1983 and $185.4 billion in 1984. A student comments, "The government must have acted during 1984 to raise taxes or cut spending or both." Do you agree? Briefly explain.

Solving the Problem

Step 1: **Review the chapter material.** This problem is about the federal budget as an automatic stabilizer, so you may want to review the section "How the Federal Budget Can Serve as an Automatic Stabilizer," which begins on page 553.

Step 2: **Explain how changes in the budget deficit can occur without Congress and the president acting.** If Congress and the president take action to raise taxes or cut spending, the federal budget deficit will decline. But the deficit will also decline automatically when GDP increases, even if the government takes no action. When GDP increases, rising household incomes and firm profits result in higher tax revenues. Increasing GDP also usually means falling unemployment, which reduces government spending on unemployment insurance and other transfer payments. So, you should disagree with the comment. A falling deficit does not mean that the government *must* have acted to raise taxes or cut spending.

Extra Credit: Although you don't have to know it to answer the question, GDP did increase from $3.5 trillion in 1983 to $3.9 trillion in 1984.

MyEconLab **Your Turn:** For more practice, do related problem 6.6 on page 568 at the end of this chapter.

Should the Federal Budget Always Be Balanced?

Although many economists believe that it is a good idea for the federal government to have a balanced budget when the economy is at potential GDP, few economists believe that the federal government should attempt to balance its budget every year. To see why economists take this view, consider what the government would have to do to keep the budget balanced during a recession, when the federal budget automatically moves into deficit. To bring the budget back into balance, the government would have to raise taxes or cut spending, but these actions would reduce aggregate demand, thereby making the recession worse. Similarly, when GDP increases above its potential level, the budget automatically moves into surplus. To eliminate this surplus, the government would have to cut taxes or increase government spending. But these actions would increase aggregate demand, thereby pushing GDP further beyond potential GDP and increasing the risk of higher inflation. To balance the budget every year, the government might have to take actions that would destabilize the economy.

Some economists argue that the federal government should normally run a deficit, even at potential GDP. When the federal budget is in deficit, the U.S. Treasury sells bonds to investors to raise the funds necessary to pay the government's bills. Borrowing to pay the bills is a bad policy for a household, a firm, or the government when the bills are for current expenses, but it is not a bad policy if the bills are for long-lived capital goods. For instance, most families pay for a new home by taking out a 15- to 30-year mortgage. Because houses last many years, it makes sense to pay for a house out of the income the family makes over a long period of time rather than out of the income received in the year the house is bought. Businesses often borrow the funds to buy machinery, equipment, and factories by selling 30-year corporate bonds. Because these capital goods generate profits for the businesses over many years, it makes sense to pay for them over a period of years as well. By similar reasoning, when the federal government contributes to the building of a new highway, bridge, or subway, it may want to borrow funds by selling Treasury bonds. The alternative is to pay for these long-lived capital goods out of the tax revenues received in the year the goods were purchased. But that means that the taxpayers in that year have to bear the whole burden of paying for the projects, even though taxpayers for many years in the future will be enjoying the benefits.

The Federal Government Debt

Every time the federal government runs a budget deficit, the Treasury must borrow funds from investors by selling Treasury securities. For simplicity, we will refer to all Treasury securities as "bonds." When the federal government runs a budget surplus, the Treasury pays off some existing bonds. Figure 16.14 on page 553 shows that there are many more years of federal budget deficits than years of federal budget surpluses. As a result, the total number of Treasury bonds outstanding has grown over the years. The total value of U.S. Treasury bonds outstanding is referred to as the *federal government debt* or, sometimes, as the *national debt*. Each year the federal budget is in deficit, the federal government debt grows. Each year the federal budget is in surplus, the debt shrinks.

Figure 16.15 shows federal government debt as a percentage of GDP in the years since 1901. The ratio of debt to GDP increased during World Wars I and II and the Great Depression, reflecting the large government budget deficits of those years. After the end of World War II, GDP grew faster than the debt until the early 1980s, which caused the ratio of debt to GDP to fall. The large budget deficits of the 1980s and early 1990s sent the debt-to-GDP ratio climbing. The budget surpluses of 1998 to 2001 caused the debt-to-GDP ratio to fall, but it rose again with the return of deficits beginning in 2002. The large deficits beginning in 2008 caused the ratio to spike up to its highest level since 1947.

Is Government Debt a Problem?

Debt can be a problem for a government for the same reasons that debt can be a problem for a household or a business. If a family has difficulty making the monthly mortgage payment, it will have to cut back spending on other goods and services. If the family is unable to make the payments, it will have to *default* on the loan and will probably lose its house. The federal government is not in danger of defaulting on its debt. Ultimately, the government can raise the funds it needs through taxes to make the interest payments on the debt. If the debt becomes very large relative to the economy, however, the government may have to raise taxes to high levels or cut back on other types of spending to make the interest payments on the debt. Interest payments are currently about 10 percent of total federal expenditures. At this level, tax increases or significant cutbacks in other types of federal spending are not required.

In the long run, a debt that increases in size relative to GDP, as was happening after 2008, can pose a problem. As we discussed previously, crowding out of investment spending may occur if an increasing debt drives up interest rates. Lower investment spending means a lower capital stock in the long run and a reduced capacity of the economy to produce goods and services. This effect is somewhat offset if some of the government debt was incurred to finance improvements in *infrastructure*, such as

Figure 16.15

The Federal Government Debt, 1901–2011

The federal government debt increases whenever the federal government runs a budget deficit. The large deficits incurred during World Wars I and II, the Great Depression, and the 1980s and early 1990s increased the ratio of debt to GDP. The large deficits of 2009 to 2011 caused the ratio to spike up to its highest level since 1947.

Data from U.S. Bureau of the Census, *Historical Statistics of the United States, Colonial Times to 1970*, Washington, DC: U.S. Government Printing Office, 1975; Budget of the United States Government, Fiscal Year 2003, Historical Printing Office, 2002; Federal Reserve Bank of St. Louis, *National Economic Trends*, October 2011; and Congressional Budget Office.

bridges, highways, and ports; to finance education; or to finance research and development. Improvements in infrastructure, a better-educated labor force, and additional research and development can add to the productive capacity of the economy.

The Effects of Fiscal Policy in the Long Run

Some fiscal policy actions are intended to meet the short-run goal of stabilizing the economy. Other fiscal policy actions are intended to have long-run effects by expanding the productive capacity of the economy and increasing the rate of economic growth. Because these policy actions primarily affect aggregate supply rather than aggregate demand, they are sometimes referred to as *supply-side economics*. Most fiscal policy actions that attempt to increase aggregate supply do so by changing taxes to increase the incentives to work, save, invest, and start a business.

The Long-Run Effects of Tax Policy

Tax wedge The difference between the pretax and posttax return to an economic activity.

The difference between the pretax and posttax return to an economic activity is known as the **tax wedge**. The tax wedge applies to the *marginal tax rate*, which is the fraction of each additional dollar of income that must be paid in taxes. For example, the U.S. federal income tax has several tax brackets, which are the income ranges within which a tax rate applies. In 2011, for a single taxpayer, the tax rate was 10 percent on the first $8,500 earned during a year. The tax rate rose for higher income brackets, until it reached 35 percent on income earned above $379,150. Suppose you are paid a wage of $20 per hour. If your marginal income tax rate is 25 percent, then your after-tax wage is $15, and the tax wedge is $5. When discussing the model of demand and supply in Chapter 3, we saw that increasing the price of a good or service increases the quantity supplied. So, we would expect that reducing the tax wedge by cutting the marginal tax rate on income would result in a larger quantity of labor supplied because the after-tax wage would be higher. Similarly, we saw in Chapter 10 that a reduction in the income tax would increase the after-tax return to saving, causing an increase in the supply of loanable funds, a lower equilibrium interest rate, and an increase in investment spending. In general, economists believe that the smaller the tax wedge for any economic activity—such as working, saving, investing, or starting a business—the more of that economic activity that will occur. When workers, savers, investors, or entrepreneurs change their behavior as a result of a tax change, economists say that there has been a *behavioral response* to the tax change.

We can look briefly at the effects on aggregate supply of cutting each of the following taxes:

- *Individual income tax.* As we have seen, reducing the marginal tax rates on individual income will reduce the tax wedge faced by workers, thereby increasing the quantity of labor supplied. Many small businesses are *sole proprietorships*, whose profits are taxed at the individual income tax rates. Therefore, cutting the individual income tax rates also raises the return to entrepreneurship, encouraging the opening of new businesses. Most households are also taxed on their returns from saving at the individual income tax rates. Reducing marginal income tax rates, therefore, also increases the return to saving.

- *Corporate income tax.* The federal government taxes the profits earned by corporations under the corporate income tax. In 2011, most corporations faced a marginal corporate tax rate of 35 percent. Cutting the marginal corporate income tax rate would encourage investment spending by increasing the return corporations receive from new investments in equipment, factories, and office buildings. Because innovations are often embodied in new investment goods, cutting the corporate income tax can potentially increase the pace of technological change.

- *Taxes on dividends and capital gains.* Corporations distribute some of their profits to shareholders in the form of payments known as *dividends*. Shareholders also may benefit from higher corporate profits by receiving *capital gains*. A capital gain is the increase in the price of an asset, such as a share of stock. Rising profits usually result in rising stock prices and capital gains to shareholders. Individuals pay taxes on both dividends and capital gains (although the tax on capital gains can be postponed if the stock is not sold). As a result, the same earnings are, in effect, taxed twice: once when a corporation pays the corporate income tax on its profits and a second time when the profits are received by individual investors in the form of dividends or capital gains. Economists debate the costs and benefits of a separate tax on corporate profits. With the corporate income tax remaining in place, one way to reduce the "double taxation" problem is to reduce the taxes on dividends and capital gains. These taxes were, in fact, reduced in 2003, and in 2011, the marginal tax rates on dividends and capital gains were still well below the top marginal tax rate on individual income. Lowering the tax rates on dividends and capital gains increases the supply of loanable funds from households to firms, increasing saving and investment and lowering the equilibrium real interest rate.

Tax Simplification

In addition to the potential gains from cutting individual taxes, there are also gains from tax simplification. The complexity of the tax code has created a whole industry of tax preparation services, such as H&R Block. At almost 3,000 pages long, the tax code is extremely complex. The Internal Revenue Service estimates that taxpayers spend more than 6.4 billion hours each year filling out their tax forms, or about 45 hours per tax return. Households and firms have to deal with more than 480 tax forms to file their federal taxes. It is not surprising that there are more H&R Block offices around the country than Starbucks coffeehouses.

If the tax code were greatly simplified, the economic resources currently used by the tax preparation industry would be available to produce other goods and services. In addition to wasting resources, the complexity of the tax code may also distort the decisions made by households and firms. For example, the tax rate on dividends has clearly affected whether corporations pay dividends. When Congress passed a reduction in the tax on dividends in 2003, many firms—including Microsoft—began paying dividends for the first time. A simplified tax code would increase economic efficiency by reducing the number of decisions households and firms make solely to reduce their tax payments.

The Economic Effect of Tax Reform

We can analyze the economic effects of tax reduction and simplification by using the aggregate demand and aggregate supply model. Figure 16.16 shows that without tax changes, the long-run aggregate supply curve will shift from $LRAS_1$ to $LRAS_2$. This shift represents the increases in the labor force and the capital stock and the technological change that would occur even without tax reduction and simplification. To focus on the effect of tax changes on aggregate supply, we will ignore any shifts in the short-run aggregate supply curve, and we will assume that the aggregate demand curve remains unchanged, at AD_1. In this case, equilibrium moves from point A to point B, with real GDP increasing from Y_1 to Y_2 and the price level decreasing from P_1 to P_2.

If tax reduction and simplification are effective, the economy will experience increases in labor supply, saving, investment, and the formation of new firms. Economic efficiency will also be improved. Together these factors will result in an increase in the quantity of real GDP supplied at every price level. We show the effects of the tax changes in Figure 16.16 by a shift in the long-run aggregate supply curve to $LRAS_3$. With aggregate demand remaining unchanged, the equilibrium in the economy moves from point A to point C (rather than to point B, which is the equilibrium without tax changes), with real GDP increasing from Y_1 to Y_3 and the price level decreasing from P_1 to P_3. Notice that compared with the equilibrium without tax changes (point B), the equilibrium with tax changes (point C) occurs at a lower price level and a higher level of real GDP. We can conclude that the tax changes have benefited the economy by increasing output and employment while at the same time reducing the price level.

Figure 16.16

The Supply-Side Effects of a Tax Change

The economy's initial equilibrium is at point *A*. With no tax change, the long-run aggregate supply curve shifts to the right, from $LRAS_1$ to $LRAS_2$. Equilibrium moves to point *B*, with the price level falling from P_1 to P_2 and real GDP increasing from Y_1 to Y_2. With tax reductions and simplifications, the long-run aggregate supply curve shifts further to the right, to $LRAS_3$, and equilibrium moves to point *C*, with the price level falling to P_3 and real GDP increasing to Y_3.

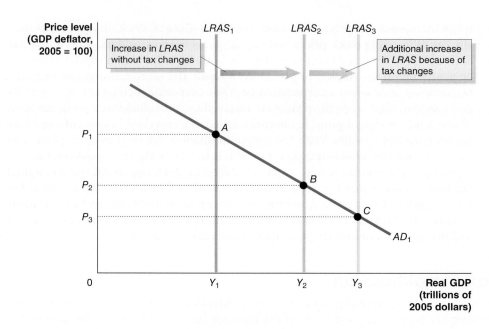

Clearly, our analysis is unrealistic because we have ignored the changes in aggregate demand and short-run aggregate supply that will occur. How would a more realistic analysis differ from the simplified one in Figure 16.16? The change in real GDP would be the same because in the long run, real GDP is equal to its potential level, which is represented by the long-run aggregate supply curve. The results for the price level would be different, however, because we would expect both aggregate demand and short-run aggregate supply to shift to the right. The likeliest case is that the price level would end up higher in the new equilibrium than in the original equilibrium. However, because the position of the long-run aggregate supply curve is further to the right as a result of the tax changes, the increase in the price level will be smaller; that is, the price level at point *C* is likely to be lower than P_2, even if it is higher than P_3, although—as we will discuss in the next section—not all economists would agree. We can conclude that a successful policy of tax reductions and simplifications will benefit the economy by increasing output and employment and, at the same time, may result in smaller increases in the price level.

How Large Are Supply-Side Effects?

Most economists would agree that there are supply-side effects to reducing taxes: Decreasing marginal income tax rates will increase the quantity of labor supplied, cutting the corporate income tax will increase investment spending, and so on. The magnitude of the effects is the subject of considerable debate, however. For example, some economists argue that the increase in the quantity of labor supplied following a tax cut will be limited because many people work a number of hours set by their employers and lack the opportunity to work additional hours. Similarly, some economists believe that tax changes have only a small effect on saving and investment. In this view, saving and investment are affected much more by changes in income or changes in expectations of the future profitability of new investment due to technological change or improving macroeconomic conditions than they are by tax changes.

Economists who are skeptical of the magnitude of supply-side effects believe that tax cuts have their greatest effect on aggregate demand rather than on aggregate supply. In their view, focusing on the effect of tax cuts on aggregate demand, while ignoring any effect on aggregate supply, yields accurate forecasts of future movements in real GDP and the price level, which indicates that the supply-side effects must be small. If tax changes have only small effects on aggregate supply, it is unlikely that they will reduce the size of price increases to the extent shown in the analysis in Figure 16.16.

Ultimately, the debate over the size of the supply-side effects of tax policy can be resolved only through careful study of the effects of differences in tax rates on labor supply and on saving and investment decisions. Some recent studies have arrived at conflicting conclusions, however. For example, a study by Nobel Laureate Edward Prescott of Arizona State University concludes that the differences between the United States and Europe with respect to the average number of hours worked per week and the average number of weeks worked per year are due to differences in taxes. The lower marginal tax rates in the United States compared with Europe increase the return to working for U.S. workers and result in a larger quantity of labor supplied. But another study by Alberto Alesina and Edward Glaeser of Harvard University and Bruce Sacerdote of Dartmouth College argues that the more restrictive labor market regulations in Europe explain the shorter work weeks and longer vacations of European workers and that differences in taxes have only a small effect.

As in other areas of economics, differences among economists in their estimates of the supply-side effects of tax changes may narrow over time as they conduct more studies.

Continued from page 531

Economics in Your Life

What Would You Do with $500?

At the beginning of the chapter, we asked how you would respond to a $500 tax rebate and what effect this tax rebate would likely have on equilibrium real GDP in the short run. This chapter has shown that tax cuts increase disposable income and that when there is a permanent increase in disposable income, consumption spending increases. So, you will likely respond to a permanent $500 increase in your disposable income by increasing your spending. How much your spending increases depends in part on your overall financial situation. As mentioned in the chapter, people who are able to borrow usually try to smooth out their spending over time and don't increase spending much in response to a one-time increase in their income. But if you are a student struggling to get by on a low income and you are unable to borrow against the higher income you expect to earn in the future, you may well spend most of the rebate. This chapter has also shown that tax cuts have a multiplier effect on the economy. That is, an increase in consumption spending sets off further increases in real GDP and income. So, if the economy is not already at potential GDP, this tax rebate will likely increase equilibrium real GDP in the short run.

Conclusion

In this chapter, we have seen how the federal government uses changes in government purchases and taxes to achieve its economic policy goals. We have seen that economists debate the effectiveness of discretionary fiscal policy actions intended to stabilize the economy. Congress and the president share responsibility for economic policy with the Federal Reserve. In Chapter 17, we will discuss further some of the challenges that the Federal Reserve encounters as it carries out monetary policy. In Chapters 18 and 19, we will look more closely at the international economy, including how monetary and fiscal policy are affected by the linkages between economies.

Read *An Inside Look at Policy* on the next page for a discussion of the arguments for and against using infrastructure spending to increase employment.

Obama Proposes Additional Spending to Stimulate the Economy

U.S. NEWS & WORLD REPORT

Are Infrastructure Projects the Answer to America's Jobs Problem?

Infrastructure spending is expected to be one of the chief components of the jobs plan that President Obama will unveil in September. The idea of spending on public works projects like road-building as economic stimulus has been a mainstay of jobs proposals from both congressional Democrats and the White House in recent years. But opponents question its efficiency at creating jobs—and its cost.

a According to data from Moody's Analytics, which performs economic analysis and forecasting, infrastructure spending is more effective, dollar for dollar, than many forms of tax cuts at boosting jobs growth. But after passing legislation, going through the appropriations process, identifying projects, planning, and hiring workers, the time it takes the federal government bureaucracy to get that money out the door can mean delayed or even diminished economic impact. Add to that a particularly slow-moving Congress with a propensity for partisan divides that slow or halt much legislation—and the current climate of budget-cutting—and a potentially promising policy move could be greatly undercut or never enacted.

Many Republican lawmakers have in the past decried spending on infrastructure. When President Obama introduced the idea of a national infrastructure bank in September 2010, Representative Eric Cantor called it "yet another government stimulus effort" and House Speaker John Boehner called it "more of the same failed 'stimulus' spending," alluding to the 2009 American Recovery and Reinvestment Act that the president introduced to counteract the Great Recession. That $787-billion stimulus package created far fewer jobs than the White House had initially predicted, a point that stimulus critics often make. But not all Republicans are opposed to infrastructure spending; Texas Senator Kay Bailey Hutchison, for example, co-sponsored a bill with Massachusetts Democrat John Kerry in March, proposing an infrastructure bank.

b The theory behind infrastructure spending is the multiplier effect: the idea that every dollar in government expenditures can increase GDP by more than one dollar by starting economic chain reactions: the government pays firms for goods and services and those firms then pay employees who then spend their paychecks.

Moody's Analytics estimates that the multiplier effect for increases in government spending is generally larger than the multiplier for tax cuts. Any additional dollar spent on permanent tax cuts adds to GDP by significantly less than a dollar. Making the Bush tax cuts permanent, for example, would add to GDP by $0.29 for every dollar of revenue reduction, according to calculations from Moody's. Infrastructure spending would add by $1.59 for every dollar spent, while extending unemployment insurance and temporarily increasing food stamps would add even more.

c The mitigating factor, then, is the speed (or lack thereof) with which infrastructure spending works. In past recessions, infrastructure projects have taken so long to get off the ground that their effects were only felt after recovery had begun, says Alan Viard, resident scholar at the American Enterprise Institute, a conservative think tank. "Dollar for dollar, [tax cuts and direct government payments] may not stimulate the economy as much as infrastructure spending, but they can be timed effectively. . . . If we expect [economic weakness] to last long enough for new infrastructure spending to come online, we've really got pretty serious problems. . . ."

It is difficult to dispute that tax cuts and direct government payments could provide rapid stimulus, but like any policy, those also have their downsides. "It's true that if you want an instant stimulus, you'd send people checks. . . . And a certain amount of that would be lost. Some would go to savings and paying back debt, and a fair amount would go to buying things that are not made in the U.S.," says Ross Eisenbrey, vice president of the liberal Economic Policy Institute. . . .

Source: "Are Infrastructure Projects the Answer to America's Jobs Problem? Disappointing stimulus package gives ammunition to the policy's opponents," by Danielle Kurtzleban from *U.S. News & World Report*, August 22, 2011. Copyright © 2011 by Wright's Media. Reprinted by permission.

Key Points in the Article

Proponents of spending on infrastructure as a means of stimulating the economy argue that for each dollar spent, infrastructure spending is more effective than tax cuts at creating jobs. They also estimate that the multiplier effect for increases in government spending is larger than the multiplier effect for tax cuts. Those opposed to using infrastructure spending as a way to increase employment argue that the 2009 American Recovery and Reinvestment Act created considerably fewer jobs than had been predicted. An important factor in determining job creation through infrastructure spending is the time needed for the spending to occur and to have its full effect on the economy. Although infrastructure spending may stimulate the economy more than tax cuts, it may also take a long time for Congress to approve spending programs and for the programs actually to take effect.

Analyzing the News

a As you read in this chapter, expansionary fiscal policy involves increasing government purchases or decreasing taxes to increase aggregate demand. The Obama administration introduced the American Recovery and Reinvestment Act in 2009, a stimulus package designed to combat the recession that began in December 2007. A portion of this stimulus package was designated for infrastructure spending, and the administration believed that it would have a greater economic effect than the less-than-successful tax rebate program implemented by the Bush administration in 2008. According to Moody's Analytics, an economic analysis and forecasting company, each dollar of infrastructure spending has a greater effect on job growth than does each dollar in tax cuts, but infrastructure spending is subject to potentially significant time delays because Congress needs to approve the spending, infrastructure projects need to be identified and planned, and workers need to be hired. The amount of time it takes to actually implement these projects can delay or even weaken their economic effect.

b An increase in infrastructure spending is subject to the multiplier effect, where every dollar spent will increase GDP by more than one dollar. The figure below shows aggregate demand increasing from AD_1 to AD when infrastructure spending is first increased. The amount of the increase is equal to the initial increase in government spending. Due to the multiplier effect, aggregate demand continues to increase, from AD to AD_2. The increase in spending therefore results in a larger increase in real GDP. Moody's Analytics estimates that the multiplier for infrastructure spending is 1.59, so for every $1 increase in spending, real GDP will increase by $1.59.

c The length of time it takes for infrastructure spending to affect the economy can make a large difference in the overall effectiveness of the spending. If the spending begins only after a relatively long period of time, the economy may have already begun to recover by the time the additional spending can have an effect. In this case, the expansionary fiscal policy could expand aggregate demand by too great an amount, leading to an eventual increase in inflation.

Thinking Critically About Policy

1. President Obama's economic team calculated the effects of its economic stimulus package using estimates of the government spending multiplier. Some economists, though, argue that administration economists have overestimated the sizes of the government purchases and tax multipliers. Other economists have argued that the sizes of these multipliers were underestimated. Why do economists have difficulty in reaching agreement on the sizes of these multipliers?

2. The Obama administration's stimulus spending resulted in a large increase in the federal budget deficit. Administration economists, however, were relatively unconcerned that crowding out would reduce the effect of the stimulus spending on real GDP. Briefly explain what crowding out is and why the administration was relatively unconcerned about it as it implemented the stimulus package.

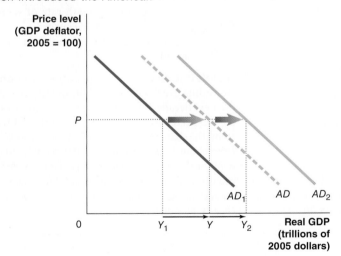

The effect on aggregate demand of infrastructure spending.

Chapter Summary and Problems

Key Terms

Automatic stabilizers, p. 532

Budget deficit, p. 553

Budget surplus, p. 553

Crowding out, p. 546

Cyclically adjusted budget deficit or surplus, p. 554

Fiscal policy, p. 532

Multiplier effect, p. 541

Tax wedge, p. 558

 16.1 **What Is Fiscal Policy?** pages 906–910
LEARNING OBJECTIVE: Define fiscal policy.

Summary

Fiscal policy involves changes in federal taxes and purchases that are intended to achieve macroeconomic policy objectives. **Automatic stabilizers** are government spending and taxes that automatically increase or decrease along with the business cycle. Since World War II, the federal government's share of total government expenditures has been between two-thirds and three-quarters. Federal government *expenditures* as a percentage of GDP rose from 1950 to the early 1990s and fell between 1992 and 2001, before rising again. Federal government *purchases* have declined as a percentage of GDP since the end of the Korean War in the early 1950s. The largest component of federal expenditures is transfer payments. The largest sources of federal government revenue are individual income taxes, followed by social insurance taxes, which are used to fund the Social Security and Medicare systems.

 Visit www.myeconlab.com to complete these exercises online and get instant feedback.

Review Questions

1.1 What is fiscal policy? Who is responsible for fiscal policy?

1.2 What is the difference between fiscal policy and monetary policy?

1.3 What is the difference between federal purchases and federal expenditures? Are federal purchases higher today as a percentage of GDP than they were in 1960? Are federal expenditures as a percentage of GDP higher?

Problems and Applications

1.4 In 2009, Congress and the president enacted "cash for clunkers" legislation that paid people buying new cars up to $4,500 if they traded in an older, low-gas-mileage car. Was this piece of legislation an example of fiscal policy? Does it depend on what goals Congress and the president had in mind when they enacted the legislation?

Based on Justin Lahart, "Trade-in Program Tunes Up Economic Engine," *Wall Street Journal*, August 4, 2009.

1.5 Based on the discussion in this chapter, which source of government revenue shown in Figure 16.4 on page 534 do you think is likely to increase the most in the future? Briefly explain.

1.6 **[Related to the** Making the Connection **on page 535]** According to a Congressional Budget Office report:

> By the end of this decade, an increasing number of baby boomers will have reached retirement age.... CBO therefore estimates that, unless changes are made to Social Security, spending for the program will rise from 4.8 percent of GDP today to 6.1 percent by 2035.

Who are the baby boomers? Why should their retirement cause an increase in the growth rate of spending by the federal government on Social Security?

From Congressional Budget Office, *CBO's 2011 Long-Term Budget Outlook*, June 2011, p. 53.

1.7 **[Related to the** Making the Connection **on page 535]** According to a Congressional Budget Office report, "During the next decade alone, the number of people over the age of 65 is expected to rise by more than a third. Over the longer term, the share of people age 65 or older is projected to grow from about 13 percent now to 20 percent in 2035...." Briefly explain the implications of these facts for federal government spending as a percentage of GDP in 2035.

From Congressional Budget Office, *CBO's 2011 Long-Term Budget Outlook*, June 2011, p. 7.

16.2 **The Effects of Fiscal Policy on Real GDP and the Price Level,** pages 910–913
LEARNING OBJECTIVE: Explain how fiscal policy affects aggregate demand and how the government can use fiscal policy to stabilize the economy.

Summary

To fight recessions, Congress and the president can increase government purchases or cut taxes. This expansionary policy causes the aggregate demand curve to shift out more than it otherwise would, raising the level of real GDP and the price level. To fight rising inflation, Congress and the president can decrease government purchases or raise taxes. This contractionary policy causes the aggregate demand curve to shift out less than it otherwise would, reducing the increase in real GDP and the price level.

MyEconLab Visit www.myeconlab.com to complete these exercises online and get instant feedback.

Review Questions

2.1 What is an expansionary fiscal policy? What is a contractionary fiscal policy?

2.2 If Congress and the president decide that an expansionary fiscal policy is necessary, what changes should they make in government spending or taxes? What changes should they make if they decide that a contractionary fiscal policy is necessary?

Problems and Applications

2.3 Briefly explain whether you agree with the following statements: "An expansionary fiscal policy involves an increase in government purchases or an increase in taxes. A contractionary fiscal policy involves a decrease in government purchases or a decrease in taxes."

2.4 Identify each of the following as (i) part of an expansionary fiscal policy, (ii) part of a contractionary fiscal policy, or (iii) not part of fiscal policy.
  a. The corporate income tax rate is increased.
  b. Defense spending is increased.

  c. The Federal Reserve lowers the target for the federal funds rate.
  d. Families are allowed to deduct all their expenses for day care from their federal income taxes.
  e. The individual income tax rate is decreased.
  f. The state of New Jersey builds a new highway in an attempt to expand employment in the state.

2.5 Use an aggregate demand and aggregate supply graph to illustrate the situation where the economy begins in equilibrium at potential GDP and then the demand for housing sharply declines. What actions can Congress and the president take to move the economy back to potential GDP? Show the results of these actions on your graph.

2.6 **[Related to the** Don't Let This Happen to You **on page 538]** Is it possible for Congress and the president to carry out an expansionary fiscal policy if the money supply does not increase? Briefly explain.

2.7 A political commentator argues: "Congress and the president are more likely to enact an expansionary fiscal policy than a contractionary fiscal policy because expansionary policies are popular and contractionary policies are unpopular." Briefly explain whether you agree.

 Fiscal Policy in the Dynamic Aggregate Demand and Aggregate Supply Model, pages 539–540

LEARNING OBJECTIVE: Use the dynamic aggregate demand and aggregate supply model to analyze fiscal policy.

Summary

We can use the *dynamic aggregate demand and aggregate supply model* introduced in Chapter 13 to look more closely at expansionary and contractionary fiscal policies. The dynamic aggregate demand and aggregate supply model takes into account that (1) the economy experiences continuing inflation, with the price level rising every year, and (2) the economy experiences long-run growth, with the *LRAS* curve shifting to the right every year. In the dynamic model, an expansionary fiscal policy tries to ensure that the aggregate demand curve will shift far enough to the right to bring about macroeconomic equilibrium, with real GDP equal to potential GDP. A contractionary fiscal policy attempts to offset movements in aggregate demand that would cause macroeconomic equilibrium to occur at a level of real GDP that is greater than potential real GDP.

MyEconLab   Visit **www.myeconlab.com** to complete these exercises online and get instant feedback.

Review Questions

3.1 What are the key differences between how we illustrate an expansionary fiscal policy in the basic aggregate demand and aggregate supply model and in the dynamic aggregate demand and aggregate supply model?

3.2 What are the key differences between how we illustrate a contractionary fiscal policy in the basic aggregate demand and aggregate supply model and in the dynamic aggregate demand and aggregate supply model?

Problems and Applications

3.3 Use the graph to answer the following questions.

a. If the government takes no policy actions, what will be the values of real GDP and the price level in 2013?
b. What actions can the government take to bring real GDP to its potential level in 2013?
c. If the government takes no policy actions, what will be the inflation rate in 2013? If the government uses fiscal

policy to keep real GDP at its potential level, what will be the inflation rate in 2013?

3.4 The hypothetical information in the following table shows what the situation will be in 2015 if the Fed does *not* use fiscal policy:

Year	Potential GDP	Real GDP	Price Level
2014	$15.0 trillion	$15.0 trillion	110.0
2015	$15.4 trillion	$15.0 trillion	111.5

a. If Congress and the president want to keep real GDP at its potential level in 2015, should it use an expansionary policy or a contractionary policy? In your answer, be sure to explain whether Congress and the president should be increasing or decreasing government purchases and taxes.

b. If Congress and the president are successful in keeping real GDP at its potential level in 2015, state whether each of the following will be higher, lower, or the same as it would have been if they had taken no action:
  i Real GDP
  ii Potential real GDP
  iii The inflation rate
  iv The unemployment rate

c. Draw an aggregate demand and aggregate supply graph to illustrate your answer. Be sure that your graph contains *LRAS* curves for 2014 and 2015; *SRAS* curves for 2014 and 2015; *AD* curves for 2014 and 2015, with and without fiscal policy action; and equilibrium real GDP and the price level in 2015, with and without fiscal policy.

3.5 Use a dynamic aggregate demand and aggregate supply graph to illustrate the change in macroeconomic equilibrium from 2015 to 2016, assuming that the economy experiences deflation during 2016. In order for deflation to take place in 2016, does the economy also have to be experiencing a recession?

<table><tr><td>**16.4**</td><td>**The Government Purchases and Tax Multipliers**, pages 540–545</td></tr></table>

LEARNING OBJECTIVE: Explain how the government purchases and tax multipliers work.

Summary

Because of the **multiplier effect**, an increase in government purchases or a cut in taxes will have a multiplied effect on equilibrium real GDP. The *government purchases multiplier* is equal to the change in equilibrium real GDP divided by the change in government purchases. The *tax multiplier* is equal to the change in equilibrium real GDP divided by the change in taxes. Increases in government purchases and cuts in taxes have a positive multiplier effect on equilibrium real GDP. Decreases in government purchases and increases in taxes have a negative multiplier effect on equilibrium real GDP.

 MyEconLab   Visit **www.myeconlab.com** to complete these exercises online and get instant feedback.

Review Questions

4.1 Why does a $1 increase in government purchases lead to more than a $1 increase in income and spending?

4.2 Define *government purchases multiplier* and *tax multiplier*.

Problems and Applications

4.3 [Related to the Chapter Opener on page 531] Why would the Caldecott tunnel in Northern California and similar construction projects elsewhere in the country be expected to help the economy in the short run? A spokesperson for the California state agency in charge of the project mentioned that the Caldecott tunnel project would have a "ripple effect" on employment. What does the spokesperson mean by a ripple effect?

4.4 In *The General Theory of Employment, Interest, and Money*, John Maynard Keynes wrote:

> If the Treasury were to fill old bottles with banknotes, bury them at suitable depths in disused coal mines which are then filled up to the surface with town rubbish, and leave it to private enterprise . . . to dig the notes up again . . . there need be no more unemployment and, with the help of the repercussions, the real income of the community . . . would probably become a good deal greater than it is.

Which important macroeconomic effect is Keynes discussing here? What does he mean by "repercussions"? Why does he appear unconcerned about whether government spending is wasteful?

4.5 Suppose that real GDP is currently $13.1 trillion, potential real GDP is $13.5 trillion, the government purchases multiplier is 2, and the tax multiplier is –1.6.
  a. Holding other factors constant, by how much will government purchases need to be increased to bring the economy to equilibrium at potential GDP?
  b. Holding other factors constant, by how much will taxes have to be cut to bring the economy to equilibrium at potential GDP?
  c. Construct an example of a *combination* of increased government spending and tax cuts that will bring the economy to equilibrium at potential GDP.

4.6 [Related to Solved Problem 16.4 on page 544] Briefly explain whether you agree with the following statement:

> Real GDP is currently $14.7 trillion, and potential real GDP is $14.4 trillion. If Congress and the president would decrease government purchases by $300 billion or increase taxes by $300 billion, the economy could be brought to equilibrium at potential GDP.

4.7 A Federal Reserve publication discusses an estimate of the tax multiplier that gives it a value of 1.2 after one year and 2.8 after two years. Briefly explain why the tax multiplier might have a larger value after two years than after one year.

From Sylvain Leduc, "Fighting Downturns with Fiscal Policy," Federal Reserve Bank of San Francisco Economic Letter, June 19, 2009.

4.8 If the short-run aggregate supply (*SRAS*) curve were a horizontal line at the current price level, what would be the effect on the size of the government purchases and tax multipliers?

The Limits of Using Fiscal Policy to Stabilize the Economy, pages 545–552

LEARNING OBJECTIVE: Discuss the difficulties that can arise in implementing fiscal policy.

Summary

Poorly timed fiscal policy can do more harm than good. Getting the timing right with fiscal policy can be difficult because obtaining approval from Congress for a new fiscal policy can be a very long process and because it can take months for an increase in authorized spending to actually take place. Because an increase in government purchases may lead to a higher interest rate, it may result in a decline in consumption, investment, and net exports. A decline in private expenditures as a result of an increase in government purchases is called **crowding out**. Crowding out may cause an expansionary fiscal policy to fail to meet its goal of keeping the economy at potential GDP.

 MyEconLab   Visit www.myeconlab.com to complete these exercises online and get instant feedback.

Review Questions

5.1 Which can be changed more quickly: monetary policy or fiscal policy? Briefly explain.

5.2 What is meant by crowding out? Explain the difference between crowding out in the short run and in the long run.

Problems and Applications

5.3 Some economists argue that because increases in government spending crowd out private spending, increased government spending will reduce the long-run growth rate of real GDP.

a. Is this most likely to happen if the private spending being crowded out is consumption spending, investment spending, or net exports? Briefly explain.

b. In terms of its effect on the long-run growth rate of real GDP, would it matter if the additional government

spending involves (i) increased spending on highways and bridges or (ii) increased spending on national parks? Briefly explain.

5.4 In 2011, an article in the *Economist* argued that "heavy public debt risks more than just crowding out private investment. It can, in the extreme, bring on insolvency." What does the article mean by "heavy public debts"? How might heavy public debts lead to insolvency?

From "Running Out of Road," *Economist*, June 16, 2011.

5.5 We saw that in calculating the stimulus package's effect on real GDP, economists in the Obama administration estimated that the government purchases multiplier has a value of 1.57. John F. Cogan, Tobias Cwik, John B. Taylor, and Volker Wieland argue that the value is only 0.61.

a. Briefly explain how the government purchases multiplier can have a value less than 1.

b. Why does an estimate of the size of the multiplier matter in evaluating the effects of an expansionary fiscal policy?

Based on John Cogan, Tobias Cwik, John Taylor, and Volker Wieland, "New Keynesian Versus Old Keynesian Government Spending Multipliers," *Journal of Economic Dynamics and Control*, Control, Vol. 34, No. 3, March 2010, pp. 281–295.

5.6 [**Related to the** Making the Connection **on page 550**] Why would recessions accompanied by a financial crisis be more severe than recessions that do not involve bank crises? Were the large budget deficits of $1.4 trillion in fiscal year 2009 and $1.3 trillion in fiscal year 2010 primarily the result of the stimulus package of 2009? Briefly explain.

5.7 Suppose that at the same time Congress and the president pursue an expansionary fiscal policy, the Federal Reserve pursues an expansionary monetary policy. How might an expansionary monetary policy affect the extent of crowding out in the short run?

16.6   **Deficits, Surpluses, and Federal Government Debt,** pages 553–558

LEARNING OBJECTIVE: Define federal budget deficit and federal government debt and explain how the federal budget can serve as an automatic stabilizer.

Summary

A **budget deficit** occurs when the federal government's expenditures are greater than its tax revenues. A **budget surplus** occurs when the federal government's expenditures are less than its tax revenues. A budget deficit automatically increases during recessions

and decreases during expansions. The automatic movements in the federal budget help to stabilize the economy by cushioning the fall in spending during recessions and restraining the increase in spending during expansions. The **cyclically adjusted budget deficit or surplus** measures what the deficit or surplus would be if the economy were at potential GDP. The federal government debt is the value of outstanding bonds issued by the U.S. Treasury. The national debt is a problem if interest payments on it require taxes to be raised substantially or require other federal expenditures to be cut.

MyEconLab   Visit **www.myeconlab.com** to complete these exercises online and get instant feedback.

Review Questions

6.1 In what ways does the federal budget serve as an automatic stabilizer for the economy?

6.2 What is the cyclically adjusted budget deficit or surplus? Suppose that the economy is currently at potential GDP, and the federal budget is balanced. If the economy moves into recession, what will happen to the federal budget?

6.3 Why do few economists argue that it would be a good idea to balance the federal budget every year?

6.4 What is the difference between the federal budget deficit and federal government debt?

Problems and Applications

6.5 In a column in the *Financial Times*, the prime minister and the finance minister of the Netherlands argue that the European Union, an organization of 27 countries in Europe, should appoint "a commissioner for budgetary discipline." They believe that "The new commissioner should be given clear powers to set requirements for the budgetary policy of countries that run excessive deficits." What is an "excessive" budget deficit? Does judging whether a deficit is excessive depend in part on whether the country is in a recession? How can budgetary policies be used to reduce a budget deficit?

From Mark Rutte and Jan Kees de Jager, "Expulsion from the Eurozone Has to Be the Final Penalty," *Financial Times*, September 7, 2011.

6.6 [**Related to** Solved Problem 16.6 **on page 555**] The federal government's budget surplus was $189.4 billion in 2000 and $41.8 billion in 2001. What does this information tell us about fiscal policy actions that Congress and the president took during those years?

6.7 The federal government calculates its budget on a fiscal year that begins each year on October 1 and ends the following September 30. At the beginning of the 2005 fiscal year, the Congressional Budget Office (CBO) forecast that the federal budget deficit would be $368 billion. The actual budget deficit for fiscal 2005 was only $319 billion. Federal expenditures were $37 billion less than the CBO had forecast, and federal revenue was $12 billion more than the CBO had forecast.
   a. Is it likely that the economy grew faster or more slowly during fiscal 2005 than the CBO had expected? Explain your reasoning.
   b. Suppose that Congress and the president were committed to balancing the budget each year. Does what happened during 2005 provide any insight into difficulties they might run into in trying to balance the budget every year?

6.8 [**Related to the** Making the Connection **on page 554**] The following is from a message by President Hoover to Congress, dated May 5, 1932:

> I need not recount that the revenues of the Government as estimated for the next fiscal year show a decrease of about $1,700,000,000 below the fiscal year 1929, and inexorably require a broader basis of taxation and a drastic reduction of expenditures in order to balance the Budget. Nothing is more necessary at this time than balancing the Budget.

Do you think President Hoover was correct in saying that, in 1932, nothing was more necessary than balancing the federal government's budget? Explain.

6.9 According to an article in the *Wall Street Journal*, "Federal Reserve Chairman Ben Bernanke warned Congress and the White House that the U.S. economy will suffer if they don't move soon to rein in the federal budget deficit." How might the economy suffer from large federal deficits? How can Congress and the president "rein in" the federal budget deficit?

From Jon Hilsenrath and Brian Blackstone, "Bernanke Urges Deficit Reduction, Sees Growth This Year," *Wall Street Journal*, June 4, 2009.

6.10 An editorial in the *Wall Street Journal* declares, "We don't put much stock in future budget forecasts because they depend on so many variables." What variables would a forecast of future federal budget deficits depend on? What is it about these variables that makes future budget deficits difficult to predict?

From "Fiscal Revelation," *Wall Street Journal*, February 6, 2007.

6.11 An article in the *Economist* described the situation in Japan in mid-2009: "Nor is there much sign that Japan's gaping budget deficits have crowded out private investment. [Interest rates] on long-term Japanese bonds . . . are still only 1.45%, even as gross public debt is heading for 200% of GDP." Why would "gaping budget deficits" be expected to lead to crowding out? Why does the fact that interest rates in Japan have not risen indicate that crowding out may not yet be a problem?

From "Damage Assessment," *Economist*, May 14, 2009.

6.12 A political columnist wrote the following:

> Today . . . the main purpose [of government's issuing bonds] is to let craven politicians launch projects they know the public, at the moment, would rather not fully finance. The tab for these projects will not come due, probably, until after the politicians have long since departed for greener (excuse the expression) pastures.

Do you agree with this commentator's explanation for why some government spending is financed through tax receipts and other government spending is financed through borrowing, by issuing bonds? Briefly explain.

"The Bond Issue Won't Be Repaid by Park Tolls," by Paul Carpenter from the *Morning Call*, May 26, 2002. Copyright © 2002 by the Morning Call. Reprinted by permission. All rights reserved.

16.7

The Effects of Fiscal Policy in the Long Run, pages 558–561

LEARNING OBJECTIVE: Discuss the effects of fiscal policy in the long run.

Summary

Some fiscal policy actions are intended to have long-run effects by expanding the productive capacity of the economy and increasing the rate of economic growth. Because these policy actions primarily affect aggregate supply rather than aggregate demand, they are sometimes referred to as *supply-side economics*. The difference between the pretax and posttax return to an economic activity is known as the **tax wedge**. Economists believe that the smaller the tax wedge for any economic activity—such as working, saving, investing, or starting a business—the more of that economic activity will occur. Economists debate the size of the supply-side effects of tax changes.

MyEconLab   Visit **www.myeconlab.com** to complete these exercises online and get instant feedback.

Review Questions

7.1 What is meant by "supply-side economics"?

7.2 What is the "tax wedge"?

Problems and Applications

7.3 It seems that both households and businesses would benefit if the federal income tax were simpler and tax forms were easier to fill out. Why then have the tax laws become increasingly complicated?

7.4 Some economists and policymakers have argued in favor of a "flat tax." A flat tax would replace the current individual income tax system, with its many tax brackets, exemptions, and deductions, with a new system containing a single tax rate and few, or perhaps no, deductions and exemptions. Suppose a political candidate hired you to develop two arguments in favor of a flat tax. What two arguments would you advance? Alternatively, if you were hired to develop two arguments against a flat tax, what two arguments would you advance?

7.5 Suppose that an increase in marginal tax rates on individual income affects both aggregate demand and aggregate supply. Briefly describe the effect of the tax increase on equilibrium real GDP and the equilibrium price level. Will the changes in equilibrium real GDP and the price level be larger or smaller than they would be if the tax increase affected only aggregate demand? Briefly explain.

7.6 Writing in the *Wall Street Journal*, Martin Feldstein, an economist at Harvard University, argues that "behavioral responses" of taxpayers to the cuts in marginal tax rates enacted in 1986 resulted in "an enormous rise in the taxes paid, particularly by those who experienced the greatest reductions in marginal tax rates." How is it possible for cuts in marginal tax rates to result in an increase in total taxes collected? What does Feldstein mean by a "behavioral response" to tax cuts?

Based on Martin Feldstein, "The Tax Reform Evidence from 1986," *Wall Street Journal*, October 24, 2011.

Appendix

A Closer Look at the Multiplier

In this chapter, we saw that changes in government purchases and changes in taxes have a multiplied effect on equilibrium real GDP. In this appendix, we will build a simple economic model of the multiplier effect. When economists forecast the effect of a change in spending or taxes, they often rely on *econometric models*. As we saw in the appendix to Chapter 12, an econometric model is an economic model written in the form of equations, where each equation has been statistically estimated, using methods similar to those used in estimating demand curves, as briefly described in Chapter 3. In this appendix, we will start with a model similar to the one we used in the appendix to Chapter 12.

An Expression for Equilibrium Real GDP

We can write a set of equations that includes the key macroeconomic relationships we have studied in this and previous chapters. It is important to note that in this model, we will be assuming that the price level is constant. We know that this is unrealistic because an upward-sloping *SRAS* curve means that when the aggregate demand curve shifts, the price level will change. Nevertheless, our model will be approximately correct when changes in the price level are small. It also serves as an introduction to more complicated models that take into account changes in the price level. For simplicity, we also start out by assuming that taxes, T, do not depend on the level of real GDP, Y. We also assume that there are no government transfer payments to households. Finally, we assume that we have a closed economy, with no imports or exports. The numbers (with the exception of the *MPC*) represent billions of dollars:

(1) $C = 1{,}000 + 0.75(Y - T)$	Consumption function
(2) $I = 1{,}500$	Planned investment function
(3) $G = 1{,}500$	Government purchases function
(4) $T = 1{,}000$	Tax function
(5) $Y = C + I + G$	Equilibrium condition

The first equation is the consumption function. The marginal propensity to consume, or *MPC*, is 0.75, and 1,000 is the level of autonomous consumption, which is the level of consumption that does not depend on income. We assume that consumption depends on disposable income, which is $Y - T$. The functions for planned investment spending, government spending, and taxes are very simple because we have assumed that these variables are not affected by GDP and, therefore, are constant. Economists who use this type of model to forecast GDP would, of course, use more realistic planned investment, government purchases, and tax functions.

Equation (5)—the equilibrium condition—states that equilibrium GDP equals the sum of consumption spending, planned investment spending, and government purchases. To calculate a value for equilibrium real GDP, we need to substitute equations (1) through (4) into equation (5). This substitution gives us the following:

$$Y = 1{,}000 + 0.75(Y - 1{,}000) + 1{,}500 + 1{,}500$$
$$= 1{,}000 + 0.75Y - 750 + 1{,}500 + 1{,}500.$$

We need to solve this equation for Y to find equilibrium GDP. The first step is to subtract $0.75Y$ from both sides of the equation:

$$Y - 0.75Y = 1{,}000 - 750 + 1{,}500 + 1{,}500.$$

Then, we solve for Y:

$$0.25Y = 3,250$$

or

$$Y = \frac{3,250}{0.25} = 13,000.$$

To make this result more general, we can replace particular values with general values represented by letters:

$C = \overline{C} + MPC(Y - T)$	Consumption function
$I = \overline{I}$	Planned investment function
$G = \overline{G}$	Government purchases function
$T = \overline{T}$	Tax function
$Y = C + I + G$	Equilibrium condition

The letters with bars above them represent fixed, or *autonomous*, values that do not depend on the values of other variables. So, $\overline{C}$ represents autonomous consumption, which had a value of 1,000 in our original example. Now, solving for equilibrium, we get:

$$Y = \overline{C} + MPC(Y - \overline{T}) + \overline{I} + \overline{G}$$

or

$$Y - MPC(Y) = \overline{C} - (MPC \times \overline{T}) + \overline{I} + \overline{G}$$

or

$$Y(1 - MPC) = \overline{C} - (MPC \times \overline{T}) + \overline{I} + \overline{G}$$

or

$$Y = \frac{\overline{C} - (MPC \times \overline{T}) + \overline{I} + \overline{G}}{1 - MPC}.$$

A Formula for the Government Purchases Multiplier

To find a formula for the government purchases multiplier, we need to rewrite the last equation for changes in each variable rather than levels. Letting Δ stand for the change in a variable, we have

$$\Delta Y = \frac{\Delta \overline{C} - (MPC \times \Delta \overline{T}) + \Delta \overline{I} + \Delta \overline{G}}{1 - MPC}.$$

If we hold constant changes in autonomous consumption spending, planned investment spending, and taxes, we can find a formula for the government purchases multiplier, which is the ratio of the change in equilibrium real GDP to the change in government purchases:

$$\Delta Y = \frac{\Delta G}{1 - MPC}$$

or

$$\text{Government purchases multiplier} = \frac{\Delta Y}{\Delta G} = \frac{1}{1 - MPC}.$$

For an MPC of 0.75, the government purchases multiplier will be

$$\frac{1}{1 - 0.75} = 4.$$

A government purchases multiplier of 4 means that an increase in government spending of $10 billion will increase equilibrium real GDP by 4 × $10 billion = $40 billion.

A Formula for the Tax Multiplier

We can also find a formula for the tax multiplier. We start again with this equation:

$$\Delta Y = \frac{\Delta \overline{C} - (MPC \times \Delta \overline{T}) + \Delta \overline{I} + \Delta \overline{G}}{1 - MPC}.$$

Now we hold constant the values of autonomous consumption spending, planned investment spending, and government purchases, but we allow the value of taxes to change:

$$\Delta Y = \frac{- MPC \times \Delta T}{1 - MPC}.$$

Or:

$$\text{The tax multiplier} = \frac{\Delta Y}{\Delta T} = \frac{-MPC}{1 - MPC}.$$

For an *MPC* of 0.75, the tax multiplier will be:

$$\frac{-0.75}{1 - 0.75} = -3.$$

The tax multiplier is a negative number because an increase in taxes causes a decrease in equilibrium real GDP, and a decrease in taxes causes an increase in equilibrium real GDP. A tax multiplier of −3 means that a decrease in taxes of $10 billion will increase equilibrium real GDP by −3 × −$10 billion = $30 billion. In this chapter, we discussed the economic reasons for the tax multiplier being smaller than the government spending multiplier.

The "Balanced Budget" Multiplier

What will be the effect of equal increases (or decreases) in government purchases and taxes on equilibrium real GDP? At first, it might appear that the tax increase would exactly offset the government purchases increase, leaving real GDP unchanged. But we have just seen that the government purchases multiplier is larger (in absolute value) than the tax multiplier. We can use our formulas for the government purchases multiplier and the tax multiplier to calculate the net effect of increasing government purchases by $10 billion at the same time that taxes are increased by $10 billion:

$$\text{Increase in real GDP from the increase in government purchases} = \$10 \text{ billion} \times \frac{1}{1 - MPC}$$

$$\text{Decrease in real GDP from the increase in taxes} = \$10 \text{ billion} \times \frac{-MPC}{1 - MPC}$$

So, the combined effect equals

$$\$10 \text{ billion} \times \left[\left(\frac{1}{1 - MPC} \right) + \left(\frac{-MPC}{1 - MPC} \right) \right]$$

or

$$\$10 \text{ billion} \times \left(\frac{1 - MPC}{1 - MPC} \right) = \$10 \text{ billion}.$$

The balanced budget multiplier is, therefore, equal to $(1 - MPC)/(1 - MPC)$, or 1. Equal dollar increases and decreases in government purchases and in taxes lead to the same dollar increase in real GDP in the short run.

The Effects of Changes in Tax Rates on the Multiplier

We now consider the effect of a change in the tax *rate*, as opposed to a change in a fixed amount of taxes. Changing the tax rate actually changes the value of the multiplier. To see this, suppose that the tax rate is 20 percent, or 0.2. In that case, an increase in household income of $10 billion will increase *disposable income* by only $8 billion [or 10 billion $\times (1 - 0.2)$]. In general, an increase in income can be multiplied by $(1 - t)$ to find the increase in disposable income, where t is the tax rate. So, we can rewrite the consumption function as:

$$C = \overline{C} + MPC(1 - t)Y.$$

We can use this expression for the consumption function to find an expression for the government purchases multiplier, using the same method we used previously:

$$\text{Government purchases multiplier} = \frac{\Delta Y}{\Delta G} = \frac{1}{1 - MPC(1 - t)}.$$

We can see the effect of changing the tax rate on the size of the multiplier by trying some values. First, assume that $MPC = 0.75$ and $t = 0.2$. Then:

$$\text{Government purchases multiplier} = \frac{\Delta Y}{\Delta G} = \frac{1}{1 - 0.75(1 - 0.2)} = \frac{1}{1 - 0.6} = 2.5.$$

This value is smaller than the multiplier of 4 that we calculated by assuming that there was only a fixed amount of taxes (which is the same as assuming that the marginal tax *rate* was zero). This multiplier is smaller because spending in each period is now reduced by the amount of taxes households must pay on any additional income they earn. We can calculate the multiplier for an *MPC* of 0.75 and a lower tax rate of 0.1:

$$\text{Government purchases multiplier} = \frac{\Delta Y}{\Delta G} = \frac{1}{1 - 0.75(1 - 0.1)} = \frac{1}{1 - 0.675} = 3.1.$$

Cutting the tax rate from 20 percent to 10 percent increased the value of the multiplier from 2.5 to 3.1.

The Multiplier in an Open Economy

Up to now, we have assumed that the economy is closed, with no imports or exports. We can consider the case of an open economy by including net exports in our analysis. Recall that net exports equal exports minus imports. Exports are determined primarily by factors—such as the exchange value of the dollar and the levels of real GDP in other countries—that we do not include in our model. So, we will assume that exports are fixed, or autonomous:

$$\text{Exports} = \overline{\text{Exports}}$$

Imports will increase as real GDP increases because households will spend some portion of an increase in income on imports. We can define the *marginal propensity to import (MPI)* as the fraction of an increase in income that is spent on imports. So, our expression for imports is

$$\text{Imports} = MPI \times Y.$$

We can substitute our expressions for exports and imports into the expression we derived earlier for equilibrium real GDP:

$$Y = \overline{C} + MPC(1 - t)Y + \overline{I} + \overline{G} + [\overline{Exports} - (MPI \times Y)],$$

where the expression $[\overline{Exports} - (MPI \times Y)]$ represents net exports. We can now find an expression for the government purchases multiplier by using the same method we used previously:

$$\text{Government purchases multiplier} = \frac{\Delta Y}{\Delta G} = \frac{1}{1 - [MPC(1 - t) - MPI]}.$$

We can see the effect of changing the value of the marginal propensity to import on the size of the multiplier by trying some values of key variables. First, assume that $MPC = 0.75$, $t = 0.2$, and $MPI = 0.1$. Then:

$$\text{Government purchases multiplier} = \frac{\Delta Y}{\Delta G} = \frac{1}{1 - (0.75(1 - 0.2) - 0.1)} = \frac{1}{1 - 0.5} = 2.$$

This value is smaller than the multiplier of 2.5 that we calculated by assuming that there were no exports or imports (which is the same as assuming that the marginal propensity to import was zero). This multiplier is smaller because spending in each period is now reduced by the amount of imports households buy with any additional income they earn. We can calculate the multiplier with $MPC = 0.75$, $t = 0.2$, and a higher MPI of 0.2:

$$\text{Government purchases multiplier} = \frac{\Delta Y}{\Delta G} = \frac{1}{1 - (0.75(1 - 0.2) - 0.2)} = \frac{1}{1 - 0.4} = 1.7.$$

Increasing the marginal propensity to import from 0.1 to 0.2 decreases the value of the multiplier from 2 to 1.7. We can conclude that countries with a higher marginal propensity to import will have smaller multipliers than countries with a lower marginal propensity to import.

Bear in mind that the multiplier is a short-run effect which assumes that the economy is below the level of potential real GDP. In the long run, the economy is at potential real GDP, so an increase in government purchases causes a decline in the nongovernment components of real GDP but leaves the level of real GDP unchanged.

The analysis in this appendix is simplified compared to what would be carried out by an economist forecasting the effects of changes in government purchases or changes in taxes on equilibrium real GDP in the short run. In particular, our assumption that the price level is constant is unrealistic. However, looking more closely at the determinants of the multiplier has helped us see more clearly some important macroeconomic relationships.

16A | A Closer Look at the Multiplier, pages 570–574

LEARNING OBJECTIVE: Apply the multiplier formula.

 MyEconLab   Visit **www.myeconlab.com** to complete these exercises online and get instant feedback.

Problem and Applications

16A.1 Assuming a fixed amount of taxes and a closed economy, calculate the value of the government purchases multiplier, the tax multiplier, and the balanced budget multiplier if the marginal propensity to consume equals 0.6.

16A.2 Calculate the value of the government purchases multiplier if the marginal propensity to consume equals 0.8, the tax rate equals 0.25, and the marginal propensity to import equals 0.2.

16A.3 Use a graph to show the change in the aggregate demand curve resulting from an increase in government purchases if the government purchases multiplier equals 2. Now, on the same graph, show the change in the aggregate demand curve resulting from an increase in government purchases if the government purchases multiplier equals 4.

16A.4 Using your understanding of multipliers, explain why an increase in the tax rate would decrease the size of the government purchases multiplier. Similarly, explain why a decrease in the marginal propensity to import would increase the size of the government purchases multiplier.

Inflation, Unemployment, and Federal Reserve Policy

Chapter Outline and Learning Objectives

Why Does CarMax Worry about Monetary Policy?

The Federal Reserve is continually balancing the risks of inflation against the risks of unemployment. A contractionary monetary policy that would help rein in inflation risks pushing the economy into recession. An expansionary policy that can reduce the effects of recession risks increasing inflation. Consider the following example of the Fed's balancing act: In an attempt to cool the inflationary effect of a booming housing market, the Fed raised the target for the federal funds rate to 5.25 percent in June 2006 and kept it there until September 2007. At that point, a rapidly declining housing market led the Fed to begin cutting the federal funds rate, although well into 2008, the Fed remained worried that rising oil and commodity prices could increase the inflation rate.

Behind the roller-coaster ride of GDP, unemployment, and inflation are individual firms and workers. In 1991, former executives from Circuit City, the now-defunct consumer electronics store, started CarMax, using a new business model. They believed customers would buy from dealers who offered a large selection of cars with non-negotiable prices. Salespeople would earn flat commissions so there would be no incentive to coax customers to buy the most expensive models. Today, CarMax has more than 100 "superstore" locations.

Monetary policy affects the performance of both new and used car companies.

When the Federal Reserve raised interest rates in 2006 and kept them high through mid-2007, it meant higher costs for consumers who borrow money to buy cars.

By late 2008, the Fed had slashed the federal funds rate to near-zero levels. Although car dealers were hit hard by the recession, CarMax's sales began to recover in 2009. Many consumers who balked at buying new cars viewed used cars as an affordable alternative, and low-interest loans reduced the monthly payments they would make. Though interest rates remained low and incomes had risen in 2010 and 2011, CarMax sales began to slip. Unemployment remained high, and consumer confidence was low. As CEO Thomas Folliard noted: "When you look at the product that we sell, it almost always requires a loan, and somebody has . . . to be confident in signing up for [a loan, which can be] six and seven years long now on cars."

In this chapter, we will further explore the Fed's attempts to balance its goals of price stability and high employment. **AN INSIDE LOOK AT POLICY** on **page 600** discusses how the Fed attempts to reduce unemployment without causing a significant increase in inflation.

Based on Caitlin Nish, "Economy Crimps CarMax Sales," *Wall Street Journal*, September 22, 2011; and Michael Myser, "The Wal-Mart of Used Cars," *Business 2.0*, October 2, 2006.

Economics in Your Life

Is It Wise to Delay a Job Search?

Your friend was recently laid off from her entry-level job as a computer analyst. You call to console her, but she does not seem very upset. "Our state offers workers up to 99 weeks of unemployment compensation. I have almost two years before I have to find a new job. With my education and job experience, I should be able to find a new job by then without much trouble." Your friend did well in school, but you are not sure that waiting almost two years to find a new job is a good idea. What advice would you give someone who has decided to wait nearly two years to look for a new job? As you read this chapter, see if you can answer this question. You can check your answer against the one we provide on **page 599** at the end of this chapter.

A n important consideration for the Federal Reserve as it carries out monetary policy is that in the short run, there can be a trade-off between unemployment and inflation: Lower unemployment rates can result in higher inflation rates. In the long run, however, this trade-off disappears, and the unemployment rate is independent of the inflation rate. In this chapter, we will explore the relationship between inflation and unemployment in both the short run and the long run, and we will discuss what this relationship means for monetary policy. We will also provide an overview of how monetary policy has evolved over the years and conclude with a discussion of the debate over Fed policy during the 2007–2009 recession.

The Discovery of the Short-Run Trade-off between Unemployment and Inflation

Ordinarily, unemployment and inflation are the two great macroeconomic problems the Fed must deal with in the short run. As we saw in Chapter 13, when aggregate demand increases, unemployment usually falls, and inflation rises. When aggregate demand decreases, unemployment usually rises and inflation falls. As a result, there is a *short-run trade-off* between unemployment and inflation: Higher unemployment is usually accompanied by lower inflation, and lower unemployment is usually accompanied by higher inflation. As we will see later in this chapter, this trade-off exists in the short run—a period that may be as long as several years—but disappears in the long run.

Although today the short-run trade-off between unemployment and inflation plays a role in the Fed's monetary policy decisions, this trade-off was not widely recognized until the late 1950s. In 1957, New Zealand economist A. W. Phillips plotted data on the unemployment rate and the inflation rate in Great Britain and drew a curve showing their average relationship. Since that time, a graph showing the short-run relationship between the unemployment rate and the inflation rate has been called a **Phillips curve**. (Phillips actually measured inflation by the percentage change in wages rather than by the percentage change in prices. Because wages and prices usually move together, this difference is not important to our discussion.) Figure 17.1 shows a graph similar to the one Phillips prepared. Each point on the Phillips curve represents a possible combination of the unemployment rate and the inflation rate that might be observed in a given year. Point *A* represents a year in which the inflation rate is 4 percent and the unemployment rate is 5 percent, and point *B* represents a year in which the inflation rate

Phillips curve A curve showing the short-run relationship between the unemployment rate and the inflation rate.

Figure 17.1

The Phillips Curve

A. W. Phillips was the first economist to show that there is usually an inverse relationship between unemployment and inflation. Here we can see this relationship at work: In the year represented by point *A*, the inflation rate is 4 percent and the unemployment rate is 5 percent. In the year represented by point *B*, the inflation rate is 2 percent and the unemployment rate is 6 percent.

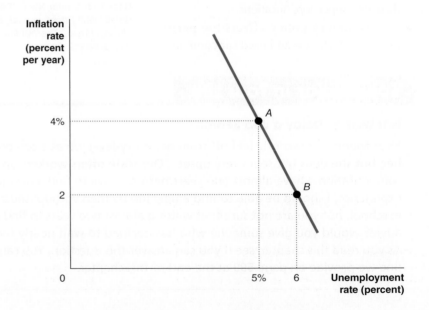

is 2 percent and the unemployment rate is 6 percent. Phillips documented that there is usually an *inverse relationship* between unemployment and inflation. During years when the unemployment rate is low, the inflation rate tends to be high, and during years when the unemployment rate is high, the inflation rate tends to be low.

Explaining the Phillips Curve with Aggregate Demand and Aggregate Supply Curves

The inverse relationship between unemployment and inflation that Phillips discovered is consistent with the aggregate demand and aggregate supply analysis we developed in Chapter 13. Figure 17.2 shows why this inverse relationship exists.

Panel (a) shows the aggregate demand and aggregate supply model from Chapter 13, and panel (b) shows the Phillips curve. For simplicity, in panel (a), we are using the basic aggregate demand and aggregate supply model, and we are assuming that the long-run aggregate supply curve and the short-run aggregate supply curve do not shift. To take a hypothetical example, assume that the economy in 2013 is at point *A*, with real GDP of $14.0 trillion and a price level of 100. If there is weak growth in aggregate demand, in 2014, the economy moves to point *B*, with real GDP of $14.3 trillion and a price level of 102. The inflation rate is 2 percent and the unemployment rate is 6 percent, which corresponds to point *B* on the Phillips curve in panel (b). If there is strong growth in aggregate demand, in 2014, the economy moves to point *C*, with real GDP of $14.6 trillion and a price level of 104. Strong aggregate demand growth results in a higher inflation rate of 4 percent but a lower unemployment rate of 5 percent. This combination of higher inflation and lower unemployment is shown as point *C* on the Phillips curve in panel (b).

To summarize, the aggregate demand and aggregate supply model indicates that slow growth in aggregate demand leads to both higher unemployment and lower inflation. This relationship explains why there is a short-run trade-off between unemployment and inflation, as shown by the downward-sloping Phillips curve. The *AD–AS*

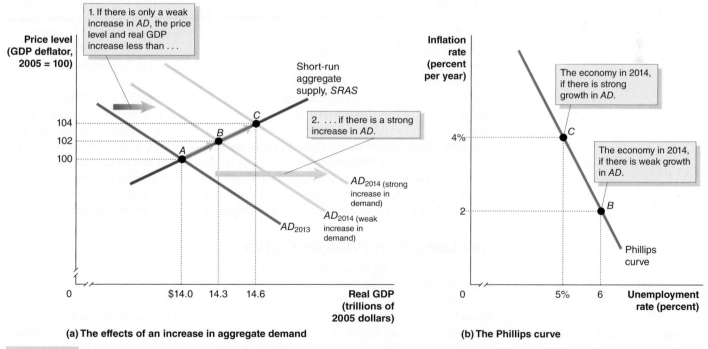

(a) The effects of an increase in aggregate demand

(b) The Phillips curve

Figure 17.2 Using Aggregate Demand and Aggregate Supply to Explain the Phillips Curve

In panel (a), the economy in 2013 is at point *A*, with real GDP of $14.0 trillion and a price level of 100. If there is weak growth in aggregate demand, in 2014, the economy moves to point *B*, with real GDP of $14.3 trillion and a price level of 102. The inflation rate is 2 percent and the unemployment rate is 6 percent, which corresponds to point *B* on the Phillips curve in panel (b). If there is strong

growth in aggregate demand, in 2014, the economy moves to point *C*, with real GDP of $14.6 trillion and a price level of 104. Strong aggregate demand growth results in a higher inflation rate of 4 percent but a lower unemployment rate of 5 percent. This combination of higher inflation and lower unemployment is shown as point *C* on the Phillips curve in panel (b).

model and the Phillips curve are different ways of illustrating the same macroeconomic events. The Phillips curve has an advantage over the aggregate demand and aggregate supply model, however, when we want to analyze explicitly *changes* in the inflation and unemployment rates.

Is the Phillips Curve a Policy Menu?

Structural relationship A relationship that depends on the basic behavior of consumers and firms and that remains unchanged over long periods.

During the 1960s, some economists argued that the Phillips curve represented a *structural relationship* in the economy. A **structural relationship** depends on the basic behavior of consumers and firms and remains unchanged over long periods. Structural relationships are useful in formulating economic policy because policymakers can anticipate that these relationships are constant—that is, the relationships will not change as a result of changes in policy.

If the Phillips curve were a structural relationship, it would present policymakers with a reliable menu of combinations of unemployment and inflation. Potentially, policymakers could use expansionary monetary and fiscal policies to choose a point on the curve that had lower unemployment and higher inflation. They could also use contractionary monetary and fiscal policies to choose a point that had lower inflation and higher unemployment. Because many economists and policymakers in the 1960s viewed the Phillips curve as a structural relationship, they believed it represented a *permanent trade-off between unemployment and inflation*. As long as policymakers were willing to accept a permanently higher inflation rate, they would be able to keep the unemployment rate permanently lower. Similarly, a permanently lower inflation rate could be attained at the cost of a permanently higher unemployment rate. As we discuss in the next section, however, economists came to realize that the Phillips curve did *not*, in fact, represent a permanent trade-off between unemployment and inflation.

Is the Short-Run Phillips Curve Stable?

During the 1960s, the basic Phillips curve relationship seemed to hold because a stable trade-off appeared to exist between unemployment and inflation. In the early 1960s, the inflation rate was low, and the unemployment rate was high. In the late 1960s, the unemployment rate had declined, and the inflation rate had increased. Then in 1968, in his presidential address to the American Economic Association, Milton Friedman of the University of Chicago argued that the Phillips curve did *not* represent a *permanent* trade-off between unemployment and inflation. At almost the same time, Edmund Phelps of Columbia University published an academic paper making a similar argument. Friedman and Phelps noted that economists had come to agree that the long-run aggregate supply curve was vertical (a point we discussed in Chapter 13). If this observation were true, the Phillips curve could not be downward sloping in the long run. A critical inconsistency exists between a vertical long-run aggregate supply curve and a long-run Phillips curve that is downward sloping. Friedman and Phelps argued, in essence, that there is no trade-off between unemployment and inflation in the long run.

The Long-Run Phillips Curve

Natural rate of unemployment The unemployment rate that exists when the economy is at potential GDP.

To understand the argument that there is no permanent trade-off between unemployment and inflation, first recall that the level of real GDP in the long run is also referred to as *potential GDP*. At potential GDP, firms will operate at their normal level of capacity, and everyone who wants a job will have one, except the structurally and frictionally unemployed. Friedman defined the **natural rate of unemployment** as the unemployment rate that exists when the economy is at potential GDP. The actual unemployment rate will fluctuate in the short run but will always come back to the natural rate in the long run. In the same way, the actual level of real GDP will fluctuate in the short run but will always come back to its potential level in the long run.

In the long run, a higher or lower price level has no effect on real GDP because real GDP is always at its potential level in the long run. In the same way, in the long run, a higher or lower inflation rate will have no effect on the unemployment rate because the

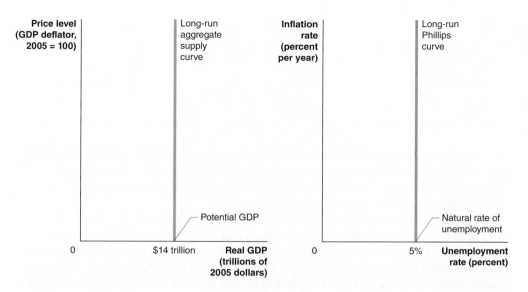

Figure 17.3

A Vertical Long-Run Aggregate Supply Curve Means a Vertical Long-Run Phillips Curve

Milton Friedman and Edmund Phelps argued that there is no trade-off between unemployment and inflation in the long run. If real GDP automatically returns to its potential level in the long run, the unemployment rate must return to the natural rate of unemployment in the long run. In this figure, we assume that potential GDP is $14 trillion and the natural rate of unemployment is 5 percent.

unemployment rate is always equal to the natural rate in the long run. Figure 17.3 illustrates Friedman's conclusion that the long-run aggregate supply curve is a vertical line at the potential real GDP, and *the long-run Phillips curve is a vertical line at the natural rate of unemployment.*

The Role of Expectations of Future Inflation

If the long-run Phillips curve is a vertical line, *no trade-off exists between unemployment and inflation in the long run.* This conclusion seemed to contradict the experience of the 1950s and 1960s, which showed a stable trade-off between unemployment and inflation. Friedman argued that the statistics from those years actually showed only a short-run trade-off between inflation and unemployment.

The short-run trade-off existed—but only because workers and firms sometimes expected the inflation rate to be either higher or lower than it turned out to be. Differences between the expected inflation rate and the actual inflation rate could lead the unemployment rate to rise above or dip below the natural rate. To see why, consider a simple case of Ford negotiating a wage contract with the United Auto Workers (UAW) union. Remember that both Ford and the UAW are interested in the real wage, which is the nominal wage corrected for inflation. Suppose, for example, that Ford and the UAW agree on a wage of $31.50 per hour to be paid during 2015. Both Ford and the UAW expect that the price level will increase from 100 in 2014 to 105 in 2015, so the inflation rate will be 5 percent. We can calculate the real wage Ford expects to pay and the UAW expects to receive as follows:

$$\text{Real wage} = \frac{\text{Nominal wage}}{\text{Price level}} \times 100 = \frac{\$31.50}{105} \times 100 = \$30.$$

But suppose that the actual inflation rate turns out to be higher or lower than the expected inflation rate of 5 percent. Table 17.1 shows the effect on the actual real wage. If the price level rises only to 102 during 2015, the inflation rate will be 2 percent, and the actual real wage will be $30.88, which is higher than Ford and the UAW had expected. With a higher real wage, Ford will hire fewer workers than it had planned to at

Nominal Wage	Expected Real Wage	Actual Real Wage	
	Expected $P_{2015} = 105$	Actual $P_{2015} = 102$	Actual $P_{2015} = 108$
	Expected inflation = 5%	Actual inflation = 2%	Actual inflation = 8%
$31.50	$\frac{\$31.50}{105} \times 100 = \$30$	$\frac{\$31.50}{102} \times 100 = \$30.88$	$\frac{\$31.50}{108} \times 100 = \$29.17$

Table 17.1

The Effect of Unexpected Price Level Changes on the Real Wage

Table 17.2	If . . .	then . . .	and . . .
The Basis for the Short-Run Phillips Curve	actual inflation is greater than expected inflation,	the actual real wage is less than the expected real wage,	the unemployment rate falls.
	actual inflation is less than expected inflation,	the actual real wage is greater than the expected real wage,	the unemployment rate rises.

the expected real wage of $30. If the inflation rate is 8 percent, the actual real wage will be $29.17, and Ford will hire more workers than it had planned to hire. If Ford and the UAW expected a higher or lower inflation rate than actually occurred, other firms and workers probably made the same assumption.

If actual inflation is higher than expected inflation, actual real wages in the economy will be lower than expected real wages, and many firms will hire more workers than they had planned to hire. Therefore, the unemployment rate will fall. If actual inflation is lower than expected inflation, actual real wages will be higher than expected, many firms will hire fewer workers than they had planned to hire, and the unemployment rate will rise. Table 17.2 summarizes this argument.

Friedman and Phelps concluded that *an increase in the inflation rate increases employment (and decreases unemployment) only if the increase in the inflation rate is unexpected.* Friedman argued that in 1968, the unemployment rate was 3.6 percent rather than 5 percent only because the inflation rate of 4 percent was above the 1 percent to 2 percent inflation that workers and firms had expected: "There is always a temporary trade-off between inflation and unemployment; there is no permanent trade-off. The temporary trade-off comes not from inflation per se, but from unanticipated inflation."

Making the Connection

Do Workers Understand Inflation?

A higher inflation rate can lead to lower unemployment if *both* workers and firms mistakenly expect the inflation rate to be lower than it turns out to be. But this same result might be due to firms forecasting inflation more accurately than workers do or to firms understanding better the effects of inflation. Some large firms employ economists to help them gather and analyze information that is useful in forecasting inflation. Many firms also have human resources or employee compensation departments that gather data on wages paid at competing firms and analyze trends in compensation. Workers generally rely on much less systematic information about wages and prices. Workers also often fail to realize a fact we discussed in Chapter 9: *Expected inflation increases the value of total production and the value of total income by the same amount.* Therefore, although not all wages will rise as prices rise, inflation will increase the average wage in the economy at the same time that it increases the average price.

Will wage increases keep up with inflation?

Robert Shiller, an economist at Yale University, conducted a survey on inflation and discovered that, although most economists believe an increase in inflation will lead quickly to an increase in wages, a majority of the general public thinks otherwise. As part of the survey, Shiller asked how "the effect of general inflation on wages or salary relates to your own experience and your own job." The most popular response was: "The price increase will create extra profits for my employer, who can now sell output for more; there will be no effect on my pay. My employer will see no reason to raise my pay."

Shiller also asked the following question:

> Imagine that next year the inflation rate unexpectedly doubles. How long would it probably take, in these times, before your income is increased enough so that you can afford the same things as you do today? In other words, how long will it be before a full inflation correction in your income has taken place?

Eighty-one percent of the public answered either that it would take several years for the purchasing power of their income to be restored or that it would never be restored.

If workers fail to understand that rising inflation leads over time to comparable increases in wages, then when inflation increases, in the short run, firms can increase wages by less than inflation without needing to worry about workers quitting or their morale falling. Once again, we have a higher inflation rate, leading in the short run to lower real wages and lower unemployment. In other words, we have an explanation for a downward-sloping short-run Phillips curve.

Based on Robert J. Shiller, "Why Do People Dislike Inflation?" in *Reducing Inflation: Motivation and Strategy* by Christina D. Romer and David H. Romer, eds., (Chicago: University of Chicago Press, 1997).

Your Turn: Test your understanding by doing related problems 1.12 and 1.13 on page 603 at the end of this chapter.   MyEconLab

---

The Short-Run and Long-Run Phillips Curves

17.2 LEARNING OBJECTIVE

Explain the relationship between the short-run and long-run Phillips curves.

If there is both a short-run Phillips curve and a long-run Phillips curve, how are the two curves related? We can begin answering this question with the help of Figure 17.4, which represents macroeconomic conditions in the United States during the 1960s. In the late 1960s, workers and firms were still expecting the inflation rate to be about 1.5 percent, as it had been from 1960 to 1965. Expansionary monetary and fiscal policies, however, had moved the short-run equilibrium up the short-run Phillips curve to an inflation rate of 4.5 percent and an unemployment rate of 3.5 percent. This very low unemployment rate was possible only because the real wage rate was unexpectedly low.

Once workers and firms began to expect that the inflation rate would continue to be about 4.5 percent, they changed their behavior. Firms knew that only nominal wage increases of more than 4.5 percent would increase real wages. Workers realized that unless they received a nominal wage increase of at least 4.5 percent, their real wage would be falling. Higher expected inflation rates had an effect throughout the economy. For example, as we saw in Chapter 14, when banks make loans, they are interested in the *real interest rate* on the loan. The real interest rate is the nominal interest rate minus the expected inflation rate. If banks need to receive a real interest rate of 3 percent on home mortgage loans and expect the inflation rate to be 1.5 percent, they will charge a nominal interest rate of 4.5 percent. If banks revise their expectations of the inflation rate to 4.5 percent, they will increase the nominal interest rate they charge on mortgage loans to 7.5 percent.

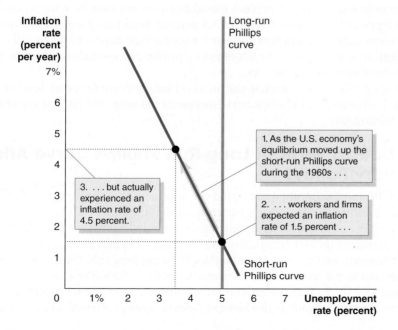

Figure 17.4

The Short-Run Phillips Curve of the 1960s and the Long-Run Phillips Curve

In the late 1960s, U.S. workers and firms were expecting the 1.5 percent inflation rates of the recent past to continue. However, expansionary monetary and fiscal policies moved the short-run equilibrium up the short-run Phillips curve to an inflation rate of 4.5 percent and an unemployment rate of 3.5 percent.

Figure 17.5

Expectations and the Short-Run Phillips Curve

By the end of the 1960s, workers and firms had revised their expectations of inflation from 1.5 percent to 4.5 percent. As a result, the short-run Phillips curve shifted up, which made the short-run trade-off between unemployment and inflation worse.

Shifts in the Short-Run Phillips Curve

The new, higher expected inflation rate can become *embedded* in the economy, meaning that workers, firms, consumers, and the government all take the inflation rate into account when making decisions. The short-run trade-off between unemployment and inflation now takes place from this higher, less favorable level, as shown in Figure 17.5.

As long as workers and firms expected the inflation rate to be 1.5 percent, the short-run trade-off between unemployment and inflation was the more favorable one shown by the lower Phillips curve. Along this Phillips curve, an inflation rate of 4.5 percent was enough to drive down the unemployment rate to 3.5 percent. Once workers and firms adjusted their expectations to an inflation rate of 4.5 percent, the short-run trade-off deteriorated to the one shown by the higher Phillips curve. At this higher expected inflation rate, the real wage rose, causing some workers to lose their jobs, and the economy's equilibrium returned to the natural rate of unemployment of 5 percent—but now with an inflation rate of 4.5 percent rather than 1.5 percent. On the higher short-run Phillips curve, an inflation rate of 7.5 percent would be necessary to reduce the unemployment rate to 3.5 percent. An inflation rate of 7.5 percent would keep the unemployment rate at 3.5 percent only until workers and firms revised their expectations of inflation up to 7.5 percent. In the long run, the economy's equilibrium would return to the 5 percent natural rate of unemployment.

As Figure 17.6 shows, there is a short-run Phillips curve for every level of expected inflation. Each short-run Phillips curve intersects the long-run Phillips curve at the expected inflation rate.

How Does a Vertical Long-Run Phillips Curve Affect Monetary Policy?

By the 1970s, most economists accepted the argument that the long-run Phillips curve is vertical. In other words, economists realized that the common view of the 1960s had been wrong: It was *not* possible to buy a permanently lower unemployment rate at the cost of a permanently higher inflation rate. The moral is that *in the long run, there is no trade-off between unemployment and inflation.* In the long run, the unemployment rate always returns to the natural rate, no matter what the inflation rate is.

Figure 17.7 shows that the inflation rate is stable only when the unemployment rate is equal to the natural rate. If the Federal Reserve were to attempt to use expansionary

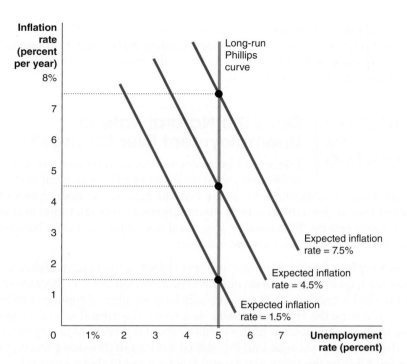

Figure 17.6

A Short-Run Phillips Curve for Every Expected Inflation Rate

There is a different short-run Phillips curve for every expected inflation rate. Each short-run Phillips curve intersects the long-run Phillips curve at the expected inflation rate.

monetary policy to push the economy to a point such as *A*, where the unemployment rate is below the natural rate, the result would be increasing inflation as the economy moved up the short-run Phillips curve. If the economy remained below the natural rate long enough, the short-run Phillips curve would shift up as workers and firms adjusted to the new, higher inflation rate. During the 1960s and 1970s, the short-run Phillips curve did shift up, presenting the economy with a more unfavorable short-run trade-off between unemployment and inflation.

If the Federal Reserve used contractionary policy to push the economy to a point such as *B*, where the unemployment rate is above the natural rate, the inflation rate would decrease. If the economy remained above the natural rate long enough, the short-run Phillips curve would shift down as workers and firms adjusted to the new, lower inflation rate. Only at a point such as *C*, where the unemployment rate is equal

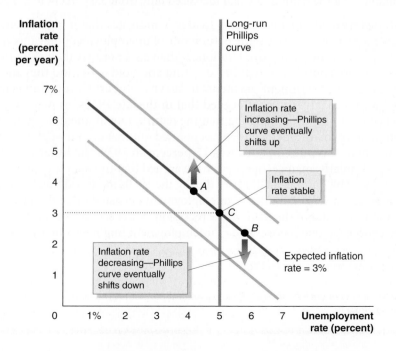

Figure 17.7

The Inflation Rate and the Natural Rate of Unemployment in the Long Run

The inflation rate is stable only if the unemployment rate equals the natural rate of unemployment (point *C*). If the unemployment rate is below the natural rate (point *A*), the inflation rate increases, and, eventually, the short-run Phillips curve shifts up. If the unemployment rate is above the natural rate (point *B*), the inflation rate decreases, and, eventually, the short-run Phillips curve shifts down.

Nonaccelerating inflation rate of unemployment (NAIRU) The unemployment rate at which the inflation rate has no tendency to increase or decrease.

to the natural rate, will the inflation rate be stable. As a result, the natural rate of unemployment is sometimes called the **nonaccelerating inflation rate of unemployment (NAIRU)**. We can conclude that *in the long run, the Federal Reserve can affect the inflation rate but not the unemployment rate.*

An increase in the number of younger and less skilled workers in an economy can make the natural rate of unemployment increase.

> **Making the Connection**
>
> ## Does the Natural Rate of Unemployment Ever Change?
>
> Life would be easier for the Federal Reserve if it knew exactly what the natural rate of unemployment was and if that rate never changed. Unfortunately for the Fed, the natural rate does change over time. Remember that at the natural rate of unemployment, only frictional and structural unemployment remain. Frictional or structural unemployment can change—thereby changing the natural rate—for several reasons:
>
> - *Demographic changes.* Younger and less skilled workers have higher unemployment rates, on average, than do older and more skilled workers. Because of the baby boom, the United States had an unusually large number of younger and less skilled workers during the 1970s and 1980s. As a result, the natural rate of unemployment rose from about 5 percent in the 1960s to about 6 percent in the 1970s and 1980s. As the number of younger and less skilled workers declined as a fraction of the labor force during the 1990s, the natural rate returned to about 5 percent.
>
> - *Labor market institutions.* As we discussed in Chapter 9, labor market institutions such as the unemployment insurance system, unions, and legal barriers to firing workers can increase the economy's unemployment rate. Because many European countries have generous unemployment insurance systems, strong unions, and restrictive policies on firing workers, the natural rate of unemployment in most European countries has been well above the rate in the United States. In 2011, some economists believed that many workers in the United States had become less mobile because of the bursting of the housing bubble. These economists argued that because workers either were unable to sell their homes or were unwilling to do so because they did not want to sell for a low price, they were less likely to move from a geographic area of high unemployment to one of lower unemployment. Economists at JPMorgan Chase estimated that this lack of mobility might have increased the natural rate of unemployment to about 6 percent. Economists at the Congressional Budget Office disagreed, estimating that the natural rate had increased only from 5.0 percent to 5.2 percent.
>
> - *Past high rates of unemployment.* Evidence indicates that if high unemployment persists for a period of years, the natural rate of unemployment may increase. When workers have been unemployed for longer than a year or two, their skills deteriorate, they may lose confidence that they can find and hold a job, and they may become dependent on government payments to survive. Robert Gordon, an economist at Northwestern University, has argued that in the late 1930s, so many U.S. workers had been out of work for so long that the natural rate of unemployment may have risen to more than 15 percent. He has pointed out that even though the unemployment rate in the United States was 17 percent in 1939, the inflation rate did not change. Similarly, many economists have argued that the high unemployment rates experienced by European countries during the 1970s increased their natural rates of unemployment. As high rates of unemployment persisted more than two and a half years after the end of the 2007–2009 recession, some economists and policymakers were concerned that natural rate of unemployment might eventually rise.
>
> Based on Congressional Budget Office: "The Budget and Economic Outlook: Fiscal Years 2011 to 2021," January 2011; and "Damage Assessment," *Economist*, May 14, 2009.

MyEconLab   **Your Turn:** Test your understanding by doing related problems 2.9 and 2.10 on page 604 at the end of this chapter.

Solved Problem 17.2

Changing Views of the Phillips Curve

Writing in a Federal Reserve publication, Bennett McCallum, an economist at Carnegie Mellon University, argues that during the 1970s, the Fed was "acting under the influence of 1960s academic ideas that posited the existence of a long-run and exploitable Phillips-type tradeoff between inflation and unemployment rates." What does McCallum mean by a "long-run and exploitable Phillips-type tradeoff"? How would the Fed have attempted to exploit this long-run trade-off? What would be the consequences for the inflation rate?

Solving the Problem

Step 1: **Review the chapter material.** This problem is about the relationship between the short-run and long-run Phillips curves, so you may want to review the section "The Short-Run and Long-Run Phillips Curves," which begins on page 583.

Step 2: **Explain what a "long-run exploitable Phillips-type tradeoff" means.** A "long-run exploitable Phillips-type tradeoff" means a Phillips curve that in the long run is downward sloping rather than vertical. An "exploitable" trade-off is one that the Fed could take advantage of to *permanently* reduce unemployment, at the expense of higher inflation, or to permanently reduce inflation, at the expense of higher unemployment.

Step 3: **Explain how the inflation rate will accelerate if the Fed tries to exploit a long-run trade-off between unemployment and inflation.** As we have seen, during the 1960s, the Fed conducted expansionary monetary policies to move up what it thought was a stationary short-run Phillips curve. By the late 1960s, these policies resulted in very low unemployment rates. In the long run, there is no stable trade-off between unemployment and inflation. Attempting to permanently keep the unemployment rate at very low levels leads to a rising inflation rate, which is what happened in the late 1960s and early 1970s.

Based on Bennett T. McCallum, "Recent Developments in Monetary Policy Analysis: The Roles of Theory and Evidence," Federal Reserve Bank of Richmond, *Economic Quarterly*, Winter 2002, p. 73.

Your Turn: For more practice, do related problem 2.6 on page 604 at the end of this chapter. MyEconLab

---

Expectations of the Inflation Rate and Monetary Policy

17.3 LEARNING OBJECTIVE

Discuss how expectations of the inflation rate affect monetary policy.

How long can the economy remain at a point that is on the short-run Phillips curve but not on the long-run Phillips curve? It depends on how quickly workers and firms adjust their expectations of future inflation to changes in current inflation. The experience in the United States over the past 60 years indicates that how workers and firms adjust their expectations of inflation depends on how high the inflation rate is. There are three possibilities:

- **Low inflation.** When the inflation rate is low, as it was during most of the 1950s, the early 1960s, the 1990s, and the 2000s, workers and firms tend to ignore it. For example, if the inflation rate is low, a restaurant may not want to pay for printing new menus that would show slightly higher prices.

- **Moderate but stable inflation.** For the four-year period from 1968 to 1971, the inflation rate in the United States stayed in the narrow range between 4 percent and

5 percent. This rate was high enough that workers and firms could not ignore it without seeing their real wages and profits decline. It was also likely that the next year's inflation rate would be very close to the current year's inflation rate. In fact, workers and firms during the 1960s acted as if they expected changes in the inflation rate during one year to continue into the following year. People are said to have *adaptive expectations* of inflation if they assume that future rates of inflation will follow the pattern of rates of inflation in the recent past.

- *High and unstable inflation.* Inflation rates above 5 percent during peacetime have been rare in U.S. history, but the inflation rate was above 5 percent every year from 1973 through 1982. Not only was the inflation rate high during these years, it was also unstable—rising from 6 percent in 1973 to 11 percent in 1974, before falling below 6 percent in 1976 and rising again to 13.5 percent in 1980. In the mid-1970s, Nobel Laureates Robert Lucas of the University of Chicago and Thomas Sargent of New York University argued that the gains to accurately forecasting inflation had dramatically increased. Workers and firms that failed to correctly anticipate the fluctuations in inflation during these years could experience substantial declines in real wages and profits. Therefore, Lucas and Sargent argued, people should use all available information when forming their expectations of future inflation. Expectations formed by using all available information about an economic variable are called **rational expectations**.

Rational expectations Expectations formed by using all available information about an economic variable.

The Effect of Rational Expectations on Monetary Policy

Lucas and Sargent pointed out an important consequence of rational expectations: An expansionary monetary policy would not work. In other words, there might not be a trade-off between unemployment and inflation, even in the short run. By the mid-1970s, most economists had accepted the idea that an expansionary monetary policy could cause the actual inflation rate to be higher than the expected inflation rate. This gap between actual and expected inflation would cause the actual real wage to fall below the expected real wage, and the unemployment rate would be pushed below the natural rate. The economy's short-run equilibrium would move up the short-run Phillips curve.

Lucas and Sargent argued that this explanation of the Phillips curve assumed that workers and firms either ignored inflation or used adaptive expectations in making their forecasts of inflation. If workers and firms have rational expectations, they will use all available information, *including knowledge of the effects of Federal Reserve policy*. If workers and firms know that an expansionary monetary policy will raise the inflation rate, they should use this information in their forecasts of inflation. If they do, an expansionary monetary policy will not cause the actual inflation rate to be above the expected inflation rate. Instead, the actual inflation rate will equal the expected inflation rate, the actual real wage will equal the expected real wage, and the unemployment rate will not fall below the natural rate.

Figure 17.8 illustrates this argument. Suppose the economy begins at point *A*, where the short-run Phillips curve intersects the long-run Phillips curve. The actual and expected inflation rates are both equal to 1.5 percent, and the unemployment rate equals the natural rate of 5 percent. Then suppose the Fed engages in an expansionary monetary policy. If workers ignore inflation or if they form their expectations adaptively, the expansionary monetary policy will cause the actual inflation rate to be higher than the expected inflation rate, and the short-run equilibrium will move from point *A* on the short-run Phillips curve to point *B*. The inflation rate will rise to 4.5 percent, and the unemployment rate will fall to 3.5 percent. The decline in unemployment will be only temporary, however. Eventually, workers and firms will adjust to the fact that the actual inflation rate is 4.5 percent, not the 1.5 percent they had expected. The short-run Phillips curve will shift up, and the unemployment rate will return to 5 percent at point *C*.

Lucas and Sargent argued that if workers and firms have rational expectations, they will realize that the Fed's expansionary policy will result in an inflation rate of

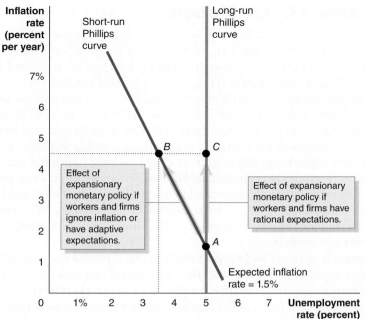

Figure 17.8

**Rational Expectations
and the Phillips Curve**

If workers and firms ignore inflation, or
if they have adaptive expectations, an expansionary monetary policy will cause the
short-run equilibrium to move from point *A*
on the short-run Phillips curve to point *B*;
inflation will rise, and unemployment will
fall. If workers and firms have rational expectations, an expansionary monetary
policy will cause the short-run equilibrium
to move up the long-run Phillips curve from
point *A* to point *C*. Inflation will still rise, but
there will be no change in unemployment.

4.5 percent. Therefore, as soon as the Fed announces its new policy, workers and firms
should adjust their expectations of inflation from 1.5 percent to 4.5 percent. There will
be no temporary decrease in the real wage, leading to a temporary increase in employment and real GDP. Instead, the short-run equilibrium will move immediately from
point *A* to point *C* on the long-run Phillips curve. The unemployment rate will never
drop below 5 percent, and the *short-run* Phillips curve will be vertical.

Is the Short-Run Phillips Curve Really Vertical?

The claim by Lucas and Sargent that the short-run Phillips curve is vertical and that
an expansionary monetary policy cannot reduce the unemployment rate below the
natural rate surprised many economists. An obvious objection to the argument of
Lucas and Sargent was that the record of the 1950s and 1960s seemed to show that
there was a short-run trade-off between unemployment and inflation and that, therefore, the short-run Phillips curve was downward sloping and not vertical. Lucas and
Sargent argued that the apparent short-run trade-off was actually the result of *unexpected* changes in monetary policy. During those years, the Fed did not announce
changes in policy, so workers, firms, and financial markets had to *guess* when the Fed
had begun using a new policy. In that case, an expansionary monetary policy might
cause the unemployment rate to fall because workers and firms would be taken by
surprise, and their expectations of inflation would be too low. Lucas and Sargent
argued that a policy that was announced ahead of time would not cause a change in
unemployment.

Many economists have remained skeptical of the argument that the short-run
Phillips curve is vertical. The two main objections raised are that (1) workers and firms
actually may not have rational expectations, and (2) the rapid adjustment of wages and
prices needed for the short-run Phillips curve to be vertical will not actually take place.
Many economists doubt that people are able to use information on the Fed's monetary
policy to make reliable forecasts of the inflation rate. If workers and firms do not know
what effect an expansionary monetary policy will have on the inflation rate, the actual
real wage may still end up being lower than the expected real wage. Also, firms may
have contracts with their workers and suppliers that keep wages and prices from adjusting quickly. If wages and prices adjust slowly, then even if workers and firms have
rational expectations, an expansionary monetary policy may still be able to reduce the
unemployment rate in the short run.

Real Business Cycle Models

During the 1980s, some economists, including Nobel Laureates Finn Kydland of Carnegie Mellon University and Edward Prescott of Arizona State University, argued that Robert Lucas was correct in assuming that workers and firms formed their expectations rationally and that wages and prices adjust quickly but that Lucas was wrong in assuming that fluctuations in real GDP are caused by unexpected changes in the money supply. Instead, Kydland and Prescott argued that fluctuations in "real" factors, particularly *technology shocks*, explain deviations of real GDP from its potential level. Technology shocks are changes to the economy that make it possible to produce either more output—a positive shock—or less output—a negative shock—with the same number of workers, machines, and other inputs. Real GDP will be above its previous potential level following a positive technology shock and below its previous potential level following a negative technology shock. Because these models focus on real factors—rather than on changes in the money supply—to explain fluctuations in real GDP, they are known as **real business cycle models**.

Real business cycle models Models that focus on real rather than monetary explanations of fluctuations in real GDP.

The approach of Lucas and Sargent and the real business cycle models are sometimes grouped together under the label *the new classical macroeconomics* because these approaches share the assumptions that people have rational expectations and that wages and prices adjust rapidly. Some of the assumptions of the new classical macroeconomics are similar to those held by economists before the Great Depression of the 1930s. John Maynard Keynes, in his 1936 book *The General Theory of Employment, Interest, and Money*, referred to these earlier economists as "classical economists." Like the classical economists, the new classical macroeconomists believe that the economy will normally be at its potential level.

Economists who find the assumptions of rational expectations and rapid adjustment of wages and prices appealing are likely to accept the real business cycle model approach. Other economists are skeptical of these models because the models explain recessions as being caused by negative technology shocks. Negative technology shocks are uncommon and, apart from the oil price increases of the 1970s, real business cycle theorists have had difficulty identifying shocks that would have been large enough to cause recessions. Some economists have begun to develop real business cycle models that allow for the possibility that changes in the money supply may affect the level of real GDP. If real business cycle models continue to develop along these lines, they may eventually converge with the approaches the Fed uses.

17.4 LEARNING OBJECTIVE

Use a Phillips curve graph to show how the Federal Reserve can permanently lower the inflation rate.

Federal Reserve Policy from the 1970s to the Present

We have already seen that the high inflation rates of the late 1960s and early 1970s were due in part to the Federal Reserve's attempts to keep the unemployment rate below the natural rate. By the mid-1970s, the Fed also had to deal with the inflationary impact of the Organization of the Petroleum Exporting Countries (OPEC) oil price increases. By the late 1970s, as the Fed attempted to deal with the problem of high and worsening inflation rates, it received conflicting policy advice. Many economists argued that the inflation rate could be reduced only at the cost of a temporary increase in the unemployment rate. Followers of the Lucas–Sargent rational expectations approach, however, argued that a painless reduction in the inflation rate was possible. Before analyzing the actual policies used by the Fed, we can look at why the oil price increases of the mid-1970s made the inflation rate worse.

The Effect of a Supply Shock on the Phillips Curve

As we saw in Chapter 13, the increases in oil prices in 1974 resulting from actions by OPEC caused the short-run aggregate supply curve to shift to the left. This shift is shown in panel (a) of Figure 17.9. (For simplicity, in this panel, we use the basic

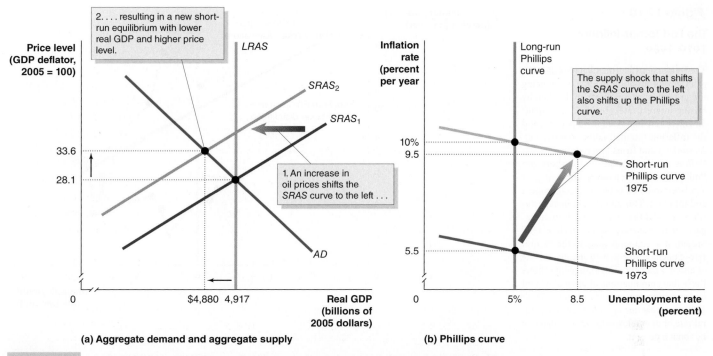

Figure 17.9 A Supply Shock Shifts the *SRAS* Curve and the Short-Run Phillips Curve

When OPEC increased the price of a barrel of oil from less than $3 to more than $10, in panel (a), the *SRAS* curve shifted to the left. Between 1973 and 1975, real GDP declined from $4,917 billion to $4,880 billion, and the price level rose from 17.1 to 33.6. Panel (b) shows that the supply shock shifted up the Phillips curve.

In 1973, the U.S. economy had an inflation rate of about 5.5 percent and an unemployment rate of about 5 percent. By 1975, the inflation rate had risen to about 9.5 percent and the unemployment rate to about 8.5 percent.

rather than dynamic *AD–AS* model.) The result was a higher price level and a lower level of real GDP. On a Phillips curve graph—panel (b) of Figure 17.9—we can shift the short-run Phillips curve up to show that the inflation rate and unemployment rate both increased.

As the Phillips curve shifted up, the economy moved from an unemployment rate of about 5 percent and an inflation rate of about 5.5 percent in 1973 to an unemployment rate of 8.5 percent and an inflation rate of about 9.5 percent in 1975. This combination of rising unemployment and rising inflation placed the Federal Reserve in a difficult position. If the Fed used an expansionary monetary policy to fight the high unemployment rate, the *AD* curve would shift to the right, and the economy's equilibrium would move up the short-run Phillips curve. Real GDP would increase, and the unemployment rate would fall—but at the cost of higher inflation. If the Fed used a contractionary monetary policy to fight the high inflation rate, the *AD* curve would shift to the left, and the economy's equilibrium would move down the short-run Phillips curve. As a result, real GDP would fall, and the inflation rate would be reduced—but at the cost of higher unemployment. In the end, the Fed chose to fight high unemployment with an expansionary monetary policy, even though that decision worsened the inflation rate.

Paul Volcker and Disinflation

By the late 1970s, the Federal Reserve had gone through a two-decade period of continually increasing the rate of growth of the money supply. In August 1979, President Jimmy Carter appointed Paul Volcker as chairman of the Board of Governors of the Federal Reserve System. Along with most other economists, Volcker was convinced that high inflation rates were damaging the economy. To reduce inflation, Volcker began reducing the annual growth rate of the money supply. This contractionary monetary policy raised interest rates, causing a decline in aggregate demand. Figure 17.10 uses the

Figure 17.10

The Fed Tames Inflation, 1979–1989

The Fed, under Chairman Paul Volcker, began fighting inflation in 1979 by reducing the growth of the money supply, thereby raising interest rates. By 1982, the unemployment rate had risen to 10 percent, and the inflation rate had fallen to 6 percent. As workers and firms lowered their expectations of future inflation, the short-run Phillips curve shifted down, improving the short-run trade-off between unemployment and inflation. This adjustment in expectations allowed the Fed to switch to an expansionary monetary policy, which by 1987 brought the economy back to the natural rate of unemployment, with an inflation rate of about 4 percent. The orange line shows the actual combinations of unemployment and inflation for each year from 1979 to 1989. Note that during these years, the natural rate of unemployment was estimated to be about 6 percent.

Disinflation A significant reduction in the inflation rate.

Phillips curve model to analyze the movements in unemployment and inflation from 1979 to 1989.

The Fed's contractionary monetary policy shifted the economy's short-run equilibrium down the short-run Phillips curve, lowering the inflation rate from 11 percent in 1979 to 6 percent in 1982—but at a cost of raising the unemployment rate from 6 percent to 10 percent. As workers and firms lowered their expectations of future inflation, the short-run Phillips curve shifted down, improving the short-run trade-off between unemployment and inflation. This adjustment in expectations allowed the Fed to switch to an expansionary monetary policy. By 1987, the economy was back to the natural rate of unemployment, which during these years was about 6 percent. The orange line in Figure 17.10 shows the actual combinations of unemployment and inflation for each year from 1979 to 1989.

Under Volcker's leadership, the Fed had reduced the inflation rate from more than 10 percent to less than 5 percent. The inflation rate has generally remained below 5 percent ever since. A significant reduction in the inflation rate is called **disinflation**. In fact, this episode is often referred to as the "Volcker disinflation." The disinflation had come at a very high price, however. From September 1982 through June 1983, the unemployment rate was above 10 percent, the first time this had happened since the end of the Great Depression of the 1930s.

Some economists argue that the Volcker disinflation provided evidence against the view that workers and firms have rational expectations. Volcker's announcement in October 1979 that he planned to use a contractionary monetary policy to bring down the inflation rate was widely publicized. If workers and firms had rational expectations, we might have expected them to have quickly reduced their expectations of future inflation. The economy should have moved smoothly down the long-run Phillips curve. As we have seen, however, the economy moved down the existing short-run Phillips curve, and only after several years of high unemployment did the Phillips curve shift down. Apparently, workers and firms had adaptive expectations—only changing their expectations of future inflation after the current inflation rate had fallen.

Robert Lucas and Thomas Sargent argue, however, that a less painful disinflation would have occurred if workers and firms had *believed* Volcker's announcement that he was fighting inflation. The problem was that previous Fed chairmen had made similar promises throughout the 1970s, but inflation had continued to get worse. By 1979, the

Don't Let This Happen to You

Don't Confuse Disinflation with Deflation

Disinflation refers to a decline in the *inflation rate*. *Deflation* refers to a decline in the *price level*. Paul Volcker and the Federal Reserve brought about a substantial disinflation in the United States during the years between 1979 and 1983. The inflation rate fell from over 11 percent in 1979 to below 5 percent in 1984. Yet even in 1984, there was no deflation: The price level was still rising—but at a slower rate.

The last period of significant deflation in the United States was in the early 1930s, during the Great Depression. The following table shows the consumer price index for each of those years.

Because the price level fell each year from 1929 to 1933, there was deflation.

Year	Consumer Price Index	Deflation Rate
1929	17.1	—
1930	16.7	−2.3%
1931	15.2	−9.0
1932	13.7	−9.9
1933	13.0	−5.1

MyEconLab

Your Turn: Test your understanding by doing related problem 4.5 on page 606 at the end of this chapter.

credibility of the Fed was at a low point. Some support for Lucas's and Sargent's argument comes from surveys of business economists at the time, which showed that they also reduced their forecasts of future inflation only slowly, even though they were well aware of Volcker's announcement of a new policy.

Solved Problem 17.4

Using Monetary Policy to Lower the Inflation Rate

Consider the following hypothetical situation: The economy is currently at the natural rate of unemployment of 5 percent. The actual inflation rate is 6 percent, and, because it has remained at 6 percent for several years, this is also the rate that workers and firms expect to see in the future. The Federal Reserve decides to reduce the inflation rate permanently to 2 percent. How can the Fed use monetary policy to achieve this objective? Be sure to use a Phillips curve graph in your answer.

Solving the Problem

Step 1: Review the chapter material. This problem is about using a Phillips curve graph to show how the Fed can fight inflation, so you may want to review the section "Paul Volcker and Disinflation," which begins on page 591.

Step 2: Explain how the Fed can use monetary policy to reduce the inflation rate. To reduce the inflation rate significantly, the Fed will have to raise the target for the federal funds rate. Higher interest rates will reduce aggregate demand, raise unemployment, and move the economy's equilibrium down the short-run Phillips curve.

Step 3: Illustrate your argument with a Phillips curve graph. How much the unemployment rate would have to rise to drive down the inflation rate from 6 percent to 2 percent depends on the steepness of the short-run Phillips curve.

Here we have assumed that the unemployment rate would have to rise from 5 percent to 7 percent.

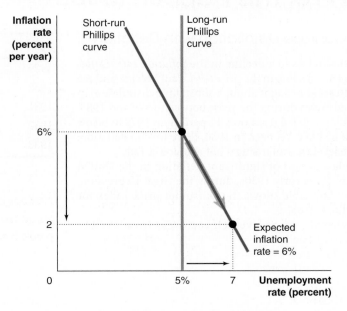

Step 4: **Show on your graph the reduction in the inflation rate from 6 percent to 2 percent.** For the decline in the inflation rate to be permanent, the expected inflation rate has to decline from 6 percent to 2 percent. We can show this decline on our graph:

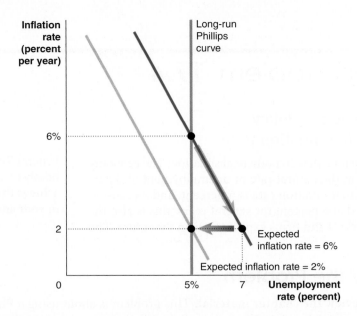

Once the short-run Phillips curve has shifted down, the Fed can use an expansionary monetary policy to push the economy back to the natural rate of unemployment. This policy is similar to the one carried out by the Fed after Paul Volcker became chairman in 1979. The downside to these policies of disinflation is that they lead to significant increases in unemployment.

Extra Credit: A follower of the new classical macroeconomics approach would have a more optimistic view of the consequences of using monetary policy to lower the inflation rate from 6 percent to 2 percent. According to this approach, the Fed's policy announcement should cause people to immediately revise downward their expectations of future inflation from 6 percent to 2 percent. The economy's short-run equilibrium would move directly down the long-run Phillips curve from an inflation rate of 6 percent to an inflation rate of 2 percent, while keeping the unemployment rate constant at 5 percent. For the reasons discussed in this chapter, many economists are skeptical that disinflation can be brought about so painlessly.

Your Turn: For more practice, do related problems 4.7 and 4.8 on page 606 at the end of this chapter.

MyEconLab

Alan Greenspan, Ben Bernanke, and the Crisis in Monetary Policy

President Ronald Reagan appointed Alan Greenspan to succeed Paul Volcker as Fed chairman in 1987. Greenspan served a term of more than 18 years. When he stepped down in January 2006, President George W. Bush appointed Ben Bernanke to take his place. Like Volcker, Greenspan and Bernanke were determined to keep the inflation rate low. Table 17.3 shows that the average annual inflation rate was lower during Greenspan's term and Bernanke's term through late 2011 than it had been during the terms of their three most immediate predecessors. Under Greenspan's leadership of the Fed, inflation was reduced nearly to the low levels experienced during the term of Chairman William McChesney Martin in the 1950s and 1960s. Greenspan's term was marked by only two short and mild recessions, in 1990–1991 and 2001. When Greenspan left office in 2006, he was widely applauded by economists, policymakers, and the media.

But with the severity of the 2007–2009 recession, some critics questioned whether decisions made by the Fed under Greenspan's leadership might have played a role in bringing on the crisis. We will discuss those arguments after briefly reviewing two other developments in monetary policy during the past 20 years:

- *Deemphasizing the money supply.* Greenspan's term was notable for the Fed's continued movement away from using the money supply as a monetary policy target. We saw in Chapter 14 that during the 1980s and 1990s, the close relationship between growth in the money supply and inflation broke down. Before 1987, the Fed would announce annual targets for how much M1 and M2 would increase during the year. In February 1987, near the end of Paul Volcker's term, the Fed announced that it would no longer set targets for M1. In July 1993, Alan Greenspan announced that the Fed also would no longer set targets for M2. Instead, the Federal Open Market Committee (FOMC) has relied on setting targets for the federal funds rate to meet its goals of price stability and high employment.

- *The importance of Fed credibility.* The Fed learned an important lesson during the 1970s: Workers, firms, and investors in stock and bond markets have to view Fed announcements as credible if monetary policy is to be effective. As inflation

Table 17.3

The Record of Fed Chairmen and Inflation

Federal Reserve Chairman	Term	Average Annual Inflation Rate During Term
William McChesney Martin	April 1951–January 1970	2.2%
Arthur Burns	February 1970–January 1978	6.5
G. William Miller	March 1978–August 1979	9.1
Paul Volcker	August 1979–August 1987	6.2
Alan Greenspan	August 1987–January 2006	3.1
Ben Bernanke	January 2006–	2.4

Note: Data for Bernanke are through October 2011.
Data from U.S. Bureau of Labor Statistics; and Federal Reserve Board of Governors.

worsened throughout the late 1960s and the 1970s, the Fed announced repeatedly that it would take actions to reduce inflation. In fact, policies were either not implemented or were ineffective, and inflation rose. These repeated failures to follow through on announced policies had greatly reduced the Fed's credibility by the time Paul Volcker took office in August 1979. The contractionary monetary policy that the Fed announced in October 1979 had less effect on the expectations of workers, firms, and investors than it would have had if the Fed's credibility had been greater. It took a severe recession to convince people that this time, the inflation rate really was coming down. Only then were workers willing to accept lower nominal wage increases, banks willing to accept lower interest rates on mortgage loans, and investors willing to accept lower interest rates on bonds.

Over the past two decades, the Fed has taken steps to enhance its credibility. Most importantly, whenever a change in Fed policy has been announced, the change has actually taken place. In addition, Greenspan revised the previous Fed policy of keeping secret the target for the federal funds rate. Since February 1994, any change in the target rate has been announced at the conclusion of the FOMC meeting at which the change is made. In addition, the minutes of the FOMC meetings are now made public after a brief delay. In February 2000, the Fed helped make its intentions for future policy clearer by announcing at the end of each FOMC meeting whether it considered the economy in the future to be at greater risk of higher inflation or of recession. In 2011, Ben Bernanke held a press conference following an FOMC meeting, which was the first time a Fed chair had done so.

The Decision to Intervene in the Failure of Long-Term Capital Management Greenspan's ability to help guide the economy through a long period of economic stability and his moves to enhance Fed credibility were widely applauded. However, two actions by the Fed during Greenspan's term have been identified as possibly contributing to the financial crisis that increased the length and severity of the 2007–2009 recession. One was the decision during 1998 to help save the hedge fund Long-Term Capital Management (LTCM). Hedge funds raise money, typically from wealthy investors, and use sophisticated investment strategies that often involve significant risk. Hedge funds generally rely heavily on borrowing in order to leverage their investments, thereby increasing potential returns. LTCM included as partners Robert Merton and Myron Scholes, who had both been awarded the Nobel Prize in Economics.

In the spring of 1998, LTCM suffered heavy losses on several of its investments, partly because the Russian government announced it would no longer make payments on some of its bonds, causing their value to plummet. Other financial firms that had loaned money to LTCM feared that the hedge fund would go bankrupt and began to push for repayment of their loans. We saw in Chapter 14 that a run on a financial firm can cause widespread problems in the financial system. If LTCM had been forced to quickly sell all of its investments, the prices of the securities it owned would have declined, causing problems for other financial firms that held the same securities. The Fed was concerned that a sudden failure of LTCM might lead to failures of other financial firms. With the support of Alan Greenspan, William McDonough, president of the Federal Reserve Bank of New York, held a meeting between the management of LTCM and the other financial firms to which LTCM owed money. The other firms were persuaded to give LTCM enough time to slowly sell off—or "unwind"—its investments to keep the prices of those investments from falling too rapidly and to avoid a financial panic.

The Fed's actions succeeded in avoiding wider damage from LTCM's failure, but some critics argued that the Fed's intervention had negative consequences in the long run because it allowed the owners of LTCM and the firms that had loaned LTCM money to avoid the full consequences of LTCM's failed investments. These critics argued that the Fed's intervention set the stage for other firms—particularly highly leveraged investment banks and hedge funds—to take on excessive risk, with the expectation that the Fed would intervene on their behalf should they suffer heavy losses on the investments.

Although some critics see the Fed's actions in the case of LTCM as encouraging the excessive risk taking that helped result in the financial crisis of 2007–2009, other observers doubt that the behavior of managers of financial firms were much affected by the Fed's actions.

The Decision to Keep the Target for the Federal Funds Rate at 1 Percent from June 2003 to June 2004 In response to the popping of the dot-com stock bubble in the spring of 2000, the beginning of a recession in March 2001, and the terrorist attacks of September 11, 2001, the Fed successively lowered the target for the federal funds rate. The target rate was cut in a series of steps from 6.5 percent in May 2000 to 1 percent in June 2003. The target remained at 1 percent until it was raised to 1.25 percent in June 2004. The Fed's decision to continue cutting the target for the federal funds rate for more than 18 months after the end of the recession in November 2001 and to keep the rate at 1 percent for another year has been criticized. At the time, the FOMC argued that although the recession of 2001 was mild, the very low inflation rates of late 2001 and 2002 raised the possibility that the U.S. economy could slip into a period of deflation. As we discussed in Chapter 15, deflation can damage the economy by raising real interest rates and by causing consumers to postpone purchases, based on the expectation that future prices will be lower than current prices.

Critics argued, though, that by keeping interest rates low for an extended period, the Fed helped to fuel the housing bubble that eventually deflated beginning in 2006, with disastrous results for the economy. We have seen that the origins of the housing bubble are complex and that contributing factors included the increase in securitization of mortgages, the willingness of banks and other lenders to give loans to subprime and Alt-A borrowers, and the widespread use of adjustable-rate mortgages that allowed borrowers to qualify for larger loans than would have been possible using conventional mortgages. Economists will continue to debate whether the Fed's policy of keeping the target for the federal funds rate very low for an extended period caused the housing bubble.

Has the Fed Lost Its Independence?

The financial crisis of 2007–2009 led the Fed to move well beyond the federal funds rate as the focus of monetary policy. With the target federal funds rate having been driven to zero without much expansionary effect on the economy, some observers began to speak of a "crisis in monetary policy." We reviewed the Fed's new policy initiatives in Chapters 14 and 15. Like other policies that represent a sharp break with the past, the Fed's actions had both supporters and critics. At this point, we can review the debate over whether the Fed's policy actions reduced its independence. The Fed worked closely with the Treasury Department in arranging to inject funds into the commercial banking system by taking partial ownership of some banks and in several other policy actions. Typically, the chairman of the Fed has formulated policy independently of the secretary of the Treasury, who is a political appointee and can be replaced at any time by the president of the United States. Close collaboration between the Fed and the Treasury, were it to continue, raises the question of whether the Fed will be able to pursue policies independent from those of the administration in power. In addition, by 2011, the Fed's extensive interventions in the financial system had led members of Congress to scrutinize—and in many cases, criticize—Fed policy to an unusual degree. Some observers worried that this intense congressional oversight might limit the Fed's freedom of action in the future.

The main reason to keep the Fed—or any country's central bank—independent of the rest of the government is to avoid inflation. Whenever a government is spending more than it is collecting in taxes, it must borrow the difference by selling bonds. The governments of many developing countries have difficulty finding anyone other than their central bank to buy their bonds. The more bonds the central bank buys, the faster the money supply grows, and the higher the inflation rate will be. Even in developed countries, governments that control their central banks may be tempted to sell bonds to the central bank rather than to the public.

Figure 17.11

The More Independent the Central Bank, the Lower the Inflation Rate

For 16 high-income countries, the greater the degree of central bank independence from the rest of the government, the lower the inflation rate. Central bank independence is measured by an index ranging from 1 (minimum independence) to 4 (maximum independence). During these years, Germany had a high index of independence of 4 and a low average inflation rate of just over 3 percent. New Zealand had a low index of independence of 1 and a high average inflation rate of over 7 percent.

"Central Bank Independence and Macroeconomic Performance: Some Comparative Evidence" by Alberto Alesina and Lawrence H. Summer from the *Journal of Money, Credit and Banking*, Vol. 25, No. 2, May 1993. Copyright © 1993 by the Ohio State University. Reprinted by permission.

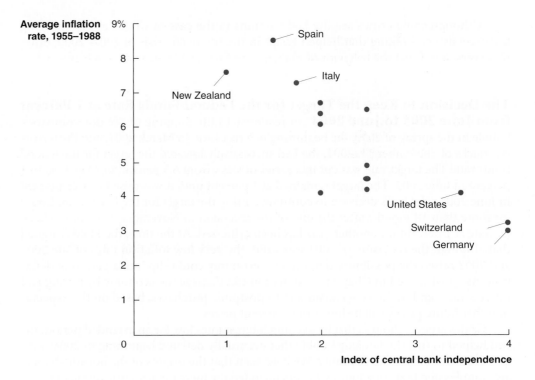

Another fear is that if the government controls the central bank, it may use that control to further its political interests. It is difficult in any democratic country for a government to be reelected at a time of high unemployment. If the government controls the central bank, it may be tempted just before an election to increase the money supply and drive down interest rates to increase production and employment. In the United States, for example, a president who had direct control over the Fed might be tempted to increase the money supply just before running for reelection, even if doing so led in the long run to higher inflation and accompanying economic costs.

We might expect that the more independent a country's central bank is, the lower the inflation rate in the country and the less independent a country's central bank, the higher the inflation rate. In a classic study, Alberto Alesina and Lawrence Summers, who were both at the time economists at Harvard University, tested this idea by comparing the degree of central bank independence and the inflation rate for 16 high-income countries during the years 1955–1988. Figure 17.11 shows the results.

Countries with highly independent central banks, such as the United States, Switzerland, and Germany, had lower inflation rates than countries whose central banks had little independence, such as New Zealand, Italy, and Spain. In the past few years, New Zealand and Canada have granted their banks more independence, at least partly to better fight inflation.

Whether the changes in the Fed's policies and procedures during and after the 2007–2009 recession will have lasting effects on its independence remains to be seen.

Continued from page 577

Economics in Your Life

Is It Wise to Delay a Job Search?

At the beginning of the chapter, we posed this question: What advice would you give someone who has decided to wait nearly two years to look for a new job? As we discussed in the chapter, evidence shows that many of those who are unemployed for longer than a year or two find it more difficult to find new employment than if they searched for a new job soon after they were laid off. The longer workers are unemployed, especially in a high-technology field, the more their skills deteriorate. By delaying her job search, your friend risks being unemployed for longer than two years. Eventually, she may have to be retrained or take additional courses in a different field in order to find a job. Tell your friend to start her job search right away!

Conclusion

The workings of the contemporary economy are complex. The attempts by the Federal Reserve to keep the U.S. economy near the natural rate of unemployment with a low rate of inflation have not always been successful. Economists continue to debate the best way for the Fed to proceed.

An Inside Look at Policy on the next page discusses the challenges the Federal Reserve faces in trying to reduce unemployment without increasing inflation.

Can the Fed Balance the Trade-off between Unemployment and Inflation?

NEWSWEEK

Ben Bernanke's Bet on Jobs and Inflation

Federal Reserve Chairman Ben Bernanke glided smoothly through his first regular news conference the other day—an event both remarkable and unremarkable. It was remarkable for symbolizing the Fed's ongoing transformation from a citadel of secrecy into an agency that tries to explain itself to the public. "The original attitude . . . was that it was no one's business what they did—and if you wanted to figure it out, do so yourself," says economist Allan Meltzer, author of a history of the Fed. Until now, there had been no news conferences, a legacy of the tight-lipped past.

a What was unremarkable is that reporters' questions focused on an old issue: How much can the Fed reduce unemployment without stoking inflation? Bernanke's bet is: a lot. He's embraced super-easy credit to cut the appalling 8.8 percent jobless rate; that's 13.5 million people, nearly half out of work for six months or more. Since late 2008, the Fed has held short-term interest rates near zero. To cut long-term rates, the Fed is buying gobs of Treasury bonds and mortgage securities: $1.725 trillion from late 2008 to March 2010; an additional $600 billion from last November through June. These purchases are known as QE1 and QE2, for "quantitative easing."

But there's a growing debate about whether all the pump-priming is helping recovery or simply fostering inflation. The economy's fate may hang on who's right. Studies by Fed economists are, not surprisingly, supportive. One estimated that QE1 and QE2 lowered long-term interest rates by about 0.5 percentage points and saved nearly 3 million jobs; the jobless rate otherwise could have approached 11 percent. Many private economists are less impressed; they suspect the benefits of QE1 faded with QE2. . . .

b Meanwhile, inflation creeps up. Over the past year, the consumer price index rose 2.7 percent; six months earlier, the year-over-year gain was only 1.2 percent. Bernanke blames higher oil and food prices, reflecting temporary factors (the war in Libya, poor harvests) that may be reversed. The danger of an inflationary wage-price spiral, goes this argument, is negligible because unemployment is high and pay is stagnant.

Maybe. But inflation's dynamics might be changing. Here's why. The recession caused enormous factory and business closures; now, there's less capacity to meet rising demand. Companies have more power to raise prices; a depreciating dollar compounds the effect by making imports more expensive. . . .

The problem might become more widespread. The Fed regularly measures manufacturers' production capacity. From 2007 to 2010, it fell 5.4 percent. That's the largest drop since the statistics began being kept in 1948; the only other annual decline occurred in 2003 and was a scant 0.25 percent.

c The Fed is attacked from both the left (for doing too little to create jobs) and the right (for doing too much and tempting inflation), notes former Fed vice chairman Donald Kohn. Bernanke aims for a middle course. One argument for a less secretive Fed is this: Investors, managers and workers who better understand the Fed's goals won't futilely try to defy them. The Fed's very commitment to low inflation will restrain wages and prices. Up to a point, this may be true. But public relations alone won't control behavior. Actions outrank intentions.

The lesson of the 1970s' great inflation (13 percent in 1980) is that once prices begin to rise consistently, they feed on themselves. The fallout is disastrous. People and companies can't plan for the future; recessions become more frequent. Unexpectedly high inflation would probably doom today's cheap credit policy. The Fed would have to raise rates. Criticism from both left and right would intensify. So, much is riding on Bernanke's bet: If he loses, we all lose.

Key Points in the Article

In an effort to reduce the unemployment rate and increase real GDP, the Fed held its target for the federal funds rate close to zero for three years beginning in late 2008. The Fed also successfully lowered long-term interest rates with its quantitative easing programs. While Fed economists argue that the Fed's policies helped save nearly 3 million jobs, some economists are concerned that these policies did more to increase inflation than to assist the recovery. From mid-2010 to mid-2011, the consumer price index rose 2.7 percent, with the largest increase coming in the last six months. Some observers criticized Fed Chairman Ben Bernanke for not doing enough to lower unemployment, while others criticized him for doing too much and fanning the flames of inflation. Bernanke argues, however, that the Fed's recent policy actions will help reduce the unemployment rate without causing a significant increase in the inflation rate.

Analyzing the News

a Fed Chairman Ben Bernanke argues that Fed policies that have reduced both short-term and long-term interest rates will be successful in lowering the high unemployment rate while keeping inflation in check. But some economists are convinced that monetary policy actions are doing less to improve the job situation and more to generate inflation. As you read in this chapter, A. W. Phillips discovered an inverse short-run relationship between the unemployment rate and the inflation rate. The figure below shows the short-run Phillips curve relationship from July 2008 through July 2011. For the months from July 2008 to July 2009, the Phillips curve relationship appears to fit the data well, as the unemployment rate rose from 5.8 percent to 9.5 percent while the inflation rate, measured by the percent change of the consumer price index, fell from 5.6 percent to −2.10 percent.

b The figure below also shows that from July 2009 to July 2011, the short-run Phillips curve relationship is less clear, as the unemployment rate remained between 9 and 10 percent, while the inflation rate rose from −2.10 percent to 3.63 percent. The article states that the dynamics of inflation may be changing and prices may rise due to reduced capacity coupled with increasing demand. As you learned in this chapter, if a higher inflation rate becomes expected in the economy, the short-run Phillips curve will shift up, and the short-run trade-off between unemployment and inflation will take place at a higher inflation rate. In the figure, the data from July 2010 to July 2011 could be indicating that workers and firms are expecting the inflation rate to increase.

c Some critics argue that the Fed has not done enough to create jobs and others claim that the Fed's actions will generate inflation. However, Bernanke is sticking with the policy decisions he believes will boost employment while keeping inflation under control. By announcing these policies and moving forward with them, the Fed maintains its credibility and therefore has a better chance of meeting its goals.

Thinking Critically about Policy

1. Suppose that the unemployment rate in mid-2011 was the same as it actually was, but the inflation rate during those months averaged 10 percent rather than the rate shown in the figure. What effect might the higher inflation rates have had on the Fed's monetary policy?

2. Suppose the unemployment rate is currently equal to the nonaccelerating inflation rate of unemployment (NAIRU) of 5 percent, and the inflation rate is 0 percent. If the Fed wants to raise the inflation rate permanently to 2 percent, what should it do? Explain your answer using a Phillips curve graph.

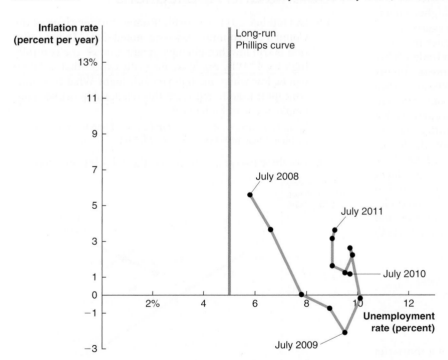

The short-run Phillips curve can be seen in the data for the period from July 2008 to July 2011.

Chapter Summary and Problems

Key Terms

Disinflation, p. 592

Natural rate of unemployment, p. 580

Nonaccelerating inflation rate of unemployment (NAIRU), p. 586

Phillips curve, p. 578

Rational expectations, p. 588

Real business cycle models, p. 590

Structural relationship, p. 580

 17.1
The Discovery of the Short-Run Trade-off between Unemployment and Inflation, pages 578–583
LEARNING OBJECTIVE: Describe the Phillips curve and the nature of the short-run trade-off between unemployment and inflation.

Summary

The **Phillips curve** illustrates the short-run trade-off between the unemployment rate and the inflation rate. The inverse relationship between unemployment and inflation shown by the Phillips curve is consistent with the aggregate demand and aggregate supply analysis developed in Chapter 13. The aggregate demand and aggregate supply (*AD–AS*) model indicates that slow growth in aggregate demand leads to both higher unemployment and lower inflation, and rapid growth in aggregate demand leads to both lower unemployment and higher inflation. This relationship explains why there is a short-run trade-off between unemployment and inflation. Many economists initially believed that the Phillips curve was a **structural relationship** that depended on the basic behavior of consumers and firms and that remained unchanged over time. If the Phillips curve were a stable relationship, it would present policymakers with a menu of combinations of unemployment and inflation from which they could choose. Nobel Laureate Milton Friedman argued that there is a **natural rate of unemployment**, which is the unemployment rate that exists when the economy is at potential GDP and to which the economy always returns. As a result, there is no trade-off between unemployment and inflation in the long run, and the long-run Phillips curve is a vertical line at the natural rate of unemployment.

MyEconLab   Visit **www.myeconlab.com** to complete these exercises online and get instant feedback.

Review Questions

1.1 What is the Phillips curve? Draw a graph of a short-run Phillips curve.

1.2 What actions should the Fed take if it wants to move from a point on the short-run Phillips curve representing high unemployment and low inflation to a point representing lower unemployment and higher inflation?

1.3 Why did economists during the early 1960s think of the Phillips curve as a "policy menu"? Were they correct to think of it in this way? Briefly explain.

1.4 Why did Milton Friedman argue that the Phillips curve did not represent a permanent trade-off between unemployment and inflation? In your answer, be sure to explain what Friedman meant by the "natural rate of unemployment."

Problems and Applications

1.5 In October 2011, Christina Romer, former chair of the Council of Economic Advisers, noted that, "Today, inflation is still low, but unemployment is stuck at a painfully high level." Why might we normally expect that inflation will be low when unemployment is high? What economic concept is used to represent this relationship between unemployment and inflation?

From Christina D. Romer, "Dear Ben: It's Time for Your Volcker Moment," *New York Times*, October 29, 2011.

1.6 Use these two graphs to answer the following questions:

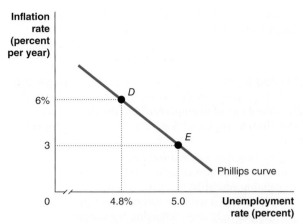

a. Briefly explain which point on the Phillips curve graph represents the same economic situation as point *B* on the aggregate demand and aggregate supply graph.

b. Briefly explain which point on the Phillips curve graph represents the same economic situation as point *C* on the aggregate demand and aggregate supply graph.

1.7 Given that the Phillips curve is derived from the aggregate demand and aggregate supply model, why do we use the Phillips curve analysis? What benefits does the Phillips curve analysis offer compared to the aggregate demand and aggregate supply model?

1.8 Briefly explain whether you agree with the following statement: "Any economic relationship that changes as economic policy changes is not a structural relationship."

1.9 In macroeconomics courses in the 1960s and early 1970s, some economists argued that one of the U.S. political parties was willing to have higher unemployment in order to achieve lower inflation and that the other major political party was willing to have higher inflation in order to achieve lower unemployment. Why might such views of the trade-off between inflation and unemployment have existed in the 1960s? Why are such views rare today?

1.10 General Juan Perón, the former dictator of Argentina, once said of the labor market in his country, "Prices have gone up the elevator, and wages have had to use the stairs." In this situation, what was happening to real wages in Argentina? Was unemployment likely to have been relatively high or relatively low?

From Robert J. Shiller, "Why Do People Dislike Inflation?" in Christina D. Romer and David H. Romer, eds., *Reducing Inflation: Motivation and Strategy*, (Chicago: University of Chicago Press, 1997).

1.11 This chapter argues that if the price level increases over time, the average wage should increase by the same amount. Why is this true?

1.12 **[Related to the** Making the Connection **on page 582]** Robert Shiller asked a sample of the general public and a sample of economists the following question: "Do you agree that preventing high inflation is an important national priority, as important as preventing drug abuse or preventing deterioration in the quality of our schools?" Fifty-two percent of the general public, but only 18 percent of economists, fully agreed. Why does the general public believe inflation is a bigger problem than economists do?

1.13 **[Related to the** Making the Connection **on page 582]** When Shiller asked a sample of the general public what they thought caused inflation, the most frequent answer he received was "greed." Do you agree that greed causes inflation? Briefly explain.

1.14 **[Related to the** Chapter Opener **on page 577]** Why might a firm such as CarMax, which we discussed in the chapter opener, pay more attention than firms in, say, the restaurant or clothing industries, to the Federal Reserve raising or lowering interest rates? In other words, why are movements in interest rates particularly important to CarMax?

17.2 **The Short-Run and Long-Run Phillips Curves,** pages 583–587

LEARNING OBJECTIVE: Explain the relationship between the short-run and long-run Phillips curves.

Summary

There is a short-run trade-off between unemployment and inflation only if the actual inflation rate differs from the inflation rate that workers and firms had expected. There is a different short-run Phillips curve for every expected inflation rate. Each short-run Phillips curve intersects the long-run Phillips curve at the expected inflation rate. With a vertical long-run Phillips curve, it is not possible to buy a permanently lower unemployment rate at the cost of a permanently higher inflation rate. If the Federal Reserve attempts to keep the economy below the natural rate of unemployment, the inflation rate will increase. Eventually, the expected inflation rate will also increase, which causes the short-run Phillips curve to shift up and pushes the economy back to the natural rate of unemployment. The reverse happens if the Fed attempts to keep the economy above the natural rate of unemployment. In the long run, the Federal Reserve can affect the inflation rate but not the unemployment rate.

Review Questions

2.1 Suppose that the expected inflation rate increases from 4 percent to 6 percent. What will happen to the short-run Phillips curve?

2.2 What is the relationship between the short-run Phillips curve and the long-run Phillips curve?

2.3 Why is it inconsistent to believe that the long-run aggregate supply curve is vertical and the long-run Phillips curve is downward sloping?

Problems and Applications

2.4 Use the following information to draw a graph showing the short-run and long-run Phillips curves:

Natural rate of unemployment = 5 percent
Current rate of unemployment = 4 percent
Expected inflation rate = 4 percent
Current inflation rate = 6 percent

Be sure your graph shows the point where the short-run and long-run Phillips curves intersect.

2.5 In 1968, Herbert Stein, who would later serve on President Nixon's Council of Economic Advisers, wrote, "Some who would opt for avoiding inflation would say that in the long run such a policy would cost little, if any, additional unemployment." Was Stein correct? Did most economists in 1968 agree with him? Briefly explain.

From Herbert Stein, *The Fiscal Revolution in America*, (Chicago: University of Chicago Press, 1969), p. 382.

2.6 **[Related to** Solved Problem 17.2 **on page 587]** In a speech in September 1975, then Fed Chairman Arthur Burns said the following:

> There is no longer a meaningful trade-off between unemployment and inflation. In the current environment, a rapidly rising level of consumer prices will not lead to the creation of new jobs. . . . Highly expansionary monetary and fiscal policies might, for a short time, provide some additional thrust to economic activity. But inflation would inevitably accelerate—a development that would create even more difficult economic problems than we have encountered over the past year.

How do Burns's views in this speech compare with the views at the Fed in the late 1960s? Why do you think he specifically says that "in the current environment" there is no trade-off between unemployment and inflation?

From Arthur F. Burns, "The Real Issues of Inflation and Unemployment," in Federal Reserve Bank of New York, *Federal Reserve Readings on Inflation*, February 1979.

2.7 In testifying before Congress, former Federal Reserve Chairman Alan Greenspan remarked, "The challenge of monetary policy is to interpret data on the economy and financial markets with an eye to anticipating future inflationary forces and to countering them by taking action in advance." Why should the Fed take action in anticipation of inflation becoming worse? Why not just wait until the increase in the inflation rate has occurred?

From Nicoletta Batini and Andrew G. Haldane, "Forward-Looking Rules for Monetary Policy," in John B. Taylor, ed., *Monetary Policy Rules*, (Chicago: University of Chicago Press, 1999), p. 157.

2.8 In Congressional testimony, Federal Reserve Chairman Ben Bernanke said:

> Another significant factor influencing medium-term trends in inflation is the public's expectations of inflation. These expectations have an important bearing on whether transitory influences on prices, such as changes in energy costs, become embedded in wage and price decisions and so leave a lasting imprint on the rate of inflation.

What did Bernanke mean when he said that the public's expectations of inflation could "become embedded in wage and price decisions"? What would be the effect on the short-run Phillips curve of the public coming to expect a higher inflation rate?

From "Testimony of Chairman Ben S. Bernanke before the Joint Economic Committee, U.S. Congress," March 28, 2007.

2.9 **[Related to the** Making the Connection **on page 586]** In 2011, an article in the *Economist* magazine argued that the natural rate of unemployment in the United States may have risen as high as 7.5 percent. The article suggested that:

> Lowering this new natural rate of unemployment will require structural reforms, such as changing education to ensure that people enter work equipped with the sort of skills firms are willing to fight over, adjusting the tax system and modernising the welfare safety net, and more broadly creating a climate conducive to entrepreneurship and innovation.

Why should policymakers be concerned with lowering the natural rate of unemployment? How would the "structural reforms" listed in the article contribute to lowering the natural rate of unemployment? Would the Fed be able to implement any of these reforms? Briefly explain.

From "The Great Mismatch," *Economist*, September 10, 2011.

2.10 **[Related to the** Making the Connection **on page 586]** An article in a publication of the Federal Reserve Bank of San Francisco described the natural rate of unemployment in 2011:

> Recent labor market developments, including mismatches in the skills of workers and jobs, extended unemployment benefits, and very high rates of long-term joblessness, may be impeding the return to "normal" unemployment rates of around 5%. An examination of alternative measures of labor market conditions suggests that the "normal" unemployment rate may have risen as much as 1.7 percentage points to about 6.7%, although much of this increase is likely to prove temporary.

a. Explain why each of the factors mentioned—mismatches in the skills of workers and jobs, extended unemployment benefits, and very high rates of long-term joblessness—might increase the natural rate of unemployment.

b. Draw short-run and long-run Phillips curves that illustrate the effects of the natural rate of unemployment increasing from 5.0 percent to 6.7 percent. Briefly explain your graph.

c. The article states that, "Even with such an increase (in the natural rate of unemployment), sizable labor market slack is expected to persist for years." What is "labor market slack"? Show on your short-run Phillips curve in part b. the situation where the economy is experiencing labor market slack.

From Justin Weidner and John C. Williams, "What Is the New Normal Unemployment Rate?" *FRBSF Economic Letter*, February 14, 2011.

17.3 Expectations of the Inflation Rate and Monetary Policy, pages 587–590

LEARNING OBJECTIVE: Discuss how expectations of the inflation rate affect monetary policy.

Summary

When the inflation rate is moderate and stable, workers and firms tend to have *adaptive expectations*. That is, they form their expectations under the assumption that future inflation rates will follow the pattern of inflation rates in the recent past. During the high and unstable inflation rates of the mid- to late 1970s, Robert Lucas and Thomas Sargent argued that workers and firms would have *rational expectations*. **Rational expectations** are formed by using all the available information about an economic variable, including the effect of the policy being used by the Federal Reserve. Lucas and Sargent argued that if people have rational expectations, expansionary monetary policy will not work. If workers and firms know that an expansionary monetary policy is going to raise the inflation rate, the actual inflation rate will be the same as the expected inflation rate. Therefore, the unemployment rate won't fall. Many economists remain skeptical of Lucas and Sargent's argument in its strictest form. **Real business cycle models** focus on "real" factors—technology shocks—rather than changes in the money supply to explain fluctuations in real GDP.

 MyEconLab   Visit www.myeconlab.com to complete these exercises online and get instant feedback.

Review Questions

3.1 Why do workers, firms, banks, and investors in financial markets care about the future rate of inflation? How do they form their expectations of future inflation? Do current conditions in the economy have any bearing on how they form their expectations?

3.2 What does it mean to say that workers and firms have rational expectations?

3.3 Why did Robert Lucas and Thomas Sargent argue that the Phillips curve might be vertical in the short run? What difference would it make for monetary policy if they were right?

Problems and Applications

3.4 During a time when the inflation rate is increasing each year for a number of years, are adaptive expectations or rational expectations likely to give the more accurate forecasts? Briefly explain.

3.5 An article in the *Economist* magazine contains the following: "Robert Lucas . . . showed how incorporating

expectations into macroeconomic models muddled the framework economists prior to the 'rational expectations revolution' thought they saw so clearly." What economic framework did economists change as the result of Lucas's arguments? Do all economists agree with Lucas's main conclusions about the effectiveness of monetary policy? Briefly explain.
From "How to Know What Causes What," *Economist*, October 10, 2011.

3.6 Would a monetary policy intended to bring about disinflation cause a greater increase in unemployment if workers and firms have adaptive expectations or if they have rational expectations? Briefly explain.

3.7 If both the short-run and long-run Phillips curves are vertical, what will be the effect on the inflation rate and the unemployment rate of an expansionary monetary policy? Use a Phillips curve graph to illustrate your answer.

3.8 An article in the *Wall Street Journal* contains the following about the views of William Poole, who was then the president of the Federal Reserve Bank of St. Louis:

Mr. Poole said both inflation expectations and the output gap—the spare room the economy has between what it's producing and what it could potentially produce—go into the inflation process. But "inflation expectations . . . trump the gap. If inflation expectations were to rise, that development by itself would tend to drag the inflation rate up . . . and it might take a very long time before the (output gap) would be able to offset what's going on with inflation expectations."

a. Use the short-run and long-run Phillips curves to explain what Poole meant in saying that both inflation expectations and the output gap affect the current inflation rate.

b. In terms of Phillips curve analysis, what are the implications of Poole's claim that "it might take a very long time before the (output gap) would be able to offset what's going on with inflation expectations"?

c. Why might inflation expectations be slow to respond to the output gap?
"Fed Policy Maker Warns of Rising Inflation," by Greg Ip from *Wall Street Journal*, June 6, 2006. Copyright © 2011 by Dow Jones & Company, Inc. Reproduced with permission of Dow Jones & Company, Inc.

17.4 Federal Reserve Policy from the 1970s to the Present, pages 590–598

LEARNING OBJECTIVE: Use a Phillips curve graph to show how the Federal Reserve can permanently lower the inflation rate.

Summary

Inflation worsened through the 1970s. Paul Volcker became Fed chairman in 1979, and, under his leadership, the Fed used contractionary monetary policy to reduce inflation. A significant reduction in the inflation rate is called **disinflation**. This contractionary

monetary policy pushed the economy down the short-run Phillips curve. As workers and firms lowered their expectations of future inflation, the short-run Phillips curve shifted down, improving the short-run trade-off between unemployment and inflation. This change in expectations allowed the Fed to switch to an expansionary monetary policy to bring the economy back to the natural rate of unemployment. During Alan Greenspan's term as Fed chairman, inflation remained low, and the credibility of the Fed increased. In recent years, some economists have argued that monetary policy decisions during Greenspan's term may have contributed to the problems the financial system experienced during the 2007–2009 recession. Some economists and policymakers fear that actions taken by the Fed during the 2007–2009 recession may have reduced its independence.

MyEconLab   Visit **www.myeconlab.com** to complete these exercises online and get instant feedback.

Review Questions

4.1 What was the "Volcker disinflation"? What happened to the unemployment rate during the period of the Volcker disinflation?

4.2 Why is the credibility of the Fed's policy announcements particularly important?

4.3 Why do most economists believe that it is important for a country's central bank to be independent of the rest of the country's central government?

Problems and Applications

4.4 According to an article in *Business Week*, many workers who retired in the year 2000 expected to live off the interest they would receive from bank certificates of deposit or money market mutual funds. "Then came disinflation—and a steep fall in interest rates." What is disinflation, and why should it lead to a fall in interest rates?

From Peter Coy, "The Surprise Threat to Nest Eggs," *Business Week*, July 28, 2003.

4.5 **[Related to the** Don't Let This Happen to You **on page 593]** Look again at the table on prices during the early 1930s on page 593. Was there disinflation during 1933? Briefly explain.

4.6 Suppose the current inflation rate and the expected inflation rate are both 4 percent. The current unemployment rate and the natural rate of unemployment are both 5 percent. Use a Phillips curve graph to show the effect on the economy of a severe supply shock. If the Federal Reserve keeps monetary policy unchanged, what will happen eventually to the unemployment rate? Show this on your Phillips curve graph.

4.7 **[Related to** Solved Problem 17.4 **on page 593]** Suppose the inflation rate has been 15 percent for the past four years. The unemployment rate is currently at the natural rate of unemployment of 5 percent. The Federal Reserve decides that it wants to permanently reduce the inflation rate to 5 percent. How can the Fed use monetary policy to achieve this objective? Be sure to use a Phillips curve graph in your answer.

4.8 **[Related to** Solved Problem 17.4 **on page 593]** In 1995, some economists argued that the natural rate of unemployment was 6 percent. Then Fed Chairman Alan Greenspan was convinced that the natural rate was actually about 5 percent. If Greenspan had accepted the view that the natural rate was 6 percent, how might monetary policy have been different during the late 1990s?

4.9 During the recession of 2007–2009, some economists were concerned that the U.S. economy might begin experiencing deflation. An article in the Federal Reserve Bank of San Francisco's *Economic Letter* stated: "A popular version of the well-known Phillips curve model of inflation predicts that we are on the cusp of a deflationary spiral in which prices will fall at ever increasing rates over the next several years."
  a. How might a deflationary spiral occur in the Phillips curve model?
  b. Why do you think that a deflationary spiral did not actually occur during or after the recession of 2007–2009?

From John C. Williams, "The Risk of Deflation," *FRBSF Economic Letter*, March 27, 2009.

4.10 According to an article in the *Wall Street Journal*, "J.P. Morgan Chase economist Michael Feroli finds that in the past two decades it has taken a far larger drop in the jobless rate to boost inflation by one percentage point than it did in the previous 25 years." If this economist is correct, has the short-run Phillips curve become steeper during the past 25 years or less steep? If true, would this fact have any implications for monetary policy? Briefly explain.

From Greg Ip, "Fed Sees Inflation Rise as Fleeting," *Wall Street Journal*, August 4, 2006.

4.11 Robert Lucas has been quoted as saying: "In practice, it is much more painful to put a modern economy through a deflation than the monetary theory we have would lead us to expect. I take this to mean that we have 'price stickiness.'" What does Lucas mean by "the monetary theory we have"? What events may have led Lucas to conclude that it is more painful to reduce the inflation rate than theory would predict? Why does he conclude that the U.S. economy apparently has "price stickiness"?

From Paul A. Samuelson and William A. Barnett, eds., *Inside Economist's Mind: Conversations with Eminent Economists*, (Malden, MA: Blackwell Publishing, 2007).

4.12 During the 2012 presidential election campaign, Texas Governor Rick Perry criticized the actions of Fed Chair Ben Bernanke. Perry argued that, "Printing more money to play politics at this particular time in American history is almost . . . treasonous in my opinion." An article in the *Wall Street Journal* commented that despite Perry's remarks, ". . . Bernanke is willing to embrace the political independence embedded in his role to do what Fed officials think the economy needs." How is "political independence" embedded in the role of Fed chair? Why did Congress initially decide to make the Fed independent of the rest of the federal government?

From Sudeep Reddy, "Rick Perry's Attack on Bernanke Highlights Political Risks Facing the Fed," *Wall Street Journal*, August 16, 2011.

Chapter Outline and Learning Objectives

A Strong Dollar Hurts McDonald's Profits

The McDonald's Big Mac is one of the most widely available products in the world. McDonald's has 32,000 outlets in 118 countries, serving 60 million customers per day. The company's stock was one of only two in the Dow Jones Industrial Average to post a gain in 2008, which was a bad year for most U.S. firms. During the recession of 2007–2009, McDonald's prospered as many consumers switched to eating out at fast-food restaurants rather than at restaurants that provide table service. The success of McDonald's continued into 2010, with the company's stock price increasing 22.5 percent, more than double the 11 percent gain in the Dow Jones Industrial Average.

With expansion in the U.S. market limited, McDonald's has grown in recent years mostly by expanding in foreign markets. About 34 percent of its sales come from the United States; 40 percent from Europe; 20 percent from the Middle East, Asia, and Africa; and about 6 percent from Canada and Latin America. Because McDonald's has restaurants in so many different countries, it receives revenue in many different currencies. As a result, the company's revenue and profits are affected by fluctuations in the value of the dollar in exchange for other currencies. In some years, converting revenue from foreign currencies yields more dollars than in other years. For example, in August 2011, global revenues for McDonald's increased by 11.3 percent from the previous year when measured in local currency—pounds in Great Britain, euros in France, yen in Japan. But when measured in terms of dollars, the company's revenues rose by only 5.4 percent. Why the discrepancy? The value of the dollar had increased relative to most other currencies. So, converting pounds, euros, and yen into dollars yielded fewer dollars for McDonald's.

What explains fluctuations in the exchange rate between the dollar and other currencies? In this chapter and the next, we will look more closely at how exchange rates are determined and at other important issues involving the international financial system. Read **AN INSIDE LOOK** on **page 630** for a discussion of the effects of a decrease in the value of the U.S. dollar relative to other currencies.

Based on Dimitra Defotis, "McDonald's Shares Hit New High; Sales Strong in EU," *Barron's*, July 22, 2011; and McDonald's, "Financial Press Release," September 9, 2011.

Economics in Your Life

The South Korean Central Bank and Your Car Loan

Suppose that you are shopping for a new car, which you plan to finance with a loan from a local bank. One morning, as you head out the door to visit another automobile dealership, you hear the following newsflash on the radio: "The Bank of Korea, South Korea's central bank, announces it will sell its large holdings of U.S. Treasury bonds." What effect will the Bank of Korea's decision to sell its U.S. Treasury bonds likely have on the interest rate you pay on your car loan? As you read this chapter, see if you can answer this question. You can check your answer against the one we provide on **page 629** at the end of this chapter.

I n Chapter 7, we looked at the basics of international trade. In this chapter, we look more closely at the linkages among countries at the macroeconomic level. Countries are linked by trade in goods and services and by flows of financial investment. We will see how policymakers in all countries take these linkages into account when conducting monetary policy and fiscal policy.

The Balance of Payments: Linking the United States to the International Economy

Today, consumers, firms, and investors routinely interact with consumers, firms, and investors in other economies. A consumer in France may use computer software produced in the United States, watch a television made in South Korea, and wear a sweater made in Italy. A firm in the United States may sell its products in dozens of countries around the world. An investor in London may sell a U.S. Treasury bill to an investor in Mexico City. Nearly all economies are **open economies** and have extensive interactions in trade or finance with other countries. Open economies interact by trading goods and services and by making investments in each other's economies. A **closed economy** has no interactions in trade or finance with other countries. No economy today is completely closed, although a few countries, such as North Korea, have very limited economic interactions with other countries.

A good way to understand the interactions between one economy and other economies is through the **balance of payments**, which is a record of a country's trade with other countries in goods, services, and assets. Just as the U.S. Bureau of Economic Analysis is responsible for collecting data on the GDP, it is also responsible for collecting data on the balance of payments. Table 18.1 shows the balance of payments for the United States in 2010. Notice that the table contains three "accounts": the *current account*, the *financial account*, and the *capital account*.

The Current Account

The **current account** records *current*, or short-term, flows of funds into and out of a country. The current account for the United States includes exports and imports of goods and services (recall from Chapter 8 that the difference between exports and imports of goods and services is called *net exports*); income received by U.S. residents from investments in other countries; income paid on investments in the United States owned by residents of other countries (the difference between investment income received and investment income paid is called *net income on investments*); and the difference between transfers made to residents of other countries and transfers received by U.S. residents from other countries (called *net transfers*). If you make a donation to a charity caring for orphans in Afghanistan, it would be included in net transfers. Any payments received by U.S. residents are positive numbers in the current account, and any payments made by U.S. residents are negative numbers in the current account.

The Balance of Trade Part of the current account is the **balance of trade**, which is the difference between the value of the goods a country exports and the value of the goods a country imports. The balance of trade is the largest item in the current account and is often a topic that politicians and the media discuss. If a country exports more goods than it imports, it has a *trade surplus*. If a country exports less than it imports, it has a *trade deficit*. In 2010, the United States had a trade deficit of $646 billion. In the same year, Japan had a trade surplus of $76 billion, and China had a trade surplus of $183 billion. Figure 18.1 shows imports and exports of goods between the United States and its trading partners and between Japan and its trading partners. The data show that the United States ran a trade deficit in 2010 with all its major trading partners and with every region of the world except for Latin America. Japan ran trade deficits with China,

Open economy An economy that has interactions in trade or finance with other countries.

Closed economy An economy that has no interactions in trade or finance with other countries.

Balance of payments The record of a country's trade with other countries in goods, services, and assets.

Current account The part of the balance of payments that records a country's net exports, net income on investments, and net transfers.

Balance of trade The difference between the value of the goods a country exports and the value of the goods a country imports.

CURRENT ACCOUNT

		Table 18.1
		The Balance of Payments, 2010 (billions of dollars)

CURRENT ACCOUNT		
Exports of goods	$1,289	
Imports of goods	−1,935	
Balance of trade		−646
Exports of services	549	
Imports of services	−403	
Balance of services		146
Income received on investments	663	
Income payments on investments	−498	
Net income on investments		165
Net transfers		−136
Balance on current account		−471

The sum of the balance of trade and the balance of services equals net exports.

FINANCIAL ACCOUNT		
Increase in foreign holdings of assets in the United States	1,259	
Increase in U.S. holdings of assets in foreign countries	−1,005	
Balance on financial account		254

BALANCE ON CAPITAL ACCOUNT	0
Statistical discrepancy	217
Balance of payments	0

Data from U.S. Bureau of Economic Analysis, "U.S. International Transactions: Second Quarter 2011," September 15, 2011.

the Middle East, and Africa, and it ran trade surpluses with other regions. (Note that exports from the United States to Japan in panel (a) of Figure 18.1 should equal imports by Japan from the United States in panel (b). These two numbers are different because international trade statistics are not measured exactly.)

Net Exports Equals the Sum of the Balance of Trade and the Balance of Services In previous chapters, we saw that *net exports* is a component of aggregate expenditures. Net exports is not explicitly shown in Table 18.1, but we can calculate it by adding together the balance of trade and the balance of services. The *balance of services* is the difference between the value of the services a country exports and the value of the services a country imports. Notice that, technically, net exports is *not* equal to the current account balance because this account also includes net income on investments and net transfers. But these other two items are relatively small, so, as we will see later in this chapter, it is often a convenient simplification to think of net exports as being equal to the current account balance.

The Financial Account

The **financial account** records purchases of assets a country has made abroad and foreign purchases of assets in the country. The financial account records long-term flows of funds into and out of a country. There is a *capital outflow* from the United States when an investor in the United States buys a bond issued by a foreign company or government or when a U.S. firm builds a factory in another country. There is a *capital inflow* into the United States when a foreign investor buys a bond issued by a U.S. firm or by the government or when a foreign firm builds a factory in the United States. Notice that we

Financial account The part of the balance of payments that records purchases of assets a country has made abroad and foreign purchases of assets in the country.

(a) Trade flows for the United States (in billions of dollars)

(b) Trade flows for Japan (in billions of dollars)

Figure 18.1 Trade Flows for the United States and Japan, 2010

Panel (a) shows that in 2010, the United States ran a trade deficit with all its major trading partners and with every region of the world except for Latin America. Panel (b) shows that Japan ran trade deficits with China, Latin America, and the Middle East, and it ran trade surpluses with the United States, Europe, and Asia. In each panel, the green arrows represent exports from the United States or Japan, and the red arrows represent imports.

Note: Japanese data are converted from yen to dollars at the average 2010 exchange rate of 87.8 yen per dollar.
Data from U.S. Bureau of Economic Analysis, "U.S. International Transactions: Second Quarter 2011," September 15, 2011.

Net foreign investment The difference between capital outflows from a country and capital inflows, also equal to net foreign direct investment plus net foreign portfolio investment.

are using the word *capital* here to apply not just to physical assets, such as factories, but also to financial assets, such as shares of stock. When firms build or buy facilities in foreign countries, they are engaging in *foreign direct investment*. When investors buy stock or bonds issued in another country, they are engaging in *foreign portfolio investment*.

Another way of thinking of the balance on the financial account is as a measure of *net capital flows*, or the difference between capital inflows and capital outflows. (Here we are omitting a few transactions included in the capital account, as discussed in the next section.) A concept closely related to net capital flows is **net foreign investment**, which is equal to capital outflows minus capital inflows. Net capital flows and net foreign investment are always equal but have opposite signs: When net capital flows are positive, net foreign investment is negative, and when net capital flows are negative, net foreign investment is positive. Net foreign investment is also equal to net foreign direct investment plus net foreign portfolio investment. Later in this chapter, we will use the relationship between the balance on the financial account and net foreign investment to understand an important aspect of the international economic system.

The Capital Account

Capital account The part of the balance of payments that records relatively minor transactions, such as migrants' transfers and sales and purchases of nonproduced, nonfinancial assets.

A third, less important, part of the balance of payments is called the *capital account*. The **capital account** records relatively minor transactions, such as migrants' transfers—which consist of goods and financial assets people take with them when they leave or enter a country—and sales and purchases of nonproduced, nonfinancial assets. A nonproduced, nonfinancial asset is a copyright, patent, trademark, or right to natural resources. The definitions of the financial account and the capital account are often misunderstood because the capital account prior to 1999 recorded all the transactions included now in both the financial account and the capital account. In other words, capital account transactions went from being a very important part of the balance of payments to being a relatively unimportant part. Because the balance on what is now called the capital account is so small—only $152 million in 2010—for simplicity we will ignore it in the remainder of this chapter.

Why Is the Balance of Payments Always Zero?

The sum of the current account balance, the financial account balance, and the capital account balance equals the balance of payments. Table 18.1 shows that the balance of payments for the United States in 2010 was zero. It's not just by chance that this balance was zero; *the balance of payments is always zero*. Notice that the current account balance in 2010 was –$471 billion. The balance on the financial account (which has the opposite sign to the balance on the current account) was $254 billion. To make the balance on the current account equal the balance on the financial account, the balance of payments includes an entry called the *statistical discrepancy*. (Remember that we are ignoring the balance on the capital account. If we included it, we would say that the statistical discrepancy takes on a value equal to the difference between the current account balance and the sum of the balance on the financial account and the balance on the capital account.)

Why does the U.S. Department of Commerce include the statistical discrepancy entry to force the balance of payments to equal zero? If the sum of the current account balance and the financial account balance does not equal zero, some imports or exports of goods and services or some capital inflows or capital outflows were not measured accurately.

To better understand why the balance of payments must equal zero every year, consider the following: In 2010, the United States spent $471 billion more on goods, services, and other items in the current account than it received. What happened to that $471 billion? We know that every dollar of that $471 billion was used by foreign individuals or firms to invest in the United States or was added to foreign holdings of dollars. We know this because logically there is nowhere else for the dollars to go: If the dollars weren't spent on U.S. goods and services—and we know they weren't because in that case they would have shown up in the current account—they must have been spent on investments in the United States or not spent at all. Dollars that aren't spent are added to foreign holdings of dollars. Changes in foreign holdings of dollars are known

Don't Let This Happen to You

Don't Confuse the Balance of Trade, the Current Account Balance, and the Balance of Payments

The terminology of international economics can be tricky. Remember that the *balance of trade* includes only trade in goods; it does not include services. This observation is important because the United States, for example, usually imports more *goods* than it exports, but it usually exports more *services* than it imports. As a result, the U.S. trade deficit is almost always larger than the current account deficit. The *current account balance* includes the balance of trade, the balance of services, net investment income, and net transfers. Net investment income and net transfers are much smaller than the balance of trade and the balance of services.

Even though the *balance of payments* is equal to the sum of the current account balance and the financial account balance—and must equal zero—you may sometimes see

references to a balance of payments "surplus" or "deficit." These references have two explanations. The first is that the person making the reference has confused the balance of payments with either the balance of trade or the current account balance. This is a very common mistake. The second explanation is that the person is not including official reserve transactions in the financial account. If we separate changes in U.S. holdings of foreign currencies and changes in foreign holdings of U.S. dollars from other financial account entries, the current account balance and the financial account balance do not have to sum to zero, and there can be a balance of payments surplus or deficit. This may sound complicated—and it is! But don't worry. How official reserve transactions are accounted for is not crucial to understanding the basic ideas behind the balance of payments.

MyEconLab

Your Turn: Test your understanding by doing related problem 1.6 on page 632 at the end of this chapter.

as *official reserve transactions*. Foreign investment in the United States and additions to foreign holdings of dollars both show up as positive entries in the U.S. financial account. Therefore, a current account deficit must be exactly offset by a financial account surplus, leaving the balance of payments equal to zero. Similarly, a country that runs a current account surplus, such as China or Japan, must run a financial account deficit of exactly the same size. If a country's current account surplus is not exactly equal to its financial account deficit, or if a country's current account deficit is not exactly equal to its financial account surplus, some transactions must not have been accounted for. The statistical discrepancy is included in the balance of payments to compensate for these uncounted transactions.

Solved Problem 18.1

Understanding the Arithmetic of Open Economies

Test your understanding of the relationship between the current account and the financial account by evaluating the following assertion by a political commentator:

> The industrial countries are committing economic suicide. Every year, they invest more and more in

developing countries. Every year, more U.S., Japanese, and European manufacturing firms move their factories to developing countries. With extensive new factories and low wages, developing countries now export far more to the industrial countries than they import.

Solving the Problem

Step 1: **Review the chapter material.** This problem is about the relationship between the current account and the financial account, so you may want to review the section "Why Is the Balance of Payments Always Zero?" which begins on page 613.

Step 2: **Explain the errors in the commentator's argument.** The argument sounds plausible. It would be easy to find statements similar to this one in recent books and articles by well-known political commentators. But the argument contains an important error: The commentator has failed to understand the relationship between the current account and the financial account. The commentator asserts that developing countries are receiving large capital inflows from industrial countries. In other words, developing countries are running financial account surpluses. The commentator also asserts that developing countries are exporting more than they are importing. In other words, they are running current account surpluses. As we have seen in this section, it is impossible to run a current account surplus *and* a financial account surplus simultaneously. A country that runs a current account surplus *must* run a financial account deficit and vice versa.

Extra Credit: Most emerging economies that have received large inflows of foreign investment during the past two decades, such as South Korea, Thailand, and Malaysia, have run current account deficits: They import more goods and services than they export. Emerging economies, such as Singapore, that run current account surpluses also run financial account deficits: They invest more abroad than other countries invest in them.

The point here is not obvious; if the point was obvious, it wouldn't confuse so many intelligent politicians, journalists, and political commentators. Unless you understand the relationship between the current account and the financial account, you won't be able to understand a key aspect of the international economy.

MyEconLab   **Your Turn:** For more practice, do related problems 1.7, 1.8, and 1.9 on page 632 at the end of this chapter.

The Foreign Exchange Market and Exchange Rates

A firm that operates entirely within the United States will price its products in dollars and will use dollars to pay its suppliers' bills, wages and salaries to its workers, interest to its bondholders, and dividends to its shareholders. A multinational corporation such as McDonald's, in contrast, may sell its products in many different countries and receive payments in many different currencies. Its suppliers and workers may also be spread around the world and may have to be paid in local currencies. Corporations may also use the international financial system to borrow in a foreign currency. For example, during a period of rapid expansion in East Asian countries such as Thailand and South Korea during the late 1990s, many large firms received dollar loans from foreign banks. When firms make extensive use of foreign currencies, they must deal with fluctuations in the exchange rate.

The **nominal exchange rate** is the value of one country's currency in terms of another country's currency. Economists also calculate the *real exchange rate*, which corrects the nominal exchange rate for changes in prices of goods and services. We discuss the real exchange rate later in this chapter. The nominal exchange rate determines how many units of a foreign currency you can purchase with $1. For example, the exchange rate between the U.S. dollar and the Japanese yen can be expressed as ¥100 = $1. (This exchange rate can also be expressed as how many U.S. dollars are required to buy 1 Japanese yen: $0.01 = ¥1.) The market for foreign exchange is very active. Every day, the equivalent of more than $3 trillion worth of currency is traded in the foreign exchange market. The exchange rates that result from this trading are reported on a number of online sites devoted to economic news and in the business or financial sections of most newspapers.

Banks and other financial institutions around the world employ currency traders, who are linked together by computer. Rather than exchange large amounts of paper currency, they buy and sell deposits in banks. A bank buying or selling dollars will actually be buying or selling dollar bank deposits. Dollar bank deposits exist not just in banks in the United States but also in banks around the world. Suppose that the Crédit Agricole bank in France wants to sell U.S. dollars and buy Japanese yen. The bank may exchange U.S. dollar deposits that it owns for Japanese yen deposits owned by the Deutsche Bank in Germany. Businesses and individuals usually obtain foreign currency from banks in their own country.

18.2 LEARNING OBJECTIVE

Explain how exchange rates are determined and how changes in exchange rates affect the prices of imports and exports.

Nominal exchange rate The value of one country's currency in terms of another country's currency.

Making the Connection | Exchange Rate Listings

Many online sites, such as wsj.com, Bloomberg.com, or finance.yahoo.com, as well as the financial pages of most newspapers list the exchange rates between the dollar and other important currencies. The exchange rates in the following table are for October 13, 2011. The euro is the common currency used by 17 European countries, including France, Germany, and Italy.

	Exchange Rate between the Dollar and the Indicated Currency	
Currency	Units of Foreign Currency per U.S. Dollar	U.S. Dollars per Unit of Foreign Currency
Canadian dollar	1.023	0.978
Japanese yen	76.870	0.013
Mexican peso	13.449	0.074
British pound	0.635	1.574
Euro	0.727	1.375

Notice that the expression for the exchange rate stated as units of foreign currency per U.S. dollar is the *reciprocal* of the exchange rate stated as U.S. dollars per unit of

You can find information on exchange rates on many online sites that report economic news and in the financial pages of most newspapers.

foreign currency. So, the exchange rate between the U.S. dollar and the British pound can be stated as either 0.635 British pounds per U.S. dollar or 1/0.635 = 1.574 U.S. dollars per British pound.

Banks are the most active participants in the market for foreign exchange. Typically, banks buy currency for slightly less than the amount for which they sell it. This spread between the buying and selling prices allows banks to cover their expenses from currency trading and to make a profit. Therefore, when most businesses and individuals buy foreign currency from a bank, they receive fewer units of foreign currency per dollar than would be indicated by the exchange rate shown on online business sites or printed in the newspaper.

Based on *Wall Street Journal*, October 13, 2011.

MyEconLab   **Your Turn:** Test your understanding by doing related problem 2.6 on page 633 at the end of this chapter.

The market exchange rate is determined by the interaction of demand and supply, just as other prices are. Let's consider the demand for U.S. dollars in exchange for Japanese yen. There are three sources of foreign currency demand for the U.S. dollar:

1. Foreign firms and households that want to buy goods and services produced in the United States.

2. Foreign firms and households that want to invest in the United States either through foreign direct investment—buying or building factories or other facilities in the United States—or through foreign portfolio investment—buying stocks and bonds issued in the United States.

3. Currency traders who believe that the value of the dollar in the future will be greater than its value today.

Equilibrium in the Market for Foreign Exchange

Figure 18.2 shows the demand and supply of U.S. dollars for Japanese yen. Notice that as we move up the vertical axis in Figure 18.2, the value of the dollar increases relative to the value of the yen. When the exchange rate is ¥150 = $1, the dollar is worth 1.5 times as much relative to the yen as when the exchange rate is ¥100 = $1. Consider, first, the demand curve for dollars in exchange for yen. The demand curve has the normal downward slope. When the value of the dollar is high, the quantity of dollars demanded will be low. A Japanese investor will be more likely to buy a $1,000 bond issued by the U.S. Treasury when the exchange rate is ¥100 = $1 and the investor pays only ¥100,000

Figure 18.2

Equilibrium in the Foreign Exchange Market

When the exchange rate is ¥150 to the dollar, it is above its equilibrium level, and there will be a surplus of dollars. When the exchange rate is ¥100 to the dollar, it is below its equilibrium level, and there will be a shortage of dollars. At an exchange rate of ¥120 to the dollar, the foreign exchange market is in equilibrium.

to buy \$1,000 than when the exchange rate is ¥150 = \$1 and the investor must pay ¥150,000. Similarly, a Japanese firm is more likely to buy \$150 million worth of micro-chips from Intel Corporation when the exchange rate is ¥100 = \$1 and the microchips can be purchased for ¥15 billion than when the exchange rate is ¥150 = \$1 and the microchips cost ¥22.5 billion.

Consider, now, the supply curve of dollars in exchange for yen. The supply curve has the normal upward slope. When the value of the dollar is high, the quantity of dollars supplied in exchange for yen will be high. A U.S. investor will be more likely to buy a ¥200,000 bond issued by the Japanese government when the exchange rate is ¥200 = \$1 and he needs to pay only \$1,000 to buy ¥200,000 than when the exchange rate is ¥100 = \$1 and he must pay \$2,000. The owner of a U.S. electronics store is more likely to buy ¥20 million worth of television sets from the Sony Corporation when the exchange rate is ¥200 = \$1 and she only needs to pay \$100,000 to purchase the televi-sions than when the exchange rate is ¥100 = \$1 and she must pay \$200,000.

As in any other market, equilibrium occurs in the foreign exchange market where the quantity supplied equals the quantity demanded. In Figure 18.2, ¥120 = \$1 is the equilibrium exchange rate. At exchange rates above ¥120 = \$1, there will be a surplus of dollars and downward pressure on the exchange rate. The surplus and the downward pressure will not be eliminated until the exchange rate falls to ¥120 = \$1. If the exchange rate is below ¥120 = \$1, there will be a shortage of dollars and upward pressure on the exchange rate. The shortage and the upward pressure will not be eliminated until the ex-change rate rises to ¥120 = \$1. Surpluses and shortages in the foreign exchange market are eliminated very quickly because the volume of trading in major currencies such as the dollar and the yen is very large, and currency traders are linked together by computer.

Currency appreciation occurs when the market value of a country's currency in-creases relative to the value of another country's currency. **Currency depreciation** oc-curs when the market value of a country's currency decreases relative to the value of another country's currency.

Currency appreciation An increase in the market value of one currency relative to another currency.

Currency depreciation A decrease in the market value of one currency relative to another currency.

How Do Shifts in Demand and Supply Affect the Exchange Rate?

Shifts in the demand and supply curves cause the equilibrium exchange rate to change. Three main factors cause the demand and supply curves in the foreign exchange market to shift:

1. Changes in the demand for U.S.-produced goods and services and changes in the demand for foreign-produced goods and services
2. Changes in the desire to invest in the United States and changes in the desire to in-vest in foreign countries
3. Changes in the expectations of currency traders about the likely future value of the dollar and the likely future value of foreign currencies

Shifts in the Demand for Foreign Exchange Consider how the three factors listed above will affect the demand for U.S. dollars in exchange for Japanese yen. Dur-ing an economic expansion in Japan, the incomes of Japanese households will rise, and the demand by Japanese consumers and firms for U.S. goods will increase. At any given exchange rate, the demand for U.S. dollars will increase, and the demand curve will shift to the right. Similarly, if interest rates in the United States rise, the desirability of invest-ing in U.S. financial assets will increase, and the demand curve for dollars will also shift to the right. **Speculators** are currency traders who buy and sell foreign exchange in an attempt to profit from changes in exchange rates. If a speculator becomes convinced that the value of the dollar is going to rise relative to the value of the yen, the speculator will sell yen and buy dollars. If the current exchange rate is ¥120 = \$1, and the speculator is convinced that it will soon rise to ¥140 = \$1, the speculator could sell ¥600,000,000 and receive \$5,000,000 (= ¥600,000,000/¥120) in return. If the speculator is correct

Speculators Currency traders who buy and sell foreign exchange in an attempt to profit from changes in exchange rates.

and the value of the dollar rises against the yen to ¥140 = $1, the speculator will be able to exchange $5,000,000 for ¥700,000,000 (=$5,000,000 × ¥140), for a profit of ¥100,000,000.

To summarize, the demand curve for dollars shifts to the right when incomes in Japan rise, when interest rates in the United States rise, or when speculators decide that the value of the dollar will rise relative to the value of the yen.

During a recession in Japan, Japanese incomes will fall, reducing the demand for U.S.-produced goods and services and shifting the demand curve for dollars to the left. Similarly, if interest rates in the United States fall, the desirability of investing in U.S. financial assets will decrease, and the demand curve for dollars will shift to the left. Finally, if speculators become convinced that the future value of the dollar will be lower than its current value, the demand for dollars will fall, and the demand curve will shift to the left.

Shifts in the Supply of Foreign Exchange The factors that affect the supply curve for dollars are similar to those that affect the demand curve for dollars. An economic expansion in the United States increases the incomes of Americans and increases their demand for goods and services, including goods and services made in Japan. As U.S. consumers and firms increase their spending on Japanese products, they must supply dollars in exchange for yen, which causes the supply curve for dollars to shift to the right. Similarly, an increase in interest rates in Japan will make financial investments in Japan more attractive to U.S. investors. These higher Japanese interest rates will cause the supply of dollars to shift to the right, as U.S. investors exchange dollars for yen. Finally, if speculators become convinced that the future value of the yen will be higher relative to the dollar than it is today, the supply curve of dollars will shift to the right as traders attempt to exchange dollars for yen.

A recession in the United States will decrease the demand for Japanese products and cause the supply curve for dollars to shift to the left. Similarly, a decrease in interest rates in Japan will make financial investments in Japan less attractive and cause the supply curve of dollars to shift to the left. If traders become convinced that the future value of the yen will be lower relative to the dollar, the supply curve will also shift to the left.

Adjustment to a New Equilibrium The factors that affect the demand and supply for currencies are constantly changing. Whether the exchange rate increases or decreases depends on the direction and size of the shifts in the demand curve and supply curve. For example, as Figure 18.3 shows, if the demand curve for dollars in exchange for Japanese yen shifts to the right by more than the supply curve shifts, the equilibrium exchange rate will increase.

Figure 18.3

Shifts in the Demand and Supply Curve Resulting in a Higher Exchange Rate

Holding other factors constant, an increase in the supply of dollars will decrease the equilibrium exchange rate. An increase in the demand for dollars will increase the equilibrium exchange rate. In the case shown in this figure, the demand curve and the supply curve have both shifted to the right. Because the demand curve has shifted to the right by more than the supply curve, the equilibrium exchange rate has increased from ¥120 to $1 at point A to ¥130 to $1 at point B.

Making the Connection	**What Explains the Fall and Rise and Fall of the Dollar?**

An American vacationing in Paris during the spring of 2002 could have bought a meal for €50 and paid the equivalent of $44 for it. In the summer of 2008, that same €50 meal would have cost the equivalent of $79. A few months later, in early 2009, it would have cost only $64. In the fall of 2011, it would have cost $69. Clearly, during these years, the value of the dollar in exchange for the euro was going through substantial fluctuations. And it wasn't just against the euro that the dollar was losing value, then regaining some of it, and then losing it again. The graph below shows fluctuations for the period from 1990 to late 2011 in an index of the value of the dollar against an average of other major currencies, such as the euro, the British pound, the Canadian dollar, and the Japanese yen. The shaded areas indicate recessions.

The graph indicates that although the dollar gained value against other currencies for a brief period during late 2008 and early 2009, and again during mid-2010, overall it has lost value since 2002. What explains the decline in the value of the dollar? We have just seen that an increase in the demand by foreign investors for U.S. financial assets can increase the value of the dollar, and a decrease in the demand for U.S. financial assets can decrease the value of the dollar. The increase in the value of the dollar in the late 1990s, as shown in the graph, was driven by strong demand from foreign investors for U.S. stocks and bonds, particularly U.S. Treasury securities. This increase in demand was not primarily due to higher U.S. interest rates but to problems in the international financial system that we will discuss in Chapter 19. Many investors saw U.S. financial assets as a safe haven in times of financial problems because the investors believed the U.S. Treasury was unlikely to default on its bonds.

Data from Federal Reserve Bank of St. Louis.

Conditions began to change in 2002, however, for a couple of reasons. First, as we saw in Chapter 15, the Fed began aggressively cutting the target for the federal funds rate to deal with the recession of 2001 and the initially slow recovery that followed. By May 2003, the target for the federal funds rate was at a historically low level of 1 percent. Low U.S. interest rates mean that investors are likely to buy foreign assets rather than U.S. assets, which depresses the demand for dollars and lowers the exchange value of the dollar. Although the Fed did begin raising the target for the federal funds rate in 2004, it resumed cutting the target in the fall of 2007. Low U.S. interest rates have played a role in the declining value of the dollar. Second, many investors and some central banks became convinced that the value of the dollar was too high in 2002 and that it was likely to decline in the future. As we will see later in this chapter, the United States has run large current account deficits since the early 2000s. Many investors believed that the substantial increase in the supply of dollars in exchange for foreign currencies that resulted from these current account deficits would ultimately result in a significant decline in the value of the dollar. Once investors become convinced that the value of a country's currency will decline, they become reluctant to hold that country's financial assets. A decreased willingness by foreign investors to buy U.S. financial assets decreases the demand for dollars and lowers the exchange value of the dollar.

What explains the increase in the value of the dollar in late 2008 and early 2009 and again in mid-2010? The increase was largely the result of the deepening of the financial crisis in the fall of 2008. Just as during the financial crisis of the late 1990s, many investors saw U.S. Treasury securities as a safe haven and demanded dollars in order to invest in them. By the summer of 2009, the easing in the financial crisis resulted in the dollar resuming its decline. Worries that some European governments—particularly Greece—might default on their government bonds caused a temporary increase in the value of the dollar during mid-2010. A smaller increase in the value of the dollar during 2011 caused the problems for McDonald's mentioned in the chapter opener.

The fall in the value of the dollar over the long run has been bad news for U.S. tourists traveling abroad and for anyone in the United States buying foreign goods and services. It has been good news, however, for U.S. firms exporting goods and services to other countries.

MyEconLab **Your Turn:** Test your understanding by doing related problems 2.14 and 2.15 on page 634 at the end of this chapter.

Some Exchange Rates Are Not Determined by the Market

To this point, we have assumed that exchange rates are determined in the market. This assumption is a good one for many currencies, including the U.S. dollar, the euro, the Japanese yen, and the British pound. Some currencies, however, have *fixed exchange rates* that do not change over long periods. For example, for more than 10 years, the value of the Chinese yuan was fixed against the U.S. dollar at a rate of 8.28 yuan to the dollar. As we will discuss in more detail in Chapter 19, a country's central bank has to intervene in the foreign exchange market to buy and sell its currency to keep the exchange rate fixed.

How Movements in the Exchange Rate Affect Exports and Imports

When the market value of the dollar increases, the foreign currency price of U.S. exports rises, and the dollar price of foreign imports falls. For example, suppose that initially the market exchange rate between the U.S. dollar and the euro is $1 = €1. In that case, an Apple iPhone that has a price of $200 in the United States will have a price of €200 in France. A bottle of French wine that has a price of €50 in France will have a price of $50 in the United States. Now suppose the market exchange rate between the U.S. dollar and the euro changes to $1.20 = €1. Because it now takes more dollars to buy a euro, the dollar has *depreciated* against the euro, and the euro has *appreciated* against the dollar. The depreciation of the dollar has decreased the euro price of the iPhone from €200 to $200/(1.20 dollars/euro) = €167. The dollar price of the French wine has risen from $50 to €50 × 1.20 dollars/euro = $60. As a result, we would expect more iPhones to be sold in France and less French wine to be sold in the United States.

To generalize, we can conclude that a depreciation in the domestic currency will increase exports and decrease imports, thereby increasing net exports. As we saw in previous chapters, net exports is a component of aggregate demand. If real GDP is currently below potential GDP, then, holding all other factors constant, a depreciation in the domestic currency should increase net exports, aggregate demand, and real GDP. An appreciation in the domestic currency should have the opposite effect: Exports should fall, and imports should rise, which will reduce net exports, aggregate demand, and real GDP.

Don't Let This Happen to You

Don't Confuse What Happens When a Currency Appreciates with What Happens When It Depreciates

One of the most confusing aspects of exchange rates is that they can be expressed in two ways. We can express the exchange rate between the dollar and the yen either as how many yen can be purchased with $1 or as how many dollars can be purchased with ¥1. That is, we can express the exchange rate as ¥100 = $1 or as $0.01 = ¥1. When a currency appreciates, it increases in value relative to another currency. When it depreciates, it decreases in value relative to another currency.

If the exchange rate changes from ¥100 = $1 to ¥120 = $1, the dollar has appreciated and the yen has depreciated because it now takes more yen to buy $1. If the exchange rate changes from $0.01 = ¥1 to $0.015 = ¥1,

however, the dollar has depreciated and the yen has appreciated because it now takes more dollars to buy ¥1. This situation can appear somewhat confusing because the exchange rate seems to have "increased" in both cases. To determine which currency has appreciated and which has depreciated, it is important to remember that an appreciation of the domestic currency means that it now takes *more* units of the foreign currency to buy one unit of the domestic currency. A depreciation of the domestic currency means it takes *fewer* units of the foreign currency to buy one unit of the domestic currency. This observation holds no matter which way we express the exchange rate.

MyEconLab

Your Turn: Test your understanding by doing related problem 2.5 on page 633 at the end of the chapter.

Solved Problem 18.2

The Effect of Changing Exchange Rates on the Prices of Imports and Exports

In June 2011, the average price of goods imported into the United States from Canada fell 2.1 percent. Is it likely that the value of the U.S. dollar appreciated or depreciated versus the Canadian dollar during this period? Is it likely that the average price in Canadian dollars of goods exported from the United States to Canada during June 2011 rose or fell?

Solving the Problem

Step 1: **Review the chapter material.** This problem is about changes in the value of a currency, so you may want to review the section "How Movements in the Exchange Rate Affect Exports and Imports" on page 620.

Step 2: **Explain whether the value of the U.S. dollar appreciated or depreciated against the Canadian dollar.** We know that if the U.S. dollar appreciates against the Canadian dollar, it will take more Canadian dollars to purchase 1 U.S. dollar, and, equivalently, fewer U.S. dollars will be required to purchase 1 Canadian dollar. A Canadian consumer or business will need to pay more Canadian dollars to buy products imported from the United States: A good or service that had been selling for 100 Canadian dollars will now sell for more than 100 Canadian dollars. A U.S. consumer or business will have to pay fewer U.S. dollars to buy products imported from Canada: A good or service that had been selling for 100 U.S. dollars will now sell for fewer than 100 U.S. dollars. We can conclude that if the price of goods imported into the United States from Canada fell, the value of the U.S. dollar must have appreciated versus the Canadian dollar.

Step 3: **Explain what happened to the average price in Canadian dollars of goods exported from the United States to Canada.** If the U.S. dollar appreciated relative to the Canadian dollar, the average price in Canadian dollars of goods exported from the United States to Canada will have risen.

Your Turn: For more practice, do related problem 2.10 on page 634 at the end of this chapter.   MyEconLab

The Real Exchange Rate

Real exchange rate The price of domestic goods in terms of foreign goods.

We have seen that an important factor in determining the level of a country's exports to and imports from another country is the relative prices of each country's goods. The relative prices of two countries' goods are determined by two factors: the relative price levels in the two countries and the nominal exchange rate between the two countries' currencies. Economists combine these two factors in the **real exchange rate**, which is the price of domestic goods in terms of foreign goods. Recall that the price level is a measure of the average prices of goods and services in an economy. We can calculate the real exchange rate between two currencies as

$$\text{Real exchange rate} = \text{Nominal exchange rate} \times \left(\frac{\text{Domestic price level}}{\text{Foreign price level}} \right).$$

Notice that changes in the real exchange rate reflect both changes in the nominal exchange rate and changes in the relative price levels. For example, suppose that the exchange rate between the U.S. dollar and the British pound is \$1 = £1, the price level in the United States is 100, and the price level in the United Kingdom is also 100. Then the real exchange rate between the dollar and the pound is

$$\text{Real exchange rate} = 1 \text{ pound/dollar} \times \left(\frac{100}{100} \right) = 1.00.$$

Now suppose that the nominal exchange rate increases to 1.1 pounds per dollar, while the price level in the United States rises to 105 and the price level in the United Kingdom remains 100. In this case, the real exchange rate will be

$$\text{Real exchange rate} = 1.1 \text{ pound/dollar} \times \left(\frac{105}{100} \right) = 1.15.$$

The increase in the real exchange rate from 1.00 to 1.15 tells us that the prices of U.S. goods and services are now 15 percent higher than they were relative to British goods and services.

Real exchange rates are reported as index numbers, with one year chosen as the base year. As with the consumer price index, the main value of the real exchange rate is in tracking changes over time—in this case, changes in the relative prices of domestic goods in terms of foreign goods.

18.3 LEARNING OBJECTIVE

Explain the saving and investment equation.

The International Sector and National Saving and Investment

Having studied what determines the exchange rate, we are now ready to explore further the linkages between the U.S. economy and foreign economies. As we saw in Figure 7.1 on page 207, until 1970, U.S. imports and exports were usually 4 percent to 5 percent of GDP. Imports and exports are now two to three times as large a fraction of U.S. GDP. Imports have also consistently been larger than exports, meaning that net exports have been negative.

Net Exports Equal Net Foreign Investment

If your spending is greater than your income, what can you do? You can sell some assets—maybe those 20 shares of stock in the Walt Disney Company your grandparents gave you—or you can borrow money. A firm can be in the same situation: If a firm's costs are greater than its revenues, it has to make up the difference by selling assets or by borrowing. A country is in the same situation when it imports more than it exports: The country must finance the difference by selling assets—such as land, office buildings, or factories—or by borrowing.

In other words, for any country, a current account deficit must be exactly offset by a financial account surplus. When a country sells more assets to foreigners than it buys from foreigners, or when it borrows more from foreigners than it lends to foreigners—as it must if it is running a current account deficit—the country experiences a net capital inflow and a financial account surplus. Remember that net exports is roughly equal to the current account balance. Remember also that the financial account balance is roughly equal to net capital flows, which are in turn equal to net foreign investment but with the opposite sign. To review these two points, look again at Table 18.1 on page 611, which shows that the current account balance is determined mainly by the balance of trade and the balance of services, and the financial account is equal to net capital flows. Also, remember the definition of net foreign investment.

When imports are greater than exports, net exports are negative, and there will be a net capital inflow as people in the United States sell assets and borrow to pay for the surplus of imports over exports. Therefore, net capital flows will be equal to net exports (but with the opposite sign), and net foreign investment will also be equal to net exports (and with the same sign). Because net exports are usually negative for the United States, in most years, the United States must be a net borrower from abroad, and U.S. net foreign investment will be negative.

We can summarize this discussion with the following equations:

$$\text{Current account balance} + \text{Financial account balance} = 0$$

or

$$\text{Current account balance} = -\text{Financial account balance}$$

or

$$\text{Net exports} = \text{Net foreign investment.}$$

This equation tells us, once again, that countries such as the United States that import more than they export must borrow more from abroad than they lend abroad: If net exports are negative, net foreign investment will also be negative by the same amount. Countries such as Japan and China that export more than they import must lend abroad more than they borrow from abroad: If net exports are positive, net foreign investment will also be positive by the same amount.

Domestic Saving, Domestic Investment, and Net Foreign Investment

As we saw in Chapter 10, the total saving in any economy is equal to saving by the private sector plus saving by the government sector, which we called *public saving*. When the government runs a budget surplus by spending less than it receives in taxes, it is saving. When the government runs a budget deficit, public saving is negative. Negative saving is also known as *dissaving*. We can write the following expression for the level of saving in the economy:

$$\text{National saving} = \text{Private saving} + \text{Public saving}$$

or

$$S = S_{\text{private}} + S_{\text{public}}.$$

Private saving is equal to what households have left of their income after spending on consumption goods and paying taxes (for simplicity, we assume that transfer payments are zero):

$$\text{Private saving} = \text{National income} - \text{Consumption} - \text{Taxes}$$

or

$$S_{\text{private}} = Y - C - T.$$

Public saving is equal to the difference between government spending and taxes:

$$\text{Government saving} = \text{Taxes} - \text{Government spending}$$

or

$$S_{\text{public}} = T - G.$$

Finally, remember the basic macroeconomic equation for GDP or national income:

$$Y = C + I + G + NX.$$

We can use this last equation, our definitions of private and public saving, and the fact that net exports equal net foreign investment to arrive at an important relationship, known as the **saving and investment equation**:

Saving and investment equation An equation that shows that national saving is equal to domestic investment plus net foreign investment.

National saving = Domestic investment + Net foreign investment

or

$$S = I + NFI.$$

This equation is an *identity* because it must always be true, given the definitions we have used.

The saving and investment equation tells us that a country's saving will be invested either domestically or overseas. If you save $1,000 and use the funds to buy a bond issued by General Motors, GM may use the $1,000 to renovate a factory in the United States (I) or to build a factory in China (NFI) as a joint venture with a Chinese firm.

Solved Problem 18.3

Arriving at the Saving and Investment Equation

Use the definitions of private and public saving, the equation for GDP or national income, and the fact that net exports must equal net foreign investment to arrive at the saving and investment equation.

Solving the Problem

Step 1: **Review the chapter material.** This problem is about the saving and investment equation, so you may want to review the section "Domestic Saving, Domestic Investment, and Net Foreign Investment," which begins on page 623.

Step 2: **Derive an expression for national saving (S) in terms of national income (Y), consumption (C), and government purchases (G).** We can bring together the four equations we need to use:

1. $S_{\text{private}} = Y - C - T$
2. $S_{\text{public}} = T - G$
3. $Y = C + I + G + NX$
4. $NX = NFI$

Because national saving (S) appears in the saving and investment equation, we need to find an equation for it in terms of the other variables. Adding equation 1 plus equation 2 yields national saving:

$$S = S_{\text{private}} + S_{\text{public}} = (Y - C - T) + (T - G) = Y - C - G.$$

Step 3: **Use the result from Step 2 to derive an expression for national saving in terms of investment (I) and net exports (NX).** Because GDP (Y) does not appear in the saving and investment equation, we need to substitute the expression for it given in equation (3):

$$S = (C + I + G + NX) - C - G$$

and simplify:

$$S = I + NX.$$

Step 4: Use the results of Steps 2 and 3 to derive the saving and investment equation. Finally, substitute net foreign investment for net exports:

$$S = I + NFI.$$

Your Turn: For more practice, do related problem 3.8 on page 635 at the end of this chapter.   MyEconLab

---

A country such as the United States that has negative net foreign investment must be saving less than it is investing domestically. To see this, rewrite the saving and investment equation by moving domestic investment to the left side:

$$S - I = NFI.$$

If net foreign investment is negative—as it is for the United States nearly every year—domestic investment (I) must be greater than national saving (S).

The level of saving in Japan has been well above domestic investment. The result has been high levels of Japanese net foreign investment. For example, Japanese automobile companies Toyota, Honda, and Nissan have all constructed factories in the United States. Sony purchased the Columbia Pictures film studio. Japan has made many similar investments in countries around the world, which has sometimes caused resentment in those countries. There were some protests in the United States in the 1980s, for example, when Japanese investors purchased the Pebble Beach golf course in California and the Rockefeller Center complex in New York City.

Japan needs a high level of net exports to help offset a low level of domestic investment. When exports of a product begin to decline and imports begin to increase, governments are often tempted to impose tariffs or quotas to reduce imports. (See Chapter 7 to review tariffs and quotas and their negative effects on the economy.) In fact, many Japanese firms have been urging the Japanese government to impose trade restrictions on imports from China.

The Effect of a Government Budget Deficit on Investment

18.4 LEARNING OBJECTIVE

Explain the effect of a government budget deficit on investment in an open economy.

The link we have just developed among saving, investment, and net foreign investment can help us understand some of the effects of changes in a government's budget deficit. When the government runs a budget deficit, national saving will decline unless private saving increases by the amount of the budget deficit, which is unlikely. As the saving and investment equation ($S = I + NFI$) shows, the result of a decline in national saving must be a decline in either domestic investment or net foreign investment. Why, though, does an increase in the government budget deficit cause a fall in domestic investment or net foreign investment?

To understand the answer to this question, remember that if the federal government runs a budget deficit, the U.S. Treasury must raise an amount equal to the deficit by selling bonds. To attract investors, the Treasury may have to raise the interest rates on its bonds. As interest rates on Treasury bonds rise, other interest rates, including those on corporate bonds and bank loans, will also rise. Higher interest rates will discourage some firms from borrowing funds to build new factories or to buy new equipment or computers. Higher interest rates on financial assets in the United States will attract foreign investors. Investors in Canada, Japan, or China will have to buy U.S. dollars to be able to purchase bonds in the United States. This greater demand for dollars will increase their value relative to foreign currencies. As the value of the dollar rises, exports from the United States will fall, and imports to the United States will rise. Net exports and, therefore, net foreign investment will fall.

Figure 18.4

The Twin Deficits, 1978–2010

During the early 1980s, large federal budget deficits occurred at the same time as large current account deficits, but twin deficits did not occur in most other periods during these years.

Data from U.S. Bureau of Economic Analysis.

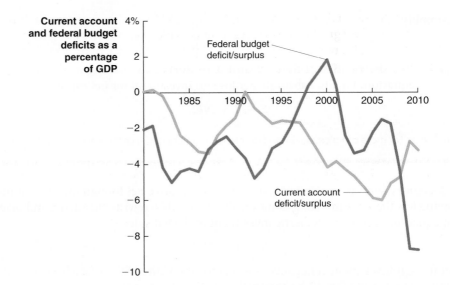

When a government budget deficit leads to a decline in net exports, the result is sometimes referred to as the *twin deficits*, which refers to the possibility that a government budget deficit will also lead to a current account deficit. The twin deficits idea first became widely discussed in the United States during the early 1980s, when the federal government ran a large budget deficit that resulted in high interest rates, a high exchange value of the dollar, and a large current account deficit.

Figure 18.4 shows that in the early 1980s, the United States had large federal budget deficits and large current account deficits. The figure also shows, however, that the twin deficits idea does not match the experience of the United States after 1990. The large federal budget deficits of the early 1990s occurred at a time of relatively small current account deficits, and the budget surpluses of the late 1990s occurred at a time of then-record current account deficits. Both the current account deficit and the federal budget deficit increased in the early 2000s, but the federal budget deficit declined in the mid-2000s much more than did the current account deficit. Beginning in 2008, the federal budget deficit soared, more than doubling as a percentage of GDP, while the current account deficit declined.

The experience of other countries also shows only mixed support for the twin deficits idea. Germany ran large budget deficits and large current account deficits during the early 1990s, but both Canada and Italy ran large budget deficits during the 1980s without running current account deficits. The saving and investment equation shows that an increase in the government budget deficit will not lead to an increase in the current account deficit, provided that either private saving increases or domestic investment declines. According to the twin deficits idea, when the federal government ran budget surpluses in the late 1990s, the current account should also have been in surplus, or at least the current account deficit should have been small. In fact, the increase in national saving due to the budget surpluses was more than offset by a sharp decline in private saving, and the United States ran very large current account deficits.

Making the Connection | **Why Is the United States Called the "World's Largest Debtor"?**

The following graph shows the current account balance as a percentage of GDP for the United States for the period 1950–2010. The United States has had a current account deficit every year since 1982, with the exception of 1991. Between 1950 and 1975, the United States ran a current account deficit in only five years. Many economists believe that the current account deficits of the 1980s were closely related to the federal budget deficits of those years. High interest rates attracted foreign investors to U.S. bonds, which raised the exchange rate between the dollar and foreign currencies. The high exchange rate reduced U.S. exports and increased imports, leading to current account deficits.

Data from U.S. Bureau of Economic Analysis.

As the federal budget deficit narrowed in the mid-1990s and disappeared in the late 1990s, the foreign exchange value of the dollar remained high—and large current account deficits continued—because foreign investors persisted in investing in the United States, despite low interest rates. In the late 1990s, a number of countries around the world, such as South Korea, Indonesia, Brazil, and Russia, suffered severe economic problems. In a process known as a *flight to quality*, many investors sold their investments in those countries and bought investments in the United States. In addition, the strong performance of the U.S. stock market through the spring of 2000 attracted many investors. Finally, the sharp decline in private saving in the United States that began during the late 1990s also contributed to the U.S. current account deficit. The fall in the value of the dollar after 2008 helped reduce the size of the current account deficit, although the deficit still remained substantial.

Do persistent current account deficits represent a problem for the United States? Current account deficits result in U.S. net foreign investment being negative. Each year, foreign investors accumulate many more U.S. assets than U.S. investors accumulate foreign assets. At the end of 2010, foreign investors owned about $2.5 trillion more of U.S. assets—such as stocks, bonds, and factories—than U.S. investors owned of foreign assets, which is why the United States is sometimes called "the world's largest debtor." But the continued willingness of foreign investors to buy U.S. stocks and bonds and foreign companies to build factories in the United States can be seen as a vote of confidence in the strength of the U.S. economy and the buying power of U.S. consumers. When private saving rates declined in the United States to historically low levels in the mid-2000s, only the continued flow of funds from foreign investors made it possible for the United States to maintain the high levels of domestic investment required for economic growth. Beginning in 2009, private saving rates increased, but public saving turned sharply negative as the federal budget deficit soared. Domestic investment in the United States remains reliant on funds from foreign investment.

Your Turn: Test your understanding by doing related problem 4.7 on page 636 at the end of this   MyEconLab
chapter.

18.5 LEARNING OBJECTIVE

Compare the effectiveness of monetary policy and fiscal policy in an open economy and in a closed economy.

Monetary Policy and Fiscal Policy in an Open Economy

When we discussed monetary policy and fiscal policy in Chapters 15 and 16, we did not emphasize that the United States is an open economy. Now that we have explored some of the links among economies, we can look at the difference between how monetary policy and fiscal policy work in an open economy as opposed to in a closed economy. Economists refer to the ways in which monetary policy and fiscal policy affect the domestic economy as *policy channels*. An open economy has more policy channels than does a closed economy.

Monetary Policy in an Open Economy

When the Federal Reserve engages in an expansionary monetary policy, it buys Treasury securities to lower interest rates and stimulate aggregate demand. In a closed economy, the main effect of lower interest rates is on domestic investment spending and purchases of consumer durables. In an open economy, lower interest rates will also affect the exchange rate between the dollar and foreign currencies. Lower interest rates will cause some investors in the United States and abroad to switch from investing in U.S. financial assets to investing in foreign financial assets. This switch will lower the demand for the dollar relative to foreign currencies and cause its value to decline. A lower exchange rate will decrease the price of U.S. products in foreign markets and increase the price of foreign products in the United States. As a result, net exports will increase. This additional policy channel will increase the ability of an expansionary monetary policy to affect aggregate demand.

When the Fed wants to reduce aggregate demand to reduce inflation, it engages in a contractionary monetary policy. The Fed sells Treasury securities to increase interest rates and reduce aggregate demand. In a closed economy, the main effect is once again on domestic investment spending and purchases of consumer durables. In an open economy, higher interest rates will lead to a higher foreign exchange value of the dollar. The prices of U.S. products in foreign markets will increase, and the prices of foreign products in the United States will fall. As a result, net exports will fall. The contractionary policy will have a larger effect on aggregate demand, and therefore it will be more effective in slowing down the growth in economic activity. To summarize: *Monetary policy has a greater effect on aggregate demand in an open economy than in a closed economy.*

Fiscal Policy in an Open Economy

To engage in an expansionary fiscal policy, the federal government increases its purchases or cuts taxes. Increases in government purchases directly increase aggregate demand. Tax cuts increase aggregate demand by increasing household disposable income and business income, which results in increased consumption spending and investment spending. An expansionary fiscal policy may result in higher interest rates. In a closed economy, the main effect of higher interest rates is to reduce domestic investment spending and purchases of consumer durables. In an open economy, higher interest rates will also lead to an increase in the foreign exchange value of the dollar and a decrease in net exports. Therefore, in an open economy, an expansionary fiscal policy may be less effective because the *crowding out effect* may be larger. In a closed economy, only consumption and investment are crowded out by an expansionary fiscal policy. In an open economy, net exports may also be crowded out.

The government can fight inflation by using a contractionary fiscal policy to slow the growth of aggregate demand. A contractionary fiscal policy cuts government purchases or raises taxes to reduce household disposable income and consumption spending. It also reduces the federal budget deficit (or increases the budget surplus), which may lower interest rates. Lower interest rates will increase domestic investment and purchases of consumer durables, thereby offsetting some of the reduction in government spending and increases in taxes. In an open economy, lower interest rates will also reduce the foreign exchange value of the dollar and increase net exports. Therefore, in an open economy, a contractionary fiscal policy will have a smaller effect on aggregate demand and therefore will be less effective in slowing down an economy. In summary: *Fiscal policy has a smaller effect on aggregate demand in an open economy than in a closed economy.*

Continued from page 609

Economics in Your Life

The South Korean Central Bank and Your Car Loan

At the beginning of the chapter, we posed this question: What effect will the Bank of Korea's decision to sell its U.S. Treasury bonds likely have on the interest rate that you pay on your car loan? To sell its holdings of Treasury bonds, South Korea's central bank may have to offer them at a lower price. When the prices of bonds fall, the interest rates on them rise. As the interest rates on U.S. Treasury bonds increase, the interest rates on corporate bonds and bank loans, including car loans, may also increase. So, the decision of the Bank of Korea has the potential to increase the interest rate you pay on your car loan. In practice, the interest rate on your car loan is likely to be affected only if the Bank of Korea sells a very large number of bonds and if investors consider it likely that other foreign central banks may soon do the same thing. The basic point is important, however: Economies are interdependent, and interest rates in the United States are not determined entirely by the actions of people in the United States.

Conclusion

At one time, U.S. policymakers—and economics textbooks—ignored the linkages between the United States and other economies. In the modern world, these linkages have become increasingly important, and economists and policymakers must take them into account when analyzing the economy. In Chapter 19, we will discuss further how the international financial system operates.

Read *An Inside Look* on the next page for a discussion of the falling value of the U.S. dollar against major foreign currencies through the first half of 2011.

Struggling Economy Contributes to a Weak Dollar

U.S. NEWS & WORLD REPORT

What a Weak Dollar Means for Consumers

The value of U.S. currency might seem trivial in the face of soaring gas prices and high unemployment, but the ripple effects of a chronically weak greenback impacts consumers both here and abroad. The U.S. Dollar Index, which tracks a basket of foreign currencies, has fallen almost 5 percent year-to-date. Despite a recent rebound, just last month it tumbled to levels not seen since the worst days of the financial crisis in 2008.

But how did the dollar drop to this point, and more importantly, how much should you worry?

The answer is complicated, but it has much to do with fundamental supply-and-demand dynamics, says Adolfo Laurenti, deputy chief economist at Chicago-based financial services firm Mesirow Financial. Stronger economies tend to attract investors, putting pressure on the supply of that country's currency and driving up its value. "The stronger the country's economy, the more people want to go and invest in that country and the stronger the currency is expected to be," Laurenti says. On the flip side, investors tend to avoid struggling economies, which lessens demand for investment in the country and weakens its currency.

(a) The Federal Reserve's bond buying programs have also had a hand in pushing the dollar lower by driving interest rates to all-time lows. While meant to reduce the cost of borrowing to spur economic growth, low interest rates have stunted yields on financial products such as bonds, reducing demand for investments denominated in dollars and weakening the currency.

"What we're seeing now is that other economies, as they come out of recession faster than we are and [are] experiencing more robust growth than we are, their central banks are starting to tighten and raise interest rates making those countries look more attractive," says J. Bradford Jensen, associate professor of international business and economics at the McDonough School of Business at Georgetown University. "They might sell U.S. dollar-denominated assets to purchase assets in other currencies, which puts downward pressure on the dollar."

(b) The specter of inflation also remains on investors' minds. "The Fed's bond buying created very low interest rates and created fear for many investors that future inflation will go up," Laurenti says. "Higher inflation expectations and lower yields on financial assets tend to bring weaker currency, and that's exactly what we are seeing for the dollar."

(c) But investors aren't the only ones who have to worry about the impact of inflation. Consumers, too, are bound to see the cost of goods inching up if the dollar remains weak. Although weaker currency helps exporters by making U.S.-produced goods more attractive in the global market, it also makes imports more expensive. U.S. companies can only absorb those higher costs for so long before they start passing hikes on to consumers.

"If you buy goods from abroad and their price continues to escalate, sooner or later, those rising costs will need to be offset in the United States by passing higher costs to the consumer," Laurenti says. "That would, in turn, generate higher inflation." Higher inflation erodes the purchasing power of consumers, which could put strain on the U.S. consumer spending-driven economy.

A weak dollar is a double-edged sword, says Axel Merk, founder of Merk Investments and author of *Sustainable Wealth*. U.S. exporters might see a bump in quarterly earnings as a result of a weaker dollar, but the benefits will be short-lived, he says. The fundamental issue, Merk says, is that advanced economies rarely compete on the prices of goods, because they can't. "When you think of low-end consumer goods that compete on price, you think of Vietnam," he says. "We have no chance to compete with Vietnam. We have to compete in high tech. We have to compete on value added."

Key Points in the Article

Through 2011, the Federal Reserve had kept interest rates at historically low levels in an effort to stimulate growth. As a result, the value of the dollar had declined relative to foreign currencies. At the same time, the central banks of some countries that were experiencing faster recoveries from the recession had begun to tighten their monetary policies by raising interest rates. Higher interest rates made those economies more attractive to investors and strengthened their currencies relative to the dollar. If the dollar remains weak, consumers will likely feel the effect in the form of rising prices for imported products. These rising prices will increase the U.S. inflation rate, reducing the purchasing power of consumers.

Analyzing the News

a In an effort to boost economic growth in the United States, the Federal Reserve has purchased very large quantities of Treasury bonds, which has helped to push U.S. interest rates to record low levels. The low interest rates have lowered the demand for dollar-denominated investments. A decrease in the demand for U.S. financial assets by foreign investors decreases the demand for U.S. dollars, which in turn decreases the dollar's value against foreign currencies. Figure 1 below shows movements in the value of the dollar since 2002. The index used to measure the value of the dollar is an average of the exchange rates between the dollar and the currencies of major trading partners of the United States. Beginning in 2002, the dollar has declined gradually over time, rising in 2008 and 2009, and then declining again through the middle of 2011.

b As you read in this chapter, lower interest rates result in a decline in the demand for financial assets by foreign investors. Figure 2 shows the exchange rate between the dollar and the euro. A decrease in the demand for U.S. assets by foreign investors causes a decrease in the demand for dollars in exchange for euros, so that the demand curve for the dollar shifts from D_1 to D_2. As a result, the exchange rate falls from €0.80 per \$1 to €0.75 per \$1. The low interest rates resulting from the Fed's bond-buying programs also have some investors concerned about the possibility that the U.S. inflation rate will increase in the future. Expectations of higher inflation combined with lower yields on financial securities have the potential to weaken the value of a currency relative to other currencies. Adolfo Laurenti of the financial services company Mesirow Financial believes this is what has happened to the U.S. dollar.

c Concerns about rising inflation can affect consumers as well as investors. A weak dollar makes imports more expensive in the United States. If the dollar remains weak, U.S. companies that sell imported products and those that use imports in the manufacture of products will likely need to pass these higher costs along to U.S. consumers by raising prices. The result would be higher inflation and reduced consumer purchasing power.

Thinking Critically

1. How would a decrease in the value of the U.S. dollar relative to other currencies affect future U.S. trade deficits?
2. Suppose the value of the U.S. dollar increased. Which sectors of the U.S. economy would benefit from such an adjustment? Briefly explain.

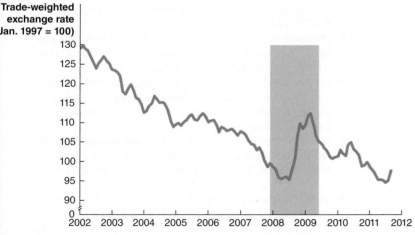

Figure 1

The weak U.S. economy led to a decline of the U.S. dollar. The shaded area indicates a recession.
Data from Trade weighted exchange index, St. Louis Federal Reserve; and Board of Governors of the Federal Reserve System.

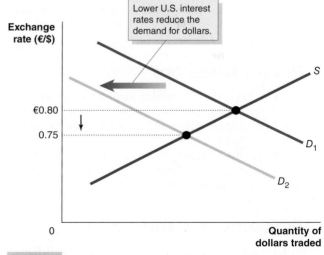

Figure 2

Lower interest rates reduce the value of the dollar against the euro.

Chapter Summary and Problems

Key Terms

Balance of payments, p. 610

Balance of trade, p. 610

Capital account, p. 612

Closed economy, p. 610

Currency appreciation, p. 617

Currency depreciation, p. 617

Current account, p. 610

Financial account, p. 611

Net foreign investment, p. 612

Nominal exchange rate, p. 615

Open economy, p. 610

Real exchange rate, p. 622

Saving and investment equation, p. 624

Speculators, p. 617

18.1 The Balance of Payments: Linking the United States to the International Economy, pages 610–614

LEARNING OBJECTIVE: Explain how the balance of payments is calculated.

Summary

Nearly all economies are **open economies** that trade with and invest in other economies. A **closed economy** has no transactions in trade or finance with other economies. The **balance of payments** is the record of a country's trade with other countries in goods, services, and assets. The **current account** records a country's net exports, net investment income, and net transfers. The **financial account** shows investments a country has made abroad and foreign investments received by the country. The **balance of trade** is the difference between the value of the goods a country exports and the value of the goods a country imports. **Net foreign investment** is the difference between capital outflows from a country and capital inflows. The **capital account** is a part of the balance of payments that records relatively minor transactions. Apart from measurement errors, the sum of the current account and the financial account must equal zero. Therefore, the balance of payments must also equal zero.

 MyEconLab   Visit www.myeconlab.com to complete these exercises online and get instant feedback.

Review Questions

1.1 What is the relationship among the current account, the financial account, and the balance of payments?

1.2 What is the difference between net exports and the current account balance?

1.3 Explain whether you agree with the following statement: "The United States has run a balance of payments deficit every year since 1982."

Problems and Applications

1.4 In 2010, France had a current account deficit of €41.0 billion (approximately $54.4 billion). Did France experience a net capital outflow or a net capital inflow during 2010? Briefly explain.

1.5 Use the information in the following table to prepare a balance of payments account, like the one shown in Table 18.1 on page 611. Assume that the balance on the capital account is zero.

Increase in foreign holdings of assets in the United States	$1,181
Exports of goods	856
Imports of services	−256
Statistical discrepancy	?
Net transfers	−60
Exports of services	325
Income received on investments	392
Imports of goods	−1,108
Increase in U.S. holdings of assets in foreign countries	−1,040
Income payments on investments	−315

1.6 **[Related to the** Don't Let This Happen to You **on page 613]** In 2010, Germany had a trade surplus of $204 billion and a current account balance of $188 billion. Explain how Germany's current account surplus could be smaller than its trade surplus. In 2010, would we expect that Germany's balance on financial account would have been −$188 billion? Briefly explain.

1.7 **[Related to** Solved Problem 18.1 **on page 614]** Is it possible for a country to run a trade deficit and a financial account deficit simultaneously? Briefly explain.

1.8 **[Related to** Solved Problem 18.1 **on page 614]** Suppose we know that a country has been receiving large inflows of foreign investment. What can we say about the country's current account balance?

1.9 **[Related to** Solved Problem 18.1 **on page 614]** The United States ran a current account surplus every year during the 1960s. What must have been true about the U.S. financial account balance during those years?

1.10 The only year since 1982 that the United States has run a current account surplus was 1991. In that year, Japan made a large payment to the United States to help pay for the Gulf War. Explain the connection between these two facts. (*Hint:* Where would Japan's payment to the United States appear in the balance of payments?)

1.11 According to this chapter, the U.S. trade deficit is almost always larger than the U.S. current account deficit. Why is this true?

1.12 An article in the *New York Times* observes that, "China is quickly shifting from being a country known for exports to one capable of making huge investments in global financial markets, analysts say." Is there a connection between China's exports and its financial investments in other countries? Your answer should mention China's current account and its financial account.

From David Barboza, "China's Growing Overseas Portfolio," *New York Times*, May 9, 2011.

 18.2 **The Foreign Exchange Market and Exchange Rates,** pages 615–622

LEARNING OBJECTIVE: Explain how exchange rates are determined and how changes in exchange rates affect the prices of imports and exports.

Summary

The **nominal exchange rate** is the value of one country's currency in terms of another country's currency. The exchange rate is determined in the foreign exchange market by the demand and supply of a country's currency. Changes in the exchange rate are caused by shifts in demand or supply. The three main sets of factors that cause the supply and demand curves in the foreign exchange market to shift are changes in the demand for U.S.-produced goods and services and changes in the demand for foreign-produced goods and services; changes in the desire to invest in the United States and changes in the desire to invest in foreign countries; and changes in the expectations of currency traders—particularly **speculators**—concerning the likely future values of the dollar and the likely future values of foreign currencies. **Currency appreciation** occurs when a currency's market value increases relative to another currency. **Currency depreciation** occurs when a currency's market value decreases relative to another currency. The **real exchange rate** is the price of domestic goods in terms of foreign goods. The real exchange rate is calculated by multiplying the nominal exchange rate by the ratio of the domestic price level to the foreign price level.

MyEconLab Visit **www.myeconlab.com** to complete these exercises online and get instant feedback.

Review Questions

2.1 If the exchange rate between the Japanese yen and the U.S. dollar expressed in terms of yen per dollar is ¥75 = $1, what is the exchange rate when expressed in terms of dollars per yen?

2.2 Suppose that the current exchange rate between the dollar and the euro is €0.7 = $1. If the exchange rate changes to €0.8 = $1, has the euro appreciated or depreciated against the dollar?

2.3 Why do foreign households and foreign firms demand U.S. dollars in exchange for foreign currency? Why do U.S. households and U.S. firms supply U.S. dollars in exchange for foreign currency?

2.4 What are the three main sets of factors that cause the supply and demand curves in the foreign exchange market to shift?

Problems and Applications

2.5 [Related to the Don't Let This Happen to You **on page 621**] If we know the exchange rate between Country A's currency and Country B's currency and we know the exchange rate between Country B's currency and Country C's currency, then we can compute the exchange rate between Country A's currency and Country C's currency.

a. Suppose the exchange rate between the Japanese yen and the U.S. dollar is currently ¥75 = $1 and the exchange rate between the British pound and the U.S. dollar is £0.62 = $1. What is the exchange rate between the yen and the pound?

b. Suppose the exchange rate between the yen and dollar changes to ¥85 = $1 and the exchange rate between the pound and dollar changes to £0.55 = $1. Has the dollar appreciated or depreciated against the yen? Has the dollar appreciated or depreciated against the pound? Has the yen appreciated or depreciated against the pound?

2.6 [Related to the Making the Connection **on page 615**] In January 1, 2002, there were 15 member countries in the European Union. Twelve of those countries eliminated their own individual currencies and began using a new common currency, the euro. For a three-year period from January 1, 1999, through December 31, 2001, these 12 countries priced goods and services in terms of both their own currencies and the euro. During that period, the value of their currencies was fixed against each other and against the euro. So during that time, the dollar had an exchange rate against each of these currencies and against the euro. The information in the following table shows the fixed exchange rates of four European currencies against the euro and their exchange rates against the U.S. dollar on March 2, 2001. Use the information below to calculate the exchange rate between the dollar and the euro (in euros per dollar) on March 2, 2001.

Currency	Units per Euro (fixed)	Units per U.S. Dollar (as of March 2, 2001)
German mark	1.9558	2.0938
French franc	6.5596	7.0223
Italian lira	1,936.2700	2,072.8700
Portuguese escudo	200.4820	214.6300

2.7 Graph the demand and supply of U.S. dollars for euros and label each axis. Show graphically and explain the effect of an increase in interest rates in Europe by the European Central Bank (ECB) on the demand and supply of dollars and the resulting change in the exchange rate of euros for U.S. dollars.

2.8 Graph the demand and supply of U.S. dollars for euros and label each axis. Suppose that higher federal budget deficits result in higher U.S. interest rates. Use your graph to show the effect higher U.S. interest rates on the demand and supply of dollars and the resulting change in the exchange rate of euros for U.S. dollars. Why might the change in the exchange rate lead to a current account deficit?

2.9 Use the graph to answer the following questions.

a. Briefly explain whether the dollar appreciated or depreciated against the yen.

b. Which of the following events could have caused the shift in demand shown in the graph?
   i. Interest rates in the United States have declined.
   ii. Income rises in Japan.
   iii. Speculators begin to believe the value of the dollar will be higher in the future.

2.10 **[Related to** Solved Problem 18.2 **on page 621]** When a country's currency appreciates, is this generally good news or bad news for the country's consumers? Is it generally good news or bad news for the country's businesses? Explain your reasoning.

2.11 An article about U.S. wheat exports is titled "Wheat Gains as Export Demand May Rise on Dollar Drop..."
   a. What does the title mean by a "dollar drop"?
   b. Why would the dollar's drop increase the demand for U.S. wheat exports?

   From Whitney McFerron, "Wheat Gains as Export Demand May Rise on Dollar Drop, EU Rain," www.businessweek.com, October 27, 2011.

2.12 **[Related to the** Chapter Opener **on page 609]** An article describing global sales for McDonald's contains the following information: "However, global sales in dollar

terms declined 4.6 per cent for the month, but would have increased 3.2 per cent in constant currencies."
   a. What does the article mean by "constant currencies"?
   b. If global sales for McDonald's declined in dollar terms but would have risen in constant currencies, what must have happened during this period to the value of the dollar in exchange for other currencies? Briefly explain.

   From Jonathan Birchall, "Strong Sales to Hit McDonald's Profits," *Financial Times*, July 27, 2011.

2.13 The following is from an article from Reuters:

   The dollar rallied broadly for its best day in more than a month on Thursday and the euro tumbled to an eight-month low as mounting concerns about the global economy drove investors to seek safety and liquidity.

   What assets were investors purchasing to seek safety and liquidity, and why did the purchases lead to a dollar rally?

   From Gertrude Chavez-Dreyfuss, "Dollar Gains as Global Gloom Spurs Flight to Safety," Reuters.com, September 23, 2011.

2.14 **[Related to the** Making the Connection **on page 619]** The humorist Dave Barry once wrote the following: "In economic news, the Federal Reserve Board, responding to recession fears and the continued weakening of the dollar, votes unanimously to be paid in euros." Granted that Barry was joking, what advantages would there be to U.S. citizens being paid in euros at a time when the dollar was "weakening"? Why did the dollar lose value against most other currencies beginning in 2002?

   From Dave Barry, *Dave Barry's History of the Millenium (So Far)*, (New York: Berkeley Books, 2008), pp. 230–231.

2.15 **[Related to the** Making the Connection **on page 619]** The following is from an article in the *Wall Street Journal*:

   [Peter] Schiff's Darien, Conn., broker-dealer firm, Euro Pacific Capital Inc., advised its clients to bet that the dollar would weaken significantly and that foreign stocks would outpace their U.S. peers. Instead, the dollar advanced against most currencies, magnifying the losses from foreign stocks Mr. Schiff steered his investors into.

   What does it mean to say that "the dollar advanced against most currencies"? Why would this advance magnify the losses to U.S. investors from investing in foreign stocks?

   From Scott Patterson, Joanna Slater, and Craig Karmin, "Right Forecast by Schiff, Wrong Plan?" *Wall Street Journal*, January 30, 2009.

18.3 **The International Sector and National Saving and Investment,** pages 622–625

LEARNING OBJECTIVE: Explain the saving and investment equation.

Summary

A current account deficit must be exactly offset by a financial account surplus. The financial account is equal to net capital flows, which is equal to net foreign investment but with the opposite sign. Because the current account balance is roughly equal to net

exports, we can conclude that net exports will equal net foreign investment. National saving is equal to private saving plus government saving. Private saving is equal to national income minus consumption and minus taxes. Government saving is the difference between taxes and government spending. As we saw in previous chapters, GDP (or national income) is equal to the sum of investment, consumption, government spending, and net exports. We can use this fact, our definitions of private and government saving, and the fact that net exports equal net foreign investment to arrive at an important relationship known as the **saving and investment equation**: $S = I + NFI$.

Review Questions

3.1 Explain the relationship between net exports and net foreign investment.

3.2 What is the saving and investment equation? If national saving declines, what will happen to domestic investment and net foreign investment?

3.3 If a country saves more than it invests domestically, what must be true of its net foreign investment?

Problems and Applications

3.4 Writing in the *Wall Street Journal*, David Wessel makes the following observation:

> Trend one: The U.S. has been buying more than $1 billion a day more from the rest of the world than it has been selling.... Trend two: Foreigners have been investing more than $1 billion a day of their savings in U.S. stocks, bonds, office towers, factories, and companies.

Is it coincidence that both of Wessel's "trends" involve $1 billion per day? Briefly explain.

"Pain from the Dollar's Decline Will Mostly Be Felt Overseas," by David Wessel from *Wall Street Journal*, June 13, 2002. Copyright © 2011 by Dow Jones & Company, Inc. Reproduced with permission of Dow Jones & Company, Inc.

3.5 In 2010, domestic investment in Japan was 20.6 percent of GDP, and Japanese net foreign investment was 1.3 percent of GDP. What percentage of GDP was Japanese national saving?

3.6 In 2010, France's net foreign investment was negative. Which was larger in France in 2010: national saving or domestic investment? Briefly explain.

3.7 Briefly explain whether you agree with the following statement: "Because in 2010 national saving was a smaller percentage of GDP in the United States than in the United Kingdom, domestic investment must also have been a smaller percentage of GDP in the United States than in the United Kingdom."

3.8 **[Related to** Solved Problem 18.3 **on page 624]** Look again at Solved Problem 18.3, in which we derived the saving and investment equation $S = I + NX$. In deriving this equation, we assumed that national income was equal to Y. But Y only includes income *earned* by households. In the modern U.S. economy, households receive substantial transfer payments—such as Social Security payments and unemployment insurance payments—from the government. Suppose that we define national income as being equal to $Y + TR$, where TR equals government transfer payments, and we also define government spending as being equal to $G + TR$. Show that after making these adjustments, we end up with the same saving and investment equation.

3.9 Use the saving and investment equation to explain why the United States experienced large current account deficits in the late 1990s.

3.10 Former congressman and presidential candidate Richard Gephardt once proposed that tariffs be imposed on imports from countries with which the United States has a trade deficit. If this proposal were enacted and if it were to succeed in reducing the U.S. current account deficit to zero, what would be the likely effect on domestic investment spending within the United States? Assume that no other federal government economic policy is changed. (*Hint*: Use the saving and investment equation to answer this question.)

3.11 According to a May 2009 article from *Reuters*:

> Net capital inflows into the United States were $23.2 billion in March, reversing a revised net outflow of $91.1 billion in the previous month.... It shows that money was returning into U.S. dollars.... The dollar extended gains against the euro, which last traded down 0.5 percent at $1.3572.

From the U.S. point of view, do the changes mentioned in the first sentence represent an increase or a decrease in net foreign investment? Why would this change in net foreign investment show that "money was returning into U.S. dollars" and cause the exchange value of the dollar to rise?

"U.S. Net Capital Inflows for March at $23.2 Billion," by Wanfeng Zhou from *Reuters*, May 15, 2009. All rights reserved. Republication or redistribution of Thomson Reuters content, including by framing or similar means, is expressly prohibited without the prior written consent of Thomson Reuters. Thomson Reuters and its logo are registered trademarks of the Thomson Reuters group of companies around the world. Copyright © 2011 by Thomson Reuters. Thomson Reuters journalists are subject to an Editorial Handbook which requires fair presentation and disclosure of relevant interests.

18.4 | **The Effect of a Government Budget Deficit on Investment,** pages 625–627

LEARNING OBJECTIVE: Explain the effect of a government budget deficit on investment in an open economy.

Summary

When the government runs a budget deficit, national saving will decline unless private saving increases by the full amount of the budget deficit, which is unlikely. As the saving and investment equation ($S = I + NFI$) shows, the result of a decline in national saving must be a decline in either domestic investment or net foreign investment.

Review Questions

4.1 What happens to national saving when the government runs a budget surplus? What is the twin deficits idea?

Did it hold for the United States in the 1990s? Briefly explain.

4.2 Why were the early and mid-1980s particularly difficult times for U.S. exporters?

4.3 Why is the United States sometimes called the "World's largest debtor"?

Problems and Applications

4.4 Tim Condon, an economist at the European bank ING, was quoted in the *Wall Street Journal* in 2011 as predicting that "China's current account or saving-investment surplus [will be in] the 1–2% of GDP range…" Is he correct in referring to China's current account as being the same as its saving-investment surplus? Briefly explain. If the Chinese government runs a large budget deficit, what will be the likely effect on its current account?

From Josh Chin, "Economists React: Chinese Imports Way Up in August," *Wall Street Journal*, September 12, 2011.

4.5 According to an article in the *Wall Street Journal*:

Economists at China International Capital Corp., or CICC, say the companies that will suffer most from a stronger yuan are textile and apparel makers and office equipment

producers…. That could also mean a sting for clothing retailers such as Wal-Mart Stores Inc. that buy a lot from China….

a. Does a "stronger yuan" mean that the yuan will exchange for more or fewer dollars?

b. How can both Chinese companies, such as apparel makers, and foreign companies, such as Wal-Mart and Carrefour, be hurt by a stronger yuan?

c. What effect will a stronger yuan be likely to have on the Chinese current account? What effect is it likely to have on the U.S. current account?

From Jason Dean, Norihiko Shirouzu, Clare Ansberry and Kersten Zhang, "Yuan Impact: General Manufacturing," *Wall Street Journal*, June 21, 2010.

4.6 The text states, "The budget surpluses of the late 1990s occurred at a time of then-record current account deficits." Holding everything else constant, what would the likely impact have been on domestic investment in the United States if the current account had been balanced instead of being in deficit?

4.7 **[Related to the** Making the Connection **on page 626]** Why might "the continued willingness of foreign investors to buy U.S. stocks and bonds and foreign companies to build factories in the United States" result in the United States running a current account deficit?

18.5 **Monetary Policy and Fiscal Policy in an Open Economy,** pages 628–629

LEARNING OBJECTIVE: Compare the effectiveness of monetary policy and fiscal policy in an open economy and in a closed economy.

Summary

When the Federal Reserve engages in an expansionary monetary policy, it buys government bonds to lower interest rates and increase aggregate demand. In a closed economy, the main effect of lower interest rates is on domestic investment spending and purchases of consumer durables. In an open economy, lower interest rates will also cause an increase in net exports. When the Fed wants to slow the rate of economic growth to reduce inflation, it engages in a contractionary monetary policy. With a contractionary policy, the Fed sells government bonds to increase interest rates and reduce aggregate demand. In a closed economy, the main effect is once again on domestic investment and purchases of consumer durables. In an open economy, higher interest rates will also reduce net exports. We can conclude that monetary policy has a greater impact on aggregate demand in an open economy than in a closed economy. To engage in an expansionary fiscal policy, the government increases government spending or cuts taxes. An expansionary fiscal policy can lead to higher interest rates. In a closed economy, the main effect of higher interest rates is on domestic investment spending and spending on consumer durables. In an open economy, higher interest rates will also reduce net exports. A contractionary fiscal policy will reduce the budget deficit and may lower interest rates. In a closed economy, lower interest rates increase domestic investment and spending on consumer durables.

In an open economy, lower interest rates also increase net exports. We can conclude that fiscal policy has a smaller impact on aggregate demand in an open economy than in a closed economy.

 MyEconLab Visit **www.myeconlab.com** to complete these exercises online and get instant feedback.

Review Questions

5.1 What is meant by a "policy channel"?

5.2 Why does monetary policy have a greater effect on aggregate demand in an open economy than in a closed economy?

5.3 Why does fiscal policy have a smaller effect on aggregate demand in an open economy than in a closed economy?

Problems and Applications

5.4 An article in the *Economist* magazine describes Ireland as "an extraordinarily open economy." Is fiscal policy in Ireland likely to be more or less effective than it would be in a less open economy? Briefly explain.

From "Celtic Cross," *Economist*, May 26, 2011.

5.5 Suppose that Federal Reserve policy leads to higher interest rates in the United States.
  a. How will this policy affect real GDP in the short run if the United States is a closed economy?
  b. How will this policy affect real GDP in the short run if the United States is an open economy?
  c. How will your answer to part b. change if interest rates also rise in the countries that are the major trading partners of the United States?

5.6 An economist remarks, "In the 1960s, fiscal policy would have been a better way to stabilize the economy, but now I believe that monetary policy is better." What has changed about the U.S. economy that might have led the economist to this conclusion?

5.7 Suppose the federal government increases spending without also increasing taxes. In the short run, how will this action affect real GDP and the price level in a closed economy? How will the effects of this action differ in an open economy?

Chapter Outline and Learning Objectives

Airbus Deals with Fluctuating Exchange Rates

In 1967, France, Germany, and the United Kingdom formed Airbus as a firm to develop and manufacture passenger aircraft. The new firm was formally organized as a manufacturing subsidiary of the European Aeronautic Defense and Space Company (EADS), located in France. The first Airbus plane, the A300, was introduced at the Paris Air Show in 1969. Over the following decades, Airbus manufactured more than 6,000 passenger aircraft and sold them to airlines around the world.

In October 2009, Airbus delivered its first A380 super-jumbo jetliner to Air France. Although the sale was cause for celebration among Airbus executives, it had a downside. Even though Airbus is a European firm and Air France is a European airline, the worldwide aerospace industry conducts business in U.S. dollars. Because Airbus received dollars from Air France rather than euros, Airbus had to convert the dollars it received into euros. Between 2001, when Air France agreed to buy 10 A380 jetliners from Airbus, and 2009, the exchange value of the euro increased by about 60 percent against the U.S. dollar—or, in other words, the value of the dollar had decreased against the euro. Therefore, when Airbus converted the dollars it received from Air France into euros, it received many fewer euros than it would have if the value of the dollar hadn't declined against the euro.

Airbus's main competitor is Boeing, which conducts its buying and selling in dollars. As a result, Boeing is not subject to losses resulting from fluctuations in exchange rates. Unlike Airbus, Air France has suffered less from exchange rate changes because it receives much of its revenue in euros, while the costs of planes, fuel, and other inputs purchased by Air France are priced in dollars. So, an increase in the value of the euro against the dollar increases Air France's profits.

In 2011, EADS announced that its first-half profits decreased by 41 percent due to the appreciation of the euro relative to the U.S. dollar. As a result, Airbus announced that it was considering pricing its aircraft in euros.

In this chapter, we will look more closely at the international financial system and at what determines fluctuations in exchange rates. **AN INSIDE LOOK AT POLICY** on **page 656** discusses a bill that the U.S. Senate passed to raise tariffs on Chinese imports in response to claims that the Chinese yuan was undervalued.

Based on Daniel Michaels, "Strong Euro Weighs on Airbus, Suppliers," *Wall Street Journal*, October 30, 2009; and David Pearson, "EADS Hit By Currency Swings," *Wall Street Journal*, July 29, 2011.

Economics in Your Life

Exchange Rate Risk in Your Life

Suppose that you decide to take a job in Spain. You plan to work there for the next 10 years, build up some savings, and then return to the United States. As you prepare for your move, you read that economists expect the average productivity of Spanish firms to grow faster than the average productivity of U.S. firms over the next 10 years. If economists are correct, then, all else being equal, will the savings that you accumulate (in euros) be worth more or less in U.S. dollars than it would have been worth without the relative gains in Spanish productivity? As you read this chapter, see if you can answer this question. You can check your answer against the one we provide on **page 655** at the end of this chapter.

A key fact about the international economy is that exchange rates among the major currencies fluctuate. These fluctuations have important consequences for firms, consumers, and governments. In Chapter 18, we discussed the basics of how exchange rates are determined. We also looked at the relationship between a country's imports and exports, as well as at capital flows into and out of a country. In this chapter, we will look further at the international financial system and at the role central banks play in the system.

Understand how different exchange rate systems operate.

Floating currency The outcome of a country allowing its currency's exchange rate to be determined by demand and supply.

Exchange rate system An agreement among countries about how exchange rates should be determined.

Managed float exchange rate system The current exchange rate system, under which the value of most currencies is determined by demand and supply, with occasional government intervention.

Fixed exchange rate system A system under which countries agree to keep the exchange rates among their currencies fixed for long periods.

Exchange Rate Systems

A country's exchange rate can be determined in several ways. Some countries simply allow the exchange rate to be determined by demand and supply, just as other prices are. A country that allows demand and supply to determine the value of its currency is said to have a **floating currency**. Some countries attempt to keep the exchange rate between their currency and another currency constant. For example, China kept the exchange rate constant between its currency, the yuan, and the U.S. dollar, from 1994 until 2005, when it announced it would allow greater exchange rate flexibility. When countries can agree on how exchange rates should be determined, economists say that there is an **exchange rate system**. Currently, many countries, including the United States, allow their currencies to float most of the time, although they occasionally intervene to buy and sell their currency or other currencies to affect exchange rates. In other words, many countries attempt to *manage* the float of their currencies. As a result, the current exchange rate system is a **managed float exchange rate system**.

Historically, the two most important alternatives to the managed float exchange rate system were the *gold standard* and the *Bretton Woods system*. These were both **fixed exchange rate systems**, where exchange rates remained constant for long periods. Under the gold standard, a country's currency consisted of gold coins and paper currency that the government was committed to redeem for gold. When countries agree to keep the value of their currencies constant, there is a fixed exchange rate system. The gold standard was a fixed exchange rate system that lasted from the nineteenth century until the 1930s.

Under the gold standard, exchange rates were determined by the relative amounts of gold in each country's currency, and the size of a country's money supply was determined by the amount of gold available. To rapidly expand its money supply during a war or an economic depression, a country would need to abandon the gold standard. In response to the Great Depression, by the mid-1930s, most countries, including the United States, had abandoned the gold standard. Although during the following decades there were occasional discussions about restoring the gold standard, no serious attempt to do so occurred.

A conference held in Bretton Woods, New Hampshire, in 1944 set up an exchange rate system in which the United States pledged to buy or sell gold at a fixed price of $35 per ounce. The central banks of all other members of the new Bretton Woods system pledged to buy and sell their currencies at a fixed rate against the dollar. By fixing their exchange rates against the dollar, these countries were fixing the exchange rates among their currencies as well. Unlike under the gold standard, neither the United States nor any other country was willing to redeem its paper currency for gold domestically. The United States would redeem dollars for gold only if they were presented by a foreign central bank. Fixed exchange rate regimes can run into difficulties because exchange rates are not free to adjust quickly to changes in demand and supply for currencies. As we will see in the next section, central banks often encounter difficulty if they are required to keep an exchange rate fixed over a period of years. By the early 1970s, the difficulty of keeping exchange rates fixed led to the end of the Bretton Woods system. The appendix to this chapter contains additional discussion about the gold standard and the Bretton Woods system.

Don't Let This Happen to You

Remember That Modern Currencies Are Fiat Money

Although the United States has not been on the gold standard since 1933, many people still believe that somehow gold continues to "back" U.S. currency. The U.S. Department of the Treasury still owns billions of dollars worth of gold bars, most of which are stored at the Fort Knox Bullion Depository in Kentucky. (Even more gold is stored in a basement of the Federal Reserve Bank of New York, which holds about one-quarter of the world's gold supply—almost 10 percent of all the gold ever mined. This gold, however, is entirely owned by foreign governments and international agencies.) The gold in Fort Knox no longer has any connection to the amount of paper money issued by the Federal Reserve. As we saw in Chapter 14, U.S. currency—like the currencies of other countries—is *fiat money*, which means it has no value except as money. The link between gold and money that existed for centuries has been broken in modern economies.

MyEconLab

Your Turn: Test your understanding by doing related problem 1.3 on page 658 at the end of this chapter.

The Current Exchange Rate System

The current exchange rate system has three important aspects:

1. The United States allows the dollar to float against other major currencies.
2. Seventeen countries in Europe have adopted a single currency, the **euro**.
3. Some developing countries have attempted to keep their currencies' exchange rates fixed against the dollar or another major currency.

We begin our discussion of the current exchange rate system by looking at the changing value of the dollar over time. In discussing the value of the dollar, we can look further at what determines exchange rates in the short run and in the long run.

19.2 LEARNING OBJECTIVE

Discuss the three key features of the current exchange rate system.

Euro The common currency of many European countries.

The Floating Dollar

Since 1973, the value of the U.S. dollar has fluctuated widely against other major currencies. Panel (a) of Figure 19.1 shows the exchange rate between the U.S. dollar and the Canadian dollar between January 1973 and October 2011, and panel (b) shows the

Figure 19.1   **Candian Dollar–U.S. Dollar and Yen–U.S. Dollar Exchange Rates, 1973–2011**

Panel (a) shows that from the end of the Bretton Woods system in 1973 through October 2011, the U.S. dollar gained slightly in value against the Canadian dollar. Panel (b) shows that during the same period, the U.S. dollar lost value against the Japanese yen.

Data from Federal Reserve Board of Governors.

exchange rate between the U.S. dollar and the Japanese yen for the same period. Remember that the dollar increases in value when it takes more units of foreign currency to buy $1, and it falls in value when it takes fewer units of foreign currency to buy $1. From January 1973 to October 2011, the U.S. dollar lost more than 74 percent in value against the yen, while it gained about 2 percent in value against the Canadian dollar.

In 2011, many individual Canadians purchased second homes in Arizona, thanks to the favorable exchange rate.

Making the Connection | The Canadian Province of . . . Arizona?

In 2011, there seemed to be a lot of Canadians buying houses in Phoenix and other cities in Arizona. For many years, some Canadians have found buying a second home in Arizona or Florida a good way to avoid the harsh Canadian winters. As Figure 19.1 shows, the value of the U.S. dollar has been declining relative to the Canadian dollar for most of the period since 2000. Although the value of the U.S. dollar soared by more than 30 percent relative to the Canadian dollar during the height of the financial crisis in 2008, it continued to decline during most of the period after the crisis had ended. The falling value of the U.S. dollar was a great help to Canadian buyers of U.S. homes.

In late 2001, it took 1.60 Canadian dollars to purchase 1 U.S. dollar. So, a Canadian purchasing a house in Phoenix priced at $125,000 would have had to pay $200,000 in Canadian dollars. In the summer of 2011, it took only 0.95 Canadian dollars to purchase 1 U.S. dollar. The stronger Canadian dollar meant that a Canadian could now purchase a house in Phoenix priced at $125,000 for only $118,750 in Canadian dollars. In other words, the decline in the value of the U.S. dollar resulted in a more than 40 percent reduction in the price of the house in Canadian dollars. As one Canadian who was buying a vacation home in Desert Ridge, Arizona, put it: "It's purchasing power, plain and simple. In the days when our dollar was 60 or 65 [U.S.] cents, I wouldn't even be talking to you. The strong Canadian dollar has created a lot of opportunities for Canadians." In addition to the decline in the value of the U.S. dollar, many Canadians found Arizona to be an ideal place to buy a second home because overbuilding in the state during the housing bubble had resulted in many property owners being willing to accept sharply lower prices (in U.S. dollars). Little wonder that by 2011, restaurants and bars in Arizona began staging Canada Day celebrations to attract the growing Canadian population.

In addition to individual Canadians looking to buy second homes in Arizona, some Canadian investors bought multiple properties, hoping to resell them for a profit in the future after local housing prices had risen and after the value of the U.S. dollar had increased relative to the Canadian dollar. Some Canadian manufacturers have also shifted operations to the United States. For example, E.H. Price, a firm that produces ventilation systems for commercial buildings and is headquartered in Winnipeg, Canada, doubled the size of its operations in the United States, where nearly half of its sales were. The rising value of the Canadian dollar would have priced its products out of the U.S. market if it had continued manufacturing the products in Canada.

Of course, further fluctuations in the value of the U.S. dollar could pose problems for Canadians buying and investing in the United States. For example, if the value of the U.S. dollar were to continue to decline, then Canadians who bought second homes in the United States or Canadian investors buying multiple U.S. homes would take a loss in terms of Canadian dollars should they decide to sell. An increase in the value of the U.S. dollar would be good news for Canadian owners of U.S. houses but bad news for Canadian manufacturers if they intended to export goods to Canada from their U.S. plants.

Based on Chana R. Schoenberger, "Canadians Warm to Phoenix," *Wall Street Journal*, October 8, 2011; Julie Schmit, "Foreign Buyers Lifting U.S. Home Sales," *USA Today*, July 14, 2011; and Barrie McKenna, "For Canadian Manufacturers, Foreign Assets Tantalizingly Cheap," *(Toronto) Globe and Mail*, June 12, 2011.

MyEconLab **Your Turn:** Test your understanding by doing related problem 2.6 on page 659 at the end of this chapter.

What Determines Exchange Rates in the Long Run?

Over the past 40 years, why has the value of the U.S. dollar fallen against the Japanese yen but risen slightly against the Canadian dollar? In the short run, the two most important causes of exchange rate movements are changes in interest rates—which cause investors to change their views of which countries' financial investments will yield the highest returns—and changes in investors' expectations about the future values of currencies. Over the long run, other factors are also important in explaining movements in exchange rates.

The Theory of Purchasing Power Parity It seems reasonable that, in the long run, exchange rates should be at a level that makes it possible to buy the same amount of goods and services with the equivalent amount of any country's currency. In other words, the purchasing power of every country's currency should be the same. The idea that in the long run, exchange rates move to equalize the purchasing powers of different currencies is referred to as the theory of **purchasing power parity**.

> **Purchasing power parity** The theory that in the long run, exchange rates move to equalize the purchasing powers of different currencies.

To make the theory of purchasing power parity clearer, consider a simple example. Suppose that a Hershey candy bar has a price of $1 in the United States and £1 in the United Kingdom and that the exchange rate is £1 = $1. In that case, at least with respect to candy bars, the dollar and the pound have equivalent purchasing power. If the price of a Hershey bar increases to £2 in the United Kingdom but stays at $1 in the United States, the exchange rate will have to change to £2 per $1 in order for the pound to maintain its relative purchasing power. As long as exchange rates adjust to reflect purchasing power, it will be possible to buy a Hershey bar for $1 in the United States or to exchange $1 for £2 and buy the candy bar in the United Kingdom.

If exchange rates are not at the values indicated by purchasing power parity, it appears that there are opportunities to make profits. For example, suppose a Hershey candy bar sells for £2 in the United Kingdom and $1 in the United States, and the exchange rate between the dollar and the pound is £1 = $1. In this case, it would be possible to exchange £1 million for $1 million and use the dollars to buy 1 million Hershey bars in the United States. The Hershey bars could then be shipped to the United Kingdom, where they could be sold for £2 million. The result of these transactions would be a profit of £1 million (minus any shipping costs). In fact, if the dollar–pound exchange rate does not reflect the purchasing power for many products—not just Hershey bars—this process could be repeated until extremely large profits were made. In practice, though, as people attempted to make these profits by exchanging pounds for dollars, they would bid up the value of the dollar until it reached the purchasing power exchange rate of £2 = $1. Once the exchange rate reflected the purchasing power of the two currencies, there would be no further opportunities for profit. This mechanism appears to guarantee that exchange rates will be at the levels determined by purchasing power parity.

Three real-world complications, though, keep purchasing power parity from being a complete explanation of exchange rates, even in the long run:

1. *Not all products can be traded internationally.* Where goods are traded internationally, profits can be made whenever exchange rates do not reflect their purchasing power parity values. However, more than half of all goods and services produced in the United States and most other countries are not traded internationally. When goods are not traded internationally, their prices will not be the same in every country. For instance, suppose that the exchange rate is £1 for $1, but the price for having a cavity filled by a dentist is twice as high in the United States as it is in the United Kingdom. In this case, there is no way to buy up the low-priced British service and resell it in the United States. Because many goods and services are not traded internationally, exchange rates will not reflect exactly the relative purchasing powers of currencies.

2. *Products and consumer preferences are different across countries.* We expect the same product to sell for the same price around the world, but if a product is similar but not identical to another product, their prices might be different. For example, a 3-ounce Hershey candy bar may sell for a different price in the United States than

does a 3-ounce Cadbury candy bar in the United Kingdom. Prices of the same product may also differ across countries if consumer preferences differ. If consumers in the United Kingdom like candy bars more than do consumers in the United States, a Hershey candy bar may sell for more in the United Kingdom than in the United States.

3. **Countries impose barriers to trade.** Most countries, including the United States, impose *tariffs* and *quotas* on imported goods. A **tariff** is a tax imposed by a government on imports. A **quota** is a government-imposed limit on the quantity of a good that can be imported. For example, the United States has a quota on imports of sugar. As a result, the price of sugar in the United States is much higher than the price of sugar in other countries. Because of the quota, there is no legal way to buy up the cheap foreign sugar and resell it in the United States.

Tariff A tax imposed by a government on imports.

Quota A numerical limit that a government imposes on the quantity of a good that can be imported into the country.

Making the Connection | **The Big Mac Theory of Exchange Rates**

In a lighthearted attempt to test the accuracy of the theory of purchasing power parity, the *Economist* magazine regularly compares the prices of Big Macs in different countries. If purchasing power parity holds, you should be able to take the dollars required to buy a Big Mac in the United States and exchange them for the amount of foreign currency needed to buy a Big Mac in any other country. The following table is for July 2011, when Big Macs were selling for an average price of $4.07 in the United States. The "implied exchange rate" shows what the xchange rate would be if purchasing power parity held for Big Macs. For example, a Big Mac sold for 20.0 pesos in Argentina and $4.07 in the United States, so for purchasing power parity to hold, the exchange rate should have been 20.0 pesos/$4.07, or 4.91 pesos = $1. The actual exchange rate in July 2011 was 4.13 pesos = $1. So, on Big Mac purchasing power parity grounds, the Argentine peso was *overvalued* against the dollar by 19 percent $(((4.91 - 4.13)/4.13) \times 100 = 19$ percent$)$. That is, if Big Mac purchasing power parity held, it would have taken 19 percent more Argentine pesos to buy a dollar than it actually did.

Is the price of a Big Mac in Buenos Aires the same as the price of a Big Mac in New York?

Could you take advantage of this difference between the purchasing power parity exchange rate and the actual exchange rate to become fabulously wealthy by buying up low-priced Big Macs in New York and reselling them at a higher price in Buenos Aires? Unfortunately, the low-priced U.S. Big Macs would be a soggy mess by the time you got them to Buenos Aires. The fact that Big Mac prices are not the same around the world illustrates one reason purchasing power parity does not hold exactly: Many goods are not traded internationally.

Country	Big Mac Price	Implied Exchange Rate	Actual Exchange Rate
Mexico	32.0 pesos	7.86 pesos per dollar	11.70 pesos per dollar
Japan	320 yen	78.62 yen per dollar	78.40 yen per dollar
United Kingdom	2.39 pounds	0.59 pound per dollar	0.61 pound per dollar
Switzerland	6.50 Swiss francs	1.60 Swiss francs per dollar	0.81 Swiss francs per dollar
Indonesia	22,534 rupiahs	5,537 rupiahs per dollar	8,523 rupiahs per dollar
Canada	4.73 Canadian dollars	1.16 Canadian dollars per U.S. dollar	0.95 Canadian dollars per U.S. dollar
China	14.7 yuan	3.61 yuan per dollar	6.45 yuan per dollar

Data from "Currency Comparisons, to Go," *Economist*, July 28, 2011.

MyEconLab **Your Turn:** Test your understanding by doing related problem 2.11 on page 659 at the end of this chapter.

Solved Problem 19.2

Calculating Purchasing Power Parity Exchange Rates Using Big Macs

Fill in the missing values in the following table. Remember that the implied exchange rate shows what the exchange rate would be if purchasing power parity held for Big Macs. Assume that the Big Mac is selling for $4.07 in the United States. Explain whether the U.S. dollar is overvalued or undervalued relative to each currency and predict what will happen in the future to each exchange rate. Finally, calculate the implied exchange rate between the Polish zloty and the Brazilian real (plural: reais) and explain which currency is undervalued in terms of Big Mac purchasing power parity.

Country	Big Mac Price	Implied Exchange Rate	Actual Exchange Rate
Brazil	9.50 reais		1.54 reais per dollar
Poland	8.63 zlotys		2.80 zlotys per dollar
South Korea	3,700 won		1,056 won per dollar
Malaysia	7.20 ringgits		2.97 ringgits per dollar

Solving the Problem

Step 1: **Review the chapter material.** This problem is about the theory of purchasing power parity, as illustrated by prices of Big Macs, so you may want to review the sections "The Theory of Purchasing Power Parity," which begins on page 643, and the Making the Connection "The Big Mac Theory of Exchange Rates" on page 644.

Step 2: **Fill in the table.** To calculate the purchasing power parity exchange rate, divide the foreign currency price of a Big Mac by the U.S. price. For example, the implied exchange rate between the Brazilian real and the U.S. dollar is 9.50 reais/$4.07, or 2.33 reais per dollar.

Country	Big Mac Price	Implied Exchange Rate	Actual Exchange Rate
Brazil	9.50 reais	2.33 reais per dollar	1.54 reais per dollar
Poland	8.63 zlotys	2.12 zlotys per dollar	2.80 zlotys per dollar
South Korea	3,700 won	909 won per dollar	1,056 won per dollar
Malaysia	7.20 ringgits	1.77 ringgits per dollar	2.97 ringgits per dollar

Step 3: **Explain whether the U.S. dollar is overvalued or undervalued against the other currencies.** The dollar is overvalued if the actual exchange rate is greater than the implied exchange rate, and it is undervalued if the actual exchange rate is less than the implied exchange rate. In this case, the dollar is overvalued against the zloty, the won, and the ringgit, but it is undervalued against the real. So, we would predict that in the future the value of the dollar should rise against the real but fall against the zloty, the won, and the ringgit.

Step 4: **Calculate the implied exchange rate between the zloty and the real.** The implied exchange rate between the zloty and the real is 8.63 zlotys/9.50 reais, or 0.91 zlotys per real. We can calculate the actual exchange rate by taking the ratio of zlotys per dollar to reais per dollar: 2.80 zlotys/1.54 reais, or 1.82 zlotys per real. Therefore, the zloty is undervalued relative to the real because our Big Mac purchasing power parity calculation tells us that it should take fewer zlotys to buy a real than it actually does.

Data from "Currency Comparisons, to Go," *Economist*, July 28, 2011.

Your Turn: For more practice, do related problem 2.12 on page 659 at the end of this chapter.   MyEconLab

The Four Determinants of Exchange Rates in the Long Run We can take into account the shortcomings of the theory of purchasing power parity to develop a more complete explanation of how exchange rates are determined in the long run. There are four main determinants of exchange rates in the long run:

1. *Relative price levels.* The purchasing power parity theory is correct in arguing that in the long run, the most important determinant of exchange rates between two countries' currencies is their relative price levels. If prices of goods and services rise faster in Canada than in the United States, the value of the Canadian dollar has to decline to maintain demand for Canadian products. Over the past 30 years, prices in Canada have risen slightly faster than average prices in the United States, while prices in Japan have risen more slowly. The relationship among inflation rates helps explain why the U.S. dollar has increased slightly in value against the Canadian dollar while losing value against the Japanese yen.

2. *Relative rates of productivity growth.* When the productivity of a firm increases, the firm is able to produce more goods and services using fewer workers, machines, or other inputs. The firm's costs of production fall, and usually so do the prices of its products. If the average productivity of Japanese firms increases faster than the average productivity of U.S. firms, Japanese products will have relatively lower prices than U.S. products, which increases the quantity demanded of Japanese products relative to U.S. products. As a result, the value of the yen should rise against the dollar. For most of the period from the early 1970s to the early 1990s, Japanese productivity increased faster than U.S. productivity, which contributed to the fall in the value of the dollar versus the yen. However, between 1992 and 2011, U.S. productivity increased faster than Japanese productivity.

3. *Preferences for domestic and foreign goods.* If consumers in Canada increase their preferences for U.S. products, the demand for U.S. dollars will increase relative to the demand for Canadian dollars, and the U.S. dollar will increase in value relative to the Canadian dollar. During the 1970s and 1980s, many U.S. consumers increased their preferences for Japanese products, particularly automobiles and consumer electronics. This greater preference for Japanese products helped to increase the value of the yen relative to the dollar.

4. *Tariffs and quotas.* The U.S. sugar quota forces firms such as Hershey Foods Corporation to buy expensive U.S. sugar rather than less expensive foreign sugar. The quota increases the demand for dollars relative to the currencies of foreign sugar producers and, therefore, leads to a higher exchange rate. Changes in tariffs and quotas have not been a significant factor in explaining trends in the U.S. dollar–Canadian dollar or U.S. dollar–yen exchange rates.

Because these four factors change over time, the value of one country's currency can increase or decrease by substantial amounts in the long run. These changes in exchange rates can create problems for firms. A decline in the value of a country's currency lowers the foreign currency prices of the country's exports and increases the prices of imports. An increase in the value of a country's currency has the reverse effect. Firms can be both helped and hurt by exchange rate fluctuations.

The Euro

A second key aspect of the current exchange rate system is that most Western European countries have adopted a single currency. After World War II, many of the countries of Western Europe wanted to more closely integrate their economies. In 1957, Belgium, France, West Germany, Italy, Luxembourg, and the Netherlands signed the Treaty of Rome, which established the European Economic Community, often referred to as the European Common Market. Tariffs and quotas on products being shipped within the European Common Market were greatly reduced. Over the years, Britain, Sweden, Denmark, Finland, Austria, Greece, Ireland, Spain, and Portugal joined the European Economic Community, which was renamed the European Union (EU) in 1991. By 2011, 27 countries were members of the EU.

Figure 19.2

Countries Adopting the Euro

The 17 member countries of the European Union that have adopted the euro as their common currency as of 2011 are shaded with red hash marks. The members of the EU that have not adopted the euro are colored tan. Countries in white are not members of the EU.

EU members decided to move to a common currency beginning in 1999. Three of the 15 countries that were then members of the EU—the United Kingdom, Denmark, and Sweden—decided to retain their domestic currencies. The move to a common currency took place in several stages. On January 1, 1999, the exchange rates of the 12 participating countries (risen to 17 in 2011) were permanently fixed against each other and against the common currency, the *euro*. At first the euro was a pure *unit of account*. No euro currency was actually in circulation, although firms began quoting prices in both the domestic currency and euros. On January 1, 2002, euro coins and paper currency were introduced, and on June 1, 2002, the old domestic currencies were withdrawn from circulation. Figure 19.2 shows the countries in the EU that had adopted the euro as of 2011. These countries are sometimes referred to as the "euro zone."

A new European Central Bank (ECB) was also established. Although the central banks of the member countries continue to exist, the ECB has assumed responsibility for monetary policy and for issuing currency. The ECB is run by a governing council that consists of a six-member executive board—appointed by the participating governments—and the governors of the central banks of the 17 member countries that have adopted the euro. The ECB represents a unique experiment in allowing a multinational organization to control the domestic monetary policies of independent countries.

Making the Connection | **Can the Euro Survive?**

The euro was first introduced as a currency at the beginning of 2002. The period from then until the beginning of the global economic downturn at the end of 2007 was one of relative economic stability in most of Europe. With low interest rates, low inflation rates, and expanding employment and production, the advantages of the euro seemed obvious. The countries using the euro no longer had to deal with problems caused by fluctuating exchange rates. Having a common currency also makes it easier for consumers and firms to buy and sell across borders. It is no longer

German Chancellor Angela Merkel, then Greek Prime Minister George Papandreou, left, and French President Nicolas Sarkozy debated how to handle Greece's financial rescue.

necessary for someone in France to exchange francs for marks in order to do business in Germany. Having a single currency reduces costs and increases competition. Some of the lower-income European countries seemed to particularly prosper under the euro. The Spanish economy grew at a rate of 3.9 percent between 1999 and 2007. The unemployment rate in Spain had been nearly 20 percent in the mid-1990s, but it had dropped to 7.9 percent in 2007. Ireland and Greece also experienced rapid growth during these years.

But by 2008, with the global recession gathering force, some economists and policymakers were starting to question whether the euro was making the economic crisis worse. The countries using the euro are not able to pursue independent monetary policies, which are instead determined by the ECB from its headquarters in Frankfurt, Germany. Countries that were particularly hard hit by the recession—for example, Spain, where the unemployment rate had more than doubled to 18 percent by 2009 and was nearly 21 percent in 2011—were unable to pursue a more expansionary policy than the ECB was willing to implement for the euro zone as a whole. Similarly, countries could not attempt to revive their exports by allowing their exchange rates to depreciate because (1) most of their exports were to other euro zone countries, and (2) the value of the euro was determined by factors affecting the euro zone as a whole.

Problems in the euro zone were made worse by a *sovereign debt* crisis that developed in 2010. Sovereign debt refers to bonds issued by a government. The recession of 2007–2009 caused large increases in government spending and reductions in tax revenues in a number of European countries, particularly Greece, Ireland, Spain, Portugal, and Italy. The resulting government budget deficits were paid for by issuing government bonds. By the spring of 2010, many investors had come to doubt the ability of Greece, in particular, to make the interest payments on the bonds. If Greece defaulted and stopped making interest payments on its bonds, investors would be likely to stop buying bonds issued by several other European governments, and the continuation of the euro would be called into question. The ECB helped Greece avoid a default by directly buying its bonds. The bank extended similar help to Spain, Ireland, and Italy. The International Monetary Fund and the European Union put together aid packages meant to keep Greece and other countries from defaulting. In exchange for the aid, these countries were required to cut government spending and raise taxes even though doing so resulted in significant protests from unions, students, and other groups. In late 2011, it was not yet clear whether the actions the European Union had taken would be sufficient to keep Greece and possibly other countries from defaulting on their bonds.

During the years of the gold standard, countries couldn't run expansionary monetary policies and were unable to have their exchange rates depreciate. During the Great Depression of the 1930s, these drawbacks to remaining on the gold standard led one country after another to abandon it, and by the mid-1930s, the gold standard had collapsed. In 2011, some economists and policymakers were predicting a similar abandonment of the euro. There were significant reasons, though, that no government had yet been willing to consider reverting from the euro to its own currency. Because many euro zone countries export a significant fraction of GDP to other euro zone countries, exchange rate stability has been important to their economic stability, making these countries reluctant to abandon the euro. In addition, some of the European countries hit hardest by the recession, particularly Spain and Ireland, were suffering from the bursting of housing bubbles. More expansionary monetary policies or depreciating exchange rates were unlikely to result in economic recovery until the effects of the collapse in residential construction had run its course. So, it was unclear that the constraints imposed by the euro were holding back recovery in Europe. Finally, because so many contracts and agreements among households, firms, and governments in Europe were written in euros, abandoning the euro was likely to be disruptive to the financial system and to trade.

The ultimate fate of the euro will help to answer the question of whether independent countries with diverse economies can successfully maintain a joint monetary policy and a single currency.

Based on Jack Ewing, Stephen Castle, and Liz Alderman, "Debt Plan Is Delayed in Europe," *New York Times*, October 20, 2011; Terence Roth, "Setting Up the Greek Default," *Wall Street Journal*, October 11, 2011; and "Solving the Euro-Zone Crisis," *Economist*, October 6, 2011.

Your Turn: Test your understanding by doing related problem 2.15 on page 660 at the end of this chapter.

MyEconLab

Pegging against the Dollar

A final key aspect of the current exchange rate system is that some developing countries have attempted to keep their exchange rates fixed against the dollar or another major currency. Having a fixed exchange rate can provide important advantages for a country that has extensive trade with another country. When the exchange rate is fixed, business planning becomes much easier. For instance, if the South Korean won increases in value relative to the dollar, Hyundai, the Korean car manufacturer, may have to raise the dollar price of cars it exports to the United States, thereby reducing sales. If the exchange rate between the Korean won and the dollar is fixed, Hyundai's planning is much easier.

In the 1980s and 1990s, an additional reason developed for having fixed exchange rates. During those decades, the flow of foreign investment funds to developing countries, particularly those in East Asia, increased substantially. It became possible for firms in countries such as Korea, Thailand, Malaysia, and Indonesia to borrow dollars directly from foreign investors or indirectly from foreign banks. For example, a Thai firm might borrow U.S. dollars from a Japanese bank. If the Thai firm wants to build a new factory in Thailand with the borrowed dollars, it has to exchange the dollars for the equivalent amount of Thai currency, the baht. When the factory opens and production begins, the Thai firm will be earning the additional baht it needs to exchange for dollars to make the interest payments on the loan. A problem arises if the value of the baht falls against the dollar. Suppose that the exchange rate is 25 baht per dollar when the firm takes out the loan. A Thai firm making an interest payment of $100,000 per month on a dollar loan could buy the necessary dollars for 2.5 million baht. But if the value of the baht declines to 50 baht to the dollar, it would take 5 million baht to buy the dollars necessary to make the interest payment. These increased payments might be a crushing burden for the Thai firm. The government of Thailand would have a strong incentive to avoid this problem by keeping the exchange rate between the baht and the dollar fixed.

Finally, in the 1980s and 1990s, some countries feared the inflationary consequences of a floating exchange rate. When the value of a currency falls, the prices of imports rise. If imports are a significant fraction of the goods consumers buy, a fall in the value of the currency may significantly increase the inflation rate. During the 1990s, an important part of Brazil's and Argentina's anti-inflation policies was a fixed exchange rate against the dollar. (As we will see, though, there are difficulties with following a fixed exchange rate policy, and, ultimately, both Brazil and Argentina abandoned fixed exchange rates.)

The East Asian Exchange Rate Crisis of the Late 1990s
When a country keeps its currency's exchange rate fixed against another country's currency, it is **pegging** its currency. It is not necessary for both countries involved in a peg to agree to it. When a developing country has pegged the value of its currency against the dollar, the responsibility for maintaining the peg has been entirely with the developing country.

Countries attempting to maintain a peg can run into problems, however. We saw in Chapter 4 that when the government fixes the price of a good or service, the result can be persistent surpluses or shortages. Figure 19.3 shows the exchange rate between the dollar and the Thai baht. The figure is drawn from the Thai point of view, so we measure the exchange rate on the vertical axis as dollars per baht. The figure represents the situation in the 1990s, when the government of Thailand pegged the exchange rate

Pegging The decision by a country to keep the exchange rate fixed between its currency and another country's currency.

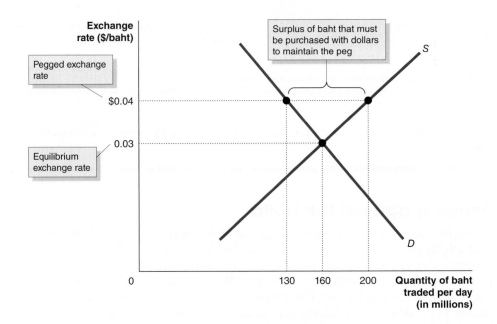

Figure 19.3

By 1997, the Thai Baht Was Overvalued against the Dollar

The government of Thailand pegged the value of the baht against the dollar to make it easier for Thai firms to export to the United States and to protect Thai firms that had taken out dollar loans. The pegged exchange rate of $0.04 per baht was well above the equilibrium exchange rate of $0.03 per baht. In the example in this figure, the overvalued exchange rate created a surplus of 70 million baht, which the Thai central bank had to purchase with dollars.

between the dollar and the baht above the equilibrium exchange rate, as determined by demand and supply. A currency pegged at a value above the market equilibrium exchange rate is said to be *overvalued*. A currency pegged at a value below the market equilibrium exchange rate is said to be *undervalued*.

Pegging made it easier for Thai firms to export products to the United States and protected Thai firms that had taken out dollar loans. The pegged exchange rate was 25.19 baht to the dollar, or about $0.04 to the baht. By 1997, this exchange rate was well above the market equilibrium exchange rate of 35 baht to the dollar, or about $0.03 to the baht. The result was a surplus of baht on the foreign exchange market. To keep the exchange rate at the pegged level, the Thai central bank, the Bank of Thailand, had to buy these baht with dollars. In doing so, the Bank of Thailand gradually used up its holdings of dollars, or its *dollar reserves*. To continue supporting the pegged exchange rate, the Bank of Thailand borrowed additional dollar reserves from the International Monetary Fund (IMF). The Bank of Thailand also raised interest rates to attract more foreign investors to investments in Thailand, thereby increasing the demand for the baht. The Bank of Thailand took these actions even though allowing the value of the baht to decline against the dollar would have helped Thai firms exporting to the United States by reducing the dollar prices of their goods. The Thai government was afraid of the negative consequences of abandoning the peg even though the peg had led to the baht being overvalued.

Although higher domestic interest rates helped attract foreign investors, they made it more difficult for Thai firms and households to borrow the funds they needed to finance their spending. As a consequence, domestic investment and consumption declined, pushing the Thai economy into recession. International investors realized that there were limits to how high the Bank of Thailand would be willing to push interest rates and how many dollar loans the IMF would be willing to extend to Thailand. These investors began to speculate against the baht by exchanging baht for dollars at the official, pegged exchange rate. If, as they expected, Thailand was forced to abandon the peg, they would be able to buy back the baht at a much lower exchange rate, making a substantial profit. Because these actions by investors make it more difficult to maintain a fixed exchange rate, they are referred to as *destabilizing speculation*. Figure 19.4 shows the results of this destabilizing speculation. The decreased demand for baht shifted the demand curve for baht from D_1 to D_2, increasing the quantity of baht the Bank of Thailand needed to buy in exchange for dollars.

Foreign investors also began to sell off their investments in Thailand and exchange the baht they received for dollars. This *capital flight* forced the Bank of Thailand to run through its dollar reserves. Dollar loans from the IMF temporarily allowed Thailand to defend the pegged exchange rate. Finally, on July 2, 1997, Thailand abandoned its

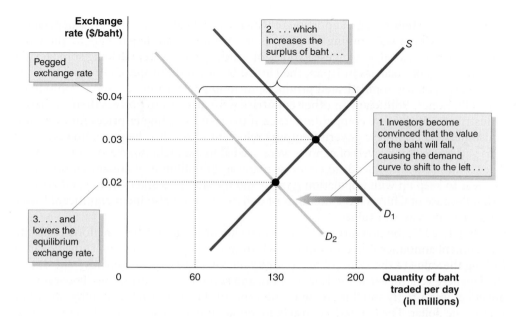

Exchange rate ($/baht)

Pegged exchange rate

$0.04

0.03

0.02

2. ... which increases the surplus of baht ...

S

1. Investors become convinced that the value of the baht will fall, causing the demand curve to shift to the left ...

D_1

D_2

3. ... and lowers the equilibrium exchange rate.

0   60   130   200   Quantity of baht traded per day (in millions)

Figure 19.4

Destabilizing Speculation against the Thai Baht

In 1997, the pegged exchange rate of $0.04 = 1$ baht was above the equilibrium exchange rate of $0.03 = 1$ baht. As investors became convinced that Thailand would have to abandon its pegged exchange rate against the dollar and allow the value of the baht to fall, they decreased their demand for baht, causing the demand curve to shift from D_1 to D_2. The new equilibrium exchange rate became $0.02 = 1$ baht. To defend the pegged exchange rate, the Bank of Thailand had to increase the quantity of baht it purchased in exchange for dollars from 70 million per day to 140 million. The *destabilizing speculation* by investors caused Thailand to abandon its pegged exchange rate in July 1997.

pegged exchange rate against the dollar and allowed the baht to float. Thai firms that had borrowed dollars were now faced with interest payments that were much higher than they had planned. Many firms were forced into bankruptcy, and the Thai economy plunged into a deep recession.

Many currency traders became convinced that other East Asian countries, such as South Korea, Indonesia, and Malaysia, would have to follow Thailand and abandon their pegged exchange rates. The result was a wave of speculative selling of these countries' currencies. These waves of selling—sometimes referred to as *speculative attacks*—were difficult for countries to fight off. Even if a country's currency was not initially overvalued at the pegged exchange rate, the speculative attacks would cause a large reduction in the demand for the country's currency. The demand curve for the currency would shift to the left, which would force the country's central bank to quickly run through its dollar reserves. Within a few months, South Korea, Indonesia, the Philippines, and Malaysia abandoned their pegged currencies. All these countries also plunged into recession.

The Decline in Pegging Following the disastrous events experienced by the East Asian countries, the number of countries with pegged exchange rates declined sharply. Most countries that continue to use pegged exchange rates are small and trade primarily with a single, much larger, country. So, for instance, several Caribbean countries continue to peg against the dollar, and several former French colonies in Africa that formerly pegged against the French franc now peg against the euro. Overall, the trend has been toward replacing pegged exchange rates with managed floating exchange rates.

The Chinese Experience with Pegging As we discussed in Chapter 11, in 1978, China began to move away from central planning and toward a market system. The result was a sharp acceleration in economic growth. Real GDP per capita grew at a rate of 6.5 percent per year between 1979 and 1995 and at the very rapid rate of more than 9 percent per year between 1996 and 2010. An important part of Chinese economic policy was the decision in 1994 to peg the value of the Chinese currency, the yuan, to the dollar at a fixed rate of 8.28 yuan to the dollar. Pegging against the dollar ensured that Chinese exporters would face stable dollar prices for the goods they sold in the United States. By the early 2000s, many economists argued that the yuan was undervalued against the dollar, possibly significantly so. Many U.S. firms claimed that the undervaluation of the yuan gave Chinese firms an unfair advantage in competing with U.S. firms.

To support the undervalued exchange rate, the Chinese central bank had to buy large amounts of dollars with yuan. By 2005, the Chinese government had accumulated more than $700 billion, a good portion of which it had used to buy U.S. Treasury bonds. In addition, China was coming under pressure from its trading partners to allow the yuan to increase in value. Chinese exports of textile products were driving some textile producers out of business in Japan, the United States, and Europe. China had also begun to export more sophisticated products, including televisions, personal computers, and cell phones. Politicians in other countries were anxious to protect their domestic industries from Chinese competition, even if the result was higher prices for domestic consumers. The Chinese government was reluctant to revalue the yuan, however, because it believed high levels of exports were needed to maintain rapid economic growth. The Chinese economy needs to create as many as 20 million new nonagricultural jobs per year to keep up with population growth and the shift of workers from rural areas to cities. Because of China's large holdings of dollars, it would also incur significant losses if the yuan increases in value.

By July 2005, the pressure on China to revalue the yuan had become too great. The government announced that it would switch from pegging the yuan against the dollar to linking the value of the yuan to the average value of a basket of currencies—the dollar, the Japanese yen, the euro, the Korean won, and several other currencies. The immediate effect was a fairly small increase in the value of the yuan from 8.28 to the dollar to 8.11 to the dollar. The Chinese central bank declared that it had switched from a peg to a managed floating exchange rate. Some economists and policymakers were skeptical, however, that much had actually changed because the initial increase in the value of the yuan had been small and because the Chinese central bank did not explain the details of how the yuan would be linked to the basket of other currencies. By late 2011, the value of the yuan had slowly increased to 6.38 to the dollar. Despite this increase, some economists and policymakers still believed that the yuan was overvalued and urged the Chinese government to allow its currency to become more responsive to changes in demand and supply in the foreign exchange markets.

Making the Connection | Crisis and Recovery in South Korea

Korea spent the first part of the twentieth century as a colony of Japan. In 1945, at the end of World War II, Korea was divided into Communist North Korea and democratic South Korea. North Korea's invasion of South Korea in June 1950 set off the Korean War, which devastated South Korea, before ending in 1953. Despite these difficult beginnings, by the 1960s, the South Korean economy was growing rapidly. As one of the *newly industrializing countries*, South Korea was a model for other developing countries.

To make it easier for firms such as Hyundai to export to the United States and to protect firms that had taken out dollar loans, the South Korean government pegged the value of its currency, the won, to the U.S. dollar. Following Thailand's decision in July 1997 to abandon its peg, large-scale destabilizing speculation took place against the won. Foreign investors scrambled to sell their investments in Korea and to convert their won into dollars. South Korea was unable to defend the peg and allowed the won to float in October 1997.

Like other countries that underwent exchange rate crises, South Korea had attempted to maintain the value of the won by raising domestic interest rates. The result was a sharp decline in aggregate demand and a severe recession. However, unlike other East Asian countries—particularly Thailand and Indonesia—that made only slow progress in recovering from exchange rate crises, South Korea bounced back rapidly. The figure on the next page shows that after experiencing falling real GDP through 1999, South Korea quickly returned to high rates of growth.

Why was the performance of South Korea so much better than that of other East Asian countries? Jahyeong Koo and Sherry L. Kiser, economists at the Federal Reserve Bank of Dallas, cite several factors:

- South Korea benefited from a $21 billion loan from the IMF in December 1997. This loan helped stabilize the value of the won.

- Even though South Korean banks were badly hurt in the crisis and cut back their loans, South Korean firms were able to obtain financing for investment projects from the stock and bond markets.

- The South Korean labor market was flexible enough to allow wage reductions, which offset some of the negative effect of the crisis on corporate profits.

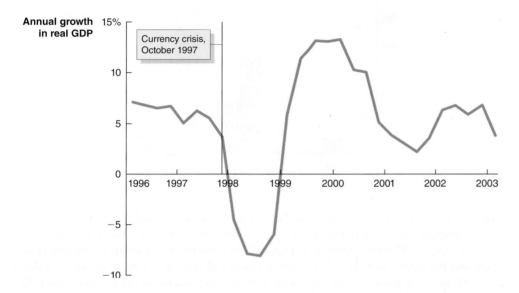

In 2011, some South Korean firms were still paying off debts originally incurred in the late 1990s, and the Korean banking system had yet to fully recover. But South Korea was able to emerge from its exchange rate crisis without suffering the political and social upheavals that occurred in countries such as Indonesia.

Based on Korea National Statistical Office; and Jahyeong Koo and Sherry L. Kiser, "Recovery from a Financial Crisis: The Case of South Korea," *Federal Reserve Bank of Dallas, Economic and Financial Review*, Fourth Quarter 2001.

Your Turn: Test your understanding by doing related problem 2.25 on page 661 at the end of this chapter.

MyEconLab

International Capital Markets

19.3 LEARNING OBJECTIVE

Discuss the growth of international capital markets.

One important reason exchange rates fluctuate is that investors seek out the best investments they can find anywhere in the world. For instance, if Chinese investors increase their demand for U.S. Treasury bills, the demand for dollars will increase, and the value of the dollar will rise. But if interest rates in the United States decline, foreign investors may sell U.S. investments, and the value of the dollar will fall.

Shares of stock and long-term debt, including corporate and government bonds and bank loans, are bought and sold on *capital markets*. Before 1980, most U.S. corporations raised funds only in U.S. stock and bond markets or from U.S. banks. U.S. investors rarely invested in foreign capital markets. In the 1980s and 1990s, European governments removed many restrictions on foreign investments in their financial markets. It became possible for U.S. and other foreign investors to freely invest in Europe and for European investors to freely invest in foreign markets. Improvements in communications and computer technology made it possible for U.S. investors to receive better and more timely information about foreign firms and for foreign investors to receive better information about U.S. firms. The growth in economies around the world also made more savings available to be invested.

Although at one time the U.S. capital market was larger than all other capital markets combined, this is no longer true. Today there are large capital markets in Europe

Figure 19.5

Growth of Foreign Portfolio Investment in the United States

Between 1995 and 2007, there was a large increase in foreign purchases of stocks and bonds issued by U.S. corporations and of bonds issued by the federal government. In 2010, the slow recovery in the United States from the 2007–2009 recession increased the degree of risk that foreign investors saw in holding these securities. Foreign purchases of U.S. government bonds soared, however.

Data from International Monetary Fund, *International Capital Markets*, August 2001; and U.S. Department of the Treasury, Treasury Bulletin, September 2011.

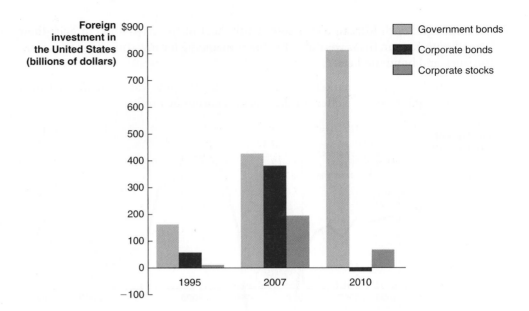

and Japan, and there are smaller markets in Latin America and East Asia. The three most important international financial centers today are New York, London, and Tokyo. Each day, the *Wall Street Journal* provides data not just on the Dow Jones Industrial Average and the Standard & Poor's 500 stock indexes of U.S. stocks but also on the Nikkei 225 average of Japanese stocks, the FTSE 100 index of stocks on the London Stock Exchange, and the DJ STOXX 50 index of European stocks. By 2011, corporations, banks, and governments had raised more than $1 trillion in funds on global financial markets.

Beginning in the 1990s, the flow of foreign funds into U.S. stocks and bonds—or *portfolio investments*—increased substantially. As Figure 19.5 shows, foreign purchases of stocks and bonds issued by corporations and bonds issued by the federal government increased dramatically between 1995 and 2007. In 2010, however, foreign purchases of U.S. corporate stocks and bonds declined sharply, as the slow recovery in the United States from the recession of 2007–2009 increased the degree of risk foreign investors saw in holding these securities. Foreign purchases of U.S. government bonds soared, however, as fears that some European governments might default on their bonds led investors to a *flight to safety*, in which they sold other investments to buy U.S. government bonds. The fact that the United States continued to run large current account deficits also fueled some of the demand for U.S. government bonds. These current account deficits led to an accumulation of dollars by foreign central banks and foreign investors who used the dollars to purchase U.S. government bonds.

Figure 19.6 shows the distribution during 2010 of foreign portfolio investment in the United States by country. Investors in the United Kingdom accounted for about half of all foreign purchases of U.S. stocks and bonds. The two other countries with the largest shares of foreign purchases were Japan, with 18 percent, and China, with 7 percent.

Figure 19.6

The Distribution of Foreign Purchases of U.S. Stocks and Bonds by Country, 2010

Investors in the United Kingdom accounted for about half of all foreign purchases of U.S. stocks and bonds, while investors in Japan accounted for 18 percent, and investors in China accounted for 7 percent.

Data from U.S. Department of the Treasury, *Treasury Bulletin*, September 2011.

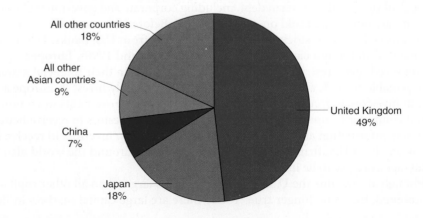

The globalization of financial markets has helped increase growth and efficiency in the world economy. Now it is possible for the savings of households around the world to be channeled to the best investments available. It is also possible for firms in nearly every country to tap the savings of foreign households to gain the funds needed for expansion. No longer are firms forced to rely only on the savings of domestic households to finance investment.

But the globalization of financial markets also has a downside, as the events of 2007–2009 showed. Because financial securities issued in one country are held by investors and firms in many other countries, if those securities decline in value, the financial pain will be widely distributed. For example, the sharp decline in the value of mortgage-backed securities issued in the United States hurt not only U.S. investors and financial firms but investors and financial firms in many other countries as well.

Continued from page 639

Economics in Your Life

Exchange Rate Risk in Your Life

At the beginning of the chapter, we posed this question: If economists are correct about the relative rates of average productivity growth between Spain and the United States in the next decade, then, all else being equal, will the savings that you accumulate (in euros) be worth more or less in U.S. dollars than it would have been worth without the relative gains in Spanish productivity? To answer this question, we saw in this chapter that when the average productivity of firms in one country increases faster than the average productivity of firms in another country, the value of the faster-growing country's currency should—all else being equal—rise against the slower-growing country's currency. Of course, Spain is only 1 of the 17 countries using the euro, so the impact of productivity increases in Spain on the value of the euro may not be large. But the savings that you accumulate in euros while you are in Spain are likely to be worth more in U.S. dollars than they would have been worth without the gains in Spanish productivity.

Conclusion

Fluctuations in exchange rates continue to cause difficulties for firms and governments. From the gold standard to the Bretton Woods system to currency pegging, governments have attempted to find a workable system of fixed exchange rates. Fixing exchange rates runs into the same problems as fixing any other price: As demand and supply shift, surpluses and shortages will occur unless the price adjusts. Seventeen countries in Europe are attempting to avoid this problem by using a single currency. Economists are looking closely at the results of that experiment.

Read *An Inside Look at Policy* on the next page for a discussion of a Senate bill aimed at raising tariffs on goods from China in response to claims that country's currency was undervalued.

Can Tariffs Offset the Effect of Overvaluation?

ASSOCIATED PRESS

China Slams U.S. Currency Bill as Threat to Trade

China criticized an American currency bill as a threat to a shaky global economic recovery and warned Wednesday that trade ties will be "severely damaged" if it becomes law.

Beijing rejected the measure passed Tuesday by the Senate as a form of damaging protectionism at a time when other nations are trying to sustain free trade. The bill would allow Washington to raise tariffs on Chinese imports that critics say are unfairly cheap due to Beijing's exchange-rate controls and are destroying U.S. jobs.

"It is completely harmful and unbeneficial," said Foreign Ministry spokesman Ma Zhaoxu in a statement. Ma said it would do nothing to reduce U.S. unemployment and would disrupt global efforts to revive economic growth.

Tuesday's 63–35 Senate vote showed a bipartisan consensus in favor of tougher action against Beijing after years of diplomatic pressure and a gradual rise in China's currency, the yuan, that critics say is inadequate.

Still, the bill is unlikely to become law because it lacks the support of the majority Republican leadership in the lower House of Representatives, who are reluctant to take up the measure. The White House and President Barack Obama have not come out against the bill but have shown they are uncomfortable with it.

U.S. manufacturers complain that Beijing's controls keep the yuan undervalued by up to 40 percent. They say that gives China's exporters an unfair price advantage and hurts foreign competitors, eroding American employment. The currency bill's supporters say it would support creation of 1 million jobs in the United States.

American critics of the bill have warned Beijing might retaliate, hurting U.S. companies in China's relatively robust markets, which are a rare bright spot for exporters amid weak demand elsewhere.

If it becomes law, "Sino–U.S. economic and trade relations will inevitably be severely damaged," Commerce Ministry spokesman Shen Dayang said in a statement.

Some opponents of the measure argue that currency sanctions would do little to help the U.S. job market because Chinese goods would simply be replaced by goods from other low-wage countries such as Vietnam and Bangladesh.

Ma, the Foreign Ministry spokesman, said the measure violates World Trade Organization rules.

"It not only cannot solve the problems in the U.S. economy or unemployment, but will seriously impede Sino–U.S. economic and trade ties and impede the joint efforts that China, the U.S. and the international community have made to enable a strong recovery and the growth of the global economy," Ma said.

The officials gave no details of a possible response but have warned in the past that unilateral trade action could damage the full array of U.S.–Chinese cooperation. That ranges from efforts to protect U.S. intellectual property rights in China to assuring the security of Taiwan and keeping the Korean Peninsula peaceful. . . .

The currency legislation would set in motion the imposition of higher tariffs on a country if the U.S. Treasury Department decides its currency is "misaligned" and the country does not act to correct it. Currently, Treasury must resolve that a country is willfully manipulating its currency, a higher bar to reach, before sanctions can be considered.

The bill also makes it easier for specific industries to petition the Commerce Department for redress if they believe an exchange rate is giving a foreign competitor the equivalent of an export subsidy.

Beijing has said repeatedly it is pushing ahead reforms of its exchange rate controls but says it will set the pace. Chinese leaders have warned that an abrupt rise in the yuan could lead to job losses and fuel unrest.

The yuan's value has been allowed to rise by about 5 percent against the dollar over the past year in tightly controlled trading. The rise has quickened in recent weeks.

On Wednesday, China's central bank issued a statement defending its currency controls as an "important contribution" to international financial stability.

Source: "China Slams U.S. Currency Bill as Threat to Trade," by Joe McDonald from the *Associated Press*, October 12, 2011. Copyright © 2005 by the Associated Press. Reproduced with permission of the YGS Group.

Key Points in the Article

China was the main target of a U.S. Senate bill to raise tariffs. Many politicians claimed that China had manipulated its currency to give Chinese exporters an unfair advantage over U.S. companies. Politicians and U.S. manufacturers supporting the bill argued that the Chinese yuan was undervalued by up to 40 percent, leading to job losses in the United States. Some opponents of the bill claimed that the sanctions would do little to help employment in the United States because the targeted Chinese products would just be replaced by goods from other countries. China said that the bill violates World Trade Organization rules and might retaliate should the bill become law. However, the bill was not expected to pass in the House of Representatives, nor did it get support from the Obama White House.

Analyzing the News

ⓐ In October 2011, the U.S. Senate passed a bill that would allow U.S. companies to apply for tariffs on imports from countries that deliberately undervalued their currencies in order to become more competitive. As you read in this chapter, a currency is said to be *undervalued* if it is pegged at a value below the market equilibrium exchange rate. Many politicians claimed that China kept its currency

undervalued in order to keep the prices of its exports low. The figure below shows the value of the yuan against the U.S. dollar. After 2005, the appreciation of the yuan against the dollar was relatively modest in comparison with the growing U.S. trade deficits with China. As you read in this chapter, the Chinese central bank has managed to keep the yuan at relatively low levels by buying large amounts of U.S. dollars with yuan. An increase in the U.S. trade deficit with China caused an increase in the supply of dollars in the foreign exchange market. Without any government intervention, the exchange rate between the U.S. dollar and the yuan might have dropped below 6 yuan per dollar. By increasing the demand for dollars in exchange for yuan, the Chinese government was able to keep the exchange rate between 6 and 7 yuan per dollar.

ⓑ U.S. manufacturers supporting the tariff bill claim that the Chinese yuan is undervalued by up to 40 percent, and this has given Chinese exporters an unfair advantage in competing with U.S. firms, leading to job losses. Supporters of the bill claim it would help create 1 million jobs in the United States. Critics have warned that Chinese retaliation could hurt U.S. companies that currently export to China and lead to unemployment in those exporting industries.

ⓒ The U.S. Treasury is required by law to investigate whether any country unfairly manipulates its currency. If it became law, the Senate bill would impose higher tariffs on countries if the Treasury Department determined that a currency is "misaligned" and the country took no corrective action. The bill also would make it easier for manufacturing firms to petition for sanctions if they believe a country is undervaluing its currency and giving foreign manufacturers what amounts to an export subsidy. China is the largest creditor of the United States, with holdings of more than $1.1 trillion in Treasury securities as of August 2011.

Thinking Critically about Policy

1. Supporters of the tariff bill discussed in this article claim that the yuan is undervalued, and tariffs on Chinese products would save jobs in the United States. Would passage of the bill hurt anyone in the United States? Briefly explain.

2. China is currently the largest creditor of the United States, with holdings of more than $1 trillion in U.S. Treasury securities in 2011. Suppose the Senate tariff bill were signed into law and China retaliated by selling all of its holdings of U.S. Treasury securities. How would interest rates in the United States be affected? How would the exchange rate of the U.S. dollar be affected? Briefly explain.

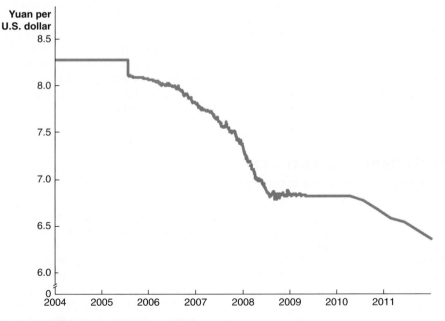

Historically, the exchange rate between the yuan and the dollar has been stable.
Data from the Federal Reserve Bank of St. Louis.

Chapter Summary and Problems

Key Terms

19.1 **Exchange Rate Systems, pages 640–641**

LEARNING OBJECTIVE: Understand how different exchange rate systems operate.

Summary

When countries agree on how exchange rates should be determined, economists say that there is an **exchange rate system**. A **floating currency** is the outcome of a country allowing its currency's exchange rate to be determined by demand and supply. The current exchange rate system is a **managed float exchange rate system**, under which the value of most currencies is determined by demand and supply, with occasional government intervention. A **fixed exchange rate system** is a system under which countries agree to keep the exchange rates among their currencies fixed. Under the gold standard, the exchange rate between two currencies was automatically determined by the quantity of gold in each currency. By the end of the Great Depression of the 1930s, every country had abandoned the gold standard. Under the Bretton Woods system, which was in place between 1944 and the early 1970s, the United States agreed to exchange dollars for gold at a price of $35 per ounce. The central banks of all other members of the system pledged to buy and sell their currencies at a fixed rate against the dollar.

 Visit **www.myeconlab.com** to complete these exercises online and get instant feedback.

Review Questions

1.1 What is an exchange rate system? What is the difference between a fixed exchange rate system and a managed float exchange rate system?

1.2 How were exchange rates determined under the gold standard? How did the Bretton Woods system differ from the gold standard?

Problems and Applications

1.3 **[Related to the** Don't Let This Happen to You **on page 641]** Briefly explain whether you agree with the following statement: "The Federal Reserve is limited in its ability to issue paper currency by the amount of gold the federal government has in Fort Knox. To issue more paper currency, the government first has to buy more gold."

1.4 The United States and most other countries abandoned the gold standard during the 1930s. Why would the 1930s have been a particularly difficult time for countries to have remained on the gold standard? (*Hint:* Think about the macroeconomic events of the 1930s and about the possible problems with carrying out an expansionary monetary policy while remaining on the gold standard.)

1.5 If a country is using the gold standard, what is likely to happen to the country's money supply if new gold deposits are discovered in the country, as happened in the United States with the gold discoveries in California in 1849? Is this change in the money supply desirable? Briefly explain.

1.6 After World War II, why might countries have preferred the Bretton Woods system to reestablishing the gold standard? In your answer, be sure to note the important ways in which the Bretton Woods system differed from the gold standard.

19.2 **The Current Exchange Rate System, pages 641–653**

LEARNING OBJECTIVE: Discuss the three key features of the current exchange rate system.

Summary

The current exchange rate system has three key aspects: (1) The U.S. dollar floats against other major currencies, (2) most countries in Western Europe have adopted a common currency, and (3) some developing countries have fixed their currencies' exchange rates against the dollar or against another major currency. Since 1973, the value of the U.S. dollar has fluctuated widely against other major currencies. The theory of **purchasing power parity** states that in the long run, exchange rates move to equalize the purchasing power of different currencies. This theory helps to explain some of the long-run movements in the value of the U.S. dollar relative to other currencies. Purchasing power parity does not provide a complete explanation of movements in exchange rates for several reasons, including the existence of *tariffs* and *quotas*. A **tariff** is a tax imposed by a government on imports. A **quota** is a government-imposed limit on the quantity of a good that can be imported. Currently, 17 European Union member countries use a common currency, known as the **euro**. The experience of the countries using the euro will provide economists with information on the costs and benefits to countries of using the same currency.

When a country keeps its currency's exchange rate fixed against another country's currency, it is **pegging** its currency. Pegging can result in problems similar to the problems countries encountered with fixed exchange rates under the Bretton Woods system. If investors become convinced that a country pegging its exchange rate will eventually allow the exchange rate to decline to a lower level, the demand curve for the currency will shift to the left. This illustrates the difficulty of maintaining a fixed exchange rate in the face of destabilizing speculation.

MyEconLab   Visit **www.myeconlab.com** to complete these exercises online and get instant feedback.

Review Questions

2.1 What is the theory of purchasing power parity? Does the theory give a complete explanation for movements in exchange rates in the long run? Briefly explain.

2.2 Briefly describe the four determinants of exchange rates in the long run.

2.3 Which European countries currently use the euro as their currency? Why did these countries agree to replace their previous currencies with the euro?

2.4 What does it mean when one currency is "pegged" against another currency? Why do countries peg their currencies? What problems can result from pegging?

2.5 Briefly describe the Chinese experience with pegging the yuan.

Problems and Applications

2.6 [**Related to the** Making the Connection **on page 642**] In the *Toronto Sun*, columnist Bob Elliot wrote: "Is there advantage to playing for the [Toronto] Blue Jays over the Boston Red Sox or New York Yankees? . . . The exchange numbers say it's better to play for the Jays—as long as you are paid in Canadian funds." Why would it be better for a baseball player on a Canadian team to be paid in Canadian dollars rather than U.S. dollars? What do the "exchange numbers" have to do with your answer? Does it matter whether the player lives in Canada or in the United States? Briefly explain.

From Bob Elliott, "Jays Wishing They Signed for Canadian Coin?" *Toronto Sun*, May 11, 2011.

2.7 Consider the following headline from an article in the *Wall Street Journal*: "Strong Franc Hurts Swiss Business." What does the article mean by a "strong franc"? Why would a strong Swiss franc be bad for Swiss businesses?

From Goran Mijuk, "Strong Franc Hurts Swiss Business," *Wall Street Journal*, October 20, 2011.

2.8 Consider this statement:

It usually takes more than 75 yen to buy 1 U.S. dollar and more than 1.5 dollars to buy 1 British pound. These values show that the United States must be a much wealthier country than Japan and that the United Kingdom must be wealthier than the United States.

Do you agree with this reasoning? Briefly explain.

2.9 The following is from an article in the *Wall Street Journal*:

Honda said its profit fell to ¥60.4 billion ($796.5 million) in the three months ended Sept. 30 [2011]. . . . Troubles related to the yen . . . come as both Honda and Toyota are working to get back to normal operations in the wake of the March 11 earthquake in Japan.

a. According to the information in this article, what was the exchange rate between the yen and the dollar in September 2011? If Honda was experiencing troubles related to the yen, was it likely that the yen had been rising in value in exchange for the U.S. dollar or falling in value in exchange for the U.S. dollar? Briefly explain.

b. Was the change in the yen–dollar exchange rate that you indicated was happening in part a. good news or bad news for U.S. consumers who buy goods imported from Japan? Briefly explain.

From Mike Ramsey and Yoshio Takahashi, "Car Wreck: Honda and Toyota," *Wall Street Journal*, November 1, 2011.

2.10 According to the theory of purchasing power parity, if the inflation rate in Australia is higher than the inflation rate in New Zealand, what should happen to the exchange rate between the Australian dollar and the New Zealand dollar? Briefly explain.

2.11 [**Related to the** Making the Connection **on page 644**] Look again at the table on page 644 that shows the prices of Big Macs and the implied and actual exchange rates. Indicate which countries listed in the table have undervalued currencies versus the U.S. dollar and which have overvalued currencies.

2.12 [**Related to the** Solved Problem 19.2 **on page 645**] Fill in the missing values in the following table. Assume that the Big Mac is selling for $4.07 in the United States. Explain whether the U.S. dollar is overvalued or undervalued relative to each of the other currencies and predict what will happen in the future to each exchange rate. Finally, calculate the implied exchange rate between the Russian ruble and the New Zealand dollar and explain which currency is overvalued in terms of Big Mac purchasing power parity.

Country	Big Mac Price	Implied Exchange Rate	Actual Exchange Rate
Chile	1,850 pesos		463 pesos per dollar
Israel	15.9 shekels		3.40 shekels per dollar
Russia	75.0 rubles		27.8 rubles per dollar
New Zealand	5.10 New Zealand dollars		1.16 New Zealand dollars per U.S. dollar

Data from "Currency Comparisons, to Go," *Economist*, July 28, 2011.

2.13 Britain decided not to join other European Union countries in using the euro as its currency. One British opponent of adopting the euro argued, "It comes down to economics. We just don't believe that it's possible to manage the entire economy of Europe with just one interest rate policy. How do you alleviate recession in Germany and curb inflation in Ireland?" What interest-rate policy would be used to alleviate recession in Germany? What interest-rate policy would be used to curb inflation in Ireland? What does adopting the euro have to do with interest-rate policy?

From Alan Cowell, "Nuanced Conflict over Euro in Britain," *New York Times*, June 22, 2001.

2.14 When the euro was introduced in January 1999, the exchange rate was $1.19 per euro. In October 2011, the exchange rate was $1.38 per euro. Was this change in the dollar–euro exchange rate good news or bad news for U.S. firms exporting goods and services to Europe? Was it good news or bad news for European consumers buying goods and services imported from the United States? Briefly explain.

2.15 **[Related to the** Making the Connection **on page 647]** Jordi Galí, an economist at the Universitat Pompeu Fabra in Spain, notes that the Spanish economy was in recession during the early 1990s, but that "in 1992 and 1993 a series of [exchange rate] devaluations got us out of trouble." Was Spain able to use exchange rate devaluations to deal with the recession of 2007–2009? Briefly explain.

From "One Size Fits None," *Economist*, June 11, 2009.

2.16 Construct a numerical example that shows how an investor could have made a profit by selling Thai baht for dollars in 1997.

2.17 **[Related to the** Chapter Opener **on page 639]** When Airbus, a subsidiary of a company located in France, sold A380 super-jumbo jetliners to Air France, the transaction was made in dollars, rather than euros. What advantages are there to aerospace firms in different countries in agreeing to carry out all transactions in a single currency? What disadvantages are there?

2.18 Use the graph to answer the following questions.

a. According to the graph, is there a surplus or a shortage of baht in exchange for U.S. dollars? Briefly explain.

b. To maintain the pegged exchange rate, will the Thai central bank need to buy baht in exchange for dollars or sell baht in exchange for dollars? How many baht will the Thai central bank need to buy or sell?

2.19 For many years, Argentina suffered from high rates of inflation. As part of its program to fight inflation, in the 1990s, the Argentine government pegged the value of the Argentine peso to the U.S. dollar at a rate of one peso per dollar. In January 2002, the government decided to abandon the peg and allow the peso to float. Just before the peg was abandoned, firms in Buenos Aires posted signs urging customers to come in and shop and take advantage of the "Last 72 Hours of One to One." What was likely to happen to the exchange rate between the dollar and the peso when Argentina abandoned the peg? Why would customers find it better to shop before the peg ended than after?

Based on Larry Rohter, "Argentina Unlinks Peso from Dollar, Bracing for Devaluation," *New York Times*, January 7, 2002.

2.20 The *Economist* observed the following: "In Argentina, many loans were taken out in dollars: this had catastrophic consequences for borrowers once the peg collapsed." What does it mean that Argentina's "peg collapsed"? Why was this catastrophic for borrowers in Argentina who had taken out dollar loans?

From "Spoilt for Choice," *Economist*, June 3, 2002.

2.21 In a column in the *New York Times*, by Christina Romer, former chair of President Barack Obama's Council of Economic Advisers, made the following observations:

a. "Our exchange rate is just a price—the price of the dollar in terms of other currencies. It is not controlled by anyone."

b. ". . . a high price for the dollar, which is what we mean by a strong dollar, is not always desirable."

Briefly explain whether you agree with these two observations.

From Christina D. Romer, "Needed: Plain Talk about the Dollar," *New York Times*, May 21, 2011.

2.22 Suppose that a developing country pegs the value of its currency against the U.S. dollar. Further, suppose that the dollar appreciates against the yen and against the euro. What will be the impact on the ability of the developing country to export goods and services to Japan and Europe? Briefly explain.

2.23 Graph the demand and supply of Chinese yuan for U.S. dollars and label each axis. To maintain its pegged exchange rate, the Chinese central bank used yuan to buy large quantities of U.S. dollars. Indicate whether the pegged exchange rate was above or below the market equilibrium exchange rate and show on the graph the quantity of yuan the Chinese central bank would have to supply each trading period.

2.24 According to an article in the *Wall Street Journal* on a trip by U.S. Treasury Secretary Timothy Geithner to China:

> The message signals that [the] Treasury is beginning to look . . . toward preventing a return to ever-mounting trade deficits and the constant political tensions they generate between the U.S. and China. . . . The issue has long been a sensitive one, with U.S. manufacturers and their political allies accusing China of manipulating its currency to get an unfair edge in foreign trade.

How would a government manipulate its currency to get an "unfair" advantage in trade? Why would U.S. manufacturers be concerned about U.S. trade deficits with China?

From "U.S. to Urge China to Shop, Not Save," *Wall Street Journal*, May 29, 2009.

2.25 [Related to the Making the Connection **on page 652**] The following is from an article in the *Wall Street Journal* on changes in the Korean economy:

> The biggest is a change in where Korean companies are finding growth. It is no longer just the U.S. and Europe, markets where Samsung,

Hyundai and other big exporters have long focused on. Instead, it is in places like China, central Asia and the Middle East. . . . The broader trend is that global economic growth is less tied to the U.S., a phenomenon that has been called "decoupling."

If the trend identified in this article is correct, what are the implications for the policy of the Korean government with respect to the dollar–won exchange rate?

From "Korean Stock Rally Shows a Different Picture," *Wall Street Journal*, June 19, 2007, p. C3.

19.3 **International Capital Markets,** pages 653–655

LEARNING OBJECTIVE: Discuss the growth of international capital markets.

Summary

A key reason exchange rates fluctuate is that investors seek out the best investments they can find anywhere in the world. Since 1980, the markets for stocks and bonds have become global. Foreign purchases of U.S. corporate bonds and stocks and U.S. government bonds have increased greatly in the period since 1995. As a result, firms around the world are no longer forced to rely only on the savings of domestic households for funds.

MyEconLab   Visit **www.myeconlab.com** to complete these exercises online and get instant feedback.

Review Questions

3.1 What were the main factors behind the globalization of capital markets in the 1980s and 1990s?

3.2 Briefly describe the pattern of foreign investments in U.S. securities between 1995 and 2010.

Problems and Applications

3.3 Why are foreign investors more likely to invest in U.S. government bonds than in U.S. corporate stocks and bonds?

3.4 The text states that "the globalization of financial markets has helped increase growth and efficiency in the world economy." Briefly explain which aspects of globalization help to increase growth in the world economy.

3.5 The global financial crisis of 2007–2009 led some economists and policymakers to suggest the reinstitution of capital controls—or limits on the flow of foreign exchange and financial investments across countries—which existed in many European countries prior to the 1960s. Why would a financial crisis lead to a reconsideration of using capital controls? What problems might result from reinstituting capital controls?

Appendix

The Gold Standard and the Bretton Woods System

The Gold Standard and the Bretton Woods System

It is easier to understand the current exchange rate system by considering further two earlier systems, the gold standard and the Bretton Woods system, which together lasted from the early nineteenth century through the early 1970s.

The Gold Standard

As we saw in this chapter, under the gold standard, the currency of a country consisted of gold coins and paper currency that could be redeemed for gold. Great Britain adopted the gold standard in 1816, but as late as 1870, only a few nations had followed. In the late nineteenth century, however, Great Britain's share of world trade had increased, as had its overseas investments. The dominant position of Great Britain in the world economy motivated other countries to adopt the gold standard. By 1913, every country in Europe, except Spain and Bulgaria, and most countries in the Western Hemisphere had adopted the gold standard.

Under the gold standard, the exchange rate between two currencies was automatically determined by the quantity of gold in each currency. If there was 1/5 ounce of gold in a U.S. dollar and 1 ounce of gold in a British pound, the price of gold in the United States would be $5 per ounce, and the price of gold in Britain would be £1 per ounce. The exchange rate would therefore be $5 = £1.

The End of the Gold Standard

From a modern point of view, the greatest drawback to the gold standard was that the central bank lacked control of the money supply. The size of a country's money supply depended on its gold supply, which could be greatly affected by chance discoveries of gold or by technological change in gold mining. For example, the gold discoveries in California in 1849 and Alaska in the 1890s caused rapid increases in the U.S. money supply. Because the central bank cannot determine how much gold will be discovered, it lacks the control of the money supply necessary to pursue an active monetary policy. During wartime, countries usually went off the gold standard to allow their central banks to expand the money supply as rapidly as was necessary to pay for the war. Britain abandoned the gold standard at the beginning of World War I in 1914 and did not resume redeeming its paper currency for gold until 1925.

When the Great Depression began in 1929, governments came under pressure to abandon the gold standard to allow their central banks to pursue active monetary policies. In 1931, Great Britain became the first major country to abandon the gold standard. A number of other countries also went off the gold standard that year. The United States remained on the gold standard until 1933, and a few countries, including France, Italy, and Belgium, stayed on even longer. By the late 1930s, the gold standard had collapsed.

The earlier a country abandoned the gold standard, the easier time it had fighting the Depression with expansionary monetary policies. The countries that abandoned the gold standard by 1932 suffered an average decline in production of only 3 percent between 1929 and 1934. The countries that stayed on the gold standard until 1933 or later suffered an average decline of more than 30 percent. The devastating economic performance of the countries that stayed on the gold standard the longest during the 1930s is the key reason no attempt was made to bring back the gold standard in later years.

The Bretton Woods System

In addition to the collapse of the gold standard, the global economy suffered during the 1930s from tariff wars. The United States had started the tariff wars in June 1930 by enacting the Smoot–Hawley Tariff, which raised the average U.S. tariff rate to more than 50 percent. Many other countries raised tariffs during the next few years, leading to a collapse in world trade.

As World War II was coming to an end, economists and government officials in the United States and Europe concluded that they needed to restore the international economic system to avoid another depression. In 1947, the United States and most other major countries, apart from the Soviet Union, began participating in the General Agreement on Tariffs and Trade (GATT), under which they worked to reduce trade barriers. The GATT was very successful in sponsoring rounds of negotiations among countries, which led to sharp declines in tariffs. U.S. tariffs dropped from an average rate of more than 50 percent in the early 1930s to an average rate of less than 2 percent in 2011. In 1995, the GATT was replaced by the World Trade Organization (WTO), which has similar objectives.

The effort to develop a new exchange rate system to replace the gold standard was more complicated than establishing the GATT. A conference held in Bretton Woods, New Hampshire, in 1944 set up a system in which the United States pledged to buy or sell gold at a fixed price of $35 per ounce. The central banks of all other members of the new **Bretton Woods system** pledged to buy and sell their currencies at a fixed rate against the dollar. By fixing their exchange rates against the dollar, these countries were fixing the exchange rates among their currencies as well. Unlike under the gold standard, neither the United States nor any other country was willing to redeem its paper currency for gold domestically. The United States would redeem dollars for gold only if they were presented by a foreign central bank. The United States continued the prohibition, first enacted in the early 1930s, against private citizens owning gold, unless they were jewelers or rare coin collectors. The prohibition was not lifted until the 1970s, when it again became possible for Americans to own gold as an investment.

Under the Bretton Woods system, central banks were committed to selling dollars in exchange for their own currencies. This commitment required them to hold *dollar reserves*. If a central bank ran out of dollar reserves, it could borrow them from the newly created **International Monetary Fund (IMF)**. In addition to providing loans to central banks that were short of dollar reserves, the IMF would oversee the operation of the system and approve adjustments to the agreed-on fixed exchange rates.

Under the Bretton Woods system, a fixed exchange rate was known as a *par exchange rate*. If the par exchange rate was not the same as the exchange rate that would have been determined in the market, the result would be a surplus or a shortage. For example, Figure 19A.1 shows the exchange rate between the dollar and the British pound. The figure is drawn from the British point of view, so we measure the exchange rate on the vertical axis as dollars per pound. In this case, the par exchange rate between the dollar and the pound is above the equilibrium exchange rate as determined by supply and demand.

In this example, at the par exchange rate of $4 per pound, the quantity of pounds demanded by people who want to buy British goods and services or who want to invest in British assets is smaller than the quantity of pounds supplied by people who would like to exchange them for dollars. As a result, the Bank of England must use dollars to buy the surplus of £1 million per day. Only at an exchange rate of $2.80 per pound would the surplus be eliminated. If the par exchange rate was below the equilibrium

Bretton Woods system An exchange rate system that lasted from 1944 to 1973, under which countries pledged to buy and sell their currencies at a fixed rate against the dollar.

International Monetary Fund (IMF) An international organization that provides foreign currency loans to central banks and oversees the operation of the international monetary system.

Figure 19A.1

A Fixed Exchange Rate above Equilibrium Results in a Surplus of Pounds

Under the Bretton Woods system, if the par exchange rate was above equilibrium, the result would be a surplus of domestic currency in the foreign exchange market. If the par exchange rate was below equilibrium, the result would be a shortage of domestic currency. In the figure, the par exchange rate between the pound and the dollar is $4 = £1, whereas the equilibrium exchange rate is $2.80 = £1. This gap forces the Bank of England to buy £1 million per day in exchange for dollars.

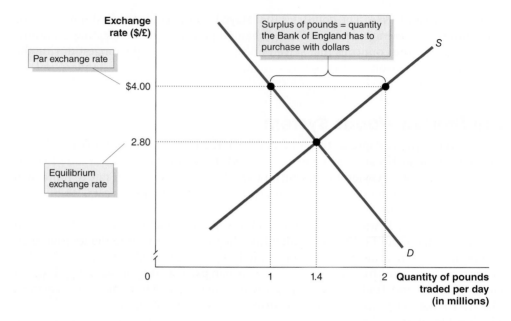

Devaluation A reduction in a fixed exchange rate.

Revaluation An increase in a fixed exchange rate.

exchange rate, there would be a shortage of domestic currency in the foreign exchange market.

A persistent shortage or surplus of a currency under the Bretton Woods system was seen as evidence of a *fundamental disequilibrium* in a country's exchange rate. After consulting with the IMF, countries in this position were allowed to adjust their exchange rates. In the early years of the Bretton Woods system, many countries found that their currencies were *overvalued* versus the dollar, meaning that their par exchange rates were too high. A reduction in a fixed exchange rate is a **devaluation**. An increase in a fixed exchange rate is a **revaluation**. In 1949, there was a devaluation of several currencies, including the British pound, reflecting the fact that those currencies had been overvalued against the dollar.

The Collapse of the Bretton Woods System

By the late 1960s, the Bretton Woods system faced two severe problems. The first was that after 1963, the total number of dollars held by foreign central banks was larger than the gold reserves of the United States. In practice, most central banks—with the Bank of France being the main exception—rarely redeemed dollars for gold. But the basis of the system was a credible promise by the United States to redeem dollars for gold if called upon to do so. By the late 1960s, as the gap between the dollars held by foreign central banks and the gold reserves of the United States grew larger and larger, the credibility of the U.S. promise to redeem dollars for gold was called into question.

The second problem the Bretton Woods system faced was that some countries with undervalued currencies, particularly West Germany, were unwilling to revalue their currencies. Governments resisted revaluation because it would have increased the prices of their countries' exports. Many German firms, such as Volkswagen, put pressure on the government not to endanger their sales in the U.S. market by raising the exchange rate of the deutsche mark against the dollar. Figure 19A.2 shows the situation faced by the German government in 1971. The figure takes the German point of view, so the exchange rate is expressed in terms of dollars per deutsche mark.

Under the Bretton Woods system, the Bundesbank, the German central bank, was required to buy and sell deutsche marks for dollars at a rate of $0.27 per deutsche mark. The equilibrium that would have prevailed in the foreign exchange market if the Bundesbank had not intervened was about $0.35 per deutsche mark. Because the par exchange rate was below the equilibrium exchange rate, the quantity of deutsche marks demanded by people wanting to buy German goods and services or wanting to invest

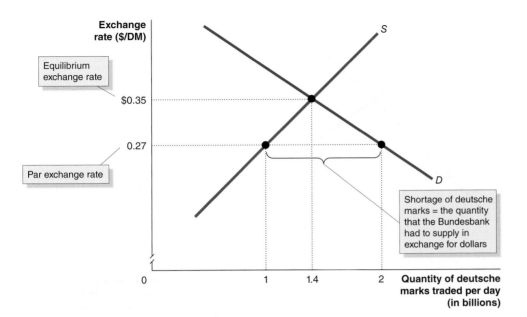

Figure 19A.2

West Germany's Undervalued Exchange Rate

The Bundesbank, the German central bank, was committed under the Bretton Woods system to defending a par exchange rate of $0.27 per deutsche mark (DM). Because this exchange rate was lower than what the equilibrium market exchange rate would have been, there was a shortage of DMs in the foreign exchange market. The Bundesbank had to supply DMs equal to the shortage in exchange for dollars. The shortage in the figure is equal to 1 billion DMs per day.

in German assets was greater than the quantity of deutsche marks supplied by people who wanted to exchange them for dollars. To maintain the exchange rate at $0.27 per deutsche mark, the Bundesbank had to buy dollars and sell deutsche marks. The number of deutsche marks supplied by the Bundesbank was equal to the shortage of deutsche marks at the par exchange rate.

By selling deutsche marks and buying dollars to defend the par exchange rate, the Bundesbank was increasing the West German money supply, risking an increase in the inflation rate. Because Germany had suffered a devastating hyperinflation during the 1920s, the fear of inflation was greater in Germany than in any other industrial country. No German government could survive politically if it allowed a significant increase in inflation. Knowing this fact, many investors in Germany and elsewhere became convinced that eventually, the German government would have to allow a revaluation of the mark.

During the 1960s, most European countries, including Germany, relaxed their *capital controls*. **Capital controls** are limits on the flow of foreign exchange and financial investment across countries. The loosening of capital controls made it easier for investors to speculate on changes in exchange rates. For instance, an investor in the United States could sell $1 million and receive about 3.7 million deutsche marks at the par exchange rate of $0.27 per deutsche mark. If the exchange rate rose to $0.35 per deutsche mark, the investor could then exchange deutsche marks for dollars, receiving $1.3 million at the new exchange rate: a return of 30 percent on an initial $1 million investment. The more convinced investors became that Germany would have to allow a revaluation, the more dollars they exchanged for deutsche marks. Figure 19A.3 shows the results.

The increased demand for deutsche marks by investors hoping to make a profit from the expected revaluation of the mark shifted the demand curve for marks to the right, from D_1 to D_2. Because of this expectation, the Bundesbank had to increase the marks it supplied in exchange for dollars, raising further the risk of inflation in Germany. As we saw in the chapter, because these actions by investors make it more difficult to maintain a fixed exchange rate, they are referred to as *destabilizing speculation*. By May 1971, the Bundesbank had to buy more than $250 million per day to support the fixed exchange rate against the dollar. Finally, on May 5, the West German government decided to allow the mark to float. In August, President Richard Nixon decided to abandon the U.S. commitment to redeem dollars for gold. Attempts were made over the next two years to reach a compromise that would restore a fixed exchange rate system, but by 1973, the Bretton Woods system was effectively dead.

Capital controls Limits on the flow of foreign exchange and financial investment across countries.

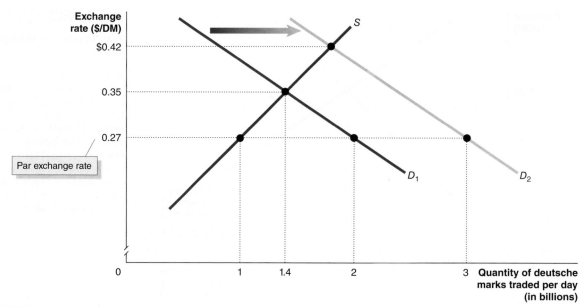

Figure 19A.3   Destabilizing Speculation against the Deutsche Mark, 1971

In 1971, the par exchange rate of $0.27 = 1 deutsche mark was below the equilibrium exchange rate of $0.35 = 1 deutsche mark. As investors became convinced that West Germany would have to revalue the deutsche mark, they increased their demand for marks, shifting the demand curve from D_1 to D_2. The new equilibrium exchange rate became $0.42 = 1 deutsche mark. This increase in demand raised the quantity of marks the Bundesbank had to supply in exchange for dollars to defend the par exchange rate from 1 billion deutsche marks to 2 billion deutsche marks per day.

Key Terms

Bretton Woods system, p. 663

Capital controls, p. 665

Devaluation, p. 664

International Monetary Fund (IMF), p. 663

Revaluation, p. 664

 The Gold Standard and the Bretton Woods System, pages 662–666

LEARNING OBJECTIVE: Explain the gold standard and the Bretton Woods system.

MyEconLab   Visit www.myeconlab.com to complete these exercises online and get instant feedback.

Review Questions

19A.1 What determined the exchange rates among currencies under the gold standard? Why did the gold standard collapse?

19A.2 Briefly describe how the Bretton Woods system operated.

19A.3 What is the difference between a devaluation and a revaluation?

19A.4 What are capital controls?

19A.5 What role did the International Monetary Fund play in the Bretton Woods system?

19A.6 What is destabilizing speculation? What role did it play in the collapse of the Bretton Woods system?

Problems and Applications

19A.7 Suppose that under the gold standard, there was 1/5 ounce of gold in a U.S. dollar and 1 ounce of gold in a British pound. Demonstrate that if the exchange rate between the dollar and the pound was $4 = £1, rather

than $5 = £1, you could make unlimited profits by buying gold in one country and selling it in the other. If the exchange rate was $6 = £1, how would your strategy change? For simplicity, assume that there was no cost to shipping gold from one country to the other.

19A.8 An article in the *Economist* observes, "When the Depression [of the 1930s] struck, this gold standard became a noose around the necks of struggling economies." In what sense was the gold standard a "noose around the necks of struggling economies" during the 1930s?

From "A Brief Post on Competitive Devaluation," *Economist*, October 31, 2011.

19A.9 According to an article in the *Economist*, when most countries left the gold standard in the 1930s, in South Africa "the mining industry flourished." Briefly explain why the end of the gold standard might be good news for the owners of gold mines.

From "Johannesburg," *Economist*, August 18, 2004.

19A.10 By the mid-1960s, the price of gold on the London market had increased to more than $35 per ounce. (Remember that it was not legal during these years for investors in the United States to own gold.) Would this have happened if foreign investors had believed that the U.S. commitment to buy and sell gold at $35 per ounce under the Bretton Woods system would continue indefinitely? Briefly explain.

19A.11 An article in the *New York Times* states that, "On Aug. 15, 1971, President Nixon unhitched the value of the dollar from the gold standard." Is the author of this article correct that the United States abandoned the gold standard in 1971? What led President Nixon to take the action described in the article?

From "Bretton Woods System" *New York Times*, October 31, 2011.

19A.12 Barry Eichengreen, an economist at the University of California, Berkeley, describes actions taken by the Federal Reserve in 1931 to try to keep the United States on the gold standard: "[T]he New York Fed raised its discount rate by a full percentage point to defend the dollar. A week later it raised the discount rate a second time, again by a full percentage point." Why would an increase in interest rates help the United States stay on the gold standard?

From Barry Eichengreen, *Exorbitant Privlege*, (Oxford: Oxford University Press, 2011), p. 36.

19A.13 One economist has argued that the East Asian exchange rate crisis of the late 1990s was due to "the simple failure of governments to remember the lessons from the breakdown of the Bretton Woods System." What are these lessons? In what sense did the East Asian governments fail to learn these lessons?

From Thomas D. Willett, "Crying for Argentina," *Milken Institute Review*, Second Quarter 2002.

19A.14 An article in the *Wall Street Journal* argues that, "The Bretton Woods system ran into trouble in the 1960s, in part because U.S. trade deficits mounted." Why would increases in the U.S. trade deficit cause problems for the Bretton Woods system?

From Jon E. Hilsenrath and Mary Kissel, "Currency Decision Marks Small Shift toward Flexibility," *Wall Street Journal*, July 22, 2005.

19A.15 An article in the *Economist* notes that after the end of the Bretton Woods system, "The Europeans did not like leaving their currencies to the whims of the markets. . . ." What does it mean for a country to leave its currency to the "whims of the markets"? What problems might a country experience as a result? What exchange rate system did most European countries ultimately adopt?

From "Forty Years On," *Economist*, August 13, 2011.

GLOSSARY

A

Absolute advantage The ability of an individual, a firm, or a country to produce more of a good or service than competitors, using the same amount of resources.

Accounting profit A firm's net income, measured as revenue minus operating expenses and taxes paid.

Adverse selection The situation in which one party to a transaction takes advantage of knowing more than the other party to the transaction.

Aggregate demand (AD) curve A curve that shows the relationship between the price level and the quantity of real GDP demanded by households, firms, and the government.

Aggregate demand and aggregate supply model A model that explains short-run fluctuations in real GDP and the price level.

Aggregate expenditure (AE) Total spending in the economy: the sum of consumption, planned investment, government purchases, and net exports.

Aggregate expenditure model A macroeconomic model that focuses on the short-run relationship between total spending and real GDP, assuming that the price level is constant.

Allocative efficiency A state of the economy in which production is in accordance with consumer preferences; in particular, every good or service is produced up to the point where the last unit provides a marginal benefit to society equal to the marginal cost of producing it.

Asset Anything of value owned by a person or a firm.

Asymmetric information A situation in which one party to an economic transaction has less information than the other party.

Autarky A situation in which a country does not trade with other countries.

Automatic stabilizers Government spending and taxes that automatically increase or decrease along with the business cycle.

Autonomous expenditure An expenditure that does not depend on the level of GDP.

B

Balance of payments The record of a country's trade with other countries in goods, services, and assets.

Balance of trade The difference between the value of the goods a country exports and the value of the goods a country imports.

Balance sheet A financial statement that sums up a firm's financial position on a particular day, usually the end of a quarter or year.

Bank panic A situation in which many banks experience runs at the same time.

Bank run A situation in which many depositors simultaneously decide to withdraw money from a bank.

Black market A market in which buying and selling take place at prices that violate government price regulations.

Bond A financial security that represents a promise to repay a fixed amount of funds.

Bretton Woods system An exchange rate system that lasted from 1944 to 1973, under which countries pledged to buy and sell their currencies at a fixed rate against the dollar.

Budget deficit The situation in which the government's expenditures are greater than its tax revenue.

Budget surplus The situation in which the government's expenditures are less than its tax revenue.

Business cycle Alternating periods of economic expansion and economic recession.

C

Capital Manufactured goods that are used to produce other goods and services.

Capital account The part of the balance of payments that records relatively minor transactions, such as migrants' transfers and sales and purchases of nonproduced, nonfinancial assets.

Capital controls Limits on the flow of foreign exchange and financial investment across countries.

Cash flow The difference between the cash revenues received by a firm and the cash spending by the firm.

Catch-up The prediction that the level of GDP per capita (or income per capita) in poor countries will grow faster than in rich countries.

Centrally planned economy An economy in which the government decides how economic resources will be allocated.

Ceteris paribus ("all else equal") condition The requirement that when analyzing the relationship between two variables—such as price and quantity demanded—other variables must be held constant.

Circular-flow diagram A model that illustrates how participants in markets are linked.

Closed economy An economy that has no interactions in trade or finance with other countries.

Commodity money A good used as money that also has value independent of its use as money.

Comparative advantage The ability of an individual, a firm, or a country to produce a good or service at a lower opportunity cost than competitors.

Competitive market equilibrium A market equilibrium with many buyers and many sellers.

Complements Goods and services that are used together.

Consumer price index (CPI) An average of the prices of the goods and services purchased by the typical urban family of four.

Consumer surplus The difference between the highest price a consumer is willing to pay for a good or service and the price the consumer actually pays.

Consumption Spending by households on goods and services, not including spending on new houses.

Consumption function The relationship between consumption spending and disposable income.

Contractionary monetary policy The Federal Reserve's increasing interest rates to reduce inflation.

Corporate governance The way in which a corporation is structured and the effect that structure has on the corporation's behavior.

Corporation A legal form of business that provides owners with protection from losing more than their investment should the business fail.

Coupon payment An interest payment on a bond.

Crowding out A decline in private expenditures as a result of an increase in government purchases.

Currency appreciation An increase in the market value of one currency relative to another currency.

Currency depreciation A decrease in the market value of one currency relative to another currency.

Current account   The part of the balance of payments that records a country's net exports, net income on investments, and net transfers.

Cyclically adjusted budget deficit or surplus   The deficit or surplus in the federal government's budget if the economy were at potential GDP.

Cyclical unemployment   Unemployment caused by a business cycle recession.

D

Deadweight loss   The reduction in economic surplus resulting from a market not being in competitive equilibrium.

Deflation   A decline in the price level.

Demand curve   A curve that shows the relationship between the price of a product and the quantity of the product demanded.

Demand schedule   A table that shows the relationship between the price of a product and the quantity of the product demanded.

Demographics   The characteristics of a population with respect to age, race, and gender.

Devaluation   A reduction in a fixed exchange rate.

Direct finance   A flow of funds from savers to firms through financial markets, such as the New York Stock Exchange.

Discount loans   Loans the Federal Reserve makes to banks.

Discount rate   The interest rate the Federal Reserve charges on discount loans.

Discouraged workers   People who are available for work but have not looked for a job during the previous four weeks because they believe no jobs are available for them.

Disinflation   A significant reduction in the inflation rate.

Dividends   Payments by a corporation to its shareholders.

Dumping   Selling a product for a price below its cost of production.

E

Economic efficiency   A market outcome in which the marginal benefit to consumers of the last unit produced is equal to its marginal cost of production and in which the sum of consumer surplus and producer surplus is at a maximum.

Economic growth   The ability of an economy to produce increasing quantities of goods and services.

Economic growth model   A model that explains growth rates in real GDP per capita over the long run.

Economic model   A simplified version of reality used to analyze real-world economic situations.

Economic profit   A firm's revenues minus all of its implicit and explicit costs.

Economic surplus   The sum of consumer surplus and producer surplus.

Economic variable   Something measurable that can have different values, such as the incomes of doctors.

Economics   The study of the choices people make to attain their goals, given their scarce resources.

Efficiency wage   A higher-than-market wage that a firm pays to increase worker productivity.

Entrepreneur   Someone who operates a business, bringing together the factors of production—labor, capital, and natural resources—to produce goods and services.

Equity   The fair distribution of economic benefits.

Euro   The common currency of many European countries.

Excess reserves   Reserves that banks hold over and above the legal requirement.

Exchange rate system   An agreement among countries about how exchange rates should be determined.

Expansion   The period of a business cycle during which total production and total employment are increasing.

Expansionary monetary policy   The Federal Reserve's decreasing interest rates to increase real GDP.

Explicit cost   A cost that involves spending money.

Exports   Goods and services produced domestically but sold in other countries.

External economies   Reductions in a firm's costs that result from an increase in the size of an industry.

F

Factor market   A market for the factors of production, such as labor, capital, natural resources, and entrepreneurial ability.

Factors of production   The inputs used to make goods and services.

Federal funds rate   The interest rate banks charge each other for overnight loans.

Federal Open Market Committee (FOMC)   The Federal Reserve committee responsible for open market operations and managing the money supply in the United States.

Federal Reserve   The central bank of the United States.

Fee-for-service   A system under which doctors and hospitals receive a separate payment for each service that they provide.

Fiat money   Money, such as paper currency, that is authorized by a central bank or governmental body and that does not have to be exchanged by the central bank for gold or some other commodity money.

Final good or service   A good or service purchased by a final user.

Financial account   The part of the balance of payments that records purchases of assets a country has made abroad and foreign purchases of assets in the country.

Financial intermediaries   Firms, such as banks, mutual funds, pension funds, and

insurance companies, that borrow funds from savers and lend them to borrowers.

Financial markets   Markets where financial securities, such as stocks and bonds, are bought and sold.

Financial system   The system of financial markets and financial intermediaries through which firms acquire funds from households.

Fiscal policy   Changes in federal taxes and purchases that are intended to achieve macroeconomic policy objectives.

Fixed exchange rate system   A system under which countries agree to keep the exchange rates among their currencies fixed.

Floating currency   The outcome of a country allowing its currency's exchange rate to be determined by demand and supply.

Foreign direct investment (FDI)   The purchase or building by a corporation of a facility in a foreign country.

Foreign portfolio investment   The purchase by an individual or a firm of stocks or bonds issued in another country.

Fractional reserve banking system   A banking system in which banks keep less than 100 percent of deposits as reserves.

Free market   A market with few government restrictions on how a good or service can be produced or sold or on how a factor of production can be employed.

Free trade   Trade between countries that is without government restrictions.

Frictional unemployment   Short-term unemployment that arises from the process of matching workers with jobs.

G

GDP deflator   A measure of the price level, calculated by dividing nominal GDP by real GDP and multiplying by 100.

Globalization   The process of countries becoming more open to foreign trade and investment.

Government purchases Spending by federal, state, and local governments on goods and services.

Gross domestic product (GDP) The market value of all final goods and services produced in a country during a period of time, typically one year.

H

Health care The goods and services, such as prescription drugs and consultations with a doctor, that are intended to maintain or improve a person's health.

Health insurance A contract under which a buyer agrees to make payments, or *premiums*, in exchange for the provider's agreeing to pay some or all of the buyer's medical bills.

Human capital The accumulated knowledge and skills that workers acquire from education and training or from their life experiences.

I

Implicit cost A nonmonetary opportunity cost.

Imports Goods and services bought domestically but produced in other countries.

Income effect The change in the quantity demanded of a good that results from the effect of a change in the good's price on consumers' purchasing power.

Income statement A financial statement that sums up a firm's revenues, costs, and profit over a period of time.

Indirect finance A flow of funds from savers to borrowers through financial intermediaries such as banks. Intermediaries raise funds from savers to lend to firms (and other borrowers).

Industrial Revolution The application of mechanical power to the production of goods, beginning in England around 1750.

Inferior good A good for which the demand increases as income falls and decreases as income rises.

Inflation rate The percentage increase in the price level from one year to the next.

Inflation targeting Conducting monetary policy so as to commit the central bank to achieving a publicly announced level of inflation.

Interest rate The cost of borrowing funds, usually expressed as a percentage of the amount borrowed.

Intermediate good or service A good or service that is an input into another good or service, such as a tire on a truck.

International Monetary Fund (IMF) An international organization that provides foreign currency loans to central banks and oversees the operation of the international monetary system.

Inventories Goods that have been produced but not yet sold.

Investment Spending by firms on new factories, office buildings, machinery, and additions to inventories, plus spending by households and firms on new houses.

K

Keynesian revolution The name given to the widespread acceptance during the 1930s and 1940s of John Maynard Keynes's macroeconomic model.

L

Labor force The sum of employed and unemployed workers in the economy.

Labor force participation rate The percentage of the working-age population in the labor force.

Labor productivity The quantity of goods and services that can be produced by one worker or by one hour of work.

Law of demand The rule that, holding everything else constant, when the price of a product falls, the quantity demanded of the product will increase, and when the price of a product rises, the quantity demanded of the product will decrease.

Law of supply The rule that, holding everything else constant, increases in price cause increases in the quantity supplied, and decreases in price cause decreases in the quantity supplied.

Liability Anything owed by a person or a firm.

Limited liability The legal provision that shields owners of a corporation from losing more than they have invested in the firm.

Long-run aggregate supply (LRAS) curve A curve that shows the relationship in the long run between the price level and the quantity of real GDP supplied.

Long-run economic growth The process by which rising productivity increases the average standard of living.

M

M1 The narrowest definition of the money supply: The sum of currency in circulation, checking account deposits in banks, and holdings of traveler's checks.

M2 A broader definition of the money supply: It includes M1 plus savings account balances, small-denomination time deposits, balances in money market deposit accounts in banks, and noninstitutional money market fund shares.

Macroeconomics The study of the economy as a whole, including topics such as inflation, unemployment, and economic growth.

Managed float exchange rate system The current exchange rate system, under which the value of most currencies is determined by demand and supply, with occasional government intervention.

Marginal analysis Analysis that involves comparing marginal benefits and marginal costs.

Marginal benefit The additional benefit to a consumer from consuming one more unit of a good or service.

Marginal cost The additional cost to a firm of producing one more unit of a good or service.

Marginal propensity to consume (MPC) The slope of the consumption function: The amount by which consumption spending changes when disposable income changes.

Marginal propensity to save (MPS) The amount by which saving changes when disposable income changes.

Market A group of buyers and sellers of a good or service and the institution or arrangement by which they come together to trade.

Market-based reforms Changes in the market for health care that would make it more like the markets for other goods and services.

Market demand The demand by all the consumers of a given good or service.

Market economy An economy in which the decisions of households and firms interacting in markets allocate economic resources.

Market equilibrium A situation in which quantity demanded equals quantity supplied.

Market for loanable funds The interaction of borrowers and lenders that determines the market interest rate and the quantity of loanable funds exchanged.

Menu costs The costs to firms of changing prices.

Microeconomics The study of how households and firms make choices, how they interact in markets, and how the government attempts to influence their choices.

Mixed economy An economy in which most economic decisions result from the interaction of buyers and sellers in markets but in which the government plays a significant role in the allocation of resources.

Monetarism The macroeconomic theories of Milton Friedman and his followers, particularly the idea that the quantity of money should be increased at a constant rate.

Monetary growth rule A plan for increasing the quantity of money at a fixed rate that does not respond to changes in economic conditions.

Monetary policy   The actions the Federal Reserve takes to manage the money supply and interest rates to pursue macroeconomic policy goals.

Monetary policy   The actions the Federal Reserve takes to manage the money supply and interest rates to pursue macroeconomic policy objectives.

Money   Assets that people are generally willing to accept in exchange for goods and services or for payment of debts.

Moral hazard   The actions people take after they have entered into a transaction that make the other party to the transaction worse off.

Multiplier   The increase in equilibrium real GDP divided by the increase in autonomous expenditure.

Multiplier effect   The series of induced increases in consumption spending that results from an initial increase in autonomous expenditures.

N

Natural rate of unemployment   The normal rate of unemployment, consisting of frictional unemployment plus structural unemployment.

Net foreign investment   The difference between capital outflows from a country and capital inflows, also equal to net foreign direct investment plus net foreign portfolio investment.

New classical macroeconomics   The macroeconomic theories of Robert Lucas and others, particularly the idea that workers and firms have rational expectations.

New growth theory   A model of long-run economic growth that emphasizes that technological change is influenced by economic incentives and so is determined by the working of the market system.

Nominal exchange rate   The value of one country's currency in terms of another country's currency.

Nominal GDP   The value of final goods and services evaluated at current-year prices.

Nominal interest rate   The stated interest rate on a loan.

Nonaccelerating inflation rate of unemployment (NAIRU)   The unemployment rate at which the inflation rate has no tendency to increase or decrease.

Normal good   A good for which the demand increases as income rises and decreases as income falls.

Normative analysis   Analysis concerned with what ought to be.

O

Open economy   An economy that has interactions in trade or finance with other countries.

Open market operations   The buying and selling of Treasury securities by the Federal Reserve in order to control the money supply.

Opportunity cost   The highest-valued alternative that must be given up to engage in an activity.

P

Partnership   A firm owned jointly by two or more persons and not organized as a corporation.

Patent   The exclusive right to produce a product for a period of 20 years from the date the patent is applied for.

Patient Protection and Affordable Care Act (PPACA)   Health care reform legislation passed by Congress and signed by President Barack Obama in 2010.

Pegging   The decision by a country to keep the exchange rate fixed between its currency and another currency.

Perfectly competitive market   A market that meets the conditions of (1) many buyers and sellers, (2) all firms selling identical products, and (3) no barriers to new firms entering the market.

Per-worker production function   The relationship between real GDP per hour worked and capital per hour worked, holding the level of technology constant.

Phillips curve   A curve showing the short-run relationship between the unemployment rate and the inflation rate.

Positive analysis   Analysis concerned with what is.

Potential GDP   The level of real GDP attained when all firms are producing at capacity.

Present value   The value in today's dollars of funds to be paid or received in the future.

Price floor   A legally determined minimum price that sellers may receive.

Price level   A measure of the average prices of goods and services in the economy.

Principal–agent problem   A problem caused by agents pursuing their own interests rather than the interests of the principals who hired them.

Producer price index (PPI)   An average of the prices received by producers of goods and services at all stages of the production process.

Producer surplus   The difference between the lowest price a firm would be willing to accept for a good or service and the price it actually receives.

Production possibilities frontier (PPF)   A curve showing the maximum attainable combinations of two products that may be produced with available resources and current technology.

Productive efficiency   A situation in which a good or service is produced at the lowest possible cost.

Product market   A market for goods—such as computers—or services—such as medical treatment.

Property rights   The rights individuals or firms have to the exclusive use of their property, including the right to buy or sell it.

Protectionism   The use of trade barriers to shield domestic firms from foreign competition.

Purchasing power parity   The theory that in the long run, exchange rates move to equalize the purchasing powers of different currencies.

Q

Quantity demanded   The amount of a good or service that a consumer is willing and able to purchase at a given price.

Quantity supplied   The amount of a good or service that a firm is willing and able to supply at a given price.

Quantity theory of money   A theory about the connection between money and prices that assumes that the velocity of money is constant.

Quota   A numerical limit a government imposes on the quantity of a good that can be imported into the country.

R

Rational expectations   Expectations formed by using all available information about an economic variable.

Real business cycle model   A macroeconomic model that focuses on real, rather than monetary, causes of the business cycle.

Real exchange rate   The price of domestic goods in terms of foreign goods.

Real GDP   The value of final goods and services evaluated at base-year prices.

Real interest rate   The nominal interest rate minus the inflation rate.

Recession   The period of a business cycle during which total production and total employment are decreasing.

Required reserve ratio   The minimum fraction of deposits banks are required by law to keep as reserves.

Required reserves   Reserves that a bank is legally required to hold, based on its checking account deposits.

Reserves   Deposits that a bank keeps as cash in its vault or on deposit with the Federal Reserve.

Revaluation   An increase in a fixed exchange rate.

Rule of law   The ability of a government to enforce the laws of the country, particularly with respect to protecting private property and enforcing contracts.

S

Saving and investment equation An equation that shows that national saving is equal to domestic investment plus net foreign investment.

Scarcity A situation in which unlimited wants exceed the limited resources available to fulfill those wants.

Securitization The process of transforming loans or other financial assets into securities.

Security A financial asset—such as a stock or a bond—that can be bought and sold in a financial market.

Separation of ownership from control A situation in a corporation in which the top management, rather than the shareholders, control day-to-day operations.

Shortage A situation in which the quantity demanded is greater than the quantity supplied.

Short-run aggregate supply (SRAS) curve A curve that shows the relationship in the short run between the price level and the quantity of real GDP supplied by firms.

Simple deposit multiplier The ratio of the amount of deposits created by banks to the amount of new reserves.

Single-payer health care system A system, such as the one in Canada, in which the government provides health insurance to all of the country's residents.

Socialized medicine A health care system under which the

government owns most of the hospitals and employs most of the doctors.

Sole proprietorship A firm owned by a single individual and not organized as a corporation.

Speculators Currency traders who buy and sell foreign exchange in an attempt to profit from changes in exchange rates.

Stagflation A combination of inflation and recession, usually resulting from a supply shock.

Stock A financial security that represents partial ownership of a firm.

Stockholders' equity The difference between the value of a corporation's assets and the value of its liabilities; also known as *net worth*.

Structural relationship A relationship that depends on the basic behavior of consumers and firms and that remains unchanged over long periods.

Structural unemployment Unemployment that arises from a persistent mismatch between the skills and attributes of workers and the requirements of jobs.

Substitutes Goods and services that can be used for the same purpose.

Substitution effect The change in the quantity demanded of a good that results from a change in price making the good more or less expensive relative to other goods, holding constant the effect of the price change on consumer purchasing power.

Supply curve A curve that shows the relationship between the price of a product and the

quantity of the product supplied.

Supply schedule A table that shows the relationship between the price of a product and the quantity of the product supplied.

Supply shock An unexpected event that causes the short-run aggregate supply curve to shift.

Surplus A situation in which the quantity supplied is greater than the quantity demanded.

T

Tariff A tax imposed by a government on imports.

Tax incidence The actual division of the burden of a tax between buyers and sellers in a market.

Tax wedge The difference between the pretax and posttax return to an economic activity.

Taylor rule A rule developed by John Taylor that links the Fed's target for the federal funds rate to economic variables.

Technological change A change in the quantity of output a firm can produce using a given quantity of inputs.

Terms of trade The ratio at which a country can trade its exports for imports from other countries.

Trade The act of buying and selling.

Trade-off The idea that because of scarcity, producing more of one good or service means producing less of another good or service.

Transfer payments Payments by the government to households for which the government does

not receive a new good or service in return.

U

Underground economy Buying and selling of goods and services that is concealed from the government to avoid taxes or regulations or because the goods and services are illegal.

Unemployment rate The percentage of the labor force that is unemployed.

V

Value added The market value a firm adds to a product.

Velocity of money The average number of times each dollar in the money supply is used to purchase goods and services included in GDP.

Voluntary exchange A situation that occurs in markets when both the buyer and seller of a product are made better off by the transaction.

Voluntary export restraint (VER) An agreement negotiated between two countries that places a numerical limit on the quantity of a good that can be imported by one country from the other country.

W

Wall Street Reform and Consumer Protection Act (Dodd-Frank Act) Legislation passed during 2010 that was intended to reform regulation of the financial system.

World Trade Organization (WTO) An international organization that oversees international trade agreements.

COMPANY INDEX

SUBJECT INDEX

Key terms and the page on which they are defined appear in **boldface**.

CREDITS

Photo

Front matter, *page vii*, Courtesy of the authors; *page xxxvii*, Wavebreakmedia, Ltd./Shutterstock; *page xl*, MCT/Getty Images.

Chapter 1, *page 2*, Getty Images; *page 15*, Ocean/Corbis.

Chapter 2, *page 38*, Bloomberg/Getty Images; *page 43*, Caro/Alamy; *page 53*, JupiterImages; *page 53*, MBI/Alamy; *page 53*, Mikael Damkier/Shutterstock; *page 53*, Elena Elisseeva/Shutterstock; *page 55*, Brooks Kraft/Corbis.

Chapter 3, *page 68*, Wavebreakmedia, Ltd./Shutterstock; *page 73*, British Retail Photography/Alamy; *page 77*, MCT/Getty Images.

Chapter 4, *page 100*, Janine Wiedel Photolibrary/Alamy.

Chapter 5, *page 136*, StockbrokerXtra/Glow Images; *page 151*, Official White House Photo by Pete Souza; *page 160*, Jim West/Alamy.

Chapter 6, *page 168*, Bloomberg/Getty Images; *page 172*, Mangostock/Shutterstock; *page 186*, Getty Images.

Chapter 7, *page 204*, Charles Rex Arbogast/AP Images; *page 216*, Sean Pavone Photo/Shutterstock; *page 223*, Robert F. Bukaty/AP Images; *page 226*, Joerg Boethling/Alamy.

Chapter 8, *page 240*, Jeff Kowalsky/Bloomberg/Getty Images; *page 245*, Mikael Damkier/Shutterstock; *page 245*, Eric Gevaert/Shutterstock; *page 245*, Bill Aron/PhotoEdit, Inc.; *page 245*, JupiterImages; *page 245*, Yoshio Tomii/SuperStock; *page 251*, Mohamed Nureldin Abdallah/Reuters.

Chapter 9, *page 266*, Richard Levine/Alamy; *page 280*, Chris Keane/Reuters.

Chapter 10, *page 302*, Stephen Brashear/Getty Images; *page 316*, Everett Collection; *page 322*, Paul Sakuma/AP Images.

Chapter 11, *page 336*, Zuma Press/Newscom; *page 339*, Author's Image Ltd/Alamy; *page 342*, Grant Neuenburg/Reuters/Corbis; *page 346*, Lionel Cironneau/AP Images; *page 362*, Claro Cortes IV/Reuters/Corbis.

Chapter 12, *page 374*, Justin Sullivan/Staff/Getty Images; *page 401*, Everett Collection/SuperStock.

Chapter 13, *page 418*, AGE Fotostock/SuperStock; *page 434*, Kimberly White/Corbis; *page 437*, Kevin Dietsch/UPI/Newscom; *page 453*, Lebrecht Music and Arts/Photo Library/Alamy.

Chapter 14, *page 454*, Marco Di Lauro/Getty Images; *page 459*, Brooks Kraft/Corbis; *page 461*, James L. Amos/Photo Researchers, Inc.; *page 474 (far left and third from right)*, Lynne Sladky/AP Images; *page 474 (center left and center right)*, Ezio Petersen/UPI/Landov; *page 474 (third from left and far right)*, Eightfish/Alamy; *page 474 (bottom left)*, Imagebroker/Alamy; *page 479*, Bettmann/Corbis.

Chapter 15, *page 490*, Matt Nager/Bloomberg/Getty Images; *page 503*, NetPhotos/Alamy; *page 514*, Iofoto/Shutterstock; *page 518*, Rebecca Cook/Reuters/Corbis.

Chapter 16, *page 530*, Justin Sullivan/Getty Images; *page 535*, Tom Grill/Corbis Super RF/Alamy; *page 550*, David Banks/EPA/Corbis; *page 554*, AP Images.

Chapter 17, *page 576*, Bloomberg/Getty Images; *page 582*, Corbis Super RF/Alamy; *page 586*, David J. Green-Lifestyle/Alamy.

Chapter 18, *page 608*, Imaginechina/Corbis; *page 615*, Iain Masterton/Alamy.

Chapter 19, *page 638*, Meigneux/SIPA/AP Images; *page 642*, Thomas Barwick/Getty Images; *page 644*, Bloomberg/Getty Images; *page 648*, Yves Logghe/AP Images.

THE PEARSON SERIES IN ECONOMICS

Abel/Bernanke/Croushore
*Macroeconomics**

Bade/Parkin
*Foundations of Economics**

Berck/Helfand
The Economics of the Environment

Bierman/Fernandez
Game Theory with Economic Applications

Blanchard
*Macroeconomics**

Blau/Ferber/Winkler
The Economics of Women, Men and Work

Boardman/Greenberg/Vining/Weimer
Cost-Benefit Analysis

Boyer
Principles of Transportation Economics

Branson
Macroeconomic Theory and Policy

Brock/Adams
The Structure of American Industry

Bruce
Public Finance and the American Economy

Carlton/Perloff
Modern Industrial Organization

Case/Fair/Oster
*Principles of Economics**

Caves/Frankel/Jones
World Trade and Payments: An Introduction

Chapman
Environmental Economics: Theory, Application, and Policy

Cooter/Ulen
Law & Economics

Downs
An Economic Theory of Democracy

Ehrenberg/Smith
Modern Labor Economics

Ekelund/Ressler/Tollison
*Economics**

Farnham
Economics for Managers

Folland/Goodman/Stano
The Economics of Health and Health Care

Fort
Sports Economics

Froyen
Macroeconomics

Fusfeld
The Age of the Economist

Gerber
*International Economics**

Gordon
*Macroeconomics**

Greene
Econometric Analysis

Gregory
Essentials of Economics

Gregory/Stuart
Russian and Soviet Economic Performance and Structure

Hartwick/Olewiler
The Economics of Natural Resource Use

Heilbroner/Milberg
The Making of the Economic Society

Heyne/Boettke/Prychitko
The Economic Way of Thinking

Hoffman/Averett
Women and the Economy: Family, Work, and Pay

Holt
Markets, Games and Strategic Behavior

Hubbard/O'Brien
*Economics**

  *Money, Banking, and the Financial System**

Hubbard/O'Brien/Rafferty
*Macroeconomics**

Hughes/Cain
American Economic History

Husted/Melvin
International Economics

Jehle/Reny
Advanced Microeconomic Theory

Johnson-Lans
A Health Economics Primer

Keat/Young
Managerial Economics

Klein
Mathematical Methods for Economics

Krugman/Obstfeld/Melitz
*International Economics: Theory & Policy**

Laidler
The Demand for Money

Leeds/von Allmen
The Economics of Sports

Leeds/von Allmen/Schiming
*Economics**

Lipsey/Ragan/Storer
*Economics**

Lynn
Economic Development: Theory and Practice for a Divided World

Miller
*Economics Today**

  Understanding Modern Economics

Miller/Benjamin
The Economics of Macro Issues

Miller/Benjamin/North
The Economics of Public Issues

Mills/Hamilton
Urban Economics

Mishkin
*The Economics of Money, Banking, and Financial Markets**

  *The Economics of Money, Banking, and Financial Markets, Business School Edition**

  *Macroeconomics: Policy and Practice**

Murray
Econometrics: A Modern Introduction

Nafziger
The Economics of Developing Countries

O'Sullivan/Sheffrin/Perez
*Economics: Principles, Applications and Tools**

Parkin
*Economics**

Perloff
*Microeconomics**

  *Microeconomics: Theory and Applications with Calculus**

Perman/Common/McGilvray/Ma
Natural Resources and Environmental Economics

Phelps
Health Economics

Pindyck/Rubinfeld
*Microeconomics**

Riddell/Shackelford/Stamos/ Schneider
Economics: A Tool for Critically Understanding Society

Ritter/Silber/Udell
*Principles of Money, Banking & Financial Markets**

Roberts
The Choice: A Fable of Free Trade and Protection

Rohlf
Introduction to Economic Reasoning

Ruffin/Gregory
Principles of Economics

Sargent
Rational Expectations and Inflation

Sawyer/Sprinkle
International Economics

Scherer
Industry Structure, Strategy, and Public Policy

Schiller
The Economics of Poverty and Discrimination

Sherman
Market Regulation

Silberberg
Principles of Microeconomics

Stock/Watson
Introduction to Econometrics

  Introduction to Econometrics, Brief Edition

Studenmund
Using Econometrics: A Practical Guide

Tietenberg/Lewis
Environmental and Natural Resource Economics

  Environmental Economics and Policy

Todaro/Smith
Economic Development

Waldman
Microeconomics

Waldman/Jensen
Industrial Organization: Theory and Practice

Weil
Economic Growth

Williamson
Macroeconomics

* denotes MyEconLab titles

Log onto www.myeconlab.com to learn more

We use **business examples** to explain economic concepts. This table highlights the topic and **real-world** company introduced in the chapter-opening vignette and revisited throughout the chapter. This table also lists the companies that appear in our *Making the Connection* and *An Inside Look* features.